Relevant economic statistics, selected years, 1947–1970

		1947	1949	1951	1953	1954	1955	1956	1957
1	New business incorporations (thousands)	113.0	86.0	84.0	103.0	117.0	140.0	141.0	137.0
2	Business failures (thousands)	3.0	9.0	8.0	9.0	11.0	11.0	13.0	14.0
3	Sales by manufacturers (billions of dollars)*	—	—	245.0	266.0	249.0	278.0	307.0	320.0
4	Profits by manufacturers (billions of dollars)*	—	—	27.0	24.0	21.0	29.0	30.0	28.0
5	After-tax manufacturing profits per dollar of sales (cents)*	7.0	6.0	5.0	4.0	5.0	5.0	5.0	5.0
6	Index of business sector productivity (1982 = 100)	—	—	—	—	—	—	—	—
7	Annual change in business sector productivity (%)	—	—	—	—	—	—	—	—
8	Nonagricultural employees in goods-producing industries (millions)	19.0	18.0	20.0	21.0	20.0	21.0	21.0	20.0
9	Nonagricultural employees in service-producing industries (millions)	25.0	26.0	28.0	29.0	29.0	30.0	31.0	32.0
10	Compensation of employees (billions of dollars)	130.0	143.0	182.0	210.0	209.0	226.0	245.0	258.0
11	Average weekly hours in private nonagricultural industries	40.3	39.4	39.9	39.6	39.1	39.6	39.3	38.8
12	Average hourly earnings in private nonagricultural industries (dollars)	1.13	1.28	1.45	1.61	1.65	1.71	1.80	1.89
13	Average weekly earnings in private nonagricultural industries (dollars)	46.0	50.0	58.0	64.0	65.0	68.0	71.0	73.0
14	Prime interest rate (%)	1.63	2.00	2.56	3.17	3.05	3.16	3.77	4.20
15	Ten-year Treasury bond interest rate (%)	—	—	—	2.85	2.40	2.82	3.18	3.65
16	Net farm income (billions of dollars)	15.4	12.8	15.9	13.0	12.4	11.3	11.3	11.1
17	Index of prices received by farmers (1977 = 100)	60.0	55.0	66.0	56.0	54.0	51.0	50.0	51.0
18	Index of prices paid by farmers (1977 = 100)	35.0	36.0	41.0	40.0	40.0	40.0	40.0	42.0
19	Persons below poverty level (millions)	—	—	—	—	—	—	—	—
20	Poverty rate (% of population)	—	—	—	—	—	—	—	—
21	U.S. merchandise exports (billions of dollars)	16.0	12.0	14.0	12.0	13.0	14.0	18.0	20.0
22	U.S. merchandise imports (billions of dollars)	6.0	7.0	11.0	11.0	10.0	12.0	13.0	13.0
23	Trade balance on current account (billions of dollars)	9.0	0.9	0.9	–1.3	0.2	0.4	2.7	4.8
24	International value of the U.S. dollar (March 1973 = 100)	—	—	—	—	—	—	—	—

*Series change in 1973
**Authors' estimate
Sources: *Economic Report of the President* and *Economic Indicators.*

1958	1959	1960	1961	1962	1963	1964	1965	1966	1967	1968	1969	1970
151.0	193.0	183.0	182.0	182.0	186.0	198.0	204.0	200.0	207.0	234.0	274.0	264.0
15.0	14.0	15.0	17.0	16.0	14.0	14.0	14.0	13.0	12.0	10.0	9.0	11.0
305.0	338.0	346.0	356.0	389.0	413.0	443.0	492.0	554.0	575.0	632.0	695.0	709.0
23.0	30.0	28.0	28.0	32.0	35.0	40.0	47.0	52.0	48.0	55.0	58.0	48.0
4.0	5.0	4.0	4.0	5.0	5.0	5.0	6.0	6.0	5.0	5.0	5.0	4.0
—	64.6	65.6	68.1	70.4	73.3	76.5	78.6	81.0	83.0	85.4	85.9	87.0
—	—	1.6	3.7	3.5	4.1	4.3	2.7	3.0	2.5	3.0	0.5	1.3
20.0	20.0	20.0	20.0	20.0	21.0	21.0	22.0	23.0	23.0	24.0	24.0	24.0
32.0	33.0	34.0	34.0	35.0	36.0	37.0	39.0	41.0	42.0	44.0	46.0	47.0
260.0	281.0	297.0	306.0	327.0	346.0	371.0	400.0	443.0	476.0	525.0	578.0	618.0
38.5	39.0	38.6	38.6	38.7	38.8	38.7	38.8	38.6	38.0	37.8	37.7	37.1
1.95	2.02	2.09	2.14	2.22	2.28	2.36	2.46	2.56	2.68	2.85	3.04	3.23
75.0	79.0	81.0	83.0	86.0	88.0	91.0	95.0	99.0	102.0	108.0	115.0	120.0
3.83	4.48	4.82	4.50	4.50	4.50	4.50	4.54	5.63	5.61	6.30	7.96	7.91
3.32	4.33	4.12	3.88	3.95	4.00	4.19	4.28	4.92	5.07	5.65	6.67	7.35
13.2	10.7	11.2	12.0	12.1	11.8	10.5	12.9	14.0	12.3	12.3	14.3	14.4
55.0	53.0	52.0	53.0	53.0	53.0	52.0	54.0	58.0	55.0	56.0	59.0	60.0
43.0	43.0	44.0	44.0	45.0	45.0	45.0	47.0	49.0	49.0	51.0	53.0	55.0
—	39.5	39.9	39.6	38.6	36.4	36.1	33.2	28.5	27.8	25.4	24.1	25.4
—	22.4	22.2	21.9	21.0	19.5	19.0	17.3	14.7	14.2	12.8	12.1	12.6
16.0	16.0	20.0	20.0	21.0	22.0	26.0	26.0	29.0	31.0	34.0	36.0	42.0
13.0	15.0	15.0	15.0	16.0	17.0	19.0	22.0	25.0	27.0	33.0	36.0	40.0
0.8	–1.3	2.8	3.8	3.4	4.4	6.8	5.4	3.0	2.6	0.6	0.4	2.3
—	—	—	—	—	—	—	—	—	120.0	122.0	122.0	121.0

(Continued)

(Continued)

Relevant economic statistics, selected years, 1971–1991

		1971	1972	1973	1974	1975	1976	1977	1978
1	New business incorporations (thousands)	288.0	317.0	329.0	319.0	326.0	376.0	436.0	478.0
2	Business failures (thousands)	10.0	9.0	9.0	10.0	11.0	10.0	8.0	7.0
3	Sales by manufacturers (billions of dollars)*	751.0	850.0	1,017.0	1,061.0	1,065.0	1,203.0	1,328.0	1,496.0
4	Profits by manufacturers (billions of dollars)*	53.0	63.0	81.0	92.0	80.0	105.0	115.0	133.0
5	After-tax manufacturing profits per dollar of sales (cents)*	4.0	4.0	5.0	6.0	5.0	5.0	5.0	5.0
6	Index of business sector productivity (1982 = 100)	90.2	92.6	95.0	93.3	95.5	98.3	99.8	100.4
7	Annual change in business sector productivity (%)	3.6	2.7	2.6	–1.8	2.3	3.0	1.6	0.6
8	Nonagricultural employees in goods-producing industries (millions)	23.0	24.0	25.0	25.0	23.0	23.0	24.0	26.0
9	Nonagricultural employees in service-producing industries (millions)	48.0	50.0	52.0	53.0	54.0	56.0	58.0	61.0
10	Compensation of employees (billions of dollars)	659.0	726.0	813.0	891.0	949.0	1,058.0	1,177.0	1,333.0
11	Average weekly hours in private nonagricultural industries	36.9	37.0	36.9	36.5	36.1	36.1	36.0	35.8
12	Average hourly earnings in private nonagricultural industries (dollars)	3.45	3.70	3.94	4.24	4.53	4.86	5.25	5.68
13	Average weekly earnings in private nonagricultural industries (dollars)	127.0	137.0	145.0	155.0	164.0	175.0	189.0	204.0
14	Prime interest rate (%)	5.72	5.25	8.03	10.81	7.86	6.84	6.83	9.06
15	Ten-year Treasury bond interest rate (%)	6.16	6.21	6.84	7.56	7.99	7.61	7.42	8.41
16	Net farm income (billions of dollars)	15.0	19.5	34.4	27.3	25.5	20.2	19.9	25.2
17	Index of prices received by farmers (1977 = 100)	62.0	69.0	98.0	105.0	101.0	102.0	100.0	115.0
18	Index of prices paid by farmers (1977 = 100)	58.0	62.0	71.0	81.0	89.0	95.0	100.0	108.0
19	Persons below poverty level (millions)	25.6	24.5	23.0	23.4	25.9	25.0	24.7	24.5
20	Poverty rate (% of population)	12.5	11.9	11.1	11.2	12.3	11.8	11.6	11.4
21	U.S. merchandise exports (billions of dollars)	43.0	49.0	71.0	98.0	107.0	115.0	121.0	142.0
22	U.S. merchandise imports (billions of dollars)	46.0	56.0	70.0	104.0	98.0	124.0	152.0	176.0
23	Trade balance on current account (billions of dollars)	–1.4	–5.8	7.1	2.0	18.1	4.2	–14.5	–15.4
24	International value of the U.S. dollar (March 1973 = 100)	118.0	109.0	99.0	101.0	99.0	106.0	103.0	92.0

*Series change in 1973

**Authors' estimate

Sources: *Economic Report of the President* and *Economic Indicators*.

1979	1980	1981	1982	1983	1984	1985	1986	1987	1988	1989	1990	1991
525.0	534.0	581.0	567.0	600.0	635.0	662.0	703.0	686.0	685.0	677.0	646.0	625.0**
8.0	12.0	17.0	25.0	31.0	52.0	57.0	62.0	62.0	57.0	50.0	61.0	88.0
1,742.0	1,913.0	2,145.0	2,039.0	2,114.0	2,335.0	2,331.0	2,221.0	2,378.0	2,596.0	2,745.0	2,811.0	2,737.0**
154.0	146.0	159.0	108.0	133.0	166.0	137.0	129.0	173.0	216.0	189.0	160.0	113.0**
6.0	5.0	5.0	4.0	4.0	5.0	4.0	4.0	5.0	6.0	5.0	4.0	3.0
99.3	98.6	99.9	100.0	102.2	104.6	106.1	108.3	109.4	110.4	109.5	109.7	109.9
−1.1	−0.7	1.3	0.1	2.2	2.3	1.4	2.0	1.0	0.9	−0.7	0.2	0.2
26.0	26.0	25.0	24.0	23.0	25.0	25.0	25.0	25.0	25.0	25.0	25.0	24.0
63.0	65.0	66.0	66.0	67.0	70.0	73.0	75.0	78.0	80.0	83.0	85.0	85.0
1,496.0	1,644.0	1,816.0	1,916.0	2,029.0	2,227.0	2,383.0	2,524.0	2,699.0	2,921.0	3,101.3	3,290.3	3,387.7
35.7	35.3	35.2	34.8	35.0	35.2	34.9	34.8	34.8	34.7	34.6	34.5	34.3
6.16	6.66	7.25	7.68	8.02	8.32	8.57	8.76	8.98	9.28	9.66	10.02	10.34
220.0	235.0	255.0	267.0	281.0	293.0	299.0	305.0	313.0	322.0	334.0	346.0	355.0
12.67	15.27	18.87	14.86	10.79	12.04	9.93	8.33	8.21	9.32	10.87	10.01	8.46
9.44	11.46	13.91	13.00	11.10	12.44	10.62	7.68	8.39	8.85	8.49	8.55	7.86
27.4	16.1	26.9	23.8	14.2	26.1	28.8	31.0	39.7	40.6	50.1	50.8	42.6**
132.0	134.0	139.0	133.0	135.0	142.0	128.0	125.0	127.0	130.0	140.0	149.0	140.0
123.0	138.0	150.0	159.0	161.0	165.0	163.0	159.0	162.0	170.0	178.0	184.0	189.0
26.1	29.3	31.8	34.4	35.3	33.7	33.1	32.4	32.2	31.7	31.5	33.6	—
11.7	13.0	14.0	15.0	15.2	14.4	14.0	13.6	13.4	13.0	12.8	13.5	—
184.0	224.0	237.0	211.0	202.0	220.0	216.0	224.0	250.0	320.0	361.0	390.0	417.0
212.0	250.0	265.0	248.0	269.0	332.0	338.0	369.0	410.0	447.0	477.0	498.0	490.0
−1.0	1.9	6.9	−5.9	−40.1	−99.0	−122.3	−145.4	−160.2	−126.2	−106.3	−92.1	—
88.0	87.0	103.0	117.0	125.0	138.0	143.0	112.0	97.0	93.0	99.0	89.0	90.0

MICRO-ECONOMICS

MICRO-ECONOMICS
Principles, Problems, and Policies

TWELFTH EDITION

Campbell R. McConnell
Professor of Economics, Emeritus
University of Nebraska—Lincoln

Stanley L. Brue
Professor of Economics
Pacific Lutheran University

McGraw-Hill, Inc.

New York St. Louis San Francisco Auckland
Bogotá Caracas Lisbon London Madrid
Mexico Milan Montreal New Delhi Paris
San Juan Singapore Sydney Tokyo Toronto

Microeconomics: Principles, Problems, and Policies

4 5 6 7 8 9 0 VNH VNH 9 0 9 8 7 6 5 4

ISBN 0-07-045617-8

This book was set in Century Oldstyle by York Graphic Services, Inc.
The editors were Scott D. Stratford, Michael R. Elia, and Edwin Hanson;
the designer was Joseph A. Piliero;
the production supervisor was Annette Mayeski.
New drawings were done by Vantage Art.
Von Hoffmann Press, Inc., was printer and binder.

Photo Credits

10: Jan Staller/The Image Works 32: AP/Wide World 63: Mike Maples/Woodfin Camp & Associates 84: Montes De Oca/FPG International 108: Larry Mulvehill/Science Source/Photo Researchers 124: Ormand Gigli/The Stock Market 131: William Curtsinger/Photo Researchers 156: John Madere/The Stock Market 182: Blaine Harrington III/The Stock Market 204: Jonathon Blair/Woodfin Camp & Associates 216: Debra P. Hershkowitz 236: Joel Gordon 252: FPG International 270: John Clark/The Stock Market 285: Bob Pizaro/Comstock 298: Hulton/Bettmann Newsphotos 320: Comstock 323: Wally McNamee/Woodfin Camp & Associates 358: Jon Feingersh/The Stock Market 340: Bettmann Newsphotos 374: Joel Gordon 393: Will & Demi McIntyre 416: Tim Davis/Photo Researchers 421: Michael A. Keller/The Stock Market 440: R. Michael Stuckey/Comstock 482: Andy Hernandez/SIPA Press

Library of Congress Cataloging-in-Publication Data

McConnell, Campbell R.
Microeconomics: principles, problems, and policies / Campbell R. McConnell, Stanley L. Brue.—12th ed.
p. cm.
Includes index.
ISBN 0-07-045617-8
1. Microeconomics. I. Brue, Stanley L., (date). II. Title.
HB172.M3925 1993
338.5—dc20 92-17817

ABOUT THE AUTHORS

Photo by: Curt McConnell

Campbell R. McConnell earned his Ph.D. from the University of Iowa after receiving degrees from Cornell College and the University of Illinois. He taught at the University of Nebraska–Lincoln from 1953 until his retirement in 1990. He is also coauthor of ***Contemporary Labor Economics,*** 3d ed. (McGraw-Hill) and has edited readers for the principles and labor economics courses. He is a recipient of both the University of Nebraska Distinguished Teaching Award and the James A. Lake Academic Freedom Award, and is past-president of the Midwest Economics Association. His primary areas of interest are labor economics and economic education. He has an extensive collection of jazz recordings and enjoys reading jazz history.

Photo by: Ken Dunmire

Stanley L. Brue did his undergraduate work at Augustana College (S.D.) and received his Ph.D. from the University of Nebraska—Lincoln. He teaches at Pacific Lutheran University, where he has been honored as a recipient of the Burlington Northern Faculty Achievement Award for classroom excellence and professional accomplishment. He is national President-elect and member of the International Executive Board of Omicron Delta Epsilon International Honor Society in Economics. Professor Brue is coauthor of ***Economic Scenes: Theory in Today's World,*** 5th ed. (Prentice-Hall); ***The Evolution of Economic Thought,*** 4th ed. (Harcourt Brace Jovanovich); and ***Contemporary Labor Economics,*** 3d ed. (McGraw-Hill). For relaxation, he enjoys boating on Puget Sound and skiing trips with his family.

To Mem
and to Terri and Craig

CONTENTS IN BRIEF

Preface *xvii*
Acknowledgments *xxv*

PART 1

AN INTRODUCTION TO ECONOMICS AND THE ECONOMY

1 The Nature and Method of Economics *1*
2 The Economizing Problem *19*
3 Pure Capitalism and the Circular Flow *35*
4 Understanding Individual Markets: Demand and Supply *47*
5 The Private Sectors and the Market System *67*
6 The Public Sector *88*

PART 2

MICROECONOMICS OF PRODUCT AND RESOURCE MARKETS

7 Demand and Supply: Elasticities and Applications *105*
8 Consumer Behavior and Utility Maximization *124*
9 The Costs of Production *140*
10 Price and Output Determination: Pure Competition *160*
11 Price and Output Determination: Pure Monopoly *187*
12 Price and Output Determination: Monopolistic Competition *207*
13 Price and Output Determination: Oligopoly *220*
14 Production and the Demand for Resources *240*
15 The Pricing and Employment of Resources: Wage Determination *255*
16 The Pricing and Employment of Resources: Rent, Interest, and Profits *275*
17 General Equilibrium: The Market System and Its Operation *290*

PART 3

GOVERNMENT AND CURRENT ECONOMIC PROBLEMS

18 Government and Market Failure: Public Goods, the Environment, and Information Problems *303*
19 Public Choice Theory and Taxation *323*
20 Antitrust and Regulation *343*
21 Agriculture: Economics and Policy *362*
22 Income Inequality and Poverty *378*
23 Labor Market Issues: Unionism, Discrimination, and Immigration *396*

PART 4

INTERNATIONAL ECONOMICS AND THE WORLD ECONOMY

24 International Trade: Comparative Advantage and Protectionism *421*
25 Exchange Rates, the Balance of Payments, and Trade Deficits *444*
26 The Soviet Economy in Transition *469*

Glossary *G1*

Index *I1*

KEY GRAPHS

2-1 Production Possibilities Curve *24*
3-2 Circular Flow of Output and Income *43*
4-5 Supply and Demand Model *59*
9-2 Short-Run Production Relationships *144*

9-5 Short-Run Cost Curves *148*
9-8 Long-Run Average Cost Curve *152*
10-3 Short-Run Pure Competition Model *169*
10-6 Competitive Firm's Short-Run Supply Curve *172*
10-12 Long-Run Equilibrium in Pure Competition *180*
11-3 Pure Monopoly Model *195*
12-1 Monopolistic Competition Model *210*
15-3 Competitive Labor Demand and Labor Supply *259*
24-2 Specialization and the Gains from International Trade *427*
25-3 Market for Foreign Exchange *450*

CONTENTS

Note: All chapter sections with substantial global content are indicated in light blue ink.

Preface *xvii*
Acknowledgments *xxv*

PART 1

AN INTRODUCTION TO ECONOMICS AND THE ECONOMY

1 THE NATURE AND METHOD OF ECONOMICS *1*

The Age of the Economist
Economics for citizenship. Personal applications.

Methodology
Descriptive economics. Economic theory. Policy economics: positive and normative.

Pitfalls to Objective Thinking
Bias. Loaded terminology. Definitions. Fallacy of composition. Cause and effect: post hoc fallacy.

The Economic Perspective

LAST WORD Fast-Food Lines: An Economic Perspective

Appendix to Chapter 1: Graphs and Their Meaning

2 THE ECONOMIZING PROBLEM *19*

The Foundation of Economics
Unlimited wants. Scarce resources.

Economics and Efficiency
Full employment and full production. Production possibilities table. Production possibilities curve. Optimal product-mix. Law of increasing opportunity costs.

Unemployment, Growth, and the Future
Unemployment and underemployment. A growing economy. Real-world applications.

The "Isms"
Pure capitalism. The command economy. Mixed systems. The traditional economy.

LAST WORD Operation Desert Storm and Iraq's Production Possibilities

3 PURE CAPITALISM AND THE CIRCULAR FLOW *35*

Capitalist Ideology
Private property. Freedom of enterprise and choice. Role of self-interest. Competition. Markets and prices. Limited government.

Other Characteristics
Extensive use of capital goods. Specialization and efficiency. Division of labor. Geographic specialization. Specialization and comparative advantage. Use of money.

The Circular Flow Model
Resource and product markets. Limitations.

LAST WORD Back to Barter

4 UNDERSTANDING INDIVIDUAL MARKETS: DEMAND AND SUPPLY *47*

Markets Defined

Demand
Law of demand. The demand curve. Individual and market demand. Determinants of demand. Changes in demand. Changes in quantity demanded.

Supply
Law of supply. The supply curve. Determinants of supply. Changes in supply. Changes in quantity supplied.

Supply and Demand: Market Equilibrium
Surpluses. Shortages. Equilibrium. Rationing function of prices. Changes in supply and demand. The resource market. "Other things equal" revisited.

Application: The Foreign Exchange Market
The dollar-yen market. Changing rates: depreciation and appreciation. Economic consequences.

LAST WORD The High Price of Marijuana

5 THE PRIVATE SECTORS AND THE MARKET SYSTEM *67*

Households as Income Receivers
The functional distribution of income. Personal distribution of income.

Households as Spenders
Personal taxes. Personal saving. Personal consumption expenditures.
The Business Population
Legal Forms of Business Enterprises
Sole proprietorship. Partnership. Corporation. Incorporate or not?
Industrial Distribution and Bigness
Types of industries. Big business.
The Foreign Sector
Volume, pattern, and linkages. Economic implications.
The Competitive Market System
The Five Fundamental Questions
The Market System at Work
Determining what is to be produced. Organizing production. Distributing total output. Accommodating change. Competition and control: the "invisible hand." The case for the market system.
LAST WORD The Financing of Corporate Activity

6 THE PUBLIC SECTOR *88*

Economic Functions of Government
Legal and Social Framework
Maintaining Competition
Redistribution of Income
Reallocation of Resources
Spillovers or externalities. Public goods and services. Allocating resources to public goods. Stabilization.
The Circular Flow Revisited
Government Finance
Government growth: purchases and transfers. Some causes.
Federal Finance
Federal expenditures. Federal receipts.
State and Local Finance
State expenditures and receipts. Local expenditures and receipts. Fiscal federalism.
LAST WORD Lotteries: Facts and Controversies

PART 2

MICROECONOMICS OF PRODUCT AND RESOURCE MARKETS

7 DEMAND AND SUPPLY: ELASTICITIES AND APPLICATIONS *105*

Price Elasticity of Demand
The price elasticity formula. Refinement: midpoints formula. Graphical analysis. The total-revenue test. Determinants of price elasticity of demand. Some practical applications.
Price Elasticity of Supply
Cross and Income Elasticity of Demand
Cross elasticity of demand. Income elasticity of demand.
Applications: Legal Prices
Price ceilings and shortages. Price floors and surpluses. Recapitulation.
LAST WORD The Troublesome Market for Health Care

8 CONSUMER BEHAVIOR AND UTILITY MAXIMIZATION *124*

Two Explanations of the Law of Demand
Income and substitution effects. Law of diminishing marginal utility.
Theory of Consumer Behavior
Consumer choice and budget restraint. Utility-maximizing rule. Algebraic restatement.
Marginal Utility and the Demand Curve
The Time Dimension
The value of time. Some implications.
LAST WORD The Water–Diamond Paradox
Appendix to Chapter 8: Indifference Curve Analysis

9 THE COSTS OF PRODUCTION *140*

Economic Costs
Explicit and implicit costs. Normal profits as a cost. Economic, or pure, profits. Short run and long run.
Production Costs in the Short Run
Law of diminishing returns. Fixed, variable, and total costs. Per unit, or average, costs. Marginal cost. Shifting the cost curves.
Production Costs in the Long Run
Firm size and costs. The long-run cost curve. Economies and diseconomies of scale. MES and industry structure.
LAST WORD Economies of Scale and Industrial Concentration

10 PRICE AND OUTPUT DETERMINATION: PURE COMPETITION *160*

Prelude: Four Market Models
Pure Competition: Concept and Occurrence
Demand to a Competitive Seller
Perfectly elastic demand. Average, total, and marginal revenue. Graphical portrayal.
Profit Maximization in the Short Run: Two Approaches
Total-revenue–total-cost approach. Marginal-revenue–marginal-cost approach. Marginal cost and the short-run supply curve. Recapitulation. Firm and industry: equilibrium price.
Profit Maximization in the Long Run
Assumptions and goal. Zero-profit model. Entry of firms eliminates profits. Exodus of firms

eliminates losses. Long-run supply for a constant-cost industry. Long-run supply for an increasing-cost industry. Long-run supply for a decreasing-cost industry.

Pure Competition and Efficiency
Qualifications.

LAST WORD The Theory of Contestable Markets

11 PRICE AND OUTPUT DETERMINATION: PURE MONOPOLY *187*

Pure Monopoly: An Introduction
Characteristics. Examples. Importance.

Barriers to Entry
Economies of scale. Public utilities: natural monopolies. Legal barriers: patents and licenses. Ownership of essential resources. Two implications.

Monopoly Demand
Price exceeds marginal revenue. Price maker. Price elasticity.

Output and Price Determination
Cost data. MR = MC rule. No monopoly supply curve. Misconceptions concerning monopoly pricing.

Economic Effects of Monopoly
Price, output, and resource allocation. Income distribution. Cost complications. Technological progress: dynamic efficiency.

Price Discrimination
Conditions. Illustrations. Consequences.

Regulated Monopoly.
Socially optimal price: P = MC. "Fair-return" price: P = AC. Dilemma of regulation.

LAST WORD Monopolies in the National Parks

12 PRICE AND OUTPUT DETERMINATION: MONOPOLISTIC COMPETITION *207*

Monopolistic Competition: Concept and Occurrence
Relatively large numbers. Product differentiation. Nonprice competition. Easy entry. Illustrations.

Price and Output Determination
The firm's demand curve. The short run: profits or losses. The long run: break even.

Wastes of Monopolistic Competition
Excess capacity. Redeeming features?

Nonprice Competition
Product differentiation and product development.

The Economics of Advertising
Controversy and scope. Two views. Empirical evidence.

Monopolistic competition and economic analysis.

LAST WORD The Market for Principles of Economics Textbooks

13 PRICE AND OUTPUT DETERMINATION: OLIGOPOLY *220*

Oligopoly: Concept and Occurrence
Oligopoly defined. Underlying causes.

Oligopoly Behavior: A Game Theory Overview
Mutual interdependence. Collusive tendencies. Incentive to cheat.

Four Oligopoly Models
Kinked demand: noncollusive oligopoly. Collusion and cartels. Price leadership. Cost-plus pricing.

Role of Nonprice Competition

Oligopoly and Economic Efficiency
Allocative and productive efficiency. Dynamic efficiency. Technological progress: the evidence.

Automobiles: A Case Study

LAST WORD The Beer Industry: Oligopoly Brewing?

14 PRODUCTION AND THE DEMAND FOR RESOURCES *240*

Significance of Resource Pricing

Complexities of Resource Pricing

Marginal Productivity Theory of Resource Demand
Resource demand as a derived demand. Marginal revenue product (MRP). Rule for employing resources: MRP = MRC. MRP is a demand schedule. Resource demand under imperfect competition. Market demand for a resource.

Determinants of Resource Demand
Changes in product demand. Productivity changes. Prices of other resources.

Elasticity of Resource Demand

Optimal Combination of Resources
The least-cost rule. The profit-maximizing rule. Numerical illustration.

Marginal Productivity Theory of Income Distribution

LAST WORD Input Substitution: The Case of Cabooses

15 THE PRICING AND EMPLOYMENT OF RESOURCES: WAGE DETERMINATION *255*

Meaning of Wages

General Level of Wages
Role of productivity. Real wages and productivity. Secular growth.

Wages in Particular Labor Markets
Competitive model. Monopsony model. Some union models. Wage increases and unemployment. Bilateral monopoly model. The minimum-wage controversy.

Wage Differentials
Noncompeting groups. Equalizing differences. Market imperfections.

Pay and Performance
The principal–agent problem. Equilibrium revisited.
LAST WORD Pay and Performance in Professional Baseball

16 THE PRICING AND EMPLOYMENT OF RESOURCES: RENT, INTEREST, AND PROFITS *275*

Economic Rent
Perfectly inelastic supply. Changes in demand. Land rent is a surplus. A single tax on land. Productivity differences. Alternative uses and costs.
Interest
Loanable funds theory of interest. Range of rates. Role of the interest rate.
Economic Profits
Role of the entrepreneur. Sources of economic profit. Functions of profits.
Income Shares
Current shares. Historical trends.
LAST WORD Determining the Price of Credit

17 GENERAL EQUILIBRIUM: THE MARKET SYSTEM AND ITS OPERATION *290*

Partial and General Equilibrium
General Equilibrium: A Two-Industry Model
Behind the curves. Initial conditions. Short-run adjustments. Long-run adjustments. Further adjustments. Efficiency implications.
General Equilibrium: Input-Output Analysis
Input-output table. Interdependence.
Market Interrelationships: OPEC and Oil Prices
The United States economy. The world economy.
Market Implications of an Aging Population
Product market. Labor market.
LAST WORD The English Cotton Famine

PART 3

GOVERNMENT AND CURRENT ECONOMIC PROBLEMS

18 GOVERNMENT AND MARKET FAILURE: PUBLIC GOODS, THE ENVIRONMENT, AND INFORMATION PROBLEMS *303*

Public Goods: Extending the Analysis
Demand for public goods. Optimal quantity of a public good. Benefit-cost analysis. Measurement problems.
Externalities Revisited
Individual bargaining. Liability rules and lawsuits. Direct controls and taxes. A market for externality rights. Society's optimal amount of externality reduction.
Pollution: A Closer Look
Dimensions of the problem. Causes: the law of conservation of matter and energy. Antipollution policy. Solid-waste disposal and recycling.
Information Failures
Inadequate information about sellers. Inadequate information about buyers. Qualification.
LAST WORD Used Cars: The Market for "Lemons"

19 PUBLIC CHOICE THEORY AND TAXATION *323*

Revealing Preferences through Majority Voting
Inefficient voting outcomes. The paradox of voting. Median-voter model.
Public Sector Failure
Special interests and "rent seeking." Clear benefits, hidden costs. Limited choice. Bureaucracy and inefficiency. Imperfect institutions.
Apportioning the Tax Burden
Benefits received versus ability to pay. Progressive, proportional, and regressive taxes.
Tax Incidence and Efficiency Loss
Elasticity and tax incidence. Efficiency loss of a tax. Probable incidence of U.S. taxes. The American tax structure.
Tax Issues
Taxes and reindustrialization. Cutting the budget deficit.
The Issue of Freedom
The conservative position. The liberal stance.
LAST WORD Rent Seeking, Tax Reform, and the Special-Interest Effect

20 ANTITRUST AND REGULATION *343*

Industrial Concentration: Definitions
Industrial Concentration: Beneficial or Harmful?
The case against industrial concentration. Defenses of industrial concentration.
The Antitrust Laws
Historical background. Sherman Act of 1890. Clayton Act of 1914. Federal Trade Commission Act of 1914. Celler-Kefauver Act of 1950.
Antitrust: Issues and Impact
Behavior or structure? Defining the market. Effectiveness. Restricting competition.
Natural Monopolies and Their Regulation
Natural monopoly. Problems. Legal cartel theory.

Deregulation: The Case of the Airlines
Controversy. Effects of Airline Deregulation.
Social Regulation
Distinguishing features. Costs and criticisms. Economic implications. In support of social regulation.
LAST WORD Does the United States Need an Industrial Policy?

21 AGRICULTURE: ECONOMICS AND POLICY *362*

The Economics of Agriculture
Short-run problem: price and income instability. Long-run problem: a declining industry.
The Economics of Farm Policy
Size and rationale. Background: the parity concept. Price supports. Coping with surpluses.
Criticisms of Farm Policy
Symptoms and causes. Misguided subsidies. Policy contradictions. Declining effectiveness.
The Politics of Farm Policy
Public choice theory revisited. New directions?
World Trade and Farm Policy
Policy impacts. GATT negotiations. Farm Act of 1990. Market-oriented income stabilization.
Global View: Feast or Famine?
LAST WORD The Sugar Program: A Sweet Deal

22 INCOME INEQUALITY AND POVERTY *378*

Income Inequality: The Facts
Personal income distribution. Trends in income inequality. The Lorenz curve.
Alternative Interpretations
Broadened income concept. Lifetime income.
Government and Redistribution.
Income Inequality: Causes
Equality versus Efficiency
The case for equality: maximizing utility. The case for inequality: incentives and efficiency. The equality–efficiency tradeoff.
The Dismal Economics of Poverty
Defining poverty. Who are the poor? Poverty trends. A "black underclass"? The "invisible" poor.
The Income Maintenance System
Social insurance programs. Public assistance programs. "The welfare mess."
Reform Proposals
Negative income tax. Workfare plans.
LAST WORD The Causes of Growing Income Inequality

23 LABOR-MARKET ISSUES: UNIONISM, DISCRIMINATION, AND IMMIGRATION *396*

Brief History of American Unionism
Repression phase: 1790 to 1930. Encouragement phase: 1930 to 1947. Intervention phase: 1947 to date.
Unionism's Decline
Collective Bargaining
The bargaining process. The work agreement.
The Economic Effects of Unions
The union wage advantage. Efficiency and productivity. Distribution of earnings. Unions and inflation.
Discrimination
Dimensions of discrimination. Occupational segregation: the crowding model. Costs of discrimination. Addenda.
Immigration
History and policy. Economics of immigration. Complications and modifications. Economics and beyond.
LAST WORD Racism in Professional Basketball?

PART 4

INTERNATIONAL ECONOMICS AND THE WORLD ECONOMY

24 INTERNATIONAL TRADE: COMPARATIVE ADVANTAGE AND PROTECTIONISM *421*

Importance of World Trade
Volume and pattern. Unique aspects.
The Economic Basis for Trade
Specialization and Comparative Advantage
The basic principle. Two isolated nations. Specializing according to comparative advantage. Terms of trade. The gains from trade. Increasing costs. The case for free trade restated.
Trade Barriers
Motivations: special-interest effect. Economic impact of tariffs. Economic impact of quotas.
The Case for Protection: A Critical Review
Military self-sufficiency argument. Increase domestic employment. Diversification for stability. Infant-industry argument. Protection against "dumping." Cheap foreign labor. A summing up.
International Trade Policies
Reciprocal Trade Act and GATT. Economic integration. Protectionism reborn.
LAST WORD Petition of the Candlemakers, 1845

25 EXCHANGE RATES, THE BALANCE OF PAYMENTS, AND TRADE DEFICITS *444*

Financing International Trade
American export transaction. America import transaction.

The International Balance of Payments
Current account. Capital account. Interrelationships. Official reserves. Payments deficits and surpluses. Deficits and surpluses: bad or good?

Exchange Rate Systems and Balance of Payments Adjustments
Freely floating exchange rates. Fixed exchange rates.

International Exchange Rate Systems
The gold standard: fixed exchange rates. The Bretton Woods system. The managed float.

Recent United States' Trade Deficits
Causes of the trade deficits. Effects of U.S. trade deficits. Reducing the trade deficit.

LAST WORD Buy American: The Global Refrigerator

26 THE SOVIET ECONOMY IN TRANSITION *469*

Ideology and Institutions
Marxian ideology. Institutions.

Central Planning and Its Problems
Ends and means. The coordination problem.

The Failure of Soviet Communism
Causes of the collapse.

The Gorbachev Reforms

Transition to a Market System
Privatization. Promotion of competition. Limited and reoriented role for government. Price reform: removing controls. Joining the world economy. Macroeconomic stability.

Can the Transition Be Implemented?
Technical problems. Public support: attitudes and values. The political problem: national disintegration. The simultaneity problem. Positive factors.

Role of Advanced Capitalist Nations
Foreign aid. Private investment. Membership in international institutions.

Prospects

LAST WORD Obituary: The Soviet Union

Glossary *G-1*

Index *I-1*

PREFACE

The publication of the twelfth edition of *Economics* (and its accompanying editions of *Macroeconomics* and *Microeconomics*) follows the most successful edition of this book to date. Naturally, we are pleased that *Economics* continues to be the best selling economics text in the United States. Moreover, we are pleasantly surprised that the Russian translation of *Economics* will soon be the leading economics text in the former Soviet Union; Politizdat Press has taken orders for nearly 500,000 copies. This fact dramatizes how remarkable these times are for teaching and learning economics! The message of our day is clear: People who comprehend economic principles will have a great advantage functioning in, and making sense of, the emerging world. We express our sincere thanks to each of you using *Microeconomics* for granting us a modest role in your efforts to teach or learn this globally important subject.

THE REVISION

This edition of *Microeconomics* has been thoroughly revised, polished, and updated. Many of the changes have been motivated by the comments of 36 reviewers and another 13 participants in focus groups. We are especially grateful to these scholars and acknowledge them by name at the end of this preface.

We strive only for an overview of the changes in this edition here; chapter-by-chapter details are provided in the *Instructor's Resource Manual* accompanying this book.

Consolidation of Introductory Chapters

Responding to reviewer suggestions, we have reduced the number of introductory chapters from eight to six, allowing for a quicker start into microeconomic theory. The previous edition's Chapters 5 and 7 are consolidated into new Chapter 5 and old Chapters 6 and 8 are combined into new Chapter 6. Parts of the material on taxation in old Chapter 8 are now found in new Chapter 19, which treats public choice and tax analysis. We have resisted the temptation to compress the introductory material even further, believing that most students inadequately understand the characteristics of capitalism (Chapter 3), the functioning of the market system (Chapter 5), and the extensive role of government in the modern economy (Chapter 6). A strong introduction helps students understand and apply microeconomic theory. We believe we have provided such an introduction, but now in a more expeditious form.

New Topics and Analysis

Much attention has been given to applying economics to the major issues of our day. Also, this edition contains new formal economic analyses. Examples of new discussions and analyses include:

- **Early introduction of comparative advantage theory.** In an optional new section in Chapter 3, we use production possibilities tables to illustrate comparative advantage. By combining this new material with Chapter 4's optional discussion of exchange rates, instructors can effectively introduce international economics early in the course.
- **Economics and the environment.** Chapter 18 is a new chapter on government and market failure. This chapter extends Chapter 6's discussion of externalities by examining the Coase theorem, liability rules and lawsuits, markets for externality rights, and society's optimal amount of externality abatement. A case study of pollution examines the dimensions, causes, and solutions of this problem. Special attention is given to the Superfund law, the Clean Air Act of 1990, and solid waste disposal and recycling.
- **Economics of information.** A lengthy new section of Chapter 18 looks at market failure associated with inadequate information by buyers about sellers

and by sellers about buyers. Topics such as adverse selection and moral hazard are included here. Also, Chapter 12's discussion of advertising is completely rewritten to highlight advertising's informational role. The idea of imperfect information in decision making is introduced *early* in the book; Chapter 1's Last Word uses the economic perspective to analyze how customers decide which fast-food line to enter.

- **Strategic behavior.** Game theory—specifically the prisoner's dilemma model—is presented in the discussion of oligopoly (Chapter 13). Also, Chapter 24 contains a discussion of strategic international trade policy.
- **Public choice and tax analysis.** A full chapter (Chapter 19) is devoted to public choice and tax analysis. Also, we have placed much more emphasis on public choice theory in our explanation of the persistence of agricultural subsidies in Chapter 21, a chapter which has been extensively revised and updated.
- **Principal–agent problem and pay for performance.** A new section of the chapter on wage determination (Chapter 15) explains the principal–agent problem and discusses pay for performance plans (piece rates, commissions and royalties, bonuses and profit sharing), seniority pay, and efficiency wages.
- **The economics of an aging American population.** Chapter 17 on general equilibrium traces the myriad implications of an aging American population.
- **Soviet economy in transition.** A completely rewritten chapter (Chapter 26) presents an up-to-date, thorough analysis of the present crisis and reform efforts in the former Soviet Union.
- **Other new discussions.** There are numerous other new discussions in this edition, a few examples being: cross and income elasticities; rent controls; the absence of a monopoly supply curve; the Herfindahl index; growing inequality in the distribution of income; consolidation in the airline industry; immigration reform; world trade and farm policy; the Farm Act of 1990; the economic impact of import quotas; the proposed North American free-trade zone; Uruguay Round negotiations; and the purchasing power parity theory of exchange rates.

New Last Words

Reviewers indicate that they appreciate the Last Word minireadings and their placement toward the conclusion of each chapter. These selections serve several purposes: Some provide current or historical real-world applications of economic concepts; others reveal human-interest aspects of economic problems; and still others present economic concepts or issues in a global context. Thirteen Last Words are new and others have been extensively revised and updated.

We have selected Last Word topics that are both highly relevant to the chapter's discussion *and* interesting to the reader. New topics are: fast-food lines viewed from the economic perspective (Chapter 1); the impact of Operation Desert Storm on Iraqi production possibilities (Chapter 2); the increasing use of barter (Chapter 3); the effect of supply interdiction on the price of marijuana (Chapter 4); the market for health care (Chapter 7); monopoly in the national parks (Chapter 11); product differentiation and nonprice competition in the market for economics textbooks (Chapter 12); the market for "lemons" (Chapter 18); the special interest effect as reflected in the Tax Reform Act of 1986 (Chapter 19); causes of greater income inequality (Chapter 22); possible discrimination in professional basketball (Chapter 23); the difficulties of "buying American" when many product components are imported (Chapter 25); and an obituary of the Soviet Union (Chapter 26).

Pedagogical Improvements

The principles course has become increasingly demanding for students. Globalization of economies, developments in economic theory, and modern economic problems have added new, sometimes complex material to the course. Concise and understandable explanations are more important than ever before. Accordingly, we have directed much effort toward improving the pedagogy of *Microeconomics*. We have "gone back to the basics," attempting to bolster what we believe to be this book's comparative advantages: its readability and accessibility. Examples of our pedagogical changes include:

- **Quick Reviews within each chapter.** Two or three new reviews within the body of each chapter allow the student to pause and ponder key points. We believe these Quick Reviews will also help students as they study for examinations.
- **Key Graphs.** Students often have a difficult time distinguishing which of the hundreds of graphs in economics are of fundamental importance. To direct students' attention to the essential graphs, we have designated 14 figures as Key Graphs. These graphs are specially designed and labeled to make them easily identifiable. Figures 2-1 and 4-5 are representative. A complete listing of the Key Graphs can be found in the Brief Table of Contents on page ix–x.

- **Motivational introductions.** In many chapters new introductions are added to stimulate reader interest in the chapter's contents. These introductions relate to students' everyday experiences and observations. The opening material for Chapters 2, 6, 8, 16, and 24 is illustrative.
- **Full-color layout.** The full range of colors in the designer's palette makes for a more interesting text and is used functionally to clarify many graphs and diagrams.
- **Functional use of color photos.** Unobtrusive chapter-opening photos are employed as "teasers" for the content of the Last Words, where larger photos are found. The front and back photos visually unite the beginning and ends of the chapters and are designed to spark reader interest in the Last Words.
- **Shorter paragraphs.** In keeping with trends in popular and academic publishing, we have shortened scores of long paragraphs.
- **Tighter sentences.** The two authors and a talented McGraw-Hill editor scrutinized every sentence in the book for unnecessary verbiage. Collectively, we were able to tighten hundreds of sentences without altering the overall style of writing. In economizing on words, we were careful *not* to reduce the thoroughness of our explanations. Where needed, the "extra sentence of explanation" remains a distinguishing characteristic of *Microeconomics*.
- **Numbered lists and added subheads.** We have substituted numbered and labeled lists for verbal strings of "First," "Second," and "Third." The idea here is to break material into smaller parcels to help students more readily retain the content. Similarly, we have used subheads more liberally so the organizational structure of each chapter and topic will be clearer for readers.
- **Footnote deletion.** We have significantly reduced the number of footnotes. Several lengthy explanatory footnotes have been deleted; a number of shorter footnotes have been integrated into the text. Footnotes suggesting additional reading have been judiciously pruned.
- **Added labeling in graphs.** Taking great care to avoid clutter, in a number of cases we have added labeling in figures to help guide the reader through the analysis. These labels are set in strong type so they are highly readable both within the book and on transparencies.
- **New diagrams.** Some of the added diagrams depict new graphical analyses such as the possible effects of advertising on demand and marginal revenue curves (Chapter 13), the economics of recycling (Figure 18-4), and a comparison of the effects of tariffs and quotas (Figure 24-3). Other new diagrams should help students visualize the interrelations of the concepts involved. Examples of these diagrams are Figures 12-2, 19-1, and 20-1.
- **Clarified explanations of difficult subject matter.** We have continued to look for ways to explain difficult material more clearly. Even minor improvements in language or labeling of graphs can often help students better understand the material. Improvements of this sort have been made in numerous places throughout the text. Good examples are our revised discussions of efficiency (Chapter 2), the relationship between the demand curve and total revenue (Chapter 11), the efficiency effects of oligopoly (Chapter 13), and efficiency losses of taxes (Chapter 19).

New and Enhanced Ancillaries

The ancillaries in this edition's package are discussed later in this Preface, but three new items are noteworthy.

- **Test Bank III.** New to the *Microeconomics* package is a test bank allowing an alternative testing approach to the predominantly multiple-choice questions in Test Banks I and II. Written by Professors William Walstad and Joyce Gleason, Test Bank III contains questions that emphasize "constructive response" concepts. Students are more actively involved in creating answers to these questions, which provide a valuable alternative to conventional test questions.
- **Augmented Test Bank I.** We have added approximately 1200 questions to the microeconomic version of Test Bank I.
- **Revised software.** The successful *Concept Master* software introduced with the previous edition has been completely updated. This software is directly tied to the contents of *Microeconomics.*

We trust that the outcome of this detailed revision effort is a text and package that are clearly superior to their predecessors.

FUNDAMENTAL GOALS

The basic purpose of *Microeconomics* continues to be to introduce the beginning economics student to those principles essential to an understanding of the fundamental economic problem and the policy alternatives available for dealing with this problem. We hope that the ability to reason accurately and objectively about economic matters and the development of a lasting interest in economics will be two valuable by-products of this basic objective. Our intention remains to present the principles and problems of economics in a straightforward, logical fashion. To this end, we continue to put great stress on clarity of presentation and on logical organization.

PRODUCT DIFFERENTIATION

This text embraces a number of features which perhaps distinguish it from other books in the field.

- **Comprehensive explanations at an appropriate level.** We have attempted to craft a comprehensive, analytical text that is challenging to better students, yet accessible—with appropriate hard work—to average students. We think the thoroughness and accessibility of *Microeconomics* enables the instructor to select topics for special classroom emphasis with confidence that students can independently read and comprehend other assigned material in the book.
- **Comprehensive definition of economics.** The principles course sometimes fails to provide students with a comprehensive and meaningful definition of economics. To avoid this shortcoming, all of Chapter 2 is devoted to a careful statement and development of the economizing problem and an exploration of its implications. This foundation should help put the many particular subject areas of economics in proper perspective.
- **Early integration of international economics.** Comparative advantage is discussed in detail in Chapter 3, exchange rates are explained as an application of supply and demand in Chapter 4, and the international trade sector of the American economy is highlighted in Chapter 5. This strong introduction to international economics permits "globalization" of later discussions of microeconomics, where appropriate. The Table of Contents highlights sections in all chapters with substantial global content.
- **Early treatment of government.** For better or worse, government is an integral component of modern capitalism. Its economic role, therefore, should not be treated piecemeal or as an afterthought. This text introduces the economic functions of government early and accords them systematic treatment in Chapter 6. Chapter 18 examines government and market failure in further detail and Chapter 19 looks at salient facets of public choice theory and public finance. Also, this text has several problem- and policy-oriented chapters in which government's role is explored.
- **Resurgence of the market system.** Economies the world over are making the difficult transition from planning to markets. Our emphasis on general equilibrium analysis and the market *system* is thus even more relevant in this edition than in the prior one. A major portion of Chapter 5 is devoted to the interrelationships within the market system, and Chapter 17 explicitly outlines the nature and significance of general equilibrium analysis.
- **Emphasis on the theory of the firm.** We have purposely given much attention to the theory of the firm for two reasons: First, marginal analysis is difficult for most beginning students. Short expositions usually compound these difficulties by raising more questions than they answer. Second, we have coupled analysis of the various market structures with a discussion of the impact of each market arrangement on price, output levels, resource allocation, and the rate of technological advance.
- **Chapters on economic issues.** As most students see it, Part 3 on micro-oriented problems is where the action is. We have sought to guide the action along logical lines through the application of appropriate analytical tools. Our bias in these parts is in favor of inclusiveness; each instructor can effectively counter this bias by omitting those chapters felt to be less relevant for a particular group of students.

ORGANIZATION AND CONTENT

We believe that the basic prerequisite of an understandable economics text is the logical arrangement and clear exposition of subject matter. This book has been organized so that the exposition of each particular topic and concept is directly related to the level of difficulty which in our experience the average student is likely to encounter. For this reason the relationship between production analysis and cost curves, price-output decisions of firms, and analysis of resource markets are given comprehensive and careful treatments. Simplicity here is correlated with comprehensiveness, not brevity. A three-step development of basic analytical tools is employed: (1) verbal descriptions and illustrations; (2) numerical examples; and (3) graphical presentation based on these numerical illustrations.

The material in this book is organized into four basic parts. They are: Part 1: An Introduction to Economics and the Economy; Part 2: Microeconomics of Product and Resource Markets; Part 3: Government and Current Economic Problems; and Part 4: International Economics and the World Economy. The Table of Contents lists the specific chapters in each part and details the contents within each chapter.

STUDENT FRIENDLY: STUDY AIDS

Microeconomics is highly student oriented.

1 Students who are comfortable with graphical analysis and a few related quantitative concepts are in an advantageous position to understand principles of economics. With this in mind, an appendix to Chapter 1 carefully reviews graphing, line slopes, and linear equations.

2 The introductory paragraphs of each chapter state objectives, present an organizational overview of the chapter, and relate the chapter to what has been covered before and what will follow.

3 Because a significant portion of any introductory course is devoted to terminology, terms are given special emphasis. In particular, each important term is in **boldface type** where it first appears in each chapter. We have tried to make all definitions clear and succinct. At the end of each chapter all new terms are listed in the "Terms and Concepts" section. Finally, at the end of the book is a comprehensive glossary. This glossary also is contained in the *Study Guide* which accompanies *Microeconomics.*

4 As we noted earlier, each chapter contains two or three "Quick Reviews" at appropriate places in the chapter to reinforce key points for students and help them study for examinations.

5 Figures worthy of intensive study are given special design treatment and designated as "Key Graphs."

6 The legends accompanying all diagrams are written so they are self-contained analyses of the relevant concepts shown. This is a strategic means of reinforcing student comprehension.

7 Much thought has gone into the end-of-chapter questions. Though purposely intermixed, the questions are of three general types. Some are designed to highlight the main points of each chapter. Others are "open-end" discussion, debate, or thought questions. Wherever pertinent, numerical problems which require the student to derive and manipulate key concepts and relationships are employed. Numerical problems are stressed in those chapters which deal with analytical material. Some optional "advanced analysis" questions accompany certain theory chapters. These problems usually involve the stating and manipulation of certain basic concepts in equation form. Answers to *all* end-of-chapter questions—both quantitative and essay—are provided in the *Instructor's Resource Manual.*

8 Many of the end-of-chapter questions deal with subject matter that is reinforced by the excellent computerized tutorial, *Concept Master II,* that accompanies the text. A floppy disk symbol appears in conjunction with questions whose content correlates to the tutorial program.

9 In addition to its considerable esthetic merit, the multicolor format of *Microeconomics* stresses the use of color so students will more quickly and easily perceive the ideas expressed in each diagram and chart.

INSTRUCTOR FRIENDLY: THE SUPPLEMENTS

Microeconomics is accompanied by supplements which we feel equal or surpass competing texts in terms of both quantity and quality.

Study Guide

Professor William Walstad has prepared a new revision of the *Study Guide* to accompany *Microeconomics* which many students find to be an indispensable aid. It contains for each chapter an introductory statement, a checklist of behavioral objectives, an outline, a list of important terms, fill-in questions, problems and projects, objective questions, and discussion questions. The glossary found at the end of *Microeconomics* also appears in the *Study Guide.*

In this revision, Professor Walstad has added text page references for every question (true-false, multiple-choice, and discussion); has extensively revised the chapter learning objectives to add more detail; and has added discussion sections to the chapter outlines. He has also increased the number of multiple-choice questions for each chapter, and has increased the number of problems and projects for further study. The *Guide* comprises, in our opinion, a superb "portable tutor" for the principles student.

Economic Concepts

Economic Concepts provides carefully designed programmed materials for all the key analytical areas of the principles course. Revised by Professor W. H. Pope for use with *Microeconomics,* it can be used as an effective supplement with any mainstream text.

Instructor's Resource Manual

Professor Joyce Gleason of Nebraska Wesleyan University has revised and updated the *Instructor's Resource Manual.* It comprises chapter summaries, listings of "what's new" in each chapter, teaching tips and suggestions, learning objectives, chapter outlines, data and visual aid sources with suggestions for classroom use, and questions and problems. Answers to all the text's end-of-chapter questions are also found in the *Manual.*

The new edition of the *Manual* includes a full, chapter-by-chapter overview of all changes in the revision. Also, the chapter outlines have been consolidated into a separate section of the *Manual,* so they can more readily be used as a resource in classroom lectures. We think instructors will find this *Manual* useful and timesaving.

Available again in this edition is a computerized version of the *Manual,* suitable for use with IBM-PC computers, IBM-PC compatibles, and Macintosh computers. The version for IBM-PCs and compatibles is available in both $5\frac{1}{4}$-inch and $3\frac{1}{2}$-inch formats. Users of *Microeconomics* can now print out portions of the *Manual's* contents, complete with their own additions or alterations, for use as student handouts or in whatever ways they might wish. This capability includes printing answers to all end-of-chapter questions.

As with the *Study Guide,* a separate edition of the *Instructor's Resource Manual* has been prepared to correspond with the paperback edition of the text. Users of *Economics* or *Microeconomics* will find that the material in the accompanying *Manual* correlates with the chapter sequencing in the text.

Three Test Banks

Microeconomics is supplemented by two test banks of objective, predominantly multiple-choice, questions and a new test bank of short essay and problem-type questions.

Test Bank I now comprises over 2900 questions, all written by the text authors; approximately 2200 are carried over from the previous edition and 700 have been prepared by the authors for the new edition.

Test Bank II, revised by Professor Walstad, contains approximately 2300 questions. For all test items in these two test banks, the nature of each question is identified (e.g., G, graphical; C, complex analysis) as are the pages in the text containing the material which is the basis for each question. Also, each chapter in *Test Banks I* and *II* has an outline or table of contents which groups questions by topics.

New to this edition, *Test Bank III* will emphasize "constructive response" testing to evaluate student understanding in a manner different from conventional multiple-choice and true-false questions. Prepared by Professors Walstad and Gleason, this unique resource emphasizes short-answer and essay questions designed to enhance critical thinking skills.

Adopters of *Microeconomics* will be able to use this sizable number of questions, organized into three test banks of equal quality, with maximum flexibility. The fact that the text authors and *Study Guide* authors have prepared all the test items will assure the fullest possible correlation with the content of the text.

As with the *Study Guide* and *Instructor's Resource Manual,* a separate version of the test banks has been prepared to correspond with *Microeconomics.*

Computerized testing *Test Banks I, II,* and, *III* are available in computerized versions, as well as print. Computerized test generation will be available for IBM-PCs and compatibles, and for MacIntosh computers. All these systems include the capability to produce high-quality graphics from the test banks.

These systems will also feature the ability to generate multiple tests, with versions "scrambled" to be distinctive, and will have other useful features. They will meet the various needs of the widest spectrum of computer users.

Color transparencies Full color transparencies for overhead projectors have been prepared especially for *Microeconomics.* These encompass all the figures which appear in *Microeconomics* and are available on request to adopters.

Student software For users of IBM-PCs and compatibles, a student software package *Concept Master II,* has been prepared by Professor William Gunther of the University of Alabama and Irene Gunther. The previous version of this software was widely praised by its users, and it has been improved to provide even more flexibility. It provides the most extensive and varied computer-assisted study material of any software package available.

Over twelve graphics-based tutorial programs provide an opportunity for students to study key topics in the book in an interactive fashion. The tutorial programs are linked to the text. Selected end-of-chapter questions that relate to the content of one of the tutorial programs are highlighted by a floppy disk symbol. The questions themselves are not necessarily contained within the tutorial program, but the tutorial does contain material that relates directly to the concepts underlying the highlighted questions.

In addition to the tutorial programs, students can quiz themselves with a self-testing program accompanying each test chapter. The package also features three microeconomic simulation games. Some of the simulations are elementary, and others are more complex. Wherever possible, they include a global perspective. Also included in the package are a list of key terms, a pop-up calculator for computations, and a section that uses the "Key Graphs" in the text to direct students to the appropriate tutorial lesson.

For users of Macintosh computers, there is an exciting tutorial program, *DiscoverEcon.* Developed by Professors Gerald Nelson and Wesley Seitz of the University of Illinois, this innovative package uses Apple's HYPERCARD programming environment to produce an extremely interactive learning experience. Dynamic shifts of curves, screen animation, sound effects, and simple-to-use command keys are features of this program.

Videodisks New to this edition are videodisks designed to harness this exciting new technology for classroom presentation. These videodisks offer an array of graphical illustrations of key economic concepts to further student understanding.

Videos New videotape materials have been assembled for this edition, to illustrate fundamental concepts and economic issues in a manner that will be equally effective in classroom settings or media resource centers. Among these materials is the new "MacNeil/Lehrer Quarterly Report on Economics", an exciting new series of excerpts from the acclaimed PBS news program, "The MacNeil/Lehrer Newshour". Your local McGraw-Hill representative can provide details on all new video ancillaries for the text.

DEBTS

The publication of this edition of *Microeconomics* will extend the life of *Economics* well into its fourth decade. The acceptance of *Economics,* which was generous from the outset, has expanded with each edition. This gracious reception has no doubt been fostered by the many teachers and students who have been kind enough to provide their suggestions and criticisms.

Our colleagues at the University of Nebraska–Lincoln and Pacific Lutheran University have generously shared knowledge of their specialties with us and have provided encouragement. We are especially indebted to Professors Harish Gupta, Jerry Petr, David Rosenbaum, and Norris Peterson, who have been most helpful in offsetting our comparative ignorance in their areas of specialty.

As indicated, this edition has benefited from a number of perceptive reviews. In both quantity and quality, they provided the richest possible source of suggestions for this revision. These contributors are listed at the end of this Preface.

Professors Thomas P. Barbiero and W. H. Pope of Ryerson Polytechnical Institute in their role as coauthors of the Canadian edition of *Economics* have provided innumerable suggestions for improvement. Thanks also go to Professor Lovewell who coded the new *Test Bank* items by type of questions and identified the corresponding text page number for all the items.

We are greatly indebted to the many professionals at McGraw-Hill—and in particular Phil Galea, Annette Mayeski, and Karen Jackson—for their expertise in the production and distribution of the book. Joe Piliero has given the book its unique design. Safra Nimrod and Debra Hershkowitz found suitable photos for the Last Word readings, and Cathy Hull provided the creative illustrations for several of them. Margaret Hanson's imaginative editing has been invaluable. Our greatest debts are to Scott Stratford, Edwin Hanson, and Mike Elia for their conscientious supervision of this revision. Their patience and many positive contributions are gratefully acknowledged.

Given this much assistance, we see no compelling reason why the authors should assume full responsibility for errors of omission or commission. But we bow to tradition.

Campbell R. McConnell
Stanley L. Brue

ACKNOWLEDGMENTS

We thank the following instructors for their written reviews and other comments, which greatly helped shape this edition:

Thomas P. Barbiero, *Ryerson Polytechnical Institute*
Arleigh T. Bell, *Loyola College*
Michael S. Blair, *Tarrant County Junior College*
Joseph P. Cairo, *La Salle University*
Robert Campbell, *Indiana University–Bloomington*
Gordon Crocker, *Community College of Allegheny County*
Paul G. Farnham, *Georgia State University*
Walter F. Gall, Jr., *Northeastern Junior College*
John A. Gould, *Garrett Community College*
Paul W. Grimes, *Mississippi State University*
Richard C. Harmstone, *Pennsylvania State University*
Gail A. Hawks, *Miami-Dade Community College*
R. Bradley Hoppes, *Southwest Missouri State University*
Matthew Hyle, *Winona State University*
Patrick Joyce, *Michigan Technological University*
James C. Koch, *St. Edwards University*
Fredric Kolb, *University of Wisconsin–Eau Claire*
Patrick Litzinger, *Robert Morris College*
Mark Lovewell, *Ryerson Polytechnical Institute*
George F. Muscat, *Camden County Community College*
Asghar Nazemzadeh, *University of Houston–Downtown*
Margaret O'Donnell, *University of Southwest Louisiana*
Ronald W. Olive, *New Hampshire College*
Diana Petersdorf, *University of Wisconsin–Stout*
David Priddy, *Piedmont Community College*
John J. Rapczak, *Community College of Rhode Island*
Theresa Riley, *Youngstown State University*
Peter Rupert, *SUNY–Buffalo*
Doris Sheets, *Southwest Missouri State University*
Steven P. Skinner, *Western Connecticut State University*
Robert Stuart, *Rutgers University*
Percy O. Vera, *Sinclair Community College*
Howard J. Wall, *West Virginia University*
Paul R. Watro, *Jefferson Community College*
Peter J. Watry, Jr., *Southwestern College*
Dieter Zschock, *SUNY–Stony Brook*

In addition, we thank the following instructors for participating in focus group sessions, which served as very useful complements to the reviewing process:

Barbara Brogan, *Northern Virginia Community College*
Robert F. Brooker, *Gannon University*
Christopher B. Colburn, *Old Dominion University*
Jacob Deutch, *University of Maryland–Baltimore County*
James Halteman, *Wheaton College*
Charles Jewell, *Charles County Community College*
George Kosicki, *College of the Holy Cross*
Patrick Litzinger, *Robert Morris College*
Craig MacPhee, *University of Nebraska–Lincoln*
Norris A. Peterson, *Pacific Lutheran University*
Donald Schilling, *University of Missouri–Columbia*
Robert Tansky, *St. Clair Community College*
Irvin Weintraub, *Towson State University*

MICRO-ECONOMICS

An Introduction to Economics and the Economy

The Nature and Method of Economics

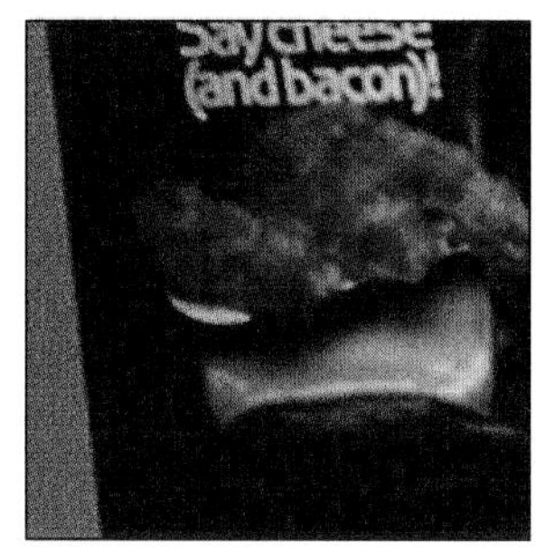

Human beings, unfortunate creatures, are plagued with wants. We want, among other things, love, social recognition, and the material necessities and comforts of life. Our striving to improve our material well-being, to "make a living," is the concern of economics. Specifically, economics is the study of our behavior in producing, distributing, and consuming material goods and services in a world of scarce resources.

But we need a more sophisticated definition of economics. We are, indeed, characterized by both biologically and socially determined wants. We seek food, clothing, shelter, and many goods and services associated with a comfortable or affluent standard of living. We are also blessed with aptitudes and surrounded by quantities of property resources—both natural and manufactured. We use available human and property resources—labor and managerial talents, tools and machinery, land and mineral deposits—to produce goods and services which satisfy these material wants. This is done through the organizational mechanism we call the *economic system.*

Quantitative considerations, however, rule out an ideal solution. The blunt fact is that the total of all our material wants is beyond the productive capacity of all available resources. Hence, absolute material abundance is not a possible outcome. This unyielding fact is the basis for our definition of economics: Economics *is concerned with the efficient use or management of limited productive resources to achieve maximum satisfaction of human material wants.* Though it may not be self-evident, all the headline-grabbing issues of the day—inflation, unemployment, the collapse of communism, government and international trade deficits, free-trade agreements among nations, poverty and inequality, pollution, and government regulation of business—are rooted in the issue of using limited resources efficiently.

In this first chapter, however, we will not plunge into problems and issues. Our immediate concern is with some basic preliminary questions: (1) Of what importance or consequence is the study of economics? (2) How should we study

economics—what are the proper procedures? What is the character of the methodology of economics? (3) What specific problems, limitations, and pitfalls might we encounter in studying economics?

THE AGE OF THE ECONOMIST

Is economics a discipline of consequence? Is the study of economics worth your time and effort? Half a century ago John Maynard Keynes (1883–1946)—clearly the most influential economist of this century—offered a telling response:

> The ideas of economists and political philosophers, both when they are right and when they are wrong, are more powerful than is commonly understood. Indeed the world is ruled by little else. Practical men, who believe themselves to be quite exempt from any intellectual influences, are usually the slaves of some defunct economist.

Most of the ideologies of the modern world which compete for our minds have been shaped by the great economists of the past—Adam Smith, David Ricardo, John Stuart Mill, Karl Marx, and John Maynard Keynes.[1] And it is currently commonplace for world leaders to receive and invoke the advice and policy prescriptions of economists.

For example: The President of the United States benefits from the ongoing counsel of his Council of Economic Advisers. The broad spectrum of economic issues facing political leaders is suggested by the contents of the annual *Economic Report of the President.* Areas covered include unemployment and inflation, economic growth and productivity, taxation and public expenditures, poverty and income maintenance, the balance of payments and the international monetary system, labor-management relations, pollution, discrimination, immigration, and competition and antitrust, among others.

Economics for Citizenship

A basic understanding of economics is essential if we are to be well-informed citizens. Most of the specific problems of the day have important economic aspects, and as voters we can influence the decisions of our political leaders in coping with these problems. What are the causes and consequences of the "twin deficits"—the Federal budget deficit and the international trade deficit—that are constantly reported by the news media? What of the depressing stories of homeless street people? Is it desirable that corporate raiders be allowed to achieve hostile takeovers of corporations? Why is inflation undesirable? What can be done to reduce unemployment? Are existing welfare programs effective and justifiable? Should we continue to subsidize farmers? Do we need further reform of our tax system? Does America need to "reindustrialize" to reassert its dominant position in world trade and finance? Has the deregulation of the airlines, trucking, and banking industries been a boon or a bane to society? Since responses to such questions are determined largely by our elected officials, intelligence at the polls requires that we have a basic working knowledge of economics. Needless to say, a sound grasp of economics is more than helpful to politicians themselves!

Personal Applications

Economics is also a vital discipline for more mundane, immediate reasons. It is of practical value in business. An understanding of the overall operation of the economic system enables the business executive to better formulate policies. The executive who understands the causes and consequences of inflation can make more intelligent business decisions during inflationary periods than otherwise. Indeed, more and more economists are appearing on the payrolls of large corporations. Their job is to gather and interpret economic information on which rational business decisions can be made. Economics also gives the individual as a consumer and worker insights on how to make wiser buying and employment decisions. What should one buy and how much? How can one "hedge" against the reduction in the dollar's purchasing power which accompanies inflation? Which occupations pay well; which are most immune to unemployment? Similarly, someone who understands the relationship between budget and trade deficits, on the one hand, and security (stock

[1]Any of the following three volumes—Robert Heilbroner, *The Worldly Philosophers,* 6th ed. (New York: Simon and Schuster, Inc., 1986); Daniel R. Fusfeld, *The Age of the Economist,* 6th ed. (Chicago: Scott, Foresman and Company, 1990); or E. Ray Canterbery, *The Making of Economics,* 3d ed. (Belmont, Calif.: Wadsworth Publishing Company, 1987)—will provide the reader with a fascinating introduction to the historical development of economic ideas.

and bond) values, on the other, can make more enlightened personal investment decisions.

In spite of its practical benefits, however, you must be forewarned that economics is mainly an academic, not a vocational, subject. Unlike accounting, advertising, corporation finance, and marketing, economics is not primarily a how-to-make-money area of study. A knowledge of economics will help you run a business or manage personal finances, but this is not its primary objective. In economics, problems are usually examined from the *social,* rather than the *personal,* point of view. The production, exchange, and consumption of goods and services are discussed from the viewpoint of society as a whole, rather than from the standpoint of one's own bankbook.

METHODOLOGY

What do economists do? What are their goals? What procedures do they employ? The title of this volume—*Microeconomics: Principles, Problems, and Policies*—contains a thumbnail answer to the first two questions. Economists formulate economic *principles* which are useful in the establishment of *policies* designed to solve economic *problems.* The procedures employed by the economist are summarized in Figure 1-1. The economist ascertains and gathers facts relevant to a specific economic problem. This task is sometimes called **descriptive** or **empirical economics** (box 1). The economist also states economic principles, that is, generalizes about the way individuals and institutions actually behave. Deriving principles is called **economic theory** or "economic analysis" (box 2).

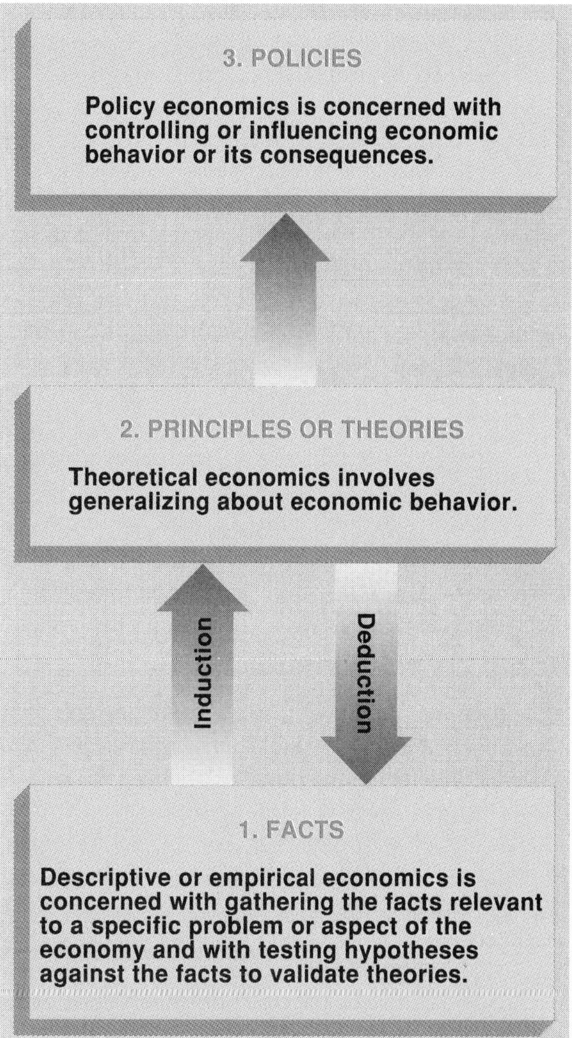

FIGURE 1-1 The relationship between facts, principles, and policies in economics

In analyzing problems or aspects of the economy, economists may use the inductive method whereby they gather, systematically arrange, and generalize on facts. Alternatively, the deductive method entails the development of hypotheses which are then tested against facts. Generalizations derived from either method of inquiry are useful not only in explaining economic behavior, but also as a basis for formulating economic policies.

As we see in Figure 1-1, economists are as likely to move from theory to facts in studying economic behavior as they are to move from facts to theory. Stated more formally, economists use both deductive and inductive methods. **Induction** distills or creates principles from facts. Here an accumulation of facts is arranged systematically and analyzed to permit the derivation of a generalization or principle. Induction moves from facts to theory, from the particular to the general. The inductive method is suggested by the left upward arrow from box 1 to box 2 in the figure.

Similarly, economists can begin with theory and proceed to the verification or rejection of this theory by an appeal to the facts. This is **deduction** or the hypothetical method. Economists may draw upon casual observation, insight, logic, or intuition to frame a tentative, untested principle called an **hypothesis.** For example, they may conjecture, on the basis of "armchair logic," that it is rational for consumers to buy more of a product when its price is low than when its price is high. The validity of this hypothesis must then be tested by the systematic and repeated examination of relevant facts. The deductive method goes from the general to the particular, from theory to facts. This method is implicit in the right downward arrow from box 2 to box 1 in Figure 1-1.

Deduction and induction are complementary, rather than opposing, techniques of investigation. Hypotheses formulated by deduction provide guidelines for the economist in gathering and systematizing empirical data. Conversely, some understanding of factual evidence—of the "real world"—is prerequisite to formulation of meaningful hypotheses.

Finally, the general knowledge of economic behavior which economic principles provides can then be used in formulating policies, that is, remedies or solutions, for correcting or avoiding the problem under scrutiny. This final aspect of the field is sometimes called "applied economics" or **policy economics** (box 3).

Continuing to use Figure 1-1 as a reference, we now examine the economist's methodology in more detail.

Descriptive Economics

All sciences are empirical; they are based on facts, that is, on observable and verifiable behavior of certain data or subject matter. In the physical sciences the factual data are inorganic. As a social science, economics examines the behavior of individuals and institutions engaged in the production, exchange, and consumption of goods and services.

Fact-gathering can be an infinitely complex task. Because the world of reality is cluttered with innumerable interrelated facts, the economist must use discretion in gathering them. One must distinguish economic from noneconomic facts and then determine which economic facts are relevant and which irrelevant for the problem under consideration. But even when this sorting process is complete, the relevant economic facts may appear diverse and unrelated.

Economic Theory

The task of economic theory or analysis is to systematically arrange, interpret, and generalize upon facts. Principles and theories—the end result of economic analysis—bring order and meaning to facts by tying them together, putting them in correct relationship to one another, and generalizing upon them. "Theories without facts may be barren, but facts without theories are meaningless."[2]

[2]Kenneth E. Boulding, *Economic Analysis: Microeconomics,* 4th ed. (New York: Harper & Row, Publishers, Incorporated, 1966), p. 5.

Principles and theories are meaningful statements drawn from facts, but facts, in turn, serve as a constant check on the validity of principles already established. Facts—how individuals and institutions actually behave in producing, exchanging, and consuming goods and services—may change with time. This makes it essential that economists continually check existing principles and theories against the changing economic environment.

Terminology Economists talk about "laws," "principles," "theories," and "models." These terms all mean essentially the same thing: generalizations, or statements of regularity, concerning the economic behavior of individuals and institutions. The term "economic law" is a bit misleading because it implies a high degree of exactness, universal application, and even moral rightness. So, to a lesser degree, does the term **principle.** And some people incorrectly associate the term "theory" with ivory-tower dreams, divorced from the facts and realities of the world. The term "model" has much to commend it. A model is a simplified picture of reality, an abstract generalization of how relevant data actually behave. In this book these four terms will be used synonymously. The choice of terms in labeling any particular generalization will be governed by custom or convenience. Thus, the relationship between the price of a product and the quantity consumers purchase will be called the "law" of demand, rather than the theory or principle of demand, because this is the customary designation.

Several other points regarding the character and derivation of economic principles are in order.

Generalizations Economic principles are **generalizations** and, as the term implies, characterized by somewhat imprecise quantitative statement. Economic facts are usually diverse; some individuals and institutions act one way and some another way. Economic principles are therefore frequently stated in terms of averages or statistical probabilities. For example, when economists say that the average household earned an income of about $35,000 in 1990, they are generalizing. It is recognized that some households earned much more and a good many others much less. Yet this generalization, properly handled and interpreted, can be very meaningful and useful.

Similarly, economic generalizations are often stated in terms of probabilities. A researcher may tell us there is a 95 percent probability that every $1.00 reduction in personal income taxes will result in a $.92 increase in consumer spending.

"Other Things Equal" Assumption Like other scientists, economists use the ***ceteris paribus*** or **other things being equal assumption** to construct their generalizations. That is, they assume all other variables except those under immediate consideration are held constant. This technique simplifies the reasoning process by isolating the relationship under consideration. For example, in considering the relationship between the price of Pepsi and the amount purchased, it helps to assume that, of all the factors which might influence the amount of Pepsi purchased (for example, the price of Pepsi, the prices of other goods such as Coke, consumer incomes and tastes), only the price of Pepsi varies. The economist can then focus on the "price of Pepsi–purchases of Pepsi" relationship without reasoning being blurred or confused by intrusion of other variables.

In the natural sciences controlled experiments usually can be performed where "all other things" are in fact held constant or virtually so. Thus, scientists can test the assumed relationship between two variables with great precision. But economics is not a laboratory science. The economist's process of empirical verification is based on "real-world" data generated by the actual operation of the economy. In this rather bewildering environment "other things" *do* change. Despite the development of complex statistical techniques designed to hold other things equal, such controls are less than perfect. As a result, economic principles are less certain and less precise in application than those of laboratory sciences.

Abstractions Economic principles, or theories, are necessarily abstractions. They do not mirror the full complexity of reality. The very process of sorting out noneconomic and irrelevant facts in the fact-gathering process involves abstracting from reality. Unfortunately, the abstractness of economic theory prompts the uninformed to identify theory as impractical and unrealistic. This is nonsense! Economic theories are practical simply because they are abstractions. The level of reality is too complex and bewildering to be very meaningful. Economists theorize to give meaning to a maze of facts which would otherwise be confusing and useless, and to put facts into a more usable, practical form. Thus, to generalize is to abstract or purposely simplify; generalization for this purpose is practical, and therefore so is abstraction.

An economic theory is a model—a simplified picture or map—of some segment of the economy. This model helps us understand reality better *because* it avoids the confusing details of reality. Theories—*good* theories—are grounded on facts and therefore are realistic. Theories which do not fit the facts are simply not good theories.

Macro and Micro There are two different levels of analysis at which the economist may derive laws concerning economic behavior. The level of **macroeconomics** deals either with the economy as a whole or with the basic subdivisions or aggregates—such as the government, household, and business sectors—which make up the economy. An aggregate is a collection of specific economic units which are treated *as if* they were one unit. Thus, we might find it convenient to lump together the over eighteen million businesses in our economy and treat them as if they were one huge unit. In dealing with aggregates, macroeconomics is concerned with obtaining an overview, or general outline, of the structure of the economy and the relationships among the major aggregates which constitute the economy. No attention is given to specific units making up the various aggregates. Macroeconomics speaks of such magnitudes as *total* output, *total* level of employment, *total* income, *aggregate* expenditures, the *general* level of prices, and so forth, in analyzing various economic problems. In short, macroeconomics examines the forest, not the trees. It gives us a bird's-eye view of the economy.

On the other hand, **microeconomics** deals with *specific* economic units and a *detailed* consideration of these individual units. At this level of analysis, the economist figuratively puts an economic unit, or very small segment of the economy, under the microscope to observe details of its operation. Here we talk in terms of an individual industry, firm, or household, and concentrate upon such magnitudes as the output or price of a specific product, the number of workers employed by a single firm, the revenue or income of a particular firm or household, or the expenditures of a given firm or family. In microeconomics we examine the trees, not the forest. Microeconomics is useful in achieving a worm's-eye view of some very specific component of our economic system.

The macro–micro distinction does not mean that the subject matter of economics is so highly compartmentalized that each topic can be readily labeled as "macro" or "micro"; many topics and subdivisions of economics are rooted in both. Indeed, there has been a convergence of macro- and microeconomics in important areas in recent years. While the problem of unemployment was treated primarily as a macroeconomic topic some twenty or twenty-five years ago ("unemployment depends on *aggregate* spending"), economists now recognize that decisions made by *individual* workers in searching for jobs and the manner in which specific product and labor markets function are also critical in determining the unemployment rate.

Graphical Expression Many of the economic models or principles presented in this book will be expressed graphically. The most important of these models are labeled "Key Graphs." You are strongly urged to read the appendix to this chapter to review graphing and other relevant quantitative relationships.

QUICK REVIEW 1-1

- ***Economics is concerned with the efficient management of scarce resources.***
- ***Induction involves observing regularities in factual data and drawing generalizations from them; deduction entails the creation of hypotheses which are then tested with factual data.***
- ***Economic theories ("laws," "principles," or "models") are generalizations, based on facts, concerning the economic behavior of individuals and institutions.***
- ***Macroeconomics deals with the economy as a whole; microeconomics focuses on specific units which comprise the economy.***

Policy Economics: Positive and Normative

As we move from the fact and principles levels (boxes 1 and 2) of Figure 1-1 to the policy level (box 3) we make a critical leap from positive to normative economics.

Positive economics deals with facts (once removed at the level of theory) and avoids value judgments. Positive economics attempts to set forth scientific statements about economic behavior. **Normative economics,** in contrast, involves someone's value judgments about what the economy should be like or what particular policy action should be recommended based on a given economic generalization or relationship.

Positive economics concerns *what is,* while normative economics embodies subjective feelings about *what ought to be.* Positive economics deals with what the economy is actually like; normative economics examines whether certain conditions or aspects of the economy are desirable or not.

Consider this example: Positive statement: "Unemployment is 7 percent of the labor force." Normative statement: "Unemployment ought to be reduced." Second positive statement: "Other things being the same, if tuition is increased, enrollment at Gigantic State University will fall." Normative statement: "Tuition should be lowered at GSU so that more students can obtain an education." Whenever words such as "ought" or "should" appear in a sentence, there is a strong chance you are dealing with a normative statement.

Most of the apparent disagreement among economists involves normative, value-based policy questions. To be sure, various economists present and support different theories or models of the economy and its component parts. But by far most economic controversy reflects differing opinions or value judgments as to what our society should be like. For example, there is greater agreement about the actual distribution of income in our society than how income should be distributed. The point we reemphasize is that value judgments or normative statements come into play at the level of policy economics.

As noted earlier, successful policy economics draws heavily on economic principles. For example, one almost universally accepted economic principle indicates that, within certain limits, there is a direct relationship between total spending and the level of employment in the economy. "If total spending increases, the volume of employment will rise. Conversely, if total spending decreases, the volume of employment will fall." This principle can be invaluable to government in determining its economic policies. If government economists note that available statistics indicate an actual slackening of total expenditures, the principle will permit them to predict the undesirable consequence of unemployment. Aware of this anticipated result, public officials can set in motion government policies designed to bolster total spending and head off or reduce expected unemployment. In short, we must be able to predict in order to effectively control. Economic principles help make prediction possible and are the basis for sound economic policy.

Economic Goals A number of **economic goals** or value judgments are widely, though not universally, accepted in our own society and in many others. These goals may be briefly listed as follows:

1 Economic Growth The production of more and better goods and services, or, more simply stated, a higher standard of living, is desired.

2 Full Employment Suitable jobs should be available for all willing and able to work.

3 Economic Efficiency We want maximum benefits at minimum cost from the limited productive resources available.

4 Price Level Stability Sizable upswings or downswings in the general price level, that is, inflation and deflation, should be avoided.

5 Economic Freedom Business executives, workers, and consumers should enjoy a high degree of freedom in their economic activities.

6 An Equitable Distribution of Income No group of citizens should face stark poverty while others enjoy extreme luxury.

7 Economic Security Provision should be made for those who are chronically ill, disabled, handicapped, laid off, aged, or otherwise unable to earn minimal levels of income.

8 Balance of Trade We seek a reasonable balance in our international trade and financial transactions.

This list of widely accepted goals[3] is the basis for several significant points.

1 Interpretation Note that this or any other statement of basic economic goals inevitably involves problems of interpretation. What are "sizable" changes in the price level? What is a "high degree" of economic freedom? What is an "equitable" distribution of income? Although most of us might accept the above goals as generally stated, we might also disagree substantially on their specific meanings and hence the types of policies needed to attain these goals. Although goals 1 to 4 and 8 are subject to reasonably accurate measurements, the inability to quantify goals 5 to 7 undoubtedly contributes to controversy over their precise meaning.

2 Complementary Certain of these goals are complementary in that when one goal is achieved, some other goal or goals will also be realized. For example, the achieving of full employment (goal 2) means elimination of unemployment, a basic cause of low incomes (goal 6) and economic insecurity (goal 7). Furthermore, the sociopolitical tensions which may accompany a highly unequal distribution of income (goal 6) are tempered somewhat when most incomes rise absolutely as a result of economic growth (goal 1).

3 Conflicting Some goals may be conflicting or mutually exclusive. For example, goals 1 and 6 may be in conflict. Some economists point out that efforts to achieve greater equality in the distribution of income may weaken incentives to work, invest, innovate, and take business risks, all of which promote rapid economic growth. They argue that government tends to equalize the distribution of income by taxing high-income people heavily and transferring those tax revenues to low-income people. The incentives of a high-income individual will be diminished because taxation reduces one's income rewards. Similarly, a low-income person will be less motivated to work and engage in other productive activities when government stands ready to subsidize that individual.

International example: Before recent events in the Soviet Union, central planning virtually eliminated unemployment with the result that this source of worker insecurity almost disappeared. However, with little fear of losing one's job, Soviet workers were quite cavalier regarding work effort and therefore productivity and efficiency in the Soviet Union were quite low. Here we have a conflict between goal 7, economic security, and goal 1, the growth of worker productivity.

4 Priorities When basic goals do conflict, society is forced to develop a system of priorities for the objectives it seeks. If full employment and price stability are to some extent mutually exclusive, that is, if full employment is accompanied by some inflation *and* price stability entails some unemployment, society must decide upon the relative importance of these two goals. There is clearly ample room for disagreement here.

Formulating Economic Policy The creation of specific policies designed to achieve the broad economic goals of our society is no simple matter. A brief examination of the basic steps in policy formulation is in order.

1 Stating Goals The first step is to make a clear statement of goals. If we say that we want "full employment," do we mean that everyone between, say, 16 and 65 years of age should have a job? Or do we mean that

[3]There are other goals which might be added. For example, improving the physical environment is a widely held goal.

everyone who wants to work should have a job? Should we allow for some "normal" unemployment caused by workers' voluntarily changing jobs?

2 Policy Options Next, we must state and recognize the possible effects of alternative policies designed to achieve the goal. This requires a clear-cut understanding of the economic impact, benefits, costs, and political feasibility of alternative programs. Thus, for example, economists currently debate the relative merits and demerits of fiscal policy (which involves changing government spending and taxes) and monetary policy (which entails altering the supply of money) as alternative means of achieving and maintaining full employment.

3 Evaluation We are obligated to both ourselves and future generations to review our experiences with chosen policies and evaluate their effectiveness; it is only through this type of evaluation that we can hope to improve policy applications. Did a given change in taxes or the supply of money alter the level of employment to the extent originally predicted? Did deregulation of a particular industry (for example, the airlines) yield the predicted beneficial results? If not, why not?

QUICK REVIEW 1-2

- ***Positive economics deals with factual statements ("what is"), while normative economics concerns value judgments ("what ought to be").***
- ***Some of society's economic goals are complementary while others are conflicting.***

PITFALLS TO OBJECTIVE THINKING

Our discussion of the economist's procedure has, up to this point, skirted some specific problems and pitfalls which frequently hinder our thinking objectively about economic problems. Consider the following impediments to valid economic reasoning.

Bias

In contrast to a neophyte physicist or chemist, the budding economist ordinarily brings into economics a bundle of biases and preconceptions about the field. For example, one might be suspicious of business profits or feel that deficit spending is invariably evil. Needless to say, biases may cloud our thinking and interfere with objective analysis. The beginning economics student must be willing to shed biases and preconceptions which are simply not warranted by facts.

Loaded Terminology

The economic terminology to which we are exposed in newspapers and popular magazines is sometimes emotionally loaded. The writer—or more frequently the particular interest group he or she represents—may have a cause to further or an ax to grind, and terms will be slanted to solicit the support of the reader. A governmental flood-control project in the Great Plains region may be called "creeping socialism" by its opponents and "intelligent democratic planning" by its proponents. We must be prepared to discount such terminology to objectively understand important economic issues.

Definitions

No scientist is obligated to use popularized or immediately understandable definitions of his or her terms. The economist may find it convenient and essential to define terms in such a way that they are clearly at odds with the definitions held by most people in everyday speech. So long as the economist is explicit and consistent in these definitions, he or she is on safe ground. For example, the term "investment" to the average citizen is associated with the buying of bonds and stocks in the securities market. How often have we heard someone talk of "investing" in General Motors stock or government bonds? But to the economist, "investment" means the purchase of real capital assets such as machinery and equipment, or the construction of a new factory building, not the purely financial transaction of swapping cash or part of a bank balance for a neatly engraved piece of paper.

Fallacy of Composition

Another pitfall in economic thinking is assuming that "what is true for the individual or part of a group is necessarily also true for the group or whole." This is a logical **fallacy of composition;** it is *not* correct. The validity of a particular generalization for an individual or part does *not* necessarily ensure its accuracy for the group or whole.

A noneconomic example may help: You are watching a football game and the home team executes an outstanding play. In the excitement, you leap to your feet to get a better view. Generalization: "If you, *an individual,* stand, then your view of the game is improved." But does this also hold true for the group—for everyone watching the game? Certainly not! If everyone stands to watch the play, everyone—including you—will probably have the same or even a worse view than when seated.

Consider two examples from economics: A wage increase for Smith is desirable because, given constant product prices, it increases Smith's purchasing power and standard of living. But if everyone realizes a wage increase, product prices may rise, that is, inflation might occur. Therefore, Smith's standard of living may be unchanged as higher prices offset her larger salary.

Second illustration: An *individual* farmer fortunate enough to reap a bumper crop is likely to realize a sharp gain in income. But this generalization does not apply to farmers as a *group.* For the individual farmer, crop prices will not be influenced (reduced) by this bumper crop, because each farmer produces a negligible fraction of the total farm output. But to farmers as a group, prices vary inversely with total output.[4] Thus, as *all* farmers realize bumper crops, the total output of farm products rises, thereby depressing crop prices. If price declines are relatively greater than the increased output, farm incomes will *fall.*

Recalling our earlier distinction between macroeconomics and microeconomics, the fallacy of composition reminds us that *generalizations which are valid at one of these levels of analysis may or may not be valid at the other.*

Cause and Effect: Post Hoc Fallacy

Still another hazard in economic thinking is to assume that simply because one event precedes another, the first is necessarily the cause of the second. This kind of faulty reasoning is known as the **post hoc, ergo propter hoc,** or **after this, therefore because of this, fallacy.**

A classic example clearly indicates the fallacy inherent in such reasoning. Suppose that early each spring the medicine man of a tribe performs his ritual by cavorting around the village in a green costume. A week or so later the trees and grass turn green. Can we safely conclude that event A, the medicine man's gyrations, has caused event B, the landscape's turning green? Obviously not. The rooster crows before dawn, but this doesn't mean the rooster is responsible for the sunrise!

It is especially important in analyzing various sets of empirical data *not* to confuse **correlation** with **causation.** *Correlation* is a technical term which indicates that two sets of data are associated in some systematic and dependable way. For example, we may find that when X increases, Y also increases. But this does not necessarily mean that X is the cause of Y. The relationship could be purely coincidental or determined by some other factor, Z, not included in the analysis.

Example: Economists have found a positive correlation between education and income. In general, people with more education earn higher incomes than do people with less education. Common sense prompts us to label education as the cause and higher incomes as the effect; more education suggest a more productive worker and such workers receive larger monetary rewards.

But, on second thought, might not causation run the other way? That is, do people with higher incomes buy more education, just as they buy more automobiles and steaks? Or is the relationship explainable in terms of still other factors? Are education and income positively correlated because the bundle of characteristics—ability, motivation, personal habits—required to succeed in education are the same characteristics required to be a productive and highly paid worker? Upon reflection, seemingly simple cause-effect relationships—"more education means more income"—may prove to be suspect or perhaps flatly incorrect.

In short, cause-and-effect relationships are typically not self-evident in economics; the economist must look carefully before concluding that event A caused event B. The fact that A preceded B is not sufficient to warrant any such conclusion.

THE ECONOMIC PERSPECTIVE

The methodology used by economists is common to all the natural and social sciences. Similarly, all scholars try to avoid the reasoning errors just discussed. Hence, economists do *not* think in a special way. But they *do* think about things from a special perspective. Economists have developed a keen alertness to certain aspects of everyday conduct and situations. Specifically, they look for *rationality* or *purposefulness* in human actions and economic institutions. This purposefulness

[4] This assumes there are no government programs which fix farm prices.

LAST WORD

FAST-FOOD LINES: AN ECONOMIC PERSPECTIVE

How might the economic perspective help us understand the behavior of fast-food consumers?

When you enter a fast-food restaurant, which line do you select? What do you do when you are in a long line in the restaurant and a new station opens? Have you ever gone to a fast-food restaurant, only to see long lines, and then leave? Have you ever had someone in front of you in a fast-food line place an order which takes a long time to fill?

The economic perspective is useful in analyzing the behavior of fast-food customers. These customers are at the restaurant because they expect the benefit or satisfaction from the food they buy to match or exceed its cost. When customers enter the restaurant they scurry to the *shortest* line, believing that the shortest line will reduce their time cost of obtaining their food. They are acting purposefully; time is limited and most people would prefer using it in some way other than standing in line.

All lines in the fast-food establishment normally are of roughly equal lengths. If one line is temporarily shorter than other lines, some people will move toward that line. These movers apparently view the time saving associated with the shorter line to exceed the cost of moving from their present line. Line changing normally results in an equilibrium line length. No further movement of customers between lines will occur once all lines are of equal length.

Fast-food customers face another cost-benefit decision when a clerk opens a new station at the counter. Should customers move to the new station or stay put? Those who do shift to the new line decide that the benefit of the time savings from the move exceeds the extra cost of physically moving. In so deciding, customers must also consider just how quickly they can get to the new station compared to others who may be contemplating the same move. (Those who hesitate in this situation are lost!)

Customers at the fast-food establishment select lines without having perfect information. For example, they do not first survey those in the lines to determine what they are ordering before deciding on which line to enter. There are two reasons for this. First, most customers would tell them "It is none of your business," and therefore no information would be forthcoming. Second, even if they could obtain the information, the amount of time necessary to get it (cost) would most likely exceed any time saving associated with finding the best line (benefit). Because information is costly to obtain, fast-food patrons select lines on the basis of imperfect information. Thus, not all decisions turn out to be as expected. For example, some people may enter a line in which the person in front of them is ordering hamburgers and fries for the forty people in the Greyhound bus parked out back! Nevertheless, at the time the customer made the decision, he or she thought that it was optimal.

Imperfect information also explains why some people who arrive at a fast-food restaurant and observe long lines decide to leave. These people conclude that the total cost (monetary plus time costs) of obtaining the fast food is too large relative to the benefit. They would not have come to the restaurant in the first place had they known the lines were so long. But, getting that information by, say, employing an advance scout with a cellular phone would cost more than the perceived benefit.

Finally, customers must decide what to order when they arrive at the counter. In making these choices they again compare costs and benefits in attempting to obtain the greatest personal well-being.

Economists believe that what is true for the behavior of customers at fast-food restaurants is true for economic behavior in general. Faced with an array of choices, consumers, workers, and businesses rationally compare costs and benefits in making decisions.

---

implies that people, individually and collectively, make choices by comparing costs and benefits. It therefore might be said that the **economic perspective** is a *cost-benefit perspective.*

Because people make economic choices from a wide array of alternatives, all choices entail sacrifices or costs. To buy a new VCR may mean not being able to afford a new personal computer. Taking a course in economics may preclude taking a course in accounting, political science, or computer science. A decision by government to provide improved health care for the elderly may mean deteriorating health care for children in poverty. Alas, costs are everywhere! Naturally, people are most aware of personal monetary costs—expenses incurred when paying tuition, buying hamburgers, hiring babysitters, renting apartments, or attending concerts. But in Chapter 2 we will see that costs occur in *all* situations in which incomes or resources are scarce relative to wants.

Economic actions of workers, producers, and consumers, of course, also produce personal economic benefits. Workers receive wages, producers garner profits, and consumers obtain satisfaction. People *compare* these benefits with costs in deciding how to spend their time, which products to buy, whether or not to work, or which goods to produce and sell. If the added benefits associated with a given course of action exceed the added costs, then it is rational to take that action. But if added costs are greater than added benefits, that action is not rational and should not be undertaken. Furthermore, when costs or benefits *change,* people *alter* their behavior accordingly.

Economists look carefully at costs and benefits to understand the everyday activities of people and institutions in the economy. This economic perspective will become increasingly evident as you advance through this book. The accompanying Last Word provides an everyday application of the economic perspective.

QUICK REVIEW 1-3

- ***Beware of logical errors such as the fallacy of composition and the post hoc fallacy when engaging in economic reasoning.***
- ***The economic perspective is a cost-benefit perspective; it helps us analyze the everyday behavior of individuals and institutions.***

CHAPTER SUMMARY

1 Economics deals with the efficient use of scarce resources in the production of goods and services to satisfy material wants.

2 Economics is studied for several reasons: **a** It provides valuable knowledge about our social environment and behavior; **b** it equips a democratic citizenry to render fundamental decisions intelligently; **c** although not chiefly a vocational discipline, economics may provide the business executive or consumer with valuable information.

3 The tasks of descriptive or empirical economics are **a** gathering those economic facts relevant to a particular problem or specific segment of the economy, and **b** testing hypotheses against facts to validate theories.

4 Generalizations stated by economists are called "principles," "theories," "laws," or "models." The derivation of these principles is the task of economic theory.

5 Induction distills theories from facts; deduction states a hypothesis and then gathers facts to determine whether the hypothesis is valid.

6 Some economic principles deal with macroeconomics (the economy as a whole or major aggregates), while others pertain to microeconomics (specific economic units or institutions).

7 Economic principles are particularly valuable as predictive devices; they are the bases for the formulation of economic policy designed to solve problems and control undesirable events.

8 Positive statements deal with facts ("what is"), while normative statements encompass value judgments ("what ought to be").

9 Economic growth, full employment, economic efficiency, price level stability, economic freedom, equity in the distribution of income, economic security, and reasonable balance in our international trade and finance are all widely accepted economic goals in our society. Some of these goals are complementary; others are mutually exclusive.

10 In studying economics the beginner may encounter numerous pitfalls. Some of the more important are **a** biases and preconceptions, **b** terminological difficulties, **c** the fallacy of composition, and **d** the difficulty of establishing clear cause-effect relationships.

11 The economic perspective envisions individuals and institutions making rational decisions based on costs and benefits.

TERMS AND CONCEPTS

economics
descriptive or empirical economics
economic theory
induction and deduction
hypothesis
principles or generalizations
ceteris paribus **or "other things being equal" assumption**

policy economics
macroeconomics and microeconomics
economic goals
positive and normative economics
correlation and causation
post hoc, ergo propter hoc or "after this, therefore because of this" fallacy
fallacy of composition
economic perspective

QUESTIONS AND STUDY SUGGESTIONS

1 Explain in detail the interrelationships between economic facts, theory, and policy. Critically evaluate: "The trouble with economics is that it is not practical. It has too much to say about theory and not enough to say about facts."

2 Analyze and explain the following quotation.[5]

> Facts are seldom simple and usually complicated; theoretical analysis is needed to unravel the complications and interpret the facts before we can understand them . . . the opposition of facts and theory is a false one; the true relationship is complementary. We cannot in practice consider a fact without relating it to other facts, and the relation is a theory. Facts by themselves are dumb; before they will tell us anything we have to arrange them, and the arrangement is a theory. Theory is simply the unavoidable arrangement and interpretation of facts, which gives us generalizations on which we can argue and act, in the place of a mass of disjointed particulars.

3 Of what significance is the fact that economics is not a laboratory science? What problems may be involved in deriving and applying economic principles?

4 Explain each of the following statements:

a "Like all scientific laws, economic laws are established in order to make successful prediction of the outcome of human actions."[6]

b "Abstraction . . . is the inevitable price of generality . . . indeed abstraction and generality are virtually synonyms."[7]

c "Numbers serve to discipline rhetoric."[8]

5 Indicate whether each of the following statements pertains to microeconomics or macroeconomics:

a The unemployment rate in the United States was 6.8 percent in August of 1991.

b The Alpo dogfood plant in Bowser, Iowa, laid off 15 workers last month.

c An unexpected freeze in central Florida reduced the citrus crop and caused the price of oranges to rise.

d Our national output, adjusted for inflation, grew by about 1 percent in 1990.

e Last week Manhattan Chemical Bank lowered its interest rate on business loans by one-half of 1 percentage point.

f The consumer price index rose by more than 6 percent in 1990.

6 Identify each of the following as either a positive or a normative statement:

a The high temperature today was 89 degrees.

b It was too hot today.

c The general price level rose by 4.4 percent last year.

d Inflation eroded living standards last year and should be reduced by government policies.

7 To what extent would you accept the eight economic goals stated and described in this chapter? What priorities would you assign to them? It has been said that we seek simply four goals: progress, stability, justice, and freedom. Is this list of goals compatible with that given in the chapter?

8 Analyze each of the following specific goals in terms of the eight general goals stated on pages 6 and 7, and note points of conflict and compatibility: **a** the lessening of environmental pollution; **b** increasing leisure; and **c** protection of American producers from foreign competition. Indicate which of these specific goals you favor and justify your position.

9 Explain and give an illustration of **a** the fallacy of composition, and **b** the "after this, therefore because of this" fallacy. Why are cause-and-effect relationships difficult to isolate in the social sciences?

10 "Economists should never be popular; men who afflict the comfortable serve equally those who comfort the afflicted and one cannot suppose that American capitalism would long prosper without the critics its leaders find such a profound source of annoyance."[9] Interpret and evaluate.

11 Use the economic perspective to explain why someone who normally is a light eater at a standard restaurant may become somewhat of a glutton at a buffet-style restaurant which charges a single price for all you can eat.

[5] Henry Clay, *Economics for the General Reader* (New York: The Macmillan Company, 1925), pp. 10–11.

[6] Oskar Lange, "The Scope and Method of Economics," *Review of Economic Studies,* vol. 13, 1945–1946, p. 20.

[7] George J. Stigler, *The Theory of Price* (New York: The Macmillan Company, 1947), p. 10.

[8] Victor R. Fuchs, *How We Live* (Cambridge, Mass.: Harvard University Press, 1983), p. 5.

[9] John Kenneth Galbraith, *American Capitalism,* rev. ed. (Boston: Houghton Mifflin Company, 1956), p. 49.

APPENDIX TO CHAPTER 1

Graphs and Their Meaning

If you glance quickly through this text, you will find graphs. Some will appear to be relatively simple, while others seem more formidable. Contrary to student folklore, graphs are *not* designed by economists to confuse students! On the contrary, graphs are employed to help students visualize and understand important economic relationships. Economists express their theories or models with graphs. The physicist and chemist sometimes illustrate their theories by building Tinker-Toy arrangements of multicolored wooden balls representing protons, neutrons, and so forth, held in proper relation to one another by wires or sticks. Economists often use graphs to illustrate their models, and by understanding these "pictures" students can more readily comprehend what economists are saying.

Most of our principles or models will explain the relationship between just two sets of economic facts; therefore, two-dimensional graphs are a convenient way of visualizing and manipulating these relationships.

Constructing a Graph

A graph is a visual representation of the relationship between two variables. Table 1 is a hypothetical illustration showing the relationship between income and consumption. Without ever having studied economics, one would expect intuitively that high-income people would consume more than low-income people. Thus we are not surprised to find in Table 1 that consumption increases as income increases.

How can the information in Table 1 be expressed graphically? Glance at the graph shown in Figure 1. Now look back at the information in Table 1 and we will explain how to represent that information in a meaningful way by constructing the graph you just examined.

What we want to show visually, or graphically, is how consumption changes as income changes. Since income is the determining factor, we represent it on the horizontal axis of the graph, as is customary. And, because consumption depends on income, we represent it on the vertical axis of the graph, as is also customary. Actually, what we are doing is representing the inde-

TABLE 1 The relationship between income and consumption

Income (per week)	*Consumption (per week)*	*Point*
$ 0	$ 50	a
100	100	b
200	150	c
300	200	d
400	250	e

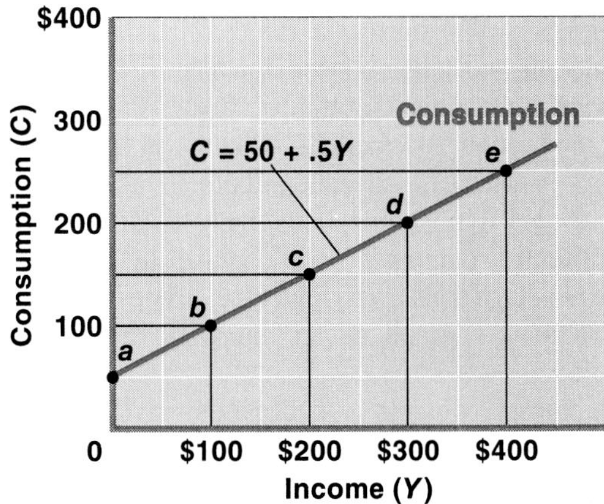

FIGURE 1 Graphing the direct relationship between consumption and income

Two sets of data which are positively or directly related, such as consumption and income, graph as an upsloping line. In this case the vertical intercept is 50 and the slope of the line is $+\frac{1}{2}$.

pendent variable on the horizontal axis and the dependent variable on the vertical axis.

Now we must arrange the vertical and horizontal scales of the graph to reflect the range of values of consumption and income, as well as mark the steps in convenient graphic increments. As you can see, the ranges in the graph cover the ranges of values in Table 1. Similarly, as so happens in this example, the increments on both scales are \$100 for approximately each half-inch.

Next, we must locate for each consumption value and the income value that it depends upon a single point which reflects the same information graphically. Our five income–consumption combinations are plotted by drawing perpendiculars from the appropriate points on the **vertical** and **horizontal axes.** For example, in plotting point *c*—the \$200 income–\$150 consumption point—perpendiculars must be drawn up from the horizontal (income) axis at \$200 and across from the vertical (consumption) axis at \$150. These perpendiculars intersect at point *c,* which locates this particular income–consumption combination. You should verify that the other income–consumption combinations shown in Table 1 are properly located in Figure 1. By assuming that the same general relationship between income and consumption prevails at all other points between the five points graphed, a line or curve can be drawn to connect these points.

Using Figure 1 as a benchmark, we can now make several additional important comments.

Direct and Inverse Relationships

Our upsloping line depicts a direct relationship between income and consumption. By a positive or **direct relationship** we mean that the two variables—in this case consumption and income—change in the *same* direction. An increase in consumption is associated with an increase in income; conversely, a decrease in consumption accompanies a decrease in income. When two sets of data are positively or directly related, they will always graph as an *upsloping* line as in Figure 1.

In contrast, two sets of data may be inversely related. Consider Table 2, which shows the relationship between the price of basketball tickets and game attendance at Gigantic State University. We observe a negative or **inverse relationship** between ticket prices and attendance; these two variables change in *opposite* directions. When ticket prices decrease, attendance increases. Conversely, when ticket prices increase, attendance decreases. In Figure 2 the six data points of Table 2 are plotted following the same procedure outlined above. Observe that an inverse relationship will always graph as a *downsloping* line.

TABLE 2 The relationship between ticket prices and attendance

Ticket price	*Attendance (thousands)*	*Point*
\$25	0	a
20	4	b
15	8	c
10	12	d
5	16	e
0	20	f

Dependent and Independent Variables

Although the task is sometimes formidable, economists seek to determine which variable is "cause" and which "effect." Or, more formally, we want to ascertain the independent and the dependent variable. By definition, the **dependent variable** is the "effect" or out-

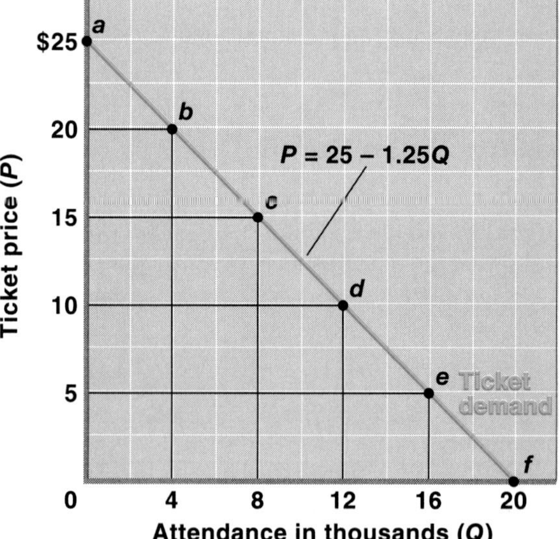

FIGURE 2 Graphing the inverse relationship between ticket prices and game attendance

Two sets of data which are negatively or inversely related, such as ticket price and the attendance at basketball games, graph as a downsloping line. The slope of this line is $-1\frac{1}{4}$.

come; it is the variable which changes because of a change in another (independent) variable.

Similarly, the **independent variable** is the "cause"; it is the variable which causes the change in the dependent variable. As noted earlier in our income–consumption example, generally, income is the independent variable and consumption the dependent variable. Income causes consumption to be what it is rather than the other way around. Similarly, ticket prices determine attendance at GSU basketball games; attendance does not determine ticket prices. Ticket price is the independent variable and the quantity purchased is the dependent variable.

You may recall from your high school courses that mathematicians always put the independent variable (cause) on the horizontal axis and the dependent variable (effect) on the vertical axis. Economists are less tidy; their graphing of independent and dependent variables is more arbitrary. Thus, their conventional graphing of the income–consumption relationship is consistent with mathematical presentation. But economists put price and cost data on the vertical axis. Hence, the economist's graphing of GSU's ticket price–attendance data conflicts with normal mathematical procedure.

Other Variables Held Constant

Our simple two-variable graphs ignore many other factors which might affect the amount of consumption which occurs at each income level or the number of people who attend GSU basketball games at each possible ticket price. When economists plot the relationship between any two variables, they invoke the *ceteris paribus* or "other things being equal" assumption discussed previously. Thus, in Figure 1 all other factors (that is, all factors other than income) which might affect the amount of consumption are presumed to be constant or unchanged. Similarly, in Figure 2 all factors other than ticket price which might influence attendance at GSU basketball games are assumed constant. In reality, we know that "other things" often change, and when they do, the specific relationships presented in our two tables and graphs will change. Specifically, we would expect the lines we have plotted to shift to new locations.

For example, what might happen to the income–consumption relationship if a stock market "crash" such at that of October 1987 occurred? The expected impact of this dramatic fall in the value of stocks would be to make people feel less wealthy and therefore less willing to consume at each income level. In short, we would anticipate a downward shift of the consumption line in Figure 1. You should plot a new consumption line, assuming that consumption is, say, $20 less at each income level. Note that the relationship remains direct, but the line has merely shifted to reflect less consumer spending at each level of income.

Similarly, factors other than ticket prices might affect GSU game attendance. If the government abandoned its program of student loans, GSU enrollment and hence attendance at games might be less at each ticket price. You should redraw Figure 2, assuming that 2000 fewer students attend GSU games at each ticket price. Question 2 at the end of this appendix introduces other variables which might cause the relationship shown in Figure 2 to shift to another position.

Slope of a Line

Lines can be described in terms of their slopes. The **slope of a straight line** between any two points is defined as the ratio of the vertical change (the rise or fall) to the horizontal change (the run) involved in moving between those points. In moving from point *b* to point *c* in Figure 1 the rise or vertical change (the change in consumption) is +$50 and the run or horizontal change (the change in income) is +$100. Therefore:

$$\text{Slope} = \frac{\text{vertical change}}{\text{horizontal change}} = \frac{+50}{+100} = +\frac{1}{2}$$

Note that our slope of $\frac{1}{2}$ is positive because consumption and income change in the same direction, that is, consumption and income are directly or positively related.

This slope of $+\frac{1}{2}$ tells us that there will be a $1 increase in consumption for every $2 increase in income. Similarly, it indicates that for every $2 decrease in income there will be a $1 decrease in consumption.

For our ticket price–attendance data the relationship is negative or inverse with the result that the slope of Figure 2's line is negative. In particular, the vertical change or fall is 5 and the horizontal change or run is 4. Therefore:

$$\text{Slope} = \frac{\text{vertical change}}{\text{horizontal change}} = \frac{-5}{+4} = -1\tfrac{1}{4}$$

This slope of $-5/+4$ or $-1\frac{1}{4}$ means that lowering the price of a ticket by $5 will increase attendance by 4000 people. Or, alternatively stated, it implies that a $1 price reduction will increase attendance by 800 persons.

In addition to its slope, the only other information needed in locating a line is the vertical intercept. By definition, the **vertical intercept** is the point at which the line meets the vertical axis. For Figure 1 the intercept is \$50. This means that, if current income was somehow zero, consumers would still spend \$50. How might they manage to consume when they have no current income? Answer: By borrowing or by selling off some of their assets. Similarly, the vertical intercept in Figure 2 shows us that at a \$25 ticket price GSU's basketball team would be playing in an empty auditorium.

Given the intercept and the slope, our consumption line can be succinctly described in equation form. In general, a linear equation is written as $y = a + bx$, where y is the dependent variable, a is the vertical intercept, b is the slope of the line, and x is the independent variable. For our income–consumption example, if C represents consumption (the dependent variable) and Y represents income (the independent variable), we can write $C = a + bY$. By substituting the values of the intercept and the slope for our specific data, we have $C = 50 + .5Y$. This equation allows us to determine consumption at *any* level of income. At the \$300 income level (point d in Figure 1), our equation predicts that consumption will be \$200 [=\$50 + (.5 × \$300)]. You should confirm that at the \$250 income level consumption will be \$175.

When economists reverse mathematical convention by putting the independent variable on the vertical axis and the dependent variable on the horizontal axis, the standard linear equation solves for the independent, rather than the dependent, variable. We noted earlier that this case is relevant for our GSU ticket price–attendance data. If P represents the ticket price and Q represents attendance, our relevant equation is $P = 25 - 1.25Q$, where the vertical intercept is 25 and the negative slope is $-1\frac{1}{4}$ or -1.25. But knowing the value for P lets us solve for Q, which is actually our dependent variable. For example, if $P = 15$, then the values in our equation become: $15 = 25 - 1.25(Q)$, or $1.25Q = 10$, or $Q = 8$. You should check this answer against Figure 2 and also use this equation to predict GSU ticket sales when price is \$7.50.

Slope of a Nonlinear Curve

We now move from the simple world of linear relationships (straight lines) to the slightly more complex world of nonlinear relationships (curves). By definition, the slope of a straight line is constant throughout. In contrast, the slope of a curve changes as we move from one point to another on the curve. For example, consider the upsloping curve AA in Figure 3a. Although its slope is positive throughout, it diminishes or flattens as we move northeast along the curve. Given

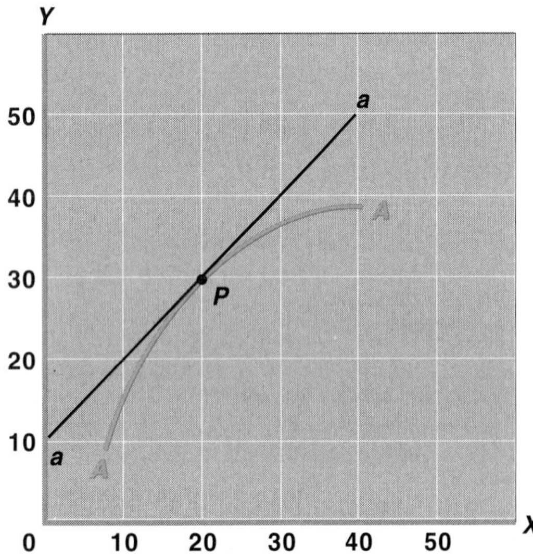

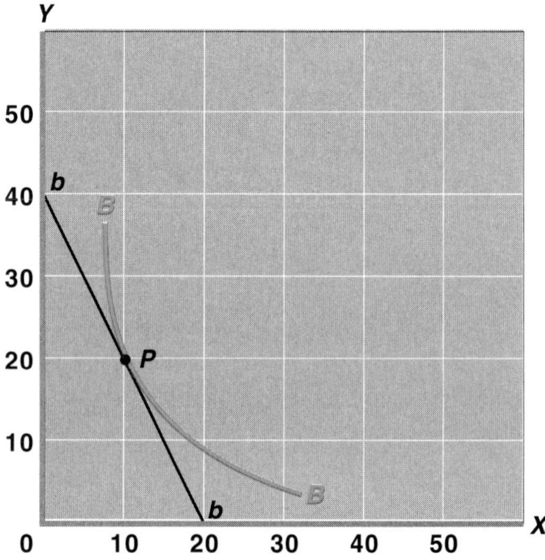

FIGURE 3 **Determining the slopes of curves**

The slope of a nonlinear curve changes as one moves from point to point on the curve. The slope at any point can be determined by drawing a straight line tangent to that point and calculating the slope of that straight line.

that the slope is constantly changing, we can only measure the slope at some particular point on the curve.

We begin by drawing a straight line which is tangent to the curve at that point where we want to measure its slope. By definition, a line is **tangent** at that point where it touches, but does not intersect, the curve. Thus, line *aa* is tangent to curve *AA* at point *P* in Figure 3a. Having done this, we can measure the slope of *AA* at point *P* by measuring the slope of the straight tangent line *aa*. Specifically, in Figure 3a, when the vertical change (rise) in *aa* is +10, the horizontal change (run) is also +10. Thus, the slope of the tangent *aa* line is 10/10 or +1 and therefore the slope of *AA* at *P* is also +1.

Now consider the downsloping curve *BB* in Figure 3b. In this case the slope of *BB* is negative and it diminishes as we move southeast along the curve. What is the slope at point *P*? Again, we draw line *bb* which is tangent to curve *BB* at *P*. Here, when the vertical change (fall) in *bb* is −10, the horizontal change is only +5. Thus, the slope of *BB* at point *P* is −10/+5 or −2. Question 6 at the end of this appendix is relevant.

APPENDIX SUMMARY

1 Graphs are a convenient and revealing means of presenting economic relationships or principles.

2 Two variables are positively or directly related when their values change in the same direction. Two variables which are directly related will plot as an upsloping line on a graph.

3 Two variables are negatively or inversely related when their values change in opposite directions. Two variables which are inversely related will graph as a downsloping line.

4 The value of the dependent variable ("effect") is determined by the value of the independent variable ("cause").

5 When "other factors" which might affect a two-variable relationship are allowed to change, the plotted relationship will likely shift to a new location.

6 The slope of a straight line is the ratio of the vertical change to the horizontal change in moving between any two points. The slope of an upsloping line is positive, while that of a downsloping line is negative.

7 The vertical (or horizontal) intercept and the slope of a line establish its location and are used in expressing the relationship between two variables as an equation.

8 The slope of a curve at any point is determined by calculating the slope of a straight line drawn tangent to that point.

APPENDIX TERMS AND CONCEPTS

vertical and horizontal axes
slope of a straight line
dependent and independent variables
vertical intercept
tangent
direct and inverse relationships

APPENDIX QUESTIONS AND STUDY SUGGESTIONS

*1 Briefly explain the use of graphs as a means of presenting economic principles. What is an inverse relationship? How does it graph? What is a direct relationship? How does it graph? Graph and explain the relationships one would expect to find between **a** the number of inches of rainfall per month and the sale of umbrellas, **b** the amount of tuition and the level of enrollment at a university, and **c** the size of a university's athletic scholarships and the number of games won by its football team.

In each case cite and explain how considerations other than those specifically mentioned might upset the expected relationship. Is your second generalization consistent with the fact that, historically, enrollments and tuition have both increased? If not, explain any difference.

2 Indicate how each of the following might affect the data shown in Table 2 and Figure 2 of this appendix:

a GSU's athletic director schedules higher-quality opponents.

b GSU's Fighting Aardvarks experience three losing seasons.

c GSU contracts to have all its home games televised.

*Note to the reader: A floppy disk symbol precedes each of the questions in this appendix. This icon is used throughout the text to indicate that a particular question relates to the content of one of the tutorial programs in the student software which accompanies this book. Please refer to the Preface for more detail about this software.

3 The following table contains data on the relationship between saving and income. Rearrange these data as required and graph the data on the accompanying grid. What is the slope of the line? The vertical intercept? Interpret the meaning of both the slope and the intercept. Write the equation which represents this line. What would you predict saving to be at the $12,500 level of income?

Income (per year)	*Saving (per year)*
$15,000	$1,000
0	−500
10,000	500
5,000	0
20,000	1,500

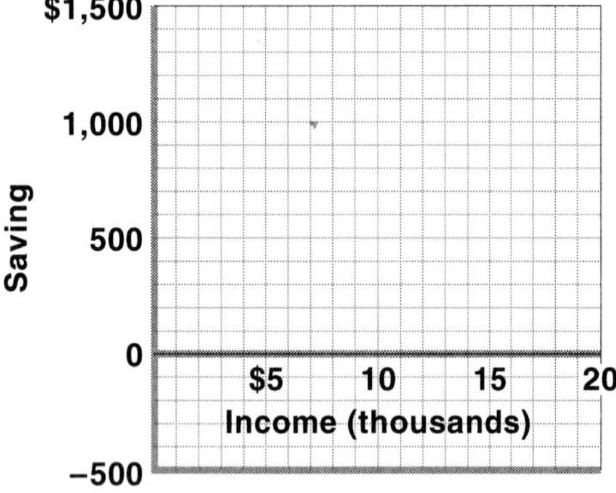

4 Construct a table from the data shown on the accompanying graph. Which is the dependent and which the independent variable? Summarize the data in equation form.

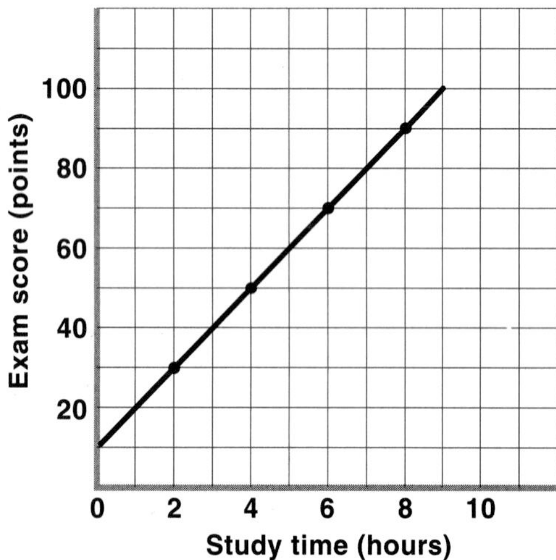

5 Suppose that when the interest rate which must be paid to borrow funds is 16 percent, businesses find it unprofitable to invest in machinery and equipment. However, when the interest rate is 14 percent, $5 billion worth of investment is profitable. At 12 percent, a total of $10 billion of investment is profitable. Similarly, total investment increases by $5 billion for each successive 2 percentage point decline in the interest rate. Indicate the relevant relationship between the interest rate and investment verbally, tabularly, graphically, and as an equation. Put the interest rate on the vertical axis and investment on the horizontal axis. In your equation use the form $i = a - bI$, where i is the interest rate, a is the vertical intercept, b is the slope of the line, and I is the level of investment. Comment on advantages and disadvantages of verbal, tabular, graphical, and equation forms of presentation.

6 The accompanying diagram shows curve *XX* and three tangents at points *A, B,* and *C.* Calculate the slope of the curve at these three points.

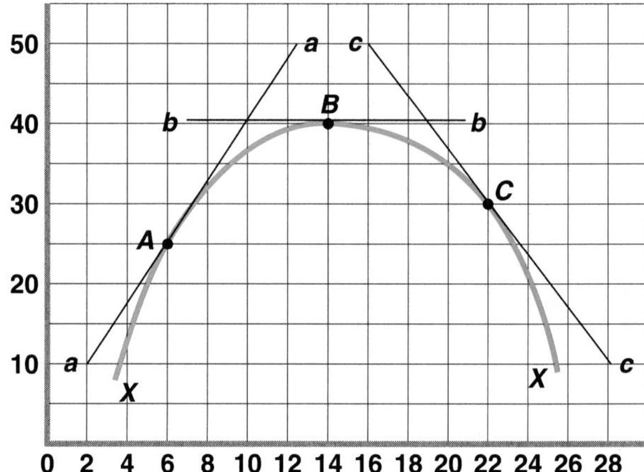

7 In the accompanying diagram, is the slope of curve *AA′* positive or negative? Does the slope increase or decrease as we move from *A* to *A′*? Answer the same two questions for curve *BB′*.

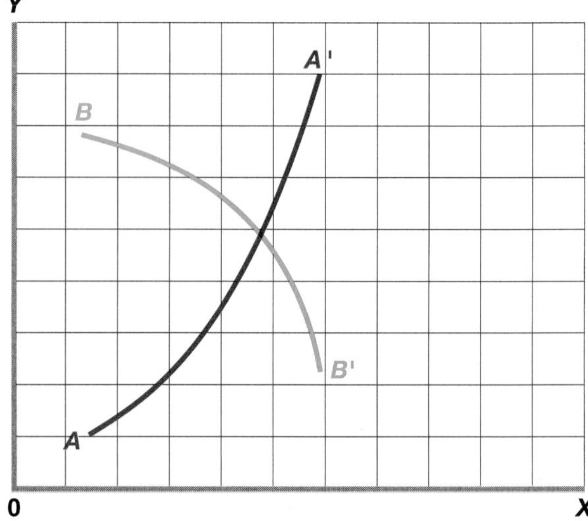

The Economizing Problem

You make decisions every day which capture the essence of economics. Suppose you have $20 and are deciding how to spend it. Should you buy a new pair of blue jeans? A couple of compact discs? A ticket for a rock concert? Similarly, what to do with the time between three and six o'clock on, say, a Thursday afternoon? Should you work extra hours on your part-time job? Do research on a term project? Prepare for an economics quiz? Watch TV? Take a nap? Money and time are both scarce and making decisions in the context of scarcity implies costs. If you choose the jeans, the cost is the forgone CDs or concert. If you nap or watch TV, the cost might be a low grade on your quiz. Scarcity, choices, and costs—these are the building blocks of the present chapter.

This chapter introduces and explores certain fundamental considerations which constitute the foundation of economic science. Basically, we expand on the definition of economics introduced in Chapter 1 and explore the essence of the economizing problem. To this end, we will illustrate, extend, and modify our definition of economics by using so-called production possibilities tables and curves. Finally, we will survey briefly different ways in which institutionally and ideologically diverse economies "solve" or respond to the economizing problem.

THE FOUNDATION OF ECONOMICS

Two fundamental facts which constitute the **economizing problem** provide a foundation for the field of economics. We must carefully state and fully understand these two facts, because everything that follows in our study of economics depends directly or indirectly upon them.

1 *Society's material wants, that is, the material wants of its citizens and institutions, are virtually unlimited or insatiable.*

2 *Economic resources—the means of producing goods and services—are limited or scarce.*

Unlimited Wants

In the first statement, precisely what is meant by "material wants"? We mean, first, the desires of consumers to obtain and use various *goods* and *services* which provide **utility,** the economist's term for pleasure or satisfaction.[1] An amazingly wide range of products fills the bill in this respect: houses, automobiles, toothpaste, compact-disc players, pizzas, sweaters, and the like. In short, innumerable products which we sometimes classify as *necessities* (food, shelter, clothing) and *luxuries* (perfumes, yachts, mink coats) all can satisfy human wants. Needless to say, what is a luxury to Smith may be a necessity to Jones, and what is a commonplace necessity today may have been a luxury a few years ago.

But services satisfy our wants as much as tangible products. A repair job on our car, the removal of our appendix, a haircut, and legal advice have in common with goods the fact that they satisfy human wants. On reflection, we realize that we indeed buy many goods, for example, automobiles and washing machines, for the services they render. The differences between goods and services are often less than they seem to be at first.

Material wants also include those which businesses and units of government seek to satisfy. Businesses want factory buildings, machinery, trucks, warehouses, communications systems, and other things that help them realize their production goals. Government, reflecting the collective wants of its citizenry or goals of its own, seeks highways, schools, hospitals, and military hardware.

As a group, these material wants are, for practical purposes, *insatiable,* or *unlimited,* meaning that material wants for goods and services cannot be completely satisfied. Our wants for a *particular* good or service can be satisfied; that is, over a short period of time we can get enough toothpaste or beer. Certainly one appendicitis operation is par for the course. But goods *in general* are another story. Here we do not, and presumably cannot, get enough. A simple experiment will help verify this point: Suppose we are asked to list those goods and services we want but do not now possess. If we ponder our unfilled material wants, chances are our list will be impressive.

Furthermore, over a period of time, wants multiply so that, as we fill some of the wants on the list, we add new ones. Material wants, like rabbits, have a high reproduction rate. The rapid introduction of new products whets our appetites, and extensive advertising tries to persuade us that we need items we might not otherwise consider buying. Not long ago, the desire for personal computers, light beer, video recorders, fax machines, and compact discs was nonexistent. Furthermore, we often cannot stop with simple satisfaction: The acquisition of an Escort or Geo has been known to whet the appetite for a Porsche or Mercedes.

At any given time the individuals and institutions which constitute society have innumerable unfulfilled material wants. Some—food, clothing, shelter—have biological roots. But some are also influenced by the conventions and customs of society: The specific kinds of food, clothing, and shelter we seek are frequently determined by the general social and cultural environment in which we live. Over time, wants change and multiply, fueled by development of new products and extensive advertising and sales promotion.

Again, let us stress that the overall objective of all economic activity is the attempt to satisfy these diverse material wants.

Scarce Resources

In considering the second fundamental fact, *economic resources are limited or scarce,* what do we mean by "economic resources"? In general, we mean all natural, human, and manufactured resources that go into the production of goods and services. This covers a lot of ground: factory and farm buildings and all equipment, tools, and machinery used to produce manufactured goods and agricultural products; a variety of transportation and communication facilities; innumerable types of labor; and land and mineral resources of all kinds. Economists broadly classify such resources as either (1) *property* resources—land or raw materials and capital; or (2) *human* resources—labor and entrepreneurial ability.

Resource Categories Let's examine these various resource categories.

Land By **land** the economist means much more than do most people. Land is all natural resources—all "gifts of nature"—usable in the productive process. Such resources as arable land, forests, mineral and oil deposits, and water resources come under this classification.

Capital **Capital,** or investment goods, is all manufactured aids to production, that is, all tools, machinery,

[1] This definition leaves a variety of wants—recognition, status, love, and so forth—for the other social sciences to worry about.

equipment, and factory, storage, transportation, and distribution facilities used in producing goods and services and getting them to the ultimate consumer. The process of producing and purchasing capital goods is known as **investment.**

Two other points are pertinent. First, *capital goods* ("tools") differ from *consumer goods* in that the latter satisfy wants directly, whereas the former do so indirectly by facilitating production of consumable goods. Second, the term "capital" as here defined does *not* refer to money. True, business executives and economists often talk of "money capital," meaning money available to purchase machinery, equipment, and other productive facilities. But money, as such, produces nothing; hence, it is not considered an economic resource. *Real capital*—tools, machinery, and other productive equipment—is an economic resource; *money* or *financial capital* is not.

Labor **Labor** is a broad term the economist uses for all the physical and mental talents of men and women which are available and usable in producing goods and services. (This excludes a special set of human talents—entrepreneurial ability—which, because of their special significance in a capitalistic economy, we will consider separately.) Thus the services of a logger, retail clerk, machinist, teacher, professional football player, and nuclear physicist all fall under the general heading of labor.

Entrepreneurial Ability Finally, there is the special human resource which we label **entrepreneurial ability,** or, more simply, *enterprise.* We can assign four related functions to the entrepreneur.

1 The entrepreneur takes the initiative in combining the resources of land, capital, and labor to produce a good or service. Both a sparkplug and a catalyst, the entrepreneur is at once the driving force behind production and the agent who combines the other resources in what is hoped will be a profitable venture.

2 The entrepreneur makes basic business-policy decisions, that is, those nonroutine decisions which set the course of a business enterprise.

3 The entrepreneur is an innovator—the one who attempts to introduce on a commercial basis new products, new productive techniques, or even new forms of business organization.

4 The entrepreneur is a risk bearer. This is apparent from a close examination of the other three entrepreneurial functions. The entrepreneur in a capitalistic system has no guarantee of profit. The reward for his or her time, efforts, and abilities may be attractive profits *or* losses and eventual bankruptcy. In short, the entrepreneur risks not only time, effort, and business reputation, but his or her invested funds and those of associates or stockholders.

Resource Payments We will see shortly how these resources are provided to business institutions in exchange for money income. The income received from supplying property resources—raw materials and capital equipment—is called *rental* and *interest income,* respectively. The income accruing to those who supply labor is called *wages* and includes salaries and various wage and salary supplements in the form of bonuses, commissions, royalties, and so forth. Entrepreneurial income is called *profits,* which, of course, may be a negative figure—that is, losses.

These four broad categories of economic resources, or *factors of production* or *inputs* as they are often called, leave room for debate when it comes to classifying specific resources. For example, suppose you receive a dividend on some newly issued Exxon stock which you own. Is this an interest return for the capital equipment the company bought with the money you provided in buying Exxon stock? Or is this return a profit which compensates you for the risks involved in purchasing corporate stock? What about the earnings of a one-person general store where the owner is both entrepreneur and labor force? Are the owner's earnings considered wages or profit income? The answer to both queries is "some of each." The point is that while we might quibble about classifying a given flow of income as wages, rent, interest, or profits, all income can be fitted under one of these general headings.

Relative Scarcity Economic resources, or factors of production, have one fundamental characteristic in common: *They are scarce or limited in supply.* Our "spaceship earth" contains only limited amounts of resources to use in producing goods and services. Quantities of arable land, mineral deposits, capital equipment, and labor (time) are all limited; that is, they are available only in finite amounts. Because of the scarcity of productive resources and the constraint this scarcity puts on productive activity, output will necessarily be limited. Society will *not* be able to produce and consume all the goods and services it might want. Thus, in the United States—one of the most affluent nations—output per person was limited to $22,419 in 1991. In the poorest nations annual output per person is as low as $200 or $300!

ECONOMICS AND EFFICIENCY

We have arrived once again at the basic definition of economics first stated at the beginning of Chapter 1. *Economics is the social science concerned with the problem of using or administering scarce resources (the means of producing) to attain the greatest or maximum fulfillment of society's unlimited wants (the goal of producing).* Economics is concerned with "doing the best with what we have." If our wants are virtually unlimited and our resources scarce, we cannot satisfy all of society's material wants. The next best thing is to achieve the greatest possible satisfaction of these wants.

Full Employment and Full Production

Economics is a science of efficiency—efficiency in the use of scarce resources. Society wants to use its limited resources efficiently; that is, it wants to get the maximum amount of useful goods and services produced with its available resources. To achieve this it must realize both full employment and full production.

Full Employment By **full employment** we mean that all available resources should be employed. No workers should be involuntarily out of work; the economy should provide employment for all who are willing and able to work. Nor should capital equipment or arable land sit idle. Note we say all *available* resources should be employed. Each society has certain customs and practices which determine what particular resources are available for employment. For example, legislation and custom provide that children and the very aged should not be employed. Similarly, it is desirable for productivity to allow farmland to lie fallow periodically.

Full Production But the employment of all available resources is insufficient to achieve efficiency. Full production must also be realized. By **full production** we mean that all employed resources should be used to make the most valued contributions to the domestic output. If we fail to realize full production, economists say that our resources are *underemployed.*

Full production implies that two kinds of efficiency—allocative and productive efficiency—are achieved.

Allocative efficiency means that resources are devoted to goods most wanted by society; for example, compact discs and cassettes, rather than 45 rpm or long-play records. Society wants resources apportioned to word processors, not mechanical typewriters, and to xerox, not mimeograph, machines. Nor do we want Iowa's farmland planted to cotton and Alabama's to corn when the opposite assignment would provide the nation with substantially more of both products from the same amount of land.

Productive efficiency means that the least costly production techniques are used to produce wanted goods and services. Efficiency requires that Tauruses and Grand Ams be produced with computerized and roboticized assembly techniques rather than with the primitive assembly lines of the 1920s. Nor do we want our farmers harvesting wheat with scythes or picking corn by hand when elaborate harvesting equipment will do the job at a much lower cost per bushel.

In summary, allocative efficiency means that resources are apportioned among firms and industries to obtain the particular mix of products society wants the most. Productive efficiency means that each good or service in this optimal product mix is produced in the least costly fashion. Full production means producing the "right" goods (allocative efficiency) in the "right" way (productive efficiency).

QUICK REVIEW 2-1

- ***Human material wants are virtually unlimited.***
- ***Economic resources—land, capital, labor, and entrepreneurial ability—are scarce or limited.***
- ***Economics is concerned with the efficient management of these scarce resources to achieve the maximum fulfillment of our material wants.***
- ***Economic efficiency entails full employment and full production.***

Production Possibilities Table

The nature of the economizing problem can be clarified by the use of a production possibilities table. This device reveals the core of the economizing problem: *Because resources are scarce, a full-employment, full-production economy cannot have an unlimited output of goods and services. As a result, choices must be made on which goods and services to produce and which to forgo.*

Assumptions Several specific assumptions will set the stage for our illustration.

1 Efficiency The economy is operating at full employment and achieving full production.

2 Fixed Resources The available supplies of the factors of production are fixed in both quantity and quality. But, of course, they can be shifted or reallocated, within limits, among different uses; for example, a relatively unskilled laborer can work on a farm, at a fast-food restaurant, or in a gas station.

3 Fixed Technology The state of the technological arts is constant; that is, technology does not change during the course of our analysis. The second and third assumptions are another way of saying that we are looking at our economy at a specific point in time, or over a very short period of time. Over a relatively long period it would be unrealistic to rule out technological advances and the possibility that resource supplies might vary.

4 Two Products To simplify our illustration further, suppose our economy is producing just two products—industrial robots and pizza—instead of the innumerable goods and services actually produced. Pizza is symbolic of **consumer goods,** those goods which directly satisfy our wants; industrial robots are symbolic of **capital goods,** those goods which satisfy our wants *indirectly* by permitting more efficient production of consumer goods.

Necessity of Choice It is evident from our assumptions that a choice must be made among alternatives. Available resources are limited. Consequently, the total amounts of robots and pizza that our economy can produce are limited. *Limited resources mean a limited output.* Since resources are limited in supply and fully employed, any increase in the production of robots will mean shifting resources away from the production of pizza. And the reverse holds true: If we step up the production of pizza, needed resources must come at the expense of robot production. *Society cannot have its cake and eat it, too.* Facetiously put, there's no such thing as a "free lunch." This is the essence of the economizing problem.

Let's generalize by noting in Table 2-1 alternative combinations of robots and pizza which our economy might choose. Though the data in this and the following **production possibilities tables** are hypothetical, the points illustrated have tremendous practical significance. At alternative A, our economy would be devoting all its resources to the production of robots (capital goods). At alternative E, all available resources would go to pizza production (consumer goods). Both these alternatives are clearly unrealistic extremes; any economy typically strikes a balance in dividing its total output between capital and consumer goods. As we move from alternative A to E, we step up the production of consumer goods (pizza), by shifting resources away from capital goods (robot) production.

TABLE 2-1 **Production possibilities of pizza and robots with full employment, 1993 *(hypothetical data)***

Type of product	*Production alternatives*				
	A	*B*	*C*	*D*	*E*
Pizza (in hundred thousands)	**0**	**1**	**2**	**3**	**4**
Robots (in thousands)	**10**	**9**	**7**	**4**	**0**

Remembering that consumer goods directly satisfy our wants, any movement toward alternative E looks tempting. In making this move, society increases the current satisfaction of its wants; but there is a cost involved. This shift of resources catches up with society over time as its stock of capital goods dwindles—or at least ceases to expand at the current rate—with the result that the potential for greater future production is impaired. In short, in moving from alternative A toward E, society chooses "more now" at the expense of "much more later."

In moving from E toward A, society chooses to forgo current consumption. This sacrifice of current consumption frees resources which can now be used to increase production of capital goods. By building up its stock of capital in this way, society can anticipate greater production and, therefore, greater consumption in the future.

At any point in time, a full-employment, full-production economy must sacrifice some of product X to obtain more of product Y. The basic fact that economic resources are scarce prohibits such an economy from having more of both X and Y.

Production Possibilities Curve

To ensure our understanding of the production possibilities table, let's view these data graphically. We employ a simple two-dimensional graph, arbitrarily putting the output of robots (capital goods) on the vertical

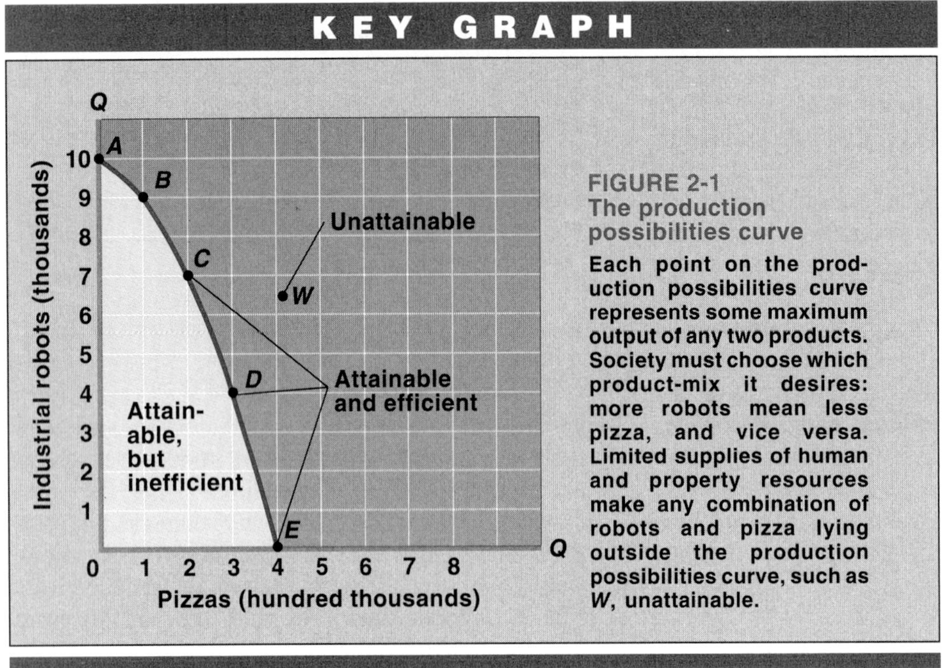

FIGURE 2-1
The production possibilities curve
Each point on the production possibilities curve represents some maximum output of any two products. Society must choose which product-mix it desires: more robots mean less pizza, and vice versa. Limited supplies of human and property resources make any combination of robots and pizza lying outside the production possibilities curve, such as *W*, unattainable.

axis and the output of pizza (consumer goods) on the horizontal axis, as in Figure 2-1 (Key Graph). Following the plotting procedure discussed in the appendix to Chapter 1, we can locate the "production possibilities" curve, as shown in Figure 2-1.

Each point on the production possibilities curve represents some maximum output of the two products. Thus the curve is, in effect, a frontier. To realize the various combinations of pizza and robots which fall on the production possibilities curve, society must achieve full employment and full production. All combinations of pizza and robots *on* the curve represent maximum quantities attainable only as the result of the most efficient use of all available resources. Points lying *inside* the curve are also attainable, but are not as desirable as points on the curve. These points imply a failure to achieve full employment and full production. Points lying *outside* the production possibilities curve, like point *W*, would be superior to any point on the curve; but such points are unattainable, given the current supplies of resources and technology. The production barrier of limited resources prohibits production of any combination of capital and consumer goods lying outside the production possibilities curve.

Optimal Product-Mix

If all outputs on the production possibilities curve reflect full employment and full production, which combination will society prefer? Consider, for example, points *C* and *D* in Figure 2-1. Which output-mix is superior or "best"? This is a nonscientific or normative matter; it reflects the values of society as expressed by its control group—the dictatorship, the party, the electorate, the citizenry, the individual institutions, or some combination thereof. What the economist can say is this: If a society's production possibilities are as in Table 2-1 *and* if that society seeks the product-mix indicated by, say, alternative *C*, it is *not* using its resources efficiently if it realizes a total output composed only of 6 units of robots and 1 unit of pizza. And the economist can also say that the society cannot hope to achieve a domestic output of 8 units of robots and 3 units of pizza with its available resources. These are quantitative, objective, positive statements. But, although the economist may have opinions as an individual, as a social scientist he or she cannot say that combination *C* is "better" or "worse" than combination *D*. This is a qualitative or normative matter.

Law of Increasing Opportunity Costs

We have stressed that resources are scarce relative to the virtually unlimited wants which these resources can be used to satisfy. As a result, choices among alternatives must be made. Specifically, more of X (pizza) means less of Y (robots). *The amount of other products which must be forgone or sacrificed to obtain some amount of any given product is called the opportunity cost of that good.* In our case the amount of Y (robots) which must be forgone or given up to get another unit of X (pizza) is the *opportunity cost,* or simply the *cost,* of that unit of X.

In moving from possibility A to B in Table 2-1, we find that the cost of 1 unit of pizza is 1 unit of robots. But, as we now pursue the concept of cost through the additional production possibilities—B to C, C to D, and so forth—an important economic principle is revealed. In shifting from alternative A to alternative E, the sacrifice or cost of robots involved in getting each additional unit of pizza *increases.* In moving from A to B, just 1 unit of robots is sacrificed for 1 more unit of pizza; but going from B to C sacrifices 2 units of robots for 1 more unit of pizza; then 3 of robots for 1 of pizza; and finally 4 for 1. Conversely, you should confirm that in moving from E to A the cost of an additional robot is $\frac{1}{4}$, $\frac{1}{3}$, $\frac{1}{2}$, and 1 unit of pizza respectively for each of the four shifts.

Note that this discussion of opportunity cost is couched in terms of an *added* or *marginal* unit of a good rather than *total,* or cumulative, opportunity cost. For example, the opportunity cost of the third unit of pizza in Table 2-1 is 3 units of robots (=7 − 4). But the total opportunity cost of 3 units of pizza is 6 units of robots (=10 − 4 or 1 + 2 + 3).

Concavity Graphically, the **law of increasing opportunity costs** is reflected in the shape of the production possibilities curve. Specifically, the curve is *concave* or bowed out from the origin. As verified by the white lines in Figure 2-1, when the economy moves from *A* toward *E,* it must give up successively larger amounts of robots (1, 2, 3, 4) as shown on the vertical axis to acquire equal increments of pizza (1, 1, 1, 1) as shown on the horizontal axis. This means that the slope of the production possibilities curve becomes steeper as we move from *A* to *E* and such a curve, by definition, is concave as viewed from the origin.

Rationale What is the economic rationale for the law of increasing opportunity costs? *Why* does the sacrifice of robots increase as we get more pizza? The answer is rather complex, but, simply stated, it amounts to this: *Economic resources are not completely adaptable to alternative uses.* As we step up pizza production, resources which are less and less adaptable to this use must be induced, or "pushed," into this line of production. If we start at *A* and move to *B,* we can first pick resources whose productivity of pizza is greatest in relation to their productivity of robots. But as we move from *B* to *C, C* to *D,* and so on, resources highly productive of pizza become increasingly scarce. To get more pizza, resources whose productivity in robots is great in relation to their productivity in pizza will be needed. It will take more and more of such resources—and hence a greater sacrifice of robots—to achieve a given increase of 1 unit in the production of pizza. This lack of perfect flexibility, or interchangeability, on the part of resources and the resulting increase in the sacrifice of one good that must be made in acquiring of more and more units of another good is the rationale for the law of increasing opportunity costs. In this case, these costs are stated as sacrifices of goods and not in terms of dollars and cents.

QUICK REVIEW 2-2

The production possibilities curve illustrates four basic concepts:

- ***The* scarcity *of resources is implicit in that all combinations of output lying outside the production possibilities curve are unattainable.***
- **Choice *is reflected in the need for society to select among the various attainable combinations of goods lying on the curve.***
- ***The downward slope of the curve implies the notion of* opportunity cost.**
- ***The concavity of the curve reveals* increasing opportunity costs.**

UNEMPLOYMENT, GROWTH, AND THE FUTURE

It is important to understand what happens when the first three assumptions underlying the production possibilities curve are released.

Unemployment and Underemployment

The first assumption was that our economy is characterized by full employment and full production. How would our analysis and conclusions be altered if idle resources were available (unemployment) or if employed resources were used inefficiently (underemployment)? With full employment and full production, our five alternatives represent a series of maximum outputs; they illustrate combinations of robots and pizzas which might be produced when the economy is operating at full capacity. With *un*employment or *under*employment, the economy would produce less than each alternative shown in Table 2-1.

Graphically, a situation of unemployment or underemployment can be illustrated by a point *inside* the original production possibilities curve, which has been reproduced in Figure 2-2. Point *U* is such a point. Here the economy is falling short of the various maximum combinations of pizza and robots reflected by all the points *on* the production possibilities curve. The arrows in Figure 2-2 indicate three of the possible paths back to full employment and full production. A move toward full employment and full production will entail a greater output of one or both products.

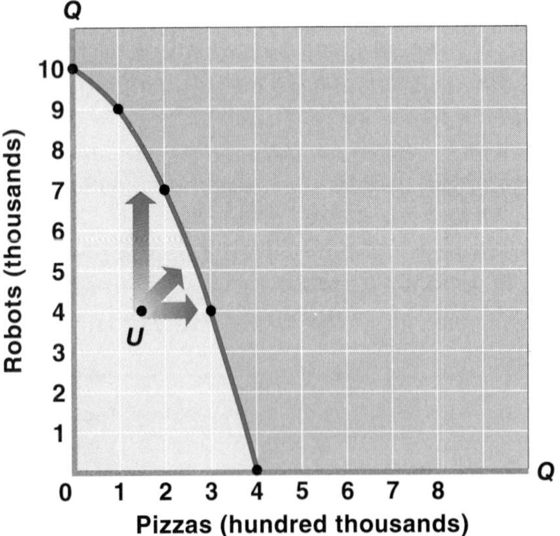

FIGURE 2-2 Unemployment and the production possibilities curve

Any point inside the production possibilities curve, such as *U*, indicates unemployment or underemployment. By moving toward full employment and full production, the economy can produce more of either or both of the two products, as the arrows indicate.

A Growing Economy

When we drop the remaining assumptions that the quantity and quality of resources and technology are fixed, the production possibilities curve will shift position; that is, the potential total output of the economy will change.

Expanding Resource Supplies Let's now abandon the simplifying assumption that our total supplies of land, labor, capital, and entrepreneurial ability are fixed in both quantity and quality. Common sense tells us that over time a nation's growing population will bring about increases in supplies of labor and entrepreneurial ability.[2] Also, labor quality usually improves over time. For example, the percentage of the labor force with a high school education rose from 30 percent in 1960 to 40 percent in 1989. Historically, our stock of capital has increased at a significant, though unsteady, rate. And although we are depleting some of our energy and mineral resources, new sources are being discovered. The drainage of swamps and the development of irrigation programs add to our supply of arable land.

Assuming continuous full employment and full production, the net result of these increased supplies of the factors of production will be the ability to produce more of both robots and pizza. Thus, in the year 2013, the production possibilities of Table 2-1 for 1993 may be obsolete, having given way to those shown in Table 2-2. Observe that the greater abundance of resources results in a greater potential output of one or both products at each alternative; economic growth, in the sense of an expanded potential output, has occurred.

But note that such a favorable shift in the production possibilities curve does not guarantee that the economy will actually operate at a point on that new curve. The economy might fail to realize fully its new potentialities. Some 125 million jobs will give us full employment now, but ten or twenty years from now our labor force, because of a growing population, will be larger, and 125 million jobs will not be sufficient for

[2]This does not mean that population growth as such is always desirable. Overpopulation can be a constant drag on the living standards of many less developed countries. In advanced countries overpopulation can have adverse effects on the environment and the quality of life.

TABLE 2-2 **Production possibilities of pizza and robots with full employment, 2013 *(hypothetical data)***

Type of product	*Production alternatives*				
	A′	*B′*	*C′*	*D′*	*E′*
Pizza (in hundred thousands)	**0**	**2**	**4**	**6**	**8**
Robots (in thousands)	**14**	**12**	**9**	**5**	**0**

full employment. In short, the production possibilities curve may shift, but the economy may fail to produce at a point on that new curve.

Technological Advance Our other simplifying assumption is a constant or unchanging technology. We know that technology has progressed remarkably over a long period. An advancing technology entails new and better goods *and* improved ways of producing these goods. For now, let's think of technological advance as comprising merely improvements in capital facilities—more efficient machinery and equipment. Such technological advance alters our earlier discussion of the economizing problem by improving productive efficiency, thus allowing society to produce more goods with fixed resources. As with increases in resource supplies, technological advance permits the production of more robots *and* more pizza.

When the supplies of resources increase or an improvement in technology occurs, the production possibilities curve of Figure 2-2 shifts outward and to the right, as illustrated by the *A′B′C′D′E′* curve in Figure 2-3. **Economic growth**—*the ability to produce a larger total output—is reflected in a rightward shift of the production possibilities curve; it is the result of increases in resource supplies, improvements in resource quality, and technological progress.* The consequence of growth is that our full-employment economy can enjoy a greater output of *both* robots and pizza. While a static, no-growth economy must sacrifice some of X to get more Y, a dynamic, growing economy can have larger quantities of both X and Y.

Economic growth does *not* typically mean proportionate increases in a nation's capacity to produce various products. Note in Figure 2-3 that, while the economy can produce twice as much pizza, the increase in robot production is only 40 percent. On Figure 2-3 you should pencil in two new production possibilities curves: one to show the situation where a better technique for producing robots has been developed, the technology for producing pizza being unchanged, and the other to illustrate an improved technology for pizza, the technology for producing robots being constant.

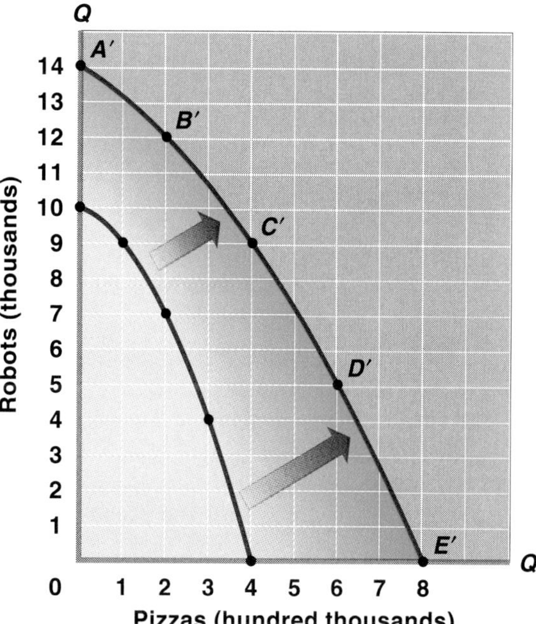

FIGURE 2-3 **Economic growth and the production possibilities curve**

The expanding resource supplies, improved resource quality, and technological advances which characterize a growing economy move the production possibilities curve outward and to the right. This permits the economy to enjoy larger quantities of both types of goods.

Present Choices and Future Possibilities *An economy's current choice of position on its production possibilities curve is a basic determinant of the future location of that curve.* Let's designate the two axes of the production possibilities curve as "goods for the future" and "goods for the present," as in Figures 2-4a and b. "Goods for the future" are such things as capital goods, research and education, and preventive medicine, which increase the quantity and quality of property resources, enlarge the stock of technological information, and improve the quality of human resources. As we have already seen, "goods for the future" are the ingredients of economic growth. "Goods for the present" are pure consumer goods such as foodstuffs, clothing, "boom boxes," and automobiles.

Now suppose there are two economies, Alphania and Betania, which are identical in every respect ex-

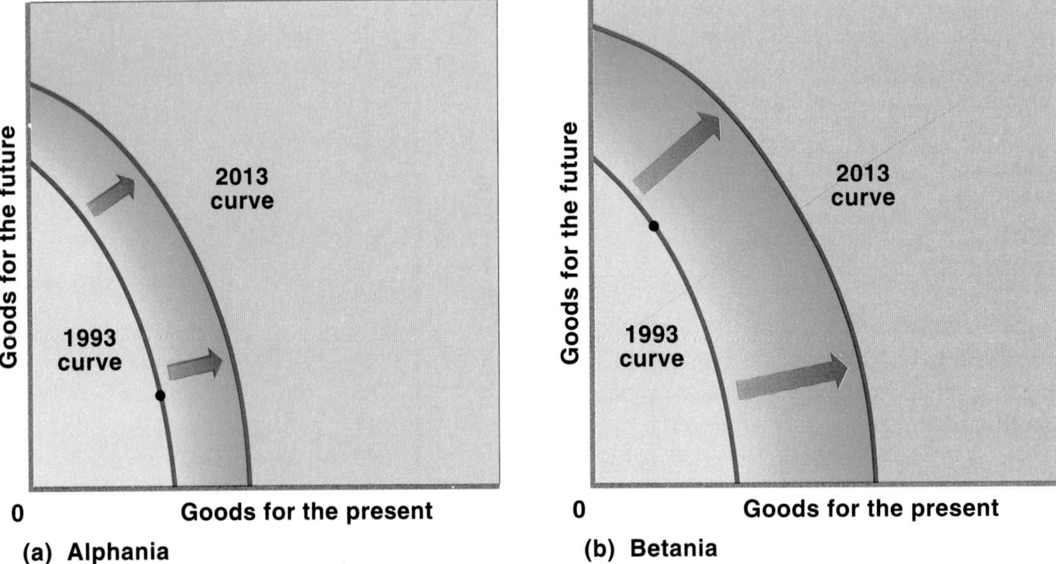

FIGURE 2-4 An economy's present choice of position on its production possibilities curve helps determine the curve's future location

A current choice favoring "present goods," as rendered by Alphania in (a), will cause a modest rightward shift of the curve. A current choice favoring "future goods," as rendered by Betania in (b), will result in a greater rightward shift of the curve.

cept that Alphania's current (1993) choice of position on its production possibilities curve strongly favors "present goods" as opposed to "future goods." The dot in Figure 2-4a indicates this choice. Betania, on the other hand, makes a current (1993) choice which stresses large amounts of "future goods" and lesser amounts of "present goods" (Figure 2-4b).

Now, all other things being the same, we can expect the future (2013) production possibilities curve of Betania to be farther to the right than that of Alphania. That is, by currently choosing an output more conducive to technological advance and to increases in the quantity and quality of property and human resources, Betania will tend to achieve greater economic growth than Alphania, whose current choice of output places less emphasis on those goods and services which cause the production possibilities curve to shift rightward. In terms of capital goods, Betania is choosing to make larger current additions to its "national factory"—that is, to invest more of its current output—than Alphania. The payoff or benefit from this choice is more rapid growth—greater future productive capacity—for Betania. The opportunity cost is fewer consumer goods in the present.

QUICK REVIEW 2-3

- ***Unemployment and underemployment (the inefficient use of employed resources) cause the economy to operate at a point inside its production possibilities curve.***
- ***Expanding resource supplies, improvements in resource quality, and technological progress cause economic growth, that is, an outward shift of the production possibilities curve.***
- ***An economy's present choice of output—particularly of capital and consumer goods—helps determine the future location of its production possibilities curve.***

Real-World Applications

There are many possible applications of the production possibilities curve.

1 Microeconomic Budgeting While our discussion is in macroeconomic terms—that is, in terms of the output of the entire economy—the concepts of scarcity, choice, and opportunity cost also apply at the microeconomic level. You should reread the first paragraph of this chapter at this point.

2 Going to War In beginning to produce war goods for World War II (1939–1945), the United States found itself with considerable unemployment. Our economy was able to produce an almost unbelievably large quantity of war goods and at the same time increase the output of consumer goods (Figure 2-2). The Soviet Union, on the other hand, entered World War II at almost capacity production; that is, the Soviet economy was operating close to full employment. Its military preparations entailed considerable shifting of resources from production of civilian goods with a drop in the standard of living.

Curiously, the United States' position during the Vietnam War was similar to that of the Soviet Union during World War II. Our economy was at full employment in the mid-1960s and the Johnson administration accelerated military spending for Vietnam while simultaneously increasing expenditures on domestic "war on poverty" programs. This attempt to achieve simultaneously more pizza and more robots—or, more accurately, more guns and more butter—in a full-employment economy was doomed to failure. The attempt to spend beyond our capacity to produce—to realize a point like *W* in Figure 2-1—contributed significantly to the double-digit inflation of the 1970s.

3 Discrimination Discrimination based on race, gender, age, or ethnic background impedes the efficient allocation or employment of human resources, keeping the economy operating at some point inside its production possibilities curve. Discrimination prevents blacks, women, and others from obtaining jobs in which society can use efficiently their skills and talents. Elimination of discrimination would help move the economy from some point inside the production possibilities curve toward a point on the curve.

4 Productivity Slowdown Since the mid-1960s the United States has experienced a rather alarming decline in the rate of growth of labor productivity; that is, the growth of output per worker-hour has diminished. Some economists feel a major cause of this decline is that the rate of increase in the mechanization of labor has slowed because of insufficient investment. One proposed remedy is to increase investment as compared to consumption. That is, a *D* to *C* type of shift in Figure 2-1 is recommended. Special tax incentives to make business investment more profitable are an appropriate policy to facilitate this shift. The expectation is that the restoration of a more rapid rate of productivity growth will accelerate the growth of the economy (that is, the rightward shift of the production possibilities curve) through time.

5 Growth: Japan versus United States The growth impact of a nation's decision on how much of its domestic output will be devoted to investment and how much to consumption is illustrated vividly in comparing Japan and the United States. Recently, Japan has been investing over 25 percent of its domestic output in productive machinery and equipment compared to only about 10 percent for the United States. The consequences are in accord with our earlier discussion. Over the 1960–1990 period Japan's domestic output expanded at about 6.4 percent per year compared to only 3.2 percent for the United States. In other words, Japan's production possibilities curve shifted outward more rapidly than the United States' curve. This is reflected in living standards. In 1980 the per capita output of Japan was \$16,711 as compared to \$17,643 for the United States. By 1989 these figures had changed to \$22,884 and \$21,404 respectively.

6 International Trade Aspects The message of the production possibilities curve is that a nation cannot live beyond its means or production potential. When the possibility of international trade is taken into account, this statement must be modified in two ways.

Trade and Growth We will discover in later chapters that a nation can circumvent the output constraint imposed by its domestic production possibilities curve through international specialization and trade. International specialization and trade have the same impact as having more and better resources or discovering improved production techniques. Both have the effect of increasing the quantities of both capital and consumer goods available to society. International specialization and trade are the equivalent of economic growth.

Trade Deficits Within the context of international trade, a nation can achieve a combination of goods outside its domestic production possibilities curve (such as point *W* in Figure 2-1) by incurring a *trade deficit.* A nation may buy and receive an amount of imported goods from other nations which exceeds the amount of goods it exports. The United States has been doing just that recently. In 1990 the United States had a trade deficit of approximately $108 billion. In other words, we imported $108 billion more worth of goods than we exported. The net result was that in 1990 the United States enjoyed some $108 billion of output over what it produced domestically.

This looks like a very favorable state of affairs. Unfortunately, there is a catch. To finance its deficit—to pay for its excess of imports over exports—the United States must go into debt to its international trading partners *or* it must give up ownership of some of its assets to those other nations. Analogy: How can you live beyond your current income? Answer: Borrow from your parents, the sellers of goods, or a financial institution. Or, alternatively, sell some of your real assets (your car or stereo) or financial assets (stocks or bonds) which you own. This is what the United States has been doing.

A major consequence of our large and persistent trade deficits is that foreign nationals hold larger portions of American private and public debt and own larger amounts of our business corporations, agricultural land, and real estate. To pay our debts and repurchase those assets we must in the future live well *within* our means. We must settle for some combination of goods within our production possibilities curve so that we can export more than we import—that is, incur a *trade surplus*—to pay off our world debts and reacquire ownership of those assets. On the other hand, to the extent that some of our imports are capital goods, our future production possibilities curve will be farther rightward than it might otherwise be.

7 Famine in Africa Modern industrial societies take economic growth—more-or-less continuous rightward shifts of the production possibilities curve—for granted. But, as the recent catastrophic famine in Ethiopia, Chad, the Sudan, and other African nations indicates, in some circumstances the production possibilities curve may shift leftward. In addition to drought, an important cause of the African famine is ecological degradation or, more simply, poor land-use practices. Land has been deforested, overfarmed, and overgrazed, causing the production possibilities of these highly agriculturally oriented countries to diminish. In fact the per capita national outputs of most of these nations declined in the 1980s.

8 Operation Desert Storm This chapter's Last Word chronicles how the Gulf War devastated Iraq's property and human resources and had the effect of shifting its production possibilities curve inward.

THE "ISMS"

A society can use many different institutional arrangements and coordinating mechanisms to respond to the economizing problem. Historically, the industrially advanced economies of the world have differed essentially on two grounds: (1) the ownership of the means of production, and (2) the method by which economic activity is coordinated and directed. Let's briefly examine the main characteristics of two "polar" types of economic systems.

Pure Capitalism

Pure, or **laissez faire, capitalism** is characterized by the private ownership of resources and the use of a system of markets and prices to coordinate and direct economic activity. In such a system each participant is motivated by his or her own self-interests; each economic unit seeks to maximize its income through individual decision making. The market system functions as a mechanism through which individual decisions and preferences are communicated and coordinated. The fact that goods and services are produced and resources are supplied under competitive conditions means there are many independently acting buyers and sellers of each product and resource. As a result, economic power is widely dispersed. Advocates of pure capitalism argue that such an economy is conducive to efficiency in the use of resources, output and employment stability, and rapid economic growth. Hence, there is little or no need for government planning, control, or intervention. Indeed, the term *laissez faire* roughly translates as "let it be," that is, keep government from interfering with the economy, because such interference will disturb the efficiency with which the market system functions. Government's role is therefore limited to protecting private property and establishing an appropriate legal framework in which free markets function.

The Command Economy

The polar alternative to pure capitalism is the **command economy** or **communism,** characterized by public ownership of virtually all property resources and the rendering of economic decisions through central economic planning. All major decisions concerning the level of resource use, the composition and distribution of output, and the organization of production are determined by a central planning board. Business firms are governmentally owned and produce according to state directives. Production targets are determined by the planning board for each enterprise and the plan specifies the amounts of resources to be allocated to each enterprise so that it might realize its production goals. The division of output between capital and consumer goods is centrally decided and capital goods are allocated among industries in terms of the central planning board's long-term priorities.

Mixed Systems

Real-world economies are arrayed between the extremes of pure capitalism and the command economy. The United States economy leans toward pure capitalism, but with important differences. Government plays an active role in our economy in promoting economic stability and growth, in providing certain goods and services which would be underproduced or not produced at all by the market system, and in modifying the distribution of income. In contrast to the wide dispersion of economic power among many small units which characterizes pure capitalism, American capitalism has spawned powerful economic organizations in the form of large corporations and strong labor unions. The ability of these power blocs to manipulate and distort the functioning of the market system to their advantage is a further reason for governmental involvement in the economy. While the former Soviet Union historically approximated the command economy, it relied to some extent upon market-determined prices and had some vestiges of private ownership. Recent reforms in the former Soviet Union, China, and most of the eastern European nations are designed to move these command economies toward more capitalistic, market-oriented systems.

But note that private ownership and reliance on the market system do not always go together, nor do public ownership and central planning. For example, the *fascism* of Hitler's Nazi Germany has been dubbed **authoritarian capitalism** because the economy was subject to a high degree of governmental control and direction, but property was privately owned. In contrast, the Yugoslavian economy was **market socialism,** characterized by public ownership of resources coupled with increasing reliance on free markets to organize and coordinate economic activity. The Swedish economy is also a hybrid system. Although over 90 percent of business activity is in private hands, government is deeply involved in achieving economic stability and in redistributing income. Similarly, the capitalistic Japanese economy entails a great deal of planning and "coordination" between government and the business sector. Table 2-3 summarizes the various ways economic systems can be categorized based on the two criteria we are using. Keep in mind that the real-world examples in this framework are only rough approximations.

The Traditional Economy

Table 2-3 is couched in terms of industrially advanced or at least semideveloped economies. Many less developed countries have **traditional** or **customary economies.** Production methods, exchange, and distribution of income are all sanctioned by custom. Heredity and caste circumscribe economic roles of individuals and socioeconomic immobility is pronounced. Technological change and innovation may be closely constrained because they clash with tradition and threaten the social fabric. Economic activity is often secondary to religious and cultural values and society's desire to perpetuate the status quo. In deciding to pursue economic development, traditional economies must face the question as to which model in Table 2-3 will result in growth and simultaneously be the most compatible with other economic and noneconomic goals valued by that society.

The point is that there is no unique or universally accepted way to respond to the economizing problem. Various societies, having different cultural and historical backgrounds, different mores and customs, and

TABLE 2-3 Comparative economic systems

Ownership of resources	Coordinating mechanism: Market system	Coordinating mechanism: Central planning
Private	United States	Nazi Germany
Public	Yugoslavia	Soviet Union

LAST WORD

OPERATION DESERT STORM AND IRAQ'S PRODUCTION POSSIBILITIES

War can seriously diminish a nation's production possibilities.

The quick and decisive military victory of the United States and its allies in Operation Desert Storm has had a devastating economic impact on Iraq. Forty-three days of intensive Allied bombing inflicted great physical damage to Iraq's productive facilities and infrastructure. Civilian factories, roads, bridges, railroads, power plants, water purification plants, and communication facilities were all severely impaired. Commerce and communications have been greatly disrupted. Furthermore, despite Iraq's greatly diminished productive potential, the United Nations has ordered it to pay up to 30 percent of its future oil revenues as war reparations to Kuwait and others harmed by the war. This means that a significant portion of Iraq's future domestic output will be unavailable for its consumers or to rebuild its productive facilities.

Devastation to Iraq's human resources was also severe. One estimate suggests that as many as 100,000 to 120,000 Iraqi troops plus 5,000 to 20,000 civilians were killed in the war. Another 20,000 lost their lives in the postwar rebellion against Saddam Hussein. Finally, an estimated 15,000 to 30,000 Kurds and other displaced people have died in camps and on the road. A Harvard medical team has predicted that 170,000 Iraqi children will die because of delayed effects of the Persian Gulf war. In particular, typhoid, cholera, diarrhea, malnutrition and other health problems will cause the death rate of children under age 5 to be two or three times higher than before the war. Without electric power water treatment plants are silent; sewage cannot be pumped or treated. Backed-up pipes now drain into rivers and canals from which people have no choice but to bathe and drink. Further, there is no power to run irrigation pumps and little gasoline is available for harvesting machines. Food harvests are in doubt and refrigeration is no longer available to store existing food supplies.

In short, Iraq invaded Kuwait to bring Kuwait's oil resources under its control and by so doing increase Iraq's production possibilities. Instead, Iraq's physical and human resources—and hence its production possibilities—have been seriously diminished by Operation Desert Storm.

contrasting ideological frameworks—not to mention resources which differ both quantitatively and qualitatively—use different institutions in dealing with the reality of relative scarcity. The former Soviet Union, the United States, and Great Britain, for example, are all—in terms of their accepted goals, ideology, technologies, resources, and culture—attempting to achieve efficiency in the use of their respective resources. The best method for responding to the unlimited wants–scarce resources dilemma in one economy may be inappropriate for another economic system.

CHAPTER SUMMARY

1 Economics centers on two basic facts: first, human material wants are virtually unlimited; second, economic resources are scarce.

2 Economic resources may be classified as property resources—raw materials and capital—or as human resources—labor and entrepreneurial ability.

3 Economics is concerned with the problem of administering scarce resources in the production of goods and services to fulfill the material wants of society. Both full employment and full production of available resources are essential if this administration is to be efficient.

4 At any time a full-employment, full-production economy

must sacrifice the output of some types of goods and services to achieve increased production of others. Because resources are not equally productive in all possible uses, shifting resources from one use to another gives rise to the law of increasing opportunity costs; that is, the production of additional units of product X entails the sacrifice of increasing amounts of product Y.

5 Over time, technological advance and increases in the quantity and quality of human and property resources permit the economy to produce more of all goods and services. Society's choice as to the composition of current output is a determinant of the future location of the production possibilities curve.

6 The various economic systems of the world differ in their ideologies and also in their responses to the economizing problem. Critical differences center on **a** private versus public ownership of resources, and **b** the use of the market system versus central planning as a coordinating mechanism.

TERMS AND CONCEPTS

economizing problem
utility
land, capital, labor, and entrepreneurial ability
investment
full employment
full production
allocative efficiency
productive efficiency
consumer goods
capital goods
production possibilities table (curve)
law of increasing opportunity costs
economic growth
pure or laissez faire capitalism
command economy or communism
authoritarian capitalism
market socialism
traditional or customary economies

QUESTIONS AND STUDY SUGGESTIONS

1 "Economics is the study of the principles governing the allocation of scarce means among competing ends when the objective of the allocation is to maximize the attainment of the ends."[3] Explain. Why is the problem of unemployment a part of the subject matter of economics?

2 Critically analyze: "Wants aren't insatiable. I can prove it. I get all the coffee I want to drink every morning at breakfast." Explain: "Goods and services are scarce because resources are scarce." Analyze: "It is the nature of all economic problems that absolute solutions are denied us."

3 What are economic resources? What are the major functions of the entrepreneur? "Economics is . . . neither capitalist nor socialist: it applies to every society. Economics would disappear only in a world so rich that no wants were unfulfilled for lack of resources. Such a world is not imminent and may be impossible, for time is always limited."[4] Carefully evaluate and explain these statements. Do you agree that time is an economic resource?

4 Distinguish between allocative efficiency and productive efficiency. Give an illustration of a achieving allocative, but not productive, efficiency; and b achieving productive, but not allocative, efficiency.

[3]George J. Stigler, *The Theory of Price* (New York: The Macmillan Company, 1947), p. 12.

[4]Joseph P. McKenna, *Intermediate Economic Theory* (New York: Holt, Rinehart and Winston, Inc., 1958), p. 2.

5 Comment on the following statement from a newspaper article: "Our junior high school serves a splendid hot meal for $1 without costing the taxpayers anything, thanks in part to a government subsidy."

6 The following is a production possibilities table for war goods and civilian goods:

Type of production	Production alternatives				
	A	B	C	D	E
Automobiles (in millions)	**0**	**2**	**4**	**6**	**8**
Guided missiles (in thousands)	**30**	**27**	**21**	**12**	**0**

a Show these production possibilities data graphically. What do the points on the curve indicate? How does the curve reflect the law of increasing opportunity costs? Explain. If the economy is currently at point *C*, what is the cost of 1 million more automobiles in terms of guided missiles? Of 1000 more guided missiles in terms of automobiles?

b Label point *G* inside the curve. What does it indicate? Label point *H* outside the curve. What does this point indicate? What must occur before the economy can attain the level of production indicated by point *H*?

c Upon what specific assumptions is the production possibilities curve based? What happens when each of these assumptions is released?

d Suppose improvement occurs in the technology of producing guided missiles but not in the production of automobiles. Draw the new production possibilities curve. Now assume that a technological advance occurs in producing automobiles but not in producing guided missiles. Draw the new production possibilities curve. Finally, draw a production possibilities curve which reflects technological improvement in the production of both products.

7 What is the opportunity cost of attending college?

8 Suppose you arrive at a store expecting to pay $100 for an item, but learn that a store two miles away is charging $50 for it. Would you drive there and buy it? How does your decision benefit you? What is the opportunity cost of your decision? Now suppose that you arrive at a store expecting to pay $6000 for an item, but learn that it costs $5950 at the other store. Do you make the same decision as before? Perhaps surprisingly, you should! Explain why.

9 "The present choice of position on the production possibilities curve is a major factor in economic growth." Explain.

10 Contrast the means by which pure capitalism, market socialism, and a command economy attempt to cope with economic scarcity.

11 Explain how an international trade deficit may permit an economy to acquire a combination of goods in excess of its domestic production potential. Explain why nations try to avoid having trade deficits.

Pure Capitalism and the Circular Flow

Fact: In the past few years the media have inundated us with stories of how the centrally planned economies are trying to alter their systems in the direction of capitalism. Question: Precisely what are the features and institutions of capitalism which these nations are trying to emulate?

Fact: You have virtually nothing whatsoever to do with the production of the vast majority of goods and services you consume. Question: Why is it that production is so specialized in modern economies?

Fact: Nearly every day you exchange paper dollars—whose intrinsic value is virtually nil—for a wide variety of products of considerable value. Question: Why do such seemingly irrational monetary transactions occur?

The foregoing questions are just some addressed in the pages that follow. Our initial task is to describe the capitalist ideology and to explain how pure, or laissez faire, capitalism would function.

Strictly speaking, pure capitalism has never existed and probably never will. Why, then, do we bother to consider the operation of such an economy? Because it provides us with a useful first approximation of how the economies of the United States and many other industrially advanced nations function. And approximations or models, when properly handled, can be very useful. In other words, pure capitalism constitutes a simplified model which we will then modify and adjust in later chapters to correspond more closely to the reality of these modern economies.

In explaining the operation of pure capitalism, we will discuss: (1) the institutional framework and basic assumptions which make up the capitalist ideology; (2) certain institutions and practices common to all modern economies; (3) capitalism and the circular flow of income; (4) how product and resource prices are determined; and (5) the market system and the allocating of economic resources. The first three topics are explored in the present chapter; the latter two will be discussed in Chapters 4 and 5.

CAPITALIST IDEOLOGY

Unfortunately, there is no neat, universally accepted definition of capitalism. We therefore must examine in some detail the basic tenets of pure capitalism to clearly understand what it entails. In short, the framework of capitalism embraces the following institutions and assumptions: (1) private property, (2) freedom of enterprise and choice, (3) self-interest as the dominant motive, (4) competition, (5) reliance on the price or market system, and (6) a limited role for government.

Private Property

Under a capitalistic system, property resources are owned by private individuals and private institutions rather than by government. **Private property,** coupled with the freedom to negotiate binding legal contracts, permits private persons or businesses to obtain, control, employ, and dispose of property resources as they see fit. The institution of private property is sustained over time by the *right to bequeath,* that is, by the right of a property owner to designate the recipient of this property at the time of death.

Needless to say, there are broad legal limits to this right of private ownership. For example, the use of one's resources for the production of illicit drugs is prohibited. Nor is public ownership nonexistent. Even in pure capitalism, public ownership of certain "natural monopolies" may be essential to the achievement of efficiency in the use of resources.

Freedom of Enterprise and Choice

Closely related to private ownership of property is freedom of enterprise and choice. Capitalism charges its component economic units with the responsibility of making certain choices, which are registered and made effective through the free markets of the economy.

Freedom of enterprise means that under pure capitalism, private business enterprises are free to obtain economic resources, to organize these resources in the production of a good or service of the firm's own choosing, and to sell it in the markets of their choice. No artificial obstacles or restrictions imposed by government or other producers block an entrepreneur's choice to enter or leave a particular industry.

Freedom of choice means that owners of property resources and money capital can employ or dispose of these resources as they see fit. It also means that laborers are free to enter any lines of work for which they are qualified. Finally, it means that consumers are at liberty, within the limits of their money incomes, to buy that collection of goods and services they feel is most appropriate in satisfying their wants.

Freedom of *consumer* choice may well be the most profound of these freedoms. The consumer is in a particularly strategic position in a capitalistic economy; in a sense, the consumer is sovereign. The range of free choices for suppliers of human and property resources is circumscribed by the choices of consumers. The consumer ultimately decides what the capitalistic economy should produce, and resource suppliers must make their free choices within these constraints. Resource suppliers and businesses are not really "free" to produce goods and services consumers do not desire.

Again, broad legal limitations prevail in the expression of all these free choices.

Role of Self-Interest

The primary driving force of capitalism is the promotion of one's **self-interest;** each economic unit attempts to do what is best for itself. Hence, entrepreneurs aim to maximize their firm's profits or, as the case might be, minimize losses. And, other things being equal, owners of property resources attempt to achieve the highest price obtainable from the rent or sale of these resources. Given the amount and irksomeness of the effort involved, those who supply human resources will also try to obtain the highest possible incomes from their employment. Consumers, in purchasing a given product, will seek to obtain it at the lowest price. Consumers also apportion their expenditures to maximize their utility or satisfaction. In short, capitalism presumes self-interest as the fundamental *modus operandi* for the various economic units as they express their free choices. The motive of self-interest gives direction and consistency to what might otherwise be an extremely chaotic economy.

Note that pursuit of economic self-interest should not be confused with selfishness. The stockholder who receives corporate dividends may contribute a portion to the United Way or leave bequests to grandchildren. Similarly, a local church official may compare price and quality among various brands in buying new pews for the church.

Competition

Freedom of choice exercised in terms of promoting one's own monetary returns is the basis for **competi-**

tion, or economic rivalry, as a fundamental feature of capitalism. Competition, as economists see it, entails:

1 The presence of large numbers of independently acting buyers and sellers operating in the market for any particular product or resource.

2 The freedom of buyers and sellers to enter or leave particular markets.

Large Numbers The essence of competition is the widespread diffusion of economic power within the two major aggregates—businesses and households—which comprise the economy. When many buyers and sellers are present in a particular market, no one buyer or seller will be able to demand or offer a quantity of the product sufficiently large to noticeably influence its price. Let's examine this statement in terms of the selling or supply side of the product market.

We know that when a product becomes unusually scarce, its price will rise. An unseasonable frost in Florida may seriously curtail the output of citrus crops and sharply increase the price of oranges. Similarly, *if* a single producer, or a small group of producers acting together, can somehow control or restrict the total supply of a product, then price can be raised to the seller's advantage. By controlling supply, the producer can "rig the market" on his or her own behalf. Now the essence of competition is that there are so many independently acting sellers that each, *because he or she is contributing an almost negligible fraction of the total supply,* has virtually no influence over the supply or, therefore, over product price.

For example, suppose there are 10,000 farmers, each of whom is supplying 100 bushels of corn in the Kansas City grain market when the price of corn is $4 per bushel. Could a single farmer who feels dissatisfied with the existing price cause an artificial scarcity of corn and thereby boost the price above $4? The answer clearly is "No." Farmer Jones, by restricting output from 100 to 75 bushels, exerts virtually no effect on the total supply of corn. In fact, the total amount supplied is reduced only from 1,000,000 to 999,975 bushels. This obviously is not much of a shortage! Supply is virtually unchanged, and, therefore, the $4 price persists. In brief, competition means that each seller is providing a drop in the bucket of total supply. Individual sellers can make no noticeable dent in total supply; hence, a seller cannot *as an individual producer* manipulate product price. This is what is meant when it is said that an individual competitive seller is "at the mercy of the market." The same rationale applies to the demand side of the market. Buyers are plentiful and act independently. Thus single buyers cannot manipulate the market to their advantage.

The widespread diffusion of economic power underlying competition controls the use and limits the potential abuse of that power. Economic rivalry prevents economic units from wreaking havoc on one another as they attempt to further their self-interests. Competition imposes limits on expressions of self-interest by buyers and sellers. Competition is a basic regulatory force in capitalism.

Entry and Exit Competition also assumes that it is simple for producers to enter or leave a particular industry; there are no artificial legal or institutional obstacles to prohibit expansion or contraction of specific industries. This aspect of competition is prerequisite to the flexibility which is essential if an economy is to remain efficient over time. Freedom of entry is necessary for the economy to adjust appropriately to changes in consumer tastes, technology, or resource supplies. (This is further explored in Chapter 5.)

Markets and Prices

The basic coordinating mechanism of a capitalist economy is the market or price system. *Capitalism is a market economy.* Decisions rendered by buyers and sellers of products and resources are made effective through a system of markets. Indeed, by definition, a **market** is simply a mechanism or arrangement which brings buyers or "demanders" and sellers or "suppliers" of a good or service into contact with one another. A McDonald's, a gas station, a grocery supermarket, a Sotheby's art auction, the New York Stock Exchange, and worldwide foreign exchange markets are but a few illustrations. The preferences of sellers and buyers are registered on the supply and demand sides of various markets, and the outcome of these choices is a system of product and resource prices. These prices are guideposts on which resource owners, entrepreneurs, and consumers make and revise their free choices in furthering their self-interests.

Just as competition is the controlling mechanism, so a system of markets and prices is a basic organizing force. The market system is an elaborate communication system through which innumerable individual free choices are recorded, summarized, and balanced against one another. Those who obey the dictates of the market system are rewarded; those who ignore them are penalized by the system. Through this communication system, society decides what the economy should produce, how production can be efficiently organized, and how the fruits of productive endeavor are distributed among the individual economic units which make up capitalism.

Not only is the market system the mechanism through which society decides how it allocates its resources and distributes the resulting output, but it is through the market system that these decisions are carried out.

Economic systems based on the ideologies of socialism and communism also depend on market systems, but not to the same degree or in the same way as pure capitalism. Socialistic and communistic societies use markets and prices primarily to implement decisions made wholly or in part by a central planning authority. In capitalism, the market system functions both as a device for registering innumerable choices of free individuals and businesses *and* as a mechanism for carrying out these decisions.

In Chapters 4 and 5 we will analyze the mechanics and operation of the market system.

Limited Government

A competitive capitalist economy promotes a high degree of efficiency in the use or allocation of its resources. There is allegedly little real need for governmental intervention in the operation of such an economy beyond its role of imposing broad legal limits on the exercise of individual choices and the use of private property. The concept of pure capitalism as a self-regulating and self-adjusting economy precludes any significant economic role for government. However, as we will find in Chapter 6, a number of limitations and potentially undesirable outcomes associated with capitalism and the market system have resulted in an active economic role for government.

QUICK REVIEW 3-1

- ***Pure capitalism rests on the private ownership of property and freedom of enterprise and choice.***
- ***Economic entities—businesses, resource suppliers, and consumers—seek to further their own self-interests.***
- ***The coordinating mechanism of capitalism is a competitive system of prices or markets.***
- ***The efficient functioning of the market system under capitalism allegedly precludes significant government intervention.***

OTHER CHARACTERISTICS

Private property, freedom of enterprise and choice, self-interest as a motivating force, competition, and reliance on a market system are all institutions and assumptions more or less exclusively associated with pure capitalism. In addition, there are certain institutions and practices which are characteristic of all modern economies: (1) the use of advanced technology and large amounts of capital goods, (2) specialization, and (3) the use of money. Specialization and an advanced technology are prerequisites to efficient employment of any economy's resources. The use of money is a mechanism which allows society more easily to practice and reap the benefits of specialization and advanced productive techniques.

Extensive Use of Capital Goods

All modern economies—whether they approximate the capitalist, socialist, or communist ideology—are based on advanced technology and the extensive use of capital goods. Under pure capitalism it is competition, coupled with freedom of choice and the desire to further one's self-interest, which provides the means for achieving technological advance. The capitalistic framework is felt to be highly effective in harnessing incentives to develop new products and improved techniques of production, because monetary rewards accrue directly to the innovator. Pure capitalism therefore presupposes extensive use and relatively rapid development of complex capital goods: tools, machinery, large-scale factories, and facilities for storage, transportation, and marketing.

Why are the existence of an advanced technology and the extensive use of capital goods important? Because the most direct method of producing a product is usually the least efficient.[1] Even Robinson Crusoe avoided the inefficiencies of direct production in favor of **roundabout production.** It would be ridiculous for a farmer—even a backyard farmer—to go at production with bare hands. It pays huge dividends in terms of more efficient production and, therefore, a more abundant output, to fashion tools of production, that is, capital equipment, to aid in the productive process. There is a better way of getting water out of a well than to dive in after it!

[1]Remember that consumer goods satisfy wants directly, while capital goods do so indirectly through the more efficient future production of consumer goods.

But there is a catch involved. Recall our discussion of the production possibilities curve and the basic nature of the economizing problem. With full employment and full production, resources must be diverted from the production of consumer goods to be used in the production of capital goods. We must currently tighten our belts as consumers to free resources for the production of capital goods which will increase productive efficiency and give us a greater output of consumer goods in the future.

Specialization and Efficiency

The extent to which society relies on **specialization** is astounding. The vast majority of consumers produce virtually none of the goods and services they consume and, conversely, consume little or nothing of what they produce. The hammer-shop laborer who spends a lifetime stamping out parts for jet engines may never "consume" an airplane trip. The assembly-line worker who devotes 8 hours a day to installing windows in Corsicas may own a Honda. Few households seriously consider any extensive production of their own food, shelter, and clothing. Many farmers sell their milk to the local dairy and then buy margarine at the Podunk general store. Society learned long ago that self-sufficiency breeds inefficiency. The jack-of-all-trades may be a very colorful individual, but is certainly not efficient.

Division of Labor

In what specific ways might human specialization—the **division of labor**—enhance productive efficiency?

1 Specialization permits individuals to take advantage of existing differences in their abilities and skills. If caveman A is strong, swift, and accurate with a spear, and caveman B is weak and slow, but patient, this distribution of talents can be most efficiently used by making A a hunter and B a fisherman.

2 Even if the abilities of A and B are identical, specialization may be advantageous. By devoting all one's time to a single task, the doer is more likely to develop the appropriate skills and to discover improved techniques than when apportioning time among a number of diverse tasks. One learns to be a good hunter by hunting!

3 Finally, specialization—devoting all one's time to, say, a single task—avoids the loss of time involved in shifting from one job to another.

For all these reasons the division of labor results in greater productive efficiency in the use of human resources.

Geographic Specialization

Specialization also is desirable on a regional and international basis. Oranges could be grown in Nebraska, but because of the unsuitability of the land, rainfall, and temperature, the costs involved would be exceedingly high. Florida could achieve some success in the production of wheat, but for similar reasons such production would be relatively costly. As a result, Nebraskans produce those products—wheat in particular—for which their resources are best adapted, and Floridians do the same, producing oranges and other citrus fruits. In so doing, both produce surpluses of their specialties. Then, very sensibly, Nebraskans and Floridians swap some of their surpluses. Specialization permits each area to turn out those goods which its resources can most efficiently produce. In this way both Nebraska and Florida can enjoy a larger amount of both wheat and oranges than would otherwise be the case.

Similarly, on an international basis the United States specializes in such items as commercial aircraft and computers which it sells abroad in exchange for video recorders from Japan, bananas from Honduras, shoes from Italy, and woven baskets from Thailand. In short, human and geographical specialization are both essential in achieving efficiency in the use of resources.

Specialization and Comparative Advantage[2]

These simple illustrations clearly show that specialization is economically desirable because it results in more efficient production. Indeed, the point is almost self-explanatory. But, because the concept of specialization is so vital to understanding the production and exchange processes of modern economies, let's tackle a more exacting illustration of the gains which accrue from specialization.

Comparative Costs Let's pursue our Nebraska–Florida example of specialization at a more advanced level, relying on an already familiar concept—the production possibilities table—as a basic analytical device. Suppose production possibilities data for the Nebraska and Florida economies are as in Tables 3-1 and 3-2, respectively.

These production possibilities tables are "different" from those of Chapter 2 in that we here assume

[2]This section may be skipped by instructors who wish to defer detailed treatment of comparative advantage to Part 4 on the world economy.

TABLE 3-1 Nebraska's production possibilities table *(hypothetical data; in tons)*

Product	Production alternatives			
	A	*B*	*C*	*D*
Wheat	0	20	40	60
Oranges	15	10	5	0

constant costs rather than increasing costs. Each state must give up a constant, rather than an increasing, amount of one product in securing constant increments of the other product. This will simplify our discussion without impairing the validity of our conclusions.

Specialization and trade are mutually beneficial or "profitable" to the two states (individuals, regions, nations) if the comparative costs of the two products within the two states differ.

What's the comparative cost of oranges and wheat in Nebraska? Table 3-1 shows that 5 tons of oranges must be forgone or sacrificed to produce 20 tons of wheat. Or more simply, it costs 1 ton of oranges to get 4 tons of wheat in Nebraska ($1O = 4W$). Because of our constant-cost assumption, this comparative-cost relationship will not change as we expand the output of either product. Similarly, in Table 3-2 at a cost of 10 tons of oranges, Floridians can obtain 30 tons of wheat, that is, in Florida the comparative-cost ratio for the two products is: $1O$ equals $3W$.

The comparative cost of the two products within the two states is clearly different. Economists describe this situation by saying that Florida has a comparative-cost advantage, or more simply, **comparative advantage,** in oranges; that is, Florida must forgo less wheat (3 tons) to get 1 ton of oranges than is the case in Nebraska where 1 ton of oranges costs 4 tons of wheat. Comparatively speaking, oranges are cheap in Florida. *A state or nation has a comparative advantage in some product when it can produce it at a lower opportunity cost than can any other state or nation.* Nebraska, on the other hand, has a comparative (cost) advantage in wheat. While it costs $\frac{1}{3}$ ton of oranges to get 1 ton of wheat in Florida, by comparison 1 ton of wheat only costs $\frac{1}{4}$ ton of oranges in Nebraska. Comparatively speaking wheat is cheap in Nebraska.

TABLE 3-2 Florida's production possibilities table *(hypothetical data; in tons)*

Product	Production alternatives			
	A	*B*	*C*	*D*
Wheat	0	30	60	90
Oranges	30	20	10	0

Given these comparative-cost differences, we can demonstrate that if both states specialize according to their comparative advantage, they can achieve a larger total output of oranges and wheat than otherwise. That is, they can get a larger total output with the same total input of resources through specialization and thus will be using their scarce resources more efficiently.

Terms of Trade Given Florida's cost ratio of $1O$ equals $3W$, it stands to reason that Floridians would be pleased to specialize in oranges, if they could obtain *more than* 3 tons of wheat for a ton of oranges through trade with Nebraska. Similarly, recalling Nebraska's $1O$ equals $4W$ cost ratio, it will be advantageous to Nebraskans to specialize in wheat, provided they can get 1 ton of oranges for *less than* 4 tons of wheat.

Suppose through negotiation the two states agree on an exchange rate of 1 ton of oranges for $3\frac{1}{2}$ tons of wheat.[3] Note that these **terms of trade** will be mutually beneficial in that both states can "do better" through trade than they can at home. Floridians get $3\frac{1}{2}$ tons of wheat by sending 1 ton of oranges to Nebraska, whereas they can get only 3 tons of wheat by reallocating resources from oranges to wheat production at home. It would cost Nebraskans 4 tons of wheat to obtain 1 ton of oranges by reallocating their domestic resources, whereas 1 ton of oranges can be obtained through trade with Florida at the smaller cost of only $3\frac{1}{2}$ tons of wheat.

Gains from Specialization and Trade Table 3-3 helps us pinpoint the size of the gains in total output from specialization and trade. Suppose that before specialization and trade, production alternative B was the optimum product-mix for each state (as shown in column 1). That is, Nebraskans preferred 20 tons of wheat and 10 tons of oranges (Table 3-1) and Floridians preferred 30 tons of wheat and 20 tons of oranges (Table 3-2) to all other alternatives available within the respective state economies. Both states now specialize according to comparative advantage, Nebraska producing 60 tons of wheat and no oranges (alternative D) and Florida producing no wheat and 30 tons of oranges (alternative A) as reflected in column 2 of Table 3-3. Using our $1O$ equals $3\frac{1}{2}W$ terms of trade, assume that

[3]In Chapter 24 we will find that market forces—supply and demand—will determine the rate at which the two products are exchanged.

TABLE 3-3 Regional specialization according to comparative advantage and the gains from trade *(hypothetical data; in tons)*

State	(1) Outputs before specialization	(2) Outputs after specialization	(3) Amounts	(4) Outputs available after trade	(5) = (4) − (1) Gains from specialization and trade
Nebraska	20 wheat	60 wheat	−35 wheat	25 wheat	5 wheat
	10 oranges	0 oranges	+10 oranges	10 oranges	0 oranges
Florida	30 wheat	0 wheat	+35 wheat	35 wheat	5 wheat
	20 oranges	30 oranges	−10 oranges	20 oranges	0 oranges

Nebraska exchanges 35 tons of its wheat for 10 tons of Florida oranges. Nebraskans will now have 25 tons of wheat and 10 tons of oranges, while Floridians will thus obtain 35 tons of wheat and 20 tons of oranges. Column 3 of Table 3-3 summarizes this trade. Compared with their optimum product-mixes prior to specialization and trade, *both* states now enjoy the same amount of oranges and 5 additional tons of wheat! These extra 10 tons of wheat, equally divided between the two state economies in this instance, represent the *gains from specialization and trade.* You can confirm these figures in column 5 of Table 3-3 where we have subtracted the *before*-specialization outputs of column 1 from the outputs realized *after* specialization in column 4.

The point is that *resource allocation has been improved through specialization according to comparative advantage.* The same total inputs of resources have resulted in a larger total output. By having Nebraska and Florida allocate all their resources to wheat and oranges respectively, the same total inputs of resources have given rise to more output, indicating that resources are being more efficiently used or allocated.

You may recall that we asserted in Chapter 2 that specialization and trade permit a nation or state to overcome the production constraints imposed by its production possibilities curve. In other words, specialization and trade have the same effect as economic growth. Although the domestic production possibilities frontiers of the two states have not been pushed to the right, specialization and trade have circumvented the constraints of the production possibilities curve. *The economic effects of specialization and trade between states (regions, nations) are tantamount to having more or better resources or to achieving technological progress.*

Disadvantages Despite these efficiency advantages, specialization does have certain drawbacks.

1 The potential monotony and drudgery of specialized work are well known. Imagine the boredom of our assembly-line worker who is still putting windows in Corsicas.

2 Specialization and mutual interdependence vary directly with one another. The less one produces for oneself, the more one depends on the output of others.

3 A third problem centers on the exchanging of the surpluses which specialization entails. An examination of this problem leads us into a discussion of the use of money in the domestic and world economies.

Use of Money

Virtually all economies, advanced or primitive, are money-using. Money performs many functions, but first and foremost it is a **medium of exchange.**

In our Nebraska–Florida example, Nebraskans must trade or exchange wheat for Florida's oranges if both states are to share in the benefits of specialization. If trade was highly inconvenient or prohibited for some reason, gains from specializing would be lost to society. Consumers want a wide variety of products and, in the absence of trade, would tend to devote their human and material resources to many diverse types of production. If exchange could not occur or was very inconvenient to transact, Nebraska and Florida would be forced to be more self-sufficient, and the advantages of specialization would not occur. *In short, a convenient means of exchanging goods is a prerequisite of specialization.*

Now exchange can, and sometimes does, occur on the basis of **bartering,** that is, swapping goods for goods. But bartering as a means of exchange can pose serious problems for the economy. Specifically, exchange by barter requires a *coincidence of wants* between the two transactors. In our example, we assumed that Nebraskans had excess wheat to trade and that they wanted oranges. And we assumed Floridians had excess oranges to swap and that they wanted wheat. So exchange occurred. But if this coincidence of wants did not exist, trade would be stymied.

Suppose Nebraska does not want any of Florida's oranges but is interested in buying potatoes from

Idaho. Ironically, Idaho wants Florida's oranges but not Nebraska's wheat. And, to complicate matters, suppose that Florida wants some of Nebraska's wheat but none of Idaho's potatoes. The situation is summarized in Figure 3-1.

In no case do we find a coincidence of wants. Trade by barter clearly would be difficult. To overcome such a stalemate, modern economies use *money,* which is simply a convenient social invention to facilitate exchange of goods and services. Historically, cattle, cigarettes, shells, stones, pieces of metal, and many other diverse commodities have been used, with varying degrees of success, as a medium for facilitating exchange. But to be money, an item needs to pass only one test: *It must be generally acceptable by buyers and sellers in exchange.* Money is socially defined; whatever society accepts as a medium of exchange *is* money. Most modern economies use pieces of paper as money. We shall assume that this is the case with the Nebraska–Florida–Idaho economy; they use pieces of paper which they call "dollars" as money. Can the use of paper dollars as a medium of exchange overcome our stalemate?

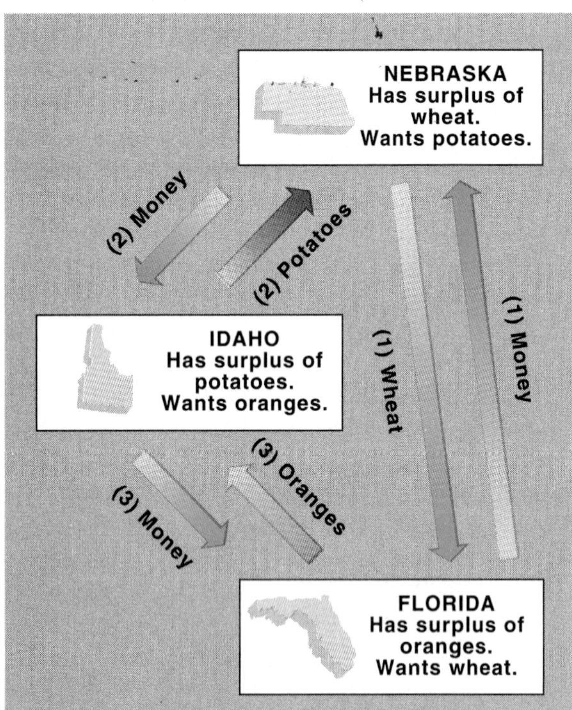

FIGURE 3-1 Money facilitates trade where wants do not coincide

By the use of money as a medium of exchange, trade can be accomplished, as indicated by the arrows, despite a noncoincidence of wants. By facilitating exchange, the use of money permits an economy to realize the efficiencies of specialization.

Indeed it can, with trade occurring as shown in Figure 3-1:

1 Floridians can exchange money for some of Nebraska's wheat.

2 Nebraskans can take the money realized from the sale of wheat and exchange it for some of Idaho's potatoes.

3 Idahoans can then exchange the money received from the sale of potatoes for some of Florida's surplus oranges.

The willingness to accept paper money (or any other kind of money, for that matter) as a medium of exchange has permitted a three-way trade which allows each state to specialize in one product and obtain the other product(s) its residents desire, despite the absence of a coincidence of wants between any two of the parties. Barter, resting as it does on a coincidence of wants, would have impeded this exchange and in so doing would have induced the three states not to specialize. Of course, the efficiencies of specialization would then have been lost to those states. Strange as it may first seem, two exchanges—surplus product for money and then money for a wanted product—are simpler than the single product-for-product exchange which bartering entails. Indeed, in this example, product-for-product exchange would not be likely to occur at all.

On a global basis the fact that different nations have different currencies complicates international specialization and exchange. However, the existence of foreign exchange markets permits Americans, Japanese, Germans, Britons, and Mexicans to exchange dollars, yen, marks, pounds, and pesos for one another to complete the desired international exchanges of goods and services.

A final example: Imagine a Detroit laborer producing crankshafts for Oldsmobiles. At the end of the week, instead of receiving a piece of paper endorsed by the company comptroller, or a few pieces of paper engraved in green and black, the laborer receives from the company paymaster four Oldsmobile crankshafts. Inconvenient as this is, and with no desire to hoard crankshafts, the laborer ventures into the Detroit business district, to spend this hard-earned income on a bag of groceries, a pair of jeans, and a movie. Obviously, the worker is faced with some inconvenient and time-consuming trading, and may not be able to negoti-

KEY GRAPH

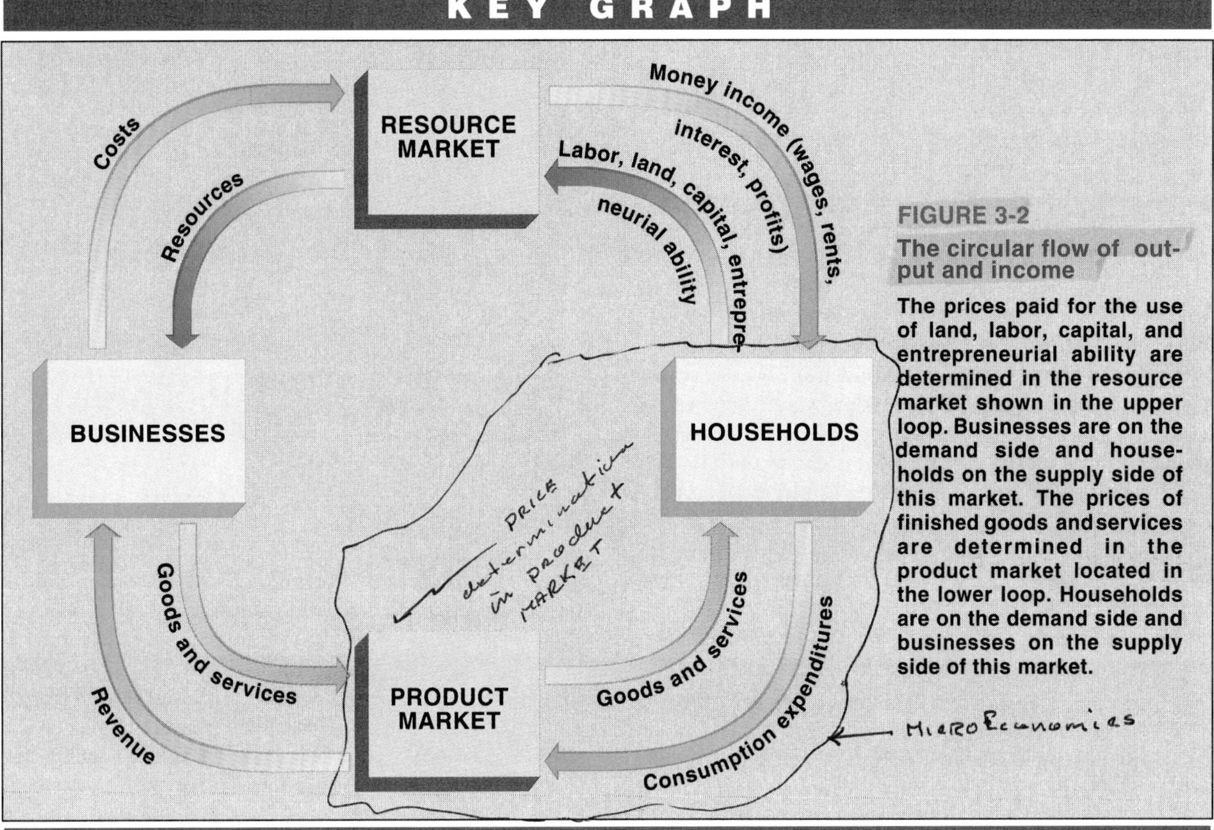

FIGURE 3-2
The circular flow of output and income

The prices paid for the use of land, labor, capital, and entrepreneurial ability are determined in the resource market shown in the upper loop. Businesses are on the demand side and households on the supply side of this market. The prices of finished goods and services are determined in the product market located in the lower loop. Households are on the demand side and businesses on the supply side of this market.

ate any exchanges at all. Finding a clothier with jeans who happens to be in the market for an Oldsmobile crankshaft can be a formidable task. And, if the jeans do not trade evenly for crankshafts, how do the transactors "make change"? Examples such as this demonstrate that money is one of the great social inventions of civilization.

QUICK REVIEW 3-2

- ***Advanced economies achieve greater efficiency in production through the use of large quantities of capital goods.***
- ***Specialization enhances efficiency; by specializing in accordance with comparative advantage a nation or region can realize an output greater than those on its production possibilities curve.***
- ***The use of money facilitates the exchange of goods which specialization entails.***

THE CIRCULAR FLOW MODEL

Our discussion of specialization and the related need for a monetary system to facilitate exchange brings us back to the role of markets and prices in a capitalistic economy. The remainder of this chapter is devoted to the market system, and examines the two basic types of markets of pure capitalism and the transactions occurring within them.

Resource and Product Markets

Figure 3-2 (Key Graph) shows two groups of *decision makers*—households and businesses. (Government will be added as a third decision maker in Chapter 6.) The *coordinating mechanism* which brings the decisions of households and businesses into alignment with one another is the market system, in particular resource and product markets.

LAST WORD

BACK TO BARTER

Despite the advantages of using money, there is evidence that bartering is a "growth industry."

Because money facilitates exchange, it may seem odd that a considerable and growing volume of both domestic and international trade occurs through barter.

Suppose you own a small firm selling equipment to television stations. The economy is in recession; business is slow; your cash flow is down; and your inventories are much higher than desired. What do you do? You approach a local TV station which needs new equipment. But it, too, is feeling the effects of recession. Its advertising revenues are down and it also faces a cash-flow crunch. So a deal is struck. You provide $50,000 worth of equipment in exchange for $50,000 worth of "free" advertising. Advantage to seller: You move unwanted inventory, eliminating warehousing and insurance costs. You also receive valuable advertising time. The TV station gets needed equipment and pays for it with advertising time slots which would otherwise be unfilled. Both parties gain and no money changes hands.

Internationally, a firm might encounter an obstacle in selling its goods to a nation which does not have "hard" (exchangeable) currencies such as dollars, marks, or yen. Barter circumvents this problem. Example: Arcon Manufacturing of North Carolina sold its grain silos to a Nicaraguan firm, knowing that the buyer had no hard currency for making payment. Arcon took payment in sesame seeds, which it delivered to a Middle Eastern food manufacturer which was able to pay Arcon in hard currency. PepsiCo swaps cola syrup for Russian vodka. Coca-Cola has traded its syrup for Egyptian oranges, Turkish tomato paste, Polish beer, and Hungarian soft-drink bottles. Recently, large American oil companies such as Chevron and Amoco

The upper half of the diagram portrays the **resource market.** Here, households, which directly or indirectly (through their ownership of business corporations) own all economic resources, *supply* these resources to businesses.[4] Businesses, of course, will *demand* resources because they are the means by which firms produce goods and services. The interaction of demand and supply for the immense variety of human and property resources establishes the price of each. The payments which businesses make in obtaining resources are costs to businesses, but simultaneously constitute flows of wage, rent, interest, and profit income to the households supplying these resources.

Now consider the **product market** shown in the bottom half of the diagram. The money income received by households from the sale of resources does not, as such, have real value. Consumers cannot eat or wear coins and paper money. Hence, through the expenditure of money income, households express their *demand* for a vast array of goods and services. Simultaneously, businesses combine the resources they have obtained to produce and *supply* goods and services in these same markets. The interaction of these demand and supply decisions determines product prices (Chapter 4). Note, too, that the flow of consumer expenditures for goods and services constitutes sales revenues or receipts from the viewpoint of businesses.

The **circular flow model** implies a complex, interrelated web of decision making and economic activity. Note that households and businesses participate in both basic markets, but on different sides of each. Businesses are on the buying or demand side of resource markets, and households, as resource owners and suppliers, are on the selling or supply side. In the product market, these positions are reversed; households, as consumers, are on the buying or demand side, and businesses are on the selling or supply side. Each group of economic units both buys and sells.

[4]For present purposes think of businesses simply as organizational charts, that is, institutions on paper apart from the capital, raw materials, labor, and entrepreneurial ability which breathe life into them and make them "going concerns."

have negotiated "joint ventures" with the former Soviet Union based on barter. The Soviets get updated capital equipment, new technologies, and increased oil production; American oil companies take their earnings in oil rather than currency.

Estimates differ on the volume of barter transactions within the United States. One estimate is that 175,000 businesses engaged in barter transactions of almost $1 billion in 1990, a fivefold increase in dollar volume since 1980. A higher estimate indicates that in 1990 some 220,000 firms conducted $5.3 billion worth of barter transactions.

The increasing popularity of barter has partly resulted from the development of "exchange companies" which coordinate barter transactions. The exchange company provides trade credits to members who make goods or services available; these accounts are debited when members make purchases. For its services the exchange company charges a membership fee and receives a percentage of the value of each transaction. At present there are over 400 barter exchanges in America.

Barter does involve time-consuming negotiation and it could undermine and distort the flow of open multilateral trade (Figure 3-1). Yet, as our illustrations make clear, barter is a means of bringing about mutually advantageous transactions which otherwise would not have occurred.

Furthermore, the specter of scarcity haunts these transactions. Because households have only limited amounts of resources to supply to businesses, the money incomes of consumers will be limited. This means that each consumer's income will go only so far. A limited number of dollars clearly will not permit the purchase of all the goods and services the consumer might like to buy. Similarly, because resources are scarce, the output of finished goods and services is also necessarily limited. Scarcity and choice permeate our entire discussion.

To summarize: In a monetary economy, households, as resource owners, sell their resources to businesses and, as consumers, spend the money income received buying goods and services. Businesses must buy resources to produce goods and services; their finished products are then sold to households in exchange for consumption expenditures or, as businesses view it, revenues. The net result is a counterclockwise *real* flow of economic resources and finished goods and services, and a clockwise *money* flow of income and consumption expenditures. These flows are simultaneous and repetitive.

Limitations

Our model simplifies in many ways. Intrahousehold and intrabusiness transactions are concealed. Government and the "rest of the world" are ignored as decision makers. The model subtly implies constant flows of output and income, while in fact these flows are unstable over time. Nor is the circular flow a perpetual motion machine; production exhausts human energies and absorbs physical resources, the latter giving rise to problems of environmental pollution. Finally, our model does not explain how product and resource prices are actually determined, which is examined in Chapter 4.

CHAPTER SUMMARY

1 The capitalistic system is characterized by private ownership of resources and the freedom of individuals to engage in economic activities of their choice to advance their material well-being. Self-interest is the driving force of such an economy, and competition functions as a regulatory or control mechanism.

2 Capitalistic production is not organized in terms of a government plan, but rather features the market system as a means of organizing and making effective the myriad individual decisions which determine what is produced, the methods of production, and the sharing of output. The capitalist ideology envisions government playing a minor and relatively passive economic role.

3 Specialization according to comparative advantage and an advanced technology based on the extensive use of capital goods are features common to all modern economies.

4 Functioning as a medium of exchange, money circumvents problems of bartering and thereby permits greater specialization both domestically and internationally.

5 An overview of the operation of the capitalistic system can be gained through the circular flow of income. This simplified model locates the product and resource markets and presents the major income-expenditure flows and resources-output flows which constitute the lifeblood of the capitalistic economy.

TERMS AND CONCEPTS

private property
freedom of enterprise
freedom of choice
self-interest
competition
market
roundabout production
comparative advantage
specialization and division of labor
terms of trade
medium of exchange
bartering
resource and product markets
circular flow model

QUESTIONS AND STUDY SUGGESTIONS

1 "Capitalism may be characterized as an automatic self-regulating system motivated by the self-interest of individuals and regulated by competition."[5] Explain and evaluate.

2 Explain how the market system is a means of communicating and implementing decisions concerning allocation of the economy's resources.

3 What advantages result from "roundabout" production? What problem is involved in increasing a full-employment, full-production economy's stock of capital goods? Illustrate this problem in terms of the production possibilities curve. Does an economy with unemployed resources face the same problem?

4 What are the advantages of specialization in the use of human and material resources? The disadvantages? Explain: "Exchange is the necessary consequence of specialization."

5 Answer question 7 at the end of Chapter 24.

6 What problems does barter entail? Indicate the economic significance of money as a medium of exchange. "Money is the only commodity that is good for nothing but to be gotten rid of. It will not feed you, clothe you, shelter you, or amuse you unless you spend or invest it. It imparts value only in parting."[6] Explain this statement.

7 Describe the operation of pure capitalism as portrayed by the circular flow model. Locate resource and product markets and emphasize the fact of scarcity throughout your discussion. Specify the limitations of the circular flow model.

[5]Howard R. Bowen, *Toward Social Economy* (New York: Holt, Rinehart and Winston, Inc., 1948), p. 249.

[6]Federal Reserve Bank of Philadelphia, "Creeping Inflation," *Business Review,* August 1957, p. 3.

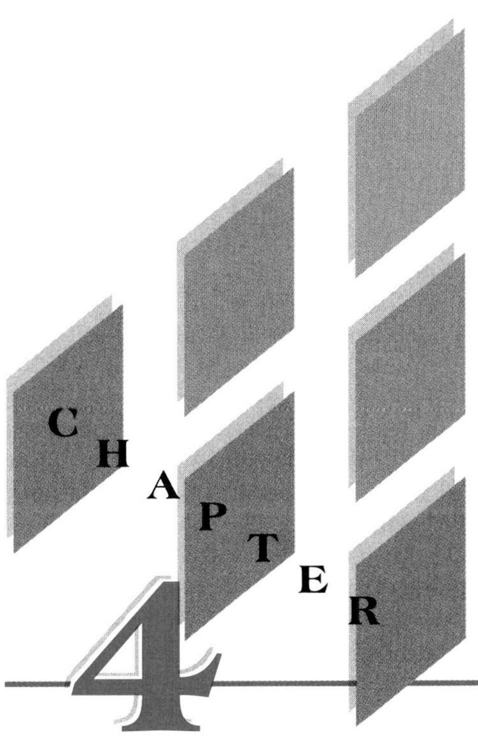

Chapter 4 Understanding Individual Markets: Demand and Supply

Teach a parrot to say, "Demand and supply," and you have an economist! There is a strong element of truth in this quip. The simple tools of demand and supply can take us far in understanding not only specific economic issues, but also the operation of the entire economic system.

In this chapter we will examine the nature of markets and how prices and outputs are determined. Our circular flow model in Chapter 3 identified the participants in both product and resource markets. But we assumed there that product and resource prices were "given"; no attempt was made to explain how prices are "set" or determined. We now build on the circular flow model by discussing the concept of a market more fully.

MARKETS DEFINED

A **market** is *an institution or mechanism which brings together buyers ("demanders") and sellers ("suppliers") of particular goods and services.* Markets exist in many forms. The corner gas station, the fast-food outlet, the local music store, a farmer's roadside stand—all are familiar markets. The New York Stock Exchange and the Chicago Board of Trade are highly organized markets where buyers and sellers of stocks and bonds and farm commodities, respectively, from all over the world are brought into contact with one another. Similarly, auctioneers bring together potential buyers and sellers of art, livestock, used farm equipment, and sometimes real estate. The all-American quarterback and his agent bargain with the owner of an NFL team. A graduating finance major interviews with Citicorp or Chase Manhattan at the university placement office. All these situations which link potential buyers with potential sellers constitute markets. As our examples imply, some markets are local while others are national or international in scope. Some are highly personal, involving face-to-face contact between demander and supplier; others are impersonal in that buyer and seller never see or know one another.

This chapter concerns the functioning of *purely competitive markets.* Such markets presume large numbers of independently acting buyers and sellers interested in exchanging a standardized product. These markets are not the music store or corner gas station where products have price tags, but competitive markets such as a central grain exchange, a stock market, or a market for foreign currencies where the equilibrium price is "discovered" by the interacting decisions of buyers and sellers. Similarly, we see how prices are established in resource markets by demand decisions of competing businesses and supply decisions of competing households (Figure 3-2). We shall concentrate on the *product market,* then later in the chapter examine the *resource market.* Our goal is to explain the mechanics of prices.

DEMAND

Demand is *a schedule which shows the various amounts of a product consumers are willing and able to purchase at each price in a series of possible prices during a specified period of time.*[1] Demand portrays a series of alternative possibilities which can be set down in tabular form. It shows the quantities of a product which will be demanded at various possible prices, *all other things being equal.*

We usually view demand from the vantage point of price; that is, we read demand as showing the amounts consumers will buy at various possible prices. It is equally correct and sometimes more useful to view demand from the reference point of quantity. Instead of asking what quantities can be sold at various prices, we ask what prices can be gotten from consumers for various quantities of a good. Table 4-1 is a hypothetical **demand schedule** for a single consumer purchasing bushels of corn.

This tabular portrayal of demand reflects the relationship between the price of corn and the quantity the consumer would be willing and able to purchase at each of these prices. Note that we say willing and *able,* because willingness alone is not effective in the market. I may be willing to buy a Porsche, but if this willingness is not backed by the necessary dollars, it will not be effective and, therefore, not reflected in the market. In Table 4-1, if the price of corn were $5 per bushel, our consumer would be willing and able to buy 10 bushels per week; if it were $4, the consumer would be willing and able to buy 20 bushels per week; and so forth.

The demand schedule does not tell us which of the five possible prices will actually exist in the corn market. This depends on demand *and supply.* Demand is simply a tabular statement of a buyer's plans, or intentions, with respect to the purchase of a product.

To be meaningful the quantities demanded at each price must relate to a specific period—a day, a week, a month. To say "a consumer will buy 10 bushels of corn at $5 per bushel" is meaningless. To say "a consumer will buy 10 bushels of corn *per week* at $5 per bushel" is clear and meaningful. Without a specific time period we would not know whether demand for a product was large or small.

[1]In adjusting this definition to the resource market, substitute the word "resources" for "product" and "businesses" for "consumers."

TABLE 4-1 **An individual buyer's demand for corn *(hypothetical data)***

Price per bushel	*Quantity demanded per week*
$5	10
4	20
3	35
2	55
1	80

Law of Demand

A fundamental characteristic of demand is this: All else being constant, as price falls, the quantity demanded rises. Or, other things being equal, as price increases, the corresponding quantity demanded falls. In short, there is a negative or *inverse* relationship between price and quantity demanded. Economists call this inverse relationship the **law of demand.**

The "other things being constant" assumption is critical here. Many factors other than the price of the product under consideration affect the amount purchased. For example, the quantity of Nikes purchased will depend not only on the price of Nikes, but also on the prices of such substitute shoes as Reeboks, Adidas, and L.A. Gear. The law of demand in this case says that fewer pairs of Nikes will be purchased if the price of Nikes rises *and the prices of Reeboks, Adidas, and L.A. Gear all remain constant.* In short, if the *relative price* of Nikes increases, fewer Nikes will be bought. If the prices of Nikes and all other competing shoes increase by some amount—say $5—consumers might buy more, less, or the same amount of Nikes.

On what foundation does the law of demand rest? There are several levels of analysis on which to argue the case.

1 Common sense and simple observation are consistent with the law of demand. People ordinarily *do* buy more of a given product at a low price than they do at a high price. Price is an obstacle which deters consumers from buying. The higher this obstacle, the less of a product they will buy; the lower the price obstacle, the more they will buy. A high price discourages consumers from buying, and a low price encourages them to buy. The fact that businesses have "sales" is concrete

evidence of their belief in the law of demand. "Bargain days" are based on the law of demand. Businesses reduce their inventories by lowering prices, not by raising them.

2 In any given time period each buyer of a product will derive less satisfaction or benefit or utility from each successive unit of a product. The second "Big Mac" will yield less satisfaction to the consumer than the first; and the third still less added benefit or utility than the second. Because consumption is subject to **diminishing marginal utility**—consuming successive units of a particular product yields less and less extra satisfaction—consumers will only buy additional units if price is reduced.

3 The law of demand also can be explained in terms of income and substitution effects. The **income effect** indicates that, at a lower price, you can afford more of the good without giving up other goods. In other words, a decline in the price of a product will increase the purchasing power of your money income, enabling you to buy more of the product than before. A higher price will have the opposite effect.

The **substitution effect** suggests that, at a lower price, you have the incentive to substitute the cheaper good for similar goods which are now relatively more expensive. Consumers tend to substitute cheap products for dear products.

For example, a decline in the price of beef will increase the purchasing power of consumer incomes, enabling them to buy more beef (the income effect). At a lower price, beef is relatively more attractive and is substituted for pork, mutton, chicken, and fish (the substitution effect). The income and substitution effects combine to make consumers able and willing to buy more of a product at a low price than at a high price.

The Demand Curve

This inverse relationship between product price and quantity demanded can be represented on a simple graph wherein, by convention, we measure quantity demanded on the horizontal axis and price on the vertical axis. We locate on the graph those five price–quantity possibilities shown in Table 4-1 by drawing perpendiculars from the appropriate points on the two axes. Thus, in plotting the "$5-price–10-quantity-demanded" possibility, we draw a perpendicular from the horizontal (quantity) axis at 10 to meet a perpendicular drawn from the vertical (price) axis at $5. If this is done for all five possibilities, the result is a series of points as shown in Figure 4-1. Each point represents a specific price and the corresponding quantity the consumer will purchase at that price.

Now, assuming the same inverse relationship between price and quantity demanded at all points between the ones graphed, we can generalize on the inverse relationship between price and quantity demanded by drawing a curve to represent *all* price–quantity-demanded possibilities within the limits shown on the graph. The resulting curve is called a **demand curve,** labeled *DD* in Figure 4-1. It slopes

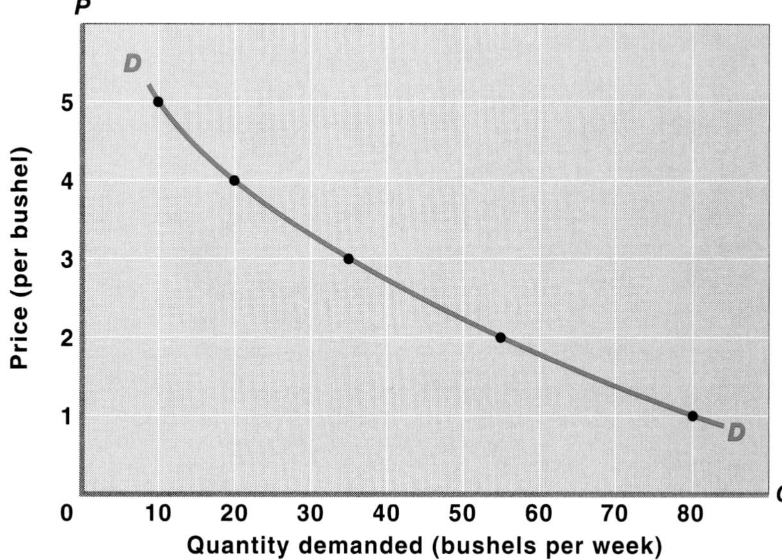

FIGURE 4-1 An individual buyer's demand curve for corn

An individual's demand schedule graphs as a downsloping curve such as *DD*, because price and quantity demanded are inversely related. Specifically, the law of demand generalizes that consumers will buy more of a product as its price declines.

downward and to the right because the relationship it portrays between price and quantity demanded is negative or inverse. The law of demand—people buy more at a low price than at a high price—is reflected in the downward slope of the demand curve.

What is the advantage of graphing our demand schedule? After all, Table 4-1 and Figure 4-1 contain exactly the same data and reflect the same relationship between price and quantity demanded. The advantage of graphing is that we can represent clearly a given relationship—in this case the law of demand—more simply than if we relied on verbal and tabular presentation. A single curve on a graph, if understood, is simpler to state *and manipulate* than tables and lengthy verbal descriptions. Graphs are invaluable tools in economic analysis. They permit clear expression and handling of sometimes complex relationships.

Individual and Market Demand

Until now we have assumed just one consumer. Competition assumes many buyers are in the market. The transition from an *individual* to a *market* demand schedule can be accomplished easily by summing the quantities demanded by each consumer at the various possible prices. If there were just three buyers in the market, as is shown in Table 4-2, it would be easy to determine the total quantities demanded at each price. Figure 4-2 shows the same summing procedure graphically, using only the $3 price to illustrate the adding-up process. Note that we are simply summing the three individual demand curves *horizontally* to derive the total demand curve.

TABLE 4-2 Market demand for corn, three buyers (hypothetical data)

Price per bushel	*Quantity demanded*						*Total quantity demanded per week*
	First buyer		*Second buyer*		*Third buyer*		
$5	10	+	12	+	8	=	30
4	20	+	23	+	17	=	60
3	35	+	39	+	26	=	100
2	55	+	60	+	39	=	154
1	80	+	87	+	54	=	221

Competition, of course, entails many more than three buyers of a product. So—to avoid a lengthy addition process—suppose there are 200 buyers of corn in the market, each of whom chooses to buy the same amount at each of the various prices as our original consumer does. Thus, we can determine total or market demand by multiplying the quantity-demanded data of Table 4-1 by 200, as in Table 4-3. Curve D_1 in Figure 4-3 indicates this market demand curve for the 200 buyers.

Determinants of Demand

An economist constructing a demand curve such as D_1 in Figure 4-3 assumes that price is the most important influence on the amount of any product purchased. But the economist knows that other factors can and do affect purchases. Thus, in locating a given demand curve such as D_1, it must also be assumed that "other things are equal"; that is, certain *determinants* of the amount demanded are assumed to be constant. When any of

FIGURE 4-2 The market demand curve is the sum of the individual demand curves

Graphically the market demand curve (*D* total) is found by summing horizontally the individual demand curves (D_1, D_2, and D_3) of all consumers in the market.

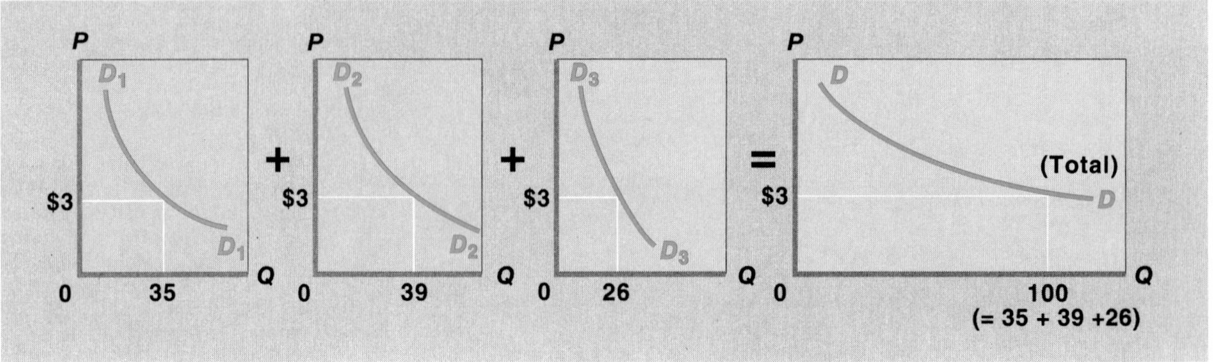

TABLE 4-3 Market demand for corn, 200 buyers *(hypothetical data)*

(1) Price per bushel	(2) Quantity demanded per week, single buyer		(3) Number of buyers in the market		(4) Total quantity demanded per week
$5	10	×	200	=	2,000
4	20	×	200	=	4,000
3	35	×	200	=	7,000
2	55	×	200	=	11,000
1	80	×	200	=	16,000

these determinants do change, the location of the demand curve will shift to the right or left of D_1. For this reason determinants of demand are referred to as *demand shifters.*

The basic determinants of market demand are: (1) the tastes or preferences of consumers, (2) the number of consumers in the market, (3) the money incomes of consumers, (4) prices of related goods, and (5) consumer expectations about future prices and incomes.

Changes in Demand

A change in one or more of the determinants of demand will change the demand schedule data in Table 4-3 and therefore the location of the demand curve in Figure 4-3. A change in the demand schedule data, or, graphically, a shift in the location of the demand curve, is called a *change in demand.*

If consumers become willing and able to buy more of this particular good at each possible price than is reflected in column 4 of Table 4-3, the result will be an *increase in demand.* In Figure 4-3, this increase in demand is reflected in a shift of the demand curve to the *right,* from D_1 to D_2. Conversely, a *decrease in demand* occurs when, because of a change in one or more of the determinants, consumers buy less of the product at each possible price than indicated in column 4 of Table 4-3. Graphically, a decrease in demand is shown as a shift of the demand curve to the *left,* for example, from D_1 to D_3 in Figure 4-3.

Let's now examine how changes in each determinant affect demand.

1 Tastes A change in consumer tastes or preferences favorable to a product—possibly prompted by

FIGURE 4-3 Changes in the demand for corn

A change in one or more of the determinants of demand—consumer tastes, the number of buyers in the market, money incomes, the prices of other goods, or consumer expectations—will cause a change in demand. An increase in demand shifts the demand curve to the right, as from D_1 to D_2. A decrease in demand shifts the demand curve to the left, as from D_1 to D_3. A change in the quantity demanded is caused by a change in the price of the product, and is shown by a movement from one point to another—as from *a* to *b*—on a fixed demand curve.

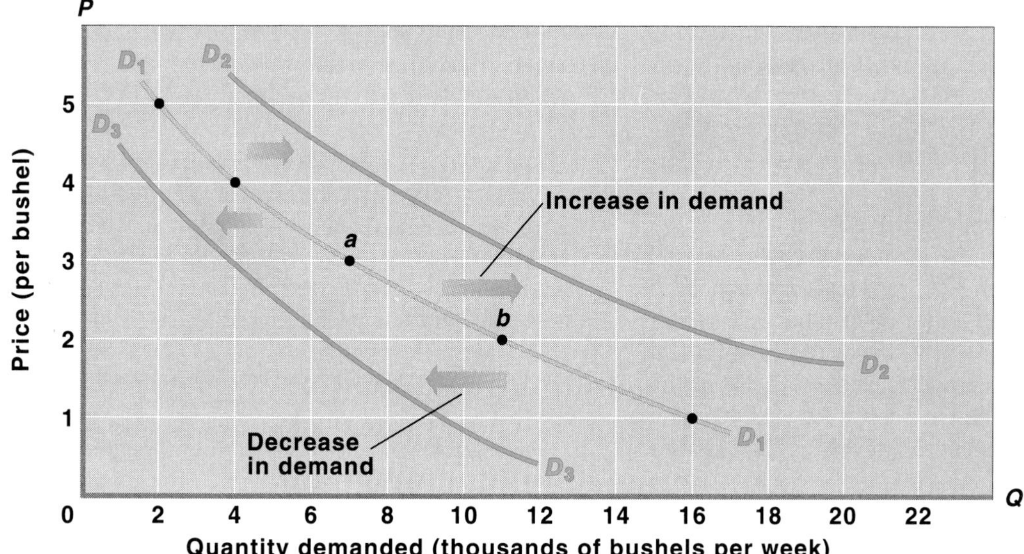

advertising or fashion changes—will mean that more will be demanded at each price; that is, demand will increase. An unfavorable change in consumer preferences will cause demand to decrease, shifting the curve to the left. Technological change in the form of a new product may prompt a revision of consumer tastes. For example, the introduction of compact discs has decreased the demand for long-playing records. Demand for oat bran has increased greatly because of health studies linking it to lower cholesterol levels.

2 Number of Buyers An increase in the number of consumers in a market will increase demand. Fewer consumers will be reflected by a decrease in demand. For example, dramatic improvements in communications have made financial markets international in scope, increasing demand for stocks, bonds, and other financial instruments. And the "baby boom" after World War II increased demand for diapers, baby lotion, and services of obstetricians. When the "baby boom" generation reached their twenties in the 1970s, the demand for housing increased dramatically. Conversely, the aging of the baby boomers in the 1980s and 1990s has been an important factor in the recent "slump" in housing demand. Also, increasing life expectancy has increased demands for medical care, retirement communities, and nursing homes. Note, too, that American trade negotiators are trying to reduce foreign trade barriers to American farm products to increase demands for those products.

3 Income The impact of changes in money income on demand is more complex. For most commodities, a rise in income will cause an increase in demand. Consumers typically buy more steaks, sunscreen, and stereos as their incomes increase. Conversely, the demand for such products will decline in response to a fall in incomes. Commodities whose demand varies *directly* with money income are called **superior, or normal, goods.**

Although most products are normal goods, there are a few exceptions. As incomes increase beyond some point, the amounts of bread or lard or cabbages purchased at each price may diminish because higher incomes allow consumers to buy more high-protein foods, such as dairy products and meat. Rising incomes may also decrease demands for used clothing and third-hand automobiles. Similarly, rising incomes may cause demands for hamburger and margarine to decline as wealthier consumers switch to T-bones and butter. Goods whose demand varies *inversely* with a change in money income are called **inferior goods.**

4 Prices of Related Goods Whether a given change in the price of a related good will increase or decrease the demand for a product will depend on whether the related good is a substitute for it or a complement to it. A substitute is a good which can be used in place of another good. A complement is a good used in conjunction with another good.

Substitutes For example, butter and margarine are **substitute goods.** When the price of butter rises, consumers will buy less butter, and this will increase the demand for margarine.[2] Conversely, as the price of butter falls, consumers will buy more butter, causing the demand for margarine to decrease. *When two products are substitutes, the price of one good and the demand for the other are directly related.* So it is with Millers and Budweiser, sugar and Nutrasweet, Toyotas and Hondas, and Coke and Pepsi.

Complements Other pairs of products are **complementary goods;** they "go together" in that they are jointly demanded. If the price of gasoline falls and, as a result, you drive your car more, this extra driving will increase your demand for motor oil. Conversely, an increase in the price of gasoline will diminish the demand for motor oil.[3] Thus gas and oil are jointly demanded; they are complements. So it is with ham and eggs, tuition and textbooks, VCRs and video cassettes, golf clubs and golf balls, cameras and rolls of film. *When two commodities are complements, the price of one good and the demand for the other are inversely related.*

Many pairs of goods, of course, are not related at all—they are *independent* goods. For such pairs of commodities as, for example, butter and golf balls, potatoes and automobiles, bananas and wristwatches, a change in the price of one would have little or no impact on the demand for the other.

5 Expectations Consumer expectations about future product prices, product availability, and future income can shift demand. Consumer expectations of higher future prices may prompt them to buy now to "beat" anticipated price rises; similarly, the expectation of rising incomes may induce consumers to be freer in

[2]Note that the consumer is moving up a stable demand curve for butter. But the demand curve for margarine shifts to the right (increases). Given the supply of margarine, this rightward shift in demand means more margarine will be purchased and that its price will also rise.

[3]While the buyer is moving up a stable demand curve for gasoline, the demand for motor oil shifts to the left (decreases). Given the supply of motor oil, this decline in the demand for motor oil will reduce both the amount purchased and its price.

current spending. Conversely, expectations of falling prices and income will decrease current demand for products. First example: If freezing weather destroys much of Florida's citrus crop, consumers may reason that forthcoming shortages of frozen orange juice will escalate its price. They may stock up on orange juice by purchasing extraordinarily large quantities now. Second example: Several years ago Johnny Carson jokingly predicted a toilet paper shortage. Many of his TV fans took this seriously and within a few days toilet paper was not to be found on the shelves of many supermarkets. Third example: A first-round NFL draft choice might splurge for a new Mercedes in anticipation of a lucrative professional football contract. Final example: Additional Federal excise taxes imposed on beer, wine, and distilled liquor on January 1, 1991, sharply increased demand in December of 1990 as consumers "bought early" to beat anticipated price increases.

In summary, an *increase* in demand—the decision by consumers to buy larger quantities of a product at each possible price—can be caused by:

1 A favorable change in consumer tastes
2 An increase in the number of buyers
3 Rising incomes if the product is a normal good
4 Falling incomes if the product is an inferior good
5 An increase in the price of a substitute good
6 A decrease in the price of a complementary good
7 Consumer expectations of higher future prices and incomes

Be sure you can "reverse" these generalizations to explain a *decrease* in demand. Table 4-4 provides additional illustrations to reinforce your understanding of the determinants of demand.

TABLE 4-4 Determinants of demand: factors that shift the demand curve

1 **Change in buyer tastes** Example: Physical fitness increases in popularity, increasing the demand for jogging shoes and bicycles

2 **Change in number of buyers** Examples: Japanese reduce import quotas on American telecommunications equipment, thereby increasing the demand for such equipment; a decline in the birthrate reduces the demand for education

3 **Change in income** Examples: An increase in incomes increases the demand for such normal goods as butter, lobster, and filet mignon, while reducing the demand for such inferior goods as cabbage, turnips, retreaded tires, and used clothing

4 **Change in the prices of related goods** Examples: A reduction in air fares reduces the demand for bus transportation (substitute goods); a decline in the price of compact disc players increases the demand for compact discs (complementary goods)

5 **Change in expectations** Example: Inclement weather in South America causes the expectation of higher future coffee prices, thereby increasing the current demand for coffee

Changes in Quantity Demanded

A "change in demand" must not be confused with a "change in quantity demanded." A **change in demand** is a shift in the entire demand curve either to the right (an increase in demand) or to the left (a decrease in demand). The consumer's state of mind concerning purchases of this product has been altered. The cause: a change in one or more of the determinants of demand. The term "demand" refers to a schedule or curve; therefore, a "change in demand" means that the entire schedule has changed and that graphically the curve has shifted its position.

In contrast, a **change in the quantity demanded** designates the movement from one point to another point—from one price-quantity combination to another—on a fixed demand curve. The cause of a change in quantity demanded is a change in the price of the product under consideration. In Table 4-3 a decline in the price from $5 to $4 will increase the quantity of corn demanded from 2000 to 4000 bushels.

The distinction between a change in demand and a change in the quantity demanded can be seen in Figure 4-3. The shift of the demand curve D_1 to either D_2 or D_3 is a "change in demand." But the movement from point *a* to point *b* on curve D_1 is a "change in the quantity demanded."

You should decide whether a change in demand or a change in quantity demanded is involved in each of the following illustrations:

1 Consumer incomes rise, with the result that more jewelry is purchased.
2 A barber raises the price of haircuts and experiences a decline in volume of business.
3 The price of Toyotas goes up, and, as a consequence, the sales of Chevrolets increase.

QUICK REVIEW 4-1

- ***A market is any arrangement which facilitates purchase and sale of goods, services, or resources.***
- ***The law of demand indicates that, other things being constant, the quantity of a good purchased will vary inversely with its price.***

- ***The demand curve will shift because of changes in a consumer tastes, b the number of buyers in the market, c incomes, d the prices of substitute or complementary goods, and e expectations.***
- ***A "change in quantity demanded" refers to a movement from one point to another on a stable demand curve; a "change in demand" designates a shift in the entire demand curve.***

SUPPLY

Supply *is a schedule which shows the amounts of a product a producer is willing and able to produce and make available for sale at each price in a series of possible prices during a specified period.*[4] This **supply schedule** portrays a series of alternative possibilities, such as shown in Table 4-5, for a single producer of corn. Supply tells us the quantities of a product which will be supplied at various prices, all other factors held constant.

Our definition of supply indicates that supply is usually viewed from the vantage point of price. That is, we read supply as showing the amounts producers will offer at various prices. It is equally correct and more useful in some instances to view supply from the reference point of quantity. Instead of asking what quantities will be offered at various prices, we can ask what prices will be required to induce producers to offer various quantities of a good.

Law of Supply

Table 4-5 shows a positive or *direct* relationship between price and quantity supplied. As price rises, the corresponding quantity supplied rises; as price falls, the quantity supplied also falls. This particular relationship is called the **law of supply.** Producers will produce and offer for sale more of their product at a high price than at a low price. This again is basically a commonsense matter.

Price is a deterrent from the consumer's standpoint. The obstacle of a high price means that the consumer, being on the paying end of this price, will buy a relatively small amount of the product; the lower the price obstacle, the more the consumer will buy. The supplier is on the receiving end of the product's price.

[4]In talking of the resource market, our definition of supply reads: a schedule which shows the various amounts of a resource which its owners are willing to supply in the market at each possible price in a series of prices during a specified time.

TABLE 4-5 An individual producer's supply of corn *(hypothetical data)*

Price per bushel	*Quantity supplied per week*
$5	60
4	50
3	35
2	20
1	5

To a supplier, price is revenue per unit and therefore an inducement or incentive to produce and sell a product. Given production costs, a higher product price means greater profits for the supplier and thus an incentive to increase the quantity supplied.

Consider a farmer who can shift resources within limits among alternative products. As price moves up in Table 4-5, the farmer will find it profitable to take land out of wheat, oats, and soybean production and put it into corn. Furthermore, higher corn prices will make it possible for the farmer to cover the costs associated with more intensive cultivation and the use of larger quantities of fertilizers and pesticides. All these efforts result in more output of corn.

Now consider a manufacturing concern. Beyond some point manufacturers usually encounter increasing production costs per added unit of output. Therefore, a higher product price is necessary to cover these rising costs. Costs rise because certain productive resources—in particular, the firm's plant and machinery—cannot be expanded quickly. As the firm increases the amounts of more readily variable resources such as labor, materials, and component parts, the fixed plant will at some point become crowded or congested. Productive efficiency will decline and the cost of successive units of output will increase. Producers must receive a higher price to produce these more costly units. Price and quantity supplied are directly related.

The Supply Curve

As with demand, it is convenient to represent graphically the concept of supply. Our axes in Figure 4-4 are the same as those in Figure 4-3, except for the change of "quantity demanded" to "quantity supplied" on the horizontal axis. The graphing procedure is the same, but the quantity data and relationship involved are different. The market supply data graphed in Figure 4-4 as S_1 are shown in Table 4-6, which assumes there are 200 suppliers in the market having the same supply

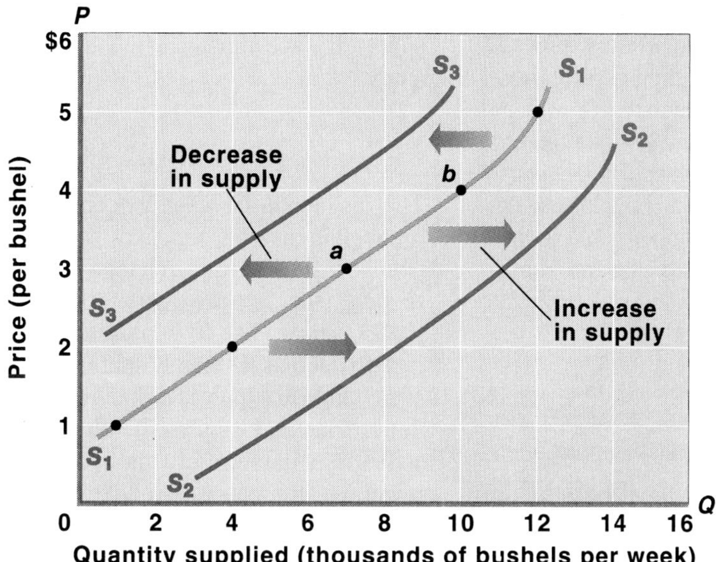

FIGURE 4-4 Changes in the supply of corn

A change in one or more of the determinants of supply—resource prices, productive techniques, the prices of other goods, taxes and subsidies, price expectations, or the number of sellers in the market—will cause a change in supply. An increase in supply shifts the supply curve to the right, as from S_1 to S_2. A decrease in supply is shown graphically as a shift of the curve to the left, as from S_1 to S_3. A change in the quantity supplied is caused by a change in the price of the product and is shown by a movement from one point to another—as from *a* to *b*—on a fixed supply curve.

schedules as the producer previously portrayed in Table 4-5.

Determinants of Supply

In constructing a supply curve, the economist assumes that price is the most significant influence on the quantity supplied of any product. But, as with the demand curve, the supply curve is anchored on the "other things are equal" assumption. The supply curve is drawn assuming that certain determinants of the amount supplied are given and do not change. If any of these determinants of supply do change, the supply curve will shift.

The basic determinants of supply are (1) resource prices, (2) the technique of production, (3) taxes and subsidies, (4) prices of other goods, (5) price expectations, and (6) the number of sellers in the market. A change in any one or more of these determinants or *supply shifters* will cause the supply curve for a product to shift either to the right or the left. A shift to the *right,* from S_1 to S_2 in Figure 4-4, designates an *increase in supply:* Producers are now supplying larger quantities of the product at each possible price. A shift to the *left,* S_1 to S_3 in Figure 4-4, indicates a *decrease in supply:* Suppliers are offering less at each price.

TABLE 4-6 Market supply of corn, 200 producers *(hypothetical data)*

(1) Price per bushel	*(2) Quantity supplied per week, single producer*		*(3) Number of sellers in the market*		*(4) Total quantity supplied per week*
$5	60	×	200	=	12,000
4	50	×	200	=	10,000
3	35	×	200	=	7,000
2	20	×	200	=	4,000
1	5	×	200	=	1,000

Changes in Supply

Let's consider how changes in each of these determinants affect supply.

1 Resource Prices As indicated in our explanation of the law of supply, the relationship between production costs and supply is an intimate one. A firm's supply curve is based on production costs; a firm must receive higher prices for additional units of output because those extra units cost more to produce. It follows that a decrease in resource prices will lower production costs and increase supply, that is, shift the supply curve to the right. If prices of seed and fertilizer decrease, we can expect the supply of corn to increase. Conversely, an increase in resource prices will raise production costs and reduce supply, that is, shift the supply curve to the left. Increases in the prices of iron ore and coke will increase the cost of producing steel and reduce its supply.

2 Technology A technological improvement means new knowledge permits us to produce a unit of output with fewer resources. Given the prices of these resources, this will lower production costs and increase supply. Recent breakthroughs in superconductivity portend the possibility of transporting electric power with little or no loss. Currently, about 30 percent of electric power transmitted by copper cable is lost. Consequence? Significant cost reductions and supply increases might occur in a wide range of products where energy is an important input.

3 Taxes and Subsidies Businesses treat most taxes as costs. Therefore, an increase in sales or property taxes will increase costs and reduce supply. Conversely, subsidies are "taxes in reverse." If government subsidizes the production of a good, it in effect lowers costs and increases supply.

4 Prices of Other Goods Changes in the prices of other goods can also shift the supply curve for a product. A decline in the price of wheat may cause a farmer to produce and offer more oats at each possible price. Conversely, a rise in the price of wheat may make farmers less willing to produce and offer oats in the market. A firm manufacturing athletic equipment might reduce its supply of basketballs in response to a rise in the price of soccer balls.

5 Expectations Expectations concerning the future price of a product can affect a producer's current willingness to supply that product. It is difficult, however, to generalize how the expectation of higher prices will affect the present supply of a product. Farmers might withhold some of their current corn harvest from the market, anticipating a higher corn price in the future. This will cause a decrease in the current supply of corn. Similarly, if the price of IBM stock is expected to rise significantly in the near future, the supply offered today for sale might decrease. On the other hand, in many types of manufacturing, expected price increases may induce firms to add another shift of workers or expand their production facilities, causing supply to increase.

6 Number of Sellers Given the scale of operations of each firm, the larger the number of suppliers, the greater the market supply. As more firms enter an industry, the supply curve will shift to the right. The smaller the number of firms in an industry, the less the market supply will be. This means that as firms leave an industry, the supply curve will shift to the left.

Table 4-7 provides a checklist of the determinants of supply; the accompanying illustrations deserve careful study.

Changes in Quantity Supplied

The distinction between a "change in supply" and a "change in quantity supplied" parallels that between a change in demand and a change in quantity demanded. A **change in supply** means the entire supply curve shifts. An increase in supply shifts the curve to the right; a decrease in supply shifts it to the left. The cause of a change in supply is a change in one or more of the determinants of supply. The term "supply" refers to a schedule or curve. A "change in supply" therefore must mean that the entire schedule has changed and that the curve has shifted.

A **change in the quantity supplied** refers to the movement from one point to another on a stable supply curve. The cause of such a movement is a change in the price of the specific product under consideration. In Table 4-6 a decline in the price of corn from $5 to $4 decreases the quantity of corn supplied from 12,000 to 10,000 bushels.

Shifting the supply curve from S_1 to S_2 or S_3 in Figure 4-4 entails "changes in supply." The movement

TABLE 4-7 Determinants of supply: factors that shift the supply curve

1 Change in resource prices **Examples: A decline in the price of fertilizer increases the supply of wheat; an increase in the price of irrigation equipment reduces the supply of corn**

2 Change in technology **Example: The development of a more effective insecticide for corn rootworm increases the supply of corn**

3 Changes in taxes and subsidies **Examples: An increase in the excise tax on cigarettes reduces the supply of cigarettes; a decline in subsidies to state universities reduces the supply of higher education**

4 Change in prices of other goods **Example: A decline in the prices of mutton and pork increases the supply of beef**

5 Change in expectations **Example: Expectations of substantial declines in future oil prices cause oil companies to increase current supply**

6 Change in number of suppliers **Examples: An increase in the number of firms producing personal computers increases the supply of personal computers; formation of a new professional football league increases the supply of professional football games**

from point *a* to point *b* on S_1, however, is a "change in quantity supplied."

You should determine which of the following involves a change in supply and which a change in quantity supplied:

1 Because production costs decline, producers sell more automobiles.

2 The price of wheat declines, causing the number of bushels of corn sold per month to increase.

3 Fewer oranges are offered for sale because their price has decreased in retail markets.

4 The Federal government doubles its excise tax on liquor.

QUICK REVIEW 4-2

- ***The law of supply states that, other things being unchanged, the quantity of a good supplied varies directly with its price.***
- ***The supply curve will shift because of changes in a resource prices, b technology, c taxes or subsidies, d prices of other goods, e expectations regarding future product prices, and f the number of suppliers.***
- ***A "change in supply" means a shift in the supply curve; a "change in quantity supplied" designates the movement from one point to another on a given supply curve.***

SUPPLY AND DEMAND: MARKET EQUILIBRIUM

We may now bring the concepts of supply and demand together to see how interaction of the buying decisions of households and the selling decisions of producers will determine the price of a product and the quantity actually bought and sold in the market. In Table 4-8, columns 1 and 2 reproduce the market supply schedule for corn (from Table 4-6), and columns 2 and 3, the market demand schedule for corn (from Table 4-3). Note that in column 2 we are using a common set of prices. We assume competition—a large number of buyers and sellers.

TABLE 4-8 **Market supply and demand for corn** *(hypothetical data)*

(1) Total quantity supplied per week	*(2) Price per bushel*	*(3) Total quantity demanded per week*	*(4) Surplus (+) or shortage (−) (arrows indicate effect on price)*
12,000	$5	2,000	+10,000 ↓
10,000	4	4,000	+ 6,000 ↓
7,000	3	7,000	0
4,000	2	11,000	− 7,000 ↑
1,000	1	16,000	−15,000 ↑

Surpluses

Of the five[5] possible prices at which corn might sell in this market, which will actually prevail as the market price for corn? Let us derive our answer through the simple process of trial and error. For no particular reason, we start with $5. Could this be the prevailing market price for corn? The answer is "No," because producers are willing to produce and offer in the market some 12,000 bushels of corn at this price while buyers are willing to buy only 2000 bushels at this price. The relatively high price of $5 encourages farmers to produce a great deal of corn, but discourages most consumers from buying it. Other products appear as "better buys" when corn is high-priced. The result here is a 10,000-bushel **surplus** or *excess supply* of corn in the market. This surplus, shown in column 4, is the excess of quantity supplied over quantity demanded at the price of $5. Corn farmers find themselves with unwanted inventories of output.

A price of $5—even if it existed temporarily in the corn market—could not persist over a period of time. The very large surplus of corn would prompt competing sellers to bid down the price to encourage buyers to take this surplus off their hands.

Suppose price goes down to $4. Now the situation has changed considerably. The lower price has encouraged buyers to take more of this product off the market and, at the same time, has induced farmers to use a smaller amount of resources in producing corn. The surplus has diminished to 6000 bushels. However, a surplus or excess supply still exists and competition among sellers will once again bid down the price of corn. We can conclude, then, that prices of $5 and $4 will be unstable because they are "too high." The market price for corn must be something less than $4.

Shortages

Let's now jump to the other end of our price column and examine $1 as the possible market price for corn.

[5] Of course, there are many possible prices; our example shows only five of them.

Observe in column 4 that at this price, quantity demanded is in excess of quantity supplied by 15,000 units. This relatively low price discourages farmers from devoting their resources to corn production and encourages consumers to attempt to buy more than is available. The result is a 15,000-bushel **shortage** of, or *excess demand* for, corn. This price of $1 cannot persist as the market price. Competition among buyers will bid up the price to something greater than $1. At a price of $1, many consumers who are willing and able to buy at this price will be left out in the cold. Many potential consumers will express a willingness to pay a price above $1 to ensure getting some of the available corn.

Suppose this competitive bidding up of price by buyers boosts the price of corn to $2. This higher price has reduced, but not eliminated, the shortage of corn. For $2, farmers are willing to devote more resources to corn production, and some buyers who were willing to pay $1 for a bushel of corn will choose not to buy at $2. But a shortage of 7000 bushels still exists at $2. We can conclude that competitive bidding among buyers will push market price above $2.

Equilibrium

By trial and error we have eliminated every price but $3. At a price of $3, *and only at this price,* the quantity which farmers are willing to produce and supply in the market is identical with the amount consumers are willing and able to buy. As a result, there is neither a shortage nor a surplus of corn at this price. A surplus causes price to decline and a shortage causes price to rise.

With neither a shortage nor a surplus at $3, there is no reason for the actual price of corn to move away from this price. The economist calls this price the *market-clearing* or **equilibrium price,** equilibrium meaning "in balance" or "at rest." At $3, quantity supplied and quantity demanded are in balance; that is, **equilibrium quantity** is 7000 bushels. Hence $3 is the only stable price of corn under the supply and demand conditions shown in Table 4-8. Or, stated differently, the price of corn will be established where the supply decisions of producers and the demand decisions of buyers are mutually consistent. Such decisions are consistent with one another only at a price of $3. At any higher price, suppliers want to sell more than consumers want to buy and a surplus will result; at any lower price, consumers want to buy more than producers are willing to offer for sale, as shown by the consequent shortage. Discrepancies between supply and demand intentions of sellers and buyers will prompt price changes which will bring these two sets of plans into accord with one another.

A graphical analysis of supply and demand should yield the same conclusions. Figure 4-5 (Key Graph) puts the market supply and market demand curves for corn on the same graph, the horizontal axis now measuring both quantity demanded and quantity supplied. At any price above the equilibrium price of $3, quantity supplied will exceed quantity demanded. This surplus will cause a competitive bidding down of price by sellers eager to rid themselves of their surplus. The falling price will cause less corn to be offered and will simultaneously encourage consumers to buy more.

Any price below the equilibrium price will entail a shortage; quantity demanded will exceed quantity supplied. Competitive bidding by buyers will push the price up toward the equilibrium level. And this rising price will simultaneously cause producers to increase the quantity supplied and ration buyers out of the market, thereby eliminating the shortage. *Graphically, the intersection of the supply curve and the demand curve for the product will indicate the equilibrium point.* In this case equilibrium price and quantity are $3 per bushel and 7000 bushels.

Rationing Function of Prices

The ability of the competitive forces of supply and demand to establish a price where selling and buying decisions are synchronized or coordinated is called the **rationing function of prices.** In this case, the equilibrium price of $3 clears the market, leaving no burdensome surplus for sellers and no inconvenient shortage for potential buyers. The composite of freely made individual buying and selling decisions sets this price which clears the market. In effect, the market mechanism of supply and demand says that any buyer willing and able to pay $3 for a bushel of corn will be able to acquire one; those who are not, will not. Similarly, any seller willing and able to produce bushels of corn and offer them for sale at $3 will be able to do so; those who are not, will not.

Changes in Supply and Demand

We know that demand might change because of fluctuations in consumer tastes or incomes, changes in consumer expectations, or variations in the prices of related goods. Supply might vary in response to changes

KEY GRAPH

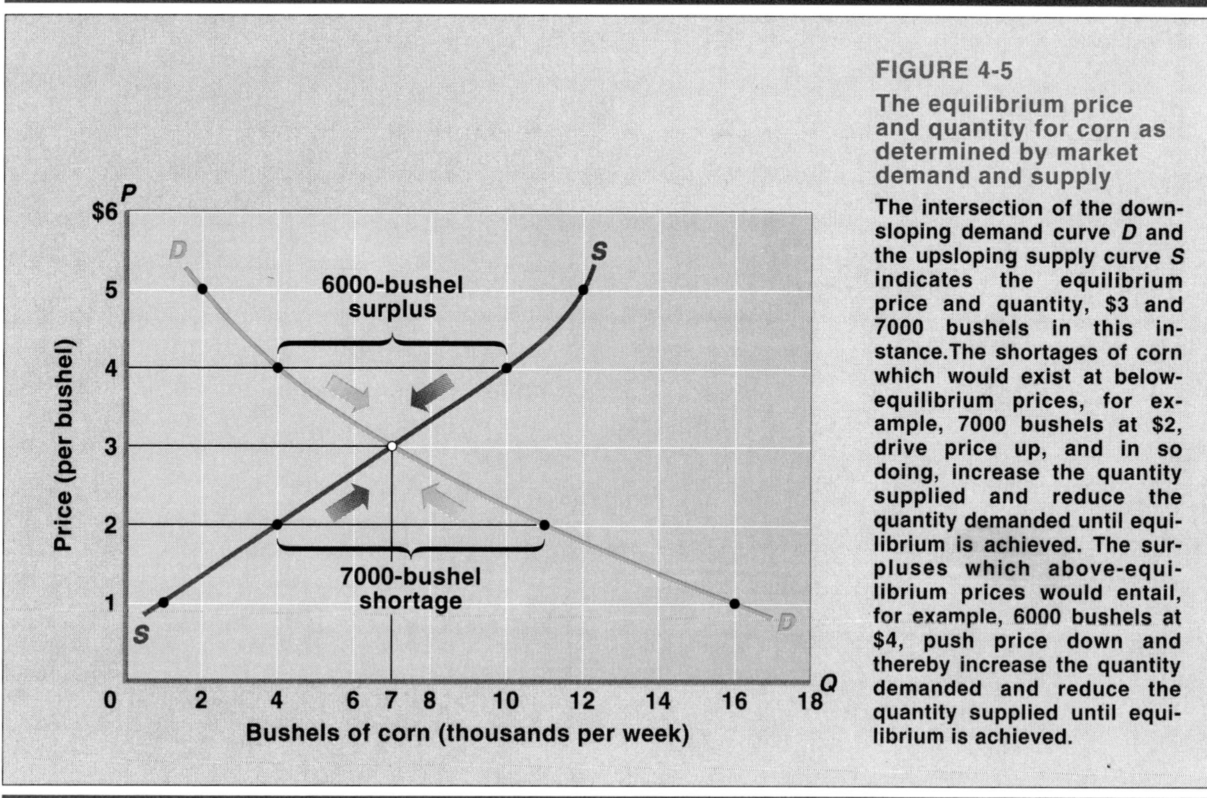

FIGURE 4-5

The equilibrium price and quantity for corn as determined by market demand and supply

The intersection of the downsloping demand curve *D* and the upsloping supply curve *S* indicates the equilibrium price and quantity, $3 and 7000 bushels in this instance. The shortages of corn which would exist at below-equilibrium prices, for example, 7000 bushels at $2, drive price up, and in so doing, increase the quantity supplied and reduce the quantity demanded until equilibrium is achieved. The surpluses which above-equilibrium prices would entail, for example, 6000 bushels at $4, push price down and thereby increase the quantity demanded and reduce the quantity supplied until equilibrium is achieved.

in technology, resource prices, or taxes. Our analysis would be incomplete if we did not consider the effect of changes in supply and demand on equilibrium price.

Changing Demand First, we analyze the effects of a change in demand, assuming supply is constant. Suppose demand increases, as shown in Figure 4-6a. What is the effect on price? Since the new intersection of the supply and demand curves is at a higher point on both the price and quantity axes, an increase in demand, other things (supply) being equal, will have a *price-increasing effect* and a *quantity-increasing effect.* (The value of graphical analysis is now apparent; we need not fumble with columns of figures in determining the effect on price and quantity but only compare the new with the old point of intersection on the graph.)

A decrease in demand, shown in Figure 4-6b, reveals both *price-decreasing* and *quantity-decreasing effects.* Price falls, and quantity also declines. *In brief, we find a direct relationship between a change in demand and resulting changes in both equilibrium price and quantity.*

Changing Supply Let's now analyze the effect of a change in supply on price, assuming that demand is constant. If supply increases, as in Figure 4-6c, the new intersection of supply and demand is located at a lower equilibrium price. Equilibrium quantity, however, increases. If supply decreases, product price will rise. Figure 4-6d illustrates this situation. Here, price increases but quantity declines.

In short, an increase in supply has a *price-decreasing* and a *quantity-increasing effect.* A decrease in supply has a *price-increasing* and a *quantity-decreasing effect. There is an inverse relationship between a change in supply and the resulting change in equilibrium price, but the relationship between a change in supply and the resulting change in equilibrium quantity is direct.*

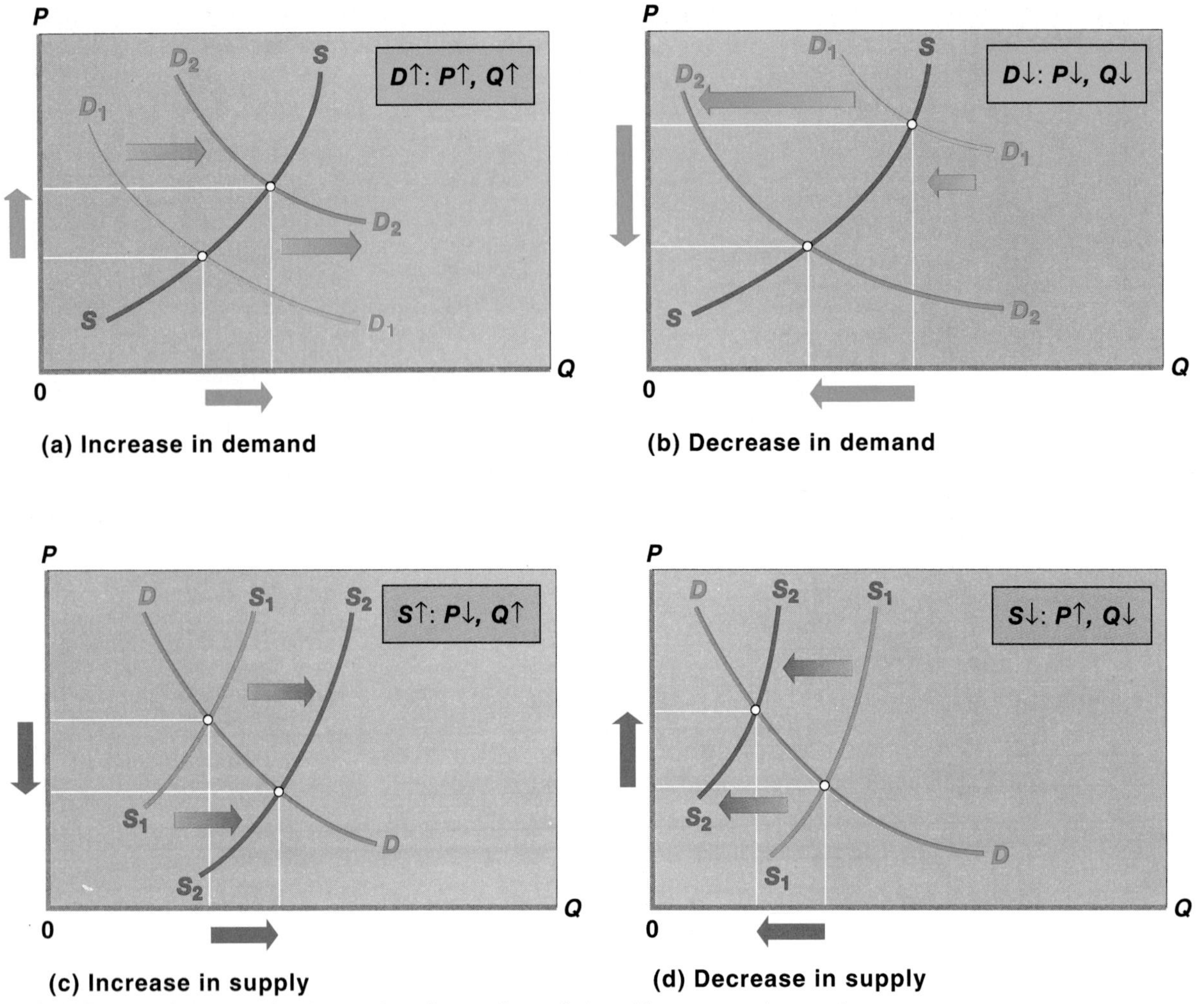

FIGURE 4-6 Changes in demand and supply and the effects on price and quantity

The increase in demand of (a) and the decrease in demand of (b) indicate a direct relationship between a change in demand and the resulting changes in equilibrium price and quantity. The increase in supply of (c) and the decrease in supply of (d) show an inverse relationship between a change in supply and the resulting change in equilibrium price, but a direct relationship between a change in supply and the accompanying change in equilibrium quantity.

Complex Cases A host of more complex cases might arise, involving changes in both supply and demand.

1 Supply Increase; Demand Decrease Assume first that supply increases and demand decreases. What effect does this have on equilibrium price? This example couples two price-decreasing effects, and the net result will be a price fall greater than what would result from either change alone. How about equilibrium quantity? Here the effects of the changes in supply and demand are opposed: The increase in supply increases equilibrium quantity, but the decrease in demand reduces the equilibrium quantity. The direction of the change in quantity depends on the relative sizes of the changes in supply and demand.

2 Supply Decrease; Demand Increase Another possibility is for supply to decrease and demand to increase. Two price-increasing effects are involved here.

We can predict an increase in equilibrium price greater than that caused by either change separately. The effect on equilibrium quantity is again indeterminate, depending on the relative size of the changes in supply and demand. If the decrease in supply is relatively larger than the increase in demand, the equilibrium quantity will be less than initially. But if the decrease in supply is relatively smaller than the increase in demand, the equilibrium quantity will increase as a result of these changes. You should trace through these two cases graphically to verify these conclusions.

3 Supply Increase; Demand Increase What if supply and demand both increase? What is the effect on equilibrium price? It depends. Here we must compare two conflicting effects on price—the price-decreasing effect of the increase in supply and the price-increasing effect of the increase in demand. If the increase in supply is greater than the increase in demand, the equilibrium price will decrease. If the opposite holds, equilibrium price will increase.

The effect on equilibrium quantity is certain: Increases in supply and in demand both have quantity-increasing effects. This means that equilibrium quantity will increase by an amount greater than either change alone.

4 Supply Decrease; Demand Decrease A decrease in both supply and demand can be similarly analyzed. If the decrease in supply is greater than the decrease in demand, equilibrium price will rise. If the reverse holds true, equilibrium price will fall. Because decreases in supply and demand both have quantity-decreasing effects, it can be predicted with certainty that equilibrium quantity will be less than that which prevailed initially.

Special cases might arise where a decrease in demand and a decrease in supply, on the one hand, and an increase in demand and an increase in supply, on the other, exactly cancel out. In both these cases, the net effect on equilibrium price will be zero; price will not change. You should also work out these more complex cases in terms of supply and demand curves to verify all these results.

The Resource Market

As in the product market, resource supply curves are typically upsloping, and resource demand curves are downsloping.

Resource supply curves reflect a *direct* relationship between resource price and quantity supplied, because it is in the interest of resource owners to supply more of a particular resource at a high price than at a low price. High income payments in a particular occupation or industry encourage households to supply more human and property resources. Low-income payments discourage resource owners from supplying resources in this particular occupation or industry and encourage them to supply their resources elsewhere. There is strong evidence, incidentally, that most college students choose their major (their occupation) on the basis of prospective financial rewards.

On the demand side, businesses buy less of a given resource as its price rises, and they substitute other relatively low-priced resources for it. Entrepreneurs will find it profitable to substitute low- for high-priced resources as they try to minimize costs. More of a particular resource will be demanded at a low price than at a high price. The result? A downsloping demand curve for the various resources.

Just as supply decisions of businesses and the demand decisions of consumers determine prices in the product market, so the supply decisions of households and demand decisions of businesses set prices in the resource market.

"Other Things Equal" Revisited

Recall from Chapter 1 that as a substitute for their inability to conduct controlled experiments, economists invoke the "other things being equal" assumption in their analyses. We have seen in the present chapter that a number of forces bear on both supply and demand. Hence, in locating specific supply and demand curves, such as D_1 and S in Figure 4-6a, economists isolate the impact of what they judge to be the most important influence on the amounts supplied and demanded—the price of the specific product under consideration. In thus representing the laws of demand and supply by downsloping and upsloping curves respectively, the economist assumes that the determinants of demand (incomes, tastes, and so forth) and supply (resource prices, technology, and other factors) are constant or unchanging. That is, price and quantity demanded are inversely related, *other things being equal.* And price and quantity supplied are directly related, *other things being equal.*

If you forget the "other things equal" assumption, you can encounter situations which *seem* to be in conflict with the laws of demand and supply. For example, suppose Ford sells 200,000 Escorts in 1990 at $8000; 300,000 at $8500 in 1991; and 400,000 in 1992 at $9000. Price and the number purchased vary *directly,* and these real-world data seem to be at odds with the law of demand. But there is really not a conflict here; these data do *not* refute the law of demand. The catch is that the law of demand's "other things equal" assumption has been violated over the three years in the example. Specifically, because of, for example, growing incomes, population growth, and relatively high gasoline prices which increase the attractiveness of compact cars, the demand curve for Escorts has increased over the years—shifted to the right as from D_1 to D_2 in Figure 4-6a—causing price to rise and, simultaneously, a larger quantity to be purchased.

Conversely, consider Figure 4-6d. Comparing the original S_1D and the new S_2D equilibrium positions, *less* of the product is being sold or supplied at a higher price; that is, price and quantity supplied seem to be *inversely* related, rather than *directly* related as the law of supply indicates. The catch again is that the "other things equal" assumption underlying the upsloping supply curve has been violated. Perhaps production costs have gone up or a specific tax has been levied on this product, shifting the supply curve from S_1 to S_2. These examples also emphasize the importance of our earlier distinction between a "change in quantity demanded (or supplied)" and a "change in demand (supply)."

QUICK REVIEW 4-3

- ***In competitive markets price adjusts to the equilibrium level at which quantity demanded equals quantity supplied.***
- ***A change in demand alters both equilibrium price and equilibrium quantity in the same direction as the change in demand.***
- ***A change in supply causes equilibrium price to change in the opposite direction, but equilibrium quantity to change in the same direction, as the change in supply.***
- ***Over time equilibrium price and quantity may change in directions which seem at odds with the laws of demand and supply because the "other things equal" assumption is violated.***

APPLICATION: THE FOREIGN EXCHANGE MARKET[6]

We close this chapter by applying our understanding of demand and supply to the **foreign exchange market,** the market where various national currencies are exchanged for one another. At the outset two points merit emphasis.

1 Real-world foreign exchange markets conform closely to the kinds of markets studied in this chapter. These are competitive markets characterized by large numbers of buyers and sellers dealing in a standardized "product" such as the American dollar, the German mark, the British pound, or the Japanese yen.

2 The price or exchange value of a nation's currency is an unusual price in that it links *all* domestic (United States) prices with *all* foreign (say, Japanese or German) prices. Exchange rates enable consumers in one country to translate prices of foreign goods into units of their own currency by multiplying the foreign product price by the exchange rate. For example, if the dollar-yen exchange rate is 1 cent per yen, a Sony cassette player priced at 20,000 yen will cost an American $200 (=20,000 × 1¢). But if the exchange rate is 2 cents per yen, the Sony will cost an American $400 (=20,000 × 2¢). Similarly, all other Japanese products will double in price to American buyers. As we shall see, a change in exchange rates has important implications for a nation's levels of domestic production and employment.

The Dollar–Yen Market

Skirting technical details, we now examine how the foreign exchange market for dollars and yen might work. When nations trade they need to exchange their currencies. American exporters who sell to Japan want to be paid in dollars, not yen; but Japanese importers of American goods possess yen, not dollars. This problem is resolved by Japanese offering or supplying yen in exchange for dollars. Conversely, American importers need to pay Japanese exporters with yen, not dollars. To do so they go to the foreign exchange market as demanders of yen. We can think of Japanese importers as suppliers of yen and American importers as demanders of yen. The interaction of the demand for yen and the supply of yen will establish the dollar price of yen. Suppose the equilibrium dollar price of yen—the dollar–yen exchange rate—is $1 = ¥100. That is, a

[6]Some instructors may choose to skip this section.

LAST WORD

THE HIGH PRICE OF MARIJUANA

In late 1990 and early 1991 the Drug Enforcement Agency reported that the price of marijuana reached historic highs.

At the start of this decade the price of a "lid" (an ounce) of marijuana ranged from $200 to $400 in the United States. In comparison an ounce of gold was selling for $370.

Simple supply and demand explains this "reefer madness." On the demand side marijuana is by far the nation's most commonly used illegal drug. It is estimated that about one-third of all American adults—some 66 million people—have used pot at least once during their lives. However, the demand for marijuana is declining. In 1979 over 35 percent of all young adults (aged 18–25) used pot at least once a month. By 1990 this figure had declined to less than 13 percent. Stated differently, over 22 million people smoked marijuana in 1979 compared to slightly over 10 million in 1990. Other things the same, a declining demand should mean lower, not higher, pot prices.

But other things have not been the same. For a variety of reasons substantial reductions in marijuana supply have occurred. First, law enforcement in Mexico—a major exporter of pot to the United States—has improved. Second, many pot producers have shifted their resources to alternative drugs. In particular, Colombia's incredibly profitable cocaine industry has expanded and attracted resources from marijuana. It is also cheaper and easier to smuggle small quantities of cocaine compared to bulky truck- and plane-loads of marijuana. Third, the interdiction of pot smugglers has improved; less marijuana is coming over our borders. Finally, within the United States efforts to apprehend marijuana growers and destroy their crops have been increasingly effective.

How to explain the high price of pot? Quite simply: Supply has fallen much more dramatically than has demand.

---

dollar will buy 100 yen (the "dollar price" of 1 yen is 1 cent) and therefore 100 yen worth of Japanese goods. Conversely, 100 yen will buy $1 worth of American goods.

Changing Rates: Depreciation and Appreciation

What might cause this exchange rate to change? The determinants of the demand for and the supply of yen are similar to those we have already discussed. From the vantage point of the United States, several things might take place to increase the demand for—and therefore the dollar price of—yen. Incomes might rise in the United States, causing Americans to buy not only more domestic goods, but also more Sony televisions, Nikon cameras, and Nissan automobiles from Japan. To do this Americans need more yen, so the demand for yen increases. Or there may be a change in American tastes which enhances our preferences for Japanese goods. For instance, when gasoline prices soared in the 1970s, many American auto buyers shifted their demands from large, gas-guzzling domestic cars to gas-efficient Japanese compact cars. In so doing the demand for yen increased.

The point is that an increase in the American demand for Japanese goods will increase the demand for yen and raise the dollar price of yen. Let's suppose the dollar price of yen rises from $1 = ¥100 (or 1¢ = ¥1) to $2 = ¥100 (or 2¢ = ¥1). When the dollar price of yen *increases,* a **depreciation** of the dollar relative to the yen has occurred. Dollar depreciation means that it takes more dollars (pennies in this case) to buy a single unit of a foreign currency (the yen). A dollar is worth less because it will buy fewer yen and therefore fewer Japanese goods.

If events opposite to those we have presumed had occurred—that is, if incomes rose in Japan and Japanese preferences for American goods strengthened—then the *supply* of yen in foreign exchange markets would increase. This increase in the supply of yen relative to demand would *decrease* the equilibrium dollar price of yen. For example, supply might increase to the extent that the dollar price of yen declines from the original $1 = ¥100, or 1¢ = ¥1, to $.50 = ¥100 or ½¢ = ¥1.

This *decrease* in the dollar price of yen means there has been an **appreciation** of the dollar relative to the yen. Appreciation means it takes fewer dollars (pennies) to buy a single yen than previously. The dollar is worth more because it can purchase more yen and therefore more Japanese goods.

Economic Consequences

The profound consequences of changes in exchange rates are easily perceived. Suppose America is operating at a point inside its production possibilities curve and the dollar depreciates, that is, the dollar price of yen rises from 1¢ = ¥1 to 2¢ = ¥1. This means that the yen and therefore *all* Japanese goods are now more expensive to Americans. Therefore, American consumers shift their expenditures from Japanese to American goods. The Chevy Corsica is now relatively more attractive than the Honda Accord to American consumers. American industries are stimulated by this shift in expenditures and their production and employment both rise. Conversely, Japanese export industries find the sales of their products diminishing, so output and employment both tend to decline. The depreciation of the dollar has caused America to become more prosperous and Japan less so.

You are urged to confirm that an appreciation of the dollar's value relative to the yen will tend to depress the American economy and stimulate the Japanese economy.

With the economic stakes so high, it is easy to understand why governments often interfere with otherwise "free" foreign exchange markets. Thus, the United States government might attempt to depreciate the dollar when our economy is at less than full employment. The problem, however, is that the consequent shift in American expenditures from foreign goods to domestic goods will lower Japanese exports and tend to depress *their* economy. The Japanese government may well be interested in offsetting the depreciation of the dollar which the Americans desire. Both the economic and political implications of exchange rates are great, and they will be considered in later chapters.

CHAPTER SUMMARY

1 A market is any institution or arrangement which brings buyers and sellers of some product or service together.

2 Demand refers to a schedule which summarizes the willingness of buyers to purchase a given product during a specific time period at each of the various prices at which it might be sold. According to the law of demand, consumers will ordinarily buy more of a product at a low price than they will at a high price. Therefore, other things being equal, the relationship between price and quantity demanded is negative or inverse and demand graphs as a downsloping curve.

3 Changes in one or more of the basic determinants of demand—consumer tastes, the number of buyers in the market, the money incomes of consumers, the prices of related goods, and consumer expectations—will cause the market demand curve to shift. A shift to the right is an increase in demand; a shift to the left, a decrease in demand. A "change in demand" is distinguished from a "change in the quantity demanded," the latter involving movement from one point to another point on a fixed demand curve because of a change in the price of the product under consideration.

4 Supply is a schedule showing the amounts of a product which producers would be willing to offer in the market during a given period at each possible price. The law of supply says that, other things equal, producers will offer more of a product at a high price than they will at a low price. As a result, the relationship between price and quantity supplied is a direct one, and the supply curve is upsloping.

5 A change in resource prices, production techniques, taxes or subsidies, the prices of other goods, price expectations, or the number of sellers in the market will cause the supply curve of a product to shift. A shift to the right is an increase in supply; a shift to the left, a decrease in supply. In contrast, a change in the price of the product under consideration will result in a change in the quantity supplied, that is, a movement from one point to another on a given supply curve.

6 Under competition, the interaction of market demand and market supply will adjust price to that point where quantity demanded and quantity supplied are equal. This is the equilibrium price. The corresponding quantity is the equilibrium quantity.

7 The ability of market forces to synchronize selling and buying decisions to eliminate potential surpluses or shortages is termed the "rationing function" of prices.

8 A change in either demand or supply will cause equilibrium price and quantity to change. There is a positive or direct relationship between a change in demand and the resulting changes in equilibrium price and quantity. Though the relationship between a change in supply and resulting change in equilibrium price is inverse, the relationship between a change in supply and equilibrium quantity is direct.

9 The concepts of supply and demand also apply to the resource market.

10 The foreign exchange market is an important application of demand and supply analysis. Foreign importers are suppliers of their currencies and American importers are demanders of foreign currencies. The resulting equilibrium exchange rates link the price levels of all nations.

11 Depreciation of the dollar reduces our imports and stimulates our domestic economy; dollar appreciation increases our imports and depresses our domestic economy.

TERMS AND CONCEPTS

market
demand
demand schedule (curve)
law of demand
diminishing marginal utility
income and substitution effects
normal (superior) good
inferior good
substitute goods
complementary goods
change in demand (supply) versus change in the quantity demanded (supplied)
supply
supply schedule (curve)
law of supply
surplus
shortage
equilibrium price and quantity
rationing function of prices
foreign exchange market
depreciation and appreciation of the dollar

QUESTIONS AND STUDY SUGGESTIONS

1 Explain the law of demand. Why does a demand curve slope downward? What are the determinants of demand? What happens to the demand curve when each of these determinants changes? Distinguish between a change in demand and a change in the quantity demanded, noting the cause(s) of each.

2 Critically evaluate: "In comparing the two equilibrium positions in Figure 4-6a, I note that a larger amount is actually purchased at a higher price. This refutes the law of demand."

3 Explain the law of supply. Why does the supply curve slope upward? What are the determinants of supply? What happens to the supply curve when each of these determinants changes? Distinguish between a change in supply and a change in the quantity supplied, noting the cause(s) of each.

4 Explain the following news dispatch from Hull, England: "The fish market here slumped today to what local commentators called 'a disastrous level'—all because of a shortage of potatoes. The potatoes are one of the main ingredients in a dish that figures on almost every café-menu—fish and chips."

5 Suppose the total demand for wheat and the total supply of wheat per month in the Kansas City grain market are as follows:

Thousands of bushels demanded	*Price per bushel*	*Thousands of bushels supplied*	*Surplus (+) or shortage (−)*
85	$3.40	72	______
80	3.70	73	______
75	4.00	75	______
70	4.30	77	______
65	4.60	79	______
60	4.90	81	______

a What will be the market or equilibrium price? What is the equilibrium quantity? Using the surplus-shortage column, explain why your answers are correct.

b Using the above data, graph the demand for wheat and the supply of wheat. Be sure to label the axes of your graph correctly. Label equilibrium price *"P"* and equilibrium quantity *"Q."*

c Why will $3.40 not be the equilibrium price in this market? Why not $4.90? "Surpluses drive prices up; shortages drive them down." Do you agree?

d Now suppose that the government establishes a ceiling price of, say, $3.70 for wheat. Explain carefully the effects of this ceiling price. Demonstrate your answer graphically. What might prompt government to establish a ceiling price?

e Assume now that the government establishes a price floor of, say, $4.60 for wheat. Explain carefully the effects of this supported price. Demonstrate your answer graphically. What might prompt the government to establish this price support?

f "Legally fixed prices strip the price mechanism of its rationing function." Explain this statement in terms of your answers to 5d and 5e.

6 Given supply, what effect will each of the following have on the demand for, and the equilibrium price and quantity of, product B?

a Product B becomes more fashionable.

b The price of product C, a good substitute for B, goes down.

c Consumers anticipate declining prices and falling incomes.

d There is a rapid upsurge in population growth.

7 Given demand, what effect will each of the following have on the supply and equilibrium price and quantity of product B?

a A technological advance in the methods of producing B.

b A decline in the number of firms in industry B.

c An increase in the prices of resources required in the production of B.

d The expectation that the equilibrium price of B will be lower in the future than it is currently.

e A decline in the price of product A, a good whose production requires substantially the same techniques and resources as does the production of B.

f The levying of a specific sales tax on B.

g The granting of a 50-cent per unit subsidy for each unit of B produced.

8 Explain and illustrate graphically the effect of:

a An increase in income on the demand curve of an inferior good.

b A drop in the price of product S on the demand for substitute product T.

c A decline in income on the demand curve of a normal good.

d An increase in the price of product J on the demand for complementary good K.

9 "In the corn market, demand often exceeds supply and supply sometimes exceeds demand." "The price of corn rises and falls in response to changes in supply and demand." In which of these two statements are the terms "supply" and "demand" used correctly? Explain.

10 How will each of the following changes in demand and/or supply affect equilibrium price and equilibrium quantity in a competitive market; that is, do price and quantity *rise, fall, remain unchanged,* or are the answers *indeterminate,* depending on the magnitudes of the shifts in supply and demand? You should rely on a supply and demand diagram to verify answers.

a Supply decreases and demand remains constant.

b Demand decreases and supply remains constant.

c Supply increases and demand is constant.

d Demand increases and supply increases.

e Demand increases and supply is constant.

f Supply increases and demand decreases.

g Demand increases and supply decreases.

h Demand decreases and supply decreases.

11 "Prices are the automatic regulator that tends to keep production and consumption in line with each other." Explain.

12 Explain: "Even though parking meters may yield little or no net revenue, they should nevertheless be retained because of the rationing function they perform."

13 Use two market diagrams to explain how an increase in state subsidies to public colleges might affect tuition and enrollments in both public and private colleges.

14 What effects would United States import quotas on Japanese automobiles have on the American price of Japanese cars *and* on the demand for, and price of, American-made cars?

15 Many states have had usury laws stipulating the maximum interest rate which lenders (commercial banks, savings and loan associations, etc.) can charge borrowers. Indicate in some detail what would happen in the loan market during periods when the equilibrium interest rate exceeds the stipulated maximum. On the basis of your analysis, do you favor usury laws?

16 Explain why labor unions—whose members are paid wage rates far above the legal minimum—strongly and actively support increases in the minimum wage.

17 "Our imports create a demand for foreign monies; foreign imports of our goods generate supplies of foreign monies." Do you agree? Other things being equal, would a decline in American incomes or a weakening of American preferences for foreign products cause the dollar to depreciate or appreciate? What would be the effects of that depreciation or appreciation on production and employment domestically and abroad?

18 **Advanced analysis:** Assume that demand for a commodity is represented by the equation $P = 10 - .2Q_d$ and supply by the equation $P = 2 + .2Q_s$, where Q_d and Q_s are quantity demanded and quantity supplied, respectively, and P is price. Using the equilibrium condition $Q_s = Q_d$, solve the equations to determine equilibrium price. Now determine equilibrium quantity. Graph the two equations to substantiate your answers.

The Private Sectors and the Market System

Chapters 5 and 6 will put meat on the bare-bones model of capitalism developed thus far. In this chapter we consider the private sectors—households, businesses, and the foreign sector. Chapter 6 is devoted to the public or governmental sector.

Our main goals in this chapter are twofold:

1 Households and businesses are the primary *decision makers* in our economy and we need to know more about them. We flesh out our discussion of a market economy by exploring the characteristics of the household, business, and foreign components of the private economy.

2 A system of markets and prices is the basic *coordinating mechanism* of a capitalistic system. We will examine how the market system synchronizes the innumerable decisions of the consumers, businesses, and resource suppliers which comprise the private sector.

HOUSEHOLDS AS INCOME RECEIVERS

The household sector of American capitalism is currently composed of some 94 million households. These households are the ultimate suppliers of all economic resources and simultaneously the major spending group in the economy. We will consider households first as income receivers and second as spenders.

There are two related approaches to studying the facts of income distribution.

1 The **functional distribution** of income indicates how society's money income is divided among wages, rents, interest, and profits. Here total income is distributed according to the function performed by the income receiver. Wages are paid to labor, rents and interest compensate property resources, and profits flow to the owners of corporations and unincorporated businesses.

2 The **personal distribution** of income shows the way total money income of society is apportioned among individual households.

The Functional Distribution of Income

The functional distribution of the nation's total earned income for 1991 is shown in Figure 5-1. Clearly the largest source of income for households is the wages and salaries paid to workers by the businesses and governmental units hiring them. In our capitalist system the bulk of total income goes to labor and not to

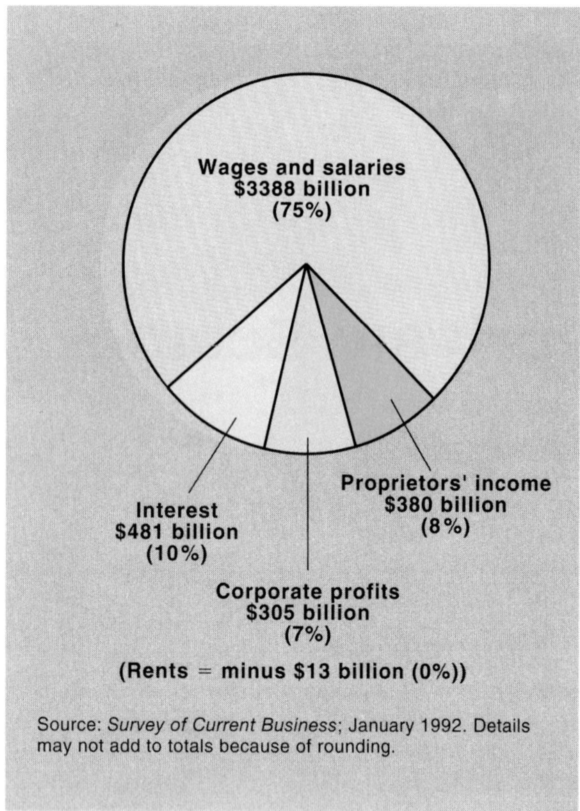

	Billions of dollars	*Percent of total*
Wages and salaries	**$3388**	**75**
Proprietors' income	**380**	**8**
Corporate profits	**305**	**7**
Interest	**481**	**10**
Rents	**−13**	**0**
Total earnings	**$4541**	**100**

FIGURE 5-1 **The functional distribution of income, 1991**

Almost three-fourths of national income is received as wages and salaries. Capitalist income—corporate profits, interest, and rents—only account for less than one-fifth of total income. (The "rents" figure is negative because depreciation exceeded rental income.)

"capital." Proprietors' income—that is, the incomes of doctors, lawyers, small business owners, farmers, and other unincorporated enterprises—is in fact a combination of wage, profit, rent, and interest incomes. The other three sources of earnings are virtually self-defining. Some households own corporate stock and receive dividend income on their holdings. Many households also own bonds and savings accounts which yield interest income. Rental income results from households providing buildings, land, and other natural resources to businesses.

Personal Distribution of Income

Figure 5-2 is an overall view of how total income is distributed among households. Here we divide families into five numerically equal groups or *quintiles* and show the percentage of total income received by each group. In 1990 the poorest 20 percent of all families received less than 5 percent of total personal income in contrast to the 20 percent they would have received if income were equally distributed. In comparison the richest 20 percent of all families received over 44 percent of personal income. Thus the richest fifth of the population received almost ten times as much income as the poorest fifth. Given these data, most economists agree there is considerable inequality in the distribution of income.

HOUSEHOLDS AS SPENDERS

How do households dispose of the income they earn? Part flows to government in the form of personal taxes, and the rest is divided between personal consumption expenditures and personal saving. Specifically, households disposed of their total personal income in 1991 as shown in Figure 5-3.[1]

Personal Taxes

Personal taxes, of which the Federal personal income tax is the major component, have risen sharply in both

[1]The income concepts used in Figures 5-1 and 5-3 are different, accounting for the quantitative discrepancy between "total income" in the two figures.

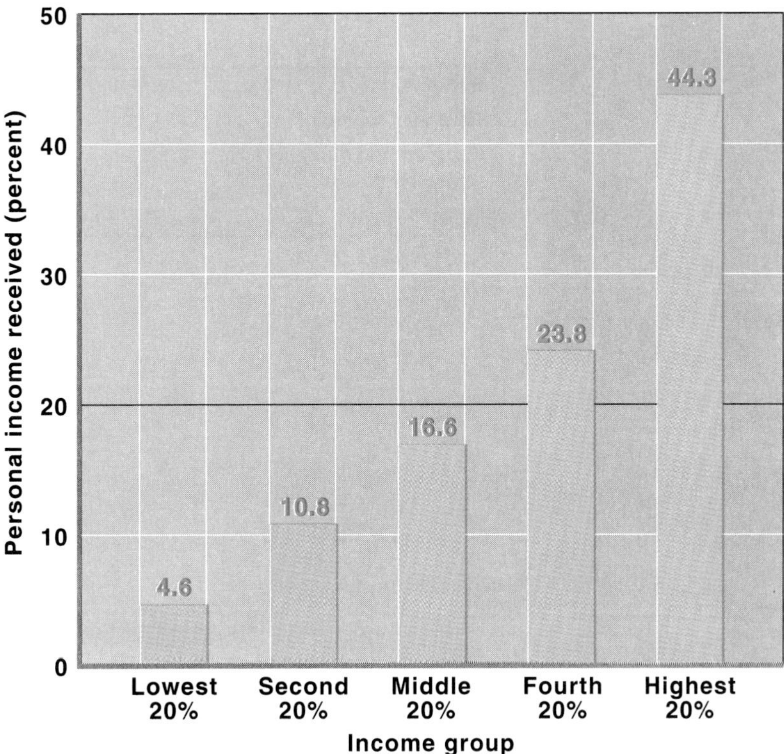

FIGURE 5-2 The distribution of income among families, 1990

Personal income is quite unequally distributed in the United States. An equal distribution would mean that all vertical bars would be equal to the horizontal line drawn at 20 percent; each 20 percent of the families would get 20 percent of total personal Income. In fact, the richest fifth of the families gets almost ten times as much income as does the poorest fifth.

absolute and relative terms since World War II. In 1941, households paid $3.3 billion, or about 3 percent of their $95.3 billion total income, in personal taxes, compared to $616 billion, or about 13 percent of that year's $4724 billion total income in 1991.

Personal Saving

Economists define saving as "that part of after-tax income which is *not* consumed"; hence, households have just two choices with their incomes after taxes—to consume or to save.

Saving is defined as that portion of current (this year's) income not paid out in taxes or in the purchase of consumer goods, but which flows into bank accounts, insurance policies, bonds and stocks, and other financial assets.

Reasons for saving are many and diverse, but they center around *security* and *speculation.* Households save to provide a nest egg for unforeseen contingencies—sickness, accident, unemployment—for retirement from the work force, to finance the education of children, or simply for the overall financial security of one's family. On the other hand, saving might well occur for speculation. One might channel part of one's income to the purchase of securities, speculating as to increases in their monetary values.

The desire or willingness to save, however, is not enough. This willingness must be accompanied by the *ability* to save, which depends basically on the size of one's income. If income is very low, households may *dissave;* that is, they may consume in excess of their after-tax incomes. They do this by borrowing and by digging into savings they may have accumulated in years when their incomes were higher. However, both saving and consumption vary directly with income; as households get more income, they divide it between saving and consumption. In fact, the top 10 percent of income receivers account for most of the personal saving in our society.

Personal Consumption Expenditures

Figure 5-3 shows that the bulk of total income flows from income receivers back into the business sector of the economy as personal consumption expenditures.

The size and composition of the economy's total output depend to a great extent on the size and composition of the flow of consumer spending. It is thus imperative that we examine how households divide their

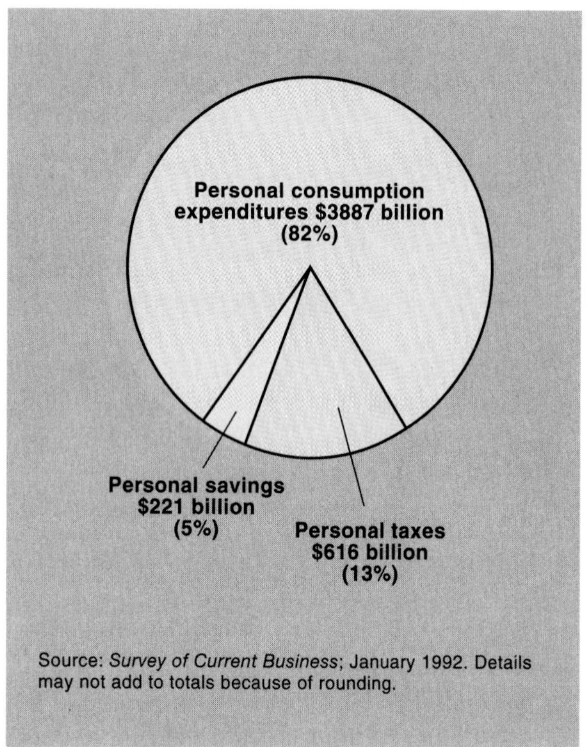

Source: *Survey of Current Business*; January 1992. Details may not add to totals because of rounding.

	Billions of dollars	*Percent of total*
Personal taxes	$ 616	13
Personal saving	221	5
Personal consumption expenditures	3887	82
Total income	$4724	100

FIGURE 5-3 The disposition of household income, 1991

Household income is apportioned between taxes, saving, and consumption, with consumption being the dominant use of income.

expenditures among the various goods and services competing for their dollars. The U.S. Department of Commerce classifies consumer spending as (1) expenditures on durables, (2) expenditures on nondurables, and (3) expenditures on services. If a product generally has an expected life of one year or more, it is called a **durable good;** if its life is less than one year, it is labeled **nondurable.** Automobiles, video recorders, washing machines, personal computers, and most furniture are good examples of consumer durables. Most food and clothing items are representative of nondurables. **Services** refer to the services which lawyers, barbers, doctors, mechanics, and others provide to consumers. Note in Table 5-1 that *ours is a service-oriented economy in that over one-half of consumer outlays are for services.*

This threefold breakdown, detailed in Table 5-1, implies that many consumer outlays are discretionary or postponable. During prosperity, durable, or "hard," goods are typically traded in or scrapped before they become utterly useless. This is ordinarily the case with automobiles and most major household appliances. But if a recession materializes, consumers tend to forgo expenditures on durables, having little choice but to put up with an old model car and outdated household appliances. The desire to conserve dollars for the nondurable necessities of food and clothing may cause a radical shrinkage of expenditures on durables. Much the same is true of many services. True, one cannot postpone an operation for acute appendicitis. But education, dental work, and a wide variety of less pressing services can be deferred or, if necessary, forgone entirely. In brief, the durable goods and services segments of personal consumption expenditures are subject to much more variation over time than are expenditures on nondurables.

QUICK REVIEW 5-1

- ***The functional distribution of income indicates how income is divided among wages, rents, interest, and profits; the personal distribution of income shows how income is apportioned among households.***
- ***Wages and salaries are the major component of the functional distribution of income. The personal distribution reveals considerable inequality.***
- ***Over 80 percent of household income is consumed, the remainder being saved or paid in taxes.***
- ***Over half of consumer spending is for services.***

TABLE 5-1 The composition of personal consumption expenditures, 1991*

Types of consumption	*Amount (billions of dollars)*		*Percent of total*	
Durable goods		$ 445		11
Motor vehicles and parts	$184		5	
Furniture and household equipment	172		4	
All others	90		2	
Nondurable goods		1251		32
Food	619		16	
Clothing and shoes	211		5	
Gasoline and oil	103		3	
Fuel oil and coal	12		1	
All others	307		8	
Services		2191		56
Housing	575		15	
Household operations	225		6	
Medical care	577		15	
Transportation	156		4	
Personal services, recreation, and others	658		17	
Personal consumption expenditures		$3887		100

*Excludes interest paid to businesses.

Sources: Survey of Current Business, January 1992. Details may not add to totals because of rounding.

THE BUSINESS POPULATION

Businesses constitute the second major aggregate of the private sector. To avoid confusion, we preface our discussion with some comments on terminology. In particular, we must distinguish among a plant, a firm, and an industry.

1 A **plant** is a physical establishment in the form of a factory, farm, mine, retail or wholesale store, or warehouse which performs one or more specific functions in the fabrication and distribution of goods and services.

2 A business **firm,** on the other hand, is the business organization which owns and operates these plants. Although most firms operate only one plant, many own and operate a number of plants. Multiplant firms may be "horizontal," "vertical," or "conglomerate" combinations. For example, without exception all the large steel firms of our economy—USX Corporation (United States Steel), Bethlehem Steel, Republic Steel, and the others—are **vertical combinations** of plants; that is, each company owns plants at various stages of the production process. Each steelmaker owns ore and coal mines, limestone quarries, coke ovens, blast furnaces, rolling mills, forge shops, foundries, and, in some cases, fabricating shops.

The large chain stores in the retail field— A&P, Kroger, Safeway, J.C. Penney—are **horizontal combinations** in that each plant is at the same stage of production. Other firms are **conglomerates;** they comprise plants which operate across many different markets and industries. For example, International Telephone and Telegraph, apart from operations implied by its name, is involved through affiliated plants on a large-scale basis in such diverse fields as hotels, baking products, educational materials, and insurance.

3 An **industry** is a group of firms producing the same, or at least similar, products. Though an apparently uncomplicated concept, industries are usually difficult to identify in practice. For example, how do we identify the automobile industry? The simplest answer is, "All firms producing automobiles." But automobiles are heterogeneous products. While Cadillacs and Buicks are similar products, and Buicks and Fords are similar, and Fords and Geos are similar, it is clear that Geos and Cadillacs are very dissimilar. At least most buyers think so. And what about trucks? Certainly, small pickup trucks are similar in some respects to station wagons. Is it better to speak of the "motor vehicle industry" rather than of the "automobile industry"?

This matter of delineating an industry becomes even more complex because most enterprises are multiproduct firms. American automobile manufacturers are also responsible for such diverse products as diesel locomotives, buses, refrigerators, guided missiles, and air conditioners. As you can see, industry classifications are usually somewhat arbitrary.

LEGAL FORMS OF BUSINESS ENTERPRISES

The business population is extremely diverse, ranging from giant corporations like General Motors with 1990 sales of $126 billion and 761,000 employees to neighborhood speciality shops and "mom and pop" groceries with one or two employees and sales of only $100 or $150 per day. This diversity makes it necessary to classify business firms by some criterion such as legal structure, industry or product, or size. Figure 5-4 shows how the business population is distributed among the three major legal forms: (1) the sole proprietorship, (2) the partnership, and (3) the corporation.

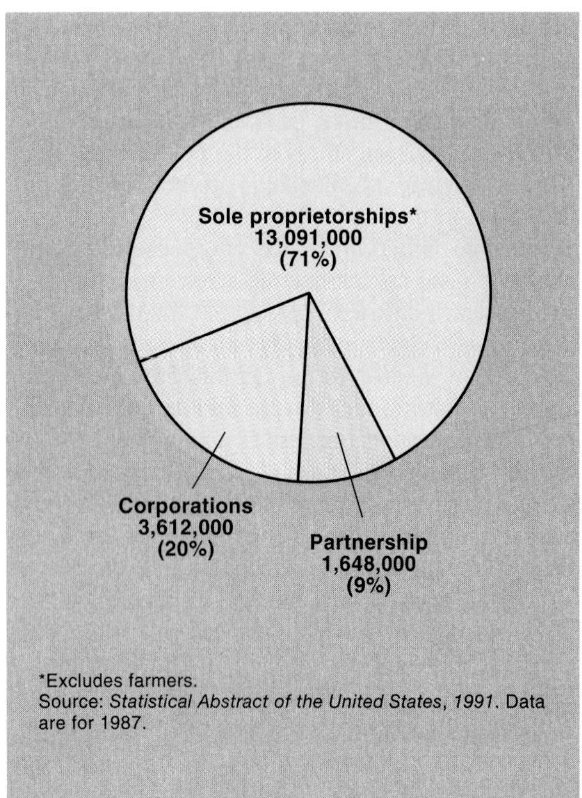

The business population by form of legal organization and volume of sales

Form	*Number of firms*	*Percent of total*	*Volume of sales (billions)*	*Percent of total*
Sole proprietorships*	13,091,000	71	$ 611	6
Partnerships	1,648,000	9	411	4
Corporations	3,612,000	20	9,185	90
Total	18,351,000	100	$10,207	100

*Excludes farmers.

FIGURE 5-4 **The business population by form of legal organization**

Although sole proprietorships dominate the business population numerically, corporations account for 90 percent of total sales.

Sole Proprietorship

A **sole proprietorship** is literally an individual in business for himself or herself. The proprietor owns or obtains the materials and capital equipment needed by the business and personally supervises its operation.

Advantages This simple type of business organization has certain distinct advantages:

1 A sole proprietorship is very easy to organize—there is virtually no legal red tape or expense.

2 The proprietor is his or her own boss and has substantial freedom of action. Since the proprietor's profit income depends on the enterprise's success, there is a strong and immediate incentive to manage the affairs of the business efficiently.

Disadvantages But the disadvantages of this form of business organization are great. They include financial restrictions on firm growth, the inability to specialize in management, and the fact that all of a proprietor's assets are potentially available to creditors.

1 With rare exceptions, the financial resources of a sole proprietorship are insufficient to permit the firm to grow into a large-scale enterprise. Finances are usually limited to what the proprietor has in his or her bank account and to what he or she can borrow. Since proprietorships often fail, commercial banks are not eager to extend much credit to them.

2 Being in complete control of an enterprise forces the proprietor to carry out all basic management functions. A proprietor must make all basic decisions concerning buying, selling, and the hiring and training of personnel, not to mention the technical aspects involved in producing, advertising, and distributing the product. In short, the potential benefits of specialization in business management are usually inaccessible to the typical small-scale proprietorship.

3 Most important of all, the proprietor is subject to *unlimited liability.* Individuals in business for themselves risk not only the assets of the firm but also their personal assets. If assets of an unsuccessful proprietorship are insufficient to satisfy the claims of creditors, those creditors can file claims against the proprietor's personal property.

Partnership

The **partnership** form of business organization is more or less a natural outgrowth of the sole proprietorship. Partnerships were developed to overcome some of the major shortcomings of proprietorships. In a partnership, two or more individuals agree to own and operate a business. Usually they pool their financial resources and business skills. Similarly, they share the risks and the profits or losses.

Advantages What are the advantages of a partnership arrangement?

1 Like the sole proprietorship, it is easy to organize. Although a written agreement is almost invariably involved, legal red tape is not great.

2 Greater specialization in management is possible because there are more participants.

3 Again, because there are several participants, the odds are that the financial resources of a partnership will be greater than those of a sole proprietorship. Partners can pool their money capital and are usually somewhat better risks in the eyes of lending institutions.

Disadvantages The partnership often does less to overcome the shortcomings of the proprietorship than first appears, and raises some new potential problems which the sole proprietorship does not have.

1 Whenever several people participate in management, this division of authority can lead to inconsistent, divided policies or to inaction when action is required. Worse yet, partners may flatly disagree on basic policy. For all these reasons, management in a partnership may be unwieldy and cumbersome.

2 The finances of partnerships are still limited, although generally superior to those of a sole proprietorship. But the financial resources of three or four partners may still not be enough for the growth of a successful enterprise.

3 The continuity of a partnership is very precarious. The withdrawal or death of a partner generally means dissolution and complete reorganization of the firm, disrupting its operations.

4 Finally, unlimited liability plagues a partnership, just as it does a proprietorship. In fact, each partner is liable for all business debts incurred, not only as a result of each partner's own management decisions, but also as a consequence of the actions of any other partner. A wealthy partner risks money on the prudence of less affluent partners.

Corporation

Corporations are legal entities, distinct and separate from the individuals who own them. As such, these governmentally designated "legal persons" can acquire resources, own assets, produce and sell products, incur debts, extend credit, sue and be sued, and carry on all those functions which any other type of enterprise performs.

Advantages The advantages of the corporate form of business enterprise have catapulted it into a dominant position in modern American capitalism. Although corporations are relatively small in number (Table 5-2), they are frequently large in size and scale of operations. Although only 20 percent of all businesses are corporations, they account for roughly 90 percent of all business sales.

1 The corporation is by far the most effective form of business organization for raising money capital. As this chapter's Last Word reveals, the corporation features unique methods of finance—the selling of stocks and bonds—which allow the firm to tap the savings of untold thousands of households. Through the securities market, corporations can pool the financial resources of extremely large numbers of people.

Financing by the sale of securities also has advantages from the viewpoint of the purchasers of these securities. First, households can now participate in enterprise and share the expected monetary reward therefrom without assuming an active part in management. In addition, an individual can spread any risks by buying the securities of several corporations. Finally, it is usually easy for the holder of corporate securities to dispose of these holdings. Organized stock exchanges facilitate transfer of securities among buyers and sellers, which increases the willingness of savers to buy corporate securities.

Corporations have easier access to bank credit than other types of business organizations. Corporations are better risks and are more likely to provide banks with profitable accounts.

2 Corporations have the distinct advantage of **limited liability.** The owners (stockholders) of a corporation risk *only* what they paid for the stock purchased. Their personal assets are not at stake if the corporation founders on the rocks of bankruptcy. Creditors can sue the corporation as a legal person, but not the owners of the corporation as individuals. Limited liability clearly eases the corporation's task in acquiring money capital.

3 Because of their advantage in attracting money capital, successful corporations find it easier to expand the size and scope of their operations and to realize associated advantages. In particular, corporations can take advantage of mass-production technologies. Similarly, size permits greater specialization in the use of human resources. While the manager of a sole proprietorship may be forced to share her time between production, accounting, and marketing functions, a corporation can hire specialized personnel in these areas and achieve greater efficiency.

4 As a legal entity, the corporation has a life independent of its owners and, for that matter, of its individual officers. Proprietorships are subject to sudden and unpredictable demise, but, legally at least, corporations are immortal. The transfer of corporate ownership through the sale of stock will not disrupt the continuity of the corporation. Corporations have a certain permanence, lacking in other forms of business organization, which is conducive to long-range planning and growth.

Disadvantages The corporation's advantages are of tremendous significance and typically override any accompanying disadvantages. Yet the following drawbacks of the corporate form of organization merit mentioning:

1 There are some red tape and legal expense in obtaining a corporate charter.

2 From the social point of view, the corporate form of enterprise lends itself to certain abuses. Because the corporation is a legal entity, unscrupulous business owners sometimes can avoid personal responsibility for questionable business activities by adopting the corporate form of enterprise. And, despite legislation to the contrary, the corporate form of organization has been a cornerstone for the issue and sale of worthless securities. Note, however, that these are potential abuses of the corporate form, not inherent defects.

3 A further disadvantage of corporations is the **double taxation** of corporate income. That part of corporate income paid out as dividends to stockholders is taxed twice—once as part of corporate profits and again as part of stockholders' personal incomes.

4 In the sole proprietorship and partnership forms, those owning the real and financial assets of the firm also directly manage or control those assets. But, in larger corporations where ownership of common stock is widely diffused over tens or hundreds of thousands of stockholders, a fundamental **separation of ownership and control** will arise. The roots of this cleavage lie in the lethargy of the typical stockholder. Most stockholders do not exercise their voting rights, or, if they do, merely sign these rights over by proxy to the corporation's present officers. And why not? Average stockholders know little or nothing about the efficiency with which "their" corporation is being managed. Because the typical stockholder may own only 1000 of 15,000,000 shares of common stock outstanding, one vote "really doesn't make a bit of difference." Not voting, or the automatic signing over of one's proxy to current corporate officials, makes those officials self-perpetuating.

The separation of ownership and control is of no fundamental consequence so long as the actions of the control (management) group and the wishes of the ownership (stockholder) group are in accord. In fact, the interests of the two groups are not always identical. Management, seeking the power and prestige which accompany control over a *large* enterprise, may favor unprofitable expansion of the firm's operations. Or a conflict of interest can develop on current dividend policies. What portion of corporate earnings after taxes should be paid out as dividends, and what amount should be retained by the firm as undistributed profits? And corporation officials may vote themselves large salaries, pensions, bonuses, and so forth, out of corporate earnings which might otherwise be used for increased dividend payments. In short, the separation of ownership and control raises important and intriguing questions about the distribution of power and authority, the accountability of corporate managers, and the possibility of intramural conflicts between managers and shareholders.

Incorporate or Not?

The need for money capital is a critical determinant of whether or not a firm incorporates. The money capital required to establish and operate a barbershop, a shoeshine stand, or a small gift shop is modest, making incorporation unnecessary. In contrast, modern technology and a much larger dollar volume of business make incorporation imperative in many lines of production. In most branches of manufacturing—automobiles, steel, fabricated metal products, electrical equipment, and household appliances—substantial money requirements for investment in fixed assets and for working capital are involved. Given these circumstances, there is no choice but to incorporate.

INDUSTRIAL DISTRIBUTION AND BIGNESS

What do the 18.4 million firms which compose the business sector of our economy produce?

Types of Industries

Table 5-2 measures the significance of the various industry classifications in several different ways. Column 2 indicates the numerical and percentage distribution of the business population among various industries. Column 3 shows in both absolute and relative terms the portion of the domestic output originating in various industries. Column 4 indicates the absolute and relative amounts of employment provided by each industry. Several points in Table 5-2 are noteworthy:

1 Many firms are engaged in agriculture, but agriculture is relatively insignificant as a provider of incomes and jobs. This implies that agriculture comprises a large number of small, competitive producers.

2 The wholesale and retail industries and the service industries (hotels, motels, and personal services) are heavily populated with firms and are simultaneously important sources of employment and incomes in the economy.

3 Table 5-2 reminds us that not all the economy's income and employment originate in private domestic enterprises. Government and foreign enterprises account for about 13 percent of the economy's domestic output and employ about 16 percent of the labor force.

4 The relatively small number of firms in manufacturing account for almost one-fifth of domestic output and total employment. These figures correctly suggest that our economy is highly industrialized, characterized by gigantic business corporations in its manufacturing industries. This point merits brief elaboration.

Big Business

To what degree does big business prevail in our economy? Casual evidence suggests that many of our major industries are dominated by corporate giants which enjoy assets and annual sales revenues of billions of dollars, employ hundreds of thousands of workers, have a hundred thousand or more stockholders, and earn annual profits after taxes running into hundreds of millions of dollars. We have already cited the vital statistics of General Motors, America's largest corporation, for 1990: sales, about $126 *billion;* assets, about $180 *billion;* employees, about 761,000. Remarkably, there are only 20 or so nations in the world whose

TABLE 5-2 Industry classes: number of firms, domestic output originating, and employment provided*

(1) Industry	*(2) Number of private businesses*		*(3) Contribution to domestic output*		*(4) Workers employed*	
	Thousands	*Percent*	*Billions*	*Percent*	*Thousands*	*Percent*
Agriculture, forestry, and fisheries	2,088	11	$ 114	2	2,863	3
Mining	258	1	80	2	735	1
Construction	2,067	11	248	5	5,204	5
Manufacturing	686	4	966	18	19,063	17
Wholesale and retail trade	3,521	18	826	16	26,150	23
Finance, insurance, and real estate	2,571	13	897	17	6,832	6
Transportation, communications, and public utilities	824	4	461	9	5,839	5
Services	7,384	38	971	19	28,208	25
Government			619	12	18,291	16
Rest of world			38	1		
Total	19,399	100	$5,220	100	113,185	100

*Column 2 is for 1987; 3 for 1989; and 4 for 1990. Includes farms.

Source: Statistical Abstract of the United States, 1991, p. 526; and *Survey of Current Business.* Details may not add to totals because of rounding.

annual domestic outputs are more than GM's annual sales!

In 1990 some 123 industrial corporations enjoyed annual sales of over $4 billion; 213 industrial firms realized sales over $2 billion. Generally, the fact that corporations, constituting only 20 percent of the business population, produce about nine-tenths of total business output, hints at the dominant role of large corporations in our economy.

But the influential position of giant corporations varies significantly from industry to industry. Big business dominates manufacturing and is pronounced in the transportation, communications, power utilities, and banking and financial industries. At the other extreme are some 2 million farmers whose total sales in 1990 were less than the economy's two largest industrial corporations! In between are a wide variety of retail and service industries characterized by relatively small firms. Despite great diversity by industry, it is reasonably accurate to say that large corporations dominate the American business landscape and grounds exist for labeling the United States a "big business" economy.

THE FOREIGN SECTOR

Our economy is deeply enmeshed in a complex web of economic relationships with the rest of the world. Evidence of the growing importance of international trade and finance is all around us. You may be wearing a T-shirt made in Thailand and a wristwatch from Japan; your stereo or television may be from Korea; your bicycle may have been manufactured in England or West Germany. Newspapers feature stories about our seemingly chronic trade deficits, the changing international value of the dollar, trade negotiations with Japan, and the indebtedness of the less developed countries to American banks. It is clear that the "rest of the world" sector has manifold effects on our domestic economy.

In this section we explore the quantitative importance of the international sector *and* will see how international trade and finance affects the American economy.

Volume, Pattern, and Linkages

The volume of United States merchandise trade with the rest of the world has increased both absolutely and relatively. In 1960 American merchandise exports and imports were each in the $25 to $30 billion range and constituted about 5 percent of our domestic output. By 1990 these figures had grown to $390 and $498 billion and 7 to 9 percent of domestic output.

Table 5-3 identifies our major trading partners. The most apparent generalization is that most of our trade is with other industrially advanced nations. Note that Canada, not Japan, is our major trade partner.

Table 5-3 also implies a complex set of financial linkages which exist between nations. Note that the

TABLE 5-3 U.S. merchandise exports and imports by area, 1990

Exports to	*Value (in billions) of dollars)*		*Percentage of total*		*Imports from*	*Value (in billions of dollars)*		*Percentage of total*	
Industrial countries	$251		64		Industrial countries	$296		59	
Canada		84		22	Canada		93		19
Japan		48		12	Japan		90		18
Western Europe		111		28	Western Europe		109		22
Australia		8		2	Australia		4		1
Developing countries	135		35		Developing countries	199		40	
OPEC		13		3	OPEC		38		8
Other		122		31	Other		161		32
Eastern Europe	4		1		Eastern Europe	2		1	
Total	$390		100		Total	$498		100	

Source: Survey of Current Business, December 1991.

Note: Data are on international transactions basis and exclude military shipments. Data will not add to totals because of rounding.

United States incurred a $108 billion *trade deficit* in 1990; that is, we imported $108 billion more merchandise than we exported in that year. Indeed, we have had large trade deficits for the last decade or so.

How are such deficits financed? How does a nation—or an individual—obtain more goods from others than is provided to them? The answer is by borrowing from them or by giving up ownership of some of your assets or wealth. This is precisely what has been happening to the United States. We have financed our trade deficits by borrowing from (selling securities to) other nations. The United States is now the world's largest debtor nation. Similarly, nations with which we have large trade deficits such as Japan (Table 5-3) are acquiring assets in America. For example, Doubleday Publishing and RCA are owned by German firms; Standard Oil is in British hands; and CBS Records and Firestone Tire are Japanese.

Economic Implications

The impacts of global trade and finance on the United States economy are numerous and important.

1 Specialization and Living Standards We emphasized in Chapter 3 that individuals and regions within a given nation specialize according to comparative advantage because productive efficiency is enhanced and living standards increased. Our illustration indicated that Nebraska grows wheat to which its resources are suited, and Florida grows oranges. By trading part of their outputs, people in both states can enjoy larger aggregate amounts of wheat and oranges than otherwise. The same reasoning applies across international boundaries. International specialization allows each nation to concentrate its resources on goods it can produce most efficiently, and to obtain through trade with other nations products it cannot produce efficiently. Such international specialization contributes to a higher "world income."

2 Competition A large and growing volume of trade usually means more competition. Not many years ago our domestic automobile industry was dominated by three large domestic producers. Imported autos were an oddity which accounted for only a miniscule portion of the market. But now about one-third of all autos sold in the United States are imports. General Motors, Ford, and Chrysler now face a much more competitive environment as they struggle for market shares with Nissan, Honda, Toyota, Hyundai, Volkswagen, Mercedes, and so on.

Is greater competition a good thing? Although domestic auto producers may not be thrilled by it, competition is good for consumers. Foreign competition provides consumers with a greater variety of goods and forces domestic producers to be more efficient.

3 Finance and Banking Dramatic improvements in communications have globalized financial markets and banking industries. Developments in the New York Stock Exchange affect stock markets in London and Tokyo and vice versa. The United States has become the world's largest debtor nation as a result of large and persistent trade deficits. Furthermore, major American banks have made billions of dollars worth of loans to less developed nations; potential default on these loans is a threat to individual American banks and a source of apprehension for our entire banking system.

4 Instability and Policy Two related points are relevant with respect to macroeconomic instability and policy. First, a nation engaged in world trade faces potential sources of instability which would not affect a nation "closed" to the world economy. Second, these new sources of instability complicate domestic stabilization policy and *may* make it less effective. For example, recessions and inflations can be highly contagious among nations. Suppose the nations of western Europe experienced a rather severe recession. As their incomes declined, they would curtail purchases of American goods. As a result, inventories of unsold American goods would rise and American firms would respond by reducing their production and employment. In short, recession in Europe might contribute to a recession in the United States.

Another example: Recall from Chapter 4 that changes in exchange rates can affect a nation's exports and imports and therefore domestic output. If the dollar were to *appreciate* vis-a-vis other currencies—that is, if it now took fewer dollars to buy units of foreign monies—domestic output and employment would tend to be depressed. If foreign currencies become relatively cheaper to Americans so do all foreign goods and Americans will respond by shifting their expenditures from domestic to foreign goods. In both instances policy makers would have to take these developments into account in formulating and applying domestic stabilization policies.

QUICK REVIEW 5-2

- ***Business firms are either sole proprietorships, partnerships, or corporations.***
- ***Although relatively small in number, corporations dominate our economy because of their limited liability and superior ability to raise money capital.***
- ***Our international trade, which is primarily with other industrially advanced nations, has increased absolutely and relative to our domestic output.***
- ***The main advantages of international trade are a it permits greater worldwide specialization, and b it enhances competition.***

THE COMPETITIVE MARKET SYSTEM

Now that we have some understanding of the economy's private decision makers, let's consider an intriguing problem. We stressed in Chapter 3 that a capitalistic system is characterized by freedom of enterprise and choice. Consumers are free to buy what they choose; businesses, to produce and sell what they choose; and resource suppliers, to make their property and human resources available in whatever occupations they choose. We may well wonder why such an economy does not collapse in chaos. If consumers want breakfast cereal, businesses choose to produce aerobic shoes, and resource suppliers want to offer their services in manufacturing computer software, production would seem to be deadlocked because of the apparent inconsistency of these free choices.

In reality, the millions of decisions made by households and businesses are highly consistent with one another. Firms do produce those particular goods and services consumers want. Households provide the kinds of labor businesses want to hire. Here we will see how a competitive market system constitutes a coordinating mechanism which overcomes the potential chaos suggested by freedom of enterprise and choice. The competitive market system is a mechanism both for communicating decisions of consumers, producers, and resource suppliers to one another and for synchronizing those decisions toward consistent production objectives.

THE FIVE FUNDAMENTAL QUESTIONS

To understand the operation of a market economy we must first recognize that there are **Five Fundamental Questions** to which *every* economy must respond:

1 *How much* is to be produced? At what level—to what degree—should available resources be employed or used in the production process?
2 *What* is to be produced? What collection of goods and services will best satisfy society's material wants?
3 *How* is that output to be produced? How should production be organized? What firms should do the producing and what productive techniques should they use?
4 *Who* is to receive the output? In particular, how should the output of the economy be shared by consumers?
5 Can the system *adapt* to change? Can the system negotiate appropriate adjustments when changes occur in consumer wants, resource supplies, and technology?

Two points are relevant. First, we will defer the "how much" question for now. Macroeconomics deals in detail with the complex question of the level of resource employment.

Second, the Five Fundamental Questions are merely an elaboration of the choices underlying Chapter 2's production possibilities curve. These questions would be irrelevant were it not for the economizing problem.

THE MARKET SYSTEM AT WORK

Chapter 3's circular flow diagram (Figure 3-2) provides the setting for our discussion. In examining how the market system answers the Fundamental Questions, we must add demand and supply diagrams as developed in Chapter 4 to represent the various product and resource markets embodied in the circular flow model.

Determining What Is to Be Produced

Given the product and resource prices established by competing buyers and sellers in both the product and resource markets, how would a purely capitalistic economy decide the types and quantities of goods to be produced? Remembering that businesses seek profits and want to avoid losses, we can generalize that those goods and services which can be produced at a profit will be produced and those whose production entails a loss will not. Two things determine profits or losses.

1 The total revenue a firm receives when it sells a product.

2 The total costs of producing the product.

Both total revenue and total costs are price-times-quantity figures. Total revenue is found by multiplying product price by the quantity of the product sold. Total costs are found by multiplying the price of each resource used by the amount employed and summing the costs of each.

Economic Costs and Profits To say that those products which can be produced profitably will be produced and those which cannot will not is only an accurate generalization if the meaning of **economic costs** is clearly understood.

Let's again think of businesses as simply organizational charts, that is, businesses "on paper," distinct from the capital, raw materials, labor, and entrepreneurial ability which make them going concerns. To become actual producing firms, these "on paper" businesses must secure all four types of resources. *Economic costs are the payments which must be made to secure and retain the needed amounts of these resources.* The per unit size of these costs—that is, resource prices—will be determined by supply and demand in the resource market. Like land, labor, and capital, entrepreneurial ability is a scarce resource and has a price tag on it. Costs therefore must include not only wage and salary payments to labor and interest and rental payments for capital and land, but also payments to the entrepreneur for the functions he or she performs in organizing and combining the other resources in the production of a commodity. The cost payment for these contributions by the entrepreneur is called a **normal profit.**

A product will be produced only when total revenue is large enough to pay wage, interest, rental, *and* normal profit costs. Now if total revenues from the sale of a product exceed all production costs, including a normal profit, the remainder will go to the entrepreneur as the risk taker and organizing force. This return above all costs is called a **pure,** or **economic, profit.** It is *not* an economic cost, because it need not be realized for the business to acquire and retain entrepreneurial ability.

Profits and Expanding Industries A few hypothetical examples will explain how the market system determines what is to be produced. Suppose the most favorable relationship between total revenue and total cost in producing product X occurs when the firm's output is 15 units. Assume, too, that the least-cost combination of resources to use in producing 15 units of X is 2 units of labor, 3 units of land, 1 of capital, and 1 of entrepreneurial ability, selling at prices of $2, $1, $3, and $3, respectively. Finally, suppose that the 15 units of X which these resources produce can be sold for $1 per unit. Will firms enter into the production of product X? Yes, because the firm will be able to pay wage, rent, interest, and normal profit costs of $13 [$=(2 \times \$2) + (3 \times \$1) + (1 \times \$3) + (1 \times \$3)$]. The difference between total revenue of $15 and total costs of $13 will be an economic profit of $2.

This economic profit is evidence that industry X is a prosperous one. Such an industry will become an **expanding industry** as new firms, attracted by these above-normal profits, are created or shift from less profitable industries.

But the entry of new firms will be a self-limiting process. As new firms enter industry X, the market supply of X will increase relative to the market demand. This will lower the market price of X (Figure 4-6c) and economic profits will in time be competed away. The market supply and demand situation prevailing when economic profits become zero will determine the total amount of X produced. At this point the industry will have achieved its "equilibrium size," at least until a further change in market demand or supply upsets that equilibrium.

Losses and Declining Industries But what if the initial market situation for product X were less favorable? Suppose conditions in the product market were such that the firm could sell the 15 units of X at a price of just 75 cents per unit. Total revenue would be $11.25 ($=15 \times 75$ cents). After paying wage, rental, and interest costs of $10, the firm would obtain a below-normal profit of $1.25. In other words, *losses* of $1.75 (=$11.25 − $13) would be incurred.

Certainly, firms would not be attracted to this unprosperous **declining industry.** On the contrary, if these losses persisted, entrepreneurs would seek the normal profits or possibly even the economic profits offered by more prosperous industries. In time existing firms in industry X would go out of business entirely or migrate to other industries where normal or better profits prevail. However, as this happens, the market supply of X will fall relative to the market demand. Product price will rise (Figure 4-6d) and losses will eventually disappear. Industry X will then stabilize itself in size. The market supply and demand situation that prevails at that point where economic profits are zero will determine the total output of product X. Again, the industry for the moment will have reached its equilibrium size.

"Dollar Votes" Consumer demand plays a crucial role in determining the types and quantities of goods produced. Consumers, unrestrained by government and with money incomes from the sale of resources, spend their dollars on those goods they are most willing and able to buy. These expenditures are **dollar votes** by which consumers register their wants through the demand side of the product market. If these votes are great enough to provide a normal profit, businesses will produce that product. An increase in consumer demand, that is, an increase in the dollar votes cast for a product, will mean economic profits for the industry producing it. These profits will signal expansion of that industry and increases in the output of the product.

Conversely, a decrease in consumer demand, that is, fewer votes cast for the product, will result in losses and, in time, contraction of the industry. As firms leave the industry, the output of the product declines. Indeed, the industry may cease to exist. The dollar votes of consumers play a key role in determining what products profit-seeking businesses will produce. As noted in Chapter 3, the capitalistic system is characterized by **consumer sovereignty** because of the strategic role consumers have in determining the types and quantities of goods produced.

A much-publicized illustration of consumer sovereignty occurred a few years ago when a substantial number of consumers rejected the "new" Coca-Cola. Despite elaborate market surveys and extensive advertising, many Coke drinkers judged the new product inferior and engaged in organized protests until the manufacturer responded by again making original "classic" Coke available.

Market Restraints on Freedom From the viewpoint of businesses, we now see that firms are not really "free" to produce what they wish. The demand decisions of consumers, by making production of some products profitable and others not, restrict the choice of businesses in deciding what to produce. Businesses must match their production choices with consumer choices or face losses and eventual bankruptcy.

Much the same holds true for resource suppliers. The demand for resources is a **derived demand**—derived, that is, from the demand for the goods and services which the resources help produce. There is a demand for autoworkers only because there is a demand for automobiles. Generally, in seeking to maximize returns from the sale of their human and property resources, resource suppliers are prompted by the market system to make their choices in accord with consumer demands. If only those firms which produce goods wanted by consumers can operate profitably, only those firms will demand resources. Resource suppliers will not be "free" to allocate their resources to the production of goods which consumers do not value highly. There will be no firms producing such products, because consumer demand is not sufficient to make it profitable.

In brief, consumers register their preferences on the demand side of the product market, and producers and resource suppliers respond appropriately in seeking to further their own self-interests. The market system communicates the wants of consumers to businesses and resource suppliers and elicits appropriate responses.

Organizing Production

How is production to be organized in a market economy? This Fundamental Question is composed of three subquestions:

1 How should resources be allocated among specific industries?

2 What specific firm should do the producing in each industry?

3 What combinations of resources—what technology—should each firm employ?

Production and Profits The preceding section has answered the first subquestion. The market system steers resources to those industries whose products consumers want badly enough to make their production profitable. It simultaneously deprives unprofitable industries of scarce resources. If all firms had sufficient time to enter prosperous industries and to leave unprosperous industries, the output of each industry would be large enough for the firms to make just normal profits. If total industry output at this point happens to be 1500 units and the most profitable output for each firm is 15 units, as in our previous example, the industry will be made up of 100 competing firms.

The second and third subquestions are closely intertwined. In a competitive market economy, the firms which do the producing are those which are willing and able to employ the economically most efficient technique of production. And what determines the most efficient technique? Economic efficiency depends on:

1 Available technology, that is, the alternative combinations of resources or inputs which will produce the desired output.

2 The prices at which needed resources can be obtained.

Least-Cost Production The combination of resources which is most efficient economically depends not only on the physical or engineering data provided by available technology but also on the relative worth of the required resources as measured by their market prices. Thus, a technique which requires just a few physical inputs of resources to produce a given output may be highly *in*efficient economically *if* the required resources are valued very highly in the market. *Economic efficiency entails getting a given output of product with the smallest input of scarce resources, when both output and resource inputs are measured in dollars-and-cents terms.* That combination of resources which will produce, say, $15 worth of product X at the lowest possible money cost is the most efficient.

An example will help. Suppose there are three techniques by which the desired $15 worth of product X can be produced. The quantity of each resource required by each production technology and the prices of the required resources are shown in Table 5-4. By multiplying the quantities of the various resources required by the resource prices in each of the three techniques, the total cost of producing $15 worth of X by each technique can be determined.

Technique No. 2 is economically the most efficient of the three techniques because it is the least costly. Technique No. 2 permits society to obtain $15 worth of output by using a smaller amount of resources—$13 worth in this instance—than the $15 worth which would be used by the two alternative techniques.

But what guarantee is there that firms will actually use technique No. 2? The answer is that firms will want to use the most efficient technique because it yields the greatest profit.

A change in *either* technology *or* resource prices may cause the firm to shift from the technology now employed. If the price of labor falls to 50 cents, technique No. 1 will now be superior to technique No. 2. Businesses will find they can lower their costs by shifting to a technology which uses more of that resource whose price has fallen. You should verify that a new technique involving 1 unit of labor, 4 of land, 1 of capital, and 1 of entrepreneurial ability will be preferable to all three techniques listed in Table 5-4, assuming the resource prices given there.

Distributing Total Output

The market system enters the picture in two ways in solving the problem of distributing total output. Generally, any given product will be distributed to consumers on the basis of their ability and willingness to pay the existing market price for it. If the price of X is $1 per unit, those buyers who are able and willing to pay that price will get a unit of this product; those who are not, will not. This is the rationing function of equilibrium prices.

The size of one's money income determines a consumer's ability to pay the equilibrium price for X and other available products. And money income depends on the quantities of the various property and human resources which the income receiver supplies and the prices which they command in the resource market. Thus, resource prices play a key role in determining the size of each household's income claim against the total output of society. Within the limits of a consumer's money income, his or her willingness to pay the equilibrium price for X determines whether or not some of this product is distributed to that person. And this will-

TABLE 5-4 Techniques for producing $15 worth of product X (*hypothetical data*)

		Units of resource		
Resource	*Price per unit of resource*	*Technique no. 1*	*Technique no. 2*	*Technique no. 3*
Labor	$2	4	2	1
Land	1	1	3	4
Capital	3	1	1	2
Entrepreneurial ability	3	1	1	1
Total cost of $15 worth of X		$15	$13	$15

ingness to buy X will depend on one's preference for X compared to available close substitutes for X and their relative prices. Thus, product prices play a key role in determining spending patterns of consumers.

There is nothing particularly ethical about the market system as a mechanism for distributing output. Households which accumulate large amounts of property resources by inheritance, through hard work and frugality, through business acumen, or by crook will receive large incomes and thus command large shares of the economy's total output. Others, offering unskilled and relatively unproductive labor resources which elicit low wages, will receive meager money incomes and small portions of total output.

Accommodating Change

Industrial societies are dynamic: Consumer preferences, technology, and resource supplies all change. This means that the particular allocation of resources which is *now* the most efficient for a *given* pattern of consumer tastes, for a *given* range of technological alternatives, and for *given* supplies of resources will become obsolete and inefficient as consumer preferences change, new techniques of production are discovered, and resource supplies alter over time. Can the market economy negotiate adjustments to these changes so that resources are still used efficiently?

Guiding Function of Prices Suppose consumer tastes change. Specifically, assume that, because of greater health consciousness, consumers decide they want more exercise bikes and fewer cigarettes than the economy currently provides. This change in consumers' taste will be communicated to producers through an increase in demand for bikes and a decline in demand for cigarettes. Bike prices will rise and cigarette prices will fall. Now, assuming firms in both industries were enjoying precisely normal profits before these changes in consumer demand, higher exercise bike prices mean economic profits for the bike industry, and lower cigarette prices mean losses for the cigarette industry. Self-interest induces new competitors to enter the prosperous bike industry. Losses will in time force firms to leave the depressed cigarette industry.

But these adjustments are both self-limiting. The expansion of the bike industry will continue only until the resulting increase in the market supply of bikes brings bike prices back down to a level where normal profits again prevail. Similarly, contraction in the cigarette industry will persist until the accompanying decline in the market supply of cigarettes brings cigarette prices up to a level where remaining firms can receive a normal profit. Or, in the extreme, the cigarette industry may cease to exist.

The point is that these adjustments in the business sector are completely appropriate to changes in consumer tastes. Society—meaning consumers—wants more exercise bikes and fewer cigarettes, and that is precisely what it is getting as the bike industry expands and the cigarette industry contracts. These adjustments, incidentally, portray the concept of consumer sovereignty at work.

This analysis assumes that resource suppliers are agreeable to these adjustments. Will the market system prompt resource suppliers to reallocate their human and property resources from the cigarette to the bike industry, thereby permitting the output of bikes to expand at the expense of cigarette production? The answer is "Yes."

The economic profits which initially follow the increase in demand for bikes will not only provide that industry with the inducement to expand but will also give it the revenue needed to obtain the resources essential to its growth. Higher bike prices will permit firms in that industry to pay higher prices for resources, thereby drawing resources from what are now less urgent alternative employments. Willingness and ability to employ more resources in the exercise bike industry will be communicated back into the resource market through an increase in the demand for resources.

The reverse occurs in the adversely affected cigarette industry. The losses which the decline in consumer demand initially entails will cause a decline in the demand for resources in that industry. Workers and other resources released from the contracting cigarette industry can now find employment in the expanding bike industry. Furthermore, the increased demand for resources in the bike industry will mean higher resource prices in that industry than those being paid in the cigarette industry, where declines in resource demand have lowered resource prices. The resulting differential in resource prices will provide the incentive for resource owners to further their self-interests by reallocating their resources from the cigarette to the bike industry. And this is the precise shift needed to permit the bike industry to expand and the cigarette industry to contract.

The ability of the market system to communicate changes in such basic data as consumer tastes and to elicit appropriate responses from both businesses and resource suppliers is called the **directing** or **guiding function of prices.** By affecting product prices and profits, changes in consumer tastes direct the expansion of some industries and the contraction of others. These adjustments carry through to the resource market as expanding industries demand more resources and contracting industries demand fewer. The resulting changes in resource prices guide resources from the contracting to the expanding industries. Without a market system, some administrative agency, presumably a governmental planning board, would have to direct business institutions and resources into specific lines of production.

Similar analysis would indicate that the market system would adjust to similar fundamental changes—for example, to changes in technology and in the relative supplies of various resources.

Initiating Progress Adjusting to changes is one thing; initiating changes, particularly desirable changes, is something else again. Is the competitive market system congenial to technological improvements and capital accumulation—the interrelated changes which lead to greater productivity and a higher level of material well-being for society? This question is not easy to answer. Our answer at this point will not consider qualifications and modifications.

Technological Advance The competitive market system contains the incentive for technological advance. New cost-cutting techniques give the innovating firm a temporary advantage over its rivals. Lower production costs mean economic profits for the pioneering firm. By passing part of its cost reduction to the consumer through a lower product price, the firm can increase sales and obtain economic profits at the expense of rival firms. Furthermore, the competitive market system provides an environment favorable to the rapid spread of a technological advance. Rivals *must* follow the lead of the most progressive firm or suffer immediate losses and eventual bankruptcy.

The lower product price which technological advance permits will cause the innovating industry to expand. This expansion may be the result of existing firms' expanding their rates of output or of new firms entering the industry lured by the economic profits initially created by technological advance. This expansion, that is, the diversion of resources from less progressive to more progressive industries, is as it should be. Sustained efficiency in the use of scarce resources demands that resources be continually reallocated from industries whose productive techniques are relatively less efficient to those whose techniques are relatively more efficient.

Capital Accumulation But technological advance typically requires increased amounts of capital goods. The entrepreneur as an innovator can command through the market system the resources necessary to produce the machinery and equipment upon which technological advance depends.

If society registers dollar votes for capital goods, the product market and the resource market will adjust to these votes by producing capital goods. The market system acknowledges dollar voting for both consumer and capital goods.

But who, specifically, will register votes for capital goods? First, the entrepreneur as a receiver of profit income can be expected to apportion part of that income to accumulation of capital goods. By doing so, an even greater profit income can be achieved in the future if innovation is successful. Furthermore, by paying interest, entrepreneurs can borrow portions of the incomes of households and use these borrowed funds in casting dollar votes for the production of more capital goods.

Competition and Control: The "Invisible Hand"

Though the market system is the organizing mechanism of pure capitalism, competition is the mechanism of control. The market mechanism of supply and demand communicates the wants of consumers (society) to businesses and through businesses to resource suppliers. It is competition, however, which forces businesses and resource suppliers to make appropriate responses.

To illustrate: We have seen that an increase in consumer demand for some product will raise that good's price above the wage, rent, interest, and normal profit costs of production. The resulting economic profits are a signal to producers that society wants more of the product. It is competition—new firms entering the industry—that simultaneously brings an expansion of output and a lowering of price back to a level just consistent with production costs. However, if the industry was dominated by, say, one huge firm (a monopolist) which was able to prohibit entry of potential competitors, that firm could continue to enjoy economic profits by preventing expansion of the industry.

But competition does more than guarantee responses appropriate to the wishes of society. It also forces firms to adopt the most efficient productive techniques. In a competitive market, the failure of some

LAST WORD

THE FINANCING OF CORPORATE ACTIVITY

One of the main advantages of corporations is their ability to finance their operations through the sale of stocks and bonds. It is informative to examine the nature of corporate finance in more detail.

Generally speaking, corporations finance their activities in three different ways. First, a very large portion of a corporation's activity is financed internally out of undistributed corporate profits. Second, like individuals or unincorporated businesses, corporations may borrow from financial institutions. For example, a small corporation which wants to build a new plant or warehouse may obtain the funds from a commercial bank, a savings and loan association, or an insurance company. Third, unique to corporations, common stocks and bonds can be issued.

A common stock is an ownership share. The purchaser of a stock certificate has the right to vote in the selection of corporate officers and to share in any declared dividends. If you own 1000 of the 100,000 shares issued by Specific Motors, Inc. (hereafter SM), then you own 1 percent of the company, are entitled to 1 percent of any dividends declared by the board of directors, and control 1 percent of the votes in the annual election of corporate officials. In contrast, a bond is not an ownership share. A bond purchaser is simply lending money to a corporation. A bond is merely an IOU, in acknowledgment of a loan, whereby the corporation promises to pay the holder a fixed amount at some specified future date and other fixed amounts (interest payments) every year up to the bond's maturity date. For example, one might purchase a ten-year SM bond with a face value of $1000 with a 10 percent stated rate of interest. This means that in exchange for your $1000 SM guarantees you a $100 interest payment for each of the next ten years and then to repay your $1000 principal at the end of that period.

There are clearly important differences between stocks and bonds. First, as noted, the bondholder is not an owner of the company, but is only a lender. Second, bonds are considered to be less risky than stocks for two reasons. On the one hand, bondholders have a "legally prior claim" upon a corporation's earnings. Dividends cannot be paid to stockholders until all interest payments due to bondholders have been paid. On the other hand, holders of SM stock do not know how much their dividends will be or how much they might obtain for their stock if they decide to sell. If Specific Motors falls on hard times, stockholders may receive no dividends at all and the value of their stock

firms to use the least costly production technique means their eventual elimination by more efficient firms. Finally, we have seen that competition provides an environment conducive to technological advance.

The operation and adjustments of a competitive market system create a curious and important identity —the identity of private and social interests. Firms and resource suppliers, seeking to further their own self-interest and operating within the framework of a highly competitive market system, will simultaneously, as though guided by an **"invisible hand,"**[2] promote the public or social interest. For example, we have seen that given a competitive environment, business firms use the least costly combination of resources in producing a given output because it is in their private self-interest to do so. To act otherwise would be to forgo profits or even to risk bankruptcy. But, at the same time, it is clearly also in the social interest to use scarce resources in the least costly, that is, most efficient, manner. Not to do so would be to produce a given output at a greater cost or sacrifice of alternative goods than is necessary.

In our more-bikes–fewer-cigarettes illustration, it is self-interest, awakened and guided by the competitive market system, which induces responses appropriate to the assumed change in society's wants. Businesses seeking to make higher profits and to avoid

[2]Adam Smith, *The Wealth of Nations* (New York: Modern Library, Inc., originally published in 1776), p. 423.

may plummet. Provided the corporation does not go bankrupt, the holder of an SM bond is guaranteed a $100 interest payment each year and the return of his or her $1000 at the end of ten years.

But this is not to imply that the purchase of corporate bonds is riskless. The market value of your SM bond may vary over time in accordance with the financial health of the corporation. If SM encounters economic misfortunes which raise questions about its financial integrity, the market value of your bond may fall. Should you sell the bond prior to maturity you may receive only $600 or $700 for it (rather than $1000) and thereby incur a capital loss.

Changes in interest rates also affect the market prices of bonds. Specifically, increases in interest rates cause bond prices to fall and vice versa. Assume you purchase a $1000 ten-year SM bond this year (1993) when the going interest rate is 10 percent. This obviously means that your bond provides a $100 fixed interest payment each year. But now suppose that by next year the interest rate has jumped to 15 percent and SM must now guarantee a $150 fixed annual payment on its new 1994 $1000 ten-year bonds. Clearly, no sensible person will pay you $1000 for your bond which pays only $100 of interest income per year when new bonds can be purchased for $1000 which pay the holder $150 per year. Hence, if you sell your 1993 bond before maturity, you will suffer a capital loss.

Bondholders face another element of risk due to inflation. If substantial inflation occurs over the ten-year period you hold a SM bond, the $1000 principal repaid to you at the end of that period will represent substantially less purchasing power than the $1000 you loaned to SM ten years earlier. You will have lent "dear" dollars, but will be repaid in "cheap" dollars.

losses, on the one hand, and resource suppliers pursuing greater monetary rewards, on the other, negotiate the changes in the allocation of resources and therefore the composition of output which society demands. The force of competition controls or guides the self-interest motive in such a way that it automatically, and quite unintentionally, furthers the best interests of society. The "invisible hand" tells us that when firms maximize their profits, society's domestic output is also maximized.

The Case for the Market System

The virtues of the market system are implicit in our discussion of its operation. Two merit emphasis.

Allocative Efficiency The basic economic argument for the market system is that it promotes an efficient allocation of resources. The competitive market system guides resources into production of those goods and services most wanted by society. It forces use of the most efficient techniques in organizing resources for production, and is conducive to the development and adoption of new and more efficient production techniques. The "invisible hand" will in effect harness self-interest so as to provide society with the greatest output of wanted goods from its available resources. This, then, suggests the maximum economic efficiency. This presumption of allocative efficiency makes most economists hesitant to advocate governmental interference with, or regulation of, free markets unless reasons for such interference are clear and compelling.

Freedom The major noneconomic argument for the market system is its great emphasis on personal freedom. One of the fundamental problems of social organization is how to coordinate the economic activities of large numbers of individuals and businesses. We recall from Chapter 2 that there are two contrasting ways of providing this coordination: one is central direction and the use of coercion; the other is voluntary cooperation through the market system. Only the market system can coordinate economic activity without coercion. The market system permits—indeed, it thrives on—freedom of enterprise and choice. Entrepreneurs and workers are not herded from industry to industry by government directives to meet production targets established by some omnipotent governmental agency. On the contrary, they are free to further their own self-interests, subject, of course, to the rewards and penalties imposed by the market system itself.

QUICK REVIEW 5-3

- ***The output mix of the competitive market system is determined by profits. Profits cause industries to expand; losses cause them to contract.***
- ***Competition forces firms to use the least costly (most efficient) production methods.***
- ***The distribution of output in a market economy is determined by consumer incomes and product prices.***
- ***Competitive markets reallocate resources in response to changes in consumer tastes, technological progress, and changes in resource supplies.***

CHAPTER SUMMARY

1 The functional distribution of income shows how society's total income is divided among wages, rents, interest, and profits; the personal distribution of income shows how total income is divided among individual households.

2 Households divide their total incomes among personal taxes, saving, and consumer goods. Consumer expenditures on durables and some services are discretionary and therefore postponable.

3 Sole proprietorships, partnerships, and corporations are the major legal forms of business enterprises. Corporations dominate the business sector because they **a** have limited liability, and **b** are in a superior position to acquire money capital for expansion.

4 Ours is a "big business" economy in that many industries are dominated by a small number of large corporations.

5 United States world trade has grown both absolutely and as a proportion of domestic output. The other industrially advanced nations are our major trading partners.

6 International trade yields significant economic benefits in the form of **a** more efficient use of world resources, and **b** enhanced competition. A potential disadvantage is that a nation's international economic interrelationships may create new sources of macroeconomic instability which complicate policy making.

7 Every economy is confronted with Five Fundamental Questions: **a** At what level should available resources be employed? **b** What goods and services are to be produced? **c** How is that output to be produced? **d** To whom should the output be distributed? **e** Can the system adapt to changes in consumer tastes, resource supplies, and technology?

8 Those products whose production and sale yield total revenue sufficient to cover all costs, including a normal profit, will be produced. Those whose production will not yield a normal profit will not be produced.

9 Economic profits designate an industry as prosperous and signal its expansion. Losses mean an industry is unprosperous and result in contraction of that industry.

10 Consumer sovereignty means that both businesses and resource suppliers channel their efforts in accordance with the wants of consumers.

11 Competition forces firms to use the least costly, and therefore the most economically efficient, productive techniques.

12 The prices commanded by the quantities and types of resources supplied by each household will determine the number of dollar claims against the economy's output which each household receives. Within the limits of each household's money income, consumer preferences and the relative prices of products determine the distribution of total output.

13 The competitive market system can communicate changes in consumer tastes to resource suppliers and entrepreneurs, thereby prompting appropriate adjustments in the allocation of the economy's resources. The competitive market system also provides an environment conducive to technological advance and capital accumulation.

14 Competition, the primary mechanism of control in the market economy, will foster an identity of private and social interests; as though directed by an "invisible hand," competition harnesses the self-interest motives of businesses and resource suppliers to simultaneously further the social interest in using scarce resources efficiently.

TERMS AND CONCEPTS

functional and personal distribution of income
durable and nondurable goods
services
plant
horizontal and vertical combinations
firm
conglomerates
industry
sole proprietorship
partnership
corporation
limited liability
double taxation
economic costs
separation of ownership and control
Five Fundamental Questions
normal versus economic profits
dollar votes
expanding industry versus declining industry
consumer sovereignty
derived demand
directing (guiding) function of prices
"invisible hand"

QUESTIONS AND STUDY SUGGESTIONS

1 Distinguish between functional and personal distributions of income. What effects do you think a change in the personal distribution of income from that shown in Figure 5-2 to one of complete equality would have on the composition of output and the allocation of resources?

2 What is the demand for consumer durable goods less stable than that for nondurables?

3 Distinguish clearly between a plant, a firm, and an industry. Why is an "industry" often difficult to define in practice?

4 What are the major legal forms of business organization? Briefly state the advantages and disadvantages of each. How do you account for the dominant role of corporations in our economy? Explain and evaluate the separation of ownership and control which characterizes the corporate form of business enterprise.

5 What are the major industries in American capitalism in terms of a the number of firms in operation, and b the amount of income and employment provided?

6 Explain and evaluate the following statements:

a "It is the consumer, and the consumer alone, who casts the vote that determines how big any company should be."

b "The very nature of modern industrial society requires labor, government, and businesses to be 'big' and their bigness renders impossible the functioning of the older, small-scale, simpler, and more flexible capitalist system."

c "The legal form which an enterprise assumes is dictated primarily by the financial requirements of its particular line of production."

d "If we want capitalism, we must also accept inequality of income distribution."

7 What is the quantitative importance of world trade to the United States? Explain: "Nations engage in international trade because it allows them to realize the benefits of specialization."

8 How have persistent United States trade deficits been financed? "Trade deficits mean we get more merchandise from the rest of the world than we provide in return. Therefore, trade deficits are economically desirable." Do you agree?

9 Suppose excessive aggregate expenditures in the United States are causing inflation. Explain the effect of a appreciation, and b depreciation of the dollar on domestic inflation.

10 Describe in detail how the market system answers the Fundamental Questions. Why must economic choices be made? Explain: "The capitalistic system is a profit and loss economy."

11 Evaluate and explain the following statements:

a "The most important feature of capitalism is the absence of a central economic plan."

b "Competition is the indispensable disciplinarian of the market economy."

c "Production methods which are inferior in the engineering sense may be the most efficient methods in the economic sense."

12 Explain fully the meaning and implications of the following quotation.

> The beautiful consequence of the market is that it is its own guardian. If output prices or certain kinds of remuneration stray away from their socially ordained levels, forces are set into motion to bring them back to the fold. It is a curious paradox which thus ensues: the market, which is the acme of individual economic freedom, is the strictest taskmaster of all. One may appeal the ruling of a planning board or win the dispensation of a minister; but there is no appeal, no dispensation, from the anonymous pressures of the market mechanism. Economic freedom is thus more illusory than at first appears. One can do as one pleases in the market. But if one pleases to do what the market disapproves, the price of individual freedom is economic ruination.[3]

13 Assume that a business firm finds that its profits will be at maximum when it produces $40 worth of product A. Suppose also that each of the three techniques shown in the following table will produce the desired output.

Resource	Price per unit of resource	Technique no. 1	Technique no. 2	Technique no. 3
Labor	$3	5	2	3
Land	4	2	4	2
Capital	2	2	4	5
Entrepreneurial ability	2	4	2	4

a Given the resource prices shown, which technique will the firm choose? Why? Will production entail profits or losses? Will the industry expand or contract? When is a new equilibrium output achieved?

b Assume now that a new technique, technique No. 4, is developed. It entails the use of 2 units of labor, 2 of land, 6 of capital, and 3 of entrepreneurial ability. Given the resource prices in the table, will the firm adopt the new technique? Explain your answer.

c Suppose now that an increase in labor supply causes the price of labor to fall to $1.50 per unit, all other resource prices being unchanged. Which technique will the producer now choose? Explain.

d "The market system causes the economy to conserve most in the use of those resources which are particularly scarce in supply. Resources which are scarcest relative to the demand for them have the highest prices. As a result, producers use these resources as sparingly as is possible." Evaluate this statement. Does your answer to question 13c bear out this contention? Explain.

14 Foreigners frequently point out that, comparatively speaking, Americans are very wasteful of food and material goods and very conscious, and overly economical, in their use of time. Can you provide an explanation for this observation?

[3]Robert L. Heilbroner, *The Worldly Philosophers,* 3d ed. (New York: Simon & Schuster, Inc., 1967), p. 42.

Chapter 6 The Public Sector

The economic activities of government affect your well-being every day of your life. If you attend a public college or university, taxpayers heavily subsidize your education. When you receive a check from your part-time or summer job, you see significant deductions for income and social security taxes. The ground beef in your Big Mac has been examined by government inspectors to prevent contamination and to ensure quality. Laws requiring seat belts and motorcycle helmets—not to mention the sprinkler system government mandates in your dormitory—are all intended to enhance your safety. If you are a woman or a member of a minority group, an array of legislation is designed to enhance your education, housing, and employment opportunities.

All real-life economies are "mixed"; government and the market system share the responsibility of responding to the Five Fundamental Questions. Our economy is predominantly a market economy, yet the economic activities of government are of great significance. In this chapter we will (1) state and illustrate the major economic functions of the public sector; (2) add government to the circular flow model; and (3) examine the major expenditures and sources of tax revenue for Federal, state, and local governments.

ECONOMIC FUNCTIONS OF GOVERNMENT

The economic functions of government are many and varied. The economic role of government is so broad that it is virtually impossible to establish an all-inclusive list of its economic functions. The following breakdown of government's economic activities will serve as a pattern for our discussion, although some overlapping is unavoidable.

First, some economic functions of government strengthen and facilitate the operation of the market system. The two major activities of government in this area are:

1 Providing the legal foundation and a social environment conducive to the effective operation of the market system.

2 Maintaining competition.

Through a second group of functions, government supplements and modifies the operation of the market system. The three major functions of government here involve:

3 Redistributing income and wealth.
4 Adjusting the allocation of resources to alter the composition of the domestic output.
5 Stabilizing the economy, that is, controlling unemployment and inflation caused by business fluctuations, and promoting economic growth.

In reality most government activities and policies have *some* impact in all these areas. For example, a program to redistribute income to the poor affects the allocation of resources in that the poor buy somewhat different goods and services than the wealthy. A decline in, say, government military spending to lessen inflationary pressures also reallocates resources from public to private uses.

LEGAL AND SOCIAL FRAMEWORK

Government provides the legal framework and certain basic services prerequisite to the effective operation of a market economy. The necessary legal framework includes providing for the legal status of business enterprises, defining the rights of private ownership, and providing for enforcement of contracts. Government also establishes legal "rules of the game" governing the relationships of businesses, resource suppliers, and consumers with one another. Through legislation, government can referee economic relationships, detect foul play, and exercise authority in imposing appropriate penalties.

Basic services provided by government include police powers to maintain internal order, a system of standards for measuring the weight and quality of products, and a monetary system to facilitate exchange of goods and services.

The Pure Food and Drug Act of 1906 and its various amendments are an excellent example of how government has strengthened the operation of the market system. This act sets rules of conduct governing producers in their relationships with consumers. It prohibits the sale of adulterated and misbranded foods and drugs, requires net weights and ingredients of products to be specified on their containers, establishes quality standards which must be stated on labels of canned foods, and prohibits deceptive claims on patent-medicine labels. All these measures are designed to prevent fraudulent activities on the part of producers and, simultaneously, to increase the public's confidence in the integrity of the market system. Similar legislation pertains to labor-management relations and relations of business firms to one another.

The presumption is that this type of government activity will improve resource allocation. Supplying a medium of exchange, ensuring product quality, defining ownership rights, and enforcing contracts tend to increase the volume of exchange. This widens markets and permits greater specialization in the use of both property and human resources. Such specialization means a more efficient allocation of resources. However, some argue that government has overregulated interactions of businesses, consumers, and workers, stifling economic incentives and impairing productive efficiency.

MAINTAINING COMPETITION

Competition is the basic regulatory mechanism in a capitalistic economy. It is the force which subjects producers and resource suppliers to the dictates of consumer sovereignty. With competition, the supply and demand decisions of *many* sellers and buyers determine market prices. Individual producers and resource suppliers can only adjust to the wishes of buyers as tabulated and communicated by the market system. Profits and survival await the competitive producers who obey the market system; losses and eventual bankruptcy are the lot of those who deviate from it. With competition, buyers are the boss, the market is their agent, and businesses are their servants.

The growth of **monopoly** drastically alters this situation. *Monopoly exists when the number of sellers becomes small enough for each seller to influence total supply and therefore the price of the commodity being sold.*

When monopoly supplants competition, sellers can influence, or "rig," the market in their own self-interests, to the detriment of society as a whole. Through their ability to influence total supply, monopolists can artificially restrict the output of products and enjoy higher prices and, frequently, persistent economic profits. These above-competitive prices and profits directly conflict with the interests of consumers. Monopolists are not regulated by the will of society as are competitive sellers. Producer sovereignty supplants consumer sovereignty to the degree that monopoly supplants competition. Resources are then allocated in terms of the profit-seeking interests of monopolistic sellers rather than in terms of the wants of society as a whole. Monopoly causes a misallocation of economic resources.

In the United States, government has attempted to control monopoly primarily in two ways.
1 In the case of "natural monopolies"—industries in

which technological and economic realities rule out competitive markets—government has created public commissions regulating prices and service standards. Transportation, communications, and electric and other utilities are industries which are regulated in varying degrees. At local levels of government, public ownership of electric and water utilities is common.

2 In the vast majority of markets, efficient production can be attained with a high degree of competition. The Federal government has therefore enacted a series of antimonopoly or antitrust laws, beginning with the Sherman Act of 1890, to maintain and strengthen competition as an effective regulator of business behavior.

Even if the legal foundation of capitalistic institutions is assured and competition is maintained, there is still a need for certain additional economic functions on the part of government. *The market economy has certain biases and shortcomings which compel government to supplement and modify its operation.*

REDISTRIBUTION OF INCOME

The market system is an impersonal mechanism, and the distribution of income to which it gives rise may entail more inequality than society desires. The market system yields very large incomes to those whose labor, by virtue of inherent ability and acquired education and skills, commands high wages. Similarly, those who possess—through hard work or easy inheritance—valuable capital and land receive large property incomes.

But others in our society have less ability and have received modest amounts of education and training. These same people typically have accumulated or inherited no property resources. Hence, their incomes are very low. Furthermore, many of the aged, the physically and mentally handicapped, and husbandless women with dependent children earn only very small incomes or, like the unemployed, no incomes at all through the market system. In short, the market system involves considerable inequality in the distribution of money income (recall Figure 5-2) and therefore in the distribution of total output among individual households. Poverty amidst overall plenty in our economy persists as a major economic and political issue.

Government responsibility for ameliorating income inequality is reflected in a variety of policies and programs.

1 *Transfer payments* provide relief to the destitute, aid to the dependent and handicapped, and unemployment compensation to the unemployed. Similarly, our social security and Medicare programs provide financial support for the retired and aged sick. All these programs transfer income from government to households which would otherwise have little or none.

2 Government also alters the distribution of income by *market intervention,* that is, by modifying the prices established by market forces. Price supports for farmers and minimum-wage legislation are illustrations of government price fixing designed to raise incomes of specific groups.

3 Finally, the personal income tax has been used historically to take a larger proportion of the incomes of the rich than the poor. However, recent revisions of the personal income tax have significantly reduced its redistributive impact.

REALLOCATION OF RESOURCES

Economists recognize two major cases of *market failure,* that is, situations in which the competitive market system would either (1) produce the "wrong" amounts of certain goods and services, or (2) fail to allocate any resources whatsoever to the production of certain goods and services whose output is economically justified. The first case involves "spillovers" or "externalities" and the second "public" or "social" goods.

Spillovers or Externalities

One of the virtues of a competitive market system is that it would result in an efficient allocation of resources. The "right" or optimal amount of resources would be allocated to each of the various goods and services produced. Hence, the equilibrium output in a competitive market is also identified as the optimal output.

But the conclusion that competitive markets automatically bring about allocative efficiency rests on the hidden assumption that *all* the benefits and costs of production and consumption of each product are fully reflected in the market demand and supply curves respectively. It is assumed that there are no *spillovers* or *externalities* associated with the production or consumption of any good or service.

A *spillover*[1] occurs when some of the benefits or costs of production or consumption of a good "spill over" onto third parties, that is, to parties other than the

[1]Spillovers may go by other names—for example, external economies and diseconomies, neighborhood effects, and social benefits and costs.

immediate buyer or seller. Spillovers are also termed *externalities* because they are benefits and costs accruing to some individual or group external to the market transaction.

Spillover Costs When production or consumption of a commodity inflicts costs on a third party without compensation, there exists a **spillover cost.** Obvious examples of spillover costs involve environmental pollution. When a chemical manufacturer or meat-packing plant dumps its wastes into a lake or river, swimmers, fishermen, and boaters—not to mention communities' water supplies—suffer spillover costs. When a petroleum refinery pollutes the air with smoke or a paint factory creates distressing odors, the community bears spillover costs for which it is not compensated.

Figure 6-1a illustrates how spillover or external costs affect the allocation of resources. When spillover costs occur—when producers shift some of their costs onto the community—their production costs are lower than otherwise. The supply curve does not include or "capture" all the costs which can be legitimately associated with production of the good. Hence, the producer's supply curve, *S,* understates total costs of production and therefore lies to the right of the supply curve which would include all costs, S_t. By polluting, that is, by creating spillover costs, the firm enjoys lower production costs and the supply curve *S.* The result, shown in Figure 6-1a, is that equilibrium output Q_e is larger than optimal output Q_o. This means resources are *overallocated* to the production of this commodity.

Correcting for Spillover Costs Government can take several actions to correct the overallocation of resources associated with spillover costs and "internalize" the external costs. Two basic types of corrective action are common: legislative action and specific taxes.

1 Legislation In our examples of air and water pollution, we find that the most direct action is to pass *legislation* prohibiting or limiting pollution. Such legislation forces potential polluters to bear costs of properly disposing of industrial wastes. Firms must buy and install smoke-abatement equipment or facilities to purify water contaminated by manufacturing processes. Such action forces potential offenders, under the threat of legal action, to bear *all* costs associated with their production. In short, legislation can shift the supply curve *S* toward S_t in Figure 6-1b, bringing equilibrium and optimal outputs into equality.

2 Specific Taxes A second, less direct action is based upon the fact that taxes are a cost and therefore a determinant of a firm's supply curve (Chapter 4). Government might levy a *specific tax* which equals or ap-

FIGURE 6-1 Spillover costs and the overallocation of resources

With spillover costs in (a) we find that the lower costs borne by businesses, as reflected in *S,* fail to reflect all costs, as embodied in S_t. Consequently, the equilibrium output Q_e is greater than the efficient or optimal output Q_o. This overallocation of resources can be corrected by legislation or, as shown in (b), by imposing a specific tax, *T,* which raises the firm's costs and shifts its supply curve from *S* to S_t.

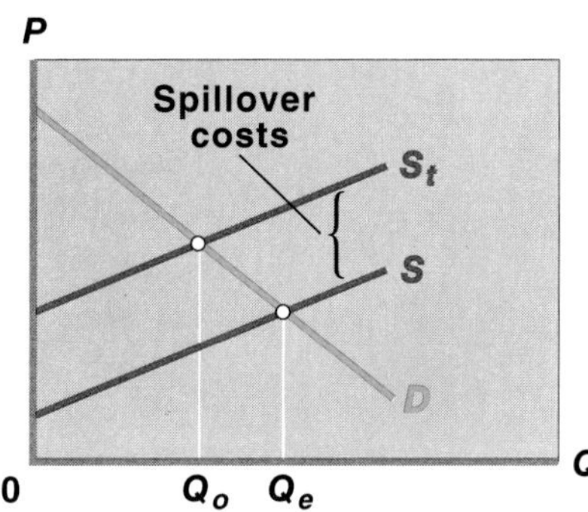

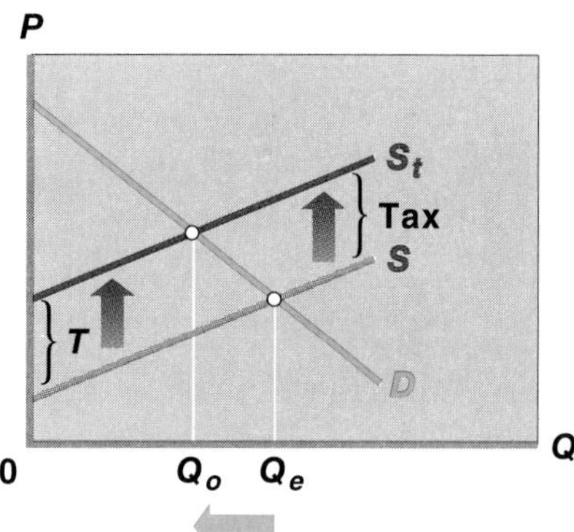

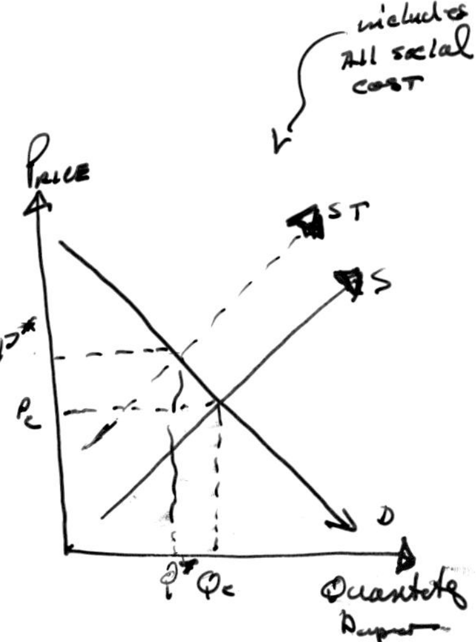

proximates the spillover costs per unit of output. Through this tax, government attempts to shove back onto the offending firm those external or spillover costs which private industry would otherwise avoid. A specific tax equal to T per unit in Figure 6-1b will increase the firm's costs, shifting the supply curve from S to S_t. The result is that the equilibrium output Q_e will decline so that it corresponds with the optimal output Q_o and the overallocation of resources will be eliminated.

Spillover Benefits But spillovers may also take the form of benefits. Production or consumption of certain goods and services may confer spillover or external benefits on third parties or the community at large for which payment or compensation is not required. For example, measles and polio immunization shots result in direct benefits to the immediate consumer. But immunization against these contagious diseases yields widespread and substantial spillover benefits to the entire community.

Education is another example of **spillover benefits.** Education benefits individual consumers: "More educated" people generally achieve higher incomes than "less educated" people. But education also confers sizable benefits upon society. The economy as a whole benefits from a more versatile and more productive labor force, on the one hand, and smaller outlays in crime prevention, law enforcement, and welfare programs, on the other. Significant, too, is the fact that political participation correlates positively with the level of education in that the percentage of persons who vote increases with educational attainment.

Figure 6-2a shows the impact of spillover benefits on resource allocation. The existence of spillover benefits means that the market demand curve, which reflects only private benefits, understates total benefits. The market demand curve fails to capture all the benefits associated with the provision and consumption of goods and services which entail spillover benefits. Thus D in Figure 6-2a indicates the benefits which private individuals derive from education; D_t is drawn to include these private benefits *plus* the additional spillover benefits accruing to society at large. While market demand D and supply S_t would yield an equilibrium output of Q_e, this output would be less than the optimal output Q_o. The market system would not produce enough education; resources would be *underallocated* to education.

Correcting for Spillover Benefits How might the underallocation of resources associated with the presence of spillover benefits be corrected?

1 Increase Demand One approach is to increase demand by providing consumers with purchasing power which can be used *only* to obtain the particular good or service producing spillover benefits. Example: Our food stamp program is designed to improve the diets of low-income families. The food stamps which government provides to such families can be spent

Positive Externalities

FIGURE 6-2 Spillover benefits and the underallocation of resources

Spillover benefits in (a) cause society's total benefits from a product, as shown by D_t, to be understated by the market demand curve, D. As a result, the equilibrium output Q_e is less than the optimal output Q_o. This can be corrected by a subsidy to consumers, as shown in (b), which increases market demand from D to D_t. Alternatively, the underallocation can be eliminated by providing producers with a subsidy of U, which increases their supply curve from S_t to S_t'.

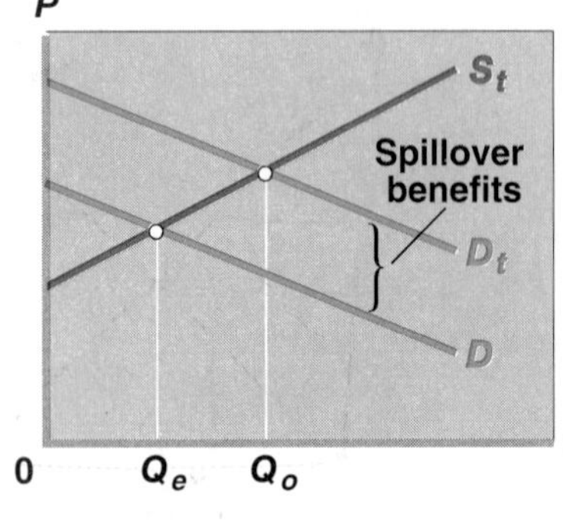

(a) The case of spillover benefits

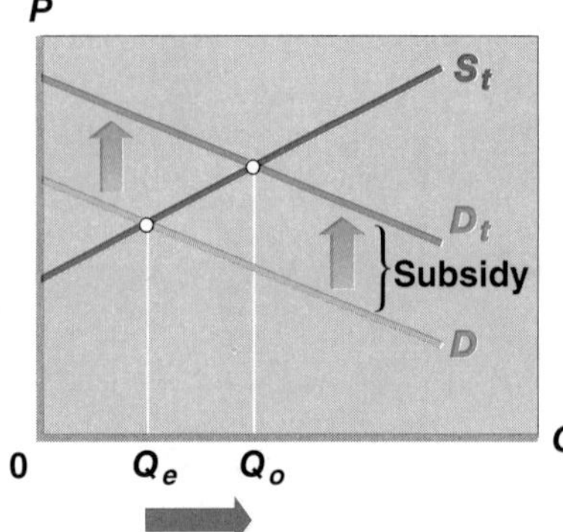

(b) Correcting the underallocation of resources: demand side

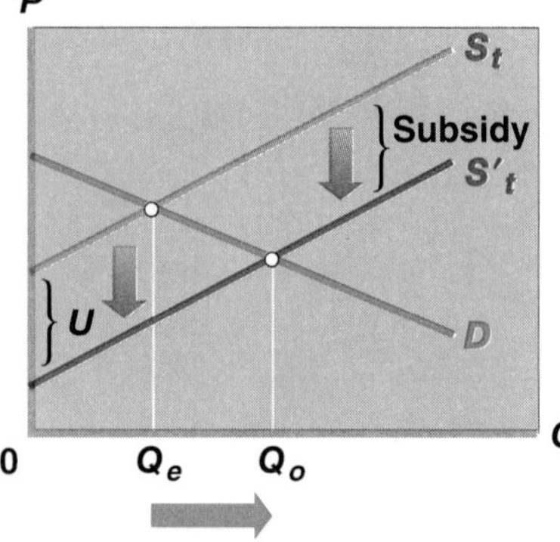

(c) Correcting the underallocation of resources: supply side

only on food. Stores accepting food stamps are reimbursed with money by the government. Part of the rationale for this program is that improved nutrition will help disadvantaged children perform better in school and disadvantaged adults to be better employees. In brief, the program is designed to help disadvantaged people become productive participants in the economy, an outcome benefiting society as a whole. In terms of Figure 6-2b the program increases the demand for food from from D to D_t, thereby alleviating or eliminating the underallocation of resources.

2 Increase Supply An alternative approach works through the supply side of the market. Instead of subsidizing consumers of a particular good, government may find it more convenient and administratively simpler to subsidize producers. A *subsidy* is a specific tax in reverse; taxes impose an extra cost on producers, whereas subsidies reduce their costs. In Figure 6-2c a subsidy of U per unit to producers will reduce costs and shift the supply curve downward from S_t to S_t', and output will increase from Q_e to the optimal level Q_o. Hence, the underallocation of resources will be corrected. Public subsidization of higher education, mass immunization programs, and public hospitals and health clinics are cases in point.

3 Government Provision A third policy option arises if spillover benefits are extremely large: Government may simply choose to finance or, in the extreme, to own and operate such industries. This option leads us into a discussion of public goods and services.

Public Goods and Services

Private goods, which are produced through the market system, are *divisible* in that they come in units small enough to be afforded by individual buyers. Furthermore, private goods are subject to the **exclusion principle,** the idea that those willing and able to pay the equilibrium price get the product, but those unable or unwilling to pay are excluded from the benefits provided by that product.

Certain goods and services—**public** or **social goods**—would not be produced at all by the market system because their characteristics are essentially opposite those of private goods. Public goods are *indivisible,* involving such large units that they cannot be sold to individual buyers. Individuals can buy hamburgers, computers, and automobiles through the market, but not Patriot missiles, highways, and air-traffic control.

More importantly, the exclusion principle does *not* apply; there is no effective way of excluding individuals from the benefits of public goods once those goods come into existence. Obtaining the benefits of private goods is predicated upon *purchase;* benefits from public goods accrue to society from the *production* of such goods.

Illustrations The classic public goods example is a lighthouse on a treacherous coast or harbor. The construction of a lighthouse would be economically justified if benefits (fewer shipwrecks) exceeded production costs. But the benefit accruing to each individual user would not justify the purchase of such a large and indivisible product. In any event, once in operation, its warning light is a guide to *all* ships. There is no practical way to exclude certain ships from its benefits. Therefore, why should any ship owner voluntarily pay for the benefits received from the light? The light is there for all to see, and a ship captain cannot be excluded from seeing it if the ship owner chooses not to pay. Economists call this the **free-rider problem;** *people can receive benefits from a good without contributing to its costs.*

Given the inapplicability of the exclusion principle, there is no economic incentive for private enterprises to supply lighthouses. If the services of the lighthouse cannot be priced and sold, it will be unprofitable for private firms to devote resources to lighthouses. Here is a service which yields substantial benefits but for which the market would allocate no resources. National defense, flood-control, public health, and insect-abatement programs are other public goods. If society is to enjoy such goods and services, they must be provided by the public sector and financed by compulsory charges in the form of taxes.

Large Spillover Benefits While the inapplicability of the exclusion principle sets off public from private goods, many other goods and services are provided by government even though the exclusion principle *could* be applied. Such goods and services as education, streets and highways, police and fire protection, libraries and museums, preventive medicine, and sewage disposal could be subject to the exclusion principle, that is, they could be priced and provided by private producers through the market system. But, as noted earlier, these are all services with substantial spillover benefits and would be underproduced by the market system. Therefore, government undertakes or sponsors their provision to avoid the underallocation of resources which would otherwise occur. Such goods and services are sometimes called *quasi-public goods.* One can understand the long-standing controversies surrounding the status of medical care and housing. Are these private goods to be provided through the market system, or are they quasi-public goods to be provided by government?

Allocating Resources to Public Goods

Given that the price system would fail to allocate resources for public goods and would underallocate resources for quasi-public goods, what is the mechanism by which such goods get produced?

Public goods are purchased through the government on the basis of group, or collective, choices, in contrast to private goods, which are purchased from private enterprises on the basis of individual choices. The types and quantities of the various public goods produced are determined in a democracy by political means, that is, by voting. The quantities of the various public goods consumed are a matter of public policy.[2] These group decisions, made in the political arena, supplement the choices of households and businesses in answering the Five Fundamental Questions.

Given these group decisions, precisely how are resources reallocated from production of private goods to production of public goods? In a full-employment economy, government must free resources from private employment to make them available for production of public goods. The apparent means of releasing resources from private uses is to reduce private demand for them. This is accomplished by levying taxes on businesses and households, diverting some of their incomes—some of their potential purchasing power—out of the income-expenditure streams. With lower incomes, businesses and households must curtail their investment and consumption spending. *Taxes diminish private demand for goods and services, and this decrease in turn prompts a drop in the private demand for resources.* By diverting purchasing power from private spenders to government, taxes free resources from private uses.

Government expenditure of the tax proceeds can then reabsorb these resources in the provision of public goods and services. Corporation and personal income taxes release resources from production of investment goods—printing presses, boxcars, warehouses—and consumer goods—food, clothing, and television sets. Government expenditures can reabsorb these resources in production of guided missiles, military aircraft, and new schools and highways. Government purposely reallocates resources to bring about significant changes in the composition of the economy's total output.

Stabilization

Historically, the most recent function of government is that of stabilizing the economy—assisting the private economy to achieve both the full employment of resources and a stable price level. At this point we will only outline (rather than fully explain) the stabilization function of government.

The level of output depends directly on total or aggregate expenditures. A high level of total spending means it will be profitable for industries to produce large outputs. This condition, in turn, will necessitate that both property and human resources be employed at high levels. But aggregate spending may either fall short of, or exceed, that particular level which will provide for full employment and price stability. Two possibilities, unemployment or inflation, may then occur.

1 Unemployment The level of total spending in the private sector may be too low for full employment. Thus, the government may choose to augment private spending so that total spending—private *and* public—will be sufficient to generate full employment. Government can do this by using the same techniques—government spending and taxes—as it uses to reallocate resources to production of public goods. Specifically, government might increase its own spending on public goods and services on the one hand, and reduce taxes to stimulate private spending on the other.[3]

2 Inflation The second possibility is that the economy may attempt to spend in excess of its productive capacity. If aggregate spending exceeds the full-employment output, the excess spending will pull up the price level. Excessive aggregate spending is inflationary. Government's obligation here is to eliminate the excess spending. It can do this primarily by cutting its own expenditures and by raising taxes to curtail private spending.

[2]There are differences between *dollar voting,* which dictates ouput in the private sector of the economy, and *political voting,* which determines ouput in the public sector. The rich person has many more votes to cast in the private sector than does the poor person. In the public sector, each—at least in theory—has an equal say. Furthermore, the children who cast their votes for bubble gum and comic books in the private sector are banned by virtue of their age from the registering of social choices.

[3]In macroeconomics we learn that government can also use monetary policy—changes in the nation's money supply and interest rates—to help achieve economic stability.

QUICK REVIEW 6-1

- ***Government enhances the operation of the market system by providing an appropriate legal foundation and promoting competition.***
- ***Transfer payments, direct market intervention, and the tax system are ways government can lessen income inequality.***
- ***Government can correct the overallocation of resources associated with spillover costs through legislation or specific taxes; the underallocation of resources associated with spillover benefits can be offset by government subsidies.***
- ***Government must provide public goods because they are indivisible and the exclusion principle does not apply to them.***
- ***Government spending and tax revenues can be manipulated to stabilize the economy.***

THE CIRCULAR FLOW REVISITED

Government is thoroughly integrated into the real and monetary flows which comprise our economy. It is informative to reexamine the redistributional, allocative, and stabilization functions of government in terms of Chapter 3's circular flow model. In Figure 6-3 flows (1) through (4) restate Figure 3-2. Flows (1) and (2) show business expenditures for the resources provided by households. These expenditures are costs to businesses, but represent wage, rent, interest, and profit income to households. Flows (3) and (4) portray households making consumer expenditures for the goods and services produced by businesses.

Now consider the numerous modifications which stem from the addition of government. Flows (5)

FIGURE 6-3 The circular flow and the public sector

Government expenditures, taxes, and transfer payments affect the distribution of income, the allocation of resources, and the level of economic activity.

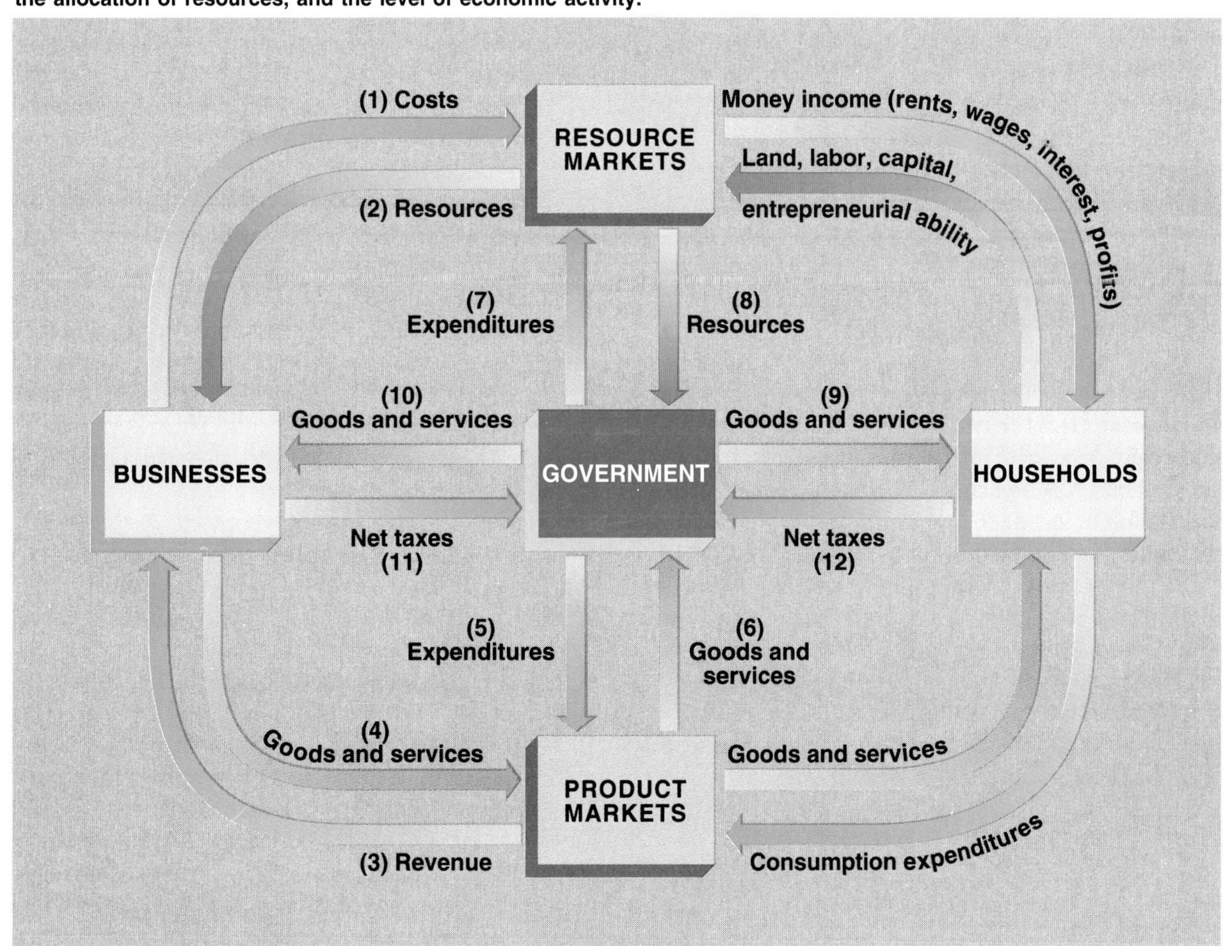

through (8) tell us that government makes purchases in both product and resource markets. Specifically, flows (5) and (6) represent government purchasing such things as paper clips, computers, and military hardware from private businesses. Flows (7) and (8) reflect government purchases of resources. The Federal government employs and pays salaries to members of Congress, the armed forces, Justice Department lawyers, various bureaucrats, and so on. State and local governments hire teachers, bus drivers, police, and firefighters. The Federal government might lease or purchase land to expand a military base; a city may buy land to build a new elementary school.

Government then provides public goods and services to both households and businesses as shown by flows (9) and (10). The financing of public goods and services requires tax payments by businesses and households as reflected in flows (11) and (12). We have labeled these flows as *net* taxes to acknowledge that they also include "taxes in reverse" in the form of transfer payments to households and subsidies to businesses. Thus, flow (11) entails not merely corporate income, sales, and excise taxes flowing from businesses to government, but also various subsidies to farmers, shipbuilders, and some airlines.[4] Similarly, government also collects taxes (personal income taxes, payroll taxes) directly from households and makes available transfer payments, for example, welfare payments and social security benefits as shown by flow (12).

Our expanded circular flow model clearly shows us how government can alter the distribution of income, reallocate resources, and change the level of economic activity. The structure of taxes and transfer payments can have a significant impact on income distribution. In flow (12) a tax structure which draws tax revenues primarily from well-to-do households combined with a system of transfer payments to low-income households will result in greater equality in the distribution of income.

Flows (6) and (8) imply an allocation of resources which differs from that of a purely private economy. Government buys goods and labor services which differ from those purchased by households.

Finally, all governmental flows suggest means by which government might attempt to stabilize the economy. If the economy was experiencing unemployment, an increase in government spending with taxes and transfers held constant would increase aggregate spending, output, and employment. Similarly, given the level of government expenditures, a decline in taxes or an increase in transfer payments would increase spendable incomes and boost private spending. Conversely, with inflation the opposite government policies would be in order: reduced government spending, increased taxes, and reduced transfers.

[4]Most business subsidies are "concealed" in the form of low-interest loans, loan guarantees, tax concessions, or the public provision of facilities at prices less than costs.

GOVERNMENT FINANCE

How large is the public sector? What are the main economic programs of Federal, state, and local governments? How are these programs financed?

Government Growth: Purchases and Transfers

We can get a general impression of the size and growth of government's economic role by examining government purchases of goods and services and government transfer payments. The distinction between these two kinds of outlays is significant.

1 **Government purchases** are "exhaustive" in that they directly absorb or employ resources and the resulting production is part of the domestic output. For example, the purchase of a missile absorbs the labor of physicists and engineers along with steel, explosives, and a host of other inputs.

2 **Transfer payments** are "nonexhaustive" in that they do not directly absorb resources or account for production. Social security benefits, welfare payments, veterans' benefits, and unemployment compensation are examples of transfer payments. Their key characteristic is that recipients make no current contribution to output in return for these payments.

Figure 6-4 compares *government purchases* of goods and services with the domestic output, that is, with the total amount of goods and services produced in the economy for the 1929–1991 period. Total government purchases rose significantly relative to domestic output over the 1929–1940 period, but then skyrocketed during World War II. However, since the early 1950s government spending for goods and services has hovered around 20 percent of the domestic output. Of course, the domestic output has expanded dramatically over the 1929–1991 period so that the *absolute* volume of government spending has increased greatly. Government expenditures on goods and services to-

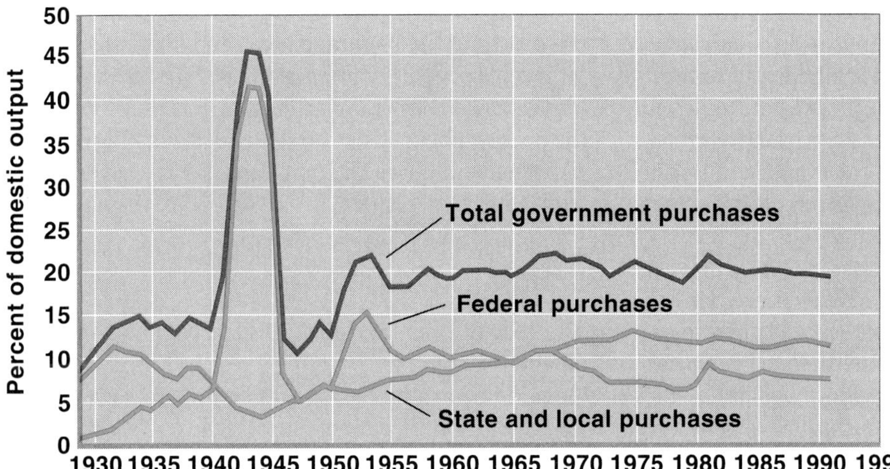

FIGURE 6-4 Government purchases as a percent of domestic output, 1929–1991

Government purchases rose relative to domestic output over the 1929–1940 period, only to increase dramatically during World War II. Since the early 1950s total government purchases have been approximately 20 percent of the domestic output.

taled $1087 billion in 1991 as compared to only $9 billion in 1929!

When transfer payments are added, our impression of government's role and its growth change considerably. Transfers have grown rapidly since the 1960s, rising from $29 billion or 5 percent of the domestic output in 1960, to $759 billion or 13 percent of the domestic output in 1991. The net result is that tax revenues required to finance both government purchases *and* transfers are equal to approximately one-third of the domestic output. In 1990 an average tax bill of about $13,000 was imposed on every family in the United States. In 1991 the average taxpayer spent about 2 hours and 49 minutes of each 8-hour workday to pay taxes. However, the size of our public sector is small compared to other industrialized countries. Taxes in Sweden, Norway, France, Great Britain, and West Germany are 51, 46, 45, 39, and 37 percent of domestic output respectively, compared to about 30 percent in the United States.

Some Causes

Let's now consider some specific factors which account for the historical growth and present size of government spending and taxes.

1 War and Defense Hot and cold wars have tended to sustain Federal expenditures at high levels for the past four decades. War, national defense, and military-space research are among the major causes of the growth of government spending and taxation which has occurred since 1940.

2 Population Growth There are over twice as many Americans today as there were a scant sixty years ago. This means there are more people for whom public goods and services must be provided. Even with a constant level of government spending per person, total government spending would have increased dramatically in recent decades.

3 Urbanization and the Demand for Public Goods The increasing urbanization of our economy has necessitated massive expenditures on streets, public transportation facilities, police and fire protection, and sewers. Also, the public has demanded more and better public goods and services to "match" the rising standard of living provided by the private sector of the economy. We want bigger and better highways to accommodate more and better automobiles. We seek more and better educational facilities to upgrade the labor force for the more demanding jobs of private industry.

4 Environmental Quality Population growth and urbanization have contributed to serious and well-publicized problems of environmental quality. Society has become highly aware that the production and consumption of vast quantities of goods can lead to serious external or spillover costs in air, water, and land pollution. Government has inherited a central role in coping with these environmental problems.

5 Egalitarianism Since the mid-1960s there has occurred a sharp expansion of programs designed to alleviate poverty and reduce income inequality. Social security, unemployment compensation, welfare, Medicare, food stamps, and public housing are examples. These programs accounted for about 3 percent of domestic output twenty years ago. They now require approximately 13 percent of domestic output.

FEDERAL FINANCE

Now we will disaggregate the public sector into Federal, state, and local units of government to compare their expenditures and taxes. Table 6-1 tells the story for the Federal government.

Federal Expenditures

Although Table 6-1 reveals a wide variety of Federal expenditures, three important areas of spending stand out: (1) income security, (2) national defense, and (3) interest on the public debt. The *income security* category reflects the myriad income-maintenance programs for the aged, the disabled, the unemployed, the handicapped, the medically indigent, and families with no breadwinner. *National defense* constitutes about one-fourth of the Federal budget and underscores the high costs of military preparedness. *Interest on the public debt* has grown dramatically in recent years because the public debt itself has grown. The remaining categories of expenditures listed in Table 6-1 are largely self-explanatory.

Federal Receipts

The receipts side of Table 6-1 clearly shows that the personal income tax, payroll taxes, and the corporate income tax are the basic revenue getters, accounting for 45, 37, and 9 cents of each dollar collected.

Personal Income Tax The **personal income tax** is the kingpin of our national tax system and merits special comment. This tax is levied on *taxable income,* that is, on the incomes of households and unincorporated businesses after certain exemptions ($2,150 for each household member) and deductions (business expenses, charitable contributions, home mortgage interest payments, certain state and local taxes) are taken into account.

The Federal personal income tax is a *progressive tax,* that is, people with higher incomes pay a larger percentage of their income as taxes than do persons with lower incomes. The progressivity is achieved through a system of higher tax rates which apply to successive layers or brackets of income.

Columns 1 and 2 of Table 6-2 portray the mechanics of the income tax for a married couple filing a joint return. Note that the 15 percent rate applies to all taxable income up to $34,000, at which point any *additional* income up to $82,150 is taxable at the 28 percent rate.

TABLE 6-1 The Federal budget, 1990

Tax receipts	*Billions of dollars*	*Percent of total*	*Expenditures*	*Billions of dollars*	*Percent of total*
Personal income tax	**$ 467**	**45**	**Income security**	**$ 494**	**39**
Payroll taxes	**380**	**37**	**National defense**	**299**	**24**
Corporate income taxes	**94**	**9**	**Interest on public debt**	**184**	**15**
Excise taxes	**35**	**3**	**Commerce, housing, and transportation**	**97**	**8**
Customs duties	**17**	**2**	**Education, training, and health**	**96**	**8**
Estate and gift taxes	**12**	**1**	**Agriculture, natural resources, and environment**	**46**	**4**
All other	**26**	**3**	**All other (net)**	**36**	**3**
Total receipts	**$1031**	**100**	**Total expenditures**	**$1252**	**100**

Source: Economic Report of the President. Because of rounding, figures may not add up to totals.

TABLE 6-2 **Federal personal income tax rates, 1991***

(1) Total taxable income	(2) Marginal tax rate (4) ÷ (3)	(3) Change in income Δ(1)	(4) Change in taxes Δ(5)	(5) Total tax	(6) Average Tax rate (5) ÷ (1)
$ 0	0%	—	—	—	—
34,000	15	$34,000	$ 5,100	$ 5,100	15%
82,150	28	48,150	13,482	18,582	22.6
Over 82,150	31	—	—	—	—

*Data are for a married couple filing a joint return.

Any additional taxable income above $82,150 is taxed at 31 percent.

The tax rates shown in column 2 of Table 6-2 are marginal tax rates. A **marginal tax rate** is the tax paid on additional or incremental income. By definition, it is the *increase* in taxes paid (column 4) divided by the *increase* in income (column 3). Thus, if our couple's taxable income increased from $0 to $34,000 the increase in taxes paid would be $5,100 (=.15 × $34,000) as shown in column 4. If the couple's taxable income rose by an additional $48,150 (column 3)—that is, from $34,000 to $82,150—a higher marginal tax rate of 28 percent would apply so that an additional tax of $13,482 (=.28 × $48,150) would have to be paid (column 4).

The marginal tax rates of column 2 overstate the personal income tax bite because the rising rates apply only to income falling within each successive tax bracket. To get a better picture of the tax burden one must consider average tax rates. The **average tax rate** is the total tax paid divided by total taxable income. In column 6 of Table 6-2 for the $0 to $34,000 tax bracket the average tax rate is $5,100 (column 4) divided by $34,000 (column 1) or 15 percent, the same as the marginal tax rate. But the couple earning $82,150 does *not* pay 28 percent of its income as taxes as the marginal tax rate would suggest. Rather, its average tax rate is only about 22.6 percent (=$18,582 ÷ $82,150). The reason is that the first $34,000 of income it taxed at 15 percent and only the next $48,150 is subject to the 28 percent rate. You should calculate the average tax rate for a couple earning $182,500. What we observe here is that, if the marginal tax rate is higher than the average tax rate, the average tax rate will rise.[5]

By definition, a tax whose average tax rate rises as income increases is called a *progressive tax.* Such a tax claims both a larger absolute amount and a larger proportion of income as income rises. Thus we can say that our current personal income tax is mildly progressive.

[5]The arithmetic is the same as what you may have encountered in school. You must get a score on an additional or "marginal" examination higher than your existing average grade to pull your average up!

Payroll Taxes Social security contributions, or **payroll taxes,** are the premiums paid on the compulsory insurance plans—old age insurance and Medicare—provided for by existing social security legislation. These taxes are paid by both employers and employees. Improvements in, and extensions of, our social security programs, plus growth of the labor force, have resulted in very significant increases in payroll taxes in recent years. In 1992 employees and employers each paid a tax of 7.65 percent on the first $55,500 of an employee's annual earnings.

Corporate Income Tax The Federal government also taxes corporate income. This **corporate income tax** is levied on a corporation's profits—the difference between its total revenue and its total expenses. The basic rate is 34 percent, which applies to annual profits over $335,000. A firm with profits of $1,335,000 would pay corporate income taxes of $340,000. Firms making annual profits less than $335,000 are taxed at lower rates.

Excise Taxes Commodity or consumption taxes may take the form of **sales taxes** or **excise taxes.** The difference between the two is basically one of coverage. Sales taxes fall on a wide range of products, whereas excises are taxes on a small, select list of commodities. As Table 6-1 suggests, the Federal government collects excise taxes on such commodities as alcoholic beverages, tobacco, and gasoline. Beginning in 1991 a new excise tax applies to certain luxury goods. A 10 percent tax is now levied on that portion of the price above $30,000 for cars, $100,000 for boats, $250,000 for aircraft, and $10,000 for furs and jewelry. If your rich uncle were to buy you a $60,000 Mercedes for graduation, he would have to pay a tax of $3,000. The Federal government does *not* levy a general sales tax; sales taxes are the bread and butter of most state governments.

TABLE 6-3 Consolidated budget of all state governments, 1990

Tax receipts	*Billions of dollars*	*Percent of total*	*Expenditures*	*Billions of dollars*	*Percent of total*
Sales, excise, and gross receipts taxes	$147	49	Public welfare	$ 83	25
Personal income taxes	96	32	Education	75	23
Corporate income taxes	22	7	Highways	44	13
Property taxes	6	2	Health and hospitals	42	13
Death and gift taxes	4	1	Public safety	30	9
Licenses, permits, and others	25	8	All others	59	18
Total receipts	$300	100	Total expenditures	$333	100

Source: Bureau of the Census, *State Government Finances in 1990.* Because of rounding, figures may not add up to totals.

STATE AND LOCAL FINANCE

While the Federal government finances itself largely through personal and corporate income taxation and payroll taxes, state and local governments rely heavily on sales and property taxes, respectively. Although there is considerable overlap in the types of expenditures made by the three levels of government, public welfare is the main outlay of state governments, followed closely by education. For local governments, education is the dominant expenditure.

State Expenditures and Receipts

Note in Table 6-3 that the basic sources of tax revenue at the state level are sales and excise taxes, which account for about 49 percent of all state tax revenues. State personal income taxes, which entail much more modest rates than those of the Federal government, are the second most important source of revenue. Taxes on corporate income, property, inheritances, and licenses and permits constitute the remainder of state tax revenue.

On the expenditure side, the major outlays of state governments are for (1) public welfare, (2) education, (3) highway maintenance and construction, and (4) health and hospitals.

Note that the budget statement shown in Table 6-3 contains aggregated data, telling us little about the finances of individual states. States vary tremendously in the types of taxes employed. Thus, although personal income taxes are a major source of revenue for all state governments combined, four states do not use the personal income tax. Furthermore, great variations in the size of tax receipts and disbursements exist among the states.

Local Expenditures and Receipts

The receipts and expenditures shown in Table 6-4 are for all units of local government, including counties, municipalities, townships, and school districts. One major source of revenue and a single basic use of reve-

TABLE 6-4 Consolidated budget of all local governments, 1990

Tax receipts	*Billions of dollars*	*Percent of total*	*Expenditures*	*Billions of dollars*	*Percent of total*
Property taxes	$150	75	Education	$217	43
Sales and excises	31	15	Welfare, health, and hospitals	66	13
Personal and corporate income taxes	11	6	Environment and housing	56	11
Licenses, permits, and others	9	4	Public safety	50	10
			Transportation	34	7
			All others	81	16
Total receipts	$201	100	Total expenditures	$504	100

Source: Bureau of the Census, *Government Finances in 1989–1990.* Because of rounding, figures may not add up to totals.

LAST WORD

LOTTERIES: FACTS AND CONTROVERSIES

State lotteries, which began in 1963, are a potentially important source of public revenue. What are the characteristics of lotteries? And what are the arguments for and against this means of enhancing state revenues?

In 1990 some 33 states and the District of Columbia had lotteries which sold over $20 billion worth of tickets. The average lottery returns about 50 percent of its gross revenues to ticket purchasers as prizes and 40 percent goes to the state treasury. The remaining 10 percent is for designing and promoting the lottery and for commissions to retail outlets which sell tickets. Although states sponsoring lotteries currently obtain only 3 to 4 percent of their total revenues in this way, per capita sales of lottery tickets increased by 12 percent per year over the 1975–1989 period.

Lotteries have been controversial. Critics make the following arguments. First, the 40 percent of gross revenues from lotteries which goes to the state governments is in effect a 40 percent tax on ticket purchases. This tax is higher than the taxes on cigarettes and liquor. Furthermore, research indicates that the "lottery tax" is highly regressive in that there is little relationship between ticket purchases and household incomes. This means that low-income families spend a larger proportion of their incomes on lotteries than do high-income families. The 10 percent of the adults who patronize lotteries most heavily account for one-half of total ticket sales. Second, critics argue that it is ethically wrong for the state to sponsor gambling. Gambling is generally regarded as immoral and, in other forms, is illegal in most states. It is also held that lotteries may whet the appetite for gambling and generate compulsive gamblers who will impoverish themselves and their families. Third, lotteries may be sending the message that luck and fate—rather than education, hard work, and saving and investing—are the route to success and wealth in America.

But there are counterarguments. It is contended, in the first place, that lottery revenue should not be regarded as a tax. Tax collections are compulsory and involve coercion; the purchase of a lottery ticket is voluntary and entails free consumer choice. A second and related argument is that within wide limits it is not appropriate to make moral judgments about how people should spend their incomes. Individuals allegedly achieve the maximum satisfaction from their incomes by spending without interference. If some people derive satisfaction from participating in lotteries, they should be free to do so. Third, faced with tax revenue shortfalls and intense pressure not to raise taxes, lotteries are a relatively painless source of revenue to finance important state services such as education and welfare programs. Finally, lotteries are competitive with illegal gambling and thereby may be socially beneficial in curtailing the power of organized crime.

Two observations seem certain at the moment. One is that total lottery revenue will continue to increase. More and more states are establishing lotteries and people seem to enjoy gambling, particularly when they feel their losses are being used for "good causes." The other point is that this source of revenue will remain controversial.

Source: Based on Charles T. Clotfelter and Philip J. Cook, "On the Economics of State Lotteries," *Journal of Economic Perspectives*, Fall, 1990, pp. 105–119.

---

nue stand out: The bulk of the revenue received by local government comes from **property taxes** and most local revenue is spent for education. Other, less important sources of funds and types of disbursements are self-explanatory.

The gaping deficit shown in Table 6-4 is largely removed when nontax resources of income are taken into account: In 1990 the tax revenues of local governments were supplemented by some $209 billion in intergovernmental grants from Federal and state governments. Furthermore, local governments received an additional $52 billion as proprietary income, that is, as revenue from government-owned hospitals and utilities. Finally, lotteries—the subject of this chapter's Last Word—are a growing source of nontax revenue for two-thirds of the states.

QUICK REVIEW 6-2

- ***Government purchases are about 20 percent of the domestic output; the addition of transfers increases government spending to almost one-third of domestic output.***
- ***Income security and national defense are the main Federal expenditures; personal income, payroll, and corporate income taxes are the primary sources of revenue.***
- ***States rely primarily on sales and excise taxes for revenue; their spending is largely for education, welfare, and health.***
- ***Education is the dominant expenditure for local governments and most of their revenue is derived from property taxes.***

Fiscal Federalism

Historically, the tax collections of both state and local governments have fallen substantially short of their expenditures. These revenue shortfalls are largely filled by Federal transfers or grants. It is not uncommon for 15 to 20 percent of all revenue received by state and local governments to come from the Federal government. In addition to Federal grants to state and local governments, the states also make grants to local governmental units. This system of intergovernmental transfers is called **fiscal federalism.** Concern over large and persistent Federal budget deficits has precipitated declines in Federal grants in recent years, causing state and local governments to increase tax rates, impose new taxes, and restrain expenditures.

CHAPTER SUMMARY

1 Government enhances the operation of the market system by **a** providing an appropriate legal and social framework, and **b** acting to maintain competition.

2 Government alters the distribution of income by direct market intervention and through the tax-transfer system.

3 Spillovers or externalities cause the equilibrium output of certain goods to vary from the optimal output. Spillover costs result in an overallocation of resources which can be corrected by legislation or specific taxes. Spillover benefits are accompanied by an underallocation of resources which can be corrected by subsidies to either consumers or producers.

4 Government must provide public goods because such goods are indivisible and entail benefits from which nonpaying consumers cannot be excluded.

5 The manipulation of taxes and its expenditures is one basic means by which government can reduce unemployment and inflation.

6 The circular flow model helps us envision how government performs its redistributional, allocative, and stabilizing functions.

7 Although the absolute level of total government purchases of goods and services has increased greatly, such purchases have been about 20 percent of the domestic output in the entire post-World War II period.

8 Government purchases are exhaustive or resource-absorbing; transfer payments are not. Government purchases and transfers combined amount to about one-third of the domestic output.

9 Wars and national defense, population growth, urbanization, environmental problems, and egalitarianism have been among the more important causes of the historical growth of the public sector.

10 The main categories of Federal spending are for income security, national defense, and interest on the public debt; revenues come primarily from personal income, payroll, and corporate income taxes.

11 The primary sources of revenue for the states are sales and excise taxes; public welfare, education, highways, and health and hospitals are the major state expenditures.

12 At the local level, most revenue comes from the property tax, and education is the most important expenditure.

13 Under our system of fiscal federalism, state and local tax revenues are supplemented by sizable revenue grants from the Federal government.

TERMS AND CONCEPTS

monopoly
spillover costs and spillover benefits
exclusion principle
public or social goods
free-rider problem
government purchases
transfer payments
personal income tax
marginal and average tax rates
payroll taxes
corporate income tax
sales and excise taxes
property taxes
fiscal federalism

QUESTIONS AND STUDY SUGGESTIONS

1 Carefully evaluate this statement: "The public, as a general rule . . . gets less production in return for a dollar spent by government than from a dollar spent by private enterprise."

2 Enumerate and briefly discuss the main economic functions of government.

3 Explain why, in the absence of spillovers, equilibrium and optimal outputs are identical in competitive markets. What divergences arise between equilibrium and optimal output when a spillover costs and b spillover benefits are present? How might government correct for these discrepancies? "The presence of spillover costs suggests underallocation of resources to that product and the need for governmental subsidies." Do you agree? Explain how zoning and seat belt laws might be used to deal with a problem of spillover costs.

4 UCLA researchers have concluded that injuries caused by firearms cost about $429 million a year in hospital expenses alone. Because the majority of those shot are poor and without insurance, almost 86 percent of hospital costs must be borne by taxpayers. Use your understanding of externalities to recommend appropriate policies.

5 What are the basic characteristics of public goods? Explain the significance of the exclusion principle. By what means does government provide public goods?

6 Use your understanding of the characteristics of private and public goods to determine whether the following should be produced through the market system or provided by government: a bread; b street lighting; c bridges; d parks; e swimming pools; f medical care; g mail delivery; h housing; i air traffic control; j libraries.

7 Explain how government might manipulate its expenditures and tax revenues to reduce a unemployment and b the rate of inflation.

8 "Most governmental actions simultaneously affect the distribution of income, the allocation of resources, and the levels of unemployment and prices." Use the circular flow model to confirm this assertion for each of the following: a the construction of a new high school in Blackhawk County; b a 2 percent reduction in the corporate income tax; c an expansion of preschool programs for disadvantaged children; d a $50 billion increase in spending for space research; e the levying of a tax on air polluters; and f a $1 increase in the minimum wage.

9 Draw a production possibilities curve with public goods on the vertical axis and private goods on the horizontal axis. Assuming the economy is initially operating on the curve, indicate the means by which the production of public goods might be increased. How might the output of public goods be increased if the economy is initially functioning at a point inside the curve?

10 Describe and account for the historical growth of the public sector of the economy. In your response carefully distinguish between government purchases and transfer payments.

11 What is the most important source of revenue and the major type of expenditure at the Federal level? At the state level? At the local level?

12 Briefly describe the mechanics of the Federal personal income tax. Use the concepts of marginal and average tax rates to explain why it is a progressive tax.

13 Assume that the structure of a personal income tax is such that you would pay a tax of $2000 if your taxable income was $16,000 and a tax of $3000 if your taxable income was $20,000. What is the average tax rate at the $16,000 and $20,000 levels of taxable income? What marginal tax rate applies to taxable income which falls between $16,000 and $20,000? Is this tax progressive? Explain.

14 Calculate the average and marginal tax rates for the following table. Is this tax progressive? How do you know? What generalization can you offer concerning the relationship between marginal and average tax rates?

Income	*Tax*	*Average tax rate*	*Marginal tax rate*
$ 0	$ 0	______	
100	10	______	______
200	30	______	______
300	60	______	______
400	100	______	______
500	150	______	______

15 The Federal government recently increased its excise taxes on gasoline, alcoholic beverages, and tobacco. What effect might these increases have on the revenues which states receive from their excises on these same products?

16 What is "fiscal federalism"? Why does it exist?

Microeconomics of Product and Resource Markets

Demand and Supply: Elasticities and Applications

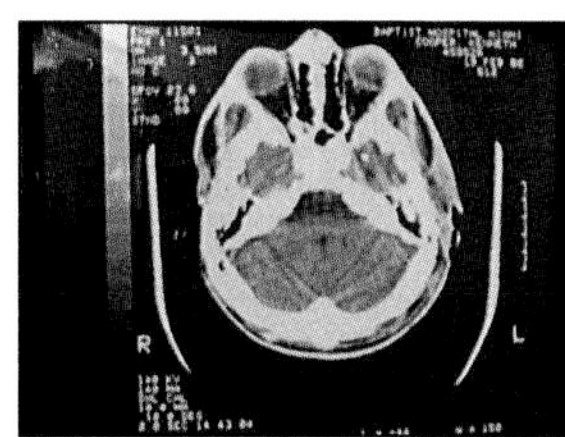

Scarce resources and unlimited wants are the foundation of economic science. The efficient management of scarce resources is a major goal of our economic system. There are two major facets to achieving efficient resource use. The first centers on the full employment of available resources.

The second aspect of the economizing problem—the one to which we now turn—deals with the efficient use of employed resources. This is the task we undertake in Part 2.

A major characteristic of capitalistic economies is their heavy reliance on the market system for allocating resources. Major topics of discussion, then, are individual prices and the market system. Specifically, our goal in this and ensuing chapters is to acquire an understanding of the operation and relative efficiency of the *market* or *price system* in allocating resources within the framework of capitalism. In achieving this primary goal, we will analyze *individual* prices under a variety of contrasting market arrangements.

In Chapter 4 we examined demand and supply analysis. If your recollection of that material is hazy, you might reread that chapter or at least examine the chapter summary. In this chapter we will extend our understanding of demand and supply. Specifically, this chapter's tasks are threefold.

1 We will examine the concept of price elasticity as it applies to both demand and supply.

2 We will generalize the elasticity concept by introducing both cross and income elasticity of demand.

3 Finally, as an application of demand and supply analysis, we will examine the potential effects of legally fixed prices on individual markets.

PRICE ELASTICITY OF DEMAND

The law of demand means consumers will respond to a price decline by buying more of a product. But the degree of consumer responsiveness to a price change may vary considerably from product to product. We also will find that consumer responsiveness typically varies substantially between different price ranges for the same product.

The responsiveness, or sensitivity, of consumers to a change in the price of a product is measured by the concept of **price elasticity of demand.** Demand for some products is such that consumers are relatively responsive to price changes; modest price changes lead to very considerable changes in the quantity purchased. The demand for such products is said to be *relatively elastic* or simply *elastic.* For other products, consumers are relatively unresponsive to price changes; substantial price changes result only in modest changes in the amount purchased. In such cases demand is *relatively inelastic* or simply *inelastic.*

The Price Elasticity Formula

Economists measure the degree of elasticity or inelasticity by the coefficient E_d in this price elasticity formula:

$$E_d = \frac{\text{percentage change in quantity demanded of product X}}{\text{percentage change in price of product X}}$$

These *percentage* changes are calculated by dividing the change in price by the original price and the consequent change in quantity demanded by the original quantity demanded. Thus, our formula restated:

$$E_d = \frac{\text{change in quantity demanded of X}}{\text{original quantity demanded of X}} \div \frac{\text{change in price of X}}{\text{original price of X}}$$

Use of Percentages Why use percentages rather than absolute amounts in measuring consumer responsiveness? The answer is twofold.

1 If we use absolute changes, our impression of buyer responsiveness will be arbitrarily affected by the choice of units. To illustrate: If the price of product X falls from $3 to $2 and consumers increase their purchases from 60 to 100 pounds, it appears that consumers are quite sensitive to price changes and therefore that demand is elastic. After all, a price change of "one" has caused a change in the amount demanded of "forty." But by changing the monetary unit from dollars to pennies (why not?), we find a price change of "one hundred" causes a quantity change of "forty," giving the impression of inelasticity. Using percentage changes avoids this problem. The given price decline is 33 percent whether measured in terms of dollars ($1/$3) or pennies (100¢/300¢).

2 The other reason for using percentages is that we can more meaningfully compare consumer responsiveness to changes in the prices of different products. It makes little sense to compare the effects on quantity demanded of a $1 increase in the price of a $10,000 auto with a $1 increase in the price of a $1 can of Coors. Here the price of the auto is rising by .0001 percent while the beer price is up by 100 percent! If we increased the price of both products by 1 percent—$100 for the car and 1¢ for the can—we would obtain a sensible comparison of consumer sensitivity to the price changes.

Ignore Minus Sign We know from the downsloping demand curve that price and quantity demanded are inversely related. This means that the price elasticity coefficient of demand will always yield a *negative* number. For example, if price declines, then quantity demanded will increase. This means that the numerator in our formula will be positive and the denominator negative, yielding a negative coefficient. Conversely, for an increase in price, the numerator will be negative but the denominator positive, again yielding a negative coefficient.

Economists usually ignore the minus sign and simply present the *absolute value* of the elasticity coefficient to avoid an ambiguity which might otherwise arise. It can be confusing to say that an elasticity coefficient of −4 is greater than one of −2; this possible confusion is avoided when we say a coefficient of 4 indicates greater elasticity than one of 2. Hence, in what follows we ignore the minus sign in the coefficient of price elasticity of demand and merely show the absolute value. Incidentally, the noted ambiguity does not arise with supply because price and quantity are positively related.

Interpretations Now let's interpret our formula. Demand is **elastic** if a given percentage change in price results in a *larger* percentage change in quantity demanded. Example: If a 2 percent decline in price results in a 4 percent increase in quantity demanded, demand is elastic. In such cases where demand is elastic, the elasticity coefficient will be greater than 1; in this case it will be 2.

If a given percentage change in price is accompanied by a relatively smaller change in quantity demanded, demand is **inelastic.** Illustration: If a 3 percent decline in price leads to only a 1 percent increase in amount demanded, demand is inelastic. Specifically, the elasticity coefficient is .33 in this instance. It is apparent that the elasticity coefficient will always be less than 1 when demand is inelastic.

The borderline case separating elastic and inelastic demands occurs where a percentage change in price and the accompanying percentage change in quantity demanded are equal. For example, a 1 percent drop in price causes a 1 percent increase in amount sold. This special case is termed **unit elasticity,** because the elasticity coefficient is exactly 1, or unity.

When economists say demand is "inelastic," they do not mean consumers are completely unresponsive to a price change. The term **perfectly inelastic** demand refers to the extreme situation where a price change results in no change whatsoever in the quantity demanded. Approximate examples: an acute diabetic's demand for insulin or an addict's demand for heroin. A demand curve parallel to the vertical axis—such as D_1 in Figure 7-1—shows this graphically. Conversely, when economists say demand is "elastic," they do not mean that consumers are completely responsive to a price change. In the extreme situation, where a small price reduction would cause buyers to increase their purchases from zero to all they could obtain, we say that demand is **perfectly elastic.** A perfectly elastic demand curve is a line parallel to the horizontal axis such as D_2 in Figure 7-1. We will see in Chapter 10 that such a demand curve applies to a firm selling in a purely competitive market.

FIGURE 7-1 Perfectly inelastic and elastic demand

A perfectly inelastic demand curve, D_1, graphs as a line parallel to the vertical axis; a perfectly elastic demand curve, D_2, is drawn parallel to the horizontal axis.

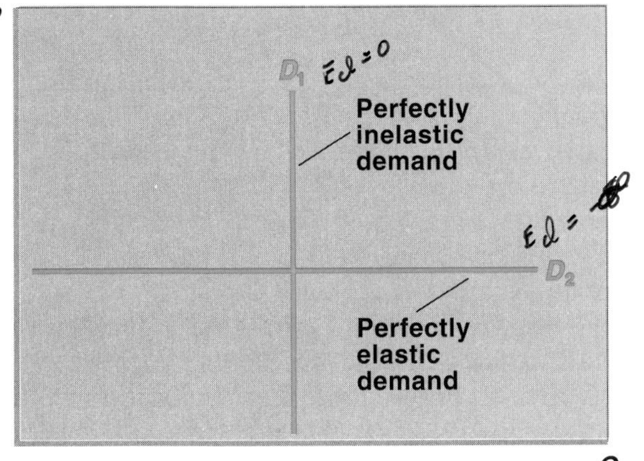

Refinement: Midpoints Formula

The hypothetical demand data shown in Table 7-1 are useful in explaining an annoying problem which arises in applying the price elasticity formula. In calculating the elasticity coefficient for the \$5–\$4 price range, should we use the \$5–4 units price–quantity combination or the \$4–5 units combination as a point of reference in calculating percentage changes in price and quantity which the elasticity formula requires? Our choice will influence the outcome.

Using the \$5–4 unit reference point, the percentage decrease in price is 20 percent and the percentage increase in quantity, 25 percent. Substituting in the formula, the elasticity coefficient is 25/20, or 1.25, indicating that demand is somewhat elastic. But, using the \$4–5 unit reference point, the percentage increase in price is 25 percent and the percentage decline in quantity 20 percent. The elasticity coefficient is therefore 20/25, or 0.80, meaning demand is slightly inelastic. Which is it? Is demand elastic or inelastic?

A workable solution to this problem is achieved by using *averages* of the two prices and two quantities under consideration for reference points. In the \$5–\$4 price-range case, the price reference is \$4.50 and the quantity reference, 4.5 units. The percentage change in price is now about 22 percent and the percentage change in quantity also about 22 percent, giving us an elasticity coefficient of 1. Instead of gauging elasticity at either one of the extremes of this price–quantity range, this solution estimates elasticity at the midpoint of the \$5–\$4 price range. We now can refine our earlier statement of the elasticity formula to read:

$$E_d = \frac{\text{change in quantity}}{\text{sum of quantities}/2} \div \frac{\text{change in price}}{\text{sum of prices}/2}$$

Substituting data for the \$5–\$4 price range, we get

$$E_d = \frac{1}{9/2} \div \frac{1}{9/2} = 1$$

TABLE 7-1 Price elasticity of demand as measured by the elasticity coefficient and the total revenue test *(hypothetical data)*

(1) Total quantity demanded per week	(2) Price per unit	(3) Elasticity coefficient, E_d	(4) Total revenue (1) × (2)	(5) Total revenue test
1	$8		$ 8	
		5.00		Elastic
2	7		14	
		2.60		Elastic
3	6		18	
		1.57		Elastic
4	5		20	
		1.00		Unit elastic
5	4		20	
		0.64		Inelastic
6	3		18	
		0.38		Inelastic
7	2		14	
		0.20		Inelastic
8	1		8	

This indicates that *at* the $4.50–4.5 price–quantity point the price elasticity of demand is unity. Here a 1 percent price change would result in a 1 percent change in quantity demanded.

In column 3 you should verify the elasticity calculations for the $1–$2 and $7–$8 price ranges. The interpretation of the coefficient for the $1–$2 range is that a 1 percent change in price will change quantity demanded by .20 percent. For the $7–$8 range a 1 percent change in price will change quantity demanded by 5 percent.

Graphical Analysis

In Figure 7-2a we have plotted our demand curve from Table 7-1. This portrayal brings two points into focus.

Elasticity and Price Range First, elasticity typically varies over the different price ranges of the same demand schedule or curve. For all straight-line and most other demand curves demand is more elastic in the upper left portion ($5–$8 price range) than in the lower right portion ($4–$1 price range). This is a consequence of the arithmetic properties of the elasticity measure. Specifically, in the upper left portion the percentage change in quantity is large because the original quantity from which the percentage quantity change is derived is small. Similarly, in this portion the percentage change in price is small because the original price from which the percentage price change is calculated is large. The relatively large percentage change in quantity divided by the relatively small change in price yields an elastic demand.

The reverse holds true for the lower right portion of the demand curve. Here the percentage change in quantity is small because the original quantity from which the percentage change is determined is large. Similarly, the percentage change in price is large because the original price from which the relative price change is calculated is small. The small percentage change in quantity divided by the relatively large percentage change in price results in an inelastic demand.

Assignment: Draw two linear demand curves which are parallel to one another. Demonstrate that for any given price change demand is more elastic on the curve closer to the origin.

Elasticity versus Slope The second point is that the graphical appearance, that is, the slope, of a demand curve is *not* a sound basis for judging its elasticity. The catch is that the slope—the flatness or steepness—of a demand curve is based on *absolute* changes in price and quantity, while elasticity involves *relative* or *percentage* changes in price and quantity.

Observe in Figure 7-2a that our demand curve is linear, which by definition means the slope is constant throughout. But we have already demonstrated that such a curve is elastic in its high-price ($8–$5) range and inelastic in its low-price ($4–$1) range.

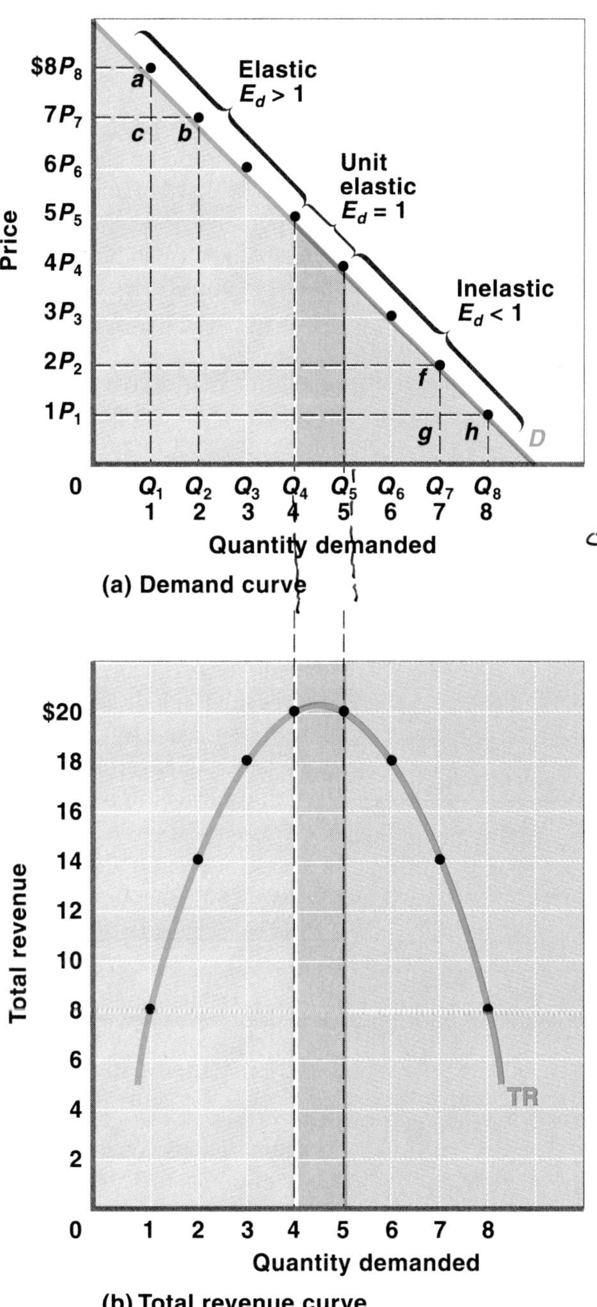

FIGURE 7-2 Price elasticity of demand and its relation to total revenue

As shown in (a), the typical demand curve is elastic in high price ranges and inelastic in low price ranges. In (b) total revenue rises in the elastic range as price is reduced. Where demand elasticity is unity, a change in price will not change total revenue. In this range total revenue is maximized. Price reductions in the inelastic range of the demand curve cause total revenue to fall.

QUICK REVIEW 7-1

- ***Price elasticity of demand measures the extent to which consumers alter the quantity of a product purchased when its price changes.***
- ***Price elasticity of demand is the ratio of the percentage change in quantity demanded to the percentage change in price. The average of the prices and quantities are used in calculating the percentage changes.***
- ***When price elasticity is greater than 1, demand is elastic; when less than 1, it is inelastic. When equal to 1, demand is of unit elasticity.***
- ***Demand is typically elastic in the high-price (low-quantity) range and inelastic in the low-price (high-quantity) range of the demand curve.***

The Total-Revenue Test

Perhaps the easiest way to infer whether demand is elastic or inelastic is to employ the **total-revenue test.** In this test we observe what happens to total revenue—total expenditures from the buyer's viewpoint—when the product price changes.

1 Elastic Demand If demand is *elastic,* a *decrease* in price will result in an *increase* in total revenue. Even though a lesser price is being received per unit, enough additional units are now being sold to more than make up for the lower price. This is shown in Figure 7-2a for the \$8–\$7 price range of our demand curve from Table 7-1. (Ignore Figure 7-2b for the moment.) Total revenue, of course, is price times quantity. Hence, the area shown by the rectangle OP_8aQ_1 is total revenue (\$8) when price is P_8 (\$8) and quantity demanded is Q_1 (1 unit). When price declines to P_7 (\$7), causing the quantity demanded to increase to Q_2 (2 units), total revenue changes to OP_7bQ_2 (\$14), which is obviously larger than OP_8aQ_1. It is larger because the *loss* in revenue from the lower price per unit (area P_7P_8ac) is *less* than the *gain* in revenue due to the larger sales (area Q_1cbQ_2) accompanying the lower price. Specifically, the \$1 price reduction applies to the original 1 unit (Q_1) for a loss of \$1. But the lower price increases sales by 1 unit (Q_1 to Q_2) with a resulting gain in revenue of \$7. Hence, the *net increase* in total revenue is \$6 (=\$7 − \$1).

This reasoning is reversible: If demand is elastic, a price *increase* will cause total revenue to *decrease.* The *gain* in total revenue caused by the higher unit price (area P_7P_8ac) is *less* than the *loss* in revenue associated with the accompanying fall in sales (Q_1cbQ_2). ***If demand is elastic, a price change will cause total revenue to change in the opposite direction.***

2 Inelastic Demand If demand is *inelastic*, a price *decrease* will cause total revenue to *decrease*. The modest increase in sales which occurs will not offset the decline in revenue per unit, and the net result is that total revenue declines. This is true for the \$2–\$1 price range of our demand curve, as shown in Figure 7-2a. Initially, total revenue is OP_2fQ_7 (\$14) when price is P_2 (\$2) and quantity demanded is Q_7 (7 units). If we reduce price to P_1 (\$1), quantity demanded will increase to Q_8 (8 units). Total revenue will change to OP_1hQ_8 (\$8), which is clearly less than OP_2fQ_7. It is smaller because the loss in revenue from the lower unit price (area P_1P_2fg) *is larger* than the *gain* in revenue from the accompanying increase in sales (area Q_7ghQ_8). The \$1 decline in price applies to 7 units (Q_7) with a consequent revenue loss of \$7. The sales increase accompanying this lower price is 1 unit (Q_7 to Q_8) which results in a revenue gain of \$1. The overall result is a *net decrease* in total revenue of \$6 (=\$1 − \$7).

Again, our analysis is reversible: If demand is inelastic, a price increase will increase total revenue. ***If demand is inelastic, a price change will cause total revenue to change in the same direction.***

3 Unit Elasticity In the special case of *unit elasticity*, an increase or decrease in price will leave total revenue unchanged. Loss in revenue from a lower unit price will be exactly offset by the gain in revenue from the accompanying increase in sales. Conversely, the gain in revenue from a higher unit price will be exactly offset by the revenue loss associated with the accompanying decline in the amount demanded.

In Figure 7-2a we find that at the \$5 price 4 units will be sold to yield total revenue of \$20. At \$4 a total of 5 units will be sold, again resulting in \$20 of total revenue. The \$1 price reduction causes the loss of \$4 in revenue on the 4 units that could have been sold for \$5 each. This is exactly offset by a \$4 revenue gain which results from the sale of 1 more unit at the lower \$4 price.

Graphical Portrayal The relationship between price elasticity of demand and total revenue can be demonstrated graphically by comparing Figures 7-2a and 7-2b. In Figure 7-2b we have graphed the eight total revenue–quantity demanded points from columns 1 and 4 of Table 7-1.

Lowering price over the \$8–\$5 price range increases total revenue. We know from the elasticity coefficient calculations in Table 7-1 that demand is *elastic* in this range so any given percentage decline in price results in a larger percentage increase in the quantity demanded. The lower price per unit is more than offset by the increase in sales and, consequently, total revenue rises.

The \$5–\$4 price range is characterized by *unit* elasticity. Here the percentage decline in price causes an equal percentage increase in the quantity demanded. The price cut is exactly offset by increased purchases so total revenue is unchanged.

Finally, our coefficient calculations tell us that in the \$4–\$1 price range demand is *inelastic*, which means that any given percentage decline in price will be accompanied by a smaller percentage increase in sales, causing total revenue to diminish. Question 2 at the end of this chapter is recommended at this point.

Our logic is reversible. A price *increase* in the elastic \$8–\$5 price range will reduce total revenue. Similarly, a price *increase* in the inelastic \$4–\$1 range causes total revenue to increase.

Reprise Table 7-2 provides a convenient summary of the characteristics of price elasticity of demand and merits careful study.

Determinants of Price Elasticity of Demand

There are no ironclad generalizations concerning determinants of the elasticity of demand. The following points, however, are valid and helpful.

1 Substitutability Generally, the larger the number of good substitute products available, the greater the elasticity of demand. We will find later that in a purely competitive market, where by definition there are many perfect substitutes for the product of any given seller, the demand curve to that single seller will be perfectly elastic. If one competitive seller of wheat or corn raises its price, buyers will turn to the readily available perfect substitutes of its many rivals. At the other extreme, the diabetic's demand for insulin or an addict's demand for heroin is highly inelastic.

TABLE 7-2 Price elasticity of demand: a summary

Absolute value of elasticity coefficient	*Terminology*	*Description*	*Impact on total revenue (expenditures) of a price:*	
			Increase	*Decrease*
Greater than 1 ($E_d > 1$)	"Elastic" or "relatively elastic"	Quantity demanded changes by a larger percentage than does price	Total revenue decreases	Total revenue increases
Equal to 1 ($E_d = 1$)	"Unit" or "unitary elastic"	Quantity demanded changes by the same percentage as does price	Total revenue is unchanged	Total revenue is unchanged
Less than 1 ($E_d < 1$)	"Inelastic" or "relatively inelastic"	Quantity demanded changes by a smaller percentage than does price	Total revenue increases	Total revenue decreases

Necessity $0 < E_I < 1$ Inferior Good $E_I < 0$
Luxury $1 < E_I$

The elasticity of demand for a product depends on how narrowly the product is defined. Demand for Texaco motor oil is more elastic than is the overall demand for motor oil. Many other brands are readily substitutable for Texaco's oil, but there is no good substitute for motor oil.

2 Proportion of Income Other things being equal, the higher the price of a good relative to one's budget, the greater will be the elasticity of demand for it. A 10 percent increase in the price of pencils or chewing gum will amount to only a few pennies, with little response in the amount demanded. A 10 percent increase in the price of automobiles or housing means price increases of perhaps \$1500 and \$10,000 respectively. These increases are significant fractions of the annual incomes of many families, and quantities purchased could be expected to diminish significantly.

3 Luxuries versus Necessities The demand for "necessities" tends to be inelastic; for "luxuries," elastic. Bread and electricity are generally regarded as necessities; we can't get along without them. A price increase will not reduce significantly the amount of bread consumed or the amounts of lighting and power used in a household. Note the very low price elasticities of these goods in Table 7-3. A more extreme case: You will not decline an operation for acute appendicitis because the physician's fee has just gone up!

On the other hand, French cognac and emeralds are luxuries which, by definition, can be forgone. If the price of cognac or emeralds rises, you need not buy and will encounter no hardship.

The demand for salt is highly inelastic on several counts. It is a "necessity"; there are few good substitutes available; and, finally, salt is a negligible item in the family budget.

4 Time Generally, product demand is more elastic the longer the time period under consideration because many consumers are creatures of habit. When the price of a product rises, it takes time to find and experiment with other products to see if they are acceptable. Consumers may not immediately reduce their purchases very much when the price of beef rises by 10 percent, but in time they may shift to chicken or fish, for which they have now "developed a taste." Another consideration is product durability. Studies show that "short-run" demand for gasoline is more inelastic at 0.2 than is "long-run" demand at 0.7. In the long run, large, gas-guzzling automobiles wear out and, with rising gasoline prices, are replaced by smaller, higher-mileage cars.

An empirical study of commuter rail transportation in the Philadelphia area estimates that "long-run" elasticity of demand is almost three times as great as "short-run" elasticity. Specifically, short-run commuter responses (defined as those occurring immediately at the time of a fare change) are inelastic at 0.68. In contrast, the long-run response (defined as those occurring over a four-year period) is elastic at 1.84. The greater long-run elasticity occurs because over time

TABLE 7-3 Selected price elasticities of demand

Product or service	*Price elasticity of demand*	*Product or service*	*Price elasticity of demand*
Housing	.01	Milk	.63
Electricity (household)	.13	Household appliances	.63
Bread	.15	Movies	.87
Telephone service	.26	Beer	.90
Medical care	.31	Shoes	.91
Eggs	.32	Motor vehicles	1.14
Legal services	.37	China, glassware, tableware	1.54
Automobile repair	.40	Restaurant meals	2.27
Clothing	.49	Lamb and mutton	2.65

Main sources: H. S. Houthakker and Lester D. Taylor, *Consumer Demand in the United States: Analyses and Projections,* 2d ed. (Cambridge, Mass.: Harvard University Press, 1970); P. S. George and G. A. King, *Consumer Demand for Food Commodities in the United States with Projections for 1980* (Berkeley: University of California Press, 1971); and Ahsan Mansur and John Whalley, "Numerical Specification of Applied General Equilibrium Models: Estimation, Calibration, and Data," in Herbert E. Scarf and John B. Shoven, *Applied General Equilibrium Analysis* (New York: Cambridge University Press, 1984).

potential rail commuters can make choices concerning automobile purchases, car pooling, and the locations of residences and employment. These different elasticities led to the prediction that the commuter system, with about 100,000 riders, could immediately *increase* daily revenues by $8000 by increasing the price of a one-way ticket by $.25 or about 9 percent. Why? Because short-run demand is inelastic. But in the long run the same 9 percent fare increase is estimated to *reduce* total revenue per day by over $19,000 because demand is elastic. This implies that a fare increase which is profitable in the short run may lead to financial difficulties in the long run.[1]

Table 7-3 shows estimated price elasticities of demand for a number of products. You should use the elasticity determinants just discussed to explain or rationalize each of these elasticity coefficients.

QUICK REVIEW 7-2

- ***A price change will cause total revenue to vary in the opposite direction when demand is elastic and in the same direction when demand is inelastic.***
- ***Price elasticity of demand is greater a the larger the number of substitutes available; b the higher the price of a product relative to one's budget; c the greater the extent to which the product is a luxury; and d the longer the time period involved.***

[1]Richard Voith, "Commuter Rail Ridership: The Long and the Short Haul," *Business Review* (Federal Reserve Bank of Philadelphia), November–December 1987, pp. 13–23.

Some Practical Applications

The concept of price elasticity of demand has great practical significance, as seen in the following examples.

1 Wage Bargaining The United Automobile Workers once contended that automobile manufacturers should raise wages and simultaneously cut automobile prices. Arguing that the elasticity of demand for automobiles was about 4, the UAW concluded that a price cut would help check inflation, boost the total revenue of manufacturers, and preserve or even increase the profits of producers. A spokesman for the Ford Motor Company, however, claimed that available studies suggest an elasticity of demand for automobiles in the 0.5–1.5 range. He held that price cuts would therefore shrink profits or result in losses for manufacturers. In this case, elasticity of demand for automobiles was a strategic factor in labor-management relations and wage bargaining.

2 Bumper Crops Studies indicate that demand for most farm products is highly inelastic, perhaps 0.20 or 0.25. As a result, increases in the output of farm products due to a good growing season or to productivity increases depress both the prices of farm products and total revenues (incomes) of farmers. For farmers as a group, the inelastic nature of demand for their products means that a bumper crop may be undesirable. For policy makers it means that higher total farm income depends on the restriction of farm output.

3 Automation The impact of automation, that is, of rapid technological advance, on the level of employment depends in part on the elasticity of demand for the product being manufactured. Suppose a firm installs new laborsaving machinery, resulting in technological unemployment of 500 workers. Suppose too that part of the cost reduction resulting from this technological advance is passed on to consumers in the form of reduced product prices. The effect of this price reduction on the firm's sales and therefore the quantity of labor it requires will depend on the elasticity of product demand. An elastic demand might increase sales to the extent that some of, all, or even more than the 500 displaced workers are reabsorbed by the firm. An inelastic demand will mean that few, if any, displaced workers will be reemployed, because the increase in the volume of the firm's sales and output will be small.

4 Airline Deregulation Deregulating the airlines in the late 1970s initially increased the profits of many carriers. The reason was that deregulation increased competition among the airlines, lowering air fares. Lower fares, coupled with an elastic demand for air travel, increased revenues. Because additional costs associated with flying full, as opposed to partially empty, aircraft are minimal, revenues increased ahead of costs and profits were enhanced. Unfortunately for the airlines, this profitability was not to last, for three reasons: The competitive scramble for new routes competed profits away; rising fuel prices increased operating costs; and persistent "fare wars" cut into profits.

5 Excise Taxes Government pays attention to elasticity of demand when selecting goods and services on which to levy excise taxes. Assume a $1 tax is currently levied on a product and 10,000 units are sold. Tax revenue is $10,000. If the tax is now raised to $1.50, and the consequent higher price reduces sales to 5,000 because of an elastic demand, tax revenue will *decline* to $7,500. A higher tax on a product, the demand for which is elastic, will bring in less tax revenue. Hence, legislatures will seek out products for which demand is inelastic—liquor, gasoline, and cigarettes—when levying excises. It is not by chance that the Federal government increased taxes on these three categories of goods in 1991 in trying to reduce the budget deficit.

6 Cocaine and Street Crime The fact that the demand for crack-cocaine by addicts is highly inelastic poses some awkward tradeoffs in law enforcement. The approach typically used in attempting to reduce cocaine addiction is restricting supply, that is, making the drug less readily available by cracking down on its shipment into the United States. But what will happen if this policy is successful? Given the highly inelastic demand, the street price to addicts will rise sharply while the amount purchased will decrease only slightly. From the drug dealers' viewpoint this means greatly increased revenues and profits. From the addicts' viewpoint it means greater total expenditures on cocaine. Because much of the income which addicts spend on cocaine comes from crime—shoplifting, burglary, prostitution, muggings—these crimes will increase as addicts increase their total expenditures for cocaine. Here, the effort of law-enforcement authorities to control the spread of drug addiction may increase the amount of crime committed by addicts.

In recent years the controversial proposal to legalize drugs has been widely debated. Proponents contend that drugs should be treated like alcohol; they should be made legal for adults and regulated for purity and potency. The current war on drugs, it is argued, has been unsuccessful and the associated costs—including enlarged police forces, the construction of more prisons, an overburdened court system, and untold human costs—have increased markedly. Legalization would allegedly reduce drug trafficking greatly by taking the profit out of it. Crack-cocaine, for example, is cheap to produce and could be sold at a low price in a legal market. Because the demand of addicts is highly inelastic, the amount consumed at the lower price will only increase modestly. Total expenditures for cocaine by addicts will decline and so will the street crime which finances these expenditures.

Opponents of legalization take the position that, in addition to the addict's inelastic demand, there is another segment to the market where demand may be more elastic. This is the segment populated by occasional users or "dabblers." Dabblers will use cocaine when its price is low, but abstain or substitute, say, alcohol when cocaine's price is high. For this group the lower price of cocaine associated with legalization will increase consumption by dabblers and in time turn many of them into addicts. This will increase street crime and enlarge all the social costs associated with drug use.

7 Minimum Wage The Federal minimum wage prohibits employers from paying covered workers less than $4.25 per hour. Critics contend that an above-equilibrium minimum wage moves employers back up their downsloping labor demand curves and causes unemployment, particularly among teenage workers. On the other hand, workers who remain employed at the minimum wage will receive higher incomes than otherwise. The amount of income lost by the unemployed and the income gained by those who keep their jobs will clearly depend on the elasticity of demand for teenage labor. Research studies suggest that demand for teenage labor is quite inelastic, possibly as low as 0.15 or 0.25. If these estimates are correct, it means that income gains associated with the minimum wage exceed income losses. The case made by critics of the minimum wage would be stronger if the demand for teenage workers were elastic.

More examples could be cited but you can see that elasticity of demand is vitally important to businesses, farmers, labor, and government policy makers.

PRICE ELASTICITY OF SUPPLY

The concept of price elasticity also applies to supply. If producers are responsive to price changes, supply is elastic. If they are relatively insensitive to price changes, supply is inelastic.

The elasticity formula is pertinent in determining the degree of elasticity or inelasticity of supply. The only required alteration is substitution of "percentage change in quantity *supplied*" for "percentage change in quantity *demanded*."

$$E_s = \frac{\text{percentage change in quantity supplied of product X}}{\text{percentage change in price of product X}}$$

For reasons explained earlier, the midpoints of the changes in quantity supplied and price are used in calculations. Suppose price were to increase from $4 to $6, causing quantity supplied to rise from 8 to 12. The percentage change in quantity supplied would be $\frac{4}{10}$, or 40 percent, and the percentage change in price would be $\frac{2}{5}$, or 40 percent. Substituting in our formula, we determine elasticity of supply to be $\frac{40}{40}$ or +1.00. Note that, because price and quantity supplied are directly related, the coefficient will always be positive.

The main determinant of the **price elasticity of supply** is the amount of *time* which a producer has to respond to a given change in product price. We can expect a greater output response—and therefore greater elasticity of supply—the longer the amount of time a producer has to adjust to a given price change. A producer's response to an increase in the price of product X depends on its ability to shift resources from the production of other products (whose prices we assume remain constant) to the production of X. And shifting resources takes time: the greater the time, the greater the resource "shiftability." Hence, the greater will be the output response and the elasticity of supply.

In analyzing the impact of time on elasticity of supply, economists distinguish between the immediate market period, the short run, and the long run.

1 The Market Period The immediate **market period** is so short a time that producers cannot respond to a change in demand and price. Suppose a small truck farmer brings an entire season's output of tomatoes—one truckload—to market. The supply curve will be perfectly inelastic; the farmer will sell the truckload whether the price is high or low. Why? Because he cannot offer more tomatoes than his one truckload if the price of tomatoes should be higher than he had anticipated. Though he might like to offer more, tomatoes cannot be produced overnight. Another full growing season is needed to respond to a higher-than-expected price by producing more than one truckload. Similarly, because the product is perishable, the farmer cannot withhold it from the market. If the price is lower than anticipated, he will still sell the entire truckload. Costs of production, incidentally, will not be important in this decision. Though the price of tomatoes may fall far short of production costs, the farmer will nevertheless sell out to avoid a total loss through spoilage. In a very short time, then, our farmer's supply of tomatoes is fixed; only one truckload can be offered no matter how high the price. The perishability of the product

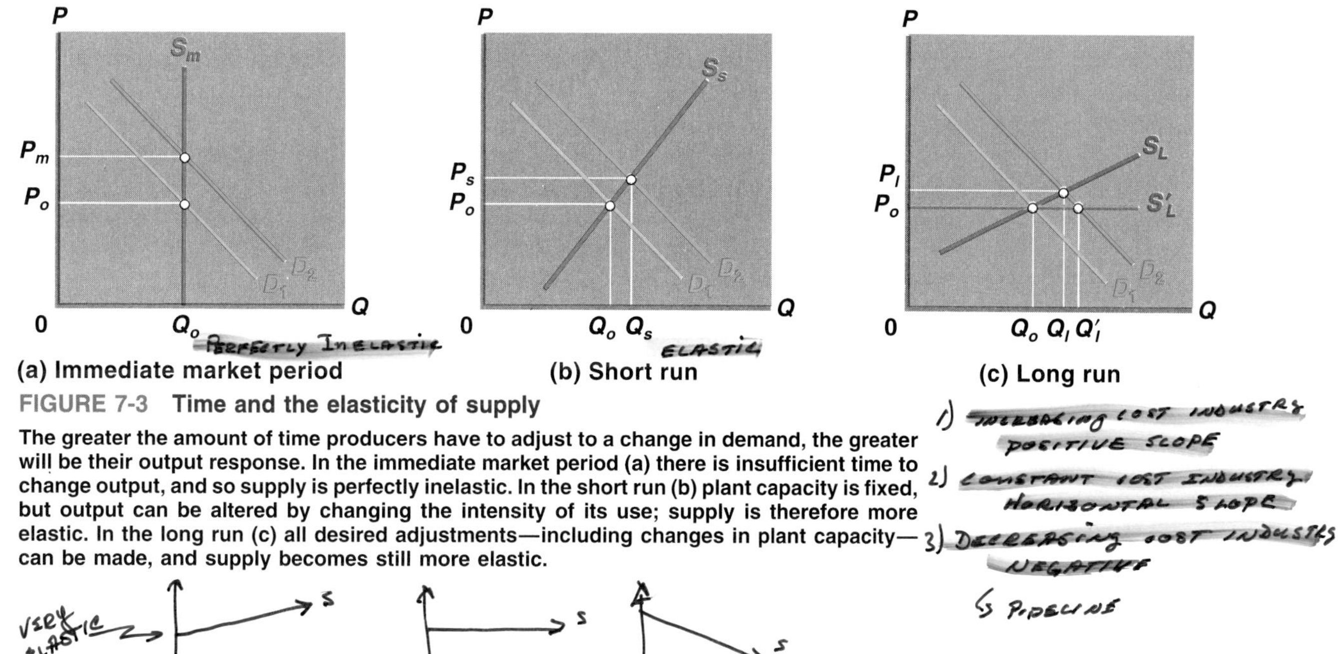

FIGURE 7-3 Time and the elasticity of supply

The greater the amount of time producers have to adjust to a change in demand, the greater will be their output response. In the immediate market period (a) there is insufficient time to change output, and so supply is perfectly inelastic. In the short run (b) plant capacity is fixed, but output can be altered by changing the intensity of its use; supply is therefore more elastic. In the long run (c) all desired adjustments—including changes in plant capacity—can be made, and supply becomes still more elastic.

forces the farmer to sell all, no matter how low the price.

Figure 7-3a illustrates the truck farmer's perfectly inelastic supply curve in the market period. Note that this and other truck farmers cannot respond to an assumed increase in demand; they do not have time to increase the amount supplied. The price increase from P_o to P_m simply rations a fixed supply to buyers, but elicits no increase in output.[2]

2 The Short Run In the **short run,** the plant capacity of individual producers and the industry is presumed fixed. But firms *do* have time to use their plants more or less intensively. Thus, in the short run, our truck farmer's plant—comprised of land and farm machinery—is fixed. But he does have time in the short run to cultivate tomatoes more intensively by applying more labor and more fertilizer and pesticides to the crop. The result is a greater output response to the presumed increase in demand; this greater output response is reflected in a more elastic supply of tomatoes, as shown by S_s in Figure 7-3b. Note that the increase in demand is met by a larger quantity adjustment (Q_o to Q_s) and a smaller price adjustment (P_o to P_s) than in the market period; price is therefore lower than in the market period.

3 The Long Run The **long run** is a time period sufficiently long so that firms can make all desired resource adjustments; individual firms can expand (or contract) their plant capacities, and new firms can enter (or existing firms can leave) the industry. In the "tomato industry" our truck farmer can acquire additional land and buy more machinery and equipment. Furthermore, more farmers may be attracted to tomato production by increased demand and higher price. These adjustments mean an even greater supply response, that is, an even more elastic supply curve S_L. The result, shown in Figure 7-3c, is a small price effect (P_o to P_l) and a large output effect (Q_o to Q_l) in response to the increase in demand.

The dark supply curve in Figure 7-3c entails a new long-run equilibrium price, P_l, somewhat higher than the original price, P_o, in Figure 7-3a. The presumption is that tomato farming is an **increasing-cost industry,** meaning simply that the industry's expansion causes prices of relevant resources to rise. Increased demand for fertilizer and farm equipment has pushed their prices up somewhat; expanded demand for land has increased its market or rental value. In short, it is realis-

[2]The supply curve need not be perfectly inelastic (vertical) in the market period. If the product is not perishable, producers may choose, at low current prices, to store some of their product for future sale. This will cause the market supply curve to have some positive slope.

tic to expect the expansion of an industry to result in "increasing costs." Hence, while P_o was sufficient for profitable production in Figure 7-3a, a higher price, P_l, is required for profitable production in the enlarged industry.

If the tomato industry hired very small or negligible portions of relevant resources, then its increased demand for these inputs would leave their prices unchanged. In this **constant-cost industry** case the long-run supply curve would be perfectly elastic, as shown by the light red curve S'_L in Figure 7-3c. The new price would be equal to the original price, P_o, in Figure 7-3a.

There is no total-revenue test for elasticity of supply. Supply shows a positive or direct relationship between price and amount supplied; that is, the supply curve is upsloping. Thus, regardless of the degree of elasticity or inelasticity, price and total revenue will always move together.

CROSS AND INCOME ELASTICITY OF DEMAND

In addition to price elasticity, two other elasticity concepts are significant.

Cross Elasticity of Demand

We have seen that *price elasticity of demand* measures the effect of a change in a product's price on the quantity of *that* product demanded. The concept of **cross elasticity of demand** measures how sensitive consumer purchases of *one* product (say X) are to a change in the price of some *other* product (say Y). Our formula for the coefficient of cross elasticity of demand is similar to simple price elasticity except that we are relating the percentage change in the consumption of X to a percentage change in the price of Y:

$$E_{xy} = \frac{\text{percentage change in quantity demanded of X}}{\text{percentage change in price of Y}}$$

This elasticity concept allows us to quantify and more fully understand substitute and complementary goods as introduced in Chapter 4.

If cross elasticity of demand is *positive*—that is, the quantity demanded of X varies directly with a change in the price of Y—then X and Y are *substitute goods.* For example, an increase in the price of butter (Y) will cause consumers to buy more margarine (X). The larger the positive coefficient, the greater the substitutability between the two products.

When cross elasticity is *negative,* then we know that X and Y "go together" and are *complementary goods.* Thus an increase in the price of cameras will decrease the amount of film purchased. The larger the negative coefficient, the greater the complementarity between the two goods.

A zero or near-zero coefficient suggests that the two products are unrelated or *independent goods.* For example, we would not expect a change in the price of butter to have any significant impact on the purchases of film.

Income Elasticity of Demand

The concept of **income elasticity of demand** measures the percentage change in the quantity of a product demanded which results from some percentage change in consumer incomes:

$$E_i = \frac{\text{percentage change in quantity demanded}}{\text{percentage change in income}}$$

For most goods the income elasticity coefficient will be *positive.* Again recalling Chapter 4, those products of which more is purchased as incomes increase are called *normal* or *superior* goods. But the positive elasticity coefficient varies greatly among products. For example, the income elasticity of demand for automobiles has been estimated to be about +3.00, while for most farm products it is only about +0.20.

A *negative* income elasticity coefficient designates an *inferior good.* Retreaded tires, cabbage, bus tickets, used clothing, and muscatel wine are likely candidates. Consumers *decrease* their purchases of such products as incomes *increase.*

The practical significance of income elasticity coefficients is that they help us predict which industries are likely to be prosperous, expanding industries and which will probably be unprosperous, declining industries. Specifically, other things being equal, a high positive income elasticity implies that that industry will share more than proportionately in the overall income growth of the economy. A small positive or, worse yet, a negative coefficient implies a declining industry. For example, the indicated high positive income elasticity of demand for automobiles portends a greater likelihood of long-run prosperity for that industry in comparison to agriculture's low coefficient which suggests chronic problems.

APPLICATIONS: LEGAL PRICES

Supply and demand analysis and the elasticity concept will be applied repeatedly in the remainder of this book. Let's strengthen our understanding of these analytical tools and their significance by examining some of the implications of legal prices.

On occasion the general public and government feel that the forces of supply and demand result in prices that are either unfairly high to buyers or unfairly low to sellers. In such instances government may intervene by legally limiting how high or low the price may go.

Price Ceilings and Shortages

A **price ceiling** *is the maximum legal price a seller may charge for a product or service.* The rationale for ceiling prices on specific products is that they purportedly enable consumers to obtain some "essential" good or service they could not afford at the equilibrium price. Rent controls and usury laws (which specify maximum interest rates which may be charged to borrowers) are examples. More generally, ceiling prices or general price controls have been used in attempting to restrain the overall rate of inflation in the economy. Price controls were invoked during World War II and to a lesser extent during the Korean conflict. Similarly, President Nixon froze prices, wages, and rents in the early 1970s.

FIGURE 7-4 Price ceilings result in persistent shortages

Because a price ceiling such as P_c results in a persistent product shortage, indicated by the distance Q_sQ_d, government must undertake the job of rationing the product to achieve an equitable distribution.

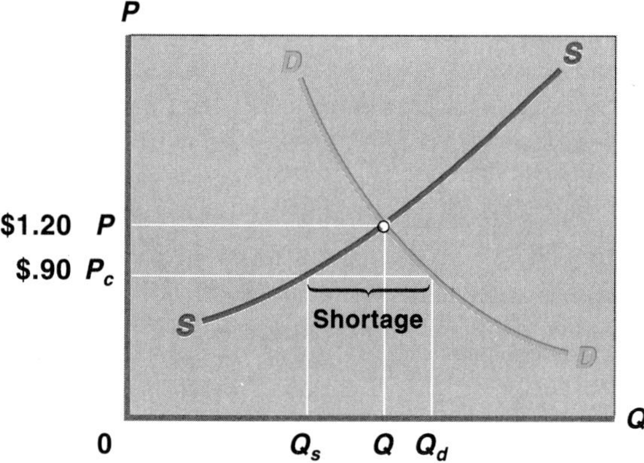

World War II Price Controls Let's turn back the clock to World War II and analyze the effects of a ceiling price on butter. The booming wartime prosperity of the early 1940s was shifting demand for butter to the right so that, as in Figure 7-4, the equilibrium or market price P was, say, \$1.20 per pound. On the one hand, the rapidly rising price of butter was contributing to inflation and, on the other, rationing out of the butter market those families whose money incomes were not keeping up with the soaring cost of living. To help stop inflation and to keep butter on the tables of the poor, government imposed a ceiling price P_c of, say, \$0.90 per pound. Note that to be effective a ceiling price must be *below* the equilibrium price. A ceiling price of \$1.50 would have no immediate impact on the butter market.

What will be the effects of this ceiling price? The rationing ability of the free market will be rendered ineffective. At the ceiling price there will be a persistent shortage of butter. The quantity of butter demanded at P_c is Q_d and the quantity supplied is only Q_s; a persistent excess demand or shortage in the amount Q_sQ_d occurs. The size of this shortage varies directly with the price elasticities of supply and demand.

The important point is that the legal price P_c prevents the usual market adjustment where competition among buyers would bid up price, thereby inducing more production and rationing some buyers out of the market until the shortage disappears at the equilibrium price and quantity, P and Q.

By preventing these market-clearing adjustments from occurring, the ceiling price poses problems born of the market disequilibrium.

1 How is the available supply Q_s to be apportioned among buyers who want amount Q_d? Should supply be distributed on a first-come, first-served basis, that is, to those willing and able to stand in line the longest? Or should the grocer distribute butter on the basis of favoritism? An unregulated shortage is hardly conducive to the equitable distribution of butter. To avoid catch-as-catch-can distribution, government must establish some formal system of rationing the product to consumers. This was done during World War II by issuing ration coupons to individuals on an equitable basis. An

effective rationing system entails the printing of ration coupons equal to Q_s pounds of butter and their equitable distribution among consumers so that the rich family of four and the poor family of four will both get the same number of coupons.

2 But the use of ration coupons does not prevent a second problem from arising. Specifically, the curve in Figure 7-4 tells us there are many buyers who are willing to pay more than the ceiling price. And, of course, it is more profitable for grocers to sell above the ceiling price. Thus, despite the sizable enforcement bureaucracy which accompanied World War II price controls, illegal *black markets*—markets where products were bought and sold at prices above the legal limits—flourished for many goods. Counterfeiting of ration coupons was also a problem.

Rent Controls Some 200 American cities—including New York City, Boston, and San Francisco—have rent controls. Such legislation is well-intended. Its goals are to protect low-income families from escalating rents caused by perceived housing shortages and to make housing more affordable to the poor.

What are the actual economic effects? On the demand side, it is true that below-equilibrium rents will mean that more families are willing to consume rental housing; the quantity of rental housing demanded will increase at the lower price. The problem occurs on the supply side. Price controls make it less attractive for landlords to offer housing on the rental market. In the short run they may sell their apartments or convert them to condominiums. In the long run low rents make it unprofitable for owners to maintain or renovate their rental units. Rent controls are one cause of the many abandoned apartment buildings found in larger cities. Also, potential new investors in housing such as insurance companies and pension funds will find it more profitable to invest in office buildings, shopping malls, or motels where rents are not controlled,

In brief, rent controls distort market signals so that resources are misallocated: Too few resources are allocated to rental housing, too many to alternative uses. Ironically, although rent controls are often legislated to mitigate the effects of perceived housing shortages, in fact, controls are a primary cause of such shortages.

Credit Card Interest Ceilings In recent years several bills have been introduced in Congress to impose a nationwide interest rate ceiling on credit card accounts. In fact, several states now have such laws and others have legislation under consideration. The usual rationale for interest rate ceilings is that the banks and retail stores issuing such cards are presumably "gouging" users and, in particular, lower-income users by charging interest rates that average about 18 percent. In late 1991 President Bush sought such ceilings on the grounds that lower interest rates would stimulate consumer spending and help the economy recover from recession.

What might be the responses to the legal imposition of below-equilibrium interest rates on credit cards? According to a study by the Federal Reserve,[3] profits on bank-issued credit cards have been low, while retail store cards have generally entailed losses for their issuers. Hence, lower interest income associated with a legal interest ceiling would require adjustments by issuers to reduce costs or enhance revenues. What forms might these responses take?

1 Card issuers might tighten credit standards to reduce nonpayment losses and collection costs. In particular, low-income people and young people who have not yet established their creditworthiness would find it more difficult to obtain credit cards.

2 The annual fee charged card holders might be increased as might the fee charged merchants for processing credit card sales. Similarly, card users might be charged a fee for every transaction.

3 Card users now have a "grace period" when the credit provided is interest-free. This period might be shortened or eliminated.

4 Finally, retail stores which issue cards might increase their merchandise prices to help offset the decline of interest income. This would mean that customers who pay cash would in effect be subsidizing customers who use credit cards. Empirical studies of states which now have ceilings on credit card interest rates have confirmed our first and final predictions.

Rock Concerts Below-equilibrium pricing should not be associated solely with government policies. Superstars such as Madonna or Michael Jackson frequently price their concert tickets below the market-clearing price. Tickets are usually rationed on a first-come, first-served basis and black market "scalping" is common. Why should rock stars want to subsidize their fans—at least those fortunate enough to obtain tickets—with below-equilibrium prices? Why not set

[3]Glenn B. Canner and James T. Fergus, "The Economic Effects of Proposed Ceilings on Credit Card Interest Rates," *Federal Reserve Bulletin*, January 1987, pp. 1–13.

ticket prices at a higher, market-clearing level and realize more income from a tour?

The answer is that long lines of fans waiting hours or days for bargain-priced tickets catch the attention of the press, as does an occasional attempt by ticketless fans to "crash" a sold-out concert. The millions of dollars worth of free publicity undoubtedly stimulates record and CD sales from which much of any rock group's income is derived. Hence, the "gift" of below-equilibrium ticket prices a rock star gives to fans also benefits the star. The gift also imposes costs upon fans—the opportunity cost of time spent waiting in line to buy tickets.

Price Floors and Surpluses

Price floors—*minimum prices fixed by government which are above equilibrium prices*—have generally been invoked when society has felt that the free functioning of the market system has not provided a sufficient income for certain groups of resource suppliers or producers. Minimum-wage legislation and the support of agricultural prices are the two most widely discussed examples of government price floors. Let's examine price floors as applied to a specific farm commodity.

FIGURE 7-5 Price floors result in persistent surpluses

A price floor such as P_f gives rise to a persistent product surplus, indicated by the distance Q_dQ_s. Government must either purchase these surpluses or take measures to eliminate them by restricting product supply or increasing product demand.

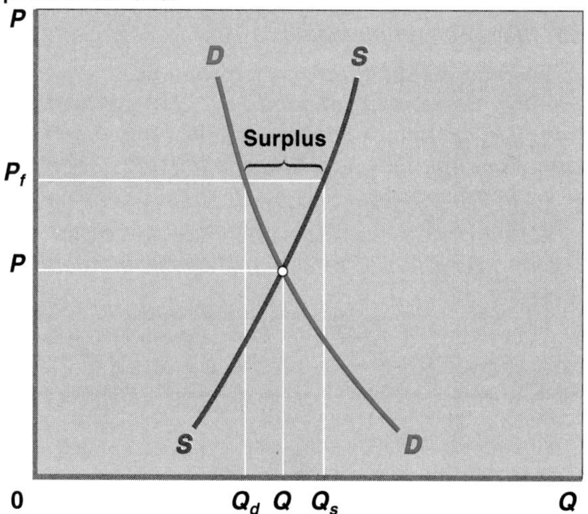

Suppose the going market price for corn is $2 per bushel, and as a result of this price, many farmers realize extremely low incomes. Government decides to lend a helping hand by establishing a legal floor price of $3 per bushel.

What will be the effects? At any price above the equilibrium price, quantity supplied will exceed quantity demanded; that is, there will be a persistent excess supply or surplus of the product. Farmers will be willing to produce and offer for sale more than private buyers are willing to purchase at the price floor. The size of this surplus will vary directly with the elasticity of demand and supply. The greater the elasticity of demand and supply, the greater the resulting surplus. As is the case with a ceiling price, the rationing ability of the free market has been disrupted by imposing a legal price.

Figure 7-5 illustrates the effect of a price floor. Let *SS* and *DD* be the supply and demand curves for corn. Equilibrium price and quantity are P and Q, respectively. If government imposes a price floor of P_f, farmers will produce Q_s, but private buyers will only take Q_d off the market at that price. The surplus is measured by the excess of Q_s over Q_d.

Government may cope with the surplus a price floor entails in two basic ways.

1 It might restrict supply (for example, acreage allotments by which farmers agree to take a certain amount of land out of production) or increase demand (for example, researching new uses for agricultural products). In these ways the difference between the equilibrium price and the price floor and thereby the size of the resulting surplus might be reduced.

2 If these efforts are not wholly successful, then government must purchase the surplus output (thereby subsidizing farmers) and store or otherwise dispose of it (Chapter 21).

Recapitulation

Price ceilings and floors rob the free-market forces of supply and demand of their ability to bring the supply decisions of producers and the demand decisions of buyers into accord with one another. Freely determined prices automatically ration products to buyers; legal prices do not. Therefore, government must accept the administrative problem of rationing which stems from price ceilings and the problem of buying or eliminating surpluses which price floors entail. Legal prices entail controversial tradeoffs. Alleged benefits of price ceilings and floors to consumers and producers

LAST WORD

THE TROUBLESOME MARKET FOR HEALTH CARE

Changes in demand and supply help explain why health care costs have risen dramatically.

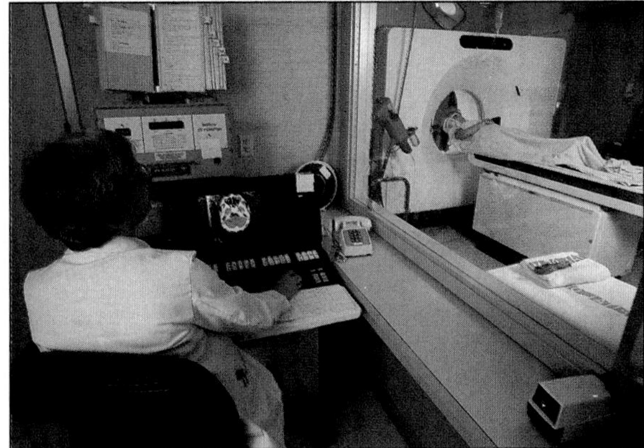

Health care costs in the United States are currently over 12 percent of GDP, up from about 5 percent in 1960. In 1990 we spent about $662 billion on health care, compared to $359 billion and $299 billion on education and national defense, respectively. The Department of Health and Human Services projects that $1.6 trillion—over 16 percent of domestic output—will be spent on health care by the turn of the century. Although it is a complex problem, an analysis of factors at work on the demand and supply sides of the health care market yield important insights as to why medical costs have soared.

Let's first consider the demand side. First, medical care is a normal good so the demand for medical care has increased as per capita incomes have grown. Second, our population is aging and older people encounter more frequent and prolonged spells of illness. Third, social and lifestyle factors such as high rates of violence and drug abuse as compared to most other countries create demands for medical services. Fourth, the way we pay for health care has greatly increased demand. About three-fourths of all medical costs are paid, not as an out-of-pocket expense by individual users, but by private and public insurance. This has had two demand-increasing effects. On the one hand, Medicare and Medicaid, respectively, finance health care for the aged and the poor, thereby bringing many people into the health care market who might not otherwise have been there. On the other hand, individ-

respectively must be set against costs associated with consequent shortages and surpluses.

Furthermore, our discussions of World War II price controls, rent controls, and interest rate ceilings on credit cards show that governmental interference with the market can have unintended, undesirable side effects. Rent controls may discourage housing construction and repair. Instead of protecting low-income families from high interest charges, interest rate ceilings may simply make credit unavailable to them.

QUICK REVIEW 7-3

- ***Price elasticity of supply is the ratio of the percentage change in quantity supplied to the percentage change in price. The elasticity of supply varies directly with the amount of time producers have to respond to the price change.***
- ***Cross elasticity of demand is the percentage change in the quantity demanded of one product divided by the percentage change in the price of another product. If the cross elasticity coefficient is positive, the two products are substitutes; if negative, they are complements.***
- ***Income elasticity is the percentage change in quantity demanded divided by the percentage change in income. A positive coefficient indicates a normal or superior good. The coefficient is negative for an inferior good.***
- ***Legal prices—ceilings and floors—negate the rationing function of prices and cause unintended side effects.***

CHAPTER SUMMARY

1 Price elasticity of demand measures consumer response to price changes. If consumers are relatively sensitive to price changes, demand is elastic. If they are relatively unresponsive to price changes, demand is inelastic.

2 The price elasticity formula measures the degree of elasticity or inelasticity of demand. The formula is

uals pay a fixed insurance fee and then, aside from a modest deductible, medical care is "free" to the individual. In most markets the buyer or demander is confronted with a price that reflects the opportunity cost of that good or service. The price provides a direct economic incentive to restrict the use of that product. But through insurance one's health care is prepaid, creating an incentive to overuse the system. We demand medical services and procedures which we might forgo if directly confronted with their price.

The costs of health care services underlying the supply of health care have greatly increased, tending to reduce or slow the growth of supply. In the first place, new technological advances have made medical care much more costly. For example, increasingly sophisticated body scanners have usurped x-ray machines. A \$20 or \$40 x-ray has given way to a scan costing as much as \$1000 or \$2500. Fearful of becoming technologically obsolete, hospitals want to offer the most sophisticated equipment and procedures. Doctors and hospital administrators both realize that to pay for such equipment it must be used extensively. Second, in a litigious society such as ours physicians are prone to recommend more tests and procedures than might be medically warranted to protect themselves from malpractice suits. Third, doctors are paid on a fee-for-service basis. More surgery is performed in the United States on a fee basis than in foreign countries, where doctors are paid annual salaries unrelated to the number of procedures performed. A recent study concluded that doctors who own x-ray or ultrasound machines did four to four-and-one-half times as many tests as doctors who referred their patients to radiologists. Finally, economists have long argued that the American Medical Association has kept admissions to medical schools and hence the supply of physicians artificially low. All of this increases costs and restricts the supply of health care.

As the demand for medical care has increased relative to supply, prices have soared. The consequences are predictable. Some 35 million Americans—13 percent of the population—lack health insurance. Companies and their workers are increasingly at odds over the sharing of health insurance costs. Politicians are debating the creation of a national health insurance program. Finally, the increasing acuteness of our health care problems is forcing us to face the hard fact that medical care is a scarce service which must be rationed. Can we continue to provide \$5000 per-day intensive care to a comatose ninety-year-old who is unlikely to be restored to reasonable health?

$$E_d = \frac{\text{percentage change in quantity demanded of X}}{\text{percentage change in price of X}}$$

The averages of prices and quantities under consideration are used as reference points in determining percentage changes in price and quantity. If E_d is greater than 1, demand is elastic. If E_d is less than 1, demand is inelastic. Unit elasticity is the special case in which E_d equals 1. A perfectly inelastic demand curve is portrayed by a line parallel to the vertical axis; a perfectly elastic demand curve is shown by a line above and parallel to the horizontal axis.

3 Elasticity varies at different price ranges on a demand curve, tending to be elastic in the northwest segment and inelastic in the southeast segment. Elasticity cannot be judged by the steepness or flatness of a demand curve on a graph.

4 If price and total revenue move in opposite directions, demand is elastic. If price and total revenue move in the same direction, demand is inelastic. Where demand is of unit elasticity, a change in price will leave total revenue unchanged.

5 The number of available substitutes, the size of an item in one's budget, whether the product is a luxury or necessity, and time are all determinants of elasticity of demand.

6 The elasticity concept also applies to supply. Elasticity of supply depends on the shiftability of resources between alternative employments. This shiftability in turn varies directly with the time producers have to adjust to a given price change.

7 Cross elasticity gauges how sensitive the purchases of one product are to changes in the price of another product. It is measured by the percentage change in the quantity demanded of product X divided by the percentage change in the price of product Y.

8 Income elasticity indicates the responsiveness of consumer purchases to a change in income. It is measured by the percentage change in the quantity demanded of the product divided by the percentage change in income.

9 Legally fixed prices upset the rationing function of equilibrium prices. Effective price ceilings result in persistent product shortages and, if an equitable distribution of the product is sought, government will have to ration the product to consumers. Price floors lead to product surpluses; government must purchase these surpluses *or* eliminate them by imposing restrictions on production or by increasing private demand.

TERMS AND CONCEPTS

price elasticity of demand
elastic versus inelastic demand
perfectly inelastic demand
perfectly elastic demand
total-revenue test
price elasticity of supply
market period
increasing- and constant-cost industries
cross elasticity of demand
short run and long run
income elasticity of demand
price ceiling
price floor

QUESTIONS AND STUDY SUGGESTIONS

1 Answer questions 1, 3, and 10 at the end of Chapter 4.

2 Graph the accompanying demand data and then use both the elasticity coefficient and the total-revenue test to determine price elasticity of demand for each possible price change. What can you conclude about the relationship between the slope of a curve and its elasticity? Explain in a nontechnical way *why* demand is elastic in the northwest segment of the demand curve and inelastic in the southeast segment. Graph the total revenue data below the demand curve and generalize on the relationship between price elasticity and total revenue.

Product price	*Quantity demanded*
$5	1
4	2
3	3
2	4
1	5

3 In some industries, for example, the petroleum industry, producers justify their reluctance to lower prices by arguing that demand for their products is inelastic. Explain.

4 How will the following changes in price affect total revenue (expenditures)—that is, will total revenue *increase, decline,* or *remain unchanged?*

- **a** Price falls and demand is inelastic.
- **b** Price rises and demand is elastic.
- **c** Price rises and supply is elastic.
- **d** Price rises and supply is inelastic.
- **e** Price rises and demand is inelastic.
- **f** Price falls and demand is elastic.
- **g** Price falls and demand is of unit elasticity.

5 What are the major determinants of price elasticity of demand? Use these determinants in judging whether demand for each of the following products is elastic or inelastic: **a** oranges; **b** cigarettes; **c** Winston cigarettes; **d** gasoline; **e** butter; **f** salt; **g** automobiles; **h** football games; **i** diamond bracelets; and **j** this textbook.

6 Empirical estimates suggest the following demand elasticities: 0.6 for physicians' services; 4.0 for foreign travel; and 1.2 for radio and television receivers. Use the generalizations for the determinants of elasticity developed in this chapter to explain each of these figures.

7 What effect would a rule stating that university students must live in university dormitories have on the price elasticity of demand for dormitory space? What impact might this in turn have on room rates?

8 You are sponsoring an outdoor rock concert. Your major costs—for the band, land rent, and security—are largely independent of attendance. Use the concept of price elasticity of demand to explain how you might establish ticket prices to maximize profits.

9 "If the demand for farm products is highly price inelastic, a bumper crop may reduce farm incomes." Evaluate and illustrate graphically.

10 You are chairperson of a state tax commission responsible for establishing a program to raise new revenue through excise taxes. Would elasticity of demand be important to you in determining those products on which excises should be levied? Explain.

11 In May 1990 Vincent van Gogh's painting "Portrait of Dr. Gachet" sold at auction for $82.5 million. Portray this sale in a demand and supply diagram and comment on the elasticity of supply.

12 In the 1970s the Organization of Petroleum Exporting Countries (OPEC) became operational as a cartel which reduced the world supply of oil, greatly increasing OPEC's revenues and profits. What can you infer regarding the elasticity of demand for oil? Would you expect countries exporting bananas or pineapples to be able to emulate OPEC? Explain.

13 In 1987 the average price of a home rose from $97,000 in April to $106,800 in May. During the same period home sales fell from 724,000 to 616,000 units. If we assume that mortgage interest rates and all other factors affecting home sales are constant, what do these figures suggest about the elasticity of demand for housing?

14 In the 1950s the local Boy Scout troop in Jackson, Wyoming, decided to gather and sell at auction elk antlers shed by thousands of elk wintering in the area. Buyers were mainly local artisans who used the antlers to make belt buckles, buttons, and tie clasps. Price per pound was 6¢ and the troop took in $500 annually. In the 1970s a fad developed in Asia which involved grinding antlers into powder to sprinkle on food for purported aphrodisiac benefits. In 1979 the price per pound of elk antlers in the Jackson auction was $6 per pound and the Boy Scouts earned $51,000! Show graphically and explain these dramatic increases in price and total revenue. Assuming no shift in the supply curve of elk antlers, use the midpoints formula to calculate the coefficient for the elasticity of supply.

15 Suppose the cross elasticity of demand for products A and B is +3.6 and for products C and D it is −5.4. What can you conclude about how products A and B and products C and D are related?

16 The income elasticities of demand for movies, dental services, and clothing have been estimated to be +3.4, +1.0, and +0.5, respectively. Interpret these coefficients. What does it mean if the income elasticity coefficient is negative?

17 Why is it desirable for ceiling prices to be accompanied by government rationing? And for price floors to be accompanied by surplus-purchasing or output-restricting or demand-increasing programs? Show graphically why price ceilings entail shortages and price floors result in surpluses. What effect, if any, does elasticity of demand and supply have on the size of these shortages and surpluses? Explain.

18 New York City has had rent controls since 1941. What effect do you think they have had on the amount of housing demanded? On the construction of new housing? Explain: "Rent controls are a kind of self-fulfilling prophecy. They are designed to cope with housing shortages, but instead create such shortages." Can you predict the economic consequences of laws which impose ceilings on interest rates? Show diagrammatically the expected effect of the minimum wage upon employment of low-wage workers.

Consumer Behavior and Utility Maximization[1]

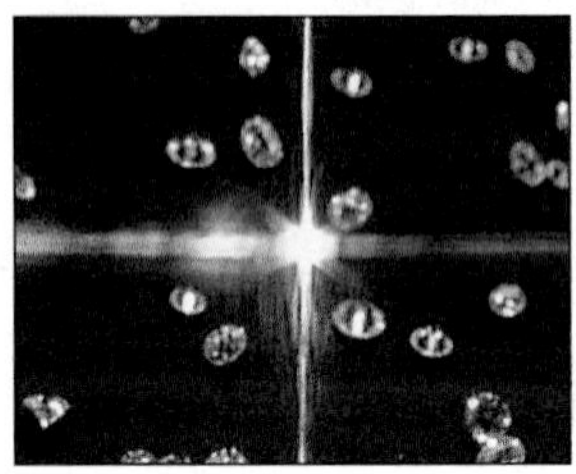

You have probably seen the bumper sticker which asserts: "I'd rather be shopping!" Indeed, we seem to be a nation of shoppers. Fact: Consumers spent about $3.9 trillion on goods and services in 1991. Fact: Americans consume 92 percent of their after-tax incomes. Fact: Consumption per person was $15,383 in the United States in 1991.

One concern of microeconomics is explaining consumer spending. If you were to compare the shopping carts of two consumers leaving a supermarket, you would observe striking differences. Why does Paula have potatoes, parsnips, pomegranates, and Pepsi in her cart, while Sam has sugar, saltines, soap, and 7-Up in his? Why didn't Paula also buy pork and pimentos? Why didn't Sam have soup and spaghetti on his grocery list? In this chapter, we will learn how individual consumers allocate their money incomes among the various goods and services available to them. Why does a consumer buy some specific bundle of goods rather than any one of a number of other collections of goods available? As we examine these issues we will also strengthen our understanding of the law of demand.

TWO EXPLANATIONS OF THE LAW OF DEMAND

The law of demand may be treated as a commonsense notion. A high price discourages consumers from buying; a low price encourages them to buy. We now explore two complementary explanations of the downsloping nature of the demand curve which will back up our everyday observations. (A third explanation, based on indifference curves, is more advanced and is summarized in the appendix to this chapter.)

Income and Substitution Effects

In Chapter 4 the law of demand—the downsloping demand curve—was explained in terms of income and substitution effects. Whenever a product's price decreases, two things happen to cause the amount demanded to increase.

[1]Some instructors may choose to omit this chapter. This can be done without impairing the continuity and meaning of ensuing chapters.

1 Income Effect The **income effect** is the impact of a change in the price of a product on a consumer's real income and consequently on the quantity of that product demanded. If the price of a product—say, steak—declines, the real income or purchasing power of anyone buying that product will increase. This increase in real income will be reflected in increased purchases of many products, including steak. With a constant money income of $20 per week you can buy 10 pounds of steak at $2 per pound. But if the price of steak falls to $1 per pound and you buy 10 pounds, $10 per week is freed to buy more of this and other commodities. A decline in the price of steak increases the consumer's real income, enabling him or her to purchase more steak.[2] This is called the *income effect.*

2 Substitution Effect The **substitution effect** is the impact a change in a product's price has on its relative expensiveness, and consequently on the quantity demanded. The lower price of a product means it is now cheaper relative to all other products. Consumers will substitute the cheaper product for other products which are now relatively more expensive. In our example, as the price of steak falls—prices of other products being unchanged—steak will become more attractive to the buyer. At $1 per pound it is a "better buy" than at $2. The lower price will induce the consumer to substitute steak for some of the now relatively less attractive items in the budget. Steak may well be substituted for pork, chicken, veal, fish, and other foods. A lower price increases the relative attractiveness of a product and the consumer will buy more of it. This is the *substitution effect.*

The income and substitution effects combine to make a consumer able and willing to buy more of a specific good at a low price than at a high price.

Law of Diminishing Marginal Utility

A second explanation of the downsloping demand curve is that, although consumer wants in general may be insatiable, wants for specific commodities can be fulfilled. In a given span of time, where buyers' tastes are unchanged, consumers can get as much of specific goods and services as they want. The more of a specific product consumers obtain, the less they will want more units of the same product.

This can be most readily seen for durable goods. A consumer's want for an automobile, when he or she has none, may be very strong; the desire for a second car is much less intense; for a third or fourth, very weak. Even the wealthiest families rarely have more than a half-dozen cars, although their incomes would allow them to purchase a whole fleet of them.

Terminology Economists theorize that specific consumer wants can be fulfilled with succeeding units of a commodity in the **law of diminishing marginal utility.** Recall that a product has utility if it can satisfy a want. **Utility** is want-satisfying power. Two characteristics of this concept must be emphasized.

1 "Utility" and "usefulness" are not synonymous. Paintings by Picasso may be useless in a functional sense and yet be of tremendous utility to art connoisseurs.

2 Implied in the first point is the fact that utility is a subjective notion. The utility of a specific product will vary widely from person to person. A bottle of muscatel wine may yield substantial utility to the Skid Row alcoholic, but zero or negative utility to the local temperance union president. Eyeglasses have great utility to someone who is extremely far- or near-sighted, but no utility to a person having 20-20 vision.

By *marginal* utility we simply mean the extra utility, or satisfaction, a consumer gets from one additional unit of a specific product. In any short time wherein the consumer's tastes do not change, the marginal utility derived from successive units of a given product will decine.[3] A consumer will eventually become relatively saturated, or "filled up," with that particular product. The fact that marginal utility will decline as the consumer acquires additional units of a specific product is known as the law of diminishing marginal utility.

Because it is a subjective concept, utility is not susceptible to precise quantitative measurement. But for purposes of illustration, assume we can measure satisfaction with units we will call "utils." This mythical unit of satisfaction is a convenient pedagogical device allowing us to quantify consumer behavior. Thus, in Table 8-1, we can illustrate the relationship between the quantity obtained of a product—say, fast-food hamburgers—and the accompanying extra utility derived from each successive unit. Here we assume that the law of diminishing marginal utility sets in with the first hamburger consumed. Each successive hamburger

[2]We assume here that steak is a *normal* or *superior* good.

[3]For a time the marginal utility of successive units of a product may increase. A third can of beer may yield a larger amount of extra satisfaction than the first or second. But beyond some point, we can expect the marginal utility of added units to decline. With beer, this decline may be abrupt.

TABLE 8-1 The law of diminishing marginal utility as applied to hamburgers (*hypothetical data*)

Unit of hamburgers	*Marginal utility, utils*	*Total utility, utils*
First	10	10
Second	6	16
Third	2	18
Fourth	0	18
Fifth	−5	13

yields less and less extra utility than the previous one as the consumer's want for hamburgers comes closer and closer to fulfillment. *Total utility* can be found for any number of hamburgers by cumulating the marginal-utility figures as indicated in Table 8-1. This is so because marginal utility is the change in total utility associated with the consumption of one more unit of a good. Thus, the third hamburger has a marginal utility of 2 utils; 3 hamburgers yield a total utility of 18 utils (=10 + 6 + 2). Notice that marginal utility becomes zero for the fourth hamburger and negative for the fifth.

Relation to Demand and Elasticity How does the law of diminishing marginal utility explain why the demand curve for a specific product is downsloping? If successive units of a good yield smaller and smaller amounts of marginal, or extra, utility, then the consumer will buy additional units of a product only if its price falls. The consumer for whom these utility data are relevant may buy 2 hamburgers at a price of $1. But, owing to diminishing marginal utility from additional hamburgers, a consumer will choose *not* to buy more at this price, because giving up money really means giving up other goods, that is, alternative ways of getting utility. Therefore, additional hamburgers are "not worth it" unless the price (sacrifice of other goods) declines. (When marginal utility becomes negative, McDonald's or Burger King would have to pay *you* to consume another hamburger!) From the seller's viewpoint, diminishing marginal utility forces the producer to lower the price so buyers will take more of the product. This rationale supports the notion of a downsloping demand curve.

The amount by which marginal utility declines as more units of a product are consumed will determine its price elasticity of demand. Other things being equal, if marginal utility falls sharply as successive units are consumed, we would expect demand to be inelastic. Conversely, modest declines in marginal utility as consumption increases imply an elastic demand.

QUICK REVIEW 8-1

- ***The law of demand can be explained in terms of the income effect (a decline in price increases the consumer's purchasing power) and the substitution effect (a product whose price falls is substituted for other products).***
- ***Utility is the benefit or satisfaction a person receives from consuming a good or service.***
- ***The law of diminishing marginal utility indicates that the gains in satisfaction will decline as successive units of a given product are consumed.***
- ***Diminishing marginal utility provides a rationale for a the law of demand and b differing price elasticities.***

THEORY OF CONSUMER BEHAVIOR

As well as providing a basis for explaining the law of demand, the idea of diminishing marginal utility is critical in explaining how consumers should allocate their money income among the many goods and services available for purchase.

Consumer Choice and Budget Restraint

The situation of the typical consumer is something like this:

1 Rational Behavior The consumer is a rational person, trying to dispose of his or her money income so as to derive the greatest amount of satisfaction, or utility, from it. Consumers want to get "the most for their money" or, more technically, to maximize total utility.

2 Preferences The consumer has rather clear-cut preferences for various goods and services available in the market. We assume buyers have a good idea of how much marginal utility they will get from successive units of the various products they might purchase.

3 Budget Restraint The consumer's money income is limited. Because a consumer supplies limited amounts of human and property resources to businesses, the money income received will be limited. With few possible exceptions—the Rockefellers, Bob Hope, Michael Jackson, and Saudi Arabia's King Fahd—all consumers are subject to a *budget restraint.*

4 Prices The goods and services available to consumers have price tags on them. They are scarce in relation to the demand for them, or, stated differently, their production uses scarce and therefore valuable resources. In our examples we will suppose that product prices are not affected by the amounts of specific goods which the individual consumer buys; pure competition exists on the buying or demand side of the market.

If a consumer has limited dollars and the products he or she wants have price tags on them, the consumer can purchase only a limited amount of goods. The consumer cannot buy everything wanted when each purchase exhausts a portion of a limited money income. It is precisely this point which brings the economic fact of scarcity home to the individual consumer.

> In making his choices, our typical consumer is in the same position as the Western prospector . . . who is restocking for his next trip into the back country and who is forced by the nature of the terrain to restrict his luggage to whatever he can carry on the back of one burro. If he takes a great deal of one item, say baked beans, he must necessarily take much less of something else, say bacon. His job is to find that collection of products which, in view of the limitations imposed on the total, will best suit his needs and tastes.[4]

The consumer must compromise; he or she must choose among alternative goods to obtain with limited money income the most satisfying mix of goods and services.

Utility-Maximizing Rule

Of all the collections of goods and services a consumer can obtain within his or her budget, which specific collection will yield the maximum utility or satisfaction? The rule to be followed in maximizing satisfaction is that *the consumer's money income should be allocated so that the last dollar spent on each product purchased yields the same amount of extra (marginal) utility.* We shall call this the **utility-maximizing rule.** When the consumer is "balancing his margins" in accordance with this rule, there will be no incentive to alter his or her expenditure pattern. The consumer will be in *equilibrium* and, barring a change in tastes, income, or the prices of the various goods, will be worse off—total utility will decline—by any alteration in the collection of goods purchased.

Numerical Example An illustration will help explain this rule. For simplicity's sake we limit our discussion to just two products, but the analysis can readily be extended to any number of goods. Suppose consumer Brooks is trying to decide which combination of two products—A and B—she should purchase with her limited daily income of $10. Brooks's preferences for these two products and their prices will be basic data determining the combinations of A and B which will maximize her satisfactions. Table 8-2 summarizes Brooks's preferences for products A and B. Column 2a shows the amount of extra or marginal utility she will derive from each successive unit of A. Column 3a reflects her preferences for product B. In each case the relationship between the number of units of the product obtained and the corresponding marginal utility reflects the law of diminishing marginal utility. Diminishing marginal utility is assumed to begin with the first unit of each product purchased.

Marginal Utility per Dollar Before we apply the utility-maximizing rule to these data, we must put the

TABLE 8-2 The utility-maximizing combination of products A and B obtainable with an income of $10* (*hypothetical data*)

(1)	*(2)* *Product A: price = $1*		*(3)* *Product B: price = $2*	
Unit of product	*(a) Marginal utility, utils*	*(b) Marginal utility per dollar (MU/price)*	*(a) Marginal utility, utils*	*(b) Marginal utility per dollar (MU/price)*
First	10	10	24	12
Second	8	8	20	10
Third	7	7	18	9
Fourth	6	6	16	8
Fifth	5	5	12	6
Sixth	4	4	6	3
Seventh	3	3	4	2

*It is assumed in this table that the amount of marginal utility received from additional units of each of the two products is independent of the quantity of the other product. For example, the marginal utility schedule for product A is independent of the amount of B obtained by the consumer.

[4] E. T. Weiler, *The Economic System* (New York: The Macmillan Company, 1952), p. 89.

marginal-utility information of two columns 2a and 3a on a per-dollar-spent basis. A consumer's choices will be influenced not only by the extra utility which successive units of product A will yield, but also by how many dollars (and therefore how many units of alternative good B) she must give up to obtain those added units of A.

The rational consumer must compare the extra utility from each product with its cost. Suppose you prefer a pizza whose marginal utility is, say, 36 utils to a movie whose marginal utility is just 24 utils. But if the pizza's price is \$12 and the movie only \$6, you would choose the movie rather than the pizza! Why? Because the marginal utility per dollar spent would be 4 utils for the movie (4 = 24 ÷ \$6) compared to only 3 utils for the pizza (3 = 36 ÷ \$12). You could buy two movies for \$12 and, assuming the marginal utility of the second movie is, say, 16 utils, total utility would be 40 utils. Forty units of satisfaction from two movies is clearly superior to 36 utils from the same \$12 expenditure on one pizza. *To make the amounts of extra utility derived from differently priced goods comparable, marginal utility must be put on a per-dollar-spent basis.* This is done in columns 2b and 3b. These figures are obtained by dividing the marginal-utility data of columns 2a and 3a by the assumed prices of A and B—\$1 and \$2, respectively.

Decision-Making Process Now we have Brooks's preferences—on unit and per dollar bases—and the price tags of A and B before us. Brooks stands patiently with \$10 to spend on A and B. In what order should she allocate her dollars on units of A and B to achieve the highest degree of utility within the limits imposed by her money income? What specific combination of A and B will she have obtained at the time that she exhausts her \$10?

Concentrating on columns 2b and 3b of Table 8-2, we find that Brooks should first spend \$2 on the first unit of B, because its marginal utility per dollar of 12 utils is higher than A's of only 10 utils. But now Brooks finds herself indifferent about whether she should buy a second unit of B or the first unit of A, because the marginal utility per dollar of both is 10. So she buys both of them. Brooks now has 1 unit of A and 2 of B. With this combination of goods the last dollar spent on each yields the same amount of extra utility. Does this combination of A and B therefore represent the maximum amount of utility which Brooks can obtain? The answer is "No." This collection of goods only costs \$5 [=(1 × \$1) + (2 × \$2)]; Brooks has \$5 remaining, which she can spend to achieve a still higher level of total utility.

Examining columns 2b and 3b again, we find Brooks should spend the next \$2 on a third unit of B because marginal utility per dollar for the third unit of B is 9 compared to 8 for the second unit of A. But now, with 1 unit of A and 3 of B, we find she is again indifferent to a second unit of A and a fourth unit of B. Again assume Brooks purchases one more unit of each. Marginal utility per dollar is now the same at 8 utils for the last dollar spent on each product, *and* Brooks's money income of \$10 is exhausted [(2 × \$1) + (4 × \$2)]. *The utility-maximizing combination of goods attainable by Brooks is 2 units of A and 4 of B.*[5] By summing the marginal utility information of columns 2a and 3a we find that Brooks is realizing 18 (=10 + 8) utils of satisfaction from the 2 units of A and 78 (=24 + 20 + 18 + 16) utils of satisfaction from the 4 units of B. Her \$10, optimally spent, yields 96 (=18 + 78) utils of satisfaction. Table 8-3 summarizes this step-by-step process for maximizing consumer utility and merits your careful study.

Inferior Options There are other combinations of A and B which are obtainable with \$10. But none will yield a level of total utility as high as 2 units of A and 4 of B. For example, 4 units of A and 3 of B can be obtained for \$10. However, this combination violates the utility-maximizing rule; total utility here is only 93 utils, clearly inferior to the 96 utils yielded by 2 of A and 4 of B. Furthermore, there are other combinations of A and B (such as 4 of A and 5 of B *or* 1 of A and 2 of B) where the marginal utility of the last dollar spent is the same for both A and B. But all such combinations are either unobtainable with Brooks's limited money income (as 4 of A and 5 of B) or fail to exhaust her money income (as 1 of A and 2 of B) and therefore do not yield her the maximum utility attainable.

Problem: Suppose that Brooks's money income was \$14 rather than \$10. What now would be the utility-maximizing combination of A and B? Are A and B normal or inferior goods?

Algebraic Restatement

Our rule merely says that a consumer will maximize her satisfaction when she allocates her money income

[5]To simplify, we assume in this example that Brooks spends her entire income; she neither borrows nor saves. Saving can be regarded as a utility-yielding commodity and incorporated in our analysis. It is treated thus in question 5 at the end of the chapter.

TABLE 8-3 Sequence of purchases in achieving consumer equilibrium

	Potential choice	*Marginal utility per dollar*	*Purchase decision*	*Income remaining*
1	First unit of A	10	First unit of B for $2	$8 = $10 − $2
	First unit of B	12		
2	First unit of A	10	First unit of A for $1 and second unit of B for $2	$5 = $8 − $3
	Second unit of B	10		
3	Second unit of A	8	Third unit of B for $2	$3 = $5 − $2
	Third unit of B	9		
4	Second unit of A	8	Second unit of A for $1 and fourth unit of B for $2	$0 = $3 − $3
	Fourth unit of B	8		

so that the last dollar spent on product A, the last on product B, and so forth, yield equal amounts of additional, or marginal, utility. Now the marginal utility per dollar spent on A is indicated by MU of product A/price of A (column 2b of Table 8-2) and the marginal utility per dollar spent on B by MU of product B/price of B (column 3b of Table 8-2). Our utility-maximizing rule merely requires that these ratios be

$$\frac{\text{MU of product A}}{\text{price of A}} = \frac{\text{MU of product B}}{\text{price of B}}$$

and, of course, the consumer must exhaust her available income. Our tabular illustration has shown us that the combination of 2 units of A and 4 of B fulfills these conditions in that

$$\frac{8}{1} = \frac{16}{2}$$

and the consumer's $10 income is spent.

If the equation is not fulfilled, there will be some reallocation of the consumer's expenditures between A and B, from the low to the high marginal-utility-per-dollar product, which will increase the consumer's total utility. For example, if the consumer spent $10 on 4 of A and 3 of B, we would find that

$$\frac{\text{MU of A: 6 utils}}{\text{price of A: \$1}} < \frac{\text{MU of B: 18 utils}}{\text{price of B: \$2}}$$

The last dollar spent on A provides only 6 utils of satisfaction, and the last dollar spent on B provides 9 (=18 ÷ $2). On a per dollar basis, units of B provide more extra satisfaction than units of A. Hence, the consumer will increase total satisfaction by purchasing more of B and less of A. As dollars are reallocated from A to B, the marginal utility from additional units of B will decline as the result of moving *down* the diminishing marginal-utility schedule for B, and the marginal utility of A will rise as the consumer moves *up* the diminishing marginal-utility schedule for A. At some new combination of A and B—specifically, 2 of A and 4 of B—the equality of the two ratios and therefore consumer equilibrium will be achieved. As we already know, the net gain in utility is 3 utils (=96 − 93).

MARGINAL UTILITY AND THE DEMAND CURVE

It is a simple step from the utility-maximizing rule to the construction of a downsloping demand curve. Recall that the basic determinants of an individual's demand curve for a specific product are (1) preferences or tastes, (2) money income, and (3) prices of other goods. The utility data of Table 8-2 reflect our consumer's preferences. We continue to suppose that her money income is $10. And, concentrating on the construction of a simple demand curve for product B, we assume that the price of A—representing "other goods"—is $1.

Deriving the Demand Curve We can now derive a simple demand schedule for B by considering alternative prices at which B might be sold and determining the quantity our consumer will purchase. We have already determined one such price-quantity combination in explaining the utility-maximizing rule: Given tastes, income, and prices of other goods, the rational consumer will purchase 4 units of B at $2. Now assume the price of B falls to \$1. The marginal-utility-per-dollar data of column 3b of Table 8-2 will double, because the price of B has been halved; the new data for column 3b are in fact identical to those in column 3a. The purchase of 2 units of A and 4 of B is no longer an equilibrium combination. By applying the same reasoning used to develop the utility-maximizing rule, we now find Brooks's utility-maximizing position is 4 units of A and 6 of B. We sketch Brooks's demand curve for B as in Table 8-4, confirming a downsloping demand curve.

Income and Substitution Effects Revisited At the beginning of this chapter we indicated that increased purchases of a good whose price had fallen could be understood in terms of the substitution and income effects. Although our analysis does not let us sort out these two effects quantitatively, we can see intuitively how each is involved in the increased purchase of product B.

The *substitution effect* can be understood by referring back to our utility-maximizing rule. Before the price of B declined, Brooks was in equilibrium in that $MU_A(8)/P_A(\$1) = MU_B(16)/P_B(\$2)$, when purchasing 2 units of A and 4 units of B. But after B's price falls from \$2 to \$1, $MU_A\ (8)/P_A(\$1) < MU_B(16)/P_B(\$1)$ or, more simply stated, the last dollar spent on B now yields more utility (16 utils) than does the last dollar spent on A (8 utils). This indicates that a switching of expenditures from A to B is needed to restore equilibrium; that is, a *substitution* of now cheaper B for A will occur in the bundle of goods which Brooks purchases.

What about the *income effect?* The assumed decline in the price of B from \$2 to \$1 increases Brooks's real income. Before the price decline, Brooks was in equilibrium when buying 2 of A and 4 of B. But at the lower \$1 price for B, Brooks would have to spend only \$6 rather than \$10 on this same combination of goods. She has \$4 left over to spend on more of A, more of B, or more of both. In short, the price decline of B has caused Brooks's *real* income to increase so that she can now obtain larger amounts of A and B with the same \$10 *money* income. The portion of the 2-unit increase in her purchase of B due to this increase in real income is the income effect.

TABLE 8-4 The demand schedule for product B

Price per unit of B	*Quantity demanded*
\$2	4
1	6

QUICK REVIEW 8-2

- ***The theory of consumer behavior assumes that, with limited money incomes and given product prices, consumers make rational choices on the basis of well-defined preferences.***
- ***A consumer maximizes utility by allocating money income so that the marginal utility per dollar spent is the same for every good purchased.***
- ***A downsloping demand curve can be derived by changing the price of one product in the consumer-behavior model.***

THE TIME DIMENSION

The theory of consumer behavior has been generalized to take the economic value of *time* into account. Both consumption and production activities have a common characteristic—they take time. Time is a valuable economic resource; by working—by using an hour in productive activity—one may earn \$6, \$10, \$50, or more, depending on one's education and skills. By using that hour for leisure or in consumption activities, one incurs the opportunity cost of forgone income; you sacrifice the \$6, \$10, or \$50 you could have earned by working.

The Value of Time

In the marginal-utility theory of consumer behavior economists traditionally have assumed that consumption is an instantaneous act. However, it is logical to argue that "prices" of consumer goods should include, not merely market price, but also the value of the time required in consumption of the good. In other words, the denominators of our earlier marginal-utility/price ratios are incomplete because they do not reflect the "full price"—market price *plus* the value of consumption time—of the product.

Imagine a consumer who is considering the purchase of a round of golf, on the one hand, and a concert, on the other. The market price of the golf game is \$15 and the concert is \$20. But the golf game is more time-intensive than the concert. Suppose you will spend four hours on the golf course, but only two hours at the concert. If your time is worth \$7 per hour—as evidenced by the \$7 wage rate you can obtain by working—then the "full price" of the golf game is \$43 (the \$15 market price *plus* \$28 worth of time). Similarly, the "full price" of the concert is \$34 (the \$20 market price

LAST WORD

THE WATER–DIAMOND PARADOX

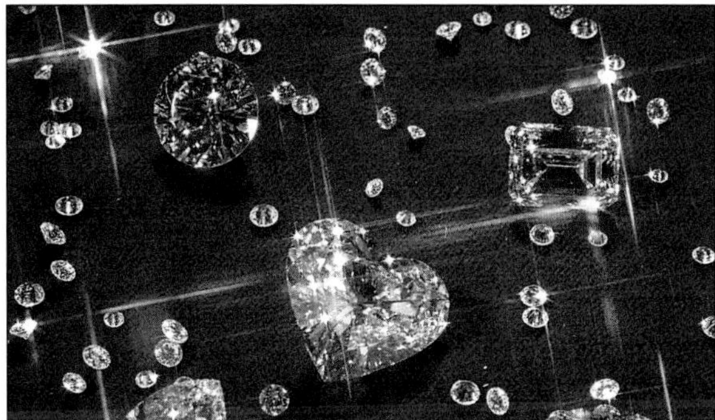

Water is clearly one of the most useful products in the world; our very survival depends on it. Yet water is very cheap. In contrast, diamonds—which are merely decorative and have little practical value—are very expensive. Why do prices apparently fail to measure the usefulness of goods? Our theory of consumer behavior and the distinction between total and marginal utility help resolve this paradox.

The explanation of the water–diamond paradox lies in two related considerations. First, the supplies of the two products are much different. Water is plentiful and, as a consequence, its price is low and we therefore consume large quantities of it. In doing so we extend our use of water to uses wherein the utility from the last unit of water—water's marginal utility—is very low. For example, we water our lawns, make ice cubes, and wash our cars. In contrast, diamonds are rare and costly to mine, cut, and polish. Therefore, their supply is restricted and they are available only at a high price. The marginal utility of diamonds is therefore very large.

The second consideration relates back to the utility-maximizing rule which states that consumers should purchase any good until the ratio of its marginal utility to price is the same as that for all other goods. Although the *marginal* utility of water may be low because it is plentiful and its price is low, the *total* utility derived from its consumption is exceedingly large because of the great quantity consumed. Conversely, the total utility derived from diamonds is low because the very high price which reflects the scarcity of diamonds causes consumers to purchase relatively few of them. In short, the total utility derived from water is relatively great and the total utility derived from diamonds is relatively small, but it is *marginal* utility which is relevant to the price people are willing to pay for a good. Water yields much more total utilty to us than do diamonds, even though the utility of an additional gallon of water is much less than the utility of an additional diamond. Society would gladly give up *all* of the diamonds in the world if that were necessary to obtain *all* of the water in the world. But society would rather have an *additional* diamond than an *additional* gallon of water, given the abundant stock of water available.

plus \$14 worth of time). We find that, contrary to what market prices alone indicate, the "full price" of the concert is really *less* than the "full price" of the golf game.

If we now assume that the marginal utilities derived from successive golf games and concerts are identical, traditional theory would indicate that one should consume more golf games than concerts because the market price of the former is lower (\$15) than the latter (\$20). But when time is taken into account, the situation is reversed and golf games are more expensive (\$43) than concerts (\$34). Hence, it is rational in this case to consume more concerts than golf games.

Some Implications

By taking time into account, we can explain certain observable phenomena which traditional theory does not. It may be rational for the unskilled worker or retiree whose time has little or no market value to ride a bus from Peoria to Pittsburgh. But the corporate executive, whose time is very valuable, will find it cheaper to fly, even though bus fare is only a fraction of plane fare. It is sensible for the retiree, living on a modest social security check and having ample time, to spend many hours shopping for bargains. It is equally intelligent for the highly paid physician, working 55 hours per week, to patronize the hospital cafeteria and to buy a new television set over the phone.

Foreigners feel affluent Americans are "wasteful" of food and other material goods, but "overly economical" in the use of time. Americans who visit less developed countries find that time is used casually or "squandered," while material goods are very highly prized and carefully used. These differences are not a paradox or a case of radically different temperaments. The differences are primarily a rational reflection that the high labor productivity characteristic of an advanced society gives time a high market value, whereas the opposite is true in a less developed country.

A final point: As labor productivity has increased historically with the growth of our economy, time has become more valuable in the labor market. Or, stated differently, time used on pure leisure and various consumer activities has become more expensive. Thus we make a great effort to use nonwork time more "productively." Where possible, we try to increase the pleasure or utility yield per hour by consuming more per unit of time. In some cases this means making consumption more goods-intensive; for example, by buying or renting a motorized golf cart, the time required for a round of golf can be reduced. One watches the news on television because it takes less time than reading the newspaper. In other instances, we consume two or more items simultaneously. After dinner, the consumer "may find himself drinking Brazilian coffee, smoking a Dutch cigar, sipping a French cognac, reading *The New York Times,* listening to a Brandenburg Concerto and entertaining his Swedish wife—all at the same time, with varying degrees of success."[6]

But the yield from certain uses of time—pure idleness, cultural pursuits, and the "cultivation of mind and spirit"—cannot be readily increased. Hence, time tends to be shifted from these uses to areas where the yield is greater. This helps explain why, although economic development may bring affluence in the form of goods, it also increases the relative scarcity of time and creates a more hectic life-style. Economic growth, it is argued, cannot produce abundance in all respects; total affluence—an abundance of *both* goods and time—is a logical fallacy. Advanced economies are goods-rich and time-poor, while less developed countries are time-rich and goods-poor.

[6]Staffan B. Linder, *The Harried Leisure Class* (New York: Columbia University Press, 1970), p. 79.

CHAPTER SUMMARY

1 The law of demand can be explained in terms of the income and substitution effects or the law of diminishing marginal utility.

2 The income effect says that a decline in the price of a product will enable the consumer to buy more of it with a fixed money income. The substitution effect points out that a lower price will make a product relatively more attractive and therefore increase the consumer's willingness to substitute it for other products.

3 The law of diminishing marginal utility states that beyond some point, additional units of a specific good will yield ever-declining amounts of extra satisfaction to a consumer.

4 We may assume that the typical consumer is rational and acts on the basis of well-defined preferences. Because income is limited and goods have prices on them, the consumer cannot purchase all the goods and services he or she might like to have. The consumer should therefore select that attainable combination of goods which will maximize his or her utility or satisfaction.

5 The consumer's utility will be maximized when income is allocated so that the last dollar spent on each product purchased yields the same amount of extra satisfaction. Algebraically, the utility-maximizing rule is fulfilled when

$$\frac{\text{MU of product A}}{\text{price of A}} = \frac{\text{MU of product B}}{\text{price of B}}$$

and the consumer's income is spent.

6 The utility-maximizing rule and the demand curve are logically consistent. Because marginal utility declines, a lower price will be needed to induce the consumer to buy more.

7 The theory of consumer choice has been generalized by taking into account the value of the time required in the consumption of various goods and services.

TERMS AND CONCEPTS

income effect
substitution effect
law of diminishing marginal utility
utility
utility-maximizing rule

QUESTIONS AND STUDY SUGGESTIONS

1 Explain the law of demand through the income and substitution effects, using a price increase as a point of departure for your discussion. Explain the law of demand in terms of diminishing marginal utility.

2 Mrs. Peterson buys loaves of bread and quarts of milk each week at prices of \$1 and 80 cents, respectively. At present she is buying these two products in amounts such that the marginal utilities from the last units purchased of the two products are 80 and 70 utils, respectively. Is she buying the utility-maximizing combination of bread and milk? If not, how should she reallocate her expenditures between the two goods?

3 You are choosing between two goods, X and Y, and your marginal utility from each is as shown below. If your income is \$9 and the prices of X and Y are \$2 and \$1 respectively, what quantities of each will you purchase in maximizing utility? Specify the amount of total utility you will realize. Assume that, other things remaining unchanged, the price of X falls to \$1. What quantities of X and Y will you now purchase? Using the two prices and quantities you have derived for X, graph your demand curve for X.

Units of X	MU_x	*Units of Y*	MU_y
1	10	1	8
2	8	2	7
3	6	3	6
4	4	4	5
5	3	5	4
6	2	6	3

4 "Nothing is more useful than water: but it will purchase scarce any thing; scarce any thing can be had in exchange for it. A diamond, on the contrary, has scarce any value in use; but a very great quantity of other goods may frequently be had in exchange for it."[7] Explain.

[7]Adam Smith, *The Wealth of Nations* (New York: Modern Library, Inc., originally published in 1776), p. 28.

5 Columns 1 through 4 of the table at the bottom of this page show the marginal utility, measured in terms of utils, which Mr. Black would get by purchasing various amounts of products A, B, C, and D. Column 5 shows the marginal utility Black gets from saving. Assume that the prices of A, B, C, and D are \$18, \$6, \$4, and \$24, respectively, and that Black has a money income of \$106.

a What quantities of A, B, C, and D will Black purchase in maximizing his satisfactions?

b How many dollars will Black choose to save?

c Check your answers by substituting them into the algebraic statement of the utility-maximizing rule.

6 "In the long run it may be irrational to purchase goods on the basis of habit; but in the short run habitual buying may prove to be a very sensible means of allocating income." Do you agree? Explain.

7 How can time be incorporated into the theory of consumer behavior? Foreigners frequently point out that Americans are very wasteful of food and other material goods and very conscious of, and overly economical in, their use of time. Can you explain this observation?

8 Explain:

a "Before economic growth, there were too few goods; after growth, there is too little time."

b "It is irrational for an individual to take the time to be completely rational in economic decision making."

9 In the last decade or so there has been a dramatic expansion of small retail convenience stores—such as Kwik Shops, 7-Elevens, Gas 'N Shops—although their prices are generally much higher than those in the large supermarkets. Can you explain their success?

10 **Advanced analysis:** Let $MU_a = z = 10 - x$ and $MU_b = z = 21 - 2y$, where z is marginal utility measured in utils, x is the amount spent on product A, and y is the amount spent on B. Assume the consumer has \$10 to spend on A and B; that is, $x + y = 10$. How is this \$10 best allocated between A and B? How much utility will the marginal dollar yield?

Column 1		*Column 2*		*Column 3*		*Column 4*		*Column 5*	
Units of A	*MU*	*Units of B*	*MU*	*Units of C*	*MU*	*Units of D*	*MU*	*No. of dollars saved*	*MU*
1	72	1	24	1	15	1	36	1	5
2	54	2	15	2	12	2	30	2	4
3	45	3	12	3	8	3	24	3	3
4	36	4	9	4	7	4	18	4	2
5	27	5	7	5	5	5	13	5	1
6	18	6	5	6	4	6	7	6	$\frac{1}{2}$
7	15	7	2	7	$3\frac{1}{2}$	7	4	7	$\frac{1}{4}$
8	12	8	1	8	3	8	2	8	$\frac{1}{8}$

APPENDIX TO CHAPTER 8

Indifference Curve Analysis

A more advanced explanation of consumer behavior and equilibrium is based upon (1) budget lines and (2) indifference curves.

The Budget Line: What Is Attainable

A **budget line** *shows various combinations of two products which can be purchased with a given money income.* If the price of product A is \$1.50 and the price of B \$1.00, then the consumer could purchase all the combinations of A and B shown in Table 1 with \$12 of money income. At one extreme the consumer might spend all of his or her income on 8 units of A and have nothing left to spend on B. Or, by giving up 2 units of A and thereby "freeing" \$3, the consumer could have 6 units of A and 3 of B. And so on to the other extreme, at which the consumer could buy 12 units of B at \$1.00 each, spending his or her entire money income on B with nothing left to spend on A.

Figure 1 shows the budget line graphically. The slope of the budget line measures the ratio of the price of B to the price of A; more precisely, the absolute value of the slope is $P_B/P_A = \$1.00/\$1.50 = 2/3$. This is the mathematical way of saying that the consumer must forgo 2 units of A (measured on the vertical axis) at \$1.50 each to have \$3 to spend on 3 units of B (measured on the horizontal axis). In moving down the budget or price line, 2 of A (at \$1.50 each) must be given up to obtain 3 of B (at \$1.00 each). This yields a slope of $\frac{2}{3}$.

TABLE 1 **The budget line: combinations of A and B attainable with an income of \$12 (*hypothetical data*)**

Units of A (price = \$1.50)	*Units of B (price = \$1.00)*	*Total expenditures*
8	0	\$12 (=\$12 + \$0)
6	3	\$12 (=\$9 + \$3)
4	6	\$12 (=\$6 + \$6)
2	9	\$12 (=\$3 + \$9)
0	12	\$12 (=\$0 + \$12)

Two other characteristics of the budget line merit comment.

1 Income Changes The location of the budget line varies with money income. An *increase* in money income will shift the budget line to the *right;* a *decrease* in money income will move it to the *left.* To verify these statements, recalculate Table 1 assuming that money income is (*a*) \$24 and (*b*) \$6 and plot the new budget lines in Figure 1.

2 Price Changes A change in product prices will also shift the budget line. A decline in the prices of both products—the equivalent of a real income increase—will shift the curve to the right. You can verify this by recalculating Table 1 and replotting Figure 1 assuming that $P_A = \$.75$ and $P_B = \$.50$. Conversely, an increase

FIGURE 1 **A consumer's budget line**

The budget line shows all the various combinations of any two products which can be purchased, given the prices of the products and the consumer's money income.

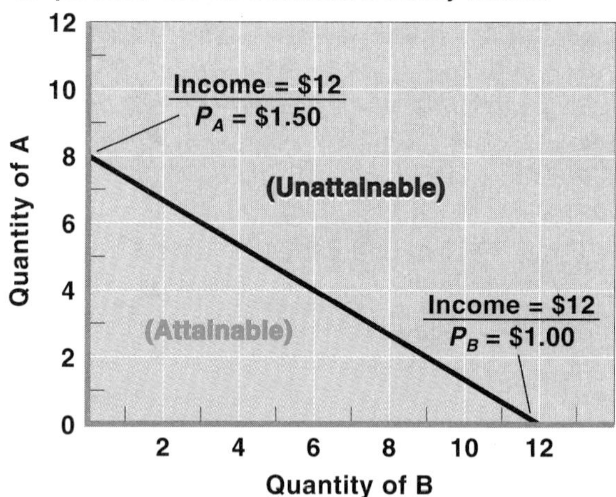

in the prices of A and B will shift the curve to the left. Again, assume $P_A = \$3$ and $P_B = \$2$ and rework Table 1 and Figure 1 to substantiate this statement. Note in particular what happens if we change P_B while holding P_A (and money income) constant. The reader should verify that, if we lower P_B from \$1.00 to \$.50, the budget line will fan outward to the right. Conversely, by increasing P_B from \$1.00 to \$1.50, the line will fan inward to the left. In both instances the line remains "anchored" at 8 units on the vertical axis because P_A has not changed.

Indifference Curves: What Is Preferred

Budget lines reflect "objective" market data involving income and prices. The budget line reveals combinations of A and B which are attainable, given money income and prices. Indifference curves, on the other hand, embody "subjective" information about consumer preferences for A and B. An **indifference curve** *shows all combinations of products A and B which will yield the same level of satisfaction or utility to the consumer.* Table 2 and Figure 2 present a hypothetical indifference curve involving products A and B. The consumer's subjective preferences are such that he or she will realize the same total utility from each combination of A and B shown in the table or curve; hence, the consumer will be indifferent as to which combination is actually obtained.

It is essential to understand several characteristics of indifference curves.

1 Downsloping Indifference curves are downsloping because both product A and product B yield utility to the consumer. Hence, in moving from combination *j* to combination *k*, the consumer is obtaining more of B and increasing his or her total utility; therefore, some of A must be taken away to decrease total utility by a precisely offsetting amount. In brief, "more of B" necessitates "less of A" so that the quantities of A and B are inversely related. Any curve which reflects inversely related variables is downsloping.

TABLE 2 **An indifference schedule (*hypothetical data*)**

Combination	*Units of A*	*Units of B*
j	12	2
k	6	4
l	4	6
m	3	8

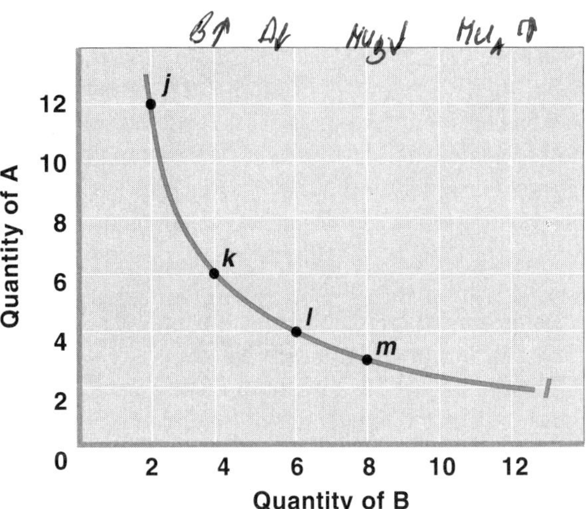

FIGURE 2 **A consumer's indifference curve**

Every point on an indifference curve represents some combination of products A and B which is equally satisfactory to the consumer; that is, each combination of A and B embodies the same level of total utility.

2 Convex to Origin But, as viewed from the origin, a downsloping curve can be concave (bowed outward) or convex (bowed inward). A concave curve has an increasing (steeper) slope as one moves down the curve, while a convex curve has a diminishing (flatter) slope as one moves down it. (Recall that the production possibilities curve of Figure 2-1 is concave, reflecting the law of increasing opportunity costs.) Note in Figure 2 that *the indifference curve is convex as viewed from the origin.* That is, the slope diminishes or becomes flatter as we move from *j* to *k*, to *l*, to *m*, and so on down the curve. Technically, the slope of the indifference curve measures the **marginal rate of substitution** (MRS) because it shows the rate, at the margin, at which the consumer will substitute one good for the other (B for A) to remain equally satisfied. The diminishing slope of the indifference curve means the willingness to substitute B for A *diminishes* as one moves down the curve.

The rationale for this convexity, that is, for a diminishing MRS, is that a consumer's subjective willingness to substitute B for A (or vice versa) will depend on the amounts of B and A he or she has to begin with. Consider Table 2 and Figure 2 once again, beginning at point *j*. Here, in relative terms, the consumer has a substantial amount of A and very little of B. This means that "at the margin" B is very valuable (that is, its marginal utility is high), while A is less valuable at the margin (its marginal utility is low). The consumer will then be willing to give up a substantial amount of A to get, say, 2 more units of B. In this particular case, the consumer is willing to forgo 6 units of A to get 2 more units of B; the MRS is $\frac{6}{2}$, or 3. But at point *k* the consumer now has less A and more B. Now A will be somewhat more valuable, and B somewhat less valuable, at the margin. Considering the move from point *k* to point *l*, the consumer is only willing to give up 2 units of A to get 2 more units of B so the MRS is now only $\frac{2}{2}$, or 1. Having still less of A and more of B at point *l*, the consumer is only willing to give up 1 unit of A in return for 2 more of B and and the MRS falls to $\frac{1}{2}$.

In general, as the amount of B *increases,* the marginal utility of additional units of B *decreases.* Similarly, as the quantity of A *decreases,* its marginal utility *increases.* In Figure 2 we see that in moving down the curve the consumer will be willing to give up smaller and smaller amounts of A to offset acquiring each additional unit of B. The result is a curve with a diminishing slope, one which is convex when viewed from the origin. The MRS declines as one moves southeast along the indifference curve.

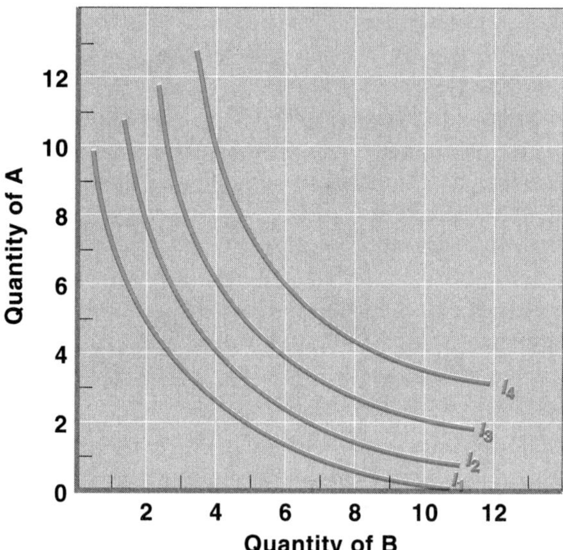

FIGURE 3 An indifference map

An indifference map is comprised of a set of indifference curves. Each successive curve further from the origin indicates a higher level of total utility. That is, any combination of products A and B shown by a point on I_4 is superior to any combination of A and B shown by a point on I_3, I_2, or I_1.

3 Indifference Map The single indifference curve of Figure 2 reflects some constant (but unspecified) level of total utility or satisfaction. It is possible—and useful for our analysis—to sketch a whole series of indifference curves or, in other words, an **indifference map** as shown in Figure 3. Each curve reflects a different level of total utility. Specifically, each curve to the *right* of our original curve (labeled I_3 in Figure 3) reflects combinations of A and B which yield *more* utility than I_3. Each curve to the *left* of I_3 reflects *less* total utility than I_3. *As we move out from the origin each successive indifference curve entails a higher level of utility.* This can be demonstrated by drawing a line in a northeasterly direction from the origin and noting that its points of intersection with each successive curve entail larger amounts of *both* A and B and therefore a higher level of total utility.

Equilibrium at Tangency

Noting that the axes of Figures 1 and 3 are identical, we can now determine the consumer's **equilibrium position** by combining the budget line and the indifference map as shown in Figure 4. By definition, the budget line indicates all combinations of A and B the consumer can attain, given his or her money income and the prices of A and B. Of these attainable combinations, the consumer will most prefer that combination which yields the greatest satisfaction or utility. Specifically, *the utility-maximizing combination will be the one lying on the highest attainable indifference curve.*

In terms of Figure 4 the consumer's utility-maximizing or equilibrium combination of A and B is at point *X* where the budget line is *tangent* to I_3. Why not point *Y*? Because *Y* is on a lower indifference curve, I_2. By trading "down" the budget line—by shifting dollars from purchases of A to purchases of B—the consumer can get on an indifference curve further from the origin and thereby increase total utility from the same income. Why not *Z*? Same reason: Point *Z* is on a lower indifference curve, I_1. By trading "up" the budget line—by reallocating dollars from B to A—the consumer can get on higher indifference curve I_3 and increase total utility.

How about point *W* on indifference curve I_4? While it is true that *W* yields a higher level of total utility than does *X*, point *W* is beyond (outside) the budget line and hence *not* attainable to the consumer. Point *X* is the best or optimal *attainable* combination of products A and B. At this point we note that, by definition of tangency, the slope of the highest attainable indifference curve equals the slope of the budget line. Because the slope of the indifference curve reflects the MRS and

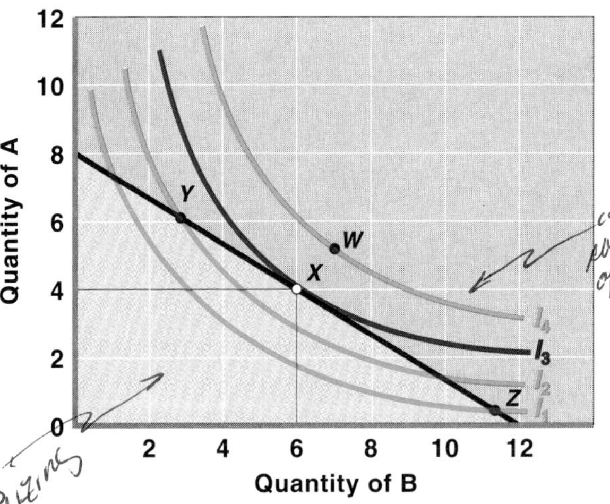

FIGURE 4 The consumer's equilibrium position

The consumer's equilibrium position is at point *X*, where the budget line is tangent to the highest attainable indifference curve, I_3. In this case the consumer will buy 4 units of A at \$1.50 per unit and 6 of B at \$1 per unit with a \$12 money income. Points *Z* and *Y* also represent attainable combinations of A and B, but yield less total utility as is evidenced by the fact they are on lower indifference curves. While *W* would entail more utility than *X*, it is outside the budget line and therefore unattainable.

the slope of the budget line is P_B/P_A, the optimal or equilibrium position is where

$$\text{MRS} = P_B/P_A$$

Digression: The Measurement of Utility

There is an important difference between the marginal-utility theory and the indifference curve theory of consumer demand. The marginal-utility theory assumes that utility is *numerically* measurable. That is, the consumer is assumed to be able to say *how much* extra utility he or she derives from an extra unit of A or B. Given the prices of A and B, the consumer must be able to measure the marginal utility derived from successive units of A and B to realize the utility-maximizing (equilibrium) position as previously indicated by

$$\frac{\text{Marginal utility of A}}{\text{price of A}} = \frac{\text{marginal utility of B}}{\text{price of B}}$$

The indifference curve approach poses a less stringent requirement for the consumer: He or she need only specify whether a given combination of A and B yields more, less, or the same amount of utility than some other combination of A and B. The consumer need only say, for example, that 6 of A and 7 of B yield more (or less) satisfaction than 4 of A and 9 of B; indifference curve analysis does *not* require the consumer to specify *how much* more (or less) satisfaction will be realized.

When the equilibrium situations in the two approaches are compared we find that (1) in the indifference curve analysis the MRS equals P_B/P_A; however, (2) in the marginal-utility approach the ratio of marginal utilities equals P_B/P_A. We therefore deduce that the MRS is equivalent in the marginal-utility approach to the ratio of marginal utilities of the two goods.[8]

Deriving the Demand Curve

We noted earlier that, given the price of A, an increase in the price of B will cause the budget line to fan inward to the left. This fact can now be used to derive a demand curve for product B. In Figure 5a we reproduce Figure 4 showing our initial consumer equilibrium at point *X*. The budget line involved in determining this equilibrium position assumes a money income of \$12 and that P_A = \$1.50 and P_B = \$1.00. Let's examine what happens to the equilibrium position if we increase P_B to \$1.50, holding money income and the price of A constant.

The result is shown in Figure 5a. The budget line fans to the left, yielding a new equilibrium point of tangency with indifference curve I_2 at point X'. At X' the consumer is buying 3 units of B and 5 of A compared to 4 of A and 6 of B at *X*. Our interest is in B and we note that we have sufficient information to locate the demand curve for product B. We know that at equilibrium point *X* the price of B is \$1.00 and 6 units are purchased; at equilibrium point X' the price of B is \$1.50 and 3 units are purchased.

These data are shown graphically as a demand curve for B in Figure 5b. Note that the horizontal axes of Figure 5a and b are identical; both measure the quantity demanded of B. Hence, we can drop gray perpendiculars from Figure 5a down to the horizontal axis of Figure 5b. On the vertical axis of Figure 5b we locate the two chosen prices of B. Connecting these prices

[8]Technical footnote: If we begin with the utility-maximizing rule, $\text{MU}_A/P_A = \text{MU}_B/P_B$, then multiply through by P_B and divide through by MU_A, we obtain $P_B/P_A = \text{MU}_B/\text{MU}_A$. In indifference curve analysis we know that the optimal or equilibrium position is where MRS = P_B/P_A. Hence, MRS also equals MU_B/MU_A.

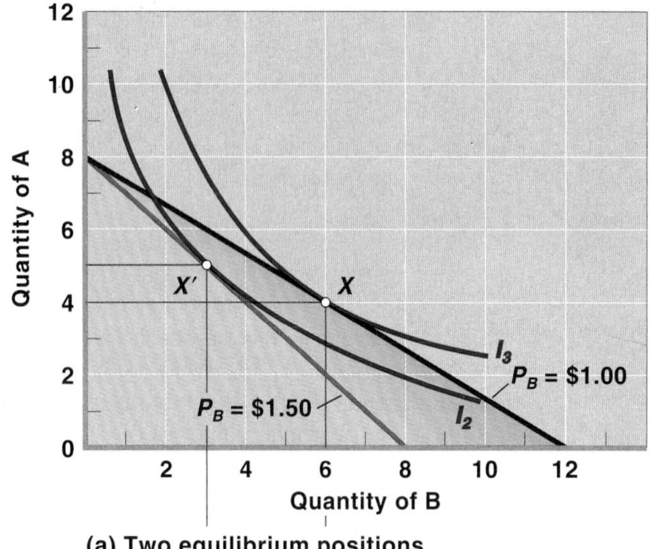

(a) Two equilibrium positions

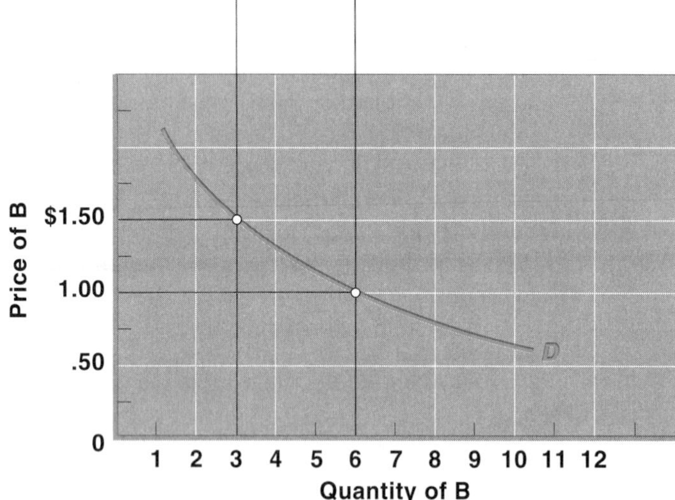

(b) The demand curve for product B

FIGURE 5 Deriving the demand curve
When the price of B is increased from \$1.00 to \$1.50 in (a) the equilibrium position moves from *X* to *X′*, decreasing the quantity of B demanded from 6 to 3 units. The demand curve for B is determined in (b) by plotting the \$1.00–6 units and the \$1.50–3 units price-quantity combinations for B.

with the relevant quantities demanded, we locate two points on the demand curve for B. By simple manipulation of the price of B in an indifference curve–budget line context, a downsloping demand curve for B can be derived. We have derived the law of demand under the correct assumption of "other things being equal" since *only* the price of B has been changed. The price of A as well as the consumer's income and tastes have remained constant when deriving the consumer's demand curve for product B.

APPENDIX SUMMARY

1 The indifference curve approach to consumer behavior is based on the consumer's budget line and indifference curves.

2 The budget line shows all combinations of two products which the consumer can purchase, given money income and product prices.

3 A change in product prices or money income will shift the budget line.

4 An indifference curve shows all combinations of two products which will yield the same level of total utility to the consumer. Indifference curves are downsloping and convex to the origin.

5 An indifference map consists of a number of indifference curves; the further from the origin, the higher the level of utility associated with each curve.

6 The consumer will select that point on the budget line which puts him or her on the highest attainable indifference curve.

7 Changing the price of one product shifts the budget line and determines a new equilibrium position. A downsloping demand curve can be determined by plotting the price-quantity combinations associated with the old and new equilibrium positions.

APPENDIX TERMS AND CONCEPTS

budget line
indifference curve
marginal rate of substitution
indifference map
equilibrium position

APPENDIX QUESTIONS AND STUDY SUGGESTIONS

1 What information is embodied in a budget line? What shifts will occur in the budget line when money income **a** increases and **b** decreases? What shifts will occur in the budget line as the product price shown on the horizontal axis **a** increases and **b** decreases?

2 What information is contained in an indifference curve? Why are such curves **a** downsloping and **b** convex to the origin? Why does total utility increase as the consumer moves to indifference curves further from the origin? Why can't indifference curves intersect?

3 Using Figure 4, explain why the point of *tangency* of the budget line with an indifference curve is the consumer's equilibrium position. Explain why any point where the budget line *intersects* an indifference curve will *not* be equilibrium. Explain: "The consumer is in equilibrium where MRS = P_B/P_A."

4 Assume that the data in the accompanying table indicate an indifference curve for Mr. Chen. Graph this curve, putting A on the vertical and B on the horizontal axis. Assuming the prices of A and B are \$1.50 and \$1.00, respectively, and that Chen has \$24 to spend, add the resulting budget line to your graph. What combination of A and B will Chen purchase? Does your answer meet the MRS = P_B/P_A rule for equilibrium?

Units of A	*Units of B*
16	6
12	8
8	12
4	24

5 Explain graphically how indifference analysis can be used to derive a demand curve.

6 **Advanced analysis:** Demonstrate that the equilibrium condition MRS = P_B/P_A is the equivalent of the utility-maximizing rule $MU_A/P_A = MU_B/P_B$.

The Costs of Production

Product prices are determined by the interaction of demand and supply. In preceding chapters we examined factors underlying demand. As observed in Chapter 4, the basic factor underlying the ability and willingness of firms to supply a product in the market is the cost of production. Production of any good requires economic resources which, because of their relative scarcity, bear price tags. The amount of any product a firm is willing to supply depends on the prices (costs) and the productivity of the resources essential to its production, on the one hand, and the price the product will bring in the market, on the other.

This chapter considers the general nature of production costs. Product prices are introduced in the following chapters, and supply decisions of producers are then explained.

ECONOMIC COSTS

Costs exist because resources are scarce and have alternative uses. To use a bundle of resources in producing some particular good means that certain alternative production opportunities have been forgone. *Costs in economics deal with forgoing the opportunity to produce alternative goods and services.* The **economic,** or **opportunity cost** of any resource in producing a good is its value or worth in its best alternative use.

This conception of costs is embodied in the production possibilities curve of Chapter 2. Note that at point *C* in Table 2-1 the opportunity cost of producing 100,000 *more* pizzas is the 3,000 industrial robots which must be forgone. The steel used for armaments is not available for manufacturing automobiles or apartment buildings. And if an assembly-line worker can produce automobiles or washing machines, then the cost to society in employing this worker in an automobile plant is the contribution the worker would otherwise have made in producing washing machines. The cost to you in reading this chapter is the alternative uses of your time—studying for a biology exam or going to a movie—which you must forgo while you read it.

Explicit and Implicit Costs

Let's now consider costs from the firm's viewpoint. Given the notion of opportunity costs, we can say that *economic costs are those payments a firm must make, or incomes it must provide, to resource suppliers to attract these resources away from alternative production oppor-*

tunities. These payments or incomes may be either explicit or implicit.

The monetary payments—the "out-of-pocket" or cash expenditures a firm makes to "outsiders" who supply labor services, materials, fuel, transportation services, and power—are called **explicit costs.** Explicit costs are payments to nonowners of the firm for the resources they supply.

But, in addition, a firm may use certain resources the firm itself owns. Our concept of opportunity costs tells us that, regardless of whether a resource is owned or hired by an enterprise, there is a cost involved in using that resource in a specific employment. The costs of such self-owned, self-employed resources are nonexpenditure or **implicit costs.** To the firm, those implicit costs are the money payments the self-employed resources could have earned in their best alternative employments.

Example: Suppose Holly operates a corner grocery as a sole proprietor. She owns outright her store building and supplies all her own labor and money capital. Though her enterprise has no explicit rental or wage costs, implicit rents and wages are incurred. By using her own building for a grocery, Holly sacrifices the $800 monthly rental income she otherwise could have earned by renting it to someone else. Similarly, by using her money capital and labor in her own enterprise, Holly sacrifices the interest and wage incomes she otherwise could have earned by supplying these resources in their best alternative employments. And, finally, by running her own enterprise, Holly forgoes earnings she could have realized by supplying her managerial efforts to another firm.

Normal Profits as a Cost

The minimum payment required to keep Holly's entrepreneurial talents engaged in this enterprise is called a **normal profit.** As is true of implicit rent or implicit wages, her normal return for performing entrepreneurial functions is an implicit cost. If this minimum, or normal, return is not realized, the entrepreneur will withdraw her efforts from this line of production and reallocate them to a more attractive line of production. Or she may cease being an entrepreneur and become a wage or salary earner.

The economist includes as costs all payments—explicit and implicit, the latter including a normal profit—required to attract and retain resources in a given line of production.

Economic, or Pure, Profits

Economists and accountants use the term "profits" differently. *Accounting profits are the firm's total revenue less its explicit costs.* But economists define profits differently. **Economic profits** *are total revenue less all costs (explicit and implicit, the latter including a normal profit to the entrepreneur).* Therefore, when an economist says a firm is just covering its costs, it means that all explicit and implicit costs are being met and that the entrepreneur is receiving a return just large enough to retain his or her talents in the present line of production.

If a firm's total receipts exceed all its economic costs, any residual accrues to the entrepreneur. This residual is called an *economic,* or *pure, profit.* In short:

$$\text{Economic profits} = \text{total revenue} - \text{opportunity cost of all inputs}$$

An economic profit is *not* a cost, because by definition it is a return in excess of the normal profit required to retain the entrepreneur in this particular line of production.

Figure 9-1 shows the relationships between various cost and profit concepts and merits close examination. You should also consider question 2 at the end of this chapter.

Short Run and Long Run

The costs a firm or industry incurs in producing any given output will depend on the types of adjustments it can make in the amounts of the various resources it

FIGURE 9-1 Economic and accounting profits

Economic profits are equal to total revenue less opportunity costs. Opportunity costs are the sum of explicit and implicit costs and include a normal profit to the entrepreneur. Accounting profits are equal to total revenue less accounting (explicit) costs.

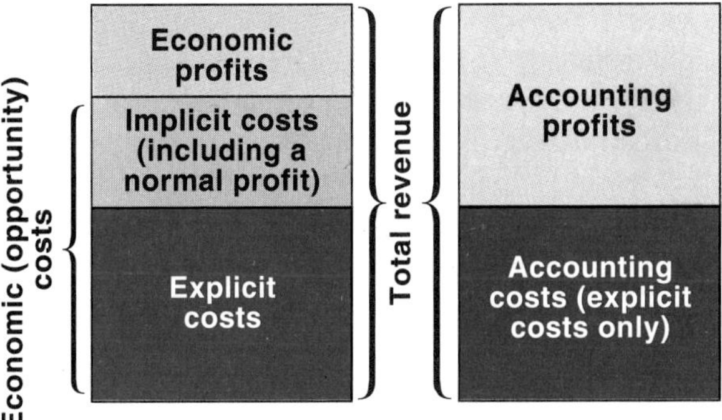

employs. The quantities employed of many resources —most labor, raw materials, fuel, and power—can be varied easily and quickly. Other resources require more time for adjustment. The capacity of a manufacturing plant, that is, the size of the factory building and the amount of machinery and equipment therein, can only be varied over a considerable period of time. In some heavy industries it may take several years to alter plant capacity.

Short Run: Fixed Plant These differences in the time necessary to vary quantities of various resources used in the productive process make it essential to distinguish between the short run and the long run. The **short run** is a period of time too brief for an enterprise to alter its plant capacity, yet long enough to permit a change in the level at which the fixed plant is used. The firm's plant capacity is fixed in the short run, but output can be varied by applying larger or smaller amounts of labor, materials, and other resources to that plant. Existing plant capacity can be used more or less intensively in the short run.

Long Run: Variable Plant From the viewpoint of existing firms, the **long run** is a period of time extensive enough for these firms to change the quantities of *all* resources employed, including plant capacity. From the industry's viewpoint, the long run also encompasses enough time for existing firms to dissolve and leave the industry or for new firms to be created and enter the industry. *While the short run is a "fixed-plant" time period, the long run is a "variable-plant" time period.*

Illustrations If a General Motors plant hired 100 extra workers or added an entire shift of workers, this would be a short-run adjustment. If the same GM plant added a new wing to its building and installed more equipment, this would be a long-run adjustment.

Note that the short run and the long run are *conceptual* rather than specific calendar time periods. In light manufacturing industries, changes in plant capacity may be negotiated almost overnight. A small T-shirt firm can increase its plant capacity in a few days or less by ordering and installing a couple of new cutting tables and several extra sewing machines. But heavy industry is a different story. It may take Exxon several years to construct a new oil refinery.

We will now analyze production costs in the short-run, or fixed-plant, period. Following this we consider costs in the long-run, or variable-plant, period.

QUICK REVIEW 9-1

- ***Explicit costs are money payments a firm makes to outside suppliers of resources; implicit costs are the opportunity costs associated with a firm's use of resources it owns.***
- ***Economic profits are total revenue less all explicit and implicit costs, including a normal profit.***
- ***In the short run a firm's plant capacity is fixed; in the long run a firm can vary its plant size.***

PRODUCTION COSTS IN THE SHORT RUN

A firm's costs of producing any output will depend not only on prices of needed resources, but also on technology—the quantity of resources it takes to produce that output. It is the latter, technological aspect of costs which we now consider. In the short run a firm can change its output by adding variable resources to a fixed plant. But how does output change as more and more variable resources are added to the firm's fixed resources?

Law of Diminishing Returns

The answer is provided in general terms by the **law of diminishing returns,** also called the "law of diminishing marginal product" and the "law of variable proportions." This law states that *as successive units of a variable resource (say, labor) are added to a fixed resource (say, capital or land), beyond some point the extra, or marginal, product attributable to each additional unit of the variable resource will decline.* If additional workers are applied to a given amount of capital equipment, as is the case in the short run, eventually output will rise by smaller and smaller amounts as more workers are employed.

Rationale Suppose a farmer has a fixed amount of land—80 acres—planted in corn. If the farmer does not cultivate the cornfields at all, the yield will be 40 bushels per acre. If the land is cultivated once, output may rise to 50 bushels per acre. A second cultivation may increase output to 57 bushels per acre, a third to 61, and a fourth to 63. Further cultivations will add little or nothing to total output. Successive cultivations add less and less to the land's yield. If this were not so, the world's needs for corn could be fulfilled by extremely intense cultivation of this single 80-acre plot of land.

Indeed, if diminishing returns did not occur, the world could be fed out of a flowerpot.

The law of diminishing returns also holds true in nonagricultural industries. Assume a small planing mill is manufacturing wood furniture frames. It has a given amount of equipment—lathes, planers, saws, sanders. If this firm hired just one or two workers, total output and productivity (output per worker) would be very low. These workers would perform many different jobs, and the advantages of specialization would be lost. Time would also be lost in switching from one job to another, and machines would stand idle much of the time. In short, the plant would be understaffed, and production inefficient because there is too much capital relative to labor.

These difficulties would disappear as more workers were added. Equipment would be more fully used, and workers could now specialize on a single job. Time would no longer be lost from job switching. Thus, as more workers are added to the initially understaffed plant, the extra or marginal product of each will tend to rise due to more efficient production.

But this cannot go on indefinitely. As still more workers are added, problems of overcrowding will arise. Workers must wait in line to use the machinery, so now *workers* are under-used. Total output increases at a diminishing rate because, given the fixed plant size, each worker will have less capital equipment to work with as more and more labor is hired. The extra, or marginal, product of additional workers declines because the plant is more intensively staffed. There now is more labor in proportion to the fixed amount of capital goods. In the extreme case, the continuous addition of labor to the plant would use up all standing room, and production would be brought to a standstill.

Note that the law of diminishing returns assumes that all units of variable inputs—workers in this case—are of equal quality. Each successive worker is presumed to have the same innate ability, motor coordination, education, training, and work experience. Marginal product ultimately diminishes, not because successive workers are qualitatively inferior, but because more workers are being used relative to the amount of capital goods available.

Numerical Example Table 9-1 presents a numerical illustration of the law of diminishing returns. Column 2 indicates the **total product** resulting from combining each level of labor input in column 1 with a fixed amount of capital goods.

Column 3, **marginal product,** shows the *change* in total output associated with each additional input of labor. Note that with no labor inputs, total product is zero; an empty plant will yield no output. The first two workers reflect increasing returns, their marginal products being 10 and 15 units of output respectively. But then, beginning with the third worker, marginal product—the increase in total product—diminishes continuously and actually becomes zero with the eighth worker and negative with the ninth.

Average product or output per worker (also called "labor productivity") is shown in column 4. It is calculated by dividing total product (column 2) by the corresponding number of workers (column 1).

TABLE 9-1 The law of diminishing returns *(hypothetical data)*

(1) Inputs of the variable resource (labor)	*(2) Total product*	*(3) Marginal product Δ2/Δ1*		*(4) Average product (2)/(1)*
0	0			—
		10	Increasing marginal returns	
1	10			10
		15		
2	25			$12\frac{1}{2}$
		12	Diminishing marginal returns	
3	37			$12\frac{1}{3}$
		10		
4	47			$11\frac{3}{4}$
		8		
5	55			11
		5		
6	60			10
		3		
7	63			9
		0	Negative marginal returns	
8	63			$7\frac{7}{8}$
		−1		
9	62			$6\frac{8}{9}$

KEY GRAPH

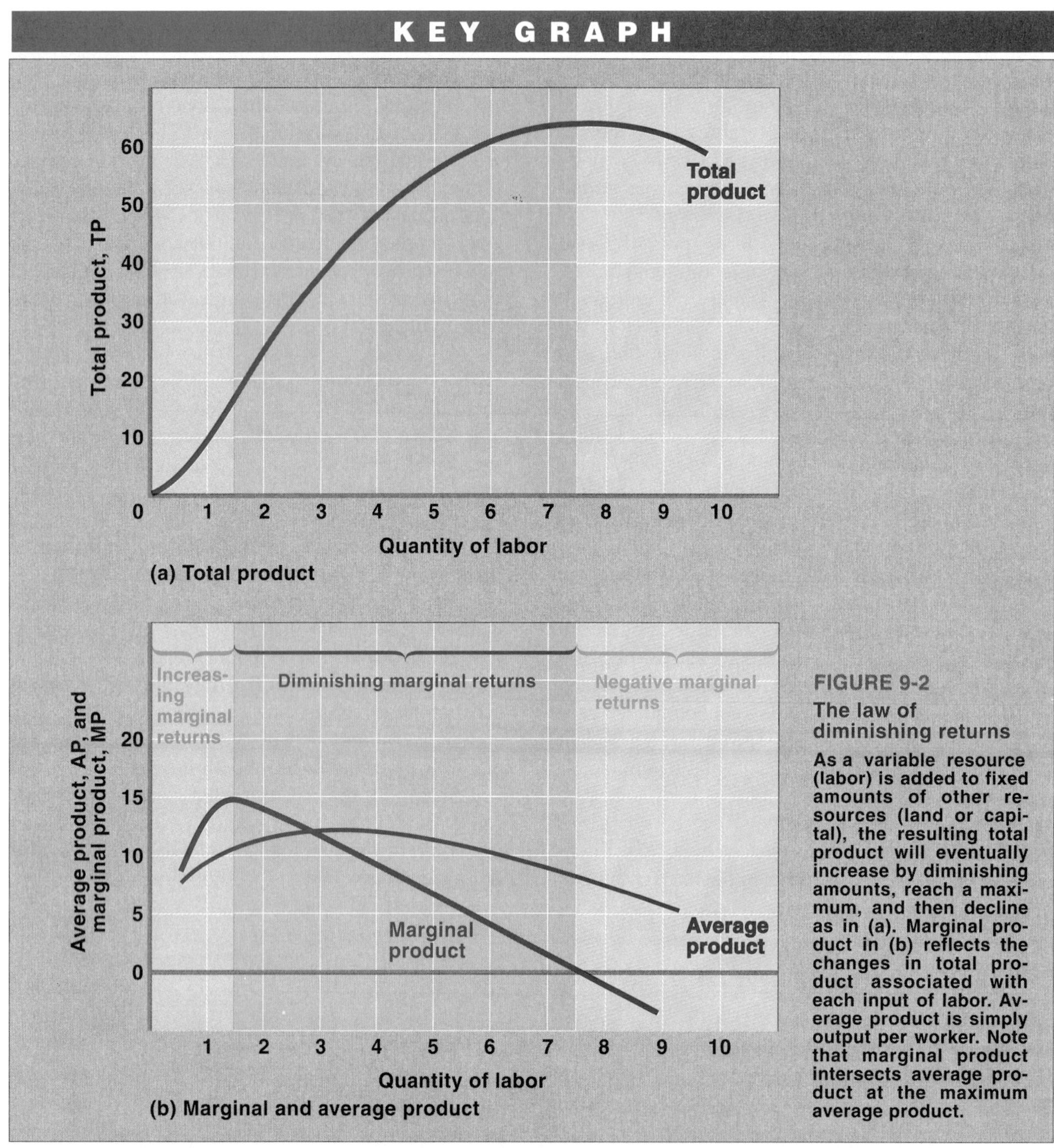

FIGURE 9-2
The law of diminishing returns
As a variable resource (labor) is added to fixed amounts of other resources (land or capital), the resulting total product will eventually increase by diminishing amounts, reach a maximum, and then decline as in (a). Marginal product in (b) reflects the changes in total product associated with each input of labor. Average product is simply output per worker. Note that marginal product intersects average product at the maximum average product.

Graphical Portrayal Figure 9-2a and b (Key Graph) shows the law of diminishing returns graphically and will help you understand the relationships between total, marginal, and average product. Note first that total product goes through three phases: It rises initially at an increasing rate; then it increases but at a decreasing rate; finally it reaches a maximum and declines.

Geometrically, marginal product is the slope of the total product curve. Stated differently, marginal product measures the rate of change in total product associated with each successive worker. Hence, the three phases of total product are also reflected in marginal product. Where total product is increasing at an increasing rate, marginal product is necessarily rising.

Here extra workers are adding larger and larger amounts to total product. Similarly, where total product is increasing but at a decreasing rate, marginal product is positive but falling. Each additional worker adds less to total product than did preceding workers. When total product is at a maximum, marginal product is zero. When total product declines, marginal product becomes negative.

Average product also reflects the same general "increasing-maximum-diminishing" relationship between variable inputs of labor and output as does marginal product. But note the relationship between marginal product and average product: Where marginal product exceeds average product, the latter must rise. And wherever marginal product is less than average product, average product must be declining. It follows that marginal product intersects average product where the latter is at a maximum.

This relationship is a mathematical necessity. If you add a number to a total which is greater than the current average of that total, the average must rise. And if you add a number to a total which is less than the current average of that total, the average falls. You raise your average course grade only when your score on an additional (marginal) examination is greater than the average of all your past scores. If your grade on an additional exam is below your current average, your average will be pulled down. In our production example, so long as the amount an additional worker adds to total product exceeds the average product or "productivity" of all workers already employed, average product will rise. Conversely, when an extra worker adds an amount to the total product which is less than the present average product, then that worker will lower average product or "productivity."

The law of diminishing returns is embodied in the shapes of all three curves. But, as our earlier definition of the law of diminishing returns indicates, economists are most concerned with marginal product. The stages of increasing, diminishing, and negative marginal product (returns) are shown in Figure 9-2. Glancing back at columns 1 and 3 of Table 9-1, we observe increasing returns for the first two workers, decreasing returns for workers 3 through 8, and negative returns for the ninth worker.

Fixed, Variable, and Total Costs

The production data described by the law of diminishing returns must be coupled with resource prices to determine the total and per unit costs of producing various levels of output. We have emphasized that in the short run some resources—those associated with the firm's plant—are fixed. Others are variable. This means that in the short run costs can be classified as either fixed or variable.

Fixed Costs **Fixed costs** *are those costs which in total do not vary with changes in output.* Fixed costs are associated with the very existence of a firm's plant and therefore must be paid even if its output is zero. Such costs as interest on a firm's bonded indebtedness, rental payments, a portion of depreciation on equipment and buildings, insurance premiums, and the salaries of top management and key personnel are generally fixed costs. In column 2 of Table 9-2 we assume that the firm's total fixed costs are \$100. By definition, this fixed-cost figure prevails at all levels of output, including zero. Fixed costs cannot be avoided in the short run.

Variable Costs **Variable costs** *are those costs which change with the level of output.* They include payments for materials, fuel, power, transportation services, most labor, and similar variable resources. In column 3 of Table 9-2 we find that the total of variable costs changes directly with output. But note that *the increases in variable costs associated with each one-unit increase in output are not constant.* As production begins, variable costs will for a time increase by a *decreasing* amount; this is true through the fourth unit of output. Beyond the fourth unit, however, variable costs rise by *increasing* amounts for each successive unit of output.

The reason for this lies in the law of diminishing returns. Because of increasing marginal product, smaller and smaller increases in the amounts of variable resources will be needed for a time to get each successive unit of output produced. Because all units of the variable resources are priced the same, total variable costs will increase by decreasing amounts. But when marginal product begins to decline as diminishing returns are encountered, larger and larger additional amounts of variable resources are needed to produce each successive unit of output. Total variable costs will therefore increase by increasing amounts.

Total Cost **Total cost** is the *sum of fixed and variable costs at each level of output.* It is shown in column 4 of Table 9-2. At zero units of output, total cost is equal to the firm's fixed costs. Then for each unit of production—1 through 10—total cost varies by the same amounts as does variable cost.

TABLE 9-2 Total- and average-cost schedules for an individual firm in the short run *(hypothetical data)*

Total-cost data				*Average-cost data*			
(1) Total product (Q)	*(2) Total fixed cost (TFC)*	*(3) Total variable cost (TVC)*	*(4) Total cost (TC) TC = TFC + TVC*	*(5) Average fixed cost (AFC)* $AFC = \frac{TFC}{Q}$	*(6) Average variable cost (AVC)* $AVC = \frac{TVC}{Q}$	*(7) Average total cost (ATC)* $ATC = \frac{TC}{Q}$	*(8) Marginal cost (MC)* $MC = \frac{\text{change in TC}}{\text{change in Q}}$
0	$100	$ 0	$ 100				
1	100	90	190	$100.00	$90.00	$190.00	$ 90
2	100	170	270	50.00	85.00	135.00	80
3	100	240	340	33.33	80.00	113.33	70
4	100	300	400	25.00	75.00	100.00	60
5	100	370	470	20.00	74.00	94.00	70
6	100	450	550	16.67	75.00	91.67	80
7	100	540	640	14.29	77.14	91.43	90
8	100	650	750	12.50	81.25	93.75	110
9	100	780	880	11.11	86.67	97.78	130
10	100	930	1030	10.00	93.00	103.00	150

Figure 9-3 shows graphically the fixed-, variable-, and total-cost data of Table 9-2. Note that total variable cost is measured vertically from the horizontal axis and total fixed cost is added vertically to total variable cost in locating the total-cost curve.

The distinction between fixed and variable costs is very significant to the business manager. Variable costs are those which businesses can control or alter in the short run by changing production levels. In contrast, fixed costs are beyond the business executive's present control; they are incurred in the short run and must be paid regardless of output level.

Per Unit, or Average, Costs

Producers are certainly interested in their total costs, but they are equally concerned with *per unit,* or *average, costs.* In particular, average-cost data are more usable for making comparisons with product price, which is always stated on a per unit basis. Average fixed cost, average variable cost, and average total cost are shown in columns 5 to 7 of Table 9-2. We must understand how these unit-cost figures are derived and how they vary as output changes.

1 AFC **Average fixed cost** (AFC) is found by dividing total fixed cost (TFC) by the corresponding output *(Q).* That is,

$$\text{AFC} = \frac{\text{TFC}}{Q}$$

While total fixed costs are, by definition, independent of output, AFC will decline so long as output increases. As output increases, a given total fixed cost of $100 is being spread over a larger and larger output. When output is just 1 unit, total fixed costs and AFC are equal at $100. But at 2 units of output, total fixed costs of $100 become $50 worth of fixed costs per unit; then $33.33, as $100 is spread over 3 units; and $25, when spread over 4 units. This is commonly refered to as "spreading the overhead." We find in Figure 9-4 that AFC graphs as a continually declining amount as total output is increased.

2 AVC **Average variable cost** (AVC) is calculated by dividing total variable cost (TVC) by the corresponding output *(Q):*

$$\text{AVC} = \frac{\text{TVC}}{Q}$$

AVC declines initially, reaches a minimum, and then increases again. Graphically, this is a U-shaped or saucer-shaped AVC curve, as shown in Figure 9-4.

Because total variable cost reflects the law of diminishing returns, so must the AVC figures, which are derived from total variable cost. Due to increasing re-

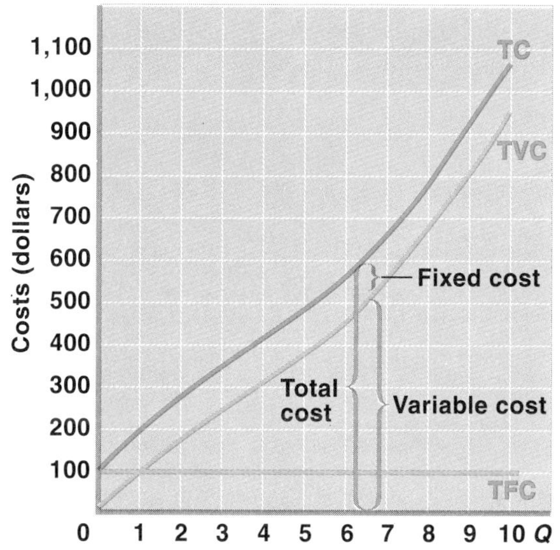

FIGURE 9-3 Total cost is the sum of fixed and variable costs

Total variable costs (TVC) change with output. Fixed costs are independent of the level of output. The total cost (TC) of any output is the vertical sum of the fixed and variable costs of that output.

turns, it takes fewer and fewer additional variable resources to produce each of the first 4 units of output. As a result, variable cost per unit will decline. AVC hits a minimum with the fifth unit of output, and beyond this point AVC rises as diminishing returns require more and more variable resources to produce each additional unit of output.

In simpler terms, at low levels of output production will be relatively inefficient and costly, because the firm's fixed plant is understaffed. Not enough variable resources are being combined with the firm's plant; production is inefficient, and per unit variable costs are therefore relatively high. As output expands, however, greater specialization and better utilization of the firm's capital equipment will yield more efficiency, and variable cost per unit of output will decline. As more variable resources are added, a point will be reached where diminishing returns are incurred. The firm's capital equipment will now be staffed more intensively, and therefore each added input will not increase output by as much as preceding inputs. This means AVC will increase.

You can verify the U or saucer shape of the AVC curve by returning to Table 9-1. Assume the price of labor is $10 per unit. By dividing average product (output per worker) into $10 (price per worker), you will determine labor cost per unit of output. Because we have assumed labor to be the only variable input, labor cost per unit of output *is* variable cost per unit of output or AVC. When average product is initially low, AVC will be high. As workers are added, average product rises and AVC falls. When average product is at its maximum, AVC will be at its minimum. Then, as still more workers are added and average product declines, AVC will rise. The "hump" of the average-product curve is reflected in the saucer or U shape of the AVC curve. A glance ahead at Figure 9-6 will confirm this graphically.

FIGURE 9-4 The average-cost curves

Average total cost (ATC) is the vertical sum of average variable cost (AVC) and average fixed cost (AFC). AFC necessarily falls as a given amount of fixed costs is apportioned over a larger and larger output. AVC initially falls because of increasing marginal returns but then rises because of diminishing marginal returns.

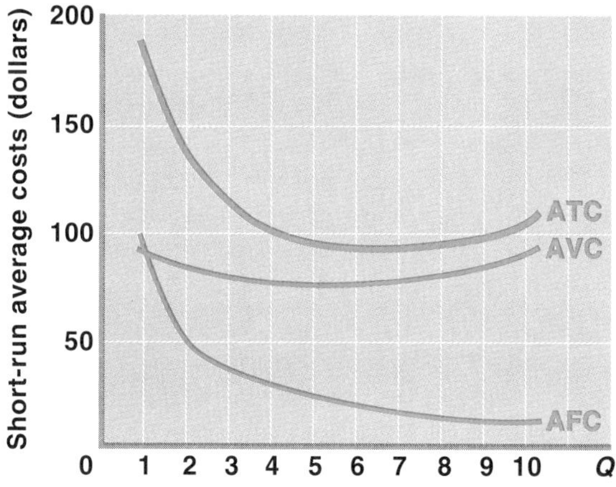

3 ATC **Average total cost** (ATC) is found by dividing total cost (TC) by total output *(Q)* or by adding AFC and AVC for each of the ten levels of output:

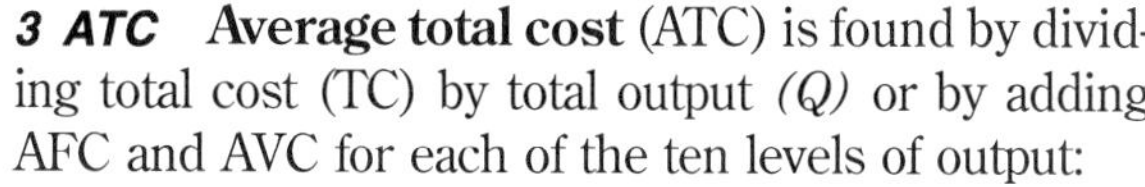

$$ATC = \frac{TC}{Q} = AFC + AVC$$

These data are shown in column 7 of Table 9-2. ATC is found by adding vertically the AFC and AVC curves, as in Figure 9-4. Thus the vertical distance between the ATC and AVC curves reflects AFC at any level of output.

Marginal Cost

One final and very crucial cost concept remains—marginal cost. **Marginal cost** (MC) *is the extra, or additional, cost of producing one more unit of output.* MC can

KEY GRAPH

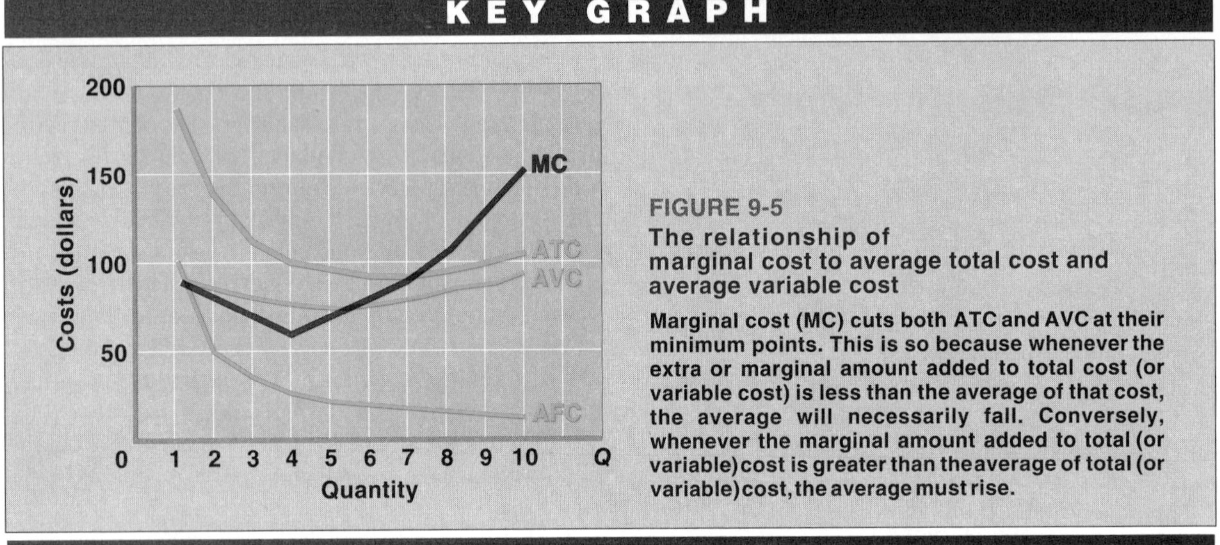

FIGURE 9-5
The relationship of marginal cost to average total cost and average variable cost

Marginal cost (MC) cuts both ATC and AVC at their minimum points. This is so because whenever the extra or marginal amount added to total cost (or variable cost) is less than the average of that cost, the average will necessarily fall. Conversely, whenever the marginal amount added to total (or variable) cost is greater than the average of total (or variable) cost, the average must rise.

be determined for each additional unit of output by noting the *change* in total cost which that unit's production entails.

$$MC = \frac{\text{change in TC}}{\text{change in } Q}$$

Our data are structured so that the "change in Q" is always "1," so we have defined MC as the cost of *one* more unit of output.

Calculations In Table 9-2, production of the first unit of output increases total cost from \$100 to \$190. Therefore, the additional, or marginal, cost of that first unit is \$90. The marginal cost of the second unit is \$80 (=\$270 − \$190); the MC of the third is \$70 (=\$340 − \$270); and so forth. MC for each of the 10 units of output is shown in column 8 of Table 9-2.

MC can also be calculated from the total-variable-cost column because the only difference between total cost and total variable cost is the constant amount of fixed costs (\$100). Thus, the *change* in total cost and the *change* in total variable cost associated with each additional unit of output are always the same.

Marginal Decisions Marginal cost is a strategic concept because it designates those costs over which the firm has the most direct control. Specifically, MC indicates those costs incurred in producing the last unit of output and, simultaneously, the cost which can be "saved" by reducing total output by the last unit. Average-cost figures do *not* provide this information. For example, suppose the firm is undecided whether to produce 3 or 4 units of output. At 4 units Table 9-2 indicates that ATC is \$100. But the firm does not increase its total costs by \$100 by producing, nor does it "save" \$100 by not producing, the fourth unit. Rather, the change in costs involved here is only \$60, as the MC column of Table 9-2 reveals.

A firm's decisions as to what output level to produce are typically marginal decisions, that is, decisions to produce a few more or a few less units. Marginal cost reveals the change in costs which one more or one less unit of output entails. When coupled with marginal revenue, which we will find in Chapter 10 indicates the change in revenue from one more or one less unit of output, marginal cost allows a firm to determine if it is profitable to expand or contract its production level. The analysis in the next four chapters centers on these marginal calculations.

Graphical Portrayal Marginal cost is shown graphically in Figure 9-5 (Key Graph). Note that marginal cost declines sharply, reaches a minimum, and then rises rather sharply. This mirrors the fact that variable cost, and therefore total cost, increases first by decreasing amounts and then by increasing amounts (see Figure 9-3 and columns 3 and 4 of Table 9-2).

MC and Marginal Product The marginal-cost curve's shape is a reflection of, and the consequence of, the law of diminishing returns. The relationship between marginal product and marginal cost can be seen by looking back to Table 9-1. If each successive unit of a variable resource (labor) is hired at a constant price, the marginal cost of each extra unit of output will *fall* so long as the marginal product of each additional worker is *rising*. This is so because marginal cost is the (constant) price or cost of an extra worker divided by his or her marginal product. Hence, in Table 9-1, suppose each worker can be hired for $10. Because the first worker's marginal product is 10 and hiring this worker increases the firm's costs by $10, the marginal cost of each of these 10 extra units of output will be $1 (=$10 ÷ 10). The second worker also increases costs by $10, but the marginal product is 15, so that the marginal cost of each of these 15 extra units of output is $.67 (=$10 ÷ 15). In general, so long as marginal product is rising, marginal cost will be falling.

But as diminishing returns set in—in this case, with the third worker—marginal cost will begin to rise. Thus, for the third worker, marginal cost is $.83 (=$10 ÷ 12); $1.00 for the fourth worker; $1.25 for the fifth; and so on. *Given the price (cost) of the variable resource, increasing returns will be reflected in a declining marginal cost and diminishing returns in a rising marginal cost.* The MC curve is a mirror reflection of the marginal product curve. As seen in Figure 9-6, when marginal product is rising, marginal cost is necessarily falling. When marginal product is at its maximum, marginal cost is at its minimum. And when marginal product is falling, marginal cost is rising.

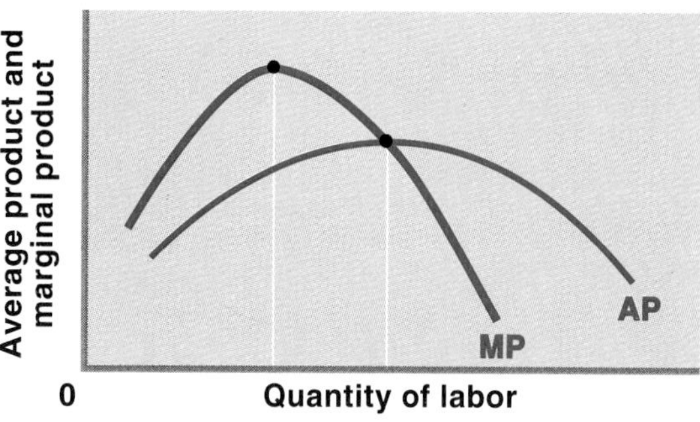

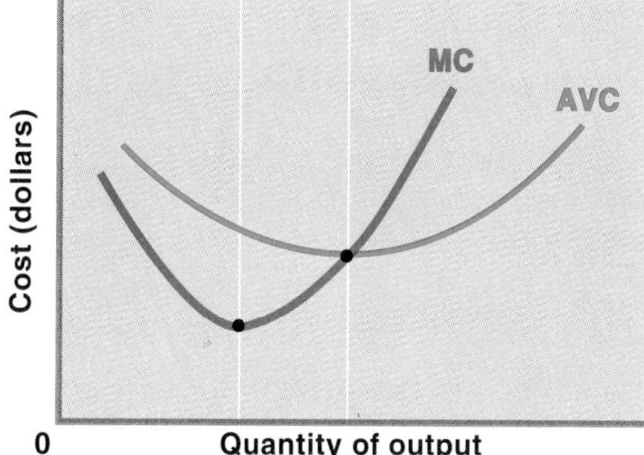

FIGURE 9-6 The relationship between productivity curves and cost curves

The marginal cost (MC) and average-variable-cost (AVC) curves are mirror images of the marginal product (MP) and average-product (AP) curves respectively. Assuming labor is the only variable input and that its price (the wage rate) is constant, MC is found by dividing the wage rate by MP. Thus, when MP is rising, MC is falling; when MP reaches its maximum, MC is at its minimum; and when MP is diminishing, MC is rising. A similar relationship holds between AP and AVC.

Relation of MC to AVC and ATC The marginal cost curve intersects both the AVC and ATC curves at their minimum points. As noted earlier, this marginal-average relationship is a mathematical necessity, which a simple illustration will reveal. Suppose a professional baseball pitcher has allowed his opponents an average of 3 runs per game in the first three games he has pitched. Now, whether his average falls or rises as a result of pitching a fourth (marginal) game will depend on whether the additional runs he allows in that extra game are fewer or more than his current 3-run average. If he allows fewer than 3 runs—for example, 1—in the fourth game, his total runs will rise from 9 to 10, and his average will fall from 3 to $2\frac{1}{2}$ (=10 ÷ 4). Conversely, if he allows more than 3 runs—say, 7—in the fourth game, his total will increase from 9 to 16 and his average will rise from 3 to 4 (=16 ÷ 4).

So it is with costs. When the amount added to total cost (marginal cost) is less than the average of total cost, ATC will fall. Conversely, when marginal cost exceeds ATC, ATC will rise. This means in Figure 9-5 that so long as MC lies below ATC, the latter will fall, and where MC is above ATC, ATC will rise. Therefore, at the point of intersection where MC equals ATC, ATC has just ceased to fall but has not yet begun to rise. This, by definition, is the minimum point on the ATC curve. *The marginal-cost curve intersects the average-total-cost curve at the latter's minimum point.*

Because MC can be defined as the addition either to total cost *or* to total variable cost resulting from one more unit of output, this same rationale explains why the MC curve also crosses the AVC curve at the latter's minimum point. No such relationship exists for the MC curve and the average-fixed-cost curve, because the two are not related; marginal cost includes only those costs which change with output, and fixed costs by definition are independent of output.

Shifting the Cost Curves

Changes in either resource prices or technology will cause cost curves to shift. If fixed costs had been higher—say, $200 rather than the $100 we assumed in Table 9-2—then the AFC curve in Figure 9-5 would be shifted upward. The ATC curve would also be at a higher position because AFC is a component of ATC. But the positions of the AVC and MC curves would be unaltered because their locations are based on the prices of variable rather than fixed resources. Thus, if the price (wage) of labor or some other variable input rose, the AVC, ATC, and MC curves would all shift upward, but the position of AFC would remain unchanged. Reductions in the prices of fixed or variable resources will entail cost curve shifts exactly opposite to those just described.

If a more efficient technology were discovered, then the productivity of all inputs would increase. The cost figures in Table 9-2 would all be lower. To illustrate, if labor is the only variable input and wages are $10 per hour and average product is 10 units, then AVC would be $1. But if a technological improvement increases the average product of labor to 20 units, then AVC will decline to $.50. More generally, an upward shift in the productivity curves shown in the top portion of Figure 9-6 will mean a downward shift in the cost curves portrayed in the bottom portion of that diagram.

QUICK REVIEW 9-2

- ***The law of diminishing returns indicates that, beyond some point, output will increase by diminishing amounts as a variable resource (labor) is added to a fixed resource (capital).***
- ***In the short run the total cost of any level of output is the sum of fixed and variable costs (TC = TFC + TVC).***
- ***Average fixed, average variable, and average total costs are fixed, variable and total cost per unit of output; marginal cost is the cost of producing one more unit of output.***
- ***Average fixed cost declines continuously as output increases; average variable cost and average total cost are U-shaped, reflecting increasing and then diminishing returns; marginal cost falls but then rises, intersecting both average variable and average total cost at their minimum points.***

PRODUCTION COSTS IN THE LONG RUN

In the long run an industry and the individual firms it comprises can undertake all desired resource adjustments. The firm can alter its plant capacity; it can build a larger plant or revert to a smaller plant than assumed in Table 9-2. The industry can also change its plant size; the long run allows sufficient time for new firms to enter or existing firms to leave an industry. The impact of the entry and exodus of firms into and from an industry will be discussed in the next chapter; here we are concerned only with changes in plant capacity made by a single firm. We will couch our analysis in terms of ATC, making no distinction between fixed and variable costs because all resources, and therefore all costs, are variable in the long run.

Firm Size and Costs

Suppose a single-plant manufacturing enterprise begins on a small scale and then, as the result of successful operations, expands to successively larger plant sizes. What happens to average total costs as this occurs? For a time successively larger plants will bring lower average total costs. However, eventually the building of a still larger plant may cause ATC to rise.

Figure 9-7 illustrates this situation for five possible plant sizes. ATC-1 is the average-total-cost curve for the smallest of the five plants, and ATC-5 for the largest. The relationship of the five plant sizes to one another is clearly that stated above. Constructing a larger plant will entail lower minimum per unit costs through plant size 3. But beyond this point a larger plant will mean a higher level of minimum average total costs.

The Long-Run Cost Curve

The vertical lines perpendicular to the output axis in Figure 9-7 are crucial. They indicate those outputs at which the firm should change plant size to realize the lowest attainable per unit costs of production. In Figure 9-7 we see that for all outputs up to 20 units, the lowest per unit costs are attainable with plant size 1. However, if the firm's volume of sales expands to some level greater than 20 but less than 30 units, it can achieve lower per unit costs by constructing a larger plant—plant size 2. Although *total* cost will be higher at the greater levels of production, the cost *per unit* of output

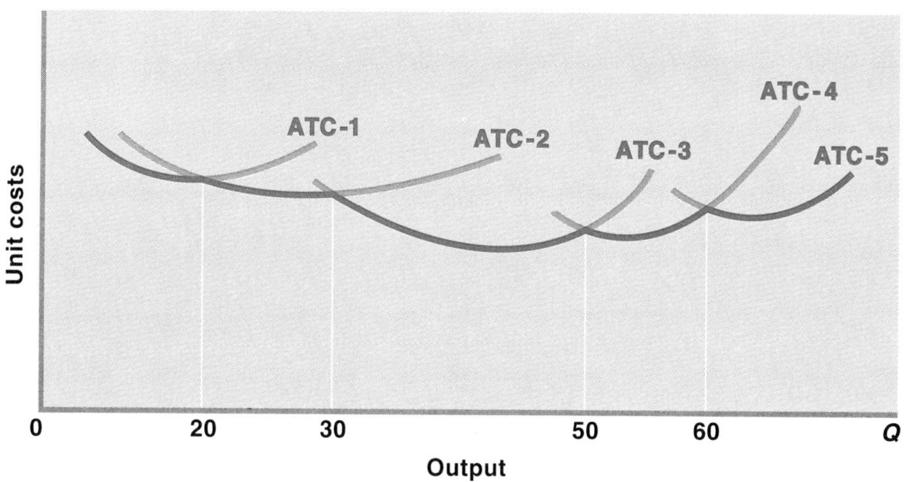

FIGURE 9-7 The long-run average-cost curve: five possible plant sizes
The long-run average-cost curve is made up of segments of the short-run cost curves (ATC-1, ATC-2, etc.) of the various-sized plants from which the firm might choose. Each point on the bumpy planning curve shows the least unit cost attainable for any output when the firm has had time to make all desired changes in its plant size.

will be less than before. For any output between 30 and 50 units, plant size 3 will yield the lowest per unit costs. For the 50- to 60-unit range of output, plant size 4 must be built to achieve the lowest unit costs. Lowest per unit costs for any output over 60 units demand construction of the still larger plant size 5.

Tracing these adjustments, we can conclude that the long-run ATC curve for the enterprise will comprise segments of the short-run ATC curves for the various plant sizes which can be constructed. *The long-run ATC curve shows the least per unit cost at which any output can be produced after the firm has had time to make all appropriate adjustments in its plant size.* In Figure 9-7 the heavy, bumpy curve is the firm's long-run ATC curve or, as it is often called, the firm's planning curve.

In most lines of production the choice of plant sizes is much wider than that in our illustration. In fact, in many industries the number of possible plant sizes is virtually unlimited, and in time quite small changes in the volume of output (sales) will lead to changes in plant size. Graphically, this implies an unlimited number of short-run ATC curves, as suggested by Figure 9-8 (Key Graph). The minimum ATC of producing each possible level of output is shown by the long-run ATC curve. Rather than being comprised of *segments* of short-run ATC curves as in Figure 9-7, the long-run ATC curve is made up of all the *points of tangency* of the theoretically unlimited number of short-run ATC curves from which the long-run ATC curve is derived. Hence, the planning curve is smooth rather than bumpy.

Economies and Diseconomies of Scale

We have accepted the contention that for a time larger and larger plant size will entail lower unit costs but that beyond some point successively larger plants will mean higher average total costs. Exactly why is the long-run ATC curve U-shaped? Note, first, that the law of diminishing returns does *not* apply here, because it presumes one resource is fixed in supply while the long run assumes all resources are variable. Also, our discussion assumes resource prices are constant. We can explain the U-shaped long-run average-cost curve in terms of economies and diseconomies of large-scale production.

Economies of Scale **Economies of scale** or, more commonly, economies of mass production, explain the downsloping part of the long-run ATC curve, as indicated in Figure 9-9a. As plant size increases, a number

KEY GRAPH

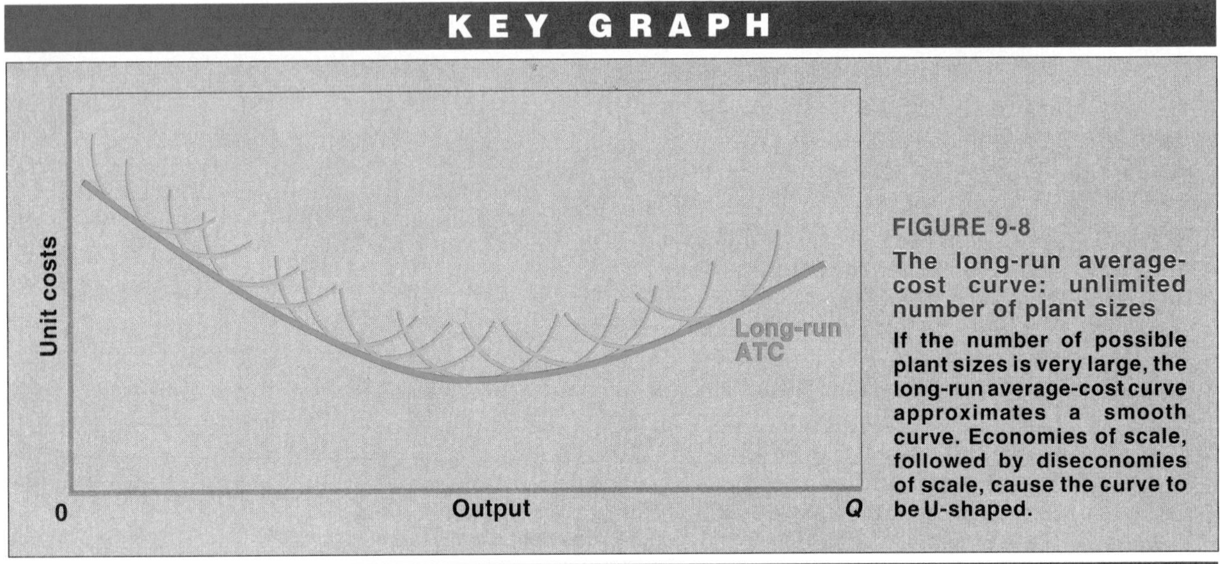

FIGURE 9-8
The long-run average-cost curve: unlimited number of plant sizes
If the number of possible plant sizes is very large, the long-run average-cost curve approximates a smooth curve. Economies of scale, followed by diseconomies of scale, cause the curve to be U-shaped.

of factors will for a time lead to lower average costs of production.

1 Labor Specialization Increased specialization in the use of labor is feasible as a plant increases in size. Hiring more workers means jobs can be divided and subdivided. Each worker may now have just one task to perform instead of five or six distinct operations in the productive process. Workers can work full time on those particular operations at which they have special skills. In a small plant skilled machinists may spend half their time performing unskilled tasks, leading to higher production costs.

Further, large scale allows dividing of work operations, which helps workers become very proficient at the specific tasks assigned them. The jack-of-all trades burdened with five or six jobs will not likely be very efficient in any of them. When allowed to concentrate on one task, the same worker may become highly efficient.

Finally, greater specialization eliminates the loss of time which accompanies the shifting of workers from one job to another.

2 Managerial Specialization Large-scale production also means better use of, and greater specialization in, management. A supervisor who can handle twenty workers will be under-used in a small plant hiring only ten people. The production staff can be doubled with no increase in administrative costs.

Nor will small firms be able to use management specialists to best advantage. In a small plant a sales specialist may have to divide his or her time between several executive functions—for example, marketing, personnel, and finance. A larger scale of operations will mean that the marketing expert can supervise sales and product distribution full time, while appropriate specialists perform other managerial functions. Greater efficiency and lower unit costs are the net result.

3 Efficient Capital Small firms often cannot employ the most technologically efficient productive equipment. In many lines of production this machinery is available only in very large and extremely expensive units. Furthermore, effective utilization of this equipment demands a high volume of production, so only large-scale producers can afford and operate the best available equipment.

In the automobile industry the most efficient fabrication method employs robotics and elaborate assembly-line equipment. Effective use of this equipment demands an annual output of an estimated 200,000 to 400,000 automobiles (Chapter 13). Only very large-scale producers can afford to purchase and use this equipment efficiently. The small-scale producer is

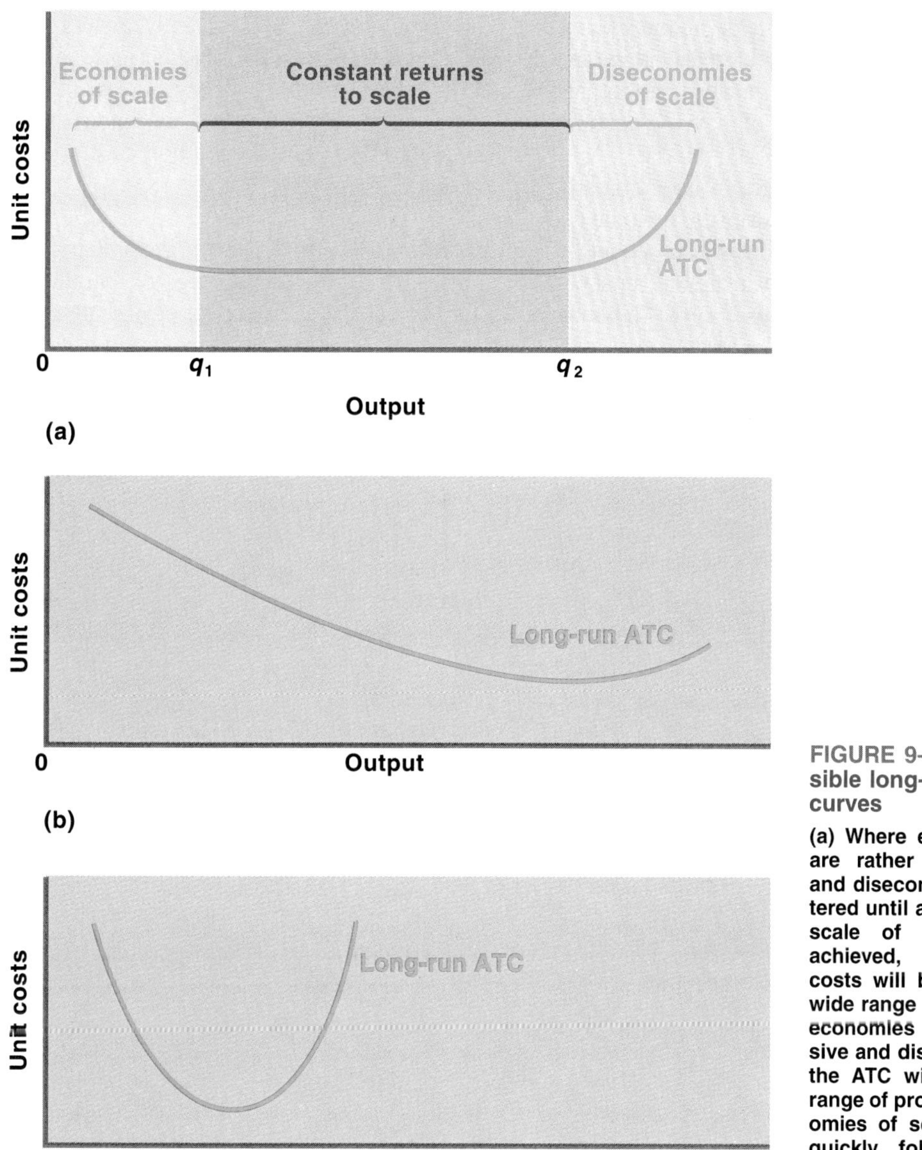

FIGURE 9-9 Various possible long-run average-cost curves

(a) Where economies of scale are rather rapidly exhausted and diseconomies not encountered until a considerably large scale of output has been achieved, long-run average costs will be constant over a wide range of output. (b) When economies of scale are extensive and diseconomies remote, the ATC will fall over a wide range of production. (c) If economies of scale are exhausted quickly, followed immediately by diseconomies, minimum unit costs will be encountered at a relatively low output.

faced with a dilemma. To fabricate automobiles using other equipment is inefficient and therefore more costly per unit. The alternative of purchasing the most efficient equipment and underusing it with a small level of output is also inefficient and costly.

4 By-Products The large-scale producer can better use by-products than a small firm. The large meat-packing plant makes glue, fertilizer, pharmaceuticals, and a host of other products from animal remnants which would be discarded by smaller producers.

All these technological considerations—greater specialization in labor and management, the ability to use the most efficient equipment, and effective use of by-products—contribute to lower unit costs for the producer able to expand its scale of operations. From a slightly different perspective, an increase in *all* resources of, say, 10 percent will cause a more-than-proportionate increase in output of, say, 20 percent. The necessary result will be a decline in ATC.

It is of interest that the notion of economies of scale has been invoked in debate over the national defense budget. When the Pentagon was proposing a fleet of 132 B-2 Stealth bombers, the estimated cost per plane was $580 million. But a proposed cut to 75 bombers by the Secretary of Defense caused the cost per plane to surge to over $800 million. The per plane cost increase was allegedly due to the loss of scale economies associated with the smaller order.

Diseconomies of Scale But in time the expansion of a firm *may* lead to diseconomies and therefore higher per unit costs.

The main factor causing **diseconomies of scale** lies with managerial problems in efficiently controlling and coordinating a firm's operations as it becomes a large-sclae producer. In a small plant a single key executive may make all the basic decisions for the plant's operation. Because of the firm's smallness, the executive is close to the production line and can readily comprehend the firm's operations, easily digest information gained from subordinates, and make clear and efficient decisions.

This neat picture changes, however, as a firm grows. There are many management levels between the executive suite and the assembly line; top management is far removed from the actual production operations of the plant. One person cannot assemble, understand, and digest all the information essential to rational decision making in a large-scale enterprise. Authority must be delegated to innumerable vice-presidents, second vice-presidents, and so forth. This expansion in depth and width of the management hierarchy leads to problems of communication, coordination, and bureaucratic red tape, and the possibility that decisions of various subordinates will fail to mesh. The result is impaired efficiency and rising average costs.

Also, in massive production facilities workers may feel alienated from their jobs and have little commitment to productive efficiency. Opportunities to shirk—to avoid work in favor of on-the-job leisure—may be greater in large plants than in small ones. Large plants susceptible to worker alienation and shirking may require additional worker supervision, which increases costs.

Again, thought of differently, an increase in *all* resources of 10 percent will cause a less-than-proportionate increase in output of, say, 5 percent. As a consequence, ATC will increase. Diseconomies of scale are illustrated by the rising portion of the long-run cost curve in Figure 9-9a.

Constant Returns to Scale In some instances there may exist a rather wide range of output between the output level at which economies of scale are exhausted and the point at which diseconomies of scale are encountered. That is, there will be a range of **constant returns to scale** over which long-run average cost is constant. The q_1q_2 output range of Figure 9-9a is relevant. Here a given percentage increase in *all* inputs of 10 percent will cause a proportionate 10 percent increase in output. Thus, ATC does not change.

Relevance In many American manufacturing industries economies of scale have been of great significance. Firms which have expanded their scale of operations to realize economies of mass production have survived and flourished. Those unable to achieve this expansion are in the unenviable position of being high-cost producers, doomed to a marginal existence or ultimate insolvency.

There is some difference of opinion among economists as to the relevance of diseconomies of scale. Some feel that the existence and continued growth of such gigantic corporations as General Motors, AT&T, Exxon, and Prudential Life Insurance cast doubt on the concept. In practice, computerized information and communication systems have often been developed and applied to overcome or forestall the decision-making problems embodied in the notion of diseconomies of scale. Where these efforts are successful, the long-run average-cost curve would fall and then become more or less constant as economies of scale are exhausted.

But there is case study and anecdotal evidence to suggest that diseconomies of scale are a fact of industrial life and, when encountered, can be significant. Large firms often design their organizational structures in the hope of avoiding diseconomies of scale. Among its many subdivisions, General Motors has established five automobile-producing divisions (Chevrolet, Buick, Oldsmobile, Pontiac, and Cadillac), each of which is largely autonomous and competing. GM's recent Saturn automobile project entailed the creation of a separate company. In short, a degree of decentralization has been sought which will allow full attainment of economies of scale yet help avoid diseconomies of scale.

Some economists contend that small companies have fueled much of the technological innovation and job creation of the last fifteen or twenty years. They also point out that huge American corporations in such industries as steel, automobiles, and consumer electronics have failed to meet cost and quality competition of foreign firms, some of which are smaller. It is also relevant that some of the more successful big companies such as Johnson & Johnson (pharmaceuticals) and Hewlett-Packard (computers) have organized themselves into groups of smaller, essentially independent firms.

Former executives of large corporations attest to the reality of diseconomies of scale. A former General Motors president commented thus on GM's Chevrolet division:

> Chevrolet is such a big monster that you twist its tail and nothing happens at the other end for months and months. It is so gigantic that there isn't any way to really run it. You just sort of try to keep track of it.

Similarly, a former GM vice-president provided this insider's view of Chevrolet:

> One of the biggest . . . problems was in the manufacturing staff. It was overburdened with layer upon layer of management. . . . A plant manager reported to a city manager who reported to a regional manager who reported to a manager of plants who reported to me, the general manager. Consequently, the manager of the Chevrolet Gear and Axle plant on Detroit's near east side who was only a few miles away from my office, was almost light years away in terms of management reporting channels.

Adams and Brock[1] recently examined the steel and automobile industries, concluding that the hierarchical, bureaucratic managements which accompany the large size of firms in those industries tend to inhibit efficiency. They also note that in recent years many large and highly diversified corporations have divested themselves of various divisions and subsidiaries to enhance managerial efficiency.

[1]Walter Adams and James W. Brock, *The Bigness Complex* (New York: Pantheon Books, 1986), chap. 3. The above two quotations are cited in Adams and Brock.

MES and Industry Structure

Economies and diseconomies of scale are an important determinant of an industry's structure. Here it is helpful to introduce the concept of **minimum efficient scale** (MES) which is the smallest level of output at which a firm can minimize long-run average costs. In Figure 9-9a this occurs at Oq_1 units of output. Because of the extended range of constant returns to scale, firms producing substantially larger outputs could also realize the minimum attainable average costs. Specifically, firms would be equally efficient within the q_1q_2 range. We would therefore not be surprised to find an industry with such cost conditions to be populated by firms of quite different sizes. The meatpacking, furniture, wood products, and small appliance industries provide approximate examples. With an extended range of constant returns to scale, relatively large and relatively small firms could coexist in an industry and be equally viable.

Compare this with Figure 9-9b where economies of scale are extensive and diseconomies are remote. Here the long-run average-cost curve will decline over a long range of output, the case in the automobile, aluminum, steel, and other heavy industries. Given consumer demand, efficient production will be achieved only with a small number of industrial giants. Small firms cannot realize the minimum efficient scale and will not be viable. In the extreme, economies of scale might extend beyond the market's size, resulting in what is termed a natural monopoly (Chapter 11). A **natural monopoly** is a market situation where unit costs are minimized by having one firm produce the particular good or service.

Where economies of scale are few and diseconomies quickly encountered, minimum efficient size occurs at a small level of output as shown in Figure 9-9c. In such industries a given level of consumer demand will support a large number of relatively small producers. Many retail trades and some types of farming fall into this category. So do certain types of light manufacturing, such as the baking, clothing, and shoe industries. Fairly small firms are as efficient as, or more efficient than, large-scale producers in such industries.

The point is that the shape of the long-run average-cost curve, as determined by economies and diseconomies of scale, can be significant in determining the structure and competitiveness of an industry. Whether

LAST WORD

ECONOMIES OF SCALE AND INDUSTRIAL CONCENTRATION

Is market concentration explainable in terms of economies of scale?

It is sometimes argued that industrial concentration—the dominance of a market by a small number of firms—is justified on the basis of economies of scale. If a firm's long-run average-cost curve declines over an extended range of output, total consumption of the product may only support a few efficient (minimum unit cost) producers (Figure 9-9b).

Research studies suggest that industrial concentration is generally *not* warranted on the basis of economies of scale. The minimum efficient scale (MES)—the smallest plant size at which minimum unit cost would be attained—has been determined for a number of industries, twelve of which are listed in the accompanying table. Column 2 compares the MES output with domestic consumption of each product to determine the percentage of total consumption which a single MES plant could produce. We find, for example, that a cigarette manufacturer of minimum efficient scale could produce about 6.6 percent of the domestic consumption of cigarettes.

By dividing the percentage of domestic consumption which an MES plant could produce into 100 percent (total domestic consumption), one can calculate the number of efficient plants which consumption will support. Thus we observe in column 3 that 15 MES plants (=100 percent ÷ 6.6 percent) are compatible with domestic cigarette consumption.

In a few industries—small diesel engines, turbogenerators, electric motors, and refrigerators—some level of concentration is required to realize scale economies. But for most of the industries shown, the minimum efficient plant sizes are small compared to the domestic market for each product. This suggests that economies of scale do *not* provide a rationale or justification for a high degree of concentration in most of the studied industries. The fact that the four largest firms in the beer industry actually provide 77 percent of

an industry is "competitive"—populated by a relatively large number of small firms—or "concentrated"—dominated by a few large producers—is sometimes a reflection of an industry's technology and the resulting shape of its long-run average-cost curve.

But we must be cautious in making this statement because industry structure does not depend on cost conditions alone. Government policies, geographic size of a market, managerial ability, and other factors must be considered in explaining the structure of a given industry. Indeed, this chapter's Last Word presents empirical evidence suggesting that many industries are much more concentrated than can be justified on the basis of economies of scale.

QUICK REVIEW 9-3

- ***Most firms have U-shaped long-run average-cost curves, reflecting economies and then diseconomies of scale.***
- ***Economies of scale are the consequence of greater specialization of labor and management, more efficient capital equipment, and the use of by-products.***
- ***Diseconomies of scale are caused by problems of coordination and communication which arise in large firms.***
- ***Minimum efficient scale is the lowest level of output at which a firm's long-run average costs are at a minimum.***

Minimum efficient plant sizes as a percentage of domestic consumption

(1) *Industry*	(2) *Minimum efficient scale as a percentage of domestic consumption*	(3) *Number of efficient plants compatible with domestic consumption*
Diesel engines (small)	25.5%	4
Turbogenerators	23.0	4
Electric motors	15.0	7
Refrigerators	14.1	7
Cellulosic synthetic fiber	11.1	9
Passenger automobile production	11.0	9
Commercial aircraft	10.0	10
Cigarettes	6.6	15
Printing paper	4.4	23
Beer brewing	3.4	29
Bicycles	2.1	48
Petroleum refining	1.9	53

Source: F. M. Scherer, *Industrial Market Structure and Economic Performance,* 2d ed. (Boston: Houghton Mifflin Company, 1980), pp. 96–97.

domestic beer output and the four largest cigarette manufacturers control 90 percent of the domestic cigarette market (Table 13-1) is not explainable solely in terms of economies of scale.

There are some qualifications which must be appended. The data cited in the table refer only to *production* economies. Multiplant firms—and therefore higher levels of industrial concentration than those suggested by column 3 of the table—may be justified on the basis of other nonproduction advantages. For example, a large multiplant firm may be able to economize on management services by drawing on a common pool of accountants, lawyers, and financial planners to serve all of its plants. Similarly, a multiplant firm may realize economies in advertising, raising money capital, or in product distribution. On the other hand, it is conceivable that diseconomies could be associated with some aspects of multiplant operation. In any event, even when adjustments are made for such factors, the general conclusion remains that economic concentration in many industries cannot be justified on the basis of economies of scale.

CHAPTER SUMMARY

1 Economic costs include all payments which must be received by resource owners to ensure continued supply of these resources in a particular line of production. This definition includes explicit costs, which flow to resource suppliers separate from a given enterprise, and also implicit costs, the remuneration of self-owned and self-employed resources. One of the implicit cost payments is a normal profit to the entrepreneur for functions performed.

2 In the short run a firm's plant capacity is fixed. The firm can use its plant more or less intensively by adding or subtracting units of variable resources, but the firm does not have sufficient time to alter plant size.

3 The law of diminishing returns describes what happens to output as a fixed plant is used more intensively. The law states that as successive units of a variable resource such as labor are added to a fixed plant, beyond some point the resulting marginal product associated with each additional worker will decline.

4 Because some resources are variable and others fixed, costs can be classified as variable or fixed in the short run. Fixed costs are independent of the level of output; variable costs vary with output. The total cost of any output is the sum of fixed and variable costs at that output.

5 Average fixed, average variable, and average total costs are fixed, variable, and total costs per unit of output. Average fixed costs decline continuously as output increases, because a fixed sum is being spread over a larger and larger number of units of production. Average variable costs are

U-shaped, reflecting the law of diminishing returns. Average total cost is the sum of average fixed and average variable costs; it too is U-shaped.

6 Marginal cost is the extra, or additional, cost of producing one more unit of output. Graphically, the marginal cost curve intersects the ATC and AVC curves at their minimum points.

7 Lower resource prices shift cost curves downward as does technological progress. Higher input prices shift cost curves upward.

8 The long run is a period of time sufficiently long for a firm to vary the amounts of all resources used, including plant size. In the long run all costs are variable. The long-run ATC, or planning, curve is composed of segments of the short-run ATC curves, representing the various plant sizes a firm can construct in the long run.

9 The long-run ATC curve is generally U-shaped. Economies of scale are first encountered as a small firm expands. A number of considerations—particularly greater specialization in the use of labor and management, ability to use the most efficient equipment, and more complete utilization of by-products—contribute to these economies of scale. Diseconomies of scale stem from the managerial complexities which accompany large-scale production. The relative importance of economies and diseconomies of scale in an industry is often an important determinant of the structure of that industry.

TERMS AND CONCEPTS

economic (opportunity) cost
explicit and implicit costs
normal and economic profits
short run and long run
law of diminishing returns
total, marginal, and average product
fixed costs
variable costs
total costs
average fixed cost
average variable cost
average total cost
marginal cost
economies and diseconomies of scale
constant returns to scale
minimum efficient scale
natural monopoly

QUESTIONS AND STUDY SUGGESTIONS

1 Distinguish between explicit and implicit costs, giving examples of each. What are the explicit and implicit costs of going to college? Why does the economist classify normal profits as a cost? Are economic profits regarded as a cost of production?

2 Gomez runs a small firm which makes pottery. He hires one helper at $12,000 per year, pays annual rent of $5,000 for his shop, and materials cost $20,000 per year. Gomez has $40,000 of his own funds invested in equipment (pottery wheels, kilns, and so forth) which could earn him $4,000 per year if alternatively invested. Gomez has been offered $15,000 per year to work as a potter for a competitor. He estimates his entrepreneurial talents are worth $3,000 per year. Total annual revenue from pottery sales is $72,000. Calculate accounting profits and economic profits for Gomez's pottery.

3 Which of the following are short-run and which are long-run adjustments? a Wendy's builds a new restaurant; b Acme Steel Corporation hires 200 more workers; c A farmer increases the amount of fertilizer used on his corn crop; and d An Alcoa plant adds a third shift of workers.

4 Why can the distinction between fixed and variable costs be made in the short run? Classify the following as fixed or variable costs: advertising expenditures, fuel, interest on company-issued bonds, shipping charges, payments for raw materials, real estate taxes, executive salaries, insurance premiums, wage payments, depreciation and obsolescence charges, sales taxes, and rental payments on leased office machinery. "There are no fixed costs in the long run; all costs are variable." Explain.

5 List the fixed and variable costs associated with owning and operating an automobile. Suppose you are considering whether to drive your car or fly 1000 miles to Florida for spring break. Which costs—fixed, variable, or both—would you take into account in making your decision? Would any implicit costs be relevant? Explain.

6 Use the following data to calculate marginal product and average product. Plot total, marginal, and average product and explain in detail the relationship between each pair of curves. Explain why marginal product first rises, then declines, and ultimately becomes negative. What bearing does the law of diminishing returns have on short-run costs? Be specific. "When marginal product is rising, marginal cost is falling. And when marginal product is diminishing, marginal cost is rising." Illustrate and explain graphically and through a numerical example.

Inputs of labor	*Total product*	*Marginal product*	*Average product*
1	15	15	15
2	34	19	17
3	51	17	17
4	65	14	16.25
5	74	9	14 4/5
6	80	6	13 1/3
7	83	3	11 4/7
8	82	-1	10 1/4

7 A firm has fixed costs of $60 and variable costs as indicated in the table below. Complete the table. When finished, check your calculations by referring to question 4 at the end of Chapter 23.

a Graph fixed cost, variable cost, and total cost. Explain how the law of diminishing returns influences the shapes of the variable-cost and total-cost curves.

b Graph AFC, AVC, ATC, and MC. Explain the derivation and shape of each of these four curves and the relationships they bear to one another. Specifically, explain in nontechnical terms why the MC curve intersects both the AVC and ATC curves at their minimum points.

c Explain how the locations of each of the four curves graphed in question 7b would be altered if (1) total fixed cost had been $100 rather than $60, and (2) total variable cost had been $10 less at each level of output.

8 Indicate how each of the following would shift the a marginal cost curve, b average variable cost curve, c average fixed cost curve, and d average total cost curve of a manufacturing firm. In each case specify the direction of the shift.

a A reduction in business property taxes

b An increase in the nominal wages of production workers

c A decrease in the price of electricity

d An increase in insurance rates on plant and equipment

e An increase in transportation costs

9 Suppose a firm has only three possible plant size options as shown in the accompanying figure. What plant size will the firm choose in producing a 50, b 130, c 160, and d 250 units of output? Draw the firm's long-run average-cost curve on the diagram and define this curve.

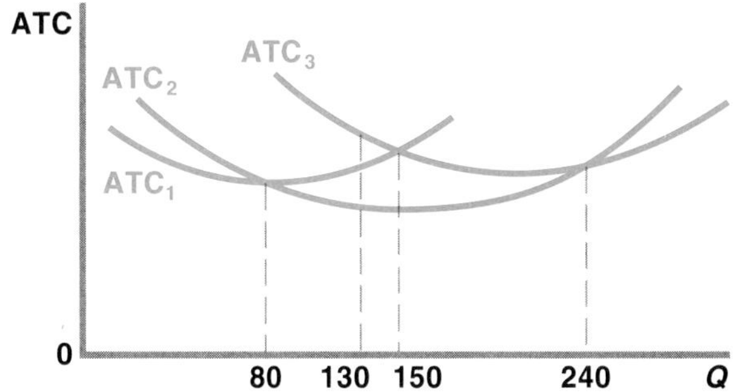

Total product	*Total fixed cost*	*Total variable cost*	*Total cost*	*Average fixed cost*	*Average variable cost*	*Average total cost*	*Marginal cost*
0	$______	$ 0	$______	$______	$______	$______	
							$______
1	______	45	______	______	______	______	
							______
2	______	85	______	______	______	______	
							______
3	______	120	______	______	______	______	
							______
4	______	150	______	______	______	______	
							______
5	______	185	______	______	______	______	
							______
6	______	225	______	______	______	______	
							______
7	______	270	______	______	______	______	
							______
8	______	325	______	______	______	______	
							______
9	______	390	______	______	______	______	
							______
10	______	465	______	______	______	______	

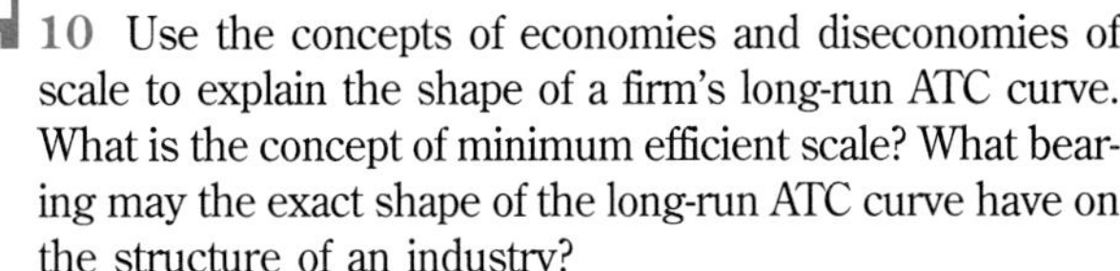
10 Use the concepts of economies and diseconomies of scale to explain the shape of a firm's long-run ATC curve. What is the concept of minimum efficient scale? What bearing may the exact shape of the long-run ATC curve have on the structure of an industry?

CHAPTER 10 Price and Output Determination: Pure Competition

Chapters 7 to 9 have given us the basic tools of analysis for understanding how product price and output are determined. But a firm's decisions concerning price and production will vary depending on the character of the industry in which it is operating. There is no such thing as an "average" or "typical" industry. Detailed examination of the business sector of our economy reveals an almost infinite number of different market situations; no two industries are alike. At one extreme we find a single producer dominating a market; at the other thousands of firms, each supplying a minute fraction of market output. Between these extremes lies an unlimited variety of market structures.

PRELUDE: FOUR MARKET MODELS

Any attempt to examine each specific industry would be an impossible task. We seek a more realistic objective—to define and discuss several basic market structures, or models. In so doing, we will acquaint ourselves with the *general* way in which price and output are determined in most of the market types characterizing our economy.

Economists envision four relatively distinct market situations: (1) pure competition, (2) pure monopoly, (3) monopolistic competition, and (4) oligopoly. They will be considered in this order here and in the next three chapters. These four market models differ in the number of firms in the industry, whether the product is standardized or differentiated, and how easy or difficult it is for new firms to enter the industry.

The main characteristics of these four models are outlined below and in Table 10-1 with more detailed definitions to follow.

1 In **pure competition** there are a very large number of firms producing a standardized product (for example, wheat or peanuts). New firms can enter the industry very easily.

2 At the other extreme, **pure monopoly** (Chapter 11) is a market in which one firm is the sole seller of a product or service (a local electric company). Entry of additional firms is blocked so that the firm *is* the industry. Because there is only one product, there is no product differentiation.

3 **Monopolistic competition** (Chapter 12) is characterized by a relatively large number of sellers producing differentiated products (women's clothing, furniture, books). Differentiation is the basis for product promotion and development. Entry to a monopolistically competitive industry is quite easy.

Finally, in **oligopoly** (Chapter 13) there are a few sellers; this "fewness" means that pricing and output decisions are interdependent. Each firm is affected by the decisions of rivals and must take these decisions into account in determining its own price-output behavior. Products may be standardized (steel or aluminum) or differentiated (automobiles and computers). Generally, entry to oligopolistic industries is very difficult.

These definitions and the characteristics outlined in Table 10-1 will come into sharper focus as we examine each model in detail.

We will find it convenient occasionally to distinguish between the characteristics of a purely competitive market and those of all other basic market structures—pure monopoly, monopolistic competition, and oligopoly. To facilitate such comparisons we will employ **imperfect competition** as a generic term to designate all those market structures deviating from the purely competitive market model.

PURE COMPETITION: CONCEPT AND OCCURRENCE

Let's focus our attention on pure competition, beginning with an elaboration of our definition.

1 Very Large Numbers A basic feature of a purely competitive market is the presence of a large number of independently acting sellers, usually offering their products in a highly organized market. Markets for farm commodities, the stock market, and the foreign exchange market are illustrative.

2 Standardized Product Competitive firms produce a standardized or homogeneous product. Given price, the consumer is indifferent as to the seller from which the product is purchased. In a competitive market the products of firms, B, C, D, and E, are viewed by the buyer as perfect substitutes for that of firm A. Because of product standardization, there is no reason for *nonprice competition,* that is, competition based on differences in product quality, advertising, or sales promotion.

3 "Price Taker" In a purely competitive market *individual firms* exert no significant control over product price. This characteristic follows from the preceding two. Under pure competition each firm produces such a small fraction of total output that increasing or decreasing its output will not perceptibly influence total supply or, therefore, product price. Assume there are 10,000 competing firms, each currently producing 100

TABLE 10-1 Characteristics of the four basic market models

	Market Model			
Characteristic	*Pure competition*	*Monopolistic competition*	*Oligopoly*	*Pure monopoly*
Number of firms	A very large number	Many	Few	One
Type of product	Standardized	Differentiated	Standardized or differentiated	Unique; no close substitutes
Control over price	None	Some, but within rather narrow limits	Circumscribed by mutual interdependence; considerable with collusion	Considerable
Conditions of entry	Very easy, no obstacles	Relatively easy	Significant obstacles present	Blocked
Nonprice competition	None	Considerable emphasis on advertising, brand names trademarks, etc.	Typically a great deal, particularly with product differentiation	Mostly public relations advertising
Examples	Agriculture	Retail trade, dresses, shoes	Steel, automobiles, farm implements, many household appliances	Local utilities

units of output. Total supply is therefore 1,000,000. Now suppose one of these firms cuts its output to 50 units. This will not affect price, because this restriction of output by a single firm has almost no impact on total supply. Specifically, the total quantity supplied declines from 1,000,000 to 999,950. This is not enough of a change in total supply to affect product price noticeably. In short, the individual competitive producer is a **price taker;** the competitive firm cannot adjust market price, but can only adjust to it.

Stated differently, the individual competitive producer is at the mercy of the market; product price is a given datum over which the producer exerts no influence. The firm gets the same price per unit for a large output as it does for a small output. To ask a price higher than the going market price would be futile. Consumers will not buy from firm A at $2.05 when its 9999 competitors are selling an identical, and therefore perfect substitute, product at $2 per unit. Conversely, because firm A can sell as much as it chooses at $2 per unit, there is no reason for it to charge a lower price, say, $1.95, for to do so would shrink its profits.

4 Free Entry and Exit New firms can freely enter and existing firms can freely leave purely competitive industries. No significant obstacles—legal, technological, financial, or other—exist to prohibit new firms from forming and selling their outputs in competitive markets.

Relevance Pure competition is quite rare in practice. This does not mean, however, that an analysis of how competitive markets work is irrelevant:

1 A few industries more closely approximate the competitive model than any other market structure. For example, much can be learned about American agriculture by understanding the operation of competitive markets.

2 Pure competition provides the simplest context in which to apply the revenue and cost concepts developed in previous chapters. Pure competition is a clear and meaningful starting point for any discussion of price and output determination.

3 In the concluding section of this chapter we will discover that the operation of a purely competitive economy gives us a standard, or norm, against which the efficiency of the real-world economy can be compared and evaluated.

In short, pure competition is a market model of considerable analytical and some practical importance.

Our analysis of pure competition has four major objectives. First, we will examine demand from the competitive seller's viewpoint. Second, we consider how a competitive producer adjusts to market price in the short run. Next, the nature of long-run adjustments in a competitive industry is explored. Finally, we evaluate the efficiency of competitive industries from the standpoint of society.

DEMAND TO A COMPETITIVE SELLER

Because each competitive firm offers a negligible fraction of total supply, the individual firm cannot perceptibly influence the market price which the forces of total demand and supply have established. The competitive firm does *not* have a price policy, that is, the ability to adjust price. Rather, the firm can merely *adjust to* the market price, which it must regard as a given datum determined by the market. As noted, the competitive seller is a *price taker,* rather than a *price maker.*

Perfectly Elastic Demand

Stated technically, the demand curve of the individual competitive firm is *perfectly elastic.* Columns 1 and 2 of Table 10-2 show a perfectly elastic demand curve

TABLE 10-2 The demand and revenue schedules for an individual purely competitive firm (hypothetical data)

Firm's demand or average-revenue schedule		*Revenue data*	
(1) Product price (average revenue)	*(2) Quantity demanded (sold)*	*(3) Total revenue*	*(4) Marginal revenue*
$131	0	$ 0	
131	1	131	$131
131	2	262	131
131	3	393	131
131	4	524	131
131	5	655	131
131	6	786	131
131	7	917	131
131	8	1048	131
131	9	1179	131
131	10	1310	131

where market price is assumed to be $131. Note that the firm cannot obtain a higher price by restricting output; nor need it lower price to increase its sales volume.

We are *not* saying that the *market* demand curve is perfectly elastic in a competitive market. Instead, it is typically a downsloping curve as a glance ahead at Figure 10-7b reveals. In fact, the total-demand curves for most agricultural products are quite *in*elastic, even though agriculture is the most competitive industry in our economy. However, the demand schedule faced by the *individual firm* in a purely competitive industry is perfectly elastic.

The distinction comes about in this way. For the industry—for all firms producing a particular product—a larger sales volume can be realized only by accepting a lower product price. All firms, acting independently but simultaneously, can and do affect total supply and therefore market price. But not so for the individual firm. If a *single* producer increases or decreases output, the outputs of all other competing firms being constant, the effect on total supply and market price is negligible. The single firm's demand or sales schedule is therefore perfectly elastic, as shown in Figures 10-1 and 10-7a. This is an instance in which the fallacy of composition is worth remembering. What is true for the industry or group of firms (a downsloping, less than perfectly elastic, demand curve) is *not* true for the individual, purely competitive firm (a perfectly elastic demand curve).

Average, Total, and Marginal Revenue

The firm's demand schedule is simultaneously a revenue schedule. What appears in column 1 of Table 10-2 as price per unit to the purchaser is revenue per unit, or **average revenue,** to the seller. To say that a buyer must pay $131 per unit is to say that the revenue per unit, or average revenue, received by the seller is $131. Price and average revenue are the same thing seen from different points of view.

Total revenue for each sales level can be determined by multiplying price by the corresponding quantity the firm can sell. Multiply column 1 by column 2, and the result is column 3. In this case, total revenue increases by a constant amount, $131, for each additional unit of sales. Each unit sold adds exactly its price to total revenue.

When a firm is pondering a change in its output, it will consider how its revenue will *change* as a result of that shift in output. What will be the additional revenue from selling another unit of output? **Marginal revenue** is the change in total revenue, that is, the extra revenue, which results from selling one more unit of output. In column 3 of Table 10-2 total revenue is obviously zero when zero units are being sold. The first unit of output sold increases total revenue from zero to $131. Marginal revenue—the increase in total revenue from the sale of the first unit of output—is therefore

under PERFECT COMPETITION PRICE AND MARGINAL REVENUE ARE EQUAL

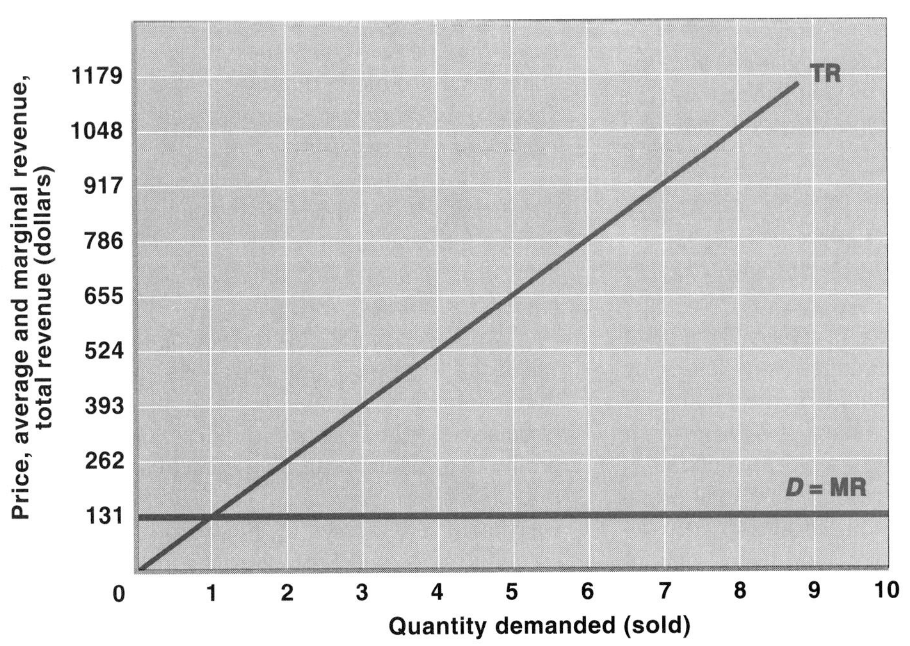

FIGURE 10-1 Demand, marginal revenue, and total revenue of a purely competitive firm

Because it can sell additional units of output at a constant price, the marginal-revenue curve (MR) of a purely competitive firm coincides with its perfectly elastic demand curve (*D*). The firm's total-revenue curve (TR) is a straight upsloping line.

$131. The second unit sold increases total revenue from $131 to $262, so marginal revenue is again $131. Note in column 4 that marginal revenue is a constant figure of $131, because total revenue increases by a constant amount with every extra unit sold.

Under purely competitive conditions, product price is constant to the individual firm; added units therefore can be sold without lowering product price. Each additional unit of sales adds exactly its price—$131 in this case—to total revenue, and marginal revenue *is* this increase in total revenue. Marginal revenue is constant under pure competition because additional units can be sold at a constant price.

Graphical Portrayal

The competitive firm's demand curve and total- and marginal-revenue curves are shown graphically in Figure 10-1. The demand or average-revenue curve is perfectly elastic. The marginal-revenue curve coincides with the demand curve because product price is constant to the competitive firm. Each extra unit of sales increases total revenue by $131. Total revenue is a straight line up to the right. Its slope is constant—it is a straight line—because marginal revenue is constant.

QUICK REVIEW 10-1

- ***In a purely competitive industry there are a large number of firms producing a homogeneous product and no significant entry barriers.***
- ***The competitive firm's demand curve is perfectly elastic at the market price.***
- ***Marginal and average revenue coincide with the firm's demand curve; total revenue rises by the amount of product price for each additional unit sold.***

PROFIT MAXIMIZATION IN THE SHORT RUN: TWO APPROACHES

In the short run the competitive firm has a fixed plant and maximizes its profits or minimizes its losses by adjusting its output through changes in the amounts of variable resources (materials, labor, and so forth) it employs. The economic profits it seeks are defined as the difference between total revenue and total costs. Indeed, this is the direction of our analysis. The revenue data of the previous section and the cost data of Chapter 9 must be brought together so the profit-maximizing output for the firm can be determined.

There are two complementary approaches to determining the level of output at which a competitive firm will realize maximum profits or minimum losses. The first compares total revenue and total costs; the second compares marginal revenue and marginal costs. Both approaches apply not only to a purely competitive firm but also to firms operating in any of the other three basic market structures. To understand output determination under pure competition, we will use both approaches, emphasizing the marginal approach. Also, hypothetical data in both tabular and graphical form will be employed to clarify the two approaches.

Total-Revenue–Total-Cost Approach

Given the market price of its product, the competitive producer is faced with three related questions: (1) Should we produce? (2) If so, what amount? (3) What profit (or loss) will be realized?

At first, the answer to question 1 seems obvious: "You should produce if it is profitable to do so." But the situation is more complex than this. In the short run part of the firm's total costs is variable costs, and the remainder is fixed costs. The latter have to be paid "out of pocket" even when the firm is closed down. In the short run a firm takes a loss equal to its fixed costs when it produces zero units of output. This means that, although there may be no level of output at which the firm can realize a profit, the firm might still produce if it can realize a loss less than the fixed-cost loss it will face in closing down. Thus, the correct answer to the "Should we produce?" question is: *The firm should produce in the short run if it can realize either (1) a profit or (2) a loss less than its fixed costs.*

Assuming the firm *will* produce, the second question becomes relevant: "How much should be produced?" The answer here is evident: *In the short run the firm should produce that output at which it maximizes profits or minimizes losses.*

We now examine three cases demonstrating the validity of these two generalizations and answer our third query by indicating how profits and losses can be calculated. In the first case the firm will maximize its profits by producing. In the second case it will minimize its losses by producing. In the third case the firm will minimize its losses by closing down. We will assume the same short-run cost data for all three cases and explore the firm's production decisions when faced with three different product prices.

Profit-Maximizing Case In all three cases we employ cost data with which we are already familiar. Col- 3 through 5 of Table 10-3 repeat the fixed-, variable-, and total-cost data developed in Table 9-2. Assuming that market price is $131, we derive total revenue for each output level by multiplying output by price, as we did in Table 10-2. These data are presented in column 2. Then in column 6 the profit or loss encountered at each output is found by subtracting total cost (column 5) from total revenue (column 2). Now we have all the data needed to answer the three questions.

Should the firm produce? Yes, because it can realize a profit by doing so. How much? Nine units, because column 6 tells us this is the output at which total economic profits will be at a maximum. The size of that profit in this **profit-maximizing case?** $299.

Figure 10-2a compares total revenue and total cost graphically. Total revenue is a straight line, because under pure competition each additional unit adds the same amount—its price—to total revenue (Table 10-2).

Total costs increase with output; more production requires more resources. But the rate of increase in total costs varies with the relative efficiency of the firm. Specifically, the cost data reflect Chapter 9's law of diminishing returns. For a time the rate of increase in total cost is less and less as the firm uses its fixed resources more efficiently. Then, after a time, total cost begins to rise by ever-increasing amounts because of the inefficiencies accompanying more intensive use of the firm's plant.

Comparing total cost with total revenue in Figure 10-2a, note that a **break-even point** occurs at about 2 units of output. If our data were extended beyond 10 units of output, another such point would be incurred where total cost would catch up with total revenue, as shown in Figure 10-2a. Any output outside these points will entail losses. Any output within these break-even points will produce an economic profit. Maximum profit is achieved where the vertical difference between total revenue and total cost is greatest. For our particular data this is at 9 units of output and the resulting maximum profit is $299.

Loss-Minimizing Case Assuming no change in costs, the firm may not realize economic profits if the market yields a price considerably below $131. Suppose the market price is only $81. As column 6 of Table 10-4 indicates, at this price all levels of output will lead to losses. But the firm will *not* close down because, by producing, it realizes a loss considerably less than the $100 fixed-cost loss it would incur by closing down, that is, producing zero units of output. Specifically, in this **loss-minimizing case,** the firm will minimize its losses by producing 6 units of output. The resulting $64 loss is clearly preferable to the $100 loss which closing down would involve. By producing 6 units the firm earns a total revenue of $486, sufficient to pay all the firm's variable costs ($450) and also a substantial portion—$36 worth—of the firm's $100 of fixed costs.

In general terms, whenever total revenue exceeds total *variable* costs, the firm will produce because all variable costs as well as some portion of total fixed costs can be paid out of revenue. If the firm closed down, all of its total fixed costs would have to be paid out of the entrepreneur's pocket. By producing some output, the firm's loss will be less than its total fixed cost. Note that there are several other outputs which entail a loss less than the firm's $100 fixed costs; but at 6 units of output the loss is minimized.

TABLE 10-3 The profit-maximizing output for a purely competitive firm: total-revenue–total-cost approach (price = $131)

(1) Total product	*(2) Total revenue*	*(3) Total fixed cost*	*(4) Total variable cost*	*(5) Total cost*	*(6) Total economic profit (+) or loss (−), = (2) − (5)*
0	$ 0	$100	$ 0	$ 100	$−100
1	131	100	90	190	− 59
2	262	100	170	270	− 8
3	393	100	240	340	+ 53
4	524	100	300	400	+124
5	655	100	370	470	+185
6	786	100	450	550	+236
7	917	100	540	640	+277
8	1048	100	650	750	+298
9	1179	100	780	880	+299
10	1310	100	930	1030	+280

Close-Down Case Assume finally that the market price is a mere $71. Given short-run costs, column 9 of Table 10-4 indicates that at all levels of output, losses will exceed the $100 fixed-cost loss the firm will incur by closing down. Thus, in this **close-down case,** the firm will minimize its losses by halting production, that is, by producing zero units of output.

Figure 10-2b demonstrates the loss-minimizing and close-down cases graphically. In the loss-minimiz-

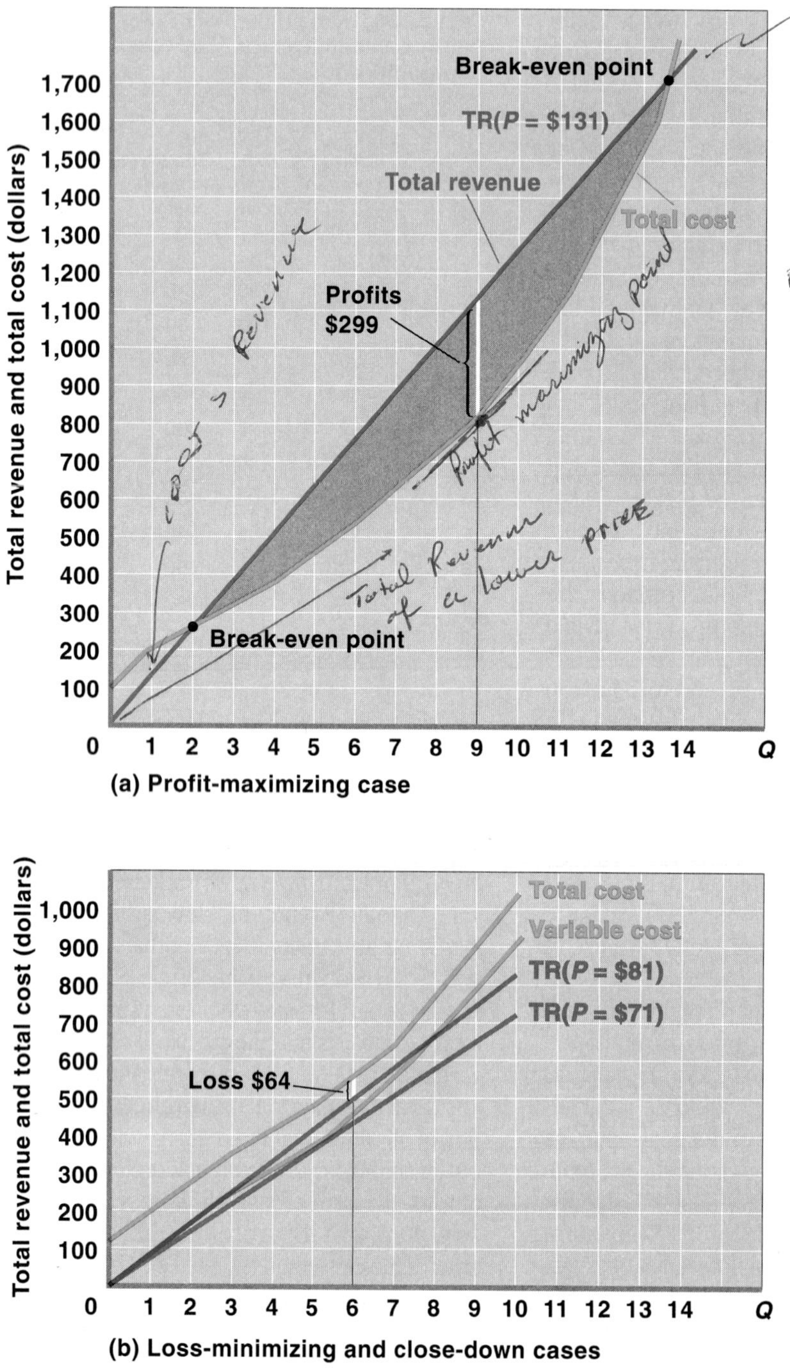

Break-even point
TR(*P* = $131)
Total revenue
Total cost
Profits $299
Break-even point
Total revenue and total cost (dollars)
(a) Profit-maximizing case

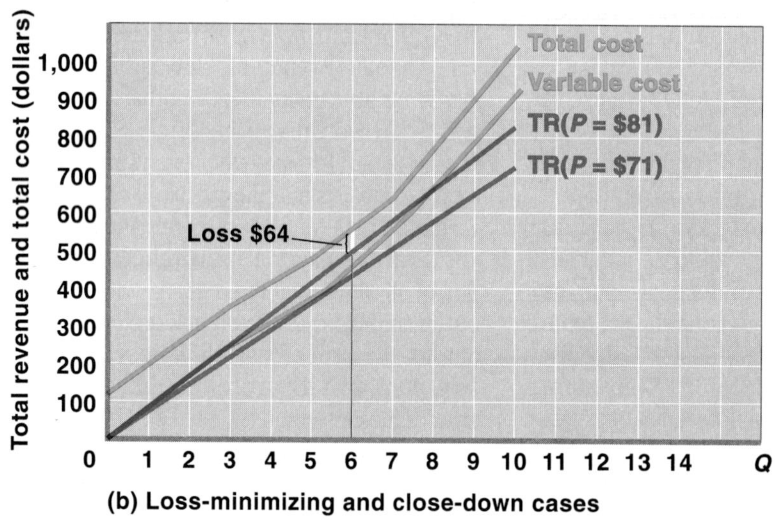

(b) Loss-minimizing and close-down cases

FIGURE 10-2 The profit-maximizing (a), loss-minimizing, and close-down cases (b), as shown by the total-revenue–total-cost approach

A firm's profits are maximized in (a) at that output at which total revenue exceeds total cost by the maximum amount. A firm will minimize its losses in (b) by producing at that output at which total cost exceeds total revenue by the smallest amount. However, if there is no output at which total revenue exceeds variable costs, the firm will minimize losses in the short run by closing down.

ing case, the total revenue line TR (P = $81) exceeds total variable cost by the maximum amount at 6 units of output. Here total revenue is $486, and the firm recovers all its $450 of variable costs and also $36 worth of its fixed costs. The firm's minimum loss is $64, superior to the $100 fixed-cost loss involved in closing down. In the close-down case, the total-revenue line TR (P = $71) lies below the total-variable-cost curve at all points; there is no output at which variable costs can be recovered. By producing the firm would incur losses exceeding its fixed costs. The firm's best choice is to close down and pay its $100 fixed-cost loss out of pocket.

TABLE 10-4 **The loss-minimizing outputs for a purely competitive firm: total-revenue–total-cost approach (prices = $81 and $71)** *(hypothetical data)*

Product price = $81						*Product price = $71*		
(1) Total product	*(2) Total revenue*	*(3) Total fixed cost*	*(4) Total variable cost*	*(5) Total cost*	*(6) Total economic profit (+) or loss (−), = (2) − (5)*	*(7) Total revenue*	*(8) Total cost*	*(9) Total economic profit (+) or loss (−), = (7) − (8)*
0	$ 0	$100	$ 0	$ 100	$−100	$ 0	$ 100	$−100
1	81	100	90	190	−109	71	190	−119
2	162	100	170	270	−108	142	270	−128
3	243	100	240	340	− 97	213	340	−127
4	324	100	300	400	− 76	284	400	−116
5	405	100	370	470	− 65	355	470	−115
6	486	100	450	550	− 64	426	550	−124
7	567	100	540	640	− 73	497	640	−143
8	648	100	650	750	−102	568	750	−182
9	729	100	780	880	−151	639	880	−241
10	810	100	930	1030	−220	710	1030	−320

QUICK REVIEW 10-2

- ***In the short run a firm should produce if it can achieve a profit or attain a loss which is smaller than its total fixed costs.***
- ***Profits are maximized where the excess of total revenue over total cost is greatest.***
- ***Losses are minimized where the excess of total cost over total revenue is smallest and is some amount less than total fixed costs.***
- ***If losses at all levels of output exceed total fixed costs, the firm should close down in the short run.***

Marginal-Revenue–Marginal Cost Approach

An alternative means for determining the amounts a competitive firm would offer in the market at each possible price is for the firm to determine and compare the amounts that each *additional* unit of output will add to total revenue, on the one hand, and to total cost, on the other. The firm should compare the *marginal revenue* (MR) and the *marginal cost* (MC) of each successive unit of output. Any unit of output whose marginal revenue exceeds its marginal cost should be produced, because on each such unit the firm gains more in revenue from its sale that it adds to costs in producing that unit. Hence, the unit of output is adding to total profits or, as the case may be, subtracting from losses. Similarly, if the marginal cost of a unit of output exceeds its marginal revenue, the firm should avoid producing that unit. It will add more to costs than to revenue; such a unit will not "pay its way."

MR = MC Rule In the initial stages of production, where output is relatively low, marginal revenue will usually (but not always) exceed marginal cost. It is therefore profitable to produce through this range of output. But at later stages of production, where output is relatively high, rising marginal costs will cause the reverse to be true. Marginal cost will exceed marginal revenue. Obviously, to maximize profits, producing units of output in this range is to be avoided.

Separating these two production ranges will be a unique point at which marginal revenue equals marginal cost. This point is the key to the output-determining rule: *The firm will maximize profits or minimize losses by producing at that point where marginal revenue equals marginal cost.* For convenience we call this profit-maximizing guide the **MR = MC rule.** For most sets of MR and MC data, there will be no nonfractional level of output at which MR and MC are precisely equal. In such instances the firm should produce the last complete unit of output whose MR exceeds its MC.

TABLE 10-5 The profit-maximizing output for a purely competitive firm: marginal-revenue-equals-marginal-cost approach (price = $131) *(hypothetical data)*

(1) Total product	*(2) Average fixed cost*	*(3) Average variable cost*	*(4) Average total cost*	*(5) Marginal cost*	*(6) Price = marginal revenue*	*(7) Total economic profit (+) or loss (−)*
0						$−100
1	$100.00	$90.00	$190.00	$ 90	$131	− 59
2	50.00	85.00	135.00	80	131	− 8
3	33.33	80.00	113.33	70	131	+ 53
4	25.00	75.00	100.00	60	131	+124
5	20.00	74.00	94.00	70	131	+185
6	16.67	75.00	91.67	80	131	+236
7	14.29	77.14	91.43	90	131	+277
8	12.50	81.25	93.75	110	131	+298
9	11.11	86.67	97.78	130	131	+299
10	10.00	93.00	103.00	150	131	+280

Three Characteristics Three features of this MR = MC rule merit comment.

1 The rule assumes that the firm will choose to produce rather than close down. Shortly, we will note that marginal revenue must be equal to, or must exceed, average variable cost, or the firm will find it preferable to close down rather than produce the MR = MC output.

2 The MR = MC rule is an accurate guide to profit maximization for all firms, be they purely competitive, monopolistic, monopolistically competitive, or oligopolistic. The rule's application is *not* limited to the special case of pure competition.

3 The MR = MC rule can be conveniently restated in a slightly different form when being applied to a purely competitive firm. Product price is determined by the market forces of supply and demand, and although the competitive firm can sell as much or as little as it chooses at that price, the firm cannot manipulate the price itself. In technical terms the demand, or sales, schedule faced by a competitive seller is perfectly elastic at the going market price. The result is that product price and marginal revenue are equal; that is, each extra unit sold adds precisely its price to total revenue as shown in Table 10-2 and Figure 10-1. Thus, under pure competition—and *only* under pure competition—we may substitute price for marginal revenue in the rule, so that it reads as follows: *To maximize profits or minimize losses the competitive firm should produce at that point where price equals marginal cost* (*P* = MC). This ***P* = MC rule** is simply a special case of the MR = MC rule.

Now let's apply the MR = MC or, because we are considering pure competition, the *P* = MC rule, using the same three prices as in our total-revenue–total-cost approach to profit maximization.

Profit-Maximizing Case Table 10-5 reproduces the unit- and marginal-cost data derived in Table 9-2. It is, of course, the marginal-cost data of column 5 in Table 10-5 which we will compare with price (equal to marginal revenue) for each unit of output. Suppose first that market price, and therefore marginal revenue, is $131, as shown in column 6.

What is the profit-maximizing output? We see that every unit of output up to and including the ninth adds more to total revenue than to cost. Price, or marginal revenue, exceeds marginal cost on all the first 9 units of output. Each unit therefore adds to the firm's profits and should be produced. The tenth unit, however, will not be produced, because it would add more to costs ($150) than to revenue ($131).

Profit Calculations The level of economic profits realized by the firm can be calculated from the unit-cost data. Multiplying price ($131) times output (9), we find total revenue to be $1179. Total cost of $880 is found by multiplying average total cost ($97.78) by output (9).[1]

[1]In most instances the unit-cost data are rounded figures. Therefore, economic profits calculated from them will typically vary by a few cents from the profits determined in the total-revenue–total-cost approach. We here ignore the few-cents differentials and make our answers consistent with the results of the total-revenue–total-cost approach.

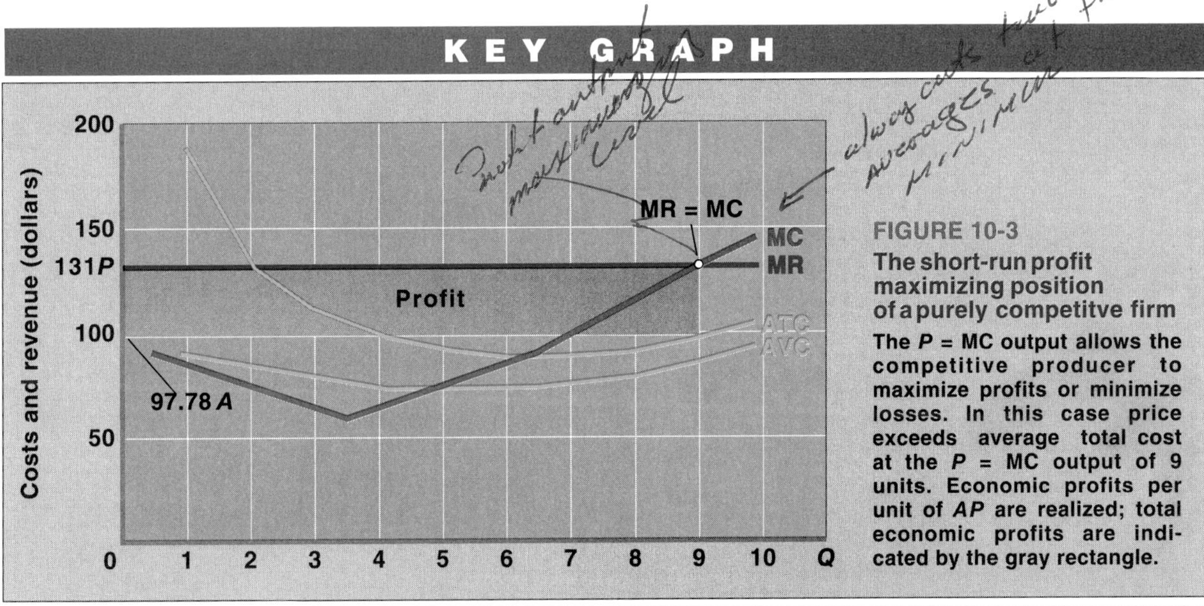

FIGURE 10-3
The short-run profit maximizing position of a purely competitve firm
The P = MC output allows the competitive producer to maximize profits or minimize losses. In this case price exceeds average total cost at the P = MC output of 9 units. Economic profits per unit of AP are realized; total economic profits are indicated by the gray rectangle.

The difference of \$299 (=\$1179 − \$880) is economic profits.

Another means of calculating economic profits is to determine profit *per unit* by subtracting average total cost (\$97.78) from product price (\$131) and multiplying the difference (per unit profits of \$33.22) by the level of output (9). By verifying the figures in column 7 of Table 10-5 you will find that any output other than that indicated to be most profitable by the MR (=P) = MC rule will mean either losses or profits less than \$299.

Graphical Portrayal Figure 10-3 (Key Graph) compares price and marginal cost graphically. Here per unit economic profit is indicated by the distance AP. When multiplied by the profit-maximizing output, the resulting total economic profit is shown by the gray rectangular area.

Note that the firm is seeking to maximize its *total* profits, not its *per unit* profits. Per unit profits are largest at 7 units of output, where price exceeds average total cost by \$39.57 (= \$131 − \$91.43). But by producing only 7 units, the firm would be forgoing the production of two additional units of output which would clearly contribute to total profits. The firm is happy to accept lower per unit profits if the additional profits associated with the extra units of sales more than compensate for the lower per unit profits.

Loss-Minimizing Case Now let's assume that market price is \$81 rather than \$131. Should the firm produce? If so, how much? And what will the resulting profits or losses be? The answers, respectively, are "Yes," "Six units," and "A loss of \$64."

Column 6 of Table 10-6 shows the new price (equal to marginal revenue) beside the same unit- and marginal-cost data presented in Table 10-5. Comparing columns 5 and 6, we find that the first unit of output adds \$90 to total cost but only \$81 to total revenue. One might conclude: "Don't produce—close down!" But this would be hasty. Remember that in the very early stages of production, marginal product is low, making marginal cost unusually high. The price–marginal-cost relationship improves with increased production. On the next 5 units—2 through 6—price exceeds marginal cost. Each of these 5 units adds more to revenue than to cost, more than compensating for the "loss" taken on the first unit. Beyond 6 units, however, MC exceeds MR (=P). The firm should therefore produce at 6 units. In general, the profit-seeking producer should always compare marginal revenue (or price under pure competition) with the *rising* portion of the marginal-cost schedule or curve.

Loss Determination Will production be profitable? No, because at 6 units of output average total costs of \$91.67 exceed price of \$81 by \$10.67 per unit. Multiply by the 6 units of ouput, and we find the firm's total loss is \$64. Then why produce? Because this loss is less than the firm's \$100 of fixed costs—the \$100 loss the firm would incur in the short run by closing down. The firm receives enough revenue per unit (\$81) to cover

TABLE 10-6 The loss-minimizing outputs for a purely competitive firm: marginal-revenue-equals-marginal-cost approach (prices = $81 and $71) ***(hypothetical data)***

(1) Total product	(2) Average fixed cost	(3) Average variable cost	(4) Average total cost	(5) Marginal cost	(6) $81 price = marginal revenue	(7) Profit (+) or loss (−), $81 price	(8) $71 price = marginal revenue	(9) Profit (+) or loss (−), $71 price
0						$−100		$−100
1	$100.00	$90.00	$190.00	$90	$81	−109	$71	−119
2	50.00	85.00	135.00	80	81	−108	71	−128
3	33.33	80.00	113.33	70	81	− 97	71	−127
4	25.00	75.00	100.00	60	81	− 76	71	−116
5	20.00	74.00	94.00	70	81	− 65	71	−115
6	16.67	75.00	91.67	80	81	− 64	71	−124
7	14.29	77.14	91.43	90	81	− 73	71	−143
8	12.50	81.25	93.75	110	81	−102	71	−182
9	11.11	86.67	97.78	130	81	−151	71	−241
10	10.00	93.00	103.00	150	81	−220	71	−320

its average variable costs of $75 and also provide $6 per unit, or a total of $36, to apply against fixed costs. Therefore, the firm's loss is only $64 (=$100 − $36), rather than $100.

Graphical Portrayal This case is shown graphically in Figure 10-4. Whenever price exceeds the minimum average variable cost but falls short of average total cost, the firm can pay part of, but not all, its fixed costs by producing. In this instance total variable costs are shown by the area *OVGF.* Total revenue, however, is *OPEF,* greater than total variable costs by *VPEG.* This excess of revenue over variable costs can be applied against total fixed costs, represented by area *VACG.* If it produces 6 units the firm's loss is only area *PACE;* if it closes down, its loss would be its fixed costs shown by the larger area *VACG.*

Close-Down Case Suppose now that the market yields a price of only $71. It will now pay the firm to close down, to produce nothing, because there is no output at which the firm can cover its average variable costs, much less its average total cost. In other words, the smallest loss it can realize by producing is greater than the $100 worth of fixed costs it will lose by closing down. The best action is to close down.

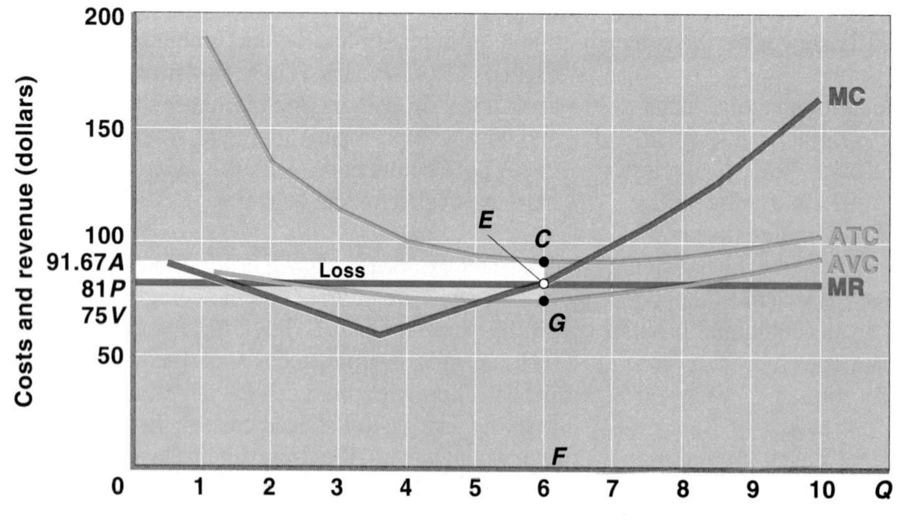

FIGURE 10-4 The short-run loss-minimizing position of a purely competitive firm

If price exceeds the minimum AVC but is less than ATC, the *P* = MC output of 6 units will permit the firm to minimize its losses. In this instance losses are *AP* per unit; total losses are shown by the area *PACE.*

This can be verified by comparing columns 3 and 8 of Table 10-6 and can be seen in Figure 10-5. Price comes closest to covering average variable costs at the MR (=P) = MC output of 5 units. But even here, price or revenue per unit would fall short of average variable cost by \$3 (=\$74 − \$71). By producing at the MR (=P) = MC output, the firm would lose its \$100 worth of fixed costs *plus* \$15 (\$3 on each of the 5 units) worth of variable costs, for a total loss of \$115. This clearly compares unfavorably with the \$100 fixed-cost loss the firm would incur by closing down and thereby producing no output. In short, it will pay the firm to close down rather than operate at a \$71 price or, for that matter, at any price less than the minimum average variable cost of \$74.

The close-down case obligates us to modify our MR (=P) = MC rule for profit maximization or loss minimization. *A competitive firm will maximize profits or minimize losses in the short run by producing at that output at which* MR (=P) = MC, *provided that price exceeds minimum average variable cost.*

Marginal Cost and the Short-Run Supply Curve

You will recognize that we have simply selected three different prices and asked how much the profit-seeking competitive firm, faced with certain costs, would choose to offer or supply in the market at each of these prices. This information—product price and corresponding quantity supplied—constitutes the supply schedule for the competitive firm.

Table 10-7 summarizes the supply schedule data for the three prices chosen—\$131, \$81, and \$71. You are urged to apply the MR (=P) = MC rule (modified by the close-down case) to verify the quantity-supplied data for the \$151, \$111, \$91, and \$61 prices and calculate the corresponding profits or losses. We confirm that the supply schedule is upsloping. Here price must be \$74 (equal to minimum average variable cost) or greater before any output is supplied. And because the marginal cost of successive units of output is increasing, the firm must get successively higher prices for it to be profitable to produce these additional units of output.

TABLE 10-7 The supply schedule of a competitive firm confronted with the cost data of Table 10-5 (hypothetical data)

Price	Quantity supplied	Maximum profit (+) or minimum loss (−)
\$151	10	\$____
131	9	+299
111	8	____
91	7	____
81	6	− 64
71	0	−100
61	0	____

Figure 10-6 (Key Graph) generalizes on our application of the MR (=P) = MC rule. We have drawn the appropriate cost curves and from the vertical axis have extended a series of marginal-revenue lines from some possible prices the market might set for the firm. The crucial prices are P_2 and P_4. Our close-down case reminds us that at any price *below* P_2—that price equal to

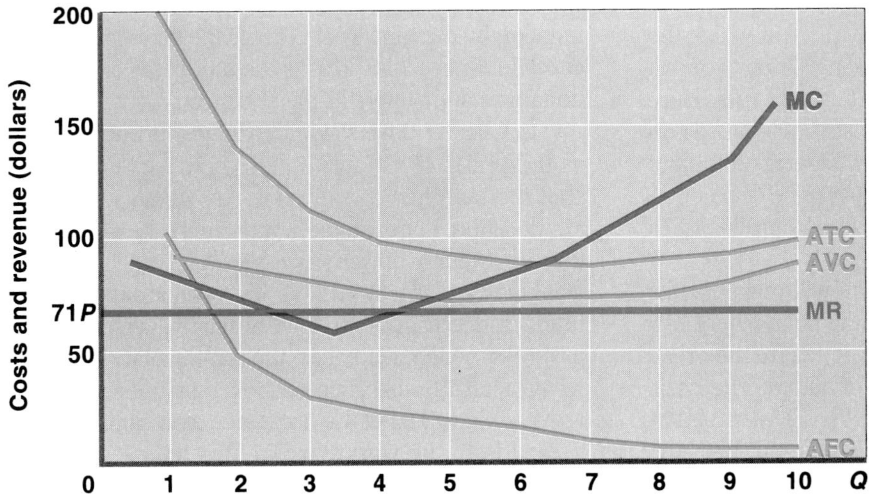

FIGURE 10-5 The short-run close-down position of a purely competitive firm

If price falls short of minimum AVC, the competitive firm will minimize its losses in the short run by closing down. There is no level of output at which the firm can produce and realize a loss smaller than its fixed costs.

KEY GRAPH

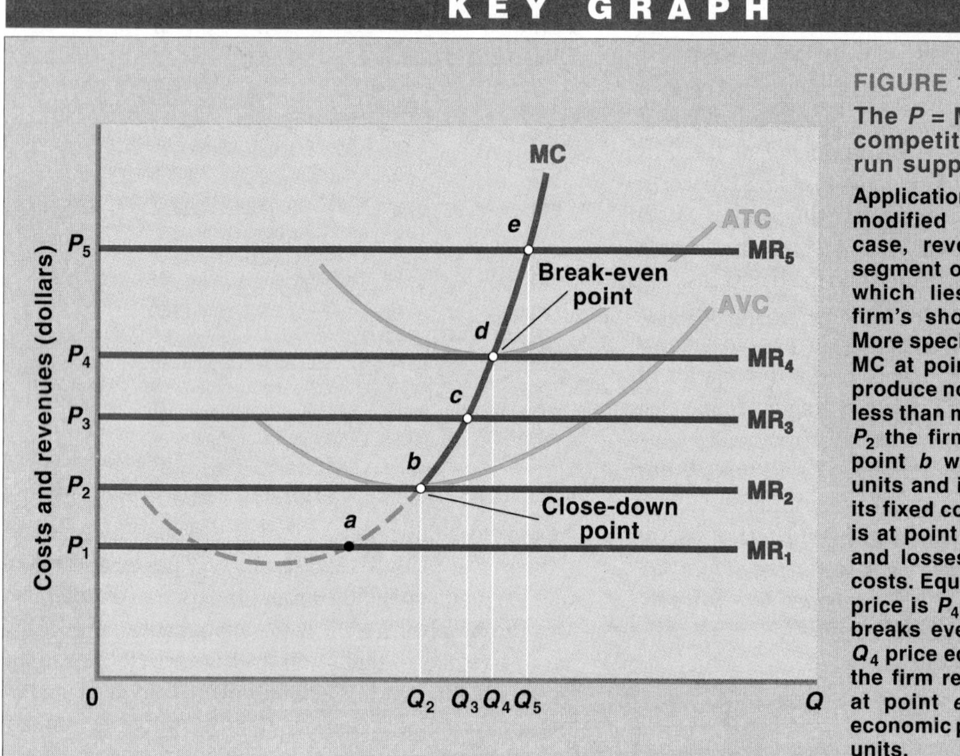

FIGURE 10-6

The P = MC rule and the competitive firm's short-run supply curve

Application of the P = MC rule, as modified by the close-down case, reveals that the (solid) segment of the firm's MC curve which lies above AVC is the firm's short-run supply curve. More specifically, at price P_1, P = MC at point *a*, but the firm will produce no output because P_1 is less than minimum AVC. At price P_2 the firm is in equilibrium at point *b* where it produces Q_2 units and incurs a loss equal to its fixed costs. At P_3 equilibrium is at point *c* where output is Q_3 and losses are less than fixed costs. Equilibrium is at point *d* if price is P_4; in this case the firm breaks even because at output Q_4 price equals ATC. At price P_5 the firm reaches an equilibrium at point *e* and maximizes its economic profit by producing Q_5 units.

the minimum average variable cost—the firm should close down and supply nothing. Actually, by producing Q_2 units of output *at* a price of P_2, the firm will just cover its variable costs, and its loss will be equal to its fixed costs. The firm therefore would be indifferent as to closing down *or* producing Q_2 units of output. But at any price below P_2, such as P_1, the firm will close down and supply zero units of output.

P_4 is strategic because it is the price at which the firm will just break even by producing Q_4 units of output, as indicated by the MR (=P) = MC rule. Here total revenue will just cover total costs (including a normal profit). At P_3 the firm supplies Q_3 units of output and minimizes its losses. At any other price between P_2 and P_4 the firm will minimize its losses by producing to the point where MR (=P) = MC.

At any price above P_4 the firm will maximize its economic profits by producing to the point where MR (=P) = MC. Thus at P_5 the firm will realize the greatest profits by supplying Q_5 units of output. The basic point is that each of the various MR (=P) = MC intersection points shown as *b,c,d,* and *e* in Figure 10-6 indicates a possible product price (on the vertical axis) and the corresponding quantity which the profit-seeking firm would supply at that price (on the horizontal axis). These points, by definition, locate the supply curve of the competitive firm. Because nothing would be produced at any price below the minimum average variable cost, we can conclude that *the portion of the firm's marginal-cost curve which lies above its average-variable-cost curve is its* **short-run supply curve.** The solid segment of the marginal cost curve is the short-run supply curve in Figure 10-6. This is the link between production costs and supply in the short run.

In Chapter 9 we saw that changes in such factors as the prices of variable inputs or in technology will shift the marginal cost or short-run supply curve to a new location. For example, a wage increase would shift the supply curve upward as viewed from the horizontal axis (leftward as viewed from the vertical axis), constituting a decrease in supply. Similarly, technological progress which increases the productivity of labor would shift the marginal cost or supply curve downward as viewed from the horizontal axis (rightward as viewed from the vertical axis). This represents an increase in supply. You should determine how (1) a specific tax on the product and (2) a per unit subsidy on this product would shift the supply curve.

QUICK REVIEW 10-3

- ***Profits are maximized or losses minimized at that output at which marginal revenue or price equals marginal cost.***
- ***At any price below minimum average variable cost the firm will minimize losses by closing down.***
- ***The segment of the firm's marginal cost curve which lies above average variable cost is its short-run supply curve.***

Recapitulation

Let's pause to summarize the main points made concerning short-run competitive pricing. Table 10-8 is a convenient check sheet on the total-revenue–total-cost and MR = MC approaches to determining the competitive firm's profit-maximizing output. This table warrants careful study.

Firm and Industry: Equilibrium Price

Now, having developed the competitive firm's short-run supply curve by applying the MR (=*P*) = MC rule, we must determine which of the various price possibilities will actually be the equilibrium price.

From Chapter 4 we know that in a purely competitive market, equilibrium price is determined by *total,* or market, supply and total demand. To derive total supply, the supply schedules or curves of the individual competitive sellers must be summed. Thus in Table 10-9, columns 1 and 3 repeat the individual competitive firm's supply schedule just derived in Table 10-7. We now conveniently assume that there are a total of 1000 competitive firms in this industry, each having the same total and unit costs as the single firm we discussed. This lets us calculate the total- or market-supply schedule (columns 2 and 3) by multiplying the quantity-supplied figures of the single firm (column 1) by 1000.

TABLE 10-9 Firm and market supply and market demand *(hypothetical data)*

(1) Quantity supplied, single firm	(2) Total quantity supplied, 1000 firms	(3) Product price	(4) Total quantity demanded
10	10,000	$151	4,000
9	9,000	131	6,000
8	8,000	111	8,000
7	7,000	91	9,000
6	6,000	81	11,000
0	0	71	13,000
0	0	61	16,000

Market Price and Profits To determine equilibrium price and output, this total-supply data must be compared with total-demand data. Let's assume total-demand data are as shown in columns 3 and 4 of Table 10-9. Comparing the total quantity supplied and total quantity demanded at the seven possible prices, we determine that equilibrium price is $111 and equilibrium quantity 8000 units for the industry—8 units for each of the 1000 identical firms.

Will these conditions of market supply and demand make this a prosperous or an unprosperous industry? Multiplying product price ($111) by output (8), we find the total revenue of each firm is $888. Total cost is $750, found by multiplying average total cost of $93.75 by 8, or simply by looking at column 5 of Table 10-3. The $138 difference is the economic profit of each

TABLE 10-8 Summary of competitive output determination in the short run

	Total-revenue–total-cost approach	*Marginal-revenue–marginal-cost approach*
Should the firm produce?	**Yes, if TR exceeds TC or if TC exceeds TR by some amount less than total fixed cost.**	**Yes, if price is equal to, or greater than, minimum average variable cost.**
What quantity should be produced to maximize profits?	**Produce where the excess of TR over TC is a maximum or where the excess of TC over TR is a minimum (and less than total fixed costs).**	**Produce where MR or price equals MC.**
Will production result in economic profit?	**Yes, if TR exceeds TC. No, if TC exceeds TR.**	**Yes, if price exceeds average total cost. No, if average total cost exceeds price.**

firm. Another way of calculating economic profits is to determine *per unit* profit by subtracting average total cost ($93.75) from product price ($111) and multiplying the difference (per unit profits of $17.25) by the firm's equilibrium level of output (8). For the industry, total economic profit is $138,000. This, then, is a prosperous industry.

Graphical Portrayal Figure 10-7a and b shows this analysis graphically. The individual supply curves of each of the 1000 identical firms—one of which is shown as *s* in Figure 10-7a—are summed horizontally to get the total supply curve *S* of Figure 10-7b. Given total demand *D*, equilibrium price is $111, and equilibrium quantity for the industry is 8000 units. This equilibrium price is given and unalterable to the individual firm; that is, each firm's demand curve is perfectly elastic at the equilibrium price, indicated by *d*. Because price is given and constant to the individual firm, the marginal-revenue curve coincides with the demand curve. This $111 price exceeds average total cost at the firm's equilibrium MR (=*P*) = MC output, resulting in a situation of economic profits similar to that already portrayed in Figure 10-3.

Assuming no changes in cost or market demands, these diagrams reveal a genuine *short-run* equilibrium situation. There are no shortages or surpluses in the market to cause price or total quantity to change. Nor can any of the firms in the industry improve their profits by altering their output. Note, too, that higher unit and marginal costs, on the one hand, or a weaker market demand situation, on the other, could pose a loss situation similar to Figure 10-4. You are urged to sketch, in Figure 10-7a and b, how higher costs and a less favorable demand could cause a short-run equilibrium situation entailing losses.

Firm versus Industry Figure 10-7a and b underscores a point made earlier: Product price is a given datum to the *individual* competitive firm, but at the same time, the supply plans of all competitive producers *as a group* are a basic determinant of product price. If we recall the fallacy of composition, we find there is no inconsistency here. Though each firm, supplying a negligible fraction of total supply, cannot affect price, the sum of the supply curves of all the firms in the industry constitutes the industry supply curve, and this curve does have an important bearing on price. *Under competition, equilibrium price is a given datum to the individual firm and simultaneously is the result of the production (supply) decisions of all firms taken as a group.*

FIGURE 10-7 Short-run competitive equilibrium for a firm (a) and the industry (b)

The horizontal sum of the 1000 firms' supply curves (*s*) determines the industry supply curve (*S*). Given industry demand (*D*), the short-run equilibrium price and output for the industry are $111 and 8000 units. Taking the equilibrium price as given datum, the representative firm establishes its profit-maximizing output at 8 units and, in this case, realizes the economic profit shown by the gray area.

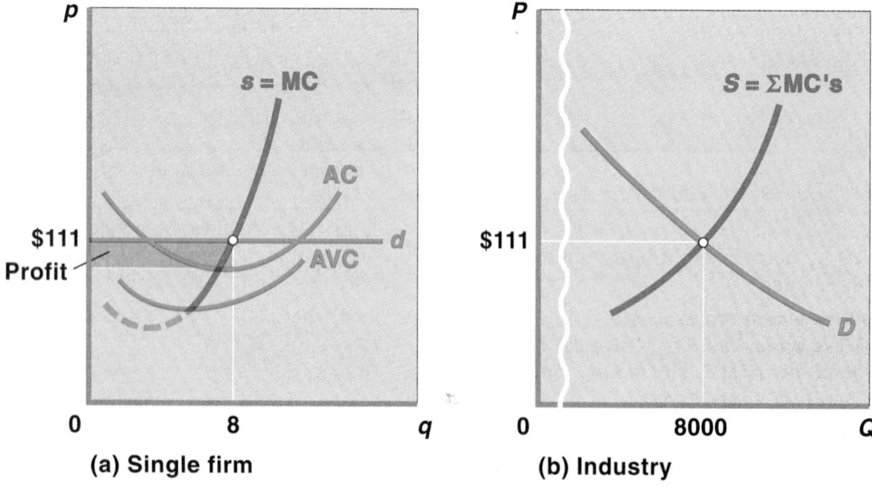

PROFIT MAXIMIZATION IN THE LONG RUN

The long run permits firms to make certain adjustments which time does not allow in the short run. In the short run there are a given number of firms in an industry, each of which has a fixed, unalterable plant. True, firms may close down in the sense that they produce zero units of output in the short run; but they do not have sufficient time to liquidate their assets and go out of business. By contrast, in the long run firms already in an industry have sufficient time either to expand or contract their plant capacities. More importantly, the number of firms in the industry may either increase or decrease as new firms enter or existing firms leave. We now examine how these long-run adjustments modify our conclusions concerning short-run output and price determination.

Assumptions and Goal

We will make certain simplifying assumptions, none of which will impair the general validity of our conclusions.

1 Entry and Exodus We will suppose that the only long-run adjustment is the entry and exodus of firms. Furthermore, for simplicity's sake we ignore the short-run adjustments already analyzed, in order to grasp the nature of long-run competitive adjustments.

2 Identical Costs We also assume that all firms in the industry have identical cost curves. This lets us discuss an "average," or "representative," firm knowing that all other firms in the industry are similarly affected by any long-run adjustments which occur.

3 Constant-Cost Industry We assume for the moment that the industry under discussion is a constant-cost industry. This means that the entry and exodus of firms will *not* affect resource prices or, therefore, the locations of the unit-cost schedules of individual firms.

We will describe long-run competitive adjustments both verbally and through graphical analysis. The basic conclusion we seek to explain is as follows: *After all long-run adjustments are completed, that is, when long-run equilibrium is achieved, product price will be exactly equal to, and production will occur at, each firm's point of minimum average total cost.*

This conclusion follows from two basic facts: (1) Firms seek profits and shun losses, and (2) under competition, firms are free to enter and leave industries. If price initially exceeds average total costs, the resulting economic profits will attract new firms to the industry. But this industry expansion will increase product supply until price is brought back down into equality with average total cost. Conversely, if price is initially less than average total cost, resulting losses will cause firms to leave the industry. As they leave, total product supply will decline, bringing price back up into equality with average total cost.

Zero-Profit Model

Our conclusion can best be demonstrated and its significance evaluated by assuming that the average or representative firm in a purely competitive industry is initially in long-run equilibrium. This is shown in Figure 10-8a, where price and minimum average total cost are equal at, say, $50. Economic profits here are zero; the industry is in equilibrium or "at rest," because there is no tendency for firms to enter or leave the industry. The going market price is determined by total, or industry, demand and supply, as shown by D_1 and S_1 in Figure 10-8b. (The market supply schedule, incidentally, is a *short-run* schedule; the industry's long-run supply schedule will be developed in our discussion.) By examining the quantity axes of the two graphs, we note that if all firms are identical, there must be 1000 firms in the industry, each producing 100 units, to achieve the industry's equilibrium output of 100,000 units.

Entry of Firms Eliminates Profits

Now our model is set up. Let's upset the long-run equilibrium of Figure 10-8 and trace subsequent adjustments. Suppose a change in consumer tastes increases product demand from D_1 to D_2. This favorable shift in demand will make production profitable; the new price of $60 exceeds average total cost of $50. *These economic profits will lure new firms into the industry.* Some entrants will be newly created firms; others will shift from less prosperous industries.

As firms enter, the market supply of the product will increase, causing product price to gravitate downward from $60 toward the original level. Assuming, as we are, that entry of new firms has no effect on costs, economic profits will persist, and entry will therefore

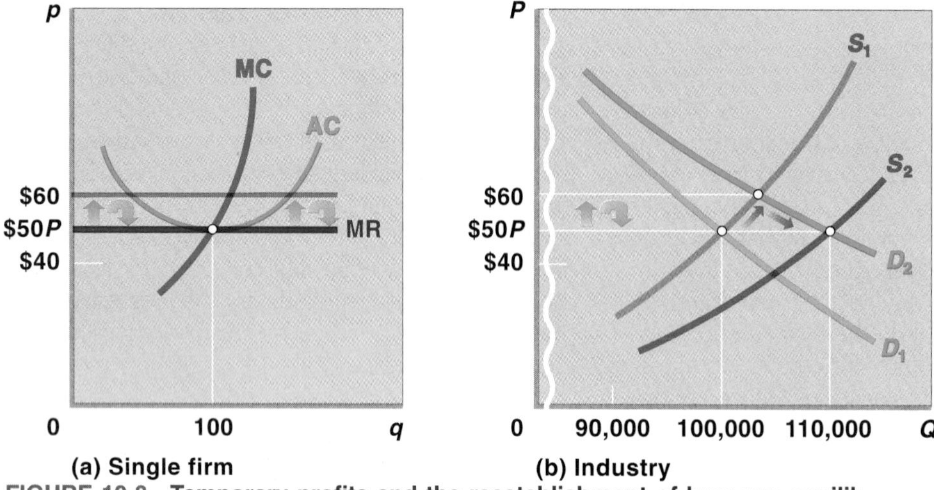

FIGURE 10-8 Temporary profits and the reestablishment of long-run equilibrium in a representative firm (a) and the industry (b)

A favorable shift in demand (D_1 to D_2) will upset the original equilibrium and produce economic profits. But profits will cause new firms to enter the industry, increasing supply (S_1 to S_2) and lowering product price until economic profits are once again zero.

continue until short-run market supply has increased to S_2. At this point, price is again equal to minimum average total cost at $50. The economic profits caused by the boost in demand have been competed away to zero, and as a result, the previous incentive for more firms to enter the industry has disappeared. Long-run equilibrium is restored at this point.

Figure 10-8 tells us that upon reestablishment of long-run equilibrium, industry output is 110,000 units and that each firm in the now expanded industry is producing 100 units. We can conclude that the industry is now composed of 1100 firms; that is, 100 new firms have entered the industry.

Exodus of Firms Eliminates Losses

To strengthen our understanding of long-run competitive equilibrium, let's reverse our analysis. In Figure 10-9a and b, the $50 price and curves S_1 and D_1 show the initial long-run equilibrium situation used as a point of departure in our previous analysis of how the entry of firms eliminates economic profits.

Now suppose that consumer demand falls from D_1 to D_3. This forces price down to $40, making production unprofitable. *In time resulting losses will induce firms to leave the industry.* The reason is that owners can realize a normal profit elsewhere as opposed to the below-normal profit (losses) now confronting them. As capital equipment wears out and contractual obligations expire, some firms will simply fold. As this exodus of firms proceeds, however, industry supply will decrease, moving from S_1 toward S_3. As this occurs, price will begin to rise from $40 back toward $50. Assuming costs are unchanged by the exodus of firms, losses will force firms to leave the industry until supply has declined to S_3, at which point price is again exactly $50, barely consistent with minimum average total cost. The exodus continues until losses are eliminated and long-run equilibrium is again restored.

Observe in Figure 10-9a and b that total quantity supplied is now 90,000 units and each firm is producing 100 units. The industry is now populated by only 900 firms rather than the original 1000 since losses have forced 100 firms out of business.

You may have noted that we have sidestepped the question of which firms will leave the industry when losses occur by assuming all firms have identical cost curves. In the "real world" entrepreneurial talents differ so that, even if resource prices and technology are the same for all firms, inferior entrepreneurs would incur higher costs and therefore be the first to leave the industry when product demand declined. Similarly, other resources may be heterogeneous and also give rise to cost differences. For example, firms with less productive labor forces will be high-cost producers and likely candidates to quit the industry when product demand decreases.

Our prestated conclusion has now been verified. Competition, reflected in the entry and exodus of firms, forces price into equality with the minimum long-run average total cost of production, and each firm produces at the point of minimum long-run average total

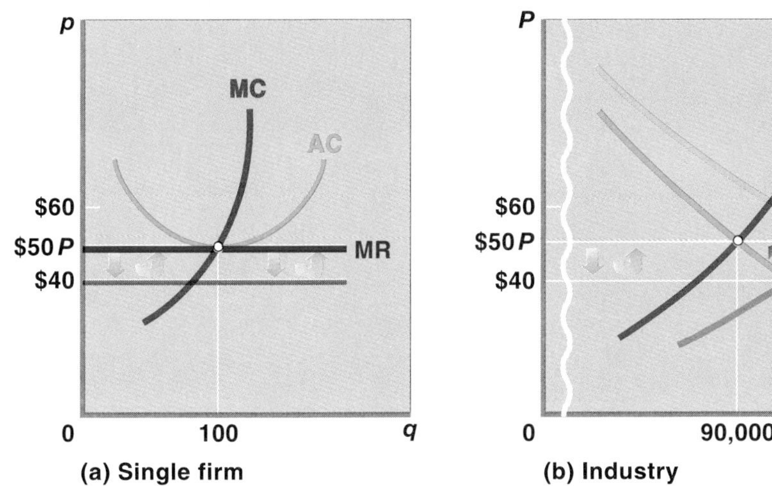

FIGURE 10-9 Temporary losses and the reestablishment of long-run equilibrium in a representative firm (a) and the industry (b)

An unfavorable shift in demand (D_1 to D_3) will upset the original equilibrium and produce losses. But losses will cause firms to leave the industry, decreasing supply (S_1 to S_3) and increasing product price until all losses have disappeared.

cost. Note, too, that these expanding- and declining-industry cases explain the functioning of consumer sovereignty, a concept we discussed in Chapter 5.

Long-Run Supply for a Constant-Cost Industry

What is the character of the **long-run supply curve** which evolves from this analysis of the expansion or contraction of a competitive industry? Although our discussion deals with the long run, we have noted that the market supply curves of Figures 10-8b and 10-9b are short-run industry supply curves. However, the analysis itself permits us to sketch the nature of the long-run supply curve for this competitive industry. The crucial factor in determining the shape of the industry's long-run supply curve is the effect, if any, which changes in the number of firms in the industry will have on the costs of the individual firms in the industry.

Constant-Cost Industry In the foregoing analysis of long-run competitive equilibrium we assumed the industry under discussion was a **constant-cost industry.** This means that industry expansion through the entry of new firms will not affect resource prices or, therefore, production costs. Graphically, the entry of new firms does *not* change the position of the long-run average-cost curves of individual firms in the industry. When will this be the case? For the most part, when the industry's demand for resources is small in relation to the total demand for those resources. This is most likely to occur when the industry employs unspecialized resources which are being demanded by many other industries. In short, when the particular industry's demand for resources is a negligible component of total demand, the industry can expand without significantly affecting resource prices and costs.

Perfectly Elastic Supply What will the long-run supply curve for a constant-cost industry look like? The answer is contained in our previous discussion of the long-run adjustments toward equilibrium which profits or losses will initiate. Here we assumed that entrance or departure of firms would not affect costs. The result was that entry or exodus of firms would alter industry output but always bring product price back to the original $50 level, where it is just consistent with the unchanging minimum average total cost of production. Specifically, we discovered that the industry would supply 90,000, 100,000, or 110,000 units of output, all at a price of $50 per unit. *The long-run supply curve of a constant-cost industry is perfectly elastic.*

This is demonstrated graphically in Figure 10-10, where the data from Figures 10-8 and 10-9 are retained. Suppose that industry demand is originally D_1, industry output is Q_1 (100,000), and product price is Q_1P_1 ($50). This situation, referring to Figure 10-8, is one of long-run equilibrium. Now assume that demand increases to D_2, upsetting this equilibrium. The resulting economic profits will attract new firms. Because this is a constant-cost industry, entry will continue and indus-

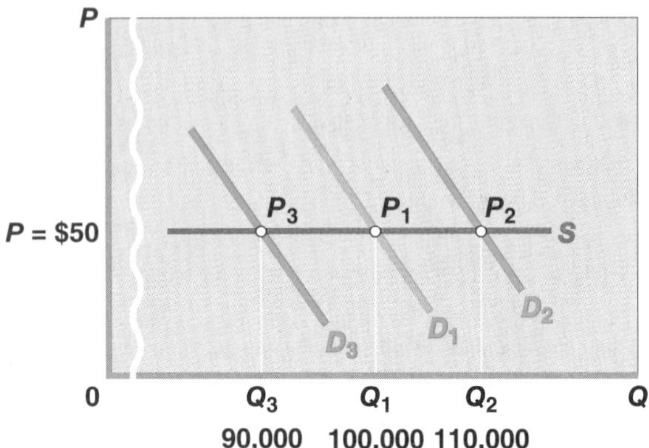

FIGURE 10-10 The long-run supply curve for a constant-cost industry is perfectly elastic

Because the entry or exodus of firms does not affect resource prices or, therefore, unit costs, an increase in demand (D_1 to D_2) will cause an expansion in industry output (Q_1 to Q_2) but no alteration in price ($Q_1P_1 = Q_2P_2$). Similarly, a decrease in demand (D_1 to D_3) will cause a contraction of output (Q_1 to Q_3) but no change in price ($Q_1P_1 = Q_3P_3$). This means that the long-run industry supply curve (S) will be perfectly elastic.

try output will expand until price is driven back down to the unchanged minimum average-total-cost level. This will be at price Q_2P_2 ($50) and output Q_2 (110,000).

This analysis, now referring to Figure 10-9, is reversible. A decline in short-run industry demand from D_1 to D_3 will cause an exodus of firms and ultimately restore equilibrium at price Q_3P_3 ($50) and output Q_3 (90,000). A line connecting all points, such as these three, shows the various price–quantity supplied combinations most profitable when firms have had enough time to make *all* desired adjustments to assumed changes in industry demand. By definition, this line is the industry's long-run supply curve. In a constant-cost industry this line, S in Figure 10-10, is perfectly elastic.

Long-Run Supply for an Increasing-Cost Industry

But constant-cost industries are a special case. Most industries are **increasing-cost industries** in that their average cost curves shift upward as the industry expands and downward as the industry contracts. Usually, the entry of new firms will bid up resource prices and therefore raise unit costs for individual firms in the industry. When an industry is using a significant portion of some resource whose total supply is not readily increased, the entry of new firms will increase resource demand in relation to supply and boost resource prices. This is particularly so in industries using specialized resources whose initial supply is not readily augmented. Higher resource prices will result in higher long-run average costs for firms in the industry. The higher costs take the form of an upward shift in the long-run average-cost curve for the representative firm.

Two-Way Profit Squeeze The net result is that when an increase in product demand causes economic profits and attracts new firms to the industry, a two-way squeeze on profits will occur to eliminate those profits. On the one hand, the entry of new firms will increase market supply and lower product price and, on the other, the entire average-total-cost curve of the representative firm will shift upward. The equilibrium price will now be higher than it was originally. The industry will only produce a larger output at a higher price because industry expansion has increased average total costs, and in the long run product price must cover these costs. Greater output will be forthcoming at a higher price, or, more technically, the industry supply curve for an increasing-cost industry will be upsloping. Instead of getting either 90,000, 100,000, or 110,000 units at the same price of $50, in an increasing-cost industry 90,000 units might be forthcoming at $45; 100,000 at $50; and 110,000 at $55. The higher price is required to induce more production because costs per unit of output increase as the industry expands.

This can be seen graphically in Figure 10-11. Original market demand, industry output, and price are D_1, Q_1 (100,000), and Q_1P_1 ($50) respectively. An increase in demand to D_2 will upset this equilibrium and lead to economic profits. As new firms enter, (1) industry supply will increase, driving product price down to minimum average cost, and (2) resource prices will rise, causing average total costs of production to rise. Because of these average-total-cost increases, the new long-run equilibrium price will be established at some level *above* the original price, such as Q_2P_2 ($55). Conversely, a decline in demand from D_1 to D_3 will make production unprofitable and cause firms to leave the industry. The resulting decline in the demand for resources relative to their supply will lower resource prices and reduce average total costs of production. The new equilibrium price will be established at some level *below* the original price, such as Q_3P_3 ($45). Connecting these three equilibrium positions, we derive an upsloping long-run supply curve shown by S in Figure 10-11.

Long-Run Supply for a Decreasing-Cost Industry

In some industries firms may experience lower costs as the industry expands. Such industries are **de-**

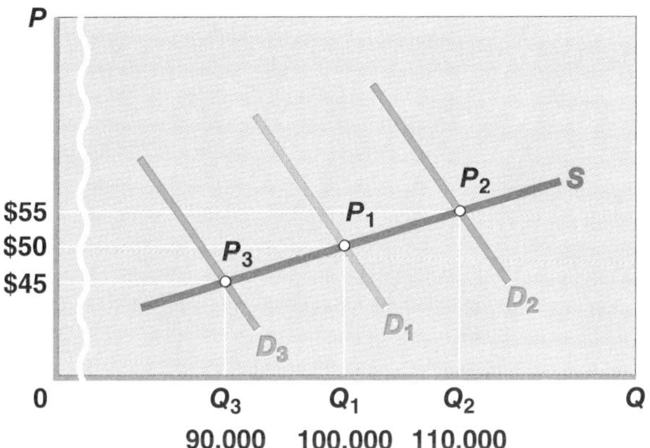

FIGURE 10-11 **The long-run supply curve for an increasing-cost industry is upsloping**

In an increasing-cost industry the entry of new firms in response to an increase in demand (D_3 to D_1 to D_2) will bid up resource prices and thereby increase unit costs. As a result, an increased industry output (Q_3 to Q_1 to Q_2) will be forthcoming only at higher prices ($Q_2P_2 > Q_1P_1 > Q_3P_3$). The long-run industry supply curve (S) is therefore upsloping.

creasing-cost industries. Classic example: As more mines are established in a given locality, each firm's costs in pumping out water seepage may decline. With more mines pumping, seepage into each is less, and pumping costs are therefore reduced. Furthermore, with only a few mines in an area, industry output might be so small that only relatively primitive and therefore costly transportation facilities are available. But as the number of firms and industry output expand, a railroad might build a spur into the area and thereby significantly reduce transportation costs.

You are urged to replicate the analysis underlying Figure 10-11 to show that the long-run supply curve of a decreasing-cost industry will be *downsloping.*

PURE COMPETITION AND EFFICIENCY

Whether a purely competitive industry is one of constant or increasing costs, the final long-run equilibrium position for each firm will have the same basic characteristics. As shown in Figure 10-12 (Key Graph) price (and marginal revenue) will settle where they are equal to minimum average cost. However, we discovered in Chapter 9 that the marginal-cost curve intersects, and is therefore equal to, average cost at the point of minimum average cost. In the long-run equilibrium position, "everything is equal." MR (=*P*) = minimum AC = MC.

This triple equality tells us that, although a competitive firm may realize economic profits or losses in the short run, it will barely break even by producing in accordance with the MR (=*P*) = MC rule in the long run. Also, this triple equality suggests certain conclusions of great social significance concerning the efficiency of a purely competitive economy.

Economists agree that, subject to certain limitations and exceptions, a purely competitive economy will lead to the most efficient use of society's scarce resources. *A competitive price economy will allocate the limited amounts of resources available to society so as to maximize the satisfactions of consumers.* Actually, efficient use of limited resources requires that two conditions—which we have called allocative efficiency and productive efficiency—are fulfilled.

First, to achieve **allocative efficiency** resources must be apportioned among firms and industries to obtain the particular mix of products which is most wanted by society (consumers). Allocative efficiency is realized when it is impossible to alter the composition of total output to achieve a net gain for society.

Second, **productive efficiency** requires that each good in this optimum product mix be produced in the least costly way. To facilitate our discussion of how these conditions would be achieved under purely competitive conditions, let's examine the second point first.

1 Productive Efficiency: P = Minimum AC We know that, in the long run, competition forces firms to produce at the point of minimum average total cost of production and to charge that price which is just consistent with these costs. This is a most desirable situation from the consumer's point of view. It means that firms must use the best available (least-cost) technology or they will not survive. Stated differently, the minimum amount of resources will be used to produce any given output.

For example, glance back at the final equilibrium position shown in Figure 10-9a. Each firm in the industry is producing 100 units of output by using $5000 (equal to average cost of $50 *times* 100 units) worth of resources. If that same output had been produced at a total cost of, say, $7000, resources would be being used inefficiently. Society would be faced with the net loss of $2000 worth of alternative products. Note, too, that consumers benefit from the lowest product price possible under the cost conditions currently prevailing. Finally, the costs involved in each instance are only those costs essential in producing a product. Because products are standardized in competitive industries, there will be no selling or promotional costs added to production costs in determining product price.

KEY GRAPH

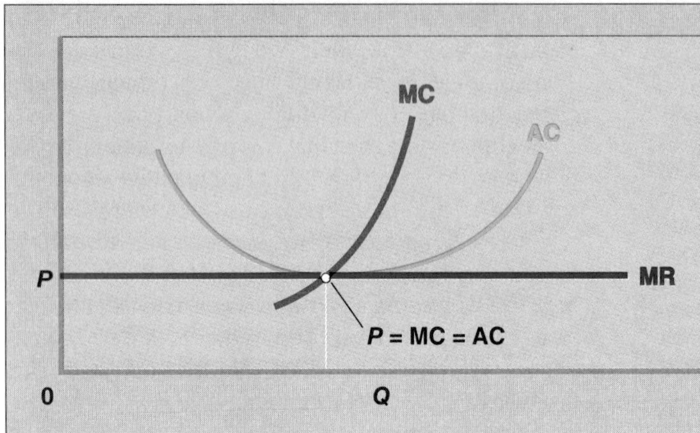

FIGURE 10-12
The long-run equilibrium position of a competitive firm, P = minimum AC = MC

The equality of price and minimum average cost indicates that the firm is using the most efficient known technology and is charging the lowest price P and producing the greatest output Q consistent with its costs. The equality of price and marginal cost indicates that resources are being allocated in accordance with consumer preferences.

2 Allocative Efficiency: P = MC But the competitive production of *any* collection of goods does not necessarily make for an efficient allocation of resources. Production must not only be technologically efficient, but must also be the "right goods," goods consumers want most. The competitive market system functions so that resources are allocated to produce a total output whose composition best fits consumer preferences.

We must first grasp the social meaning of competitive product and resource prices. *The money price of any product—product X—is society's measure, or index, of the relative worth of that product at the margin.* Similarly, recalling the notion of opportunity costs, *the marginal cost of producing X measures the value, or relative worth, of the other goods the resources used in producing an extra unit of X could otherwise have produced.* In short, product price measures the benefit, or satisfaction, which society gets from additional units of X, and the marginal cost of an additional unit of X measures the sacrifice, or cost to society, of other goods in using resources to produce more of X.

Underallocation: $P > MC$ Now, under competition, the production of each product will occur up to that precise point at which price is equal to marginal cost (Figure 10-12). The profit-seeking competitor will realize the maximum possible profit only by equating price and marginal cost. To produce short of the MR (=P) = MC point will mean less than maximum profits to the individual firm and an *under*allocation of resources to this product from society's standpoint. The fact that price exceeds marginal cost indicates that society values additional units of X more highly than the alternative products the appropriate resources could otherwise produce.

To illustrate, if the price of a shirt is $10 and its marginal cost is $8, producing an additional shirt will cause a net increase in total output of $2. Society will gain a shirt valued at $10, while the alternative products sacrificed by allocating more resources to shirts would only be valued at $8. Whenever society can gain something valued at $10 by giving up something valued at $8, the initial allocation of resources must have been inefficient.

Overallocation: $P < MC$ For similar reasons, the production of X should not go beyond the output at which price equals marginal cost. To do so would entail less than maximum profits for producers and an *over*allocation of resources to X from the standpoint of society. To produce X at some point at which marginal cost exceeds price means resources are being used in the production of X by sacrificing alternative goods society values more highly than the added units of X. For example, if the price of a shirt is $10 and its marginal cost $13, then the production of one less shirt would result in a net increase in society's total output of $3. Society would lose a shirt valued at $10, but reallocating the freed resources to their best alternative uses would increase the output of some other good valued at $13. Again, whenever society is able to give up something valued at $10 in return for something valued at $13, the original allocation of resources must have been inefficient.

Efficient Allocation Our conclusion is that *under pure competition, profit-motivated producers will pro-*

duce each commodity up to that precise point at which price and marginal cost are equal. This means that resources are efficiently allocated under competition. Each good is produced to the point at which the value of the last unit is equal to the value of the alternative goods sacrificed by its production. To alter the production of X would necessarily reduce consumer satisfactions. To produce X beyond the P = MC point would sacrifice alternative goods whose value to society exceeds that of the extra units of X. To produce X short of the P = MC point would sacrifice units of X which society values more than the alternative goods resources can produce.

Dynamic Adjustments A further attribute of purely competitive markets is their ability to restore efficiency in the use of resouces when disrupted by dynamic changes in the economy. In a competitive economy, any changes in consumer tastes, resource supplies, or technology will automatically set in motion appropriate realignments of resources. As we have already explained, an increase in consumer demand for product X will increase its price. Disequilibrium will occur in that, at its present output, the price of X will now exceed its marginal cost. This will create economic profits in industry X and stimulate its expansion. Its profitability will permit the industry to bid resources away from now less pressing uses. Expansion in this industry will end only when the price of X again equals its marginal cost, that is, when the value of the last unit produced once again equals the value of the alternative goods society forgoes in producing that last unit of X.

Similarly, changes in supplies of particular resources or in production techniques will upset existing price–marginal-cost equalities by either raising or lowering marginal cost. These inequalities will cause business executives, in either pursuing profits or shunning losses, to reallocate resources until price once again equals marginal cost in each line of production. In so doing, they correct any inefficiencies in the allocation of resources which changing economic data may temporarily impose on the economy.

"Invisible Hand" Revisited A final point: The highly efficient allocation of resources which a purely competitive economy fosters comes about because businesses and resource suppliers freely seek to further their own self-interests. That is, the "invisible hand" (Chapter 5) is at work in a competitive market system. In a competitive economy, businesses employ resources until the extra, or marginal, costs of production equal the product price. This not only maximizes profits for individual producers but simultaneously results in a pattern of resource allocation which maximizes consumer satisfaction. The competitive market system organizes the private interests of producers along lines which are fully in accord with society's interest in using scarce resources efficiently.

QUICK REVIEW 10-4

- ***In the long run the entry of firms will compete away profits and the exodus of firms will eliminate losses so that price equals minimum average cost.***
- ***The long-run supply curves of constant-, increasing-, and decreasing-cost industries are perfectly elastic, upsloping, and downsloping, respectively.***
- ***In purely competitive markets both productive efficiency (price equals minimum average cost) and allocative efficiency (price equals marginal cost) are achieved in the long run.***

Qualifications

Our conclusion that a purely competitive market system results in both productive and allocative efficiency must be qualified in several important respects.

The Income Distribution Problem The contention that pure competition will allocate resources efficiently is predicated on some given distribution of money income. Money income is distributed among households in some specific way, and this distribution results in a certain structure of demand. The competitive market system then brings about an efficient allocation of resources or, stated differently, an output of goods and services whose composition maximizes fulfillment of these particular consumer demands.

But if the distribution of money income is altered so that the structure of demand changes, would the competitive market system negotiate a new allocation of resources? The answer is "Yes"; the market system would reallocate resources and therefore change the composition of output to maximize the fulfillment of this new pattern of consumer wants. The question, then, is which of these two "efficient" allocations of resources is the "most efficient"? Which allocation of resources yields the greatest level of satisfaction to society?

There is no *scientific* answer to this question because we cannot measure and compare the satisfaction derived by various individuals from goods and services. If all people were alike in their capacities to ob-

LAST WORD

THE THEORY OF CONTESTABLE MARKETS

The concept of contestable markets suggests that the market power of imperfectly competitive producers may be severely constrained by potential industry entrants.

As noted in this chapter, the outcomes of purely competitive markets set standards of efficiency by which imperfectly competitive markets are judged. Both allocative and productive efficiency are realized when an industry is purely competitive. Princeton's William Baumol argues that the *potential* entry of firms to industries which are *not* purely competitive may also bring about the efficient results associated with pure competition.

Baumol has developed the notion of a *contestable market,* which means a market in which firm entry and exit are costless or virtually so. Envision a contestable market which is oligopolistic, that is, comprised of three or four large firms. The contestability of the market means that it is subject to "hit and run" entry by other firms because they can enter and leave virtually without cost. It follows that any economic profits or production inefficiencies on the part of the several firms in the industry will attract new entrants. (Productive inefficiencies imply that profits are being forgone by existing producers and new entrants can realize such profits by producing efficiently.) Hence, in contestable markets the mere presence of potential competition will force existing firms to produce efficiently and to charge prices which yield only a normal profit. Stated differently, incumbent firms are forced to behave as would purely competitive firms to forestall entry of other firms. We thus realize the socially desirable outcomes of purely competitive markets in contestable markets even though the latter are populated by only a few firms. The important factor which promotes these outcomes is not the number of firms in the industry, but costless entry and exit.

The most cited example of a contestable market is the airline industry. Assume there are just two airlines flying the Omaha–Chicago route. If entry and exit were costly, the market would *not* be contestable and the two incumbent airlines might realize substantial economic profits from their protected market position.

But in fact additional airlines can enter and leave this particular segment of the air transportation market with minimal cost. The reason is that the relevant capital equipment—the airplanes themselves—are highly mobile. Hence, if an additional airline were to enter and find the Omaha–Chicago route to be unprofitable, it could simply "pull out" by flying its equipment to some other route. The important point is that the awareness of the possibility of costless entry will compel the two airlines currently flying the Omaha–Chicago route to provide their transportation services efficiently and at prices which yield only a normal profit.

The main policy implication of contestable markets is that the focus of antimonopoly policy should shift from the current structure or competitive conditions within an industry to the conditions of entry. The primary criticism of contestable market theory is that its applicability is extremely limited. Critics contend that there are few, if any, industries—including the aforementioned airline industry—where entry and exit are costless.

tain satisfaction from income, economists could recommend that income be distributed equally and that the allocation of resources appropriate to *that* distribution would be the "best" or "most efficient" of all. But, people differ in their education, experiences, and environment, not to mention their inherited mental and physical characteristics. Such differences can be used to argue for an unequal distribution of income.

The distribution of income associated with the workings of a purely competitive market system is in fact quite unequal (Chapter 22) and therefore may lead to the production of trifles for the rich while denying basic needs of the poor. Many economists believe that the distribution of income which pure competition provides should be modified by public action. They maintain that allocative efficiency is hardly a virtue if it is a response to an income distribution which offends prevailing standards of equity.

Market Failure: Spillovers and Public Goods Under competition each producer will assume only those costs which it *must* pay. This correctly implies that in some lines of production there are significant costs producers can and do avoid, usually by polluting the environment. Recall from Chapter 6 that these avoided costs accrue to society and are aptly called *spillover* or *external costs.* On the other hand, consumption of certain goods and services, such as chest x-rays and measles vaccinations, yields widespread satisfactions, or benefits, to society as a whole. These satisfactions are called *external* or *spillover benefits.*

The profit-seeking activities of producers will bring about an allocation of resources which is efficient from society's point of view only if marginal cost embodies *all* the costs which production entails and product price accurately reflects *all* the benefits which society gets from a good's production. Only in this case will competitive production at the MR $(=P)$ = MC point balance the *total* sacrifices and satisfactions of society and result in an efficient allocation of resources. To the extent that price and marginal cost are not accurate indexes of sacrifices and satisfactions—to the extent that spillover costs and benefits exist—production at the MR $(=P)$ = MC point will *not* signify an efficient allocation of resources (see Figures 6-1 and 6-2).

Remember, too, the point of the lighthouse example in Chapter 6: The market system does not provide for social or public goods, that is, for goods to which the exclusion principle does *not* apply. Despite its other virtues, the competitive price system ignores an important class of goods and services—national defense, flood-control programs, and so forth—which can and do yield satisfaction to consumers but which cannot be priced and sold through the market system.

Productive Techniques Purely competitive markets may not always entail the use of the most efficient productive techniques or encourage development of improved techniques. There are both a static (or "right now") aspect and a dynamic (or "over time") aspect of this criticism.

Natural Monopolies The static aspect involves the *natural monopoly* problem introduced in Chapter 9. In certain lines of production, existing technology may be such that a firm must be a large-scale producer to realize the lowest unit costs of production. Given consumer demand, this suggests that a relatively small number of large-scale producers is needed if production is to be carried on efficiently. Existing mass-production economies might be lost if such an industry were populated by the large number of small-scale producers pure competition requires.

Technological Progress The dynamic aspect of this criticism concerns the willingness and ability of purely competitive firms to undertake technological advance. The progressiveness of pure competition is debated by economists. Some authorities believe that a purely competitive economy would *not* foster a very rapid rate of technological progress. They argue, first, that the incentive for technological advance may be weak under pure competition because the profit rewards accruing to an innovating firm from a cost-reducing technological improvement will be quickly competed away by rival firms adopting the new technique. Second, the small size of the typical competitive firm and the fact that it tends to "break even" in the long run raise serious questions whether such producers could finance substantial programs of organized research. We will return to this controversy in Chapter 13.

Range of Consumer Choice A purely competitive economy might not provide a sufficient range of consumer choice or foster development of new products. This criticism, like the previous one, has both a static and a dynamic aspect. Pure competition, it is contended, means product standardization, whereas other market structures—for example, monopolistic competition and, frequently, oligopoly—encompass a wide range of types, styles, and quality gradations of any product. This product differentiation widens the consumer's range of free choice and simultaneously allows the buyer's preferences to be more completely fulfilled. Similarly, critics of pure competition point out that, just as pure competition is not likely to be progressive in developing new productive techniques, neither is this market structure conducive to improving existing products or creating completely new ones.

The question of the progressiveness of various market structures in terms of both productive techniques and product development will recur in the following three chapters.[2]

[2]Instructors who want to consider agriculture as a case study in pure competition should insert Chapter 21 at this point.

CHAPTER SUMMARY

1 The market models of **a** pure competition, **b** pure monopoly, **c** monopolistic competition, and **d** oligopoly are classifications into which most industries can be fitted with reasonable accuracy.

2 A purely competitive industry comprises a large number of independent firms producing a standardized product. Pure competition assumes that firms and resources are mobile among different industries.

3 No single firm can influence market price in a competitive industry; the firm's demand curve is perfectly elastic and price therefore equals marginal revenue.

4 Short-run profit maximization by a competitive firm can be analyzed by a comparison of total revenue and total cost or through marginal analysis. A firm will maximize profits by producing that output at which total revenue exceeds total cost by the greatest amount. Losses will be minimized by producing where the excess of total cost over total revenue is at a minimum and less than total fixed costs.

5 Provided price exceeds minimum average variable cost, a competitive firm will maximize profits or minimize losses in the short run by producing that output at which price or marginal revenue equals marginal cost. If price is less than average variable cost, the firm will minimize its losses by closing down. If price is greater than average variable cost but less than average total cost, the firm will minimize its losses by producing the $P = \text{MC}$ output. If price exceeds average total cost, the $P = \text{MC}$ output will provide maximum economic profits for the firm.

6 Applying the MR ($=P$) = MC rule at various possible market prices leads to the conclusion that the segment of the firm's short-run marginal-cost curve lying above average variable cost is its short-run supply curve.

7 In the long run, competitive price will equal the minimum average cost of production because economic profits will cause firms to enter a competitive industry until those profits have been competed away. Conversely, losses will force the exodus of firms from the industry until product price once again barely covers unit costs.

8 The long-run supply curve is perfectly elastic for a constant-cost industry, upsloping for an increasing-cost industry, and downsloping for a decreasing-cost industry.

9 The long-run equality of price and minimum average cost means that competitive firms will use the most efficient known technology and charge the lowest price consistent with their production costs.

10 The equality of price and marginal cost implies that resources will be allocated in accordance with consumer tastes. The competitive price system will reallocate resources in response to a change in consumer tastes, technology, or resource supplies to maintain allocative efficiency over time.

11 Economist recognize four possible deterrents to allocative efficiency in a competitive economy. **a** There is no reason why the competitive market system will result in an optimal distribution of income. **b** In allocating resources, the competitive model does not allow for spillover costs and benefits or for the production of public goods. **c** A purely competitive industry may preclude the use of the best-known productive techniques and foster a slow rate of technological advance. **d** A competitive system provides neither a wide range of product choice nor an environment conducive to the development of new products.

TERMS AND CONCEPTS

pure competition
pure monopoly
monopolistic competition
oligopoly
imperfect competition
price taker
average, total, and marginal revenue
profit-maximizing case
break-even point
loss-minimizing case
close-down case
MR ($=P$) = MC rule
short-run supply curve
long-run supply curve
increasing-cost industry
constant-cost industry
decreasing-cost industry
allocative efficiency
productive efficiency

QUESTIONS AND STUDY SUGGESTIONS

1 Briefly indicate the basic characteristics of pure competition, pure monopoly, monopolistic competition, and oligopoly. Under which of these market classifications does each of the following most accurately fit? **a** a supermarket in your home town; **b** the steel industry; **c** a Kansas wheat farm; **d** the commercial bank in which you or your family has an account; **e** the automobile industry. In each case justify your classification.

2 Strictly speaking, pure competition never has existed and probably never will. Then why study it?

3 Use the following demand schedule to determine total and marginal revenues for each possible level of sales.

Product price	*Quantity demanded*	*Total revenue*	*Marginal revenue*
$2	0	$____	
2	1	____	$____
2	2	____	____
2	3	____	____
2	4	____	____
2	5	____	____

a What can you conclude about the structure of the industry in which this firm is operating? Explain.
b Graph the demand, total-revenue, and marginal-revenue curves for this firm.
c Why do the demand and marginal-revenue curves coincide?
d "Marginal revenue is the change in total revenue." Do you agree? Explain verbally and graphically, using the data in the table.

4 Assume the following unit-cost data are for a purely competitive producer:

Total product	*Average fixed cost*	*Average variable cost*	*Average total cost*	*Marginal cost*
0				
1	$60.00	$45.00	$105.00	$45
2	30.00	42.50	72.50	40
3	20.00	40.00	60.00	35
4	15.00	37.50	52.50	30
5	12.00	37.00	49.00	35
6	10.00	37.50	47.50	40
7	8.57	38.57	47.14	45
8	7.50	40.63	48.13	55
9	6.67	43.33	50.00	65
10	6.00	46.50	52.50	75

a At a product price of $32, will this firm produce in the short run? Why, or why not? If it does produce, what will be the profit-maximizing or loss-minimizing output? Explain. Specify the amount of economic profit or loss per unit of output.
b Answer the questions of 4a assuming product price is $41.
c Answer the questions of 4a assuming product price is $56.
d Complete the short-run supply schedule for the firm, and indicate the profit or loss incurred at each output (columns 1 to 3).

(1) Price	*(2) Quantity supplied, single firm*	*(3) Profit (+) or loss (−)*	*(4) Quantity supplied, 1500 firms*
$26	____	$____	____
32	____	____	____
38	____	____	____
41	____	____	____
46	____	____	____
56	____	____	____
66	____	____	____

e Explain: "That segment of a competitive firm's marginal-cost curve which lies above its average-variable-cost curve constitutes the short-run supply curve for the firm." Illustrate graphically.
f Now assume there are 1500 identical firms in this competitive industry; that is, there are 1500 firms, each of which has the same cost data shown here. Calculate the industry supply schedule (column 4).
g Suppose the market demand data for the product are as follows:

Price	*Total quantity demanded*
$26	17,000
32	15,000
38	13,500
41	12,000
46	10,500
56	9,500
66	8,000

What will equilibrium price be? What will equilibrium output be for the industry? For each firm? What will profit or loss be per unit? Per firm? Will this industry expand or contract in the long run?

5 Why is the equality of marginal revenue and marginal cost essential for profit maximization in all market structures? Explain why price can be substituted for marginal revenue in the MR = MC rule when an industry is purely competitive.

6 Explain: "A competitive producer must look to average variable cost in determining whether or not to produce in the short run, to marginal cost in deciding on the best volume of production, and to average total cost to calculate profits or losses." Why might a firm produce at a loss in the short run rather than close down?

7 Using diagrams for both the industry and a representative firm, illustrate competitive long-run equilibrium. Employing these diagrams, show how a an increase, and b a decrease, in market demand will upset this long-run equilibrium. Trace graphically and describe verbally the adjustment processes by which long-run equilibrium is restored. Assume the industry is one of constant costs.

8 Distinguish carefully between constant-cost, increasing cost, and decreasing-cost industries. Answer question 7 assuming that the industry is one of increaasing costs. Compare the long-run supply curves of constant-cost, increasing-cost and decreasing-cost industries.

9 Suppose a decrease in demand occurs in a competitive increasing-cost industry. Contrast the product price and industry output existing after all long-run adjustments are completed with those which originally prevailed.

10 In long-run equilibrium, $P = AC = MC$. Of what significance for economic efficiency is the equality of P and AC? The equality of P and MC? Distinguish between productive efficiency and allocative efficiency in your answer.

11 Explain why some economists believe that an unequal distribution of income might impair the allocative efficiency of a competitive market system. What other criticisms can be made of a purely competitive economy?

Price and Output Determination: Pure Monopoly

You deal with monopolies—sole sellers of products and services—daily. When you mail a letter, you are using the services of the United States Postal Service, a governmentally sponsored monopoly. Similarly, when you use your telephone, turn on your lights, or subscribe to cable TV, you are patronizing monopolies.

We now jump from pure competition to the opposite end of the industry spectrum (Table 10-1) and examine the characteristics, bases, price-output behavior, and social desirability of monopoly. How is a pure monopoly defined? What conditions underlie its existence? How does a monopolist's price-output behavior compare with that of a purely competitive industry? Do monopolists achieve the allocative and productive efficiency associated with pure competition? If not, can government policies improve the price-output behavior of a pure monopolist?

PURE MONOPOLY: AN INTRODUCTION

Absolute or **pure monopoly** exists when *a single firm is the sole producer of a product for which there are no close substitutes.* Let's first examine the characteristics of pure monopoly and then provide examples.

Characteristics

1 Single Seller A pure, or absolute, monopolist is a one-firm industry. A single firm is the only producer of a specific product or the sole supplier of a service; the firm and the industry are synonymous.

2 No Close Substitutes Thus, the monopolist's product is unique in that there are no good, or close, substitutes. From the buyer's viewpoint, there are no reasonable alternatives. The buyer must buy the product from the monopolist or do without it.

3 "Price Maker" We saw that the individual firm operating under pure competition exercises no influence over product price; it is a "price taker." This is so because it contributes only a negligible portion of total supply. In contrast, the pure monopolist is a *price maker;* the firm exercises considerable control over price because it is responsible for, and therefore controls, the total quantity supplied. Given a downsloping demand curve for its product, the monopolist can change product price by manipulating the quantity of the product supplied. If it is advantageous, the monopolist will use this power.

4 Blocked Entry A pure monopolist has no immediate competitors because there are barriers to entry. Economic, technological, legal, or other obstacles must exist to keep new competitors from coming into the industry if monopoly is to persist. Entry under conditions of pure monopoly is totally blocked.

5 Advertising The fact there are no close substitutes for the monopolized product has interesting implications for advertising. Depending on the type of product or service offered, a monopolist may or may not engage in extensive advertising and sales promotion. For example, a pure monopolist selling a luxury good such as diamonds might advertise heavily to increase demand for the product. The result might be that more people will buy diamonds rather than take vacations. Local public utilities, on the other hand, normally see no point in large expenditures for advertising: People wanting water, gas, electric power, and local telephone service already know from whom they must buy these necessities.

Examples

In most cities governmentally owned or regulated public utilities—gas and electric companies, the water company, the cable TV company, and the telephone company—are all monopolies or virtually so. There are no close substitutes for services provided by these public utilities. Of course, there is almost always *some* competition. Candles or kerosene lights are very imperfect substitutes for electricity; telegrams, letters, and courier services can be substituted for the telephone. But such substitutes are either costly, inconvenient, or unappealing.

The classic example of a private, unregulated monopoly is the De Beers diamond syndicate which effectively controls 80 to 90 percent of the world's diamond supply. But in the United States major manufacturing monopolies are rare and frequently transient in that in time new competitors emerge to erode their single-producer status.

> . . . monopoly in the sense of a single seller is virtually nonexistent in nationwide U.S. manufacturing industries of appreciable size. The rate at which near-monopolies have faded appears to have exceeded the rate of new appearance by a substantial margin. In 1962 Gillette made 70 percent of domestic razor blade sales, but its position was eroded, first by the appearance of Wilkinson's stainless steel blades and then by Bic's aggressive marketing of disposable razors. Eastman Kodak's 90 percent share of amateur film sales and 65 percent share of all film sales, including instant photo packs, was sharply challenged in the 1980s by import competition from Fuji. General Motors' share of diesel locomotive sales probably remains near 75 percent. For decades Western Electric supplied roughly 85 percent of U.S. telephone equipment, but its position faded rapidly owing to technological changes of the 1970s and the antitrust-induced divestiture in 1984 of affiliated Bell Telephone local operating companies, ending a captive market situation. IBM's 72 to 82 percent share of the digital computer market during the 1960s fell as new rivals captured mini- and microcomputer applications. Xerox's 75 to 80 percent share of electrostatic copier revenues declined with the erosion of its patent position during the 1970s. . . . During much of the 1960s and 1970s, Boeing controlled roughly two-thirds of noncommunist world jet airliner placements. With the rise of Europe's Airbus Consortium, Boeing's share declined to 50 percent in the late 1980s.[1]

Professional sports leagues embody monopoly power by granting member clubs franchises to be the sole suppliers of their services in designated geographic areas. Aside from Chicago, New York, and one or two other extremely large metropolitan areas, larger American cities are served by a single professional baseball, football, hockey, or basketball team. If you want to see a live major-league professional basketball game in Phoenix or Seattle, you must patronize the Suns and the Sonics respectively.

Monopoly may also be geographic. A small town may have only one airline or railroad. The local bank, movie, or bookstore may approximate a monopoly in a small, isolated community.

Importance

Analysis of pure monopoly is important for at least two reasons.

1 A not insignificant amount of economic activity—perhaps 5 or 6 percent of domestic output—is carried out under conditions approaching pure monopoly.

2 A study of pure monopoly yields valuable insights concerning the more common market structures of

[1]F. M. Scherer and David Ross, *Industrial Market Structure and Economic Performance,* 3d ed. (Chicago: Rand McNally College Publishing Company, 1990), p. 82.

monopolistic competition and oligopoly, discussed in Chapters 12 and 13. These two market situations combine in differing degrees characteristics of pure competition and pure monopoly.

BARRIERS TO ENTRY

The absence of competitors characterizing pure monopoly is largely explainable in terms of factors which prohibit additional firms from entering an industry. These **barriers to entry** are also pertinent in explaining the existence of oligopoly and monopolistic competition between the market extremes of pure competition and pure monopoly.

In pure monopoly, entry barriers effectively block all potential competition. Somewhat less formidable barriers permit the existence of oligopoly, a market dominated by a few firms. Still weaker barriers result in the fairly large number of firms which characterizes monopolistic competition. The virtual absence of entry barriers helps explain the very large number of competing firms which is the basis of pure competition. The point is that barriers to entry are pertinent not only to the extreme case of pure monopoly but also to the "partial monopolies" so characteristic of our economy.

Economies of Scale

Modern technology in some industries is such that efficient, low-cost production can be achieved only if producers are extremely large both absolutely and in relation to the market. Where economies of scale are very significant, a firm's long-run average-cost schedule will decline over a wide range of output (Figure 9-9b). Given market demand, the achieving of low unit costs and therefore low unit prices for consumers depends on the existence of a small number of firms or, in the extreme case, only one firm.

The automobile, aluminum, and basic steel industries are a few of many heavy industries which reflect such conditions. If three firms currently enjoy all available economies of scale and each has roughly one-third of a market, it is easy to see why new competitors may find it extremely difficult to enter this industry. New firms entering the market as small-scale producers will have little or no chance to survive and expand. As small-scale entrants they cannot realize the cost economies enjoyed by the existing "Big Three" and therefore will be unable to realize the profits necessary for survival and growth. New competitors in the basic steel and automobile industries will not come from the successful operation and expansion of small "backyard" producers. They simply will not be efficient enough to survive.

The other option is to start out big, that is, to enter the industry as a large-scale producer. In practice, this is extremely difficult. It is very difficult for a new and untried enterprise to secure the money capital needed to obtain capital facilities comparable to those of the Big Three in the automobile industry. The financial obstacles in the way of starting big are so great in many cases as to be prohibitive.

Public Utilities: Natural Monopolies

In a few industries, economies of scale are particularly pronounced; they extend throughout the range of market demand. This can be envisioned graphically by looking ahead to Figure 11-6. At the same time competition is impractical, inconvenient, or simply unworkable. Such industries are called *natural monopolies,* and most of the so-called public utilities—electric and gas companies, bus firms, cable television, and water and communication facilities—fit into this category. These industries are generally given exclusive franchises by government. But in return for this sole right to supply electricity, water, or bus service to a given geographic area, government reserves the right to regulate the operations of such monopolies to prevent abuses of the monopoly power it has granted.

As an illustration, it would be exceedingly wasteful if a community had several firms supplying water or electricity. Technology is such in these industries that large-scale and extensive capital expenditures on generators, pumping and purification equipment, water mains, and transmission lines are required. This problem is aggravated because capital equipment must be sufficient to meet peak demands which occur on hot summer days when lawns are being watered and air conditioners operated. The point is that unit costs of production decline with the number of cubic feet of water or kilowatt hours of electricity supplied by each firm, that is, as the firm expands its size. The presence of several water and electricity suppliers would divide the total market and reduce the sales of each competitor. Each firm would be pushed back up its declining long-run average-cost curve. Firms would be too small to achieve minimum long-run average costs and therefore electricity and water rates would be unnecessarily high.

In addition, competition could be extremely inconvenient. The presence of a half-dozen telephone companies in an area could mean having six telephones and six telephone books—not to mention six telephone bills—to ensure communication with all other residents in the same area.

Because natural monopolies can lower their average costs by expanding output, they try to increase sales by price cutting. As a result, cutthroat price competition breaks out when several firms exist in these public utilities industries. The result will be losses, bankruptcy of weaker rivals, and eventual merger of survivors. The evolving pure monopoly will be anxious to recoup past losses and to profit fully from its new position of market dominance by charging monopoly prices for its goods or services.

To spare society such disadvantageous results, government will usually grant an exclusive franchise to a single firm to supply water, natural gas, electricity, telephone service, or bus transportation. In return, government reserves the right to designate the monopolist's geographic area of operation, to regulate the quality of its services, and to control the prices it charges. The result is a regulated or government-sponsored monopoly—monopoly designed to achieve low unit costs but regulated so that consumers will benefit from these cost economies. Some of the problems associated with regulation are considered later in this chapter and in Chapter 20.

Legal Barriers: Patents and Licenses

We have already noted that government frequently gives exclusive franchises to natural monopolies. Government also creates legal entry barriers in awarding patents and licenses.

Patents By granting an inventor the exclusive right to produce or license a product for seventeen years, American patent laws aim to protect the inventor from having the product or process usurped by rival enterprises which have not shared in the time, effort, and money outlays which have gone into its development. By the same token patents provide the inventor with a monopoly position for the life of the patent.

Patent control figured prominently in the growth of many modern-day industrial giants such as National Cash Register, General Motors, Xerox, Polaroid, General Electric, and du Pont. The United Shoe Machinery Company is a notable example of patent control being abused to achieve monopoly power. In this case United Shoe became the exclusive supplier of certain essential shoemaking machines through patent control. It extended its monopoly power to other types of shoemaking machinery by requiring all lessees of its patented machines to sign a "tying agreement" in which shoe manufacturers agreed also to lease all other shoemaking machinery from United Shoe. This allowed United Shoe to monopolize the market until partially effective antitrust action was taken by the government in 1955.

Research underlies the development of patentable products. Firms which gain a measure of monopoly power by their own research or by purchasing the patents of others are in a strategic position to consolidate and strengthen their market position. The profits from one important patent can finance the research required to develop new patentable products. The pharmaceutical industry is a case in point. Patents on prescription drugs have produced large monopoly profits which have helped finance the discovery of new patentable medicines. Monopoly power achieved through patents may well be cumulative.

Licenses Entry into an industry or occupation may be limited by government through the issuing of licenses. At the national level the Federal Communications Commission licenses radio and television stations. In many large cities one needs a municipal license to drive a taxicab. The consequent restriction of the supply of cabs creates monopolistic earnings for cab owners and drivers. In a few instances government might license itself to provide some product and thereby create a public monopoly. For example, the sale of liquor in some states is exclusively through state-owned retail outlets. Similarly, many states have in effect "licensed" themselves to run lotteries (Chapter 6). This chapter's Last Word discusses how generous contracts granted to national park concessionaires have resulted in monopoly power and monopoly profits.

Ownership of Essential Resources

The institution of private property can be used by a monopoly as an effective obstacle to potential rivals. A firm owning or controlling a resource essential to the production process can prohibit the creation of rival firms. The Aluminum Company of America retained its monopoly position in the aluminum industry for many years by virtue of its control of all basic sources of bauxite, the major ore used in aluminum fabrication. At one time the International Nickel Company of Canada (now called Inco) controlled approximately 90 percent of the world's known nickel reserves. As noted earlier, most of the world's known diamond mines are owned or effectively controlled by the De Beers Company of South Africa. Similarly, it is very difficult for new professional sports leagues to evolve when existing leagues have contracts with the best players and leases on the major stadiums and arenas.

Two Implications

Our discussion of barriers to entry suggests two noteworthy points about monopoly.

1 Relatively Rare Barriers to entry are rarely complete. This is merely another way of stating our earlier point that pure monopoly is relatively rare. Although research and technological advance may strengthen the market position of a firm, technology may also undermine existing monopoly power. Existing patent advantages may be circumvented by the development of new and distinct, yet substitutable, products. New sources of strategic resources may be found. It is probably only a modest overstatement to say that monopoly in the sense of a one-firm industry persists over time only with the sanction or aid of government, as with the postal service's monopoly on the delivery of first-class mail.

2 Desirability We have implied that monopolies may be desirable or undesirable from the standpoint of economic efficiency. The public utilities and economies-of-scale arguments suggest that market demand and technology may be such that efficient low-cost production presupposes the existence of monopoly. On the other hand, our comments on resource ownership, patents, and licensing as sources of monopoly imply more undesirable connotations of business monopoly.

MONOPOLY DEMAND

Let's begin our analysis of the price-output behavior of a pure monopolist by making three assumptions.

1 Our monopolist's status is secured by patents, economies of scale, or resource ownership.

2 The firm is *not* governmentally regulated.

3 The firm is a single-price monopolist; it charges the same price for all units of output.

The crucial difference between a pure monopolist and a purely competitive seller lies on the demand side of the market. Recall from Chapter 10 that the purely competitive seller faces a perfectly elastic demand schedule at the market price determined by industry supply and demand. The competitive firm is a "price taker" which can sell as much or as little as it wants at the going market price. It follows that each additional unit sold will add a constant amount—its price—to the firm's total revenue. In other words, marginal revenue for the competitive seller is constant and equal to product price. This means that total revenue increases by a constant amount, that is, by the constant price of each unit sold. (Refer back to Table 10-2 and Figure 10-1 for price, marginal-revenue, and total-revenue relationships for the purely competitive firm.)

The monopolist's demand curve—indeed, the demand curve of *any* imperfectly competitive seller—is much different. Because the pure monopolist *is* the industry, its demand, or sales, curve is the industry demand curve.[2] And the industry demand curve is not perfectly elastic, but rather is downsloping, as illustrated by columns 1 and 2 of Table 11-1.

There are three implications of a downsloping demand curve which must be understood.

Price Exceeds Marginal Revenue

A downsloping demand curve means that a pure monopoly can increase its sales only by charging a lower unit price for its product. *Because the monopolist must lower price to boost sales, marginal revenue is less than price (average revenue) for every level of output except the first.* The reason? Price cuts will apply not only to the extra output sold but also to *all* other units of output which otherwise could have been sold at a higher price. Each additional unit sold will add to total revenue its price *less* the sum of the price cuts which must be taken on all prior units of output.

In Figure 11-1 we have extracted two price–quantity combinations—$142-3 and $132-4—from the monopolist's demand curve. By lowering price from $142 to $132, the monopolist can sell one more unit and thus gain as revenue the fourth unit's price of $132. This gain is designated as the gray rectangle. But to sell this fourth unit for $132, the monopolist must lower price on the first three units from $142 to $132. This $10 reduction on 3 units results in a $30 revenue loss indicated by the light red rectangle in Figure 11-1. The *net* change in total revenue, or marginal revenue, from selling the fourth unit is $102, the $132 gain minus the $30 loss.

[2]Recall in Chapter 10 that we presented separate diagrams for the purely competitive industry *and* for a single firm in that industry. Because with pure monopoly the firm and the industry are one and the same, we need only a single diagram.

TABLE 11-1 **Revenue and cost data of a pure monopolist *(hypothetical data)***

Revenue data				*Cost data*			
(1) Quantity of output	*(2) Price (average revenue)*	*(3) Total revenue*	*(4) Marginal revenue*	*(5) Average total cost*	*(6) Total cost*	*(7) Marginal cost*	*(8) Profit (+) or loss (−)*
0	$172	$ 0			$ 100		$−100
			$162			$ 90	
1	162	162		$190.00	190		− 28
			142			80	
2	152	304		135.00	270		+ 34
			122			70	
3	142	426		113.33	340		+ 86
			102			60	
4	132	528		100.00	400		+128
			82			70	
5	122	610		94.00	470		+140
			62			80	
6	112	672		91.67	550		+122
			42			90	
7	102	714		91.43	640		+ 74
			22			110	
8	92	736		93.73	750		− 14
			2			130	
9	82	738		97.78	880		−142
			−18			150	
10	72	720		103.00	1030		−310

This same point is evident in Table 11-1, where we observe that the marginal revenue of the second unit of output is $142 rather than its $152 price, because a $10 price cut must be taken on the first unit to increase sales from 1 to 2 units. Similarly, to sell 3 units the firm must lower price from $152 to $142. The resulting marginal revenue will be just $122—the $142 addition to total revenue which the third unit of sales provides less $10 price cuts on the first 2 units of output. It is this rationale which explains why the marginal-revenue data of column 4 of Table 11-1 fall short of product price in column 2 for all levels of output except the first. Because marginal revenue is, by definition, the increase in total revenue associated with each additional unit of output, the declining marginal-revenue figures mean that total revenue will increase at a diminishing rate as shown in column 3 of Table 11-1.

FIGURE 11-1 **Price and marginal revenue under pure monopoly**

A pure monopolist—or, in fact, any imperfect competitor with a downsloping demand curve—must reduce price to sell more output. As a consequence, marginal revenue will be less than price. In our example, by reducing price from $142 to $132 the monopolist gains $132 from the sale of the fourth unit. But from this gain must be subtracted $30 which reflects the $10 price cut which has been made on each of the first three units. Hence, the fourth unit's marginal revenue is $102 (=$132 − $30), considerably less than its $132 price.

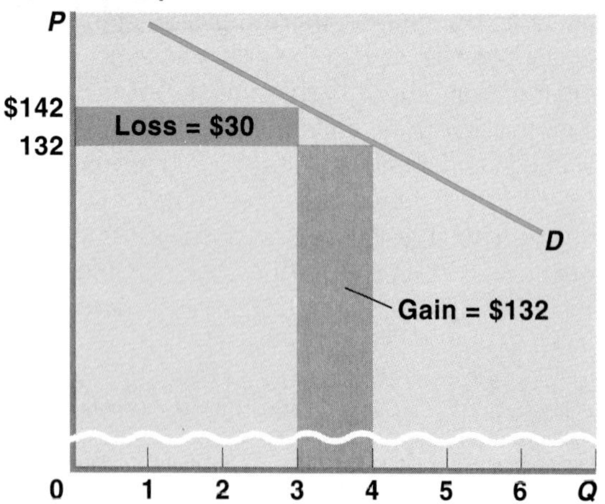

The relationships between the demand, marginal-revenue, and total-revenue curves, which were introduced in Chapter 7, are portrayed graphically in Figure 11-2a and b. In drawing this diagram we have extended the demand and revenue data of columns 1 through 4 of Table 11-1 by continuing to assume that successive $10 price cuts will each elicit one additional unit of sales. That is, 11 units can be sold at $62, 12 at $52, and so forth.

In addition to the fact that the marginal-revenue curve lies *below* the demand curve, note the special relationship between total revenue and marginal revenue. Because marginal revenue is, by definition, the change in total revenue, we observe that so long as total revenue is increasing, marginal revenue is positive. When total revenue reaches its maximum, marginal revenue is zero. When total revenuc is diminishing, marginal revenue is negative.

Price Maker

In all imperfectly competitive markets in which downsloping demand curves are relevant—that is, purely monopolistic, oligopolistic, and monopolistically competitive markets—firms have a price policy. By virtue of their ability to influence total supply, the output decisions of these firms necessarily affect product price.

This is most evident in pure monopoly, where one firm controls total output. Faced with a downsloping demand curve, in which each output is associated with some unique price, the monopolist unavoidably determines price in deciding what volume of output to produce. The monopolist simultaneously chooses both price and output. In columns 1 and 2 of Table 11-1 we find that the monopolist can sell only an output of 1 unit at a price of $162, only an output of 2 units at a price of $152 per unit, and so forth.

This does not mean that the monopolist is "free" of market forces in establishing price and output or that the consumer is completely at the monopolist's mercy. In particular, the monopolist's downsloping demand curve means that it cannot raise price without losing sales, or gain sales without charging a lower price.

Price Elasticity

The total-revenue test for price elasticity of demand is the basis for our third conclusion. Recall from Chapter 7 that the total-revenue test tells us that, when demand is elastic, a decline in price will increase total revenue. Similarly, when demand is inelastic, a decline in price will reduce total revenue. Beginning at the top of the demand curve in Figure 11-2, observe that for all price reductions from $172 down to approximately $82, total revenue increases (and marginal revenue therefore is positive). This means that demand is elastic in this price range. Conversely, for price reductions below $82, total revenue decreases (marginal revenue is negative), which indicates that demand is inelastic.

Our generalization is that a monopolist will never choose a price-quantity combination where price declines cause total revenue to decrease (marginal revenue to be negative). *The profit-maximizing monopolist will always want to avoid the inelastic segment of its demand curve in favor of some price-quantity combination in the elastic segment.* By lowering price into the inelastic range, total revenue will decline. But the lower price is associated with a larger output and therefore increased total costs. Lower revenue and higher costs mean diminished profits.

QUICK REVIEW 11-1

- ***A pure monopolist is the sole supplier of a product or service for which there are no close substitutes.***
- ***Monopolies exist because of entry barriers such as economies of scale, patents and licenses, and the ownership of essential resources.***
- ***The monopolist's demand curve is downsloping, causing the marginal revenue curve to lie below it.***
- ***Price declines in the elastic range of the monopolist's demand curve will increase total revenues, and marginal revenue will be positive; in the inelastic portion of the demand curve price declines will decrease total revenue, and marginal revenue will be negative.***

OUTPUT AND PRICE DETERMINATION

What specific price-quantity combination on its demand curve will a profit-maximizing monopolist choose? To answer this we must add production costs to our understanding of monopoly demand.

Cost Data

On the cost side, we will assume that, although the firm is a monopolist in the product market, it hires resources competitively and employs the same technology as our competitive firm in the preceding chapter. This lets us use the cost data developed in Chapter 9 and applied in Chapter 10 to compare the price-output decisions of a pure monopoly with those of a pure competitor. Columns 5 through 7 of Table 11-1 restate the pertinent cost concepts of Table 9-2.

MR = MC Rule

A profit-seeking monopolist will employ the same rationale as a profit-seeking firm in a competitive industry. It will produce each successive unit of output so long as it adds more to total revenue than it does to total cost. The firm will produce up to that output at which marginal revenue equals marginal cost (MR = MC).

A comparison of columns 4 and 7 in Table 11-1 indicates that the profit-maximizing output is 5 units;

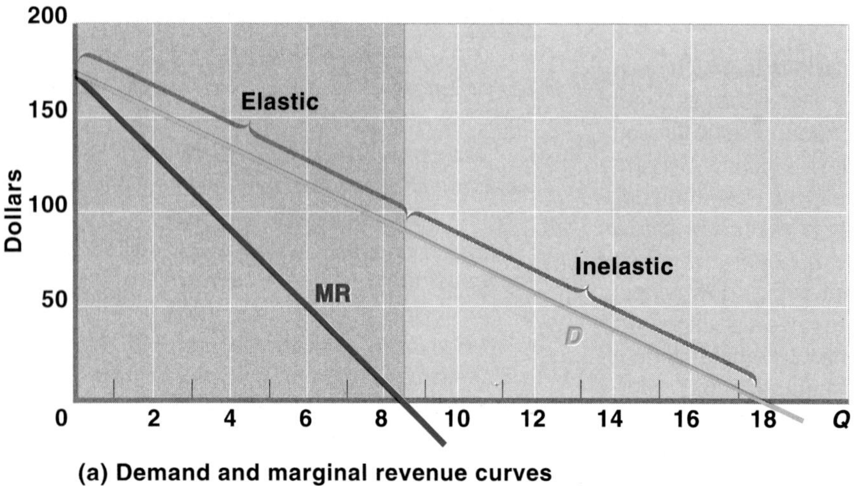

(a) Demand and marginal revenue curves

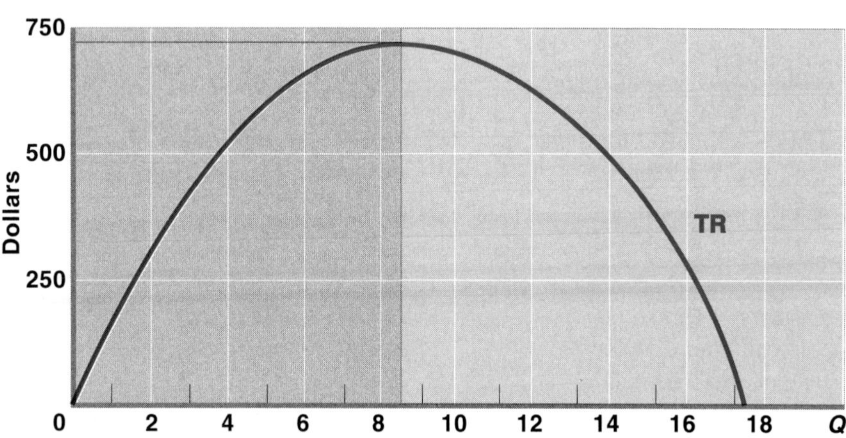

(b) Total revenue curve

FIGURE 11-2 Demand, marginal revenue, and total revenue of an imperfectly competitive firm

Because it must lower price to increase its sales, an imperfectly competitive firm's marginal-revenue curve (MR) lies below its downsloping demand curve (*D*). Total revenue (TR) increases at a decreasing rate, reaches a maximum, and then declines. Note that, because MR is the change in TR, a unique relationship exists between MR and TR. In moving down the elastic segment of the demand curve, TR is increasing and, hence, MR is positive. When TR reaches its maximum, MR is zero. And in moving down the inelastic segment of the demand curve, TR is declining, so MR is negative. A monopolist or other imperfectly competitive seller will never choose to lower price into the inelastic segment of its demand curve because by doing so it will simultaneously reduce total revenue and increase production costs, thereby lowering profits.

the fifth unit is the last unit of output whose marginal revenue exceeds its marginal cost. What price will the monopolist charge? The downsloping demand curve of columns 1 and 2 in Table 11-1 indicates that there is only one price at which 5 units can be sold: $122.

This analysis is presented graphically in Figure 11-3 (Key Graph), where the demand, marginal-revenue, average-total-cost, and marginal-cost data of Table 11-1 have been drawn. Comparing marginal revenue and marginal cost confirms that the profit-maximizing

KEY GRAPH

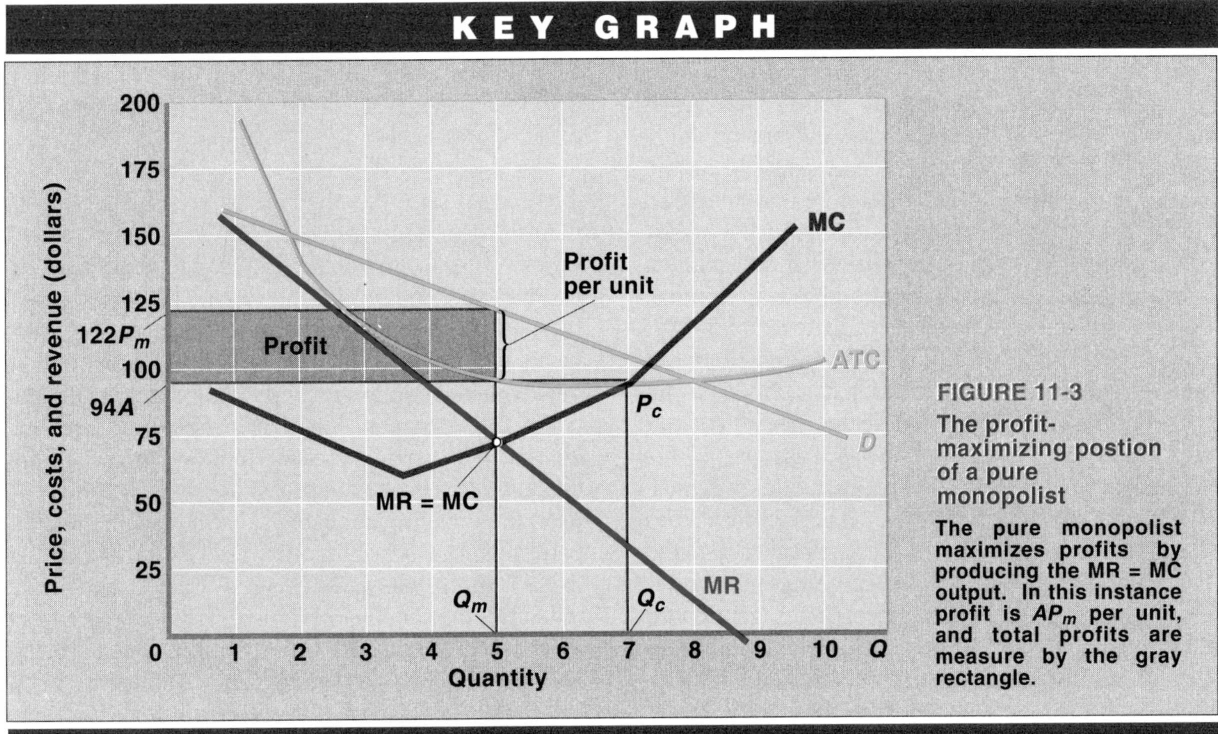

FIGURE 11-3
The profit-maximizing postion of a pure monopolist
The pure monopolist maximizes profits by producing the MR = MC output. In this instance profit is AP_m per unit, and total profits are measure by the gray rectangle.

output is 5 units or, more generally, Q_m. The unique price at which Q_m can be sold is found by extending a perpendicular line up from the profit-maximizing point on the output axis and then at right angles from the point at which it hits the demand curve to the vertical axis. The indicated price is P_m. To charge a price higher than P_m, the monopolist must move up the demand curve, meaning that sales will fall short of the profit-maximizing level Q_m. Specifically, the firm will fail to produce units of output whose marginal revenue exceeds their marginal cost. If the monopolist charges less than P_m, it would involve a sales volume in excess of the profit-maximizing output.

Columns 2 and 5 of Table 11-1 indicate that, at 5 units of output, product price of $122 exceeds average total cost of $94. Economic profits are therefore $28 per unit; total economic profits are then $140 (= 5 × $28). In Figure 11-3, per unit profit is indicated by the distance AP_m, and total economic profits—the gray area—are found by multiplying this unit profit by the profit-maximizing output Q_m.

The same profit-maximizing combination of output and price can also be determined by comparing the total revenue and total costs incurred at each possible level of production. You should employ columns 3 and 6 of Table 11-1 to verify the conclusions reached through our marginal-revenue–marginal-cost analysis. Similarly, an accurate graphing of total revenue and total cost against output will also show the greatest differential (the maximum profit) at 5 units of output.

No Monopoly Supply Curve

Recall that the supply curve of a purely competitive firm is that portion of its marginal-cost curve lying above average variable costs (Figure 10-6). The supply curve is determined by applying the $P =$ MC profit-maximization rule. At any given market-determined price the purely competitive seller will maximize profits by equating that price (which is equal to marginal revenue) with marginal cost. When market price increases or decreases, the competitive firm will move up or down its marginal-cost curve because it is profitable to produce more or less output. We find each price to be uniquely associated with a specific output, thus defining the supply curve.

At first glance we would suspect that the pure monopolist's marginal-cost curve would also be its supply curve. But this is *not* the case. *The pure monopolist has no supply curve.* The reason is that there is no unique relationship between price and quantity supplied. The price and amount supplied depend on the location of the demand (and therefore marginal-revenue) curves. Like the competitive firm, the monopolist equates marginal revenue and marginal cost, but for the monopolist marginal revenue is less than price. Because the monopolist does *not* equate marginal cost to price, it is possible for different demand conditions to bring about different profit-maximizing prices for the same output. To convince yourself of this, go back to Figure 11-3 and pencil in a steeper (less elastic) demand curve, drawing its corresponding marginal-revenue curve so that it intersects marginal cost at the same point as does the present marginal-revenue curve. With the steeper demand curve, this new MR = MC output will yield a higher price. Conclusion: There is no single, unique price associated with output level Q_m, and therefore no supply curve for the pure monopolist.

Misconceptions Concerning Monopoly Pricing

Our analysis explodes some popular fallacies concerning monopoly behavior.

1 Not Highest Price Because a monopolist can manipulate output and price, it is often alleged that it "will charge the highest price it can get." This is a misguided assertion. There are many prices above P_m in Figure 11-3, but the monopolist shuns them because they entail a smaller-than-maximum profit. *Total* profits are the difference between *total* revenue and *total* costs, and each of these two determinants of profits depends on quantity sold as much as on price and unit cost.

2 Total, Not Unit, Profits The monopolist seeks maximum *total* profits, not maximum *unit* profits. In Figure 11-3 a careful comparison of the vertical distance between average cost and price at various possible outputs indicates that per unit profits are greater at a point slightly to the left of the profit-maximizing output Q_m. This is seen in Table 11-1, where unit profits are \$32 at 4 units of output compared with \$28 at the profit-maximizing output of 5 units. Here the monopolist accepts a lower-than-maximum per unit profit because additional sales more than compensate for lower unit profits. A profit-seeking monopolist would rather sell 5 units at a profit of \$28 per unit (for a total profit of \$140) than 4 units at a profit of \$32 per unit (for a total profit of only \$128).

3 Losses Pure monopoly does *not* guarantee economic profits. True, the likelihood of economic profits is greater for a pure monopolist than for a purely competitive producer. In the long run the latter is doomed by the free and easy entry of new firms to a normal profit; barriers to entry permit the monopolist to perpetuate economic profits in the long run.[3] Unlike the competitive situation, entry barriers keep out potential entrants who would increase supply, drive price down, and eliminate economic profits.

Like the pure competitor, the monopolist will not persistently operate at a loss. Faced with losses, the firm's owners will move their resources to alternative industries offering higher returns. Thus we can expect the monopolist to realize a normal profit or better in the long run. However, if the demand and cost situation faced by the monopolist is sufficiently less favorable than shown in Figure 11-3, short-run losses will be realized. Despite its dominance in the market, the monopolist shown in Figure 11-4 realizes a loss of an amount shown by the light red area by virtue of weak demand and relatively high costs. Yet it continues to operate for the time being because its total loss is less than its fixed costs. More precisely, observe that at Q_m the monopolist's price P_m exceeds its average variable cost. Although the government's rail corporation AMTRAK has a virtual monopoly in long-distance passenger train service, it frequently operates at a loss.

ECONOMIC EFFECTS OF MONOPOLY

Let's now evaluate pure monopoly from the standpoint of society as a whole. We will examine (1) price, output, and resource allocation; (2) income distribution; (3) some uncertainties caused by difficulties in making

[3]A related point is that the distinction between the short run and the long run is less important under monopoly than it is under pure competition. With pure competition the entry or exit of firms guarantees that economic profits will be zero in the long run. But with pure monopoly barriers to entry prevent the competing away of economic profits by new firms.

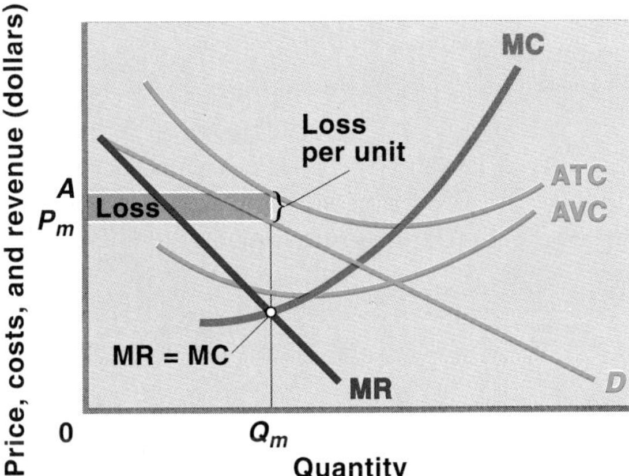

FIGURE 11-4 The loss-minimizing position of a pure monopolist

If demand *D* is weak and costs are high, the pure monopolist may be unable to make a profit. Because P_m exceeds AVC at Q_m, it will minimize losses in the short run by producing at that output where MR = MC. Loss per unit is AP_m, and total losses are indicated by the light red rectangle.

cost comparisons between competitive and monopolistic firms; and (4) technological progress.

Price, Output, and Resource Allocation

In Chapter 10 we concluded that pure competition would result in both "productive efficiency" and "allocative efficiency." Productive efficiency is realized because free entry and exodus of firms would force firms to operate at the optimal rate of output where unit costs of production would be at a minimum. Product price would be at the lowest level consistent with average total costs. In Figure 11-3 the competitive firm would sell Q_c units of output at a price of Q_cP_c.

Allocative efficiency is reflected in the fact that production under competition would occur up to that point at which price (the measure of a product's value to society) would equal marginal cost (the measure of the alternative products forgone by society in producing any given commodity).

Figure 11-3 indicates that, *given the same costs,* a purely monopolistic firm will produce much less desirable results. The pure monopolist will maximize profits by producing an output of Q_m and charging a price of P_m. *The monopolist will find it profitable to sell a smaller output and to charge a higher price than would a competitive producer.*[4] Output Q_m is short of the Q_c point where average total costs are minimized (the intersection of MC and ATC). In column 5 of Table 11-1, ATC at the monopolist's 5 units of output is $94.00 compared to the $91.43 which would result under pure competition. Also, at Q_m units of output, product price is considerably greater than marginal cost. This means that society values additional units of this monopolized product more highly than it does the alternative products resources could otherwise produce. The monopolist's profit-maximizing output results in an underallocation of resources; the monopolist finds it profitable to restrict output and therefore employ fewer resources than are justified from society's standpoint.

[4]In Figure 11-3 the price-quantity comparison of monopoly and pure competition is from the vantage point of the single purely competitive *firm* of Figure 10-7a. An equally illuminating approach is to start with the purely competitive *industry* of Figure 10-7b, reproduced below. Recall that the competitive industry's supply curve *S* is the horizontal sum of the marginal-cost curves of all the firms in the industry. Comparing this with industry demand *D*, we get the purely competitive price and output of P_c and Q_c. Now suppose that this industry becomes a pure monopoly as a result of a wholesale merger or one firm's somehow buying out all its competitors. Assume, too, that no changes in costs or market demand result from this dramatic change in the industry's structure. What were formerly, say, 100 competing firms are now a pure monopolist consisting of 100 branch plants.

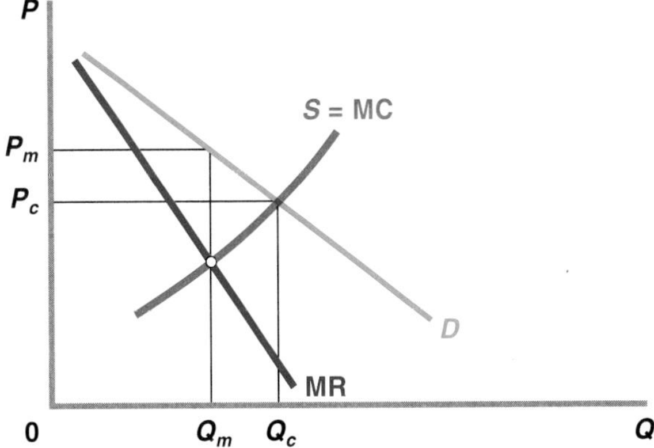

The industry supply curve is now the marginal-cost curve of the monopolist, the summation of the MC curves of its many branch plants. The important change, however, is on the market demand side. From the viewpoint of each individual competitive firm, demand was perfectly elastic, and marginal revenue was therefore equal to price. Each firm equated MC to MR (and therefore to *P*) in maximizing profits (Chapter 10). But industry demand and individual demand are the same to the pure monopolist; the firm *is* the industry, and thus the monopolist correctly envisions a downsloping demand curve *D*. This means that marginal revenue MR will be less than price; graphically the MR curve lies below the demand curve. In choosing the profit-maximizing MC = MR position, the monopolist selects an output Q_m which is smaller, and a price P_m which is greater, than if the industry were organized competitively.

Income Distribution

Business monopoly probably contributes to inequality in income distribution. By virtue of their market power, monopolists charge a higher price than would a purely competitive firm with the same costs; monopolists in effect can levy a "private tax" on consumers and thereby realize substantial economic profits. These monopolistic profits, it should be noted, are not widely distributed because corporate stock ownership is largely concentrated in the hands of upper income groups. The owners of monopolistic enterprises tend to be enriched at the expense of the rest of society.

Cost Complications

Our evaluation of pure monopoly has led us to conclude that, *given identical costs,* a purely monopolistic firm will find it profitable to charge a higher price, produce a smaller output, and foster an allocation of economic resources inferior to that of a purely competitive industry. These contrasting results are rooted in the entry barriers characterizing monopoly.

Now we must recognize that costs may *not* be the same for purely competitive and monopolistic producers. Unit costs incurred by a monopolist may be either larger or smaller than those facing a purely competitive firm. Several potentially conflicting considerations are involved: (1) economies of scale, (2) the notion of "X-inefficiency," (3) monopoly-preserving expenditures, and (4) the "very long-run" perspective which allows for technological progress. We examine the first three issues in this section and technological progress in the ensuing section.

Economies of Scale Revisited The assumption that unit costs available to the purely competitive and the purely monopolistic firm are the same may not hold in practice. Given production techniques and therefore production costs, consumer demand may not be sufficient to support a large number of competing firms producing at an output which permits each one to realize all *existing* economies of scale. In such instances a firm must be large in relation to the market—it must be monopolistic—to produce efficiently (at low unit cost).

This is shown diagrammatically in Figure 11-5. The argument is that with pure competition or its approximation each firm would have only a small share of the market such as Q_c. This small share forces each firm back up the long-run average-cost curve so that unit costs are high (AC_c). Economies of scale are *not* being realized and average costs are therefore high.

But with monopoly (or oligopoly) the single (or each of the few) firm(s) can achieve existing scale economies and lower unit costs. In other words, a monopolist or oligopolist may realize output Q_m with the consequent lower average cost of AC_m. Presumably these lower costs—even after allowing for an economic profit—translate into a lower product price than competitive firms could charge.

How important is this exception? Most economists feel that it applies mostly to public utilities and is not significant enough to undermine our general conclusions concerning the restrictive nature of monopoly. Evidence suggests that the large corporations in many manufacturing industries now have more monopoly power than can be justified on the grounds that they are merely availing themselves of existing economies of scale. Again, Chapter 9's Last Word provides relevant evidence suggesting that most industries could be quite competitive at smaller firm sizes without sacrificing economies of scale.

X-Inefficiency While economies of scale *might* argue for monopoly in a few cases, the notion of X-inefficiency suggests that monopoly costs might be *higher* than those associated with more competitive industries. What is X-inefficiency? Why might it plague monopolists more than competitors?

All the average-cost curves used in this and other chapters are based on the assumption that the firm chooses from *existing* technologies the most efficient one or, in other words, that technology which permits the firm to achieve the minimum average cost for each level of output. **X-inefficiency** occurs when a firm's actual costs of producing any output are greater than the minimum possible costs. In Figure 11-5 X-inefficiency is represented by unit costs of AC_x (as opposed to AC_c) for output Q_c and average costs of AC'_x (rather than AC_m) for output Q_m. Any point above the average-cost curve in Figure 11-5 is attainable but reflects internal inefficiency or "bad management" on the part of the firm.

Why does X-inefficiency occur when it reduces profits? The answer is that managers may often have goals—firm growth, an easier work life, avoidance of business risk, providing jobs for incompetent friends and relatives—which conflict with cost minimization. Or X-inefficiency may arise because a firm's workers

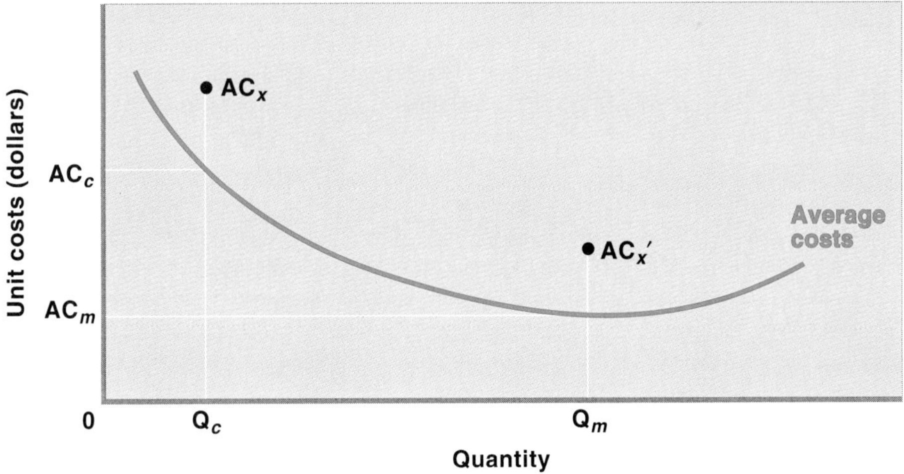

FIGURE 11-5 Economies of scale and X-inefficiency

This diagram serves to demonstrate two unrelated points. First, given the existence of extensive economies of scale, we note that a monopolist can achieve low unit costs of AC_m at Q_m units of output. In contrast, if the market were divided among a number of competing firms so that each produced only Q_c, then scale economies would be unrealized and unit costs of AC_c would be high. The second point is that X-inefficiency—the inefficient internal operation of a firm—results in higher-than-necessary costs. For example, unit costs might be AC_x rather than AC_c for Q_c units of output and AC_x' rather than AC_m for the Q_m level of output.

are poorly motivated. Or a firm may simply become lethargic and relatively inert, relying on rules-of-thumb in decision making as opposed to relevant calculations of costs and revenues.

For our purposes the relevant question is whether monopolistic firms are more susceptible to X-inefficiency than are competitive producers. Presumably this is the case. Theoretically, firms in competitive industries are continually under pressures from rivals which force them to be internally efficient to survive. But monopolists and oligopolists are sheltered from competitive forces by entry barriers and such an environment leads to X-inefficiency. Empirical evidence on X-inefficiency is largely anecdotal and sketchy, but it does suggest that X-inefficiency is greater the smaller the amount of competition. A reasonable estimate is that X-inefficiency may be 5 percent or more of costs for monopolists, but only 3 percent for an "average" oligopolistic industry in which the four largest firms produce 60 percent of total output.[5] In the words of one authority: "The evidence is fragmentary, but it points in the same direction. X-inefficiency exists, and it is more apt to be reduced when competitive pressures are strong than when firms enjoy insulated market positions."[6]

[5]William G. Shepherd, *The Economics of Industrial Organization,* 3d ed. (Englewood Cliffs, N.J.: Prentice-Hall, Inc., 1990), p. 129. For a rather extensive review of case study evidence of X-inefficiency, see Scherer and Ross, pp. 668–672.

Rent-Seeking Expenditures Economists use the term **rent-seeking behavior** in referring to activities designed to transfer income or wealth to a particular firm or resource supplier at someone else's or society's expense. We have seen that a monopolist can earn economic profits even in the long run. Therefore, it is no surprise a firm may go to considerable expense to acquire or maintain monopoly privileges granted by government. A monopolist's barrier to entry may depend on legislation or an exclusive license provided by government as in radio and television broadcasting. To sustain or enhance the consequent economic profits, the monopolist may spend large amounts on legal fees, lobbying, and public relations advertising to persuade government to grant or sustain its privileged position. These expenditures add nothing to the firm's output, but clearly increase its costs. Rent-seeking expenditures mean that monopoly might entail higher costs and a greater efficiency loss than suggested by Figure 11-3.

[6]Scherer and Ross, p. 672.

Technological Progress: Dynamic Efficiency

We have noted that our condemnation of monopoly must be qualified where *existing* mass-production economies might be lost if an industry comprises a large number of small, competing firms. Now we must consider the issue of **dynamic efficiency,** or whether monopolists are more likely to develop more efficient production techniques over time than competitive firms. Are monopolists more likely to improve productive technology, thereby lowering (shifting downward) their average-cost curves, than are competitive producers? Although we will concentrate on changes in productive techniques, the same question applies to product improvement. Do monopolists have greater means and incentives to improve their products and thus enhance consumer satisfaction? This is fertile ground for honest differences of opinion.

The Competitive Model Competitive firms certainly have the incentive—indeed, a market mandate—to employ the most efficient *known* productive techniques. Their very survival depends on being efficient. But competition deprives firms of economic profit—an important means and a major incentive to develop *new* and improved productive techniques or *new* products. The profits of technological advance may be short-lived to the innovating competitor. An innovating firm in a competitive industry will find that its rivals will soon duplicate or imitate any technological advance it may achieve; rivals will share the rewards but not the costs of successful technological research.

The Monopoly Model In contrast—thanks to entry barriers—a monopolist may persistently realize substantial economic profits. Hence, the pure monopolist will have greater financial resources for technological advance than competitive firms. But what about the monopolist's incentives for technological advance? Here the picture is clouded.

There is one imposing argument suggesting that the monopolist's incentives to develop new techniques or products will be weak: The absence of competitors means there is no automatic stimulus to technological advance in a monopolized market. Because of its sheltered market position, the pure monopolist can afford to be inefficient and lethargic. The keen rivalry of a competitive market penalizes the inefficient; an inefficient monopolist does not face this penalty simply because it has no rivals. The monopolist has every reason to be satisfied with the status quo, to become complacent. It might well pay the monopolist to withhold or "file" technological improvements in both productive techniques and products to exploit existing capital equipment fully. New and improved techniques and products may be suppressed by monopolists to avoid losses caused by the sudden obsolescence of existing machinery and equipment. And, even when improved techniques are belatedly introduced by monopolists, the accompanying cost reductions will accrue to the monopolist as increases in profits and only partially, if at all, to consumers in the form of lower prices and increased output.

Proponents of this view point out that in a number of industries which approximate monopoly—for example, steel and aluminum—interest in research has been minimal. Such advances as have occurred have come largely from outside the industry or from smaller firms which make up the "competitive fringe" of the industry.

Basically, there are at least two counterarguments:

1 Technological advance lowers unit costs and thereby expands profits. As our analysis of Figure 11-3 implies, lower costs will give rise to a profit-maximizing position which involves a larger output and a lower price than previously. Any expansion of profits will not be of a transitory nature; barriers to entry protect the monopolist from profit encroachment by rivals. In short, technological progress is profitable to the monopolist and therefore will be undertaken.

2 Research and technological advance may be one of the monopolist's barriers to entry; hence, the monopolist must persist and succeed in technological advance or fall prey to new competitors, including those located abroad. Technological progress, it is argued, is essential to the maintenance of monopoly.

A Mixed Picture What can be offered by way of a summarizing generalization on the economic efficiency of pure monopoly? In a static economy, where economies of scale are equally accessible to purely competitive and monopolist firms, pure competition will be superior to pure monopoly in that pure competition forces use of the best-known technology and allocates resources according to the wants of society. However, when economies of scale available to the monopolist are not attainable by small competitive producers, or in a dynamic context in which changes in the rate of technological advance must be considered, the inefficiencies of pure monopoly are somewhat less evident.

QUICK REVIEW 11-2

- ***The monopolist maximizes profits (or minimizes losses) at the output where MR = MC and charges the price on its demand curve which corresponds to this output.***
- ***Given identical costs, a monopolist will be less efficient than a purely competitive firm because the monopolist produces less output and charges a higher price.***
- ***The inefficiencies of monopoly may be offset or lessened by economies of scale and technological progress, but intensified by the presence of X-inefficiency and rent-seeking expenditures.***

PRICE DISCRIMINATION

Up to now we have assumed that the monopolist charges a uniform price to all buyers. Under certain conditions the monopolist can exploit its market position more fully and thus increase profits by charging different prices to different buyers. In so doing the seller is engaging in price discrimination. **Price discrimination** *occurs when a given product is sold at more than one price and these price differences are not justified by cost differences.*

Conditions

The opportunity to engage in price discrimination is not readily available to all sellers. In general, price discrimination is workable when three conditions are realized.

1 Monopoly Power The seller must be a monopolist or, at least, possess some degree of monopoly power, that is, some ability to control output and price.

2 Market Segregation The seller must be able to segregate buyers into separate classes where each group has a different willingness or ability to pay for the product. This separation of buyers is usually based on different elasticities of demand as later illustrations will make clear.

3 No Resale The original purchaser cannot resell the product or service. If buyers in the low-price segment of the market can easily resell in the high-price segment, the monopolist's price discrimination strategy creates competitive sellers with the monopolist in the high-price segment of the market. This competition will reduce price in the high-price segment and undermine the monopolist's price discrimination policy. This correctly suggests that service industries such as the transportation industry or legal and medical services, where resale is impossible, are especially susceptible to price discrimination.

Illustrations

Price discrimination is widely practiced in our economy. The sales representative who must communicate important information to corporate headquarters has a highly inelastic demand for long-distance telephone service and pays the high daytime rate. The college student making a periodic "reporting in" call to the folks at home has an elastic demand and defers the call to take advantage of lower evening or weekend rates. Electric utilities frequently segment their markets by end uses, such as lighting and heating. The absence of reasonable substitutes means that the demand for electricity for illumination is inelastic and the price per kilowatt hour for this use is high. But the availability of natural gas and petroleum as alternatives to electrical heating makes the demand for electricity less inelastic for this purpose and the price charged is lower. Similarly, industrial users of electricity are typically charged lower rates than residential users because the former may have the alternative of constructing their own generating equipment while the individual household does not.

Movie theaters and golf courses vary their charges on the basis of time (higher rates in the evening and on weekends when demand is strong) and age (ability to pay). Railroads vary the rate charged per ton mile of freight according to the market value of the product being shipped. The shipper of 10 tons of television sets or costume jewelry will be charged more than the shipper of 10 tons of gravel or coal. Airlines charge high fares to traveling executives, whose demand for travel is inelastic, and offer a variety of lower fares in the guise of "family rates" and "standby fares" to attract vacationers and others whose demands are more elastic. Hotels, restaurants, theaters, and pharmacies frequently give discounts to retired people. In international trade, price discrimination is called "dumping." A South Korean electronics manufacturer, for example, might sell TV sets for $100 less in the United States than it charges domestically.

Consequences

The economic consequences of price discrimination are twofold.

1 It is not surprising that a monopolist will be able to increase its profits by practicing price discrimination.

2 Other things being equal, a discriminating monopolist will produce a larger output than a nondiscrimination monopolist.

1 More Profits The simplest way to understand why price discrimination can yield additional profits is to look again at our monopolist's downsloping demand curve in Figure 11-3. Although the profit-maximizing uniform price is \$122, the segment of the demand curve lying above the profit area in Figure 11-3 tells us there are buyers willing to pay *more than* P_m (\$122) rather than forgo the product.

If the monopolist can identify and segregate each of these buyers and charge the maximum price each would pay, the sale of any given level of output will be more profitable. In columns 1 and 2 of Table 11-1 we note that buyers of the first 4 units of output would be willing to pay more than the equilibrium price of \$122. If the seller could practice perfect price discrimination by extracting the maximum price each buyer would pay, total revenue would increase from \$610 (=\$122 × 5) to \$710 (=\$122 + \$132 + \$142 + \$152 + \$162) and profits would increase from \$140 (=\$610 − \$470) to \$240 (=\$710 − \$470).

2 More Production Other things being the same, the discriminating monopolist will choose to produce a larger output than the nondiscriminating monopolist. Recall that when the nondiscriminating monopolist lowers price to sell additional output, the lower price will apply not only to the additional sales but also to *all* prior units of output. As a result, marginal revenue is less than price and, graphically, the marginal-revenue curve lies below the demand curve. The fact that marginal revenue is less than price is a disincentive to increased production.

But when a perfectly discriminating monopolist lowers price, the reduced price applies *only* to the additional unit sold and *not* to prior units. Hence, price and marginal revenue are equal for any unit of output. Graphically, the perfectly discriminating monopolist's marginal-revenue curve will coincide with its demand curve and the disincentive to increased production is removed. As indicated in Table 11-1, because marginal revenue now equals price, the monopolist will find that it is profitable to produce 7, rather than 5, units of output. The additional revenue from the sixth and seventh units is \$214 (=\$112 + \$102). Thus total revenue for 7 units is \$924 (=\$710 + \$214). Total costs for 7 units are \$640, so profits are \$284.

Ironically, although price discrimination increases the monopolist's profit compared to a nondiscriminating monopolist, it also results in greater output and thus less allocative inefficiency. In our example, the output level of 7 units matches that which would occur in pure competition. That is, allocative efficiency (P = MC) is achieved.

Questions 5 and 6 at the end of this chapter may be helpful in comparing the price and output decisions of a nondiscriminating and a discriminating monopolist.

REGULATED MONOPOLY

Most purely monopolistic industries are natural monopolies and subject to regulation. In particular, the prices or rates public utilities—telephone companies, natural gas and electricity suppliers—can charge are determined by a Federal, state, or local regulatory commission or board.

Figure 11-6 shows the demand and long-run cost conditions of a natural monopoly. Because of the advantages of larger firm size, demand cuts the average-cost curve at a point where long-run average cost is still falling. It would be inefficient to have many firms in

FIGURE 11-6 Regulated monopoly

Price regulation can improve the social consequences of a natural monopoly. The socially optimal price P_r will result in an efficient allocation of resources but is likely to entail losses and therefore call for permanent public subsidies. The "fair-return" price P_f will allow the monopolist to break even, but will not fully correct the underallocation of resources.

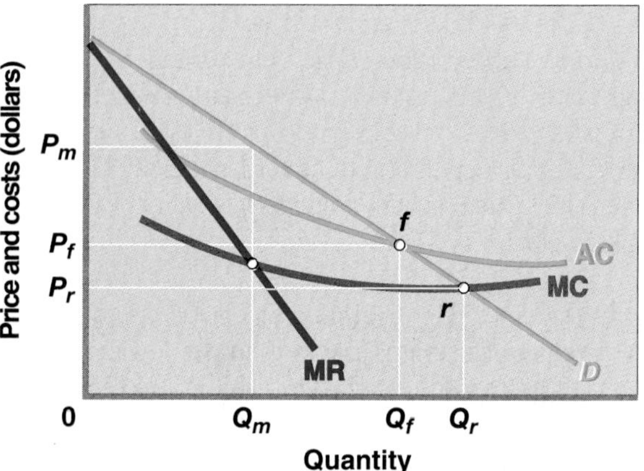

such an industry because, by dividing the market, each firm would move further to the left on its average-cost curve so unit costs would be substantially higher. The relationship between market demand and costs is such that the attainment of low unit costs presumes only one producer.

We know by application of the MR = MC rule that P_m and Q_m are the profit-maximizing price and output which the unregulated monopolist would choose. Because price exceeds average total cost at Q_m, the monopolist enjoys a substantial economic profit. Furthermore, price exceeds marginal cost, indicating an underallocation of resources to this product or service. Can government regulation bring about better results from society's point of view?

Socially Optimal Price: $P = \text{MC}$

If the objective of our regulatory commission is to achieve allocative efficiency, it should attempt to establish a legal (ceiling) price for the monopolist equal to *marginal cost.* Remembering that each point on the market demand curve designates a price-quantity combination, and noting that marginal cost cuts the demand curve only at point r, it is clear that P_r is the only price equal to marginal cost. The imposition of this maximum or ceiling price causes the monopolist's effective demand curve to become $P_r rD$; the demand curve becomes perfectly elastic, and therefore $P_r =$ MR, out to point r, where the regulated price ceases to be effective.

The important point is that, given the legal price P_r, the monopolist will maximize profits or minimize losses by producing Q_r units of output, because it is at this output that MR $(= P_r) =$ MC. By making it illegal to charge more than P_r per unit, the regulatory agency has eliminated the monopolist's incentive to restrict output to benefit from a higher price.

In short, by imposing the legal price P_r and letting the monopolist choose its profit-maximizing or loss-minimizing output, the allocative results of pure competition can be simulated. Production takes place where $P_r =$ MC, and this equality indicates an efficient allocation of resources to this product or service.[7] This price which achieves allocative efficiency is called the **socially optimal price.**

"Fair-Return" Price: $P = \text{AC}$

But the socially optimal price P_r may pose a problem of losses for the regulated firm. The price which equals marginal cost may be so low that average total costs are not covered, as is shown in Figure 11-6. The inevitable result is losses. The reason for this lies in the basic character of public utilities. Because they are required to meet "peak" demands (both daily and seasonally) for their product or service, they have substantial excess productive capacity when demand is relatively "normal." This high level of investment in capital facilities means that unit costs of production are likely to decline over a wide range of output. In technical terms, the market demand curve in Figure 11-6 cuts marginal cost at a point to the left of the marginal-cost–average-total-cost intersection, so the socially optimal price is necessarily below AC. Therefore, to enforce a socially optimal price on the regulated monopolist would mean short-run losses, and in the long run, bankruptcy for the utility.

What to do? One option would be a public subsidy to cover the loss which marginal-cost pricing would entail. Another possibility is condoning price discrimination and hoping that the additional revenue gained will permit the firm to cover costs.

In practice, regulatory commissions have pursued a third option; they tend to back away somewhat from the objective of allocative efficiency and marginal-cost pricing. Most regulatory agencies in the United States are concerned with establishing a **"fair-return" price.** This is so because, as the courts have seen it, a socially optimal price would lead to losses and eventual bankruptcy and thereby deprive the monopoly's owners of their private property without "due process of law." Indeed, the Supreme Court has held that regulatory agencies must permit a "fair return" to owners.

Remembering that total costs include a normal or "fair" profit, we see that the "fair" or "fair-return" price in Figure 11-6 would be P_f, where price equals *average* cost. Because the demand curve cuts average cost only at point f, clearly P_f is the only price which permits a fair return. The corresponding output at regulated price P_f will be Q_f. Total revenue of $0P_f fQ_f$ will equal total costs of the same amount and the firm will realize a normal profit.

Dilemma of Regulation

Comparing results of the socially optimal price ($P =$ MC) and the fair-return price ($P =$ AC) suggests a policy dilemma, sometimes termed the **dilemma of regu-**

[7]While "allocative efficiency" is achieved, "productive efficiency" would only be achieved by chance. In Figure 11-6 we note that production takes place at Q_r which is less than the output at which average costs are minimized. Can you redraw Figure 11-6 to show those special conditions where both allocative and productive efficiency are realized?

LAST WORD

MONOPOLIES IN THE NATIONAL PARKS

Few people recognize that the facilities found in our national parks are operated by government-sponsored monopolies.

In the early years of the National Park Service (NPS), officials felt that it was necessary to provide services—modern campgrounds, restaurants, motels and lodges, shops and stores, and ski lifts—to attract visitors. To achieve this, the NPS negotiated long-term contracts on highly favorable terms to private concessionaires. For example, in 1963 the Curry Company, a subsidiary of entertainment giant Music Corporation of America, was granted virtually exclusive rights to do business in Yosemite National Park for a fee of 0.75 percent of gross revenues. In 1988 the NPS collected only $590,000 on the basis of gross sales by Curry of almost $79 million. Critics estimate Curry's 1988 profits were from $10 to $20 million. Across the nation NPS fees averaged only about 2.5 percent of gross revenues. At the Grand Canyon the government received $1.2 million on the basis of concessionaire revenues of almost $49 million. In 1990 the 75 largest concessionaires paid the government just $12.3 million or 2.5 percent on sales of $486 million.

Critics contend, first, that this is an outrageous, wholly unjustified granting of monopoly power by the NPS. Second, environmentalists argue that concessionaires are opposed to policies designed to protect the parks from deterioration through overuse. For example, they say the Curry Company has been successful in stalling a plan to restrict greatly automobile traffic and to remove some motel rooms and employee housing from Yosemite because of potentially adverse effects on sales revenues.

The concessionaires defend current arrangements, contending that they have resulted in a high level of visitor services under adverse conditions of short visitor seasons and high construction and operating costs. Furthermore, the private concessionaires assert they are able to maintain and modify facilities without the inevitable delays associated with governmental bureaucracies. In short, concessionaires hold that the present system has worked in the public interest.

Many concessionaire agreements are soon coming up for renewal and the NPS is seeking to shorten the duration of contracts and to raise its fees to 22 percent of gross revenues.

lation. When price is set to achieve the most efficient allocation of resources (P = MC), the regulated utility is likely to suffer losses. Survival of the firm would presumably depend on permanent public subsidies out of tax revenues. On the other hand, although a fair-return price (P = AC) allows the monopolist to cover costs, it only partially resolves the underallocation of resources which the unregulated monopoly would foster. That is, the fair-return price would only increase output from Q_m to Q_f, while the socially optimal output is Q_r. Despite this problem, regulation can improve on the results of monopoly from the social point of view. Price regulation can simultaneously reduce price, increase output, and reduce the economic profits of monopolies.

QUICK REVIEW 11-3

- ***Price discrimination occurs when a seller charges different prices which are not based on cost differentials.***
- ***The conditions necessary for price discrimination are: a monopoly power; b the segregation of buyers on the basis of different demand elasticities; and c the inability of buyers to resell the product.***
- ***Monopoly price can be reduced and output increased through government regulation.***
- ***The socially optimal price (P = MC) achieves allocative efficiency but may result in losses; the fair-return price (P = AC) yields a normal profit but falls short of allocative efficiency.***

CHAPTER SUMMARY

1 A pure monopolist is the sole producer of a commodity for which there are no close substitutes.

2 Barriers to entry, in the form of **a** economies of scale, **b** natural monopolies, **c** patent ownership and research, and **d** ownership or control of essential resources, help explain the existence of pure monopoly and other imperfectly competitive market structures. Barriers to entry which are formidable in the short run may prove to be surmountable in the long run.

3 The pure monopolist's market situation differs from a competitive firm's in that the monopolist's demand curve is downsloping, causing the marginal-revenue curve to lie below the demand curve. Like the competitive seller, the pure monopolist will maximize profits by equating marginal revenue and marginal cost. Barriers to entry may permit a monopolist to acquire economic profits even in the long run. Note, however, that **a** the monopolist does not charge "the highest price it can get"; **b** the maximum total profit sought by the monopolist rarely coincides with maximum unit profits; **c** high costs and a weak demand may prevent the monopolist from realizing any profit at all; and **d** the monopolist will want to avoid the inelastic range of its demand curve.

4 Given the same costs, the pure monopolist will find it profitable to restrict output and charge a higher price than would a competitive seller. This restriction of output causes resources to be misallocated, as is evidenced by the fact that price exceeds marginal cost in monopolized markets.

5 Monopoly also tends to increase income inequality.

6 The costs of monopolists and competitive producers may not be the same. On the one hand, economies of scale may make lower unit costs accessible to monopolists but not to competitors. On the other hand, X-inefficiency—the failure to produce with the least-costly combination of inputs—is more common to monopolists than to competitive firms and monopolists may make sizable expenditures to maintain monopoly privileges conferred by government.

7 Economists disagree as to how conducive pure monopoly is to technological advance. Some feel pure monopoly is more progressive than pure competition because its ability to realize economic profits helps finance technological research. Others, however, argue that absence of rival firms and the monopolist's desire to exploit fully its existing capital facilities weaken the monopolist's incentive to innovate.

8 A monopolist can increase its profits by practicing price discrimination, provided it can segregate buyers on the basis of different elasticities of demand and the product or service cannot be readily transferred between the segregated markets. Other things being equal, the discriminating monopolist will produce a larger output than will the nondiscriminating monopolist.

9 Price regulation can be invoked to eliminate wholly or partially the tendency of monopolists to underallocate resources and to earn economic profits. The "socially optimal" price is determined where the demand and marginal-cost curves intersect; the "fair-return" price is determined where the demand and average-cost curves intersect.

TERMS AND CONCEPTS

pure monopoly
barriers to entry
X-inefficiency
rent-seeking behavior
dynamic efficiency
price discrimination
socially optimal price
fair-return price
the dilemma of regulation

QUESTIONS AND STUDY SUGGESTIONS

1 "No firm is completely sheltered from rivals; all firms compete for consumer dollars. Pure monopoly, therefore, does not exist." Do you agree? Explain.

2 Discuss the major barriers to entry. Explain how each barrier can foster monopoly or oligopoly. Which barriers, if any, do you feel give rise to monopoly that is socially justifiable?

3 How does the demand curve faced by a purely monopolistic seller differ from that confronting a purely competitive firm? Why does it differ? Of what significance is the difference? Why is the pure monopolist's demand curve not perfectly inelastic?

4 Use the demand schedule below to calculate total revenue and marginal revenue. Plot the demand, total-revenue, and marginal-revenue curves and carefully explain the relationships between them. Explain why the marginal revenue of the fourth unit of output is \$3.50, even though its price is \$5.00. Use Chapter 7's total-revenue test for price elasticity to designate the elastic and inelastic segments of your graphed demand curve. What generalization can you make regarding the relationship between marginal revenue and elasticity of demand? Suppose that somehow the marginal cost of successive units of output were zero. What output would the profit-seeking firm produce? Finally, use your

analysis to explain why a monopolist would never produce in that range of its demand curve which is inelastic.

Price	Quantity demanded	Price	Quantity demanded
$7.00	0	$4.50	5
6.50	1	4.00	6
6.00	2	3.50	7
5.50	3	3.00	8
5.00	4	2.50	9

5 Suppose a pure monopolist is faced with the demand schedule shown below and the same cost data as the competitive producer discussed in question 4 at the end of Chapter 10. Calculate total and marginal revenue and determine the profit-maximizing price and output for this monopolist. What is the level of profits? Verify your answer graphically and by comparing total revenue and total cost. If this firm could engage in perfect price discrimination, what would be the level of output? Of profits?

Price	Quantity demanded	Total revenue	Marginal revenue
$115	0	$____	
			$____
100	1	____	
			____
83	2	____	
			____
71	3	____	
			____
63	4	____	
			____
55	5	____	
			____
48	6	____	
			____
42	7	____	
			____
37	8	____	
			____
33	9	____	
			____
29	10	____	

6 Draw a diagram showing the relevant demand, marginal-revenue, average-cost, and marginal-cost curves and the equilibrium price and output for a nondiscriminating monopolist. Use the same diagram to show the equilibrium position of a monopolist able to practice perfect price discrimination. Compare equilibrium outputs, total revenues, and economic profits in the two cases. Comment on the economic desirability of price discrimination.

7 Assume a pure monopolist and a purely competitive firm have the same unit costs. Contrast the two with respect to **a** price, **b** output, **c** profits, **d** allocation of resources, and **e** impact upon the distribution of income. Since both monopolists and competitive firms follow the MC = MR rule in maximizing profits, how do you account for the different results? Why might the costs of a purely competitive firm and a monopolist *not* be the same? What are the implications of such cost differences?

8 Carefully evaluate the following widely held viewpoint. Can you offer any arguments to the contrary?

> A monopoly is usually not under pressure to *invent* new products or methods. Nor does it have strong incentives to *innovate:* to apply those new inventions in practice and bring new products to the market. *The monopoly may choose to invent and innovate, but it will do so only at its own pace.* Because the new product cuts the value of the existing products, the monopoly will tend to hold back on innovation. Typically it innovates only when a smaller competitor forces its hand. Even if its capital is outdated or its products mediocre, a monopolist may prefer to protect and continue them rather than to replace them with better ones.[8]

9 Critically evaluate and explain:

a "Because they can control product price, monopolists are always assured of profitable production by simply charging the highest price consumers will pay."

b "The pure monopolist seeks that output which will yield the greatest per unit profit."

c "An excess of price over marginal cost is the market's way of signaling the need for more production of a good."

d "The more profitable a firm, the greater its monopoly power."

e "The monopolist has a price policy; the competitive producer does not."

f "With respect to resource allocation, the interests of the seller and of society coincide in a purely competitive market but conflict in a monopolized market."

g "In a sense the monopolist makes a profit for not producing; the monopolist produces profits more than it does goods."

10 Assume a monopolistic publisher has agreed to pay an author 15 percent of the total revenue from the sales of a text. Will the author and the publisher want to charge the same price for the text? Explain.

11 Suppose a firm's demand curve lies below its average-total-cost curve at all levels of output. Can you conceive of any circumstance in which production might be profitable?

12 Are colleges and universities engaging in price discrimination when they charge full tuition to some students and provide financial aid to others? What are the advantages and disadvantages of this practice?

13 Explain verbally and graphically how price (rate) regulation may improve the performance of monopolies. In your answer distinguish between **a** socially optimal (marginal-cost) pricing and **b** fair-return (average-cost) pricing. What is the "dilemma of regulation"?

14 It has been proposed that natural monopolists should be allowed to determine their profit-maximizing outputs and prices and then government should tax their profits away and distribute them to consumers in proportion to their purchases from the monopoly. Is this proposal as socially desirable as requiring monopolists to equate price with marginal cost or average cost?

[8]William G. Shepherd, *Public Policies Toward Business,* 8th ed. (Homewood, Ill.: Richard D. Irwin, Inc., 1991), p. 36.

Price and Output Determination: Monopolistic Competition

If you live in a town or city of any reasonable size, you have a wide array of choices in buying many products. Suppose you want to purchase a sweater. You might patronize a discount store whose newspaper flier advertises an imported acrylic for $12. Or you might select a fleece pullover with your college's logo and colors advertised in your campus newspaper for $20 on sale at your bookstore. Alternatively, you might buy a cotton knit for $45 from any one of a number of mail-order catalogs. Or you could shop at an "upscale" clothier and pay $80 or $90 or more for a wool sweater. These product choices reflect the world of monopolistic competition where competition is not only based on price, but also on product quality, services, and advertising.

Pure competition and pure monopoly are the exception, not the rule, in our economy. Most market structures fall somewhere between these two extremes. In Chapter 13 we will discuss oligopoly, a market structure close to pure monopoly. In this chapter we examine monopolistic competition. Monopolistic competition correctly suggests a blending of monopoly and competition; more specifically, monopolistic competition involves a very considerable amount of competition mixed with a small dose of monopoly power.

Our objectives are to (1) define and discuss the nature and prevalence of monopolistic competition, (2) analyze and evaluate the price-output behavior of monopolistically competitive firms, and (3) explain and assess the role of nonprice competition, that is, competition based on product quality and advertising, in monopolistically competitive industries.

MONOPOLISTIC COMPETITION: CONCEPT AND OCCURRENCE

Let's recall and expand on our definition of monopolistic competition.

Relatively Large Numbers

Monopolistic competition refers to that market situation in which a relatively large number of small producers or sellers offer similar but not identical products. The contrasts between this and pure competition are important. Monopolistic competition does not require the presence of hundreds or thousands of firms but only a fairly large number—say 25, 35, 60, or 70.

Several important characteristics of monopolistic competition follow from the presence of relatively large numbers.

1 Small Market Share Each firm has a comparatively small percentage of the total market, so each has a very limited amount of control over market price.

2 No Collusion The presence of a relatively large number of firms also ensures that collusion—concerted action by firms to restrict output and rig price—is all but impossible.

3 Independent Actions Finally, with numerous firms in the industry, there is no feeling of mutual interdependence among them; each firm determines its policies without considering possible reactions of rival firms. This is a very reasonable way to act in a market in which one's rivals are numerous. After all, the 10 or 15 percent increase in sales which firm X may realize by cutting price will be spread so thinly over its 20, 40, or 60 rivals that, for all practical purposes, the impact on their sales will be imperceptible. Rivals' reactions can be ignored because the impact of one firm's actions on each of its many rivals is so small that these rivals will have no reason to react.

Product Differentiation

Also in contrast to pure competition, monopolistic competition has the fundamental feature of **product differentiation.** Purely competitive firms produce a standardized or homogeneous product; monopolistically competitive producers turn out variations of a given product. In fact, product differentiation may take a number of different forms.

1 Product Quality Product differentiation may take the form of physical or qualitative differences in products themselves. "Real" differences in functional features, materials, design, and workmanship are vitally important aspects of product differentiation. Personal computers, for example, differ in terms of hardware capacity, software, graphics, and how "user-friendly" they are. There are scores of competing principles of economics texts which differ in content, organization, presentation and readability, pedagogical aids, and graphics and design. Any good-sized city will have a variety of retail stores selling men's and women's clothing varying greatly in styling, materials, and quality of workmanship. Similarly, one fast-food hamburger chain may feature lean beef, while a competitor stresses the juiciness of its hamburgers.

2 Services Services and conditions surrounding the sale of a product are important aspects of product differentiation. One grocery store may stress the helpfulness of its clerks who bag your groceries and carry them to your car. A "warehouse" competitor may leave bagging and carrying to its customers, but feature lower prices. "One-day" clothes cleaning may be preferred to cleaning of equal quality which takes three days. The "snob appeal" of a store, the courteousness and helpfulness of clerks, the firm's reputation for servicing or exchanging its products, and credit availability are all service aspects of product differentiation.

3 Location Products may also be differentiated as to location and accessibility. Small minigroceries or convenience stores successfully compete with large supermarkets, even though they have a more limited range of products and charge higher prices. They compete on the basis of location—being close to customers and on busy streets—and by staying open 24 hours a day. Similarly, a gas station's proximity to the interstate highway gives it a locational advantage which may allow it to sell gasoline at a higher price than could a gas station in a city 2 or 3 miles from the interstate.

4 Promotion and Packaging Product differentiation may also arise from perceived differences created through advertising, packaging, and the use of brand names and trademarks. A celebrity's name associated with jeans or perfume may enhance those products in the minds of buyers. Many consumers regard toothpaste packaged in a "pump" container as preferable to the same toothpaste in a conventional tube. While there are many aspirin-type products, product promotion and advertising may convince many consumers that Bayer or Anacin is superior and worth a higher price than a generic substitute.

One important implication of product differentiation is that, despite the presence of a relatively large number of firms, monopolistically competitive producers do have limited control over the prices of their products. Consumers prefer the products of specific sellers and *within limits* will pay more to satisfy those preferences. Sellers and buyers are no longer linked at random, as in a purely competitive market.

Nonprice Competition

Under monopolistic competition economic rivalry centers not only on price, but also on such nonprice factors as product quality, advertising, and conditions associated with the sale of a product. Because products are differentiated, they can be varied over time and the differentiating features of each firm's product will be susceptible to advertising and other forms of sales promotion. Great emphasis is placed on trademarks and brand names to convince consumers that a firm's product is better than its rivals.

Easy Entry

Entry into monopolistically competitive industries tends to be relatively easy. The fact that monopolistically competitive producers are typically small-sized firms, both absolutely and relatively, suggests that economies of scale and capital requirements are few. On the other hand, compared with pure competition, added financial barriers may result from the need to develop a product different from one's rivals and the obligation to advertise it. Existing firms may hold patents on their products and copyrights on their brand names and trademarks, enhancing the difficulty and cost of successfully imitating them.

TABLE 12-1 Percentage of output* produced by firms in selected low-concentration manufacturing industries

Industry	*Four largest firms*	*Eight largest firms*	*Twenty largest firms*
Men's and boys' suits and coats	25%	37%	57%
Mattresses and bedsprings	23	31	43
Prefab metal buildings	21	31	50
Women's and misses' suits and coats	19	28	40
Book publishing	17	30	56
Upholstered furniture	17	25	39
Wood furniture	16	23	37
Metal house furniture	16	26	44
Paperboard boxes	15	26	43
Bolts, nuts, and rivets	13	23	38
Fur goods	12	19	33
Metal doors	11	17	30
Women's and misses' dresses	6	10	17

*As measured by value of industry shipments. Data are for 1982.

Source: Bureau of the Census, *1982 Census of Manufacturers.*

Illustrations

Table 12-1 lists a group of manufacturing industries which approximate monopolistic competition. In addition, retail stores in metropolitan areas are generally monopolistically competitive; grocery stores, gasoline stations, barber shops, dry cleaners, clothing stores, and so forth, operate under conditions similar to those we have described.

PRICE AND OUTPUT DETERMINATION

We now analyze the price-output behavior of a monopolistically competitive firm. We assume initially that the firms in the industry are producing *given* products and engaging in a *given* amount of promotional activity. Later we note how product variation and advertising modify our discussion.

The Firm's Demand Curve

Our explanation is couched in terms of Figure 12-1 (Key Graph). The basic feature of this diagram, which sets it off from our analyses of pure competition and pure monopoly, is the elasticity of the firm's individual demand, or sales, curve. *The demand curve faced by a monopolistically competitive seller is highly, but not perfectly, elastic.* It is much more elastic than the demand curve of the pure monopolist, because the monopolistically competitive seller is faced with many rivals producing close-substitute goods. The pure monopolist, of course, has no rivals at all. Yet, for two reasons, the monopolistically competitive seller's sales curve is not perfectly elastic as is the purely competitive producer's: First, the monopolistically competitive firm has fewer rivals, and, second, the products of these rivals are close but not perfect substitutes.

Generally speaking, the precise degree of elasticity embodied in the monopolistically competitive firm's demand curve will depend on the exact number of rivals and the degree of product differentiation. The larger the number of rivals and the weaker the product differentiation, the greater will be the elasticity of each seller's demand curve, that is, the closer the situation will be to pure competition.

KEY GRAPHS

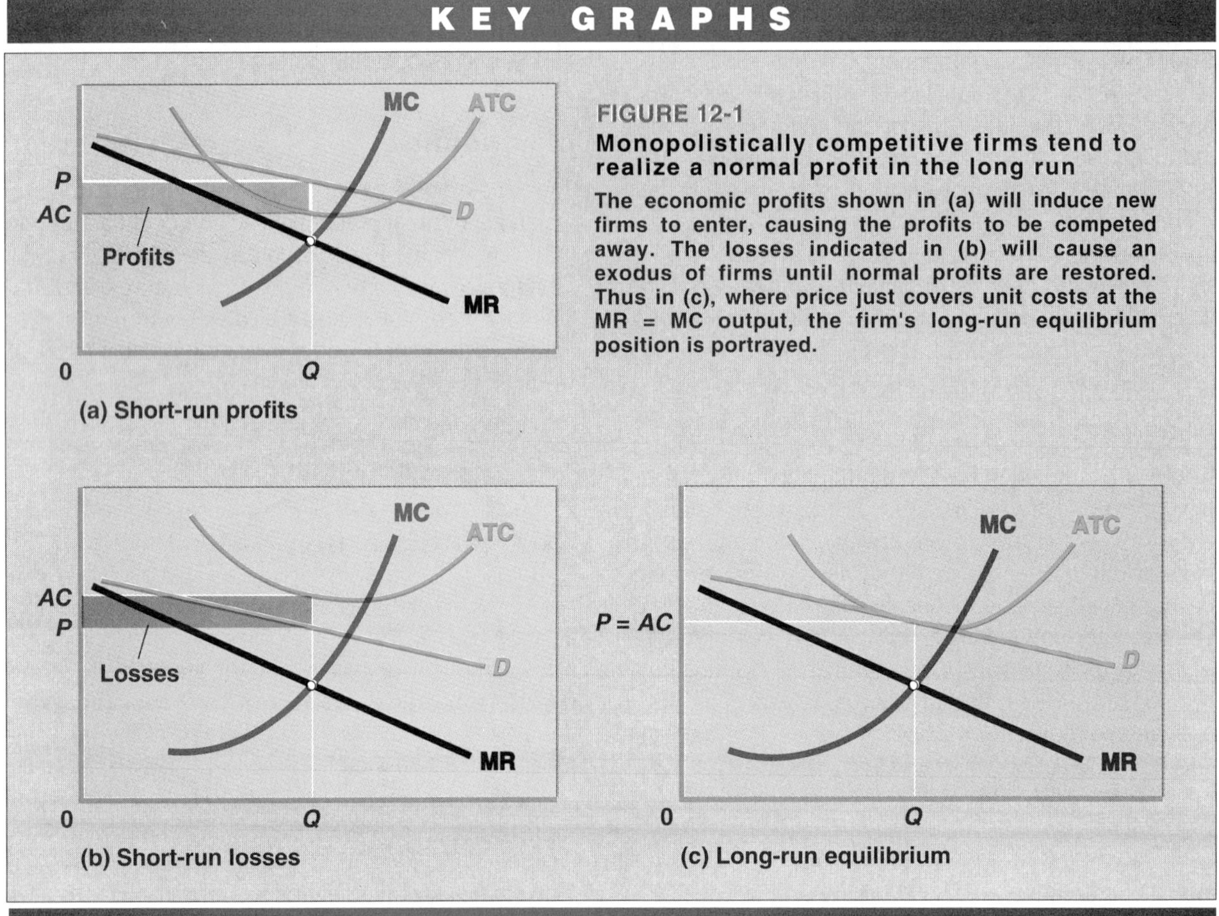

FIGURE 12-1
Monopolistically competitive firms tend to realize a normal profit in the long run
The economic profits shown in (a) will induce new firms to enter, causing the profits to be competed away. The losses indicated in (b) will cause an exodus of firms until normal profits are restored. Thus in (c), where price just covers unit costs at the MR = MC output, the firm's long-run equilibrium position is portrayed.

The Short Run: Profits or Losses

The firm will maximize its profits or minimize its losses in the short run by producing that output designated by the equality of marginal cost and marginal revenue, for reasons with which we are now familiar. Our firm of Figure 12-1a produces an output *Q*, charges a price *P*, and realizes a total profit of the size indicated in gray. But a less favorable cost and demand situation may exist, putting the monopolistically competitive firm in the position of realizing losses in the short run. This is illustrated by the light red area in Figure 12-1b. In the short run the monopolistically competitive firm may either realize an economic profit or be faced with losses.

The Long Run: Break Even

In the long run, however, the *tendency* is for monopolistically competitive firms to earn a normal profit or, in other words, to break even.

Profits: Firms Enter In the short-run profits case, Figure 12-1a, economic profits will attract new rivals, because entry is relatively easy. As new firms enter, the demand curve faced by the typical firms will fall (shift to the left) and become more elastic. Why? Because each firm has a smaller share of the total demand and now faces a larger number of close-substitute products. This in turn tends to cause the economic profits to disappear. When the demand curve is tangent to the average-cost curve at the profit-maximizing output, as shown in Figure 12-1c, the firm is just breaking even. Output *Q* is the equilibrium output for the firm; as Figure 12-1c clearly indicates, any deviation from that output will entail average costs which exceed product price and, therefore, losses for the firm. Furthermore, economic profits have been competed away, and there is no incentive for more firms to enter.

Losses: Firms Leave In the short-run losses case, Figure 12-1b, an exodus of firms would occur in the long run. Faced with fewer substitute products and blessed with an expanded share of total demand, surviving firms will find that their losses disappear and gradually give way to approximately normal profits. (For simplicity's sake we have assumed constant costs; shifts in the cost curves as firms enter or leave would complicate our discussion slightly, but would not alter the conclusions.)

Complications We have been careful to say that the representative firm in a monopolistically competitive market *tends* to break even, or earn a normal profit, in the long run. Certain complicating factors prevent us from being more definite than this.

1 Some firms may achieve a measure of product differentiation which cannot be duplicated by rivals even over a long span of time. A given gasoline station may have the only available location at the busiest intersection in town. Or a firm may hold a patent giving it a slight and more-or-less permanent advantage over imitators. Such firms may realize a sliver of economic profits even in the long run.

2 Remember that entry is not completely unrestricted. Because of product differentiation, there are likely to be greater financial barriers to entry than otherwise would be the case. This again suggests that some economic profits may persist even in the long run.

3 A final consideration may work in the opposite direction, causing losses—below-normal profits—to persist in the long run. The proprietors of a corner delicatessen persistently accept a return less than they could earn elsewhere because their business is a "way of life" to them. The suburban barber ekes out a meager existence, because cutting hair is "all he wants to do." With all things considered, however, the long-run normal profit equilibrium of Figure 12-1c is a reasonable portrayal of reality.

WASTES OF MONOPOLISTIC COMPETITION

Recalling our evaluation of competitive pricing in Chapter 10, we know that economic efficiency requires the triple equality of price, marginal cost, and average cost. The equality of price and marginal cost is necessary for the realization of *allocative efficiency,* that is, the allocation of the right amount of resources to the product. The equality of price with minimum average total cost suggests the achievement of *productive efficiency* or the use of the most efficient (least-cost) technology; this equality means consumers will enjoy the largest volume of the product and the lowest price which least-cost conditions allow.

Excess Capacity

In monopolistically competitive markets neither allocative nor productive efficiency is realized. An examination of Figure 12-2, which enlarges the relevant portion of Figure 12-1c and adds detail, suggests that the monopolistic element in monopolistic competition causes a modest underallocation of resources to goods produced under this market structure. Price (*a*) exceeds marginal cost (*b*) in long-run equilibrium, indicating that society values additional units of this commodity more than the alternative products the needed resources can otherwise produce.

Furthermore, in contrast to purely competitive firms, we observe in Figure 12-2 that monopolistically competitive firms produce somewhat short of the most efficient (least unit cost) output. Production entails higher unit costs (*a*) than the minimum attainable (*c*). This means a somewhat higher price (*a*) than would result under competition (*c*). Consumers do *not* benefit from the largest output and lowest price which cost conditions permit. Indeed, monopolistically competitive firms must charge a higher than competitive price in the long run to achieve a normal profit. Viewed differently, if each firm could produce at the most efficient output, fewer firms could produce the same total output, and the product could be sold at a lower price. Monopolistically competitive industries tend to be overcrowded with firms, each of which is underutilized, that is, operating short of optimal capacity. This is typified by many kinds of retail establishments, for example, the thirty or forty gasoline stations, all operating with excess capacity, that populate a medium-sized city. These are the so-called **wastes of monopolistic competition,** the underutilized plants and consumers penalized through higher than competitive prices for this underutilization.

Redeeming Features?

In many monopolistically competitive industries, however, the price and output results are not drastically different from those of pure competition. The highly elastic nature of each firm's demand curve guarantees that results are nearly competitive.

Furthermore, the product differentiation characterizing monopolistic competition means buyers can select from many variations of the same general product, better satisfying the diverse tastes of consumers.

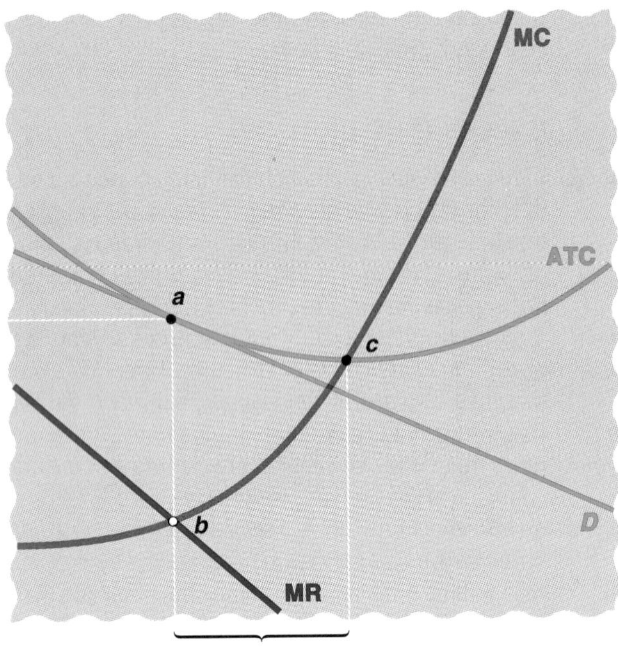

FIGURE 12-2 The inefficiency aspects of monopolistic competition

In long-run equilibrium a monopolistically competitive firm achieves neither allocative nor productive efficiency. An underallocation of resources is reflected in the fact that the product price of *a* exceeds marginal cost of *b*. Productive efficiency is not realized because production occurs where unit costs of *a* exceed the minimum attainable unit cost of *c*.

In fact, there is a tradeoff between product differentiation and the production of a given product at the minimum average cost. The stronger the product differentiation (the less elastic the demand curve), the further to the left of the minimum average costs will production take place. But the greater the product differentiation, the more likely diverse tastes will be fully satisfied. The greater the excess capacity problem, the wider the range of consumer choice.

QUICK REVIEW 12-1

- ***Monopolistic competition refers to industries which comprise a relatively large number of firms, operating noncollusively, in the production of differentiated products.***
- ***In the short run a monopolistically competitive firm will maximize profits or minimize losses by producing that output at which marginal revenue equals marginal cost.***
- ***In the long run easy entry and exodus of firms generates a strong tendency for firms to break even.***
- ***A monopolistically competitive firm's equilibrium output is such that price exceeds marginal cost (indicating that resources are underallocated to the product) and price exceeds minimum average total cost (implying that consumers do not get the product at the lowest unit cost and price attainable).***

NONPRICE COMPETITION

For reasons cited above, we can conclude that the situation portrayed in Figure 12-1c and Figure 12-2 may not be the most beneficial to society. It is also not very satisfying to the monopolistically competitive producer which barely captures a normal profit for its efforts. We can therefore expect monopolistically competitive producers to try to improve on the long-run equilibrium position.

How can this be accomplished? The answer lies in product differentiation. Each firm has a product distinguishable in some more-or-less tangible way from those of its rivals. The product is presumably subject to further variation, that is, to product development. The emphasis on real product differences and the creation of perceived differences also may be achieved through advertising and related sales promotion. In short, the profit-realizing firm of Figure 12-1a will not stand by and watch new competitors encroach on its profits by duplicating or imitating its product, copying its advertising, and matching its services to consumers. Rather, the firm will attempt to sustain these profits and stay ahead of competitors through further product development and by enhancing the quantity and quality of advertising. In this way it might prevent the long-run tendency of Figure 12-1c from becoming a reality. True, product development and advertising will add to the firm's costs, but they can also increase the demand for its product. If demand increases by more than enough to compensate for development and promotional costs, the firm will have improved its profit position. As Figure 25-1c suggests, the firm may have little or no prospect of increasing profits by price cutting. So why not practice **nonprice competition?**

Product Differentiation and Product Development

The likelihood that easy entry will promote product variety and product improvement is possibly a redeeming feature of monopolistic competition which may offset, wholly or in part, the "wastes" associated with this market structure. There are two considerations here: (1) product differentiation at a point in time, and (2) product improvement over a period of time.

1 Differentiation Product differentiation means that at any point in time the consumer will be offered a wide range of types, styles, brands, and quality gradations of any given product. Compared with the situation of pure competition, this suggests possible advantages to the consumer. The range of choice is widened, and variations and shadings of consumer tastes are more fully met by producers.

But skeptics warn that product differentiation is a mixed blessing. Product proliferation may reach the point where the consumer becomes confused and rational choice becomes time-consuming and difficult. Variety may add spice to the consumer's life, but only up to a point. A woman shopping for lipstick may be bewildered by the vast array of products available. Revlon alone offers 157 shades of lipstick, of which 41 are "pink"! Worse yet, some observers fear that the consumer, faced with a myriad of similar products, may judge product quality by price; the consumer may irrationally assume that price is necessarily an index of product quality.

2 Development Product competition is vital to technological innovation and product betterment over a period of time. Such product development may be cumulative in two different ways. First, a successful product improvement by one firm obligates rivals to imitate or, if they can, improve on this firm's temporary market advantage or suffer the penalty of losses. Second, profits realized from a successful product improvement can finance further improvements.

Again, however, there are criticisms of the product development which may occur under monopolistic competition. Critics point out that many product alterations are more apparent than real, consisting of frivolous and superficial changes which do *not* improve the product's durability, efficiency, or usefulness. A more exotic container, bright packaging, or "shuffling the chrome" is frequently the focus for product development. It is argued, too, that particularly with durable and semidurable consumer goods, development may follow a pattern of "planned obsolescence," where firms improve their product only by that amount necessary to make the average consumer dissatisfied with last year's model.

Do the advantages of product differentiation, properly discounted, outweigh the "wastes" of monopolistic competition? It is difficult to say, short of examining specific cases; and even then, concrete conclusions are difficult to come by.

THE ECONOMICS OF ADVERTISING

A monopolistically competitive producer may gain at least a temporary edge on rivals by altering its product. It may also seek the same result by attempting to influence consumer preferences through advertising and sales promotion. Advertising *may* be a mechanism through which a firm can increase its share of the market and enhance consumer loyalty to its particular product.

Controversy and Scope

In fact, there is considerable disagreement as to the economic and social desirability of advertising. Since advertising and promotional expenditures in the United States were estimated to be almost $129 billion in 1990, the issues involved are significant. This amount exceeded by a wide margin the amount all state and local governments spent on public welfare. Hence, if advertising is generally wasteful, any potential virtues of monopolistically competitive markets are thereby dimmed, and the need for corrective public policies is indicated.

Two Views

The controversy over advertising has generated two diametrically opposed views of advertising.[1] In outlin-

[1]The ensuing discussion draws upon Robert B. Eklund, Jr., and David S. Saurman, *Advertising and the Market Process* (San Francisco: Pacific Research Institute for Public Policy, 1988).

ing these two positions, bear in mind that advertising is not confined to monopolistic competition. Product differentiation and heavy advertising are also characteristic of many oligopolistic industries (Chapter 13). Hence, our comments are equally germane to these industries.

The **traditional view** envisions advertising as a redundant and economically wasteful expenditure which generates economic concentration and monopoly power. The **new perspective** on advertising sees it as an efficient means for both providing information to consumers and enhancing competition. Let's contrast these two views in three critical areas.

1 Persuasion or Information? The traditional view holds that the main purpose of advertising is to manipulate or persuade consumers, that is, to alter their preferences in favor of the advertiser's product. A television beer commercial or a newspaper cigarette ad conveys little or no useful information to consumers. Advertising is often based on misleading and extravagant claims which confuse and frequently insult the intelligence of consumers, not enlighten them. Indeed, advertising may well persuade consumers in some cases to pay high prices for much-acclaimed but inferior products, forgoing better but unadvertised products selling at lower prices.

The new perspective contends that consumers need extensive information about product characteristics and prices to make rational (efficient) decisions. Advertising is alleged to be a low-cost means of providing that information. Suppose you are in the market for a CD player and there was no newspaper or magazine advertising of this product. To make a rational choice you might have to spend several days visiting electronics stores to determine the prices and features of various brands. This entails both direct costs (gasoline, parking fees) and indirect costs (the value of your time). Advertising, it is argued, reduces your "search time" and minimizes these costs.

2 Concentration or Competition? Does advertising generate monopoly or stimulate competition? The traditional view envisions some firms as being more successful than others in establishing "brand loyalty" through advertising, that is, in persuading consumers to buy their products. As a consequence, such firms are able to increase their sales, expand their market share, and enjoy enlarged profits. Enhanced profits permit still more advertising and further enlargement of the firm's market share and profits. In short, successful advertising leads to the expansion of some firms at the expense of others and therefore to increased industrial concentration. Consumers in time lose the advantages of competitive markets and face the disadvantages of monopolized markets. Furthermore, potential new entrants to the industry will be faced with the need to incur large advertising expenditures to establish their product in the marketplace; hence, advertising expenditures may be a formidable barrier to entry.

The traditional view is portrayed graphically in Figure 12-3a. By successfully generating brand loyalty through advertising, the firm's demand curve shifts rightward from D_1 to D_2, implying a larger market share. The fact that curve D_2 is less elastic than D_1 indicates a lessening of competition; successful advertising has convinced consumers that there exist fewer good substitutes for this firm's product. The less elastic demand curve also means that the producer can charge higher prices with less loss of sales.

The new perspective sees advertising as a force which enhances competition. By providing information about the wide variety of substitute products available to buyers, advertising diminishes monopoly power. In fact, advertising is frequently associated with the introduction of new products designed to compete with existing brands. Could the Hyundai and Isuzu automobiles have gained a foothold in the American market without advertising? How about Act II microwave popcorn and Softsoap?

In terms of Figure 12-3b, advertising, in a world of costly and imperfect knowledge, makes consumers more aware of the range of substitutable products available to them and provides them with valuable information on the prices and characteristics of these goods. Before advertising, consumers may have only been aware that products B and C were good substitutes for A. But advertising provides them with the knowledge that D, E, and F are also substitutable for A. As a consequence of the advertising of all firms in the industry, the demand curve of firm A shifts leftward, as from D_3 to D_4 in Figure 12-3b, and becomes more elastic. Both of these changes reflect enhanced competition.

3 Wasteful or Efficient? The traditional view contends that advertising is economically wasteful. First, it makes markets less competitive and therefore obstructs the realization of either allocative or productive efficiency. Second, advertising allegedly diverts human and property resources from higher-valued uses. For example, timber, which is sorely needed in the produc-

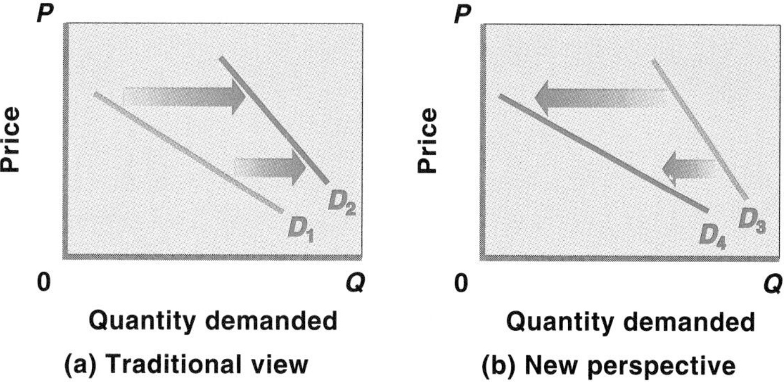

FIGURE 12-3 Advertising and a firm's demand curve: two views

The traditional view of advertising sees advertising as a device which increases the successful advertiser's market share and enhances brand loyalty. The result is greater market concentration as the demand curve of the successful advertiser shifts rightward and becomes more inelastic as shown by the D_1 to D_2 movement in panel (a). The new perspective regards advertising as a means of increasing consumer awareness of substitute products, thereby enhancing competition. Consequently, advertising in an industry will cause a firm's demand curve to shift leftward and become more elastic as portrayed by the movement from D_3 to D_4 in panel (b).

tion of housing, is squandered on unsightly billboards and on producing the paper used for the ubiquitous advertising supplements in local newspapers. Advertising allegedly constitutes an inefficient use of scarce resources. Finally, advertising expenditures contribute to higher costs which are ultimately reflected in higher prices to consumers.

The new perspective, as we have seen, views advertising as an efficiency-enhancing activity. It is an inexpensive means of providing useful information to consumers and thus lowers search costs. By enhancing competition advertising is conducive to both greater allocative and productive efficiency. Finally, by facilitating the successful introduction of new products advertising is conducive to technological progress.

Empirical Evidence

There are important empirical studies which lend credence to both of these views. For example, Comanor and Wilson have examined the role of advertising in forty-one industries manufacturing consumer goods. They concluded that advertising is generally anticompetitive. Specifically, they report that "the heavy volume of advertising expenditures in some industries serves as an important barrier to new competition in the markets served by these industries."[2] Prices of heavily advertised goods exceed their marginal costs, reflecting a misallocation of resources. Furthermore, for many of the studied industries expenditures for advertising were found to be "excessive" and wasteful of scarce resources.

In contrast, Eckard has concluded that advertising is a procompetitive force. He reasons that, if advertising promotes monopoly power, then industries which advertise most heavily should be the ones which increase their prices the most and their outputs the least over time (recall Figure 11-3). Examining price and output changes of some 150 major industries over the 1963–1977 period, Eckard found that generally those industries with higher-than-average levels of advertising had *lower*-than-average rates of price increases and had *higher*-than-average rates of output increase. Conclusion: Rather than contributing to monopoly power, advertising generally enhances competition.[3]

There are also other industry studies which suggest that advertising enhances competition and has economically desirable results. For example, a study of the eyeglasses industry compared prices in states where professional codes of ethics permitted optometrists to advertise with those where codes prohibited or restricted advertising. The conclusion was that prices of eyeglasses were 25 to 40 percent higher in states

[2]William S. Comanor and Thomas A. Wilson, *Advertising and Market Power* (Cambridge, Mass.: Harvard University Press, 1974), p. 239.

[3]E. Woodrow Eckard, Jr., "Advertising, Concentration, and Consumer Welfare," *Review of Economics and Statistics,* May 1988, pp. 340–343.

LAST WORD

THE MARKET FOR PRINCIPLES OF ECONOMICS TEXTBOOKS*

The market for principles texts embraces a number of the characteristics of monopolistic competition.

Currently there are fifty or more economics texts which could be used in the principles course. If you undertook the arduous task of comparing a number of them, you would find considerable differences. While there is some variation in subject matter, most leading texts cover the same core topics. Books do vary considerably as to the rigor and detail with which material is presented. They also vary as to reading level. Some books have a one-color format, others a multicolor presentation. Books vary greatly in the use of such pedagogical devices as photos, "boxed features," cartoons, learning objectives, intrachapter summaries, and glossaries. Publishers seek the mix of these features which will be most appealing to instructors and students.

Texts are also differentiated by their accompanying "packages" of ancillary materials. These include study guides, videos, and computer tutorial and simulation programs to aid student understanding. Instructor manuals, test banks, and overhead transparencies are designed to save instructor time and enhance teacher productivity. Were you to trace the introduction and development of these various pedagogical aids and instructional materials, you would find that when any one of them was introduced and proved attractive to adopters, that feature would be quickly incorporated into future editions of most other old and new books.

Product differentiation is accompanied by considerable nonprice competition. Texts are advertised by direct mail and in widely read economics journals. Publishers provide potential adopters with free copies and use "trade fair" booths at economics conventions to publicize their wares. Sales representatives of the various publishers—who receive bonuses for exceeding sales quotas—prowl the halls of academia to make

*Based on Timothy Tregarthen, "The Market for Principles of Economics Texts," *The Margin,* March 1987, pp. 14–15; and Joseph E. Stiglitz, "On the Market for Principles of Economics Textbooks: Innovation and Product Differentiation," *Journal of Economic Education,* Spring 1988, pp. 171–177.

where advertising was restricted.[4] A similar study of retail drug prices, comparing states where advertising was permitted with those in which it was not, found that prescription drug prices were about 5 percent lower in states which permitted advertising.[5] Finally, a study of the toy industry yielded the conclusion that television advertising had the effect of bringing about substantial price reductions:

> Advertising cuts distribution margins on advertised brands for two reasons: *first,* advertising causes goods to turn over rapidly so they can be sold profitably with smaller markups; and *second,* advertising creates product identity—which, in differentiated products, permits the public to compare prices between stores, thus setting a limit on the retailer's freedom to mark up. Products which are both heavily advertised and are fast sellers will be pulled through the distribution channels with the lowest markups of all.[6]

[4]Lee and Alexandra Benham, "Regulating the Professions: A Perspective on Information Control," *Journal of Law and Economics,* October 1975, pp. 421–447.

[5]John F. Cady, *Restricted Advertising and Competition: The Case of Retail Drugs* (Washington, D.C.: American Enterprise Institute, 1976).

[6]Robert L. Steiner, "Does Advertising Lower Consumer Prices?" *Journal of Marketing,* October 1973, p. 21.

professors aware of the distinguishing features and alleged advantages of their particular text. Over 1 million students take principles courses each year so the battle for market shares is vigorous.

Price competition probably plays a secondary role in the textbook market. First, unlike most markets, the product is chosen for the consumer by a second party. Your instructor—who gets a free text from the publisher and may not even be aware of its retail price—decides the text you must read for the course. Second, instructors usually put textbook quality above price. It would prove very costly to students to use an inaccurate, poorly written text which might impair the teaching-learning process. The significant exception is that over the years more and more instructors have opted for lower-priced paperbacks which split micro and macro components of the course. Thus, a student taking only one semester of economics can avoid the higher cost of a two-semester hardback.

While there are no artificial barriers to entering the market, the widespread use of multicolor formats and the obligation to provide an array of student-instructor ancillary items poses a significant financial barrier. It may take an investment of $1 million or more for a publisher to enter the market with a text and ancillaries comparable to those already on the market. Even so, it is not uncommon to find two or three new entries in the market every year.

In summary, the economics textbook market is characterized by product differentiation and nonprice competition. Price competition is muted and the only entry barrier is financial.

Evidence on the economic effects of advertising is mixed because studies are usually plagued by data problems and difficulties in determining cause and effect. Suppose it is found that firms which do a great deal of advertising seem to have considerable monopoly power and large profits. Does this mean that advertising creates barriers to entry which in turn generate monopoly power and profits? Or do entry barriers associated with factors remote from advertising cause monopoly profits which in turn allow firms to spend lavishly in advertising their products? In any event, at this time there is simply no consensus on the economic implications of advertising.

QUICK REVIEW 12-2

- ***Monopolistically competitive firms may seek economic profits through product differentiation, product development, and advertising.***
- ***The traditional view of advertising alleges that it is a persuasive rather than informative activity; it promotes economic concentration and monopoly power; and it is a source of economic waste and inefficiency.***
- ***According to the new perspective, advertising is a low-cost source of information for consumers; a means of increasing competition by making consumers aware of substitutable products; and a source of greater efficiency in the use of resources.***

Monopolistic Competition and Economic Analysis

Our discussion of nonprice competition correctly implies that the equilibrium situation of a monopolistically competitive firm is actually more complex than the previous graphical analysis indicates. Figure 12-1a, b, and c *assumes* a given product and a given level of advertising expenditures. But we now know these are not given in practice. The monopolistically competitive firm must actually juggle three variable factors—price, product, and promotion—in seeking maximum profits. What specific variety of product, selling at what price, and supplemented by what level of promotional activity, will result in the greatest level of profits attainable? This complex situation is not easily expressed in a simple, meaningful economic model. At best we can note that each possible combination of price, product, and promotion poses a different demand and cost (production plus promotion) situation for the firm, some one of which will allow it maximum profits. In practice, this optimal combination cannot be readily forecast but must be sought by trial and error. Even here, certain limitations may be imposed by the actions of rivals. A firm may not eliminate its advertising expenditures for fear its share of the market will decline sharply, benefiting its rivals who do advertise. Similarly, patents held by rivals will rule out certain desirable product variations.

CHAPTER SUMMARY

1 The distinguishing features of monopolistic competition are: **a** There are enough firms so that each has little control over price, mutual interdependence is absent, and collusion is virtually impossible; **b** products are characterized by real and perceived differences and by varying conditions surrounding their sale; **c** economic rivalry entails both price and nonprice competition; and **d** entry to the industry is relatively easy. Many aspects of retailing, and some industries where economies of scale are few, approximate monopolistic competition.
2 Monopolistically competitive firms may earn economic profits or incur losses in the short run. The easy entry and exodus of firms give rise to a tendency for them to earn a normal profit in the long run.
3 The long-run equilibrium position of the monopolistically competitive producer is less socially desirable than that of a purely competitive firm. Under monopolistic competition, price exceeds marginal cost, suggesting an underallocation of resources to the product, and price exceeds minimum average total cost, indicating that consumers do not get the product at the lowest price which cost conditions would allow. However, because the firm's demand curve is highly elastic, these "wastes" of monopolistic competition should not be overemphasized.
4 Product differentiation provides a means by which monopolistically competitive firms can offset the long-run tendency for economic profits to approximate zero. Through product development and advertising outlays, a firm may strive to increase the demand for its product more than nonprice competition increases its costs.
5 Although subject to certain dangers and problems, product differentiation affords the consumer a greater variety of products at any point in time and improved products over time. Whether these features fully compensate for the "wastes" of monopolistic competition is a complex and unresolved question.
6 The traditional and new perspective views of advertising differ as to whether advertising **a** is persuasive or informative, **b** promotes monopoly or competition, and **c** impairs or improves efficiency in resource use. Empirical evidence reveals no consensus as to whether advertising is an anti- or procompetitive force.
7 In practice the monopolistic competitor seeks that specific combination of price, product, and promotion which will maximize its profits.

TERMS AND CONCEPTS

monopolistic competition
product differentiation
traditional and new perspective views of advertising
wastes of monopolistic competition
nonprice competition

QUESTIONS AND STUDY SUGGESTIONS

1 How does monopolistic competition differ from pure competition? From pure monopoly? Explain fully what product differentiation entails.
2 Compare the elasticity of the monopolistically competitive producer's demand curve with that of **a** a pure competitor, and **b** a pure monopolist. Assuming identical long-run costs, compare graphically the prices and outputs which would result under pure competition and monopolistic competition. Contrast the two market structures in terms of allocative and productive efficiency. Explain: "Monopolistically competitive industries are characterized by too many firms, each of which produces too little."
3 "Monopolistic competition is monopoly up to the point at which consumers become willing to buy close-substitute products and competitive beyond that point." Explain.
4 "Competition in quality and in service may be quite as effective in giving the buyer more for her money as is price competition." Do you agree? Explain why monopolistically competitive firms frequently prefer nonprice to price competition.
5 Critically evaluate and explain:

a "In monopolistically competitive industries economic profits are competed away in the long run; hence, there is no valid reason to criticize the performance and efficiency of such industries."

b "In the long run monopolistic competition leads to a monopolistic price but not to monopolistic profits."

6 Compare the traditional and new perspective view of advertising. Which do you feel is more accurate?
7 Do you agree with the following statements?

a "The amount of advertising which a firm does is likely to vary inversely with the real differences in its product."

b "If each firm's advertising expenditures merely tend to cancel the effects of its rivals' advertising, it is clearly irrational for these firms to maintain large advertising budgets."

8 Carefully evaluate the two views expressed in the following statements:

a "It happens every day. Advertising builds mass demand. Production goes up—costs come down. More people can buy—more jobs are created. These are the ingredients of economic growth. Each stimulates the next in a cycle of productivity and plenty which constantly creates a better life for you."

b "Advertising constitutes 'inverted education'—a costly effort to induce people to buy without sufficient thought and deliberation and therefore to buy things they don't need. Furthermore, advertising outlays vary directly with the level of consumer spending."

Which view do you feel is the more accurate? Justify your position.

Chapter 13 Price and Output Determination: Oligopoly

In many of our manufacturing, mining, and wholesaling industries, a few firms are dominant. Such industries are called oligopolies. It is with these industries that the present chapter is concerned. Specifically, we have five objectives. (1) We first define oligopoly, assess its occurrence, and note the reasons for its existence. (2) Our major goal is to survey the possible courses of price-output behavior which oligopolistic industries might follow. (3) The role of nonprice competition, that is, competition based on product development and advertising, in oligopolistic industries is discussed. (4) Next, some comments on the economic efficiency and social desirability of oligopoly are offered. (5) Finally, many of the salient points just discussed are underscored in a brief case study of the automobile industry.

OLIGOPOLY: CONCEPT AND OCCURRENCE

What are the basic characteristics of oligopoly? How frequently is it encountered in our economy? Why has this industry structure developed?

Oligopoly Defined

Oligopoly exists when a few large firms, producing a homogeneous or differentiated product, dominate a market. "Fewness" means that the firms are mutually interdependent in that each must consider the possible reactions of its rivals to its price, advertising, and product development decisions.

But what specifically is meant by "a few" firms? This is necessarily vague, because the market model of oligopoly covers much ground, ranging between pure monopoly, on the one hand, and monopolistic competition, on the other. Thus oligopoly encompasses the aluminum industry, in which three firms dominate an entire national market, and the situation in which ten or fifteen gasoline stations may enjoy roughly equal shares of the petroleum products market in a medium-sized town. Generally, when we hear of the "Big Three," "Big Four" or "Big Six," we can be relatively certain that the indicated industry is oligopolistic.

Homogeneous or Differentiated Products Oligopolies may be **homogeneous** or **differentiated;** that is, the firms in an oligopolistic industry may produce standardized or differentiated products. Many industrial products—steel, zinc, copper, aluminum, lead, cement, industrial alcohol—are virtually standardized products in the physical sense and are produced under oligopolistic conditions. On the other hand, many consumer goods industries—automobiles, tires, detergents, greeting cards, breakfast cereals, cigarettes, and a host of household appliances—are differentiated oligopolies.

Concentration Ratios Economists often use **concentration ratios** as an approximate measure of the structure of an industry. The data in Table 13-1 show the four-firm concentration ratios—the percentage of total industry sales accounted for by the four largest firms—for a number of oligopolistic industries. Note, for example, that 90 percent of the cigarettes and 79 percent of the household detergents produced in the United States are manufactured by the four largest firms in each industry.

Generally, when the largest four firms control 40 percent or more of the total market, the industry is oligopolistic. Using this benchmark, roughly one-half of all United States manufacturing industries are oligopolies.

While concentration ratios provide useful insights on the competitiveness or monopolization of various industries, they are subject to several shortcomings.

1 Localized Markets Concentration ratios pertain to the nation as a whole, while relevant markets for some products are actually highly localized because of high transportation costs. For example, the concentration ratio for ready-mix concrete is only 6 percent, suggesting a highly competitive industry. But the sheer bulk of this product limits the relevant market to a given town or metropolitan area and in such localized markets we typically find oligopolistic suppliers. We have already suggested that, at the local level, some aspects of the retail trade—particularly in small- and medium-sized towns—are characterized by oligopoly.

2 Interindustry Competition Definitions of industries are somewhat arbitrary and we must be aware of **interindustry competition,** that is, competition between two products associated with different industries. Table 13-1's high concentration ratios for the aluminum and copper industries understate the degree of competition because aluminum and copper compete in many applications—for example, in the market for electrical transmission lines.

3 World Trade The data are for American products and therefore often overstate monopoly power because they do not take into account the **import competition** of foreign suppliers. The automobile industry is a highly relevant illustration. While Table 13-1 tells us that four American firms account for 92 percent of the domestic production of motor vehicles, it ignores the fact that about 35 percent of the automobiles purchased in the United States are imports.

4 Herfindahl Index Another problem associated with concentration ratios is that they fail to measure accurately the distribution of market power among the several dominant firms. For example, suppose that in the long-distance telephone industry one firm controlled all service. In a second industry—say, the automobile industry—assume four firms exist and each has 25 percent of the market. For both industries the four-firm concentration ratio would be 100 percent. But the telecommunications industry would be a pure monopoly, while the auto industry would be an oligopoly

TABLE 13-1 Concentration ratios in selected high-concentration manufacturing industries

Industry	*Percentage of industry output* produced by four largest firms*
Primary lead	100
Household refrigerators and freezers	94
Motor vehicles	92
Household laundry equipment	91
Electric lamps (bulbs)	91
Cigarettes	90
Small arms ammunition	87
Primary copper	87
Cereal breakfast foods	86
Flat glass	85
Greeting card publishing	84
Turbines and generators	84
Household vacuum cleaners	80
Household detergents	79
Beer and malt beverages	77
Telephones	76
Gypsum products	76
Sewing machines	72
Tires and inner tubes	66
Primary aluminum	64
Aircraft	64

*As measured by value of shipments. Data are for 1982.

Source: Bureau of the Census. *Concentration Ratios in Manufacturing.*

characterized perhaps by significant economic rivalry. Most economists would agree that market power would be substantially greater in the telecommunications than in the auto industry, a fact not reflected in the identical 100 percent concentration ratios.

The **Herfindahl index** deals with this problem. This index is *the sum of the squared market shares of each firm in the industry.* By squaring the market shares, much greater weight is given to larger firms than smaller ones. In the hypothetical case of the single-firm telecommunications industry, the index would be 100^2 or 10,000. For the supposed four-firm auto industry the index would be $25^2 + 25^2 + 25^2 + 25^2$ or 2500. To generalize, the larger the Herfindahl index, the greater the degree of market power within an industry. As we will find in Chapter 20, antitrust officials sometimes use the Herfindahl index in deciding whether to approve or reject proposed corporate mergers.

5 Performance Finally, concentration ratios tell us nothing about the actual market performance of various industries. Industries X and Y may have identical four-firm concentration ratios of 85 percent. Industry X may be characterized by vigorous price competition and technological progress, evidenced by improved product and production techniques. In contrast, firms of industry Y may price their products collusively and be technologically stagnant. From society's viewpoint the "competitive" performance of industry X is clearly superior to the "monopolistic" performance of Y, a fact concealed by the identical concentration ratios.

Underlying Causes

Why are certain industries composed of only a few firms? The answer lies primarily in cost economies, other barriers to entry, and mergers.

Economies of Scale We saw in Chapter 9 that, where economies of scale are substantial (see Figure 9-9b), reasonably efficient production will be possible only with a small number of producers. In other words, efficiency requires that the productive capacity of each firm be large relative to the total market. Indeed, it is an unstable situation for an industry to have a large number of high-cost firms, each of which is failing to realize existing economies of scale.

In Figure 9-7, for example, a firm currently operating with the small and inefficient plant size indicated by ATC-1 will recognize that this short-run position is unsatisfactory; it can realize substantially lower unit costs and a larger profit by expanding its plant to ATC-2. The same can be said for the move to ATC-3. However, given a reasonably stable market demand, all the many firms with small (ATC-1) plant sizes cannot now survive. Profitable expansion to larger plant sizes by some will necessarily come at the expense of rivals. The realization of economies of scale by some firms implies that the number of rival producers is simultaneously being reduced through failure or merger.

Historically, in many industries technological progress has made more and more economies of scale attainable over time. Many industries started out with a primitive technology, few economies of scale, and many competitors. But as technology improved and economies of scale became increasingly pronounced, the less alert or less aggressive firms fell by the wayside and a few producers emerged. For example, estimates suggest that over eighty firms populated the automobile industry in its infancy. Over the years, development of mass-production techniques reduced the field through failure and combination. Now the Big Three—General Motors, Ford, and Chrysler—account for over 90 percent of domestically produced automobile sales.

Why aren't new firms created to enter the automobile industry? The answer is that to achieve the low unit costs essential to survival, any new entrants must necessarily start out as large producers. This may require several billions of dollars worth of investment in machinery and equipment alone. Economies of scale can be a formidable barrier to entry. They explain not only the evolution of oligopoly in many industries, but also why such industries are not likely to become more competitive. However, recall from Chapter 9's Last Word that the degree of concentration in many industries exceeds that warranted by economies of scale.

Other Barriers The development or persistence of some oligopolies can be traced at least in part to other entry barriers. In the electronics, chemical, and aluminum industries, ownership of patents and control of strategic raw materials have been important. And prodigious advertising outlays may be an added financial barrier to entry, as some economists argue has been the case in the cigarette industry.

The Urge to Merge The final factor in explaining oligopoly or fewness is merger. The motivation for merger has diverse roots. Of immediate relevance is the fact that the combining of two or more formerly competing firms by merger may increase their market share substantially, enabling the new and larger production unit to achieve greater economies of scale.

Another significant motive underlying the "urge to merge" is the market power which may accompany merger. A firm that is larger both absolutely and relative to the market may have greater ability to control the market for, and the price of, its product than does a smaller, more competitive producer. Also, the large size which merger entails may give the firm the advantage of being a "big buyer" and permit it to demand and obtain lower prices (costs) from input suppliers than previously.

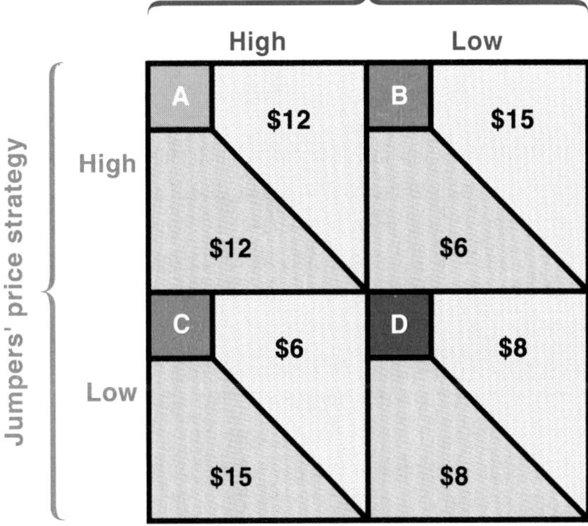

FIGURE 13-1 The profit payoffs for a two-firm oligopoly

Both firms would realize the largest profit of $12 million if each adhered to a high-price policy (cell A). But if they are acting independently or competitively, either might achieve a higher profit of $15 million by adopting a low-price policy against its rival's high-price policy (cells B and C). Such independent pricing causes the outcome to gravitate to cell D, where profits are only $8 million. Collusion can be used to establish mutual high prices and increase each firm's profits from $8 million (cell D) to $12 million (cell A). But cells B and C remind us of the temptation to cheat on a collusive agreement.

OLIGOPOLY BEHAVIOR: A GAME THEORY OVERVIEW

Oligopoly pricing behavior has the characteristics of a game of strategy such as poker, chess, or bridge. The best way to play your hand in a poker game depends on the way rivals play theirs. Players must pattern their actions according to the actions and expected reactions of rivals. Let's use a simple **game theory model** to grasp the basics of oligopolistic pricing behavior. To simplify we assume a **duopoly**—a two-firm oligopoly—exists.

Consider Figure 13-1 which shows the price-profit or profit-payoffs matrix for two firms which produce athletic shoes. Pricing policies or strategies for the firms—say, Leapers and Jumpers—are shown along the top and left margins, respectively. Entries in the matrix show the profit payoffs to the two firms associated with any given combination of pricing strategies. Leapers' profit (in millions) is shown in the northeast gold portion of each cell and Jumpers' profit is in the southwest green portion. For example, if both firms adopt a high-price strategy (cell A), each will realize a $12 million profit. Alternatively, if Jumpers follows a high-price policy and Leapers a low-price policy (cell B), Jumpers profit will be only $6 million and Leapers' will be $15 million.

Although the data of Figure 13-1 are hypothetical, the profit figures are not arbitrarily chosen. In reality, if Jumpers committed itself to a high price and did not vary from it, Leapers could increase its profits by choosing a low price and gaining market share at Jumpers' expense. The same rationale applies if Leapers commits to a high price and Jumpers opts for a low price.

Mutual Interdependence

The most evident point demonstrated by Figure 13-1 is the **mutual interdependence** of oligopolists. Each firm's profits will depend not only on its own pricing strategy, but also on that of its rivals. As we have just observed, if Jumpers adopts a high-price policy, its profit will be $12 million *provided* Leapers also employs a high-price strategy (cell A). But if Leapers uses a low-price strategy against Jumpers' high-price strategy (cell B), Leapers will increase its market share and thereby its profits from $12 to $15 million. Leapers' higher profits come at the expense of Jumpers, whose profits fall from $12 to $6 million. Jumpers' high-price strategy is only a "good" strategy *if* Leapers employs the same strategy. Indeed, a good, workable definition of oligopoly is that *oligopoly exists when the number of firms in an industry is so small that each must consider the reactions of rivals in formulating its price policy.*

Collusive Tendencies

A second point is that oligopoly often leads to **collusion,** meaning some sort of formal or informal arrangement to coordinate pricing strategies or fix prices. To illustrate in terms of Figure 13-1, suppose that initially both firms are independently following high-price strategies. Each realizes a $12 million profit (cell A).

Observe that *either* Leapers or Jumpers could increase its profits by switching to a low-price strategy (cell B or C). If Leapers uses a low-price strategy against Jumpers' high-price strategy, its profits will increase to $15 million and Jumpers' will fall to $6 million. But by comparing cells B and D, we note that when Leapers shifts to a low-price policy, Jumpers would be better off if it also adopted a low-price policy. By doing so its profit would increase from $6 million (cell B) to $8 million (cell D).

Similarly, starting again at cell A, if Jumpers switched to a low-price policy against Leapers' high-price strategy, Jumpers' profit would increase to $15 million and Leapers' would fall to $6 million (cell C). And, again, Leapers could increase its profit from $6 (cell C) to $8 million (cell D) by also switching to a low-price policy.

What we find is that independent action by oligopolists will likely lead to mutual "competitive" low-price strategies. Independent oligopolists compete with respect to price and this leads to lower prices and lower profits. This is clearly beneficial to consumers, but not to the oligopolists who experience lower profits than if both had used high-price strategies (cell A).

How can oligopolists avoid the low-profit outcome of cell D? The answer is *not* to establish prices competitively or independently, but rather to collude. Specifically, the two firms must agree to establish and maintain a high-price policy. Each firm thus will increase its profits from $8 million (cell D) to $12 million (cell A). We will discuss a variety of specific collusive practices later in this chapter.

Incentive to Cheat

The payoff matrix also explains why an oligopolist might be strongly tempted to cheat on a collusive agreement. Suppose that as a result of collusion Jumpers and Leapers both agree to high-price policies with each earning $12 million in profits (cell A). The temptation to cheat on this pricing agreement arises because either firm can increase its profits to $15 million by lowering its price (cell B or C). If Jumpers agrees to a high-price policy but secretly "cheats" on that agreement by actually charging low prices, the outcome moves from cell A to cell C. Result? Jumpers' profit rises to $15 million and Leapers' falls to $6 million. The same reasoning applies to Leapers, which could move the outcome from cell A to cell B by cheating.

QUICK REVIEW 13-1

- ***Oligopolistic industries comprise a "few" firms producing either homogeneous or differentiated products.***
- ***The four-firm concentration ratio shows the percentage of an industry's sales accounted for by the four largest firms; the Herfindahl index measures the degree of market power in an industry by summing the squares of the market shares held by each firm.***
- ***Oligopolies result from scale economies, the control of patents or strategic resources, or mergers.***
- ***Game theory reveals that a oligopolies are mutually interdependent in their pricing policies; b collusion will enhance oligopoly profits; and c there is a persistent temptation for oligopolists to cheat on a collusive agreement.***

FOUR OLIGOPOLY MODELS

To gain further insights on oligopolistic price-output behavior we will examine four rather distinct models: (1) the kinked demand curve, (2) collusive pricing, (3) price leadership, and (4) cost-plus pricing.

Why not a single model as in our discussions of the other market structures? There is no standard portrait of oligopoly for two major reasons.

1 Oligopoly encompasses a greater range and diversity of market situations than other market structures. It includes "tight oligopoly" in which two or three firms dominate an entire market, as well as the "loose oligopoly" in which six or seven firms share, say, 70 or 80 percent of a market while a "competitive fringe" of firms share the remainder. It includes both product differentiation and standardization. It encompasses cases where firms act in collusion and those where they act independently. It embodies situations in which barriers to entry are very strong and those in which they are not quite so strong. In short, the diversity of oligopoly precludes development of a simple market

model which provides a general explanation of oligopolistic behavior.

2 The element of mutual interdependence added by fewness is a significant complication. The inability of a firm to predict with certainty the reactions of its rivals makes it virtually impossible to estimate the demand and marginal-revenue data faced by an oligopolist. Without such data, firms cannot determine their profit-maximizing price and output even in theory, as we will presently see.

Despite these analytical difficulties, two interrelated characteristics of oligopolistic pricing have been observed. First, oligopolistic prices are inflexible, or "sticky." Prices change less frequently in oligopoly than under pure competition, monopolistic competition, and in some instances, pure monopoly. Second, when oligopolistic prices do change, firms are likely to change their prices together; oligopolistic price behavior suggests the presence of incentives to act in concert or collusively in setting and changing prices.

Kinked Demand: Noncollusive Oligopoly

Imagine an oligopolistic industry comprising just three firms, A, B, and C, each having about one-third of the total market for a differentiated product. Assume the firms are "independent" in that they do not engage in collusive practices in setting prices. Suppose, too, that the going price for firm A's product is PQ and its current sales are Q, as shown in Figure 13-2a.

Now the question is, "What does the firm's demand, or sales, curve look like?" Mutual interdependence, and the uncertainty of rivals' reactions which interdependence entails, make this question difficult to answer. The location and shape of an oligopolist's demand curve depend on how the firm's rivals will react to a price change introduced by A. There are two plausible assumptions about the reactions of A's rivals.

Match Price Changes One possibility is that firms B and C will exactly match any price change initiated by A. In this case, A's demand and marginal-revenue curves will look like D_1D_1 and MR_1MR_1 in Figure 13-2a. If A cuts price, its sales will increase very modestly, because its two rivals will follow suit to prevent A from gaining any price advantage over them. The small increase in sales which A (and its two rivals) will realize is at the expense of other industries; A will gain no sales from B and C. If A raises the going price, its sales will fall only modestly, because B and C match its price increase, so A does not price itself out of the market. The industry now loses some sales to other industries, but A loses no customers to B and C.

Ignore Price Changes The other possibility is that firms B and C will ignore any price change invoked by A. In this case, the demand and marginal-revenue curves faced by A will resemble D_2D_2 and MR_2MR_2 in Figure 13-2a. The demand curve in this case is considerably more elastic than under the assumption that B and C will match A's price changes. The reasons are clear. If A lowers its price and its rivals do not, A will gain sales significantly at the expense of its two rivals because it will be underselling them. Conversely, if A raises its price and its rivals do not, A will lose many customers to B and C, which are now underselling it. Because of product differentiation, however, A's sales do not fall to zero when it raises its price; some of A's customers will pay the higher price because they have strong preferences for A's product.

A Mixed Strategy Now, which is the most logical assumption for A to make on how its rivals will react to any price change it might initiate? The answer is "some of each"! Common sense and observation of oligopolistic industries suggest that price declines will be matched as a firm's competitors act to prevent the price cutter from taking their customers. But price increases will be ignored, because rivals of the price-increasing firm stand to gain the business lost by the price booster. In other words, the dark blue D_2P segment of the "rivals ignore" demand curve seems relevant for price increases, and the dark blue PD_1 segment of the "rivals follow" demand curve is more realistic for price cuts. It is logical, or at least a good guess, that an oligopolist faces a **"kinked" demand curve** like D_2PD_1 as shown in Figure 13-2b. (Ignore the MC_1 and MC_2 curves for now.) The curve is highly elastic above the going price, but much less elastic or even inelastic below the current price.

Note also that if it is correct to suppose that rivals will follow a price cut but ignore an increase, the marginal-revenue curve of the oligopolist will also have an odd shape. It, too, will be made up of two segments—the brown MR_2f part of the marginal-revenue curve appropriate to D_2D_2 and the brown gMR_1 chunk of the marginal-revenue curve appropriate to D_1D_1 in Figure 13-2a. Because of the sharp differences in elasticity of demand above and below the going price, there is a gap, or what we can treat as a vertical segment, in the

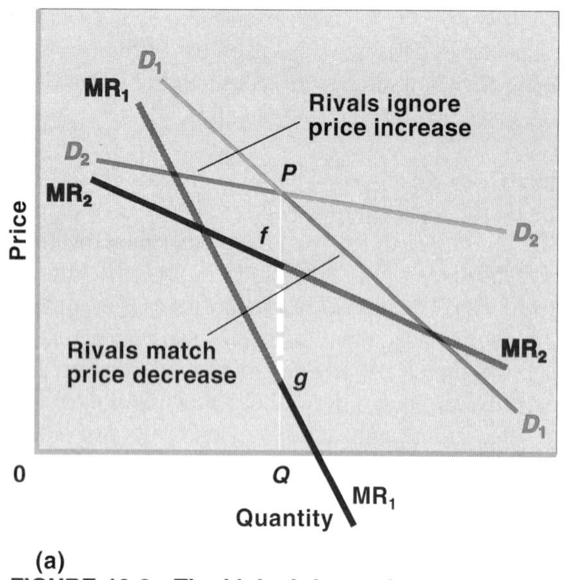

(a)

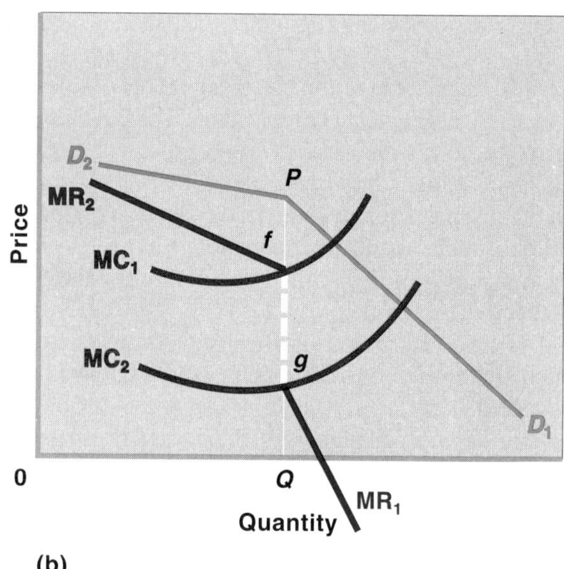

(b)

FIGURE 13-2 The kinked demand curve

The nature of a noncollusive oligopolist's demand and marginal-revenue curves as shown in (a) will depend on whether its rivals will match (D_1D_1 and MR_1MR_1) or ignore (D_2D_2 and MR_2MR_2) any price changes which it may initiate from the current price *PQ*. In all likelihood an oligopolist's rivals will ignore a price increase but follow a price cut. This causes the oligopolist's demand curve to be kinked (D_2PD_1) and the marginal-revenue curve to have a vertical break, or gap (*fg*) as shown in (b). Furthermore, because any shift in marginal costs between MC_1 and MC_2 will cut the vertical (dashed) segment of the marginal-revenue curve, no change in either price *PQ* or output *Q* will occur.

marginal-revenue curve. In Figure 13-2b the marginal-revenue curve is shown by the two brown lines connected by the dashed vertical segment, or gap.

Price Inflexibility This analysis goes far to explain why price changes may be infrequent in noncollusive oligopolistic industries.

1 The kinked-demand schedule gives each oligopolist good reason to believe that any change in price will be for the worse. Many of a firm's customers will desert it if it raises its price. If it lowers its price, its sales at best will increase very modestly. Even if a price cut increases its total revenue somewhat, the oligopolist's costs may well increase by a more-than-offsetting amount. If the brown PD_1 segment of its sales schedule is *inelastic* in that E_d is less than 1, the firm's profits will surely fall. A price decrease will lower the firm's total revenue, and the production of a somewhat larger output will increase total costs.

Worse yet, a price cut by A may be *more* than met by B and C; A's initial price cut may precipitate a **price war;** so the amount sold by A may actually decline as its rivals charge still lower prices. These are all good reasons on the demand side of the picture why noncollusive oligopolies might follow live-and-let-live or don't-upset-the-applecart price policies. If the resulting profits are satisfactory to the several firms at the existing price, it may seem prudent to them not to alter that price.

2 The other reason for price inflexibility under noncollusive oligopoly works from the cost side of the picture. The broken marginal-revenue curve accompanying the kinked demand curve suggests that, within limits, substantial cost changes will have no effect on output and price. Any shift in marginal cost between MC_1 and MC_2 as shown in Figure 13-2b will result in no change in price or output; MR will continue to equal MC at output *Q* at which price *PQ* will be charged.

Shortcomings The kinked-demand analysis has two major criticisms. First, *it does not explain how the going price gets to be at PQ (Figure 13-2) in the first place.* Rather, it only helps to explain why oligopolists may be reluctant to deviate from an existing price which yields them a "satisfactory" or "reasonable" profit. The kinked demand curve explains price inflexibility but not price itself.

Second, oligopoly prices are not as rigid—particularly in an upward direction—as the kinked-demand theory implies. During inflationary periods such as the 1970s and the early 1980s, oligopolistic producers raised their prices frequently and substantially. Such price increases might be better explained in terms of collusive oligopoly.

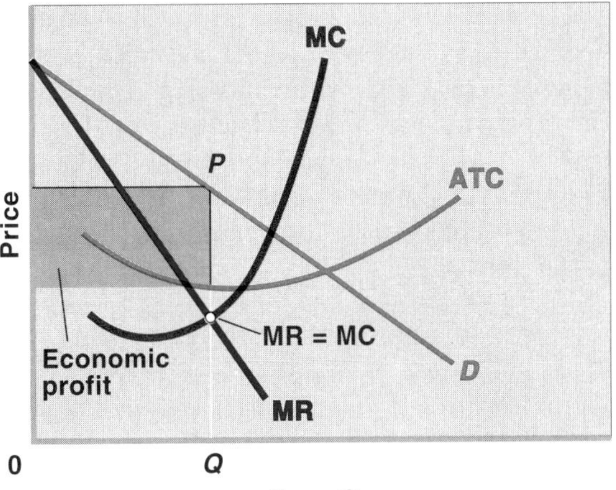

FIGURE 13-3 Collusion and the tendency toward joint-profit maximization

If oligopolistic firms face identical or highly similar demand and cost conditions, they may choose to behave collusively and maximize joint profits. The price and output results are essentially the same as those of pure (unregulated) monopoly; each oligopolist charges price *PQ* and produces output *Q*.

Collusion and Cartels

Our game theory model has suggested that oligopoly is conducive to collusion. *Collusion* occurs when firms in an industry reach an overt or covert agreement to fix prices, divide or share the market, or otherwise restrict competition among themselves. The disadvantages and uncertainties of the noncollusive, kinked-demand model to producers are obvious. There is always the danger of a price war breaking out. In particular, in a general business recession each firm will find itself with excess capacity, and can reduce per unit costs by increasing its market share. Then, too, a new firm may surmount entry barriers and initiate aggressive price cutting to gain a foothold in the market. In addition, the kinked demand curve's tendency toward rigid prices may adversely affect profits if general inflationary pressures increase costs. Stated differently, collusive control over price may permit oligopolists to reduce uncertainty, increase profits, and perhaps even prohibit entry of new rivals.

Price and Output Where will price and output be established under **collusive oligopoly?** Assume once again there are three firms—A, B, and C—producing in this instance homogeneous products. Each firm has identical cost curves. Each firm's demand curve is indeterminate unless we know how its rivals will react to any price change. Therefore, suppose each firm assumes its two rivals will match either a price cut or a price increase. In other words, each firm's demand curve is of the D_1D_1 type in Figure 13-2a. Assume further that the demand curve for each firm is identical. Given identical cost and identical demand and marginal revenue data, we can say that Figure 13-3 represents the position of each of our three oligopolistic firms.

What price and output combination should each firm choose? If firm A were a pure monopolist, the answer would be clear: Establish output at *Q*, where marginal revenue equals marginal cost, charge the corresponding price *PQ*, and enjoy the maximum profit attainable. However, firm A *does* have two rivals selling identical products, and if A's assumption that its rivals will match its price proves to be incorrect, the consequences could be disastrous for A. Specifically, if B and C actually charge prices below *PQ*, then firm A's demand curve will shift sharply to the left as its potential customers turn to its rivals, which are now selling the same product at a lower price. Of course, A can retaliate by cutting its price too; but this will move all three firms down their demand curves, lowering their profits, and perhaps even driving them to some point where average cost exceeds price and losses are incurred.

So the question becomes, "Will B and C want to charge a price below *PQ*?" Under our assumptions, and recognizing that A will have little choice except to match any price they may set below *PQ*, the answer is "No." Faced with the same demand and cost circumstances, B and C will find it in their interest to produce *Q* and charge *PQ*. This is a curious situation; each firm finds it most profitable to charge the same price *PQ*, but only if its rivals will actually do so! How can the three firms realize the *PQ*-price and *Q*-quantity solution in which each is keenly interested? How can this be made a reality so that all three can avoid the less profitable outcomes associated with either higher or lower prices?

The answer is evident: The firms will all be motivated to collude—to "get together and talk it over"—and agree to charge the same price *PQ*. In addition to reducing the omnipresent possibility of price warring, each firm will obtain the maximum profit. And for society, the result is the same as if the industry were a pure monopoly composed of three identical plants (see Chapter 11).

Overt Collusion: the OPEC Cartel Collusion may assume a variety of forms. The most comprehensive form of collusion is the **cartel** which typically involves a formal written agreement with respect to both price and production. Output must be controlled—that is, the market must be shared—to maintain the agreed-upon price.

The most spectacularly successful international cartel of recent decades has been OPEC (the Organization of Petroleum Exporting Countries). Comprising thirteen nations, OPEC was extremely effective in the 1970s in restricting oil supply and raising prices. The cartel was able to raise world oil prices from $2.50 to $11.00 per barrel within a six-month period in 1973–1974. By early 1980 price hikes had brought the per barrel price into the $32 to $34 range. The result was enormous profits for cartel members, a substantial stimulus to worldwide inflation, and serious international trade deficits for oil importers.

OPEC was highly effective in the 1970s for several reasons. First, it dominated the world market for oil. If a nation imported oil, it was almost obligated to do business with OPEC. Second, world demand for oil was strong and expanding in the 1970s. Finally, the "short-run" demand for oil was highly inelastic because the economies of oil-importing nations such as the United States were locked into gas-guzzling automobiles and energy-intensive housing and capital equipment. This inelasticity meant that a small restriction of output by OPEC would result in a relatively large price increase. Thus, as shown in Figure 13-4, in 1973–1974 and again in 1979–1980 OPEC was able to achieve dramatic increases in oil prices and only incur a very modest decline in sales. Given this inelastic demand, higher prices meant greatly increased total revenues to OPEC members. The accompanying smaller output meant lower total costs. The combination of more total revenue and lower total costs resulted in greatly expanded profits. (We discuss the serious weakening of the OPEC cartel in the 1980s later in this chapter.)

FIGURE 13-4 The OPEC cartel and the world oil market

Because of the inelasticity of the demand for oil, in 1973–1974 and again in 1979–1980 the OPEC cartel was able to obtain a dramatic increase in the price of oil (P_1 to P_2) accompanied by only a very modest decline in production and sales (Q_1 to Q_2). Total revenue thus rose.

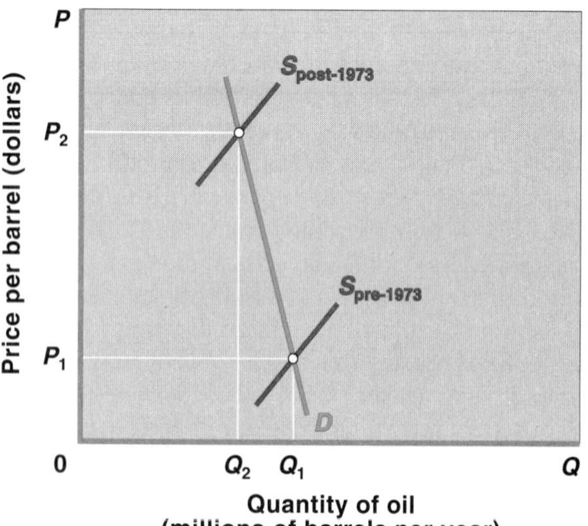

Covert Collusion: The Electrical Equipment Conspiracy Cartels are illegal in the United States and hence collusion has been covert or secret. In 1960 an extensive price-fixing and market-sharing scheme involving heavy electrical equipment such as transformers, turbines, circuit breakers, and switchgear was uncovered. Elaborate covert schemes were developed by such participants as General Electric, Westinghouse, and Allis-Chalmers to rig prices and divide the market.

> The manner in which prices were fixed, bids controlled, and markets allocated may be illustrated by *power switch gear assemblies* . . . five companies and twelve individuals were involved. It was charged that at least twenty-five meetings were held between the middle of November 1958 and October 1959 in various parts of the country. . . .
>
> At these periodic meetings, a scheme or formula for quoting nearly identical prices to electric utility companies, private industrial corporations and contractors was used by defendant corporations, designated by their representatives as a "phase of the moon" or "light of the moon" formula. Through cyclic rotating positioning inherent in the formula one defendant corporation would quote the low price, others would quote intermediate prices and another would quote the high price; these positions would be periodically rotated among the defendant corporations. . . . This formula was designed to permit each

> defendant corporation to know the exact price it and every other defendant corporation would quote on each prospective sale.
>
> At these periodic meetings, a cumulative list of sealed bid business secured by all of the defendant corporations was also circulated and the representatives present would compare the relative standing of each corporation according to its agreed upon percentage of the total sales pursuant to sealed bids. The representatives present would then discuss particular future bid invitations and designate which defendant corporation should submit the lowest bid therefore, the amount of such bid, and the amount of the bid to be submitted by others.[1]

Twenty-nine manufacturers and forty-six company officials were indicted in this "great electrical conspiracy" which violated our antitrust laws. Substantial fines, jail penalties, and lawsuits by victimized buyers were the final outcome.

In innumerable other instances collusion is even more subtle. **Gentlemen's agreements** frequently are struck at cocktail parties, on the golf course, or at trade association meetings where competing firms reach a verbal agreement on product price, leaving market shares to the ingenuity of each seller as reflected in nonprice competition. Although they too collide with the antitrust laws, the elusive character of gentlemen's agreements makes them more difficult to detect and prosecute successfully.

Obstacles to Collusion In practice cartels and similar collusive arrangements are difficult to establish and maintain. Let's briefly consider several important barriers to collusion.

1 Demand and Cost Differences When oligopolists' costs and product demands differ, it is more difficult to agree on price. Where products are differentiated and changing frequently over time, this would be the case. Indeed, even with highly standardized products, we would expect that firms might have somewhat different market shares and would operate with differing degrees of productive efficiency. Thus it is likely that even homogeneous oligopolists would have different demand and cost curves.

In either event, differences in costs and demand will mean that the profit-maximizing price for each firm will differ, there will be no single price readily acceptable to all. Price collusion therefore depends on the ability to achieve compromises and concessions—to arrive at a degree of "understanding" which in practice is often difficult to attain. For example, the MR = MC positions of firms A, B, and C may call for them to charge \$12, \$11, and \$10 respectively, but this price cluster or range may be unsatisfactory to one or more of the firms. Firm A may feel that differences in product quality justify only a \$1.50, rather than a \$2, price differential between its product and that of firm C. In short, cost and demand differences make it difficult for oligopolists to agree on a single price or a "proper" cluster of prices; these differentials are therefore an obstacle to collusion.

2 Number of Firms Other things being equal, the larger the number of firms, the more difficult it is to achieve a cartel or other form of price collusion. Agreement on price by three or four producers that control an entire market is much more readily accomplished than it is when ten firms each have roughly 10 percent of the market, or where the Big Three have, say, 70 percent of the market, while a "competitive fringe" of eight or ten smaller firms battles for the remainder.

3 Cheating As our game theory model made clear, there is a more-or-less persistent temptation for collusive oligopolists to engage in clandestine price cutting, that is, to make secret price concessions to get additional business.

The difficulty with cheating is that buyers paying a high price may get wind of the lower-priced sales and demand similar treatment. Or buyers receiving price concessions from one oligopolist may use this concession as a wedge to get even larger price concessions from the firm's rivals. The attempt of buyers to play sellers against one another may precipitate price warring among the firms. In short, although it is potentially profitable, secret price concessions threaten the maintenance of collusive oligopoly over time. Collusion is more likely to persist when cheating is deterred because it is easy to detect and punish.

4 Recession Recession is usually an enemy of collusion because slumping markets increase average costs. In technical terms, as the oligopolists' demand and marginal-revenue curves shift to the left (Figure 13-3), each firm moves back to a higher point on its average-cost curve. Firms find they have substantial excess productive capacity, sales are down, unit costs are up, and profits are being squeezed. Under these

[1]Jules Backman, *The Economics of the Electrical Machinery Industry* (New York: New York University Press, 1962), pp. 135–138, abridged. Reprinted by permission.

conditions, businesses may feel they can better avoid serious profit reductions by price cutting in the hope of gaining sales at the expense of rivals.

5 Potential Entry The enhanced prices and profits which result from collusion may attract new entrants, including foreign firms. Such entry would increase market supply and reduce prices and profits. Therefore, successful collusion requires that colluding oligopolists can block entry of new producers.

6 Legal Obstacles: Antitrust Our antitrust laws (Chapter 10) prohibit cartels and the kind of price-fixing collusion we have been discussing. Therefore, less obvious means of price rigging—such as price leadership—have evolved in the United States.

OPEC in Disarray The highly successful OPEC oil cartel of the 1970s fell into disarray in the 1980s. The reasons for OPEC's decline relate closely to the obstacles to collusion we have just enumerated.

First, the dramatic runup of oil prices in the 1970s stimulated the search for new oil reserves, and soon non-OPEC nations, which OPEC could not block from entering world markets, became part of the world oil industry. Great Britain, Norway, Mexico, and the former Soviet Union have all become major world oil suppliers. As a result, OPEC's share of world oil production fell sharply.

Second, on the demand side, oil conservation, worldwide recession in the early 1980s, and expanded use of alternative energy sources (such as coal, natural gas, and nuclear power) all reduced the demand for oil. The combination of greater production by non-OPEC nations and a decline in world demand generated an "oil glut" and seriously impaired OPEC's ability to control world oil prices.

Third, OPEC has had a serious cheating problem stemming from the relatively large number of members (thirteen) and the diversity of their economic circumstances. Saudi Arabia is the dominant cartel member; it has the largest oil reserves and is probably the lowest-cost producer. Saudi Arabia has favored a "moderate" pricing policy because it has feared that very high oil prices would hasten development of alternative energy sources (such as solar power and synthetic fuels) and increase the attractiveness of existing substitutes such as coal and natural gas. These developments would greatly reduce the value of its vast oil reserves. Saudi Arabia also has a small population and a very high per capita domestic output. But other members—for example, Nigeria and Venezuela—are very poor, have large populations, and are burdened with large external debts. Still others—Iran, Iraq, and Libya—have had large military commitments. All of these members have had immediate needs for cash. Hence, there has been substantial cheating whereby some members have exceeded assigned production quotas and have sold oil at prices below those agreed to by the cartel. Thus, although OPEC's official oil price reached $34 per barrel in 1979, it is currently about $17 per barrel.

Price Leadership

Price leadership is a type of gentlemen's agreement by which oligopolists can coordinate their price behavior without engaging in outright collusion. Formal agreements and clandestine meetings are ***not*** involved. Rather, a practice evolves whereby the "dominant" firm—usually the largest or the most efficient in the industry—initiates price changes, and all other firms more-or-less automatically follow that price change. The importance of price leadership is evidenced in the fact that such industries as farm machinery, anthracite coal, cement, copper, gasoline, newsprint, tin cans, lead, sulfur, rayon, fertilizer, glass containers, steel, automobiles, and nonferrous metals are practicing, or have in the recent past practiced, price leadership.

Cigarette Pricing Consider the cigarette industry, a classic example of tight price leadership. In this instance the Big Three, producing from 68 to 90 percent of total output, evolved a highly profitable practice of price leadership which resulted in virtually identical prices over the entire 1923 to 1941 period.

> In 1918 American Tobacco tried to lead a price rise, but Reynolds (the largest seller) refused to follow. In 1921, American cut its price and Reynolds retaliated with a further cut, which American and the other sellers matched. This experience apparently had a profound educational impact on American and the other major brand sellers, none of whom challenged Reynolds' leadership again for a decade. Between 1923 and 1941, virtual price identity prevailed continuously among the Big Three's standard brands, although certain other cigarettes of similar size and quality sold in smaller quantities at premium prices, and premium-priced Philip Morris grew through heavy advertising to a 6 percent market share. During this period there were eight standard brand list price changes. Reynolds led six of them, five upward and one downward, and was followed each time, in

> most cases within twenty-four hours of its announcement. The other two changes were downward revisions during 1933 led by American and followed by the other standard brand vendors. American also attempted to lead a price increase in 1941, but Reynolds again refused to follow and the change was rescinded. Throughout this period, the return on invested capital realized by Reynolds, American, and Ligget & Myers averaged 18 percent after taxes—roughly double the rate earned by American manufacturing industry as a whole.[2]

Since 1946 cigarette pricing has been somewhat less rigid, reflecting both successful antitrust action and the development of increasingly heterogeneous product lines. But overall there has been little evidence of enhanced price rivalry.

Leadership Tactics The examination of price leadership in a variety of industries suggests that the price leader is likely to observe the following tactics.

1 Because price changes always carry some risk that rivals will not follow, price adjustments will be made infrequently. The price leader will *not* respond pricewise to minuscule day-to-day changes in cost and demand conditions. Price will be changed only when cost and demand conditions have been altered significantly and on an industry-wide basis by, for example, industrywide wage increases, an increase in taxes, or an increase in the price of some basic input such as energy. In the automobile industry price adjustments traditionally have been made when new models are introduced each fall.

2 Impending price adjustments are often communicated by the price leader to the industry through speeches by major executives, trade publication interviews, and so forth. By publicizing "the need to raise prices" the price leader can elicit a consensus among its competitors for the actual increase.

3 The price leader does not necessarily choose the price which maximizes short-run profits for the industry. The reason for this is that the industry may want to discourage new firms from entering. If barriers to entry are based on cost advantages (economies of scale) of existing firms, these cost barriers may be surmounted by new entrants *if* product price is set high enough. New firms which are relatively inefficient because of their small size may survive and grow if the industry's price is very high. To discourage new competitors and maintain the current oligopolistic structure of the industry, price may be established below the short-run profit-maximizing level.

Cost-Plus Pricing

A final view of oligopolistic price behavior centers on what is variously known as ***markup, rule-of-thumb,*** or **cost-plus pricing.** In this case the oligopolist uses a formula or procedure to estimate cost per unit of output and a markup is applied to cost to determine price. Unit costs, however, vary with output and therefore the firm must assume some typical or target level of output. For example, the firm's average-cost figure may be that which is realized when the firm is operating at, say, 75 or 80 percent of capacity. A markup, usually in the form of a percentage, is applied to average cost in determining price. An appliance manufacturer may estimate unit costs of dishwashers to be $250, to which a 50 percent markup is applied. This yields a $375 price to retailers.

The markup is 50 percent rather than 25 or 100 percent because the firm is seeking some target profit or rate of return on its investment. To illustrate, consider the pricing technique used by General Motors for over four decades prior to the advent of aggressive foreign competition in the mid-1970s.

> GM started with the goal of earning, on the average over the years, a return of approximately 15 percent after taxes on total invested capital. Not knowing how many autos would be sold and hence unit costs (including prorated fixed costs), it calculated costs on the assumption of operation at 80 percent of conservatively rated capacity. A standard price was calculated by adding to unit cost a sufficient profit margin to yield the desired 15 percent after-tax return. The rule would be adjusted across the product line to take account of actual and potential competition, business conditions, long-run strategic goals and other factors. Actual profit then depended on the number of vehicles sold. Between 1960 and 1979, GM's actual return on stockholders' equity fell below 15 percent in only four years, all marked by recession and/or OPEC-induced gasoline price shocks. The average return was 17.6 percent. After 1979, however, recession and intensifying import competition caused GM frequently to fall short of its target.[3]

Two final points. First, this method of pricing is consistent with collusion or price leadership. If producers in an industry have roughly similar costs, adherence to a common pricing formula will result in highly

[2]F. M. Scherer and David Ross, *Industrial Market Structure and Economic Performance,* 3d ed. (Boston: Houghton Mifflin Company, 1990), p. 250.

[3]Ibid., p. 262.

similar prices and price changes. As we will find in the case study which concludes this chapter, General Motors used cost-plus pricing *and* was until recently the price leader in the automobile industry.

Second, cost-plus pricing has special advantages for multiproduct firms which would otherwise be faced with the difficult and costly process of estimating demand and cost conditions for perhaps hundreds of different products. In practice, it is virtually impossible to allocate correctly certain common overhead costs such as power, lighting, insurance, and taxes to specific products.

ROLE OF NONPRICE COMPETITION

We have noted that, for several reasons, oligopolists have an aversion to price competition. This aversion may lead to some more-or-less informal type of collusion on price. In the United States, however, price collusion is usually accompanied by nonprice competition. It is typically through nonprice competition that each firm's share of the total market is determined. This emphasis on nonprice competition has its roots in two basic facts.

1 Less Easily Duplicated Price cuts can be quickly and easily met by a firm's rivals. Because of this the possibility of significantly increasing one's share of the market through price competition is small; rivals will promptly cancel any potential gain in sales by matching price cuts. And, of course, the risk is always present that price competition will precipitate disastrous price warring. Nonprice competition is less likely to get out of hand. Oligopolists seem to feel that more permanent advantages can be gained over rivals through nonprice competition because product variations, improvements in productive techniques, and successful advertising gimmicks cannot be duplicated so quickly and completely as price reductions.

2 Greater Financial Resources There is a more evident reason for the tremendous emphasis which oligopolists put on nonprice competition: Manufacturing oligopolists are typically blessed with substantial financial resources with which to support advertising and product development. Thus, although nonprice competition is a basic characteristic of both monopolistically competitive and oligopolistic industries, the latter are typically in a financial position to indulge in nonprice competition more fully.

OLIGOPOLY AND ECONOMIC EFFICIENCY

Is oligopoly an "efficient" market structure from society's standpoint? How does the price–output behavior of the oligopolist compare with that of a purely competitive firm? Because there are a variety of oligopoly models—kinked demand, collusion, price leadership, and cost-plus pricing—it is difficult to make such a comparison.

Allocative and Productive Efficiency

Many economists believe that the outcome of oligopolistic markets is approximately that shown in Figure 13-3. Note that, as compared to the benchmark of pure competition (Figure 10-12), production occurs where price exceeds marginal cost and short of that output where average total cost is minimized. In terms of the terminology of Chapters 10 and 11, neither allocative efficiency (P = MC) nor productive efficiency (P = minimum ATC) is likely to occur under oligopoly.

One may even argue that oligopoly is actually less desirable than pure monopoly simply because pure monopoly in the United States is frequently subject to government regulation to mitigate abuses of market power. Informal collusion among oligopolists may yield price and output results similar to pure monopoly, yet at the same time maintain the outward appearance of several independent and "competing" firms.

Two qualifications are relevant. First, in recent years foreign competition has generated more rivalry in a number of oligopolistic markets—autos and steel come immediately to mind—and has tended to undermine such cozy arrangements as price leadership and cost-plus pricing and stimulate more competitive pricing. Second, recall that oligopolistic firms may purposely keep prices below the short-run, profit-maximizing level to deter entry where entry barriers are less formidable.

Dynamic Efficiency

What about the "very long run" perspective where we allow for innovation in terms of improvements in product quality and more efficient production methods?

Competitive View One view is that competition provides a compelling incentive to be technologically progressive. If a given competitive firm does not seize the initiative, one or more rivals will introduce an improved product or a cost-reducing production technique which may drive it from the market. In short, as a matter of short-term profits and long-term survival, competitive firms are under persistent pressure to improve products and lower costs through innovation.

Some adherents of this **competitive view** allege that oligopolists may often have a strong incentive to impede innovation and restrain technological progress. The larger corporation wants to maximize profits by exploiting fully all its capital assets. Why rush to develop and introduce a new product (for example, fluorescent lights) when that product's success will render obsolete all equipment designed to produce an existing product (incandescent bulbs)? Furthermore, it is not difficult to cite oligopolistic industries in which interest in research and development has been modest at best: The steel, cigarette, and aluminum industries are cases in point.

Schumpeter–Galbraith View In contrast, the **Schumpeter–Galbraith view** holds that large oligopolistic firms with market power are necessary for rapid technological progress.

High R&D Costs It is argued, first, that modern research to develop new products and new productive techniques is incredibly expensive. Therefore, only large oligopolistic firms can finance extensive research and development (R&D) activities.

Barriers and Profits Second, the existence of barriers to entry gives the oligopolist some assurance that it will realize any profit rewards from successful R&D endeavors. In Galbraith's words:

> The modern industry of a few large firms [is] an excellent instrument for inducing technical change. It is admirably equipped for financing technical development. Its organization provides strong incentives for undertaking development and for putting it into use. . . . In the modern industry shared by a few large firms, size and the rewards accruing to market power combine to insure that resources for research and technical development will be available. The power that enables the firm to have some influence on prices insures that the resulting gains will not be passed on to the public by imitators (who have stood none of the costs of development) before the outlay for development can be recouped. In this way market power protects the incentive to technical development.[4]

Bluntly put, small competitive firms have neither the *means* nor the *incentives* to be technologically progressive; large oligopolists do.

If the Schumpeter–Galbraith view is correct, it suggests that over time oligopolistic industries will foster rapid product improvement, lower unit production costs, lower prices, and perhaps a greater output and more employment than would the same industry organized competitively. There is anecdotal and case-study evidence suggesting that many oligopolistic manufacturing industries—television and other electronics products, home appliances, automobile tires—have been characterized by substantial improvements in product quality, falling relative prices, and expanding levels of output and employment.

Technological Progress: The Evidence

Which view is more nearly correct? Empirical studies have yielded ambiguous results. The consensus, however, seems to be that giant oligopolies are probably *not* a fountainhead of technological progress. A pioneering study[5] of sixty-one important inventions made from 1880 to 1965 indicates that over half were the work of independent inventors disassociated from corporate industrial research laboratories. Such substantial advances as air conditioning, power steering, the ballpoint pen, cellophane, the jet engine, insulin, xerography, the helicopter, and the catalytic cracking of petroleum have this individualistic heritage. Other equally important advances have come from small- and medium-sized firms.

According to this study, about two-thirds—forty out of sixty-one—of the basic inventions of this century have been initiated by independent inventors or the research activities of relatively small firms. This is not to deny that in a number of oligopolistic industries—for example, the aircraft, chemical, petroleum, and electronics industries—research activity has been pursued vigorously and fruitfully. But even here the picture is clouded by the fact that a very substantial portion of the research carried on in the aircraft-missile, electronics, and communications industries is heavily subsidized with public funds.

Some leading researchers in this field have tentatively concluded that technological progress in an industry may be determined more by the industry's sci-

[4]John Kenneth Galbraith, *American Capitalism*, rev. ed. (Boston: Houghton Mifflin Company, 1956), pp. 86–88. Also see Joseph Schumpeter, *Capitalism, Socialism, and Democracy* (New York: Harper & Row Publishers, Inc., 1942).

[5]John Jewkes, David Sawers, and Richard Stillerman, *The Sources of Invention*, rev. ed. (New York: St. Martin's Press, Inc., 1968).

entific character and "technological opportunities" than by its market structure. There may simply be more ways to progress in the electronics and computer industries than in the brickmaking and cigarette industries, regardless of whether they are organized competitively or oligopolistically.

QUICK REVIEW 13-2

- ***The kinked demand curve model is based on the assumption that an oligopolist's rivals will match a price cut but ignore a price increase. This model is consistent with observed price rigidity found in some oligopolistic industries.***
- ***A cartel is a collusive association of firms which establishes a formal agreement to determine price and to divide the market among participants.***
- ***Price leadership occurs when one firm—usually the largest or most efficient—determines price, and rival firms establish identical or highly similar prices.***
- ***Cost-plus pricing means that a firm establishes price by adding a percentage markup to the average cost of its product.***
- ***Oligopoly is conducive to neither allocative or productive efficiency. There is disagreement as to whether oligopoly is conducive to technological progress.***

AUTOMOBILES: A CASE STUDY[6]

The automobile industry provides an informative case study of oligopoly, illustrating many of the points made in this chapter. It also indicates that market structure is not permanent and, in particular, that foreign competition can upset the oligopolists' "quiet life."

Market Structure Although there were over eighty auto manufacturers in the early 1920s, several mergers (most notably the combining of Chevrolet, Pontiac, Oldsmobile, Buick, and Cadillac into General Motors), many failures during the Great Depression of the 1930s, and the increasing importance of entry barriers —all reduced numbers in the industry. Currently, three large firms—General Motors (GM), Ford, and Chrysler—dominate the market for domestically produced automobiles.

These firms are gigantic: According to *Fortune* magazine, GM, Ford, and Chrysler were the first, third, and eleventh largest manufacturing companies in the United States in 1990 as measured by sales. All three are leading truck manufacturers, produce household appliances, are involved in defense contracting and finance and banking, and have extensive overseas interests. GM has a virtual monopoly in producing buses and diesel locomotives in the United States.

Entry Barriers Entry barriers are substantial, as evidenced by the fact that it has been about six decades since an American firm successfully entered the automobile industry. The primary barrier is economies of scale. It is estimated that the minimum efficient scale for a producer is about 300,000 units of output per year. However, given the uncertainties of consumer tastes, experts feel a truly viable firm must produce at least two different models. Hence, to have a reasonable prospect of success a new firm would have to produce about 600,000 autos per year.

The estimated cost of an integrated plant (involving the production of engines, transmissions, other components, and product assembly) might be as much as $1.2 to $1.4 billion. Other entry barriers include the need for extensive advertising and far-flung dealer networks (GM has over 15,500 dealers and Chrysler has 10,500) which provide spare parts and repair service. A newcomer also would face the expensive task of overcoming existing brand loyalties. Given that the domestic automobile industry spent $2.6 billion on advertising in 1990, this is no small matter.

Price Leadership and Profits The indicated industry structure—a few firms with high entry barriers—has been fertile ground for collusive or coordinated pricing. GM traditionally was the price leader. Each fall, with the introduction of new models, GM would establish prices for its basic models and Ford and Chrysler would set the prices of their comparable models accordingly. (Details of how GM established its prices were outlined in the earlier section on cost-plus pricing.)

In the past several decades automobile prices have moved up steadily and at a rate in excess of the overall rate of inflation. And despite large periodic declines in demand and sales, automobile prices have displayed considerable downward rigidity, although import competition and recession have caused rebates and financing subsidies to become common in recent years.

[6]This section draws heavily on Walter Adams and James W. Brock, "The Automobile Industry," in Walter Adams (ed.), *The Structure of American Industry,* 8th ed. (New York: The Macmillan Company, 1990), pp. 101–127.

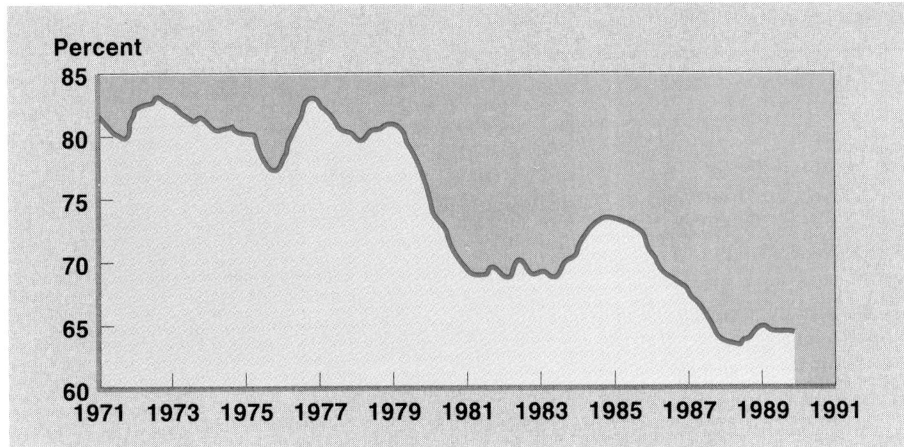

FIGURE 13-5 Big Three sales as a share of the United States automobile market

Although GM, Ford, and Chrysler commanded about 80 percent of domestic car sales in the 1970s, that share fell sharply in the late 1970s and early 1980s and is now less than 65 percent.

Over the years price leadership has proved to be very profitable. Over the 1947–1977 period the Big Three earned an average profit rate significantly greater than that of all United States manufacturing corporations taken as a whole.

Styling and Technology In addition to advertising, nonprice competition has centered on styling and technological advance. In practice the former has been stressed over the latter. As early as the 1920s GM recognized that the replacement market was becoming increasingly important compared to the market for first-time purchasers. Therefore, its strategy—later adopted by other manufacturers—became one of annual styling changes accompanied by model proliferation. The purpose is to achieve higher sales and profits by encouraging consumers to replace their autos with greater frequency and to encourage buyers to shift their purchase from basic to "upscale" models.

As summarized by Adams and Brock, technological progress represents a mixed picture over time:

> First, the rate, breadth, and depth of product innovation were greatest in the era prior to World War II, when the field was populated by many independent producers. Competition was intense, and new people with new ideas could put their ideas (the bad along with the good) into commercial practice. . . .
>
> Second, with the demise of a vigorous independent sector, and with the consolidation of the industry into a tight oligopoly, the pace of genuine product innovation slackened. Innovations like front-wheel drive, disc brakes, fuel injection, utilitarian minivans and fuel-efficient subcompacts, and four-wheel steering languished in the hands of the Big Three. . . .
>
> Third, while the domestic oligopoly luxuriated in complacency and the cosmetic style game, foreign producers took the lead in aggressively exploiting the frontiers of automobile technology. . . . This lead persists to the present day, with foreign producers commercializing such recent product innovations as four-wheel steering, electronically controlled active suspensions, multivalve engines, and ceramic engine componentry.
>
> Fourth, with regard to *process* innovation, the domestic oligopoly's performance is hardly more enviable. Here, too, foreign firms—especially the Japanese—have exhibited far more entrepreneurship in seeking out and implementing improved manufacturing techniques. . . . In their devotion to production, and in their relentless willingness to experiment, the Japaneses seem to have been far more astute students of Henry Ford than the chieftains of the U.S industry, who succumbed to satisfaction with the status quo.
>
> In the 1980s the Big Three have struggled to advance, both in product innovation as well as in production technology. They have progressed on both fronts—examples are the successful Ford Taurus program, GM's "Saturn" project, billions of dollars in cost reductions, and productivity gains on the factory floor.[7]

Foreign Competition In the last two decades the automobile market in the United States has become more competitive than the tight oligopolistic structure of the domestic industry would suggest. GM, Ford, and Chrysler have been challenged by foreign (particularly Japanese) producers. As Figure 13-5 shows, the Big Three's share of the United States market has declined

[7]Ibid., pp. 117–119.

LAST WORD

THE BEER INDUSTRY: OLIGOPOLY BREWING?

The beer industry was once populated by hundreds of firms and an even larger number of brands. But this industry has increasingly become concentrated and is now an oligopoly.

The brewing industry has undergone profound changes since World War II which have increased the degree of concentration in the industry. In 1947 slightly over 400 independent brewing companies existed in the United States. By 1967 the number had declined to 124 and by 1980 only 33 survived. While the five largest brewers sold only 19 percent of the nation's beer in 1947, the Big Five brewers currently sell 93 percent of the nation's domestically produced beer as shown in the accompanying table. The Big Two—Anheuser-Busch and Miller—produce 68 percent. Why the change?

Market share for domestically produced beer, 1990

Firm	*Market share*
Anheuser-Busch	45%
Miller	23
Coors	10
Stroh	8
Heileman	7
All others	7
	100%

Changes on the demand side of the market have contributed to the "shake-out" of small brewers from the industry. First, there is evidence that in the 1970s consumer tastes shifted from the stronger-flavored beers of the small brewers to the light, dry products of the larger brewers. Second, there has been a relative shift from the consumption of beer in taverns to consumption in the home. The significance of this change is that taverns were usually supplied with kegs from local brewers to avoid the relatively high cost of shipping kegs. But the acceptance of metal containers for home consumption made it possible for large, distant brewers to compete with the local brewers because the former could now ship their products by truck or rail without breakage.

from 80 percent as recently as 1979 to less than 65 percent currently.

The reasons for growth of foreign competition are manifold.

1 Rising Gas Prices The OPEC-inspired increases in gasoline prices in the 1970s prompted a shift in consumer demand toward smaller, fuel-efficient imports from Japan and Germany. Many analysts contend that domestic producers seriously misjudged the scope and apparent permanence of this shift.

2 Quality In addition, many consumers perceive that imports have quality advantages. A 1990 consumer survey with respect to perceived automobile quality found seven Japanese models, two German models, and only one American-made car in the top ten. The American car ranked fifth.

3 Costs Finally, lower overseas wages and higher labor productivity have given the Japanese and Koreans a substantial cost advantage on compact cars.

The response of the domestic automobile industry to enhanced foreign competition has been essentially threefold.

1 Protection The industry—with the support of organized labor—successfully lobbied government for protection. The result, beginning in 1981, was "voluntary" import quotas on Japanese cars which effectively restrained competition. Reduced foreign competition allowed domestic manufacturers to boost their prices

Developments on the supply side of the market have been even more profound. In particular, technological advances have speeded up the bottling or closing lines so that, for example, the number of cans of beer which could be filled and closed per minute increased from 900 to 1500 between 1965 and the late 1970s. Currently the most modern canning lines can close 2000 cans per minute. Large plants are also able to reduce labor costs through the automating of brewing and warehousing. Furthermore, plant construction costs per barrel are about one-third less for a 4.5-million-barrel plant than for a 1.5-million-barrel plant. As a consequence of these and other economies, it is estimated that unit production costs decline sharply up to the point at which a plant produces 1.25 million barrels per year. Average costs continue to decline, but less significantly, up to the 4.5-million-barrel capacity at which all scale economies seem to be exhausted. Evidence of the importance of scale economies is reflected in statistics which show that over time there has been a steady decline in breweries producing less than 2 million barrels per year. Because the construction of a modern 4-million-barrel capacity brewery costs about $250 million, economies of scale may now constitute a significant barrier to entry.

Although mergers have occurred, they have not been a fundamental cause of increased concentration in the brewing industry. Rather, mergers have been largely the result of failing small breweries selling out.

On the other hand, the ascendancy of the Miller Brewing Company from the seventh to the second largest producer in the 1970s was due in large measure to advertising and product differentiation. When Miller was acquired by the Philip Morris Company in 1970, the new management made two salient changes. First, Miller High Life beer was "repositioned" into that segment of the market where potential sales were the greatest. Sold previously as the "champagne of beers," High Life had appealed heavily to upper-income consumers and women who only drank beer occasionally. Miller's new television ads featured young blue-collar workers who were inclined to be greater beer consumers. Second, Miller then developed its low-calorie Lite beer which was extensively promoted with the infusion of Philip Morris advertising dollars. Lite proved to be the most popular new product in the history of the beer industry and contributed significantly to Miller's dramatic rise in the industry.

Currently, the beer industry does not appear to have engaged in economically undesirable behavior. There has been no evidence of collusion and current excess productive capacity prompts the large brewers to compete for market shares. The fact that historically there has been considerable turnover in the ranking of the largest firms is further evidence of competition. Miller, ranked eighth in 1968, rose to number two in 1977 and has maintained that position. In comparison, Schlitz and Pabst were the second and third largest brewers in the mid-1970s, but now are only "also rans."

Source: This synopsis is based on Kenneth G. Elzinga, "The Beer Industry," in Walter Adams (ed.), *The Structure of American Industry,* 8th ed. (New York: Macmillan Publishing Co., Inc. 1990), pp. 128–160. Updated.

to consumers. For example, one authoritative estimate suggests that the import quotas strengthened the domestic oligopoly to the extent that on the average domestic producers earned an additional $400 in profits on each car sold in 1983. Given that the output of domestic producers was 7 million cars in 1983, the aggregate increase in profits of domestic manufacturers was $2.8 billion.[8] These estimates clearly indicate that American consumers have a great stake in free international trade and the competition it generates (Chapter 24).

[8]"Carving Up the Car Buyer," *Newsweek,* March 5, 1984, pp. 72–73. The estimates are those of Robert Crandall of The Brookings Institution. The import quotas further hurt American consumers by restricting the supply and increasing the prices of Japanese cars.

But the Japanese in turn have responded to import quotas and the uncertainties inherent in the changing dollar–yen exchange rate by building automobile plants in the United States. These so-called "transplants" now produce about 10 percent of the cars sold in the United States. The success of Japanese production in America is reflected in the fact that they built eight new factories in the United States in the 1980s, precisely the number closed by the Big Three in the 1987–1989 period. It is significant that the Japanese have not sacrificed their production cost advantage by producing in the United States. The transplants embody state-of-the-art equipment, Japanese industrial relations techniques, and in some cases nonunion workers. The result is an automobile built for $500 to $800 less than in most of the Big Three's plants.

2 Joint Ventures The second response of domestic producers has been to co-opt and mitigate foreign competition by initiating an elaborate network of joint ownership arrangements and joint ventures with foreign producers. Chrysler owns about one-fourth of Mitsubishi and imports both compact cars and parts from the latter. Mitsubishi in turn is a part owner of Korea's Hyundai Motor Company. General Motors has a joint production arrangement with Toyota in California and has significant ownership shares in other lesser-known Japanese auto manufacturers. Ford owns about one-fourth of Mazda. These arrangements cast a cloud of doubt on the contention that foreign competition has had an important "disciplining" effect on American auto manufacturers.

Adams and Brock, two astute observers of the industry, point out that ". . . a decade of joint ventures in the automotive industry has secured an interlocking system of mutually acceptable accords, and may well have forged the groundwork for cartelizing the world automobile industry."[9]

[9]Walter Adams and James W. Brock, "Joint Ventures, Antitrust, and Transnational Cartelization," *Northwestern Journal of International Law & Business,* Winter 1991, p. 465.

3 Altered Pricing Another effect of Japanese competition has been to alter the GM price leadership pattern which characterized the industry for many decades. In 1977–1978 the dollar significantly declined in value relative to the yen, meaning that each dollar earned by the Japanese on auto sales in the United States translated into a smaller amount of yen profits. Led by Toyota, the Japanese raised their prices in four steps during the 1978 model year. American producers generally followed these increases. Again in 1985–1988 a depreciating dollar further increased Japanese car prices but, perhaps alarmed by declining market shares, the Big Three only boosted prices by about one-third of the Japanese increases. In short, the price leadership role of GM has been clouded by a new group of foreign rivals.

We have now finished our analysis of the four basic product market models—pure competition, pure monopoly, monopolistic competition, and oligopoly. You should reexamine Table 10-1 to ensure that you clearly understand the main characteristics of each of these models.

CHAPTER SUMMARY

1 Oligopolistic industries are characterized by the presence of a few firms, each of which has a significant fraction of the market. Firms thus situated are mutually interdependent; the behavior of any one firm directly affects, and is affected by, the actions of rivals. Products may be virtually uniform or significantly differentiated. Underlying reasons for the evolution of oligopoly are economies of scale, other entry barriers, and the advantages of merger.

2 Concentration ratios can be used as a measure of oligopoly and market power. By giving more weight to larger firms, the Herfindahl index is designed to measure market dominance in an industry.

3 Game theory **a** shows the mutual interdependence of oligopolists' price policies; **b** reveals the tendency to act collusively; and **c** explains the temptation to cheat on collusive agreements.

4 Important models of oligopoly include: **a** the kinked-demand model, **b** collusive oligopoly, **c** price leadership, and **d** cost-plus pricing.

5 Noncollusive oligopolists may face a kinked demand curve. This curve and the accompanying marginal-revenue curve help explain the price rigidity which characterizes such markets; they do not, however, explain the level of price.

6 The uncertainties inherent in noncollusive pricing are conducive to collusion. There is a tendency for collusive oligopolists to maximize joint profits—that is, to behave somewhat like pure monopolists. Demand and cost differences, the presence of a "large" number of firms, "cheating" through secret price concessions, recessions, and the antitrust laws are all obstacles to collusive oligopoly.

7 Price leadership is a less formal means of collusion where the largest or most efficient firm in the industry initiates price changes and the other firms follow.

8 With cost-plus or markup pricing, oligopolists estimate their unit costs at some target level of output and add a percentage "markup" to determine price.

9 Market shares in oligopolistic industries are usually determined on the basis of nonprice competition. Oligopolists emphasize nonprice competition because **a** advertising and product variations are less easy for rivals to match, and **b** oligopolists frequently have ample resources to finance nonprice competition.

10 It is unlikely that either allocative or productive efficiency is realized in oligopolistic markets. The competitive view envisions oligopoly as being inferior to more competitive market structures in promoting product improvement and cost-decreasing innovations. The Schumpeter–Galbraith view is that oligopolists have both the incentive and financial resources to be technologically progressive.

TERMS AND CONCEPTS

oligopoly
homogeneous and differentiated oligopoly
concentration ratios
interindustry competition
import competition
Herfindahl index
game theory model
duopoly
mutual interdependence
collusion
kinked demand curve
price war
collusive oligopoly
gentlemen's agreements
cartel
price leadership
cost-plus pricing
competitive and Schumpeter–Galbraith views

QUESTIONS AND STUDY SUGGESTIONS

1 Why do oligopolies exist? List five or six oligopolists whose products you own or regularly purchase. What distinguishes oligopoly from monopolistic competition?

2 "Fewness of rivals means mutual interdependence, and mutual interdependence means uncertainty as to how those few rivals will react to a price change by any one firm." Explain. Of what significance is this for determining demand and marginal revenue? Other things being equal, would you expect mutual interdependence to vary directly or inversely with the degree of product differentiation? With the number of firms? Explain.

3 What is the meaning of a four-firm concentration ratio of 60 percent? 90 percent? What are the shortcomings of concentration ratios as measures of market power?

4 Suppose that in industry A five firms have annual sales of 30, 30, 20, 10, and 10 percent of total industry sales. For the five firms in industry B the figures are 60, 25, 5, 5, and 5 percent. Calculate the Herfindahl index for each industry and compare their likely competitiveness.

5 Explain the general character of the data in the following profits-payoff matrix for oligopolists C and D. All profit figures are in thousands.

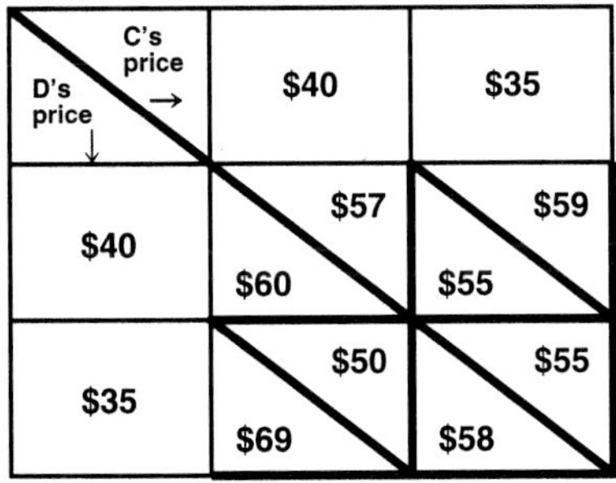

D's price ↓ \ C's price →	$40	$35
$40	$57 / $60	$59 / $55
$35	$50 / $69	$55 / $58

a Use the table to explain the mutual interdependence which characterizes oligopolistic industries.
b Assuming no collusion, what is the likely outcome of this game?
c Given your answer to question **b,** explain why price collusion is mutually profitable. Why might there be a temptation to cheat on the collusive agreement?

6 What assumptions concerning a rival's responses to price changes underlie the kinked demand curve? Why is there a gap in the marginal-revenue curve? How does the kinked demand curve help explain oligopolistic price rigidity? What are the shortcomings of the kinked-demand model?

7 Why might price collusion occur in oligopolistic industries? Assess the economic desirability of collusive pricing. Explain: "If each firm knows that the price of each of its few rivals depends on its own price, how can the prices be determined?" What are the main obstacles to collusion? Apply these obstacles to the weakening of OPEC in the 1980s.

8 Assume the demand curve shown in question 4 in Chapter 11 applies to a pure monopolist which has a constant marginal cost of $4. What price and output will be most profitable for the monopolist? Now assume the demand curve applies to a two-firm industry (a "duopoly") and that each firm has a constant marginal cost of $4. If the firms collude, what price and quantity will maximize their joint profits? Demonstrate why it might be profitable for one of the firms to cheat. If the other firm becomes aware of this cheating, what will happen?

9 Explain how price leadership might evolve and function in an oligopolistic industry. Is cost-plus pricing compatible with collusion?

10 "Oligopolistic industries have both the means and the inclination for technological progress." Do you agree? Explain.

11 "If oligopolists really want to compete, they should do so by cutting their prices rather than by squandering millions of dollars on advertising and other forms of sales promotion." Do you agree? Why don't oligopolists usually compete by cutting prices?

12 Using Figure 13-3, explain how a collusive oligopolist might increase its profits by offering secret price concessions to buyers. On the diagram, indicate the amount of additional profits which the firm may realize. What are the risks involved in such a policy?

13 Review the case study of the automobile industry and identify aspects of industry structure and behavior which are oligopolistic. What responses have domestic producers made to increasing foreign competition?

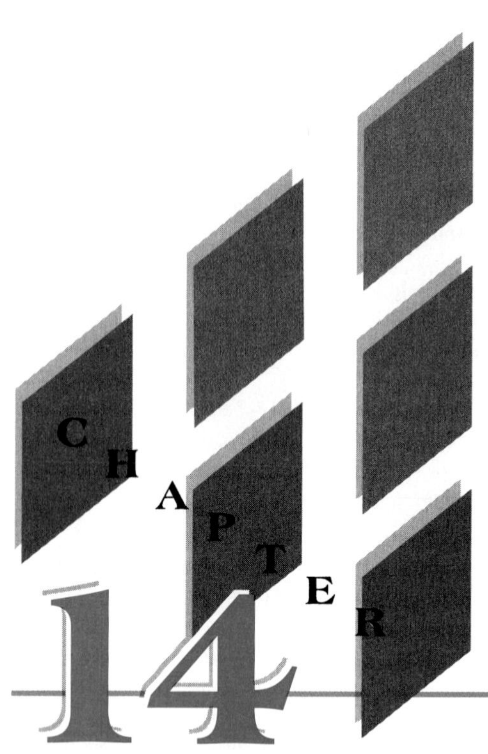

Production and the Demand for Resources

We explored the pricing and output of goods and services under a variety of product market structures in the preceding four chapters. The purely competitive cucumber farmer considers the market price and decides how many acres to plant. The monopolistically competitive local restaurant decides on the best combination of price, quality, and advertising to maximize its profits. The automobile manufacturer pays close attention to the business strategies of rivals and sets its price and production plans accordingly. The local telephone monopoly files requests for rate increases before the state utility board, and then provides service to all customers.

Although firms and market structures differ greatly, firms in general have something in common. In producing their product—be it cucumbers, sandwiches, automobiles, or telephone service—they must hire productive resources. Among other resources, the cucumber farmer needs land, tractors, fertilizer, and pickers. The restaurant buys kitchen equipment and hires cooks and waiters. The auto manufacturer purchases production materials and hires executives, accountants, engineers, and assembly-line workers. The telephone company leases land, buys telephone poles and wires, and hires operators and billing clerks.

In this chapter and in Chapters 15 and 16, we turn from the pricing and production of goods to the pricing and employment of resources needed in production. Land, labor, capital, and entrepreneurial resources directly or indirectly are owned and supplied by households. In terms of our circular flow model of the economy (Chapters 3 and 6), we now shift attention from the bottom loop of the diagram, where firms supply and households demand products, to the top loop, where households supply and businesses demand resources. This reversal of roles in part necessitates a separate discussion of resource pricing.

SIGNIFICANCE OF RESOURCE PRICING

There are several related reasons to study resource pricing.

1 Money Incomes The most basic fact about resource prices is that they are a major determinant of money or nominal incomes. The expenditures businesses make in acquiring economic resources flow as wage, rent, interest, and profit incomes to those households which supply the human and property resources at their disposal.

2 Resource Allocation Just as product prices ration finished goods and services to consumers, so resource prices allocate scarce resources among various industries and firms. An understanding of how resource prices affect resource allocation is particularly significant since, in a dynamic economy, the efficient allocation of resources over time calls for continuing shifts in resources among alternative uses.

3 Cost Minimization To the firm, resource prices are costs, and to realize maximum profits a firm must produce the profit-maximizing output with the most efficient (least costly) combination of resources. Given technology, resource prices play the major role in determining the quantities of land, labor, capital, and entrepreneurial ability that will be combined in the productive process (Table 5-1).

4 Policy Issues Finally, there are a myriad of ethical questions and public policy issues surrounding the resource market. In particular, the amoral nature of resource prices results in considerable inequality in the personal distribution of income. Should a special tax be levied on "excess" profits? Is it desirable for government to establish a wage floor in the form of a legal minimum wage? What about legal ceilings on interest rates? Are current government subsidies to farmers justifiable? Chapter 22 will explore the facts and ethics of income distribution.

COMPLEXITIES OF RESOURCE PRICING

Economists generally agree on the basic principles of resource pricing. Yet there is considerable disagreement as to the variations in these principles which are made when they are applied to specific resources and particular markets. While economists generally agree that the pricing and employment of economic resources, or factors of production, are a supply and demand phenomenon, they also recognize that in particular markets resource supply and demand may assume unique and often complex dimensions. This is further complicated when the operation of supply and demand forces is altered or even largely supplanted by the policies and practices of government, business firms, or labor unions, not to mention a host of other institutional considerations.

Our major objective in this chapter is to explain the basic factors underlying the demand for economic resources. We will couch our discussion in terms of labor, recognizing that the principles outlined also generally apply to land, capital, and entrepreneurial ability. In Chapter 15 our understanding of resource demand will be combined with a discussion of labor supply in analyzing wage rates. Then in Chapter 16 the supply side of the markets for property resources will be incorporated to analyze the prices of, and returns to, land, capital, and entrepreneurial talent.

MARGINAL PRODUCTIVITY THEORY OF RESOURCE DEMAND

The least complicated approach to resource demand is one which assumes a firm hires a specific resource in a competitive market and in turn sells its product in a competitive market. The simplicity of this situation lies in the fact that under competition the firm as a "price taker" can dispose of as little or as much output as it chooses at the going market price. The firm is selling such a negligible fraction of total output that it exerts no influence whatever on product price. Similarly, in the resource market, competition means that the firm is hiring such a small fraction of the total supply of the resource that its price is unaffected by the quantity the firm purchases.

Resource Demand as a Derived Demand

Having specified these simplified conditions, we note that the demand for resources is a **derived demand;** it is derived from the finished goods and services which resources help produce. Resources usually do not directly satisfy consumer wants, but do so indirectly by producing goods and services. No one wants to consume an acre of land, a John Deere tractor, or the labor services of a farmer, but households do want to consume the various food and fiber products these resources help produce.

Marginal Revenue Product (MRP)

The derived nature of resource demand implies that the strength of the demand for any resource will depend on (1) the productivity of the resource in helping to create a good, and (2) the market value or price of the good it is producing. A resource which is highly productive in turning out a commodity highly valued by society will be in great demand. On the other hand, demand will be very weak for a relatively unproductive resource which is only capable of producing some good not in great demand by households. There will be no demand for a resource which is phenomenally efficient in producing something no one wants to purchase!

Productivity The roles of productivity and product price in determining resource demand can be clearly seen in Table 14-1. Here we assume a firm adds one variable resource—labor—to its fixed plant. Columns 1 through 3 remind us that the law of diminishing returns will apply in this situation, causing the **marginal product** (MP) of labor to fall beyond some point. (It might be helpful to review the section, "Law of Diminishing Returns," in Chapter 9 at this point.) For simplicity, we assume that diminishing marginal productivity sets in with the first worker hired.

Product Price But the derived demand for a resource also depends on the price of the commodity it produces. Column 4 adds this price information. Note that product price is constant, in this case at $2, because we are supposing a competitive product market.

Multiplying column 2 by column 4, we get the total-revenue data of column 5. From these total-revenue data we can compute **marginal revenue product** (MRP)—*the increase in total revenue resulting from the use of each additional variable input (labor, in this case)*. This is indicated in column 6.

Rule for Employing Resources: MRP = MRC

The MRP schedule—columns 1 and 6—is the firm's demand schedule for labor. To explain this, we must first discuss the rule which guides a profit-seeking firm in hiring any resource. *To maximize profits, a firm should hire additional units of any given resource so long as each successive unit adds more to the firm's total revenue than it does to its total costs.*

Economists have special terms designating what each additional unit of labor or other variable resource adds to total cost and what it adds to total revenue. We noted that, by definition, MRP measures how much each successive worker adds to total revenue. The amount which each additional unit of a resource adds to the firm's total (resource) cost is called **marginal resource cost** (MRC). Thus we can restate our rule for hiring resources as follows: *It will be profitable for a firm to hire additional units of a resource up to the point at which that resource's MRP is equal to its MRC.* If the number of workers a firm is currently hiring is such that the MRP of the last worker exceeds his or her MRC, the firm can clearly profit by hiring more workers. But if the number being hired is such that the

TABLE 14-1 The demand for a resource: pure competition in the sale of the product *(hypothetical data)*

(1) Units of resource	(2) Total product	(3) Marginal product (MP), or Δ(2)	(4) Product price	(5) Total revenue, or (2) × (4)	(6) Marginal revenue product (MRP), or Δ(5)
0	0		$2	$ 0	
		7			$14
1	7		2	14	
		6			12
2	13		2	26	
		5			10
3	18		2	36	
		4			8
4	22		2	44	
		3			6
5	25		2	50	
		2			4
6	27		2	54	
		1			2
7	28		2	56	

MRC of the last worker exceeds the MRP, the firm is hiring workers who are not "paying their way," and it can thereby increase its profits by laying off some workers. You may have recognized that this **MRP = MRC rule** is very similar to the MR = MC profit-maximizing rule employed throughout our discussion of price and output determination. The rationale of the two rules is the same, but the point of reference is now *inputs* of resources, rather than *outputs* of product.

MRP Is a Demand Schedule

Just as product price and marginal revenue are equal in a purely competitive product market, so *resource price and marginal resource cost are equal when a firm is hiring a resource competitively.* In a purely competitive labor market the wage rate is set by the total, or market, supply of, and the market demand for, labor. Because it hires such a small fraction of the total supply of labor, a single firm cannot influence this wage rate. This means that total resource cost increases by exactly the amount of the going wage rate for each additional worker hired; the wage rate and MRC are equal. It follows that so long as it is hiring labor competitively, *the firm will hire workers to the point at which their wage rate (or MRC) is equal to their MRP.*[1]

In terms of the data in column 6 of Table 14-1, if the wage rate is $13.95, the firm will hire only one worker. This is so because the first worker adds $14 to total revenue and slightly less—$13.95—to total costs. For each successive worker, however, MRC exceeds MRP, indicating that it will not be profitable to hire any of those workers. If the wage rate is $11.95, by the same reasoning we discover that it will pay the firm to hire both the first and second workers. Similarly, if the wage rate is $9.95, three will be hired. If $7.95, four. If $5.95, then five. And so forth. It is evident that *the MRP schedule constitutes the firm's demand for labor, because each point on this schedule (curve) indicates the number of workers which the firm would hire at each possible wage rate which might exist.* This is shown graphically in Figure 14-1.

The rationale employed here is familiar to us. Recall in Chapter 10 that we applied the price-equals-marginal-cost or P = MC rule for the profit-maximizing *output* to discover that the portion of the competitive firm's short-run marginal-cost curve lying above average variable cost is the short-run *product supply* curve (Figure 10-6). Presently we are applying the MRP = MRC rule for the profit-maximizing *input* to the firm's MRP curve and determining that this curve is the input or *resource demand* curve.

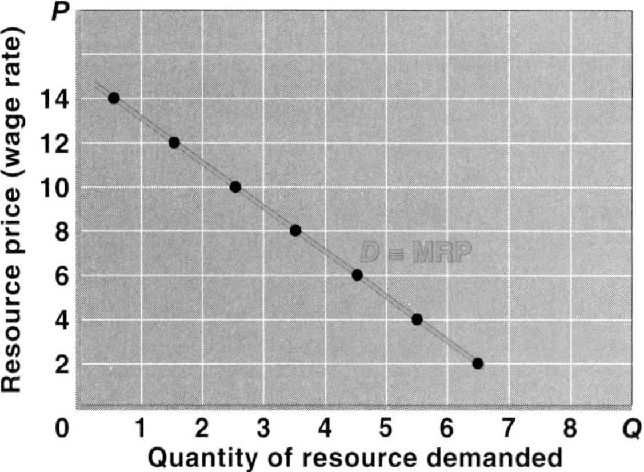

FIGURE 14-1 The purely competitive seller's demand for a resource

The MRP curve is the resource demand curve. The location of the curve depends on the marginal productivity of the resource and the price of the product. Under pure competition product price is constant; therefore, diminishing marginal productivity is the sole reason why the resource demand curve is downsloping.

Resource Demand under Imperfect Competition

Our analysis of labor demand becomes more complex when we assume that the firm is selling its product in an imperfectly competitive market. Pure monopoly, oligopoly, and monopolistic competition in the product market all mean that the firm's product demand curve is downsloping; the firm must accept a lower price to increase its sales.

Table 14-2 takes this into account. The productivity data of Table 14-1 are retained in columns 1–3, but we now assume in column 4 that product price must be lowered to sell the marginal product of each successive worker. The MRP of the purely competitive seller falls for one reason: Marginal product diminishes. But the MRP of the imperfectly competitive seller falls for two reasons: Marginal product diminishes *and* product price falls as output increases.

It must be emphasized that the lower price accompanying every increase in output applies in each case not only to the marginal product of each successive worker but also to all prior units which otherwise could have sold at a higher price. To illustrate: The second worker's marginal product is 6 units. These 6 units can be sold for $2.40 each or, as a group, for $14.40. But this is *not* the MRP of the second worker. To sell these 6

[1]The logic here is the same as that which allowed us to change the MR = MC profit-maximization rule to P = MC for the purely competitive seller of Chapter 10.

TABLE 14-2 The demand for a resource: imperfect competition in the sale of the product *(hypothetical data)*

(1) Units of resource	*(2) Total product*	*(3) Marginal product (MP), or Δ(2)*	*(4) Product price*	*(5) Total revenue, or (2) × (4)*	*(6) Marginal revenue product (MRP), or Δ(5)*
0	0		$2.80	$ 0	
		7			$18.20
1	7		2.60	18.20	
		6			13.00
2	13		2.40	31.20	
		5			8.40
3	18		2.20	39.60	
		4			4.40
4	22		2.00	44.00	
		3			2.25
5	25		1.85	46.25	
		2			1.00
6	27		1.75	47.25	
		1			−1.05
7	28		1.65	46.20	

units, the firm must take a 20-cent price cut on the 7 units produced by the first worker—units which could have been sold for $2.60 each. Thus, the MRP of the second worker is only $13.00 [= $14.40 − (7 × 20 cents)]. Similarly, the third worker's MRP is $8.40. Although the 5 units this worker produces are worth $2.20 each in the market, the third worker does not add $11.00 to the firm's total revenue when account is taken of the 20-cent price cut which must be taken on the 13 units produced by the first two workers. In this case the third worker's MRP is only $8.40 [= $11.00 − (13 × 20 cents)]. The other figures in column 6 are similarly explained.

The net result is that the MRP curve—the resource demand curve—of the imperfectly competitive producer tends to be less elastic than that of a purely competitive producer. At a wage rate or MRC of $11.95, both the purely competitive and the imperfectly competitive seller will hire two workers. But at $9.95, the competitive firm will hire three and the imperfectly competitive firm only two. And at $7.95, the purely competitive firm will take on four employees and the imperfect competitor only three. This difference in elasticity can be readily seen by graphing the MRP data of Table 14-2 as in Figure 14-2 and comparing them with Figure 14-1.[2]

[2]Note that the points in Figures 14-1 and 14-2 are plotted halfway between each number of workers because MRP is associated with the *addition* of one more worker. Thus, in Figure 14-2, for example, the MRP of the second worker ($13.00) is plotted not at 1 or 2, but rather at 1½. This "smoothing" technique also allows us to present a continuously downsloping curve rather than one which moves downward in discrete steps as each worker is hired.

It is not surprising that the imperfectly competitive producer is less responsive to wage cuts in terms of workers employed than is the purely competitive producer. The imperfect competitor's relative reluctance to employ more resources and thereby produce more output when resource prices fall is merely the resource market reflection of the imperfect competitor's tendency to restrict output in the product market. Other things being equal, the imperfectly competitive seller will produce less of a product than would a purely com-

FIGURE 14-2 The imperfectly competitive seller's demand for a resource

An imperfectly competitive seller's resource demand curve slopes downward because marginal product diminishes and product price falls as output increases.

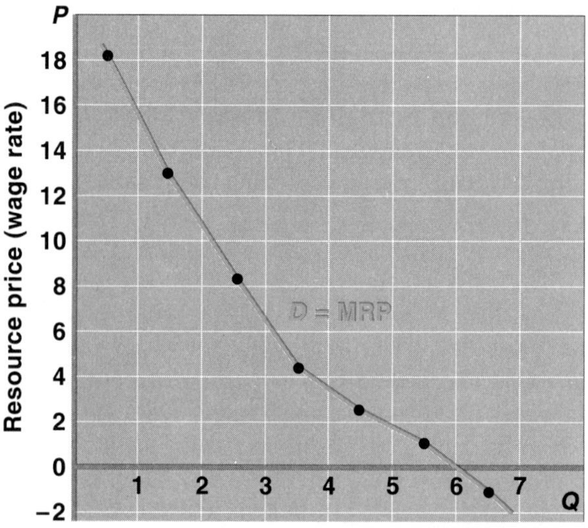

petitive seller. In producing this smaller output, it will demand fewer resources.

But one important qualification exists. We noted in Chapters 11 and 13 that the market structures of pure monopoly and oligopoly *might* lead to technological progress and a higher level of production, more employment, and lower prices in the long run than would a purely competitive market. The resource demand curve in these cases would not be restricted.

Market Demand for a Resource

We can now derive the market demand curve for a resource. You will recall that the total, or market, demand curve for a product is developed by summing horizontally the demand curves of all individual buyers in the market. Similarly, the market demand curve for a particular resource can be derived in essentially the same fashion, that is, by summing the individual demand or MRP curves for all firms hiring that resource.

QUICK REVIEW 14-1

- ***A resource will be employed in the profit-maximizing amount where its marginal revenue product equals its marginal resource cost (MRP = MRC).***
- ***Application of the MRP = MRC rule to a firm's MRP curve demonstrates that the MRP curve is the firm's resource demand curve.***
- ***The resource demand curve of a purely competitive seller is downsloping solely because the marginal product of the resource diminishes; the resource demand curve of an imperfectly competitive seller is downsloping because marginal product diminishes and product price falls as output is increased.***

DETERMINANTS OF RESOURCE DEMAND

What will alter the demand for a resource, that is, shift the demand curve? What are the determinants of labor demand? The very derivation of resource demand immediately suggests two related factors—the resource's productivity and the market price of the product it is producing. And our previous analysis of changes in product demand (Chapter 4) suggests another factor—changes in the prices of other resources.

Changes in Product Demand

Because resource demand is a derived demand, any change in the demand for the product will affect product price and therefore the MRP of the resource. Other things being equal, *a change in the demand for the product that a particular type of labor is producing will shift labor demand in the same direction.*

In Table 14-1, assume an increase in product demand which boosts product price from \$2 to \$3. If you calculate the new labor demand curve and plot it in Figure 14-1, you will find it lies to the right of the old curve. Similarly, a drop in product demand and price will shift the labor demand curve to the left.

Real-world examples: The 1987 stock market crash resulted in a decline in the volume of stocks traded daily and a consequent decline in the demand for stockbrokers, causing widespread layoffs on Wall Street. Similarly, the increases in the prices of oil, natural gas, and electricity which have occurred since the mid-1970s increased the demand for woodburning stoves. An interesting labor market impact was an increase in the demand for chimney sweeps. Finally, in late 1987 McDonald's used television commercials to attract housewives and retirees to work in its 1600 company-owned restaurants. Why did this recruitment campaign begin in 1987 rather than a decade or two earlier? A major reason was that more and more women were working outside the house and thus had less time for meal preparation. The result was an increase in the demand for restaurant meals and an increase in the demand for fast-food workers which could not be entirely filled by teenagers, the traditional source of labor for fast-food restaurants.

Productivity Changes

Other things being unchanged, *a change in the productivity of labor will shift the labor demand curve in the same direction.* If we were to double the MP data of column 3 in Table 14-1 we would find that the MRP data would also double, indicating an increase in labor demand.

The productivity of any resource can be altered in several ways.

1 The marginal productivity data for, say, labor will depend on the quantities of other resources with which it is combined. The greater the amount of capital and land resources with which labor is combined, the greater will be the marginal productivity and the demand for labor.

2 Technological improvements will have the same effect. The better the quality of the capital, the greater the productivity of labor. Steelworkers employed with a given amount of real capital in the form of modern oxygen furnaces are more productive than when employed with the same amount of real capital embodied in old open-hearth furnaces.

3 Improvements in the quality of the variable resource itself—labor—will increase marginal productivity and therefore the demand for labor. In effect, we have a new demand curve for a different, more skilled, kind of labor.

All these considerations, incidentally, are important in explaining why the average level of (real) wages is higher in the United States than in many other nations. American workers are generally healthier and better trained than those of these other nations, and in most industries they work with a larger and more efficient stock of capital goods and more abundant natural resources. This spells a strong demand for labor. On the supply side of the market, labor is *relatively* scarce compared with some other nations. A strong demand and a relatively scarce supply result in high wage rates. This will be discussed further in Chapter 15.

Prices of Other Resources

Just as changes in the prices of other products will change the demand for a specific commodity, so changes in the prices of other resources can be expected to alter the demand for a particular resource. Just as the effect of a change in the price of product X on the demand for product Y depends on whether X and Y are substitute or complementary goods (Chapter 4), so the effect of a change in the price of resource A on the demand for resource B will depend on their substitutability or their degree of complementarity.

Substitute Resources Suppose in a certain production process that technology is such that labor and capital are substitutable for one another. In other words, a firm can produce some given output with a relatively small amount of labor and a relatively large amount of capital or vice versa. Now assume a decline in the price of machinery occurs. The resulting impact on the demand for labor will be the net result of two opposed effects: the substitution effect and the output effect.

1 Substitution Effect The decline in the price of machinery will prompt the firm to substitute machinery for labor. This is the obvious adjustment to make if the firm seeks to produce any given output in the least costly fashion. At given wage rates, smaller quantities of labor will now be employed. In short, this **substitution effect** will decrease the demand for labor.

2 Output Effect Because the price of machinery has fallen, the costs of producing various outputs will also have declined. With lower costs, the firm will find it profitable to produce and sell a larger output. This greater output will increase the demand for all resources, including labor. For a reduction in the price of machinery, this **output effect** will increase the demand for labor.

The substitution and output effects clearly work in opposite directions. For a decline in the price of machinery, the substitution effect decreases and the output effect increases the demand for labor. The net impact on labor demand will depend on the relative sizes of the two opposed effects. If the substitution effect outweighs the output effect, the reduction in the price of capital reduces the demand for labor. If the reverse holds true, the demand for labor will increase. *If the substitution effect outweighs the output effect, a change in the price of a substitute resource will change the demand for labor in the same direction. If the output effect exceeds the substitution effect, a change in the price of a substitute resource will change the demand for labor in the opposite direction.*

Complementary Resources Recall from Chapter 4 that certain products, such as cameras and film or computers and software, are complementary goods in that they "go together" and are jointly demanded. Resources may also be complementary; an increase in the quantity of one of them used in the production process will require an increase in the amount used of the other as well, and vice versa. For example, suppose a small manufacturer of metal products uses punch presses as its basic piece of capital equipment. Each press is designed to be operated by one worker; the machine is not automated—it won't run itself—and a second worker would be wholly redundant.

Assume that a significant technological advance in the production of these presses substantially reduces their costs. Now there can be no negative substitution effect because labor and capital must be used in fixed proportions, one person for one machine. Capital cannot be substituted for labor. But there is a positive output effect for labor. Other things being equal, the reduction in the price of capital goods means lower production costs. It will therefore be profitable to produce a larger output. In doing so the firm will use both more capital and more labor. When labor and capital are complementary, a decline in the price of machinery will increase the demand for labor through the output effect. Conversely, in the case of an increase in the price of capital, the output effect will reduce the demand for labor. *A change in the price of a complementary resource will cause the demand for labor to change in the opposite direction.*

Recapitulation: The demand curve for labor will *increase* (shift rightward) when:

1 The demand for (and therefore the price of) the product produced by that labor increases
2 The productivity (MP) of labor increases
3 The price of a substitute input decreases, provided the output effect is greater than the substitution effect
4 The price of a substitute input increases, provided the substitution effect exceeds the output effect
5 The price of a complementary input decreases

ELASTICITY OF RESOURCE DEMAND

The factors just discussed are responsible for shifts in the location of resource demand curves. Such changes in demand must be distinguished from a change in the quantity of a resource demanded. The latter does not entail a shift in the resource demand curve but rather a movement from one point to another on a stable resource demand curve, because of a change in the price of the specific resource under consideration. In Table 14-1 and Figure 14-1 we note that an increase in the wage rate from $5.95 to $7.95 will reduce the quantity of labor demanded from five to four workers.

What determines the sensitivity of producers to changes in resource prices? Or, more technically, what determines the elasticity of resource demand? Several generalizations provide important insights in answering this question.

1 Rate of MP Decline A purely technical consideration—the rate at which the marginal product of the variable resource declines—is crucial. *If the marginal product of labor declines slowly as it is added to a fixed amount of capital, the MRP, or demand curve for labor, will decline slowly and tend to be highly elastic.* A small decline in the price of such a resource will yield a relatively large increase in the amount demanded. Conversely, if the marginal productivity of labor declines sharply, the MRP, or labor demand curve, will decline rapidly. This means that a relatively large decline in the wage rate will be accompanied by a very modest increase in the amount of labor hired; resource demand will be inelastic.

2 Ease of Resource Substitutability The degree to which resources are substitutable is also a determinant of elasticity. *The larger the number of good substitute resources available, the greater will be the elasticity of demand for a particular resource.* If a furniture manufacturer finds that five or six different types of wood are equally satisfactory in making coffee tables, a rise in the price of any one type of wood may cause a very sharp drop in the amount demanded as the producer substitutes other woods. At the other extreme, it may be impossible to substitute; bauxite is absolutely essential in the production of aluminum ingots. Thus, the demand for it by aluminum producers is inelastic.

Note that *time* can play an important role in the input substitution process. For example, a firm's truck drivers may obtain a substantial wage increase with little or no immediate decline in employment. But over time, as the firm's trucks wear out and are replaced, the company may purchase larger trucks and thereby be able to deliver the same total output with fewer drivers. Alternatively, as the firm's trucks depreciate, it might turn to entirely different means of transportation. As a second example, recently developed commercial aircraft have been specifically designed to require only two pilots rather than the customary three.

3 Elasticity of Product Demand The elasticity of demand for any resource will depend on the elasticity of demand for the product it helps produce. *The greater the elasticity of product demand, the greater the elasticity of resource demand.* The derived nature of resource demand would lead us to expect this relationship. A small rise in the price of a product with great elasticity of demand will sharply reduce output and therefore bring about a relatively large decline in the amounts of various resources demanded. This correctly implies that the demand for the resource is elastic. Remember that the resource demand curve of Figure 14-1 is more elastic than the resource demand curve shown in Figure 14-2. The difference arises because in Figure 14-1 we assume a perfectly elastic product demand curve, while Figure 14-2 is based on a downsloping or less than perfectly elastic product demand curve.

4 Labor Cost–Total Cost Ratio *The larger the proportion of total production costs accounted for by a resource, the greater will be the elasticity of demand for that resource.* In the extreme, if labor costs were the only production cost, then a 20 percent increase in wage rates would shift the firm's cost curves upward by 20 percent. Given the elasticity of product demand, this substantial increase in costs would cause a relatively large decline in sales and a sharp decline in the amount of labor demanded. Labor demand would be elastic. But if labor costs were only 50 percent of production costs, then a 20 percent increase in wage rates would only increase costs by 10 percent. Given the same elasticity of product demand, a relatively small decline in sales and therefore in the amount of labor would result. The demand for labor would be inelastic.

QUICK REVIEW 14-2

- ***A resource demand curve will shift because of changes in product demand, changes in the productivity of the resource, and changes in the prices of other inputs.***
- ***If resources A and B are substitutable, a decline in the price of A will decrease the demand for B provided the substitution effect exceeds the output effect. But if the output effect exceeds the substitution effect, the demand for B will increase.***
- ***If resources C and D are complements, a decline in the price of C will increase the demand for D.***
- ***The elasticity of demand for a resource will be less the more rapid the decline in marginal product; the smaller the number of substitutes; the smaller the elasticity of product demand; and the smaller the proportion of total cost accounted for by the resource.***

OPTIMAL COMBINATION OF RESOURCES

So far we have centered our discussion on one variable input, namely, labor. But in the long run firms can vary the amounts of *all* the resources they use. It is therefore important to consider what combination of resources a firm will choose when all are variable. While our analysis will be based on two resources, it can be extended to any number one chooses to consider.

We will consider two interrelated questions:

1 What is the least-cost combination of resources to use in producing *any* given level of output?

2 What combination of resources will maximize a firm's profits?

The Least-Cost Rule

A firm is producing *any* given output with the **least-cost combination of resources** when the last dollar spent on each resource entails the same marginal product. That is, *the cost of any output is minimized when the marginal product per dollar's worth of each resource used is the same.* With just two resources, labor and capital, the cost-minimizing position occurs where

$$\frac{\text{MP of labor}}{\text{price of labor}} = \frac{\text{MP of capital}}{\text{price of capital}} \qquad (1)$$

You can see why fulfilling this condition means least-cost production. Suppose that the prices of capital and labor are both \$1 per unit, but that capital and labor are currently employed in such amounts that the marginal product of labor is 10 and the marginal product of capital is 5. Our equation immediately tells us this is *not* the least costly combination of resources: MP_L/P_L is 10/1 and MP_C/P_C is 5/1.

If the firm spends a dollar less on capital and shifts that dollar to labor, it will lose the 5 units of output produced by the marginal dollar's worth of capital, but will gain the 10 units of output from the extra dollar's worth of labor. *Net* output will increase by 5 (= 10 − 5) units for the same total cost. This shifting of dollars from capital to labor will push the firm down its MP curve for labor and back up its MP curve for capital, moving the firm toward a position of equilibrium where equation (1) is fulfilled. At that point the MP of both labor and capital might be, for example, 7.

Whenever the same total cost results in a greater total output, the cost per unit—and therefore the total cost of any given level of output—is being reduced. To be able to produce a *larger* output with a *given* total-cost outlay is the same thing as being able to produce a *given* output with a *smaller* total-cost outlay. From a slightly different perspective, if the firm buys \$1 less of capital, its output will fall by 5 units. By spending only \$.50 on labor the firm will increase its output by a compensating 5 units (= $\frac{1}{2}$ of the marginal product of a dollar's worth of labor). Thus, the firm will realize the same total output at a \$.50 lower total cost.

The cost of producing any given output can be reduced so long as $MP_L/P_L \neq MP_C/P_C$. But when dollars have been shifted among capital and labor to the point where equation (1) holds, there are no further changes in the amounts of capital and labor employed which will further reduce costs. The least-cost combination of capital and labor is being realized for that output.

All long run[3] *cost curves developed in Chapter 9 and applied in the ensuing product market chapters implicitly assume that each possible level of output is being produced with the least costly combination of inputs.* If this were not so, then presumably there would exist lower attainable positions for the cost curves, and consequently there would be some other (larger) output and lower price at equilibrium. In terms of Chapter 11 a firm which combines resources in violation of the least-cost rule would incur X-inefficiency.

The producer's least-cost rule is analogous to the consumer's utility-maximizing rule of Chapter 8. In achieving the utility-maximizing collection of goods, the consumer considers both his or her preferences as reflected in diminishing marginal-utility data *and* prices of the various products. Similarly, a producer wants to minimize costs, just as the consumer seeks to maximize utility. In pursuing this combination of resources, the producer must consider both the productivity of the resource as reflected in diminishing marginal productivity data *and* prices (costs) of the various resources. A firm may well find it profitable to employ very small amounts of an extremely productive resource if its price is particularly high. Conversely, a firm might hire large amounts of a relatively unproductive resource if its price is sufficiently low.

The Profit-Maximizing Rule

Minimizing cost is not sufficient for maximizing profit. There are many different levels of output which a firm can produce in the least costly way, but there is only one unique output which will maximize profits. Recalling our earlier analysis of product markets, this profit-maximizing *output* is where marginal revenue equals marginal cost (MR = MC). We now derive a comparable rule from the standpoint of resource *inputs.*

In deriving the demand schedule for labor early in this chapter we determined that the profit-maximizing quantity of labor to employ is that quantity at which the wage rate, or price of labor (P_L), equals the marginal *revenue* product of labor (MRP_L) or, more simply, $P_L = \text{MRP}_L$.

The same rationale applies to any other resource —for example, capital. Capital will also be employed in the profit-maximizing amount when its price equals its marginal revenue product, or $P_C = \text{MRP}_C$. Thus, in general, we can say that when hiring resources *in competitive markets,* a firm will realize the **profit-maximizing combination of resources** when each input is employed up to the point at which its price equals its marginal revenue product:

$$P_L = \text{MRP}_L$$

$$P_C = \text{MRP}_C$$

Dividing both sides of each equation by their respective prices, we have

$$\frac{\text{MRP}_L}{P_L} = \frac{\text{MRP}_C}{P_C} = 1 \qquad (2)$$

Note in equation (2) that it is not sufficient that the MRPs of the two resources be *proportionate to* their prices; the MRPs must be *equal to* their prices and the ratios therefore equal to 1. For example, if $\text{MRP}_L =$ \$15, $P_L =$ \$5, $\text{MRP}_C =$ \$9, and $P_C =$ \$3, the firm would be underemploying both capital and labor even though the ratios of MRP to resource price were identical for both resources. The firm could expand its profits by hiring additional amounts of both capital and labor until it had moved down their downsloping MRP curves to the points at which MRP_L was equal to \$5 and MRP_C was \$3. The ratios would now be 5/5 and 3/3 and equal to 1.[4]

[3]We specify long run because application of the least-cost rule assumes that quantities of both labor and capital are variable.

[4]It is not difficult to demonstrate that equation (2) is consistent with (indeed, the equivalent of) the $P = \text{MC}$ rule for determining the profit-maximizing output of Chapter 10. We begin by taking the reciprocal of equation (2):

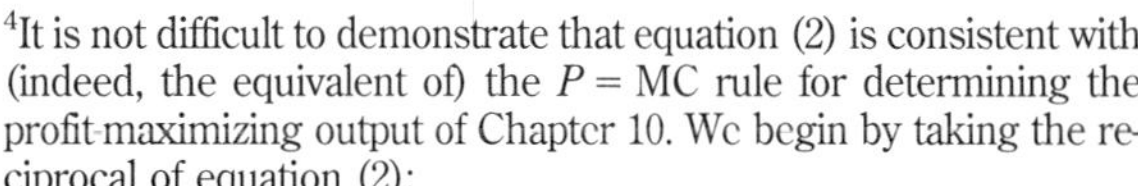

$$\frac{P_L}{\text{MRP}_L} = \frac{P_C}{\text{MRP}_C} = 1$$

Recall that, assuming pure competition in the product market, marginal revenue product, MRP, is found by multiplying marginal product, MP, by product price, P_x. Thus we can write:

$$\frac{P_L}{\text{MP}_L \cdot P_x} = \frac{P_C}{\text{MP}_C \cdot P_x} = 1$$

Multiplying through by product price, P_x, we get:

$$\frac{P_L}{\text{MP}_L} = \frac{P_C}{\text{MP}_C} = P_x$$

The two ratios measure marginal cost. That is, if we divide the cost of an additional input of labor or capital by the associated marginal product we have the addition to total cost, that is, the *marginal cost,* of each additional unit of output. For example, if the price of an extra worker (P_L) is \$10 and that worker's marginal product (MP_L) is 5 units, then the marginal cost of each of those 5 units is \$2. The same reasoning applies to capital. We thus obtain:

$$MC_x = P_x$$

Our conclusion is that equation (2) in the text, showing the profit-maximizing combination of *inputs,* is the equivalent of our earlier $P = \text{MC}$ rule which identified the profit-maximizing *output.*

Although we have separated the two for discussion purposes, the profit-maximizing position of equation (2) subsumes the least-cost position of equation (1). (Note that if we divide the MRP numerators in equation [2] by product price we obtain equation [1].) A firm which is maximizing its profits *must* be producing the profit-maximizing output with the least costly combination of resources. If it is *not* using the least costly combination of labor and capital, then it could produce the same output at a smaller total cost and realize a larger profit. Thus, a necessary condition for profit maximization is the fulfillment of equation (1). But equation (1) is not a sufficient condition for profit maximization. It is quite possible for a firm to produce the "wrong" output, that is, an output which does not maximize profits, but to produce that output with the least costly combination of resources.

Numerical Illustration

A numerical illustration may help us in grasping the least-cost and profit-maximizing rules. In columns 2, 3, 2′, and 3′ of Table 14-3 we show the total products and marginal products for various amounts of labor and capital which are assumed to be the only inputs needed in producing product X. Both inputs are subject to the law of diminishing returns.

We also assume that labor and capital are supplied in competitive resource markets at $8 and $12 respectively and that product X is sold competitively at $2 per unit. For both labor and capital we can determine the total revenue associated with each input level by multiplying total product by the $2 product price. These data are shown in columns 4 and 4′. This allows us to calculate the marginal revenue product of each successive input of labor and capital as shown in columns 5 and 5′.

Producing at Least Cost What is the least-cost combination of labor and capital to use in producing, say, 50 units of output? Answer: 3 units of labor and 2 units of capital. Note from columns 3 and 3′ that in hiring 3 units of labor $MP_L/P_L = 6/8 = 3/4$ and for 2 units of capital $MP_C/P_C = 9/12 = 3/4$, so equation (1) is fulfilled. And columns 2 and 2′ indicate that this combination of labor and capital does, indeed, result in the specified 50 (= 28 + 22) units of output. How can we verify that costs are actually minimized? First, note that the total cost of employing 3 units of labor and 2 of capital is $48 [= (3 × $8) + (2 × $12)] or, alternatively stated, cost per unit of output is $.96 (= $48/50).

Observe that there are other combinations of labor and capital which will yield 50 units of output. For example, 5 units of labor and 1 unit of capital will produce 50 (= 37 + 13) units, but we find that total cost is now higher at $52 [= (5 × $8) + (1 × $12)], meaning that average unit cost has risen to $1.04 (= $52/50). By employing 5 units of labor and 1 of capital the least-cost rule would be violated in that $MP_L/P_L = 4/8$ is less than $MP_C/P_C = 13/12$, indicating that more capital and less labor should be employed to produce this output.

Similarly, 50 units of output also could be produced with 2 units of labor and 3 of capital. The total cost of the 50 units of output would again be $52 [= (2 × $8) + (3 × $12)], or $1.04 per unit. Here equation (1) is not fulfilled in that $MP_L/P_L = 10/8$

TABLE 14-3 The least-cost and profit-maximizing combination of labor and capital *(hypothetical data)**

Labor (price = $8)					*Capital (price = $12)*				
(1) Quantity	*(2) Total product*	*(3) Marginal product*	*(4) Total revenue*	*(5) Marginal revenue product*	*(1′) Quantity*	*(2′) Total product*	*(3′) Marginal product*	*(4′) Total revenue*	*(5′) Marginal revenue product*
0	0	0	$ 0	$ 0	0	0	0	$ 0	$ 0
1	12	12	24	24	1	13	13	26	26
2	22	10	44	20	2	22	9	44	18
3	28	6	56	12	3	28	6	56	12
4	33	5	66	10	4	32	4	64	8
5	37	4	74	8	5	35	3	70	6
6	40	3	80	6	6	37	2	74	4
7	42	2	84	4	7	38	1	76	2

*To simplify, it is assumed in this table that the productivity of each resource is independent of the quantity of the other. For example, the total and marginal product of labor is assumed not to vary with the quantity of capital employed.

which exceeds $MP_C/P_C = 6/12$. This inequality suggests that the firm should use more labor and less capital.

To recapitulate: While there may be several combinations of labor and capital capable of producing any given output—in this case 50 units—only that combination which fulfills equation (1) will minimize costs.

Maximizing Profits Will 50 units of output maximize the firm's profits? Answer: No, because the profit-maximizing rule stated in equation (2) is *not* fulfilled when employing 3 units of labor and 2 of capital. We know that to maximize profits any given input should be employed until its price equals its marginal revenue product ($P_L = MRP_L$ and $P_C = MRP_C$). But for 3 units of labor we find in column 5 that labor's MRP is \$12 while its price is only \$8. This means it is profitable to hire more labor. Similarly, for 2 units of capital we observe in column 5′ that MRP is \$18 and capital's price is only \$12, indicating that more capital should be employed. When hiring 3 units of labor and 2 of capital to produce 50 units of output, the firm is underemploying both inputs. Labor and capital are both being used in less than profit-maximizing amounts.

The marginal revenue products of labor and capital are equal to their prices and equation (2) is fulfilled when the firm is employing 5 units of labor and 3 units of capital. This is therefore the profit-maximizing combination of outputs.[5] The firm's total cost will be \$76, which is made up of \$40 (= 5 × \$8) worth of labor and \$36 (= 3 × \$12) worth of capital. Total revenue of \$130 is determined by multiplying total output of 65 (= 37 + 28) by the \$2 product price or, alternatively, by simply summing the total revenue attributable to labor (\$74) and to capital (\$56). The difference between total revenue and total cost is, of course, the firm's economic profit which in this instance is \$54 (= \$130 − \$76). Equation (2) is fulfilled when 5 units of labor and 3 of capital are employed: $MRP_L/P_L = 8/8 = MRP_C/P_C = 12/12 = 1$. You should experiment with other combinations of labor and capital to demonstrate that they will yield an economic profit less than \$54.

Our example also verifies our earlier assertion that a firm using the profit-maximizing combination of inputs is also necessarily producing the resulting output with the least cost. In fulfilling equation (2) the firm is automatically fulfilling equation (1). In this case for 5 units of labor and 3 of capital we observe that $MP_L/P_L = 4/8 = MP_C/P_C = 6/12$. Questions 5 and 7 at the end of this chapter are also recommended to further your understanding of the least-cost and profit-maximizing combination of inputs.[6]

MARGINAL PRODUCTIVITY THEORY OF INCOME DISTRIBUTION

Our discussion of resource pricing is the cornerstone of the controversial view that economic justice is one of the outcomes of a competitive capitalist economy. Table 14-1 tells us, in effect, that labor receives an income payment equal to the marginal contribution it makes to the firm's revenue. Bluntly stated, labor is paid what it is economically worth. Therefore, if one is willing to accept the ethical proposition "To each according to what one creates," the marginal productivity theory seems to provide a fair and equitable distribution of income. Because the marginal productivity theory equally applies to capital and land, the distribution of all incomes can be held as equitable.

At first glance an income distribution whereby workers and owners of property resources are paid in accordance with their contribution to output sounds eminently fair. But there are serious criticisms of the **marginal productivity theory of income distribution.**

1 Inequality Critics argue that the distribution of income resulting from payment according to marginal productivity may be highly unequal because productive resources are very unequally distributed in the first place. Aside from differences in genetic endowments, individuals encounter substantially different opportunities to enhance their productivity through education and training. Some may not be able to participate in production at all because of mental or physical handicaps and would obtain no income under a system of distribution based solely on marginal productivity.

[5]Given that we are dealing with discrete (nonfractional) increases in the two outputs, you should also be aware that in fact the employment of 4 units of labor and 2 of capital is equally profitable. The fifth unit of labor's MRP and its price are equal (at \$8), so that the fifth unit neither adds to, nor subtracts from, the firm's profits. The same reasoning applies to the third unit of capital.

[6]Footnote 1 in Chapter 15 modifies our least-cost and profit-maximizing rules for the situation in which a firm is hiring resources under imperfectly competitive conditions. Where there is imperfect competition in the resource market, the marginal resource cost (MRC)—the cost of an extra input—exceeds the resource price (P). Hence, we must substitute MRC for P in the denominators of equations (1) and (2).

LAST WORD

INPUT SUBSTITUTION: THE CASE OF CABOOSES

Substituting among inputs—particularly when jobs are at stake—can be quite controversial.

We have found that a firm will achieve the least-cost combination of inputs when the last dollar spent on each makes the same contribution to total output. This rule also implies that a firm is unimpeded in changing its input mix in response to technological changes or changes in input prices. Unfortunately, in the real world the substitution of new capital for old capital and the substitution of capital for labor may be controversial and difficult to achieve.

Consider the case of railroad cabooses. The railroads claim that technological advance has made the caboose obsolete. In particular, railroads want to substitute a "trainlink" which can be attached to the coupler of the last car of a train. This small black box contains a revolving strobe light and instruments which monitor train speed, airbrake pressure, and other relevant data which it transmits to the locomotive engineer. The trainlink costs only $4000 in comparison to $80,000 for a new caboose. And, of course, the trainlink replaces one member of the train crew.

The railroads cite substantial cost economies—perhaps as much as $400 million per year—from this rearrangement of capital and labor inputs. But the United Transportation Union (UTU) which represents railroad conductors and brakemen fears that the recent trend toward the demise of the caboose portends a decline in the demand for its members. The union therefore has made a concerted, but largely unsuccessful, effort to halt the elimination of cabooses on trains. The UTU argues that the elimination of cabooses will reduce railroad safety.

The union contends that, unlike humans, trainlink cannot detect broken wheels or axles nor overheated bearings. From the vantage point of the railroads this looks like featherbedding, that is, the protection of unnecessary jobs. The railroads contend that available data show no safety differences between trains using and those not using cabooses. Indeed, safety may be enhanced without cabooses because many injuries are incurred by crew who are riding in cabooses.

While cabooses are virtually extinct in Europe, they are the rule in Canada. In the United States the railway unions have lobbied successfully for legislation in four states which makes cabooses mandatory. In all other states the use of cabooses remains a matter of collective bargaining negotiations. In any event, the case of cabooses indicates clearly that input substitution is not as simple as economic analysis would suggest.

Ownership of property resources is also highly unequal. Many landlords and capitalists obtain their property by inheritance rather than through their own productive effort. Hence, income from inherited property resources conflicts with the "To each according to what one creates" proposition. This reasoning can lead one to advocate government policies to modify the income distribution resulting from payments made strictly according to marginal productivity.

2 Monopsony and Monopoly The marginal productivity theory rests on the assumption of competitive markets. We will find in Chapter 15 that labor markets, for example, are riddled with imperfections. Some employers exert monopsony power in hiring workers. And some workers, through labor unions and professional associations, brandish monopoly power in selling their services. Indeed, the process of collective bargaining over wages suggests a power struggle over the division of income. In this struggle market forces—and income shares based on marginal productivity—are pushed into the background. In short, we will find that, because of real-world market imperfections, wage rates and other resource prices frequently do *not* measure contributions to domestic output.

CHAPTER SUMMARY

1 Resource prices are a major determinant of money incomes, and simultaneously perform the function of rationing resources to various industries and firms.

2 The fact that the demand for any resource is derived from the product it helps produce means that the demand for a resource will depend on its productivity and the market value (price) of the good it is producing.

3 The marginal revenue product schedule of any resource is the demand schedule for that resource. This follows from an application of the rule that a firm hiring under competitive conditions will find it most profitable to hire a resource up to the point where the price of the resource equals its marginal revenue product.

4 The demand curve for a resource is downsloping because the marginal product of additional inputs of any resource declines in accordance with the law of diminishing returns. When a firm is selling in an imperfectly competitive market, the resource demand curve will fall for a second reason: Product price must be reduced to permit the firm to sell a larger output. The market demand for a resource can be derived by summing horizontally the demand curves of all firms hiring that resource.

5 The demand for a resource will shift as the result of **a** a change in the demand for, and therefore the price of, the product the resource is producing; **b** changes in the productivity of the resource; and **c** changes in prices of other resources.

6 If resources A and B are substitutable, a decline in the price of A will decrease the demand for B provided the substitution effect is greater than the output effect. But if the output effect exceeds the substitution effect, a decline in the price of A will increase the demand for B.

7 If resources C and D are complementary or jointly demanded, there is only an output effect and a change in the price of C will change the demand for D in the opposite direction.

8 The elasticity of resource demand will be greater **a** the slower the rate at which the marginal product of the resource declines, **b** the larger the number of good substitute resources available, **c** the greater the elasticity of demand for the product, and **d** the larger the proportion of total production costs attributable to the resource.

9 Any level of output will be produced with the least costly combination of resources when the marginal product per dollar's worth of each input is the same, that is, when

$$\frac{\text{MP of labor}}{\text{price of labor}} = \frac{\text{MP of capital}}{\text{price of capital}}$$

10 A firm will employ the profit-maximizing combination of resources when the price of each resource is equal to its marginal *revenue* product or, algebraically, when

$$\frac{\text{MRP of labor}}{\text{price of labor}} = \frac{\text{MRP of capital}}{\text{price of capital}} = 1$$

TERMS AND CONCEPTS

derived demand
marginal product
marginal revenue product
marginal resource cost
MRP = MRC rule
substitution and output effects
least-cost combination of resources
profit-maximizing combination of resources
marginal productivity theory of income distribution

QUESTIONS AND STUDY SUGGESTIONS

1 What is the significance of resource pricing? Explain in detail how the factors determining resource demand differ from those underlying product demand. Explain the meaning and significance of the notion that the demand for a resource is a *derived* demand. Why do resource demand curves slope downward?

2 Complete the following labor demand table (page 254) for a firm which is hiring labor competitively and selling its product in a competitive market.

a How many workers will the firm hire if the going wage rate is $27.95? $19.95? Explain why the firm will not hire a larger or smaller number of workers at each of these wage rates.

b Show in schedule form and graphically the labor demand curve of this firm.

c Now redetermine the firm's demand curve for labor, assuming that it is selling in an imperfectly competitive market and that, although it can sell 17 units at $2.20 per unit, it must lower product price by 5 cents to sell the marginal product of each successive worker. Compare this demand curve with that derived in question 2b. Which curve is more elastic? Explain.

Units of labor	Total product	Marginal product	Product price	Total revenue	Marginal revenue product
1	17		$2	$	
					$
2	31		2		
					$
3	43		2		
					$
4	53		2		
					$
5	60		2		
					$
6	65		2		

3 Distinguish between a change in resource demand and a change in the quantity of a resource demanded. What specific factors might lead to a change in resource demand? A change in the quantity of a resource demanded?

4 What factors determine the elasticity of resource demand? What effect will each of the following have on the elasticity *or* the location of the demand for resource C, which is being used in the production of commodity X? Where there is any uncertainty as to the outcome, specify the causes of that uncertainty.

a An increase in the demand for product X.

b An increase in the price of substitute resource D.

c An increase in the number of resources substitutable for C in producing X.

d A technological improvement in the capital equipment with which resource C is combined.

e A decline in the price of complementary resource E.

f A decline in the elasticity of demand for product X due to a decline in the competitiveness of the product market.

5 Suppose the productivity of labor and capital are as shown below. The output of these resources sells in a purely competitive market for $1 per unit. Both labor and capital are hired under purely competitive conditions at $1 and $3 respectively.

Units of capital	MP of capital	Units of labor	MP of labor
1	24	1	11
2	21	2	9
3	18	3	8
4	15	4	7
5	9	5	6
6	6	6	4
7	3	7	1
8	1	8	½

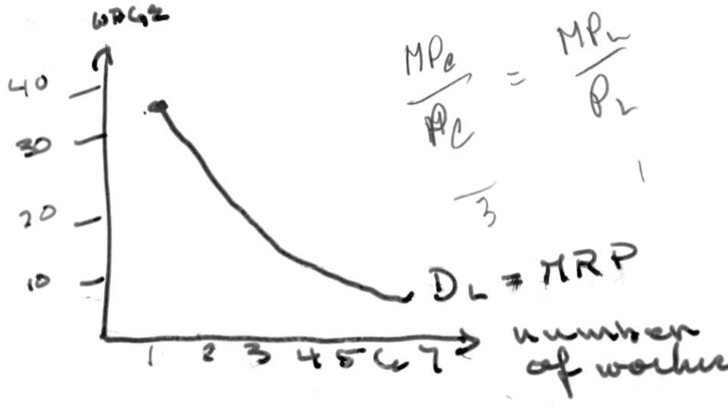

a What is the least-cost combination of labor and capital to employ in producing 80 units of output? Explain.

b What is the profit-maximizing combination of labor and capital for the firm to employ? Explain. What is the resulting level of output? What is the economic profit?

c When the firm employs the profit-maximizing combination of labor and capital determined in 5b, is this combination also the least costly way of producing the profit-maximizing output? Explain.

6 Using the substitution and output effects, explain how a decline in the price of resource A *might* cause an increase in the demand for substitute resource B. If resources C and D are complementary and used in fixed proportions, what will be the impact of an increase in the price of C on the demand for D?

7 In each of the following four cases MRP_L and MRP_C refer to the marginal revenue products of labor and capital, respectively, and P_L and P_C refer to their prices. Indicate in each case whether the conditions are consistent with maximum profits for the firm. If not, state which resource(s) should be used in larger amounts and which resource(s) should be used in smaller amounts.

a $MRP_L = \$8$; $P_L = \$4$; $MRP_C = \$8$; $P_C = \$4$.

b $MRP_L = \$10$; $P_L = \$12$; $MRP_C = \$14$; $P_C = \$9$.

c $MRP_L = \$6$; $P_L = \$6$; $MRP_C = \$12$; $P_C = \$12$.

d $MRP_L = \$22$; $P_L = \$26$; $MRP_C = \$16$; $P_C = \$19$.

8 **Advanced analysis:** Demonstrate algebraically that the condition for the profit-maximizing level of output is the equivalent of the condition for the profit-maximizing combination of inputs.

9 If each input is paid in accordance with its marginal revenue product, will the resulting distribution of income be ethically just?

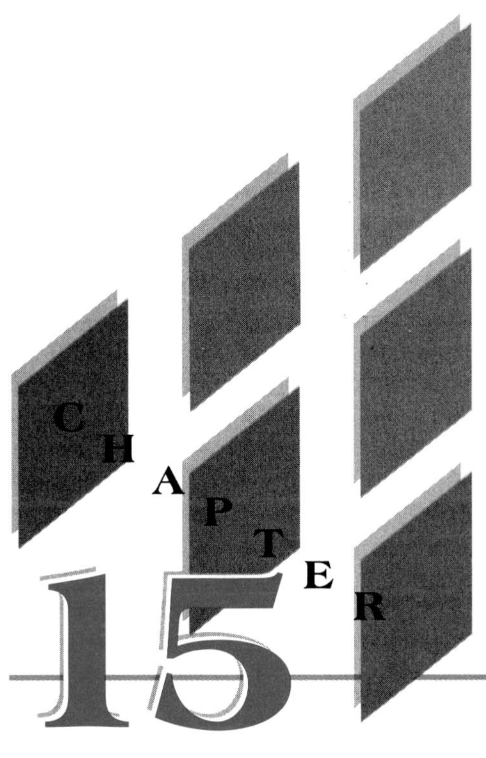

The Pricing and Employment of Resources: Wage Determination

The most important price you will encounter in your lifetime will most likely be your wage rate. It will be critical in determining your economic well-being. The following facts and questions may be of more than casual interest.

Fact: Real wages and therefore living standards have increased historically in the United States. Question: What forces account for these increases?

Fact: Union workers generally receive higher wages than nonunion workers in the same occupation. Question: How are unions able to accomplish this wage advantage?

Fact: The average salary for major league baseball players in 1991 was $890,844 compared to about $33,000 for teachers. Question: What causes differences in wages and incomes?

Fact: Most people are paid a certain hourly wage rate. But some workers are paid by the number of units produced or receive commissions and royalties. Question: What is the rationale for various compensation schemes?

Having explored the strategic factors underlying resource demand, we now introduce supply as it characterizes the markets for labor, land, capital, and entrepreneurial ability, to understand how wages, rents, interest, and profits are determined. We discuss wages before other resource prices because to the vast majority of households the wage rate is the most important price in the economy; it is the sole or basic source of income. About three-fourths of the national income is in the form of wages and salaries.

Our basic objectives in discussing wage determination are to (1) understand the forces underlying the general level of wage rates in the United states; (2) see how wage rates are determined in particular labor markets by presenting several representative labor market models; (3) analyze the impact of unions on the structure and level of wages; (4) discuss the economic effects of the minimum wage; (5) explain wage differentials; and (6) survey a number of compensation schemes which link pay to worker performance.

Throughout this chapter we will rely on the marginal productivity theory of Chapter 14 as an explanation of labor demand.

MEANING OF WAGES

Wages, or wage rates, are the price paid for the use of labor. Economists often use the term "labor" broadly to apply to payments received by (1) workers in the popular sense of the term, that is, blue- and white-collar workers of almost infinite variety; (2) professional people—lawyers, physicians, dentists, teachers; and (3) owners of small businesses—barbers, plumbers, television repairers, and a host of retailers—for the labor services they provide in operating their own businesses.

Wages may take the form of bonuses, royalties, commissions, and monthly salaries, but we will for the most part use the term "wages" to mean wage rates per unit of time—per hour, per day, and so forth. This designation will remind us that the wage rate is a price paid for the use of units of labor service. It also lets us distinguish clearly between "wages" and "earnings," the latter depending on wage rates *and* the number of hours or weeks of labor service supplied in the market.

We also distinguish between money or nominal wages and real wages. **Nominal wages** are the amount of money received per hour, per day, per week, and so on. **Real wages,** however, are the quantity of goods and services one can obtain with nominal wages; real wages are the "purchasing power" of nominal wages.

One's real wages depend on one's nominal wages and the prices of the goods and services purchased. The percentage change in real wages can be determined by subtracting the percentage change in the price level from the percentage change in nominal wages. Thus an 8 percent increase in nominal wages during a year when the price level increases by 5 percent yields a 3 percent increase in real wages. Unless otherwise indicated, our discussion will be in terms of real wage rates by assuming that the level of product prices is constant.

GENERAL LEVEL OF WAGES

Wages differ among nations, regions, various occupations, and individuals. Wage rates are vastly higher in the United States than in China or India; they are generally higher in the north and east of the United States than in the south; plumbers are paid less than NFL punters; physician Adams may earn twice as much as physician Bennett for the same number of hours of work. Wage rates also differ by gender and race.

The general or average level of wages, like the general level of prices, is a composite concept encompassing a wide range of different specific wage rates. This admittedly vague concept is a useful point of departure in making and explaining international and interregional wage comparisons. Statistical data indicate that the general level of real wages in the United States is among the highest in the world. The simplest explanation is that in the United States the demand for labor has been great in relation to supply.

Role of Productivity

We know that the demand for labor—or any other resource—depends on its productivity. In general, the greater the productivity of labor, the greater the demand for it. And, given the total supply of labor, the stronger the demand, the greater the average level of real wages. The demand for American labor has been strong because it is highly productive. The reasons for this high productivity are several:

1 Capital American workers are used in conjunction with large amounts of capital equipment. A recent estimate indicates that total physical capital (machinery and buildings) per worker is approximately $40,000.

2 Natural Resources Natural resources are abundant in relation to the size of the labor force. The United States is richly endowed with arable land, basic mineral resources, and ample sources of industrial power. The fact that American workers have large amounts of high-quality natural resources to work with is perhaps most evident in agriculture where, historically, the growth of productivity has been dramatic (Chapter 21).

3 Technology The level of technological advance is generally higher in the United States than in most foreign nations. American workers in many industries use not only more capital equipment but better (technologically superior) equipment than do the vast majority of foreign workers. Similarly, work methods are steadily being improved through detailed scientific study and research.

4 Labor Quality The health, vigor, education and training, and work attitudes of American workers are generally superior to those of the labor of most other nations. This means that, even with the same quantity and quality of natural and capital resources, American workers would be more efficient than many of their foreign counterparts.

5 Other Factors Less tangible, yet important, items underlying the high productivity of American labor are (a) the efficiency and flexibility of American management; (b) a business, social, and political environment which puts great emphasis on production and productivity; and (c) the vast size of the domestic market, which provides the opportunity for firms to realize mass-production economies.

Real Wages and Productivity

The dependence of real hourly wages on the productivity level is indicated in Figure 15-1. Note the relatively close relationship in the long run between real hourly wages and output per labor-hour. When one recalls that real income and real output are two ways of viewing the same thing, it is no surprise that *real income (earnings) per worker can increase only at about the same rate as output per worker.* More real output per hour means more real income to distribute for each hour worked. The simplest case is the classic one of Robinson Crusoe on the deserted island. The number of coconuts he can pick or fish he can catch per hour *is* his real wage per hour.

Secular Growth

But simple supply and demand analysis suggests that, even if the demand for labor is strong in the United States, increases in the supply of labor will reduce the general level of wages over time. It is certainly true that the American population and the labor force have grown significantly over the decades. However, these increases in the supply of labor have been more than offset by increases in the demand for labor stemming from the productivity-increasing factors discussed above. The result has been a long-run, or secular, increase in wage rates and employment, as suggested by Figure 15-2.

WAGES IN PARTICULAR LABOR MARKETS

We now turn from the general level of wages to specific wage rates. What determines the wage rate received by some specific type of worker? Demand and supply analysis again provides a revealing approach. Our analysis covers some half-dozen basic market models.

Competitive Model

A purely **competitive labor market** has the following characteristics:

1 Many firms are competing with one another in hiring a specific type of labor.
2 Numerous qualified workers with identical skills are independently supplying this type of labor service.
3 "Wage taker" behavior pertains to both firms and workers in that neither can exert control over the market wage rate.

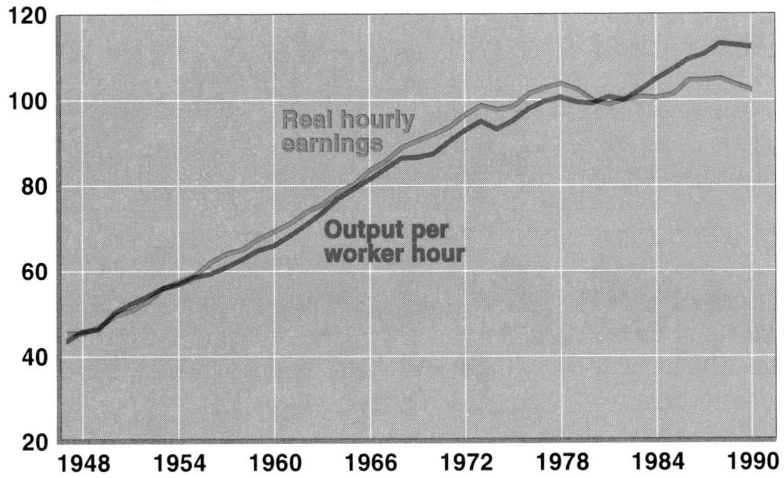

FIGURE 15-1 Output per hour and real average hourly earnings

Over a long period of years there has been a close relationship between real hourly earnings and output per worker-hour. *(Department of Labor, Monthly Labor Review.)*

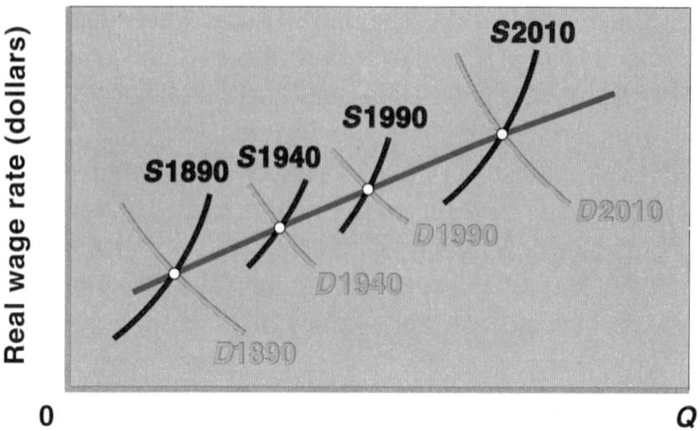

FIGURE 15-2 The secular trend of real wages in the United States

The productivity of American labor has increased substantially in the long run, causing the demand for labor to increase in relation to the supply. The result has been increases in real wages.

Market Demand Suppose there are many—say, 200—firms demanding a particular type of semiskilled or skilled labor. These firms need not be in the same industry; industries are defined in terms of the products they produce and not of the resources they employ. Thus, firms producing wood-frame furniture, window and door frames, and cabinets will all demand carpenters. The total, or market, demand for the labor in question can be determined by summing horizontally the labor demand curves (the MRP curves) of the individual firms, as suggested in Figure 15-3a and b (Key Graph).

Market Supply On the supply side of the picture, we assume there is no union; workers compete individually for available jobs. The supply curve for a particular type of labor will be upsloping, reflecting the fact that, in the absence of unemployment, hiring firms as a group will be forced to pay higher wage rates to obtain more workers. This is so because firms must bid these workers away from other industries, occupations, and localities. Within limits, workers have alternative job opportunities; that is, they may work in other industries in the same locality, or they may work in their present occupations in different cities or states. In a full-employment economy the group of firms in this particular labor market must pay higher and higher wage rates to attract this type of labor away from these alternative job opportunities. Similarly, higher wages are necessary to induce individuals not currently in the labor force to seek employment.

More technically, the market supply curve rises because it is an *opportunity cost* curve. To attract workers to this particular employment the wage rate paid must cover the opportunity costs of alternative uses of time spent, either in other labor markets, in household activities, or in leisure. Higher wages attract more people to this employment—people who were not attracted by lower wages because their opportunity costs were too high.

Market Equilibrium The equilibrium wage rate and the equilibrium level of employment for this type of labor are determined at the intersection of the labor demand and labor supply curves. In Figure 15-3b the equilibrium wage rate is W_c ($6), and the number of workers hired is Q_c (1000). To the individual firm the wage rate W_c is given. Each of the many hiring firms employs such a small fraction of the total available supply of this type of labor that none can influence the wage rate. The supply of labor is perfectly elastic to the individual firm, as shown by S in Figure 15-3a.

Each individual firm will find it profitable to hire workers up to the point at which the going wage rate is equal to labor's MRP. This is merely an application of the MRP = MRC rule developed in Chapter 14. (Indeed, the demand curve in Figure 15-3a is based on Table 15-1.)

As Table 15-1 indicates, *because resource price is given to the individual competitive firm, the marginal cost of that resource* (MRC) *will be constant and equal to resource price (the wage rate)*. In this case the wage rate and hence the marginal cost of labor are constant to the individual firm. Each additional worker hired adds precisely his or her wage rate ($6 in this case) to the firm's

TABLE 15-1 The supply of labor: pure competition in the hire of labor *(hypothetical data)*

(1) Units of labor	*(2) Wage rate*	*(3) Total labor cost (wage bill)*	*(4) Marginal resource (labor) cost*
0	$6	$ 0	
1	6	6	$6
2	6	12	6
3	6	18	6
4	6	24	6
5	6	30	6
6	6	36	6

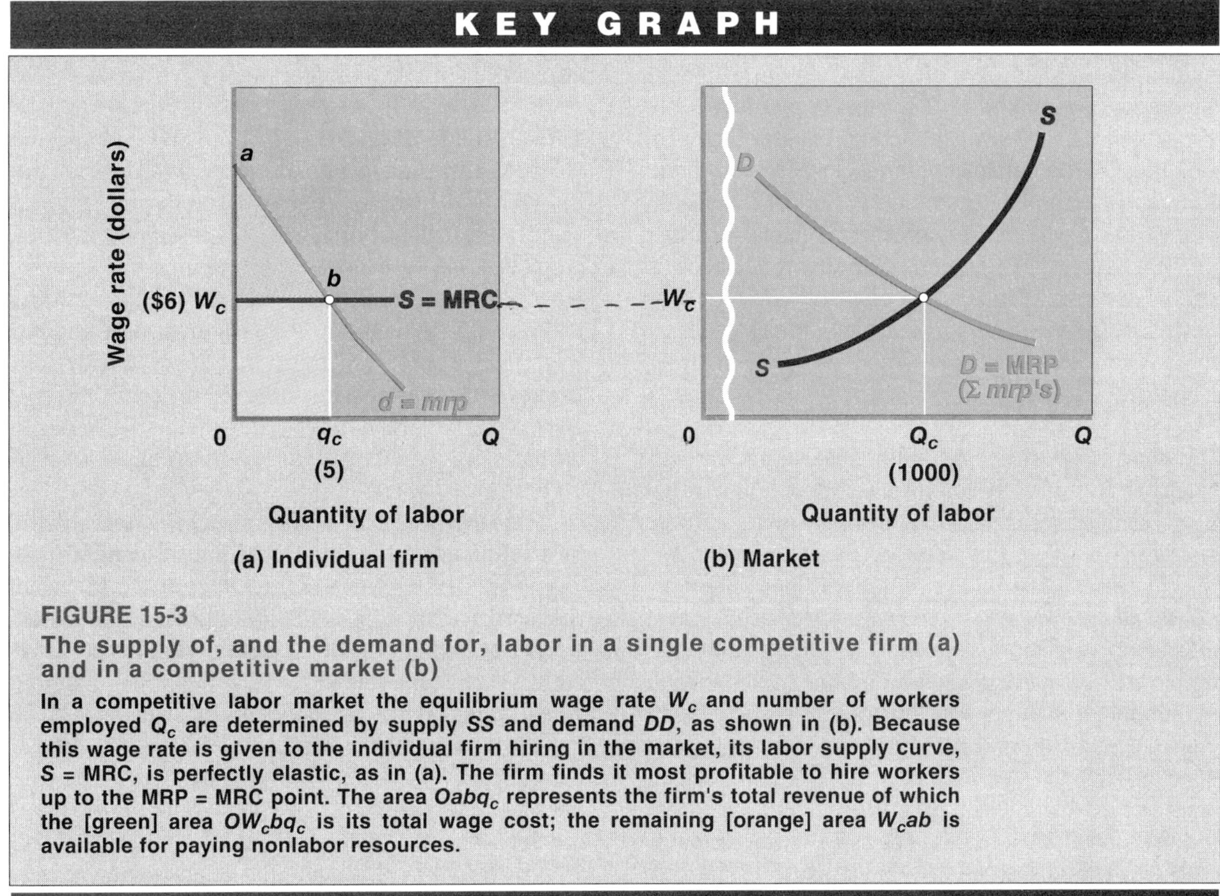

FIGURE 15-3
The supply of, and the demand for, labor in a single competitive firm (a) and in a competitive market (b)
In a competitive labor market the equilibrium wage rate W_c and number of workers employed Q_c are determined by supply *SS* and demand *DD*, as shown in (b). Because this wage rate is given to the individual firm hiring in the market, its labor supply curve, *S* = MRC, is perfectly elastic, as in (a). The firm finds it most profitable to hire workers up to the MRP = MRC point. The area $Oabq_c$ represents the firm's total revenue of which the [green] area OW_cbq_c is its total wage cost; the remaining [orange] area W_cab is available for paying nonlabor resources.

total resource cost. The firm then will maximize its profits by hiring workers to the point at which their wage rate, and therefore marginal resource cost, equals their marginal revenue product. In Figure 15-3a the "typical" firm will hire q_c (5) workers.

Note that the firm's total revenue from hiring q_c workers can be found by summing their MRPs. In this case the total revenue from the five workers is indicated by the area $0abq_c$ in Figure 15-3a. Of this total revenue, the green area $0W_cbq_c$ is the firm's total wage cost and the orange triangular area W_cab represents additional revenue available to reward other inputs such as capital, land, and entrepreneurship.

Monopsony Model

In a purely competitive labor market each employer hires too small an amount of labor to influence the wage rate. Each firm is a "wage taker"; it can hire as little or as much labor as it needs at the market wage, as reflected in its perfectly elastic labor supply curve.

Characteristics Let's now consider the case of **monopsony,** which describes an employer with monopolistic buying (hiring) power. Monopsony has the following characteristics:

1 The given firm's employment is a large portion of the total employment of a particular kind of labor.

2 This type of labor is relatively immobile, either geographically or in the sense that, if workers sought alternative employment, they would have to acquire new skills.

3 The firm is a "wage maker" in that the wage rate it must pay varies directly with the number of workers it employs.

In some instances the monopsonistic power of employers is virtually complete because there is only one major employer in a labor market. For example, the economies of some towns and cities depend almost entirely on one major firm. A silver-mining concern may be the basic source of employment in a remote Colorado town. A New England textile mill, a Wisconsin paper mill, or a farm-belt food processor may provide most of the employment in its locality. Anaconda Mining is the dominant employer in Butte, Montana. In other cases *oligopsony* may prevail; three or four firms may each hire a large portion of the supply of labor in a particular market. Our study of oligopoly correctly suggests that there is a strong tendency for oligopsonists to act in concert—much like a monopsonist—in hiring labor.

Upsloping Supply to Firm When a firm hires a considerable portion of the total available supply of a particular type of labor, its decision to employ more or fewer workers will affect the wage rate paid to that labor. Specifically, *if a firm is large in relation to the labor market, it will have to pay a higher wage rate to obtain more labor.* For simplicity's sake suppose there is only one employer of a particular type of labor in a specified geographic area. In this extreme case, the labor supply curve to that firm and the total supply curve for the labor market are identical. This supply curve, for reasons already made clear, is upsloping, indicating that the firm must pay a higher wage rate to attract more workers. This is shown by *SS* in Figure 15-4. The supply curve is in effect the average-cost-of-labor curve from the firm's perspective; each point on it indicates the wage rate (cost) per worker which must be paid to attract the corresponding number of workers.

FIGURE 15-4 The wage rate and level of employment in a monopsonistic labor market

In a monopsonistic labor market the employer's marginal resource (labor) cost curve (MRC) lies above the labor supply curve *(S)*. Equating MRC with labor demand MRP at point *b*, the monopsonist will hire Q_m workers (compared with Q_c under competition) and pay the wage rate W_m (compared with the competitive wage W_c).

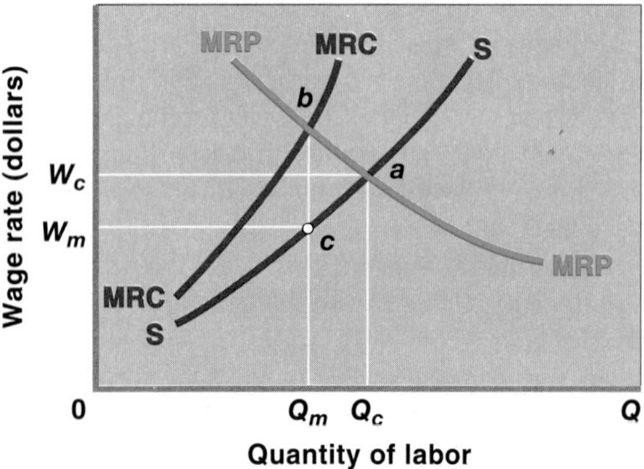

MRC Exceeds Wage Rate But the higher wages involved in attracting *additional* workers will also have to be paid to *all* workers currently employed at lower wage rates. If not, labor morale will deteriorate, and the employer will be plagued with serious problems of labor unrest because of wage-rate differentials existing for the same job. As for cost, payment of a uniform wage to all workers will mean that the cost of an extra worker—the marginal resource (labor) cost (MRC)—will exceed the wage rate by the amount necessary to bring the wage rate of all workers currently employed up to the new wage level.

Table 15-2 illustrates this point. One worker can be hired at a wage rate of \$6. But hiring a second worker forces the firm to pay a higher wage of \$7. Marginal resource (labor) cost is \$8—the \$7 paid the second worker plus a \$1 raise for the first worker. Stated differently, total labor cost is \$14 (= 2 × \$7) rather than \$13, which would be the case if the first worker was paid \$6 and the second paid \$7. Hence, the MRC of the second worker is \$8 (= \$14 − \$6), not the \$7 wage rate paid the second worker. Similarly, the marginal labor cost of the third worker is \$10—the \$8 which must be paid to attract this worker from alternative employments plus \$1 raises for the first two workers. The important point is that *to the monopsonist, marginal resource (labor) cost will exceed the wage rate.* Graphically, the MRC curve (columns 1 and 4 in Table 15-2) will lie above the average-cost, or supply, curve of labor (columns 1 and 2 in Table 15-2). This is shown graphically in Figure 15-4.

TABLE 15-3 Average hourly and weekly earnings in selected industries, September 1991

(1) Units of labor	*(2) Wage rate*	*(3) Total labor cost (wage bill)*	*(4) Marginal resource (labor) cost*
0	\$ 5	\$ 0	
			\$ 6
1	6	6	
			8
2	7	14	
			10
3	8	24	
			12
4	9	36	
			14
5	10	50	
			16
6	11	66	

Equilibrium How much labor will the firm hire, and what wage rate will it pay? To maximize profits the firm will equate marginal resource (labor) cost with the MRP.[1] The number of workers hired by the monopsonist is indicated by Q_m, and the wage rate paid, W_m, is indicated by the corresponding point on the resource supply, or average-cost-of-labor, curve.

It is particularly important to contrast these results with those which a competitive labor market would have yielded. With competition in the hire of labor, the level of employment would have been greater (Q_c), and the wage rate would have been higher (W_c). It simply does not pay the monopsonist to hire workers up to the point at which the wage rate and labor's MRP are equal. *Other things being equal, the monopsonist maximizes its profits by hiring a smaller number of workers and thereby paying a less-than-competitive wage rate.* In the process, society gets a small output,[2] and workers get a wage rate less by *bc* than their marginal revenue product. Just as a monopolistic seller finds it profitable to restrict product output to realize an above-competitive price for its goods, so the monopsonistic employer of resources finds it profitable to restrict employment in order to depress wage rates and therefore costs, that is, to realize below-competitive wage rates.[3]

[1]The fact that MRC exceeds resource price when resources are hired or purchased under imperfectly competitive (monopsonistic) conditions calls for appropriate adjustments in Chapter 14's least-cost and profit-maximizing rules for hiring resources. [See equations (1) and (2) in the "Optimal Combination of Resources" section of Chapter 14.] Specifically, we must substitute MRC for resource price in the denominators of our two equations. That is, with imperfect competition in the hiring of both labor and capital, equation (1) becomes

$$\frac{\text{MP}_L}{\text{MRC}_L} = \frac{\text{MP}_C}{\text{MRC}_C} \tag{1'}$$

and equation (2) is restated as

$$\frac{\text{MRP}_L}{\text{MRC}_L} = \frac{\text{MRP}_C}{\text{MRC}_C} = 1 \tag{2'}$$

In fact, equations (1) and (2) can be regarded as special cases of (1′) and (2′) in which firms happen to be hiring under purely competitive conditions and resource price is therefore equal to, and can be substituted for, marginal resource cost.

[2]This is analogous to the monopolist's restricting output as it sets product price and output on the basis of marginal revenue, not product demand. In this instance, resource price is set on the basis of marginal labor (resource) cost, not resource supply.

[3]Will a monopsonistic employer also be a monopolistic seller in the product market? Not necessarily. The New England textile mill may be a monopsonistic employer, yet face severe domestic and foreign competition in selling its product. In other cases—for example, the automobile and steel industries—firms have both monopsonistic and monopolistic (oligopolistic) power.

Illustrations In fact, monopsonistic labor market outcomes are not common in our economy. There are typically many potential employers for most workers, particularly when these workers are occupationally and geographically mobile. Also, as we will see momentarily, unions often counteract monopsony power in labor markets. Nevertheless, economists have found evidence of monopsony in such diverse labor markets as those for nurses, professional athletes, public school teachers, newspaper employees, and some building trades workers.

In the case of nurses the major employers in most localities are a relatively small number of hospitals. Furthermore, the highly specialized skills of nurses are not readily transferable to other occupations. It has been found in accordance with the monopsony model that, other things being equal, the smaller the number of hospitals in a town or city (that is, the greater the degree of monopsony), the lower the beginning salaries of nurses.

The market for professional athletes is also of interest. Although *potential* employers are quite numerous, the market is characterized by ingenious collusive devices which employers have used with considerable success to limit competition in the hire of labor. The National Football League, the National Basketball Association, and the American and National Baseball Leagues have established systems of rules which tie a player to one team and prevent him from selling his talents to the highest bidder on the open (competitive) market. In particular, through the new player draft, the team which selects or "drafts" a player has the exclusive right to bargain a contract with that player. Furthermore, the so-called reserve clause in each player's contract gives his team the exclusive right to purchase his services for the next season. Though recent court cases and collective bargaining agreements stipulating "free agency" for experienced players have made the labor markets for professional athletes more competitive, collusive monopsony persists.

As detailed in this chapter's Last Word, empirical studies have shown that prior to 1976 baseball players (despite very high salaries) were paid substantially less than their estimated MRPs, which is, of course, consistent with Figure 15-4. However, beginning in 1976 players were allowed to become "free agents"—in other words, they became free to sell their services to any interested team—after their sixth season of play. A comparison of the salaries of the first group of free agents with their estimated MRPs indicates that the competitive bidding of teams for free agents brought their salaries and MRPs into close accord as our competitive model suggests.

QUICK REVIEW 15-1

- ***Real wages have increased historically in the United States because labor demand has increased relative to labor supply.***
- ***Real wages per worker have increased at approximately the same rate as worker productivity.***
- ***The competitive employer is a "wage taker" and employs workers at the point where the wage rate or MRC equals MRP.***
- ***The labor supply curve to a monopsonist is upsloping, causing MRC to exceed the wage rate for each worker. Other things equal, the monopsonist will hire fewer workers and pay a lower wage rate than would a purely competitive employer.***

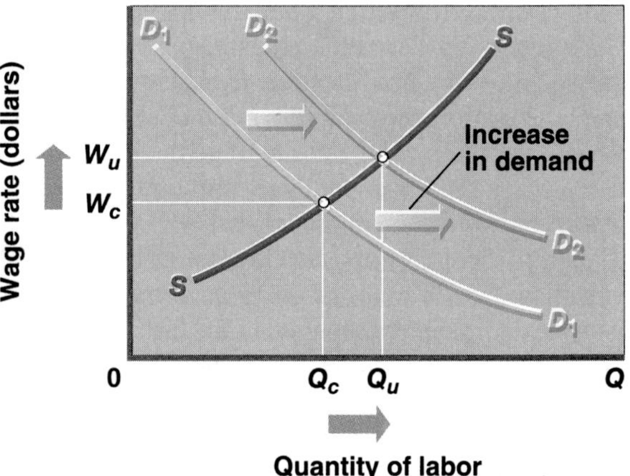

FIGURE 15-5 Unions and the demand for labor
When unions can increase the demand for labor (D_1D_1 to D_2D_2), higher wage rates (W_c to W_u) and more jobs (Q_c to Q_u) can be realized.

Some Union Models

Thus far, we have assumed that workers actively compete in the sale of their labor services. In some markets workers "sell" their labor services collectively through unions. To view the economic impact of unions in the simplest context, let's first suppose a union is formed in an otherwise competitive labor market. That is, a union is now bargaining with a relatively large number of employers.

Unions seek many goals. The basic economic objective, however, is to raise wage rates. The union can pursue this objective in several different ways.

Increasing the Demand for Labor From the union's viewpoint, the most desirable technique for raising wage rates is to increase the demand for labor. As shown in Figure 15-5, an increase in the demand for labor will result in *both* higher wage rates and more jobs. The relative sizes of these increases will depend on the elasticity of labor supply.

A union might increase labor demand by altering one or more of the determinants of labor demand (Chapter 14). Specifically, a union can attempt to (1) increase the demand for the product or service it is producing, (2) enhance labor productivity, or (3) alter the prices of other inputs.

1 Increase Product Demand Unions may attempt to increase the demand for the products they help produce—and hence increase the derived demand for their own labor services—by advertising, political lobbying, or "featherbedding."

Union television ads urging consumers to "buy the union label" are relevant. Historically, The International Ladies Garment Workers Union (ILGWU) has joined with its employers to finance advertising campaigns to bolster demand for their products. Also, the Communications Workers of America (CWA) helped finance a $2 million "Call or Buy Union" campaign to convince telephone users to choose the long-distance services and equipment of AT&T and Western Union Corporation, which together provided almost 100,000 CWA jobs.

On the political front we see construction unions lobbying for new highway or urban renewal projects. Similarly, teachers' unions and associations push for increased public spending on education. Unions connected with the aerospace industry lobby to increase military spending. And it is no accident that some unions have vigorously supported their employers in seeking protective tariffs or import quotas designed to exclude competing foreign products. The steelworkers and automobile workers both have sought such forms of protection. Thus, a decline in the supply of imported cars through tariffs or negotiated agreements between nations will increase import prices, increasing the demand for highly substitutable American-made autos and boosting the derived demand for American auto workers.

Some unions have sought to expand the demand for labor by forcing make-work, or "featherbedding," rules on employers. Prior to recent court rulings, the Railway Brotherhoods forced railroads to hire train crews of a certain minimum size; diesel engines had to have a fireman even though there was no fire.

2 Increase Productivity While many decisions affecting labor productivity—for example, decisions concerning quantity and quality of real capital—are made unilaterally by management, there is a growing interest in establishing joint labor-management committees designed to increase labor productivity.

3 Increase Prices of Substitutes Unions might enhance the demand for their own labor by increasing the prices of substitute resources. A good example is that unions—whose workers are generally paid significantly more than the minimum wage—strongly support increases in the minimum wage. An alleged reason for this position is that unions want to increase the price of potentially substitutable low-wage, nonunion labor. A higher minimum wage for nonunion workers will deter employers from substituting them for union workers, thereby bolstering the demand for union workers.

Similarly, unions can also increase the demand for their labor by supporting public actions which *reduce* the price of a complementary resource. Unions in industries using large amounts of energy might actively oppose rate increases proposed by electric or natural gas utilities. Where labor and energy are complementary, energy price increase might reduce the demand for labor through Chapter 14's output effect.

Unions recognize that their capacity to influence the demand for labor is tenuous and uncertain. As many of our illustrations imply, unions are frequently trying to forestall *declines* in labor demand rather than actually increasing it. In view of these considerations, it is not surprising that union efforts to increase wage rates have concentrated on the supply side of the market.

FIGURE 15-6 Exclusive or craft unionism

By reducing the supply of labor (S_1S_1 to S_2S_2) through the use of restrictive membership policies, exclusive unions achieve higher wage rates (W_c to W_u). However, the restriction of labor supply also reduces the number of workers employed (Q_c to Q_u).

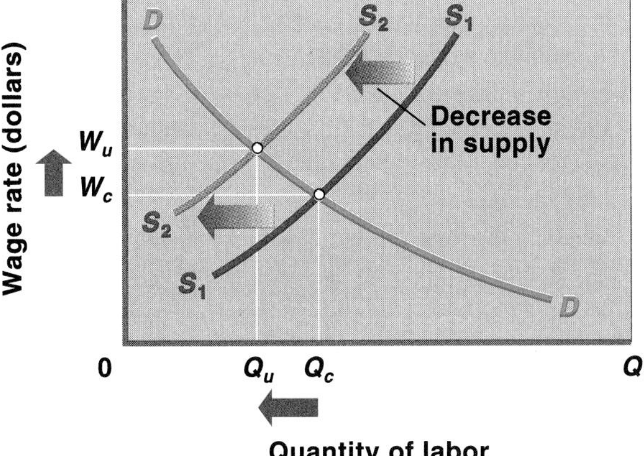

Exclusive or Craft Unionism Unions may boost wage rates by reducing the supply of labor. Historically, organized labor has favored policies designed to restrict the supply of labor to the economy as a whole to bolster the general level of wages. Labor unions have supported legislation which has (1) restricted immigration, (2) reduced child labor, (3) encouraged compulsory retirement, and (4) enforced a shorter workweek.

More relevant for present purposes, specific types of workers have adopted, through unions, techniques designed to restrict their numbers. This is especially true of *craft unions*—unions which comprise workers of a given skill, such as carpenters, bricklayers, and plumbers. These unions have frequently forced employers to agree to hire only union workers, giving the union virtually complete control of the supply of labor. Then, by following restrictive membership policies—long apprenticeships, exorbitant initiation fees, the limitation or flat prohibition of new members—the union causes an artificial restriction of the labor supply. As indicated in Figure 15-6, this results in higher wage rates. This approach to achieving wage increases is called **exclusive unionism.** Higher wages result from excluding workers from the union and therefore from the supply of labor.

Occupational licensing is another widely used means of restricting the supplies of specific kinds of labor. Here a group of workers in an occupation will pressure state or municipal governments to pass a law which provides that, say, barbers (physicians, plumbers, beauticians, egg graders, pest controllers) can practice their trade only if they meet certain specified requirements. These requirements might specify the level of education, amount of work experience, the passing of an examination, and personal characteristics ("the practitioner must be of good moral character"). The licensing board administering the law is typically dominated by members of the licensed occupation. The result is self-regulation, conducive to polices that reflect self-interest. In short, imposing arbitrary and irrelevant entrance requirements or constructing an unnecessarily stringent examination can restrict entrants to the occupation. Ostensibly, the purpose of licensing is to protect consumers from incompetent practitioners. But in fact licensing laws are frequently abused in that the number of qualified workers is artificially restricted, resulting in above-competitive wages and earnings for those in the occupation (Figure 15-6). Furthermore, licensing requirements often specify a residency requirement which tends to inhibit the interstate movement of qualified workers. It is estimated that some 600 occupations are now licensed in the United States.

Many economists feel that the very high earnings of physicians are attributable in part to the American Medical Association's ability to control licensing of doctors. Practicing physicians must be licensed and licenses are awarded only to graduates of medical schools approved by the AMA. By restricting the number of approved schools and by indirectly influencing the number of medical school acceptances, the AMA has allegedly restricted the supply of physicians relative to demand and thereby increased the incomes of licensed doctors.

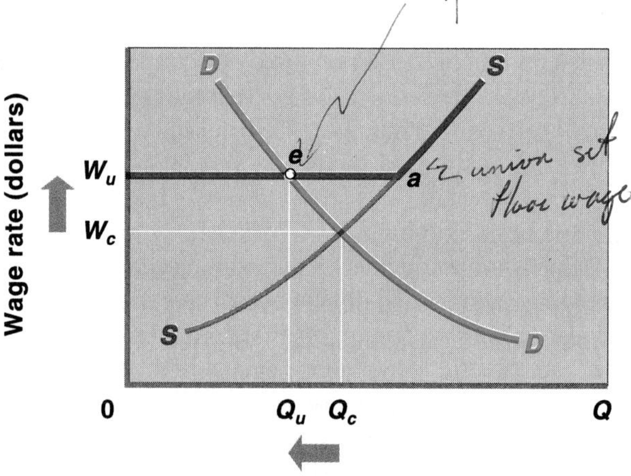

FIGURE 15-7 Inclusive or industrial unionism

By organizing virtually all available workers and thereby controlling the supply of labor, inclusive industrial unions may impose a wage rate, such as W_u, which is above the competitive wage rate W_c. The effect is to change the labor supply curve from SS to W_uaS. At the W_u wage rate, employers will cut employment from Q_c to Q_u.

Inclusive or Industrial Unionism Most unions, however, do not attempt to limit their membership. On the contrary, they seek to organize all available or potential workers. This is characteristic of the so-called *industrial unions*—unions, such as the automobile workers and steelworkers, which seek all unskilled, semiskilled, and skilled workers in an industry as members. A union can afford to be exclusive when its members are skilled craftsmen for whom substitute workers are not readily available in quantity. But a union that comprises largely unskilled and semiskilled workers will undermine its own existence by limiting its membership, causing numerous highly substitutable nonunion workers to be available for employment.

If an industrial union includes virtually all workers in its membership, firms will be under great pressure to agree to the wage rate demanded by the union. By going on strike the union can deprive the firm of its entire labor supply.

Inclusive unionism is illustrated in Figure 15-7. Initially, the competitive equilibrium wage rate is W_c, and the level of employment is Q_c. Now suppose an industrial union is formed, and it imposes a higher, above-equilibrium wage rate of, say, W_u. This wage rate changes the supply curve of labor to the firm from the preunion SS curve to the postunion W_uaS curve shown by the dark red line.[4] No workers will be forthcoming at a wage rate less than that demanded by the union. If employers decide it is better to pay this higher wage rate than to suffer a strike, they will cut back on employment from Q_c to Q_u.

By agreeing to the union's W_u wage demand, individual employers become "wage takers" at this wage and therefore face a perfectly elastic labor supply curve over the W_ua range. Because labor supply is perfectly elastic, MRC is equal to the W_u wage over this range. The Q_u level of employment results from employers equating MRC ($=W_u$) with MRP as embodied in the labor demand curve.

Note that at W_u there is an excess supply or surplus of labor in the amount *ea*. Without the union—that is, in a purely competitive labor market—these unemployed workers might accept lower wages and the wage rate would thereby fall to the W_c competitive equilibrium level. But this doesn't happen because workers are acting collectively through their union.

[4]Technically, the wage rate W_u makes the labor supply curve perfectly elastic over the W_ua range in Figure 15-7. If employers hire any number of workers in this range, the union-imposed wage rate is effective and must be paid, or the union will supply no labor at all—the employers will be faced with a strike. If employers want a number of workers over W_ua, they will have to bid up wages above the union's minimum. This will only occur if the market demand curve for labor shifts rightward so that it intersects the aS range of the labor supply curve.

Workers cannot individually offer to work for less than W_u; nor can employers contractually pay less.

Wage Increases and Unemployment

Have unions been successful in raising the wages of their members? The best evidence suggests that union members on the average achieve a 10 to 15 percent wage advantage over nonunion workers.

As Figures 15-6 and 15-7 suggest, the wage-raising actions of both exclusive and inclusive unionism cause employment to decline. A union's success in achieving above-equilibrium wage rates is tempered by the consequent decline in the number of workers employed. This unemployment effect can act as a restraining influence on union wage demands. A union cannot expect to maintain solidarity within its ranks if it seeks a wage rate so high that joblessness will result for, say, 20 or 30 percent of its members.

The unemployment impact of wage increases might be mitigated from the union's standpoint in two ways.

1 Growth The normal growth of the economy increases the demand for most kinds of labor through time. Thus a rightward shift of the labor demand curves in Figures 15-6 and 15-7 could offset, or more than offset, any unemployment effects which would otherwise be associated with the indicated wage increases. There would still be an employment restricting aspect to the union wage increases but it would take the form of a decline in the rate of growth of job opportunities, not of an absolute decline in the number of jobs.

2 Elasticity The size of the unemployment effect will depend on the elasticity of demand for labor. The more inelastic the demand, the smaller will be the amount of unemployment accompanying a given wage-rate increase. If unions have sufficient bargaining strength, they *may* obtain provisions in their collective bargaining agreements which reduce the substitutability of other inputs for labor and thereby reduce the elasticity of demand for union labor. For example, a union may force employer acceptance of rules blocking the introduction of new machinery and equipment. Or the union may bargain successfully for severance or layoff pay, which increases the cost to the firm of substituting capital for labor when wage rates are increased. Similarly, the union might gain a contract provision prohibiting the firm from subcontracting production to nonunion (lower-wage) firms, effectively restricting the substitution of cheaper labor for union workers.

For these and other reasons the unemployment restraint on union wage demands may be less pressing than our exclusive and inclusive union models suggest.

Bilateral Monopoly Model

Suppose now that a strong industrial union is formed in a labor market which is monopsonistic rather than competitive. In other words, we combine the monopsony model with the inclusive unionism model. The result is **bilateral monopoly.** The union is a monopolistic "seller" of labor in that it controls labor supply and can influence wage rates; it faces a monopsonistic employer (or combination of oligopsonistic employers) of labor who can also affect wages by altering its employment. This is not an extreme or special case. In such important industries as steel, automobiles, meatpacking, and farm machinery, "big labor"—one huge industrial union—bargains with "big business"—a few huge industrial giants.

Indeterminate Outcome This situation is shown in Figure 15-8, which merely superimposes Figure 15-7 on 15-4. The monopsonistic employer will seek the below-competitive-equilibrium wage rate W_m and the union presumably will press for some above-competitive-equilibrium wage rate such as W_u. Which of these

FIGURE 15-8 Bilateral monopoly in the labor market

When a monopsonistic employer seeks the wage rate W_m and the inclusive union it faces seeks an above-equilibrium wage rate such as W_u, the actual outcome is logically indeterminate.

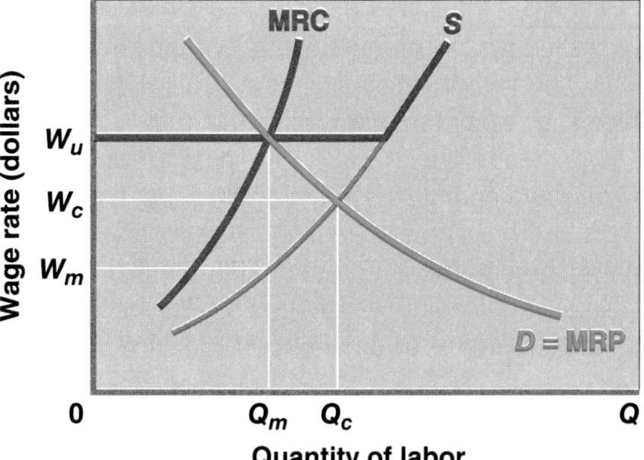

two possibilities will result? We cannot say with certainty. The outcome is logically indeterminate since economic theory does not explain what the resulting wage rate will be. We should expect the resulting wage to lie somewhere between W_m and W_u. Beyond that, about all we can say is that the party with the most bargaining power and the most effective bargaining strategy will be able to get its opponent to agree to a wage close to the one it seeks.

Desirability These comments suggest another important feature of the bilateral monopoly model. It is possible that the wage and employment outcomes might be more socially desirable than the term bilateral monopoly would imply. Monopoly on one side of the market *might* in effect cancel out the monopoly on the other side of the market, yielding competitive or near-competitive results. If either the union or management prevailed in this market—that is, if the actual wage rate were determined at either W_u or W_m—employment would be restricted to Q_m (where MRP = MRC), which is below the competitive level. But now suppose the monopoly power of the union roughly offsets the monopsony power of management, and a bargained wage rate of about W_c, which is the competitive wage, is agreed upon. Once management agrees to this wage rate, its incentive to restrict employment disappears; no longer can the employer depress wage rates by restricting employment. Thus management equates the bargained wage rate W_c (= MRC) with MRP and finds it most profitable to hire Q_c workers. In short, with monopoly on both sides of the labor market, it may be possible that the resulting wage rate and level of employment will be closer to competitive levels than if monopoly existed on only one side of the market.

The Minimum-Wage Controversy

Since the passage of the Fair Labor Standards Act in 1938, the United States has had a Federal **minimum wage.** The minimum wage has ranged from about 40 to 50 percent of the average wage paid to manufacturing workers and is currently $4.25 per hour. Roughly 90 percent of all nonsupervisory workers are covered. Our analysis of the effects of union wage-fixing raises the much-debated question of how effective minimum-wage legislation is as an antipoverty device.

Case against the Minimum Wage Critics, reasoning in terms of Figure 15-7, contend that the imposition of effective (above-equilibrium) minimum wages will simply push employers back up their MRP or labor demand curves as it is now profitable to hire fewer workers. The higher wage costs may even force some firms out of business. The result is that some of the poor, low-wage workers whom the minimum wage was designed to help will now find themselves out of work. Critics say a worker who is unemployed at a minimum wage of $4.25 per hour is clearly worse off than if he or she were employed at the market wage rate of, say, $3.50 per hour.

A second major criticism is that the minimum wage is poorly targeted as an antipoverty device. It is designed to provide a "living wage" which will allow less-skilled workers to earn enough so that they and their families can escape poverty. However, critics argue that the primary impact of the minimum wage is on teenage workers, many of whom belong to relatively affluent families.

Case for the Minimum Wage Advocates allege that critics have analyzed the impact of the minimum wage in an unrealistic context. Figure 15-7, advocates claim, assumes a competitive and static market. The imposition of a minimum wage in a monopsonistic labor market (Figure 15-8) suggests that the minimum wage can increase wage rates without causing unemployment; indeed, higher minimum wages may even result in more jobs by eliminating the monopsonistic employer's motive to restrict employment.

Furthermore, the imposition of an effective minimum wage may increase labor productivity, shifting the labor demand curve to the right and offsetting any unemployment effects which the minimum wage might otherwise induce.

But how might a minimum wage increase productivity? First, a minimum wage may have a *shock effect* on employers. Firms using low-wage workers may be inefficient in the use of labor; the higher wage rates imposed by the minimum wage will presumably shock these firms into using labor more efficiently, and so the productivity of labor rises. Second, it is argued that higher wages will increase the real incomes and therefore the health, vigor, and motivation of workers, making them more productive.

Evidence Which view is correct? The consensus of the many research studies of the minimum wage is that it does cause some unemployment, particularly among teenage (16 to 19 years) workers. It is estimated that a 10 percent increase in the minimum wage will reduce teenage employment by 1 to 3 percent. Young adults (age 20 to 24) are also adversely affected; a 10 percent increase in the minimum wage would reduce employment for this group by 1 percent or less. Blacks and women, who are disproportionately represented in low-wage occupations, tend to suffer larger declines in employment than do white males. The other side of the coin, of course, is that those who remain employed receive higher incomes and tend to escape poverty. The overall antipoverty effect of the minimum wage may thus be a mixed, ambivalent one. Those who lose their jobs are plunged deeper into poverty; those who remain employed tend to escape poverty.

WAGE DIFFERENTIALS

We have discussed the general level of wages and the role of supply and demand in a series of specific labor market situations. We now consider the wage differences which persist between different occupations and different individuals in the same occupations. Why does a corporate executive or professional athlete receive $300,000, $500,000, or even $1,000,000 or more per year while laundry workers and retail clerks get a paltry $13,000 or $14,000 per year? Why is the average annual salary almost $891,000 for major-league baseball players compared to $27,000 for acute-care nurses and $33,000 for teachers? What rationale lies behind Chrysler Corporation paying its chairman, Lee Iacocca, total compensation of over $23 million in 1987? Table 15-3 indicates the substantial **wage differentials** which exist among certain common occupational groups. Our objective is to gain some insight as to why these differentials exist.

TABLE 15-3 Average hourly and weekly earnings in selected industries, September 1991

Industry	*Average hourly gross earnings*	*Average weekly gross earnings*
Bituminous coal	$17.30	$787
Motor vehicles	15.66	689
Chemicals	14.22	616
Construction	14.14	551
Printing and publishing	11.67	446
Fabricated metals	11.32	475
Food products	9.87	409
Hotels and motels	7.23	225
Laundries and dry cleaning	7.11	241
Retail trade	7.07	204
Apparel and finished textiles	6.86	258

Source: U.S. Department of Labor, *Employment and Earnings*, November 1991.

Once again the forces of supply and demand provide a general answer. If the supply of a particular type of labor is very great in relation to the demand for it, the resulting wage rate will be low. But if demand is great and the supply relatively small, wages will be very high. Though it is a good starting point, this supply and demand explanation is not particularly revealing. To discover *why* supply and demand conditions differ in various labor markets, we must probe those factors underlying the supply and demand of particular types of labor.

If (1) all workers were homogeneous, (2) all jobs were equally attractive to workers, and (3) labor markets were perfectly competitive, all workers would receive precisely the same wage rate. As such, this is not a particularly startling statement. It suggests that in an economy having one type of labor and in effect one type of job, competition would result in a single wage rate for all workers. The statement is important in that it suggests reasons why wage rates do differ in practice. (1) Workers are not homogeneous. They differ in innate abilities and in education and training and, as a result, fall into noncompeting occupational groups. (2) Jobs vary in attractiveness; the nonmonetary aspects of various jobs are not the same. (3) Labor markets are typically characterized by imperfections.

Noncompeting Groups

Workers are not homogeneous; they differ significantly in their mental and physical capacities *and* in their education and training. At any point in time the labor force can be thought of as falling into many **noncompeting groups,** each of which may be composed of one or several occupations for which the members of this group qualify.

Ability Relatively few workers have the inherent abilities to be brain surgeons, concert violinists, research chemists, or professional athletes. The result is that supplies of these particular types of labor are very small in relation to the demand for them and consequently wages and salaries are high. These and similar groups do not compete with one another nor with other skilled or semiskilled workers. The violinist does not compete with the surgeon, nor does the garbage collector or retail clerk compete with either the violinist or the surgeon.

The concept of noncompeting groups is a flexible one; it can be applied to various subgroups and even to specific individuals in a given group. Some especially skilled surgeons can command higher fees than their run-of-the-mill colleagues performing the same operations. Michael Jordan, Larry Bird, Isiah Thomas, Patrick Ewing, and a few others demand and get salaries many times that of the average professional basketball player. In each instance their less-talented colleagues are only imperfect substitutes.

Investing in Human Capital: Education Noncompeting groups—and therefore wage differentials—also exist because of differing amounts of investment in human capital. A **human capital investment** refers to expenditures on education and training which improve the skills or, in other words, the productivity, of workers. Like business purchases of machinery and equipment, expenditures which increase one's productivity can be regarded as investments because *current* expenditures or costs are incurred with the intention that these costs will be more than compensated for by an enhanced *future* flow of earnings.

Figure 15-9 indicates, first, that individuals with larger investments in education do achieve higher incomes during their work careers than those who have made smaller education investments. A second point is that the earnings of more-educated workers rise more rapidly than those of less-educated workers. The primary reason for this is that more-educated workers usually get more on-the-job training.

Although education yields higher incomes, it also entails costs. For example, a college education entails not only direct costs (tuition, fees, books) but also indirect or opportunity costs (forgone earnings). Question: Does the higher pay received by more-educated workers compensate for these costs? The answer is "Yes." Rates of return have recently been estimated to be 10 to 13 percent for investing in a secondary education and 8 to 10 percent for higher education. Also, in recent years the pay gap between college graduates and high school graduates has been widening.

Equalizing Differences

If a group of workers in a particular noncompeting group is equally capable of performing several different jobs, one might expect that the wage rate would be identical for each of these jobs. But this is not the case. A group of high school graduates may be equally capable of becoming bank clerks or unskilled construction workers. But these jobs pay different wages. In virtually all localities, construction laborers receive higher wages than do bank clerks.

These differences can be explained on the basis of the *nonmonetary aspects* of the two jobs. The construction job involves dirty hands, a sore back, the hazard of accidents, and irregular employment, both seasonally and cyclically. The banking job means a white shirt, pleasant air-conditioned surroundings, and little fear of injury or layoff. Other things being equal, it is easy to see why workers would rather pick up a deposit slip than a shovel. The result is that contractors must pay higher wages than banks pay to compensate for the unattractive nonmonetary aspects of construction jobs. These wage differentials are called **equalizing differences** because they must be paid to compensate for nonmonetary differences in various jobs.

Market Imperfections

The notion of noncompeting groups helps explain wage differentials between various jobs for which limited numbers of workers are qualified. Equalizing differences aid in understanding wage differentials on certain jobs for which workers in the same noncompeting group are equally qualified. Market imperfections in the form of various immobilities help explain wage differences paid on identical jobs.

1 Geographic Immobilities Workers take root geographically. They are reluctant to leave friends, relatives, and associates, to force their children to change schools, to sell their houses, and to incur the costs and inconveniences of adjusting to a new job and a new community. Geographic mobility is likely to be particularly low for older workers with seniority rights and substantial claims to pension payments upon retirement. Similarly, an optometrist or dental hygienist qualified to practice in one state may not meet licensing requirements of other states, and therefore his or her ability to move geographically is impeded. Also, workers who may be willing to move may simply be ignorant of job opportunities and wage rates in other areas. As Adam Smith noted over two centuries ago, "A man is of all sorts of luggage the most difficult to be trans-

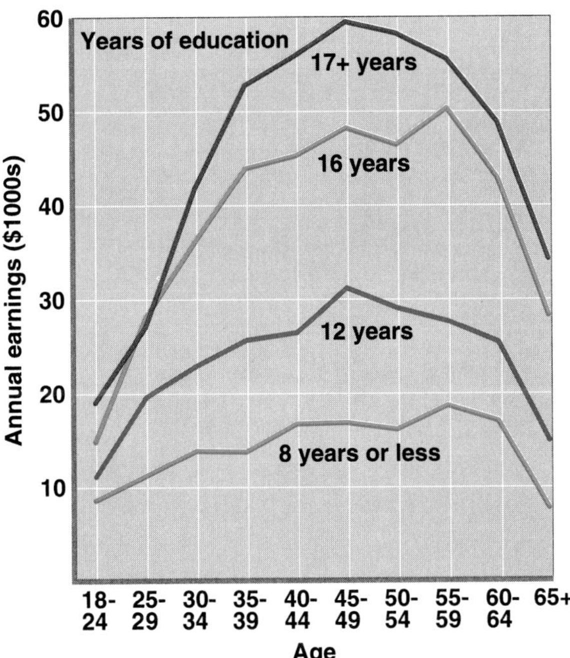

FIGURE 15-9 Education levels and individual income

Investment in education yields a return in the form of an income differential enjoyed throughout one's work-life. (*U.S. Bureau of the Census*. Data are for males in 1990.)

ported." The reluctance or inability of workers to move causes geographic wage differentials for the same occupation to persist.

2 Institutional Immobilities Geographic immobilities may be reinforced by artificial restrictions on mobility imposed by institutions. We have noted that craft unions find it to their advantage to restrict membership. After all, if carpenters and bricklayers become plentiful, the wages they can command will decline. Thus the low-paid nonunion carpenter of Brush, Colorado, may be willing to move to Chicago in the pursuit of higher wages. But his chances of successfully doing so are slim. He may be unable to get a union card; and no card, no job. The professions impose similar artificial restraints. For example, at most universities individuals lacking advanced degrees are automatically not considered for employment as teachers. Apart from one's competence as a teacher and command of the subject matter, a "union card"—an M.A. or preferably a Ph.D.—is the first requisite for employment.

3 Sociological Immobilities Finally, we must acknowledge sociological immobilities. Despite legislation to the contrary, women workers frequently receive less pay than men on the same job. The consequence of racial and ethnic discrimination is that blacks, Hispanics, and other minorities historically have been forced to accept lower wages on given jobs than fellow workers receive.

A final point: It is typical that all three of these considerations—noncompeting groups, equalizing differences, and market imperfections—will play a role in the explanation of actual wage differentials. For example, the differential between the wages of a physician and a construction worker is largely explainable on the basis of noncompeting groups. Physicians fall into a noncompeting group where, because of mental and financial requisites to entry, the supply of labor is small in relation to demand, and wages are therefore high. In construction work, where mental and financial prerequisites are much less significant, the supply of labor is great in relation to demand and wages are low when compared with those of physicians. However, were it not for the unpleasantness of the construction worker's job and the fact that his craft union pursues restrictive membership policies, the differential would probably be even greater than it is.

QUICK REVIEW 15-2

- ***Unions may achieve above-equilibrium wage rates by increasing labor demand, restricting supply (exclusive unionism) or by bargaining (inclusive unionism).***
- ***Bilateral monopoly occurs where a monopsonist bargains with an inclusive union. Wages and employment are indeterminant in this situation.***
- ***Proponents of the minimum wage argue that it is an effective means of assisting the working poor; critics contend that it is poorly targeted and causes unemployment.***
- ***Wage differentials are attributable in part to differences in worker abilities and education, nonmonetary differences in jobs, and market imperfections.***

PAY AND PERFORMANCE

The models of wage determination presented in this chapter presume that worker compensation is always

LAST WORD

PAY AND PERFORMANCE IN PROFESSIONAL BASEBALL

Professional baseball has provided an interesting "laboratory" in which the predictions of wage theory have been empirically tested.

Until 1976 professional baseball players were bound to a single team through the so-called "reserve clause" which prevented players from selling their talents on the open (competitive) market. Stated differently, the reserve clause conferred monopsony power on the team which originally drafted a player. As we have seen in the present chapter, labor market theory would lead us to predict that this monopsony power would permit teams to pay wages less than a player's marginal revenue product (MRP). However, since 1976 major league players have been able to become "free agents" at the end of their sixth season of play and at that time can sell their services to any team. Orthodox theory suggests that free agents should be able to increase their salaries and bring them more closely into accord with their MRPs. Research confirms both of the indicated predictions.

Scully* found that before baseball players could become free agents their salaries were substantially below their MRPs. Scully estimated a player's MRP as follows. First, he determined the relationship between a team's winning percentage and its revenue. Then he estimated the relationship between various possible measures of player productivity and a team's winning percentage. He found the ratio of strikeouts to walks for pitchers and the slugging averages for hitters (all nonpitchers) to be the best indicators of a player's contribution to the winning percentage. These two estimates were combined to calculate the contribution of a player to a team's total revenue.

*Gerald W. Scully, "Pay and Performance in Major League Baseball," *American Economic Review,* December 1974, pp. 915–930.

As noted, Scully calculated that prior to free agency the estimated MRPs of both pitchers and hitters were substantially greater than player salaries. Table 1 shows the relevant data for pitchers. Column 1 indicates pitcher performance as measured by lifetime strikeout-to-walk ratio. A higher ratio indicates a better pitcher. Column 2 indicates MRP after player training costs are taken into account and column 3 shows actual average salary for pitchers in each quality class. As expected, salaries were far less than MRPs. Even the lowest quality pitchers (those with a 1.60 strikeout-to-walk ratio) received on the average salaries amounting to only about 54 percent of their MRPs. Observe, too, that the gap between MRP and average salary widens

in the form of a standard hourly wage rate, for example, $5, $10, or $25 per hour. In fact, pay schemes are often more complex in composition and purpose. For example, many workers receive annual salaries rather than hourly pay. Also, pay plans are frequently designed by employers to elicit some desired level of performance by workers.

The Principal–Agent Problem

Firms hire workers because workers help produce goods or services which firms can sell for a profit. Workers may be thought of as the firm's *agents,* that is, parties who are hired to advance the interests of the firm. Similarly, firms may be regarded as *principals* or parties who hire others (agents) to help them achieve

TABLE 1 **Marginal revenue products and salaries of professional baseball pitchers, 1968–1969**

*(1) Performance**	*(2) Marginal revenue product*	*(3) Salary*
1.60	**$ 57,600**	**$31,100**
1.80	**80,900**	**34,200**
2.00	**104,100**	**37,200**
2.20	**127,400**	**40,200**
2.40	**150,600**	**43,100**
2.60	**173,900**	**46,000**
2.80	**197,100**	**48,800**
3.00	**220,300**	**51,600**
3.20	**243,600**	**54,400**
3.40	**266,800**	**57,100**
3.60	**290,100**	**59,800**

*Strikeout-to-walk ratio.

Source: Scully, op. cit., p. 923.

TABLE 2 **Estimated marginal revenue products and player costs, 1977**

(1) Pitcher	*(2) Marginal revenue product*	*(3) Annual contract cost**
Garland	**$282,091**	**$230,000**
Gullett	**340,846**	**349,333**
Fingers	**303,511**	**332,000**
Campbell	**205,639**	**210,000**
Alexander	**166,203**	**166,667**

*Includes annual salary, bonuses, the value of insurance policies and deferred payments, etc.

Source: Sommers and Quinton, op. cit., p. 432.

as player quality improves. "Star" players were exploited more than other players. The best pitchers received salaries which were only about 21 percent of their MRPs, according to Scully. The same general results apply to hitters. For example, the least productive hitters on the average received a salary equal to about 37 percent of their MRPs.

Sommers and Quinton† have assessed the economic fortunes of fourteen players who constituted the "first family" of free agents. In accordance with the predictions of labor market theory, their research indicates that the competitive bidding of free agency has brought the salaries of free agents more closely into accord with their estimated MRPs. The data for the five free-agent pitchers are shown in Table 2 where we find a surprisingly close correspondence between estimated MRPs and salaries. Although MRP and salary differences are larger for hitters, Sommers and Quinton conclude that the overturn of the monopsonistic reserve clause "has forced owners into a situation where there is a greater tendency to pay players in relation to their contribution to team revenues."

How have baseball team owners reacted to the escalating salaries under free agency? In early 1986 the players' union filed a grievance charging that the twenty-six professional baseball clubs had acted in concert against signing any of the players who became free agents in 1985. In fact, of the sixty-two players who became free agents in 1985, only two had signed contracts with a different team before the season began. In effect, the players charged that owners had attempted to restore some of the monopsony power which they previously had possessed. Such collusive action is illegal because it violates the basic collective bargaining agreement which exists between players and owners. In the fall of 1987 an arbitrator ruled that baseball owners had conspired to "destroy" the free-agent market and in 1990 the courts ordered club owners to pay $102.5 million in lost salaries to players.

†Paul M. Sommers and Noel Quinton, "Pay and Performance in Major League Baseball: The Case of the First Family of Free Agents," *Journal of Human Resources,* Summer 1982, pp. 426–435.

their goals. Principals and their agents have a common interest. The principal's (firm's) objective is profits, and agents (workers) are willing to help firms earn profits in return for payments of wage income.

But the interests of firms and workers are not identical and when these interests diverge a so-called **principal–agent problem** arises. Agents might increase their utility by **shirking** on the job, that is, by providing less than agreed-upon worker effort or by taking unauthorized work breaks. Workers may improve their well-being by increasing their leisure—through reduced work effort and work time—without forfeiting income. The night watchman in a warehouse may leave work early or spend time reading a novel as opposed to making the assigned rounds. A salaried manager may spend much time out of the office, visiting about personal interests with friends, rather than attending to urgent company business.

Firms (principals) have a profit incentive to reduce or eliminate shirking. One option is to monitor workers; but monitoring is often difficult and costly. Hiring another worker to monitor our night watchman might double the costs of having a secure warehouse. Another way of resolving a principal–agent problem is through some sort of **incentive pay plan** which ties worker compensation more closely to worker output or performance. Such incentive pay schemes include piece rates, commissions and royalties, bonuses and profit sharing, seniority pay, and efficiency wages.

Piece Rates *Piece rates* are compensation paid in proportion to the number of units a worker produces. By paying fruit pickers by the bushel and typists by the page, the principal need not be concerned with shirking or monitoring costs.

Commissions and Royalties Unlike piece rates, which link pay to units of output, commissions and royalties tie pay to the *value* of sales. Realtors, insurance agents, stockbrokers and retail salespersons commonly receive *commissions* based on the monetary value of their sales. *Royalties* are paid to recording artists and authors based on a certain percentage of sales revenue.

Bonuses and Profit Sharing *Bonuses* are payments beyond one's annual salary based on some factor such as performance of the individual or the firm. A professional baseball player may receive bonuses for a high batting average, the number of home runs, or the number of runs batted in. A manager may receive bonuses based on the profit performance of his or her unit. *Profit sharing* allocates a specified percentage of a firm's profits to its employees.

Seniority Pay Wages and earnings generally increase with job tenure. One recent explanation of this is that it is advantageous to both workers and employers to pay junior workers less than their MRPs and senior workers more than their MRPs. *Seniority pay* may be an inexpensive way of reducing shirking when monitoring costs are high. If shirkers are found out and dismissed, they will forgo the high seniority pay accruing in later years of employment. From the firm's standpoint, turnover is reduced because workers who quit will forfeit the high seniority pay. Less turnover means a more experienced and therefore more productive work force. The increased productivity of workers is the source of extra sales revenue from which the firm and the workers, respectively, enhance their profits and lifetime pay. Young workers accept wages which are initially less than their MRPs for the opportunity to participate in a labor market where in time the reverse will be true. The increased work effort and higher average productivity are appealing to workers because they are the source of higher lifetime earnings.

Efficiency Wages The notion of *efficiency wages* suggests that employers might get greater effort from their workers by paying them relatively high, above-equilibrium wage rates. Glance back at Figure 15-3 for a competitive labor market where the equilibrium wage rate is \$6. What if an employer decided to pay an above-equilibrium wage of \$7 per hour? Rather than put the firm at a cost disadvantage compared to rival firms paying only \$6, the higher wage *might* improve worker effort and productivity so that unit labor costs actually fall. For example, if each worker produces 10 units of output per hour at the \$7 wage rate compared to only 6 units at the \$6 wage rate, unit labor costs will be only \$.70 (= \$7 ÷ 10) for the high-wage firm as opposed to \$1.00 (= \$6 ÷ 6) for firms paying the equilibrium wage.

An above-equilibrium wage might enhance worker efficiency in several ways. The higher wage permits the firm to attract higher-quality workers. Worker morale should be higher. Turnover will be reduced, resulting in a more experienced work force, greater worker productivity, and also lower recruitment and training costs. Because the opportunity cost of losing a high-wage job is greater, workers are likely to put forth their best efforts with less supervision and monitoring.

Equilibrium Revisited

Labor market equilibrium is often more complex than the simple determination of wage rates and employment (Figures 15-3 through 15-8). When principal–agent problems involving shirking and monitoring costs arise, decisions must also be made with respect to the most effective compensation scheme. When we recognize that work effort and productivity are related to the form of worker compensation, the choice of pay plan is not a matter of indifference to either employer or employee.

CHAPTER SUMMARY

1 Wages are the price paid per unit of time for the services of labor.

2 The general level of wages in the United States is higher than in most foreign nations because the demand for labor is great in relation to the supply. The strong demand for American labor is based on its high productivity. Over time various productivity-increasing factors have caused the demand for labor to increase in relation to the supply, accounting for the long-run rise of real wages in the United States.

3 The determination of specific wage rates depends on the structure of the particular labor market. In a competitive market the equilibrium wage rate and level of employment are determined at the intersection of labor supply and demand.

4 Under monopsony, however, the marginal resource cost curve will lie above the resource supply curve, because the monopsonist must bid up wage rates in hiring extra workers and pay that higher wage to *all* workers. The monopsonist will hire fewer workers than under competitive conditions to achieve less-than-competitive wage rates (costs) and thereby greater profits.

5 A union may raise competitive wage rates by **a** increasing the derived demand for labor **b** restricting the supply of labor through exclusive unionism, and **c** directly enforcing an above-equilibrium wage rate through inclusive unionism.

6 In many important industries the labor market takes the form of bilateral monopoly, in which a strong union "sells" labor to a monopsonistic employer. The wage rate outcome of this labor market model is logically indeterminate.

7 On the average, unionized workers realize wage rates 10 to 15 percent higher than comparable nonunion workers.

8 Economists disagree about the desirability of the minimum wage as an antipoverty mechanism. While it causes unemployment for some low-income workers, it raises the incomes of others who retain their jobs.

9 Wage differentials are largely explainable in terms of **a** noncompeting groups arising from differences in the capacities and education of different groups of workers, **b** equalizing differences, that is, wage differences which must be paid to offset nonmonetary differences in jobs; and **c** market imperfections in the form of geographic, artificial, and sociological immobilities.

10 The principal–agent problem arises when workers shirk, that is, provide less-than-expected work effort. Firms may combat this problem by monitoring workers or by creating incentive pay schemes which link worker compensation to work effort.

TERMS AND CONCEPTS

nominal and real wages
competitive labor market
exclusive and inclusive unionism
monopsony
occupational licensing
bilateral monopoly
the minimum wage
wage differentials
noncompeting groups
human capital investment
equalizing differences
principal–agent problem
shirking
incentive pay plan

QUESTIONS AND STUDY SUGGESTIONS

1 Explain why the general level of wages is higher in the United States than in most foreign nations. What is the most important single factor underlying the long-run increase in average real wage rates in the United States?

2 Describe wage determination in a labor market in which workers are unorganized and many firms actively compete for the services of labor. Show this situation graphically, using W_1 to indicate the equilibrium wage rate and Q_1 to show the number of workers hired by the firms as a group. Compare the labor supply curve of the individual firm with that of the total market and explain any differences. In the firm's diagram identify total revenue, total wage cost, and revenue available for the payment of nonlabor resources.

a Suppose now that the formerly competing firms form an employers' association which hires labor as a monopsonist would. Describe verbally the impact upon wage rates and employment. Adjust the market graph you have just drawn, showing the monopsonistic wage rate and employment level as W_2 and Q_2, respectively.

b Using the monopsony model, explain why hospital administrators frequently complain about a "shortage" of nurses. Do you have suggestions for correcting this shortage?

3 Describe the techniques which unions might employ to raise wages. Evaluate the desirability of each from the viewpoint of **a** the union, and **b** society as a whole. Explain: "Craft unionism directly restricts the supply of labor; industrial unionism relies upon the market to restrict the number of jobs."

4 Assume a monopsonistic employer is paying a wage rate of W_m and hiring Q_m workers, as indicated in Figure 15-8. Now suppose that an industrial union is formed and that it forces the employer to accept a wage rate of W_c. Explain verbally and graphically why in this instance the higher wage rate will be accompanied by an *increase* in the number of workers hired.

5 Complete the accompanying labor supply table for a firm hiring labor competitively.

Units of labor	Wage rate	Total labor cost (wage bill)	Marginal resource (labor) cost
0	$14	$	$
1	14		
2	14		
3	14		
4	14		
5	14		
6	14		

a Show graphically the labor supply and marginal resource (labor) cost curves for this firm. Explain the relationships of these curves to one another.

b Compare these data with the labor demand data of question 2 in Chapter 14. What will the equilibrium wage rate and level of employment be? Explain.

c Now redetermine this firm's supply schedule for labor, assuming that it is a monopsonist and that, although it can hire the first worker for $6, it must increase the wage rate by $3 to attract each successive worker. Show the new labor supply and marginal labor cost curves graphically and explain their relationships to one another. Compare these new data with those of question 2 for Chapter 14. What will be the equilibrium wage rate and the level of employment? Why do these differ from your answer to question 5b?

6 A critic of the minimum wage has contended, "The effects of minimum wage legislation are precisely the opposite of those predicted by those who support them. Government can legislate a minimum wage, but cannot force employers to hire unprofitable workers. In fact, minimum wages cause unemployment among low-wage workers who can least afford to give up their small incomes." Do you agree? What bearing does the elasticity of labor demand have on this assessment? What factors might possibly offset the potential unemployment effects of a minimum wage?

7 On the average do union workers receive higher wages than comparable nonunion workers?

8 What are the basic considerations which help explain wage differentials? What long-run effect would a substantial increase in safety for underground coal miners have on their wage rates in comparison to other workers?

9 "Many of the lowest-paid people in society—for example, short-order cooks—also have relatively poor working conditions. Hence, the notion of equalizing wage differentials is disproved." Do you agree? Explain.

10 What is meant by investment in human capital? Use this concept to explain **a** wage differentials, and **b** the long-run rise of real wage rates in the United States.

11 What is meant by the principal–agent problem? Have you ever worked in a setting where this problem has arisen? If so, do you think increased monitoring would have eliminated the problem? Why don't firms simply hire more supervisors to eliminate shirking?

12 The notion of efficiency wages suggests that an above-equilibrium wage rate will elicit a more-than-offsetting increase in worker productivity. By what specific means might the higher wage cause worker productivity to rise? Why might young workers accept a seniority pay plan under which they are initially paid less than their MRPs?

The Pricing and Employment of Resources: Rent, Interest, and Profits

7.75%
1-Year Introductory Rate

Emphasis in the previous two chapters was on labor markets because wages and salaries account for about three-fourths of our national income. In this chapter we focus on three other sources of income—rent, interest, and profits—which compose the remaining one-fourth of national income.

You undoubtedly are aware of these income sources. We read stories of incredibly high land rents in urban areas such as Tokyo, where an acre of land may sell for more than $85 million. An acre of desert may cost $650,000 along the Las Vegas casino strip; meanwhile, an acre of land in the middle of the Nevada desert can be bought for about $60. *How do land prices and rents get established?*

If you put money in a three-month certificate of deposit in early 1991, you probably received an interest rate of about 7 percent. One year later that CD paid only about 3.7 percent. *What factors determine interest rates and explain why they change?*

The news media continually document the profit and loss performance of various firms and industries. The maker of Nintendo video games has reaped large profits. And the firm which produces AZT, a drug which prolongs the life of AIDS patients, doubled its profits over a three-year period. Meanwhile, some automakers and airlines have recently suffered record losses. *What are the sources of profits and losses? What functions do they serve?*

ECONOMIC RENT

To most people the term "rent" means the amount one must pay for a two-bedroom apartment or a dormitory room. To the business executive, "rent" is a payment made for use of a factory building, machinery, or warehouse facilities. Closer examination finds these commonsense definitions of rent to be confusing and ambiguous. Dormitory room rent, for example, includes interest on the money capital the univeristy has borrowed to finance the dormitory's construction, wages for custodial service, utility payments, and so forth.

Economists therefore use the term "rent" in a narrower, less ambiguous sense: **Economic rent** *is the price paid for use of land and other natural resources which are completely fixed in total supply.* The unique supply conditions of land and other natural resources—their fixed supply—make rental payments distinguishable from wage, interest, and profit payments.

Let's examine this feature and some of its implications through supply and demand analysis. To avoid complications, assume, first, that all land is the same grade or quality—in other words, each available acre of land is equally productive. Suppose, too, that all land has just one use, being capable of producing just one product—say, corn. And assume that land is being rented in a competitive market—that many corn farmers are demanding and many landowners offering land in the market.

In Figure 16-1, *SS* indicates the supply of arable farmland available in the economy as a whole and D_2 the demand of farmers for use of that land. As with all economic resources, demand is a derived demand. It is downsloping because of the law of diminishing returns and the fact that, for farmers as a group, product price must be reduced to sell additional units of output.

Perfectly Inelastic Supply

The unique feature of our analysis is on the supply side: For all practical purposes the supply of land is perfectly inelastic, as reflected in *SS*. Land has no production cost; it is a "free and nonreproducible gift of nature." The economy has so much land, and that's that. It is true, of course, that within limits existing land can be made more usable by clearing, drainage, and irrigation. But these programs are capital improvements and not changes in the amount of land as such. Furthermore, such variations in the usability of land are a very small fraction of the total amount of land in existence and do not undermine the basic argument that land and other natural resources are in virtually fixed supply.

FIGURE 16-1 The determination of land rent

Because the supply of land and other natural resources is perfectly inelastic (*SS*), demand is the sole active determinant of land rent. An increase (D_2 to D_1) or decrease (D_2 to D_3) in demand will cause considerable changes in rent (R_2 to R_1 and R_2 to R_3). If demand is very small (D_4) relative to supply, land will be a "free good."

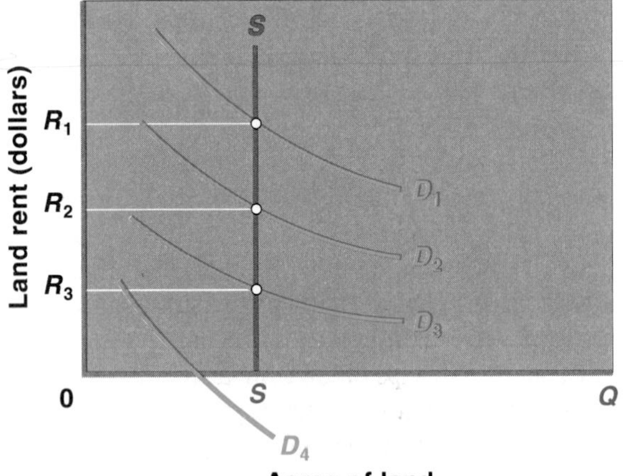

Changes in Demand

The fixed nature of the supply of land means that demand is the only active determinant of land rent; supply is passive. And what determines the demand for land? Those factors discussed in Chapter 14—the price of the product grown on the land, the productivity of land (which depends in part on the quantity and quality of the resources with which land is combined), and the prices of those other resources which are combined with land. If in Figure 16-1, the demand for land should increase from D_2 to D_1 or decline from D_2 to D_3, land rent would change from R_2 to R_1 or R_3, but the amount of land supplied would remain unchanged at 0*S*. Changes in economic rent will have no impact on the amount of land available; the supply of land is simply not augmentable. In technical terms, there is a large price effect and no quantity effect when the demand for land changes. If demand for land is only D_4, land rent will be zero; land will be a "free good" because it is not scarce enough in relation to demand for it to command a price. This situation was approximated in the free-land era of American history.

Land Rent Is a Surplus

The perfect inelasticity of the supply of land must be contrasted with the relative elasticity of such property resources as apartment buildings, machinery, and warehouses. These resources are *not* fixed in total supply. A higher price will give entrepreneurs the incentive to construct and offer larger quantities of these property resources. Conversely, a decline in their prices will induce suppliers to allow existing facilities to depreciate and not be replaced. The same general reasoning applies to the total supply of labor. Within limits, a higher average level of wages will induce more workers to enter the labor force, and lower wages will cause them to drop out of the labor force. The supplies of nonland resources are upsloping or, stated differently, the prices paid to such resources perform an **incentive**

function. A high price provides an incentive to offer more; a low price, to offer less.

Not so with land. Rent serves no incentive function, because the total supply of land is fixed. If rent is $10,000, $500, $1, or $0 per acre, the same amount of land will be available to society to make a contribution to production. Rent, in other words, could be eliminated without affecting the productive potential of the economy. For this reason economists consider rent to be a *surplus,* that is, a payment which is not necessary to ensure that land will be available to the economy as a whole.[1]

A Single Tax on Land

If land is a free gift of nature, costs nothing to produce, and would be available even in the absence of rental payments, why should rent be paid to those who by historical accident, by inheritance, or by crook happen to be landowners? Socialists have long argued that all land rents are unearned incomes. Therefore, they argue, land should be nationalized—owned by the state—so that any payments for its use can be used by the state to further the well-being of the entire population rather than being used by a landowning minority.

Henry George's Proposal In the United States, criticism of rental payments has taken the form of a **single-tax movement** which gained much support in the late nineteenth century. Spearheaded by Henry George's provocative book *Progress and Poverty* (1879), this reform movement maintained that economic rent could be taxed away completely without impairing the available supply of land or, therefore, the productive potential of the economy as a whole.

George observed that as population grew and the geographic frontier closed, landowners enjoyed larger and larger rents from their landholdings. These increments in rent were the result of a growing demand for a resource whose supply was perfectly inelastic; some landlords were receiving fabulously high incomes, not through rendering any productive effort, but solely from holding advantageously located land. Henry George stated that these increases in land rent belonged to the economy as a whole; he held that land rents should be taxed away and spent for public uses.

Indeed, George held that there was no reason to tax away only 50 percent of the landowner's unearned rental income. Why not take 70 or 90 or 99 percent? In seeking popular support for his ideas on land taxation, Henry George proposed that taxes on rental income be the *only* tax levied by government.

George's case for taxing land was based not only on equity or fairness, but also on efficiency grounds. In particular, unlike virtually every other tax, a tax on land does *not* alter or distort the allocation of resources. For example, a tax on wages will reduce after-tax wages and might weaken incentives to work. An individual who decides to participate in the labor force at a $6 before-tax wage rate may decide to drop from the labor force and go on welfare when an income tax reduces the after-tax wage rate to $4.50. Similarly, a property tax on buildings lowers returns to investors in such property, causing them in time to reallocate their money capital toward other investments. But no such reallocations of resources occur when land is taxed. The most profitable use for land before it is taxed remains the most profitable use after the tax is imposed. Of course, a landlord could withdraw land from production when a tax is imposed, but this would mean no rental income at all.

Criticisms Critics of the single tax on land make these points:

1 Current levels of government spending are such that a land tax alone would clearly not bring in enough revenue; it cannot be considered realistically as a *single* tax.

2 As noted earlier, in practice most income payments combine elements of interest, rent, wages, and profits. Land is typically improved in some manner by productive effort, and economic rent cannot be readily disentangled from payments for capital improvements. As a practical matter, it would be difficult to determine how much of any given income payment is actually rent.

3 The question of unearned income goes beyond land and land ownership. One can argue that many individuals and groups other than landowners benefit from receipt of "unearned" income associated with the overall advance of the economy. For example, consider the capital gains income received by someone who,

[1]A portion—in some instances a major portion—of wage and salary incomes may be a surplus in that these incomes exceed the minimum amount necessary to keep an indvidual in his or her current line of work. For example, in 1991 the *average* salary paid to major league baseball players was about $891,000 per year. In the next best occupational option as, say, a college coach, a player might earn only $40,000 or $50,000 per year. Most of his current income is therefore a surplus. Observe that in the twilight of their careers, professional athletes sometimes accept sizable salary reductions rather than seek employment in alternative occupations.

some twenty or twenty-five years ago, chanced to purchase (or inherit) stock in a firm which has experienced rapid growth (say, IBM or Xerox). How is this income different from the rental income of the landowner?

4 Finally, historically a piece of land is likely to have changed ownership many times. *Former* owners may have been the beneficiaries of past increases in land rent. It is hardly fair to tax *current* owners who paid the competitive market price for land.

Productivity Differences

Thus far we have assumed that all units of land are of the same grade. In practice, this is plainly not so. Different acres vary greatly in productivity. These productivity differences stem primarily from differences in soil fertility and such climatic factors as rainfall and temperature. These factors explain why Iowa soil is excellently suited to corn production, the plains of eastern Colorado are much less so, and desert wasteland of New Mexico is incapable of corn production. These productivity differences will be reflected in resource demand. Competitive bidding by farmers will establish a high rent for the very productive Iowa land. Less productive Colorado land will command a much lower rent, and New Mexico land no rent at all.

Location may be equally important in explaining differences in land rent. Other things being equal, renters will pay more for a unit of land which is strategically located with respect to materials, labor, and customers than for a unit of land whose location is remote from these markets. Witness the extremely high land rents in large metropolitan areas.

The rent differentials to which quality differences in land would give rise can be seen by viewing Figure 16-1 from a slightly different point of view. Suppose, as before, that only one agricultural product, say corn, can be produced on four grades of land, *each* of which is available in the fixed amount $0S$. When combined with identical amounts of capital, labor, and other cooperating resources, the productivity—or, more specifically, the marginal revenue productivity—of each grade of land is reflected in demand curves D_1, D_2, D_3, and D_4. Grade 1 land is the most productive, as reflected in D_1, whereas grade 4 is the least productive, as is shown by D_4. The resulting economic rents for grades 1, 2, and 3 land will be R_1, R_2, and R_3 respectively, the rent differentials mirroring differences in productivity of the three grades of land. Grade 4 land is so poor in quality that it would not pay farmers to bring it fully into production; it would be a "free" and only partially used resource.

Alternative Uses and Costs

We have also supposed, thus far, that land has only one use. Actually, we know that land normally has a number of alternative uses. An acre of Iowa farm land may be useful in raising not only corn, but also wheat, oats, milo, and cattle; or it may be useful as a house or factory site.

What is the importance of this obvious point? It indicates that, although land is a free gift of nature and has no production cost from the viewpoint of society as a whole, the rental payments of individual producers are *costs.* The total supply of land will be available to society even if no rent at all is paid for its use. But, from the standpoint of individual firms and industries, land has alternative uses, and therefore payments must be made by specific firms and industries to attract that land from those other uses. Such payments by definition are costs. Again, the fallacy of composition (Chapter 1) has entered our discussion. From the standpoint of society, there is no alternative but for land to be used by society. Therefore, to society, rents are a surplus, not a cost. But because land has alternative uses, the rental payments of corn farmers or any other individual user are a cost; such payments are required to attract land from alternative uses.

QUICK REVIEW 16-1

- ***Economic rent is the price paid for resources such as land, the supply of which is perfectly inelastic.***
- ***Land rent is a surplus in that land would be available to society even if rent were not paid.***
- ***The surplus nature of land rent was the basis for Henry George's single-tax movement.***
- ***Differential rents allocate land among alternative uses.***

INTEREST

The interest rate is the price paid for the use of money. It is the amount of money one must pay for the use of one dollar for a year. Two aspects of this income payment are notable.

1 Stated as Percentage Because it is paid in kind, interest is typically stated as a percentage of the amount of money being borrowed rather than as an absolute amount. It is less clumsy to say one is paying 12 percent interest than to proclaim that interest is "$120 per year per $1000." Furthermore, stating interest as a percentage facilitates comparison of interest paid on loans of much different absolute amounts. By expressing interest as a percentage, we can immediately compare an interest payment of, say, $432 per year per $2880 and one of $1800 per year per $12,000. In this case both interest payments are 15 percent—a fact not obvious from the absolute figures.

The **Truth in Lending Act** was passed in 1968 and requires lenders to state the costs and terms of consumer credit in concise and uniform language. In particular, the act requires that interest must be stated as an annual rate. Nevertheless, as this chapter's Last Word explains, it is not always simple to determine how much interest is being charged.

2 Money Not a Resource Money is *not* an economic resource. As such, money is not productive; it cannot produce goods and services. However, businesses "buy" the use of money, because money can be used to acquire capital goods—factory buildings, machinery, warehouses, and so forth. These facilities clearly do contribute to production. Thus, in hiring the use of money capital, business executives are ultimately buying the use of real capital goods.

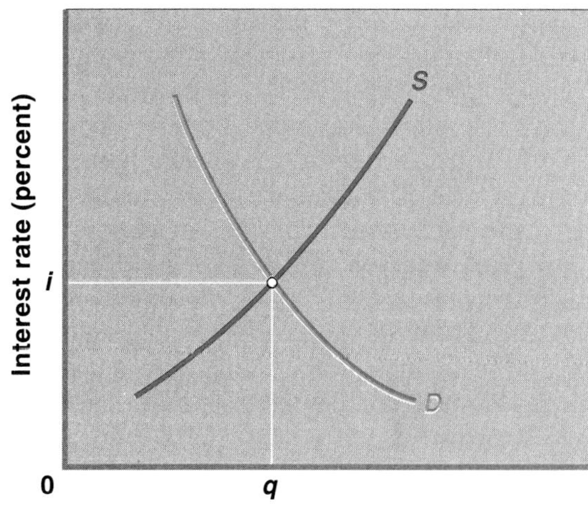

FIGURE 16-2 The market for loanable funds

The upsloping supply curve of loanable funds reflects the notion that households prefer present consumption to future consumption and, therefore, must be paid an interest rate "bribe" to induce them to save (not consume). The higher the interest rate, the larger the amount households are willing to save. The downsloping demand curve for loanable funds is based upon the fact that, other things being equal, more potential investments will be profitable at low interest rates than at high interest rates. The interaction of the two curves determines the equilibrium rate of interest.

Loanable Funds Theory of Interest

The **loanable funds theory of interest** explains the interest rate in terms of the demand for and supply of loanable funds. The equilibrium interest rate equates the quantities of loanable funds demanded and supplied.

Supply of Loanable Funds Let's first consider the loanable funds theory in a simplified form in which we assume that households or consumers are the sole suppliers and businesses are the only demanders of loanable funds. In Figure 16-2 the supply of loanable funds is shown as an upsloping curve; a larger quantity of funds will be made available at high interest rates than at low interest rates. The explanation of this is rooted in the idea that most people prefer the pleasure of indulgence today rather than the promise of indulgence at some time in the future. Most individuals prefer present consumption to future consumption because, given the uncertainties of life, present consumption seems more tangible and therefore more valuable. In short, people are impatient and subjectively prefer goods in the present over goods in the future. It follows that a consumer must be "bribed" or compensated by an interest payment to defer consumption or, in other words, to save. The upsloping supply of loanable funds curve indicates that the larger the interest rate "bribe," the more households are willing to save (or, alternatively, the less of their incomes they consume).

Demand for Loanable Funds The primary demanders of loanable funds are businesses which want to replace or add to their stocks of capital goods. Firms demand loanable funds to build new plants or warehouses, to purchase machinery and equipment, and so forth.

Consider in simplified fashion the character of such investment decisions. Suppose a firm is contemplating buying a machine which will increase output and sales to the extent that its total revenue will rise by $110 for the year. Also assume the machine costs $100 and has a useful life of just one year. Comparing the $10 earned above the cost of the machine to that cost, we find the **rate of return** on this investment is 10 percent (=$10/$100).

The firm must now compare the interest rate—the price of loanable funds—with the 10 percent rate of return to determine whether the investment is profitable and therefore should be made. For example, if funds can be borrowed at some rate less than the rate of return, say, 6 percent, then the investment is profitable and should be undertaken. But if funds are available at a 14 percent rate of interest, this investment is unprofitable and should not be made.

Why is the demand for loanable funds downsloping as shown in Figure 16-2? At higher interest rates fewer investment projects will be profitable to businesses and hence a small quantity of loanable funds will be demanded. Conversely, more investment projects will be profitable and therefore more loanable funds will be demanded at lower interest rates. Indeed, we have just seen in our example that it is profitable to purchase the $100 machine if funds can be borrowed at 6 percent, but it is not profitable if the firm must borrow at 14 percent.

Extending the Model We now want to make our portrayal of the loanable funds market more realistic in two different ways. In our first extension of the model we consider factors which might cause the supply and demand curves of loanable funds to shift and thereby change the equilibrium interest rate.

Change in Supply Consider the supply side. Anything which causes households to be more thrifty will prompt them to save more at each interest rate, shifting the supply curve rightward. For example, if the tax laws were changed to exempt interest earned on savings from taxation, we would expect the supply of loanable funds to increase and the equilibrium interest rate to decrease. Conversely, a decline in thriftiness would shift the curve leftward and increase the equilibrium interest rate. Illustration: If government expanded our social insurance to more fully cover the costs of hospitalization and retirement, the incentives of households to save might diminish.

Change in Demand On the demand side, anything which increases the rates of return on potential investments will increase the demand for loanable funds. Let's return to our earlier example where a firm would receive additional revenues of $110 by purchasing a $100 machine and, hence, realize a 10 percent return on the investment. What factors might increase or decrease the rate of return? Suppose a technological advance raises the productivity of the machine so that it produces still more output and thereby increases the firm's total revenue by $120 rather than $110. The rate of return will now be 20 percent, rather than 10 percent. Before the techological advance the firm would demand no loanable funds at, say, a 14 percent interest rate. But now it would demand $100, implying a rightward shift of the demand for loanable funds curve.

Similarly, an increase in consumer demand for the firm's product—reflecting perhaps the movement of the economy from recession to prosperity—will increase product price. Even though we assume the productivity of the machine is unchanged, the firm's additional total revenue might again rise from $110 to $120 which increases the rate of return to 20 percent. This implies that the demand for loanable funds has shifted righward. Conversely, we would expect a decline in the price of the firm's product to decrease the demand for loanable funds.

Other Transactors Second, we must recognize that there are more transactors on both the demand and supply side of the loanable funds market. For example, while households are suppliers of loanable funds, many are also demanders of those funds. Households borrow to finance large purchases such as housing, automobiles, and furniture and household appliances. Governments are also on the demand side when they borrow to finance budgetary deficits. Similarly, businesses which have revenues in excess of their current costs or expenditures may make the consequent business saving available in the market for loanable funds. Note that households and businesses are on both the supply and demand sides of the market.

Finally, in studying macroeconomics you will find that commercial banks and other financial institutions not only gather and make available the savings of households and businesses, but also create loanable funds when they lend. Thus, banks are another source of loanable funds.

There is disagreement among economists as to how much the quantity of loanable funds made available by suppliers changes in response to changes in the interest rate. Most economists view saving—a major component of the supply of loanable funds—as being relatively insensitive to changes in the interest rate. The supply curve of loanable funds therefore may be highly inelastic. But whatever the elasticity of the curve, the basic point remains: The equilibrium interest rate equates the quantities of loanable funds demanded and supplied.

Range of Rates

Although economists often speak in terms of a single interest rate, in fact there exists a whole cluster or range of interest rates. Table 16-1 lists many interest rates referred to in the media. Note that these rates range from 5 to 18 percent. Why the differences?

1 Risk Varying degrees of risk on loans are important. The greater the chance the borrower will not repay the loan, the more interest the lender will charge to compensate for this risk.

2 Maturity The length or maturity of a loan also affects the interest rate. Other things being equal, long-term loans usually command higher rates of interest than do short-term loans. The long-term lender suffers the inconvenience and possible financial sacrifice of forgoing alternative uses for his or her money for a greater period of time.

3 Loan Size Given two loans of equal length and risk, the interest rate usually will be somewhat higher on the smaller of the two loans. This is so because administrative costs of a large and a small loan are about the same absolutely.

4 Taxability Interest on certain state and municipal bonds is exempt from Federal income taxation. Because lenders are interested in their after-tax rate of interest, states and local governments can attract lenders even though they pay lower interest rates. Thus, a high-income lender may prefer a 6 percent interest rate on a tax-exempt municipal bond compared to an 8 percent taxable interest rate on a corporate bond.

5 Market Imperfections Market imperfections are also important in explaining some interest rate differentials. The small-town bank which monopolizes the local money market may charge high interest rates on consumer loans because households find it inconvenient and costly to "shop around" at banks in somewhat distant cities. The large corporation, on the other hand, can survey a number of rival investment houses in floating a new bond issue, and can secure the lowest obtainable rate.

To circumvent the difficulties involved in discussing the whole structure of interest rates, economists talk of "the" interest rate or the **pure rate of interest.** This pure rate is best approximated by the interest paid on long-term, virtually riskless bonds such as the long-term bonds of the United States government (thirty-year Treasury bonds). This interest payment can be thought of as being made solely for the use of money over an extended time period, because risk and administrative costs are negligible and the interest on such securities is not distorted by market imperfections. At the end of 1991 the pure interest rate was about 8 percent.

TABLE 16-1 Selected interest rates, October 1991

Type of interest rate	*Annual percentage*
30-year Treasury bond rate (Federal government security used to finance the public debt)	7.93%
90-day Treasury bill rate (Federal government security used to finance the public debt)	4.99
Prime interest rate (Interest rate charged by banks to their best corporate customers)	8.00
30-year mortgage rate (Fixed-interest rate on loans for houses)	8.78
4-year automobile loan rate (Bank interest rate on loans for new automobiles)	11.06
Tax-exempt municipal bond rate (Interest rate paid on a low-risk bond issued by a state or local government)	6.28
Federal funds rate (Interest rate on overnight loans between banks)	5.21
Consumer credit card rate (Interest rate charged for credit card purchases)	18.24

Role of the Interest Rate

The interest rate is an extremely important price as it simultaneously affects both the *level* and *composition* of investment goods production.

Interest and Domestic Output Other things being equal, a change in the equilibrium rate of interest will move businesses along the aggregate investment-demand curve, changing the level of investment and the equilibrium level of GDP. The interest rate is an "administered price." This means that the monetary authorities purposely manipulate the money supply to influence the interest rate and thereby the levels of output, employment, and prices. Recall that an easy (low interest rate) monetary policy increases investment and expands the economy; a tight (high interest rate) monetary policy chokes off investment and constrains the economy.

Interest and the Allocation of Capital Prices are rationing devices. The interest rate is no exception; it allocates money capital and therefore physical capital to various firms and investment projects. It rations the available supply of money or liquidity to investment projects whose rate of return or expected profitability is sufficiently high to warrant payment of the going interest rate.

If the expected rate of net profits of additional physical capital in the computer industry is 14 percent and the required funds can be secured at an interest rate of 10 percent, the computer industry will be able, in terms of profit, to borrow and expand its capital facilities. If the expected rate of net profits of additional capital in the steel industry is expected to be only 8 percent, it will be unprofitable for this industry to accumulate more capital goods at the 10 percent interest rate. *The interest rate allocates money, and ultimately physical capital, to those industries in which it will be most productive and therefore most profitable. Such an allocation of capital goods is in the interest of society as a whole.*

But the interest rate does not perform the task of rationing capital to its most productive uses perfectly. Large oligopolistic borrowers are in a better position than competitive borrowers to pass interest costs on to consumers by virtue of their ability to control output and thereby manipulate their prices. Also, the sheer size and prestige of large industrial concerns may help them obtain money capital on favorable terms, whereas the market for money capital screens out less-well-known firms whose profit expectations might actually be superior.

QUICK REVIEW 16-2

- ***Interest is the price paid for the use of money.***
- ***The equilibrium interest rate is determined by the demand for and the supply of loanable funds.***
- ***There exists a range of interest rates which is influenced by risk, maturity, loan size, taxability, and market imperfections.***
- ***The equilibrium real interest rate affects the aggregate level of investment and therefore the level of domestic output; it also allocates money and real capital to specific industries and firms.***

ECONOMIC PROFITS

As with rent, economists find it advantageous to define profits more narrowly than do accountants. To accountants, "profit" is what remains of a firm's total revenue after it has paid individuals and other firms for materials, capital and labor supplied to the firm. To the economist, this conception is too broad and therefore ambiguous. The difficulty is that this view of profits takes into account only **explicit costs:** the payments made by the firm to outsiders. It ignores **implicit costs:** the payments to similar resources owned and self-employed by a firm. In other words, this concept of profits fails to allow for implicit wage, rent, and interest costs. **Economic,** or **pure, profits** are what remain after *all* opportunity costs—both explicit and implicit wage, rent, and interest costs and a normal profit—have been subtracted from a firm's total revenue (Figure 9-1). Economic profits may be either positive or negative (losses).

For example, as the economist sees it, farmers who own their land and equipment and provide all their own labor grossly overstate their economic profits if they merely subtract their payments to outsiders for seed, insecticides, fertilizer, and gasoline from their total revenues. Actually, much or possibly all of what remain are the implicit rent, interest, and wage costs the farmers forgo in deciding to self-employ the resources they own rather than make them available in alternative employments. Interest on capital or wages for labor contributed by farmers are no more profits than are payments which would be made if outsiders had supplied these resources. Economic profits are a residual—the total revenue remaining after *all* costs are taken into account.

Role of the Entrepreneur

The economist views profits as the return to a very special type of human resource—entrepreneurial ability. The functions of the entrepreneur were summarized in Chapter 2. They entail (1) taking the initiative to combine other resources in producing a good or service; (2) making basic, nonroutine policy decisions for the firm; (3) introducing innovations in the form of new products or production processes; and (4) bearing the economic risks associated with all these functions.

Part of the entrepreneur's return is called a **normal profit.** This is the minimum return or payment necessary to retain the entrepreneur in some specific line of production. This normal profit payment is a cost (Chapter 9). However, we know that a firm's total revenue may exceed its total costs (explicit, implicit, the latter inclusive of a normal profit). This extra or excess revenue above all costs is an economic, or pure, profit. This residual—which is *not* a cost because it is in excess of the normal profit required to retain the entrepreneur in the industry—accrues to the entrepreneur. The entrepreneur is the residual claimant.

Economists offer several theories to explain why this residual of economic profit might occur. These explanations relate to:

1 The *risks* which the entrepreneur bears by functioning in a dynamic and therefore uncertain environment or by undertaking innovational activity.

2 The possibility of attaining *monopoly power.*

Sources of Economic Profit

Our understanding of economic profits and the entrepreneur's functions can be enhanced by describing an artificial economic environment within which pure profits would be zero. Then, by noting real-world deviations from this environment, we can lay bare the sources of economic profit.

In a purely competitive static economy, pure profits would be zero. By a **static economy** we mean one in which basic data—resource supplies, technological knowledge, and consumer tastes—are constant and unchanging. A static economy is a changeless one in which all determinants of cost and supply data, on the one hand, and demand and revenue data, on the other, are constant.

Given the static nature of these data, the economic future is perfectly foreseeable; economic uncertainty is nonexistent. The outcome of price and production policies is accurately predictable. Furthermore, the static nature of such a society precludes innovational change. Under pure competition any pure profits (positive or negative) which might have existed initially in various industries will disappear with the entry or exodus of firms in the long run. All costs—explicit and implicit—will therefore be covered in the long run, leaving no residual in the form of pure profits (Figure 10-12).

The notion of zero economic profits in a static, competitive economy enhances our understanding of profits by suggesting that the presence of profits is linked to the dynamic nature of real-world capitalism and its accompanying uncertainty. Furthermore, it indicates that economic profits may arise from a source apart from the directing, innovating, risk-bearing functions of the entrepreneur. And that source is the presence of some degree of monopoly power.

Uncertainty, Risk, and Profits In a dynamic economy the future is always uncertain. This means that the entrepreneur necessarily assumes risks. Profits can be thought of in part as a reward for assuming these risks.

In linking pure profits with uncertainty and risk bearing, we must distinguish between risks which are insurable and those which are not. Some types of risks —fires, floods, theft, and accidents to employees—are measurable in that actuaries can accurately estimate their average occurrence. As a result, these risks are typically insurable. Firms can avoid, or at least provide for, them by incurring a known cost in the form of an insurance premium. It is the bearing of **uninsurable risks,** then, which is a potential source of economic profits.

Basically, such uninsurable risks are uncontrollable and unpredictable changes in demand (revenue) and supply (cost) conditions facing the firm. Some of these uninsurable risks stem from unpredictable changes in the general economic environment or, more specifically, from the business cycle. Prosperity brings substantial windfall profits to most firms, whereas depression means widespread losses. In addition, changes are constantly taking place in the structure of the domestic and world economies. Even in a full-employment, noninflationary economy, changes are always occurring in consumer tastes, technology, and resource supplies. Example: Technological change has been such that vinyl long-playing records have given way to cassettes and the latter in turn have partially lost their market to compact discs. Digital audio tapes may soon challenge compact discs.

Such changes continually alter the revenue and cost data faced by individual firms and industries, leading to changes in the structure of the business population as favorably affected industries expand and adversely affected industries contract. Changes in government policies are pertinent at both levels. Appropriate fiscal and monetary policies of government may reverse a recession, whereas the establishment or elimination of a tariff may alter significantly the demand and revenue data of the affected industry.

The point is that profits and losses can be associated with the bearing of uninsurable risks stemming from cyclical, structural, and policy changes in the economy.

Uncertainty, Innovations, and Profits The uncertainties just discussed are external to the firm; they are beyond the control of the individual firm or industry. One other extremely important dynamic feature of capitalism—innovation—occurs at the initiative of the entrepreneur. Business firms deliberately introduce new methods of production and distribution to affect their costs favorably and new products to influence their revenue favorably. The entrepreneur purposely undertakes to upset existing cost and revenue data in a way which hopefully will be profitable.

But once again, uncertainty enters the picture. Despite exhaustive market surveys, new products or modifications of existing products may prove to be economic failures. Three-dimensional movies, not to mention Yugo and Fiero automobiles, and disk cameras come readily to mind. Similarly, of the many new novels, textbooks, records, and tapes which appear every year, only a handful garner large profits. Nor is it known with certainty whether a new machine will actually provide the cost economies predicted for it while it is still in the blueprint stage. Innovations purposely undertaken by entrepreneurs entail uncertainty, just as do those changes in the economic environment over which an individual enterprise has no control. In a sense, innovation as a source of profits is merely a special case of risk bearing.

Under competition and in the absence of patent laws, innovational profits will be temporary. Rival firms will imitate successful (profitable) innovations, competing away all economic profits. Nevertheless, innovational profits may always exist in a progressive economy as new, successful innovations replace older ones whose associated profits have been eroded or competed away.

Monopoly Profits Thus far, we have emphasized that profits are related to the uncertainties and uninsurable risks surrounding dynamic events which enterprises are exposed to or initiate themselves. The existence of monopoly in some form or other is a final source of economic profits. Because of its ability to restrict output and deter entry, a monopolist may persistently enjoy above-competitive prices and economic profits, provided demand is strong relative to costs (Figure 11-3).

There are both a causal relationship and a notable distinction between uncertainty, on the one hand, and monopoly, on the other, as sources of profits. The causal relationship involves the fact that an entrepreneur can reduce uncertainty, or at least manipulate its effects, by achieving monopoly power. The competitive firm is unalterably exposed to the vagaries of the market; the monopolist, however, can control the market to a degree and offset or minimize potentially adverse effects of uncertainty. Furthermore, innovation is an important source of monopoly power; the short-run uncertainty associated with the introduction of new techniques or new products may be borne for the purpose of achieving a measure of monopoly power.

The notable distinction between profits stemming from uncertainty and from monopoly has to do with the social desirability of the two sources of profits. Bearing the risks inherent in a dynamic and uncertain economic environment and the undertaking of innovations are socially desirable functions. The social desirability of monopoly profits, on the other hand, is very doubtful. Monopoly profits typically are founded on output restriction, above-competitive prices, and a contrived misallocation of resources.

Functions of Profits

Profit is the prime mover, or energizer, of the capitalistic economy. As such, profits influence both the level of resource utilization and the allocation of resources among alternative uses.

Investment and Domestic Ouput It is profits—or better, the *expectation* of profits—which induce firms to innovate. Innovation stimulates investment, total output, and employment. Innovation is a fundamental aspect of the process of economic growth, and it is the pursuit of profit which underlies most innovation. However, profit expectations are volatile, with the result that investment, employment, and the rate of growth have been unstable. Profits have functioned imperfectly as a spur to innovation and investment.

Profits and Resource Allocation Perhaps profits perform more effectively the task of allocating resources among alternative lines of production. Entrepreneurs seek profits and shun losses. The occurrence of economic profits is a signal that society wants that particular industry to expand. Profit rewards are more than an inducement for an industry to expand; they also are the financial means by which firms in such industries can add to their productive capacities.

Losses, on the other hand, signal society's desire for the afflicted industries to contract; losses penalize businesses which fail to adjust their productive efforts to those goods and services most preferred by consumers. This is not to say that profits and losses result in an allocation of resources now and forever attuned to consumer preferences. In particular, the presence of monopoly in both product and resource markets impedes the shiftability of firms and resources, as do the various geographic, artificial, and sociological immobilities discussed in Chapter 15.

QUICK REVIEW 16-3

- ***Pure or economic profits are determined by subtracting all explicit and implicit costs (including a normal profit) from a firm's total revenue.***
- ***Economic profits result from a the bearing of uninsurable risks, b innovation, and c monopoly power.***
- ***Profits and profit expectations affect the levels of investment and domestic output and also allocate resources among alternative uses.***

INCOME SHARES

The discussions of Chapters 15 and 16 would be incomplete without a brief empirical summary on the importance of wages, rent, interest, and profits as proportions or relative shares of the national income. Table 16-2 provides an historical look at income shares in terms of the income categories used in our national income accounts. Although these accounting conceptions of income do not neatly fit the economist's definitions of wages, rent, interest, and profits, they do yield some usable insights about the relative size and trends of income shares.

Current Shares

The most recent 1982–1990 figures in the table reveal the dominant role of labor income. Defining labor income narrowly as "wages and salaries," labor currently receives almost 75 percent of the national income. But some economists argue that since proprietors' income is largely composed of wages and salaries, it should be added to the official "wages and salaries" category to determine labor income. When we use this broad definition, labor's share rises to about 80 percent of national income. Interestingly, although we label our system a "capitalist economy," the capitalist share of national income—the sum of "corporate profits," "interest," and "rent"—is only about 20 percent of the national income.

Historical Trends

What can be deduced from Table 16-2 about historical trends? Let's concentrate on the dominant wage share. Using the narrow definition of labor's share as simply "wages and salaries," we note an increase from about 55 to almost 75 percent in this century.

Structural Changes Although these are several tentative explanations of these data, one prominent theory stresses the structural changes which have occurred in our economy. Two specific points are made.

1 Corporate Growth Noting the relative constancy of the capitalist share (the sum of columns 4, 5, and 6)—roughly 20 percent in both the 1900–1909 and the 1982–1990 periods—we find that the expansion of labor's share has come primarily at the expense of the share going to proprietors. This suggests that the evolution of the corporation as the dominant form of business enterprise is an important explanatory factor. Individuals who would have operated their own corner groceries in the 1920s are the hired managers of corporate supermarkets in the 1980s or 1990s.

2 Changing Industry-Mix The changing output-mix and therefore the industry-mix which have occurred historically have increased labor's share. Overall, there has been a long-term change in the composition of output and industry away from land- and capital-intensive production and toward labor-intensive production. Again, crudely stated, there has been an historical reallocation of labor from agriculture (where labor's share is quite low) to manufacturing (where labor's share is rather high) and, finally, to private and public services (where labor's share is very high). These shifts account for much of the growth of labor's share reflected in column 2 of Table 16-2.

Unions? It is tempting to explain an expanding wage share in terms of the growth of labor unions. But there are difficulties with this approach.

1 The growth of the labor movement in the United States does not fit very well chronologically with the growth of labor's share of the national income. Much of the growth of "wages and salaries" occurred between 1900 and 1939; much of the growth in the labor movement came in the last few years of the 1930s and the war years of the early 1940s.

2 Wage increases for union members may come at the expense of wages of unorganized workers. That is, in obtaining higher wages, unions restrict employment opportunities (Figures 15-6 and 15-7) in organized industries. Unemployed workers and new labor-force entrants therfore seek jobs in nonunion sectors. Resulting increases in labor supply depress wage rates in nonunion jobs. If this scenario is correct, then higher wages for union workers may be achieved, not at the expense of the capitalist share, but rather at the expense of the nonunion wage share. Overall, the total labor share—union plus nonunion—could well be unaffected by unions.

3 If the national income is disaggregated into industry sectors (as in Table 5-5) and the historical trend of the wage share in each sector is examined, we reach a curious conclusion. Generally, labor's share has grown more rapidly in those sectors where unions are weak than in sectors which are highly unionized.

TABLE 16-2 Relative shares of national income, 1900–1990 *(decade or period averages of shares for individual years)*

			Property (capital) income			
(1) Decade	*(2) Wages and salaries*	*(3) Proprietors' income*	*(4) Corporate profits*	*(5) Interest*	*(6) Rent*	*(7) Total*
1900–1909	55.0%	23.7%	6.8%	5.5%	9.0%	100%
1910–1919	53.6	23.8	9.1	5.4	8.1	100
1920–1929	60.0	17.5	7.8	6.2	7.7	100
1930–1939	67.5	14.8	4.0	8.7	5.0	100
1939–1948	64.6	17.2	11.9	3.1	3.3	100
1949–1958	67.3	13.9	12.5	2.9	3.4	100
1954–1963	69.9	11.9	11.2	4.0	3.0	100
1963–1970	71.7	9.6	12.1	3.5	3.2	100
1971–1981	75.9	7.1	8.4	6.4	2.2	100
1982–1990	73.6	7.3	8.3	10.0	1.0	100

Source: Irving Kravis, "Income Distribution: Functional Share," *International Encyclopedia of Social Sciences,* vol. 7 (New York: The Macmillan Company and Free Press, 1968), p. 134, updated.

LAST WORD

DETERMINING THE PRICE OF CREDIT

There are a variety of lending practices which can cause the effective interest rate to be quite different from what it appears to be.

Borrowing and lending—receiving and granting credit—are a way of life. Individuals receive credit when they negotiate a mortgage loan and when they use their credit cards. Conversely, individuals make loans when they open a savings account in a commercial bank or buy a government bond.

Despite the passage of the Truth in Lending Act of 1968, it remains difficult to determine exactly how much interest one pays and receives in borrowing and lending. A few illustrations will be helpful. Let's suppose that you borrow \$10,000 which you agree to repay plus \$1,000 of interest at the end of the year. In this instance the interest rate is 10 percent. To determine the interest rate (r) one merely compares interest paid with the amount borrowed:

$$r = \frac{\$1{,}000}{\$10{,}000} = 10\%$$

But in some cases a lender, say, a bank, will *discount* the interest payment at the time the loan is made. Thus, instead of giving the borrower \$10,000, the bank disounts the \$1,000 interest payment in advance, giving the borrower only \$9,000. This increases the interest rate:

$$r = \frac{\$1{,}000}{\$9{,}000} = 11\%$$

While the absolute amount of interest paid is the same, in this second case the borrower has only \$9,000 available for the year.

An even more subtle point is that, in order to simplify their calculations, many financial institutions assume a 360-day year (twelve 30-day months). This means the borrower has the use of the lender's funds for five days less than the normal year. This use of a "short year" also increases the interest rate paid by the borrower.

The interest rate paid can change dramatically if a loan is repaid in installments. Suppose a bank lends you \$10,000 and charges interest in the amount of \$1,000 to be paid at the end of the year. But the loan contract requires you to repay the \$10,000 loan in 12 equal monthly installments. The effect of this is that the average amount of the loan outstanding during the year is only \$5,000. Hence:

$$r = \frac{\$1{,}000}{\$5{,}000} = 20\%$$

Here interest is paid on the total amount of the loan (\$10,000) rather than the outstanding balance (which averages \$5,000 for the year), making for a much higher interest rate.

Another fact which influences the effective interest rate is whether or not interest is *compounded.* Suppose you deposit \$10,000 in a savings account which pays a 10 percent interest rate compounded semiannually. In other words, interest is paid on your "loan" to the bank twice a year. At the end of the first six months, \$500 of interest (10% of \$10,000 for one-half a year) is added to your account. At the end of the year, interest is calculated on \$10,500 so that the second interest payment is \$525 (10% of \$10,500 for one-half a year). Hence:

$$r = \frac{\$1{,}025}{\$10{,}000} = 10.25\%$$

This means that a bank advertising a 10 percent interest rate compounded semiannually is actually paying more interest to its customers than a competitor paying a simple (noncompounded) interest rate of 10.20 percent.

"Let the borrower beware" is a fitting motto in the world of credit.

CHAPTER SUMMARY

1 Economic rent is the price paid for the use of land and other natural resources whose total supplies are fixed.

2 Rent is a surplus since land would be available to the economy as a whole even without rental payments. The notion of land rent as a surplus gave rise to the single-tax movement of the late 1800s.

3 Differences in land rent are explainable in terms of differences in productivity due to the fertility and climatic features of land and in its location.

4 Land rent is a surplus rather than a cost to the economy as a whole; however, because land has alternative uses from the standpoint of individual firms and industries, rental payments of firms and industries are correctly regarded as costs.

5 Interest is the price paid for the use of money. The equilibrium interest rate is determined by the demand for and supply of loanable funds.

6 The equilibrium interest rate influences the level of investment and helps ration financial and physical capital to specific firms and industries. The real interest rate, not the nominal rate, is critical to the investment decision.

7 Economic, or pure, profits are the difference between a firm's total revenue and its total costs, the latter defined to include implicit costs, which include a normal profit. Profits accrue to entrepreneurs for assuming the uninsurable risks associated with organizing and directing economic resources and innovating. Profits also result from monopoly power.

8 Profit expectations influence innovating and investment activities and therefore the level of employment. The basic function of profits and losses, however, is to induce that allocation of resources which is in general accord with the tastes of consumers.

9 The largest share of the national income goes to labor. Narrowly defined as "wages and salaries," labor's relative share has increased through time. When more broadly defined to include "proprietors' income," labor's share has been about 80 percent and the capitalist share about 20 percent of national income since 1900.

TERMS AND CONCEPTS

economic rent
incentive function
single-tax movement
Truth in Lending Act
rate of return
loanable funds theory of interest
nominal versus real interest rate
pure rate of interest
explicit and implicit costs
normal profit
economic or pure profit
static economy
uninsurable risks

QUESTIONS AND STUDY SUGGESTIONS

1 How does the economist's usage of the term "rent" differ from everyday usage? "Though rent need not be paid by society to make land available, rental payments are very useful in guiding land into the most productive uses." Explain.

2 Explain why economic rent is a surplus to the economy as a whole but a cost of production from the standpoint of individual firms and industries. Explain: "Rent performs no 'incentive function' in the economy." What arguments can be made for and against a heavy tax on land?

3 If money capital is not an economic resource, why is interest paid and received for its use? What considerations account for the fact that interest rates differ greatly on various types of loans? Use these considerations to explain the relative size of the interest rates charged on the following:

a a ten-year $1000 government bond;

b a $20 pawnshop loan;

c an FHA thirty-year mortgage loan on a $97,000 house;

d a 24-month $12,000 commercial bank loan to finance an automobile; and

e a 60-day $100 loan from a personal finance company.

4 Why is the supply of loanable funds upsloping? Why is the demand for loanable funds downsloping? Explain the equilibrium interest rate and indicate factors which might cause it to change.

5 What are the major economic functions of the interest rate? Of economic profits? How might the fact that more and more businesses are financing their investment activities internally affect the efficiency with which the interest rate performs its functions?

6 Distinguish between nominal and real interest rates. Which is more relevant in making investment decisions? If the nominal interest rate is 12 percent and the inflation rate is 8 percent, what is the real rate of interest? At various times during the 1970s savers earned nominal rates of interest on their savings accounts which were less than the rate of inflation so that their savings earned negative real interest. Why, then, did they save?

7 Historically, usury laws which put below-equilibrium ceilings on interest rates have been used by some states on the grounds that such laws will make credit available to poor people who could not otherwise afford to borrow. Critics of such laws contend that it is poor people who are most likely to be hurt by such laws. Which view is correct?

8 How do the concepts of business profits and economic profits differ? Why are economic profits smaller than business profits? What are the three basic sources of economic profits? Classify each of the following in accordance with these sources:

a a firm's profits from developing and patenting a ball-point pen containing a permanent ink cartridge;

b a restaurant's profit which results from construction of a new highway past its door;

c the profit received by a firm benefiting from an unanticipated change in consumer tastes.

9 Why is the distinction between insurable and uninsurable risks significant for the theory of profits? Carefully evaluate: "All economic profits can be traced to either uncertainty or the desire to avoid it."

10 Explain the absence of economic profit in a purely competitive, static economy. Realizing that the major function of profits is to allocate resources in accordance with consumer preferences, evaluate the allocation of resources in such an economy.

11 What has happened to the wage, profit, interest, and rent shares of national income over time? Explain the alleged growth of labor's share in terms of structural changes in the economy. Have unions affected the size of labor's share?

real interest rate - rate of interest expressed in terms of dollars or constant or inflation adjusted value

Nominal interest rate - rate of interest expressed in terms of dollars of current value

interest rate = $\frac{\text{interest paid}}{\text{usable funds}}$

stated rate of interest

effective rate of interest

discount loan - interest paid at loan inception

$$\frac{i(P)}{(P) - \text{discount}}$$

discount loan with compensating balance

$$\frac{i(P)}{(P) - \text{discount} - \text{compensating value}}$$

amortized loan - usable funds $\frac{i}{P/2}$

General Equilibrium: The Market System and Its Operation

American automobile manufacturers and the United Automobile Workers have sought protective tariffs on foreign automobiles. The reason is that the immediate impact would be to increase the price of foreign cars, diverting demand toward American-made autos. The result would be beneficial in that output and employment in the American automobile industry would both increase.

But by restricting our analysis to the product and labor markets of the American auto industry in isolation, we obtain an incomplete and misleading understanding of the consequences of a tariff. The purpose of a tariff is to diminish the ability of foreign industry to sell in the American market. In this case the incomes of those associated with the Japanese, German, and Korean auto industries will decline. With smaller incomes these nations will be less able to buy from American industries exporting computers, aircraft, machine tools, and farm products. The increases in output and employment in the protected American auto industry may be fully offset by indirect declines in American exporting industries. Thus, the net benefit of the tariff in terms of American output and jobs is not at all evident.

To understand the full consequences of a policy or event, it is often necessary to look beyond its immediate impact. The purpose of general equilibrium analysis is to provide this broader multimarket view.[1]

PARTIAL AND GENERAL EQUILIBRIUM

Our discussion of prices has been compartmentalized; we have examined representative product and resource prices in isolation and largely apart from any detailed interrelationships each may bear to the other. In the jargon of the economist, we have dealt with **partial equilibrium analysis**—a study of equilibrium prices and outputs in the many specific markets which are the component *parts* of the market system.

But the economy is not merely a myriad of isolated and unrelated markets. It is an interlocking network of prices where changes in one market may elicit numerous and significant changes in other markets. Our vantage point now shifts from individual markets and prices in isolation to an analysis of the market system as a whole. Our discussion now shifts to **general equi-**

[1]As a prologue to this chapter, it might help to scan pages 78–85 of Chapter 5 and the concluding section of Chapter 10, summarizing efficiency aspects of competitive pricing.

librium analysis—an overall, big-picture view of the interrelationships among all the various markets and prices (parts) which make up the market *system.*

General equilibrium analysis provides a much broader perspective for analyzing the effects of given economic disturbances or policies than does partial equilibrium analysis. Partial equilibrium analysis shows merely "the big splash" of an initial disturbance; general equilibrium analysis traces the waves and ripples emanating from the big splash. In some instances the waves and ripples are relatively unimportant; in others they may prove to be a tidal wave which completely changes conclusions one would draw from the big splash viewed in isolation.

First, we examine a hypothetical model of two industries, making explicit use of the supply and demand tools of microeconomics. Next, an input-output table is presented and analyzed to further stress the interdependence of the various sectors of the economy. Finally, we turn to two real-world examples: the multitudinous market impacts of the oil price increases of the 1970s and some of the expected market implications of the aging of our population.

GENERAL EQUILIBRIUM: A TWO-INDUSTRY MODEL

Let's begin with a hypothetical illustration which explicitly embodies the formal tools of economic analysis. In Figure 17-1, which is a detailed version of Figure 3-2, we have two product markets, X and Y. And although each industry would actually employ many different inputs, it will facilitate our analysis to concentrate only on the labor market relevant to each industry. We assume that industry X uses type A labor and industry Y uses type B labor. We also assume that both product markets and resource (labor) markets are purely competitive.

Behind the Curves

First, let's review the concepts underlying the demand and supply curves of both product and resource markets.

The product demand curves are downsloping because of *diminishing marginal utility* (Chapter 8). Successive units of a given product yield less and less additional satisfaction or utility to buyers, so consumers will purchase more of that product only if its price falls.

The upsloping product supply curves are based on the concept of *increasing marginal costs* (Chapter 9). Because extra units of output are more costly, firms must receive a higher price before they can profitably produce this extra output.

The downsloping labor demand curves are based on the law of diminishing returns or *diminishing marginal productivity* (Chapter 14). Beyond some point, the addition of labor or any other variable resource to fixed resources will result in smaller and smaller increases in total output. Recall the link between the upsloping product supply curve and the downsloping resource demand curve. It is the diminishing marginal productivity of the resource which *causes* marginal costs to increase as output is increased. If each successive unit of labor (hired at a constant wage cost) adds less and less to output, then the cost of *each* successive unit of output must be more and more.

Finally, the upsloping labor supply curves reflect the *rising opportunity costs* of attracting additional workers (Chapter 15). A firm or an industry must pay higher and higher wage rates to obtain larger amounts of labor service.

Initial Conditions

We assume long-run equilibrium initially, so that P_{x1} and w_{a1} are the equilibrium product price and wage rate for industry X, and P_{y1} and w_{b1} represent the equilibrium price and wage for industry Y. Firms are making normal profits, and there is therefore no reason for either industry to expand or contract. The two labor markets are similarly "at rest"; there is therefore no incentive for workers to move out of or into either market.

Suppose now that something happens to upset this equilibrium. Specifically, a change occurs in consumer preferences or tastes so that consumer demand for X increases and consumer demand for Y simultaneously decreases. What will be the character of the resulting adjustments?

Short-Run Adjustments

What short-run adjustments will occur in response to these changes in consumer demand? First of all, production, which was normally profitable in industry X before demand rose from D_{x1} to D_{x2}, now results in economic profits. Firms in industry X, faced with the new higher price of P_{x2}, find it profitable to move to some point further up and to the right on their marginal-cost curves (Figure 10-6). Collectively, these mar-

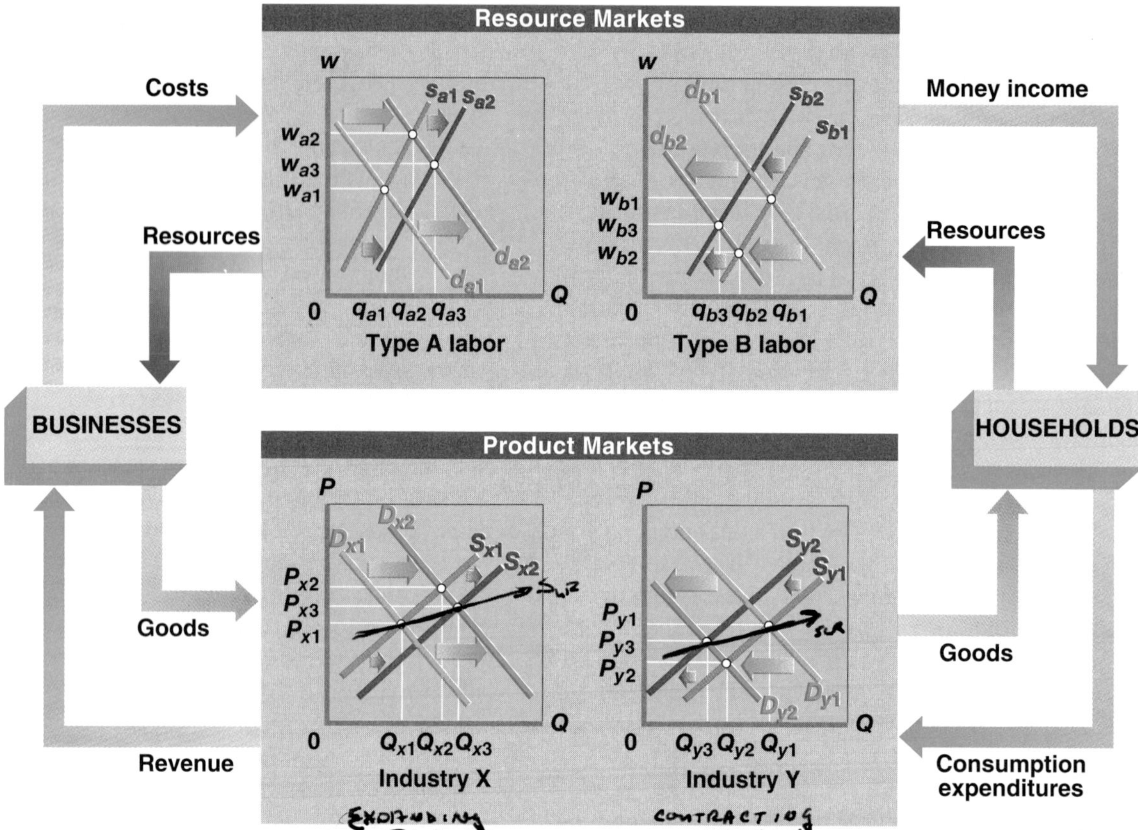

FIGURE 17-1 General equilibrium and the interaction of product and resource markets

These diagrams show the short-run and long-run adjustments resulting from an assumed increase in the demand for product X and assumed decline in the demand for product Y. Emphasis here is on product and resource market interactions, and the diagrams therefore conceal many of the less obvious repercussions. For example, the given changes in demand for X and Y will affect the demands for substitute and complementary goods and alter the distribution of income.

ginal-cost curves are the supply curve S_{x1} for the industry. Thus, in Figure 17-1 existing firms find it profitable to expand output as a group from Q_{x1} to Q_{x2}.

But to expand output, firms in industry X must acquire more resources, such as type A labor. Because the demand for resources is a *derived demand,* the expansion of output by firms in X will increase the demand for labor from d_{a1} to, say, d_{a2}. Workers in this labor market will offer more of their services, perhaps by working longer hours or more days per week, moving up s_{a1} in response to the higher wage rate w_{a2}.

An opposite set of short-run adjustments will occur in industry Y. Product demand falls to, say, D_{y2}, causing price to fall from P_{y1} to P_{y2}. At this lower price, individual firms incur losses. These firms will react by moving down and to the left on their marginal-cost curves as they seek loss-minimizing positions. The decline in demand for product Y is reflected back in the resource market. In particular, the demand for type B labor falls from d_{b1} to d_{b2}, reducing the equilibrium wage rate to w_{b2} and employment to q_{b2}.

Long-Run Adjustments

But we have only traced the first round of market adjustments. At the end of these short-run adjustments, the production of X still yields an economic profit, while losses persist in industry Y. The presumed changes in consumer demand have made X a prosperous, expanding industry and Y an unprosperous, declining industry. Given sufficient time, new firms will then enter industry X, while firms will leave industry Y.

Product Markets As new firms enter X, the industry supply curve will shift to the right from S_{x1} to S_{x2}. This increase in supply brings price back down to P_{x3}. Equilibrium output of X has further increased to Q_{x3}. If P_{x3} and Q_{x3} represent a new long-run equilibrium, as we assume is the case, we note in passing that industry X must be an increasing-cost industry. Why? Because the new long-run equilibrium entails a higher price than the initial equilibrium price P_{x1} (Figure 10-11). If this were a constant-cost industry, the new price would be the same as the original price. Note that, in the new equilibrium position, consumers are getting a larger output of X—which is precisely what they wanted. In other words, these adjustments are a manifestation of *consumer sovereignty.*

Losses in industry Y induce firms to leave the industry. As they do, industry supply will decline from S_{y1} to S_{y2}. This raises price somewhat from P_{y2} to P_{y3}. If we assume industry Y is also an increasing-cost industry, contraction of the industry will lower unit costs. Thus, in the new long-run equilibrium position at P_{y3}, price will be lower than originally, production will be normally profitable once again, and industry size will be stabilized.

Resource Markets These long-run adjustments have counterparts in the resource markets. The supply curve for type B labor, s_{b1}, is drawn on the assumption that other wage rates—for example, the wage rate received by type A labor—are given. This also holds true for the type A labor supply curve, s_{a1}. But our short-run changes in the demand for labor have increased the wage rate for type A labor and reduced the wage rate for type B labor. Some of type B labor will shift from industry Y, where job opportunities and wage rates have been declining, to industry X, where employment has been expanding and wage rates have been increasing. Thus we would expect the supply of type A labor to increase from s_{a1} to s_{a2} and the supply of type B labor to fall from s_{b1} to s_{b2}. As a result, wage rates for type A labor fall somewhat from w_{a2} to w_{a3}. For type B labor, wage rates go back up from w_{b2} to w_{b3}.

But note these two related points about these labor market adjustments. First, we are assuming that type B labor can qualify as type A labor without too much difficulty and retraining. In reality, supply shifts might take a substantial period of time. Type B workers may in fact require additional education, job retraining, and geographical relocation before becoming type A workers.

Second, because of various immobilities (Chapter 15), we would not expect the supply curve shifts to be great enough to restore the wage rates of the original equilibrium. The new equilibrium wage rate will be w_{a3} (higher than w_{a1}) for type A labor and w_{b3} (lower than w_{b1}) for type B labor. Indeed, these long-run wage adjustments are consistent with, and a factor in, the assumed increasing-cost character of industries X and Y.

Further Adjustments

But this is only the beginning of the repercussions which stem from our original change in the structure of consumer demand. There are many more subtle adjustments we might take into account.

Other Industries Consider now a third industry—industry Z. One of the determinants of the demand for product Z is the prices of related goods, and X just might be "related" to Z. If X and Z are *substitutes* (butter and margarine) the rise in the price of X will increase the demand for Z. A series of adjustments will be precipitated in the product and resource markets for Z similar to those just sketched for X. And if X and Z are *complements* (gasoline and motor oil) the higher price for X will lower the demand for Z. This would precipitate adjustments in Z like those already traced for industry Y.

Other Resources The initial changes in the demands for type A and type B labor may have an impact on other resource markets. Suppose that technology in industry X is such that labor and capital must be used in virtually fixed proportions, for example, one machine is needed for every two workers. This means that expansion in the employment of type A labor will stimulate the demand for relevant kinds of capital goods.

Income Distribution Our short-run and long-run adjustments will alter the distribution of income. Workers and entrepreneurs associated with industry X will receive higher incomes; those in industry Y, lower incomes. It is realistic to expect some differences in tastes which will be transformed into further changes in the structure of consumer demand. These new changes in demand will trigger new rounds of short-run and long-run adjustments.

We could go on, but the basic point is clear. The adjustments stemming from our initial changes in demand are much more complex and go far beyond the simple supply and demand shifts of Figure 17-1. *Any initial disturbance such as a change in demand, a change in technology, or a change in resource supply will*

TABLE 17-1 A simplified input-output table *(hypothetical data)*

	Consuming or using sectors					
Producing sectors	*(1) Metal*	*(2) Machinery*	*(3) Fuel*	*(4) Agriculture*	*(5) Households (labor)*	*(6) Total output*
(1) Metal	10	65	10	5	10	100
(2) Machinery	40	25	35	75	25	200
(3) Fuel	15	5	5	5	20	50
(4) Agriculture	15	10	50	50	525	650
(5) Labor (households)	100	200	100	550	50	1000

set off a highly complex economic chain reaction. This chapter's Last Word is a fascinating case study of the seemingly endless chain of economic repercussions triggered by the virtual suspension of American cotton exports to England during the Civil War.

Efficiency Implications

The competitive market system is conducive to efficient use of resources. We found in Chapter 10 that under pure competition both "allocative efficiency" and "productive efficiency" are realized. In nontechnical terms, the "right" amount of each good will be produced and per unit production costs for each good minimized. Furthermore, given the distribution of income, free choice by consumers allows them to spend their incomes to maximize their satisfaction or utility (Chapter 8).

But there are a number of real-world complications. In particular, the competitive market system would not allocate resources to the production of public goods. Nor would it take into account spillover benefits and costs (Chapters 6 and 18). Government would have to employ its taxation and expenditure powers to provide the economy with public goods. It would also need to use legislation or specific taxes and subsidies to correct misallocations of resources caused by spillover costs and benefits. Furthermore, the personal distribution of income which the competitive market system would yield might not be regarded by society as equitable or just, again implying the need for governmental intervention. Finally, in the real world our market system is imperfectly competitive (Chapters 11 through 13), with the result that resources are used less efficiently and resource reallocations are more sluggish and less complete than our discussion of Figure 17-1 implies.

GENERAL EQUILIBRIUM: INPUT-OUTPUT ANALYSIS

The general equilibrium model just explored emphasizes the interrelatedness of the many decision makers who comprise the economy. Further appreciation of the intricate interrelationships between various sectors or industries of the economy can be gained through **input-output analysis.**

Input-Output Table

Table 17-1 is a simplified hypothetical input-output table for an economy.[2] On the left side of the table are the five producing sectors (industries) of the economy. Column 6 shows the total output associated with each of the five sectors—the metal sector produces 100 units, the machine sector 200 units, and so on. These five sectors are also the consuming sectors of the economy and are shown in this capacity across the top of the table. Looking across each of the horizontal rows of figures, we see how the total output of each sector is disposed of, or consumed, among the five sectors. For example, of the 200 units of output of the machinery sector, 40 units go to the metal sector, 25 to the machinery sector itself (because it takes machines to make machines), and 35, 75, and 25 units go to the fuel, agriculture, and household sectors, respectively, thereby exhausting the units produced.

[2]Wassily W. Leontieff is largely responsible for input-output analysis. See his simplified discussion of "Input-Output Economics," *Scientific American,* October 1951, pp. 15–21. Table 17-1 and portions of the accompanying discussion are from Francis M. Boddy, "Soviet Economic Growth," in Robert T. Holt and John E. Turner (eds.), *Soviet Union: Paradox and Change* (New York: Holt, Rinehart and Winston, Inc., 1962), pp. 77–79, with permission of the publisher. Currently national input-output tables divide the economy into over 400 industries, producing an input-output matrix which has over 400 rows and columns.

Following through on this disposition-of-output procedure for all five sectors, note that each vertical column must and does show the units of output of each producing sector which are consumed as inputs by the five sectors. For example, we find in column 2 that to produce 200 units of machinery, inputs of 65 units of metal, 25 of machinery, 5 of fuel, 10 of agricultural products, and 200 of labor are required. In this way, the table vividly reveals the highly interdependent character of the various sectors or industries. Any given industry or sector employs the outputs of other sectors—and indeed, some of its own output—as its inputs. And the outputs of that given sector are the inputs of the other sectors. To cite a real-world example: While outputs of steel are inputs in the production of railroad cars, these railroad cars are, in turn, used to transport both finished steel and the various inputs—coke, pig iron, and so forth—which are necessary to steel production.

Interdependence

The interdependence of the economy's sectors or industries can be further demonstrated by tracing the repercussions of an assumed change in the output of a commodity.

Consider the repercussions of a 20-unit (10 percent) increase in machinery production. This means that a 10 percent increase in the production of all the outputs used as inputs in the production of machinery is required.[3] These inputs are listed in column 2 of Table 17-1. Applying the 10 percent figure, we find that 6.5 *additional* units (outputs) of metal, 2.5 units of machinery, 0.5 unit of fuel, 1 unit of agricultural products, and 20 units of labor will be needed to produce another 20 units of machinery.

But further adjustments are also required. Because each sector which supplies inputs to the machinery sector must expand *its* output, these supplying sectors in turn will require more inputs from other sectors. The additional 6.5 units of metal needed as inputs to produce the extra 20 units of machinery will in turn call for an appropriate—6.5 percent, in this case—increase in the production of all the inputs shown in column 1 to be needed in producing metal.

The same reasoning applies to the fuel, agriculture, and labor sectors. That is, the 0.5-unit increase in fuel production required in producing the extra 20 units of machinery will call for an appropriate (1 percent) increase in the production of all the inputs listed in column 3, and similarly for the agricultural and labor sectors.

Note that the production of 20 more units of machinery output requires as inputs the production of 2.5 units of machinery. This 2.5-unit increase will require "second-round" increases (of 1.25 percent here) in the inputs of all the resources shown in column 2 in the same fashion as did the initial 20-unit increase in machinery output.

The chain reaction is by no means at an end. All the repercussions cited in these examples call for still further adjustments similar to those already described. The crucial point is that, because of the high degree of interrelatedness among the sectors of the economy, a change in the figure in any one "cell" or "box" of the input-output table will precipitate an almost endless series of adjustments in other figures. In our illustration, expansion of production in one sector has nearly innumerable repercussions reaching into virtually every nook and cranny of the economy. This is why economists sometimes remark, not entirely facetiously, that "in economics everything depends on everything else."

QUICK REVIEW 17-1

- ***Partial equilibrium analysis examines adjustments in one market in isolation; general equilibrium analysis considers how an event which disturbs equilibrium in one market may affect other related markets.***
- ***Demand and supply analysis can be used to trace interactions between various product markets and between those product markets and relevant resource markets.***
- ***Input-output analysis systematically analyzes the interrelationships between an industry's output and the inputs needed to produce that output.***

MARKET INTERRELATIONSHIPS: OPEC AND OIL PRICES

Just as a rock dropped into a pond causes widening circles of ripples, any change in the economy precipitates further changes which radiate outward with gradually diminishing force. And just as these ripples some-

[3]We invoke here one of the simplifying assumptions underlying the input-output table, namely, that production occurs under conditions of constant returns to scale (Chapter 9).

times reach shore and rebound eventually to affect the initial point of impact, so too are there feedback effects of initial changes occurring in single markets in the economy. This process of reverberation continues throughout the domestic economy—indeed, throughout the world economy—as a new equilibrium is approached in all markets.

To gain further insight as to the interrelatedness of markets, let's consider one of the most dramatic series of price changes of recent history—the run-up of oil prices in the 1970s. In 1973–1974 the OPEC (Organization of Petroleum Exporting Countries) oil cartel—which then accounted for 90 percent of world oil exports—restricted production and increased oil prices by about $8 per barrel. In relative terms the price of a barrel of oil quadrupled within a few months. Then in 1979–1980 OPEC succeeded in imposing a much larger price increase of about $21 per barrel. Thus the barrel of oil which sold for $2.50 in 1972 was priced at $34 in 1980.

According to partial equilibrium analysis, the restriction of output by OPEC would simply reduce the supply of oil, increase its equilibrium price, and reduce its equilibrium output. And that would be the end of the matter. But this narrow perspective would overlook most of the important ramifications of the price increase. What were some of the more salient implications of these oil price increases? Although the two are not neatly separable, we first consider impacts on the domestic economy and then international effects.

The United States Economy

One of the initial effects of much higher oil prices was that users conserved oil and derivative products and sought substitute products. For example, many power producers converted their plants from oil to natural gas or coal. Wood-burning stoves and furnaces became popular in homes once again. High oil prices affected locational decisions as many firms moved from the Snow Belt to the Sun Belt.

The prices of products derived from oil—for example, plastics and commercial fertilizer—rose sharply, causing higher costs and many adjustments for manufacturers and farmers who used these products as inputs. The rise in gasoline prices from about $.30 per gallon in the pre-OPEC era to $.65 per gallon in 1974 had far-reaching effects on both automobile users and producers. The immediate effect of sharply higher gasoline prices was to cause drivers to curtail use of their cars. Carpools suddenly became popular. Resort owners were adversely affected as many drivers canceled or cut short vacation plans.

Demands for goods and services complementary to automobiles—car washes, motor oil, tires, and auto repairs—declined. Demand for substitutes—for example, public transportation—increased. Over time, automobile purchasers redirected their expenditures from large gas-guzzling American-made cars to compact fuel-efficient imports from Japan and Germany. The OPEC-inspired upsurge in oil and gasoline prices was an important contributor to the growing share of imports in the United States automobile market.

Households using oil for heating also took steps to conserve. Demands increased for insulation, weather-stripping, thermopane windows, and storm doors. Impacts on resource markets were predictable and, in some cases, profound. Less labor was needed in the production of domestic automobiles and more was needed in the production and installation of insulation. Less capital was used to build gas stations and more was employed in oil-drilling rigs and offshore platforms. Generally, high energy prices made the plants and equipment of some industries obsolete. In some cases this was the direct result of higher operating costs. Capital goods which were economic and usable when oil was $2 per barrel became uneconomic when oil was $10, $15, or $25 per barrel. In other instances the obsolescence reflected the impact of higher oil prices on the structure of product demand. The plants of American auto producers were heavily committed to producing large fuel-inefficient cars, the demand for which lagged as consumers shifted to more fuel-efficient imports.

Many more subtle ripples emanating from higher oil and gas prices occurred because the demands for oil and gas are inelastic. For example, elasticity of demand for gasoline is estimated to be in the .20 to .40 range, meaning that a 10 percent increase in price will only result in a 2 to 4 percent decrease in consumption. Recalling our total revenue (expenditures) test for elasticity (Chapter 7), this means that after a price increase consumers will spend more of their income on oil and gasoline and therefore will have less to spend on a whole host of other goods and services unrelated to oil and gasoline as either substitutes or complements.

The OPEC oil price increases were the equivalent of a gigantic tax levied on imported oil. American consumers and manufacturers were forced to pay this tax and the OPEC nations served as tax collectors. This "OPEC tax"—which totaled as much as $40 to $50 billion per year—had significant contractionary effects.

The net exports (exports minus imports) component of aggregate demand declined, which shifted the curve to the left. After paying the OPEC tax, both American consumers and businesses found themselves with less money to spend on domestic consumption and investment goods.

The pervasive impacts of higher oil prices were an important factor in the stagflation of the 1970s. As noted, higher energy prices confronted American producers with higher per unit production costs. Indeed, it is difficult to think of any industry whose production and transportation costs were not increased by OPEC's price boosts. In terms of the cost-push inflation model, these cost increases shifted the aggregate supply curve leftward and brought about both a higher price level and reductions in real output and employment.

Not all American industries were affected negatively by OPEC's oil price increases. American oil-producing companies in particular benefited greatly and enjoyed soaring profits. The economies of oil-producing states such as Texas and Louisiana boomed in the 1970s. Industries producing substitutes for oil also prospered. Thus the American coal industry experienced a revitalization.

The World Economy

The economic impacts of the increase in OPEC oil prices transcended national boundaries. The price boosts gave rise to gigantic transfers of real income from oil-importing nations such as the United States to OPEC and other oil-exporting countries. In real terms these transfers resulted because higher oil prices shifted the "terms of trade" against the oil-importing nations and in favor of oil-exporting nations. The United States and other oil importers were forced to exchange larger amounts of their real output to obtain a barrel of imported oil than before, lowering our domestic standard of living.

But the financial aspects of these transfers also posed problems. In particular, the United States for many years has had international trade deficits; the value of our merchandise exports has been less than our merchandise imports. Or, simply put, the United States has not been "paying its way" in international trade. The large boosts in the price of imported oil greatly intensified this problem.

Higher oil prices also affected foreign exchange markets. The international value of the dollar—the price of the dollar in terms of other currencies—is largely determined by the forces of supply and demand. When OPEC raised oil prices, the resulting increase in the United States' expenditures for its oil imports increased the supply of dollars in foreign exchange markets. This increase in the supply of dollars relative to demand reduced the international value of the dollar. Using Chapter 4's terminology, the dollar depreciated.

This depreciation had important consequences. Most importantly, it reinforced the cost-push inflation which was occurring. When the dollar's value declines, the effect is to increase the price of *all* goods Americans import. When the dollar depreciates, it takes more dollars to buy a given amount of a foreign currency and, therefore, more dollars to buy a foreign product. A British woolen suit, selling for £50 in Britain, will cost an American buyer only $100 when the dollar is worth half a pound. That same suit will cost an American $200 if the dollar depreciates to one-fourth of a pound. The decline in the international value of the dollar boosted the prices of all imports and reinforced our domestic inflation.

The impact of the oil price increases was particularly devastating for the many non-oil-producing, less developed countries (LDCs) of Africa, Asia, and Latin America. They were dependent on petroleum as an energy source in developing their economies. By having to pay much higher prices for oil, they were forced to sacrifice not only sorely needed consumer goods, but also capital goods essential for long-term economic growth. Furthermore, stagflation in the industrially advanced nations curtailed demand for LDC exports. Hence, most of the LDCs were forced to borrow. Indeed, LDC debts to wealthier nations increased almost sevenfold between 1973 and 1982.

MARKET IMPLICATIONS OF AN AGING POPULATION

Our population is getting older because of declining birth rates and greater longevity. This fact provides another application of general equilibrium analysis. Figure 17-2 gives us an overview of this demographic development. While about 9 percent of the population was 65 or over in 1960, an estimated 21 percent will be in this age group by 2030. Conversely, we see that the 18 and under group declines from approximately 36 to about 22 percent over the same period. What are the product and labor market repercussions of the "geezer boom"?

Product Market

In the product market we can expect an increase in demand for medical care because older people are ill more frequently. Similarly, demand for retirement housing and nursing home facilities will rise sharply. While the prescription drug industry is likely to prosper, industries producing children's goods—diapers, toys, baby food, and education—will be adversely affected. The housing industry is also likely to suffer. Most people marry and initially form households in their twenties and purchase and furnish their first home between ages 25 and 34. Figure 17-2 tells us that the 25–34 age group will decline significantly between 1990 and 2030. Demand for rental housing and starter homes is therefore likely to decline.

From a macroeconomic view there has been great concern recently that Americans have been consuming too much and, therefore, saving and investing too little. In the late 1980s consumption claimed about 82 percent of our national income, up from 75 percent in the late 1960s. The personal savings rate diminished from about 6 percent of national income in the late 1960s to an average of only 3.5 percent in the past five years. Significant growth in consumer installment debt accompanied these changes in consumption and saving. These developments have portrayed Americans as being irresponsible spendthrifts who will have to face future hardships as a result of their current extravagance.

FIGURE 17-2 The age distribution of the United States population

Declining birth rates and increasing longevity have reduced the percentage of younger people and increased the percentage of older people in our society. ***(Source: Census Bureau data).***

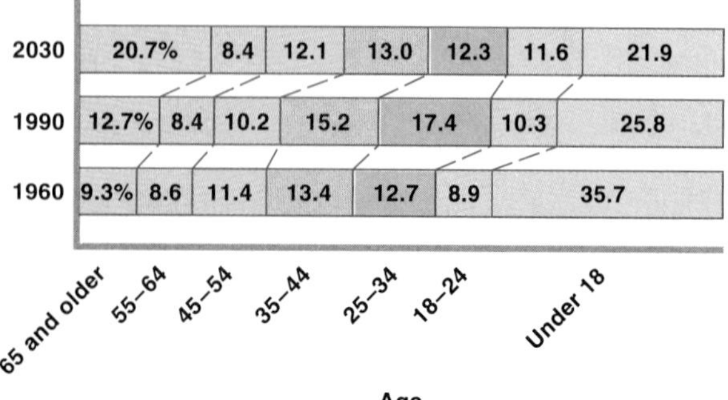

But the demographic trends described—the aging of "baby boomers" born between 1946 and 1964—may explain these developments. Young workers who are forming families and buying and furnishing houses have high levels of spending and debt relative to current income, while middle-aged workers have relatively low levels of consumption and debt relative to income. Over the 1965–1980 period, the age distribution of the labor force changed in favor of younger workers as baby boomers entered the work force in large numbers. In other words, the high-consumption and high-debt segment of the work force increased significantly, explaining much of the increases in consumption and debt and the decline in saving which occurred in the 1970s and 1980s. As these workers mature in the years ahead and enter middle age, there is reason to believe that consumption and debt will decrease, and saving will increase, approximately to earlier levels. This suggests that, in the aggregate, consumption goods industries may shrink relatively and, with increased saving, investment or capital goods markets may expand relatively.

Labor Market

The most evident development of an aging population is declining labor force growth. It is estimated that the labor force will grow by only 1.2 percent per year over the 1988–2000 period, down from 2.0 percent annually for 1976–1988. In absolute terms the net growth of the labor force is expected to be 19 million between 1988 and 2000, significantly less than the 25 million who were added in the 1976–1988 period.

There are two factors that are of primary importance in explaining the projected slowdown in labor force growth.

1 By the late 1970s most of the post-World War II baby boomers—the 76 million people born between 1946 and 1964—had already entered the labor force. The baby boom was followed by a sharp decline in birthrates in the late 1960s and early 1970s. As a result, substantially fewer new young workers will enter the labor force in the years ahead.

2 The labor force participation rate of women—the number of women working (or seeking work) as a percentage of eligible women workers—grew rapidly in the 1970s and 1980s and was a major factor causing the overall participation rate and the size of the labor force to grow. Given that the participation rate of women is already high and approaching that of men for many age

LAST WORD

THE ENGLISH COTTON FAMINE

The relevance of general equilibrium analysis is illustrated by the myriad effects of the marked decline of American cotton exports to England during the Civil War.

The Civil War led to a near suspension of English imports of American cotton, which in 1860 had accounted for about four-fifths of the English supply. The price of cotton at Liverpool rose from 8 pence per pound in June of 1860 to a peak of 31½ pence in July of 1864. The effects of this cotton famine provide some notion of the interrelationships of prices: the famine was severe (imports of cotton fell by three-fifths from 1861 to 1862) and the cotton industry was very large (employing about 500,000 people in a total labor force of 9 million), so wide effects are noticeable.

The famine led to a great decrease in the demand for cotton fabrication, and hence in the demand for the services of cotton mills and their laborers. The margin between the prices of raw cotton and cloth (taking 39-inch shirtings as an example) declined from 7 pence a pound in 1860, almost equal to the cost of the raw cotton, to 1 or 2 pence in 1862 and 1863. Wage (piece) rates fell an unknown amount, and workers' earnings fell much more when they were forced to work with the inferior Surat cotton.

Of course a large expansion took place in rival fabrics. The production of flax quadrupled between 1861 and 1864 in Ireland, and yarn imports rose greatly; even so, prices of linen goods rose about 60 percent between 1862 and 1864. Similarly, the wool industry experienced a great boom: imports of wool rose by a third during the period, and raw wool prices rose more than 40 percent, but the Yorkshire industry was overtaxed and processing margins increased by half. Some migration of cotton workers and entrepreneurs to Yorkshire, and of weavers of woolens to Lancashire, helped the latter area.

The unemployment in Lancashire caused great distress. The big decrease in consumer expenditures in the area hit shopkeepers hard, and landlords even harder: families doubled up, marriages fell by more than a third, and poor rates increased. By 1863 about one-fourth of the families requiring public assistance were not directly connected with the textile industry.

Of course the effects reached to industries for which cotton textiles was an important customer. The textile machinery industry had a bad slump until 1864, and the warehouses of the region suffered also. The Lancashire and Yorkshire Railway, unlike other English roads, had a decline in both freight and passenger traffic in 1862 and 1863.

We could cast our net farther to uncover more relationships of substitution and complementarity and buyer and seller, and subject only to the limitations of imagination and energy, we shall continue to find them. In Birmingham, to give only one example, the button and needle industries had to discharge many workers, but the edged-tool industry expanded greatly to provide tools for new cotton plantings in India and Egypt.

Perhaps this brief and highly incomplete sketch is sufficient to illustrate the basis for the economist's faith, for such it is, in the general interdependence of economic phenomena. It does not seem bold to conjecture that everyone in England was somehow affected by the cotton famine: as a consumer, in the price of clothing; as a laborer, in the altered directions of consumer spending; in the effects on transport, banking, and commerce; as a capitalist, in the return on investments in textiles and other industries.

Source: George J. Stigler, *The Theory of Price*, rev. ed. (New York: The Macmillan Company, 1952), pp. 288–289.

groups, the growth of the female participation rate is expected to slow in the future.

The slowing of labor force growth allows us to make the following labor market predictions.

1 Low Unemployment Rates It is likely that, barring a major recession, unemployment rates will be lower in the years ahead than they have been in the past decade or so. It will simply be easier for labor markets to accommodate the smaller labor force increments which lie ahead. Lower unemployment rates can be expected to be particularly helpful to minorities and other disadvantaged workers who are typically the last to be hired.

2 Higher Real Wages If, as anticipated, the growth of labor supply slows relative to the growth of labor demand, we can expect real (inflation-adjusted) wages to increase more rapidly than has been the case in the past twenty years or so. Specifically, we might anticipate that the real weekly earnings of private nonagricultural workers, which stagnated and declined in the 1970s and 1980s, will resume their secular rise in the 1990s.

3 Retaining Older Workers With fewer young people entering the labor force, employers will need to meet their needs for additional workers by retaining and attracting older workers. Rising real wages and abundant job opportunities may induce more and more older workers to embark on second and third careers.

4 Increased Immigration Employment opportunities in the United States have always attracted workers from less affluent nations. Another effect of increasingly attractive labor markets in the United States in the years ahead is that immigration—both legal and illegal—may increase. The other side of the coin is that American producers may become increasingly inclined to export production and jobs overseas as real labor costs rise in the United States.

5 Emphasis on Productivity Growth There are two basic means by which a nation can increase its domestic output: (1) use more labor inputs and (2) improve labor productivity, that is, increase output per unit of labor input. The expected slowdown in labor force growth suggests that the United States will be obligated to pay increased attention to measures and policies which enhance labor productivity if it is to sustain the growth of its real domestic output. For private industry this means spending more on machinery and equipment, research and development, and worker training. For government it means more effective measures to enhance the quantity and quality of education.

CHAPTER SUMMARY

1 General equilibrium analysis is concerned with the operation of the entire market system and the interrelationships among different markets and prices. These interrelationships are important in that they might modify or negate the immediate effects of economic disturbances or policies which partial equilibrium analysis reveals.

2 Demand and supply analysis for both product and resource markets can be used to analyze the many market adjustments triggered by an initial change in market demand or supply.

3 The input-output table provides a kind of general equilibrium analysis which reveals the overall fabric of the economy by focusing on the interdependencies existing among the various sectors or industries which it comprises.

4 The dramatic increases in oil prices in 1973–1974 and 1979–1980 provide an interesting case study of the many market responses which came into play both domestically and internationally.

5 The aging of the American population and slower labor force growth have important product and labor market implications, including an expected decline in housing demand; changes in aggregate consumption and saving; lower unemployment rates; rising real wages; increased immigration; and greater efforts to increase labor productivity.

TERMS AND CONCEPTS

partial equilibrium analysis

general equilibrium analysis

input-output analysis

QUESTIONS AND STUDY SUGGESTIONS

1 Compare partial and general equilibrium analysis. In what respect is each useful?

2 Suppose the price of movie theater tickets is $5 and the price of video cassette rentals is $3. A tax of $1 is levied on movie tickets, but not cassette rentals. Use supply and demand analysis to explain the effect of the tax on **a** the movie ticket market and **b** the video cassette market. Note any feedback effects from the video to the movie market.

3 Trace through the market system the economic effects of:

- a the development of a synthetic fiber which never wears out, fades, or stains
- b a permanent increase in the demand for leather
- c the development of a new production technique which cuts the cost of home computers by 50 percent
- d the imposition of a 20 percent excise tax on shoes
- e the discovery of an effective vaccine for the common cold

4 Use your understanding of general equilibrium analysis to trace through the market repercussions of the following developments:

- a For health reasons there has been a shift of consumer demand from red meat to seafood.
- b Because of the greater use of preventive measures, such as fluoridated water and regular dental care, demand for dental services declines.

5 Assume a drought in the Great Plains reduces the supply of wheat. Given that wheat is a basic ingredient in production of bread and that potatoes are a consumer substitute for bread, use supply and demand diagrams to explain the effects of the drought on **a** the price of wheat, **b** the supply and price of bread, and **c** the demand for and price of potatoes. Sketch the nature of the relevant resource market adjustments.

6 What is an input-output table? Using Table 17-1, trace some of the repercussions of a 5-unit (10 percent) increase in fuel production. What insights might input-output analysis provide as to the operation of a capitalistic system?

7 In early 1986 the OPEC oil cartel fell into severe disarray and per barrel oil prices fell from $28 to about $10. List some of the economic repercussions of a substantial reduction in the price of oil for the United States. In particular, trace the expected effects on our automobile, coal, steel, airline, and oil-exploration industries. What impact might a price cut have on the locational decisions of firms within the United States? What implications will the price cut have on American banks which have made large loans to less developed oil producing countries such as Mexico? What might the effects be on the world distribution of real income? On exchange rates?

8 Between 1946 and 1964 unusually high birth rates added 76 million to the population. List as many product, labor, and financial market implications of this baby boom as you can.

PART 3

Government and Current Economic Problems

free market system achieves
allocative efficiency
productive efficiency

market failures:

1) externalities
2) Public Goods
3) Income Distribution from Possesion of Factors of Production
4) Regulation of Natural Monopolies
5) Procyclical Tendencies of Savers and Lenders
6) Monopolistic Tendencies are inherent in a free market
"The urge to merge"

Government and Market Failure: Public Goods, the Environment, and Information Problems

By now you have a basic understanding of government's role in the economy. In particular, you are well aware of the five economic functions of government: (1) providing the legal foundation and social environment conducive to the effective operation of the market system, (2) maintaining competition, (3) redistributing income and wealth, (4) adjusting the allocation of resources to provide public goods and correct for externalities, and (5) stabilizing the economy. These functions were discussed in Chapter 6, where we also examined the growth of the public sector and presented the facts of government expenditures and taxes.

In this chapter and in Chapter 19 we will extend and deepen our understanding of government and also identify some of the problems which it faces in carrying out its economic functions. We begin by returning to the topic of *market failure* introduced in Chapter 6. Our recently acquired tools of marginal analysis permit us to provide a fuller discussion of public goods and externalities. Next, the pervasive externality—pollution—is discussed in some detail. Finally, we turn our attention to *information failures* in the private sector to determine their implication for government participation in the economy.

In Chapter 19 our discussion of government continues with an analysis of *government failure* and the microeconomics of taxation. The chapters which then follow in the remainder of Part 3 involve economic problems government has attempted to resolve—with varying degrees of success. Chapter 20 examines the problem of monopoly and anticompetitive business practices. Chapter 21 probes the farm problem. In Chapter 22 we look at the problems of poverty and income inequality, and Chapter 23 investigates such labor market issues as unionism, discrimination, and migration. Our analysis in this present chapter and in Chapter 19 will enhance our understanding of government's involvement in these areas.

PUBLIC GOODS: EXTENDING THE ANALYSIS

Recall that a *private* good is divisible—it comes in small enough units to be afforded by individual buyers. It is also subject to the exclusion principle—those unable or unwilling to pay are excluded from the benefits provided by the product.

A market demand curve for a private good is the *horizontal* summation of demand curves representing each individual buyer (review Table 4-2 and Figure 4-2). If Adams wants to buy 3 hot dogs at $1 each; Benson, 1 hot dog; and Conrad, 2 hot dogs; the market demand will reflect that 6 hot dogs (=3 + 1 + 2) are demanded at a $1 price. The market demand resulting from the sum of the desires of each potential individual buyer creates a possibility for sellers to gain revenue and garner a profit. The equilibrium amount of a private good produced and purchased is dictated by product price, which is jointly determined by market demand and supply. This equilibrium output is optimal in that it maximizes the combined well-being of the buyers and sellers, the only people affected by the transactions.

A serious snag develops, however, if we apply this same line of thinking to a public good. A *public good* is indivisible and one for which the exclusion principle does not apply. Once the good is provided, the producer cannot exclude nonpayers from receiving its indivisible benefits. Because they will obtain the benefit from a public good whether or not they pay for it, potential buyers will *not* reveal their true preferences for it. In other words, they will become free riders who will *not* voluntarily pay for the public good in the marketplace. *Thus, the market demand curve for a public good will be either nonexistent or significantly understated.* The demand for the product expressed in the marketplace will not generate enough revenue to cover the costs of production, even though the collective benefits of the good may exceed the relevant economic costs.

Demand for Public Goods

How might we determine society's optimal (allocatively efficient) amount of a public good—at least in theory—in view of this problem? For simplicity, suppose Adams and Benson are the only people in the economy and their true demand schedules for a particular public good, say, national defense, are those shown as columns 1 and 2 and columns 1 and 3 of Table 18-1. These demand schedules are "phantom" demand curves since the two people will not actually reveal

TABLE 18-1 Demand for a public good, two individuals *(hypothetical data)*

(1) Quantity	*(2) Adams' willingness to pay (price)*		*(3) Benson's willingness to pay (price)*		*(4) Collective willingness to pay (price)*
1	$4	+	$5	=	$9
2	3	+	4	=	7
3	2	+	3	=	5
4	1	+	2	=	3
5	0	+	1	=	1

them in the marketplace. Instead, we assume that this information has been discovered through a survey indicating Adams' and Benson's willingness to pay for each added unit of the public good, rather than go without it.

Suppose government decides to produce 1 unit of this public good. Because the exclusion principle does not apply, neither Adams nor Benson will voluntarily offer to pay for this unit because each can consume it without paying. Adams' consumption of the good does not preclude Benson from also consuming it. But the combined amount of money these two citizens are willing to pay, rather than each not having this one unit of the good, can be determined through the information in Table 18-1. Columns 1 and 2 show that Adams would be willing to pay $4 for the first unit of the public good; columns 1 and 3 show that Benson would be willing to pay $5 for it. The $9 price (column 4) these two are jointly willing to pay is the sum of the amounts each is willing to pay. Similarly, the collective price they are willing to pay for the second unit of the public good is $7 (=$3 by Adams plus $4 by Benson).

We could then employ this same procedure for the third unit, and so on. Looking at the collective willingness to pay (column 4) for each additional unit, we construct a collective demand schedule for a public good. Rather than adding the *quantities demanded* at each price as when determining the market demand for a private good, we are adding the *prices* people collectively are willing to pay for the last unit of the public good at each quantity demanded.

Figure 18-1 shows the same summing procedure graphically, using data from Table 18-1 to illustrate the adding-up process. Observe that we are summing Adams' and Benson's demand curves for the public good *vertically* to derive the collective demand curve. The height of the collective demand curve D_c at 2 units of output, for example, is $7—the sum of the amount that Adams and Benson together are willing to pay for

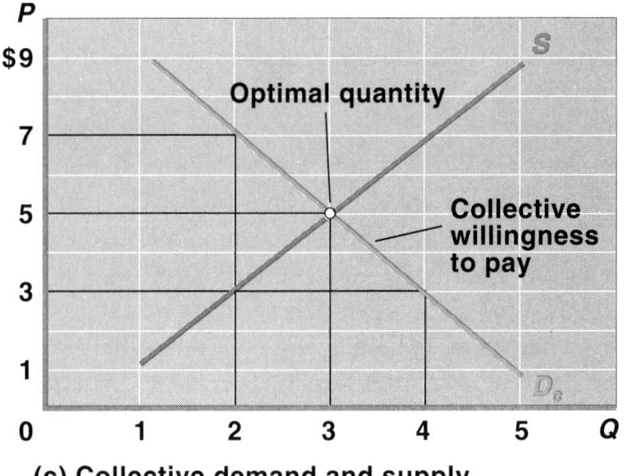

(c) Collective demand and supply

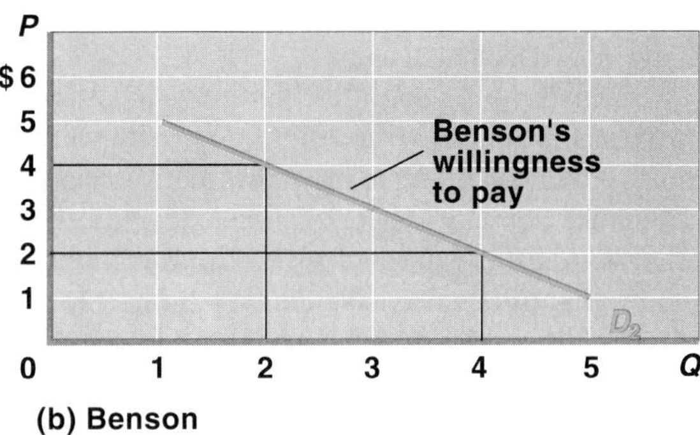

(b) Benson

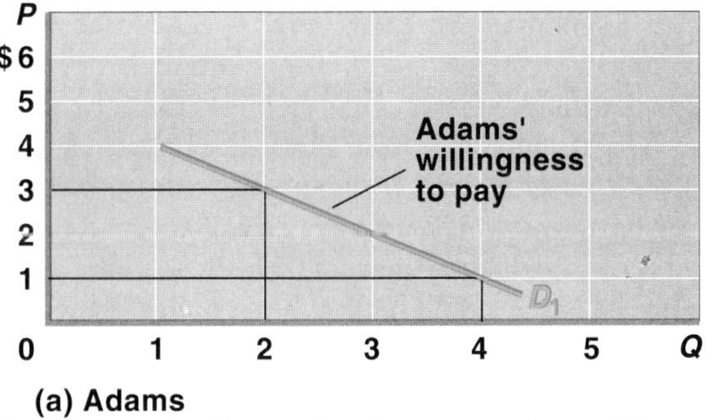

(a) Adams

FIGURE 18-1 The optimal amount of a public good

Graphically the collective demand curve D_c for the public good shown in (c) is found by summing vertically the individual demand curves D_1 and D_2 exhibited in (a) and (b). Government should provide 3 units of the public good, because at that quantity the combined marginal benefit, as measured by citizens' willingness to pay for the last unit (shown by D_c), equals the good's marginal cost (shown by S).

the second unit (=$3 + $4). Likewise, the height of the collective demand curve at 4 units of the public good is $3 (=$1 + $2).

Our collective demand curve D_c is based on the monetary value of the perceived benefits of the various extra units that are equally available to both persons for simultaneous consumption. The curve predictably slopes downward because of the law of diminishing marginal utility: Successive units of the public good will yield less added satisfaction than the previous units.

Optimal Quantity of a Public Good

The optimal quantity of the public good alluded to in Figure 18-1 can now be determined. In Figure 18-1c the supply curve for the public good is upsloping in the usual sense. The short-run law of diminishing returns, which gives rise to the upsloping supply curve, applies whether making missiles (public goods) or mufflers (private goods). In this case, the optimal quantity of the public good will be 3 units, shown by the intersection of the collective demand and supply curves.

Recalling that a supply curve reflects marginal costs, if 2 units are produced, the collective willingness to pay for that second unit (=$7) will exceed the good's marginal cost of production (=$3). This situation illustrates an underproduction of the good and therefore an *underallocation* of resources to this use.

On the other hand, the sum of the amount these two people are willing to pay for the fourth unit (=$3) of the public good is less than that unit's marginal cost (=$7). Hence, the fourth unit entails an overproduction of the good and an *overallocation* of resources to this use.

The optimal quantity of the public good is 3 units, where the combined willingness to pay for the extra unit—the combined marginal benefit to the two consumers—just matches the marginal cost of that unit ($5 = $5). This "marginal benefit equals marginal cost" principle is analogous to the MR = MC output rule and the MRP = MRC input rule for maximizing profit.

Benefit-Cost Analysis

Economic theory therefore provides some guidance to efficient decision making in the public sector. This guidance can be helpful in understanding **benefit-cost analysis.**

Concept Suppose government is contemplating a specific project, for example, a flood-control project. The basic nature of the economizing problem tells us that any decision to use more resources in the public sector will involve both a benefit and a cost. The benefit is the extra satisfaction resulting from the output of more public goods; the cost is the loss of satisfaction associated with the accompanying decline in the production of private goods (or some alternative public good). Should the resources under consideration be shifted from the private to the public sector? The answer is "Yes" *if* the benefits from the extra public goods exceed the cost resulting from having fewer private goods. The answer is "No" *if* the value or cost of the forgone private goods is greater than the benefits associated with the extra public goods.

But benefit-cost analysis can do more than indicate whether a public program is worth undertaking. It can also provide guidance as to the extent to which a given project should be pursued. Economic questions, after all, are not simply questions to be answered by "Yes" or "No," but rather, matters of "how much" or "how little." In the case of flood control we note first that a flood-control project is a public good in that the exclusion principle is not readily applicable. Now, should government undertake a flood-control project in a given river valley? And, if so, what is the proper size or scope for the project?

Illustration Table 18-2 list a series of increasingly ambitious and increasingly costly flood-control plans. To what extent, if at all, should government undertake flood control? The answers depend on costs and benefits. Costs in this case are largely the capital costs of constructing and maintaining levees and reservoirs; benefits are reduced flood damage.

A quick glance at all the plans shows that for each plan total benefits (column 4) exceed total costs (column 2), indicating that a flood-control project on this river is economically justifiable. This can be seen directly in column 6 where total annual costs (column 2) are subtracted from total annual benefits (column 4). But the question of the optimal size or scope for this project remains. This answer is determined by comparing the additional, or *marginal,* costs and the additional, or *marginal,* benefits associated with each plan. The guideline is the one we established when discussing the optimal amount of a public good: Pursue an activity or project as long as the marginal benefits (column 5) exceed the marginal costs (column 3). Stop the activity or project at, or as close as possible to, that point at which marginal benefits equal marginal costs.

In this case Plan C—the medium-sized reservoir—is the best plan. Plans A and B are too modest; in both cases marginal benefits exceed marginal costs. Plan D's marginal costs ($12,000) exceed marginal benefits ($7000) and therefore cannot be justified. Plan D isn't economically justifiable; it overallocates resources to this project. Plan C is closest to the optimum; it expands flood control so long as marginal benefits exceed marginal costs.

Regarded from a slightly different vantage point, the **marginal benefit = marginal cost rule** will determine which plan entails the maximum excess of total benefits (column 4) over total costs (column 2) or, in other words, the plan which yields the maximum *net* gain or benefit to society. We confirm directly in column 6 that the maximum net benefit (of $7000) is associated with Plan C.

Benefit-cost analysis shatters the myth that "economy in government" and "reduced government spending" are synonymous. "Economy" is concerned with efficiency in resource use. If a government program yields marginal benefits which are less than the marginal benefits attainable from alternative private uses—that is, if costs exceed benefits—then the proposed public program should *not* be undertaken. But if benefits exceed cost, then it would be uneconomical or "wasteful" *not* to spend on that government program. Economy in government does *not* mean minimization of public spending; rather, it means allocating resources between the private and public sectors until no net benefits can be realized from further reallocations.

TABLE 18-2 Benefit-cost analysis for a flood-control project

(1) Plan	(2) Total annual cost of project	(3) Marginal cost	(4) Total annual benefit (reduction in damage)	(5) Marginal benefit	(6) Net benefit or (4) − (2)
Without protection	$ 0		$ 0		$ 0
		$ 3,000		$ 6,000	
A: Levees	3,000		6,000		3,000
		7,000		10,000	
B: Small reservoir	10,000		16,000		6,000
		8,000		9,000	
C: Medium reservoir	18,000		25,000		7,000
		12,000		7,000	
D: Large reservoir	30,000		32,000		2,000

Source: Adapted from Otto Eckstein, *Public Finance,* 3d ed. (Englewood Cliffs, N.J.: Prentice-Hall, Inc., 1973), p. 23. Used with permission.

Measurement Problems

Benefit-cost analysis is helpful in promoting clear thinking about the public sector and is useful in actual studies of projects such as flood control, pollution cleanup, and highway construction. But the benefits and costs associated with public goods are partially spillovers or externalities which are difficult to measure.

Consider the possible benefits and costs associated with construction of a new freeway in a major metropolitan area. In addition to estimating the obvious costs—land purchase and construction costs—the responsible agency must also estimate the spillover cost of additional air pollution resulting from an enlarged flow of traffic. Furthermore, more traffic may call for increased expenditures for traffic police.

What about benefits? Improved transportation means a widening of markets, more competition, and a greater opportunity for the community to specialize and improve economic efficiency. But what is the monetary value of this benefit? The freeway also may make more jobs accessible to the central-city poor. Again, what is the dollar value of these benefits?

The point is that the full costs and benefits associated with government programs are not easily calculated, and benefit-cost analysis is sometimes difficult to apply. Nevertheless, this technique is widely used by government and has improved public-sector decision making.

QUICK REVIEW 18-1

- ***The demand for a public good is found by vertically adding the prices which members of the society are willing to pay for each unit of output at various output levels.***
- ***The socially optimal amount of a public good is the amount where the marginal benefit and marginal cost of the good are equal.***
- ***Benefit-cost analysis is the method of evaluating alternative projects or sizes of projects by comparing marginal benefits and marginal costs.***

EXTERNALITIES REVISITED

We can now extend our earlier analysis of government policies designed to correct the market failure we call *externalities* or *spillovers.* Recall that a spillover is a cost or benefit accruing to an individual or group—a third party—which is external to the market transaction. An example of a spillover cost is pollution; of a spillover benefit, an immunization shot. A review of Figure 6-1 will remind you an overallocation of resources to the production of a particular good results when spillover costs are present. Conversely, Figure 6-2 reveals that an underallocation of resources is associated with spillover benefits.

Economists have explored several approaches to solving the externality problem. It will be helpful to extend Chapter 6's discussion of these various options.

Individual Bargaining

In some situations externalities do not require government intervention; they can be solved through individual bargaining.

Coase Theorem According to the **Coase theorem,** named after its originator Ronald Coase, negative or positive spillovers do *not* require government intervention where (1) property ownership is clearly defined, (2) the number of people involved is small, and (3) bargaining costs are negligible. Government should confine its role under these circumstances to encouraging bargaining between affected individuals or groups. Because the economic self-interests of the parties are at stake, bargaining with one another will enable them to find an acceptable solution to the problem. Property rights place a price tag on an externality, creating an opportunity cost for both parties. Hence, a compelling incentive emerges for the parties to find ways to solve the externality problem.

Extended Example Suppose an owner of a large parcel of forest land is considering contracting with a logging company to clear-cut (totally cut) thousands of acres of old-growth fir trees. The complication is that the forest surrounds a lake with a nationally known resort on its shore. The resort is on land owned by the resort owner. The unspoiled beauty of the general area attracts vacationers from all over the nation to the resort. Should state or local government intervene to prevent the tree cutting?

According to the Coase theorem, the forest owner and the resort owner can resolve this situation without government intervention. As long as *one* of the parties to the dispute has property rights to what is at issue, an incentive will exist for *both* parties to negotiate a solution acceptable to each. In our example, the owner of the timberland holds the property rights to the land to be logged. The owner of the resort therefore has an incentive to negotiate with the forest owner to reduce the logging impact. Clearly, excessive logging of the forest surrounding the resort will reduce tourism and therefore revenues to the resort owner.

Less obvious, but equally strong, is the economic incentive of the forest owner to explore the possibility of an agreement with the resort owner. Why? The answer draws directly on the idea of opportunity cost. One important cost incurred by the owner in logging the forest is the forgone payment which the forest owner could obtain from the resort owner for agreeing *not* to clear-cut the fir trees. The resort owner should be willing to make a lump-sum or annual payment to the owner of the forest to avoid or minimize the spillover cost. Or, perhaps the resort owner will be willing to buy the forested land at a relatively high price to prevent the logging. As viewed by the forest owner, a payment to preclude logging or a purchase price above the value of the land as a tree farm are *opportunity costs* of logging the land.

We would predict a negotiated agreement which both parties would regard as better than clear-cutting the firs. According to the Coase theorem, government intervention would not be needed to correct this potential externality.

Alternative Assignment of Property Right A surprising facet of the Coase theorem is that an efficient outcome is independent of which of the two parties is assigned the property right. As an extreme example, suppose government had in advance assigned to the resort owner a "property" right consisting of a legal prohibition of tree cutting within several miles of the resort without permission of the resort owner.

Now, we would expect the owner of the forest land to seek out the resort owner to discuss the situation. And the resort owner would discover a new opportunity cost. Under the new arrangement of property rights, the resort owner could secure a payment from the owner of the timberland in exchange for allowing, say, selective cutting of some of the older trees on an annual basis. This potential payment is an opportunity cost of *not* allowing tree cutting, as viewed by the resort owner.

Once again the two parties would have an economic incentive to negotiate a mutually acceptable agreement. In so doing they would eliminate or lessen the externality.

Limitations Unfortunately, many negative externalities involve large numbers of affected parties, high bargaining costs, and community property such as air and water. Private bargaining in these situations will not remedy the spillover costs. For example, the acid-rain problem involving the United States and Canada affects millions of people spread out over two nations. The vast number of affected parties could not independently negotiate an agreement to remedy this problem. In this example, we must rely on both governments to find acceptable solutions.

Nevertheless, the Coase theorem reminds us that clearly defined property rights can be a positive factor in remedying some externalities.

Liability Rules and Lawsuits

Although private negotiation may not be a realistic solution to most externality problems, clearly established property rights may be helpful in another way. Government has established a framework of laws which define private property and protect it from damage done by other parties. These laws—and the legal tort (wrongful act) system to which they give rise—permit those suffering spillover costs to sue for damages.

Consider the following case. Suppose the Ajax Degreaser Company regularly dumps leaky barrels containing solvents into a nearby canyon owned by Bar Q ranch. Bar Q eventually discovers this dump site, and, after tracing the drums to Ajax, immediately contacts its lawyer. Ajax gets sued! Not only will Ajax have to pay for the cleanup, it may well have to pay Bar Q additional damages for despoiling its property.

Clearly defined property rights and government specified liability rules thus provide an avenue for remedying some externality problems. They do so directly by forcing the perpetrator of the harmful externality to pay damages to those injured. They do so indirectly by discouraging firms and individuals from initially generating negative externalities, for fear of being sued. Thus, it is not surprising that many significant externalities do *not* involve private property, but rather property held in common. It is the *public* bodies of water, the *public* lands, and the *public* air, where ownership is less clear, which often bear the brunt of negative externalities.

Caveat: Like private negotiations, private lawsuits to resolve externalities have their own limitations. Specifically, lawsuits are expensive, time-consuming, and have uncertain outcomes. Large legal fees and major time delays in the court system are commonplace. Also, the uncertainty associated with the court outcome reduces the effectiveness of this approach. Will the court accept your claim that your emphysema has resulted from the smoke emitted by the factory next door, or will it conclude that your ailment is unrelated to the plant's pollution? Can you prove that a specific firm in the area is the source of the contamination of your well? What are Bar Q's options if Ajax Degreaser goes out of business during the litigation?

Direct Controls and Taxes

Other approaches for achieving allocative efficiency are needed when large numbers of people are affected by a negative externality and community resources are being harmed. In Chapter 6 we addressed direct controls and specific taxes as two such policy options. A brief review of these approaches will be useful.

1 Direct Controls The most direct approach to reducing negative externalities is to pass legislation which places limits on the amount of the activity which can take place. To date, this approach has dominated public policy in the United States. Clean air legislation has been enacted to limit the amounts of nitrogen oxide, particulates, and other substances which plants can emit into the air. Clean water legislation has specified the amount of heavy metals, detergents, and other pollutants firms can place into rivers and bays. Toxic-waste laws specify special procedures and dump sites for disposing of contaminated soil and solvents. Violation of these laws brings with it fines and, occasionally, imprisonment.

The effect of direct controls is to force offending firms to incur costs associated with pollution control. Thus, the private marginal costs of producing these goods and services rises. In Figure 6-1b, the supply curve—which we now know reflects private marginal costs—shifts upward from S to S_t. Product price increases, equilibrium output falls from Q_e to Q_o, and the initial Q_eQ_o overallocation of resources is corrected.

2 Specific Taxes A second policy approach to significant and widespread spillover costs is to levy specific taxes or emission charges on the perpetrators. For example, the Federal government has placed an excise tax on manufacturers of chlorofluorocarbons (CFCs) which deplete the stratospheric ozone layer protecting the earth from excessive solar ultraviolet radiation. This substance is used widely as a coolant in refrigeration, a blowing agent for foam, and a solvent for electronics. Facing such a tax, manufacturers must decide whether to pay it or expend additional funds to purchase or develop substitute products. In either case, the marginal cost of producing CFCs will rise, ideally shifting the private supply curve in Figure 6-1b upward from S to S_t. Equilibrium price will therefore increase and equilibrium output will decline from Q_e to the allocatively efficient level Q_o.

A Market for Externality Rights

One of the more novel policy approaches suggested to remedy negative externalities is to create a **market for externality rights.** We confine our discussion to pollution, although other externalities might also lend themselves to this approach.

The rationale for creating a market for pollution rights is that the air, rivers, lakes, oceans, and public lands, such as parks and streets, are all primary objects for pollution because the *rights* to use these resources are either held "in common" by society or are unspecified by law. As a result, no specific private individual or institution has an incentive to restrict the use or maintain the purity or quality of these resources because no one has the right to realize a monetary return from doing so. We maintain the property we own—we paint and repair our homes periodically—in part because we will gain the value of these improvements at the time of resale. But, as long as "rights" to air, water, and certain land resources are commonly held and these resources are freely available, there will be no incentive to maintain them or restrict their use. Hence, these natural resources are "overconsumed" and thereby polluted.

Creating a Market The proposal is therefore made that an appropriate pollution-control agency should determine the amount of pollutants which can be discharged into the water or air of a given region each year and still maintain the quality of the water or air at some acceptable standard. For example, the agency may determine that 500 tons of pollutants can be discharged into Metropolitan Lake and "recycled" by Nature. Hence, 500 pollution rights, each entitling the owner to dump 1 ton of pollutants into the lake in the given year, are made available for sale each year. The resulting supply of pollution rights is fixed and therefore perfectly inelastic, as shown in Figure 18-2.

The demand for pollution rights—in this case D_{1993}—will take the same downsloping form as will the demand for any other input. At high prices, polluters either will stop polluting or will pollute less by acquiring pollution-abatement equipment. Thus, an equilib-

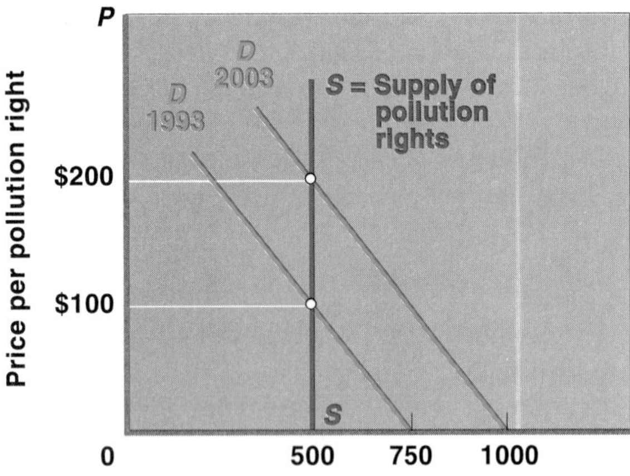

FIGURE 18-2 The market for pollution rights

Pollution can be controlled by having a public body determine the amount of pollution which the atmosphere or a body of water can safely recycle and sell these limited rights to polluters. The effect is to make the environment a scarce resource with a positive price. Economic and population growth will increase the demand for pollution rights over time, but the consequence will be an increase in the price of pollution rights rather than more pollution.

rium market price for pollution rights of $100 will be determined at which an environment-preserving quantity of pollution rights will be rationed to polluters. Note that without this market—that is, if the use of the lake as a dump site for pollutants were free—750 tons of pollutants would be discharged into the lake and it would be "overconsumed," or polluted, in the amount of 250 tons.

Over time, as human and business populations expand, demand will increase, as from D_{1993} to D_{2003}. *Without* a market for pollution rights, pollution would occur in 2003 in the amount of 500 tons beyond that which can be assimilated by Nature. *With* the market for pollution rights, price will rise from $100 to $200 and the amount of pollutants will remain at 500 tons—the amount which the lake can recycle.

Advantages This proposal has several advantages relative to direct controls. Most importantly, it reduces society's costs because pollution rights can be bought and sold. Suppose that it costs Acme Pulp Mill $20 a year to reduce a particular noxious waterborne discharge by 1 ton while it costs Zemo Chemicals $8000 a year to accomplish this same reduction. Also, assume that Zemo increases its output such that it needs to reduce its pollution discharge by 1 ton.

Without the sale of pollution rights, the cost of reducing the pollution by 1 ton would be $8000. But Zemo will find it cheaper to buy 1 ton of pollution rights for the $100 price shown in Figure 18-2 rather than cut pollution at a cost of $8000. Acme, on the other hand, will be willing to sell 1 ton of pollution rights for $100 to Zemo, incurring the $20 expense of reducing its own discharge by 1 ton. The total economic cost of reducing the 1 ton of discharge will therefore be $20 rather than $8000.

Market-based plans have other advantages. Potential polluters are confronted with an explicit monetary incentive not to pollute: They must buy pollution rights to do so. Conservation groups can fight pollution by buying up and withholding pollution rights, reducing actual pollution below governmentally determined standards. As the demand for pollution rights increases over time, the growing revenue from the sale of the given quantity of pollution rights could be devoted to environment improvement. Similarly, with time the rising price of pollution rights should stimulate the search for improved techniques to control pollution.

Administrative and political problems have dissuaded government from abandoning direct controls—uniform emission standards—for a full-scale market for pollution rights. But, as we will soon discuss, a market for air pollution rights *has* emerged. Also, recent legislation has established a system of pollution rights, or "tradeable emission allowances," as part of a plan to reduce sulfur dioxide emitted by coal-burning public utilities. These firms are the major source of acid rain.

Society's Optimal Amount of Externality Reduction

As distinct from economic goods, negative externalities such as pollution are "economic bads"; they reduce the recipient's utility rather than increase it. If something is bad, shouldn't society eliminate it entirely? Why should society allow firms or municipalities to discharge *any* impure waste into public waterways or emit *any* pollution into our air?

The answer is that reducing a negative spillover will come at a "price" and therefore society must decide on how much of a reduction it wants to "buy." Totally eliminating pollution may not be desirable, even if it were technologically feasible. Because of the law of diminishing returns, cleaning up the last 1 percent of effluents from an industrial smokestack normally is far more costly than cleaning up the previous 10 percent.

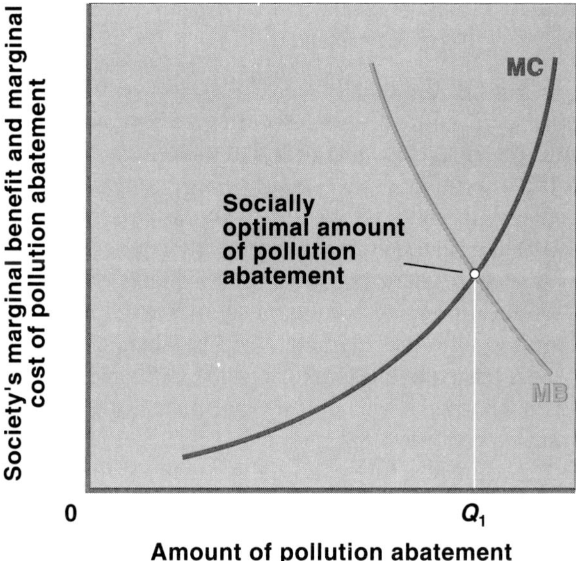

FIGURE 18-3 Society's optimal amount of pollution abatement

The optimal amount of externality reduction—in this case pollution abatement—occurs at Q_1 where society's marginal cost and marginal benefit of reducing the externality are equal. Reductions of pollution beyond Q_1 will reduce allocative efficiency by overallocating resources to pollution control.

Eliminating that 10 percent is most likely more costly than cleaning up the prior 10 percent, and so on.

Stated technically, the marginal cost (MC) to the firm and hence to society—the opportunity cost of the extra resources used—rises as more and more pollution is reduced. At some point MC may rise so high that it exceeds society's marginal benefit (MB) of further pollution abatement (reduction). Additional actions to reduce pollution will therefore lower society's well-being; total cost will rise by more than total benefit.

MC, MB, and Equilibrium Quantity Figure 18-3 helps demonstrate this point. Observe the rising marginal cost curve MC and the downsloping marginal benefit curve, MB. Society's marginal benefits of pollution abatement decline because of the law of diminishing marginal utility. That is, the benefits from reducing pollution are a reflection of utility, and marginal utility (not total utility) falls as greater amounts of pollution abatement are achieved.

Stated generally, the **optimal reduction of an externality** occurs where society's marginal cost and marginal benefit of reducing that externality are equal (MB = MC). In Figure 18-3 this amount of pollution abatement is Q_1. When MB exceeds MC, additional abatement moves society toward allocative efficiency; the added benefit of cleaner air or water exceeds the benefit of any alternative use of the required resources. When MC exceeds MB, further abatement reduces allocative efficiency; the benefits from using resources alternatively are greater than using them to further reduce pollution.

In reality, it is difficult to measure the marginal costs and benefits of pollution control. Nevertheless, Figure 18-3 is useful in demonstrating that some pollution may be socially efficient. This is so, not because pollution is desirable, per se, but because beyond some level of control, further abatement may reduce our well-being.

Shifts in Locations of Curves The locations of the marginal-cost and marginal benefit curves in Figure 18-3 are not forever fixed; they can, and probably do, shift over time. For example, suppose the technology of pollution control equipment dramatically improves. We would expect the cost of pollution abatement to fall, society's MC curve to shift rightward, and the optimal level of abatement to rise. As another example, suppose society increases its desire for cleaner air and water because of new information about adverse health effects of pollution. The MB curve in Figure 18-3 would shift rightward, and again, the optimal level of pollution control would increase beyond Q_1. Test your understanding of these statements by drawing new MC and MB curves in Figure 18-3.

POLLUTION: A CLOSER LOOK

Pollution, the most acute negative externality facing industrial society, provides a relevant illustration of several of the concepts and public policies we have just discussed. This spillover takes several forms, including air, water, and solid-waste (garbage) pollution. What are the dimensions of these problems? What are their causes? What public policies are in place to reduce them?

Dimensions of the Problem

The extent and seriousness of the pollution problem have been well documented in the popular press, and need only a review here. We know that some rivers, lakes, and bays have turned into municipal and industrial sewers. Almost half our population drinks water of dubious quality. There are an estimated 27,000 major industrial and utility sources of air pollution, which contributes to lung cancer, emphysema, pneumonia, and other respiratory diseases. Over 2 billion pounds of toxic chemicals, some of them carcinogens, are released into the air each year. Solid-waste disposal has become an acute problem for many cities as the most readily available dump sites have been filled and citizens resist the establishment of new dumps or incinerators near them.

The nations of eastern Europe are so polluted that it will take several decades, at best, for them to be cleaned up. Government has identified hundreds of dangerous toxic-waste disposal sites in the United States. Recent giant oil spills in Alaska and the Persian Gulf have seriously damaged those two important ecosystems. Passive cigarette smoke has been found to cause cancer in nonsmokers.

Possible global consequences of environmental pollution are equally disturbing. Some scientists contend that the concentrations of industry, people, structures, and cement which constitute cities might create air and heat pollution sufficient to cause irreversible and potentially disastrous changes in the earth's climate and weather patterns through the so-called greenhouse effect. Headlines warn us that our continued use of CFCs has contributed to a rising rate of skin cancer by depleting the earth's stratospheric ozone layer.

Causes: The Law of Conservation of Matter and Energy

The root of the pollution problem can best be envisioned through the **law of conservation of matter and energy.** This law holds that matter can be transformed to other matter or into energy but can never vanish. All inputs (fuels, raw materials, water, and so forth) used in the economy's production processes will ultimately result in an equivalent residual of waste. For example, unless it is continuously recycled, the cotton found in a T-shirt ultimately will be abandoned in a closet, buried in a dump, or burned in an incinerator. Even if burned it will not truly vanish; instead, it will be transformed into heat and smoke.

Fortunately, the ecological system—Nature, if you are over fifty—has the self-regenerating capacity which allows it, within limits, to absorb or recycle such wastes. But the volume of such residuals has tended to outrun this absorptive capacity.

Why has this happened? Why do we have a pollution problem? Causes are manifold, but perhaps four are paramount.

1 Population Density There is the simple matter of population growth. An ecological system which may accommodate 50 or 100 million people may begin to break down under the pressures of 200 or 300 million.

2 Rising Incomes Economic growth means that each person consumes and disposes of more output. Paradoxically, the affluent society helps to spawn the effluent society. A rising GDP (gross domestic product) means a rising GDG (gross domestic garbage). Thus a high standard of living permits Americans to own over 185 million motor vehicles. But autos and trucks are a primary source of air pollution and, concomitantly, give rise to the hard problem of disposing of some 10 or 11 million junked vehicles each year. Additionally, between 175 and 200 million tires hit the nation's scrap heap each year.

3 Technology Technological change is another contributor to pollution. For example, the addition of lead to gasoline posed a serious threat to human health, leading to the government requirement of unleaded fuel. The development and widespread use of "throw-away" containers made of virtually indestructible aluminum or plastic add substantially to the solid-waste crisis. Some detergent soap products have been highly resistant to sanitary treatment and recycling.

4 Incentives Profit-seeking manufacturers will choose the least-cost combination of inputs and will find it advantageous to bear only unavoidable costs. If they can dump waste chemicals into rivers and lakes rather than pay for expensive treatment and proper disposal, businesses will be inclined to do so. If manufacturers can discharge smoke and the hot water used to cool machinery rather than purchase expensive abatement and cooling facilities, they will tend to do so. The result is air and water pollution—both chemical and thermal—and, in the economist's jargon, the shifting of certain costs to the community at large as external or spillover costs. Enjoying lower "internal" costs than if they had not polluted the environment, the producers can sell their products more cheaply, expand their production, and realize larger profits.

But it is neither just nor accurate to lay the entire blame for pollution at the door of industry. On the one hand, a well-intentioned firm which wants to operate in a socially responsible way with respect to pollution may find itself in an untenable position. If an individual firm "internalizes" all its external or spillover costs by installing, say, water-treatment and smoke-abatement equipment, the firm will find itself at a cost disadvantage in comparison to its polluting competitors. The socially responsible firm will have higher costs and will be forced to raise its product price. The "reward" for the pollution-conscious firm is a declining market for its product, diminished profits, and, in the extreme, the prospect of bankruptcy. This means that effective action to combat pollution must be undertaken collectively through government.

On the other hand, given that an important function of government is to correct the misallocation of resources which accompanies spillover costs, it is ironic that most major cities are heavy contributors to the pollution problem. Municipal power plants are frequently major contributors to air pollution; many cities discharge inadequately treated sewage into rivers or lakes because it is cheap and convenient to do so.

Similarly, individuals avoid the costs of proper refuse pickup and disposal by burning their garbage. We also find it easier to use throw-away containers rather than recycle "return" containers. The majority of families with babies opt for the convenience of disposable diapers which glut landfills rather than using reusable cloth diapers. Smoke from woodstoves, fireplaces, and outdoor grills has become a major pollution problem in some towns and cities.

Antipollution Policy

American antipollution policy comprises a complex maze of laws, regulations, taxes, markets for pollution rights, and government-financed cleanup activity. Much of this complexity derives from the sheer number of pollution sources and the thousands of specific substances emitted into the air or placed into the water or garbage dumps. Rather than try to summarize the full range of antipollution policy, we have selected three components for examination. They are the Superfund law, the Clean Air Act of 1990, and incentives to recycle.

The Superfund Law Before passage of the **Superfund law of 1980,** companies disposed of their chemical waste by storing it next to their plants, flushing it into nearby waterways, or paying to have it hauled away. Once the toxic waste was removed from their premises, those who produced it had no further liability. Many of the individuals and firms hauling the hazardous waste improperly stored it in leaky drums or dumped it into private and public landfills.

The Superfund law established both direct controls and specific taxes in addressing the toxic waste problem. It asserted Federal control over the contaminated sites and assigned liability for the improperly dumped waste to the firms producing, transporting, and dumping it. Finally, the law imposed a tax on manufacturers of toxic chemicals, with revenues flowing into a "Superfund," to be used by the Environmental Protection Agency (EPA) to finance the cleanup of the more than 1200 toxic waste sites. Once the decontamination work is under way, the Federal government sues the allegedly responsible parties to try to recover all or part of the expense.

How has the Superfund concept worked? On the plus side of the ledger, the tax on chemical producers has raised $10 billion. On the negative side, the Superfund has become a political "public works" project. Politicians have fought among themselves to get their home state or local dump sites on the cleanup list and to establish the highest priority for cleanup efforts in their locales. Decontamination of the toxic-waste sites not only eliminates health hazards, it brings money and jobs to the local area.

Numerous studies, hearings, and appeals are required to decide on the proper scope and method of cleanup for each site. This process has taken considerable time and has had the unpleasant side-effect of draining enormous sums from the Superfund. Reports indicate that millions of dollars have gone toward dubious overhead expenses charged to the government by private contractors. Thus far, only about 20 percent of the spending from the Superfund has gone toward actual physical cleanup work.

In brief, the Superfund cleanup is off to an expensive, slow start. After eleven years, less than 70 of the more than 1200 toxic-waste sites on the Superfund list have actually been decontaminated. However, some of the most dangerous sites have been cleaned up and work on 550 other sites is now under way.

Clean Air Act of 1990 Direct controls in the form of *uniform emission standards*—limits on allowable pollution—have historically dominated American air pollution policy. The **Clean Air Act of 1990** continues this tradition, but also establishes a limited market for pollution rights. The five major provisions of this law are as follows.

1 Toxic Air Pollution Factories and businesses must install "maximum achievable control technology" to reduce emissions of 189 toxic chemicals by 90 percent by the year 2000.

2 Urban Smog The law requires that smog-causing pollution in about 100 cities with unhealthy air be reduced by 15 percent within six years and 3 percent annually after that until air quality standards are met.

3 Motor Vehicles Auto tailpipe emissions, the major cause of urban smog, must be reduced 30 percent to 60 percent by 1998. Also, the law requires the sale of cleaner blends of gasoline in the nine cities with the worst smog problems: Los Angeles, Houston, New York, Milwaukee, Baltimore, Philadelphia, Hartford, San Diego, and Chicago. In Los Angeles, 300,000 cars must be powered by alternative fuels by 1999.

4 Ozone Depletion The use of CFCs which deplete the ozone layer must be curtailed by 20 percent by 1993 and 50 percent by 1998. Although not a part of this law, the excise tax on CFCs previously discussed will help accomplish this reduction.

5 Acid Rain To stop the destruction of lakes and forests by acid rain, coal-burning electric utilities must cut their annual emissions of sulfur dioxide by about 50 percent. The law also creates a market for pollution rights similar to that shown in Figure 18-2 by allowing utilities to trade *emission credits* provided by government. Some utilities may choose to reduce sulfur dioxide emissions by more than amounts specified, selling their emission credits to other utilities that find it less costly to buy the credits than install additional pollution-control equipment.

Trading of Pollution Rights The acid-rain provisions of the Clean Air Act of 1990 complement other air pollution policies which permit exchange of pollution rights. Specifically, the EPA now permits firms to exchange pollution rights internally and externally.

Polluters are allowed to transfer air pollution rights internally between individual sources within their plants. That is, as long as they meet the overall pollution standard assigned to them, firms may increase one source of pollution by offsetting it with reduced pollution from another part of their operations.

The EPA also permits external trading of pollution rights. It has set targets for reducing air pollution in regions where the minimum standards are not being met. Previously, new pollution sources could not enter these regions unless existing polluters went out of business. In the last decade or so, the EPA has allowed firms which reduce their pollution below set standards to sell pollution rights to new or existing firms. Thus, a new firm desiring to locate in the Los Angeles area, for example, might be able to buy rights to emit 20 tons of nitrous oxide annually from an existing firm which has reduced its emissions below its allowable limit. The price of these emission rights will depend on their supply and demand.

A small, but growing market for such rights has recently emerged. The acid-rain provisions of the Clean Air Act of 1990 will greatly expand this market. In fact, in 1991 the Chicago Board of Trade established a formal market for rights to emit sulfur dioxide.

Solid-Waste Disposal and Recycling

Nowhere is the law of conservation of matter and energy more apparent than in solid-waste disposal. The 180 million tons of garbage which accumulate annually in our landfills have become a growing externality problem. Landfills in the northeast, in particular, are either completely full or rapidly filling up. Garbage from there and elsewhere is now being transported thousands of miles across state lines to dumps in other states. For instance, New Jersey exports trash to Alabama, Illinois, Indiana, Kentucky, Michigan, Ohio, Pennsylvania, Virginia, and West Virginia. On the receiving end, many people in rural areas near newly expanding dumps are understandably upset about the increased truck traffic on their highways and growing mounds of smelly garbage in local dumps. Also, some landfills are producing serious groundwater pollution.

The high opportunity cost of urban and suburban land, and the negative externalities created by dumps, make the landfill solution to solid waste increasingly expensive. An alternative garbage policy is to incinerate it in plants which produce electricity. But people object to having garbage incinerators—a source of truck traffic and air pollution—close to their homes. So where do we turn for a solution to the growing problem of solid waste?

Although garbage dumps and incinerators are likely to remain the mainstays of garbage disposal, recycling is receiving increased attention. According to the EPA, 90 percent of lead-acid batteries, 55 percent of aluminum cans, 45 percent of corrugated boxes, 30 percent of newspapers, 21 percent of plastic soft drink bottles, and 20 percent of glass beer bottles are now being recycled.

Market for Recyclable Inputs The incentives for recycling can be shown through our basic supply and demand analysis. In Figure 18-4a we have drawn a demand and supply curve for some recyclable product, say, glass.

The demand for recyclable glass derives from manufacturers of glass who use it as a resource in producing new glass. Just as a firm has a demand for labor and capital, it has a demand for raw materials useful in producing its product, and recyclable materials may be one such input. The demand curve for recyclable glass slopes downward, telling us that manufacturers will increase their purchases of recyclable glass as its price falls.

The location of the resource demand curve in Figure 18-4a depends partly on the demand for the product which the recycled glass is being used to produce. The greater the demand for the product, the greater is the demand for recyclable inputs. The location also depends on the technology and thus the cost of using original raw materials rather than recycled glass in the production process. The more costly it is to use original materials relative to recycled glass, the further to the right will be the demand curve for recyclable glass.

The supply curve for recyclable glass slopes upward in the typical fashion in that higher prices in-

FIGURE 18-4 The economics of recycling

The equilibrium price and amount of materials recycled are determined by supply and demand, as shown in (a). In (b), policies which increase the incentives for producers to buy recyclable inputs shift the demand curve rightward and raise both equilibrium price and the amount of recycling. In (c), policies which encourage households to recycle expand the equilibrium amount of recycling but also reduce the equilibrium price of recyclable inputs.

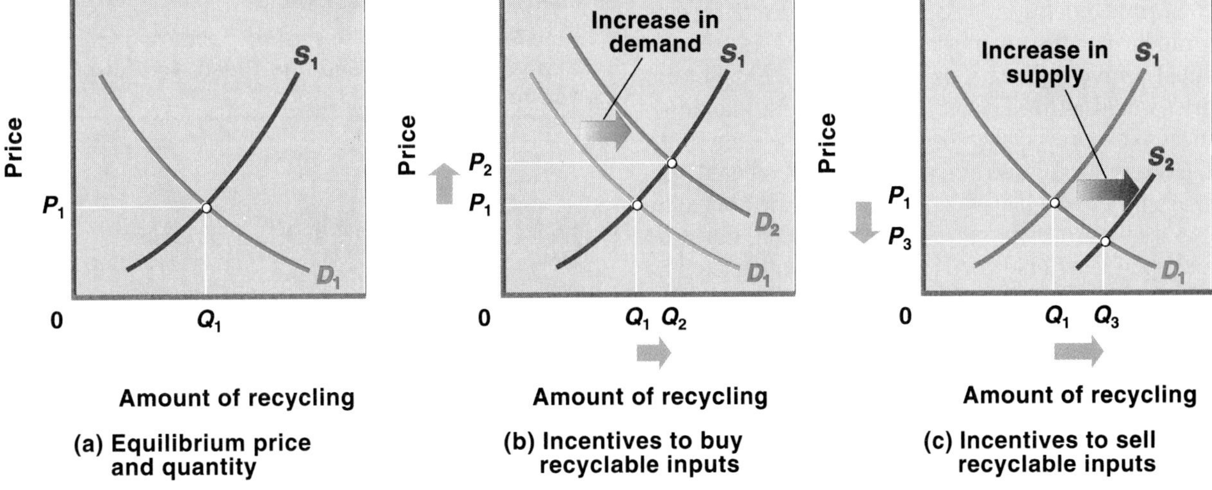

crease the incentive for households to recycle. The location of the supply curve depends on such factors as the attitudes of households toward recycling and the cost to them of alternative disposal.

The equilibrium price P_1 and quantity Q_1 in Figure 18-4a are determined at the intersection of the supply and demand curves. At price P_1 the market clears; there is neither a shortage nor a surplus of recyclable glass.

Policy Suppose government wants to encourage recycling as an alternative to land dumps or incineration. It could do this in one of two ways.

1 Demand Incentives Government could increase recycling by increasing the demand for recycled inputs. If the demand curve in Figure 18-4b shifts from D_1 rightward to D_2, equilibrium price and quantity will increase to P_2 and Q_2. An example of a specific policy which might accomplish this goal would be to place specific taxes on the inputs which are substitutable for recycled glass in the production process. Such taxes would encourage firms to use more of the untaxed recycled glass and less of the original taxed inputs. Alternatively, government could shift its purchases toward goods produced with recycled inputs and require that its contractors do the same.

Also, environmental awareness by the public itself can contribute to rightward shifts of the demand curve for recycled resources. Fearing negative consumer backlashes against their products, firms such as Procter & Gamble (disposable diapers) and McDonald's (packaging of fast foods) have undertaken multimillion dollar campaigns to use recycled plastic and paper.

2 Supply Incentives As shown in Figure 18-4c, government can also increase recycling by shifting the supply curve rightward, as from S_1 to S_2. Equilibrium price would fall from P_1 to P_3 and equilibrium quantity—in this case, recyclable glass—would rise from Q_1 to Q_3. Many local governments have implemented specific policies which fit within this framework. For example, they encourage recycling by providing curbside pickup of recyclable goods at a lower monthly fee than for pickup of normal garbage.

In a few cases, supply incentives for recyclables have been so effective that the prices of some recycled items have fallen to zero. You can envision this outcome by shifting the supply curve in Figure 18-4c further and further rightward. In fact, some cities now are *paying* manufacturers to truck away certain recyclable products such as mixed paper (negative price) rather than charging them a price. This may or may not promote allocative efficiency. On the one hand, the cost of paying firms to take away recyclable products may be lower than the cost of alternative disposal, particularly in view of the negative externalities of dumps and incinerators. If so, recycling will promote allocative efficiency.

On the other hand, a policy of paying firms to take away recyclable items need not always be economical. In some cases it may be more costly to recycle goods than to bury or incinerate them, even when externalities are considered. If so, recycling will *reduce* efficiency rather than increase it.

Government's task is to find the optimal amount of recycling compared to alternative disposal of garbage. It can do this by estimating and comparing the marginal benefit and marginal cost of recycling. And, incidentally, consumers as a group can reduce the initial accumulation of garbage by not buying products with excessive packaging.

QUICK REVIEW 18-2

- ***Policies for coping with negative externalities include a private bargaining, b liability rules and lawsuits, c direct controls, d specific taxes, and e markets for externality rights.***
- ***The optimal amount of externality reduction occurs where society's marginal cost and marginal benefit of reducing the externality are equal.***
- ***The ultimate cause of pollution is the law of conservation of matter and energy, which holds that matter can be transformed into other matter or into energy, but cannot vanish.***
- ***Recent policies to reduce pollution include the Superfund law of 1980, the Clean Air Act of 1990, and recycling.***

INFORMATION FAILURES

Thus far we have added new detail and insights concerning two types of market failure: public goods and externalities. But there is another, more subtle, market failure. This inefficiency results when either buyers or sellers have incomplete or inaccurate information and their cost of obtaining better information is prohibitive.

Market information normally is sufficient to ensure that goods and services are produced and purchased in allocatively efficient quantities. But in some instances, inadequate information precludes sorting out legitimate from illegitimate sellers, or legitimate from illegitimate buyers. In these markets, society's scarce resources will not be allocated efficiently, implying that government should intervene by increasing the information available to the market participants. Under rarer circumstances government may itself supply a good for which information problems have prohibited profitable production.

Inadequate Information About Sellers

We begin by asking how inadequate information about *sellers* and their products can cause market failure. Examining the market for gasoline and the services of surgeons will give us an answer.

Gasoline Market First, we consider the market for gasoline and assume an absurd situation. Suppose there is no system of weights and measures established by law, no government inspection of gasoline pumps, and no laws against false advertising. Each gas station therefore can use whatever measure it chooses; it can define a gallon of gas as it pleases. A station can advertise that its gas is 87 octane when in fact it is only 75. It can rig its pumps to indicate it is providing more gas than the amount being delivered.

Obviously, the consumer's cost of obtaining reliable information under these conditions is exceptionally high, if not prohibitive. Each consumer will have to buy samples of gas from various gas stations, have them tested for octane level, and pour gas into a measuring device to see how the station has calibrated the pump. Also, the consumer will need to use a hand calculator to ascertain if the machine is correctly multiplying the price per gallon by the number of gallons. And these activities will need to be repeated regularly, since the station owner can alter the product quality and the accuracy of the pump at will.

Because of the high costs of obtaining information about the seller, many customers will opt out of this chaotic market. One tankful of a 50 percent solution of gasoline and water will be enough to discourage many motorists from further driving. More realistically, the conditions described in this market will encourage consumers to vote for political candidates who promise to provide a governmental solution. The oil companies and honest gasoline suppliers will not object to this government intervention. They will realize that, by enabling this market to work, accurate information will expand their total sales.

Government has intervened in the market for gasoline and other markets having similar information difficulties. It has established a system of weights and measures, employed inspectors to check the accuracy of gasoline pumps, and passed laws against fraudulent claims and misleading advertising. There can be no doubt that these government activities have produced net benefits for society.

Licensing of Surgeons Let's look at another example of how inadequate information about sellers can create market failure. Suppose that anyone can hang out a shingle and claim to be a surgeon in much the same way that anyone can become a house painter. The market will eventually sort out the true surgeons from those who are learning by doing or are fly-by-night operators who move into and out of an area. As people die from unsuccessful surgery, lawsuits for malpractice eventually will eliminate the medical imposters. People needing surgery for themselves or their loved ones can glean information from newspaper reports and solicit information from people—or their relatives—who have undergone similar operations.

But this process of generating information for those needing surgery will take considerable time and will impose unacceptably high human and economic costs. There is a fundamental difference between an amateurish paint job on one's house and being on the receiving end of heart surgery by a bogus physician. The marginal cost of obtaining information about sellers in this market is excessively high. The risk of proceeding without good information will result in an underallocation of resources to surgery.

Government has remedied this market failure through a system of qualifying tests and licensing. This licensing enables consumers to obtain inexpensive information about a service they only infrequently buy. Government has taken a similar role in several other areas of the economy. For example, it approves new medicines, regulates the securities industry, and requires warnings on containers of potentially hazardous substances. It also requires warning labels on cigarette packages and disseminates information about communicable diseases. It issues warnings about unsafe toys and inspects restaurants for health-related violations.

Inadequate Information About Buyers

Just as inadequate information about sellers can keep markets from achieving allocative efficiency, so can inadequate information about *buyers.* These buyers can either be consumers buying products or firms buying resources.

Moral Hazard Problem Private markets may underallocate resources to a particular good or service for which there is a severe **moral hazard problem.** *The moral hazard problem is the tendency of one party to a contract to alter her or his behavior in ways which are costly to the other party.* A contract will not be profitable to a seller, for example, if the seller must incur large costs to identify those buyers most likely to alter their behavior in cost-imposing ways.

To understand this point, suppose a firm offers an insurance policy which pays a set amount of money per month to people who suffer divorces. The attraction of this insurance is that it pools the economic risk of divorce among thousands of people and, in particular, protects nonworking spouses and children from the economic hardship which divorce often brings. Unfortunately, the moral hazard problem reduces the likelihood that insurance companies can profitably provide this type of insurance contract.

After taking out this insurance, some people will alter their behavior in ways which impose heavy costs on the insurer. Specifically, married couples will have less of an incentive to get along and to iron out marital difficulties. At the extreme, some people might be motivated to obtain a divorce, collect the insurance, and then live together. The problem is that the insurance promotes *more* divorces, the very outcome it protects against. The moral hazard difficulty will force the insurer to charge such high premiums for this insurance that few policies will be bought. If the insurer could identify in advance those people most prone to alter their behavior, the firm could exclude them from buying it. But the firm's marginal cost of getting this information is too high compared to the marginal benefit. Thus, this market fails.

Divorce insurance is not available in the marketplace, but society recognizes the benefits of insuring against the hardships of divorce. It has corrected for this underallocation of "hardship insurance" through child-support laws which dictate payments—when the economic circumstances so warrant—to the spouse who retains the children. Alimony laws also play a role.

Finally, government provides "divorce insurance" of sorts through the Aid to Families with Dependent Children (AFDC) program. If a divorce leaves a spouse with children destitute, the family is eligible for AFDC payments. Government intervention does not eliminate the moral hazard problem; instead, it overcomes or offsets it. Unlike private firms, government need not earn a profit to continue the insurance.

The moral hazard concept has numerous applications. We mention them only in passing, to reinforce your understanding of the basic principle.

1 Drivers may be less cautious because they have car insurance.
2 Medical malpractice insurance may increase the amount of malpractice.
3 Guaranteed contracts for professional athletes may reduce their performance.
4 Unemployment compensation insurance may lead some workers to shirk.
5 Government insurance on bank deposits may encourage banks to make risky loans.

Adverse Selection Problem Another information problem resulting from inadequate information about buyers is the **adverse selection problem.** *The adverse selection problem arises when information known by the first party to a contract is not known by the second, and, as a result, the second party incurs major costs.* Unlike the moral hazard problem, which arises *after* a person signs a contract, the adverse selection problem arises *at the time* a person signs the contract.

In insurance, the adverse selection problem is that people most likely to receive insurance payouts are those who will buy insurance. For example, those in poorest health will seek to buy the most generous health insurance policies. Or, at the extreme, a person planning to hire an arsonist to "torch" his failing business has an incentive to buy fire insurance.

Our example of hypothetical divorce insurance sheds further light on the adverse selection problem. If the insurance firm sets the premiums on the basis of the average rate of divorce, many of the married couples about to get a divorce will buy insurance. An insurance premium based on average probabilities will make for a great insurance buy for those about to get divorced. Meanwhile, those in highly stable marriages will opt against buying it. In summary, the adverse selection problem will eliminate the pooling of risk which is the basis for profitable insurance. The insurance rates needed to cover payouts will be so high that few people will wish or be able to buy this insurance.

Where private firms underprovide insurance because of information problems, government often establishes some type of social insurance. Government can require everyone in a particular group to enter the insurance pool and therefore can overcome the adverse selection problem. Although the social security system in the United States is partly an insurance and partly a welfare program, in its broadest sense it is insurance against poverty in one's senior years. The social security insurance program overcomes the adverse selection problem by requiring nearly universal participation. People who are most likely to need the minimum benefits that social security provides automatically are participants in the program. So, too, are those not likely to need the benefits.

Workplace Safety The labor market also provides an example of how inadequate information about buyers (employers) can produce market failures.

For several reasons employers have an economic incentive to provide safe workplaces. A safe workplace reduces the amount of disruption of the production process created by job accidents and lowers the costs of recruiting, screening, training, and retaining new workers. It also reduces a firm's worker compensation insurance premiums (legally required insurance against job injuries).

But a safe workplace comes at an expense. Safe equipment, protective gear, and slower paces of work all entail costs. Thus, the firm will compare its marginal cost and marginal benefit of providing a safer workplace in deciding how much safety to provide. Will this amount of job safety achieve allocative efficiency, as well as maximize the firm's profits?

The answer is "Yes" if the labor and product markets are competitive and workers are fully aware of job risks at various places of employment. With full information, workers will avoid employers having unsafe workplaces. Hence, the supply of labor to these establishments will be greatly restricted, forcing them to boost their wages to attract a work force. These higher wages give the employer an incentive to provide socially desirable levels of workplace safety; safer workplaces will reduce wage expenses. Only firms which find it very costly to provide safer workplaces will choose to pay high compensating wage differentials, rather than reduce workplace hazards.

But a serious problem arises when workers *do not know* that particular occupations or workplaces are unsafe. Because information about the buyer is inadequate—that is, about the employer and the workplace—the firm may *not* need to pay a wage premium to attract its work force. Its incentive to remove safety hazards therefore is diminished and its profit-maximizing level of workplace safety will be less than socially desirable. In brief, the labor market will fail because of inadequate information about buyers (employers).

Government has several options for remedying this information problem.

1 It can directly provide information to workers about the injury experience of various employers, much like it publishes the on-time performance of the various airlines.

2 It can mandate that firms provide information to workers about known workplace hazards.

3 It can establish standards of workplace safety and enforce them through inspection and penalties.

The Federal government has mainly employed the "standards and enforcement" approach to improve workplace safety, but some contend that an "information" strategy might be less costly and more effective.

QUICK REVIEW 18-3

- ***Inadequate information can cause markets to fail, causing society's scarce resources to be allocated inefficiently.***
- ***The moral hazard problem is the tendency of some parties to a contract to alter their behavior in ways which are costly to the other party; for example, a person who buys insurance may incur added risk.***
- ***As it relates to insurance, the adverse selection problem is the tendency of people who are most likely to collect insurance benefits to buy large amounts of insurance.***

Qualification

People have found many ingenious ways to overcome information difficulties short of government intervention. For example, many firms offer product warranties to overcome the lack of information about themselves and their products. Franchising also helps overcome this problem. When you visit McDonald's or Holiday Inn, you know precisely what you are going to get, as opposed to Sam's Hamburger Shop or the Bates Motel.

Also, some private firms and organizations have specialized in providing information to buyers and sellers. *Consumer Reports* and the *Mobil Travel Guide* provide product information, labor unions collect and dis-

LAST WORD

USED CARS: THE MARKET FOR "LEMONS"

Inadequate product information could result in markets where sellers offer only defective goods.

A new car loses much of its market value as the buyer drives it off the sales lot. Physical depreciation alone cannot explain this large loss of value. The same new car can sit on the dealer's lot for weeks, or even months, and retain its value.

One explanation of this paradox rests on the idea of inadequate information about *used* cars.* Auto owners have much more knowledge about the mechanical condition of their vehicles than do potential buyers of used cars. At the time of the purchase, individual buyers of used cars find it difficult to distinguish between so-called "lemons"—defective cars—and vehicles of the same car make and model that operate perfectly. Therefore, a single price emerges for used cars of the same year, make and model whether they are lemons or high-quality vehicles. This price roughly reflects the average quality of the vehicles, influenced by the proportion of lemons to high-quality cars. The higher the proportion of lemons, the lower are prices of used cars.

An adverse selection problem now becomes evident. Owners of lemons have an incentive to sell their cars to unsuspecting buyers, while owners of high-quality autos will wish to keep their cars. Therefore, most used cars on the market will be of lower quality than the same car models which are *not* for sale. As people become aware of this, the demand for used cars will decline and prices of used cars will fall. These lower prices will further reduce the incentive of owners of high-quality used cars to offer them for sale. At the extreme, only lemons will appear on the market; *poor-quality products will drive out high-quality products.*

We thus have a solution to our paradox. Once a buyer drives a new car away from the dealership, the auto's value becomes the value set in the lemons' mar-

seminate information about job safety, and credit bureaus provide information to insurance companies. Brokers, bonding agencies, and intermediaries also provide information to clients.

However, economists agree that the private sector cannot remedy all information problems. In some situations government intervention is desirable to promote an efficient allocation of society's scarce resources.

CHAPTER SUMMARY

1 Graphically, the collective demand curve for a particular public good can be found by summing *vertically* each of the individual demand curves for that good. The demand curve which results from this process indicates the collective willingness to pay for the last unit of any given amount of the public good.

ket. This is true even though the probability is high that the new car is of high quality.

The instantaneous loss of new car value would be even greater were it not for several factors. Because new-car warranties are transferable to used-car buyers, purchasers of low-mileage late-model cars are protected against costly repairs. Thus, the demand for these vehicles rises. Also, prospective buyers can distinguish good cars from lemons by hiring mechanics to perform inspections. Moreover, sellers can signal potential buyers that their cars are not lemons through ads such as "Must sell, transferred abroad," "Divorce forces sale." Of course, the buyer must determine the truth of these claims. Additionally, auto rental companies routinely sell high-quality, late-model cars, increasing the ratio of good cars to lemons in the used-car market.

Government also plays a role in solving the market failure evident in the lemons' market. Many states have "lemon laws" which force auto dealers to take back defective new cars. Supposedly, dealers do not offer these lemons for sale in the used-car market until completing all needed repairs. Also, some states require dealers to either offer warranties on used cars or explicitly state that a car is offered "as is." The latter designation gives the buyer a good clue that the car may be defective.

In brief, both private and governmental initiatives temper the lemons' problem. Nevertheless, this principle is applicable to a wide variety of used products such as autos, computers, and cameras, which are complex and occasionally defective. Buying any of these used products remains a somewhat risky transaction.

The classical article on this topic is George A. Akerlof, "The Market for 'Lemons': Qualitative Uncertainty and the Market Mechanism,"** ***Quarterly Journal of Economics, **August 1970, pp. 488–500.**

2 The optimal quantity of a public good occurs where the combined willingness to pay for the last unit—the marginal benefit of the good—equals the good's marginal cost.

3 Benefit-cost analysis can provide useful guidance as to the economic desirability and most efficient scope of public goods output. The major difficulty in applying benefit-cost analysis is that the full costs and benefits of a public good or service are not easily calculated.

4 According to the Coase theorem, private bargaining is capable of solving potential externality problems where **a** the property rights are clearly defined, **b** the number of people involved is small, and **c** bargaining costs are negligible.

5 Clearly established property rights and liability rules permit some spillover costs to be prevented or remedied through private lawsuits. Lawsuits, however, are costly, time-consuming, and uncertain as to their results.

6 Direct controls and specific taxes can improve resource allocation in situations where externalities affect many people and involve community resources. Both direct controls (smokestack emission standards) and specific taxes (taxes on firms producing toxic chemicals) increase production costs and hence product price. As product price rises, the externality is reduced since less of the output is bought and sold.

7 Markets for pollution rights, in which people can buy and sell the rights to a fixed amount of pollution, place a price tag on pollution and encourage firms to reduce or eliminate it.

8 The socially optimal amount of externality abatement occurs where society's marginal cost and marginal benefit of reducing the externality are equal. This optimal amount of pollution abatement is likely to be less than a 100 percent reduction. Changes in technology or changes in society's attitudes about pollution can affect the optimal amount of pollution abatement.

9 The law of conservation of matter and energy is at the heart of the pollution problem. Matter can be transformed into other matter or into energy, but does not disappear. If not recycled, all production will ultimately end up as waste.

10 The Superfund law of 1980 places a tax on producers of chemicals and uses the proceeds to clean up toxic-waste dumps.

11 The Clean Air Act of 1990 seeks to **a** reduce toxic air pollution, **b** hasten smog reduction in urban areas, **c** limit the use of substances which are depleting the earth's ozone layer, and **d** reduce acid rain by cutting emissions of sulfur dioxide. Under the law, utilities are able to buy and sell emission credits for sulfur dioxide.

12 Recycling is a recent response to the growing garbage disposal problem. The equilibrium price and quantity of recyclable inputs depend on their demand and supply. Government can encourage recycling through either demand or supply incentives.

13 Inadequate information about sellers or buyers can cause markets to fail. The moral hazard problem occurs when people alter their behavior after they sign a contract, imposing costs on the other party. As it relates to insurance, the adverse selection problem occurs when people who are of above-average risk buy large amounts of insurance.

TERMS AND CONCEPTS

benefit-cost analysis
marginal benefit = marginal cost rule
Coase theorem
market for externality rights
optimal reduction of an externality
law of conservation of matter and energy
Superfund law of 1980
Clean Air Act of 1990
moral hazard problem
adverse selection problem

QUESTIONS AND STUDY SUGGESTIONS

1 Given the following three individual demand schedules for a particular good, and assuming these three people are the only ones in the society, determine **a** the market demand schedule on the assumption that the good is a private good, and **b** the collective demand schedule on the assumption that the good is a public good. Explain the differences, if any, in your schedules.

Individual 1		*Individual 2*		*Individual 3*	
P	Q_d	*P*	Q_d	*P*	Q_d
$8	0	$8	1	$8	0
7	0	7	2	7	0
6	0	6	3	6	1
5	1	5	4	5	2
4	2	4	5	4	3
3	3	3	6	3	4
2	4	2	7	2	5
1	5	1	8	1	6

2 Use your demand schedule for a public good determined in question 1 and the following supply schedule to ascertain the optimal quantity of this public good. Explain why this is the optimal quantity.

P	Q_s
$19	10
16	8
13	6
10	4
7	2
4	1

3 The following table shows the total costs and total benefits in billions for four different antipollution programs of increasing scope. Which program should be undertaken? Why?

Program	*Total cost*	*Total benefit*
A	$ 3	$ 7
B	7	12
C	12	16
D	18	19

4 An apple-grower's orchard provides nectar to a neighbor's bees, while a beekeeper's bees help the apple grower by pollinating the apple blossoms. Use Figure 6-2 to explain why this situation might lead to an underallocation of resources to apple growing and to beekeeping. How might this underallocation get resolved via the means suggested by the Coase theorem?

5 Explain: "Without a market for pollution rights, dumping pollutants into the air or water is costless; in the presence of the right to buy and sell pollution rights, dumping pollution creates an opportunity cost for the polluter." What is the significance of this fact to the search for better technology to reduce pollution?

6 Manipulate the MB curve in Figure 18-3 to explain the following statement: "The optimal amount of pollution abatement for some substances, say, water from storm drains, is very low; the optimal amount of abatement for other substances, say, cyanide poison, is close to 100 percent." Explain.

7 Relate the law of conservation of matter and energy to: **a** the air pollution problem; and **b** the solid-waste disposal problem.

8 What is the Superfund? How is it financed and for what purpose is it used? Are there any Superfund sites in your area? If so, determine the current status of the cleanup efforts.

9 Which provisions of the Clean Air Act of 1990 reflect the direct controls approach to pollution? Which provision directly incorporates a market for pollution rights?

10 Explain why there may be insufficient recycling of products when the externalities associated with landfills and garbage incinerators are not considered. What demand and supply incentives might government provide to promote more recycling?

11 Why is it in the interest of new home buyers *and* builders of new homes to have government building codes and building inspectors?

12 Place an *M* beside items in the following list which describe a moral hazard problem; place an *A* beside those which describe an adverse selection problem.

a A person with a terminal illness buys several life insurance policies through the mail.

b A person drives carelessly because he or she has insurance.

c A person who intends to "torch" his warehouse takes out a large fire insurance policy.

d A professional athlete who has a guaranteed contract fails to stay in shape during the off-season.

e A woman anticipating having a large family takes a job with a firm which offers exceptional child-care benefits.

Public Choice Theory and Taxation

In view of the positive role of government described in Chapter 18, it may seem surprising that government elicits so much public disenchantment and distrust. This antigovernment sentiment has diverse roots, but it stems in part from the apparent failure of costly government programs to resolve socioeconomic ills. For example, it is argued that foreign aid programs have contributed little or nothing to the economic growth of the less developed nations. We hear reports that well-financed state and Federal school enrichment programs have had no perceptible impact on the educational attainment of students. Some programs have allegedly fostered the very problems they were designed to solve: Our farm programs were originally designed to save the family farm, but in fact have heavily subsidized large corporate farms which in turn have driven family farms out of business.

There are also charges that government agencies have become mired in paperwork. It is alleged that the public bureaucracy embodies great duplication of effort; that obsolete programs persist; that various agencies work at cross purpose; and so on.

Coincident with this popular disenchantment, there has evolved a body of literature which alleges that, just as certain limitations or failures are embodied in the private sector's market system, so there are also more-or-less inherent deficiencies in the political processes, bureaucratic agencies, and tax systems within the public sector.

This chapter will examine some of these difficulties. Specifically, we scrutinize the problems society has in revealing its true preferences through majority voting. This is followed by a closely related discussion of *government failure*—the contention that certain characteristics of the public sector hinder government's ability to assist the market system in achieving an efficient allocation of resources. Next, we examine taxes and tax incidence to see how taxes are apportioned in the United States and who bears the burden. After examining two current tax issues, we end the chapter with a brief discussion of the conservative and liberal stances on government and economic freedom.

It will become apparent that this is a chapter on public choice theory—the economic analysis of government decision making; and on selected topics and problems of public finance—the study of public expenditures and revenues.

REVEALING PREFERENCES THROUGH MAJORITY VOTING

Which public goods should be produced and in what amounts? In what circumstances and through what methods should government intervene to correct for externalities? How should the tax burden of financing government be apportioned?

These and many other decisions concerning government are made collectively in the United States through a democratic process which relies heavily on majority voting. Candidates for office offer voters alternative policy packages and we elect people who we think will make the best decisions on our collective behalf. Voters "retire" officials who do not adequately represent their collective wishes and elect persons who convince them they will better reflect the collective wants of the electorate. Additionally, citizens periodically have opportunities at the state and local level to vote directly on ballot issues which involve public expenditures or new legislation.

Although this democratic process generally works well at revealing society's true preferences, it is not without its shortcomings. Just as the market fails in some cases to allocate resources efficiently, our system of voting in some instances produces inefficiencies and inconsistencies. We will now explore some of these potential voting difficulties.

Inefficient Voting Outcomes

Providing a public good having a total benefit greater than its total cost will add to society's well-being. Unfortunately, majority voting raises the possibility of voting outcomes which are economically inefficient. Voters may defeat a proposal to provide a public good even though it may yield total benefits exceeding its total cost. Conversely, majority voting raises the possibility that voters may adopt a proposal to provide a public good costing more than the benefits it could yield.

Illustration: Inefficient "No" Vote Suppose that a public good, say, national defense, can be provided at a total expense of $900. Also, suppose that there are only three individuals—Adams, Benson, and Conrad—in the society and they will share the $900 tax expense equally. That is, Adams, Benson, and Conrad will each pay $300 of tax if the good is provided. Assume, as illustrated in Figure 19-1a, that Adams is willing to pay $700 to have this good; Benson, $250; and Conrad, $200. What might be the result if a majority vote is determined on whether or not this good will be provided? Although people do not always vote strictly on the basis of their own economic interest, it is entirely likely that Benson and Conrad will vote "No" because they will incur tax expenses of $300 each while gaining benefits of only $250 and $200, respectively. The majority vote in this case will defeat the proposal even though the total benefit of $1150 (=$700 for Adams + $250 for Benson + $200 for Conrad) exceeds the total cost of $900.

Illustration: Inefficient "Yes" Vote We can easily construct an example illustrating the converse, in which the majority might favor the provision of a public good even though its total cost exceeds its total benefit. Figure 19-1b shows the details. Again, Adams, Benson, and Conrad will equally share the $900 cost of the public good; they each will be taxed $300. But, now note that Adams is only willing to pay $100 for the public good, rather than forgo it. Meanwhile, Benson and Adams are willing to pay $350 dollars each. They will vote for the public good; Adams will vote against it. The election will result in a public good costing $900 which produces total benefits of $800 (=$100 for Adams + $350 for Benson + $350 for Conrad). Society's resources will be inefficiently allocated to this public good.

The point of our examples is that an inefficiency may take the form of either an overproduction or underproduction of a specific public good, and therefore an overallocation or underallocation of resources for that particular use. In Chapter 18 we saw that government might improve allocative efficiency (resources channeled to their highest valued use) by providing public goods which the market system would not make available. Now we have extended that analysis to reveal that government might fail to provide some public goods whose production is economically justifiable while providing other goods whose creation is not economically warranted.

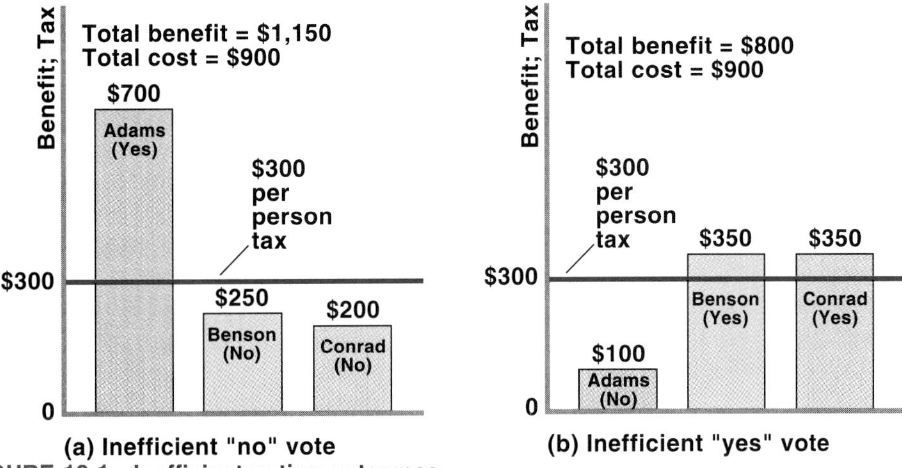

FIGURE 19-1 Inefficient voting outcomes

Majority voting can produce inefficient decisions. In (a) majority voting leads to rejection of a public good which would entail a greater total benefit than total cost. In (b) majority voting results in provision of a public good having a higher total cost than total benefit.

Our examples illustrate that people have only a single vote no matter how much they might gain or lose from a public good. In both examples shown in Figure 19-1, if buying votes were legal, Adams would be willing to purchase a vote from either Benson or Conrad, paying for it out of prospective personal gain. In the marketplace the consumer can decide *not* to buy a good, even though it is popular with others. Also, specific goods are normally available to people with strong preferences for them even though most consumers conclude that product prices exceed the marginal utilities of these goods. A consumer can buy beef tongues and fresh squid in some supermarkets, but it is doubtful these products would be available under a system which used majority voting to stock the shelves. On the other hand, one cannot easily "buy" national defense once the majority has decided it is not worth buying.

To repeat: *Because it fails to incorporate the strength of the preferences of the individual voter, majority voting may produce economically inefficient outcomes.*

Interest Groups and Logrolling Ways do exist through which inefficiencies associated with majority voting *may* get resolved. Two examples:

1 Interest Groups Those who have a strong preference for a public good may band together into an interest group and use advertisements, mailings, and the like to try to convince others of the merits of a public good. In our first example (Figure 19-1a), Adams might make a major effort to convince Benson and Conrad that it is actually in their interest to vote for national defense; that is, that national defense is actually worth more than the $250 and $200 values they now place on it. Such appeals are commonplace in contemporary American politics.

2 Political Logrolling **Logrolling**—*the trading of votes to secure favorable outcomes on decisions which otherwise would be adverse*—can turn an inefficient outcome into an efficient one. In our first example (Figure 19-1a), perhaps Benson has a strong preference for a different public good, say, a new road, which Adams and Conrad do not think is worth the tax expense. Now, an opportunity has developed for Adams and Benson to agree to trade votes to ensure provision of *both* national defense and the new road. The majority vote (Adams and Benson) in our three-person society will result in a positive vote for both national defense and the road. Without the logrolling, each would have been rejected. This logrolling will add to society's well-being if, as was true for national defense, the road creates a positive overall net benefit.

Logrolling need not increase economic efficiency. We could easily construct a scenario in which both national defense and the road individually cost more than the total benefits they each provide, and yet both would be provided because of vote trading. All that is necessary for the road and national defense to be provided is that Adams and Benson each secure net gains from their favored public good.

In other words, the tax cost imposed on Conrad by the expenditures for national defense and the road could exceed Conrad's benefits so much that it swamped the combined net benefit received by Adams and Benson from the public goods. Under conditions of majority voting and logrolling, government will provide each of the public goods and shift a large net burden to Conrad. This scenario is familiar to political scientists who call this practice "pork-barrel politics" (getting public goods for constituents from the public barrel).

Our conclusion is that logrolling can either increase or diminish economic efficiency depending on the circumstances.

The Paradox of Voting

Another difficulty with majority voting is called the **paradox of voting,** *which is a situation where society may not be able to rank its preferences consistently through majority voting.*

Preferences Consider Table 19-1 where we again assume a community consisting of just three voters: Adams, Benson, and Conrad. Suppose the community has three alternative public goods from which to choose: national defense, a road, and a weather warning system. We would expect each member of the community to arrange the order of the three alternatives according to her or his preferences and then select the preferred option. This implies that each voter will state that he or she prefers national defense to a road, and a road to a weather warning system, or whatever. We can then attempt to determine the collective preference scale of the community using a majority voting procedure. Specifically, a vote can be held between any two of the public goods and the winner of the contest matched against the third public good.

The three goods and the assumed individual preferences of the three voters are listed in the top portion of Table 19-1. In the lower part of the table, outcomes of various elections are listed. The upper portion indicates that Adams prefers national defense to the road and the road to the weather warning system. This also implies that Adams prefers national defense to the weather warning system. Benson values the road more than the weather warning system and the warning system more than national defense. Finally, Conrad's first choice is the weather warning system, second choice is national defense, and third choice is the road.

TABLE 19-1 Paradox of voting

	Preferences		
Public good	*Adams*	*Benson*	*Conrad*
National defense	**1st choice**	**3d choice**	**2d choice**
Road	**2d choice**	**1st choice**	**3d choice**
Weather warning system	**3d choice**	**2d choice**	**1st choice**

Election	*Voting outcomes winner*
(1) National defense vs. road	**National defense (preferred by Adams and Conrad)**
(2) Road vs. weather warning system	**Road (preferred by Adams and Benson)**
(3) National defense vs. weather warning system	**Weather warning system (preferred by Benson and Conrad)**

Voting Outcomes Consider the outcomes of three hypothetical elections decided through majority vote. First, let's match national defense against the road in an election. In Table 19-1 national defense will win this contest because a majority of voters, Adams and Conrad, prefer national defense to a road. This outcome is reported in row (1) of the lower part of the table, where election outcomes are summarized. Next we hold an election to see whether this community wants a road or a weather warning system. A majority of voters, Adams and Benson, prefer the road to the weather warning system, as shown in row (2).

We have determined that the majority in this community prefer national defense to a road *and* prefer a road to a weather warning system. It therefore seems logical to conclude that the community prefers national defense to a weather warning system. But it does not!

To demonstrate this point, consider a direct election between national defense and the weather warning system. In row (3) a majority of voters, Benson and Conrad, prefer the weather warning system to national defense. As indicated in Table 19-1, majority voting falsely implies that this community is irrational: it seems to prefer national defense to a road *and* a road to a weather warning system, but would rather have a weather warning system than national defense.

The problem is not one of irrational preferences, but rather one of a flawed procedure for determining those preferences. Majority voting can yield opposing outcomes depending on how the vote on public expenditures or other public issues is ordered. Majority voting thus fails under some circumstances to make *consistent* choices that reflect the community's underlying preferences. As a consequence, government might find it difficult to provide the "correct" public goods by acting in accordance with majority voting.

Median-Voter Model

One final aspect of majority voting deserves comment because of the insights it reveals into real-world phenomena. The **median-voter model** suggests that *under majority rule the median voter will in a sense determine the outcomes of elections.* The median voter is the person holding the middle position on an issue: One-half of the other voters have stronger preferences for an expenditure on a public good, amount of taxation, or the degree of government regulation, and the remaining one-half have weaker—or negative—preferences.

Example To illustrate this principle again suppose a society composed of Adams, Benson, and Conrad. Now assume that agreement has been reached among the three that as a society they need a weather warning system. Each independently is to submit a total dollar amount which he or she thinks should be spent on the warning system, given the fact that each will be taxed one-third of that amount. An election then will determine the actual size of the system. Because each person can be expected to vote for his or her own proposal, no majority will occur if all the proposals are placed on the ballot at the same time. Thus, the group decides they will first vote between two of the proposals and then match the winner of that vote against the remaining proposal.

The three proposals are as follows: Adams desires a $400 system; Benson wants an $800 system; Conrad opts for a $300 system. Which proposal will win? The median-voter model suggests it will be the $400 proposal submitted by the median voter, Adams. One-half of the other voters favors a more costly system; one-half favors a less costly system. To understand why the $400 system will be the outcome we need to conduct two elections.

First, suppose that the $400 proposal is matched against the $800 proposal. Adams naturally will vote for her $400 proposal, but how will Benson and Conrad vote? Conrad—who proposed a $300 expenditure for the warning system—will vote for the $400 proposal rather than the one for $800. Adams' $400 proposal is selected by a 2-to-1 majority vote. Next, we match the $400 proposal against the $300 proposal. Again the $400 proposal is victorious, because it gets a vote from Adams and one from Benson, who proposed the $800 expenditure and for that reason clearly prefers a $400 expenditure to a $300 one. Adams—the median voter in this case—in a sense is the person who has decided the proper level of expenditure on a weather warning system for this society.

Real-World Applicability Although this is purposely a simple illustration, the idea behind it explains much. We *do* note a tendency for public choices to match up closely with the median view. In fact, we often observe political candidates taking one set of positions to win the nomination of their political parties; that is, they appeal to the median voter *within the party* to get the nomination. They then shift their views more closely to the political center when they square off against their opponent from the opposite political party. In effect, they redirect their appeal toward the median voter *within the total population.* They also try to label their opponents as being too liberal, or too conservative, and out of touch with "mainstream America." Additionally, they conduct polls and adjust their positions on issues accordingly.

Implications Two interesting implications of the median voter model merit comment.

1 Many people will be dissatisfied by the extent of government involvement in the economy. The size of government will to a large extent be determined by the median preference, leaving many people desiring a much larger, or a much smaller, public sector. In the marketplace you can buy zero zucchinis, 2 zucchinis, or 200 zucchinis, depending on how much you enjoy zucchinis. In the public sector you get the number of Stealth bombers and interstate highways that the median voter prefers.

2 A related point is that some people may "vote with their feet" by moving into political jurisdictions where the median voter's preferences are closer to their own. Someone may move from the city to a suburb where the level of government services and therefore taxes are lower. Or they may move into an area known for its excellent, but expensive, school system. Demographic changes within political jurisdictions also occur which change the median preference.

For these reasons, and because our personal preferences for government activity are not static, the median preference within political jurisdictions can and does shift over time. Additionally, information about people's preferences is imperfect, leaving much room for politicians to mistake the true median position.

PUBLIC SECTOR FAILURE

Our discussion of the problem of achieving the optimal output of public goods and the problems in voting for that output makes it clear that the economic functions of government are not always performed effectively and efficiently. Just because the economic results of the market are not entirely satisfactory, it does not necessarily follow that the political process will yield superior results. We might agree that government has a legitimate role in dealing with instances of market failure; that is, government should make adjustments for spillover costs and benefits, provide public goods and services, provide information, and so forth. We might also accept benefit-cost analysis as an important guide to economically efficient decision making in the public sector. But a more fundamental question remains: Are there inherent problems or shortcomings within the public sector which constrain governmental decision making as a mechanism for promoting economic efficiency? In fact, casual reflection suggests that there may be significant divergence between "sound economics" and "good politics." The former calls for the public sector to pursue various programs so long as marginal benefits exceed marginal costs. Good politics, however, suggests that politicians support those programs and policies which will maximize their chance of getting elected and retained in office.

Let's now briefly consider some reasons given by public choice theorists for **public sector failure,** that is, some reasons why the public sector may function inefficiently in an economic sense.

Special Interests and "Rent Seeking"

Ideally, public decisions promote the general welfare or, at least, the interests of the vast majority of the citizenry. But in fact, government often promotes the goals of small special-interest groups to the detriment of the public at large.

Special-Interest Effect Efficient public decision making is often impaired by a **special-interest effect.** A special-interest issue is a program or policy from which a small number of people individually will receive *large* gains at the expense of a vastly larger number of persons who individually suffers *small* losses.

The small group of potential beneficiaries will be well informed and highly vocal on this issue, pressing politicians for approval. The large numbers who face very small losses will generally be uninformed and indifferent on this issue; after all, they have little at stake. Crudely put, politicians feel they will clearly lose the support of the small special-interest group which supports the program if they vote against it. But politicians will *not* lose the support of the large group of uninformed voters who will evaluate them on other issues in which these voters have a stronger interest. Furthermore, the politicians' inclination to support special-interest legislation is enhanced by the fact that such groups are often more than willing to help finance the campaigns of "right-minded" politicians. The result is that the politician will support the special-interest program, even though it may not be economically desirable from a social point of view.

Rent-Seeking Behavior This pursuit through government of a transfer of wealth at someone else's or society's expense is called **rent-seeking behavior.** As used here the term "rent" means any payment to a resource supplier, business, or other organization above that which would accrue under competitive market conditions. Corporations, trade associations, labor unions, and professional organizations employ a vast amount of resources in their attempt to secure "rent" directly or indirectly dispensed by government. Government provides this "rent" through legislation and policies which increase payments to some groups, leaving others or society at large less well off.

Examples of special-interest or rent-seeking groups realizing legislation and policies unjustified on the basis of efficiency or equity are manifold: tariffs on foreign products which limit competition and raise prices to consumers; tax loopholes which benefit only the wealthy; public work projects which cost more than the benefits they yield; occupational licensing which goes beyond that needed to protect customers; large subsidies to farmers by taxpayers; and so forth.

Clear Benefits, Hidden Costs

The contention is also made that vote-seeking politicians will not *objectively* weigh all costs and benefits of various programs, as economic rationality demands, in deciding which to support and which to reject. Because political officeholders must seek voter support every few years, politicians will favor programs with immediate and clear-cut benefits, on the one hand, and vague, difficult-to-identify, or deferred costs, on the other. Conversely, politicians will look askance at programs which embody immediate and easily identifiable costs along with future benefits which are diffuse and vague.

The point here is that such biases in the area of public choice can lead politicians to reject economically justifiable programs and to accept programs which are economically irrational. Example: A proposal to construct and expand mass-transit systems in large metropolitan areas may be economically rational on the basis of objective benefit-cost analysis (Table 18-2). But if (1) the program is to be financed by immediate increases in highly visible income or sales taxes *and* (2) benefits will accrue only a decade hence when the project is completed, the vote-seeking politician may decide to oppose the program.

Assume, on the other hand, that a proposed program of Federal aid to municipal police forces is *not* justifiable on the basis of objective benefit-cost analysis. But if costs are concealed and deferred through deficit financing, the program's modest benefits may loom so large that it gains political approval.

Limited Choice

Public choice theorists also argue that the nature of the political process is such that citizens are forced to be less selective in the choice of public goods and services than they are in the choice of private goods and services.

In the market sector, the citizen *as consumer* can reflect personal preferences very precisely by buying certain goods and forgoing others. However, in the public sector the citizen *as voter* is confronted with two or more candidates for office, each of whom represents different "bundles" of programs (public goods and services). In no case is the bundle of public goods represented by any particular candidate likely to fit precisely the wants of the particular voter. For example, voter Smith's favored candidate for office may endorse national health insurance, the development of nuclear energy, subsidies to tobacco farmers, and tariffs on imported automobiles. Citizen Smith votes for this candidate because the bundle of programs she endorses comes closest to matching Smith's preferences, even though Smith may oppose tobacco subsidies and tariffs on foreign cars.

The voter, in short, must take the bad with the good; in the public sector, one is forced to "buy" goods and services one does not want. It is as if, in going to a clothing store, you were forced to buy an unwanted pair of slacks to get a wanted pair of shoes. This is clearly a situation where resources are *not* being allocated efficiently to best satisfy consumer wants. In this sense, the provision of public goods and services is inherently inefficient.

Bureaucracy and Inefficiency

Finally, it is contended that private businesses are innately more efficient than public agencies. The reason for this is *not* that lazy and incompetent workers somehow end up in the public sector, while the ambitious and capable gravitate to the private sector. Rather, it is held that the market system creates incentives and pressures for internal efficiency which are absent in the public sector. The managers of private enterprises have a strong personal incentive—increased profits—to be efficient in their operation. Whether a private firm is in a competitive or monopolistic environment, lower costs through efficient management contribute to enlarged profits. There is no tangible personal gain—a counterpart to profits—for the government bureau chief who achieves efficiency within his or her domain.

In brief, there is simply less incentive to be cost-conscious in the public sector. Indeed, in a larger sense the market system imposes an explicit test of performance on private firms—the test of profits and losses. An efficient firm is profitable and therefore successful; it survives, prospers, and grows. An inefficient enterprise is unprofitable and unsuccessful; it declines and in time goes bankrupt and ceases to exist. But there is no similar, clear-cut test by which one can assess efficiency or inefficiency of public agencies. How can one determine whether TVA, a state university, a local fire department, the Department of Agriculture, or the Bureau of Indian Affairs is operating efficiently?

Cynics argue that, in fact, a public agency which uses its resources inefficiently may be in line for a budget increase! In the private sector, inefficiency and monetary losses lead to abandonment of certain activities—the discontinuing of certain products and services. But government, it is contended, is loath to abandon activities in which it has failed. Some suggest that the typical response of government to failure of a program is to double its budget and staff. This means that public sector inefficiency may be sustained on a larger scale.

Furthermore, returning to our earlier comments on special-interest and rent-seeking groups, it has been pointed out that public programs spawn new constituencies of bureaucrats and beneficiaries whose political clout causes programs to be sustained or expanded after they have fulfilled their goals or, alternatively, even if they have failed miserably in their mission. Relevant bureaucrats, school administrators, and teachers may band together to become a highly effective special-interest group for sustaining inefficient programs of Federal aid to education or for causing these programs to be expanded beyond the point at which marginal benefits equal marginal costs.

Some specific suggestions have been offered recently to deal with the problems of bureaucratic inefficiency. Benefit-cost analysis, of course, is one suggested approach. It has also been proposed that all legislation establishing new programs contain well-defined performance standards so the public can better judge efficiency. Further, the suggestion has been made that expiration dates—so-called "sunset laws"—be written into all new programs, forcing a thorough periodic evaluation which might indicate the need for program abandonment.

QUICK REVIEW 19-1

- ***Majority voting can produce voting outcomes which are inefficient; projects having greater total benefits than total costs can be defeated and projects having greater total costs than total benefits can be approved.***
- ***The paradox of voting occurs where voting by majority rule fails to provide a consistent ranking of society's preferences for public goods and services.***
- ***The median-voter model suggests that under majority rule the voter having the middle (median) preference will determine the outcome of an election.***
- ***Public sector failure allegedly occurs because of rent-seeking by special-interest groups, short-sighted political behavior, limited citizen choices, and bureaucratic inefficiency.***

Imperfect Institutions

One might argue that these criticisms of public sector efficiency are overdrawn and too cynical. Perhaps so. On the other hand, they are sufficiently persuasive to shake one's faith in a simplistic concept of a benevolent government responding with precision and efficiency to the wants of its citizenry. The market system of the private sector is by no means perfectly efficient; indeed, government's economic functions are attempts to correct the market system's shortcomings. But the public sector may also be subject to important deficiencies in fulfilling its economic functions. "The relevant comparison is not between perfect markets and imperfect governments, nor between faulty markets and all-knowing, rational, benevolent governments, but between inevitably imperfect institutions."[1]

One of the important implications of the fact that the market system and public agencies are both imperfect institutions is that, in practice, it can be exceedingly difficult to determine whether some particular activity can be performed with greater success in the private or the public sector. It is easy to reach agreement on opposite extremes: National defense must lie in the public sector, whereas wheat production can best be accomplished in the private sector. But what about health insurance? The provision of parks and recreation areas? Fire protection? Garbage collection? Housing? Education? It is very hard to assess each type of good or service and to say unequivocally that its provision should be assigned to either the public or the private sector. Evidence that this is so is reflected in the fact that all the goods and services mentioned above are provided in part by both private enterprises and public agencies.

APPORTIONING THE TAX BURDEN

Our attention now turns from the difficulties of making collective decisions on the types and amounts of public goods to the difficulties in deciding how those goods should be financed.

The characteristics of public goods and services make it difficult to measure precisely the manner in which their benefits are apportioned among individuals and institutions. It is virtually impossible to determine accurately the amount by which John Doe benefits from military installations, a network of highways, a public school system, the national weather bureau, and local police and fire protection.

The situation is a bit different on the taxation side of the picture. Studies reveal with somewhat greater clarity the manner in which the overall tax burden is

[1]Otto Eckstein, *Public Finance,* 3d ed. (Englewood Cliffs, N.J.: Prentice-Hall, Inc., 1973), p. 17.

apportioned. Needless to say, this is a question which affects each of us in a vital way. Although the average citizen is concerned with the overall level of taxes, chances are he or she is even more interested in exactly how the tax burden is allocated among individual taxpayers.

Benefits Received versus Ability to Pay

There are two basic philosophies on how the economy's tax burden should be apportioned.

Benefits-Received Principle The **benefits-received principle** of taxation asserts that households and businesses should purchase the goods and services of government in basically the same manner in which other commodities are bought. It is reasoned that those who benefit most from government-supplied goods or services should pay the taxes necessary for their financing. A few public goods are financed essentially on the basis of the benefits principle. For example, gasoline taxes are typically earmarked for the financing of highway construction and repairs. Those who benefit from good roads pay the cost of those roads. Difficulties immediately arise, however, when an accurate and widespread application of the benefits principle is considered:

1 How does government go about determining the benefits which individual households and businesses receive from national defense, education, and police and fire protection? Recall that public goods entail widespread spillover benefits and that the exclusion principle is inapplicable. Even in the seemingly tangible case of highway finance we find it difficult to measure benefits. Individual car owners benefit in different degrees from the existence of good roads. And those who do not own cars also benefit. Businesses would certainly benefit greatly from any widening of their markets which good roads will encourage.

2 Government efforts to redistribute income would be self-defeating if financed on the basis of the benefits principle. It would be absurd and self-defeating to ask poor families to pay the taxes needed to finance their welfare payments! It would be equally ridiculous to think of taxing only unemployed workers to finance the unemployment compensation payments which they receive.

Ability-to-Pay Principle The **ability-to-pay principle** of taxation stands in sharp contrast to the benefits principle. Ability-to-pay taxation rests on the idea that the tax burden should be geared directly to one's income and wealth. As the ability-to-pay principle has come to be applied in the United States, it contends that individuals and businesses with larger incomes should pay more taxes—both absolutely and relatively—than those with more modest incomes.

What is the rationale of ability-to-pay taxation? Proponents argue that each additional dollar of income received by a household will yield smaller and smaller increments of satisfaction or marginal utility. It is held that, because consumers act rationally, the first dollars of income received in any period of time will be spent on high-urgency goods which yield the greatest marginal utility. Successive dollars of income will go for less urgently needed goods and finally for trivial goods and services. This means that a dollar taken through taxes from a poor person who has few dollars is a greater utility sacrifice than is a dollar taken by taxes from the rich person who has many dollars. In order to balance the sacrifices which taxes impose on income receivers, it is contended that taxes should be apportioned according to the amount of income one receives.

This is appealing, but problems of application exist here too. In particular, although we might agree that the household earning $100,000 per year has a greater ability to pay taxes than the household receiving a paltry $10,000, exactly *how much more* ability to pay does the first family have compared with the second? Should the rich person simply pay the *same percentage* of his or her larger income—and hence a larger absolute amount—as taxes? Or should the rich be made to pay a *larger fraction* of this income as taxes?

The problem is there is no scientific way of measuring one's ability to pay taxes. Thus, in practice, the answer hinges on guesswork, the tax views of the political party in power, expediency, and how urgently the government needs revenue.

Progressive, Proportional, and Regressive Taxes

Any discussion of the ability-to-pay and the benefits-received principles of taxation leads ultimately to the question of tax rates and the manner in which tax rates change as one's income increases.

Definitions Taxes are classified as being progressive, proportional, or regressive. These designations focus on the relationship between tax rates and *income* simply because all taxes—regardless of whether they are levied on income or on a product or building or parcel of land—are ultimately paid out of someone's income.

1 A tax is **progressive** if its average rate *increases* as income increases. Such a tax claims not only a larger absolute amount, but also a larger fraction or percentage of income as income increases.

2 A **regressive** tax is one whose average rate *declines* as income increases. Such a tax takes a smaller and smaller proportion of income as income increases. A regressive tax may or may not take a larger absolute amount of income as income expands.

3 A tax is **proportional** when its average rate *remains the same,* regardless of the size of income.

We can illustrate these ideas in terms of the personal income tax. Suppose tax rates are such that a household pays 10 percent of its income in taxes, regardless of the size of its income. This would clearly be a proportional income tax.

Now suppose the rate structure is such that the household with an annual taxable income of less than $10,000 pays 5 percent in income taxes, the household realizing an income of $10,000 to $20,000 pays 10 percent, $20,000 to $30,000 pays 15 percent, and so forth. This, as we have already explained, would be a *progressive* income tax.

The final case is where the rates decline as taxable income rises: You pay 15 percent if you earn less than $10,000; 10 percent if you earn $10,000 to $20,000; 5 percent if you earn $20,000 to $30,000; and so forth. This is a *regressive* income tax. In general, progressive taxes are those which bear down most heavily on the rich; regressive taxes are those which hit the poor hardest.

Applications What can we say about the progressivity, proportionality, or regressivity of the major kinds of taxes used in the United States?

1 Personal Income Tax We noted in Chapter 6 that the Federal *personal income tax* is mildly progressive with marginal tax rates ranging from 15 to 31 percent. The deductibility of interest on home mortgages and property taxes, along with the exemption of interest income from state and local bonds, partly erodes the progressivity of the tax.

2 Sales Taxes At first glance a *general sales tax* with, say, a 3 percent rate would seem to be proportional. But in fact it is regressive with respect to income. A larger portion of a poor person's income is exposed to the tax than is the case with a rich person; the latter avoids the tax on the part of income which is saved, whereas the former is unable to save. Example: "Poor" Smith has an income of $15,000 and spends it all. "Rich" Jones has an income of $300,000 but spends only $200,000 of it. Assuming a 3 percent sales tax applies to the expenditures of each individual, we find Smith will pay $450 (3 percent of $15,000) in sales taxes, and Jones will pay $6000 (3 percent of $200,000). Note that whereas *all* of Smith's $15,000 income is subject to the sales tax, only two-thirds of Jones' $300,000 income is taxed. Thus, while Smith pays $450, or 3 percent, of a $15,000 income as sales taxes, Jones pays $6000, or just 2 percent, of a $300,000 income. We conclude that the general sales tax is regressive.

3 Corporate Income Tax The Federal *corporate income tax* is essentially a flat-rate proportional tax with a 34 percent tax rate. But this assumes that corporation owners (shareholders) bear the tax. Some tax experts argue that at least a part of the tax is passed through to consumers in the form of higher product prices. To the extent that this occurs, the tax is regressive like a sales tax.

4 Payroll Taxes Payroll taxes are regressive because they apply to only a fixed absolute amount of one's income. For example, in 1992, payroll tax rates were 7.65 percent, but this figure applies only to the first $55,500 of one's wage income. Thus a person earning exactly $55,500 would pay $4245.75, or 7.65 percent of his or her wage income, while someone with twice that income, or $111,000, would also pay $4245.75—only 3.825 percent of his or her wage income.

Note, too, that this regressivity is enhanced because the payroll tax excludes nonwage income. If our individual with the $111,000 wage income also received $59,000 in nonwage (dividend, interest, rent) income, then the payroll tax would amount to only 2.50 percent (=$4245.75 ÷ $170,000) of the total income.

5 Property Taxes Most economists feel that *property taxes* on buildings are regressive for essentially the same reasons as are sales taxes. First, property owners add the tax to the rents which tenants are charged. Second, property taxes, as a percentage of income, are higher for poor families than for rich families because the poor must spend a larger proportion of their incomes for housing.[2] The alleged regressivity of the property tax may be reinforced by the fact that property-tax rates are not likely to be uniform as between various political subdivisions. For example, if property values decline in, say, a decaying central-city area, property-tax rates must be increased in the city to bring in a given amount of revenue. But in a wealthy suburb, where the market value of housing is rising, a given amount of tax revenue can be maintained with lower property-tax rates.

TAX INCIDENCE AND EFFICIENCY LOSS

Determining whether a particular tax is progressive, proportional, or regressive is complicated by the fact that taxes do not always stick where they are levied. It is therefore necessary to locate as best we can the final resting place of a tax, or, **tax incidence.** The tools of elasticity of supply and demand help in this endeavor. To demonstrate, we focus on a hypothetical excise tax levied on wine producers. Do producers pay this tax, or do they shift it forward to wine consumers? This analysis will then provide a logical bridge to a discussion of other aspects of the economic burden of a tax.

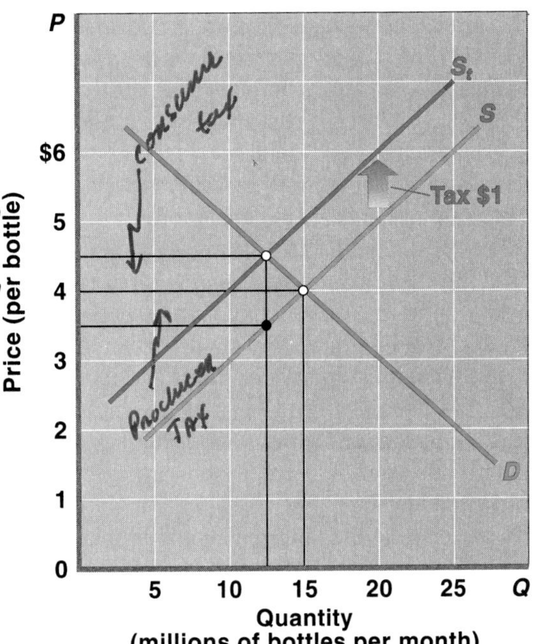

FIGURE 19-2 The incidence of an excise tax

The imposition of an excise tax of a specified amount, say, $1 per unit, shifts the supply curve upward by the amount of the tax. This results in a higher price ($4.50) to the consumer and a lower after-tax price ($3.50) to the producer. In this particular case the burden of the tax is shared equally by consumers and producers.

Elasticity and Tax Incidence

Suppose that Figure 19-2 shows the market for a certain domestic wine and that the no-tax equilibrium price and quantity are $4 per bottle and 15 million bottles. Now assume that government levies a specific sales or excise tax of $1 per bottle on this wine. What is the incidence of this tax?

Division of Burden Assuming that government imposes the tax on sellers (suppliers), it can be viewed as an addition to the supply price of the product. While sellers were willing to offer, for example, 5 million bottles of untaxed wine at $2 per bottle, they must now receive $3 per bottle—$2 plus the $1 tax—to offer the same 5 million bottles. Sellers must now get $1 more for each quantity supplied to receive the same per unit price they were getting before the tax. The tax thus shifts the supply curve upward as shown in Figure 19-2, where *S* is the "no-tax" supply curve and S_t is the "after-tax" supply curve.

Careful comparison of after-tax supply and demand with the pretax equilibrium reveals that the new equilibrium price is $4.50 per bottle, compared with the before-tax price of $4.00. In this case, one-half of the tax is paid by consumers in the form of a higher price and the other half by producers in the form of a lower after-tax price. Consumers pay 50 cents more per bottle and, after remitting the $1 tax per unit to government, producers receive $3.50, or 50 cents less than the $4.00 before-tax price. In this instance, consumers and producers share the burden of the tax equally; producers shift half the tax forward to consumers in the form of a higher price and bear the other half themselves.

Elasticities If the elasticities of demand and supply were different from those shown in Figure 19-2, the incidence of tax would also be different. Two generalizations are relevant.

[2] Controversy arises in part because empirical research, which compares the value of housing to lifetime (rather than a single year's) income, suggests that this ratio is approximately the same for all income groups.

1 *Given supply, the more inelastic the demand for the product, the larger the portion of the tax shifted forward to consumers.* The easiest way to verify this is to sketch graphically the extreme cases where demand is perfectly elastic and perfectly inelastic. In the first case the incidence of the tax is entirely on sellers; in the second, the tax is shifted entirely to consumers.

Figure 19-3 contrasts the more likely cases where demand might be relatively elastic (D_e) or relatively inelastic (D_i) in the relevant price range. In the elastic demand case of Figure 19-3a, a small portion of the tax (PP_e) is shifted forward to consumers and most of the tax (PP_a) is borne by producers. In the inelastic demand case of Figure 19-3b, most of the tax (PP_i) is shifted to consumers and only a small amount (PP_b) is paid by producers.

Note, too, that the decline in equilibrium quantity is smaller, the more inelastic the demand. This recalls one of our previous applications of the elasticity concept: Revenue-seeking legislatures place heavy excise taxes on liquor, cigarettes, automobile tires, and other products whose demand is inelastic.

2 *Given demand, the more inelastic the supply, the larger the portion of the tax borne by producers.* While the demand curves are identical, the supply curve is elastic in Figure 19-4a and inelastic in Figure 19-4b. For the elastic supply curve most of the tax (PP_e) is shifted forward to consumers and only a small portion (PP_a) is borne by producers or sellers. But where supply is inelastic, the reverse is true. The major portion of the tax (PP_b) falls on sellers and a relatively small amount (PP_i) is shifted to buyers. Quantity also declines less with an inelastic supply than it does with an elastic supply.

Gold is an example of a product for which supply is inelastic and therefore for which the burden of an excise tax would fall mainly on producers. On the other hand, because the supply of baseballs is elastic, much of an excise tax on this product would get passed forward to consumers.

Efficiency Loss of a Tax

We have just observed that an excise tax on producers in a market characterized by typical supply and demand curves is borne partly by producers and partly by consumers. Additional attention to the burden of an excise tax is now warranted. Figure 19-5 is identical to Figure 19-2 but contains additional detail important to our discussion.

Tax Revenue The $1 excise tax on wine increases the market price from $4 to $4.50 per bottle and reduces the equilibrium quantity from 15 to 12.5 million bottles. Government's tax revenue is $12.5 million (=$1 × 12.5 million bottles), an amount shown as the rectangle labeled *efac* in Figure 19-5. In this case, the elasticities of supply and demand are such that consumers and producers each pay one-half of this total

FIGURE 19-3 Demand elasticity and the incidence of an excise tax

In (a) we find that, if demand is elastic in the relevant price range, price will rise modestly (*P* to P_e) when an excise tax is levied. Hence, the producer bears most of the tax burden. But if demand is inelastic as in (b), the price to the buyer will increase substantially (*P* to P_i) and most of the tax is shifted to consumers.

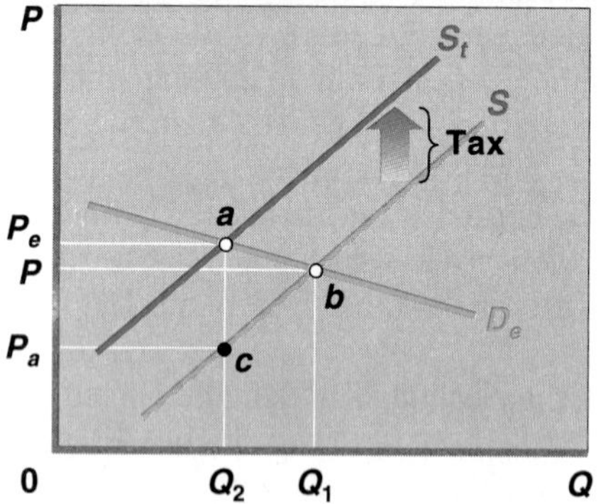

(a) Tax incidence and elastic demand

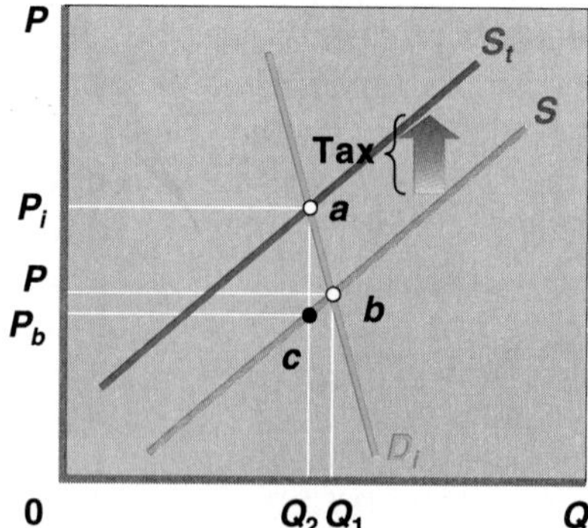

(b) Tax incidence and inelastic demand

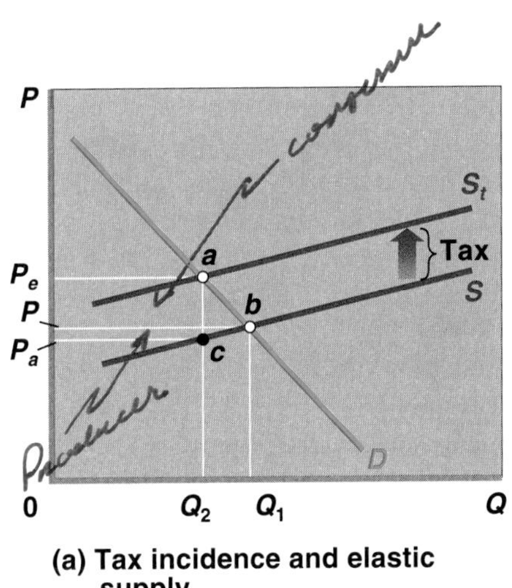

(a) Tax incidence and elastic supply

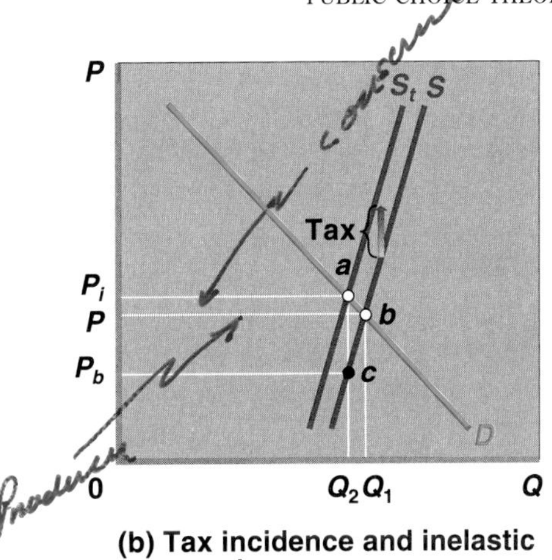

(b) Tax incidence and inelastic supply

FIGURE 19-4 Supply elasticity and the incidence of an excise tax

Part (a) indicates that with an elastic supply an excise tax results in a large price increase (P to P_e) and the tax is therefore paid largely by consumers. But if supply is inelastic as in (b), the price rise will be small (P to P_i) and sellers will have to bear most of the tax.

amount, or $6.25 million apiece (=$.50 × 12.5 million bottles). Government, of course, uses this $12.5 million of tax revenue to provide public goods and services of value. Thus there is no loss of well-being to society as a whole from this transfer from consumers and producers to government.

FIGURE 19-5 Efficiency loss of a tax

The levy of a $1 excise tax per bottle of wine increases the price per bottle to $4.50 and reduces the equilibrium quantity by 2.5 million bottles. Government's tax revenue is $12.5 million (area *efac*). The efficiency loss of the tax is the amount shown as triangle *abc*.

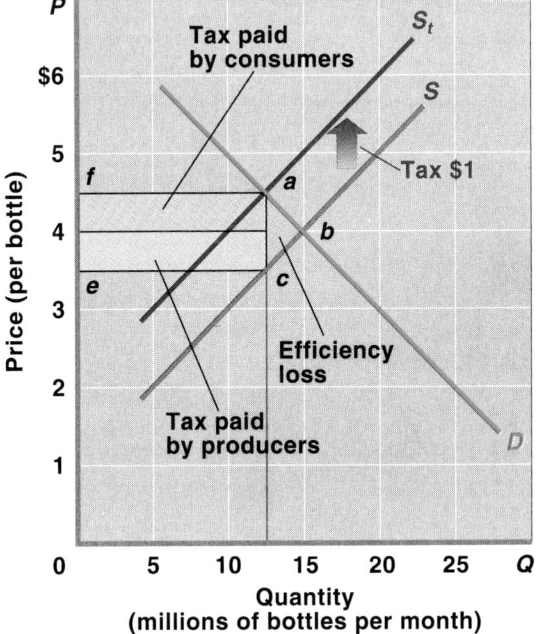

Efficiency Loss The $1 tax on wine requires consumers and producers to pay $12.5 million of taxes, but also *reduces the equilibrium amount of wine produced and consumed by 2.5 million bottles.* The fact that 2.5 million more bottles of wine were demanded and supplied prior to the tax means they provided benefits in *excess* of their costs of production. We can see this from the following simple analysis.

The *ab* segment of demand curve *D* in Figure 19-5 indicates the willingness to pay—the marginal benefit—associated with each of these 2.5 million bottles consumed prior to the tax. The *cb* segment of supply curve *S*, on the other hand, reflects the marginal cost of each of the bottles of wine. For all but the very last one of these 2.5 million bottles, the marginal benefit (shown by *ab*) exceeds the marginal cost (shown by *cb*). The reduction of well-being because these 2.5 million bottles are not produced is indicated by the triangle *abc*. This triangle shows the **efficiency loss of the tax.** *This loss is the sacrifice of net benefit accruing to society because consumption and production of the taxed product are reduced below their allocatively efficient levels.*

Role of Elasticities Most taxes create some degree of efficiency loss, but how much depends crucially on supply and demand elasticities. Glancing back to Figure 19-3, we observe that the efficiency loss triangle *abc* is greater in Figure 19-3a, where demand is relatively elastic, than in Figure 19-3b, where demand is relatively inelastic. Similarly, the area *abc* is greater in Figure 19-4a than in Figure 19-4b, indicating a larger efficiency loss where supply is more elastic.

The major principle which our analysis establishes is that the amount of efficiency loss of an excise tax or sales tax varies from market to market depending on the elasticities of supply and demand. *Other things being equal, the greater the elasticities of supply and demand, the greater the efficiency loss of a particular tax.* Two taxes which yield equal revenues do not necessarily entail equal tax burdens for society. This fact complicates government's job of determining the best way to collect its needed tax revenues. Government must consider the efficiency losses of taxes in designing an optimal tax system.

Qualifications We must add an important qualification to our analysis. Other tax goals in many instances may be more important than the goal of minimizing efficiency losses from taxes. Two examples will demonstrate this fact.

1 Government may wish to impose progressive taxes as a way to redistribute income. The 10 percent excise tax the Federal government placed on selected luxuries in 1990 is a case in point. Because the demand for luxuries is elastic, efficiency losses from this tax may be substantial. However, Congress apparently concluded that the benefits from the redistribution effects of this tax would exceed these efficiency losses.

2 Government may have intended the $1 tax on wine in Figure 19-5 to reduce consumption of wine by 2.5 million bottles. It may have concluded that consumption of alcoholic beverages produces certain negative externalities. Therefore, it might have levied this tax to adjust the market supply curve for these costs to reduce the amount of resources allocated to wine (Figure 6-1b).

Probable Incidence of U.S. Taxes

Now that we understand the concepts of tax shifting and incidence, let's look at the probable incidence of each of the various major sources of tax revenue in the United States.

Personal Income Tax The incidence of the personal income tax generally falls on the individual because there is little chance for shifting it. But there might be exceptions to this. Individuals and groups who can effectively control the price of their labor services may be able to shift a part of the tax. For example, doctors, dentists, lawyers, and other professional people who can readily increase their fees may do so because of the tax. Unions might regard personal income taxes as part of the cost of living and, as a result, bargain for higher wages. If they are successful, they may shift a portion of the tax from workers to employers who, by then increasing prices, shift the wage increase to the public. Generally, however, most experts conclude that the individual on whom the tax is initially levied bears the burden of the personal income tax. The same ordinarily holds true of payroll and inheritance taxes.

Corporate Income Tax The incidence of the corporate income tax is much less certain. The traditional view has it that a firm which is currently charging the profit-maximizing price and producing the profit-maximizing output will have no reason to change price or output when a corporate income tax is imposed. That price and output combination which yields the greatest profit before the tax will still be the most profitable after government takes a fixed percentage of the firm's profits in the form of income taxes. According to this view, the company's stockholders (owners) must bear the incidence of the tax in the form of lower dividends or a smaller amount of retained earnings.

On the other hand, some economists argue that the corporate income tax is shifted in part to consumers through higher prices and to resource suppliers through lower prices. In modern industry, where a small number of firms may control a market, producers may not be in the profit-maximizing position initially. By fully exploiting their market position currently, monopolistic firms might elicit adverse public opinion and governmental censure. Thus, they may await such events as increases in tax rates or wage increases by unions to provide an "excuse" or rationale for price increases with less fear of public criticism. When this actually occurs, a portion of the corporate income tax may be shifted to consumers through higher prices.

Both positions are plausible. Indeed, the incidence of the corporate income tax may well be shared by stockholders and the firm's customers and resource suppliers.

Sales and Excise Taxes Sales and excise taxes are the "hidden taxes" of our economy. They are hidden because such taxes are often partly or largely shifted by sellers to consumers through higher product prices. There may be some difference in the shiftability of sales taxes and excises, however. Because a sales tax covers a much wider range of products than an excise, there is little chance for consumers to resist the price boosts which sales taxes entail by reallocating their expenditures to untaxed, lower-priced products.

Excises, however, fall on a relatively short, select list of goods. Therefore, the possibility of consumers turning to substitute goods and services is greater. For example, an excise tax on theater tickets which does not apply to other types of entertainment might be difficult to pass on to consumers via price increases. Why? The answer is provided in Figure 19-3a, where demand is elastic. Price boosts on theater tickets might result in considerable substituting of alternative types of entertainment by consumers. The higher price will reduce sales so much that a seller will be better off to bear all, or a large portion of, the excise rather than the sharp decline in sales.

With other excises, however, modest price increases have smaller effects on sales. Excises on gasoline, cigarettes, and alcoholic beverages are examples. Here there are few good substitute products to which consumers can turn as prices rise. For these commodities, the seller is in a better position to shift the tax (Figure 19-3b).

Property Taxes Many property taxes are borne by the property owner simply because there is no other party to whom they can be shifted. This is typically true in the case of taxes on land, personal property, and owner-occupied residences. For example, even when land is sold, the property tax is not likely to be shifted. The buyer will discount the value of the land to allow for the future taxes which must be paid on it, and this expected taxation will be reflected in the price a buyer is willing to offer for the land.

Taxes on rented and business property are a different story. Taxes on rented property can be, and usually are, shifted wholly or in part from the owner to the tenant by the process of boosting the rent. Business property taxes are treated as a business cost and therefore are taken into account in establishing product price; thus such taxes are ordinarily shifted to the firm's customers.

Table 19-2 summarizes this discussion of the shifting and incidence of taxes.

The American Tax Structure

Is the overall tax structure—Federal, state, and local taxes combined—progressive, proportional, or regressive? This is a difficult question to answer because estimates of the distribution of the total tax burden are quite sensitive to assumptions made regarding tax incidence. To what extent are the various taxes shifted and who bears the ultimate burden? For example, we have already cited the disagreement among the experts as to the incidence of the corporate income tax.

An important study for 1985 suggested that the overall tax structure was only mildly progressive. For example, the poorest tenth of all income receivers paid about 17 percent of their income in taxes, while the richest tenth paid slightly in excess of 26 percent. The progressivity of the personal income and corporate income taxes is largely offset by the regressivity of payroll, sales, and excise taxes. This means that the tax system has only a modest effect on the distribution of income.

More recently, government agencies have examined the impact of recent tax legislation on the distribution of Federal taxes. The Tax Reform Act of 1986 greatly reduced the number of tax brackets and lowered tax rates, on the one hand, but simultaneously broadened the tax base (the amount of taxable income), on the other. Tax legislation in 1990 further adjusted tax rates and allowable deductions. In comparing the 1977 with the 1992 distribution, it was found that the recent tax changes have not greatly altered the progressivity of the Federal tax system. For example, between 1977 and 1992 the tax burden of the poorest

TABLE 19-2 The probable incidence of taxes

Type of tax	*Probable incidence*
Personal income tax	**The household or individual on which it is levied.**
Corporate income tax	**Disagreement. Some economists feel the firm on which it is levied bears the incidence; others conclude the tax is shifted, wholly or in part, to consumers and resource suppliers.**
Sales tax	**Consumers who buy the taxed products.**
Specific excise taxes	**Consumers, producers, or shared by each depending on elasticities of demand and supply.**
Property taxes	**Owners in the case of land and owner-occupied residences; tenants in the case of rented property; consumers in the case of business property.**

20 percent of the population fell slightly from 9.3 to 8.6 percent of their incomes. Meanwhile, the tax burden of the richest 20 percent fell from 27.2 to 26.8 percent over the same period. The burdens of all other income receivers increased only slightly. The slightly enhanced progressivity of the personal income tax, together with the increasing importance of the social security payroll tax, go far to explain the unchanged overall progressivity of the Federal tax system. When the largely regressive tax structures of state and local governments are combined with the Federal data, the overall tax structure is proportional or slightly progressive.

It is significant to note that, while our tax system does *not* substantially alter the distribution of income, our system of transfer payments has a pronounced effect in reducing income inequality. For example, transfers almost quadrupled the incomes of the poorest fifth of the income receivers.

QUICK REVIEW 19-2

- ***The benefits-received principle holds that government should assess taxes on individuals according to the amount of benefits they receive, regardless of their income; the ability-to-pay tax principle holds that people should be taxed according to their income, regardless of the benefits they receive from government.***
- ***As income increases, the average tax rate rises when a tax is progressive, remains the same when a tax is proportional, and falls when a tax is regressive.***
- ***The more inelastic the demand for a product, the more of an excise tax that is borne by consumers; the more inelastic the supply, the larger the portion borne by producers.***
- ***The efficiency loss of a tax is the loss of output for which marginal benefits exceed marginal costs.***
- ***Considering the probable incidences of American taxes (Table 19-2), the American tax structure is deemed to be proportional or slightly progressive.***

TAX ISSUES

While the Tax Reform Act of 1986 embodied perhaps the most sweeping changes in the Federal tax code in the past half-century, there is still considerable pressure for further changes in our tax system. These pressures reflect two quite different objectives.

Taxes and Reindustrialization

Some observers recommend that the entire tax system be recast or restructured to encourage the "reindustrialization" of the American economy. The argument essentially is that in the past two decades the productivity of American workers has stagnated relative to workers in Japan, Germany, and a number of other industrialized nations. A major consequence is that a number of our basic industries—for example, automobiles, steel, and electronics—have fallen prey to foreign competition. In aggregative terms the United States has been incurring massive balance of international trade deficits or, simply stated, our imports have greatly exceeded our exports.

Some economists contend that we must "reindustrialize" our economy by making massive new investments in machinery and equipment to offset our relative economic decline. Retooled with large amounts of modern machinery and equipment, the productivity of American workers will once again increase. But you will recall from Chapter 2's production possibilities curve that with reasonably full employment, more investment implies offsetting cuts in consumption. Some feel that a major structural overhaul of our present tax system can bring about the required increases in investment and reductions in consumption.

One proposal is that the corporate income tax should be lowered or eliminated. This allegedly would greatly enhance the expected profitability of investment and stimulate spending on new plants and equipment. But if the economy is at or close to full employment, how can the required resources be released from the production of consumer goods? A widely discussed means for achieving this is to levy a **value-added tax (VAT)** on consumer goods. VAT is much like a retail sales tax, except that the tax applies only to the difference between the value of a firm's sales and the value of its purchases from other firms. In essence, VAT would amount to a national sales tax on consumer goods. A number of European countries—for example, Great Britain and Sweden—currently use VAT as a major source of revenue.

For present purposes the point to note is that VAT penalizes consumption. One can avoid paying VAT by saving rather than consuming. And we know that saving (refraining from consumption) will release resources from consumer goods production and thereby make them available for investment goods production. In short, elimination of the corporate income tax and the installation of VAT will allegedly alter the composition of our domestic output away from consumption and toward investment with the result that our productivity growth and "competitive edge" will be restored.

Cutting the Budget Deficit

Others feel that higher tax rates or entirely new taxes are required to contain large and persistent Federal budget deficits. In recent years large Federal deficits have caused the public debt to rise sharply. Because many Federal expenditure programs are regarded to be "politically untouchable," any resolution of the deficit problem will undoubtedly entail tax increases. One option is to introduce VAT. Another option is to increase the progressivity of the personal income tax.

In 1990 Congress passed tax and spending legislation designed to reduce the Federal budget deficit by $500 billion over a five-year period. Part of this reduction is to come through reduced government spending; part, through enhanced tax revenues. These higher tax revenues will derive from modifications in various provisions of the personal income tax and higher user fees charged to those benefiting from government services. Additionally, Congress increased excise taxes on alcohol, gasoline, and cigarettes and placed an excise tax on certain luxuries such as expensive cars, yachts, and private aircraft. Nevertheless, this tax-spending package will *not* be sufficient to eliminate Federal budget deficits any time soon.

THE ISSUE OF FREEDOM

Finally, we end our discussion of government decision making by considering an important, but elusive, question: What is the nature of the relationship between the role and size of the public sector, on the one hand, and freedom, on the other? Although no attempt is made here to explore this issue in depth, we will outline two divergent views on this question.

The Conservative Position

Many conservative economists feel that, in addition to the economic costs in any expansion of the public sector, there is also a cost in the form of diminished individual freedom. Several related points constitute this position.

First, there is the "power corrupts" argument.[3] "Freedom is a rare and delicate plant . . . history confirms that the great threat to freedom is the concentration of power . . . by concentrating power in political hands, [government] is . . . a threat to freedom."

Second, one can be selective in the market system of the private sector, using one's income to buy precisely what one chooses and rejecting unwanted commodities. But, as noted earlier, in the public sector—even assuming a high level of political democracy—conformity and coercion are inherent. If the majority decides in favor of certain governmental actions—to build a reservoir, to establish a system of national health insurance, to provide a guaranteed annual income—the minority must conform. Hence, the "use of political channels, while inevitable, tends to strain the social cohesion essential for a stable society."[4] To the extent that decisions can be rendered selectively by individuals through markets, the need for conformity and coercion is lessened and this "strain" reduced. The scope of government should be strictly limited.

Finally, the power and activities of government should be dispersed and decentralized.

> If government is to exercise power, better in the county than in the state, better in the state than in Washington. If I do not like what my local community does, be it in sewage disposal, or zoning, or schools, I can move to another local community, and though few may take this step, the mere possibility acts as a check. If I do not like what my state does, I can move to another. If I do not like what Washington imposes, I have few alternatives in this world of jealous nations.[5]

The Liberal Stance

But liberal economists are skeptical of the conservative position. They hold that the conservative view is based on the **fallacy of limited decisions.** That is, conservatives implicitly assume that during any particular period there is a limited, or fixed, number of decisions to be made in the operation of the economy. If government makes more of these decisions in performing its stated functions, the private sector of the economy will necessarily have fewer "free" decisions or choices to make. This is held to be fallacious reasoning. By spon-

[3]Milton Friedman, *Capitalism and Freedom* (Chicago: The University of Chicago Press, 1962), p. 2.

[4]Ibid., p. 23.

[5]Ibid., p. 3.

LAST WORD

RENT SEEKING, TAX REFORM, AND THE SPECIAL-INTEREST EFFECT

Murray Weidenbaum, chair of President Reagan's Council of Economic Advisers, 1981–1982, looks at the Tax Reform Act of 1986 and finds numerous tax-reducing special-interest clauses.

Despite all the talk about equity, the [Tax Reform Act of 1986] contains numerous new special benefits. It would be a breach of legislative etiquette to designate the lucky recipients by name. Congress describes the "goodies" in words like "a paint and glass project which was approved by the management committee of a company on September 11, 1985." That very language was put into the Internal Revenue Code.

Another special benefit goes to "rental property which was assigned FHA [Federal Housing Administration] number 023-36602." That is really neat. It is not considered to be special-purpose legislation, because the benefit covers every taxpayer whose FHA number happens to be 023-36602. Here is my favorite: a project that was "the subject of law suits filed on June 22, 1984 and November 21, 1985." That sets an interesting precedent: getting sued now qualifies some people for being included in the tax code. See [the accompanying] table for other examples of the arbitrary distribution of federal largess in the guise of tax reform.

Source: Murray Weidenbaum, *Rendezvous with Reality.* Copyright © 1988, 1990 by Basic Books, Inc. Reprinted by permission of Basic Books, a division of HarperCollins Publishers Inc.

Some special favors in the 1986 tax bill language describing the beneficiaries

A "state which ratified the United States Constitution on May 29, 1790."

* * *

A company which entered into a binding contract "on October 3, 1984, for the purchase of 6 semi-submersible units at a cost of $425,000,000."

* * *

"Any taxpayer incorporated on September 7, 1978, which is engaged in the trade or business of manufacturing dolls and accessories."

* * *

Any project "which was the subject of a city ordinance numbered 82-115 and adopted on December 2, 1982."

* * *

Any facility where the developer "was selected on April 26, 1985."

* * *

A project to provide a roof or dome for an existing sports facility if "an 11-member task force was appointed by the county executive in June 1985, to further study the feasibility of the project."

* * *

Any project having one of the following Farmers Home Administration Code numbers:

49284553664 4927074218234
4927742022446 49270742244019
49270742276087 51460742345074
490270742387293

* * *

"Any institution of higher education . . . mandated by a state constitution in 1876."

* * *

"A corporation which was incorporated on December 29, 1969, in the State of Delaware . . . "

* * *

" . . . 10 warehouse buildings built between 1906 and 1910 and purchased under a contract dated February 17, 1926."

* * *

"A university established by charter granted by King George II of England on October 31, 1754."

Source: Tax Reform Act of 1986.

soring the production of public goods, government is, in fact, *extending* the range of free choice by permitting society to enjoy goods and services which would not be available in the absence of governmental provision.

One can cogently argue that it is largely through the economic functions of government that we have freed ourselves in some measure from ignorance, unemployment, poverty, disease, crime, discrimination, and other ills. Note, too, that in providing most public goods, government does not typically undertake production itself, but rather purchases these goods through private enterprise. When government decides to build an interstate highway, private concerns are given the responsibility of making many specific decisions and choices in connection with carrying out this decision.

One of America's leading economists has summarized the liberal view in these pointed words:

> Traffic lights coerce me and limit my freedom. Yet in the midst of a traffic jam on the unopen road, was I really "free" before there were lights? And has the algebraic total of freedom, for me or the representative motorist or the group as a whole, been increased or decreased by the introduction of well-engineered stop lights? Stop lights, you know, are also go lights . . . When we introduce the traffic light, we have, although the arch individualist may not like the new order, by cooperation and coercion created by ourselves greater freedom.[6]

[6]Paul A. Samuelson, "Personal Freedoms and Economic Freedoms in the Mixed Economy," in Earl F. Cheit (ed.), *The Business Establishment* (New York: John Wiley & Sons, Inc., 1964), p. 219.

CHAPTER SUMMARY

1 Majority voting creates a possibility of **a** an underallocation or overallocation of resources to a particular public good, and **b** inconsistent voting outcomes. The median-voter model predicts that, under majority rule, the person holding the middle position on an issue will in a sense determine the election outcome.

2 Public choice theorists cite a number of reasons why government might be inefficient in providing public goods and services. **a** There are strong reasons for politicians to support special-interest legislation. **b** Public choice may be biased in favor of programs with immediate and clear-cut benefits and difficult-to-identify costs *and* against programs with immediate and easily identified costs and vague or deferred benefits. **c** Citizens as voters have less choice as to public goods and services than they do as consumers in the private sector. **d** Government bureaucracies have less incentive to operate efficiently than do private businesses.

3 The benefits-received principle of taxation is that those who receive the benefits of goods and services provided by government should pay the taxes required to finance them. The ability-to-pay principle is that those who have greater income should be taxed absolutely and relatively more than those who have less income.

4 The Federal personal income tax is slightly progressive. The corporate income tax is essentially proportional. General sales, excise, payroll, and property taxes tend to be regressive.

5 Excise taxes affect supply and therefore equilibrium price and quantity. The more inelastic the demand for a product, the greater the portion of the tax shifted to consumers. The greater the inelasticity of supply, the larger the portion of tax borne by the seller.

6 Taxation involves loss of some output whose marginal benefit exceeds its marginal cost. The more elastic the supply and demand curves, the greater is this efficiency loss of a particular tax.

7 Sales taxes are likely to be shifted; personal income taxes are not. Specific excise taxes may or may not be shifted to consumers, depending on the elasticities of demand and supply. There is a disagreement as to whether corporate income taxes are shifted. The incidence of property taxes depends primarily whether the property is owner- or tenant-occupied.

8 The pre-TRA tax structure was only mildly progressive. TRA and recent tax changes have not greatly altered the Federal tax structure. The total tax structure is now virtually proportional for most income classes.

9 Current tax issues include **a** restructuring the tax system to promote "reindustrialization," and **b** increasing tax rates or imposing new taxes to reduce large Federal budget deficits.

10 There is disagreement as to the relationship between the size of the public sector and individual freedom.

TERMS AND CONCEPTS

public choice theory
public finance
logrolling
paradox of voting
median-voter model
public sector failure
special-interest effect
rent-seeking behavior
benefits-received principle
ability-to-pay principle
progressive tax
regressive tax
proportional tax
tax incidence
efficiency loss of a tax
value-added tax (VAT)
fallacy of limited decisions

QUESTIONS AND STUDY SUGGESTIONS

1 Explain how affirmative and negative majority votes can sometimes lead to inefficient allocations of resources to public goods. Is this problem likely to be greater under a benefits-received or an ability-to-pay tax system? Use the information in Figures 19-1a and 19-1b to show how society might be better off if Adams were allowed to buy votes.

2 Explain the paradox of voting through reference to the accompanying table which shows the ranking of three public goods by voters Larry, Curley, and Moe.

Public good	*Larry*	*Curley*	*Moe*
Courthouse	2d choice	1st choice	3d choice
School	3d choice	2d choice	1st choice
Park	1st choice	3d choice	2d choice

3 Suppose that there are only five people in a society and that each favors one of the five flood-control options shown in Table 18-2 (include no protection as one of the options). Explain which of these flood-control options will be selected using a majority rule. Will this option be the optimal size of the project from an economic perspective?

4 Carefully evaluate this statement: "The public, as a general rule . . . gets less production in return for a dollar spent by government than from a dollar spent by private enterprise."[7]

5 "To show that a perfectly functioning government can correct some problem in a free economy is not enough to justify governmental intervention, for government itself does not function perfectly." Discuss in detail.

6 How does the problem of limited choice in the public sector relate to economic efficiency? Why are public bureaucracies alleged to be less efficient than private enterprises?

7 Explain: "Politicians would make more rational economic decisions if they weren't running for reelection every few years." Do you think this statement has a bearing on the growth of our public debt?

8 Distinguish clearly between the benefits-received and the ability-to-pay principles of taxation. Which philosophy is more evident in our present tax structure? Justify your answer. To which principle of taxation do you subscribe? Why?

[7]National Association of Manufacturers, *The American Individual Enterprise System* (New York: McGraw-Hill Book Company, 1946), p. 952.

9 Precisely what is meant by a progressive tax? A regressive tax? A proportional tax? Comment on the progressivity or regressivity of each of the following taxes, indicating in each case your assumption concerning tax incidence:

a The Federal personal income tax
b A 3 percent state general sales tax
c A Federal excise tax on automobile tires
d A municipal property tax on real estate
e The Federal corporate income tax

10 Comment on the overall progressivity or regressivity of the United States tax system.

11 What is the incidence of an excise tax when demand is highly inelastic? Elastic? What effect does the elasticity of supply have on the incidence of an excise tax? What is the efficiency loss of a tax and how does it relate to elasticity of demand and supply?

12 Suppose you are a chairperson of a state tax commission responsible for establishing a program to raise new revenue through excise taxes. Would elasticity of demand be important to you in determining those products on which excises should be levied? Explain.

13 Suppose you are convinced that the long-run viability of the United States as a world industrial power necessitates that investment be increased and consumption reduced as proportions of the nation's output. What specific changes in the tax structure would you recommend to achieve this alteration of output?

14 Design what you consider to be an ideal tax system to raise revenue equal to, say, 20 percent of the nation's output.

15 "The market economy is the only system compatible with political freedom. It therefore behooves us to greatly restrain the economic scope of government." Do you agree?

16 **Advanced analysis:** Suppose that the equation for the demand curve for some product X is $P = 8 - .6Q$ and the supply curve is $P = 2 + .4Q$. What is the equilibrium price and quantity? Now suppose that an excise tax is imposed on X such that the new supply equation is $P = 4 + .4Q$. How much tax revenue will this excise tax yield the government? Graph the curves and label the area of the graph which represents the tax collection TC and the area which represents the efficiency loss of the tax EL. Briefly explain why area EL is the efficiency loss of the tax but TC is not.

Antitrust and Regulation

What do Nintendo games, razor blades, high-school yearbooks, video cassette recorders, financial aid at universities, and telecasts of college football games have in common? Answer: All have been the object of private or governmental *antitrust* suits within the past few years.

How are electricity, natural gas, local phone calls, and railroad service related? This question is easier; all are "utilities" and subject to *industrial regulation*—government regulation of prices (rates) within selected industries.

And what do workplace safety standards, infant seats, acid rain, affirmative action, and auto fuel economy have in common? Answer: All are the objects or results of *social regulation*—government regulation of the conditions under which goods are produced, their physical characteristics, and the impact of their production on society.

Antitrust, industrial regulation, and social regulation—each governmental intervention in the marketplace—are the topics of this chapter. First, we clarify some terms and summarize the debate over the desirability of industrial concentration. Next, government policy toward monopoly and anticompetitive business practices is examined, as both antitrust legislation and the regulation of natural monopolies are considered. We follow this discussion with a case study of deregulation of the airline industry. Finally, the more recent and controversial social regulation of industry is discussed.

INDUSTRIAL CONCENTRATION: DEFINITIONS

Before considering the pros and cons of industrial concentration, let's define our terminology.

In Chapter 11 we developed and applied a strict definition of monopoly. A *pure,* or *absolute,* monopoly, we said, is a one-firm industry—a situation where a unique product is being produced entirely by a single firm, and entry to the industry is blocked by insurmountable barriers.

In this chapter we will use the term *industrial concentration* to include pure monopoly and markets in which there is much potential monopoly power. **Industrial concentration** *exists whenever a single firm or a small number of firms controls the major portion of the* *output of an important industry.* One, two, or three firms dominate the particular industry, presumably resulting in higher-than-competitive prices and sustainable economic profits. This definition, which is closer to how most people understand the "monopoly problem," includes a large number of industries which we previously designated as oligopolies.

In using the term "industrial concentration" in this chapter, we refer to those industries in which firms are large in absolute terms *and* in relation to the total market. Examples are the electrical equipment industry, where General Electric and Westinghouse, large by an absolute standard, dominate the market; the automobile industry, where General Motors, Ford, and Chrysler are similarly situated; the chemical industry, dominated by du Pont, Union Carbide, and Allied Chemical; the aluminum industry, where three industrial giants—Alcoa, Reynolds, and Kaiser—reign supreme; and the cigarette industry, where the two giant firms of R. J. Reynolds and Philip Morris currently command the lion's share of this large market.

INDUSTRIAL CONCENTRATION: BENEFICIAL OR HARMFUL?

It is not at all clear whether industrial concentration is, on balance, advantageous or disadvantageous to the working of our economy.

The Case Against Industrial Concentration

The essence of the case against monopoly and oligopoly was stated in previous chapters. Let's summarize and extend those arguments.

1 Inefficient Resource Allocation Monopolists and oligopolists find it possible and profitable to restrict output and charge higher prices than if the given industry were organized competitively. Recall that with pure competition production occurs at the point where $P =$ MC. This equality specifies an efficient allocation of resources because price measures the value or benefit to society of an extra unit of output, while marginal cost reflects the cost or sacrifice of alternative goods. In maximizing profits a business monopolist equates not price, but marginal revenue with marginal cost. At this MR = MC point, price will exceed marginal cost, designating an underallocation of resources to the monopolized product. As a result, the economic well-being of society is less than it would be with pure competition.

2 Unprogressive Critics hold that industrial concentration is neither essential for achieving existing mass-production economies nor conducive to technological progress.

Empirical studies suggest that in most manufacturing industries, "fewness" is not essential for achieving economies of scale. In most industries, firms need only realize a small percentage—in many cases less than 2 or 3 percent—of the total market to achieve low-cost production; industrial concentration is *not* a prerequisite of productive efficiency.

Furthermore, the basic unit for technological efficiency is not the firm, but the individual plant. Thus one can correctly argue that productive efficiency calls for, say, a large-scale, integrated auto-manufacturing plant. But it is perfectly consistent to argue that there is no technological justification for the existence of General Motors, which is essentially a giant business corporation composed of a number of geographically distinct plants. In short, many existing firms have attained a size and structure far larger than necessary for the realization of existing economies of scale.

Nor does technological progress depend on huge corporations with substantial monopoly power. The evidence does *not* support the view that large size and market power correlate closely with technological progress. Indeed, the sheltered position of firms in highly concentrated industries is conducive to inefficiency and lethargy; there is no competitive spur to productive efficiency. Furthermore, monopolists and oligopolists tend to resist or suppress technological advances which may cause sudden obsolescence of their existing machinery and equipment.

3 Income Inequality Industrial concentration is also criticized as a contributor to income inequality. Because of entry barriers, monopolists and oligopolists can charge a price above average cost and consistently realize economic profits. These profits are realized by corporate stockholders and executives who are generally among the upper income groups.

4 Political dangers A final criticism is based on the assumption that economic power and political clout go hand in hand. It is argued that giant corporations exert undue influence over government, and this is reflected in legislation and government policies which are congenial, not to the public interest, but rather, to the preservation and growth of these industrial giants. Big businesses allegedly have exerted political power to become primary beneficiaries of defense contracts, tax loopholes, patent policy, tariff and quota protection, and other subsidies and privileges. (Recall our discussion of rent-seeking activities in Chapter 19).

Defenses of Industrial Concentration

Industrial concentration *does* have significant defenses.

1 Superior Products One defense is the contention that monopolists and oligopolists have gained their positions of market dominance by offering superior products. Large firms do not coerce consumers to buy, say, Colgate or Crest toothpaste, soft drinks from Coca-Cola and Pepsi, mainframe computers from IBM, ketchup from Heinz, or soup from Campbell. Consumers have collectively decided that these products are more desirable than those offered by other producers. Monopoly profits and large market shares therefore have been "earned" through superior performance.

2 Underestimating Competition A second defense of industrial concentration is that economists may view competition too narrowly. For example, while there may be only a few firms producing a given product, those firms may be faced with severe **interindustry competition.** That is, firms may face competition from other firms producing distinct but highly substitutable products. The fact that a handful of firms is responsible for the nation's output of aluminum belies the competition which aluminum faces in specific markets from steel, copper, wood, plastics, and a host of other products.

Foreign competition must also be taken into account. While General Motors dominates domestic automobile production, strong import competition constrains its pricing and output decisions.

Furthermore, the large profits resulting from full exploitation of a monopolist's market power is an inducement to potential competitors to enter the industry. Stated differently, **potential competition** acts as a restraint on the price and output decisions of firms now possessing market power.

3 Economies of Scale Where existing technology is highly advanced, only large producers—firms which are large both absolutely and in relation to the market—can realize low unit costs and therefore sell to consumers at relatively low prices. The traditional antimonopoly contention that industrial concentration means less output, higher prices, and an inefficient allocation of resources assumes that cost economies would be equally available to firms whether the industry's structure was highly competitive or quite monopolistic. In fact, this is frequently not the case; economies of scale may be accessible only if competition—in the sense of a large number of firms—is absent.

4 Technological Progress Recall the *Schumpeter-Galbraith view* that monopolistic industries—in particular, three- and four-firm oligopolies—are conducive to a high rate of technological progress. Oligopolistic firms have both the financial resources *and* the incentives to undertake technological research.

QUICK REVIEW 20-1

- ***Industrial concentration exists whenever a single firm or a small number of firms controls the major portion of output of an important industry.***
- ***The case against industrial concentration is that it entails allocative inefficiency, impedes technological progress, promotes income inequality, and poses political dangers.***
- ***Those who defend industrial concentration contend that it arises from superior performance and economies of scale; is countered by interindustry, foreign, and potential competition; and generates both the wherewithal and incentives for technological progress.***

THE ANTITRUST LAWS

In view of the sharp conflict of opinion over the relative merits of industrial concentration, it is not surprising that government policy toward concentration has been less than clear-cut and consistent. Although the major thrust of Federal legislation and policy has been to maintain and promote competition, we will examine later certain policies and acts which have furthered the development of monopoly and oligopoly.

Historical Background

Historically, our economy, steeped in the philosophy of free, competitive markets, has been a fertile ground for development of a suspicious, fearful public attitude toward industrial concentration. Though relatively dormant in the nation's early years, this fundamental distrust of big business came into full bloom in the decades following the Civil War. The widening of local markets into national markets as transportation facilities improved, the ever-increasing mechanization of production, and the increasingly widespread adoption of the corporate form of business enterprise were important forces causing development of "trusts"—that is, monopolies—in the 1870s and 1880s. Trusts developed in the petroleum, meatpacking, railroad, sugar, lead, coal, whiskey, and tobacco industries, among others, during this era.

Not only were questionable tactics employed in monopolizing various industries, but the resulting market power was almost invariably exerted to the detriment of all who did business with these monopolies. Farmers and small businesses, being particularly vulnerable to the growth and tactics of giant corporate monopolies, were among the first to censure their development. Consumers and labor unions were not far behind in voicing their disapproval of monopoly power.

Because of development of industries in which market forces no longer provided adequate control to ensure socially tolerable behavior, two techniques of control have been adopted as substitutes for, or supplements to, the market.

1 In those few markets where economic realities preclude the effective working of the market—that is, where there is "natural monopoly"—we have established public *regulatory agencies* to control economic behavior.

2 In most other markets in which economic and technological conditions have not made monopoly essential, social control has taken the form of antimonopoly or *antitrust legislation* designed to inhibit or prevent the growth of monopoly.

First, we will consider the major pieces of antitrust legislation which, as refined and extended by various amendments, constitute the basic law of the land with respect to corporate size and concentration.

Sherman Act of 1890

Acute public resentment of the trusts which developed in the 1870s and 1880s culminated in passage of the **Sherman Act** in 1890. This cornerstone of antitrust legislation is surprisingly brief and, at first glance, directly to the point. The core of the act is embodied in two major provisions:

In Section 1:

> Every contract, combination in the form of a trust or otherwise, or conspiracy, in restraint of trade or commerce among the several states, or with foreign nations is hereby declared to be illegal. . . .

In Section 2:

> Every person who shall monopolize, or attempt to monopolize, or combine or conspire with any person or persons, to monopolize any part of the trade or commerce among the several states, or with foreign nations, shall be deemed guilty of a misdemeanor. . . .

This act made monopoly and "restraints of trade"—for example, collusive price fixing or the dividing up of markets among competitors—criminal offenses against the Federal government. Either the Department of Justice or parties injured by monopoly or anticompetitive behavior could file suits under the Sherman Act. Firms found in violation of the act could be ordered dissolved by the courts, or injunctions could be issued to prohibit practices deemed unlawful under the act. Fines and imprisonment were also possible results of successful prosecution. Further, parties injured by illegal combinations and conspiracies could sue for **treble damages**—triple the amount of monetary injury done them. The Sherman Act seemed to provide a sound foundation for positive government action against business monopolies.

However, early court interpretations raised serious questions about the effectiveness of the Sherman Act and it became clear that a more explicit statement of the government's antitrust sentiments was in order. Indeed, the business community itself sought a clearer statement of what was legal and illegal.

Clayton Act of 1914

This needed elaboration of the Sherman Act took the form of the 1914 **Clayton Act.** The following sections of the Clayton Act were designed to strengthen and make explicit the intent of the Sherman Act:

Section 2 *outlaws price discrimination* between purchasers when such discrimination is not justified on the basis of cost differences.

Section 3 *forbids exclusive,* or **"tying," contracts** whereby a producer would sell a product only on condition that the buyer acquire other products from the same seller and not from competitors.

Section 7 *prohibits acquisition of stocks* of competing corporations when the effect is to lessen competition.

Section 8 *prohibits formation of* **interlocking directorates**—the situation where a director of one firm is also a board member of a competing firm—in large corporations where the effect would be to reduce competition.

Actually, there was little in the Clayton Act which had not already been stated by implication in the Sherman Act. The Clayton Act merely attempted to sharpen and clarify the general provisions of the Sherman Act. Furthermore, the Clayton Act sought to outlaw the techniques by which monopoly might develop and, in this sense, was a preventive measure. The Sherman Act, by contrast, was aimed more at punishing existing monopolies.

Federal Trade Commission Act of 1914

This legislation created the five-member Federal Trade Commission (FTC) and charged it with the responsibility of enforcing the antitrust laws and the Clayton Act in particular. The FTC was given the power to investigate unfair competitive practices on its own initiative or at the request of injured firms. The Commission could hold public hearings on such complaints and, if necessary, issue **cease-and-desist orders** where "unfair methods of competition in commerce" were discovered.

The **Wheeler-Lea Act** of 1938 charged the FTC with the additional responsibility of policing "deceptive acts or practices in commerce" and, as a result, the FTC also undertakes the task of protecting the public against false or misleading advertising and the misrepresentation of products.

The importance of the **Federal Trade Commission Act** is twofold: (1) the act broadened the range of illegal business behavior and (2) it established an independent antitrust agency with the authority to investigate and to initiate court cases. Today, the FTC and the U.S. Justice Department have joint responsibility in enforcing the antitrust laws.

Celler-Kefauver Act of 1950

This act amended Section 7 of the Clayton Act, which prohibits a firm from acquiring the *stock* of competitors when the acquisition would reduce competition. Firms could evade Section 7 by acquiring the physical *assets* (plant and equipment) of competing firms, rather than their stocks. The **Celler-Kefauver Act** plugged this loophole by prohibiting one firm from obtaining physical assets of another firm when the effect would be to lessen competition.

ANTITRUST: ISSUES AND IMPACT

The effectiveness of any law depends on the vigor with which the government enforces it and how the law is interpreted by the courts. The Federal government has varied considerably in its willingness to apply the antitrust acts. Administrations having a laissez-faire philosophy about industrial concentration have sometimes emasculated the acts simply by ignoring them or by cutting budget appropriations of enforcement agencies.

Similarly, the courts have run hot and cold in interpreting antitrust laws. At times, they have applied them with vigor, adhering closely to the spirit and objectives of the laws. In other cases, the courts have interpreted the acts in such ways as to render them all but completely innocuous. With this in mind let's examine two major issues which arise in interpreting antitrust laws.

Behavior or Structure?

A comparison of two landmark Court decisions reveals the existence of two distinct approaches in the application of antitrust. In the 1920 **U.S. Steel case** the courts applied the **rule of reason,** saying in effect that not every monopoly is illegal. Only those which "unreasonably" restrain trade—so-called "bad trusts"—are subject to antitrust action. The Court held in this case that mere size was not an offense; although U.S. Steel clearly *possessed* monopoly power, it was innocent because it had not resorted to illegal acts against competitors in obtaining that power, nor had it unreasonably used its monopoly power.

In the **Alcoa case** of 1945 the courts did a turnabout. The Court held that, even though a firm's behavior might be legal, mere possession of monopoly power (Alcoa had 90 percent of the aluminum ingot market) violated the antitrust laws.

These two cases point to a continuing controversy in antitrust policy. Should an industry be judged by its *behavior* (as in the U.S. Steel case) or by its *structure* (as in the Alcoa case)? "Structuralists" contend that an industry which is highly concentrated will behave like a monopolist. Thus, the economic performance of these industries will necessarily be undesirable. Such industries are therefore legitimate targets for antitrust action.

Alternatively, the "behavioralists" argue that the relationship between structure and performance is tenuous and unclear. They feel that a highly concentrated industry may be technologically progressive and have an enviable record of providing products of increasing quality at reasonable prices. Therefore, if the industry has served society well and engaged in no anticompetitive practices, it should not be accused of antitrust violation simply because it is highly concentrated. Why use antitrust to penalize efficient, well-managed firms?

Since the Alcoa decision of 1945, the courts have reverted to the rule of reason. The general sentiment among antitrust economists and those responsible for enforcing the antitrust laws has also swung away from the strict structuralist view. For example, in 1982 the government dropped its 13-year-long monopolization case against IBM on the grounds that IBM had not unreasonably restrained trade.

Defining the Market

Court decisions involving existing market power often turn on the issue of the size of the market share of the dominant firm. If the market is defined broadly, then the firm's market share will appear to be small. Conversely, if the market is defined narrowly, the market share will be large. It is the difficult task of the Court to determine the relevant market for a particular product.

For example, in the **du Pont cellophane case** of 1956 the government contended that du Pont, along with a licensee, had 100 percent of the cellophane market. But the Supreme Court defined the market broadly to include all "flexible packaging materials," that is, waxed paper, aluminum foil, and so forth, in addition to cellophane. Despite du Pont's total dominance of the "cellophane market," it only controlled about 20 percent of the market for "flexible packaging materials". The Court ruled that this did not constitute a monopoly.

Effectiveness

Have the antitrust laws been effective? This is a difficult question, but some insight can be gained by noting how the laws have been applied to existing market structures, mergers, and price fixing.

Existing Market Structures The application of antitrust laws to existing market structures has been lenient. Generally, a firm will be sued if it has more than 60 percent of the relevant market and there is evidence to suggest the firm used abusive conduct to achieve or maintain its market dominance. The most significant recent "victory" against existing market structure has been the 1982 out-of-court settlement between the government and AT&T. AT&T was charged in 1974 with violating the Sherman Act by engaging in a series of anticompetitive actions designed to maintain its domestic telephone communications monopoly. As part of the settlement, AT&T agreed to divest itself of its 22 regional telephone operating companies. Since 1982, however, the Federal government has filed no significant antitrust suits to break up existing market structure.

Mergers The treatment of mergers varies with the type of merger and its effect on industry concentration.

Merger Types Mergers are of three basic types, as shown in Figure 20-1. This diagram shows two stages of production—the input stage, and the output, or final product stage—for two distinct final-good industries: autos and beer. Each rectangle represents a particular firm.

A **horizontal merger** *is a merger between two competitors selling similar products in the same market.* In Figure 20-1 this type of merger is shown as a combination of glass producers T and U. Other hypothetical examples of horizontal mergers would be Ford Motor Company merging with General Motors or Anheuser Busch merging with Coors.

A **vertical merger**—*the merging of firms at different stages of the production process in the same industry*—is shown in Figure 20-1 as a merger between firm Z, a hops producer, and firm F, a brewery. Vertical mergers involve firms having buyer–seller relationships. Actual examples of mergers of this type are PepsiCo's mergers with Pizza Hut, Taco Bell, and Kentucky Fried Chicken. PepsiCo supplies soft drinks to each of these fast-food operations.

A **conglomerate merger** *is the merger of a firm in one industry with a firm in another unrelated industry.* In Figure 20-1 a merger between firm C, an auto manufacturer, and firm D, a brewery, fits this description. Actual examples: the merger between Philip Morris, a cigarette company, and Miller Brewing; the merger between International Telephone and Telegraph (ITT) and Sheraton Hotel Corporation.

Merger Guidelines: The Herfindahl Index The Federal government has established merger guidelines based on the Herfindahl index (Chapter 13)

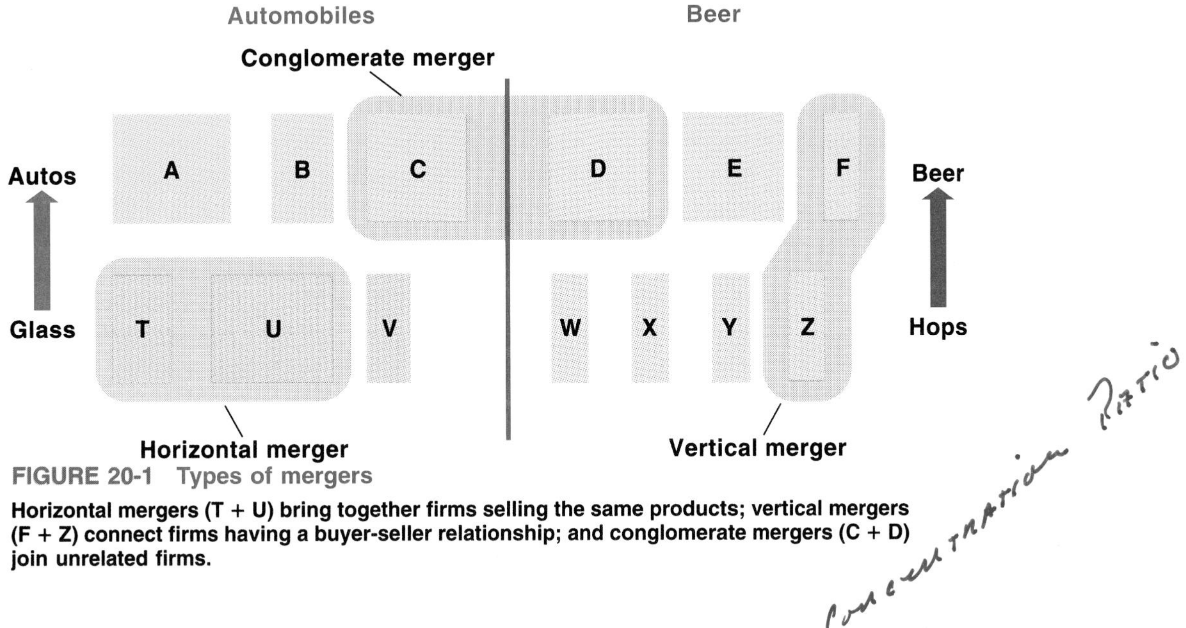

FIGURE 20-1 Types of mergers

Horizontal mergers (T + U) bring together firms selling the same products; vertical mergers (F + Z) connect firms having a buyer-seller relationship; and conglomerate mergers (C + D) join unrelated firms.

which measures the sum of the squared values of market shares within an industry. For example, an industry consisting of four firms, each with a 25 percent market share, has a Herfindahl index of 2500 ($=25^2 + 25^2 + 25^2 + 25^2$). In pure competition, where each firm's market share is minute, the index approaches 0 ($=0^2 + 0^2 + \ldots 0^2$). In pure monopoly, the index is 10,000 ($=100^2$).

Government uses Section 7 of the Clayton Act to block *horizontal* mergers which will substantially lessen competition. Generally, government is likely to challenge a horizontal merger if the post-merger Herfindahl index for the industry would be high (above 1800) and the merger has substantially increased the index (added 100 or more points). But other factors such as the impact of foreign competition and ease of entry of new firms are also considered. Also, mergers are usually allowed when one of the merging firms is on the verge of bankruptcy.

Most *vertical* mergers escape antitrust prosecution because they do not substantially lessen competition in either of the two markets. In Figure 33-1 neither the Herfindahl index in the hops industry nor that in the beer industry changes when the vertical merger between firms Z and F occurs. However, a vertical merger between large firms in highly concentrated industries may be challenged. In a 1949 case du Pont had acquired a controlling interest in General Motors' stock. General Motors subsequently purchased about two-thirds of the paint and almost half the fabrics used in auto manufacturing from du Pont. The impact was to effectively foreclose other paint and fabric manufacturers from selling to GM. The Court ordered du Pont to divest itself of GM stock and sever the tie between the two firms.

Conglomerate mergers are generally permitted. If an auto manufacturer acquires a brewery, no antitrust action is likely to be taken because neither firm has increased the market share of its own market as a result of the merger. That is, the Herfindahl index would remain unchanged in each industry.

Price fixing Price fixing is treated strictly. Evidence of price fixing, even by small firms, will elicit antitrust action as will other collusive activities such as schemes to divide up sales in a market. In the parlance of antitrust law, these activities are known as **per se violations;** they are "in and of themselves" illegal, and therefore *not* subject to the rule of reason. To gain a conviction, the government or other party making the charge need only show that there was a conspiracy to fix prices or divide up sales, not that the conspiracy succeeded or caused serious damage to other parties.

Price-fixing investigations and court actions remain common. Recent examples are:

1 A 1991 court order stopping the Ivy League

schools from engaging in a 35-year practice of not competing with each other in the amount of financial aid offered to individual students

2 A 1991 investigation of several large airlines which allegedly practiced price collusion via their computerized fare network

3 A 1990 guilty plea by Southland Corporation and Borden for rigging bids for school milk contracts in Florida

4 An agreement by Panasonic in 1989 to refund $16 million to buyers of consumer electronics, as part of a settlement for requiring wholesalers and retailers to charge minimum prices for its products

5 A 1991 investigation by the FTC into price fixing by producers of baby formula being sold to a Federal food program for low-income women and children

6 A 1990 antitrust settlement in Washington state by publishers of high-school yearbooks who rigged bids, fixed prices, and divided market territories

There are two major consequences of the government's vigor in prosecuting price fixing.

1 Price fixing is surrounded by great secrecy; it has been driven underground.

2 Collusive action is now much less formal; price leadership and the use of common cost-plus pricing formulas have often replaced formal price-fixing arrangements.

All the above statements about the application of antitrust laws are broad generalizations. Each potential antitrust case has unique circumstances which may make it an exception. Also, the strictness with which antitrust laws are interpreted has varied greatly among various administrations. The Reagan administration, for example, adopted a "lenient" enforcement posture toward existing market structures and mergers, while taking a "strict" position on price fixing. The Bush administration has continued the heavy emphasis on prosecuting price fixing. At present, there is little sentiment for breaking up existing domestic business monopolies in view of the increasing competition from equally large, or even larger, foreign firms.

Restricting Competition

Our discussion of antitrust laws and their application must not lead us to conclude that government policies are consistently procompetition. It is important to note that there are exemptions from antitrust and that a number of public policies have reduced competition.

Labor unions and agricultural cooperatives have been exempt, subject to limitations, from antitrust laws. We will see in Chapter 21 that Federal legislation and policy have provided some measure of monopolistic power for agriculture and have kept agricultural prices above competitive levels. Similarly, in a subsequent chapter we will discover that, since 1930, Federal legislation on balance has generally promoted growth of strong labor unions. This federally sponsored growth has resulted, according to some authorities, in development of union monopolies whose goal is above competitive wage rates. At state and local levels many occupational groups have been successful in establishing licensing requirements arbitrarily restricting entry to certain occupations, thereby keeping wages and earnings above competitive levels.

American **patent laws**—the first of which was passed in 1790—provide monetary incentive for innovators by granting them exclusive rights to produce and sell a new product or machine for a period of seventeen years. Patent grants protect the innovator from competitors who would otherwise quickly imitate this product and share in the profits, though not the cost and effort, of the research.

Few contest the desirability of this particular aspect of our patent laws, particularly when it is recalled that innovation can weaken and undermine existing positions of monopoly power. However, the granting of a patent frequently amounts to the granting of monopoly power in the production of the patented item. Many economists feel that the length of patent protection—seventeen years—is much too long.

The importance of patent laws in the growth of industrial concentration must not be underestimated. Du Pont, General Electric, American Telephone and Telegraph, Eastman Kodak, Alcoa, and innumerable other industrial giants have attained various measures of monopoly power in part through their ownership of certain patent rights.

Although detailed discussion of tariffs is postponed to a later chapter, at this point we must recognize that tariffs and similar trade barriers shield American producers from foreign competition. Protective tariffs are in effect discriminatory taxes against goods of foreign firms. These taxes make it difficult and often impossible for foreign producers to compete in domestic markets with American firms. The result is a less competitive domestic market and an environment frequently conducive to the growth of domestic industrial concentration.

laws which bar foreign airlines from flying domestic routes in the United States.

QUICK REVIEW 20-3

- ***Natural monopoly occurs where economies of scale are so extensive that only a single firm can produce the product at minimum cost.***
- ***The public interest theory of regulation holds that government must regulate business to prevent allocative inefficiency arising from monopoly power.***
- ***The legal cartel theory of regulation suggests that firms seek government regulation to reduce price competition and ensure stable profits.***
- ***Although deregulation of the airline industry has reduced fares and produced net social benefits, it has also created growing industry concentration.***

SOCIAL REGULATION

The "old" regulation just discussed has been labeled economic or **industrial regulation.** Here government is concerned with the overall economic performance of a few specific industries, and concern focuses on pricing and service to the public.

Beginning largely in the early 1960s, government regulation of a new type evolved and experienced rapid growth. This **social regulation** is concerned with the conditions under which goods and services are produced, the impact of production on society, and the physical characteristics of goods themselves. For example, the Occupational Safety and Health Administration (OSHA) is concerned with protecting workers against occupational injuries and illnesses and the Consumer Products Safety Commission (CPSC) specifies minimum standards for potentially unsafe products.

The main Federal regulatory commissions dealing with social regulation are listed in Table 20-2.

TABLE 20-2 **The main Federal regulatory commissions: social regulation**

Commission (year established)	*Jurisdiction*
Food and Drug Administration (1906)	**Safety and effectiveness of food, drugs, and cosmetics**
Equal Employment Opportunity Commission (1964)	**Hiring, promotion, and discharge of workers**
Occupational Safety and Health Administration (1971)	**Industrial health and safety**
Environmental Protection Agency (1972)	**Air, water, and noise pollution**
Consumer Product Safety Commission (1972)	**Safety of consumer products**

Distinguishing Features

Social regulation differs from economic regulation in several ways.

1 Social regulation is often applied "across the board" to virtually all industries and directly affects far more people. While the Interstate Commerce Commission (ICC) focuses only on specific portions of the transport industry, OSHA's rules and regulations apply to every employer.

2 The nature of social regulation involves government in the very details of the production process. For example, rather than simply specifying safety standards for products, CPSC mandates—often in detail—certain characteristics which products must have.

3 A final distinguishing feature of social regulation is its rapid expansion. Between 1970 and 1979 government created twenty new Federal regulatory agencies.

The names of the better-known regulatory agencies in Table 20-2 suggest the basic reason for their creation and growth: Much of our society had achieved a reasonably affluent level of living by the 1960s and attention shifted to improvements in the quality of life. This improvement called for safer and better products, less pollution, better working conditions, and greater equality of opportunity.

Costs and Criticisms

It is generally agreed that the overall objectives of social regulation are laudable. But there is great controversy as to whether the benefits of these regulatory efforts justify the costs.

Costs The costs of social regulation are of two types: *administrative costs,* such as salaries paid to employees of the commissions, office expenses, and the like; and *compliance costs,* which are the costs incurred by businesses and state and local governments in meeting the requirements of regulatory commissions. In 1991 total administrative costs of social regulation were about $10 billion.[2] Because compliance costs are estimated to be roughly twenty times administrative costs, the total cost of social regulation in 1991 was therefore about $200 billion. In 1991, 91,000 full-time employees worked for Federal regulatory agencies involved in social regulation.[3]

Cost estimates for specific types of regulations are also revealing. The U.S. Council on Environmental Quality has estimated that the cost of pollution control alone for the 1979–1988 period totaled over $700 billion. Federally required safety and antipollution equipment has increased the price of the typical automobile by as much as $2,200.[4] Business firms in the United States spend more than $5 billion annually to meet OSHA requirements.[5]

Criticisms Critics argue that our economy is now subject to overregulation, that regulatory activities have been carried to the point where the marginal costs of regulation exceed the marginal benefits (Chapter 18).

Uneconomic Goals It is contended, first, that many social regulation laws are poorly drawn so that regulatory objectives and standards are often stated in legal, political, or engineering terms which result in the pursuit of goals beyond the point at which marginal benefits equal marginal costs. Businesses complain that regulators press for small increments of improvement, unmindful of costs. A requirement to reduce pollution by an incremental 5 percent may cost as much as required to achieve the first 95 percent reduction.

Inadequate Information Decisions must often be made and rules promulgated on the basis of inadequate and sketchy information. CPSC officials may make sweeping decisions about the use of carcinogens in products based on limited experiments with laboratory animals.

Unintended Side Effects It is argued that regulations produce many unintended side effects which greatly boost the full cost of regulation. For example, a 1988 study concluded that Federal gas mileage standards implemented over the past several years for automobiles could cause 2200 to 3900 traffic deaths in 1989. The reason? Manufacturers have reduced the weight of vehicles as a way to meet the increasingly stringent standards. All else being equal, drivers of lighter cars have a considerably higher fatality rate than drivers of heavier vehicles.

Overzealous Personnel Finally, opponents of social regulation point out that the regulatory agencies may attract overzealous personnel who "believe" in regulation. It is often observed, for example, that the EPA staff is composed largely of "environmentalists" who are strongly inclined to punish polluters. "Treating all polluters as sinners is . . . much easier than making quantitative judgments about optimal levels of cleanliness in the air and water, but it leads to inefficient regulations, especially where government statutes imply rigid, national, uniform standards."[6]

It is further argued that the bureaucrats of the new regulatory agencies are unduly sensitive to criticism by Congress or some special interest group such as consumerists, environmentalists, or organized labor. The result is bureaucratic inflexibility and the establishment of extreme or nonsensical regulations so that no watchdog group will question the agency's commitment to its given social goal. OSHA's much-ridiculed specification of the shape of toilet seats and its proposal that farmers and ranchers provide toilet facilities within five minutes' walking distance of any point where employees are at work are cases in point. In the words of one critic:

> No realistic evaluation of . . . government regulation comfortably fits the notion of benign and wise officials making altogether sensible decisions in the society's greater interests. Instead we find waste, bias, stupidity, concentration on trivia, conflicts among the regulators and, worst of all, arbitrary and uncontrolled power.[7]

Economic Implications

1 Higher Prices If overregulation does exist, what are its consequences? Social regulation increases prod-

[2]Center for the Study of American Business, Washington University.

[3]Ibid.

[4]Robert W. Crandall, et al., *Regulating the Automobile* (Washington, D.C.: The Brookings Institution, 1986), p. 43.

[5]Murray L. Weidenbaum, *Business, Government, and the Public*, 4th ed. (Englewood Cliffs, N.J.: Prentice-Hall, 1990), p. 144.

[6]William Lilley III and James C. Miller III, "The New 'Social Regulation,'" *The Public Interest*, Spring 1977, p. 58.

[7]Murray L. Weidenbaum, "The Cost of Overregulating Business," *Tax Review*, August 1975, p. 33.

uct prices. It does this directly because compliance costs normally get passed on to consumers. Furthermore, social regulation indirectly contributes to higher product prices to the extent that it reduces labor productivity. Resources invested in antipollution equipment are not available for investment in new machinery to increase output per worker. Where wage rates are inflexible downward, declines in labor productivity increase marginal and average costs of production. In effect, product supply curves shift leftward, causing product prices to rise.

2 Slower Innovation The new regulation may have a negative impact on the rate of innovation. The fear that a new, technologically superior plant will not meet with EPA approval or that a new product may run into difficulties with CPSC may be enough to persuade a firm to produce the same old product in the same old way.

3 Reduced Competition Finally, social regulation may have an anticompetitive effect since it tends to be a relatively greater economic burden for small firms than for large firms. The costs of complying with social regulation are, in effect, fixed costs. Smaller firms produce less output over which to distribute these costs and, hence, their compliance costs per unit of output put them at a competitive disadvantage with their larger rivals. Bluntly put, the burden of social regulation is more likely to put small firms out of business and thereby contribute to the increased concentration of industry.

In Support of Social Regulation

Social regulation is not without its defenses. The problems with which social regulation contends are serious and substantial. In 1989, 10,400 workers died in job-related accidents in the United States. Particulate and ozone pollution still plagues our major cities, imposing large costs in terms of reduced property values and increased health-care expenses. Thousands of children and adults die each year in accidents involving poorly designed products. Discrimination against blacks, other minorities, females, and older workers reduces the earnings of these groups and imposes heavy costs on society as well.

Proponents of social regulation correctly point out that the relevant economic test of whether social regulation is worthwhile is not whether its costs are high or low, but rather whether benefits *exceed* costs. After years of relative neglect, society cannot expect to cleanse the environment, enhance the safety of the workplace, improve the safety of the automobile, and enhance economic opportunity without incurring substantial costs.

Furthermore, cost calculations may paint too dim a picture of social regulation. Benefits tend to be taken for granted, are more difficult to measure than costs, and may accrue to society only after an extended period.

Benefits of social regulation have in fact been substantial. Examples: It is estimated that highway fatalities would be 40 percent greater annually without auto safety features mandated through regulation.[8] Compliance with child safety-belt laws has significantly reduced the auto fatality rate for small children.[9] The National Ambient Air Quality Standards set by law have been reached in nearly all parts of the nation for sulfur dioxide, nitrogen dioxide, and lead. Affirmative action regulations have significantly increased labor demand for blacks and females.[10] Childproof lids have resulted in a 90 percent decline in child deaths caused by accidental swallowing of poisonous substances.[11]

QUICK REVIEW 20-4

- ***Social regulation is concerned with conditions under which goods and services are produced, the effect of production on society, and physical characteristics of goods themselves.***
- ***Critics of social regulation say that uneconomic policy goals, inadequate information, unintended side-effects, and overzealous personnel combine to create regulatory costs which exceed regulatory benefits.***
- ***Defenders of social regulation point to the large benefits arising from policies which keep dangerous products from the marketplace, reduce workplace injuries and death, contribute to clean air and water, and reduce employment discrimination.***

[8]Crandall, op. cit., p. 155.

[9]*Economic Report of the President, 1987* (Washington, D.C.: 1987), p. 188.

[10]Jonathon S. Leonard, "The Impact of Affirmative Action on Employment," *Journal of Labor Economics,* October 1984, pp. 439–463.

[11]U.S. Product Safety Commission estimate.

LAST WORD

DOES THE UNITED STATES NEED AN INDUSTRIAL POLICY?

Should government be more actively involved in determining the structure of industry?

There has been a growing concern in recent years that the United States' industrial preeminence has been seriously eroded. Our domestic markets have been flooded with foreign steel, automobiles, motorcycles, cameras, watches, and electronics equipment, suggesting that our competitive edge has been lost.

Noting apparent Japanese successes, many political, union, and business leaders—but only a limited number of economists—feel that the United States needs an industrial policy to reverse our alleged industrial decline. It is argued that government should undertake a more active and direct role in determining the structure and composition of American industry. Government, it is held, should use low-interest loans, loan guarantees, special tax treatment, research and development subsidies, antitrust immunity, and even foreign trade protection to accelerate the development of "high-tech" industries and to revitalize certain core manufacturing industries such as steel. Conversely, it should hasten the movement of resources out of declining "sunset" industries. Presumably the net result will be that the American economy will enjoy a higher average level of productivity and be more competitive in world markets.

Opponents of industrial policy make a number of points.

1 Deindustrialization? Has the United States in fact deindustrialized? Has our manufacturing sector experienced serious decline? Statistics suggest not. While the composition of manufacturing output has changed, manufacturing in the aggregate accounts for virtually the same percentage of the nation's output in 1991 (about 20 percent) as it did in 1950. Similarly, manufacturing's share of the nation's expenditures on new plant and equipment was about the same in 1991

Although we can expect social regulation to continue to be controversial, it is generally agreed that the contested "question is not whether (social) regulation should occur, but how and when it should be used; how we can improve the system of regulation; and whether we are fully aware of the costs and benefits involved."[12]

[12]Testimony of Juanita M. Kreps in *The Cost of Government Regulation* (Washington, D.C.: 1978), p. 7.

CHAPTER SUMMARY

1 The case against industrial concentration centers on contentions that it **a** causes a misallocation of resources; **b** retards the rate of technological advance; **c** promotes income inequality; and **d** poses a threat to political democracy.

2 The defense of industrial concentration is built around the following points: **a** firms have obtained their large market shares by offering superior products; **b** interindustry and foreign competition, along with potential competition from new industry entrants, make American industries more competitive than generally believed; **c** some degree of monopoly may be essential to realize economies

as in 1950. Employment in manufacturing has declined from 34 to 17 percent of total employment in the 1950–1991 period, but that reflects the growth of labor productivity rather than industrial demise. Output and employment in manufacturing suffered in the early and mid-1980s, but the primary cause was a very strong dollar which made foreign imports relatively cheap and American exports relatively expensive.

2 Foreign experience Advocates of an industrial policy typically cite Japan as a model. In the post-World War II era Japan has achieved rapid economic growth; it has been highly successful in penetrating world markets; and it has had a much-publicized industrial policy. Yet the overall role of industrial policy as a causal factor in Japanese industrial success is not clear. The picture is mixed.

> Japanese industrial policy has had both successes and failures. Some targeted industries, including semiconductor and machine tools, are almost certainly stronger than they would have been without government support and can be claimed as successes for Japanese industrial policy. Other industries, such as shipbuilding and steel, probably grow more quickly because of government aid, but undoubtedly would have developed without any government intervention. However, the Japanese government has also picked losers. Aluminum smelting and petrochemicals were favored industries fifteen years ago, but the public and private investments have paid off very poorly and now their capacity is being reduced. There are also several examples of successful industries that did not receive government assistance, including motorcycles and consumer electronics.*

3 Markets and politics While a proposal to create an industrial policy which subsidizes "sunrise" industries and hastens the phasing out of "sunset" industries sounds appealing, critics question the government's ability to identify future industrial "winners" and "losers." The issue here is whether private investors using capital markets have better foresight than public officials in determining industrial winners and losers. Critics argue that private investors have a greater incentive in investing their own funds to obtain accurate information on the future prospects of various industries than might government bureaucrats in investing the *taxpayers'* funds.

Furthermore, might not government use its power to allocate investment funds to buy the political support of various industries? Might not the economic goal of enhanced industrial efficiency be subverted to the political goal of getting reelected? It is feared that the creation of a new industrial policy may lead to "lemon socialism," that is, government support or ownership of declining industries and dying companies.

Those who are skeptical of industrial policy contend that government can best stimulate American industry by (1) using monetary and fiscal policy to create a favorable macroeconomic environment (high employment, low inflation, low interest rates) and (2) adjusting tax and regulatory systems to enhance incentives for investment and technological advance.

**Economic Report of the President, 1984,* p. 98.

Source: Adapted from *Economic Report of the President, 1984,* chap. 3; and Federal Reserve Bank of Kansas City, *Industrial Change and Public Policy* (1983). Updated.

of scale; and **d** monopolies and oligopolies are technologically progressive.

3 The cornerstone of antitrust policy consists of the Sherman Act of 1890 and the Clayton Act of 1914. The Sherman Act specifies that "Every contract, combination . . . or conspiracy in the restraint of interstate trade . . . is . . . illegal," and that any person who monopolizes or attempts to monopolize interstate trade is guilty of a misdemeanor.

4 The Clayton Act was designed to bolster and make more explicit the provisions of the Sherman Act. To this end the Clayton Act declared that price discrimination, tying contracts, intercorporate stockholdings, and interlocking directorates are illegal when the effect of their use is the lessening of competition.

5 The Federal Trade Commission Act of 1914 created the Federal Trade Commission to investigate antitrust violations and to prevent the use of "unfair methods of competition." Empowered to issue cease-and-desist orders, the Commission also serves as a watchdog agency for the false and deceptive representation of products.

6 The Celler-Kefauver Act of 1950 prohibits one firm from acquiring the assets of another firm where the result is a lessening of competition.

7 Major issues in applying antitrust laws include **a** the problem of determining whether an industry should be judged by its structure or its behavior and **b** defining the scope and size of the dominant firm's market.

8 Generally, antitrust officials are more likely to challenge price fixing and horizontal mergers among large firms than they are to attempt to break up existing market structures.

9 With respect to agriculture, labor, occupational licens-

ing, patents, and international trade barriers, government policies have tended to restrict competition.

10 The objective of industrial regulation is to protect the public from the market power of natural monopolies by regulating prices and quality of service. Critics contend that industrial regulation is conducive to inefficiency and rising costs and that in many instances it constitutes a legal cartel for the regulated firms. Legislation passed in the late 1970s and the 1980s has brought about varying degrees of deregulation in the airline, trucking, banking, railroad, and television broadcasting industries.

11 Airline deregulation has lowered fares and increased the efficiency of the industry, producing a sizable net benefit to society. It has also resulted in growing concentration in the industry.

12 Social regulation is concerned with product safety, safer working conditions, less pollution, and greater economic opportunity. Critics contend that businesses are overregulated in that marginal costs exceed marginal benefits, while defenders dispute that contention.

TERMS AND CONCEPTS

industrial concentration
interindustry competition
foreign competition
potential competition
Sherman Act
treble damages
Clayton Act
tying contracts
interlocking directorates
cease-and-desist order
Wheeler-Lea Act
Federal Trade Commission Act
Celler-Kefauver Act
U.S. Steel case
rule of reason
Alcoa case
du Pont cellophane case
horizontal, vertical, and conglomerate mergers
per se violations
patent laws
natural monopoly
public interest theory of regulation
legal cartel theory of regulation
Airline Deregulation Act
industrial regulation
social regulation

QUESTIONS AND STUDY SUGGESTIONS

1 You are president of General Motors or Ford. Discuss critically the case against industrial concentration. Now suppose you are a representative for a farm organization, attempting to convince a congressional committee that industrial concentration is a significant factor contributing to the farm problem. Critically evaluate the case for industrial concentration.

2 Describe the major provisions of the Sherman and Clayton acts. Who is responsible for enforcing these laws?

3 Briefly indicate the basic issue involved in the U.S. Steel, Alcoa, and du Pont cellophane cases. What issues in antitrust enforcement are implicit in these cases?

4 How would you expect antitrust authorities to react to **a** a proposed merger of Ford and General Motors; **b** evidence of secret meetings by contractors to rig bids for highway construction projects; **c** a proposed merger of a large shoe manufacturer and a chain of retail shoe stores; and **d** a proposed merger of a small life insurance company and a regional candy manufacturer.

5 Suppose a proposed merger of firms will simultaneously lessen competition and reduce unit costs through economies of scale. Do you think such a merger should be allowed?

6 In 1986 PepsiCo Inc., which then had 28 percent of the soft drink market, proposed to acquire the Seven-Up Co. Shortly thereafter the Coca-Cola Company, with 39 percent of the market, indicated it wished to acquire the Dr. Pepper Company. Seven-Up and Dr. Pepper each controlled about 7 percent of the market. In your judgment, was the government's decision to block these mergers appropriate?

7 "The antitrust laws serve to penalize efficiently managed firms." Do you agree?

8 "The social desirability of any given business enterprise should be judged not on the basis of the structure of the industry in which it finds itself, but rather on the basis of the market performance and behavior of that firm." Analyze critically.

9 What types of industries should be subjected to industrial regulation? What specific problems does industrial regulation entail? Why might an inefficient combination of capital and labor be employed by a regulated natural monopoly?

10 In view of the problems in regulating natural monopolies, compare socially optimal (marginal-cost) pricing and fair-return pricing by referring again to Figure 11-6. Assuming a government subsidy might be used to cover any loss entailed by marginal-cost pricing, which pricing policy would you favor? What problems might the subsidy entail?

11 How does social regulation differ from industrial regulation? What types of costs and benefits are associated with social regulation?

12 The following are research estimates of the average cost per life saved of three specific social regulations: 1967 automobile steering column protection rule costs $100,000 per life saved; 1979 FDA ban on DES (a suspected carcinogen) in cattle feed costs $132 million per life saved; the EPA's proposed restrictions on disposal of dioxins and solvents on land costs $3.5 billion per life saved.[13] Based on this information, do you favor each of these social regulations? If not, why not? Discuss: "Implicit within the setting of safety standards for products is the valuation of human life."

[13]*Economic Report of the President, 1987* (Washington, D.C.: 1987), p. 183.

Agriculture: Economics and Policy

An economic analysis of American agriculture can be justified on a number of grounds:

1 Agriculture is one of the nation's largest industries. Consumers spend about 16 percent of their after-tax incomes on food and other farm products (Table 5-3). Gross farm income was about $185 billion in 1991 and approximately 2 percent of the labor force is employed in agriculture.

2 Agriculture is an industry which—in the absence of government farm programs—is a real-world example of Chapter 10's purely competitive model. The industry comprises many firms selling virtually standardized products. Agriculture is an industry which can be understood by applying the demand and supply tools of competitive markets.

3 Farm markets provide revealing evidence of the intended and unintended effects of government policies which interfere with the forces of supply and demand.

4 Agriculture reflects the increasing globalization of markets. In recent decades the economic ups and downs of American agriculture have been closely tied to its ability to gain access to world markets.

5 Farm policies provide us with excellent illustrations of Chapter 19's special-interest effect and rent-seeking behavior.

THE ECONOMICS OF AGRICULTURE

Historically, farmers have frequently faced severe problems of fluctuating prices and declining incomes. We distinguish between (1) the **short-run farm problem** of year-to-year fluctuations in farm prices and incomes, and (2) the **long-run farm problem** which relates to those forces causing agriculture to be a declining industry.

Short-Run Problem: Price and Income Instability

The short-run farm problem is the result of: (1) an inelastic demand for agricultural products; (2) fluctuations in farm output; and (3) shifts in the demand curve itself.

Inelastic Demand for Agricultural Products In most developed societies, the price elasticity of demand for agricultural products is low. For farm products in the aggregate, the elasticity coefficient is estimated to be from .20 to .25. These figures suggest that the prices of agricultural products would have to fall by 40 to 50 percent for consumers to increase their purchases by a mere 10 percent. Consumers apparently put a low value on additional agricultural output compared with alternative goods.

Why is this so? You will recall that the basic determinant of elasticity of demand is substitutability. That is, when the price of a product falls, the consumer will tend to substitute *that* product for other products whose prices presumably have not fallen. But in wealthy societies this "substitution effect" (Chapter 8) is very modest for food. People simply do not switch from three to five or six meals each day in response to declines in the relative prices of agricultural products. An individual's capacity to substitute food for other products is subject to very real biological constraints.

The inelasticity of agricultural demand can also be explained in terms of diminishing marginal utility. In a wealthy society, the population by and large is well fed and well clothed; it is relatively saturated with the food and fiber of agriculture. Therefore, additional agricultural ouput involves rapidly diminishing marginal utility. Thus it takes very large price cuts to induce small increases in consumption. Curve *D* in Figure 21-1 portrays the inelastic demand for agricultural products.

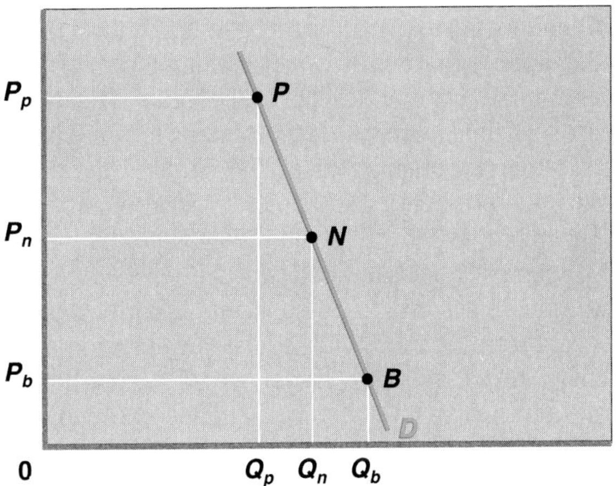

FIGURE 21-1 The effect of output changes on farm prices and incomes

Because of the inelasticity of demand for farm products, a relatively small change in output (Q_n to Q_p or Q_b) will cause relatively large changes in farm prices (P_n to P_p or P_b) and incomes (OP_nNQ_n to OP_pPQ_p or OP_bBQ_b).

Fluctuations in Output The inelastic demand for farm products causes small changes in agricultural production to be magnified into relatively larger changes in farm prices and incomes. Farmers possess only limited control over their production. First, floods, droughts, unexpected frost, insect damage, and similar disasters can mean poor crops. Conversely, an excellent growing season may mean bumper crops. Weather factors are beyond the control of farmers, yet they exert an important influence on production.

Second, the highly competitive nature of agriculture makes it virtually impossible for farmers to form a huge combination to control production. If all the millions of widely scattered and independent producers should by chance plant an unusually large or abnormally small portion of their land, extra large or small outputs would result even if the growing season were normal.

Putting the instability of farm production together with the inelastic demand for farm products in Figure 21-1, we can readily see why farm prices and incomes are highly unstable. Even if we assume that market demand for agriculture products is stable at *D*, the inelastic nature of demand will magnify small changes in output into relatively large changes in farm prices and income. For example, assume that a "normal" crop of Q_n results in a "normal" price of P_n and a "normal" farm income of OP_nNQ_n. But a bumper crop or a poor crop will cause large deviations from these normal prices and incomes; these results stem from the inelasticity of demand for farm products.

If an unusually good growing season occurs, the resulting bumper crop of Q_b will reduce farm incomes from OP_nNQ_n to OP_bBQ_b. When demand is inelastic, an increase in the quantity sold will be accompanied by a *more than* proportionate decline in price. The net result is that total revenue, that is, total farm income, will decline.

Similarly, for farmers as a group, a poor crop caused by, say, drought may boost farm incomes. A poor crop of Q_p will raise total farm income from OP_nNQ_n to OP_pPQ_p. A decline in output will cause a *more than* proportionate increase in price when demand is inelastic. Ironically, for farmers as a group, a poor crop may be a blessing and a bumper crop a hardship. Conclusion: *Given a stable market demand for farm products, the inelasticity of that demand will turn relatively small changes in output into relatively larger changes in farm prices and incomes.*

Fluctuations in Domestic Demand The other aspect of the short-run instability of farm incomes has to do with shifts in the demand curve for agricultural products. Suppose that somehow agricultural output is stabilized at the "normal" level of Q_n in Figure 21-2. Now, because of the inelasticity of the demand for farm products, short-run fluctuations in the demand for these products—prompted perhaps by cyclical changes in the economy—will cause markedly different prices and incomes to be associated with this level of production that we assume to be constant. A slight drop in demand from D_1 to D_2 will reduce farm income from OP_1aQ_n to OP_2bQ_n. A relatively small decline in demand gives farmers a drastically reduced money reward for the same amount of production. Conversely, a slight increase in demand—as from D_2 to D_1—will bring an equally sharp increase in farm income for the same volume of output. These large price-income changes are linked to the fact that demand is inelastic.

It is tempting to argue that the sharp declines in farm prices which accompany a decrease in demand will cause many farmers to close down in the short run, reducing total output and alleviating these price-income declines. But farm production is relatively insensitive to price changes, because farmers' fixed costs are high compared with their variable costs. Interest, rental, tax, and mortgage payments on buildings and equipment are the major costs faced by the farmer. These are clearly fixed charges. Furthermore, the labor supply of farmers and their families can also be regarded as a fixed cost. So long as they stay on their farms, farmers cannot reduce their costs by firing themselves! This means that their variable costs are for the small amounts of hired help they may employ, plus expenditures for seed, fertilizer, and fuel. As a result of this high volume of fixed costs, farmers are almost invariably better off when working their land than when sitting idle and attempting to pay their fixed costs out of pocket.

FIGURE 21-2 The effect of demand changes on farm prices and incomes

Because of the highly inelastic demand for agricultural products, a small shift in demand (D_1 to D_2) will cause drastically different levels of farm prices (P_1 to P_2) and farm incomes (OP_1aQ_n to OP_2bQ_n) to be associated with a given level of production Q_n.

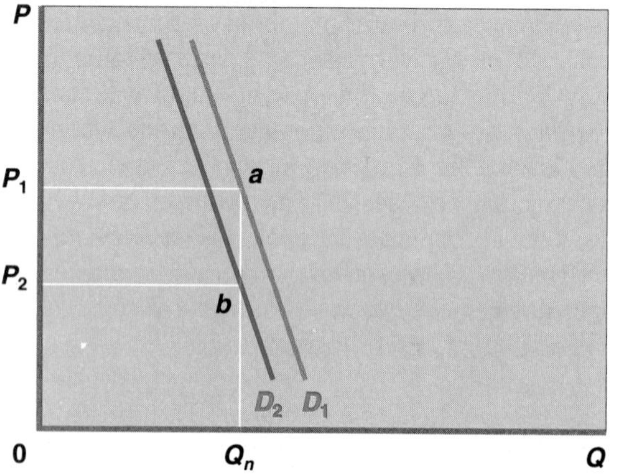

Unstable Foreign Demand American agriculture's dependence on world markets is also a source of demand volatility. The incomes of American farmers are now sensitive to changes in weather and crop production *in other countries.* Similarly, cyclical fluctuations in incomes in Europe or Japan, for example, can shift the demand for American farm products. So can changes in foreign economic policies. If the nations of western Europe decide to provide their farmers with greater protection from foreign (American) competition, American farmers will have less access to those markets and export demand will fall. International politics can also add to demand instability. Changing U.S.–U.S.S.R. political relations boosted American grain sales in the early 1970s and reduced them at the end of the decade. Changes in the international value of the dollar can be critical. Depreciation of the dollar in the 1970s increased the demand for American farm products, while appreciation of the dollar decreased foreign demand in the early 1980s.

To summarize: The increasing relative importance of exports has increased the instability of the demand for American farm products. Farm exports are affected, not only by weather, income fluctuations, and economic policies abroad, but also by international politics and fluctuations in the international value of the dollar.

Long-Run Problem: A Declining Industry

Two more characteristics of agricultural markets must be added to price inelasticity of demand to explain why agriculture has been a declining industry:

1 Over time the supply of agricultural products has increased markedly because of technological progress.

2 Demand for agricultural products has increased slowly over time because demand for them is inelastic with respect to income.

Technology and Supply Increases When a price-inelastic and slowly increasing demand for farm products is accompanied by a rapidly increasing supply, there is inexorable pressure for farm prices and incomes to fall.

A rapid rate of technological advance, particularly since World War I, has caused significant increases in the supply of agricultural products. This technological progress has many roots: the virtually complete electrification and mechanization of farms; improved techniques of land management and soil conservation; irrigation; development of hybrid crops; availability of improved fertilizers and insecticides; and improvements in breeding and care of livestock.

These technological advances have been very significant. The amount of capital used per worker increased fifteen times over the 1930–1980 period, permitting a fivefold increase in the amount of land cultivated per farmer. The simplest general index is the increasing number of people which a single farmer's output will support. In 1820 each farm worker produced enough food and fiber to support four persons; by 1947, about fourteen. By 1991 each farmer produced enough to support over one hundred people! Unquestionably, productivity in agriculture has risen significantly. Since World War II, physical productivity in agriculture has advanced at a rate *twice* as fast as that of the nonfarm economy.

It is worth noting that most technological advances have *not* been initiated by farmers but rather are the result of government-sponsored programs of research and education and the work of farm machinery producers. Land-grant colleges, experiment stations, county agents of the Agricultural Extension Service, educational pamphlets issued by the U.S. Department of Agriculture, and the research departments of farm machinery, pesticide, and fertilizer producers are the sources of technological advance in American agriculture.

Lagging Demand Increases in demand for agricultural commodities have failed to keep pace with techologically inspired increases in their supply. The reason lies in the two major determinants of agricultural demand—incomes and population.

Income Inelastic Demand In less developed countries, consumers must devote the bulk of their meager incomes to agricultural products—food and clothing—to sustain themselves. But as income expands beyond the subsistence level and the problem of hunger eventually gives way to one of obesity, consumers will increase their outlays on food at ever-declining rates. Once consumers' stomachs are filled, their thoughts turn to the amenities of life which industry, not agriculture, provides. Economic growth in the United States has boosted average per capita income far beyond the level of bare subsistence. As a result, *increases in the incomes of American consumers lead to less than proportionate increases in expenditures on farm products.*

In technical terms, the demand for farm products is *income-inelastic;* it is quite insensitive to increases in income. Estimates indicate that a 10 percent increase in real per capita after-tax income means at most an increase in consumption of farm products of only 2 percent. Certain farm products—for example, cabbage and lard—may be inferior goods. As incomes increase, purchases of these products may actually *decrease* (Chapter 4).

Population Growth Population is a somewhat different proposition. Despite the fact that, after a minimum income level is reached, each individual consumer's intake of food and fiber will become relatively fixed, more consumers obviously will mean an increase in demand for farm products. In most advanced nations demand for farm products increases at a rate roughly corresponding to the rate of population growth. But population increases, added to the relatively small increase in the purchase of farm products which occurs as incomes rise, have simply not been great enough to match concomitant increases in farm output. Indeed, it is pertinent to note that birthrates are down and United States population growth has slowed in recent decades.

Graphical Portrayal Coupled with the inelastic demand for agricultural products, these shifts in supply and demand have tended to reduce farm incomes. This is illustrated in Figure 21-3, where a large increase in supply is shown against a very modest increase in demand. Because of the inelastic demand for farm products, these shifts have resulted in a sharp decline in farm prices accompanied by relatively small increases in sales. Farm incomes therefore tend to decline. Diagrammatically, income before the increase in supply occurs (measured by rectangle $OPAQ$) will exceed farm income after supply increases (OP_1BQ_1). The income "loss" of P_1PAC is not fully offset by the income "gain" of $QCBQ_1$. In summary, *given an inelastic demand for farm products, an increase in the supply of farm products relative to the demand for them has created persistent tendencies for farm incomes to fall relative to nonfarm incomes.*

The consequences have been essentially those predicted by the purely competitive model. As farm

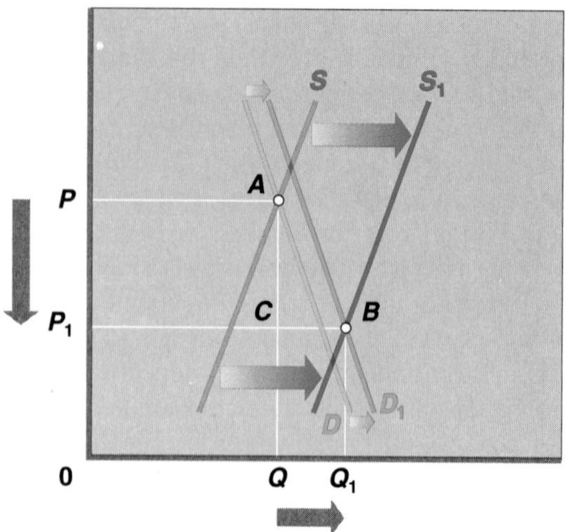

FIGURE 21-3 **A graphical summary of the long-run farm problem**

In the long run, increases in the demand for agricultural products (D to D_1) have not kept pace with the increases in supply (S to S_1) which technological advances have permitted. Coupled with the fact that agricultural demand is inelastic, these shifts have tended to depress farm prices (as from P to P_1) and income (as from $OPAQ$ to OP_1BQ_1).

incomes have fallen historically in comparison to nonfarm incomes, large numbers of farmers have left the industry as shown in Table 21-1. We would further predict that this exodus would reduce supply relative to demand until farm incomes were roughly equal to nonfarm incomes (recall Figure 10-9). However, this adjustment process is complicated by the fact that most land remains in agricultural production. Except for the minute portion of total farmland which borders on metropolitan areas, most farmland has no real alternative uses. Farmers leave, but the land they leave is acquired by other farmers and remains in production. Nevertheless, farm and nonfarm incomes have moved toward equality. The average income of farm families was $34,171 in 1990 compared to $35,376 for nonfarm families.

TABLE 21-1 **The declining farm population, selected years, 1910–1990**

	Farm population		
Year	*Millions*	*Percentage of total population*	*Number of farms (thousands)*
1910	32.1	35	6,366
1920	31.9	30	6,454
1930	30.5	25	6,295
1940	30.5	23	6,102
1950	23.0	15	5,388
1960	15.6	9	3,962
1970	9.7	5	2,954
1980	7.2	3	2,440
1985	5.4	2	2,293
1990	4.6	2	2,143

Source: Statistical Abstract of the United States; Economic Report of the President, 1992.

QUICK REVIEW 21-1

- ***Agricultural prices and incomes are volatile in the short run because an inelastic demand translates small changes in farm output and demand into larger changes in prices and incomes.***
- ***Technological progress has generated large increases in supplies of farm products over time.***
- ***Increases in demand for farm products have been modest because demand is inelastic with respect to income.***
- ***The combination of large increases in supply and small increases in demand has made agriculture a declining industry.***

THE ECONOMICS OF FARM POLICY

American agriculture has received massive subsidies which began in the 1930s. The "farm program" involves (1) farm prices, incomes, and output; (2) soil and water conservation; (3) agricultural research; (4) farm credit; (5) crop insurance; and other factors. It came into being and has persisted since the 1930s. However, the typical American farmer and the average politician have both viewed "the farm problem" as essentially a price-income problem and it is this aspect of farm policy which we will explore. We examine the economics of policy at this point, deferring political aspects until later.

Size and Rationale

Farm subsidies are massive. In aggregate terms the 1985 farm bill cost taxpayers about $80 billion during its five-year life. The farm bill passed in 1990 is expected to cost $40 to $55 billion over five years. In 1990 approximately one-fifth of net farm income was from government subsidies, down from two-fifths in 1987.

A variety of arguments have been made to justify farm subsidies.

1 Farmers are comparatively poor and should therefore receive higher prices and incomes through public help.

2 Farming—and particularly the "family farm"—is a fundamental American institution and should be nurtured as a "way of life."

3 Farmers are subject to certain extraordinary hazards—floods, droughts, and invasion by hordes of insects—to which other industries are not exposed and which cannot be fully insured.

4 While farmers are faced with highly competitive markets for their outputs, they typically buy inputs from industries which have considerable market power. In particular, most firms from which farmers buy fertilizer, farm machinery, and gasoline have some capacity to control their prices. Farmers, in contrast, are at the "mercy of the market" in selling their ouputs. Stated differently, agriculture is the last stronghold of pure competition in an otherwise imperfectly competitive economy; it warrants public aid to offset the disadvatageous terms of trade which result (see Figure 21-4).

Background: The Parity Concept

The *Agricultural Adjustment Act of 1933* established the **parity concept** as a cornerstone of agricultural policy. The simple rationale of the parity concept can be readily grasped in both real and nominal terms. In real terms, parity says that year after year for a given output of farm products, a farmer should be able to acquire a given total amount of goods and services. A given real output should always result in the same real income. "If a farmer could take a bushel of corn to town in 1912 and sell it and buy himself a shirt, he should be able to take a bushel of corn to town today and buy a shirt." In nominal terms, *the parity concept suggests that the relationship between the prices received by farmers for their output and the prices they must pay for goods and services should remain constant.* The parity concept clearly implies that, if the price of shirts tripled over some time period, then the price of corn should triple too.

Figure 21-4 indicates why farmers would benefit from having the prices of their products based on 100 percent of parity. This graph shows prices paid and received by farmers from 1910 to 1990 as percentages of the 1910 to 1914 base period. We observe that by 1990 prices paid had increased almost thirteenfold and prices received had increased almost seven times com-

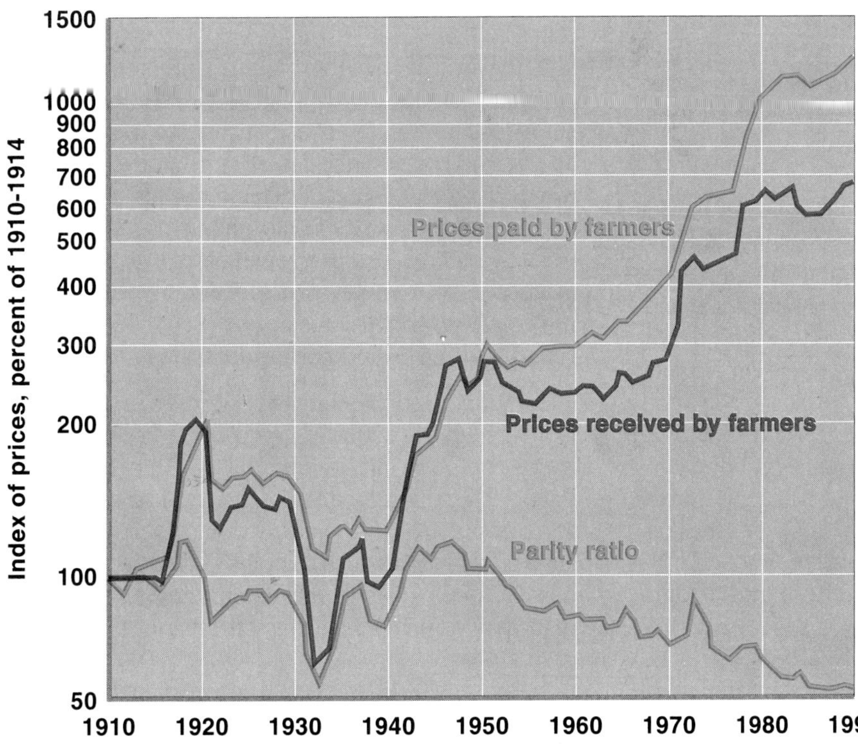

FIGURE 21-4 Prices paid and received by farmers, 1910–1990

In the past four decades the prices paid by farmers have increased ahead of prices received. As a result, the parity ratio—the ratio of prices received to prices paid—has been less than 100 percent.

pared to the base period. The **parity ratio** shown in Figure 21-4 is merely the ratio of prices received relative to prices paid. That is:

$$\text{Parity ratio} = \frac{\text{prices received by farmers}}{\text{prices paid by farmers}}$$

In 1990 the parity ratio was about 54 percent (=7 ÷ 13), indicating that prices received in 1990 were slightly more than one-half as high relative to prices paid as they were in the 1910 to 1914 period. A farm policy calling for 100 percent of parity would require substantially higher prices for farm products to bring the parity ratio up to 100.

Price Supports

The concept of parity prices provides the rationale for government *price floors* on farm products. In agriculture these minimum prices are commonly called **price supports.** The fact that, in the long run, the market prices received by farmers have not generally kept abreast of prices paid by them means that to achieve parity or some percentage thereof, the government may be required to establish above-equilibrium, or "support," prices on farm products. Although specific price support programs have been many and varied, the following discussion captures the essence of government's attempts to use price floors to stabilize and enhance farmers' incomes.

Price supports have a number of significant effects. Suppose, in Figure 21-5, that the support price is P_s compared with equilibrium price P_e.

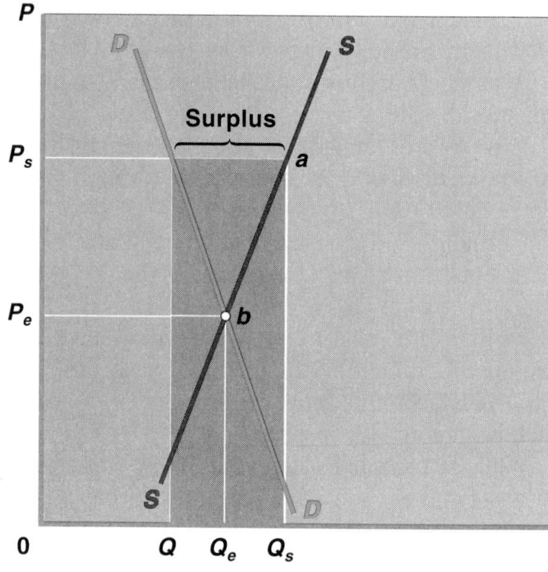

FIGURE 21-5 Effective price supports result in farm surpluses

Application of the parity concept obligates government to support farm prices at above-equilibrium levels, These supported prices result in persistent surpluses of farm products.

1 Surplus Output The most obvious effect is that product surpluses will result. Private consumers will be willing to purchase only OQ units at the supported price, while farmers will supply OQ_s units. What happens to the QQ_s surplus which results? The government must buy it to make the above-equilibrium support price effective. Huge surpluses of farm commodities accumulated in the 1950s and 1960s and stocks of many farm products remain large. For example, the government holds stocks of wheat and other grains which represent about one year's domestic consumption. As we will see, this surplus production is symptomatic of an overallocation of resources to agriculture.

2 Farmers Gain Farmers clearly gain from price supports. In Figure 21-5, gross revenues rise from the free-market level of OP_ebQ_e to the supported level of OP_saQ_s.

3 Consumer Loss Consumers of farm products lose; they will pay a higher price (P_s rather than P_e) and consume less (Q rather than Q_e) of the product. In some instances differences between the market price and the supported price can be substantial. For example, the price of a pound of sugar is four times the world market price; a quart of fluid milk is estimated to be twice as high as it would be without government programs. It is worth noting that the burden of higher food prices falls disproportionately on the poor because they spend a larger proportion of their incomes on food.

4 Societal Loss Society at large loses in two important ways. First, taxpayers will pay higher taxes to finance the government's purchase of the surplus. In Figure 21-5, this added tax burden will amount to the surplus output QQ_s, multiplied by its price P_s—as shown by the gray area. Storage costs add to this tax burden as do costs of maintaining the elaborate bureaucracy which administers the various farm programs.

Society also loses because price supports contribute to economic inefficiency by encouraging an overallocation of resources to agriculture. A price floor or support (P_s) gives rise to a greater commitment of resources to the agricultural sector than would be generated by the free market (P_e). In terms of Chapter 10's purely competitive model, the market supply curve in Figure 21-5 represents the aggregated marginal costs of all farmers producing this product. An efficient allocation of resources occurs where market price, P_e, is equal to marginal cost at point *b*. The resulting output of Q_e reflects an efficient allocation of resources. In contrast, the Q_s output associated with the P_s price support clearly represents an overallocation of resources; for all units of output in the Q_eQ_s range, marginal costs exceed the prices people would be willing to pay for these units. Hence, there is an "efficiency loss" to society.

5 International Costs The costs of farm price supports go beyond those implicit in Figure 21-5. In general, price supports generate economic distortions which transcend national boundaries. For example, above-equilibrium price supports make the American market attractive to foreign producers. But inflows of foreign agricultural products would increase supplies in the United States, aggravating our problem of agricultural surpluses. To prevent this from happening the United States is likely to impose import barriers in the form of tariffs or quotas. These barriers often restrict the production of more efficient foreign producers, while simultaneously encouraging more production from less efficient American producers. The result is a less efficient use of world agricultural resources. This chapter's Last Word suggests that this is the case for sugar.

Similarly, as the United States and other industrially advanced countries with similar agricultural programs dump surplus farm products on world markets, the prices of such products are depressed. Less developed countries—most of which are heavily dependent on world commodity markets—are hurt because their export earnings are reduced. Thus, United States subsidies for rice production have imposed significant costs on Thailand, a major rice exporter. Similarly, our cotton programs have adversely affected Egypt, Mexico, and other cotton-exporting nations.

Coping with Surpluses

An elementary knowledge of the tools of supply and demand suggests that programs designed to reduce market supply or increase market demand would help bring the market price up to the desired supported price, thereby reducing or eliminating farm surpluses (Figure 21-5).

Restricting Supply On the supply side, public policy has long been aimed at restricting farm output. In particular, "set aside" or **acreage allotment programs** have accompanied the application of price supports. In return for price supports on their crops, farmers must agree to limit the number of acres planted. Attempting to bring quantity supplied and quantity demanded into balance, the Department of Agriculture estimates the amount of each product which private buyers will take at the supported price. This amount is then translated into the number of acres of planting which will produce this amount. The total acreage figure is apportioned among states, counties, and ultimately individual farmers.

Similarly, various programs have been employed whereby the Department of Agriculture makes direct payments to farmers for removing land entirely from crop production. For example, under the *soil bank* program, the government in effect rented land from farmers. Such idle land was to be planted in cover crops or timber, not in cash crops.

Have these supply-restricting programs been successful? It is difficult to give an unqualified answer. Certainly they have not eliminated surplus farm production. The basic reason is that acreage reduction invariably results in less than proportionate declines in production. Farmers retire their worst land and keep their best in production. The tilled acres are cultivated more intensively. Better seed, more and better fertilizer and insecticides, and more labor will enhance output per acre. Nonparticipating farmers may expand their acreage in anticipation of higher prices. However, without these output controls, accumulated farm surpluses and their associated costs would have been much greater than has actually been the case.

Bolstering Demand Government has followed several paths to augment the demand for agricultural products.

1 New Uses Both government and private industry have spent considerable sums on research to uncover new uses for agricultural commodities. The production of "gasohol"—a blend of gasoline and alcohol made from grain—is a current and controversial attempt to create a new demand for agricultural output. Most experts conclude that we have been only modestly successful in such endeavors.

2 Domestic and Foreign Demand Government has initiated a variety of programs to augmuent domestic consumption of farm products. For example, the *food-stamp program* is designed to bolster low-income families' demand for food. Similarly, our **Food for Peace program** under Public Law 480 has permitted less developed countries to buy our surplus farm products with their own currencies, rather than with dollars. Furthermore, in international trade bargaining, our negotiators have pressed hard to persuade foreign nations to reduce protective tariffs and other barriers against our farm products.

Although the government's supply-restricting and demand-increasing efforts undoubtedly helped reduce the amount of surplus production, they have not been successful in eliminating surpluses. As noted earlier, farm subsidies in the 1985–1990 period totaled some $80 billion.

CRITICISMS OF FARM POLICY

After more than a half century of experience with government policies designed to stabilize and enhance farm incomes, there is considerable evidence to suggest that these programs are not working well. There is growing feeling among economists and political leaders that the traditional goals and techniques of farm policy must be reexamined and revised. Some of the more important criticisms of agricultural policy follow.

Symptoms and Causes

Our farm programs have failed to get at the causes of the farm problem. Public policy toward agriculture is designed to treat symptoms and not causes. The root *cause* of the farm problem has been a misallocation of resources between agriculture and the rest of the economy. Historically, the problem has been one of too many farmers. The effect or symptom of this misallocation of resources is relatively low farm incomes. *For the most part, public policy in agriculture has been oriented toward supporting farm prices and incomes rather than toward alleviating the resource allocation problem, which is the fundamental cause of relatively low farm incomes.*

Some critics go further and argue that price-income supports have encouraged people to stay in agriculture when they otherwise would have migrated to some nonfarm occupation. That is, the price-income orientation of the farm program has deterred the very reallocation of resources necessary to resolve the long-run farm problem.

Misguided Subsidies

Price-income support programs have most benefited those farmers who least need government assistance. Assuming the goal of our farm program is bolstering of low farm incomes, it follows that any program of government aid should be aimed at farmers at the bottom of the farm income distribution. But the poor, small-output farmer simply does not produce and sell enough in the market to get much aid from price supports. It is the large corporate farm which reaps the benefits by virtue of its large output.

In 1990, for example, the 5 percent of all farms with sales of $250,000 or more received over 38 percent of all direct government subsidies. The poorest 59 percent of all farmers—those who earned less than $20,000 from farming in 1990—received under 3 percent of all direct subsidy payments.[1] If public policy must be designed to supplement farm incomes, a strong case can certainly be made for making those benefits vary inversely, rather than directly, with one's position in the income distribution. An income-support program should be geared to *people,* not *commodities.* Many economists contend that, on equity grounds, direct income subsidies to poor farmers are highly preferable to indirect price support subsidies which go primarily to large and prosperous farmers.

A related point concerns land values. The price and income benefits which various farm programs provide are eventually capitalized into higher farmland values. By making crops more valuable, price supports have made the land itself more valuable. Sometimes this is helpful to farmers, but often it is not. Farmers rent about 40 percent of their farmland, mostly from relatively well-to-do nonfarm landlords. Thus, price supports become a subsidy to people *not* actively engaged in farming.

Policy Contradictions

The complexity and multiple objectives embedded in farm policy yield a number of conflicts and contradic-

[1]U.S. Department of Agriculture, *Economic Indicators of the Farm Sector: National Financial Summary, 1990,* p. 44.

tions. Subsidized research is aimed at increasing farm productivity and increasing the supply of farm products, while acreage reserve and "set aside" programs pay farmers to take land out of production to reduce supply. Price supports for crops mean increased feed costs for ranchers and high prices for animal products to consumers. Tobacco farmers have been subsidized at a time when serious health problems are associated with tobacco consumption. Our sugar program raises sugar prices for domestic growers by imposing import quotas which conflict with our free trade policies.

Declining Effectiveness

There is also reason to believe that farm policy has simply become less effective in accomplishing its goals, In the 1930s most farms were relatively small, semi-isolated units which employed relatively modest amounts of machinery and equipment and provided most of their own inputs. Now, however, farms are larger, highly capital-intensive, and closely integrated with both domestic and international economies.

Farmers now depend on others for seed, fertilizers, insecticides, and so forth. American agriculture uses more than twice as much physical capital (machinery and buildings) per worker as does the economy as a whole. This means that farmers now need to borrow large amounts of money to finance purchases of capital equipment and land *and* for operating capital. Despite an elaborate farm policy designed to enhance farm incomes, high interest rates can easily precipitate losses or bankruptcy for many farmers. Dependence on export markets can also undermine farm policy. A fall in foreign incomes or an increase in the international value of the dollar (which makes American farm products more expensive to foreigners) can unexpectedly reduce American farm exports and easily wipe out any positive effects of agricultural programs on farm incomes. In short, a much wider range of variables may now alter farm incomes and diminish the effectiveness of farm programs.

THE POLITICS OF FARM POLICY

In view of these criticisms, we may well ask why we have an extensive and costly farm program. Why not abandon price supports and return to free markets? Why do farm programs persist although the farm population—and the farm vote—has declined historically (Table 21-1)?

Public Choice Theory Revisited

We can respond to these questions in terms of Chapter 19's public choice theory. Recall that ***rent-seeking behavior*** involves a group—a labor union, firms in a particular industry, or farmers producing a particular product—pursuing political means to transfer income or wealth to themselves at the expense of another group or society as a whole. The ***special-interest effect*** refers to a program or policy from which a small group receives *large* benefits at the expense of a much larger group who *individually* suffer *small* losses.

Suppose a specific group of farmers—peanut or sugar growers or dairy farmers—organize themselves and establish a well-financed political action committee (PAC). The PAC's job is to promote the establishment and perpetuation of government programs which will transfer income to the group (rent-seeking behavior). Thus the PAC vigorously lobbies senators and representatives to enact or perpetuate price supports and estblish import quotas for peanuts, sugar, or milk. They do this by making political contributions to potentially sympathetic legislators. Thus, although peanut production is heavily concentrated in a few states such as Georgia, Alabama, and Texas, the PAC will make contributions to nonpeanut state legislators to gain support.

However, if an interest group—peanut or sugar growers—is small, how can it successfully line its own pockets at the expense of society as a whole? The answer: Although the aggregate costs of the group's program might be considerable, the cost imposed on *each individual* taxpayer is small (the special-interest effect). Indeed, citizen-taxpayers are likely uninformed about and indifferent to issues like these because they have little at stake. Unless you grow sugar beets or peanuts, you have probably no idea how much those programs cost you as an individual taxpayer and consumer, and you do not raise cain, so to speak, if your legislator votes for a sugar program. Civil rights, educational reform, and peace in the Middle East may seem to be much more urgent political issues to you than a program for a handful of peanut or sugar farmers.

There is also political *logrolling* (Chapter 19), the trading of votes on policies and programs to change a negative outcome into a positive outcome. Senator Foghorn votes for a program which benefits Senator Moribund's constituents and Moribund returns the favor. For example: Many members of Congress who represent low-income urban areas vote in favor of farm subsidies. In return, representatives of agricultural areas support such programs as food stamps which provide subsidized food for the poor. Thus we have a rural-urban coalition through which representatives from both areas provide benefits for their constituents and enhance their reelection chances. Such coalitions help explain why farm subsidies persist and why the food stamp program has been greatly expanded over the years.

Public choice theory also tells us that politicians are more likely to favor programs having hidden costs. As we have seen, this is often true of farm programs. In discussing Figure 21-5 we found that price supports involve, not simply an explicit transfer from taxpayer to farmer, but also the costs hidden in higher food prices, storage costs for surplus output, bureaucratic costs of administering farm programs, and costs associated with both domestic and international misallocations of resources. While the explicit or direct cost of the peanut program to taxpayers is only about $4 million a year, the price increase provided by the program carries a hidden subsidy (cost) of $190 million per year. Because the cost of the peanut program is largely indirect and hidden, the program is much more acceptable to politicians and the public than if all costs were explicit.

New Directions?

There is reason to predict that farm subsidies may decline in the future.

1 Declining Farm Population As farm population has declined, its political clout has also diminished. The farm population was about 25 percent of the total in the 1930s when many of our farm programs were established. That population now is less than 2 percent of the total. Urban lawmakers have a 9-to-1 advantage over their rural colleagues. More and more legislators are critically examining farm programs from the vantage point of their effect on consumers' grocery bills rather than farm incomes.

2 Budget Deficits Continued pressures to balance the Federal budget have brought farm subsidies under increased political scrutiny.

3 Program Excesses Program excesses have been increasingly publicized, perhaps weakening the special-interest effect. Examples: In one year in the late 1980s a large California cotton grower received $12 million is subsidy payments; the crown prince of Liechtenstein received a subsidy in excess of $2 million as a partner in a Texas rice farm; and 112 dairy farmers received $1 million each under a program designed to reduce the size of dairy herds. Also, the nonfarm population has become increasingly aware and critical of farm programs. Programs created in the 1930s to help smaller farms are being reevaluated now that agriculture is dominated by large farms increasingly like any other business.

4 Policy Conflicts It is increasingly apparent that domestic farm programs are seriously at odds with the objective of free world trade. This conflict merits more detailed consideration.

WORLD TRADE AND FARM POLICY

A more critical attitude toward farm subsidies is reflected in American negotiations designed to reduce world trade barriers to agricultural products.

Policy Impacts

Consider the impacts of current farm programs on world trade. Virtually every industrialized country—the United States, Canada, Japan, among others—intervenes in agriculture by subsidizing and providing protective trade barriers. For example, the European Community (EC)—made up of twelve western European nations—has established high prices for its domestic agricultural products. These price supports have a number of consequences.

1 To maintain high domestic prices the EC must restrict imports (supplies) of foreign farm products. It does this by imposing import tariffs and quotas, the former being excise taxes and the latter specific quantitative limits on foreign goods.

2 Although the EC was once an importer of food, high price supports have induced European farmers to produce much more output than European consumers want to purchase.

3 To rid itself of these agricultural surpluses the EC has heavily subsidized their export into world markets.

The effects on the United States are that: (1) our farmers have great difficulty in selling to EC nations because of their trade barriers; and (2) subsidized exports from the EC depress world prices for agricultural products, making these markets less attractive to our farmers.

Perhaps most importantly, from an international perspective farm programs such as those of the EC and the United States distort world agricultural trade and thereby the international allocation of agricultural resources. Encouraged by artificially high prices, farmers in industrially advanced nations produce more agricultural output than they would otherwise. The resulting surpluses flow into world markets where they depress prices. This means that farmers in countries with no farm programs—often less developed countries—face artifically low prices for their exports, which signals them to produce less. In this way farm price distortions alter production away from that based on productive efficiency or comparative advantage (Chapter 3). For example, price supports cause American agricultural resources to be allocated to sugar production, although sugar can be produced at perhaps half the cost in the Caribbean and Australia.

One estimate suggests that the benefits of free, undistorted agricultural trade to the industrially advanced economies alone would be about $35 billion per year, with the United States, the EC, and Japan as the major beneficiaries. Corollary benefits are (1) increased American farm exports, which would reduce our international balance of payments deficit; and (2) reduced expenditures on our domestic farm programs, which would help reduce the Federal budget deficit. Thus the United States has compelling economic reasons to favor the liberalization of international agricultural trade.

QUICK REVIEW 21-2

- ***The parity ratio, which is the basis for price supports, shows the ratio of prices received to prices paid by farmers.***
- ***Price supports cause surplus production which government must buy and store; raise both farmer incomes and food prices to consumers; and generate an overallocation of resources to agriculture.***
- ***Farm policy has been criticized for: delaying the exodus of resources from farming; allocating most subsidies to wealthier farmers; conflicting with other policies such as freer world trade; not effectively resolving farm problems; and being very costly.***
- ***The persistence of farm programs is explainable in terms of rent-seeking behavior, the special-interest effect, and other aspects of public choice theory.***
- ***The farm programs of the United States, the European Community, and other industrialized nations have contributed to a misallocation of the world's agricultural resources.***

GATT Negotiations

The United States—along with a number of food-exporting nations known as the Cairns Group (including Australia, New Zealand, Canada, and Argentina)—has been a leading advocate for elimination of trade barriers on agricultural products and, by implication, an advocate for the dismantling of price-support programs. Under the aegis of the General Agreement on Tariffs and Trade (GATT)—an international association of over 100 nations dedicated to the promotion of free world trade—the United States has proposed: (1) a ten-year phaseout of all agricultural tariffs; (2) elimination of agricultural export subsidies over a five-year period; and (3) a phaseout of all domestic farm supports which distort world agricultural trade. Unfortunately, under pressure from their politically powerful farm groups, the EC and Japan have rejected these proposals and negotiations have stalled.

Farm Act of 1990

Despite the failure of the GATT negotiations, recent farm legislation reflects efforts to (1) cut the cost of farm subsidies and (2) increase the role of market (as opposed to supported) prices in agricultural decision making. Specifically, the **Farm Act of 1990** reduces by 15 percent the acreage covered by price guarantees, thereby reducing the cost of subsidy programs. The potential blow to farmers is softened by allowing them to plant the affected acres in alternative crops. Farmers' decisions on these alternative crops will be based on market price signals. For example, many corn and wheat farmers may put the 15 percent reduction in price-supported land into soybeans or sunflowers, based on growing conditions and anticipated prices. In short, the new farm act simultaneously reduces farm subsidies and increases the role of market forces.

Market-Oriented Income Stabilization

From a long-term perspective it seems increasingly likely that farm policy will shift from the goal of enhancing to that of stabilizing farm incomes. The goal of *stabilization* is to reduce the sharp year-to-year fluctuations in farm incomes and prices, but to accept the long-run average of farm prices and incomes which free markets would provide. This contrasts with income *enhancement*, which seeks to provide farmers with commodity prices and incomes above those which free markets would yield. Government might moderate the boom and bust character of agricultural markets by

LAST WORD

THE SUGAR PROGRAM: A SWEET DEAL

The sugar program is a sweet deal for domestic sugar producers, but it imposes heavy costs on domestic consumers and foreign producers.

The United States' program of price supports for sugar has entailed significant costs both domestically and internationally. Recent price supports for some 12,000 American producers have maintained domestic sugar prices at almost double the world price. The estimated aggregate cost to domestic consumers is $3 billion per year.

As a consequence of our high domestic price supports, foreign sugar producers have a very strong incentive to sell their outputs in the United States. But an influx of much cheaper foreign sugar into our domestic market would undermine domestic price supports. Hence, our government has imposed import quotas on foreign sugar. As the difference between United States-supported prices and world prices has increased, import quotas have become more restrictive, with the result that imported sugar has become a declining proportion of our consumption of sweeteners. About 30 percent of our sugar was imported in 1975; currently

supporting prices and accumulating surplus stocks when prices fall significantly below the long-run trend of prices. Conversely, government would augment supply by selling from these stocks when prices rise significantly above the long-run trend.

Proponents feel that the **market-oriented income stabilization policy** has a number of advantages. First, government involvement in agriculture would be diminished in that programs of supply management through acreage reduction would be abandoned. Second, prices would reflect long-run equilibrium levels and therefore lead to an efficient allocation of resources between agriculture and the rest of the economy. By providing farmers with incomes consistent with market-clearing prices, the market system would provide the needed signals to accelerate movement of farmers to nonfarm jobs. Third, taxpayer costs would be significantly reduced. And, finally, the lower average level of farm prices would help to stimulate agricultural exports.

GLOBAL VIEW: FEAST OR FAMINE?

The American farm problem—supply outrunning demand and farm policies which foster surplus production—is not common to most other nations. Many less developed nations, not to mention the former Soviet Union, must presistently import foodstuffs. We frequently read of malnutrition, chronic food shortages, and famine in Africa and elsewhere. In the future—say, four or five decades from now—will the world be unable to feed itself?

While there is no simple response to this question, it is of interest to summarize some of the pros and cons pertinent to the issue. Pessimists, envisioning impending famine as demand increases ahead of supply, make these arguments:

1 The quantity of arable land is finite and its quality is being seriously impaired by wind and water erosion.

2 Urban sprawl and industrial expansion continue to

only 3 or 4 percent is imported. Note that our agricultural policy in the domestic sugar industry largely dictates our international trade policy with respect to that product.

The loss of the American market has had a number of very harmful effects on many of the less developed sugar-exporting countries such as the Philippines, Brazil, and a number of Central American countries. First, exclusion from the American market has significantly reduced their export earnings and national incomes. The decline in export revenues is particularly important because many of the sugar-producing countries are highly dependent on such revenues to pay interest and principal on massive external debts owed to the United States and other industrially advanced nations.

Second, barred by quotas from sale in the United States market, the sugar produced by the less developed countries has been added to world markets, where the increased supply has depressed the world price of sugar.

Third, under the impetus of domestic price supports, American sugar production has increased to the extent that the United States may soon change from a sugar-importing to a sugar-exporting nation. That is, our sugar program may soon be a source of new competition for the sugar producers of the less developed countries. Sugar price supports in the European Community have already turned that group of nations into sugar exporters.

Finally, from both a domestic and a global perspective, the sugar price support programs of the United States and other industrially advanced economies have distorted the worldwide allocation of agricultural resources. Price supports have signaled an overallocation of resources to sugar production by relatively less efficient American producers. American import quotas and consequent low world sugar prices have signaled more efficient foreign producers to restrict their production. In short, high-cost producers are producing more and low-cost producers are producing less sugar with the result being an inefficient allocation of the world's agricultural resources.

Aside from higher sugar prices to consumers, the sugar program has cost jobs in the United States. In the past decade an estimated 7000 jobs have been lost because of refinery closings due to the decline of sugar imports. The Brach Candy Company recently announced that it would probably move some 3500 jobs from Chicago to Canada where sugar prices are lower.

Based primarily on *Economic Report of the President, 1987* (Washington, D.C.: 1987), pp. 165–169. Updated.

convert prime land from agriculture to nonagricultural uses.

3 Our underground water system upon which farmers depend for irrigation is being mined at such a rapid rate that farmlands in some areas will have to be abandoned.

4 World population continues to grow; every day there are thousands of new mouths to feed.

5 Some environmentalists suggest that unfavorable long-run climatic changes will undermine future agricultural production.

Optimists offer the following counterarguments.

1 The number of acres planted to crops has been increasing and the world is far from bringing all its arable land into production.

2 Agricultural productivity continues to rise and the possibility of dramatic productivity breakthroughs lies ahead as we enter the age of genetic engineering. There is also room for substantial productivity increases in the agricultural sectors of less developed countries. For example, improved economic incentives for farm workers in China helped expand agricultural output by about one-third between 1980 and 1985.

3 The rate of growth of world population has in fact been diminishing.

4 We must reckon with the adjustment processes elicited by the market system. If food shortages were to develop, food prices would rise. Higher prices would simultaneously induce more production, constrain the amount demanded and head off the shortages.

Admittedly, the "feast or famine" debate is highly speculative; a clear picture of the world's future production capabilities and consumption needs is not easily discerned. Perhaps the main point is that American agricultural policies should take global considerations into account.

CHAPTER SUMMARY

1 In the short run, the highly inelastic nature of agricultural demand translates small changes in output and small shifts in domestic or foreign demand into large fluctuations in prices and incomes.

2 Rapid technological advance, coupled with a highly inelastic and relatively constant demand for agricultural output, has caused agriculture to be a declining industry.

3 Historically, agricultural policy has been price-centered and based on the parity concept which suggests that the relationship between prices received and paid by farmers should remain constant.

4 The use of price floors or supports has a number of economic effects: **a** surplus production occurs; **b** the incomes of farmers are increased; **c** consumers pay higher prices for farm products; **d** society at large pays higher taxes to purchase and store surplus output, and also bears the cost of an overallocation of resources to agriculture; and **e** other nations bear the costs associated with import barriers and depressed world farm commodity prices.

5 Government has pursued with limited success a variety of programs to reduce the supply of, and increase the demand for, agricultural products to reduce the surpluses associated with price supports.

6 Farm policy has been criticized for **a** confusing symptoms (low farm incomes) with causes (excess capacity); **b** providing the largest subsidies to high-income farmers; **c** contradictions among specific farm programs; and **d** declining effectiveness.

7 The persistence of agricultural subsidies can be explained in terms of public choice theory and, in particular, in terms of rent-seeking behavior, the special-interest effect, and political logrolling.

8 The United States has unsuccessfully sought through GATT to reduce barriers to international agricultural trade.

9 The Farm Act of 1990 reduces the amount of land to which price supports apply and enhances the use of market prices in agricultural decision making.

10 The United States may be moving toward a policy of stabilizing, but not enhancing, farm incomes.

TERMS AND CONCEPTS

short-run farm problem
long-run farm problem
parity concept
parity ratio
price supports
acreage allotment programs
Food for Peace program
Farm Act of 1990
market-oriented income stabilization policy

QUESTIONS AND STUDY SUGGESTIONS

1 Explain how each of the following contributes to the farm problem: **a** the inelasticity of demand for farm products, **b** rapid technological progress in farming, **c** the modest long-run growth in demand for farm commodities, **d** the competitiveness of agriculture, and **e** the relative fixity or immobility of agricultural resources. Do exports increase or reduce the instability of demand for farm products?

2 What relationship, if any, can you detect between the fact that the farmer's fixed costs of production are large and the fact that the supply of most agricultural products is generally inelastic? Be specific in your answer.

3 "The supply and demand for agricultural products are such that small changes in agricultural supply will result in drastic changes in prices. However, large changes in farm prices have modest effects on agricultural output." Carefully evaluate. *Hint:* A brief review of the distinction between *supply* and *quantity supplied* may be of assistance.

4 The key to efficient resource allocation is the shifting of resources from low-productivity to high-productivity uses. Given the high and expanding physical productivity of agricultural resources, explain why many economists want to divert resources from farming in the interest of greater allocative efficiency.

5 "Industry complains of the higher taxes it must pay to finance subsidies to agriculture. Yet the fact that the trend of agricultural prices has been downward while industrial prices have been moving upward suggests that on balance agriculture is actually subsidizing industry." Explain and evaluate.

6 "Because consumers as a whole must ultimately pay the total incomes received by farmers, it makes no real difference whether this income is paid through free farm mar-

kets or through supported prices supplemented by subsidies financed out of tax revenues." Do you agree?

7 Suppose you are president of a local chapter of one of the major farm organizations. You are directed by the chapter's membership to formulate policy statements for the chapter covering the following topics: **a** antitrust policy, **b** monetary policy, **c** fiscal policy, and **d** tariff policy. Briefly outline the policy statements which will best serve the interests of farmers. What is the rationale underlying each statement? Do you see any conflicts or inconsistencies in your policy statements?

8 Carefully demonstrate the economic effects of price supports. On what grounds do economists contend that price supports cause a misallocation of resources?

9 If in a given year the indexes of prices received and paid by farmers were 120 and 165 respectively, what would the parity ratio be? Explain the meaning of this ratio.

10 Reconcile these two statements: "The farm problem is one of overproduction." "Despite the tremendous productive capacity of American agriculture, plenty of Americans are going hungry." What assumptions about the market system are implied in your answer?

11 Use public choice theory to explain the size and persistence of subsidies to agriculture.

12 What are the effects of farm programs such as those of the United States and the European Community on **a** domestic agricultural prices; **b** world agricultural prices; **c** the international allocation of agricultural resources. Use your responses to explain the United States' proposals in the recent GATT negotiations.

13 What are the major criticisms of farm policy? Do you feel that government should attempt to enhance farm incomes, stabilize farm incomes, or allow farm incomes to be determined by free markets? Justify your position.

CHAPTER 22 Income Inequality and Poverty

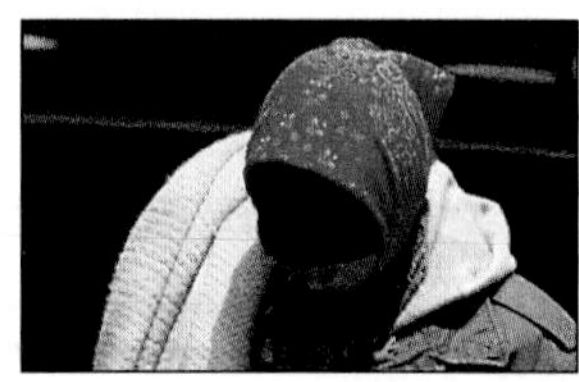

It is not difficult to muster casual evidence which suggests substantial economic disparity in the United States.

Boxer Mike Tyson was estimated to have made over $28 million in 1990; actor Jack Nicholson will reportedly earn $50 million or more for his role in the *Batman* movie.

A recent study concludes that 5.5 million American children—one in eight—go hungry and that another 6 million are nutritionally "at risk." In certain rural counties of the Deep South infant mortality rates exceed those of some less developed countries of Asia and Latin America.

The Census Bureau reports that almost 34 million Americans—over 13 percent of the population—live in poverty. Estimates indicate that 500,000 to 600,000 Americans are homeless.

The average salary in major league baseball is about $900,000 per year. Boston Red Sox pitcher Roger Clemens earns almost $5.4 million per year, which has been estimated to be $1536 per pitch.

Government data indicate that income disparity is increasing in the United States; at present the richest fifth of the population receive almost 45 percent of total income while the poorest fifth receive less than five percent.

The question of how income should be distributed has a long and controversial history in both economics and philosophy. Should our national income and wealth be more or less equally distributed than is now the case? Or, in terms of Chapter 5, is society making the proper response to the "For whom" question?

We begin by surveying some basic facts concerning the distribution of income in the United States. Next, the major causes of income inequality are considered. Third, we examine the debate over income inequality and the tradeoff between equality and efficiency implied by this debate. Fourth, we will look at the poverty problem. Finally, we consider public policy; existing income-security programs are outlined and alternative approaches to welfare reform are discussed.

INCOME INEQUALITY: THE FACTS

How equally—or unequally—is income distributed in the United States? How wide is the gulf between rich and poor? Has the degree of income inequality increased or lessened over time?

Personal Income Distribution

Average income in the United States is among the highest in the world. The average income for all families was $35,353 in 1990. But now we must examine how income is distributed around the average. In Table 22-1 we see that at the low end of the scale 9 percent of all families receive only 1 percent of total personal income. Only 3 percent of the total income went to the 17 percent of families receiving under $15,000 per year in 1990. At the top of the income pyramid 6 percent of families received incomes of $100,000 or more per year; this group received about 18 percent of total personal income. These figures suggest *there is considerable* **income inequality** *in the United States.*

Trends in Income Inequality

Over a period of years economic growth has raised incomes: *Absolutely,* the entire distribution of income has been moving upward over time. Has this changed the *relative* distribution of income? Incomes can move up absolutely, and the degree of inequality may or may not be affected. Table 22-2 is instructive on the relative distribution of income. We divide the total number of income receivers into five numerically equal groups, or *quintiles,* and show the percentage of total personal (before-tax) income received by each in selected years. It is useful to examine the data in Table 22-2 over three periods: 1929–1947, 1947–1969, and 1969–1990.

1929–1947 Period Comparison of the income distribution data for 1929 and 1947 suggests that a significant reduction in income inequality occurred between these years. Note in Table 22-2 the declining percentage of personal income going to the top quintile and the increasing percentage received by the other four quintiles. Many of the forces at work during World War II undoubtedly contributed to this decline in inequality. Warborn prosperity eliminated the many low incomes caused by the severe unemployment of the 1930s, brought a reduction of wage and salary differentials, boosted depressed farm incomes through sharp increases in farm prices, temporarily diminished discrimination in employment, and was accompanied by a decline in property incomes as a share of the national income.

1947–1969 Period Many of the forces making for greater equality during World War II became less effective after the war. During the period between 1947 and 1969, the quintile distribution continued its previous trend toward less inequality, but at a far slower pace. The income share of the lowest income group rose by

TABLE 22-1 The distribution of personal income by families, 1990

(1) Personal income class	(2) Percentage of all families in this class	(3) Percentage of total personal income received by families in this class	(4) Percentage of all families in this class and all lower classes	(5) Percentage of income received by this class and all lower classes
Under $10,000	9	1	9	1
$10,000–$14,999	8	2	17	3
$15,000–$24,999	16	8	33	11
$25,000–$34,999	16	11	49	22
$35,000–$49,999	20	19	69	41
$50,000–$74,999	18	27	87	68
$75,000–$99,999	7	14	94	82
$100,000 and over	6	18	100	100
	100	100		

Source: Bureau of the Census, *Money Income of Households, Families, and Persons in the United States: 1990,* Current Population Reports, Series P–60, No. 174, 1991.

TABLE 22-2 Percentage of total before-tax income received by each one-fifth, and by the top 5 percent, of families, selected years

Quintile	*1929*	*1935–1936*	*1947*	*1955*	*1969*	*1979*	*1990*
Lowest 20 percent	12.5	4.1	5.0	4.8	5.6	5.3	4.6
Second 20 percent		9.2	11.8	12.2	12.4	11.6	10.8
Third 20 percent	13.8	14.1	17.0	17.7	17.7	17.5	16.6
Fourth 20 percent	19.3	20.9	23.1	23.7	23.7	24.1	23.8
Highest 20 percent	54.4	51.7	43.0	41.6	40.6	41.6	44.3
Total	100.0	100.0	100.0	100.0	100.0	100.0	100.0
Top 5 percent	30.0	26.5	17.2	16.8	15.6	15.7	17.9

Source: U.S. Bureau of the Census data. Details may not add up to totals because of rounding.

.6 of a percentage point between 1947 and 1969, while that of the wealthiest quintile fell by 2.4 percentage points.

1969–1990 Period The distribution of income by quintiles has become more unequal since 1969. In 1990 the lowest 20 percent of families received only 4.6 percent of total before-tax income, compared to 5.6 percent in 1969. Meanwhile, the income share received by the highest 20 percent rose from 40.6 percent to 44.3 percent. The reasons for this latest trend in income inequality are in dispute. This chapter's Last Word considers a number of possible causes.

In summary, income inequality fell significantly between 1929 and 1947 but declined more slowly in the 1947–1969 period. More recently, income inequality has increased. But, as a direct comparison of the data for 1947 and 1990 in Table 22-2 reveals, the relative distribution in 1990 was similar to what it was over four decades ago.

The Lorenz Curve

The degree of income inequality can be seen through a **Lorenz curve** as shown in Figure 22-1. Here we *cumulate* the "percentage of families" on the horizontal axis and the "percentage of income" on the vertical axis. The theoretical possibility of a completely equal distribution of income is represented by the diagonal brown line because such a line indicates that any given percentage of families receives that same percentage of income. That is, if 20 percent of all families receive 20 percent of total income, 40 percent receive 40 percent, 60 percent receive 60 percent, and so on, all these points will fall on the diagonal line.

By plotting the 1990 data from Table 22-2 we locate the Lorenz curve to visualize the actual distribution of income. Observe that the bottom 20 percent of all families received about 4.6 percent of the income as shown by point *a*; the bottom 40 percent received 15.4 percent (=4.6 + 10.8) as shown by point *b*; and so forth. The orange area, determined by the extent to which the resulting Lorenz curve sags away from the line of perfect equality, indicates the degree of income inequality. The larger this area or gap, the greater the degree of income inequality. If the actual income distribution were perfectly equal, the Lorenz curve and the diagonal would coincide and the gap would disappear.

At the opposite extreme is the situation of complete inequality where 1 percent of families have 100 percent of the income and the rest have none. In this

FIGURE 22-1 The Lorenz curve

The Lorenz curve is a convenient means of visualizing the degree of income inequality. Specifically, the orange area between the line of perfect equality and the Lorenz curve reflects the degree of income inequality.

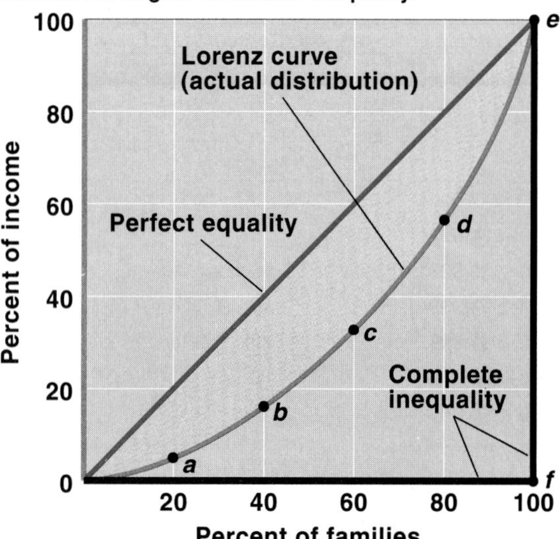

case the Lorenz curve would coincide with the horizontal and right vertical axes of the graph, forming a right angle at point *f* as indicated by the heavy black lines. This extreme degree of inequality would be indicated by the entire area southeast of the diagonal.

The Lorenz curve can be used to contrast the distribution of income at different points in time, among different groups (for example, blacks and whites), before and after taxes and transfer payments are taken into account, or among different countries. As previously observed, the data in Table 22-2 tell us that the Lorenz curve shifted slightly toward the diagonal between 1947 and 1969 and then back away from the diagonal between 1969 and 1990. Comparisons with other nations suggest that the distribution of income in the United States is quite similar to those in most other industrially advanced countries.

ALTERNATIVE INTERPRETATIONS

There has been controversy in recent years as to whether the Bureau of Census data of Tables 22-1 and 22-2 provide an accurate portrayal of the degree of income inequality. Some scholars feel that the yearly census figures are inadequate. To understand the nature of these alleged deficiencies, we must first review these data. The census figures of Tables 22-1 and 22-2 show the distribution of *nominal* income and include not only wages, salaries, dividends, and interest, but also all *cash transfer payments* such as social security and unemployment compensation benefits. The data are *before taxes* and therefore do not account for the effects of personal income and payroll (social security) taxes which are levied directly on income receivers.

Two major criticisms of the census data are, first, that the income concept employed is too narrow, and second, that the income accounting period of one year is too short.

Broadened Income Concept

Edgar K. Browning[1] has made several adjustments in the Census Bureau data, resulting in a quite different picture of income distribution. Among other adjustments, Browning estimates the market value and distribution of *in-kind transfers,* that is, transfers of goods and services under such programs as Medicare, Medicaid, housing subsidies, and food stamps. Similarly, he takes into account the value and distribution of governmentally provided education. Next, he adds capital gains such as increases in the value of stocks, bonds, and real estate. Finally, he subtracts the amounts families pay as Federal personal income and payroll taxes. The picture which emerges from these adjustments not only is a much more equal distribution of income in each year, but it also indicates a trend toward greater equality over time. The movement toward greater equality is primarily a reflection of the rapid growth of in-kind transfers in the past twenty years or so.

It should be noted that Browning has been criticized for overadjusting the census data and thereby concluding that there is greater income equality than actually exists. Indeed, our point is that income distribution data are subject to many interpretations. In this regard, a recent study by the Census Bureau has confirmed that a broader definition of income translates into reduced inequality in the distribution of income. The Census Bureau has found, however, that its broader income concept tightens the "official" income distribution by only 4 percent.[2]

Lifetime Income

Another objection to the census data is that they portray the distribution of income in a single year and thereby conceal the possibility that the *lifetime earnings* of families might be more equal. If Ben earns \$1000 in year 1 and \$100,000 in year 2, while Holly earns \$100,000 in year 1 and only \$1000 in year 2, do we have income inequality? The answer depends on the period of measurement. Annual data would reveal great income inequality; but for the two-year period we have complete equality.

This is important because there is evidence to suggest that there is considerable "churning around" in the distribution of income over time. In fact, most income receivers follow an age-earnings profile where their income starts at relatively low levels, reaches a peak during middle age, and then declines. A glance back at Figure 15-9 reveals this general pattern. It follows that, even if people received the same stream of income over their lifetimes, considerable income inequality would still exist in any given year because of

[1]Edgar K. Browning, "The Trend Toward Equality in the Distribution of Net Income," *Southern Economic Journal,* July 1976, pp. 912–923; and Browning, "How Much More Equality Can We Afford?" *The Public Interest,* Spring 1976, pp. 90–110.

[2]Bureau of the Census, *Measuring the Effect of Benefits and Taxes on Income and Poverty: 1990,* Current Population Report, Series P–60, No. 176, 1991, p. 11.

age differences. In any year the young and old would receive low incomes while the middle-aged received high incomes. This would occur despite complete equality of lifetime incomes.

Morton Paglin[3] has adjusted the quintile data of Table 22-2 for age differences. He found that (1) there is greater income equality when the time factor is taken into account and (2) there was a trend toward greater income equality during the period studied: 1947–1972. The latter conclusion is attributed to the expansion of postsecondary education.

GOVERNMENT AND REDISTRIBUTION

One of the basic functions of government is to redistribute income. As Figure 22-2 and the accompanying table reveal, the distribution of household income *before* taxes and transfers are taken into account is substantially less equal than the distribution *after* taxes and transfers are included.[4] *Government's tax system and transfer programs do reduce significantly the degree of inequality in the distribution of income.* Most of the reduction in income inequality—roughly 80 percent of it—is attributable to transfer payments. Recall from Chapter 19 that our tax system (Federal, state, and local taxes combined) is not highly progressive and, hence, the before-tax and after-tax distributions of income do not differ greatly. But transfers are vital in contributing to greater income equality. More specifically, government transfer payments account for over 75 percent of the income of the lowest quintile and have clearly been the most important means of alleviating poverty in the United States.

INCOME INEQUALITY: CAUSES

Why does the United States have the degree of income inequality evidenced in Tables 22-1 and 22-2? In general, we note that the market system is an impersonal mechanism. It has no conscience, and does not cater to ethical standards concerning what is an "equitable," or "just," distribution of income. In fact, the basically individualistic environment of the capitalist economy is very permissive of a high degree of income inequality. Factors contributing to income inequality include:

1 Ability Differences People have different mental, physical, and esthetic talents. Some have inherited the exceptional mental qualities essential to entering the high-paying fields of medicine, dentistry, and law. Others, rated as "dull normals" or "mentally retarded," are assigned to the most menial and low-paying occupations or are incapable of earning income at all. Some are blessed with the physical capacity and coordination to become highly paid professional athletes. A few have the talent to become great artists or musicians. In brief, native talents enable some individuals to make contributions to total output which command very high incomes. Others are in much less fortunate circumstances.

2 Education and Training Individuals differ significantly in the amounts of education and training they have obtained and, hence, in their capacities to earn income. In part, these differences are a matter of voluntary choice. Smith chooses to enter the labor force upon high school graduation, while Jones decides to attend college. On the other hand, such differences may be involuntary: Smith's family may simply be unable to finance a college education.

3 Tastes and Risks Incomes differ because of differences in "job tastes." Those willing to take arduous, unpleasant jobs—for example, underground mining and garbage collecting—and to work long hours with great intensity will tend to earn more. Some people boost their incomes by "moonlighting," that is, by holding two jobs. Individuals also differ in their willingness to assume risk. We refer here not only to the steeplejack and prize fighter but to the entrepreneur who assumes risk. Though most fail, the fortunate few who gamble successfully on the introduction of a new product or service may realize very substantial incomes.

4 Discrimination Simple supply and demand analysis suggests how discrimination—in this case labor market discrimination—generates income inequality. Suppose that gender discrimination restricts women to such occupations as secretaries, nurses, and teachers—once considered strictly "female" jobs. This means that the supplies of female workers will be great relative to demand in these few occupations so that

[3]Morton Paglin, "The Measurement and Trend of Inequality: A Basic Revision," *American Economic Review,* September 1975, pp. 598–609.

[4]The "before" data in this table differ from the data of Table 22-2 because the latter includes cash transfers. Also, the data in Table 22-2 are for families (a group of two persons or more related by birth, marriage, or adoption and residing together), whereas the data in Figure 22-2 are for all households (one or more persons occupying a housing unit). Finally, the data in Figure 22-2 are based on a broader concept of income than the data in Table 22-2.

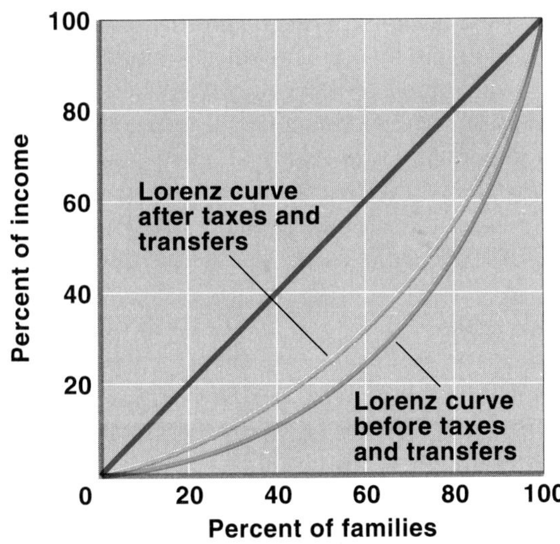

Quintile	Percent of income received, 1990	
	Before taxes and transfers	*After taxes and transfers*
Lowest 20 percent	1.1	5.1
Second 20 percent	7.9	11.1
Third 20 percent	15.5	16.5
Fourth 20 percent	24.7	23.8
Highest 20 percent	50.7	43.5

Source: Bureau of the Census, *Measuring the Effect of Benefits and Taxes on Income and Poverty: 1990*, Current Population Report, Series P-60, No. 176-RD, 1991, p. 5. The data include all money income from private sources, including realized capital gains and employer-provided health insurance. The "after taxes and transfers" data include the value of noncash transfers as well as cash transfers.

FIGURE 22-2 **The impact of government taxes and transfers on income inequality**

The distribution of personal income is significantly more equal after taxes and transfer payments are taken into account. Transfers account for most of the lessening of inequality and provide most of the income received by the lowest quintile of families.

wages and incomes will be low. Conversely, discrimination means males do not have to compete with women in "male" occupations (carpenters, pilots, accountants). This means supply is artificially limited relative to demand in these occupations, with the result that wages and incomes are high.

5 Property Ownership Ownership of property resources and receipt of property incomes are very unequal. The vast majority of households own little or no property resources, while the remaining few supply very great quantities of machinery, real estate, farmland, and so forth. A government study shows that in 1983 the top 10 percent of income receivers in the United States (those with annual incomes of $50,000 or more) owned 72 percent of all stocks, 86 percent of all tax-free bonds, 70 percent of all taxable bonds, and 50 percent of all real estate. The top 2 percent of American income receivers (with annual incomes of $100,000 or more) owned 50 percent of all stocks, 71 percent of all tax-free bonds, 39 percent of all taxable bonds, and 20 percent of all real estate.[5] Similarly, an IRS study for 1986 indicates that nearly 28.5 percent of the nation's personal wealth is held by the richest 1.6 percent of its adults. Asset holdings are much more highly concentrated than are family incomes. Basically, property incomes account for the position of those households at the very pinnacle of the income pyramid. The right of inheritance and the fact that "wealth begets wealth" reinforce the role played by unequal ownership of property resources in determining income inequality.

6 Market Power Ability to "rig the market" on one's own behalf is undoubtedly a major factor in accounting for income inequality. Certain unions and professional groups have adopted policies limiting the supplies of their productive services, thereby boosting the incomes of those "on the inside." Legislation which provides for occupational licensing for barbers, beauticians, taxi drivers, and so forth, can also exert market power favoring the licensed group. The same holds true in the product market; profit receivers in particular stand to benefit when their firm develops some degree of monopoly power.

7 Luck, Connections, and Misfortune There are other important forces which play a part in explaining income inequality. Luck, chance, and "being in the right place at the right time" have all caused individuals

[5] "Survey of Consumer Finances, 1983," *Federal Reserve Bulletin,* September 1984, pp. 679–692. Also see "Financial Characteristics of High-Income Families," *Federal Reserve Bulletin,* March 1986, pp. 163–177.

to stumble into fortunes. Discovering oil on a run-down farm or meeting the right press agent have accounted for some high incomes. Nor can personal contacts and political influence be discounted as means of attaining the higher income brackets. On the other hand, economic misfortunes such as prolonged illness, serious accident, death of the family breadwinner, and unemployment may plunge a family into poverty. The burden of such misfortunes is borne very unevenly by the population and hence contributes to the degree of income inequality.

QUICK REVIEW 22-1

- ***Income inequality has increased in the last decade; currently the top fifth of all families receive almost 45 percent of before-tax income and the bottom fifth receive under 5 percent.***
- ***The Lorenz curve portrays income inequality graphically.***
- ***Broadening the income concept and recognition of "churning" within the income distribution over time both lessen perceived income inequality.***
- ***Government taxes and transfer payments significantly reduce income inequality.***
- ***Differences in ability, education, job tastes, property ownership, and market power—along with discrimination and luck—help explain income inequality.***

EQUALITY VERSUS EFFICIENCY

The critical policy issue concerning income inequality is: What is the optimal amount? While there is no generally accepted answer to this question, much can be learned by exploring the cases for and against greater equality.

The Case for Equality: Maximizing Utility

The basic argument for an equal distribution of income is that income equality is necessary if consumer satisfaction or utility is to be maximized. The rationale for this argument is shown in Figure 22-3 where it is assumed that the money incomes of two individuals, Anderson and Brooks, are subject to diminishing marginal utility (Chapter 8). In any time period income receivers spend the first dollars received on those products they value most, that is, on products whose marginal utility is high. As their most pressing wants become satisfied, consumers then will spend additional dollars of income on less important, lower marginal utility, goods. The identical diminishing "marginal utility from income" curves reflect the assumption that Anderson and Brooks have the same capacity to derive utility from income.

Now suppose there is $10,000 worth of income (output) to be distributed between Anderson and Brooks. The best or optimal distribution would be an equal distribution which causes the marginal utility of the last dollar to be the same for both persons. We can prove this by demonstrating that, for an initially unequal distribution of income, the combined total utility of two individuals can be increased by moving toward equality.

For example, suppose that initially the $10,000 of income is distributed unequally so that Anderson gets only $2500 and Brooks receives $7500. The marginal utility from the last dollar received by Anderson is high ($0a$) and the marginal utility from Brooks' last dollar of income is low ($0b$). Clearly, redistribution of a dollar's worth of income from Brooks to Anderson—that is, toward greater equality—would increase (by $0a - 0b$) the combined total utility of the two consumers. Anderson's utility gain (the dark gray area in Figure 22-3a) exceeds Brooks' loss (the light red area in Figure 22-3b). This will continue to be so until income is equally distributed with each person receiving $5000. At this point the marginal utility of the last dollar is identical for Anderson and Brooks ($0a' = 0b'$) and further redistribution cannot increase total utility.

The Case for Inequality: Incentives and Efficiency

Although the logic of the argument for equality is sound, critics attack its fundamental assumption that there exists some fixed amount of income to be distributed. Critics of income equality argue that *the way in which income is distributed is an important determinant of the amount of income produced and available for distribution.*

Suppose in Figure 22-3 that Anderson earns $2500 and Brooks earns $7500. In moving toward equality, society (government) must *tax* away some of Brooks' income and *transfer* it to Anderson. This tax-transfer process will diminish the income rewards of high-income Brooks and raise the income rewards of low-

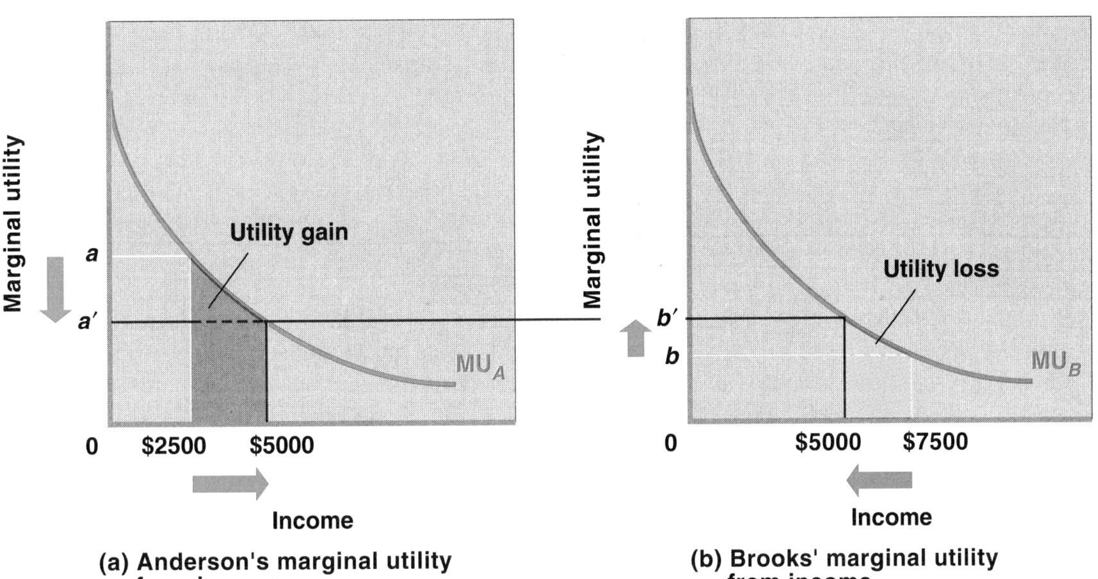

(a) Anderson's marginal utility from income

(b) Brooks' marginal utility from income

FIGURE 22-3 The utility-maximizing distribution of a given income

Proponents of income equality argue that, given identical "marginal utility from income" curves, Anderson and Brooks will maximize their combined utility when any given income (say, $10,000) is equally distributed. If income is unequally distributed ($2500 to Anderson and $7500 to Brooks), the marginal utility derived from the last dollar will be greater for Anderson (0*a*) than for Brooks (0*b*) and, hence, a redistribution toward equality will result in a net increase in total utility. The utility gain shown by the dark gray area in panel (a) exceeds the utility loss indicated by the light red area in panel (b). When equality is achieved, the marginal utility derived from the last dollar of income will be equal for both consumers (0*a*′ = 0*b*′) and, therefore, there is no further redistribution of income which will increase total utility.

income Anderson and in so doing reduce the incentives of both to *earn* high incomes. Why should Brooks work hard, save and invest, or undertake entrepreneurial risks, when the rewards from such activities will be reduced by taxation? And why should Anderson be motivated to increase his income through market activities when government stands ready to transfer income to him?

In the extreme, imagine a situation in which government levies a 100 percent tax on income and distributes the tax revenue equally to its citizenry. Why work hard? Indeed, why work at all? Why assume business risks? Why save—that is, forgo current consumption—to invest? The economic incentives to "get ahead" will have been removed and the productive efficiency of the economy—and the amount of income to be distributed—will diminish. The way the income pie is distributed affects the size of that pie! *The basic argument for income inequality is that it is essential to maintain incentives to produce output and income.*

The Equality–Efficiency Tradeoff[6]

The essence of the income (in)equality debate is that there exists a fundamental **tradeoff between equality and efficiency.**

> The contrasts among American families in living standards and in material wealth reflect a system of rewards and penalties that is intended to encourage effort and channel it into socially productive activity. To the extent that the system succeeds, it generates an efficient economy. But that pursuit of efficiency necessarily creates inequalities. And hence society faces a tradeoff between equality and efficiency.[7]

Thus the problem for a society inclined toward egalitarianism is how to achieve a given redistribution

[6]This section is based on Arthur M. Okun, *Equality and Efficiency: The Big Tradeoff* (Washington, D.C.: The Brookings Institution, 1975).

[7]Ibid., p. 1.

of income so as to minimize the adverse effects on economic efficiency. Consider this *leaky-bucket analogy.* Assume society agrees to shift income from the rich to the poor. But the money must be transferred from affluent to indigent in a leaky bucket. The leak represents an efficiency loss—the loss of output and income—due to the harmful effects of the tax-transfer process on incentives to work, to save and invest, and to accept entrepreneurial risk. It also reflects the fact that resources must be diverted to the bureaucracies which administer the tax-transfer system.

How much leakage will society accept and continue to endorse the redistribution? If cutting the income pie in more equal slices tends to shrink the pie, what amount of shrinkage will society tolerate? Is a loss of one cent on each redistributed dollar acceptable? Five cents? Twenty-five cents? Fifty cents? This is clearly a basic question which will permeate future political debates over extensions and contractions of our income-maintenance programs.

Fueling this debate over the equality–efficiency tradeoff are studies which suggest that the loss from the redistribution bucket may be quite high.

> Edgar Browning and William Johnson . . . concluded that the upper-income groups bearing the costs of the taxes would sacrifice $350 for every $100 that the poor gained—a net efficiency loss of $250. In Arthur Okun's terms, the leaks in the redistribution bucket are enormous—starting out with a bucket of $350 raised from the nonpoor, $250 is lost on the way to delivering it to the poor. For several reasons, critics of this study have found the estimate to be substantially too high. However, even if cut in half, this loss would be troublesome. Would our society be willing to accept a loss of economic efficiency of $125—or even $100—in order to equalize the distribution of income by transferring $100 to the poor? The answer is by no means clear.[8]

THE DISMAL ECONOMICS OF POVERTY

Many people are less concerned with the larger question of income distribution than they are with the more specific issue of income inadequacy. Therefore, armed with some background information on income inequality, we now turn to the poverty problem. How extensive is poverty in the United States? What are the characteristics of the poor? And what is the best strategy to take to lessen poverty?

Defining Poverty

Poverty does not lend itself to precise definition. But, in general, we might say that a family lives in poverty when its basic needs exceed its available means of satisfying them. A family's needs have many determinants: its size, its health, the ages of its members, and so forth. Its means include currently earned income, transfer payments, past savings, property owned, and so on.

The definitions of poverty developed by concerned government agencies are based on family size. In 1990 an unattached individual receiving less than $6,652 per year was living in poverty. For a family of four the poverty line was $13,359. For a family of six, it was $17,839. Applying these definitions to income data for the United States, it is found that *about 13.5 percent of the nation—some 33.6 million people—lives in poverty.*

Who Are the Poor?

Unfortunately for purposes of public policy, the poor are heterogeneous; they can be found in all geographic regions, they are whites and nonwhites, they include large numbers of both rural and urban people, they are both old and young. Yet, as Table 22-3 clearly indicates, poverty is far from randomly distributed. While the total **poverty rate** —the percentage of the population living in poverty—was 13.5 percent for the entire population, blacks and Hispanics bore a disproportionate share compared to whites. On the other hand, thanks to a generous social security system, the incidence of poverty among the elderly is less than that for the population as a whole.

TABLE 22-3 **The distribution of poverty, 1990**

Population group	*Percent in poverty*
Total population	**13.5**
Whites	**10.7**
Blacks	**31.9**
Hispanics	**28.1**
Families headed by women	**33.4**
Children under 18	**20.6**
Elderly (65 or older)	**10.9**

Source: Bureau of the Census, *Money Income and Poverty Status in the United States: 1990,* Current Population Reports, series P–60, no. 175, 1991.

[8] Robert H. Haveman, "New Policy for the New Poverty," *Challenge,* September-October 1988, p. 32.

The incidence of poverty is extremely high among female-headed families and a full one-fifth of all children under 18 years of age live in poverty. The poverty rate among black children was 45 percent in 1990.

The high poverty rates for children are especially disturbing because in a very real sense poverty breeds poverty. Poor children are at greater risk for a range of long-term problems, including poor health and inadequate education, crime, drugs, and teenage pregnancy. Many of today's impoverished children will reach adulthood unhealthy, illiterate, and unemployable. The increased concentration of poverty among children bodes poorly for reducing poverty in the near future. It also implies problems for increasing the future productivity of the labor force because poor children receive less and generally inferior education.

Recalling our previous comments on movement or "churning" within the income distribution, we know that there is considerable movement in and out of poverty. Just over half of those who are in poverty one year will remain below the poverty line the next year. On the other hand, poverty is much more persistent for some groups, in particular black families and families headed by women.

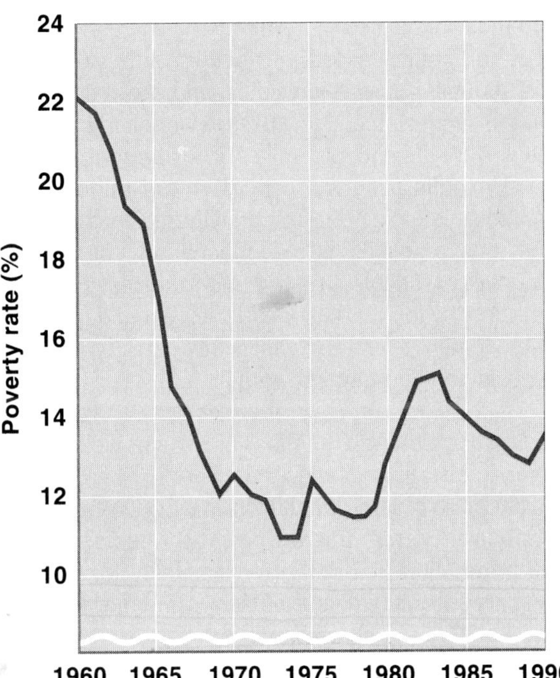

FIGURE 22-4 The U.S. poverty rate, 1960–1990

The percentage of the population living in poverty fell dramatically between 1960 and 1968, remained relatively constant for the next decade, and then climbed between 1978 and 1983. Beginning in 1984, the poverty rate once again began to decline but remained higher in 1990 than it was in the 1970s. Poverty rates for blacks have persistently exceeded those for whites.

Poverty Trends

Not revealed in Table 22-3 is the fact that the percentage of the population living in poverty was higher in 1990 than it was a decade or so ago. This disturbing reality is revealed in Figure 22-4, which traces out the percentage of people in poverty—or the poverty rate—for each year since 1960. Observe that the poverty rate fell significantly between 1960 and 1968, remained relatively unchanged from 1969–1978, and then increased sharply during the early 1980s. This recent increase in the poverty rate resulted from sluggish economic growth, high unemployment rates, and lower real levels of transfer payments. Beginning in 1984, the poverty rate gradually declined as the economy vigorously expanded toward full employment. As has been observed, the poverty rate in 1990 was 13.5 percent.

We need to add a qualification: Although the income levels used to compute the poverty rates shown in Figure 22-4 include cash transfer payments, they do *not* include the monetary value of such noncash transfers as medical care, housing assistance, and food stamps the poor receive. These noncash transfers are similar to income in that they enable the poor to purchase needed goods and services. Recently, the Census Bureau began estimating an alternative poverty rate which includes the value of noncash transfers. The poverty rate for 1990 was 9.8 percent using this expanded definition of income. But, irrespective of definitions of income, the basic point remains: poverty continues to be a persistent and difficult problem.

A "Black Underclass"?

Some observers contend that the city ghettos are spawning a "black underclass" which is trapped in a permanent cycle of poverty, broken homes, welfare, and, frequently, drugs and crime. Relevant statistics are alarming: 1 out of 2 black youths lives in poverty; 1 out of 2 black youths grows up without a father; nearly 40 percent of black teenagers are unemployed; 1 out of 4 births is to a teenager; more than 80 percent of children born to black teenagers are illegitimate; and 1 of every 21 young black men is a homicide victim.

It is argued that in the social and economic isolation of the urban ghetto a new culture—a culture of poverty and dependency—has evolved where attitudes, values, and morality are substantially different from those of mainstream America. Welfare programs—Aid to Families with Dependent Children (AFDC), food stamps, housing subsidies, and the rest—have allegedly undermined incentives to work and have created welfare-dependent families. Furthermore, the historical exodus from the central city of middle-class blacks has left drug dealers, prostitutes, hustlers, and small-time criminals as role models for youngsters. Low-quality schools grossly underprepare minority youth for the job market, while a lenient and overburdened legal system increases the attractiveness of crime as an alternative to work.

At the level of policy, the black underclass view asserts that, although there has been a significant diminution in discrimination over the past several decades and although hundreds of billions have been expended on antipoverty programs, the poverty problem persists. The implication is that the responsibility for poverty rests largely on the poor themselves and that self-help is essential to the alleviation of poverty.

Critics of the black underclass view contend that it is a simplistic and callous position which incorrectly implies that the blame for poverty rests with its victims and not with larger social and economic considerations. Critics of the underclass view also contend that central-city poverty is heterogeneous and has a multitude of causes. What is needed is a far-reaching effort to eliminate racial segregation in housing and schooling, compensatory training and education, more accessible job opportunities, and an income maintenance program which does not discourage work.

The "Invisible" Poor

These facts and figures on the extent and character of poverty may be difficult to accept. After all, ours is an affluent society. How does one square the depressing statistics on poverty with everyday observations of abundance? The answer lies mainly in the fact that much American poverty is hidden; it is largely invisible.

There are three major reasons for this invisibility. First, a sizable proportion of the people in the poverty pool change from year to year. Research has shown that as many as one-half of those in poverty are poor for only one or two years before successfully climbing out of poverty.[9] Hence, many of these people are not visible to us as being permanently downtrodden and needy. Second, the "permanently poor" are increasingly isolated. Poverty persists in the slums and ghettos of large cities and is not readily visible from the freeway or commuter train. Similarly, rural poverty and the chronically depressed areas of Appalachia, the South, and the Southwest are also off the beaten path. Third, and perhaps most important,

> The poor are politically invisible. . . . [They] do not, by far and large, belong to unions, to fraternal organizations, or to political parties. They are without lobbies of their own; they put forward no legislative program. As a group they are atomized. They have no face; they have no voice.[10]

Indeed, the American poor have been labeled "the world's least revolutionary proletariat."

THE INCOME MAINTENANCE SYSTEM

The existence of a wide variety of income-maintenance programs (Table 22-4) is evidence that alleviation of poverty has been accepted as a legitimate goal of public policy. Despite cutbacks in many programs in recent years, income-maintenance programs involve substantial monetary outlays and large numbers of beneficiaries. Total spending for income maintenance has expanded from about 4 percent of domestic production in 1940 to about 13 percent currently.

Our income-maintenance system consists of two kinds of programs: (1) social insurance programs and (2) public assistance or "welfare" programs.

Social Insurance Programs

Social insurance programs partially replace earnings lost due to retirement and temporary unemployment. "Social security" (technically Old Age, Survivors, and Disability Health Insurance or OASDHI), unemployment compensation, and Medicare are the main social insurance programs. Benefits are viewed as earned rights and do not carry the stigma of public charity. These programs are financed primarily out of Federal payroll taxes.

OASDHI and Medicare **OASDHI** is a gigantic social insurance program financed by compulsory payroll taxes levied upon both employers and employees. Ge-

[9] Greg J. Duncan, *Years of Poverty, Years of Plenty* (Ann Arbor, Mich.: University of Michigan Press, 1984).

[10] Michael Harrington, *The Other America: Poverty in the United States,* rev. ed. (New York: The Macmillan Company, 1970), p. 14.

TABLE 22-4 **Characteristics of major income-maintenance programs**

Program	Basis of eligibility	Source of funds	Form of aid	Fiscal 1990: Expenditures* (billions of dollars)	Fiscal 1990: Beneficiaries (millions)
Social Insurance Programs					
Old Age, Survivors, and Disability Health Insurance (OASDHI)	Age, disability, or death of parent or spouse; individual earnings	Federal payroll taxes on employers and employees	Cash	$248	40
Medicare	Age or disability	Federal payroll tax on employers and employees	Subsidized health insurance	98	34
Unemployment compensation	Unemployment	State and Federal payroll taxes on employers	Cash	7	14
Public Assistance Programs					
Supplemental Security Income (SSI)	Age or disability; income	Federal revenues	Cash	6	5
Aid to Families with Dependent Children (AFDC)	Certain families with children; income	Federal-state-local revenues	Cash and services	18	12
Food stamps	Income	Federal revenues	Vouchers	14	20
Medicaid	Persons eligible for AFDC or SSI and medically indigent	Federal-state-local revenues	Subsidized medical services	55	24

*Expenditures by Federal, state, and local governments; excludes administrative expenses.

Source: Social Security Bulletin, September 1991, and *Statistical Abstract of the United States, 1991.*

nerically known as "social security," the program replaces earnings lost because of a worker's retirement, disability, or death. A payroll tax of 7.65 percent is levied on both worker and employer and applies to the first $55,500 of wage income. Workers may retire at 65 with full benefits or at 62 with reduced benefits. When the worker dies, benefits accrue to the survivors. Special provisions provide benefits for disabled workers. Currently, social insurance covers over 90 percent of all employed persons in the United States. In 1989 some 40 million people received OASDHI checks averaging about $600 per month.

Medicare was appended to OASDHI in 1965. The hospital insurance it provides for the elderly and disabled is financed out of the payroll tax. Medicare also makes available a low-cost voluntary insurance program which helps pay doctor fees.

Unemployment Compensation All fifty states sponsor unemployment insurance programs. **Unemployment compensation** is financed by a modest payroll tax which varies by state and according to each firm's employment history. Any insured worker who becomes unemployed can, after a short waiting period (usually a week), become eligible for benefit payments. Almost 90 percent of all civilian workers are covered by the program. Size of payments and the number of weeks they may be received vary considerably from state to state. Generally speaking, benefits approximate one-half of a worker's after-tax wages up to a certain maximum payment. Benefits averaged $152 weekly in 1990. The number of beneficiaries and the level of total disbursements vary greatly over the business cycle.

Public Assistance Programs

Public assistance, or *welfare, programs* provide benefits for those who are unable to earn income because of permanent handicaps or dependent children. These programs are financed out of general tax revenues and are regarded as public charity. Individuals and families must demonstrate low incomes in order to qualify for aid. The Federal government finances about two-thirds of the welfare program expenditures.

Many needy persons who do not qualify for social insurance programs are assisted through other programs. Beginning in 1972 Federal grants to states for public assistance to the aged, the blind, and the disabled were terminated and a new Federally financed and administered **Supplemental Security Income (SSI) program** was created. The purpose of SSI is to establish a uniform, nationwide minimum income for these three categories of people who are unable to work. Over half the states provide additional income supplements to the aged, blind, and disabled.

The **Aid to Families with Dependent Children (AFDC) program** is state-administered, but partly financed with Federal grants. The program provides aid to families in which dependent children do not have the financial support of a parent, usually the father, because of death, disability, divorce, or desertion.

The **food stamp program** is designed to provide all low-income Americans with a "nutritionally adequate diet." Under the program eligible households receive monthly allotments of coupons which are redeemable for food. The amount of food stamps received varies inversely with a family's earned income.

Medicaid helps finance medical expenses of individuals participating in both the SSI and the AFDC programs.

QUICK REVIEW 22-2

- ***The fundamental argument for income equality is that it maximizes consumer utility; the basic argument for income inequality is that it is necessary to stimulate economic incentives.***
- ***By government standards almost 34 million people or 13.5 percent of the population live in poverty.***
- ***Our income maintenance system comprises both social insurance programs and public assistance ("welfare") programs.***

"The Welfare Mess"

There is no doubt that the income maintainence system—not to mention local relief, housing subsidies, minimum-wage legislation, veterans' benefits, private transfers through charities, pensions, and supplementary unemployment benefits—provides important means of alleviating poverty. On the other hand, the system has been subject to many criticisms in recent years.

1 Administrative Inefficiencies Critics charge that the willy-nilly growth of our welfare programs has created a clumsy and inefficient system, characterized by red tape and dependent on a huge bureaucracy for its administration. Administrative costs account for relatively large portions of the total budget of many programs.

> The amount necessary to lift every man, woman, and child in America above the poverty line has been calculated, and it is *one-third* of what is in fact spent on poverty programs. Clearly, much of the transfer ends up in the pockets of highly paid administrators, consultants, and staff as well as higher income recipients of benefits from programs advertised as antipoverty efforts.[11]

2 Inequities Serious inequities arise in welfare programs in that people with similar needs may be treated very differently.

> Benefit levels vary widely among States and among different demographic and family groups. Geographic differentials arise primarily because benefits under the two major public assistance programs—AFDC and Medicaid—are essentially controlled by the States. As a result, sharp disparities in benefit levels exist between the poorer, rural States and the wealthier, more urban areas. . . . [12]

A family in New York City might receive welfare benefits two times as great as the same family in Mississippi. Furthermore, control of the system is fragmented and some low-income families "fall between the cracks" while other families collect benefits to which they are not entitled.

3 Work Incentives A major criticism is that most of our income-maintenance programs impair incentives to work. This is because all welfare programs are constructed so that a dollar's worth of earned income yields less than a dollar of net income. As earned income increases, program benefits are reduced. An in-

[11] Thomas Sowell, *Markets and Minorities* (New York: Basic Books, Inc., Publishers, 1981), p. 122.

[12] *Economic Report of the President, 1978,* pp. 225–226.

dividual or family participating in several welfare programs may find that, when the loss of program benefits and the effect of payroll taxes on earnings are taken into account, the individual or family is absolutely worse off by working. In effect, the marginal tax rate on earned income exceeds 100 percent!

There are other criticisms. Noncash transfers interfere with freedom of consumer choice. Public assistance programs sap initiative and encourage dependency. AFDC regulations in some states promote family breakup by encouraging unemployed fathers to abandon their families so the spouse and children can qualify for benefits. AFDC benefits subsidize birth outside of marriage; nearly one-half of the mothers in the AFDC program have illegitimate children. Various welfare programs foster social divisiveness between workers and welfare recipients. For example, working mothers with small children may wonder out loud why poor mothers receiving AFDC should not also work for their money.

REFORM PROPOSALS

These criticisms have led to calls to reform the public assistance system. Although reform proposals have taken numerous forms, two broad approaches have dominated: negative income tax schemes and "workfare" plans.

Negative Income Tax

One contention is that the entire patchwork of existing welfare programs should be replaced by a **negative income tax** (NIT). The term NIT suggests that, just as the present (positive) income tax calls for families to "subsidize" the government through taxes when their incomes rise *above* a certain level, the government should subsidize households with NIT payments when household incomes fall *below* a certain level.

Comparing Plans Let's examine the two critical elements of any NIT plan. First, a NIT plan specifies a **guaranteed annual income** below which family incomes would not be allowed to fall. Second, the plan embodies a **benefit-loss rate** which indicates the rate at which subsidy benefits are reduced or "lost" as a consequence of earned income. Consider Plan One of the three plans shown in Table 22-5. In Plan One guaranteed annual income is assumed to be $8000 and the benefit-loss rate is 50 percent. If the family earns no income, it will receive a NIT subsidy of $8000. If it earns $4000, it will lose $2000 ($4000 of earnings *times* the 50 percent benefit-loss rate) of subsidy benefits and total income will be $10,000 (=$4000 of earnings *plus* $6000 of subsidy). If $8000 is earned, the subsidy will fall to $4000, and so on. Note that at $16,000 the NIT subsidy becomes zero. The level of earned income at which the subsidy disappears and at which normal (positive) income taxes apply to further increases in earned income is called the **break-even income.**

One might criticize Plan One on the grounds that a 50 percent benefit-loss rate is too high and therefore does not provide sufficient incentives to work. Hence, in Plan Two the $8000 guaranteed income is retained, but the benefit-loss rate is reduced to 25 percent. However, note that the break-even level of income increases to $32,000 and many more families would now qualify for NIT subsidies. Furthermore, a family with any given earned income will now receive a larger NIT sub-

TABLE 22-5 The negative income tax: three plans *(hypothetical data for a family of four)*

Plan One ($8000 guaranteed income and 50% benefit-loss rate)			*Plan Two ($8000 guaranteed income and 25% benefit-loss rate)*			*Plan Three ($12,000 guaranteed income and 50% benefit-loss rate)*		
Earned income	*NIT subsidy*	*Total income*	*Earned income*	*NIT subsidy*	*Total income*	*Earned income*	*NIT subsidy*	*Total income*
$ 0	$8,000	$ 8,000	$ 0	$8,000	$ 8,000	$ 0	$12,000	$12,000
4,000	6,000	10,000	8,000	6,000	14,000	8,000	8,000	16,000
8,000	4,000	12,000	16,000	4,000	20,000	16,000	4,000	20,000
12,000	2,000	14,000	24,000	2,000	26,000	24,000*	0	24,000
16,000*	0	16,000	32,000*	0	32,000			

*Indicates break-even income. Determined by dividing the guaranteed income by the benefit-loss rate.

sidy. For both of these reasons, a reduction of the benefit-loss rate to enhance work incentives will raise the cost of a NIT plan.

Examining Plans One and Two, still another critic might argue that the guaranteed annual income is too low in that it does not get families out of poverty. Plan Three raises the guaranteed annual income to $12,000 and retains the 50 percent benefit-loss rate of Plan One. While Plan Three does a better job of raising the incomes of the poor, it too yields a higher break-even income than Plan One and would therefore be more costly. Furthermore, if the $12,000 income guarantee of Plan Three were coupled with Plan Two's 25 percent benefit-loss rate to strengthen work incentives, the break-even income level would shoot up to $48,000 and add even more to NIT costs.[13]

Goals and Conflicts By comparing these three plans we find that there are conflicts or tradeoffs among the goals of an "ideal" income-maintenance plan. First, a plan should be effective in getting families out of poverty. Second, it should provide adequate incentives to work. Third, the plan's costs should be reasonable. Table 22-5 tells us that these three objectives conflict with one another and that compromises or tradeoffs are necessary.

Plan One, with a low guaranteed income and a high benefit-loss rate, keeps costs down. But the low-income guarantee means it is not very effective in eliminating poverty and the high benefit-loss rate weakens work incentives. In comparison, Plan Two has a lower benefit-loss rate and therefore stronger work incentives. But it is more costly because it involves a higher break-even income and therefore pays benefits to more families.

Compared to Plan One, Plan Three entails a higher guaranteed income and is clearly more effective in eliminating poverty. While work incentives are the same as with Plan One, the higher guaranteed income makes the plan more costly. The problem is to find the magic numbers which will provide a "decent" guaranteed income, maintain "reasonable" incentives to work, and entail "acceptable" costs. While abolishing most of our current public assistance programs in favor of the NIT might be an improvement, the NIT is fraught with internal tradeoffs and should not be regarded as a panacea. In fact, reform efforts have moved away from the NIT in recent years.

Workfare Plans

However desirable the establishment of a NIT might be, political realities are such that piecemeal changes to the income maintenance system are more likely. In fact, most critical attention has focused on AFDC, for several reasons. First, as noted earlier, AFDC may encourage family dissolution. Second, it is contended that the program encourages—or at least subsidizes—illegitimate births. Third, some critics contend that AFDC is conducive to a "culture of poverty" where poverty becomes a way of life and is passed from generation to generation. Also, according to government studies, many recipients of AFDC receive benefits fraudulently. Fifth, as more middle-class mothers with children join the labor force, a consensus is emerging that poor mothers receiving AFDC should also work for their incomes.

These criticisms have led to a variety of **workfare proposals**—also called "welfare-to-work" plans—which would alter the AFDC program by providing work, training, and education activities to help, and eventually require, welfare recipients to move from public assistance to employment. People on welfare who undertake training or enter the labor force would also receive child care and transportation subsidies. As an additional aspect of this overall approach, earnings of absentee parents—whether married or unmarried—would be taken directly from workers' paychecks to pay child support.

Several states have had some success in their experiments with the "welfare-to-work" approach to poverty. The success of these state programs helped generate support for an overhaul of the AFDC program nationally. In late 1988 Congress passed and the President signed into law the **Family Support Act of 1988,** more commonly called the *Welfare Reform Act of 1988.* This important act embraces the workfare approach and includes the following provisions:

1 Each state must establish a Job Opportunities and Basic Skills program (JOBS) through which AFDC parents will be offered basic and remedial education, literacy classes, job skills training, job readiness activities, and job placement.

2 States must provide child care and Medicaid coverage for 12 months to welfare families switching from welfare rolls to employment. The purpose is to reduce the costs of moving from welfare to work and thus to lessen the incentives to stay on welfare.

[13]You may have sensed the generalization that, given the guaranteed income, the break-even level of income varies *inversely* with the benefit-loss rate. Specifically, the break-even income can be found by dividing the guaranteed income by the benefit-loss rate. Hence, for Plan One, $8000/.50 = $16,000. Can you also demonstrate that, given the benefit-loss rate, the break-even level of income varies *directly* with the guaranteed income?

LAST WORD

THE CAUSES OF GROWING INCOME INEQUALITY

Government data indicate that the gap between rich and poor in the United States has increased in the past twenty years.

A number of interrelated hypotheses have been put forth to explain growing income disparity.

1 Industrial Restructuring One possible explanation is that our industrial mix has changed from goods to services. The service sectors have both lower average wages and greater wage variation than the goods sectors. The result is greater income inequality.

2 Import Competition A related explanation is that more competition from imports in the 1970s and 1980s severely reduced the demand for and employment of less skilled but highly paid workers in such industries as automobiles and steel. The decline in such jobs reduced the average wage for less skilled workers. It also swelled the ranks of workers in already low-paying industries, placing further downward pressure on wages in such industries.

3 Returns to Education The college wage premium—the earnings advantage enjoyed by college graduates in comparison to high-school graduates—rose significantly in the 1980s. This implies a growing wage gap between more skilled and less skilled workers. The widening premium suggests that the demand for college graduates may have increased sharply relative to the demand for less skilled workers, reflecting the emergence of new high-tech industries such as computers and biomedicine. There has also been a dramatic increase in the compensation of chief executive officers.

4 Demographic Changes The entrance of large numbers of less experienced and therefore less skilled "baby boomers" into the labor force in the 1970s and 1980s may have contributed to greater income inequality. As large numbers of younger people entered the labor force, the median age of the average worker fell. Since younger workers typically earn less than older workers, overall income inequality rose. In addition, the labor force participation of the wives of high-income husbands increased at a faster rate than for low-income husbands, adding to family income disparty. Finally, the number of unmarried or divorced women with children—who are very likely to be low income—has increased greatly.

5 Taxes and Transfers Legislation in the 1980s reduced Federal marginal tax rates such that high-income people are being taxed at rates below the levels of the 1960s and 1970s. Conversely, welfare benefits for the poor have either been cut or have not kept pace with inflation.

Conclusion: The widening of our income distribution is a complex phenomenon which is not readily explained in terms of one or two factors.

3 All states must begin offering welfare benefits to qualified two-parent families when the main wage earner is unemployed. The purpose of this provision is to reduce the incidence of family break-up associated with the AFDC program.

Supporters of the law believe that it can play an important role in helping end a "culture of welfare" in which dropping out of school, having a child, and going on welfare have allegedly become a normal way of life for part of the welfare population.

CHAPTER SUMMARY

1 The distribution of personal income in the United States reflects considerable inequality. The Lorenz curve shows the degree of income inequality graphically.
2 Income inequality lessened significantly between 1929 and the end of World War II, but inequality has increased since 1969.
3 Critics contend that **a** the use of a broadened concept of income and **b** recognition that the positions of individual families in the distribution of income change over time would reveal less income inequality than do Census data.
4 Government taxes and transfers—particularly the latter—lessen the degree of income inequality significantly.
5 Causes of income inequality include discrimination and differences in abilities, education and training, job tastes, property ownership, and market power.
6 The basic argument for income equality is that it maximizes consumer satisfaction from a given income. The main argument against income equality is that equality undermines incentives to work, invest, and assume risks, thereby reducing the amount of income available for distribution.
7 Current statistics suggest that 13.5 percent of the nation lives in poverty. Poverty is concentrated among blacks, Hispanics, female-headed families, and young children.
8 Our present income-maintenance system is composed of social insurance programs (OASDHI, Medicare, and unemployment compensation) and public assistance programs (SSI, AFDC, food stamps, and Medicaid).
9 Present welfare programs have been criticized as being administratively inefficient, fraught with inequities, and detrimental to work incentives. Reform proposals have been of two basic types: negative income tax proposals and "workfare" plans.

TERMS AND CONCEPTS

income inequality
Lorenz curve
tradeoff between equality and efficiency
poverty rate
OASDHI
Medicare
unemployment compensation
Supplemental Security Income (SSI)
food stamp program
Aid to Families with Dependent Children (AFDC)
Medicaid
negative income tax
benefit-loss rate
guaranteed annual income
break-even income
workfare proposals
Family Support Act of 1988

QUESTIONS AND STUDY SUGGESTIONS

1 What criticisms have been made of Census Bureau data on income inequality? How and to what extent does government contribute to income equality?

***2** Assume Al, Beth, Carol, David, and Ed receive incomes of $500, $250, $125, $75, and $50 respectively. Construct and interpret a Lorenz curve for this five-person economy.

3 Briefly discuss the major causes of income inequality. With respect to income inequality, is there any difference between inheriting property and inheriting a high IQ? Explain.

4 Use the "leaky-bucket analogy" to discuss the equality–efficiency tradeoff. Compared to our present income-maintenance system, do you feel that a negative income tax would reduce the leak?

5 Should a nation's income be distributed to its members according to their contributions to the production of that total income or to the members' needs? Should society attempt to equalize income *or* economic opportunities? Are the issues of "equity" and "equality" in the distribution of income synonymous? To what degree, if any, is income inequality equitable?

6 Analyze in detail: "There need be no tradeoff between equality and efficiency. An 'efficient' economy which yields an income distribution which many regard as unfair may cause those with meager income rewards to become discouraged and stop trying. Hence, efficiency is undermined. A fairer distribution of rewards may generate a higher average productive effort on the part of the population, thereby enhancing efficiency. If people think they are playing a fair economic game and this belief causes them to try harder, an economy with an equitable income distribution may be efficient as well."[14]

7 Comment on or explain:

a "To endow everyone with equal income will cer-

[14]Paraphrased from Andrew Schotter, *Free Market Economics* (New York: St. Martin's Press, 1985), pp. 30–31.

tainly make for very unequal enjoyment and satisfaction."

b "Equality is a 'superior good'; the richer we become, the more of it we can afford."

c "The mob goes in search of bread, and the means it employs is generally to wreck the bakeries."

d "Under our welfare system we have foolishly clung to the notion that employment and receipt of assistance must be mutually exclusive."

e "Some freedoms may be more important in the long run than freedom from want on the part of every individual."

f "Capitalism and democracy are really a most improbable mixture. Maybe that is why they need each other—to put some rationality into equality and some humanity into efficiency."

8 What are the essential differences between social insurance and public assistance programs? What are the major criticisms of our present income-maintenance system?

9 The table shown below contains three illustrative negative income tax (NIT) plans.

a Determine the basic benefit, the benefit-loss rate, and the break-even income for each plan.

b Which plan is the most costly? The least costly? Which plan is most effective in reducing poverty? The least effective? Which plan embodies the strongest disincentive to work? The weakest disincentive to work?

c Use your answers in part **b** to explain the following statement: "The dilemma of the negative income tax is that you cannot bring families up to the poverty level on the one hand, and simultaneously preserve work incentives and minimize program costs on the other."

10 "The father of a child has a responsibility to help support that child, irrespective of whether or not he is married to the mother. In addition, the able-bodied single mother has a responsibility to help support her child by working." Do you agree? How might these "principles" be incorporated into a welfare program? What problems might arise in implementing this program in the real world?

Plan One			*Plan Two*			*Plan Three*		
Earned income	*NIT subsidy*	*Total income*	*Earned income*	*NIT subsidy*	*Total income*	*Earned income*	*NIT subsidy*	*Total income*
$ 0	**$4,000**	**$4,000**	**$ 0**	**$4,000**	**$ 4,000**	**$ 0**	**$8,000**	**$ 8,000**
2,000	**3,000**	**5,000**	**4,000**	**3,000**	**7,000**	**4,000**	**6,000**	**10,000**
4,000	**2,000**	**6,000**	**8,000**	**2,000**	**10,000**	**8,000**	**4,000**	**12,000**
6,000	**1,000**	**7,000**	**12,000**	**1,000**	**13,000**	**12,000**	**2,000**	**14,000**

Labor-Market Issues: Unionism, Discrimination, and Immigration*

In this chapter we examine three important labor market issues: unionism, discrimination, and immigration. Although largely unrelated to each other, each issue is significant in its own right.

1 Much of the chapter consists of a detailed look at organized labor, collective bargaining, and the economic effects of unionism. What are the reasons for the historical growth and the recent decline of unionism? What impact do unions have on wages, efficiency and productivity, the distribution of earnings, and inflation?

2 We next discuss discrimination, its dimensions, and its costs.

3 Finally, we consider the much publicized issue of immigration of foreign labor to the United States. How many people enter the United States legally and illegally each year? What are the economic ramifications of this inflow of people?

BRIEF HISTORY OF AMERICAN UNIONISM

Some 17 million workers—16 percent of the employed labor force—now belong to labor unions. Bare statistics, however, may understate the importance of unions. The wage rates, hours, and working conditions of nonunionized firms and industries are influenced by those determined in organized industries. Unions are clearly important economic institutions of American capitalism.

As we consider how the labor movement evolved in the United States, we must examine government policy toward organized labor because labor legislation and union growth are intimately related. In terms of national labor policy, the American labor movement has gone through three phases: repression (1790 to 1930), encouragement (1930 to 1947), and intervention (1947 to date). Though the dates are somewhat arbitrary, these three phases serve as an excellent guide for our discussion.

Repression Phase: 1790 to 1930

Labor unions have existed in the United States for 200 years. Shoemakers, carpenters, printers, and other skilled craftsmen formed unions of some permanence in the early 1790s. As Figure 23-1 indicates, despite this early start, union growth was relatively slow and spo-

*Instructors may choose to treat the three topics in this chapter selectively.

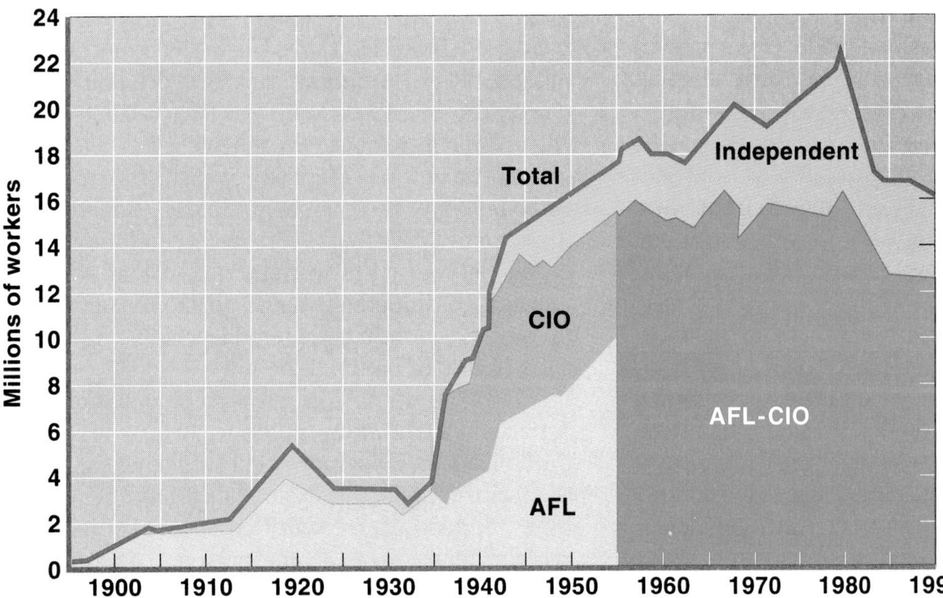

FIGURE 23-1 The growth and decline of union membership
Most of the absolute growth in organized labor has occurred since 1935. However, organized labor has been declining as a percentage of the labor force for some time and, in recent years, the absolute number of union members has also diminished. (U.S. Bureau of the Census and Bureau of Labor Statistics.)

radic until the 1930s. Two factors may account for this meager progress: (1) the hostility of the courts toward labor unions, and (2) the reluctance of American businesses to recognize and bargain with unions.

Unions and the Courts Not until the 1930s did legislation spell out the Federal government's policy toward labor unions. Lacking a national labor policy, it was up to the courts to decide on specific union-management conflicts. And, much to the dismay of organized labor, the courts were generally hostile toward unions. Their hostility had two sources. First, most judges had propertied-class backgrounds. Second, the courts are inherently conservative institutions charged with the responsibility of protecting *established* property rights. Unions, throughout the 1800s and the early decades of the 1900s, were in the unenviable position of seeking rights for labor at the expense of the *existing* rights of management.

The hostility of the courts was first given vent in the **criminal conspiracy doctrine.** This doctrine, "imported" by American courts from English common law at the turn of the nineteenth century, concluded that organizations of workers to raise wages were criminal conspiracies and hence illegal. Although unions as such were later recognized by the courts as legal organizations, the techniques employed by unions to press their demands—strikes, picketing, and boycotting—were generally held to be illegal. And, in the latter part of the 1800s, the courts employed both antitrust laws and injunctions to impede the labor movement significantly.

Although Congress passed the Sherman Act of 1890 (Chapter 20) for the expressed purpose of thwarting the growth of business monopolies, the courts interpreted the loose wording of the act to include labor unions as conspiracies in restraint of trade and frequently so applied the act.

A simpler and equally effective antiunion device was the **injunction.** An injunction, or restraining order, is a court order directing that some act not be carried out, on the ground that irreparable damage will be done to those affected by the action. The attitude of the courts toward unions was such that it was easy for employers to obtain injunctions from the courts, prohibiting unions from enforcing their demands by striking, picketing, and boycotting. Stripped of these weapons, unions were relatively powerless to obtain the status and rights they sought.

Antiunion Techniques of Management The business community, hostile to unions from their inception, developed a group of techniques to undermine unions. A simple antiunion technique was ferreting out and firing prounion workers. Too, many employers felt it their duty to inform fellow employers that the discharged workers were "troublemakers" and "labor agitators" not fit to be hired. This combination of **discriminatory**

discharge and **blacklisting** made it extremely risky for workers to seek to organize a union. One's present and future employment opportunities were at stake.

Another potent weapon in management's struggle to keep unions down was the **lockout,** management's counterpart of the strike. By closing up shop for a few weeks, employers were frequently able to bring their employees to terms and destroy any notions they might have about organizing a union. Workers of the late 1800s and early 1900s were not blessed with savings accounts or multimillion-dollar strike funds to draw upon in such emergencies.

Where workers were determined to organize, pitched battles often ensued. Rocks, clubs, shotguns, and an occasional stick of dynamite were the shadowy ancestors of collective bargaining. Some of the darkest pages of American labor history concern the violent clashes between workers and company-hired *strikebreakers.* The Homestead strike of 1892, the Pullman strike of 1894, and the Ludlow Massacre of 1914 are cases in point. Less dramatic skirmishes erupt down to the present time.

But management tactics were often more subtle than a cracked skull. The **yellow-dog contract** was one of the more ingenious antiunion devices fostered by management. In such contracts workers agreed to remain nonunion as a condition of employment. They often had little choice but to sign such contracts—no contract, no job. Violation of a yellow-dog contract exposed a worker to a lawsuit by his employer, the result of which might be a court-imposed fine or even imprisonment.

As a last resort, an employer might shower his work force with such amenities as group insurance, pension programs, and stock ownership and profit-sharing schemes to convince them that employers would look after workers' interests as effectively as unions established by "outsiders." The next step beyond company *paternalism* was employee-representation schemes or **company unions,** that is, employer-dominated "dummy" unions which, it was hoped, would discourage the establishment of genuine unions. Paternalism and company unions were decidedly effective in retarding union growth as late as the 1920s.[1]

[1]During a prolonged strike in the bituminous coal industry in 1902, a spokesman for the mine operators, George F. Baer, issued the classic statement of business paternalism: "The rights and interests of the laboring man will be protected and cared for—not by the labor agitators, but by the Christian men to whom God in His infinite wisdom has given the control of the property interests of this country."

Evolution of Business Unionism The labor movement growth which occurred in the 1800s not only was modest, but it also embraced a variety of union philosophies. The mid-1800s were in effect a laboratory in which American labor experimented with alternative forms of unionism—Marxism, utopianism, reformism, and other isms. But such unions usually floundered in the span of a few short years because of the internal conflict between the workers' interest in short-run practical goals (higher wages and shorter hours) and the long-run utopian goals (producer cooperatives, creation of a labor party) of the union leaders.

Then, in 1886, a new labor organization—the **American Federation of Labor (AFL)**—which was to dominate the labor movement for the next fifty years was formed. Under the leadership of Samuel Gompers, labor charted a conservative course which has been very influential down to the present.[2] Appropriately honored as "the father of the American labor movement," Gompers preached three fundamental ideas: (1) practical business unionism, (2) political neutrality for labor, and (3) the autonomy of each trade or craft.

1 Business Unionism Gompers was firmly convinced that "safe and sane" **business unionism** was the only course for American labor to follow. Gompers rejected long-run idealistic schemes aimed at overthrow of the capitalistic system. He spurned intellectuals and theorizers and emphasized that unions should be concerned with practical short-run economic objectives—higher pay, shorter hours, and improved working conditions. In the words of one scholar, Gompers felt that "you must offer the American working man bread and butter in the here and now instead of pie in the sky in the sweet by and by."[3]

2 Political Neutrality Gompers was convinced that government should keep its nose out of labor-management relations and collective bargaining. Although he recognized that governmental interference on behalf of labor might be a boon to union growth, Gompers was equally certain that antiunion government policies could stifle the progress of the entire labor movement.

[2]This is not to say that all unions have followed conservative paths since Gompers first espoused the virtues of business unionism. The Industrial Workers of the World, founded in 1905, advocated a decidedly revolutionary brand of left-wing unionism. In 1949 and 1950, the CIO expelled eleven affiliated unions whose leadership had come to be dominated by Communists.

[3]Charles C. Killingsworth, "Organized Labor in a Free Enterprise Economy," in Walter Adams (ed.), *The Structure of American Industry,* 3d ed. (New York: The Macmillan Company, 1961), p. 570.

Gompers cautioned organized labor not to align itself with any political party. Preoccupation with long-run political goals, he argued, causes labor to lose sight of the short-run economic objectives it should seek. Gompers admonished organized labor to reward labor's friends and punish its enemies at the polls regardless of political affiliation.

3 Trade Autonomy Finally, Gompers was firmly convinced that "autonomy of the trade," that is, unions organized on the basis of specific crafts, was the only permanent foundation for the labor movement. Unions composed of many different crafts lack the cohesiveness essential to strong, hard-hitting, business unionism. These craft unions should then be affiliated in a national federation. "One union to each trade, affiliated for one labor movement."

This philosophy—conservative business unionism, political "neutrality," and the craft principle of union organization—was destined to dominate the AFL and the entire labor movement for the next half-century. Indeed, the AFL, operating under Gompers' leadership, met with considerable success—at least for a time. AFL membership hit a high-water mark of about 4 million members by the end of World War I. Then a combination of circumstances in the 1920s forced the AFL into an eclipse (see Figure 23-1). One factor was a strong antiunion drive by employers. Also, many firms introduced employee representation plans, company unions, and a host of paternalistic schemes to convince workers that employers were better prepared to look out for their employees' interests than were labor leaders. Finally, the AFL clung tenaciously to the craft principle of union organization, ignoring the ever-increasing number of unskilled workers employed by the rapidly expanding mass-production industries—the automobile and steel industries in particular.

Encouragement Phase: 1930 to 1947

Two significant events occurred in the 1930s which revived the labor movement and inaugurated a period of rapid growth.

1 The attitude of the Federal government toward unions changed from one of indifference, not to say hostility, to one of encouragement.

2 A major structural change in the labor movement accompanied the founding of the Committee (later the Congress) of Industrial Organizations in 1936. Both events, coupled with the wartime prosperity of the 1940s, greatly swelled the ranks of organized labor.

Prolabor Legislation of the 1930s Against the background of the depressed thirties, the Federal government enacted two decidedly prolabor acts. In part, the passage of these acts reflected the strong opposition of organized labor to the previously described weapons employed by the courts and by management to suppress unions. In part, they reflected a Democratic administration replacing a Republican administration. In part, they echoed the widely held opinion that strong unions, by achieving higher wages through collective bargaining, would increase aggregate demand—or at least prevent it from falling—and help alleviate the Great Depression.

Norris–La Guardia Act of 1932 The **Norris–La Guardia Act of 1932** did much to clear the path for union growth by outlawing two of the more effective antiunion weapons. Specifically, the act

1 Made it decidedly more difficult for employers to obtain injunctions against unions

2 Declared that yellow-dog contracts were unenforceable

Wagner Act of 1935 Three years later, in 1935, the Federal government took more positive steps to encourage union growth. The **Wagner Act of 1935** (officially the National Labor Relations Act) guaranteed the "twin rights" of labor: the right of self-organization and the right to bargain collectively with employers.

The act specified a number of "unfair labor practices" on the part of management. Specifically it

1 Forbade employers from interfering with the right of workers to form unions

2 Outlawed company unions

3 Prohibited antiunion discrimination by employers in hiring, firing, and promoting

4 Outlawed discrimination against any worker who files charges or gives testimony under the act

5 Obligated employers to bargain in good faith with a union duly established by their employees

The Wagner Act was clearly "labor's Magna Charta."

A **National Labor Relations Board (NLRB)** was established by the act and charged with the authority to investigate unfair labor practices occurring under the act, to issue cease-and-desist orders in the event of violations, and to conduct worker elections in deciding which specific union, if any, workers might want to represent them.

The Wagner Act was tailored to accelerate union growth and was extremely successful in achieving this goal. The protective umbrella provided to unions by this act along with the Norris–La Guardia Act played a major role in increasing the ranks of organized labor from about 4 million in 1935 to 15 million in 1947.

Industrial Unionism: the CIO Recall that one of the causes of stagnation in the AFL during the 1920s was its unwillingness to organize the growing masses of unskilled assembly-line workers. Though the majority of AFL leaders chose to ignore unskilled workers, a vocal minority under the leadership of John L. Lewis contended that craft unionism would be ineffective as a means of organizing the hundreds of thousands of workers in the growing mass-production industries. According to Lewis and his followers, the basis for organization should be shifted from **craft unionism** to **industrial unionism,** that is, away from unions which only encompass a specific type of skilled workers (carpenters, bricklayers) to unions including all workers—both skilled and unskilled—in a given industry or group of related industries (steelworkers, autoworkers).[4] This conflict came to a head, and in 1936 Lewis and his sympathizers withdrew their unions (and were simultaneously expelled) from the AFL.

The withdrawing unions established themselves as the **Congress of Industrial Organizations (CIO).** The CIO met with startling success in organizing the automobile and steel industries. So great was this success that the AFL also moved in the direction of organizing on an industrial basis. By 1940, total union membership approximated 9 million workers.

Intervention Phase: 1947 to Date

The prolabor legislation of the 1930s, the birth of industrial unionism, and the booming prosperity of the war years brought rapid union growth (see Figure 23-1). As unions gathered strength—both numerical and financial—it became increasingly evident that they could no longer be regarded as the weak sister or underdog in negotiations with management. Just as the growing power of business monopolies brought a clamor for public control in the 1870s and 1880s, the upsurge of union power in the 1930s and 1940s brought a similar outcry for regulation. This pressure for union control came to a head in the years immediately following World War II and culminated in the passage of the **Taft-Hartley Act of 1947.**

[4]Figures 15-6 and 15-7 compare the techniques employed by craft and industrial unions in attempting to raise wages.

Taft-Hartley Act of 1947 Officially called the Labor-Management Relations Act, the provisions of this detailed piece of legislation generally fall under four headings: (1) provisions which designate and outlaw certain "unfair union practices," (2) provisions which regulate the internal administration of unions, (3) provisions which specify collective bargaining procedures and regulate the actual contents of bargaining agreements, and (4) provisions for handling of strikes imperiling the health and safety of the nation.

1 Unfair Union Practices The Wagner Act outlined a number of "unfair labor practices" on the part of management. A new and crucial feature of the Taft-Hartley Act was that it listed a number of "unfair labor practices" on the part of unions. These unfair practices, which constitute some of the most controversial sections of the act, are as follows: *(a)* Unions are prohibited from coercing employees to become union members. *(b)* **Jurisdictional strikes** (disputes between unions over the question of which has the authority to perform a specific job) are forbidden, as are **secondary boycotts** (refusing to buy or handle products produced by another union or group of workers) and certain **sympathy strikes** (strikes designed to assist some other union in gaining employer recognition or some other objective). *(c)* Unions are prohibited from charging excessive or discriminatory initiation fees or dues. *(d)* **Featherbedding,** a mild form of extortion where the union or its members receive payment for work not actually performed, is outlawed. *(e)* Unions cannot refuse to bargain in good faith with management.

2 Union Administration Taft-Hartley also imposed controls on the internal processes of labor unions: *(a)* Unions must make detailed financial reports to the National Labor Relations Board and make such information available to its members. *(b)* Welfare and pension funds must be kept separate from other union funds and jointly administered by the union and management. *(c)* Unions are prohibited from making political contributions in elections, primaries, or conventions which involve Federal offices. *(d)* Originally, union officials were required to sign non-Communist affidavits.

3 Contract Contents Other Taft-Hartley provisions are designed to control the actual collective bargaining process and the contents of the resulting work agreement: *(a)* The **closed shop** (which requires that a firm hire only workers who are already union members) is specifically outlawed for workers engaged in interstate commerce; that is, a closed-shop arrangement cannot be written into a collective bargaining agreement. *(b)* Bargaining agreements must contain termination or *reopening clauses* in which both labor and management must give the other party 60 days' notice of intent to modify or terminate the existing work agreement.

4 "Health and Safety" Strikes Finally, the Taft-Hartley Act outlines a procedure for avoiding major strikes which might disrupt the entire economy and imperil the health or safety of the nation, for example, a nationwide strike of port workers. According to this procedure, the President may obtain an injunction to delay such strikes for an 80-day "cooling off" period. Within this period striking workers are polled by the NLRB on the acceptability of the last offer of the employer. If the last offer is rejected, the union can then strike. The government's only recourse—one of questionable legality—is seizure of the industry.

Landrum-Griffin Act of 1959 Government regulation of the internal processes of labor unions was extended by passage of the **Landrum-Griffin Act** (officially the Labor-Management Reporting and Disclosure Act) in 1959. The act regulates union elections by requiring regularly scheduled elections of officers and the use of secret ballots; restrictions are placed on ex-convicts and Communists in holding union offices. Furthermore, union officials are now held strictly accountable for union funds and property. Officers handling union funds must be bonded; the embezzlement of union funds is made a Federal offense; and close restrictions are placed on a union's loans to its officers and members. The act is also aimed at preventing autocratic union leaders from infringing on the individual worker's rights to attend and participate in union meetings, to vote in union proceedings, and to nominate officers. The act permits a worker to sue his union if it denies him these rights.

UNIONISM'S DECLINE

In 1955 unity was formally reestablished in the American labor movement with the merger of the AFL and CIO. Two factors were especially important in closing the breach which had existed for almost two decades.

1 The political and legislative setbacks which labor had encountered since the prolabor era of the 1930s convinced labor leaders that unity in the labor movement was a necessary first step toward bolstering the political influence of organized labor.

2 Failure to achieve the desired rate of growth in the ranks of organized labor in the post-World War II years made it evident to organized labor that a concerted, unified effort was needed to organize currently nonunion firms and industries.

In fact, however, the period since the AFL-CIO merger has *not* been characterized by a resurgence of organized labor. The growth of union membership has failed to keep pace with the growth of the labor force. While 25 percent of the labor force was organized in the mid-1950s, currently only some 16 percent are members. Indeed, in recent years the absolute number of union members has declined significantly. Over 22 million workers were unionized in 1980; that figure had fallen to only about 17 million in 1990.

Let's consider two possible explanations as to why this has happened.

1 Structural Changes One view, the **structural-change hypothesis,** is that many structural changes unfavorable to the expansion of union membership have occurred both in our economy and in the labor force.

1 Consumer demand and therefore employment patterns have shifted away from traditional union strongholds. Generally, the industry-mix of domestic output has been shifting away from manufactured goods (where unions have been strong) to services (where unions have been weak). This change in industry-mix may be reinforced by increased competition from imports in highly unionized sectors such as automobiles and steel. Growing import competition in these industries has curtailed domestic employment and therefore union membership.

2 An unusually large proportion of the increase in employment in recent years has been concentrated among women, youths, and part-time workers, groups allegedly difficult to organize because of their less firm attachment to the labor force.

3 Spurred by high energy costs, the long-run trend for industry to shift from the Northeast and Midwest where unionism is "a way of life" to "hard to organize" areas of the South and Southwest may have impeded expansion of union membership.

4 An ironic possibility is that the relative decline of unionism may in part reflect the success unions have had in gaining a sizable wage advantage over nonunion workers in the United States and abroad. Confronted with high union wages, we would expect union employers to substitute machinery for workers, subcontract more work to nonunion suppliers, open nonunion plants in less industrialized areas, or have components produced in low-wage nations. These actions reduce the growth of employment opportunities in the union sector compared to the nonunion sector. Perhaps more important, we would also expect output and employment in low-cost nonunion firms and industries to increase at the expense of output and employment in higher-cost union firms and industries. In short, union success in raising wages may have changed the composition of industry to the disadvantage of union employment and membership.

2 Managerial-Opposition Hypothesis Another view is that intensified **managerial opposition** to unions has been a major deterrent to union growth. It is argued that in the past decade or so unions have increased the union wage advantage which they enjoy compared to nonunion workers and, as a result, union firms have become less profitable than nonunion firms. As a reaction, managerial opposition to unions has crystallized and become more aggressive. One managerial strategy has been to employ labor-management consultants who specialize in mounting aggressive antiunion drives to dissuade workers from unionizing or, alternatively, to persuade union workers to decertify their union.

It is also alleged that there has been a dramatic increase in the use of illegal antiunion tactics. In particular, it has become increasingly common to identify and dismiss leading prounion workers even though this is prohibited by the Wagner Act. Coupling these antiunion strategies with evidence that unions are devoting fewer resources to organizing the unorganized and that NLRB rulings have become increasingly antilabor, the labor movement has gone into relative and absolute eclipse.

COLLECTIVE BARGAINING

Despite the decline of unionism, collective bargaining remains an important feature of labor-management relations. Nearly 2000 major collective bargaining agreements—those involving 1000 or more workers—cover 8.5 million workers in the United States. Many million other workers are covered under collective bargaining agreements in smaller firms.

The Bargaining Process

To the outsider, collective bargaining is a dramatic clash every two or three years between labor and management. It is easy to get the impression from the newspapers that labor and management settle their differences only with strikes, picketing, and occasional acts of violence.

These impressions are largely inaccurate. Collective bargaining is a somewhat less colorful process than most people believe. In negotiating important contracts, the union is represented by top local and national officials, duly supplemented with lawyers and research economists. Management representatives include top policy-making executives, plant managers, personnel and labor relations specialists, lawyers, and staff economists.

The union usually assumes the initiative, outlining its demands. These take the form of specific adjustments in the current work agreement. The merits and demerits of these demands are then debated. Typically, a compromise solution is reached and written into a new work agreement. Strikes, picketing, and violence are clearly the exception and not the rule. About 95 percent of all bargaining contracts are negotiated without resort to work stoppages. Generally, in recent years less than one-fifth of 1 percent of all working time has been lost each year from work stoppages resulting from labor-management disputes. *Labor and management display a marked capacity for compromise and agreement.* Strikes and labor-management violence are newsworthy, whereas peaceful renewal of a work agreement hardly rates a page-5 column.

The Work Agreement

Collective bargaining agreements assume many forms. Some agreements are brief, covering two or three typewritten pages; others are highly detailed, involving 200 or 300 pages of fine print. Some agreements involve only a local union and a single plant; others set wages, hours, and working conditions for entire industries. There is no such thing as an "average" or "typical" collective bargaining agreement.

At the risk of oversimplification, collective bargaining agreements usually cover four basic areas: (1) the degree of recognition and status accorded the union and the prerogatives of management, (2) wages and hours, (3) seniority and job opportunities, and (4) a procedure for settling grievances.

Union Status and Managerial Prerogatives Unions enjoy differing degrees of recognition from management. Listed in order of the union's preference are (1) the closed shop, (2) the union shop, and (3) the open shop.

Prior to being outlawed by the Taft-Hartley Act, the closed shop afforded the greatest security to a union. Under a closed shop a worker must be a member of the union before being hired. A **union shop,** on the other hand, permits the employer to hire nonunion workers but provides that these workers must join the union in a specified period—say, thirty days—or relinquish their jobs. Some twenty states now have so-called **right-to-work laws** which make compulsory union membership, and therefore the union shop, illegal.

Under the **open shop,** management may hire union or nonunion workers. Those who are nonunion are not obligated to join the union; they may continue on their jobs indefinitely as nonunion workers. Finally, there is the **nonunion shop.** Here no union exists, and the employer makes a conscious effort to hire those workers who are least inclined to form or join a union.

The other side of the union-status coin is the issue of *managerial prerogatives.* Most work agreements contain clauses outlining certain decisions which are to be made solely by management. These managerial prerogatives usually cover such matters as size and location of plants, products to be manufactured, types of equipment and materials used in production, and production scheduling. Frequently the hiring, transfer, discipline, discharge, and promotion of workers are decisions made solely by management but are subject to the general principle of seniority and to challenge by the union through the grievance procedure.

Wages and Hours The focal point of any bargaining agreement is wages and hours. Both labor and management tend to be highly pragmatic and opportunistic in wage bargaining. The criteria, or "talking points," most frequently invoked by labor in demanding (and by management in resisting) wage boosts are (1) "what others are getting," (2) ability to pay, (3) cost of living, and (4) productivity. If a given firm's basic rates are below those of comparable firms, the union is likely to stress that wages should be increased to bring them into line with what workers in other firms are getting. Similarly, if the firm has had a very profitable year, the union is likely to demand high wages on the ground that the company has ample ability to grant such increments. Unions have often achieved considerable success in tying wages to the cost of living. About 40 percent of all union workers are covered by some kind of *cost-of-living adjustment* (COLA). Finally, unions bargain for their "fair share" of the additional revenues associated with increases in productivity.

The four wage criteria are clearly two-edged propositions. For example, the cost-of-living criterion is invoked by the union only when prices are hurrying upward; unions conveniently ignore this criterion when prices are stable or declining. Similarly, the union considers the ability-to-pay argument to be important only when profits are large. Management is equally opportunistic in the evaluation it places on the various wage-bargaining standards.

Hours of work, overtime pay, holiday and vacations provisions, and **fringe benefits**—health plans and pension benefits—are other important "economic" issues which must be addressed in the bargaining process.

Seniority and the Control of Job Opportunities The uncertainty of employment in a market economy, coupled with the fear of antiunion discrimination on the part of employers, have made workers and their unions decidedly "job-conscious." The explicit and detailed provisions covering job opportunities which most work agreements contain reflect this concern. Unions stress **seniority** as the basis for worker promotion and for layoff and recall. The worker with the longest continuous service has first chance at relevant promotions, is last to be laid off, and first to be recalled from a layoff.

Grievance Procedure Even the most detailed and comprehensive work agreement cannot anticipate all the issues and problems which might occur during its life. What if workers show up for work on a Monday morning to find that for some reason—say, a mechanical failure—the plant is closed down? Should they be given "show-up" pay amounting to, say, two or four hours' pay? Or management and the union may disagree as to whether the worker with the most seniority has the ability to perform the job to which he or she wants to be promoted. Such events and disagreements cannot be anticipated by even the most detailed collective bargaining contracts and therefore must be ironed out through a *grievance procedure.* Virtually all bargaining agreements contain an explicit grievance procedure to handle disputes which arise during the life of an agreement.

QUICK REVIEW 23-1

- ***Union growth was slowed during the repression phase (1790–1930) by a use of the criminal conspiracy doctrine and injunctions by the courts, and b employer hostility.***
- ***In the encouragement phase (1930–1947) union growth was stimulated by prounion legislation (the Norris–La Guardia and Wagner acts) and the evolution of industrial unionism.***
- ***The Taft-Hartley and Landrum-Griffin acts inaugurated the intervention phase (1947 to the present) by regulating union tactics and their internal operations.***
- ***The decline of unionism in recent decades has been attributed to a changes in the structures of the economy and the labor force, and b growing managerial opposition to unions.***
- ***Collective bargaining agreements determine a union status and managerial prerogatives, b wages and hours, c control of job opportunities, and d the resolution of grievances.***

Given the historical and legislative background of the labor movement and some understanding of collective bargaining, let's now consider the economic implications of unions.

THE ECONOMIC EFFECTS OF UNIONS

Are the economic effects of labor unions positive or negative? We will respond to this important issue by examining several questions: Do unions raise wages? Do they increase or diminish economic efficiency? Do they make the distribution of earnings more or less equal? Do unions contribute to inflation? The reader should be forewarned that there is considerable uncertainty and debate on the answers to these questions.

The Union Wage Advantage

The three union models of Chapter 15 (see Figures 15-5, 15-6, and 15-7 and the accompanying discussions) all imply that unions have the capacity to raise wages. Has unionization in fact caused wage rates to be higher than otherwise?

Empirical research overwhelmingly does suggest that *unions do raise the wages of their members relative to comparable nonunion workers,* although the size of the union wage advantage varies according to occupation, industry, race, and sex. There is also evidence to suggest that the union wage advantage increased in the 1970s. Hence, early research suggests that over the 1923–1958 period the average union–nonunion pay difference was on the order of 10 to 15 percent.

More recent studies indicate that the difference widened to 20 to 30 percent in the 1970s. Note that these are average differentials and that there is considerable variation among industries and occupations. Furthermore, the wage freezes and pay cuts ("wage give-backs") suffered by organized labor in the early and mid-1980s most likely have significantly diminished the 20 to 30 percent union wage advantage. Labor economists have speculated that the union wage advantage may have returned to the 10 to 15 percent range by the early 1990s.

These estimates of the union wage advantage tend to be understated because union workers enjoy substantially larger *fringe benefits* than nonunion workers. Union workers are more likely to have private pensions, medical and dental insurance, and paid vacations and sick leaves than nonunion workers. Where such benefits are available to both union and nonunion workers, their magnitude is greater for union workers. Thus the total compensation (wage rates plus fringe benefits) advantage of union workers is greater than the previously indicated 10 to 15 percent.

Economists also generally agree that *unions have probably had little or no impact on the average level of real wages received by labor—both organized and unorganized—taken as a whole.* At first, these two conclusions—that unions gain a wage advantage but do not affect the average level of real wages—may seem inconsistent. But they need not be if the wage gains of organized workers are at the expense of unorganized workers. As we will see (Figure 23-2), higher wages in unionized labor markets may cause employers to move back up their labor demand curves and hire fewer workers. These unemployed workers may seek employment in nonunion labor markets. The resulting increase in the supply of labor will depress wage rates in these nonunion markets. The net result may well be no change in the average level of wages.

Indeed, the tight relationship between productivity and the average level of real wages shown in Figure 15-1 correctly suggests that unions have little power to raise real wage rates for labor as a whole. But Figure 15-1 is an average relationship and therefore compatible with certain groups of (union) workers getting higher relative wages if other (nonunion) workers are simultaneously getting lower real wages.

Efficiency and Productivity

Are unions a positive or negative force insofar as economic efficiency and productivity are concerned? How do unions affect the allocation of resources? While there is much disagreement as to the efficiency aspects of unionism, it is instructive to consider some of the ways unions might affect efficiency both negatively and positively. We will consider the negative view first.

Negative View There are essentially three basic means by which unions might exert a negative impact on efficiency.

1 Featherbedding and Work Rules Some unions have undoubtedly diminished productivity growth by engaging in "make-work" or "featherbedding" practices and resisting the introduction of output-increasing machinery and equipment. These productivity-reducing practices often arise against a backdrop of technological change. Labor and management may agree to a crew size which is reasonable and appropriate at the time the agreement is concluded. But labor-saving technology may then emerge which renders the crew too large. The union is likely to resist the potential loss of jobs. For many years the Brotherhood of Locomotive Firemen and Engineers retained a fireman on train crews, even though his function was eliminated by the shift from steam to diesel engines.

Similarly, union painters sometimes eschewed the use of spray guns and in some instances limited the width of paint brushes. In more recent years, typographer unions resisted the introduction of computers in setting type. Historically, the musicians' union insisted on oversized orchestras for musical shows and required that a union standby orchestra be paid by employers using nonunion orchestras.

More generally, one can argue that unions are responsible for the establishment of work rules and practices which impede efficient production. For example, under seniority rules workers may be promoted in accordance with their employment tenure, rather than in terms of who can perform the available job with the greatest efficiency. Also, unions may impose jurisdictional restrictions on the kinds of jobs workers may perform. Sheet-metal workers or bricklayers may be prohibited from performing the simple carpentry work often associated with their jobs. Observance of such rules means, in this instance, that unneeded and underutilized carpenters must be available. Finally, it is often contended that unions constrain managerial prerogatives to establish work schedules, determine production targets, and to make freely the decisions contributing to productive efficiency.

2 Strikes A second way unions may adversely affect efficiency is through strikes. If union and management reach an impasse in their negotiations, a strike will result and the firm's production will cease for the strike's duration. The firm will forgo sales and profits and workers will sacrifice income.

Simple statistics on strike activity suggest that strikes are relatively rare and the associated aggregate economic losses are relatively minimal. In 1990, 687 major collective bargaining agreements—those covering 1000 or more workers—were negotiated. Strikes occurred in only 43 of these instances. Furthermore, many strikes last only a few days. As indicated earlier, the average amount of work-time lost each year because of strikes is only about one-fifth of 1 percent of total work-time. This loss is the equivalent of 4 hours per worker per year, which is less than 5 minutes per worker per week!

Note that economic costs associated with strikes may be greater or less than suggested by the amount of work-time lost. Costs may be greater if production of nonstruck firms is disrupted. An extended strike in the steel or rail transportation industries could have serious adverse repercussions for production and employment in many other industries and sectors of the economy.

On the other hand, costs may be less than implied by workdays lost by strikers as nonstruck firms increase their output to offset the loss of production by struck firms. While the output of General Motors will fall when its workers strike, car buyers may shift their demand to Ford and Chrysler which respond by increasing their employment and outputs. While GM and its employees are hurt by a strike, society as a whole may experience little or no decline in employment, real output, and income.

3 Labor Misallocation A third and more subtle avenue through which unions might adversely affect efficiency is the union wage advantage itself. In Figure 23-2 we have drawn (for simplicity's sake) identical labor demand curves for the unionized and nonunion sectors of the labor market for some particular kind of labor.[5] If there were no union present initially, then the wage rate which would result from the competitive hire

[5]Technical note: Our discussion assumes pure competition in both product and resource markets.

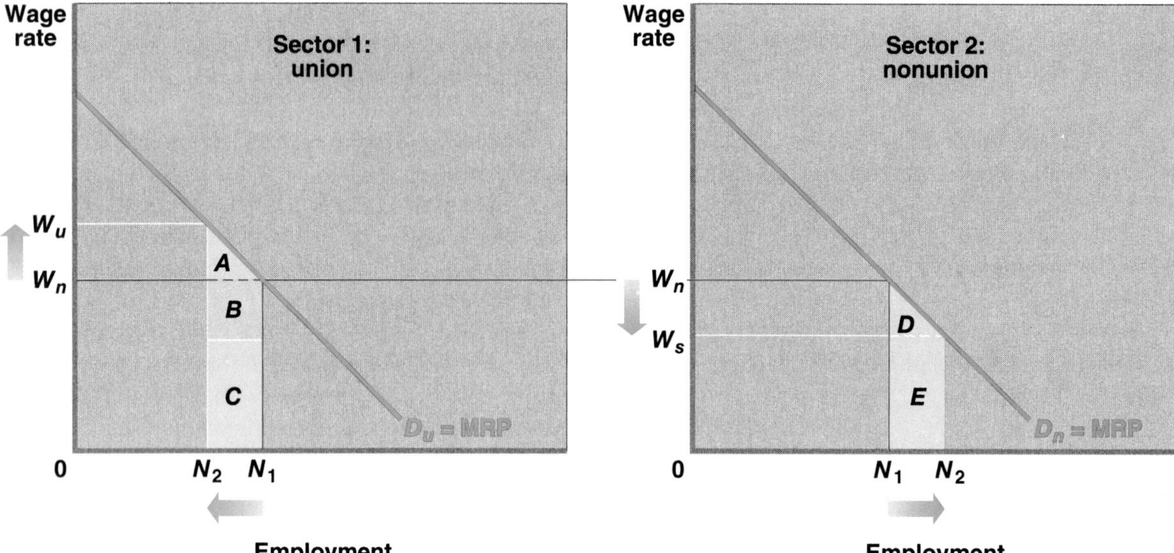

FIGURE 23-2 The effect of the union wage advantage on the allocation of labor

The higher wage W_u which the union achieves in sector I causes the displacement of N_1N_2 workers. The reemployment of these workers in nonunion sector 2 reduces the wage rate there from W_n to W_s. The associated loss of output in the union sector is area $A + B + C$, while the gain in the nonunion sector is only area $D + E$. Hence, the net loss of output is equal to area B. This suggests that the union wage advantage has resulted in the misallocation of labor and a decline in economic efficiency.

of labor would be, say, W_n. We now assume a union comes into being in sector 1 and succeeds in increasing the wage rate from W_n to W_u. As a consequence, N_1N_2 workers lose their jobs in the union sector. Assume they all move to nonunion sector 2 where they secure employment. This increase in labor supply in the nonunion sector depresses the wage rate from W_n to W_s.

Recall that the labor demand curves reflect the marginal revenue products (MRPs) of workers or, in other words, the contributions which workers make to the domestic output. This means that the shaded areas $A + B + C$ in the union sector represents the *decrease* in domestic output caused by the N_1N_2 employment decline in that sector. This $A + B + C$ area is the sum of the MRPs—the total contribution to domestic output—of the workers displaced by the W_n to W_u wage increase achieved by the union. The reemployment of these workers in nonunion sector 2 results in an *increase* in domestic output indicated by the shaded areas $D + E$. Because area $A + B + C$ exceeds area $D + E$, there is a net loss of domestic output. More precisely, because $A = D$ and $C = E$, the *net* loss attributable to the union wage advantage is equal to area B. Since the same amount of employed labor is now producing a smaller output, labor is clearly being misallocated and inefficiently used.

Viewed from a slightly different perspective, *after* the shift of N_1N_2 workers from the union to the nonunion sector has occurred, workers will be paid a wage rate equal to their MRPs in both sectors. But the MRPs of the union workers will be higher than the MRPs of the nonunion workers. The economy will always benefit from a larger domestic output when any given type of labor is reallocated from a relatively low MRP use to a relatively high MRP use. But, given the union's presence and its ability to maintain the W_u wage rate in its sector, this reallocation from sector 2 to 1 will *not* occur.

Attempts to estimate the output loss due to the allocative inefficiency associated with union wage gains suggest that the loss is relatively small. One pioneering study assumed a 15 percent union wage advantage and estimated that approximately 0.14 percent—only about one-seventh of 1 percent—of the domestic output was lost! Similarly, a more recent estimate indicates that union wage gains cost the economy 0.2 to 0.4 percent of domestic product. In 1991 this cost would amount to about \$11 to \$23 billion or \$45.00 to \$90.00 per person.

Positive View Other economists take the position that on balance unions make a positive contribution to productivity and efficiency.

1 Managerial Performance: The Shock Effect The *shock effect* is the idea that a wage increase, imposed by a union in this instance, may induce affected firms to adopt improved production and personnel methods and become more efficient. One may carry Figure 23-2's analysis of labor misallocation one step further and argue that the union wage advantage will prompt union firms to *accelerate* the substitution of capital for labor (Chapter 14) and *hasten* the search for cost-reducing (productivity-increasing) technologies. When faced with higher production costs due to the union wage advantage, employers will be pushed to reduce costs by using more machinery and by seeking improved production techniques using less of both labor and capital per unit of output. In fact, if the product market is reasonably competitive, a unionized firm with labor costs 10 to 15 percent higher than nonunion competitors will simply not survive unless productivity can be raised. In short, union wage pressure may generate managerial actions which increase national productivity.

2 Reduced Worker Turnover Unions may also contribute to rising productivity within firms through their effects on worker turnover and worker security. Unions function as a **collective voice** for members in resolving disputes and improving working conditions. That is, if a group of workers is dissatisfied with its conditions of employment, it has two potential means of response. These are the "exit mechanism" and the "voice mechanism."

The **exit mechanism** simply refers to the use of the labor market—leave or exit your present job in search of a better one—as a means of reacting to "bad" employers and "bad" working conditions.

In contrast, the **voice mechanism** involves communication by workers with the employer to improve working conditions and resolve worker grievances. It might be risky for *individual* workers to express their dissatisfaction to employers because employers may retaliate by firing them as "troublemakers." But unions can provide workers with a *collective* voice to communicate problems and grievances to management and to press for their satisfactory resolution.

More specifically, unions may help reduce worker turnover in two ways.

1 Unions provide the voice mechanism as a substitute for the exit mechanism. Unions are effective in correcting job dissatisfactions which would otherwise be "resolved" by workers through the exit mechanism of changing jobs.

2 The union wage advantage is a deterrent to job changes. Higher wages make unionized firms more attractive places to work. Several studies suggest that the decline in quit rates attributable to unionism is substantial, ranging from 31 to 65 percent.

A lower quit rate increases efficiency in several ways. First, lower turnover means a more experienced and, hence, more productive labor force. Second, fewer quits reduce the firm's recruitment, screening, and hiring costs. Finally, reduced turnover makes employers more willing to invest in the training (and therefore the productivity) of their workers. If a worker quits or "exits" at the end of, say, a year's training, the employer will get no return from the higher worker productivity attributable to that training. Lower turnover increases the likelihood that employers will receive a return on any training they provide, thereby making them more willing to upgrade their labor forces.

3 Seniority and Informal Training Much productivity-increasing training is transmitted informally. More-skilled workers may explain their functions to less-skilled workers on the job, during lunch, or during a coffee break. However, a more-skilled senior worker may want to conceal his or her knowledge from less-skilled junior workers *if* the latter can become competitive for the former's job. Because of union insistence on the primacy of seniority in such matters as promotion and layoff, worker security is enhanced. Given this security, senior workers will be more willing to pass on their job knowledge and skills to new or subordinate workers. This informal training enhances the quality and productivity of the firm's work force.

Mixed Research Findings A relatively large number of studies have measured the impact of unionization on productivity. These studies attempt to control for differences in labor quality, the amount of capital equipment used per worker, and other factors aside from unionization which might contribute to productivity differences. Unfortunately, evidence from these studies is inconclusive. For every study which finds a positive union effect on productivity, another study using different methodology or data concludes that there is a negative effect. Hence, at present there is no generally accepted conclusion regarding the overall impact of unions on labor productivity.

Distribution of Earnings

Labor unions envision themselves as institutions which enhance economic equality. Do unions in fact reduce the inequality with which earnings are distributed? The most convincing evidence suggests that unions do reduce earnings inequality.

Increasing Inequality Some economists employ Figure 23-2's analysis of labor misallocation to conclude that unions increase earnings inequality. They contend that, in the absence of the union, competition would bring wages into equality at W_n in these two sectors or submarkets. But the higher union wage realized in sector 1 displaces workers who seek reemployment in the nonunion sector. In so doing they depress nonunion wages. Instead of wage equality at W_n, we have higher wage rates of W_u for union workers and lower wages of W_s for nonunion workers. The impact of the union is clearly to increase earnings inequality. Furthermore, the fact that unionization is more extensive among the more highly skilled, higher-paid blue-collar workers than among less skilled, lower-paid blue-collar workers also suggests that the obtaining of a wage advantage by unions increases dispersion of earnings.

Promoting Equality There are other aspects of union wage policies which suggest that unionism promotes greater, not less, equality in the distribution of earnings.

1 Uniform Wages within Firms In the absence of unions employers are apt to pay different wages to individual workers on the same job. These wage differences are based on perceived differences in job performance, length of job tenure, and, perhaps, favoritism. Unions traditionally seek uniform wage rates for all workers performing a particular job. In short, while nonunion firms tend to assign wage rates to *individual workers,* unions—in the interest of worker allegiance and solidarity—seek to assign wage rate to *jobs.* To the extent that unions are successful, wage and earnings differentials based on supervisory judgments of individual worker performance are eliminated. An important side effect of this standard-wage policy is that wage discrimination against blacks, other minorities, and women is likely to be less when a union is present.

2 Uniform Wages among Firms In addition to seeking standard wage rates for given occupational classes *within* firms, unions also seek standard wage rates among firms. The rationale is that the existence of substantial wage differences among competing firms may undermine the ability of unions to sustain and enhance wage advantages. For example, if one firm in a four-firm oligopoly is allowed to pay significantly lower wages to its union workers, the union is likely to find it difficult to maintain the union wage advantage in the other three firms. In particular, during a recession high-wage firms are likely to put great pressure on the union to lower wages to the level of the low-wage firm. To avoid this kind of problem unions seek to "take wages out of competition" by standardizing wage rates among firms, thereby reducing the degree of wage dispersion.

What is the *net* effect of unionism on the distribution of earnings? Although the issue remains controversial, one authoritative study concludes that the wage effects indicated in Figure 23-2 *increase* earnings inequality by about 1 percent, but the standardization of wage rates within and among firms *decreases* inequality by about 4 percent. The net result is a 3 percent decline in earnings inequality due to unionism. Because only a small proportion of the labor force is unionized, this 3 percent reduction in inequality is substantial.

Unions and Inflation[6]

We now examine the complicated and controversial question of whether unions can increase the average level of money wages and generate cost-push or, more specifically, wage-push inflation.

Two Models There are two general models of inflation, namely, the demand-pull and the cost-push models. The demand-pull model suggests that, given aggregate supply, an increase in aggregate demand will result in a higher price level. Whether due to, say, an increase in the money supply or an increase in investment, the cause or impetus for inflation arises on the demand side of product markets which then increases the derived demands for labor and pulls up nominal wages. The important point is that in the demand-pull

[6]This section presupposes that the reader has taken a course in macroeconomic principles.

theory of inflation wage increases are an *effect* or symptom of inflation, not a *cause*. Wage increases do *not* cause inflation but are rather the *result* of excess aggregate demand. Wage increases simply transmit inflation, but do not initiate it.

In comparison, cost-push models allow union wage determination to play a causal role in inflation. Specifically, if nominal-wage increases exceed increases in labor productivity, then unit labor costs will rise. Given that labor costs comprise about three-fourths of total production costs, product prices will rise roughly in accord with the increase in unit labor costs. In terms of the aggregate supply and demand model, a decrease in aggregate supply results in a higher price level. Some economists contend that union-inspired nominal-wage increases in excess of productivity increases can be an important cause of the indicated leftward shift of the aggregate supply curve.

Tentative Conclusions Which view is correct? While there is no universally accepted conclusion, most experts downgrade union wage-setting as a causal force in inflation. We know from our experience in the early 1960s that union wage determination can be compatible with price level stability. And one can argue with considerable credibility that the major episodes of rapid inflation in the United States were started either by expansions of aggregate demand or major supply shocks which had little or nothing to do with wage increases. Hence, the "great inflation" of the 1970s was rooted in increases in government military spending in the late 1960s, on the one hand, and supply shocks associated with the OPEC oil cartel and crop shortages, on the other.

More important perhaps is the fact that the cost-push model indicates that the decrease in aggregate supply which accompanies a union-induced increase in unit labor costs causes declines in output and increases in unemployment which act to restrain union wage demands. This suggests that rising unit labor costs could not generate continuing inflation unless accommodating monetary and fiscal policies gave rise to increases in aggregate demand to offset the falling output and rising unemployment which wage inflation would create. Hence, the most reasonable judgment is that unions do *not* appear to be an initiating cause of inflation. Stated differently, unions do *not* seem to cause initial bursts of inflation or major increases in the rate of existing inflation independently of other causes.

With this survey of unionism and collective bargaining complete, we now consider two additional factors affecting American labor markets—the problem of discrimination, and the controversial immigration issue.

QUICK REVIEW 23-2

- ***Union workers receive wage rates 10 to 15 percent higher than comparable nonunion workers.***
- ***Union work rules, strikes, and the misallocation of labor associated with the union wage advantage are ways unions may reduce efficiency.***
- ***Unions may enhance productivity through the shock effect, by reducing worker turnover, and by providing the worker security prerequisite to informal on-the-job training.***
- ***On balance, unions probably reduce wage inequality by achieving wage uniformity within and among firms.***
- ***Most economists do not regard unions as an independent cause of inflation.***

DISCRIMINATION

In Chapter 22 we noted that blacks, Hispanics, and women bear a disproportionately large burden of poverty. The low incomes received by these groups are a consequence of the operation of the labor market. Thus, it is important that we consider the labor market aspects of discrimination.

Economic discrimination occurs when female or minority workers, who have the same abilities, education, training, and experience as white male workers, are accorded inferior treatment with respect to hiring, occupational access, promotion, or wage rate. Discrimination also occurs when females or minorities are denied access to education and training. Table 23-1 provides casual evidence which suggests the presence of racial discrimination. Similar data imply discrimination on the basis of gender. For example, the weekly earnings of full-time female workers is only about 70 percent that of males.

Dimensions of Discrimination

As Table 23-1 and our definition both suggest, discrimination may take several forms. Our discussion is in terms of racial and gender discrimination, but these

TABLE 23-1 **Selected measures of discrimination and inequality of opportunity, 1990**

Selected measure	*Whites*	*Blacks*
Income		
Median income of families	$36,915	$21,423
Percent of households in poverty	10.7	31.9
Percent of families with incomes of $75,000 or more	13.7	4.8
Unemployment rate (percent of civilian labor force)		
All males	4.8	11.8
All females	4.6	10.8
Teenage† males	14.2	32.1
Teenage† females	12.6	30.0
Education		
Percent of population 25 years and over completing 4 years of high school or more	78.4	64.6
Percent of population 25 years and over completing 4 years of college or more	21.8	11.8
Occupational distribution (percent of total civilian employment)		
Managerial and professional occupations	27.1	16.0
Service occupations	12.0	22.9

†Males and females, 16–19 years old.

Sources: Statistical Abstract of the United States, 1991; Economic Report of the President, 1991; and *Employment and Earnings,* February 1991.

remarks also generally apply to discrimination based on age or ethnic background.

1 **Wage discrimination** occurs when black and other minority workers are paid less than whites for doing the same work. This kind of discrimination is of declining importance because of its explicitness and the fact that it clearly violates Federal law. But, as this chapter's Last Word demonstrates, wage discrimination can sometimes be very subtle and difficult to detect.

2 **Employment discrimination** means that unemployment is concentrated among minorities. Blacks are frequently the last hired and the first fired. Hence, the unemployment rate for blacks has been roughly double that for whites (Table 23-1).

3 **Human-capital discrimination** occurs when investments in education and training are lower for blacks than for whites. The smaller amount (Table 23-1) and inferior quality of the education received by blacks have cost them the opportunity to increase their productivity and qualify for better jobs. Unfortunately, a vicious circle seems to exist here. Many blacks are poor because they have acquired little human capital. Being poor, blacks have less financial ability to invest in education and training. They also have less economic motivation to invest in human capital. Facing the very real possibility of wage, employment, and occupational discrimination, blacks tend to receive a lower rate of return on their investments in education and training.

4 **Occupational discrimination** means that minority workers have been arbitrarily restricted or prohibited from entering the more desirable, higher-paying occupations. Black executives and salespeople, not to mention electricians, bricklayers, and plumbers, are relatively few and far between. Historically, many craft unions effectively barred blacks from membership and hence from employment.

Occupational Segregation: The Crowding Model

This latter form of discrimination—**occupational segregation**—is particularly apparent in our economy. Women are disproportionately concentrated in a limited number of occupations such as nursing, public school teaching, secretarial and clerical jobs, and retail clerks. Blacks are crowed into a limited number of low-paying jobs such as laundry workers, cleaners and servants, hospital orderlies, and other manual jobs.

Assumptions The character and income consequences of occupational discrimination can be revealed

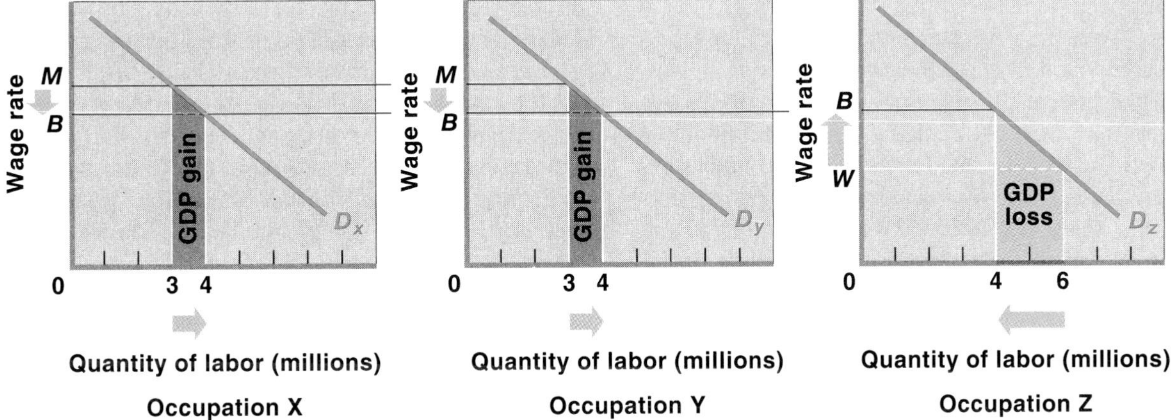

FIGURE 23-3 The simple economics of occupational discrimination

By crowding women into one occupation, men enjoy high wage rates of *OM* in occupations X and Y while women receive low wages of *OW* in occupation Z. The abandonment of discrimination will equalize wage rates at *OB and* result in a net increase in domestic output.

through a simple supply and demand model similar to that used to analyze the efficiency consequences of unions. We make the following simplifying assumptions.

1 The labor force is equally divided between male and female (or white and black) workers. Let's say there are 6 million male and 6 million female workers.

2 The economy is comprised of three occupations, each having identical labor demand curves, as shown in Figure 23-3.

3 Men and women (whites and blacks) have identical labor force characteristics; each of the three occupations could be filled equally well by men or women.

Effects of Crowding Suppose now that, as a consequence of irrational discrimination, the 6 million women are excluded from occupations X and Y and crowded into occupation Z. Men distribute themselves equally among occupations X and Y so there are 3 million male workers in each occupation and the resulting common wage rate for men is *OM*. (Assuming no barriers to mobility, any initially different distribution of males between X and Y would result in a wage differential which would prompt labor shifts from low- to high-wage occupation until wage equality was realized.) Note that women, on the other hand, are crowded into occupation Z and, because of this occupational segregation, receive a much lower wage rate *OW*. Given the reality of discrimination, this is an "equilibrium" situation. Women *cannot,* because of discrimination, reallocate themselves to occupations X and Y in the pursuit of higher wage rates.

Eliminating Discrimination But now assume that through legislation or sweeping changes in social attitudes, discrimination disappears. Women, attracted by higher wage rates, will shift from Z to X and Y. Specifically, 1 million women will shift into X and another 1 million into Y, leaving 4 million workers in Z. At this point 4 million workers will be in each occupation and wage rates will be equal to *OB* in all three occupations. Wage equality eliminates the incentive for further reallocations of labor.

This new, nondiscriminatory equilibrium is clearly to the advantage of women, who now receive higher wages, and to the disadvantage of men, who now receive lower wages. Women were initially harmed through discrimination to the benefit of men; the termination of discrimination corrects that situation.

There is also a net gain to society. Recall that the labor demand curve reflects labor's marginal revenue product (Chapter 14) or, in other words, labor's contribution to the domestic output.[7] Hence, the gray areas for occupations X and Y show the *increases* in domestic output—the market value of the marginal or extra output—realized by adding 1 million women workers in each of those two occupations. Similarly, the orange area for occupation Z shows the *decline* in domestic output caused by the shifting of the 2 million women workers from occupation Z. We note that the sum of the two additions to domestic output exceeds the sub-

[7]Technical note: This assumes pure competition in product and resource markets.

traction from domestic output when discrimination is ended. Women workers are reallocating themselves from occupation Z, where their contribution to domestic output (their MRP) is relatively low, to alternative employments in X and Y, where their contributions to domestic output (their MRPs) are relatively high. Conclusion: *Society gains from a more efficient allocation of resources when discrimination is abandoned.* Discrimination influences the distribution of a *diminished* domestic output. That is, discrimination places the nation on a point inside of its production possibilities curve.

Costs of Discrimination

Given the diverse types of discrimination, the economic costs of discrimination are difficult to estimate. However, one estimate is that if economic and social policies were successful in lowering the black unemployment rate to the level of the white rate, and if education and training opportunities were made available to the black labor force so that the average productivity of black labor became equal to that of white workers, the total output of the economy would rise by about 4 percent. For example, in 1991 the economic cost of racial discrimination alone would be about $227 billion.

Addenda

We must consider two important additions to our discussion of discrimination.

Comparable Worth Doctrine The first involves public policy. The reality of pervasive occupational segregation has given rise to the issue of comparable worth. Legislation such as the Equal Pay Act of 1963 which forced employers to pay equal wages to men and women performing the same jobs was of no help to many women because occupational segregation limited their access to jobs held by men. The essence of the **comparable worth doctrine** is that female secretaries, nurses, and clerks should receive the same salaries as male truck drivers or construction workers if the levels of skill, effort, and responsibility in these disparate jobs are comparable. The basic advantage of comparable worth is that it is a means of quickly correcting perceived pay inequities.

While the concept of comparable worth has considerable appeal, there are a number of important objections. For example, any comparison of the relative worth of various jobs is necessarily subjective and therefore arbitrary, opening the door to endless controversies and lawsuits. Second, wage setting by administrative or bureaucratic judgment, rather than supply and demand, does not bode well for long-run efficiency. To the extent that the calculated worth of specific jobs varies from their market or equilibrium value, worker shortages or surpluses will develop. Furthermore, increasing the wages of women could attract even more females to traditionally "women jobs" and prolong occupational segregation.

Nondiscriminatory Factors Not all the average income differentials found between blacks and whites *and* males and females are necessarily due to discrimination. Most researchers agree, for example, that some part of the male-female earnings differential is attributable to factors other than discrimination. For example, the work-life cycle of married women who have children historically has involved a continuous period of work until birth of the first child. Then there is a five- to ten-year period of nonparticipation or partial participation in the labor force related to childbearing and child care, followed by a more continuous period of work experience when the mother is in her late thirties or early forties. The net result is that, on the average, married women have accumulated much less labor force experience than men in the same age group. Hence, on the average females are less productive workers and are therefore paid a lower average wage rate.

Furthermore, family ties apparently provide married women with less geographical mobility in job choice than males. In fact, married women may give up good positions to move with husbands who accept jobs elsewhere. And some married women may put convenience of job location and flexibility of working hours ahead of occupational choice. Again, women may have purposely crowded into such occupations as nursing and elementary school teaching because such occupations have the greatest carryover value for productive activity within the home. Finally, in the past decades more women have entered the labor force than have men. This large increase in the supply of female workers has acted as a drag on women's wages and earnings.

All this implies that some portion of the male-female earnings differential is due to considerations other than discrimination by gender. It also suggests that the male-female wage gap will narrow in the future, now that more women are attending college, working through their childbearing years, and pursuing higher-paying professional jobs.

QUICK REVIEW 23-3

- ***Discrimination may mean a paying different wages to equally qualified workers, b higher unemployment rates for minorities, c less education and training for women and minorities, and d the concentration of minorities and women in a limited number of occupations.***
- ***The crowding model demonstrates how a men can increase their wages at the expense of women, and b occupational segregation diminishes the domestic output.***
- ***Comparable worth means that females in one occupation should receive the same wages as males in another occupation if the levels of skill, effort, responsibility and working conditions are comparable.***

IMMIGRATION

The immigration issue has long been clouded in controversy and misunderstanding. Should more or fewer people be allowed to migrate to the United States? How should the much-publicized problem of illegal entrants be handled? We will illuminate this problem by (1) briefly summarizing United States' immigration history and policy, (2) presenting a bare-bones model of the economic effects of immigration, and (3) embellishing this simple model by considering some of the more subtle costs and benefits associated with the international movement of labor.

History and Policy

During the first 140 years of our history as an independent nation, immigration to the United States was virtually unimpeded. There is little question that the great infusion of foreign labor into our labor-scarce country was a major contributing factor to our nation's economic growth. But the great flood of immigrants which came to the United States in the quarter-century prior to World War I was sharply curtailed by the war itself and by a series of restrictive immigration laws enacted in the 1920s. However, after World War II, immigration policy was liberalized and the annual inflows of **legal immigrants** were roughly 250,000 in the 1950s, 320,000 in the 1960s, and 500,000 or more during most of the 1970s and early 1980s.

These data are very imperfect, however, because they do not include **illegal immigrants.** Estimates suggest that, in recent years, as many as 500,000 illegal aliens may enter the United States each year, most coming from Mexico, the Caribbean, and Latin America. Despite this large annual influx of illegals, the total number of illegal aliens in the United States may only be about $3\frac{1}{2}$ to 5 million (estimates vary from 2 to 12 million). Many illegal aliens come to the United States for a year or so to earn a "grubstake" and then return to their native countries.

Current legislation increases the number of legal immigrants to 700,000 per year. The legislation stresses family reunification by allowing United States citizens to bring in immediate relatives—spouses, children, and parents. But there has also been a substantial increase in the number of visas made available to highly skilled professionals such as researchers, engineers, and scientists. In addition, some 10,000 visas have been earmarked for wealthy immigrants who are willing to invest at least $1 million in the United States. Emphasis is clearly on the kinds of immigrants who are likely to make significant contributions to American economic growth.

Immigration and immigration policy have been highly controversial, focusing largely on illegal immigrants. Public concern over illegal immigration gave rise to the Immigration Reform and Control Act of 1986, popularly known as the **Simpson-Rodino Act.** It has three major provisions.

1 Amnesty The law provides amnesty and grants legal status to undocumented individuals who have lived in the United States since 1982. Qualified workers receive work authorization cards and after five years of continuous residence become eligible to apply for citizenship.

2 Employer Sanctions Employers who knowingly hire illegal immigrants are subject to fines and possible imprisonment for repeated offenses.

3 Temporary Farm Labor The law allows temporary migrants or "guest workers" to enter the country to harvest perishable crops.

Economics of Immigration

We can gain some insight into the economic effects of immigration by employing a variation of the crowding model of discrimination (Figure 23-3). In Figure 23-4 we portray the demand for labor in the United States as D_u in the left diagram and the demand for labor in Mexico as D_m in the right diagram. The demand for

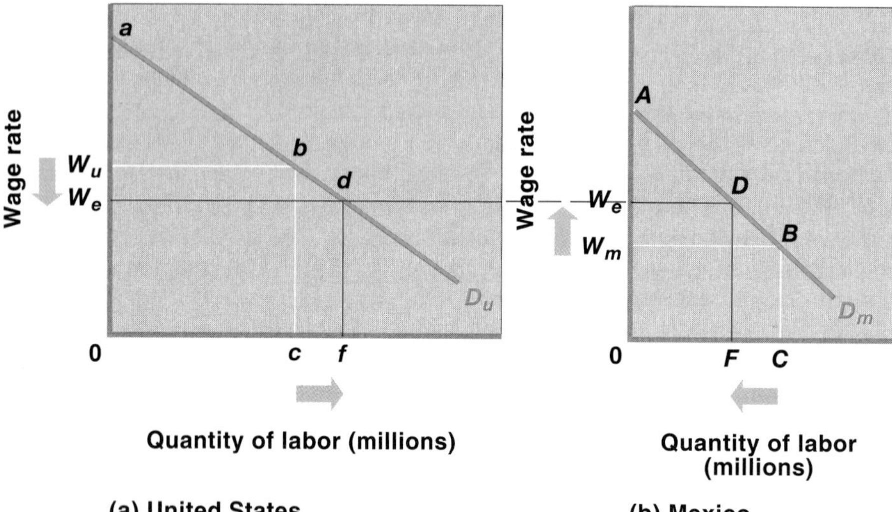

(a) United States (b) Mexico

FIGURE 23-4 The simple economics of immigration

The migration of labor to high-income United States (a) from low-income Mexico (b) will increase the domestic output, reduce the average level of wages, and increase business incomes in the United States, while having the opposite effects in Mexico. The United States' domestic output gain of *cbdf* exceeds Mexico's domestic output loss of *FDBC*; hence, there is a net increase in world output.

labor is greater in the United States, presumably because of the presence of more capital equipment and more advanced technologies which enhance the productivity of labor. (Recall from Chapter 14 that the labor demand curve is based on the marginal revenue product of labor.) Conversely, we assume that machinery and equipment are scarce in Mexico and that technology is less sophisticated; hence, labor demand is weak. We also assume that the premigration labor forces of the United States and Mexico are *Oc* and *OC* respectively, *and* that full employment exists in both countries.

Wage Rates and World Output If we further assume that (1) migration is costless; (2) it occurs solely in response to wage differentials; and (3) is unimpeded by legislation in either country, workers will migrate from Mexico to the United States until wage rates in the two countries are equal at W_e. In this case some *FC* (= *fc*) million workers will have migrated from Mexico to the United States before equilibrium is achieved. Although the average level of wage rates falls from W_u to W_e in the United States, the domestic output (the sum of the marginal revenue products of the labor force) increases from *Oabc* to *Oadf*. In Mexico, average wage rates rise from W_m to W_e, but domestic output declines from *OABC* to *OADF*.[8] Observing that the domestic output gain of *cbdf* in the United States exceeds the *FDBC* loss in Mexico, we conclude that the world's real output has increased.

Just as elimination of the barrier of sex or racial discrimination enhances economic efficiency within a country, so the elimination of legislative barriers to the international flow of labor increases worldwide economic efficiency. The world gains because freedom to migrate moves people to countries where they can make a larger contribution to world production. To repeat: Migration involves an efficiency gain. It enables the world to produce a larger real output with a given amount of resources.

Income Shares Our model also suggests that this flow of immigrants will enhance business or capitalist incomes in the United States and reduce them in Mexico. We have just noted that the before-immigration

[8]What happens to the wage bill (wage rate multiplied by the number of workers) in each of the two countries depends on the elasticity of labor demand. If the demand for labor is elastic in the W_uW_e wage range in the United States, the absolute size of the wage bill will increase. Conversely, if labor demand is inelastic in the W_uW_e wage range, the absolute size of the wage bill will decline. A similar application of the total revenue (earnings) test for elasticity applies to Mexico.

domestic output in the United States is *Oabc*. The total wage bill is OW_ubc, that is, the wage rate multiplied by the number of workers. The remaining triangular area W_uab is "business" or capitalist income. The same reasoning applies to Mexico.

Unimpeded immigration will increase business income from W_uab to W_ead in the United States and reduce it from W_mAB to W_eAD in Mexico. Business benefits from immigration in the United States; Mexican businesses are hurt by emigration. This is what we would expect intuitively; America is receiving "cheap" labor, Mexico is losing "cheap" labor. This conclusion is consistent with the historical fact that American employers have often actively recruited immigrants.

Complications and Modifications

Our model includes a number of simplifying assumptions and also omits several relevant considerations. Let's therefore release some of the more critical assumptions and introduce omitted factors, observing how our conclusions are affected.

1 Cost of Migration The international movement of workers is not costless. Costs are not only the explicit or out-of-pocket costs of geographically moving oneself and one's possessions, but also the implicit or opportunity cost of lost income during the period of movement and reestablishing oneself in the host country. Still more subtle costs are involved in adapting to a new culture, language, climate, and so forth. All such *costs* must be estimated by the potential immigrant and weighed against the expected *benefits* of higher wages in the host country. If benefits are estimated to exceed costs, it is rational to migrate. If costs exceed benefits, one should not migrate.

In Figure 23-4 the existence of migration costs means that the flow of labor from Mexico to the United States will *not* occur to the extent that wages are equalized. Wages will remain higher in the United States than in Mexico. Furthermore, the world gain from migration will be reduced.

2 Remittances and Backflows Many migrants view their moves as temporary. Their plan is to move to a wealthier country, accumulate some desired level of wealth through hard work and frugality, and return home to establish their own enterprises. During their period in the host country, migrants frequently make sizable **remittances** to their families at home. This causes a redistribution of the net gain from migration between the countries involved. In Figure 23-4 remittances by Mexican workers in the United States to their relatives would cause the *gain* in United States' domestic output to be less than that shown and the *loss* of Mexican domestic output to also be less than that shown.

Actual **backflows**—the return of migrants to their home countries—might also alter gains and losses through time. For example, if some of the Mexican workers who migrated to the United States acquired substantial labor-market or managerial skills and then returned home, their enhanced human capital might then make a substantial contribution to economic development in Mexico. Evidence suggests, however, that migrant workers who acquire skills in the receiving country tend *not* to return home. In fact, at various times the United States has been a beneficiary of "brain drains" as professional and other highly skilled workers have left western Europe and other nations for higher wages and better job opportunities in the United States.

3 Full Employment versus Unemployment Our model assumes full employment in both the sending and receiving country. Mexican workers presumably leave low-paying jobs to more-or-less immediately take higher-paying jobs in the United States. However, in many cases the factor that "pushes" immigrants from their homelands is not low wages, but chronic unemployment and underemployment. Many less developed countries are characterized by overpopulation and surplus labor; workers are either unemployed or so grossly underemployed that their marginal revenue product is zero.

Again, allowance for this possibility affects our discussion of gains and losses. Specifically, Mexico would *gain* (not lose!) by having such workers emigrate. These unemployed workers are making no contribution to Mexico's domestic output and must be sustained by transfers from the rest of the labor force. The remaining Mexican labor force will be better off by the amount of the transfers after the unemployed workers have migrated to the United States. Conversely, if the Mexican immigrant workers are unable to find jobs in the United States and are sustained through transfers from employed American workers, then the after-tax income of native American workers will decline.

4 Fiscal Aspects What impacts do immigrants have on tax revenues and government spending in the receiving country? Although evidence is scanty and

LAST WORD

RACISM IN PROFESSIONAL BASKETBALL?

Although black players earn more than white players in the NBA, researchers have discovered evidence of wage discrimination against blacks.

Casual observation would suggest an absence of racial discrimination in the National Basketball Association (NBA). About three-fourths of all NBA players—and four-fifths of all starters—are black. Teams are highly integrated. There are more black coaches in the NBA than in other professional sports. Many of the most highly paid players are black. Indeed, raw salary data for 1985–1986 show that black players earned $10,620 (2.7 percent) more than white players.

Yet recent research suggests that discrimination *does* exist. Sherer and Kahn* have adjusted 1985–1986 raw salary data for various measures of player performance (productivity) such as number of seasons played, games played per season, career points, field goal percentage, rebounds, assists per game, and so forth. These measures indicate that black players are superior to whites. Adjusting salaries to account for this superiority, Sherer and Kahn have concluded that black players earned about $80,000 or 20 percent *less* than white players.

What is the source of this discrimination? Sherer and Kahn reject the notion of racist attitudes on the part of team owners. By rejecting talented black players, racist owners would find themselves with less successful teams, declining revenues, and franchises of lesser value. Furthermore, the fact that NBA teams are highly integrated suggests that fellow employees (white players) are not the source of discrimination. Sherer and Kahn find that team customers (fans) are the source of NBA discrimination. Their research shows that home game attendance increases with the number of white players on the team. Specifically, they estimate that a team's revenue may increase by about $115,000 to $131,000 per season per additional white player, and suggest that both white players and team owners gain by serving fans' preferences to watch white players. Sherer and Kahn conclude that "As long as fans prefer to see white players, profit-oriented teams will make discriminatory salary offers."†

*Peter D. Sherer and Lawrence M. Kahn, "Racial Differences in Professional Basketball Players' Compensation," *Journal of Labor Economics,* January 1988, pp. 40–61.

†Ibid., p. 60.

subject to dispute, the consensus is that immigrants are probably net contributors to the fiscal system of the host country. They are disporportionately comprised of younger people—frequently, unattached young males—who are in the prime of life and who have received some schooling in their native country. Certainly, highly skilled migrants who already speak the host country's language are likely to be heavy net taxpayers. Less skilled workers—for example, political refugees from Haiti or Central America—may require several years of public or philanthropic aid to learn the language and become assimilated. But illegal aliens from, say, Mexico or the Caribbean are likely to be net taxpayers.

> Several studies have found that very few illegals collect unemployment compensation, go on welfare, receive food-stamps, or use medicaid. Some do use free public hospitals and send their children to pub-

lic schools, but the incremental costs involved are probably small. On the tax revenue side, it is clear that most illegals do have social security and federal income taxes withheld from their pay, although a sizable proportion apparently pay less than their legal obligation of the latter.

The very low incidence of social welfare payments to illegals is not a mystery. These payments are usually made only to the unemployed and most illegals are working. When they are not, fear of detection and deportation keeps them from applying to benefit programs. Thus, the direct social welfare costs of illegals are low.[9]

QUICK REVIEW 23-4

- ***Current policy allows about 700,000 immigrants to enter the United States each year with preference being given to "priority workers" who have special education, training, and talents.***
- ***A country receiving immigrants will experience a larger domestic output, a lower average level of wages, and an increase in business incomes. The opposite effects will occur in the donor country.***
- ***The economic effects of immigration are complicated by the costs of migration, remittances, backflows of immigrants, employment conditions, and fiscal implications.***

Economics and Beyond

Even our elementary consideration of the economic aspects of immigration makes it clear that the issues involved are complex. Much obviously depends on the character of the immigrants themselves and economic conditions in the receiving country. Many benefits would accrue to the United States from a liberal immigration policy when (1) immigrants are young, educated, and skilled; and (2) our economy is fully employed and experiencing robust growth. Benefits to Americans are less evident when (1) immigrants are unskilled and illiterate, and (2) our economy is stagnant and plagued by high unemployment. The "brain drain" to America in the 1960s and Castro's emptying out of Cuban prisons and mental hospitals in 1980 were highly contrasting episodes in American immigration history!

The immigration issue is also complicated by an assortment of essentially noneconomic issues. Do minority immigrants inflame racial problems? Does the concentration of migrants in urban areas such as New York and Miami generate social tensions and increase crime rates? Would America without fresh inflows of immigrants somehow not be America?

CHAPTER SUMMARY

1 The growth of labor unions was slow and irregular until the 1930s due to court and employer hostility.

2 The AFL dominated the American labor movement from 1886 until the CIO was formed in 1936. Its philosophy was essentially that of Samuel Gompers—business unionism, political neutrality, and craft unionism.

3 Union growth was rapid in the 1930s and 1940s. The shift toward industrial unionism, triggered by the formation of the CIO in 1936, was a significant factor in this growth. Equally important were the prolabor legislation passed by the Federal government in the 1930s and the wartime prosperity of the 1940s.

4 The Norris–La Guardia Act of 1932 rendered yellow-dog contracts unenforceable and sharply limited the use of injunctions in labor disputes. The Wagner Act of 1935—"labor's Magna Charta"—guaranteed labor the rights to organize and to bargain collectively with management.

5 The Taft-Hartley Act of 1947 brought about a shift from government-sponsored to government-regulated collective bargaining. The act **a** specifically outlaws certain "unfair practices" of unions, **b** regulates certain internal operations of unions, **c** controls the content of collective bargaining agreements, and **d** outlines a procedure for handling "national health and welfare" strikes.

6 The Landrum-Griffin Act of 1959 was designed to regulate the internal processes of unions—in particular the handling of union finances and the union's relationships with its members.

7 Unionism has declined relatively in the United States since the mid-1950s. Some labor economists attribute this to changes in the composition of domestic output and in the demographic structure of the labor force. Others contend that employers, recognizing that unionization results in lower profitability, have more aggressively sought to dissuade workers from being union members.

8 Labor and management "live together" under the terms of collective bargaining agreements. These work agreements cover four major topics: **a** union status and managerial prerogatives; **b** wages and hours; **c** seniority and job control; and **d** a grievance procedure.

9 Union workers currently enjoy wages which are 10 to 15 percent higher than comparable nonunion workers. There is little evidence to suggest that unions have been

[9]Walter Fogel, "Illegal Alien Workers in the United States," *Industrial Relations,* October 1977, p. 255. To the extent that illegal immigrants displace American workers they may impose indirect costs on our welfare and income-maintenance programs.

able to raise the average level of real wages for labor as a whole.

10 There is disagreement whether the net effect of unions on allocative efficiency and productivity is positive or negative. The negative view cites **a** inefficiencies associated with featherbedding and union-imposed work rules; **b** loss of output through strikes; and **c** the misallocation of labor to which the union wage advantage gives rise. The positive view holds that **a** through the shock effect union wage pressure spurs technological advance and mechanization of the production process; **b** as collective voice institutions unions contribute to rising productivity by reducing labor turnover; and **c** the enhanced security of union workers increases their willingness to teach their skills to less experienced workers.

11 Those who contend that unions increase earnings inequality argue that **a** unionization increases the wages of union workers but lowers the wages of nonunion workers and **b** unions are strongest among highly paid, skilled blue-collar workers but relatively weak among low-paid, unskilled blue-collar workers. But other economists contend that unions contribute to greater earnings equality because unions **a** seek uniform wages for given jobs within firms and **b** seek uniform wages among firms.

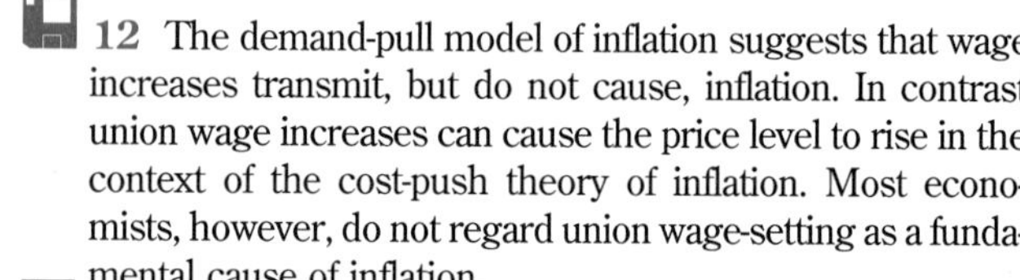

12 The demand-pull model of inflation suggests that wage increases transmit, but do not cause, inflation. In contrast union wage increases can cause the price level to rise in the context of the cost-push theory of inflation. Most economists, however, do not regard union wage-setting as a fundamental cause of inflation.

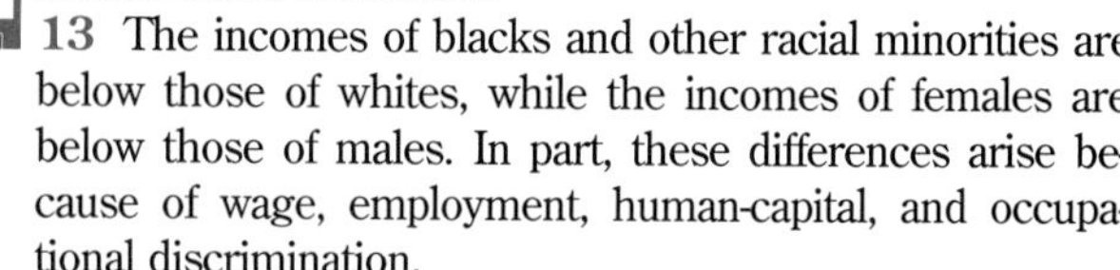

13 The incomes of blacks and other racial minorities are below those of whites, while the incomes of females are below those of males. In part, these differences arise because of wage, employment, human-capital, and occupational discrimination.

14 The crowding model of occupational segregation indicates how white males may gain higher earnings at the expense of blacks and women. The model also shows that discrimination involves a net loss of domestic output.

15 Simple supply and demand analysis suggests that the movement of migrants from a poor to a rich country will **a** increase the domestic output, **b** reduce the average level of wages, and **c** increase business incomes in the receiving country. The opposite effects will occur in the sending country, but the world as a whole can be expected to realize a larger total output.

TERMS AND CONCEPTS

criminal conspiracy doctrine
discriminatory discharge
injunction
blacklisting
lockout
yellow-dog contract
company unions
American Federation of Labor (AFL)
business unionism
Norris–La Guardia Act of 1932
Wagner Act of 1935
jurisdictional strikes
National Labor Relations Board (NLRB)
craft and industrial unionism
Congress of Industrial Organizations (CIO)
Taft-Hartley Act of 1947
secondary boycotts
sympathy strikes
featherbedding
closed shop
union shop
Landrum-Griffin Act of 1959
structural-change and managerial-opposition hypotheses
right-to-work laws
open shop
nonunion shop
fringe benefits
seniority
collective voice
exit and voice mechanisms
backflows
wage, employment, human-capital, and occupational discrimination
remittances
occupational segregation
comparable worth doctrine
legal and illegal immigrants
Simpson-Rodino Act of 1986

QUESTIONS AND STUDY SUGGESTIONS

1 Briefly describe the repression, encouragement, and intervention phases of the American labor movement.

2 It has been said that the Taft-Hartley Act was passed to achieve three major goals: a to reestablish an equality of bargaining power between labor and management to maintain industrial peace; b to protect "neutrals," that is, third parties not directly concerned with a given labor-management dispute; and c to protect the rights of individual workers in their relations with unions. Review the Taft-Hartley provisions as outlined in this chapter, and relate each to these three major goals.

3 Use the structural-change and managerial-opposition hypotheses to explain the relative decline of organized labor in the United States. In your opinion which explanation is more convincing?

4 You are the president of a newly established local

union about to bargain with an employer for the first time. List those points you would want covered explicitly in the work agreement. Assuming the economic climate which exists at this moment, what criteria would you use in backing your wage demands? Explain.

5 "There are legislative, executive, and judicial aspects to collective bargaining." Explain.

6 What is the estimated size of the union wage advantage? Explain: "Although unions get higher wages than nonunion workers, unions have not been successful in raising the average real wage of the American labor force."

7 Comment on each of the following statements:

- a "By constraining the decisions of management, unions inhibit efficiency and productivity growth."
- b "As collective voice institutions unions increase productivity by reducing worker turnover, inducing managerial efficiency, and enhancing worker security."

8 "There is an inherent cost to society that accompanies any union wage gain. That cost is the diminished efficiency with which labor resources are allocated." Explain this contention. Are you in agreement?

9 Describe the various avenues through which unions might alter the distribution of earnings. Evaluate: "Unions purport to be egalitarian institutions, but their effect is to increase earnings inequality among American workers."

10 Use both the demand-pull and the cost-push theories of inflation to discuss union wage-setting as a potential cause of inflation. Evaluate: "Union wage determination transmits and perpetuates, but does not cause, inflation." Explain the following statement: "Unionism can only be a cause of inflation if government is strongly committed to maintaining full employment."

11 Compare and account for differences in the economic status of whites and nonwhites. Distinguish between the various kinds of economic discrimination. Do you believe on balance that the distribution of education and training in our society alleviates, or contributes to, income inequality? Explain.

12 Use simple supply and demand analysis to explain the impact of occupational segregation or "crowding" upon the relative wage rates and earnings of men and women. Who gains and who loses as a consequence of eliminating occupational segregation? Is there a net gain or loss to society as a whole? "Wage differences between men and women do not reflect discrimination, but rather differences in job continuity and rational decisions with respect to education and training." Do you agree?

13 Use a simple demand and supply model to determine the gains and losses associated with the migration of population from low- to high-income countries. Explain how your conclusions are affected by **a** unemployment, **b** remittances from the host country, **c** backflows of migrants to their home countries, and **d** the personal characteristics of the migrants. If the migrants are highly skilled workers, is there any justification for the sending country to levy a "brain drain" tax on emigrants?

14 If you favor the free movement of labor within the United States, are you being inconsistent in favoring restrictions on the international movement of labor?

15 Evaluate: "If we deported 1 million illegal aliens who are in America, our total national unemployment would decline by 1 million."

16 Organized labor in the United States opposes the creation of a free trade zone with Mexico. Why?

International Economics and the World Economy

International Trade: Comparative Advantage and Protectionism

Backpackers hiking deep into wilderness areas like to think they are "leaving the world behind." Ironically, like Atlas, overnight backpackers often carry the world on their shoulders. Much of their backpacking equipment is imported—knives from Switzerland, rain gear from South Korea, cameras from Japan, pots made in England, miniature stoves from Sweden, sleeping bags containing goosedown from China, instant coffee from Brazil, compasses made in Finland, and chocolate bars with cocoa from Ghana. Some backpackers wear hiking boots from Italy, sunglasses made in France, and watches from Japan or Switzerland. Moreover, they may drive to the trailheads in Toyotas, Volvos, or BMWs, made in Japan, Sweden, and Germany, respectively.

International trade touches all of us daily, whether we are hiking in the wilderness, shopping for groceries, driving our cars, listening to music, or working at our jobs. Thus, this chapter's goals are fundamental.

First, we will look briefly at the volume and unique characteristics of international trade. Second, the principle of comparative advantage, introduced in Chapter 3, is used to explain how international specialization and trade can be mutually beneficial to participating nations. Third, we examine the economic impact of trade barriers such as tariffs and import quotas. Next, we evaluate the arguments for protectionism. The evolution of international trade policies, including the emergence of free-trade areas, is then summarized. Finally, we examine the recent resurgence of protectionism, noting causes, examples, and associated costs.

IMPORTANCE OF WORLD TRADE

The volume of world trade is sufficiently great and its characteristics so unique as to merit special consideration.

Volume and Pattern

Table 24-1 provides a rough index of the importance of world trade for several representative countries. Many nations having restricted resource bases and limited

TABLE 24-1 Exports of goods and services as a percentage of gross domestic product, selected countries, 1990

Country	Exports Percentage of GDP
The Netherlands	57
Germany	36
New Zealand	27
Canada	25
United Kingdom	24
France	22
Italy	19
Japan	11

Source: IMF, *International Financial Statistics,* 1992.

domestic markets cannot produce with reasonable efficiency the variety of goods they want to consume. For such countries, exports are the route for obtaining goods they desire and therefore exports may run from 25 to 35 percent or more of their GDPs. Other countries—the United States, for example—have rich and diversified resource bases and vast internal markets and are therefore less dependent on world trade.

1 Volume For the United States and the world the volume of international trade has been increasing both absolutely and relatively. Table 24-2 reflects the substantial growth in the dollar volume of both American exports and imports over the past three decades. Since 1960 United States' exports and imports of goods and services have more than doubled as a percentage of our GDP. Exports and imports currently are each about 10 to 11 percent of GDP. Curiously, however, the United States accounts for a diminishing percentage of total world trade. In 1947 it supplied about one-third of the world's total exports compared to about one-seventh today. World trade has increased more rapidly for other nations than it has for the United States. *But in terms of absolute volumes of imports and exports the United States is the world's leading trading nation.*

2 Dependence There can be no question as to the United States' dependence on the world economy. We are almost entirely dependent on other countries for bananas, cocoa, coffee, spices, tea, raw silk, nickel, tin, natural rubber, and diamonds. Casual observation suggests that imported goods compete strongly in many of our domestic markets: Japanese cameras and video recorders, French and Italian wines, English bicycles, and Japanese motorcycles and autos are a few cases in point. Foreign cars have made persistent gains in American markets and now account for about 35 percent of total sales in the United States. Even the great American pastime—baseball—relies heavily on imported gloves.

But world trade is a two-way street, and a host of American industries are highly dependent on foreign markets. Almost all segments of agriculture rely heavily on foreign markets—rice, wheat, cotton, and tobacco exports vary from one-fourth to more than one-half of total output. The chemical, aircraft, automobile, machine tool, coal, and computer industries are only a few of many American industries which sell significant portions of their output in international markets. Table 24-3 shows some of the major commodity exports and imports of the United States.

3 Trade Patterns An overall picture of the pattern of United States merchandise trade was given in Table 5-6. A quick review of that table provides the basis for several observations.

1 In 1990 our imports of goods from abroad were substantially in excess of our exports of goods.
2 The bulk of our export and import trade is with other developed nations, not with the less developed nations or the countries of eastern Europe.

TABLE 24-2 Trade in the U.S. economy, 1960–1991* *(dollars in billions)*

	1960		1975		1991	
	Amount	Percent of GDP	Amount	Percent of GDP	Amount	Percent of GDP
Exports of goods and services	$25.3	4.9	$136.3	8.6	$592.5	10.4
Imports of goods and services	22.8	4.4	122.7	7.7	621.9	11.0
Net exports	2.4	0.5	13.6	0.9	−29.4	0.5

*Data are on a national income accounts basis.

Source: Department of Commerce.

TABLE 24-3 Principal commodity exports and imports of the United States, 1990 *(in billions)*

Exports	*Amount*	*Imports*	*Amount*
Chemicals	$28.4	Petroleum	$62.1
Computers	25.9	Automobiles	45.9
Consumer durables	21.0	Clothing	23.9
Aircraft	18.4	Computers	23.0
Grains	14.9	Household appliances	18.7
Semiconductors	13.3	Chemicals	14.3
Generating equipment	12.7	Semiconductors	12.2
Automobiles	10.9	Iron and steel	11.3
Nonferrous metals	10.9	Toys and sporting goods	9.7
Telecommunications	9.6	Telecommunications	9.4

Source: U.S. Department of Commerce.

3 Canada is our most important trading partner quantitatively. Twenty-two percent of our exports are sold to Canadians, who in turn provide us with 19 percent of our imports.
4 There is a sizable imbalance in our trade with Japan; our imports greatly exceed our exports.
5 Our dependence on foreign oil is reflected in the excess of imports over exports in our trade with the OPEC nations.

4 Level of Output Changes in net exports—the difference between the value of a nation's exports and imports—have multiple effects on the level of domestic output in roughly the same way as do fluctuations in the various types of domestic spending. A small change in the volume of American imports and exports can have magnified repercussions on the domestic levels of output, employment, and prices.

Unique Aspects

Aside from essentially quantitative considerations, world trade has certain unique characteristics.

1 Mobility Differences Though the difference is a matter of degree, the mobility of resources is considerably less among nations than it is within nations. American workers are free to move from Iowa to Idaho or from Maine to Minnesota. Crossing international boundaries is a different story.

Immigration laws, not to mention language and cultural barriers, severely restrict migration of labor between nations. Different tax laws, different governmental regulations, different business practices, and a host of other institutional barriers limit migration of real capital over international boundaries.

International trade is a substitute for the international mobility of resources. If human and property resources do not move readily among nations, the movement of goods and services is an effective substitute.

2 Currency Differences Each nation uses a different currency. An American firm distributing Hondas or BMWs in the United States must buy yen or marks to pay the Japanese or German automobile manufactures. The possible complications which may accompany this exchange of currencies are explored in Chapter 25.

3 Politics As we will note, international trade is subject to political interferences and controls which differ markedly in degree and kind from those applying to domestic trade.

THE ECONOMIC BASIS FOR TRADE

But why do nations trade? What is the basis for trade between nations? *International trade is a way nations can specialize, increase the productivity of their resources, and realize a larger total output than otherwise.* Sovereign nations, like individuals and regions of a nation, can gain by specializing in products they can produce with greatest relative efficiency and by trading for goods they cannot produce efficiently.

While the above rationale for world trade is correct, it in a sense begs the question. A better answer to the question "Why do nations trade?" hinges on two points.

1 The distribution of economic resources—natural, human, and capital goods—among nations is quite uneven; nations are substantially different in their endowments of economic resources.

2 Efficient production of various goods requires different technologies or combinations of resources.

The character and interaction of these two points can be readily illustrated. Japan, for example, has a large, well-educated labor force; skilled labor is abundant and therefore cheap. Hence, Japan can produce efficiently (at low cost) a variety of goods whose design and production require much skilled labor; cameras, transistor radios, and video recorders are examples of such **labor-intensive** commodities.

In contrast, Australia has vast amounts of land in comparison with its human and capital resources and can cheaply produce such **land-intensive** commodities as wheat, wool, and meat. Brazil possesses the soil, tropical climate, rainfall, and ample supplies of unskilled labor needed for efficient low-cost production of coffee.

Industrially advanced nations are in a strategic position to produce cheaply a variety of **capital-intensive** goods, for example, automobiles, agricultural equipment, machinery, and chemicals.

It is important to emphasize that the economic efficiency with which nations produce various goods can and does change over time. Both the distribution of resources and technology can change, altering the relative efficiency with which goods can be produced by various countries. For example, in the past few decades South Korea has upgraded the quality of its labor force and has greatly expanded its stock of capital. Thus, although South Korea was primarily an exporter of agricultural products and raw materials a half-century ago, it now exports large quantities of manufactured goods. Similarly, the new technologies which gave rise to synthetic fibers and synthetic rubber drastically altered the resource-mix needed to produce these goods and thereby changed the relative efficiency of nations in manufacturing them.

In short, as national economies evolve, the size and quality of their labor forces may change, the volume and composition of their capital stocks may shift, new technologies will develop, and even the quality of land and quantity of natural resources may be altered. As these changes occur, the relative efficiency with which a nation can produce various goods will also change.

SPECIALIZATION AND COMPARATIVE ADVANTAGE

Let's now use the concept of comparative advantage to analyze the basis for international specialization and trade.

The Basic Principle

To understand comparative advantage, let's consider the case of a certified public accountant (CPA) who is also a skilled house painter. Suppose the CPA can paint her house in less time than the professional painter she is thinking of hiring. Also suppose the CPA can earn \$50 per hour doing her accounting and must pay the painter \$15 per hour. Let's say it will take the accountant 30 hours to paint her house; the painter, 40 hours. Finally, assume the CPA receives no special pleasure from painting.

Should the CPA take time off from her accounting to paint her own house or should she hire the painter? The CPA should hire the painter. The CPA's opportunity cost of painting her house is \$1500 (=30 hours × \$50 per hour of sacrificed income). The cost of hiring the painter is only \$600 (=40 hours × \$15 per hour paid to the painter). Although the CPA is better at both accounting and painting, her relative or comparative advantage lies in accounting. She will *lower her cost of getting her house painted* by specializing in accounting and using some of the earnings from accounting to hire the house painter.

Similarly, the house painter perhaps can reduce his cost of obtaining accounting services by specializing in painting and using some of his income to hire the CPA. Suppose it would take the painter 10 hours to prepare his income tax, while the CPA could handle this task in 2 hours. The house painter would sacrifice \$150 of income (=10 hours × \$15 per hour of sacrificed time) to get a task done which he could hire out for \$100 (=2 hours × \$50 per hour of the CPA's time). By using the CPA to prepare his tax return, the painter *lowers his cost of getting the tax return completed.*

What is true for our CPA and house painter is also true for two nations. Countries can reduce their cost of obtaining desirable goods by specializing where they have comparative advantages.

With this simple example in mind, let's turn to an international trade model to acquire an understanding of the gains from international specialization and trade.

Two Isolated Nations

Suppose the world economy is composed of just two nations, the United States and Brazil. Assume further that each can produce both wheat and coffee, but at differing levels of economic efficiency. Specifically, suppose the United States' and Brazilian domestic production possibilities curves for coffee and wheat are as shown in Figure 24-1a and b. Two characteristics of these production possibilities curves must be stressed.

1 Constant Costs We have purposely drawn the "curves" as straight lines, in contrast to the concave-from-the-origin production possibilities boundaries introduced in Chapter 2. This means the law of increasing costs has been replaced with the assumption of constant costs. This simplification will greatly facilitate our discussion. With increasing costs, the comparative costs of the two nations in producing coffee and wheat would vary with the amounts produced, and comparative advantages might even change. The assumption of constant costs permits us to complete our entire analysis without having to shift to different comparative-cost ratios with every variation in output. The constant-cost assumption will not impair the validity of our analysis and conclusions. We will consider later in our discussion the effect of the more realistic assumption of increasing costs.

2 Different Costs The production possibilities lines of the United States and Brazil are drawn differently, reflecting different resource mixes and differing levels of technological progress. Specifically, the opportunity costs of producing wheat and coffee differ between the two nations.

United States Note in Figure 24-1a that under conditions of full employment, the United States can increase its output of wheat 30 tons by forgoing 30 tons of coffee output. In other words, the slope of the production possibilities curve is $-1\ (=-1/1)$, which implies that 1 ton of wheat can be obtained for every 1 ton of coffee sacrificed. That is, in the United States the domestic exchange ratio or **cost ratio** for the two products is 1 ton of wheat for 1 ton of coffee, or $1W = 1C$. The United States, in effect, can "exchange" a ton of wheat for a ton of coffee domestically by shifting resources from wheat to coffee. Our constant-cost assumption means this exchange or cost ratio prevails for all possible moves from one point to another along the United States' production possibilities curve.

Brazil Brazil's production possibilities line in Figure 24-1b reveals a different exchange or cost ratio. In Brazil 20 tons of coffee must be given up to get 10 tons of wheat. Thus, the slope of the production possibilities curve is $-2(=-2/1)$. This means that in Brazil the domestic cost ratio for the two goods is 1 ton of wheat for 2 tons of coffee, or $1W = 2C$.

Self-Sufficiency If the United States and Brazil are isolated and therefore self-sufficient, each must choose some output-mix on its production possibilities line. Assume that point A in Figure 24-1a is the optimal

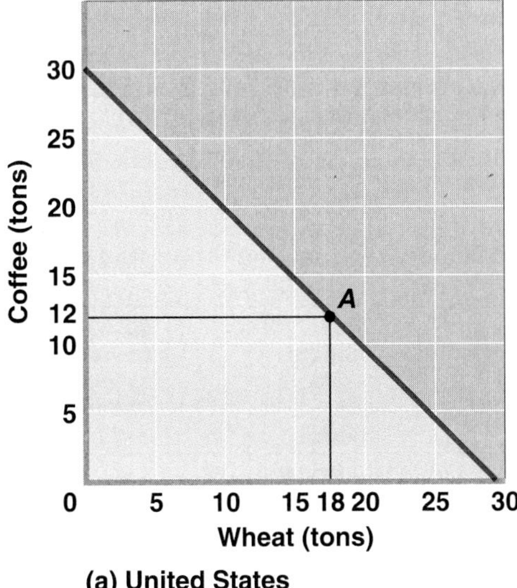

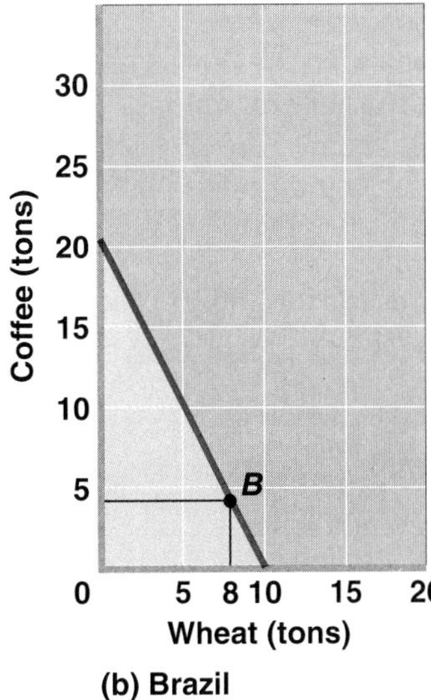

FIGURE 24-1 Production possibilities for the United States and Brazil

The two production possibilities curves show the amounts of coffee and wheat the United States (a) and Brazil (b) can produce domestically. The production possibilities for both countries are straight lines because we are assuming constant costs. The different cost ratios—1 W = 1 C for the United States and 1 W = 2C for Brazil—are reflected in the different slopes of the two lines.

output-mix in the United States. The choice of this combination of 18 tons of wheat and 12 tons of coffee is presumably rendered through the market system. Suppose Brazil's optimal product-mix is 8 tons of wheat and 4 tons of coffee, indicated by point *B* in Figure 24-1b. These choices are also reflected in column 1 of Table 24-4.

Specializing According to Comparative Advantage

Given these different cost ratios, the guideline for determining the products in which the United States and Brazil should specialize is as follows: The **principle of comparative advantage** says that *total output will be greatest when each good is produced by that nation which has the lower opportunity cost.* For our illustration, the United States' opportunity cost is lower for wheat, that is, the United States need only forgo 1 ton of coffee to produce 1 ton of wheat, whereas Brazil must forgo 2 tons of coffee for 1 ton of wheat. *The United States has a comparative (cost) advantage in wheat, and should specialize in wheat production.* The "world" (the United States and Brazil) clearly is *not* economizing in the use of its resources if a specific product (wheat) is produced by a high-cost producer (Brazil) when it could have been produced by a low-cost producer (the United States). To have Brazil produce wheat would mean that the world economy would have to give up more coffee than is necessary to obtain a ton of wheat.

Conversely, Brazil's opportunity cost is lower for coffee; it must sacrifice only $\frac{1}{2}$ ton of wheat in producing 1 ton of coffee, whereas the United States must forgo 1 ton of wheat in producing a ton of coffee. *Brazil has a comparative advantage in coffee, and should specialize in coffee production.* Again, the world would *not* be employing its resources economically if coffee were produced by a high-cost producer (the United States) rather than a low-cost producer (Brazil). If the United States produced coffee, the world would be giving up more wheat than necessary to obtain each ton of coffee. *Economizing—using given quantities of scarce resources to obtain the greatest total output—requires that any particular good be produced by that nation which has the lower opportunity cost or, in other words, the comparative advantage.* In our illustration, the United States should produce wheat and Brazil, coffee.

In column 2 of Table 24-4 we can quickly verify that specialized production in accordance with the principle of comparative advantage does, indeed, allow the world to get more output from its fixed amount of resources. By specializing completely in wheat, the United States can produce 30 tons of wheat and no coffee. Similarly, by specializing completely in coffee, Brazil produces 20 tons of coffee and no wheat. The world has more wheat—30 tons compared with 26 (=18 + 8) tons—*and* more coffee—20 tons compared with 16 (=12 + 4) tons—than in the case of self-sufficiency or unspecialized production.

Terms of Trade

But consumers of each nation want *both* wheat and coffee. Specialization implies the need to trade or exchange the two products. What will be the **terms of trade?** At what exchange ratio will the United States and Brazil trade wheat and coffee?

Because $1W = 1C$ in the United States, the United States must get *more than* 1 ton of coffee for each ton of wheat exported or it will not pay the United States to export wheat in exchange for Brazilian coffee. Stated differently, the United States must get a better price (more coffee) for its wheat in the world market than it can get domestically, or else trade will not be advantageous.

Similarly, because $1W = 2C$ in Brazil, it must be able to get 1 ton of wheat by exporting some amount *less than* 2 tons of coffee. Brazil must be able to pay a

TABLE 24-4 International specialization according to comparative advantage and the gains from trade *(hypothetical data; in tons)*

Country	*(1) Outputs before specialization*	*(2) Outputs after specialization*	*(3) Amounts exported (−) and imported (+)*	*(4) Outputs available after trade*	*(5) = (4) − (1) Gains from specialization and trade*
United States	18 wheat	30 wheat	−10 wheat	20 wheat	2 wheat
	12 coffee	0 coffee	+15 coffee	15 coffee	3 coffee
Brazil	8 wheat	0 wheat	+10 wheat	10 wheat	2 wheat
	4 coffee	20 coffee	−15 coffee	5 coffee	1 coffee

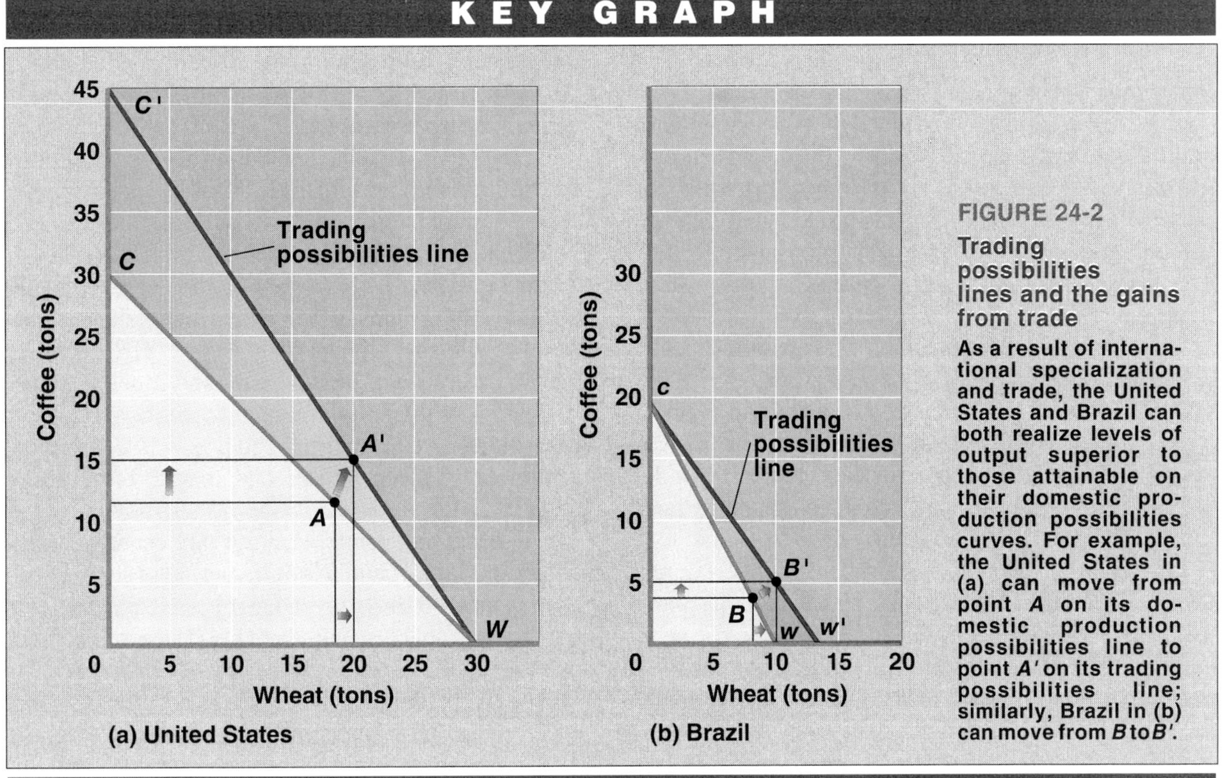

FIGURE 24-2
Trading possibilities lines and the gains from trade
As a result of international specialization and trade, the United States and Brazil can both realize levels of output superior to those attainable on their domestic production possibilities curves. For example, the United States in (a) can move from point *A* on its domestic production possibilities line to point *A'* on its trading possibilities line; similarly, Brazil in (b) can move from *B* to *B'*.

lower "price" for wheat in the world market than it must pay domestically, or it will not want to engage in international trade. Thus, the international exchange ratio or *terms of trade* must lie somewhere between

$1W = 1C$ (United States' cost conditions)

and

$1W = 2C$ (Brazil's cost conditions)

But where will the actual world exchange ratio fall between the $1W = 1C$ and $1W = 2C$ limits? This question is important, because the exchange ratio or terms of trade determine how the gains from international specialization and trade are divided among the two nations. The United States will prefer a rate close to $1W = 2C$, say, $1W = 1\frac{3}{4}C$. Americans want to get much coffee for each ton of wheat they export. Similarly, Brazil desires a rate near $1W = 1C$, say, $1W = 1\frac{1}{4}C$. Brazil wants to export as little coffee as possible for each ton of wheat it receives in exchange.

The actual exchange ratio materializing between the two limits depends on world supply and demand conditions for the two products. If overall world demand for coffee is weak relative to its supply and the demand for wheat is strong relative to its supply, the price of coffee will be low and that of wheat high. The exchange ratio will settle near the $1W = 2C$ figure preferred by the United States. Under the opposite world supply and demand conditions, the ratio will settle near the $1W = 1C$ level most favorable to Brazil.

The Gains from Trade

Suppose the international exchange ratio or terms of trade are actually $1W = 1\frac{1}{2}C$. The possibility of trading on these terms permits each nation to supplement its domestic production possibilities line with a **trading possibilities line.** This can be seen in Figure 24-2a and b (Key Graph). Just as a production possibilities line shows the options a full-employment economy has in obtaining one product by shifting resources from the production of another, so a trading possibilities lines shows the options a nation has by specializing in one product and trading (exporting) its speciality to obtain the other product. The trading possibilities lines in Figure 24-2 are drawn on the assumption that both nations specialize in accordance with comparative advantage and therefore that the United States specializes completely in wheat (point *W* in Figure 24-2a) and Brazil completely in coffee (point *c* in Figure 24-2b).

Improved Options Now, instead of being constrained by its domestic production possibilities line and having to give up 1 ton of wheat for every ton of coffee it wants as it moves up its domestic production possibilities line from point *W*, the United States, through trade with Brazil, can get $1\frac{1}{2}$ tons of coffee for every ton of wheat it exports to Brazil as it moves up the trading possibilities line *WC*′.

Similarly, we can think of Brazil as starting at point *c*, and instead of having to move down its domestic production possibilities line and having to give up 2 tons of coffee for each ton of wheat it wants, it can now export just $1\frac{1}{2}$ tons of coffee for each ton of wheat it wants by moving down its *cw*′ trading possibilities line.

Specialization and trade give rise to a new exchange ratio between wheat and coffee which is reflected in a nation's trading possibilities line. This new exchange ratio is superior for both nations to the self-sufficiency exchange ratio in the production possibilities line of each. By specializing in wheat and trading for Brazil's coffee, the United States can obtain *more than* 1 ton of coffee for 1 ton of wheat. Similarly, by specializing in coffee and trading for United States' wheat, Brazil can get 1 ton of wheat for *less than* 2 tons of coffee.

Added Output The crucial point is that by specializing according to comparative advantage and trading for those goods produced with the least relative efficiency domestically, both the United States and Brazil can realize combinations of wheat and coffee beyond their production possibilities boundaries. *Specialization according to comparative advantage results in a more efficient allocation of world resources, and larger outputs of both wheat and coffee are therefore available to the United States and Brazil.* To be more specific, suppose that at the $1W = 1\frac{1}{2}C$ terms of trade, the United States exports 10 tons of wheat to Brazil and Brazil in return exports 15 tons of coffee to the United States.

How do the new quantities of wheat and coffee available to the two nations compare with the optimal product-mixes that existed before specialization and trade? Point *A* in Figure 24-2a reminds us that the United States chose 18 tons of wheat and 12 tons of coffee originally. But, by producing 30 tons of wheat and no coffee, and by trading 10 tons of wheat for 15 tons of coffee, the United States can enjoy 20 tons of wheat and 15 tons of coffee. This new, superior combination of wheat and coffee is shown by point *A*′ in Figure 24-2a. Compared with the nontrading figures of 18 tons of wheat and 12 tons of coffee, the United States' **gains from trade** are 2 tons of wheat and 3 tons of coffee. Similarly, we assumed Brazil's optimal product-mix was 4 tons of coffee and 8 tons of wheat (point *B*) before specialization and trade. Now, by specializing in coffee—producing 20 tons of coffee and no wheat—Brazil can realize a combination of 5 tons of coffee and 10 tons of wheat by exporting 15 tons of its coffee in exchange for 10 tons of American wheat. This new position is shown by point *B*′ in Figure 24-2b. Brazil's gains from trade are 1 ton of coffee and 2 tons of wheat.

As a result of specialization and trade, both countries have more of both products. Table 24-4 is a summary statement of these figures and merits your careful study.

The fact that points *A*′ and *B*′ are economic positions superior to *A* and *B* is extremely important. Recall from Chapter 2 that a given nation can expand its production possibilities boundary by (1) expanding the quantity and improving the quality of its resources or (2) realizing technological progress. We have now discovered another means—international trade—by which a nation can circumvent the output constraint imposed by its production possibilities curve. The effects of international specialization and trade are tantamount to having more and better resources or discovering improved production techniques.

Increasing Costs

In formulating a straightforward statement of the principles underlying international trade, we have made several simplifications. Our discussion was purposely limited to two products and two nations to minimize verbiage, but multination and multiproduct examples yield similar conclusions. The assumption of constant costs, on the other hand, is a more substantive simplification. Let's therefore consider the significance of increasing costs (concave-from-the-origin production possibility curves) for our analysis.

Suppose, as in our previous constant-cost illustration, that the United States and Brazil are at positions on their production possibilities curves where their cost ratios are initially $1W = 1C$ and $1W = 2C$ respectively. As before, comparative advantage indicates that the United States should specialize in wheat and Brazil in coffee. But now, as the United States begins to expand wheat production, its $1W = 1C$ cost ratio will *fall;* it will have to sacrifice *more than* 1 ton of coffee to get 1 additional ton of wheat. Resources are no longer perfectly shiftable between alternative uses, as the constant-cost assumption implied. Resources less and less suitable to wheat production must be allocated to the American wheat industry in expanding wheat output, and this means increasing costs—the sacrifice of larger and larger amounts of coffee for each additional ton of wheat.

Similarly, Brazil, starting from its $1W = 2C$ cost ratio position, expands coffee production. But as it does, it will find that its $1W = 2C$ cost ratio begins to *rise.* Sacrificing a ton of wheat will free resources which are only capable of producing something *less than* 2 tons of coffee, because these transferred resources are less suitable to coffee production.

As the American cost ratio falls from $1W = 1C$ and Brazil's rises from $1W = 2C$, a point will be reached at which the cost ratios are equal in the two nations, for example, at $1W = 1\frac{1}{2}C$. At this point the underlying basis for further specialization and trade—differing cost ratios—has disappeared, and further specialization is therefore uneconomic. And most important, this point of equal cost ratios may be realized where the United States is still producing some coffee along with its wheat and Brazil is producing some wheat along with its coffee. *The primary effect of increasing costs is to make specialization less than complete.* For this reason we often find domestically produced products competing directly against identical or similar imported products within a particular economy.

The Case for Free Trade Restated

The compelling logic of the case for free trade is hardly new. Indeed, in 1776 Adam Smith asserted:

> It is the maxim of every prudent master of a family, never to attempt to make at home what it will cost him more to make than to buy. The taylor does not attempt to make his own shoes, but buys them of the shoemaker. The shoemaker does not attempt to make his own clothes but employs a taylor. The farmer attempts to make neither the one nor the other, but employs those different artificers. All of them find it for their interest to employ their whole industry in a way in which they have some advantage over their neighbors, and to purchase with a part of its produce, or what is the same thing, with the price of a part of it, whatever else they have occasion for.[1]

In modern jargon, the case for free trade comes down to this one potent argument. *Through free trade based on the principle of comparative advantage, the world economy can achieve a more efficient allocation of resources and a higher level of material well-being.* The resource mixes and technological knowledge of each country are different. Therefore, each nation can produce particular commodities at different real costs. Each nation should produce goods for which its opportunity costs are low relative to those of other nations and exchange these specialties for products for which its opportunity costs are high relative to those of other nations. If each nation does this, the world can realize fully the advantages of geographic and human specialization. That is, the world—and each free-trading nation—can obtain a larger real income from the fixed supplies of resources available to it. Protection—barriers to free trade—lessens or eliminates gains from specialization. If nations cannot freely trade, they must shift resources from efficient (low-cost) to inefficient (high-cost) uses to satisfy their diverse wants.

A side benefit of free trade is that it promotes competition and deters monopoly. The increased competition afforded by foreign firms forces domestic firms to adopt the lowest-cost production techniques. It also compels them to be innovative and progressive with respect to both product quality and production methods, thereby contributing to economic growth. And free trade gives consumers a wider range of products from which to choose. The reasons to favor free trade are essentially the same reasons which endorse competition. Therefore, it is not surprising that most economists embrace the case for free trade as an economically valid position.

QUICK REVIEW 24-1

- ***World trade is increasingly important to the United States and other nations of the world.***
- ***International trade enables nations to specialize, enhance the productivity of their resources, and obtain a larger output.***
- ***The principle of comparative advantage states that total world output will be greatest when each good is produced by that nation having the lowest opportunity cost.***
- ***Specialization is less than complete among nations because opportunity costs normally rise as more of a particular good is produced.***

[1]Adam Smith, *The Wealth of Nations* (New York: Modern Library, Inc., 1937), p. 424.

TRADE BARRIERS

No matter how compelling the logic of the case for free trade, barriers to free trade do exist.

1 *Tariffs* are excise taxes on imported goods: they may be imposed for purposes of revenue or protection. **Revenue tariffs** are usually applied to products not produced domestically, for example, tin, coffee, and bananas in the case of the United States. Rates on revenue tariffs are typically modest and their purpose is to provide the Federal government with tax revenues.

Protective tariffs, on the other hand, are designed to shield domestic producers from foreign competition. Although protective tariffs are usually not high enough to prohibit importation of foreign goods, they put foreign producers at a competitive disadvantage in selling in domestic markets.

2 **Import quotas** specify the maximum amounts of commodities which may be imported in any period of time. Frequently, import quotas are more effective in retarding international commerce than tariffs. A given product might be imported in relatively large quantities despite high tariffs; low import quotas, on the other hand, completely prohibit imports once quotas are filled.

3 **Nontariff barriers** (NTBs) refer to licensing requirements, unreasonable standards pertaining to product quality and safety, or simply unnecessary bureaucratic red tape in customs procedures. Japan and the European countries frequently require their domestic importers of foreign goods to obtain licenses. By restricting the issuance of licenses, imports can be effectively restricted. Great Britain bars importation of coal in this way.

4 **Voluntary export restrictions** (VERs) are a relatively new trade barrier by which foreign firms "voluntarily" limit the amount of their exports to a particular country. VERs, which have the effect of import quotas, are agreed to by exporters in the hope of avoiding more stringent trade barriers. Thus Japanese auto manufacturers agreed to a VER on exports to the United States under the threat of higher U.S. tariffs or the imposition of low import quotas.

Motivations: Special-Interest Effect

If tariffs and quotas impede free trade and diminish economic efficiency, why do we have them? While nations as a whole gain from free international trade, particular industries and groups of resource suppliers can be hurt. In our comparative advantage example, specialization and trade adversely affected the American coffee industry and the Brazilian wheat industry. Such groups may seek to preserve or improve their economic positions by persuading the government to impose tariffs or quotas to protect them from the detrimental effects of free trade. Chapter 19's special-interest effect—or concept of rent-seeking activity—is highly relevant.

> The direct beneficiaries of import relief or export subsidy are usually few in number, but each has a large individual stake in the outcome. Thus, their incentive for vigorous political activity is strong.
>
> But the costs of such policies may far exceed the benefits. It may cost the public \$40,000–\$50,000 a year to protect a domestic job that might otherwise pay an employee only half that amount in wages and benefits. Furthermore, the costs of protection are widely diffused—in the United States, among 50 States and [254] million citizens. Since the cost borne by any one citizen is likely to be quite small, and may even go unnoticed, resistance at the grass-roots level to protectionist measures often is considerably less than pressures for their adoption.[2]

Also, the costs of protectionism are hidden because tariffs and quotas are embedded in the prices of goods. Thus policy makers face fewer political restraints in responding positively to demands for protectionism.

Later in this chapter we will consider the specific arguments and appeals made to justify protection.

Economic Impact of Tariffs

Simple supply and demand analysis is useful in examining the economic effects of protective tariffs. The D_d and S_d curves in Figure 24-3 show domestic demand and supply for a product in which the United States has a comparative *dis*advantage, for example, cassette recorders. (Disregard $S_d + Q$ for now.) Without world trade, the domestic price and output would be OP_d and Oq, respectively.

Assume now that the domestic economy is opened to world trade, and that the Japanese, who have a comparative advantage in cassette recorders and dominate the world market, begin to sell their recorders in the United States. We assume that with free trade the domestic price cannot differ from the lower world price, which here is OP_w. At OP_w domestic consumption is Od, domestic production is Oa, and the difference between the two, ad, reflects imports.

[2] *Economic Report of the President, 1982,* p. 177.

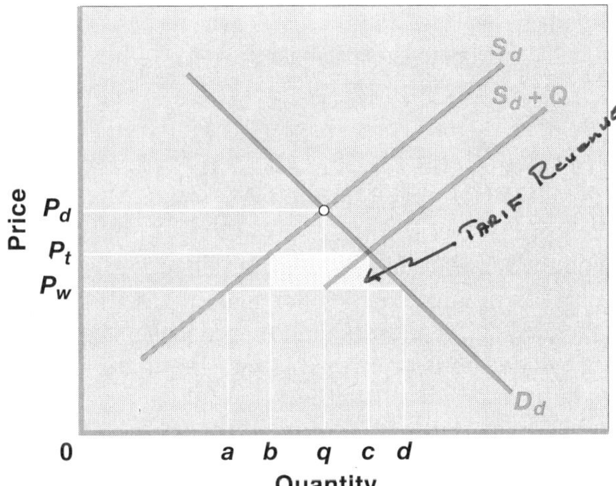

FIGURE 24-3 **The economic effects of a protective tariff or an import quota**

A tariff of P_wP_t will reduce domestic consumption from *Od* to *Oc*. Domestic producers will be able to sell more output (*Ob* rather than *Oa*) at a higher price (OP_t rather than OP_w). Foreign exporters are injured because they sell less output (*bc* rather than *ad*) in the United States. The orange area indicates the amount of tariffs paid by American consumers. An import quota of *bc* units will have the same effects as the tariff, with one exception: the orange area will go to foreign producers rather than to the U.S. Treasury.

Direct Effects Suppose now that the United States imposes a tariff of P_wP_t per unit on the imported recorders. This will raise the domestic price from OP_w to OP_t and will have several effects.

1 Decline in Consumption Consumption of recorders in the United States will decline from *Od* to *Oc* as the higher price moves buyers up their demand curve. The tariff prompts consumers to buy fewer recorders; that is, to reallocate a portion of their expenditures to less desired substitute products. American consumers are clearly injured by the tariff, since they pay P_wP_t more for each of the *Oc* units which they now buy at price P_t.

2 Increased Domestic Production American producers—who are *not* subject to the tariff—will receive a higher price of OP_t per unit. Because this new price is higher than the pretariff or world price of OP_w, the domestic recorder industry will move up its supply curve S_d, increasing domestic output from *Oa* to *Ob*. Domestic producers will enjoy both a higher price and expanded sales. These effects explain the interest of domestic producers in lobbying for protective tariffs. From a social point of view, however, the expanded domestic production of *ab* reflects the fact that the tariff permits domestic producers of recorders to bid resources away from other, more efficient, industries.

3 Decline in Imports Japanese producers will be hurt. Although the sales price of recorders is higher by P_wP_t, that increase accrues to the United States government and not to Japanese producers. The after-tariff world price, and thus the per unit revenue to Japanese producers, remains at OP_w, while the volume of United States imports (Japanese exports) falls from *ad* to *bc*.

4 Tariff Revenue Finally, note that the orange rectangle indicates the amount of revenue which the tariff yields. Specifically, total revenue from the tariff is determined by multiplying the tariff of P_wP_t per unit by the number of imported recorders, *bc*. This tariff revenue is essentially a transfer of income from consumers to government and does not represent any net change in the nation's economic well-being. The result is that government gains this portion of what consumers lose.

Indirect Effects There are more subtle effects of tariffs which go beyond our supply and demand diagram. Because of diminished sales of recorders in the United States, Japan will now earn fewer dollars with which to buy American exports. That is, American export industries—industries in which the United States has a comparative advantage—will cut production and release resources. These are highly efficient industries, as evidenced by their comparative advantage and ability to sell goods in world markets. In short, *tariffs directly promote the expansion of relatively inefficient industries which do not have a comparative advantage and indirectly cause the contraction of relatively efficient industries which do have a comparative advantage.* This means that tariffs cause resources to be shifted in the wrong direction. This is not surprising. We know that specialization and unfettered world trade based on comparative advantage would lead to the efficient use of world resources and an expansion of the world's real output. The purpose and effect of protective tariffs are to reduce world trade. Therefore, aside from their specific effects on consumers and foreign and domestic producers, tariffs diminish the world's real output.

Economic Impact of Quotas

We noted earlier than an import quota is a legal limit placed on the amount of some product which can be imported each year. Quotas have the same economic impact as a tariff with one big difference: While tariffs generate revenue for the United States government, a quota transfers that revenue to foreign producers.

Suppose in Figure 24-3 that, instead of imposing a tariff of P_wP_t per unit, the United States prohibits any Japanese imports of recorders in excess of *bc* units. In other words, an import quota of *bc* recorders is imposed on Japan. Note that we have deliberately chosen the size of this quota to be the same amount as imports would be under a P_wP_t tariff, so we are comparing "equivalent" situations. As a consequence of the quota, the supply of recorders is $S_d + Q$ in the United States. This is comprised of the domestic supply plus the constant amount *bc* (=*Q*) which importers will provide at each domestic price.[3]

Most of the economic results are the same as with a tariff. Recorder prices are higher (P_t instead of P_w) because imports have been reduced from *ad* to *bc*. Domestic consumption of recorders is down from *Od* to *Oc*. American producers enjoy both a higher price (P_t rather than P_w) and increased sales (*Ob* rather than *Oa*).

The critical difference is that the price increase of P_wP_t paid by American consumers on imports of *bc*—that is, the orange area—no longer goes to the United States Treasury as tariff (tax) revenue, but rather flows to those Japanese firms which have acquired the rights to sell recorders in the United States. For Americans, a tariff produces a better economic outcome than a quota, other things being the same. A tariff generates government revenue which can be used to cut other taxes or to finance public goods and services which benefit Americans. In contrast, the higher price created by quotas results in additional revenue for foreign producers.

It is relevant that in the early 1980s the American automobile industry with the support of its workers successfully lobbied for an import quota on Japanese autos. The Japanese government in turn apportioned this quota among its various auto producers. The restricted supply of Japanese cars in the American market allowed Japanese manufacturers to increase their prices and, hence, their profits. The American import quotas in effect provided Japanese auto manufacturers with a cartel-like arrangement which enhanced their profits. It is significant that when American import quotas were dropped in the mid-1980s, the Japanese government replaced them with its own system of export quotas for Japanese automakers.

[3]The $S_d + Q$ supply curve does not exist below price P_w because Japanese producers would not export recorders to the United States at any price *below* P_w when they can sell them to other countries *at* the world market prices of P_w.

THE CASE FOR PROTECTION: A CRITICAL REVIEW

Although free-trade advocates prevail in the classroom, protectionists sometimes dominate the halls of Congress. What arguments do protectionists make to justify trade barriers? How valid are these arguments?

Military Self-Sufficiency Argument

The argument here is not economic but of a political-military nature: Protective tariffs are needed to preserve or strengthen industries producing strategic goods and materials essential for defense or war. It plausibly contends that in an uncertain world, political-military objectives (self-sufficiency) must take precedence over economic goals (efficiency in the allocation of world resources).

Unfortunately, there is no objective criterion for weighing the relative worth of the increase in national security on the one hand, and the decrease in productive efficiency on the other, which accompany reallocation of resources toward strategic industries when such tariffs are imposed. The economist can only point out that certain economic costs are involved when tariffs are levied to enhance military self-sufficiency.

Although we might all agree that it is probably not a good idea to import our missile guidance systems from China, the self-sufficiency argument is nevertheless open to serious abuse. Virtually every industry can directly or indirectly claim a contribution to national security. Can you name an industry which did *not* contribute in some small way to World War II? Aside from abuses, are there not better ways than tariffs to provide for needed strength in strategic industries? When achieved through tariffs, self-sufficiency creates costs in the form of higher domestic prices on the output of the shielded industry. The cost of enhanced military security is apportioned arbitrarily among those consumers who buy the industry's product. A direct subsidy to strategic industries, financed out of general tax revenues, would more equitably distribute these costs.

Increase Domestic Employment

This "save American jobs" argument for tariffs becomes increasingly fashionable as an economy encounters a recession. It is rooted in macro analysis. Aggregate expenditures in an open economy are comprised of consumption expenditures (C) plus investment expenditures (I_g) plus government expenditures (G) plus net export expenditures (X_n). Net export expenditures consist of exports (X) minus imports (M). By reducing imports, M, aggregate expenditures will rise, stimulating the domestic economy by boosting income and employment. But there are important shortcomings associated with this policy.

1 Job Creation from Imports While imports may eliminate some American jobs, they create others. Imports may have eliminated jobs of American steel and textile workers in recent years, but others have gained jobs selling Hondas and imported electronics equipment. While import restrictions alter the composition of employment, they may actually have little or no effect on the volume of employment.

2 Fallacy of Composition All nations cannot simultaneously succeed in import restriction; what is true for *one* nation is not true for *all* nations. The exports of one nation must be the imports of another. To the extent that one country is able to stimulate its economy through an excess of exports over imports, another economy's unemployment problem is worsened by the resulting excess of imports over exports. It is no wonder that tariff and import quotas to achieve domestic full employment are termed "beggar my neighbor" policies. They achieve short-run domestic goals by making trading partners poorer.

3 Retaliation Nations adversely affected by tariffs and quotas are likely to retaliate, causing a competitive raising of trade barriers which will choke off trade to the end that all nations are worse off. The **Smoot-Hawley Tariff Act of 1930,** which imposed the highest tariffs ever enacted in the United States, backfired miserably. Rather than stimulate the American economy, this tariff act only induced a series of retaliatory restrictions by adversely affected nations. This caused a further contraction of international trade and lowered the income and employment levels of all nations.

4 Long-Run Feedbacks In the long run an excess of exports over imports is doomed to failure as a device for stimulating domestic employment. It is through American imports that foreign nations earn dollars with which to purchase American exports. In the long run a nation must import in order to export. The long-run impact of tariffs is not to increase domestic employment but at best to reallocate workers away from export industries and toward protected domestic industries. This shift implies a less efficient allocation of resources.

In summary, the argument that tariffs increase net exports and therefore create jobs is misleading:

> Overall employment in an economy is determined by internal conditions and macroeconomic policies, not by the existence of trade barriers and the level of trade flows. The United States created [more than 18] million payroll jobs over the course of the [1982–1990] economic expansion, a period of U.S. trade deficits and relatively open U.S. markets. During the same period the European Community (EC) created virtually no net new jobs, even though they experienced trade surpluses. The same level of employment can be obtained in the total absence of free trade as when trade is completely free. But without foreign trade a nation will be worse off economically because, in effect, it will throw away part of its productive capability—the ability to convert surplus goods into other goods through foreign trade.[4]

Diversification for Stability

Closely related to the increase-domestic-employment argument for tariff protection is the diversification-for-stability argument. The point here is that highly specialized economies—for example, Saudi Arabia's oil economy or Cuba's sugar economy—are highly dependent on international markets for their incomes. Wars, cyclical fluctuations, and adverse changes in the structure of industry will force large and frequently painful readjustments on such economies. Tariff and quota protection is therefore allegedly needed to promote greater industrial diversification and consequently less dependence on world markets for just one or two products. This will help insulate the domestic economy from international political developments, depressions abroad, and from random fluctuations in world supply and demand for one or two particular commodities, thereby providing greater domestic stability.

There is some truth in this argument. There are also serious qualifications and shortcomings.

1 The argument has little or no relevance to the United States and other advanced economies.

2 The economic costs of diversification may be great; for example, one-crop economies may be highly inefficient in manufacturing.

[4]*Economic Report of the President, 1988,* p. 131. Updated

Infant-Industry Argument

The infant-industry argument contends that protective tariffs are needed to allow new domestic industries to establish themselves. Temporarily shielding young domestic firms from the severe competition of more mature and therefore currently more efficient foreign firms will give infant industries a chance to develop and become efficient producers.

This argument for protection rests on an alleged exception to the case for free trade. The exception is that all industries have not had, and in the presence of mature foreign competition, will never have, the chance to make long-run adjustments in the direction of larger scale and greater efficiency in production. Tariff protection for infant industries will therefore correct a current misallocation of world resources now perpetuated by historically different levels of economic development between domestic and foreign industries.

Counterarguments Though the infant-industry argument has logical validity, these qualifying points must be noted.

1 In the less developed nations it is very difficult to determine which industries are the infants capable of achieving economic maturity and therefore deserving of protection.

2 Protective tariffs may persist even after industrial maturity has been realized.

3 Most economists feel that if infant industries are to be subsidized, there are better means than tariffs for doing it. Direct subsidies, for example, have the advantage of making explicit which industries are being aided and to what degree.

Strategic Trade Policy In recent years the infant-industry argument has taken a modified form in advanced economies. The contention is that government should use trade barriers strategically to reduce the risk of product development borne by domestic firms, particularly products involving advanced technology. Firms protected from foreign competition can grow more rapidly and therefore achieve greater economies of scale than unprotected foreign competitors. Thus, the protected firms can eventually dominate world markets because of lower costs. Supposedly, dominance of world markets will enable the domestic firms to return high profits to the home nation. These profits allegedly will exceed the domestic sacrifices caused by trade barriers. Also, specialization in high-technology industries supposedly is beneficial because technology advances achieved in one domestic industry often can be transferred to other domestic industries.

Japan and South Korea, in particular, have been accused of using this form of **strategic trade policy.** The problem with this strategy and therefore this argument for tariffs is that the nations put at a disadvantage by strategic trade policies tend to retaliate with tariffs of their own. The outcome may be higher tariffs worldwide, reductions in world trade, and loss of the gains from specialization and exchange.

Protection Against "Dumping"

The protection-against-dumping argument for tariffs contends that tariffs are needed to protect American firms from foreign producers which "dump" excess goods onto the American market at less than cost. Two reasons have been suggested as to why foreign firms might wish to sell in America at below cost.

1 These firms may use **dumping** to drive out American competitors, obtain monopoly power, and then raise prices. The long-term economic profits resulting from this strategy may more than offset the earlier losses which accompany the dumping.

2 Dumping may be a form of price discrimination—charging different prices to different customers. The foreign seller may find it can maximize its profits by charging a high price in its monopolized domestic market while unloading its surplus output at a lower price in the United States. The surplus output may be needed to obtain the overall per unit cost saving associated with large-scale production.

Because dumping is a legitimate concern, it is prohibited under American trade law. Where dumping occurs and is shown to injure American firms, the Federal government imposes tariffs called "antidumping duties" on the specific goods. But relative to the number of goods exported to the United States, documented cases of dumping are few. Dumping therefore does *not* justify widespread, permanent tariffs. Furthermore, allegations of dumping require careful investigation to determine their validity. Foreign producers often argue that dumping allegations and antidumping duties are an American method of restricting legitimate trade. The fact is that some foreign firms can produce certain goods at substantially less cost than American competitors, and what on the surface may seem to be dumping often is comparative advantage at work. If abused, the antidumping law can increase the price of imports and restrict competition in the American market. This reduced competition allows American firms to raise prices at consumers' expense. And even where true dumping does occur, American consumers gain from the lower-priced product—at least in the short term—much as they gain from a price war among American producers.

Cheap Foreign Labor

The cheap-foreign-labor argument holds that domestic firms and workers must be shielded from the ruinous competition of countries where wages are low. If protection is not provided, cheap imports will flood American markets and the prices of American goods—along with the wages of American workers—will be pulled down and our domestic living standards reduced.

This argument can be rebutted at several levels. The logic of the argument would suggest that it is *not* mutually beneficial for rich and poor persons to trade with one another. However, that is not the case. A low-income farm worker may pick lettuce or tomatoes for a rich landowner and both may benefit from the transaction. And don't American consumers gain when they buy a Taiwanese vest pocket radio for $12 as opposed to a qualitatively similar American-made radio selling for $20?

Also, recall that gains from trade are based on comparative advantage. Looking back at Figure 24-1, suppose the United States and Brazil have labor forces of exactly the same size. Noting the positions of the production possibilities curves, we observe that American labor is absolutely more productive because our labor force can produce more of either good. Because of this greater productivity, we can expect wages and living standards to be higher for American labor. Conversely, Brazil's less-productive labor will receive lower wages.

The cheap-foreign-labor argument would suggest that, to maintain our standard of living, America should not trade with low-wage Brazil. Suppose we follow this suggestion. Will wages and living standards rise in the United States as a result? The answer is "No." To obtain coffee America will now have to reallocate a portion of its labor from its relatively efficient wheat industry to its relatively inefficient coffee industry. As a result, the average productivity of American labor will fall as will real wages and living standards. In fact, the labor forces of *both* countries will have diminished standards of living because without specialization and trade they will have less output available to them. Compare column 4 with column 1 in Table 24-4 or points A' and B' with A and B in Figure 24-2 to confirm this point.

A Summing Up

The arguments for protection are numerous, but they are not weighty. Under proper conditions, the infant-industry argument stands as a valid exception, justifiable on economic grounds. And on political-military grounds, the self-sufficiency argument can be used to validate protection. Both arguments, however, are susceptible to severe abuses, and both neglect alternative means of fostering industrial development and military self-sufficiency. Most other arguments are semi-emotional appeals in the form of half-truths and outright fallacies. These arguments note only the immediate and direct consequences of protective tariffs. They ignore the fact that in the long run a nation must import in order to export.

There is also compelling historical evidence suggesting that free trade has led to prosperity and growth and that protectionism has had the opposite effects. Several examples follow.

1 The United States Constitution forbids individual states from levying tariffs, making America a huge free-trade area. Economic historians acknowledge this is an important positive factor in the economic development of our nation.

2 Great Britain's movement toward freer international trade in the mid-nineteenth century was instrumental in its industrialization and growth in that century.

3 As we will see, the creation of the Common Market in Europe after World War II has eliminated tariffs among member nations. Economists agree that creation of this free-trade area has been an important ingredient in the western European prosperity of recent decades.

4 More generally, the trend toward tariff reduction since the mid-1930s has been a stimulus to post-World War II expansion of the world economy.

5 We have already noted that the high tariffs imposed by our Smoot-Hawley Act of 1930 and the retaliation which it engendered worsened the Great Depression of the 1930s.

6 Studies of less developed countries overwhelmingly suggest that those which have relied on import restrictions to protect their domestic industries have realized slow growth in comparison to those pursuing more open economic policies.[5]

[5]Examples are from *Economic Report of the President 1985,* pp. 115–117.

QUICK REVIEW 24-2

- ***Trade barriers include tariffs, import quotas, nontariff barriers, and voluntary export restrictions.***
- ***A tariff on a specific product increases price, reduces consumption, increases domestic production, reduces imports, and generates tariff revenue for government; an import quota does the same, except that a quota generates revenue for foreign producers rather than the government imposing the quota.***
- ***Most arguments for trade protection are special-interest pleas which, if followed, would create gains for protected industries and their workers at the expense of much greater losses for the economy.***

INTERNATIONAL TRADE POLICIES

As Figure 24-4 makes clear, tariffs in the United States have had their ups and downs.[6] Generally, the United States was a high-tariff nation over much of its history. Note that the Smoot-Hawley Tariff Act of 1930 enacted some of the highest tariff rates ever imposed by the United States.

In view of the strong case for free trade, this high-tariff heritage may be a bit surprising. If tariffs are economically undesirable, why has Congress been willing to employ them? As suggested earlier in this chapter, the answer lies in the political realities of tariff making and, more specifically, in the special-interest effect. A small group of domestic producers who will receive large economic gains from tariffs and quotas will press vigorously for protection through well-financed and well-informed political lobbyists. The large number of consumers who individually will have small losses imposed on them will be generally uninformed and indifferent.

Indeed, the public may be won over, not only by the vigor, but also by the apparent plausibility ("Cut imports and prevent domestic unemployment") and the patriotic ring ("Buy American!") of the protectionists. Alleged tariff benefits are immediate and clear-cut to the public. The adverse effects cited by economists are obscure and widely dispersed over the economy. Then, too, the public is likely to stumble on the fallacy of composition: "If a quota on Japanese automobiles will preserve profits and employment in the American automobile industry, how can it be detrimental to the economy as a whole?" When political logrolling (Chapter 19) is added in —"You back tariffs for the apparel industry in my state and I'll do the same for the auto industry in your state"—the sum can be protective tariffs and import quotas.

[6]Technical footnote: Average tariff-rate figures understate the importance of tariffs by not accounting for the fact that some goods are *excluded* from American markets because of existing tariffs. Then, too, average figures conceal the high tariffs on particular items: watches, china, hats, textiles, scissors, wine, jewelry, glassware, wood products, and so forth.

Reciprocal Trade Act and GATT

The downward trend of tariffs since Smoot-Hawley was inaugurated with the **Reciprocal Trade Agreements Act of 1934.** Specifically aimed at tariff reduction, the act had two main features:

1 Negotiating Authority It authorized the President to negotiate agreements with foreign nations which would reduce American tariffs up to 50 percent of the existing rates. Tariff reductions were to hinge on the willingness of other nations to reciprocate by lowering tariffs on American exports.

2 Generalized Reductions By incorporating **most-favored-nation clauses** in these agreements, the resulting tariff reductions not only would apply to the specific nation negotiating with the United States, but they would be *generalized* so as to apply to all nations.

But the Reciprocal Trade Act gave rise to only bilateral (two-nation) negotiations. This approach was broadened in 1947 when twenty-three nations, including the United States, signed a **General Agreement on Tariffs and Trade (GATT).** GATT is based on three cardinal principles: (1) equal, nondiscriminatory treatment for all member nations; (2) the reduction of tariffs by *multilateral* negotiations; and (3) the elimination of import quotas. Basically, GATT is a forum for the negotiation of reductions in trade barriers on a multilateral basis. One hundred nations currently belong to GATT, and there is little doubt that it has been an important force in the trend toward liberalized trade. Under its sponsorship, seven "rounds" of negotiations to reduce trade barriers have been completed in the post-World War II period.

In 1986, the eighth "round" of GATT negotiations began in Uruguay. Proposals discussed at the "Uruguay Round" included (1) eliminating trade barriers and domestic subsidies in agriculture, (2) removing barriers to trade in services (which now account for 20 percent of international trade), (3) ending restrictions on foreign economic investments, and (4) establishing and enforcing patent, copyright, and trademark rights

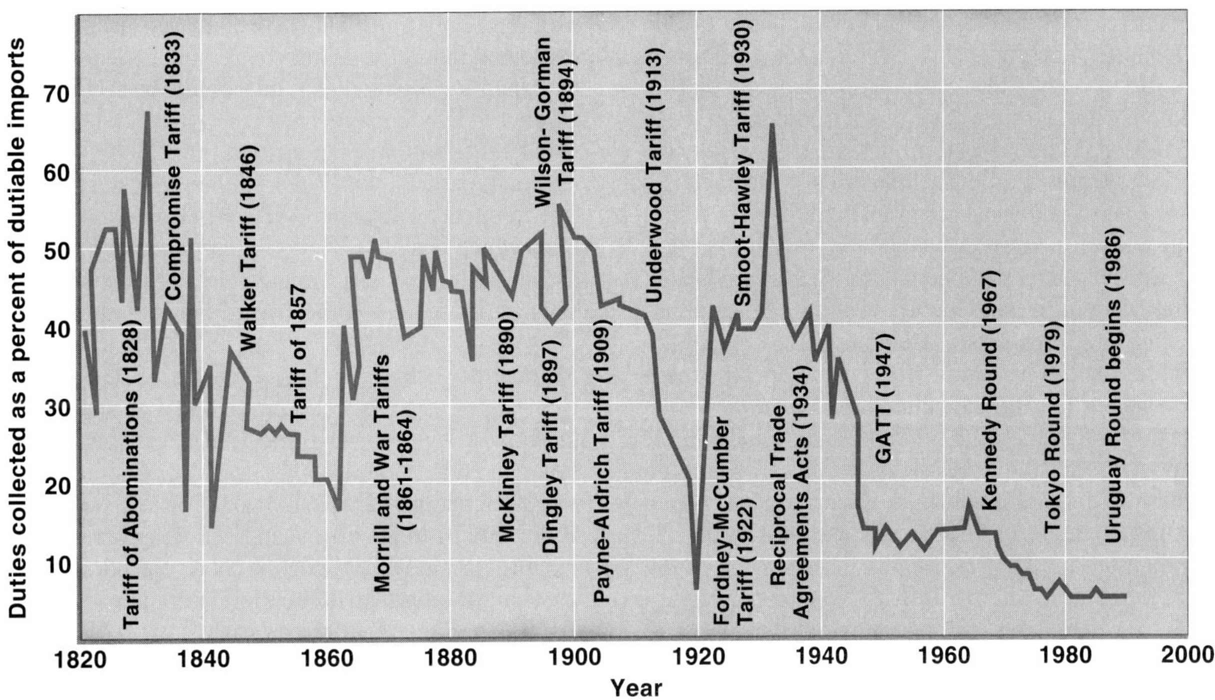

FIGURE 24-4 United States' tariff rates, 1820–1991

American tariff rates have fluctuated historically. But beginning with the Reciprocal Trade Agreements Act of 1934, the trend has been downward. (U.S. Department of Commerce data.)

—so-called *intellectual property rights*—on an international basis.

Reaching agreement on the ambitious Uruguay Round proposals has been difficult. In 1990 the negotiations temporarily collapsed, the main dispute being over European opposition to phasing out export subsidies on agricultural goods and domestic farm subsidies. **Export subsidies** are government payments which reduce the price of a good to buyers abroad; domestic farm subsidies are direct payments to farmers which boost domestic food output. Both types of subsidies artificially reduce export prices and provide unfair advantages to exporting nations. In 1991 the Uruguay Round negotiations were reconvened to try to resolve the remaining trade disagreements.

Economic Integration

Another crucial development in trade liberalization has taken the form of **economic integration**—the joining of the markets of two or more nations into a free-trade zone. Three illustrations of economic integration are the European Economic Community (EC), the U.S.–Canadian Free-Trade Agreement, and the proposed North American free-trade zone.

The Common Market The most dramatic example of economic integration is the **European Economic Community** (EC), or the **Common Market,** as it is popularly known. Begun in 1958, the EC now comprises twelve western European nations (France, Germany, Italy, Belgium, the Netherlands, Luxembourg, Denmark, Ireland, United Kingdom, Greece, Spain, and Portugal).

Goals The Common Market called for (1) gradual abolition of tariffs and import quotas on all products traded among the twelve participating nations; (2) establishment of a common system of tariffs applicable to all goods received from nations outside the Common Market; (3) free movement of capital and labor within the Market; and (4) creation of common policies with respect to other economic matters of joint concern, such as agriculture, transportation, and restrictive business practices. By 1992 most of these goals had been achieved.

Results Motives for creating the Common Market were both political and economic. The primary economic motive was to gain the advantages of freer trade for members. While it is difficult to determine the extent to which EC prosperity and growth has been due to economic integration, it is clear that integration creates the mass markets essential to Common Market industries if economies of large-scale production are to be realized. More efficient production for a large-scale market permits European industries to achieve the lower costs which small, localized markets have historically denied them.

Effects on nonmember nations, such as the United States, are less certain. On the one hand, a peaceful and increasingly prosperous Common Market makes member nations better potential customers for American exports. On the other hand, American firms encounter tariffs which make it difficult to compete in EC markets. For example, *before* the establishment of the Common Market, American, German, and French automobile manufacturers all faced the same tariff in selling their products to, say, Belgium. However, with the establishment of internal free trade among EC members, Belgian tariffs on German Volkswagens and French Renaults fell to zero, but an external tariff still applies to American Chevrolets and Fords. This clearly puts American firms and those of other nonmember nations at a serious competitive disadvantage.

The elimination of this disadvantage has been one of the United States' motivations for promoting freer trade through GATT. And, in fact, the so-called "Kennedy Round" of negotiations completed in 1967 and the "Tokyo Round" which ended in 1979 were quite successful in reducing tariffs.

U.S.–Canadian Free-Trade Agreement A second example of economic integration is the **U.S.–Canadian Free-Trade Agreement** enacted in 1989. Although three-fourths of the trade between the United States and Canada was already duty-free in 1988, the U.S.–Canadian accord is highly significant: It will create the largest free-trade area in the world. Under terms of the agreement, all trade restrictions such as tariffs, quotas, and nontariff barriers will be eliminated within a ten-year period. Canadian producers will gain increased access to a market ten times the size of Canada, while U.S. consumers will gain the advantage of lower-priced Canadian goods. In return, Canada will cut its tariffs by more than the United States because Canadian tariffs are higher than those in the United States. These reduced Canadian tariffs will help American producers and Canadian consumers.

We know from Table 5-3 that Canada is the United States' most significant trade partner quantitatively. Similarly, the United States is the main buyer of Canadian exports. Thus, the potential gain to each country from the U.S.–Canadian accord is large. It has been estimated that the free-trade agreement will generate $1 billion to $3 billion of annual gains for each nation when it is fully implemented.

The U.S.–Canadian accord has global significance. In particular, it is expected to prod multilateral tariff reductions through GATT negotiations, since nations which are not party to the free-trade agreement do not wish to be disadvantaged in a relative sense in selling their goods in the United States and Canada.

Proposed North American Free-Trade Zone The U.S.–Canadian Free-Trade Agreement has stimulated the United States, Canada, and Mexico to begin discussion of a North American free-trade zone constituting the three nations. This zone would have a combined output similar to the European Economic Community.

Free trade with Mexico is more controversial in the United States than is free trade with Canada. Critics fear a loss of American jobs as firms move to Mexico to take advantage of lower wages and less stringent regulations on pollution and workplace safety. Critics also are concerned that Japan and South Korea will build plants in Mexico to ship goods tariff-free to the United States, further hurting U.S. firms and workers.

Proponents of free trade with Mexico cite the standard free-trade argument: Specialization according to comparative advantage will enable the United States to obtain more total output from its scarce resources. Proponents also note this zone would encourage worldwide investment in Mexico, which would enhance Mexican productivity and national income. Some of this increased income will be used to buy United States' exports. Also, a higher standard of living in Mexico would help stem the flow of illegal immigrants to the United States. Finally, advocates point out that any loss of specific American jobs will occur in any event to other low-wage countries such as South Korea, Taiwan, and Hong Kong. The free-trade zone will enable and encourage American firms to be more efficient, enhancing their competitiveness with firms in Japan and the Common Market countries.

Both critics and defenders of the North American free-trade zone agree on one point: It would constitute a powerful trade bloc to counter the European Common Market. Access to the vast North American market is as important to Common Market nations as is access to the European market by the United States, Canada, and Mexico. Observers believe negotiations between the North American trade bloc and the Common Market would surely follow, eventually resulting in a free-trade agreement between the two blocs. Japan, not wishing to be left out of the world's wealthiest trade markets, would be forced to reduce its tariff and nontariff trade barriers, as well.

QUICK REVIEW 24-3

- ***The various "rounds" of the General Agreement on Tariffs and Trade (GATT) have established multinational reductions in tariffs and import quotas among the 100 signatory nations.***
- ***The European Economic Community (EC) and the U.S.–Canadian Free-Trade Agreement of 1989 have reduced trade barriers by establishing large free-trade zones.***
- ***Proponents of the proposed North American free-trade zone (United States, Canada, and Mexico) contend it will enable all three nations to increase their standards of living; critics suggest that it will result in large losses of American jobs as firms move to Mexico to take advantage of less costly Mexican labor.***

Protectionism Reborn

Despite marked progress in reducing and eliminating tariffs, much remains to be done. The previously mentioned "Uruguay Round" agenda is a case in point. In the past, GATT negotiations have focused on manufactured goods, with other aspects of international trade and finance receiving little attention. These neglected areas include agriculture, services (for example, transportation, insurance, and banking), international investment, and patents and copyrights. There is also the problem of integrating the many nonmember less developed countries into the GATT framework.

More ominously, there has recently occurred a vigorous resurgence of protectionist pressures. Nontariff barriers continue to be a serious problem; import quotas and voluntary export restrictions have been on the rise.

Causes A number of factors explain the new pressures for protection.

1 Backlash They are in part a backlash to past reductions in trade barriers. Industries and workers whose profits and jobs have been adversely affected by freer trade have sought restoration of protection.

2 Internationalized Economy A closely related point is that the American economy is much more "internationalized" than it was a decade or so ago (Table 24-2); there are simply more firms and workers potentially adversely affected by increased foreign competition.

3 Increased Competition Other nations have in fact become increasingly competitive with American producers. In the late 1970s and 1980s rates of labor productivity growth in Japan and much of western Europe exceeded those of the United States. The result was lower unit labor costs and lower relative prices for imported goods. Competition from a number of the so-called "newly industrialized countries" such as Korea, Taiwan, Hong Kong, and Singapore is also asserting itself.

4 Trade Deficits In the past several years American imports have greatly exceeded American exports. Rising imports have a negative short-run impact on production and employment in those domestic industries which directly compete with imported products. The industries and workers hurt seek government help in the form of trade barriers. Our persistent trade deficit has provided a convenient rationale for the enactment of protectionist measures to help injured industries. Furthermore, the trade deficit has rallied public support for proposals to retaliate against trading partners which restrict the sale of our products in their countries.

Examples While the United States is formally committed to work for reduction of trade barriers through GATT, we have in fact invoked a number of trade-restricting measures during the last decade.

In 1981 a "voluntary" agreement was reached with Japan to limit the number of Japanese automobiles imported to the United States. This agreement expired in 1985 but continues informally today. In 1982 import quotas were imposed on sugar, causing potentially severe problems for Central American and Caribbean nations which are heavily dependent upon sugar exports to the United States. Also in 1982, the United States negotiated a "voluntary" agreement with the Common Market nations which imposed a quota on their steel exports to the United States. Finally, the industrially advanced nations have revised the international textile agreement to tighten restrictions on textile imports from the less developed countries.

Protectionist sentiment is also evidenced in recent trade proposals and laws. The Comprehensive Trade Act of 1988 contains provisions which ease procedures for initiating unfair-trade investigations of countries with consistent patterns of unfair-trade practices (tariffs, quotas, nontariff barriers, dumping).

LAST WORD

PETITION OF THE CANDLEMAKERS, 1845

The French economist Frédéric Bastiat (1801–1850) devastated the proponents of protectionism by satirically extending their reasoning to its logical and absurd conclusions.

Petition of the Manufacturers of Candles, Waxlights, Lamps, Candlesticks, Street Lamps, Snuffers, Extinguishers, and of the Producers of Oil Tallow, Rosin, Alcohol, and, Generally, of Everything Connected with Lighting.

TO MESSIEURS THE MEMBERS OF THE CHAMBER OF DEPUTIES.

Gentlemen—You are on the right road. You reject abstract theories, and have little consideration for cheapness and plenty. Your chief care is the interest of the producer. You desire to emancipate him from external competition, and reserve the *national market* for *national industry.*

We are about to offer you an admirable opportunity of applying your—what shall we call it? your theory? No; nothing is more deceptive than theory; your doctrine? your system? your principle? but you dislike doctrines, you abhor systems, and as for principles, you deny that there are any in social economy: we shall say, then, your practice, your practice without theory and without principle.

We are suffering from the intolerable competition of a foreign rival, placed, it would seem, in a condition so far superior to ours for the production of light, that he absolutely *inundates* our *national market* with it at a price fabulously reduced. The moment he shows himself, our trade leaves us—all consumers apply to him; and a branch of native industry, having countless ramifications, is all at once rendered completely stagnant. This rival . . . is no other than the Sun.

In 1990 both houses of Congress passed protective legislation for the textile industry. The President vetoed this legislation, which would have limited the growth of textile imports to 1 percent a year. Ironically, the U.S. textile industry imports one-half of its machinery.

We should also note that, although overall American tariffs are low, the United States does have very high tariffs on some goods and imposes quantitative restrictions (quotas) on a small but important list of products. Dairy and meat products, tobacco, fruit juices, motorcycles, and cookware are all subject to significant restrictions. In addition, the footwear, machine tool, copper, shipbuilding, wine, costume jewelry, and shrimp and tuna industries, among others, have all sought additional protection during the past decade.

Costs How costly is existing U.S. trade protection to American consumers? The consumer cost of trade restrictions can be calculated by determining the effect they have on prices of protected goods. Specifically, protection will raise the price of a product in three ways.

1 The price of the imported product goes up (Figure 24-3).

What we pray for is, that it may please you to pass a law ordering the shutting up of all windows, sky-lights, dormerwindows, outside and inside shutters, curtains, blinds, bull's-eyes; in a word, of all openings, holes, chinks, clefts, and fissures, by or through which the light of the sun has been in use to enter houses, to the prejudice of the meritorious manufactures with which we flatter ourselves we have accommodated our country,—a country which, in gratitude, ought not to abandon us now to a strife so unequal.

If you shut up as much as possible all access to natural light, and create a demand for artificial light, which of our French manufactures will not be encouraged by it?

If more tallow is consumed, then there must be more oxen and sheep; and, consequently, we shall behold the multiplication of artificial meadows, meat, wool, hides, and, above all, manure, which is the basis and foundation of all agricultural wealth.

The same remark applies to navigation. Thousands of vessels will proceed to the whale fishery; and, in a short time, we shall possess a navy capable of maintaining the honor of France, and gratifying the patriotic aspirations of your petitioners, the undersigned candlemakers and others.

Only have the goodness to reflect, Gentlemen, and you will be convinced that there is, perhaps, no Frenchman, from the wealthy coalmaster to the humblest vender of lucifer matches, whose lot will not be ameliorated by the success of this our petition.

Source: Frédéric Bastiat, *Economic Sophisms* (Edinburgh: Oliver and Boyd, Tweeddale Court, 1873), pp. 49–53, abridged.

2 The higher price of imports will cause some consumers to shift their purchases to higher-priced domestically produced goods.

3 The prices of domestically produced goods may rise because import competition has declined.

Several research studies indicate the costs to consumers of protected products is strikingly high. One study examined thirty-one classes of protected products and found that total annual consumer losses from protection on these goods was about $82.6 billion.[7] Annual consumer losses from trade restrictions were particularly large for clothing ($27 billion), petroleum products ($6.9 billion), carbon steel ($6.8 billion), automobiles ($5.8 billion), and dairy products ($5.5 billion). These large costs indicate that trade barriers are an expensive means of saving jobs. Specifically, the estimated cost of trade restrictions per job saved is $750,000 in the carbon steel industry; $550,000 in the bolt, nuts, and large screws industry; $220,000 in the dairy industry; $240,000 in the orange juice industry; and $200,000 in the glassware industry. Because wages per job in these industries are only a fraction of these amounts, protectionism can hardly be called a bargain.

Other studies show that import restrictions affect low-income families proportionately more than high-income families.[8] Given that tariffs and quotas are much like sales taxes, it is no surprise that these trade restrictions are highly regressive. For example, the cost of protection was found to be seven times as large for the lowest-income group (incomes under $10,000 per year) as for the highest-income group (incomes over $60,000 per year).

But might not the gains to American producers together with the tariff revenues received by the U.S. government outweigh the high consumer costs of trade protection? The answer is a definite "No." Research studies indicate that gains from trade restrictions are substantially less than costs imposed on consumers.[9] Furthermore, net losses from trade barriers are greater than the losses estimated by the statistical studies. Tariffs and quotas produce myriad costly, difficult-to-quantify secondary effects. For example, import restraints on foreign steel drive up the price of steel to all American buyers of steel—such as American automakers. Therefore American automakers have higher costs and are less competitive in world markets.

Also, industries employ large amounts of economic resources for the purpose of influencing Congress to pass and retain protectionist laws. To the extent that these rent-seeking efforts divert resources away from more socially desirable purposes, society bears an added cost of trade restrictions.

To repeat: *The gains which trade barriers create for protected industries come at the expense of much greater losses for the economy as a whole.*

[7]Cletus C. Coughlin et al., "Protectionist Trade Policies: A Survey of Theory, Evidence and Rationale," *Review* (Federal Reserve Bank of St. Louis), January/February 1988), pp. 17–18.

[8]"The Consumer Cost of U.S. Trade Restraints," *Quarterly Review* (Federal Reserve Bank of New York), Summer 1985, pp. 1–12.

[9]Coughlin et al., op. cit., p. 19.

CHAPTER SUMMARY

1 International trade is important, quantitatively and otherwise, to most nations. World trade is vital to the United States in several respects. **a** The absolute volumes of American imports and exports exceed those of any other single nation. **b** The United States is completely dependent on trade for certain commodities and materials which cannot be obtained domestically. **c** Changes in the volume of net exports can have magnified effects on domestic levels of output and income.

2 International and domestic trade differ in that **a** resources are less mobile internationally than domestically: **b** each nation uses a different currency; and **c** international trade is subject to more political controls.

3 World trade is based on two considerations: the uneven distribution of economic resources among nations, and the fact that efficient production of various goods requires particular techniques or combinations of resources.

4 Mutually advantageous specialization and trade are possible between any two nations so long as the domestic cost ratios for any two products differ. By specializing according to comparative advantage, nations can realize larger real incomes with fixed amounts of resources. The terms of trade determine how this increase in world output is shared by the trading nations. Increasing costs impose limits on gains from specialization and trade.

5 Trade barriers take the form of protective tariffs, quotas, nontariff barriers, and "voluntary" export restrictions. Supply and demand analysis reveals that protective tariffs and quotas increase the prices and reduce the quantities demanded of affected goods. Foreign exporters find their sales diminish. Domestic producers, however, enjoy higher prices and enlarged sales. Tariffs and quotas promote a less efficient allocation of domestic and world resources.

6 When applicable, the strongest arguments for protection are the infant-industry and military self-sufficiency arguments. Most of the other arguments for protection are half-truths, emotional appeals, or fallacies which typically emphasize the immediate effects of trade barriers while ignoring long-run consequences. Numerous historical examples suggest that free trade promotes economic growth and protectionism does not.

7 The Reciprocal Trade Agreements Act of 1934 was the beginning of a trend toward lower American tariffs. In 1947 the General Agreement on Tariffs and Trade (GATT) was formed **a** to encourage nondiscriminatory treatment for all trading nations, **b** to achieve tariff reduction, and **c** to eliminate import quotas.

8 Economic integration is an important means of liberalizing trade. The outstanding illustration is the European Common Market in which internal trade barriers are abolished, a common system of tariffs is applied to nonmembers, and free internal movement of labor and capital occurs. The 1989 U.S.–Canadian Free-Trade Agreement is another example of economic integration, as is the proposed United States–Canadian–Mexican free-trade zone.

9 In recent years there has been a resurgence of protectionist pressures, but empirical evidence indicates that costs of protectionist policies outweigh benefits.

TERMS AND CONCEPTS

labor- (land-, capital-) intensive commodity
cost ratio
principle of comparative advantage
terms of trade
trading possibilities line
gains from trade
revenue and protective tariffs
import quotas
nontariff barriers
voluntary export restrictions
Smoot-Hawley Tariff Act of 1930
strategic trade policy
dumping
Reciprocal Trade Agreements Act of 1934
most-favored-nation clauses
export subsidies
economic integration
General Agreement on Tariffs and Trade (GATT)
European Economic Community (Common Market)
U.S.–Canadian Free-Trade Agreement

QUESTIONS AND STUDY SUGGESTIONS

1 In what ways are domestic and foreign trade similar? In what ways do they differ?

2 Assume that by using all its resources to produce X, nation A can produce 80 units of X; by devoting all its resources to Y, it can produce 40 Y. Comparable figures for nation B are 60 X and 60 Y. Assuming constant costs, in which product should each nation specialize? Why? Indicate the limits of the terms of trade.

3 "The United States can produce product X more efficiently than can Great Britain. Yet we import X from Great Britain." Explain.

4 State the economist's case for free trade. Given this

case, how do you explain the existence of artificial barriers to international trade?

5 Draw a domestic supply and demand diagram for a product in which the United States does not have a comparative advantage. Indicate the impact of foreign imports on domestic price and quantity. Now show a protective tariff which eliminates approximately one-half the assumed imports. Indicate the price-quantity effects of this tariff to a domestic consumers, b domestic producers, and c foreign exporters. How would the effects of a quota which gave rise to the same amount of imports differ?

6 "The most valid arguments for tariff protection are also the most easily abused." What are these arguments? Why are they susceptible to abuse? Carefully evaluate the use of artificial trade barriers, such as tariffs and import quotas, as a means of achieving and maintaining full employment.

7 The following are production possibilities tables for Japan and Hawaii. Assume that prior to specialization and trade, the optimal product-mix for Japan is alternative B and for Hawaii alternative D.

Product	*Japan's production alternatives*					
	A	*B*	*C*	*D*	*E*	*F*
Radios (in thousands)	30	24	18	12	6	0
Pineapples (in tons)	0	6	12	18	24	30

Product	*Hawaii's production alternatives*					
	A	*B*	*C*	*D*	*E*	*F*
Radios (in thousands)	10	8	6	4	2	0
Pineapples (in tons)	0	4	8	12	16	20

a Are comparative-cost conditions such that the two areas should specialize? If so, what product should each produce?

b What is the total gain in radio and pineapple output which results from this specialization?

c What are the limits of the terms of trade? Suppose actual terms of trade are 1 unit of radios for $1\frac{1}{2}$ units of pineapples and that 4 units of radios are exchanged for 6 units of pineapples. What are the gains from specialization and trade for each area?

d Can you conclude from this illustration that specialization according to comparative advantage results in more efficient use of world resources? Explain.

8 Carefully evaluate the following statements:

a "Protective tariffs limit both the imports and the exports of the nation levying tariffs."

b "The extensive application of protective tariffs destroys the ability of the international market system to allocate resources efficiently."

c "Apparent unemployment can often be reduced through tariff protection, but by the same token disguised unemployment typically increases."

d "Foreign firms which 'dump' their products onto the American market are in effect presenting the American people with gifts."

e "Given the rapidity with which technological advance is dispersed around the world, free trade will inevitably yield structural maladjustments, unemployment, and balance of payments problems for industrially advanced nations."

f "Free trade can improve the composition and efficiency of domestic output. Only the Volkswagen forced Detroit to make a compact car, and only foreign success with the oxygen process forced American steel firms to modernize."

g "In the long run foreign trade is neutral with respect to total employment."

9 In the 1981–1985 period the Japanese agreed to a voluntary export restriction which reduced American imports of Japanese automobiles by about 10 percent. What would you expect the short-run effects to have been on the American and Japanese automobile industries? If this restriction were permanent, what would be its long-run effects on a the allocation of resources, b the volume of employment, c the price level, and d the standard of living in the two nations?

10 Use "economies of scale" analysis to explain why the Common Market has enabled many European industries to compete more effectively in international markets. Explain: "Economic integration leads a double life: It can promote free trade among members, but pose serious trade obstacles for nonmembers."

11 What are the benefits and the costs of protectionist policies? Compare the two.

12 Explain the following findings from a study on the effects of the 1984 imports restraints which limited the level of steel imports to the United States: increased employment in the steel industry, 14,000; increased employment in the industries producing inputs for steel, 2,800; job losses by American steel-using firms, 52,400.[10]

[10]Arthur T. Denzau, "How Import Restraints Reduce Employment" (Washington University Center for the Study of American Business, Formal Publication #80, June 1987), as reported in Coughlin, op. cit., p. 6.

Exchange Rates, the Balance of Payments, and Trade Deficits

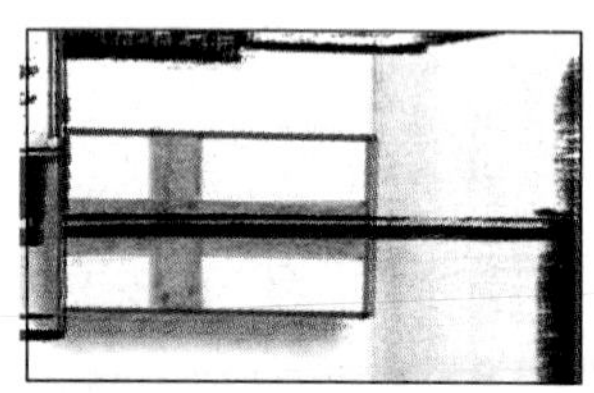

If you take an American dollar to the bank and ask to exchange it for United States currency, you will get a puzzled look. If you persist, you may get in exchange another dollar. One American dollar can buy exactly one American dollar. But, as of January 24, 1992, one United States dollar could buy 5340 Turkish lira, 1.34 Australian dollars, .56 British pounds, 1.16 Canadian dollars, 5.48 French francs, 1.61 German marks, 123.93 Japanese yen, or 5.84 Swedish krona. What explains this seemingly haphazard array of exchange rates?

In Chapter 24 we examined comparative advantage as the underlying economic basis of world trade and discussed the effects of barriers to free trade. In this chapter we first introduce the monetary or financial aspects of international trade. How are currencies of different nations exchanged when import and export transactions occur? Second, we analyze and interpret a nation's international balance of payments. What is meant by a "favorable" or "unfavorable" balance of trade? Third, the kinds of exchange rate systems which trading nations have used are explained and evaluated. In this discussion we examine the polar extremes of freely flexible and fixed exchange rates and then survey actual systems which have existed historically. Finally, we explore the balance of trade deficits the United States has encountered over the past decade.

FINANCING INTERNATIONAL TRADE

A basic feature distinguishing international from domestic payments is that two different national currencies are exchanged. When American firms export goods to British firms, the American exporter wants to be paid in dollars. But British importers have pounds sterling. The problem, then, is to exchange pounds for dollars to permit the American export transaction to occur.

This problem is resolved in *foreign exchange markets* where dollars can be used to purchase British pounds, Japanese yen, German marks, Italian lira, and so forth, and vice versa. Sponsored by major banks in New York, London, Zurich, Tokyo, and elsewhere, foreign exchange markets facilitate American exports and imports.

American Export Transaction

Suppose an American exporter agrees to sell $30,000 worth of computers to a British firm. Assume that the *rate of exchange*—the rate or price at which pounds can be exchanged for, or converted into, dollars, and vice versa—is $2 for £1. This means that the British importer must pay £15,000 to the American exporter. Let's summarize what occurs in terms of simple bank balance sheets (Figure 25-1).

a To pay for the American computers, the British buyer draws a check on its demand deposit in a London bank for £15,000. This is shown by the −£15,000 demand deposit entry in the righthand side of the balance sheet of the London bank.

b The British firm then sends this £15,000 check to the American exporter. But the American exporting firm must pay its employees and materials suppliers, as well as its taxes, in dollars, not pounds. So the exporter sells the £15,000 check or draft on the London bank to a large American bank, probably in New York City, which is a dealer in foreign exchange. The American firm is given a $30,000 demand deposit in the New York bank in exchange for the £15,000 check. Note the new demand deposit entry of +$30,000 in the New York bank.

c What does the New York bank do with the £15,000? It deposits it in a correspondent London bank for future sale. Thus, +£15,000 of demand deposits appear in the liabilities column of the balance sheet of the London bank. This +£15,000 ($30,000) is an asset as viewed by the New York bank. To simplify, we assume that the correspondent bank in London is the same bank from which the British importer obtained the £15,000 draft.

Note these salient points.

1 *American exports create a foreign demand for dollars, and the satisfaction of this demand generates a supply of foreign monies—pounds, in this case—held by American banks and available to American buyers.*

2 The financing of an American export (British import) reduces the supply of money (demand deposits) in Britain and increases the supply of money in the United States by the amount of the purchase.

American Import Transaction

But why would the New York bank be willing to give up dollars for pounds sterling? As just indicated, the New York bank is a dealer in foreign exchange; it is in the business of buying—for a fee—and, conversely, in selling—also for a fee—pounds for dollars.

Having just explained that the New York bank would buy pounds with dollars in connection with an American export transaction, we will now examine how it would sell pounds for dollars in financing an American import (British export) transaction. Suppose that an American retail concern wants to import £15,000 worth of woolens from a British mill. Again, simple commercial bank balance sheets summarize our discussion (Figure 25-2).

a Because the British exporting firm must pay its obligations in pounds rather than dollars, the American importer must exchange dollars for pounds. It does this by going to the New York bank and purchasing £15,000 for $30,000—perhaps the American importer

FIGURE 25-1 Financing a U.S. export transaction

American export transactions create a foreign demand for dollars. The satisfaction of this demand increases the supplies of foreign monies held by American banks.

LONDON BANK

Assets	Liabilities and net worth
	Demand deposit of British importer −£15,000(*a*)
	Deposit of New York bank +£15,000(*c*)

NEW YORK BANK

Assets	Liabilities and net worth
Deposit in London bank +£15,000(*c*) ($30,000)	Demand deposit of American exporter +$30,000(*b*)

LONDON BANK

Assets	Liabilities and net worth
	Demand deposit of British exporter +£15,000(*b*)
	Deposit of New York bank −£15,000(*a*)

NEW YORK BANK

Assets	Liabilities and net worth
Deposit in London bank −£15,000(*a*) ($30,000)	Demand deposit of American importer −$30,000(*a*)

FIGURE 25-2 Financing a U.S. import transaction
American import transactions create an American demand for foreign monies. The satisfaction of that demand reduces the supplies of foreign monies held by American banks.

purchases the same £15,000 which the New York bank acquired in the previous American export transaction. In Figure 25-2, this purchase reduces the American importer's demand deposit in the New York bank by $30,000 and the New York bank gives up its £15,000 deposit in the London bank.

b The American importer sends its newly purchased check for £15,000 to the British firm, which deposits it in the London bank. Note the +£15,000 deposit in the liabilities and net worth column of Figure 25-2.

We find that:

1 *American imports create a domestic demand for foreign monies (pounds sterling, in this case) and that fulfillment of this demand reduces the supplies of foreign monies held by American banks.*
2 An American import transaction increases the money supply in Britain and reduces the money supply in the United States.

By combining these two transactions, a further point comes into focus. American exports (computers) make available, or "earn," a supply of foreign monies for American banks, and American imports (British woolens) create a demand for these monies. In a broad sense, *any nation's exports finance or "pay for" its imports.* Exports provide the foreign currencies needed to pay for imports. From Britain's point of view, its exports of woolens earn a supply of dollars, which are then used to meet the demand for dollars associated with Britain's imports of computers.

Postscript: Although our examples are confined to the exporting and importing of goods, we will find that demands for and supplies of pounds also arise from transactions involving services and the payment of interest and dividends on foreign investments. Thus Americans demand pounds not only to finance imports, but also to purchase insurance and transportation services from the British, to vacation in London, to pay dividends and interest on British investments in the United States, and to make new financial and real investments in Britain.

THE INTERNATIONAL BALANCE OF PAYMENTS

We now explore the wide variety of international transactions which create a demand for and generate a supply of a given currency. This spectrum of international trade and financial transactions is reflected in the United States' international **balance of payments.** A nation's balance of payments statement records *all* transactions which take place between its residents (including individuals, businesses, and governmental units) and the residents of all foreign nations. These transactions include merchandise exports and imports, tourist expenditures, purchases and sales of shipping and insurance services, interest and dividends received or paid abroad, purchases and sales of financial or real assets abroad, and so forth. The United States' balance of payments shows the balance between all the payments the United States receives from foreign countries and all the payments which we make to them. A simplified balance of payments for the United States in 1990 is shown in Table 25-1. Let's analyze this accounting statement to see what it reveals about our international trade and finance.

TABLE 25-1 The United States' balance of payments, 1990 *(in billions)*

Current account		
(1) U.S. merchandise exports	$+390	
(2) U.S. merchandise imports	−498	
(3) Balance of trade		$−108
(4) U.S. exports of services	+133	
(5) U.S. imports of services	−107	
(6) Balance on goods and services		−82
(7) Net investment income	+12	
(8) Net transfers	−22	
(9) Balance on current account		−92
Capital account		
(10) Capital inflows to the U.S.	+117*	
(11) Capital outflows from the U.S.	−59	
(12) Balance on capital account		+58
(13) Current and capital account balance		−34
(14) Official reserves		+34
		$ 0

*Includes a $64 billion statistical discrepancy which is believed to be comprised primarily of unaccounted capital inflows.

Source: Survey of Current Business, December 1991.

Current Account

The top portion of Table 25-1 summarizes the United States' trade in currently produced goods and services and is called the **current account.** Items 1 and 2 show American exports and imports of merchandise (goods) respectively in 1990. We have designated American exports with a *plus* sign and our imports with a *minus* sign because American merchandise exports (and other export-type transactions) are **credits** in that they create or earn supplies of foreign exchange. As we saw in our discussion of how international trade is financed, any export-type transaction obligating foreigners to make "inpayments" to the United States generates supplies of foreign monies in American banks.

Conversely, American imports (and other import-type transactions) are **debits;** they use up foreign exchange. Again, our earlier discussion of trade financing indicated that American imports obligate Americans to make "outpayments" to the rest of the world which draw down available supplies of foreign currencies held by American banks.

Trade balance Items 1 and 2 in Table 25-1 tell us that in 1990 our merchandise exports of $390 billion did *not* earn enough foreign monies to finance our merchandise imports of $498 billion. Specifically, the merchandise balance of trade or, more simply, the **trade balance** refers to the difference between a country's merchandise exports and merchandise imports. If exports exceed imports, then a *trade surplus* or "favorable balance of trade" is being realized. If imports exceed exports, then a *trade deficit* or "unfavorable balance of trade" is occurring. We note in item 3 that in 1990 the United States incurred a trade deficit of $108 billion

Balance on Goods and Services Item 4 reveals that the United States not only exports autos and computers, but also sells transportation services, insurance, and tourist and brokerage services to residents of foreign countries. These service sales or "exports" totaled $133 billion in 1990. Item 5 indicates that Americans buy or "import" similar services from foreigners. These service imports were $107 billion in 1990.

The **balance on goods and services,** shown in Table 25-1 as item 6, is the difference between our ex- imports of goods and services (items 2 and 5). In 1990 our exports of goods and services fell short of our imports of goods and services by $82 billion.

Balance on Current Account Item 7 reflects that historically the United States has been a net international lender. Over time we have invested more abroad than foreigners have invested in the United States. Thus net investment income represents the excess of interest and dividend payments which foreigners have paid us for the services of our exported capital over what we paid in 1990 in interest and dividends for their capital invested in the United States. Table 25-1 shows that, on balance, our net investment income earned us $12 billion worth of foreign currencies for "exporting" the services of American money capital invested abroad.

Item 8 reflects net transfers, both public and private, from the United States to the rest of the world. Included here is American foreign aid, pensions paid to Americans living abroad, and remittances of immigrants to relatives abroad. These $22 billion of transfers are "outpayments" and exhaust available supplies of foreign exchange. As it has been facetiously put, net transfers entail the importing of "goodwill" or "thank-you notes."

By taking all transactions in the current account into consideration we obtain the **balance on current account** shown by item 9 in Table 25-1. In 1990 the United States realized a current account deficit of $92 billion. This means that our current account import transactions (items 2, 5, and 8) created a demand for a larger dollar amount of foreign currencies than our export transactions (items 1, 4, and 7) supplied.

Capital Account

The **capital account** reflects capital flows in the purchase or sale of real and financial assets which occurred in 1990. For example, Honda or Nissan might acquire an automobile assembly plant in the United States. Or, alternatively, the investments may be of a financial nature, for example, an Arabian oil sheik might purchase GM stock or Treasury bonds. In either event such transactions generate supplies of foreign currencies for the United States. They are therefore credit or inpayment items, designated with a plus sign. The United States is exporting stocks and bonds and thereby earning foreign exchange. Item 10 in Table 25-1 shows that such transactions amounted to $117 billion in 1990.

Conversely, Americans invest abroad. General Electric might purchase a plant in Hong Kong or Singapore to assemble pocket radios or telephones. Or an American might buy stock in an Italian shoe factory. Or an American bank might finance construction of a meat processing plant in Argentina. These transactions have a common feature; they all use up or exhaust supplies of foreign currencies. We therefore attach a minus sign to remind us that these are debit or outpayment transactions. The United States is importing stocks, bonds, and IOUs from abroad. Item 11 in Table 25-1 reveals that $59 billion of these transactions occurred in 1990. When items 10 and 11 are combined, the **balance on the capital account** was a *plus* $58 billion—the United States enjoyed a capital account surplus of $58 billion in 1990.

Interrelationships

The current and capital accounts are interrelated; they are essentially reflections of one another. The current account *deficit* means that American exports of goods and services were not sufficient to pay for our imports of goods and services.[1] How did we finance the difference? The answer is that the United States must either borrow from abroad or give up ownership of some of its assets to foreigners as reflected in the capital account.

A simple analogy is useful here. Suppose in a given year your expenditures exceed your earnings. How will you finance your "deficit"? You might sell some of your assets or borrow. You might sell some real assets (your car or stereo) or perhaps some financial assets (stocks or bonds) which you own. Or you might obtain a loan from your family or a bank.

Similarly, when a nation incurs a deficit in its current account, its expenditures for foreign goods and services (its imports) exceed the income received from the international sales of its own goods and services (its exports). It must somehow finance that current account deficit by selling assets and by borrowing, that is, by going into debt. And that is what is reflected in the capital account surplus. Our capital account surplus of $58 billion (item 12) indicates that in 1990 the United States "sold off" real assets (buildings, farmland) and received loans from the rest of the world in that amount to help finance our current account deficit of $92 billion.

Recap: A nation's current account deficit will be financed essentially by a net capital inflow in its capital account. Conversely, a nation's current account *surplus* would be accompanied by a net capital *outflow* in its capital account. The excess earnings from its current account surplus will be used to purchase real assets of, and make loans to, other nations.

[1]We ignore transfer payments (item 8) in making this statement.

Official Reserves

The central banks of nations hold quantities of foreign currencies called **official reserves** which are added to or drawn on to settle any *net* differences in current and capital account balances. In 1990 the surplus in our capital account was considerably less than the deficit in our current account so we had a $34 billion net deficit on the combined accounts (item 13). That is, the United States earned less foreign monies in all international trade and financial transactions than it used. This deficiency of earnings of foreign currencies was subtracted from the existing balances of foreign monies held by our central banks. The *plus* $34 billion of official reserves shown by item 14 in Table 25-1 represents this reduction of our stocks of foreign currencies. The plus sign indicates this is a credit or "export-type" transaction which represents a supply of foreign exchange.

Frequently the relationship between the current and capital account is just the opposite of that shown in Table 25-1. That is, the current account deficit is less than the capital account surplus. Hence, our central banks would experience an increase in their holdings of foreign currencies. This would show as a *minus* item in the balance of payments; it is a debit or "import-type" transaction because it represents a use of foreign exchange.

The important point here is that the three components of the balance of payments statement—the current account, the capital account, and the official reserves account—must sum to zero. Every unit of foreign exchange used (as reflected in our "minus" outpayment or debit transactions) in our international transactions must have a source (our "plus" inpayment or credit transactions).

Payments Deficits and Surpluses

Although the balance of payments must always sum to zero, economists and political officials frequently speak of **balance of payments deficits and surpluses.** In doing so they are referring to the "current and capital account balance" shown as item 13 in Table 25-1. If this is a negative item, a balance of payments deficit is being realized as was the case for the United States in 1990. In 1990 the United States earned less foreign monies from all its trade and financial transactions than it used. The United States did not "pay its way" in world trade and finance and therefore depleted its official reserves of foreign monies. If the current and capital account balance were positive, then the United States would be faced with a balance of payments surplus. The United States would have earned sufficient foreign exchange from its export-type transactions to pay for its import-type transactions. As we have just seen, it would add to its stocks of foreign monies—that is, increase its official reserve holdings.

A decrease in official reserves (shown by a positive official reserves item in Table 25-1) measures a nation's balance of payments deficit; an increase in official reserves (shown by a negative official reserves item) measures its balance of payments surplus.

Deficits and Surpluses: Bad or Good?

Having defined a variety of deficits and surpluses, we must now inquire as to their desirability. Are deficits bad, as the term implies? Is a surplus desirable, as that word suggests? The answer to both questions is "not necessarily." A large merchandise trade deficit such as the United States has been incurring in recent years is regarded by many as "unfavorable" or "adverse," as it suggests American producers are losing their competitiveness in world markets. Our industries seem to be having trouble selling their goods abroad and are simultaneously facing strong competition from imported goods. On the other hand, a trade deficit is *favorable* from the vantage point of American consumers who are currently receiving more goods as imports than they are forgoing as exports.

Similarly, the desirability of a balance of payments deficit or surplus depends on (1) the events causing them and (2) their persistence through time. For example, the large payments deficits imposed on the United States and other oil-importing nations by OPEC's dramatic runup of oil prices in 1973–1974 and 1979–1980 were very disruptive in that they forced the United States to invoke policies to curtail oil imports.

Also, any nation's official reserves are limited. Persistent or long-term payments deficits, which must be financed by drawing down those reserves, would ultimately deplete reserves. In this case that nation would have to undertake policies to correct its balance of payments. These policies might require painful macroeconomic adjustments, trade barriers and similar restrictions, or changing the international value of its currency.

KEY GRAPH

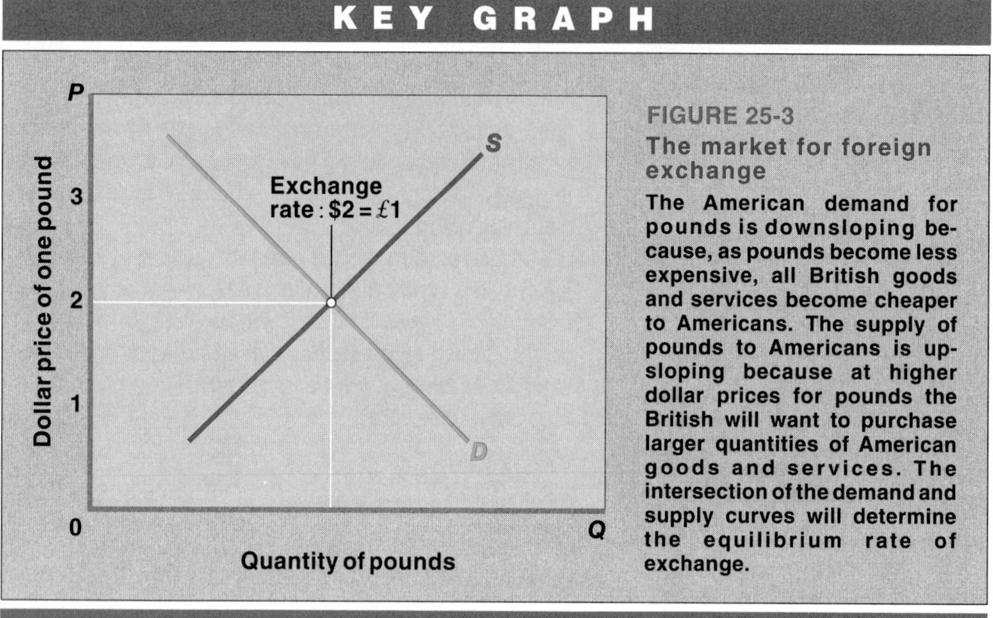

FIGURE 25-3
The market for foreign exchange
The American demand for pounds is downsloping because, as pounds become less expensive, all British goods and services become cheaper to Americans. The supply of pounds to Americans is upsloping because at higher dollar prices for pounds the British will want to purchase larger quantities of American goods and services. The intersection of the demand and supply curves will determine the equilibrium rate of exchange.

QUICK REVIEW 25-1

- *American* **exports** *create a demand for dollars and a supply of foreign currencies; American* **imports** *create a demand for foreign currencies and a supply of American dollars.*
- *The current account balance is a nation's exports of goods and services less its imports of goods and services plus its net investment income and net transfers.*
- *The capital account balance is a nation's capital inflows less its capital outflows.*
- *A balance of payments deficit occurs when the sum of the balances on current and capital accounts is negative; a balance of payments surplus arises when the sum of the balances on current and capital accounts is positive.*

EXCHANGE RATE SYSTEMS AND BALANCE OF PAYMENTS ADJUSTMENTS

Both the size and persistence of a nation's balance of payments deficits and surpluses and the kind of adjustments it must make to correct these imbalances depend on the system of exchange rates being used. There are two polar options: (1) a system of **flexible** or **floating exchange rates** where the rates at which national currencies exchange for one another are determined by demand and supply, and (2) a system of rigidly **fixed exchange rates** by which governmental intervention in foreign exchange markets or some other mechanism offsets the changes in exchange rates which fluctuations in demand and supply would otherwise cause.

Freely Floating Exchange Rates

Freely floating exchange rates are determined by the unimpeded forces of demand and supply. Let's examine the rate, or price, at which American dollars might be exchanged for, say, British pounds sterling. As indicated in Figure 25-3 (Key Graph), the demand for pounds will be downsloping; the supply of pounds, upsloping.

The downsloping *demand for pounds* shown by *D* indicates that, if pounds become less expensive to Americans, British goods will become cheaper to Americans. Americans will demand larger quantities of British goods and therefore larger amounts of pounds to buy those goods.

The *supply of pounds* is upsloping, as *S*, because, as the dollar price of pounds *rises* (that is, the pound price of dollars *falls*), the British will purchase more American goods. At higher and higher dollar prices for pounds, the British can get more American dollars and therefore more American goods per pound. Thus, American goods become cheaper to the British, inducing them to buy more of these goods. When the British buy American goods, they supply pounds to the foreign exchange market because they must exchange pounds for dollars to purchase our goods.

The intersection of the supply and demand for pounds will determine the dollar price of pounds. In this instance the equilibrium rate of exchange is \$2 to £1.

Depreciation and Appreciation An exchange rate determined by free-market forces can and does change frequently. When the dollar price of pounds increases, for example, from \$2 for £1 to \$3 for £1, the value of the dollar has **depreciated** relative to the pound. Currency depreciation means that it takes more units of a country's currency (dollars) to buy a single unit of some foreign currency (pounds).

Conversely, when the dollar price of pounds decreases—from \$2 for £1 to \$1 for £1—the value of the dollar has **appreciated** relative to the pound. Currency appreciation means that it takes fewer units of a country's currency (dollars) to buy a single unit of some foreign currency (pounds).

In our American-British illustrations, when the dollar depreciates the pound necessarily appreciates and vice versa. When the exchange rate between dollars and pounds changes from \$2 = £1 to \$3 = £1, it now takes *more* dollars to buy £1 and the dollar has depreciated. But it now takes *fewer* pounds to buy a dollar. At the initial rate it took £$\frac{1}{2}$ to buy \$1; at the new rate it only takes £$\frac{1}{3}$ to buy \$1. The pound has appreciated relative to the dollar. *If the dollar depreciates vis-à-vis the pound, the pound appreciates vis-à-vis the dollar. Conversely, if the dollar appreciates vis-à-vis the pound, the pound depreciates vis-à-vis the dollar.* These relationships are summarized in Figure 25-4.

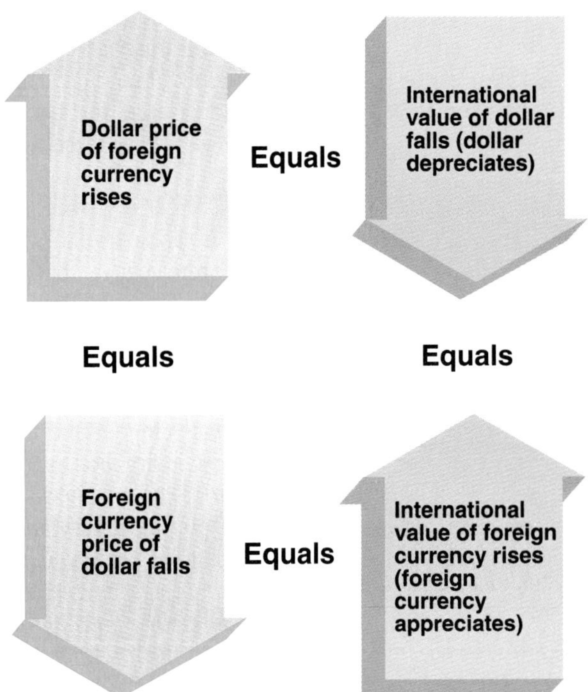

FIGURE 25-4 Currency appreciation and depreciation

An increase in the dollar price of foreign currency is equivalent to a decline in the international value of the dollar (dollar depreciates). An increase in the dollar price of foreign currency also implies a decline in the foreign currency price of dollars. That is, the international value of foreign currency rises relative to the dollar (foreign currency appreciates).

Determinants of Exchange Rates Why are the demand for and the supply of pounds located as they are in Figure 25-3? What forces will cause the demand and supply curves for pounds to change, thereby causing the dollar to appreciate or depreciate?

Changes in Tastes Any change in consumer tastes or preferences for the products of a foreign country will alter the demand for, or supply of, that nation's currency and change its exchange rate. If American technological advances in computers make them more attractive to British consumers and businesses, then they will supply more pounds in exchange markets in purchasing more American computers and the dollar will appreciate. Conversely, if British tweeds become more fashionable in the United States, our demand for pounds will increase and the dollar will depreciate.

Relative Income Changes If the growth of a nation's national income is more rapid than other countries', its currency is likely to depreciate. A country's imports vary directly with its level of income. As incomes rise in the United States, American consumers buy more domestically produced goods *and* also more foreign goods. If the United States' economy is expanding rapidly and the British economy is stagnant, American imports of British goods—and therefore U.S. demand for pounds—will increase. The dollar price of pounds will rise, meaning the dollar has depreciated.

Relative Price Changes If the domestic price level rises rapidly in the United States and remains constant in Britain, American consumers will seek out relatively low-priced British goods, increasing the demand for pounds. Conversely, the British will purchase fewer American goods, reducing the supply of pounds. This combination of an increase in the demand for, and a reduction in the supply of, pounds will cause the dollar to depreciate.

In fact, differences in relative price levels among nations—which reflect changes in price levels over time—help explain persistent differences in exchange rates. In 1992 an American dollar could buy .56 British pounds, 124 Japanese yen, or 5340 Turkish lira. One reason for these differences is that the prices of British goods and services in pounds were far lower than the prices of Japanese goods and services in yen and the prices of Turkish goods and services in lira. For example, the same market basket of products costing $500 in the United States might cost 250 pounds in England, 67,500 yen in Japan, and 2,500,000 lira in Turkey. *Generally, the higher the prices of a nation's goods and services in terms of its own currency, the greater the amount of that currency which can be obtained with an American dollar.*

Taken to its extreme, this **purchasing power parity theory** holds that differences in exchange rates *equate* the purchasing power of various currencies. That is, the exchange rates among national currencies perfectly adjust in such a way as to equal the ratios of the nations' price levels. For example, if a market basket of goods costs $100 in the United States and £50 in Great Britain, the exchange rate should be $2 = £1. Thus, a dollar spent on goods sold in Britain, Japan, Turkey, and other nations supposedly will have equal purchasing power. In practice, however, exchange rates depart significantly from purchasing power parity, even over long periods. Nevertheless, relative price levels are clearly a major determinant of exchange rates.

Relative Real Interest Rates Suppose the United States restricts the growth of its money supply (tight money policy), as it did in the late 1970s and early 1980s, to control inflation. As a result, *real* interest rates—nominal interest rates adjusted for the rate of inflation—were high in the United States compared to most other nations. Consequently, British individuals and firms found the United States an attractive place to make financial investments. This increase in the demand for American financial assets meant an increase in the supply of British pounds and the dollar therefore appreciated in value.

Speculation Suppose it is widely anticipated that the American economy will *(a)* grow faster than the British economy, *(b)* experience more rapid inflation than the British economy, and *(c)* have lower future real interest rates than Britain. All these expectations would lead one to believe that in the future the dollar will depreciate and, conversely, the pound will appreciate. Holders of dollars will thus attempt to convert them into pounds, increasing the demand for pounds. This conversion causes the dollar to depreciate and the pound to appreciate. A self-fulfilling prophecy arises: The dollar depreciates and the pound appreciates because speculators act on the supposition that these changes in currency values will in fact happen.

Flexible Rates and the Balance of Payments
Proponents of flexible exchange rates argue that such rates have a compelling virtue: *They automatically adjust so as eventually to eliminate balance of payments deficits or surpluses.* We can explain this by looking at *S* and *D* in Figure 25-5 which restate the demand for, and supply of, pounds curves from Figure 25-3. The equilibrium exchange rate of $2 = £1 correctly suggests there is no balance of payments deficit or surplus. At the $2 = £1 exchange rate the quantity of pounds demanded by Americans to import British goods, buy

FIGURE 25-5 Adjustments under flexible exchange rates, fixed exchange rates, and the gold standard

Under flexible rates an American trade deficit at the $2-for-£1 rate would be corrected by an increase in the rate to $3 for £1. Under fixed rates the *ab* shortage of pounds would be met out of international monetary reserves. Under the gold standard the deficit would cause changes in domestic price and income levels which would shift the demand for pounds (*D'*) to the left and the supply (*S*) to the right, sustaining equilibrium at the $2-for-£1 rate.

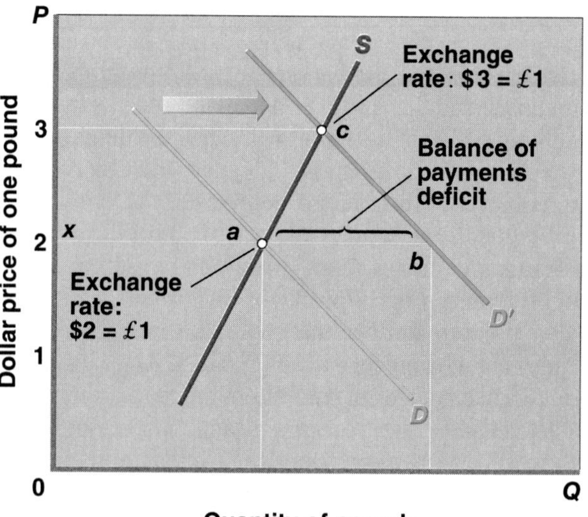

British transportation and insurance services, and pay interest and dividends on British investments in the United States equals the amount of pounds supplied by the British in buying American exports, purchasing services from Americans, and making interest and dividend payments on American investments in Britain. In brief, there would be no change in official reserves in Table 25-1.

Now suppose tastes change and Americans decide to buy more British automobiles. Or assume that the American price level has increased relative to Britain, or that interest rates have fallen in the United States compared to Britain. Any or all of these changes will cause the American demand for British pounds to increase from D to, say, D' in Figure 25-5.

We observe that *at the initial $2 = £1 exchange rate* an American balance of payments deficit has been created in the amount *ab*. That is, at the $2 = £1 rate there is a shortage of pounds in the amount *ab* to Americans. American export-type transactions will earn *xa* pounds, but Americans will want *xb* pounds to finance import-type transactions. Because this is a free competitive market, the shortage will change the exchange rate (the dollar price of pounds) from $2 = £1 to, say, $3 = £1; that is, the dollar has *depreciated.*

At this point it must be emphasized that *the exchange rate is a very special price which links all domestic (United States') prices with all foreign (British) prices.* Specifically, the dollar price of a foreign good is found by multiplying the foreign product price by the exchange rate in dollars per unit of the foreign currency. At an exchange rate of $2 = £1, a British Triumph automobile priced at 9000 will cost an American $18,000 (= 9000 × $2).

A change in the exchange rate therefore alters the prices of all British goods to Americans and all American goods to potential British buyers. Specifically, the change in the exchange rate from $2 = £1 to $3 = £1 will alter the relative attractiveness of American imports and exports in such a way as to restore equilibrium in the balance of payments of the United States. From the American point of view, as the dollar price of pounds changes from $2 to $3, the Triumph priced at £9000, which formerly cost an American $18,000, now costs $27,000 (= 9000 × $3). Other British goods will also cost more to Americans, and American imports of British goods and services will decline. Graphically, this is shown as a move from point *b* toward point *c* in Figure 25-5.

Conversely, from Britain's standpoint the exchange rate, that is, the pound price of dollars, has fallen (from £$\frac{1}{2}$ to £$\frac{1}{3}$ for $1). The international value of the pound has *appreciated.* The British previously got only $2 for £1; now they get $3 for £1. American goods are therefore cheaper to the British, and American exports to Great Britain will rise. In Figure 25-5 this is shown by the move from point *a* toward point *c.*

The two adjustments described—a decrease in American imports from Great Britain and an increase in American exports to Great Britain—are precisely those needed to correct the American balance of payments deficit. (You should reason through the operation of freely fluctuating exchange rates in correcting an initial American balance of payments *surplus* in its trade with Great Britain.)

In summary, the free fluctuation of exchange rates in response to shifts in the supply of, and demand for, foreign monies automatically corrects balance of payments deficits and surpluses.

Disadvantages Even though freely fluctuating exchange rates automatically work eventually to eliminate payments imbalances, they may involve several significant problems:

1 Uncertainty and Diminished Trade The risks and uncertainties associated with flexible exchange rates may discourage the flow of trade. Suppose an American automobile dealer contracts to purchase ten Triumph cars for £90,000. At the current exchange rate of, say $2 for £1, the American importer expects to pay $180,000 for these automobiles. But if in the three-month delivery period the rate of exchange shifts to $3 for £1, the £90,000 payment contracted by the American importer will now be $270,000.

This unheralded increase in the dollar price of pounds may easily turn the potential American importer's anticipated profits into substantial losses. Aware of the possibility of an adverse change in the exchange rate, the American importer may not be willing to assume the risks involved. The American firm therefore may confine its operations to domestic automobiles, with the result that international trade does not occur in this item.

The same rationale applies to investment. Assume that, when the exchange rate is $3 to £1, an American firm invests $30,000 (or £10,000) in a British enterprise. It estimates a return of 10 percent, that is, it anticipates earnings of $3000 or £1000. Suppose these expectations prove correct in that the British firm earns £1000 the first year on the £10,000 investment. But suppose that during the year, the value of the dollar *appreciates* to $2 = £1. The absolute return is now only $2000 (rather than $3000) and the rate of return falls from the anticipated 10 percent to only 6⅔ percent (= $2000/ $30,000). Investment is inherently risky. The added risk posed by adverse changes in exchange rates may persuade the potential American investor to avoid overseas ventures.[2]

2 Terms of Trade A nation's terms of trade will be worsened by a decline in the international value of its currency. For example, an increase in the dollar price of pounds will mean that the United States must export more goods and services to finance a given level of imports from Britain.

3 Instability Freely fluctuating exchange rates may also have destabilizing effects on the domestic economy as wide fluctuations stimulate and then depress those industries producing internationally traded goods. If the American economy is operating at full employment and the international value of its currency depreciates as in our illustration, the results will be inflationary for two reasons. Foreign demand for American goods will increase, that is, the net exports component of aggregate expenditures will increase and cause demand-pull inflation. Also, prices of all American imports will increase. Conversely, appreciation of the dollar would lower exports and increase imports, causing unemployment.

From the vantage point of policy, acceptance of floating exchange rates may complicate the use of domestic fiscal and monetary policies in seeking full employment and price stability. This is especially so for nations whose exports and imports are large relative to their GDPs (Table 24-1).

Fixed Exchange Rates

At the other extreme nations have often fixed or "pegged" their exchange rates to circumvent the disadvantages associated with floating rates. To analyze the implications and problems associated with fixed rates, assume that the United States and Britain agree to maintain a $2 = £1 exchange rate.

The basic problem is that a governmental proclamation that a dollar will be worth so many pounds does *not* mandate stability of the demand for, and supply of, pounds. As demand and supply shift over time, government must intervene directly or indirectly in the foreign exchange market if the exchange rate is to be stabilized.

In Figure 25-5 suppose the American demand for pounds increases from D to D' and an American payments deficit of ab arises. This means that the American government is committed to an exchange rate ($2 = £1) which is below the equilibrium rate ($3 = £1). How can the United States prevent the shortage of pounds—reflecting an American balance of payments deficit—from driving the exchange rate up to the equilibrium level? The answer is to alter market demand or supply or both so that they continue to intersect at the $2 = £1 rate of exchange. There are several means for achieving this.

1 Use of Reserves The most desirable means of pegging an exchange rate is to manipulate the market through the use of official reserves. International monetary *reserves* are stocks of foreign monies owned by a particular government. How do reserves originate? Let's assume that in the past the opposite market condition prevailed in which there was a surplus, rather than a shortage, of pounds, and the United States government had acquired that surplus. That is, at some earlier time the United States government spent dollars to buy surplus pounds which were threatening to reduce the $2 = £1 exchange rate to, say, $1 = £1. By now selling part of its reserve of pounds, the United States government could shift the supply of pounds curve to the right so that it intersects D' at b in Figure 25-5, thereby maintaining the exchange rate at $2 = £1.

Historically nations have used gold as "international money" or, in other words, as reserves. Thus, in our example the United States government might sell some of the gold it owns to Britain for pounds. The pounds thus acquired could be used to augment the supply earned through American trade and financial transactions to shift the supply of pounds to the right to maintain the $2 = £1 exchange rate.

It is critical that the amount of reserves be enough to accomplish the required increase in the supply of pounds. This is *not* a problem if deficits and surpluses occur more or less randomly and are of approximately

[2]At some cost and inconvenience a *trader* can circumvent part of the risk of unfavorable exchange rate fluctuations by "hedging" in the "futures market" for foreign exchange. For example, our American auto importer can purchase the needed pounds at the current $2 for £1 exchange rates to be made available three months in the future when the British cars are delivered. Unfortunately, this does not eliminate entirely exchange rate risks. Suppose the dollar price of pounds *falls* (the dollar appreciates) in the three-month delivery period and a competing importing firm did not hedge its foreign exchange purchase. This means the competitor will obtain its shipment of Triumphs at a lower price and will be able to undersell our original importer.

equivalent size. That is, last year's balance of payments surplus with Britain will increase the United States' reserve of pounds and this reserve can be used to "finance" this year's deficit. But if the United States encounters persistent and sizable deficits for an extended period, the reserves problem can become critical and force the abandonment of a system of fixed exchange rates. Or, at least, a nation whose reserves are inadequate must resort to less appealing options to maintain exchange rate stability. Let's consider these other options.

2 Trade Policies One set of policy options includes measures designed to control the flows of trade and finance directly. The United States might try to maintain the $2 = £1 exchange rate in the face of a shortage of pounds by discouraging imports (thereby reducing the demand for pounds) and by encouraging exports (thereby increasing the supply of pounds). Imports can be reduced by imposing tariffs or import quotas. Similarly, special taxes may be levied on the interest and dividends Americans receive for foreign investments. Also, the United States government might subsidize certain American exports and thus increase the supply of pounds.

The fundamental problem with these policies is that they reduce the volume of world trade and distort its composition or pattern away from that which is economically desirable. Tariffs, quotas, and the like can be imposed only at the sacrifice of some portion of the economic gains or benefits attainable from a free flow of world trade based on comparative advantage. These effects should not be underestimated; the imposition of trade barriers can elicit retaliatory responses from other nations which are adversely affected.

3 Exchange Controls: Rationing Another option is exchange controls or rationing. Under exchange controls the United States government would handle the problem of a pound shortage by requiring that all pounds obtained by American exporters be sold to it. Then, in turn, the government allocates or rations this short supply of pounds (*xa* in Figure 25-5) among various American importers who demand the quantity *xb*. In this way the American government would restrict American imports to the amount of foreign exchange earned by American exports. American demand for British pounds in the amount *ab* would be unfulfilled. Government eliminates a balance of payments deficit by restricting imports to the value of exports.

There are many objections to exchange controls.

1 Like trade controls—tariffs, quotas, and export subsidies—exchange controls distort the pattern of international trade away from that based on comparative advantage.

2 The process of rationing scarce foreign exchange necessarily involves discrimination among importers. Serious problems of equity and favoritism are implicit in the rationing process.

3 Controls impinge on freedom of consumer choice. Americans who prefer Mazdas may be forced to buy Mercuries. The business opportunities of some American importers will necessarily be impaired because imports are being constrained by government.

4 There are likely to be enforcement problems. The market forces of demand and supply indicate there are American importers who want foreign exchange badly enough to pay *more* than the $2 = £1 official rate; this sets the stage for extralegal or "black market" foreign exchange dealings.

4 Domestic Macro Adjustments A final means of maintaining a stable exchange rate is to use domestic fiscal and monetary policies to eliminate the shortage of pounds. In particular, restrictive fiscal and monetary measures will reduce the United States' national income relative to Britain's. Because American imports vary directly with our national income, our demand for British goods, and therefore for pounds, will be restrained.

To the extent that these contractionary policies reduce our price level relative to Britain's, American buyers of consumption and investment goods will divert their demands from British to American goods, also restricting the demand for pounds. Finally, a restrictive (tight) money policy will increase United States' interest rates compared to Britain and reduce American demand for pounds to make financial investments in Britain.

From Britain's standpoint lower prices on American goods and higher American interest rates will increase British imports of American goods and stimulate British financial investment in the United States. Both developments will increase the supply of pounds. The combination of a decrease in the demand for and an increase in the supply of pounds will eliminate the initial American payments deficit. In Figure 25-5 the new supply and demand curves will intersect at some new equilibrium point on the *ab* line where the exchange rate persists at $2 = £1.

This means of maintaining pegged exchange rates is hardly appealing. The "price" of exchange rate stability for the United States is falling output, employment, and price levels—in other words, a recession. Achieving a balance of payments equilibrium and realizing domestic stability are both important national economic objectives; but to sacrifice the latter for the former is to let the tail wag the dog.

QUICK REVIEW 25-2

- ***In a system where exchange rates are free to float, they are determined by the demand for, and supply of, individual national currencies.***
- ***Determinants of freely floating exchange rates—factors which shift currency supply and demand curves—include changes in tastes, changes in relative national incomes, relative price level changes, relative real interest rate changes, and speculation.***
- ***Under a system of fixed exchange rates, nations set their exchange rates and then maintain them by buying or selling reserves of foreign currencies, incurring inflation or recession, establishing trade barriers, or employing exchange controls.***

INTERNATIONAL EXCHANGE RATE SYSTEMS

There have been three different exchange rate systems which nations have employed in recent history.

The Gold Standard: Fixed Exchange Rates

Over the 1879–1934 period—except for the World War I years—an international monetary system known as the gold standard prevailed. The **gold standard** provided for fixed exchange rates. A look at its operation and ultimate downfall is instructive as to the functioning and some of the advantages and problems associated with fixed-rate systems. Currently a number of economists advocate fixed exchange rates and a few even call for a return to the international gold standard.

Conditions A nation is on the gold standard when it fulfills three conditions:

1 It must define its monetary unit in terms of a certain quantity of gold.

2 It must maintain a fixed relationship between its stock of gold and its domestic money supply.

3 It must allow gold to be freely exported and imported.

If each nation defines its monetary unit in terms of gold, the various national currencies will have a fixed relationship to one another. For example, suppose the United States defines a dollar as being worth 25 grains of gold and Britain defines its pound sterling as being worth 50 grains of gold. This means that a British pound is worth $50/25$ dollars or, simply, £1 equals $2.

Gold flows Now, ignoring costs of packing, insuring, and shipping gold between countries, under the gold standard the rate of exchange would not vary from this $2-for-£1 rate. No one in the United States would pay more than $2 for £1, because you could always buy 50 grains of gold for $2 in the United States, ship it to Britain, and sell it for £1. Nor would the English pay more than £1 for $2. Why should they, when they could buy 50 grains of gold in England for £1, send it to the United States, and sell it for $2?

In practice the costs of packing, insuring, and shipping gold must be taken into account. But these costs would only amount to a few cents per 50 grains of gold. If these costs were 3 cents for 50 grains of gold, Americans wanting pounds would pay up to $2.03 for a pound rather than buy and export 50 grains of gold to get the pound. Why? Because it would cost them $2 for the 50 grains of gold plus 3 cents to send it to England to be exchanged for £1. This $2.03 exchange rate, above which gold would begin to flow out of the United States, is called the **gold export point.**

Conversely, the exchange rate would fall to $1.97 before gold would flow into the United States. The English, wanting dollars, would accept as little as $1.97 in exchange for £1, because from the $2 which they could get by buying 50 grains of gold in England and reselling it in the United States, 3 cents must be subtracted to pay shipping and related costs. This $1.97 exchange rate, below which gold would flow into the United States, is called the **gold import point.**

Our conclusion is that *under the gold standard the flow of gold between nations would result in exchange rates which for all practical purposes are fixed.*

Domestic Macro Adjustments Figure 25-5 helps explain the kinds of adjustments the gold standard would entail. Here, initially the demand for and the supply of pounds are *D* and *S* respectively and the resulting intersection point at *a* coincides with the fixed exchange rate of $2 = £1 which results from the "in gold" definitions of the pound and the dollar. Now suppose for some reason American preferences for British goods increase, shifting the demand for pounds curve to D'. In Figure 25-5 there is now a shortage of pounds equal to *ab,* implying an American balance of payments deficit.

What will happen? Remember that the rules of the gold standard prohibit the exchange rate from moving from the fixed \$2 = £1 relationship; the rate can *not* move up to a new equilibrium of \$3 = £1 at point *c* as it would under freely floating rates. Instead, the exchange rate would rise by a few cents to the American gold export point at which gold would flow from the United States to Britain.

Recall that the gold standard requires participants to maintain a fixed relationship between their domestic money supplies and their quantities of gold. Therefore, the flow of gold from the United States to Britain would bring about a contraction of the money supply in America and an expansion of the money supply in Britain. Other things being equal, this will reduce aggregate demand and, therefore, lower real domestic output, employment, and the price level in the United States. Also, the reduced money supply will boost American interest rates.

The opposite occurs in Britain. The inflow of gold increases the money supply, causing aggregate demand, national income, employment, and the price level to all increase. The increased money supply will also lower interest rates in Britain.

In Figure 25-5 declining American incomes and prices will reduce our demand for British goods and services and therefore reduce the American demand for pounds. Lower relative interest rates in Britain will make it less attractive for Americans to invest there, also reducing the demand for pounds. For all these reasons the D' curve will shift to the left.

Similarly, higher incomes and prices in Britain will increase British demand for American goods and services and higher American interest rates will encourage the British to invest more in the United States. These developments all increase the supply of pounds available to Americans, shifting the S curve of Figure 25-5 to the right.

In short, domestic macroeconomic adjustments in America and Britain, triggered by the international flow of gold, will produce new demand and supply for pound curves which intersect at some point on the horizontal line between points *a* and *b*.

Note the critical difference in the adjustment mechanisms associated with freely floating exchange rates and the fixed rates of the gold standard. With floating rates the burden of the adjustment is on the exchange rate itself. In contrast, the gold standard involves changes in the domestic money supplies of participating nations which in turn precipitate changes in price levels, real domestic output and employment, and interest rates.

Although the gold standard boasts the advantages of stable exchange rates and the automatic correction of balance of payments deficits and surpluses, its basic drawback is that nations must accept domestic adjustments in such distasteful forms as unemployment and falling incomes, on the one hand, or inflation, on the other. In using the gold standard nations must be willing to submit their domestic economies to painful macroeconomic adjustments. Under this system a nation's monetary policy would be determined largely by changes in the demand for and supply of foreign exchange. If the United States, for example, was already moving toward recession, the loss of gold under the gold standard would reduce its money supply and intensify the problem. Under the international gold standard nations would have to forgo independent monetary policies.

Demise The worldwide Great Depression of the 1930s signaled the end of the gold standard. As domestic outputs and employment plummeted worldwide, the restoration of prosperity became the primary goal of afflicted nations. Protectionist measures such as the United States' Smoot-Hawley Tariff were enacted as nations sought to increase net exports and stimulate their domestic economies. And each nation was fearful that its economic recovery would be aborted by a balance of payments deficit which would lead to an outflow of gold and consequent contractionary effects. Indeed, nations attempted to devalue their currencies in term of gold to make their exports more attractive and imports less attractive. These devaluations undermined a basic condition of the gold standard and the system broke down.

The Bretton Woods System

Not only did the Great Depression of the 1930s lead to the downfall of the gold standard, it also prompted erection of trade barriers which greatly impaired international trade. World War II was similarly disruptive to world trade and finance. Thus, as World War II drew to a close the world trading and monetary systems were in shambles.

To lay the groundwork for a new international monetary system, an international conference of Allied nations was held at Bretton Woods, New Hampshire, in

1944. Out of this conference evolved a commitment to an *adjustable-peg system* of exchange rates, sometimes called the **Bretton Woods system.** The new system sought to capture the advantages of the old gold standard (fixed exchange rates), while avoiding its disadvantages (painful domestic macroeconomic adjustments).

Furthermore, the conference created the **International Monetary Fund** (IMF) to make the new exchange rate system feasible and workable. This international monetary system, emphasizing relatively fixed exchange rates and managed through the IMF, prevailed with modifications until 1971. The IMF continues to play a basic role in international finance and in recent years has performed a major role in ameliorating debt problems of the less developed countries.

IMF and Pegged Exchange Rates Why did the Bretton Woods adjustable-peg system evolve? We have noted that during the depressed 1930s, various countries resorted to the practice of **devaluation**—devaluing[3] their currencies to try to stimulate domestic employment. For example, if the United States was faced with growing unemployment, it might devalue the dollar by *increasing* the dollar price of pounds from \$2.50 for £1 to, say, \$3 for £1. This action would make American goods cheaper to the British and British goods dearer to Americans, increasing American exports and reducing American imports. The resulting increase in net exports, abetted by the multiplier effect, would stimulate output and employment in the United States.

But the problem is that every nation can play the devaluation game, and most gave it a whirl. The resulting rounds of competitive devaluations benefited no one; on the contrary, they actually contributed to further demoralization of world trade. Nations at Bretton Woods therefore agreed that the postwar monetary system must provide for overall exchange rate stability whereby disruptive currency devaluations could be avoided.

What was the adjustable-peg system of exchange rates like? First, as with the gold standard, each IMF member was obligated to define its monetary unit in terms of gold (or dollars), thereby establishing par rates of exchange between its currency and the currencies of all other members. Each nation was further obligated to keep its exchange rate stable vis-à-vis any other currency.

But how was this obligation to be fulfilled? The answer, as we saw in our discussion of fixed exchange rates, is that governments must use international monetary reserves to intervene in foreign exchange markets. Assume, for example, that under the Bretton Woods system the dollar was "pegged" to the British pound at \$2 = £1. Now suppose in Figure 25-5 that the American demand for pounds temporarily increases from D to D' so that a shortage of pounds of ab arises at the pegged rate. How can the United States keep its pledge to maintain a \$2 = £1 rate when the new market or equilibrium rate would be at \$3 = £1? The United States could supply additional pounds in the exchange market, shifting the supply of pounds curve to the right so that it intersects D' at b and thereby maintains the \$2 = £1 rate of exchange.

Where would the United States obtain the needed pounds? Under the Bretton Woods system there were three main sources.

1 Reserves The United States might currently possess pounds in a "stabilization fund" as the result of the opposite exchange market condition existing in the past. That is, at some earlier time the United States government may have spent dollars to purchase surplus pounds which were threatening to reduce the \$2 = £1 exchange rate to, say, \$1 = £1.

2 Gold Sales The United States government might sell some of the gold it holds to Britain for pounds. The proceeds would then be offered in the exchange market to augment the supply of pounds.

3 IMF Borrowing The needed pounds might be borrowed from the IMF. Nations participating in the Bretton Woods system were required to make contributions to the IMF on the basis of the size of their national income, population, and volume of trade. Thus, if necessary, the United States could borrow pounds on a short-term basis from the IMF by supplying its own currency as collateral.

Fundamental Imbalances: Adjusting the Peg A fixed-rate system such as Bretton Woods functions well so long as a nation's payments deficits and surpluses occur more or less randomly and are approximately equal in size. If a nation's payments surplus last year

[3]A note on terminology is in order. We noted earlier in this chapter that the dollar has *appreciated (depreciated)* when its international value has increased (decreased) as the result of changes in the demand for, or supply of, dollars in foreign exchange markets. The terms *revalue* and *devalue* are used to describe an increase or decrease, respectively, in the international value of a currency which occurs as the result of governmental action.

allows it to add a sufficient amount to its international monetary reserves to finance this year's payments deficit, no problems will arise. But what if the United States, for example, encountered a "fundamental imbalance" in its international trade and finance and was confronted with persistent and sizable payments deficits? In this case it is evident that the United States would eventually run out of reserves and be unable to maintain its fixed exchange rate.

Under the Bretton Woods system, a fundamental payments deficit was corrected by devaluation, that is, by an "orderly" reduction in the nation's pegged exchange rate. Also, the IMF allowed each member nation to alter the value of its currency by 10 percent without explicit permission from the Fund to correct a deeply rooted or "fundamental" balance of payments deficit. Larger exchange rate changes required the sanction of the Fund's board of directors. By requiring approval of significant rate changes, the Fund guarded against arbitrary and competitive currency devaluation prompted by nations seeking a temporary stimulus to their domestic economies. In our illustration, devaluing the dollar would increase American exports and lower American imports, correcting its persistent payments deficits.

The objective of the adjustable-peg system was to realize a world monetary system which embraced the best features of both a fixed exchange rate system (such as the old international gold standard) and a system of freely fluctuating exchange rates. By reducing risk and uncertainty, short-term exchange rate stability—pegged exchange rates—would presumably stimulate trade and lead to the efficient use of world resources. Periodic exchange rate adjustments—adjustments of the pegs—made in an orderly fashion through the IMF, and on the basis of permanent or long-run changes in a country's payments position, provided a mechanism by which persistent international payments imbalances could be resolved by means other than painful changes in domestic levels of output and prices.

Demise of the Bretton Woods System Under the Bretton Woods system gold and the dollar came to be accepted as international reserves. The acceptability of gold as an international medium of exchange was derived from its role under the international gold standard of an earlier era. The dollar became acceptable as international money for two reasons.

1 The United States emerged from World War II as the free world's strongest economy.

2 The United States had accumulated large quantities of gold and between 1934 and 1971 maintained a policy of buying gold from, and selling gold to, foreign monetary authorities at a fixed price of $35 per ounce. Thus the dollar was convertible into gold on demand; the dollar came to be regarded as a substitute for gold and therefore "as good as gold."

But the role of the dollar as a component of international monetary reserves contained the seeds of a dilemma. Consider the situation as it developed in the 1950s and 1960s. The problem with gold as international money was a quantitative one. The growth of the world's money stock depends on the amount of newly mined gold, less any amounts hoarded for speculative purposes or used for industrial and artistic purposes. Unfortunately, the growth of the gold stock lagged behind the rapidly expanding volume of international trade and finance. Thus the dollar came to occupy an increasingly important role as an international monetary reserve.

Economies of the world acquire dollars as reserves as the result of United States' balance of payments deficits. With the exception of some three or four years, the United States incurred persistent payments deficits throughout the 1950s and 1960s. These deficits were financed in part by drawing down American gold reserves. But for the most part United States' deficits were financed by growing foreign holdings of American dollars which were "as good as gold" until 1971.

As the amount of dollars held by foreigners soared and as our gold reserves dwindled, other nations inevitably began to question whether the dollar was really "as good as gold." The ability of the United States to maintain the convertibility of the dollar into gold became increasingly doubtful, and, therefore, so did the role of the dollar as generally accepted international monetary reserves. Hence, the dilemma: ". . . to preserve the status of the dollar as a reserve medium, the payments deficit of the United States had to be eliminated; but elimination of the deficit would mean a drying up of the source of additional dollar reserves for the system."[4] The United States had to reduce or eliminate its payments deficits to preserve the dollar's status as an international medium of exchange. But success in this endeavor would limit the expansion of international reserves or liquidity and restrict the growth of international trade and finance.

[4]Delbert A. Snider, *Introduction to International Economics,* 7th ed. (Homewood, Ill.: Richard D. Irwin, Inc., 1979), p. 352.

This problem came to a head in the early 1970s. Faced with persistent and growing United States' payments deficits, President Nixon suspended the dollar's convertibility into gold on August 15, 1971. This suspension abrogated the policy to exchange gold for dollars at $35 per ounce, which had existed for thirty-seven years. This new policy severed the link between gold and the international value of the dollar, thereby "floating" the dollar and allowing its value to be determined by market forces. The floating of the dollar withdrew American support from the old Bretton Woods system of fixed exchange rates and sounded the death knell for that system.

The Managed Float

The system of exchange rates which has since evolved is not easily described; it can probably best be labeled a system of **managed floating exchange rates.** It is recognized that changing economic conditions among nations require continuing changes in exchange rates to avoid persistent payments deficits or surpluses; exchange rates must be allowed to float. But short-term changes in exchange rates—perhaps accentuated by purchases and sales by speculators—disrupt and discourage the flow of trade and finance. Thus, it is generally agreed that the central banks of the various nations should buy and sell foreign exchange to smooth out such fluctuations in rates. That is, central banks should "manage" or stabilize short-term speculative variations in their exchange rates.

These characteristics were formalized by a leading group of IMF nations in 1976. Thus, ideally, the managed floating system will have not only the needed long-term exchange rate flexibility to correct fundamental payments imbalances, but also sufficient short-term stability of rates to sustain and encourage international trade and finance.

Actually, the current exchange rate system is more complicated than the previous paragraphs suggest. While the major currencies—German marks, American and Canadian dollars, Japanese yen, and the British pound—fluctuate or float in response to changing demand and supply conditions, most of the European Common Market nations are attempting to peg their currencies to one another. Furthermore, many less developed nations peg their currencies to the dollar and allow their currencies to fluctuate with it. Finally, some nations peg the value of their currencies to a "basket" or group of other currencies.

How well has the managed floating system worked? It has both proponents and critics.

Pros Proponents argue that the system has functioned well—far better than anticipated—during its relatively brief existence.

1 Trade Growth In the first place, fluctuating exchange rates did not lead to the diminution of world trade and finance that skeptics had predicted. In real terms world trade has grown at approximately the same rate under the managed float as it did during the decade of the 1960s under the fixed exchange rates of the Bretton Woods system.

2 Managing Turbulence Proponents argue that the managed float has weathered severe economic turbulence which might well have caused a fixed exchange regime to have broken down. Such dramatic events as worldwide agricultural shortfalls in 1972–1974, extraordinary oil-price increases in 1973–1974 and again in 1979–1980, worldwide stagflation in 1974–1976 and 1981–1983, and large U.S. budget deficits in the 1980s, all generated substantial international trade and financial imbalances. Flexible rates facilitated international adjustments to these developments, whereas the same events would have put unbearable pressures on a fixed-rate system.

Cons But there is still considerable sentiment in favor of a system characterized by greater exchange rate stability. Those favoring stable rates see problems with the current system.

1 Volatility and Adjustment Critics argue that exchange rates have been excessively volatile under the managed float. This volatility, it is argued, has occurred even when underlying economic and financial conditions of particular nations have been stable. Perhaps more importantly, the managed float has not readily resolved balance of payments imbalances as flexible rates are presumably capable of doing. Thus the United States has run persistent trade deficits in recent years, while Germany and Japan have had persistent surpluses. Changes in the international values of the dollar, mark, and yen have not yet corrected these imbalances.

2 A "Nonsystem"? Skeptics feel that the managed float is basically a "nonsystem"; the rules and guidelines circumscribing the behavior of each nation as to its exchange rate are not sufficiently clear or constraining to make the system viable in the long run. Nations will inevitably be tempted to intervene in foreign exchange markets, not merely to smooth out short-term or speculative fluctuations in the value of their currencies, but to prop up their currency if it is chronically weak or to manipulate the value of their currency to achieve domestic stabilization goals. In brief, there is fear that in time there may be more "managing" and less "floating" of exchange rates, and this may be fatal to the present loosely defined system.

An example of more "managing" and less "floating" of exchange rates occurred in February 1987 when the "Group of Seven" industrial nations **(G-7 nations)**—the United States, West Germany, Japan, Britain, France, Italy, and Canada—agreed to take actions to stabilize the value of the dollar. In the previous two years the dollar had declined rapidly because of a sizable U.S. trade deficit. Although the U.S. trade deficit remained large, it was felt that a further depreciation of the dollar might be disruptive to economic growth in several G-7 economies. The G-7 nations thus bought large quantities of dollars to prop up the dollar's value. Since 1987 the G-7 nations have periodically intervened in foreign exchange markets to help stabilize the value of the dollar. Do these actions represent an admission by the industrial economies that the system of flexible exchange rates is seriously flawed?

The jury is still out on the managed float and no clear assessment has been reached: "Flexible rates have neither attained their proponents' wildest hopes nor confirmed their opponents' worst fears. But they have seen the major industrial economies through [two decades] mined with major disturbances to the international economy."[5]

QUICK REVIEW 25-3

- ***Under the gold standard (1789–1934), nations fixed exchange rates by valuing their currencies in terms of gold, by tying their stocks of money to gold, and by allowing gold to flow between nations when balance of payment deficits and surpluses occurred.***
- ***The Bretton Woods, or adjustable-peg, system of exchange rates (1944–1971) fixed or pegged short-run exchange rates, but permitted orderly long-run adjustments of the pegs.***
- ***The managed floating system of exchange rate (1971–present) relies on foreign exchange markets to establish equilibrium exchange rates, but permits central banks to buy and sell foreign currencies to manage or stabilize short-term speculative changes in exchange rates.***

[5]Richard E. Caves and Ronald W. Jones, *World Trade and Payments*, 3d ed. (Boston: Little, Brown and Company, 1981), p. 471.

RECENT UNITED STATES' TRADE DEFICITS

As shown in Figure 25-6, the United States had large trade deficits in the 1980s and early 1990s. Specifically, our merchandise trade deficit jumped from \$25 billion in 1980 to \$160 billion in 1987, then fell to \$74 billion in 1991. In 1980 the United States had a current account surplus of \$2 billion; by 1987 this had changed to a \$160 billion deficit. By 1991 the current account deficit had narrowed to \$92 billion.

What caused these large trade deficits? What were their effects? Why have they recently diminished?

Causes of the Trade Deficits

It is generally agreed that three major factors contributed to the large trade deficits of the 1980s and early 1990s.

The Rise of the Dollar As Figure 25-7 indicates, there was a pronounced rise in the international value of the dollar between 1980 and 1985. Here the value of the dollar is compared to ten other major currencies (weighted by the amount of trade we carry on with each country). By the end of 1984 the dollar was about 65 percent above its 1980 average value and at the highest level since floating exchange rates were adopted in the early 1970s. A strong or appreciated dollar means that foreign monies are cheaper to Americans and, conversely, dollars are more expensive to foreigners. As a result, foreign goods are cheap to Americans and our imports rise. Conversely, American goods are expensive to foreigners and our exports fall.

But why did the value of the dollar surge between 1980 and 1985? The basic answer is that real interest rates in the United States—nominal interest rates less the rate of inflation—rose in the United States compared to foreign countries. High real interest rates made the United States a very attractive place for foreigners to invest. As a result, the demand for dollars to make such investments increased, causing the dollar to appreciate in value.

Real interest rates were relatively high in America for two reasons.

1 The large Federal budget deficits of the 1980s are cited by many economists as a basic cause of high interest rates. Simply put, government borrowing to finance its deficits increased the domestic demand for money and boosted interest rates.

2 In 1979 the United States shifted to a tighter money policy in its efforts to control inflation. This

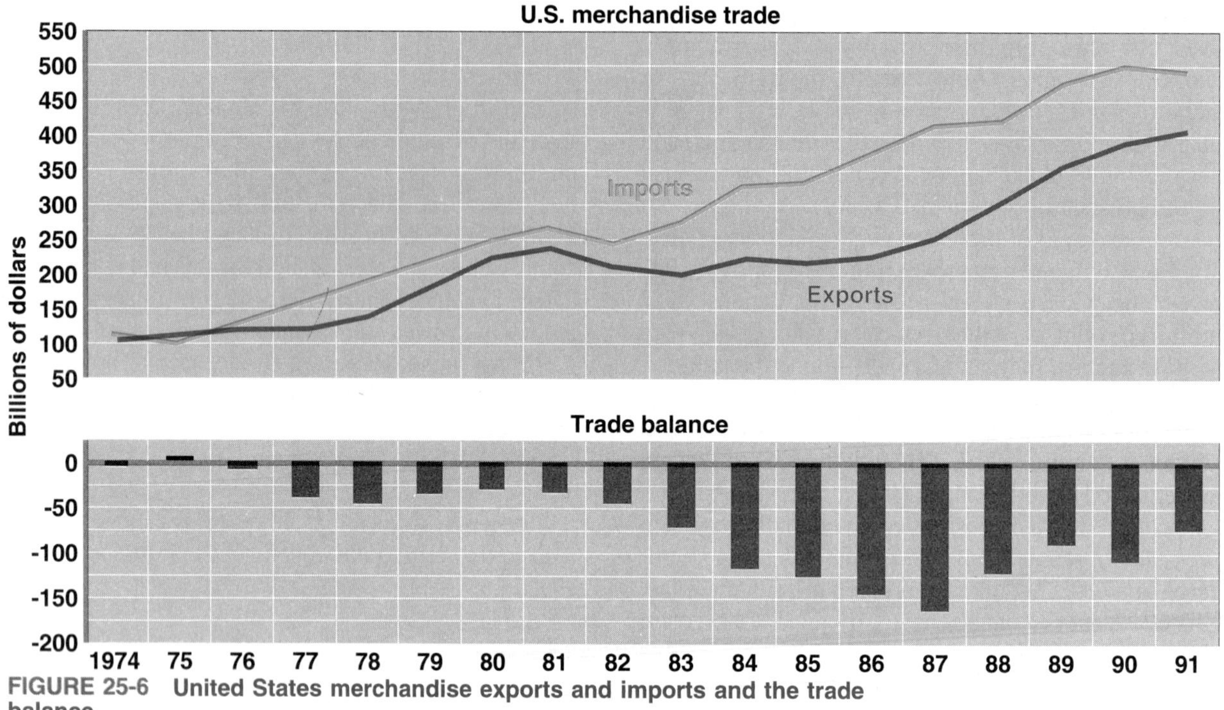

FIGURE 25-6 United States merchandise exports and imports and the trade balance

In recent years American trade deficits have been persistently large.

action increased interest rates directly by reducing the supply of money relative to its demand. Indirectly the lower rate of inflation kept the demand of foreign investors for dollars high because lower inflation means a higher *real* rate of return on investments in the United States.

By 1985 the value of the dollar had reached record heights relative to other currencies. Two factors then began to interact to reduce the dollar's value sharply over the next two years.

1 Five industrial nations—the United States, West Germany, Great Britain, France, and Japan—collectively decided to nudge the dollar downward to help correct the massive U.S. trade deficit and the trade surpluses in Japan and other nations. These five nations agreed to increase the supply of dollars in foreign exchange markets to reduce the dollar's value.

2 The demand for foreign currency in the United States rose sharply because more foreign money was needed to pay for the expanding volume of imports. This increase in the demand for yen, francs, and other foreign currencies increased the value of these currencies relative to the dollar. As shown in Figure 25-7, the value of the dollar declined sharply relative to other currencies over the 1985–1987 period.

Despite the sharp decline in the dollar between 1985 and 1987, the American trade imbalance stubbornly persisted. The major reason was that Japanese and other foreign importers did not immediately increase their dollar prices of products by as much as the decline in the international value of the dollar. Instead of increasing their prices, major importers accepted lower per unit profits on their goods. Therefore, imports to the United States for a time continued to rise, offsetting increases in American exports. Also, recall that in 1987 the G-7 nations agreed to halt the decline in the value of the dollar. Only in the second half of 1988 did the American trade deficit finally begin to shrink.

Rapid American Growth A second cause of the large trade deficits of the 1980s and 1990s is that the United States experienced a more rapid recovery from the 1980–1982 world recession than did its major trading partners. For example, American growth was about double that of Europe in 1983 and nearly triple the European rate in 1984. Although the gap in growth rates narrowed, the American growth rate continued to outpace the European rate between 1985 and 1990. This is significant because, like domestic consumption, a nation's purchases of foreign goods (its imports) vary di-

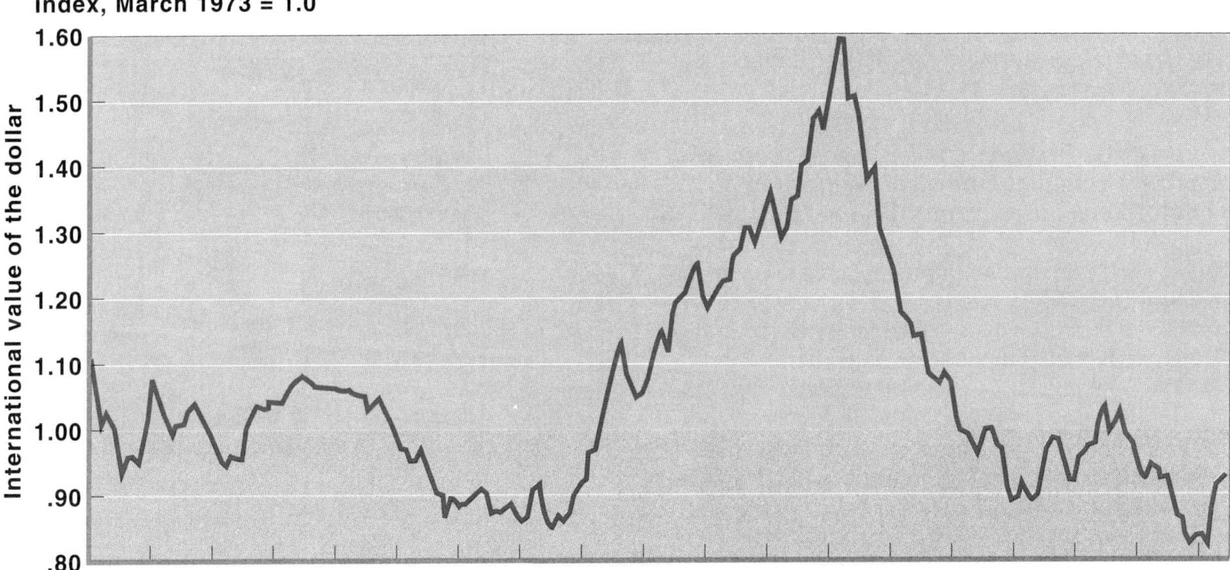

FIGURE 25-7 The international value of the dollar

Between 1980 and 1985 the value of the dollar increased greatly relative to other major currencies, tending to increase our imports and decrease our exports. The dollar fell sharply from 1985 through 1987 but trade deficits continued into the 1990s.

rectly with the level of domestic income. Because our national income expanded relatively rapidly, our imports also expanded rapidly. The slower growth of foreign national incomes meant their imports (our exports) grew slowly.

Exports to Less Developed Countries A third factor contributing to the large trade deficits was a falloff in our exports to the less developed countries (LDCs). An important source of the LDCs' external debt problem was their need to finance large international trade deficits by borrowing from the industrially advanced nations. As part of rescheduling and restructuring their debts in the 1980s, the less developed countries agreed to lessen their trade deficits. Thus they reduced their imports by using more restrictive monetary and fiscal policies to restrain the growth of their national incomes. In so doing their demands for imported goods declined. Part of those import reductions involved American goods, that is, United States exports. Many LDCs also *devalued* their currencies or, in other words, lowered the exchange rate value of their currencies by governmental decree. Devaluation restricted their imports and stimulated their exports. Thus the LDCs bought less from, and sold more to, the United States.

Effects of U.S. Trade Deficits

What have been the effects or consequences of our foreign trade deficits?

Dampened Aggregate Demand A trade deficit—more specifically, negative net exports—reduces aggregate demand and therefore, unless offset by other spending, diminishes the levels of real domestic output and employment via the multiplier effect. While this was a factor in keeping our level of employment below the full-employment rate for much of the 1980s, it also helped restrain inflation. A strong, appreciated dollar lowers the prices of all imported goods. Furthermore, a surging volume of imports exerts downward pressure on the prices of domestic goods that compete with those imports.

The constraining effect of a trade deficit is concentrated on industries which are highly dependent on export markets or are most competitive with imports. Some of the problems faced by American farmers, automobile manufacturers, and steel producers in the 1980s, for example, were related to the strong dollar and the associated trade deficits. These difficulties contributed greatly to the upsurge in political pressure for protectionist policies discussed in Chapter 24. They

LAST WORD

BUY AMERICAN: THE GLOBAL REFRIGERATOR

Humorist Art Buchwald pokes fun at those who suggest we could end our trade deficits by buying American consumer products.

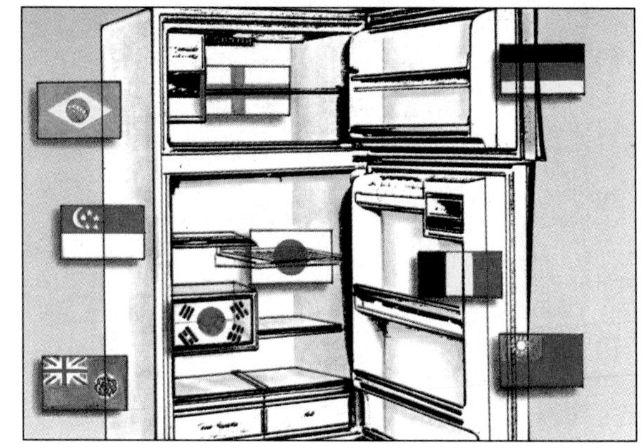

"There is only one way the country is going to get on its feet," said Baleful.

"How's that?" I asked, as we drank coffee in his office at the Baleful Refrigerator Company.

"The consumer has to start buying American," he said, slamming his fist down on the desk. "Every time an American buys a foreign refrigerator it costs one of my people his job. And every time one of my people is out of work it means he or she can't buy refrigerators."

"It's a vicious circle," I said.

Baleful's secretary came in. "Mr. Thompson, the steel broker is on the phone."

My friend grabbed the receiver. "Thompson, where is that steel shipment from Japan that was supposed to be in last weekend? . . . I don't care about weather. We're almost out of steel, and I'll have to close down the refrigerator assembly line next week. If you can't deliver when you promise, I'll find myself another broker."

"You get your steel from Japan?" I asked Baleful.

"Even with shipping costs, their price is still lower than steel made in Europe. We used to get all our sheets from Belgium, but the Japanese are now giving them a run for their money."

The buzzer on the phone alerted Baleful. He listened for a few moments and then said, "Excuse me, I have a call from Taiwan. Mark Four? Look, R&D designed a new push-button door handle and we're going to send the specs to you. Tell Mr. Chow if his people send us a sample of one and can make it for us at the same price as the old handle, we'll give his company the order."

A man came in with a plastic container and said, "Mr. Baleful, you said you wanted to see one of these before we ordered them. They are the containers for the ice maker in the refrigerator."

Baleful inspected it carefully and banged it on the floor a couple of times. "What's the price on it?"

"Hong Kong can deliver it at $2 a tray, and Dong-Fu Plastics in South Korea said they can make it for $1.70."

"It's just a plastic tray. Take the South Korea bid. We'll let Hong Kong supply us with the shelves for the freezer. Any word on the motors?"

"There's a German company in Brazil that just came out with a new motor, and it's passed all our tests, so Johnson has ordered 50,000."

"Call Cleveland Motors and tell them we're sorry, but the price they quoted us was just too high."

"Yes, sir," the man said and departed.

---

also generated interest in industrial policies designed to provide special help for allegedly "key" industries deemed critical to American industrial preeminence.

Increased American Indebtedness A trade deficit is also considered "unfavorable" because it must be financed by increased American indebtedness to foreigners. A trade deficit means we must borrow from the rest of the world to finance that deficit. This failure to "pay our way" in international trade is usually interpreted as a sign of domestic economic weakness and, hence, undesirable. However, economists point out that, at the time a trade or current account deficit is occurring, it is clearly beneficial to American consumers. After all, a trade deficit means that Americans are currently receiving more goods and services as imports from the rest of the world than we are sending to the rest of the world as exports. Trade deficits augment our domestic living standards during the period in which they occur.

A related consequence of our recent trade deficits is that in 1985 the United States' status changed from that of a net creditor to that of a *net debtor* for the first time since 1914. That is, the United States now owes foreigners more than they owe this country. Recall that current account deficits are financed primarily by net

The secretary came in again and said, "Harry telephoned and wanted to let you know the defroster just arrived from Finland. They're unloading the box cars now."

"Good. Any word on the wooden crates from Singapore?"

"They're at the dock in Hoboken."

"Thank heaven. Cancel the order from Boise Cascade."

"What excuse should I give them?"

"Tell them we made a mistake in our inventory, or we're switching to plastic. I don't care what you tell them."

Baleful turned to me. "Where were we?"

"You were saying that if the consumer doesn't start buying American, this country is going to be in a lot of trouble."

"Right. It's not only his patriotic duty, but his livelihood that's at stake. I'm going to Washington next week to tell the Senate Commerce Committee that if they don't get off the stick, there isn't going to be a domestic refrigerator left in this country. We're not going to stay in business for our health."

"Pour it to them," I urged him.

Baleful said, "Come out with me into the showroom."

I followed him. He went to his latest model, and opened the door. "This is an American refrigerator made by the American worker, for the American consumer. What do you have to say to that?"

"It's beautiful," I said. "It puts foreign imports to shame."

Source: **Art Buchwald, "Being Bullish on Buying American." Reprinted by permission. We discovered this article in** ***Master Curriculum Guide in Economics: Teaching Strategies for International Trade*** **(New York: Joint Council on Economic Education, 1988).**

capital inflows to the United States. When our exports are insufficient to pay for our imports, we finance the difference by borrowing from foreigners or, in other words, by going into debt. The financing of our recent large trade deficits has caused foreigners to accumulate a larger volume of claims against American assets than we have accumulated against foreign assets. The U.S. foreign debt burden climbed to $721 billion in 1990, making us the largest debtor nation in the world.

One implication of net debtor status is that we can no longer look forward to a net inflow of dividend and interest payments (see item 7 in Table 25-1's balance of payments) to help cover deficits in our merchandise and services trade. A second implication is that more of our corporations are foreign-owned.

The above comments on the economic effects of our trade deficit for the United States economy can be reversed as far as our industrialized trading partners are concerned. The current accounts of Japan and Germany, for example, tended to move toward surplus. These countries experienced an expansionary-inflationary stimulus and unusual growth in their export-dependent industries. They also increased their holdings of American debt.

QUICK REVIEW 25-4

- ***In the 1980s and early 1990s the United States experienced large trade deficits, caused by a strong dollar, relatively rapid American growth prior to the 1990–1991 recession, and reduced purchases of our exports by less developed nations.***
- ***These large deficits had a contractionary, anti-inflationary impact, hurt export-dependent industries, and resulted in the United States becoming a debtor nation; they also temporarily enhanced America's standard of living.***

Reducing the Trade Deficit

Two kinds of policies for reducing large trade deficits are most often cited: reduction of the Federal budget deficit and measures to accelerate economic growth abroad.

Reduction of the Budget Deficit Many economists agree that the most critical cause of our continuing trade deficits has been our large annual Federal budget deficits. It is argued that a reduction in the size of our Federal budget deficit will lower the real interest rate in the United States compared to other nations. In other words, a reduction in the government's demand for funds to finance its deficits will lower domestic interest rates and thus make financial investments in the United States less attractive to foreigners. The demand for dollars by foreigners will decline and the dollar will depreciate. Given a depreciated dollar, our exports will increase and imports will fall, correcting our trade deficit.

Would not a "managed" depreciation of the dollar by the G-7 nations produce a decline in the U.S. trade deficit, even without a reduction in our budget deficit? Perhaps so, but this point may be moot. Our trading partners have not been interested in allowing the dollar to fall appreciably below its 1988 level, unless we reduce our budget deficit. In effect, these nations contend that the United States must "get its fiscal house in order" to achieve a better balance of international trade.

Economic Growth Abroad The American trade deficit can also be reduced if nations abroad speed up their rates of economic growth. Higher levels of foreign national income increase the demand for American exports. The G-7 group of industrial nations has recognized the importance of economic growth in the nations which have trade surpluses as a way to reduce these surpluses and lower the American trade deficit. In the late 1980s, the governments of Japan and Germany established expansionary fiscal and monetary policies to bolster national income and increase the demand for goods produced in America.

Other "Remedies" There are several other possible "remedies" to the persistent United States' trade deficits.

Easy Money Policy Under appropriate circumstances, an easy money policy lowers real interest rates and reduces a trade deficit. The process works as follows. The decline in interest rates reduces the international demand for dollars, which results in a depreciation of the dollar. Dollar depreciation raises our exports and lowers our imports.

Protective Tariffs Protective tariffs can be used to reduce imports, but this strategy results in the loss of the gains from specialization and international trade. Furthermore, it may not be successful: Tariffs which reduce our *imports* foster retaliatory tariffs abroad which reduce our *exports.* Trade deficits do not disappear in this circumstance; instead, all trading partners suffer declines in their living standards.

Recession Recessions in the United States reduce disposable income and thus spending on all goods, including imports. Because exports are largely unaffected, the decline in imports trims the trade deficit. This is precisely what happened in the United States during the recession of 1990–1991. But recession is an undesirable way to reduce trade deficits; it imposes higher economic costs (lost output) on society than the costs associated with the trade deficit itself. Also, unless the fundamental causes of the deficits have in the meanwhile been remedied, imports and thus trade deficits again rise when the economy begins to recover from recession.

Increased American Competitiveness The American trade deficits can be reduced by lowering the costs of, and improving the quality of, American goods and services relative to foreign goods. Cost-saving production technologies, development of improved products, and more efficient management techniques each can contribute to a decline in the trade deficit by lowering United States demand for imported goods and increasing foreign demand for American goods.

Direct Foreign Investment Ironically, our persistent trade deficit has set off a chain of events which has begun to feed back to reduce the trade deficit itself. The vast accumulation of American dollars in foreign hands has enabled foreign individuals and firms to buy American factories or to build new plants in the United States. Furthermore, the fall in the value of the dollar has provided an incentive for foreign firms to produce in the United States rather than in their own nations.

In short, the trade deficit has given rise to an increase in *direct foreign investment* in the form of plant and equipment. Foreign-owned factories are beginning to turn out increasing volumes of goods that otherwise would have been imported. Hondas and Mazdas, produced in American factories, have replaced Hondas and Mazdas formerly imported from Japan. Other examples abound. The upshot is that the American trade deficit may shrink as imports are replaced with goods produced in foreign-owned factories in the United States.

CHAPTER SUMMARY

1 American exports create a foreign demand for dollars and make a supply of foreign exchange available to Americans. Conversely, American exports simultaneously create a demand for foreign exchange and make a supply of dollars available to foreigners. Generally, a nation's exports earn the foreign currencies needed to pay for its imports.

2 The balance of payments records all international trade and financial transactions taking place between a given nation and the rest of the world. The trade balance compares merchandise exports and imports. The balance on goods and services compares exports and imports of both goods and services. The current account balance considers not

only goods and services transactions, but also net investment income and net transfers.

3 A deficit on the current account will be largely offset by a surplus on the capital account. Conversely, a surplus on the current account will be largely offset by a deficit on the capital account. A balance of payments deficit occurs when the sum of the current and capital accounts is in deficit. A payments deficit is financed by drawing down official reserves. A balance of payments surplus occurs when the sum of the current and capital accounts is in surplus. A payments surplus results in an increase in official reserves. The desirability of a balance of payments deficit or surplus depends on its causes and its persistence over time.

4 Flexible or floating exchange rates are determined by the demand for and supply of foreign currencies. Under floating rates a currency will depreciate or appreciate as a result of changes in tastes, relative income changes, relative price changes, relative changes in real interest rates, and speculation.

5 Maintenance of fixed exchange rates requires adequate reserves to accommodate periodic payments deficits. If reserves are inadequate, nations must invoke protectionist trade policies, engage in exchange controls, or endure undesirable domestic macroeconomic adjustments.

6 Historically, the gold standard provided exchange rate stability until its disintegration during the 1930s. Under this system, gold flows between nations precipitated sometimes painful changes in price, income, and employment levels in bringing about international equilibrium.

7 Under the Bretton Woods system exchange rates were pegged to one another and were stable. Participating nations were obligated to maintain these rates by using stabilization funds, gold, or borrowings from the IMF. Persistent or "fundamental" payments deficits could be resolved by IMF-sanctioned currency devaluations.

8 Since 1971 a system of managed floating exchange rates has been in use. Rates are generally set by market forces, although governments intervene with varying frequency to alter their exchange rates.

9 Between 1980 and 1991 the United States experienced large international trade deficits. Causes include **a** a rapidly appreciating dollar between 1980 and 1985; **b** relatively rapid expansion of the American economy prior to the recession of 1990–1991; and **c** curtailed purchases of our exports by the less developed countries.

10 The effects of large trade deficits have been manifold. They have had a contractionary, anti-inflationary effect on our domestic economy. American export-dependent industries have experienced declines in output, employment, and profits, thereby generating political pressures for protection. The United States has become the world's largest debtor nation. However, the trade deficit has meant a current increase in the living standards of American consumers.

11 Two solutions to the trade deficit are **a** reduction of the budget deficit and **b** faster economic growth abroad. Other "remedies" are an easy money policy, protective tariffs, recession, improved U.S. competitiveness, and direct foreign investment.

TERMS AND CONCEPTS

balance of payments
current account
credits
debits
trade balance
balance on goods and services
balance on current account
capital account
balance on the capital account
official reserves
balance of payments deficits and surpluses
fixed exchange rates
flexible or floating exchange rates
depreciation and appreciation
purchasing power parity
gold standard
gold import and export points
Bretton Woods system
International Monetary Fund
devaluation
managed floating exchange rates
G-7 nations

QUESTIONS AND STUDY SUGGESTIONS

1 Explain how an American automobile importer might finance a shipment of Toyotas from Japan. Demonstrate how an American export of machinery to Italy might be financed. Explain: "American exports earn supplies of foreign monies which Americans can use to finance imports."

2 "A rise in the dollar price of yen necessarily means a fall in the yen price of dollars." Do you agree? Illustrate and elaborate: "The critical thing about exchange rates is that they provide a direct link between the prices of goods and services produced in all trading nations of the world." Explain the purchasing power parity theory of exchange rates.

3 The Swedish auto company Saab imports car components from Germany and exports autos to the United States. In 1990 the dollar depreciated, and the German mark appreciated, relative to the Swedish krona. Speculate as to how this hurt Saab—twice.

4 Indicate whether each of the following creates a demand for, or a supply of, French francs in foreign exchange markets:

a An American importer purchases a shipload of Bordeaux wine

b A French automobile firm decides to build an assembly plant in Los Angeles

c An American college student decides to spend a year studying at the Sorbonne

d A French manufacturer exports machinery to Morocco on an American freighter

e The United States incurs a balance of payments deficit in its transactions with France

f A United States government bond held by a French citizen matures

g It is widely believed that the international value of the franc will fall in the near future

5 Explain why the American demand for Mexican pesos is downsloping and the supply of pesos to Americans is upsloping. Assuming a system of floating exchange rates between Mexico and the United States, indicate whether each of the following would cause the Mexican peso to appreciate or depreciate:

a The United States unilaterally reduces tariffs on Mexican products

b Mexico encounters severe inflation

c Deteriorating political relations reduce American tourism in Mexico

d The United States' economy moves into a severe recession

e The Board of Governors embarks on a tight money policy

f Mexican products become more fashionable to Americans

g The Mexican government invites American firms to invest in Mexican oil fields

h The rate of productivity growth in the United States diminishes sharply

6 Explain whether or not you agree with the following statements:

a "A country which grows faster than its major trading partners can expect the international value of its currency to depreciate."

b "A nation whose interest rate is rising more rapidly than in other nations can expect the international value of its currency to appreciate."

c "A country's currency will appreciate if its inflation rate is less than that of the rest of the world."

7 "Exports pay for imports. Yet in 1990 the rest of the world exported about $108 billion more worth of goods and services to the United States than were imported from the United States." Resolve the apparent inconsistency of these two statements.

8 Answer the following questions on the basis of Scorpio's balance of payments for 1993 as shown below. All figures are in billions of dollars. What is the balance of trade? The balance on goods and services? The balance on current account? The balance on capital account? Does Scorpio have a balance of payments deficit or surplus? Would you surmise that Scorpio is participating in a system of fixed or flexible exchange rates? Are Scorpio's international transactions having a contractionary or expansionary effect on its domestic economy?

Merchandise exports	**+$40**	**Net transfers**	**+$10**
Merchandise imports	**− 30**	**Capital inflows**	**+ 10**
Service exports	**+ 15**	**Capital outflows**	**− 40**
Service imports	**− 10**	**Official reserves**	**+ 10**
Net investment income	**− 5**		

9 Explain in detail how a balance of payments deficit would be resolved under **a** the gold standard, **b** the Bretton Woods system, and **c** freely floating exchange rates. What are the advantages and shortcomings of each system?

10 Outline the major costs and benefits associated with a large trade or current account deficit. Explain: "A current account deficit means we are receiving more goods and services from abroad than we are sending abroad. How can that be called 'unfavorable'?"

11 Some people assert that the United States is facing a foreign trade crisis. What do you think they mean? What are the major causes of this "crisis"?

12 Cite and explain two reasons for the decline in the international value of the dollar between 1985 and 1987. Why did the U.S. trade deficit remain high, even though the dollar fell in value?

13 Explain how a reduction in the Federal budget deficit could contribute to a decline in the U.S. trade deficit. Why do trade deficits fall during recessions? Is recession a desirable remedy to trade deficits?

The Soviet Economy in Transition

In 1957 Communist Party Chairman Nikita Khrushchev bluntly asserted that the centrally planned Soviet economy would prove itself superior to the United States economy:

> We declare war upon you—excuse me for using such an expression—in the peaceful field of trade. We declare war. We will win over the United States. The threat to the United States is not the ICBM, but in the field of peaceful production. We are relentless in this and it will prove the superiority of our system.

But in October of 1990 Soviet President Mikhail Gorbachev announced to the world that the Soviet economy was unraveling:

> The position of the economy continues to deteriorate. The volume of production is declining. Economic links are being broken. Separatism is on the increase. The consumer market is in dire straits. The budget deficit and the solvency of the government are now at critical levels. Antisocial behavior and crime are increasing. People are finding life more and more difficult and are losing their interest in work and their belief in the future. The economy is in very great danger. The old administrative system of management has been destroyed but the impetus to work under a market system is lacking. Energetic measures must be taken, with the consent of the public, to stabilize the situation and to accelerate progress towards a market economy.

In the early 1990s there was compelling evidence that the economy of the former Soviet Union was in severe disarray. Consumers were queuing up for hours to buy food and shoddy consumer goods, frequently to find only empty store shelves. One-fifth of 1991's grain production was either unharvested or left to rot because of inadequate storage and transportation. Government rationing of consumer staples was common and black markets were flourishing. Confidence in the monetary unit—the ruble—was rapidly waning and exchange by the use of such "hard" foreign currencies as dollars, yen, and marks and by barter was be-

coming commonplace. Both government budget deficits and trade deficits were substantial and rising. Official government statistics chronicled a falling real domestic output, increasing unemployment, and a rapidly rising price level.

Economic disarray has been accompanied by political turmoil. An abortive August 1991 coup pushed Soviet President Mikhail Gorbachev into the background and brought Russian Republic President Boris Yeltsin to the fore. The Baltic states—Estonia, Latvia, and Lithuania—have declared their independence. The remaining twelve republics—with the possible exception of Georgia—are attempting to align themselves in some sort of confederation. Thus, the media refers to the remaining republics as the "Commonwealth of Independent States" or the "former Soviet Union," a practice we shall adopt in this chapter. The political situation remains highly volatile. Given the ethnic conflict between Christian Armenia and Muslim Azerbaijan, civil war is not unthinkable. Nor is the resurrection of an authoritarian system similar to the fallen communist regime.

In this final chapter we will examine the economy of the former Soviet Union and the problems it now faces. Specific questions addressed are: What were the main characteristics and goals of the Soviet planned economy? Why did it fail? What must be done to achieve the transition to the market economy envisioned in Gorbachev's remarks? What are the major obstacles in implementing the transition from central planning to a market economy? What role might the United States and other western nations play in this transition?

There are important by-products of examining an economy which has been at the opposite end of the ideological and institutional spectrum. By understanding the problems and ultimate failure of Soviet communism, we cannot help but more fully understand and appreciate the functioning of our own system. It also helps us grasp the transition problems of other eastern European nations such as Poland, Hungary, and Czechoslovakia which also seek to change from central planning to market-oriented systems. Finally, there are lessons for the less developed countries, many of which sought forced economic development by emulating the Soviet system of central planning.

IDEOLOGY AND INSTITUTIONS

To understand the Soviet planned economy we must understand its ideology and institutions.

Marxian Ideology

The Communist Party, until recently the dominant force in Soviet political and economic life, viewed itself as a dictatorship of the proletariat or working class. Based on Marxism–Leninism, the Communists envisioned their system as the inevitable successor to capitalism, the latter being plagued by internal contradictions stemming from the exploitation, injustice, and insecurity which it allegedly generates.

Especially important for our purposes is the Marxian concept of a **labor theory of value**—the idea that the economic or exchange value of any commodity is determined solely by the amount of labor time required for its production. Thanks to the capitalistic institution of private property, capitalists own the machinery and equipment necessary for production in an industrial society. The propertyless working class is therefore dependent on the capitalists for employment and for its livelihood. Given the worker's inferior bargaining position and the capitalist's pursuit of profits, the capitalist will exploit labor by paying a daily wage which is much less than the value of the worker's daily production. The capitalist can and will pay workers a subsistence wage and expropriate the remaining fruits of their labor as profits, or what Marx termed **surplus value.** In the Soviet system, surplus value was to be extracted by the state as an agency of the working class and distributed in large part through subsidies to what we would call public or quasi-public goods, for example, education, transportation, health care, and housing.

The function of communism was to overthrow capitalism and replace it with a classless society within which human exploitation is absent. The Communist Party viewed itself as the vanguard of the working class, and its actions were held to be in keeping with the goals of the proletariat. In fact, it was a strong dictatorship. Many westerners characterized the Soviet government as a dictatorship *over* the proletariat, rather than *of* the proletariat.

Institutions

The two outstanding institutional characteristics of the Soviet economy were: (1) state ownership of property resources, and (2) authoritarian central economic planning.

State Ownership **State ownership** meant the Soviet state owned all land, natural resources, transportation and communication facilities, the banking system, and virtually all industry. Most retail and wholesale enterprises and most urban housing were governmentally owned. In agriculture many farms were state-owned; most, however, were government-organized collective farms, that is, essentially cooperatives to which the state assigned land "for free use for an unlimited time." An exception to state ownership was the small plot of land which each state collective farm family had set aside for its personal use. Workers in factories also had the use of small plots of land.

Central Economic Planning **Central economic planning,** in contrast with the decentralized market economy of the United States, meant that the Soviet Union had a centralized "command" economy functioning in terms of a detailed economic plan. The Soviet economy was government-directed rather than market-directed. Choices made primarily through the market in our United States' economy were made by bureaucratic decision in the U.S.S.R. The overall character of the Soviet Five-year Plans has been succinctly described in these words:

> The Soviet economic plan is a gigantic, comprehensive blueprint that attempts to govern the economic activities and interrelations of all persons and institutions in the U.S.S.R., as well as the economic relations of the U.S.S.R. with other countries. To the extent that the plan actually controls the development of events, all the manifold activities of the Soviet economy are coordinated as if they were parts of one incredibly enormous enterprise directed from the central headquarters in Moscow.[1]

CENTRAL PLANNING AND ITS PROBLEMS

The Soviet system of central planning was put in place in the late 1920s and early 1930s. Although occasional reforms were experimented with in the 1950s and 1960s, the system remained fundamentally unchanged for almost seven decades.

Ends and Means

The following generalizations describe how Soviet planning has functioned historically.

1 Industrialization and Military Strength The economy of the former Soviet Union has been described as "totalitarianism harnessed to the task of rapid industrialization and economic growth."[2] Planning goals put heavy emphasis on rapid industrialization and military strength. This was achieved through extensive investment in heavy industries—steel, chemicals, and machine tools—and the allocation of a large percentage of domestic output to the military. As a consequence, development of consumer goods industries, the distribution and service sectors, and the infrastructure were neglected.

2 Resource Overcommitment Production increases sought in the various Soviet Five-year Plans were very ambitious, tending to overcommit the economy's available resources. As a result, not all planning targets could be achieved. And, as already suggested, Soviet planning priorities were to achieve those goals associated with heavy industry and the military at the expense of consumption.

3 Resource Mobilization Industrialization and rapid economic growth were initially achieved through mobilization of labor, capital, and raw materials. In the

[1]Harry Schwartz, *Russia's Soviet Economy,* 2d ed. (Englewood Cliffs, N.J.: Prentice-Hall, Inc., 1954), p. 146.

[2]Robert W. Campbell, *The Soviet-type Economies,* 3d ed. (Boston: Houghton Mifflin Company, 1974), p. 3. Also see Campbell's *The Socialist Economies in Transition: A Primer on Semi-Reformed Systems* (Bloomington: Indiana University Press, 1991).

early years of planning there was substantial surplus labor in agriculture which the plans reallocated to industrial production. Similarly, a larger proportion of the population was induced or coerced into the labor force. Early Soviet growth was achieved through the use of more inputs rather than using given inputs more productively. In the 1930s and again in the early post-World War II era, this strategy produced growth rates greater than the United States and other industrialized nations.

4 Allocation by Directives Soviet central planners directed the allocation of inputs among industries and firms, thereby determining the composition of output. Planning directives were substituted for the market or price system as an allocational mechanism.

5 Government Price Fixing In the former Soviet Union prices were set by government direction rather than by the forces of demand and supply. Consumer good prices were changed infrequently and, as a matter of social policy, the prices of "necessities"—for example, housing and many foodstuffs—were established at low levels. Rents on Soviet housing averaged only about 3 percent of income and did not change between 1928 and 1992! Input prices and the price of an enterprise's output were also governmentally determined and were used primarily as accounting devices to gauge a firm's progress in meeting its production target.

6 Self-Sufficiency The Soviet Union viewed itself as a single socialist nation surrounded by hostile capitalistic countries. Therefore, the central plans stressed economic self-sufficiency. Trade with western nations was greatly restricted because the ruble was not convertible into other currencies. Soviet trade was largely with the other communist bloc nations of eastern Europe.

7 Passive Macroeconomic Policies The Soviet economy has been a quantity-directed system with money and prices playing only a limited role in resource allocation. Unlike most market economies, monetary and fiscal policies were passive rather than active in the Soviet Union. In the United States and other market systems, monetary and fiscal policies are used to manipulate the aggregate levels of output, employment, and prices. Historically, unemployment in the Soviet Union has been kept very low, perhaps only 1 or 2 percent of the labor force. This is partly the result of ambitious planning targets and various admonitions to work. Low unemployment has also been due to overstaffing (managers cannot fire redundant workers), a disinterest in cost-minimization (gross output being the overriding objective), and a population whose growth rate has been steadily diminishing.

Similarly, government price determination was the primary device used to control the price level. The state banking system, *Gosbank,* issued credit or working capital to enterprises, based on what was needed to fulfill their planned production targets. But it did not use, and did not have the control mechanisms, to manipulate the money supply to achieve macroeconomic stability.

The Coordination Problem

The market system is a powerful organizing force which coordinates millions of individual decisions by consumers, resources suppliers, and businesses, and fosters a reasonably efficient allocation of scarce resources. It is not an easy matter to substitute central planning as a coordinating mechanism.

A simple example illustrates this problem. Suppose a Soviet enterprise in Minsk is producing men's shoes. Planners must establish a realistic production target for that enterprise and then see that all the necessary inputs—labor, electric power, leather, rubber, thread, nails, appropriate machinery, transportation—for production and delivery of that product are made available. When we move from a simple product such as shoes to more complex products such as television sets and farm tractors, planners' allocational problems are greatly compounded.

Because the outputs of many industries are inputs to other industries, the failure of any single industry to fulfill its output target is likely to cause a whole chain of adverse repercussions. If iron mines—for want of machinery or labor or transportation inputs—fail to supply the steel industry with the required inputs of iron ore, the steel industry in turn will be unable to fulfill the input needs of the myriad industries dependent on steel. All these steel-using industries—for example, automobiles, tractors, and transportation—will therefore be unable to fulfill their planned production goals. And so the bottleneck chain reaction goes on to all those firms which use steel parts or components as inputs.

There were some 47,000 industrial enterprises producing goods in the former Soviet Union. The central planners had to see that all the resources needed by these enterprises to fulfill their assigned production targets were somehow allocated to them.

> The literally billions of planning decisions that must be made to achieve consistency result in a complex

> and complete interlocking of macro- and micro- management . . . . The number of planned interconnections increases more rapidly than the size of the economy . . . . Even with the most sophisticated mathematical techniques and electronic computers, the task of interrelating demands and factor inputs for every possible item by every possible subcategory becomes impossible for the central planners alone.[3]

There is much evidence from Soviet sources indicating that bottlenecks occurred with alarming regularity in the 1980s and early 1990s. Moreover, bottlenecks were nothing new to the Soviet economy.

> The Byelorussian Tractor Factory, which has 227 suppliers, had its production line stopped 19 times in 1962 because of the lack of rubber parts, 18 times because of ball bearings, and 8 times because of transmission components. The pattern of breakdowns continued in 1963. During the first quarter of 1963 only about one-half of the plant's ball bearing and rubber needs were satisfied, and only half of the required batteries were available. One supplier shipped 19,000 less wheels than called for in the contract. In total, they were short of 27 different items. . . .
>
> It is not surprising that 90 enterprises out of 100 surveyed in the Chelyabinsk region blamed their underfulfillment of production plans in 1962 on supply deficiencies.[4]

QUICK REVIEW 26-1

- ***Marxian ideology is based on the labor theory of value and views capitalism as a system for expropriating profits or surplus value from workers.***
- ***The primary institutional features of the former Soviet economy were state ownership of property resources and central economic planning.***
- ***Soviet plans were characterized by a an emphasis on rapid industrialization and military power, b resource overcommitment; c growth through the use of more inputs rather than greater efficiency; d resource allocation by government directives rather than markets; e government price determination; f an emphasis on economic self-sufficiency; and g passive monetary and fiscal policies.***
- ***The basic planning problem is to direct needed resources to each enterprise so that production targets can be achieved.***

THE FAILURE OF SOVIET COMMUNISM

Soviet economic growth in the 1950s and 1960s was impressive. In the 1950s Soviet real domestic output expanded at roughly 6 percent per year compared to about 3 percent for the United States. The Soviet economy continued to grow at about 5 percent per year in the 1960s. But growth fell to an annual rate of about $2\frac{1}{2}$ or 3 percent in the 1970s and further declined to 2 percent by the mid-1980s. More recent data indicate that growth has halted and in the last few years real domestic output has declined. Official Soviet estimates indicate that real domestic output fell by 4 percent in 1990 and 14 percent in 1991.

Further evidence of economic failure is reflected in the quality of goods. In such vital manufacturing sectors as computers and machine tools it is estimated that Soviet technology lags some seven to twelve years behind that of the United States. Overall, the quality of most Soviet manufactured goods is far short of international standards. Consumer goods are of notoriously poor quality and product assortment is greatly limited. Durable goods— automobiles, refrigerators, and consumer electronics products—are primitive by world standards. Furthermore, widespread shortages of basic goods, interminable shopper queues, black markets, and corruption in the distribution of products are all characteristic of the consumer sector.

The major contributing factor to the downfall of Soviet communism has been its inability to efficiently supply the goods and services which consumers want to buy. In the early decades of Soviet communism the government established a "social contract" with its citizenry to the effect that, by enduring the consumer sacrifices associated with the high rates of saving and investment necessary for rapid industrialization and growth, the population would be rewarded with consumer abundance in the future (Figure 2-4). The failure of the system to meet consumer expectations has contributed to frustration and deteriorating morale among consumers and workers. "All future and no present, certainly as in the USSR after six decades, begins to appear after a while more like a long term confidence game than a meaningful program of economic development."[5]

Comparisons with the United States are revealing. While the United States has 565 cars and 789 tele-

[3]Barry M. Richman, *Soviet Management* (Englewood Cliffs, N.J.: Prentice-Hall, Inc., 1965), p. 17.

[4]Ibid., p. 123.

[5]Marshall I. Goldman, *USSR in Crisis: The Failure of an Economic System* (New York: W. W. Norton & Company, 1983), p. 175.

phones per 1000 people, the former Soviet Union has only 46 cars and 124 phones for each 1000 citizens. Overall, Soviet per capita consumption is less than 30 percent of that achieved in the United States. When qualitative deficiencies in Soviet goods and services and the cost of time spent searching for goods and waiting in queues are taken into account, this figure may overstate Soviet consumption levels.

Causes of the Collapse

Having chronicled the deteriorating performance of the economy of the former Soviet Union, we now consider causes. The following interrelated factors have contributed to the collapse of the Soviet system.

1 Military Burden Large Soviet military expenditures of 15 to 20 percent of domestic output—compared to 6 percent for the United States—absorbed great quantities of resources which would otherwise have been available for the production of consumer and investment goods. During the extended cold war era it was the government's policy to channel superior management and the best scientists and engineers to defense and space research, which undoubtedly adversely affected technological progress and the quality (productivity) of investment in the civilian sector.

2 Agricultural Drag By western standards agriculture in the former Soviet Union is something of a monument to inefficiency and is a drag on economic growth, engulfing some 30 percent of the labor force and roughly one-fourth of annual investment. Furthermore, output per worker is only 10 to 25 percent of the United States' level. The low productivity of Soviet agriculture is attributable to many factors: relative scarcity of good land; vagaries in rainfall and length of growing season; serious errors in planning and administration; and, perhaps most important, the failure to construct an effective incentive system.

Once a major exporter of grain and other agricultural products, the former Soviet Union has recently become one of the world's largest importers of agricultural commodities. Indeed, agricultural imports have been a serious drain on foreign currency reserves which its leadership would prefer to use in financing imports of western capital goods and technology.

3 More Inputs versus Increased Efficiency Much of the former Soviet Union's rapid growth in the early decades of central planning was the result of simply using more labor, capital, and land in the production process. But in recent years this means of increasing real domestic output has been virtually exhausted. Soviet labor force participation rates are among the highest in the world so there is little or no opportunity to recruit more workers. Furthermore, population and labor force growth have slowed significantly. While the annual average increase in the labor force was about 1.5 percent in the 1970s, it slowed to about 0.6 percent in the 1980s, and no growth is forecast for the 1990s. Similarly, the percentage of domestic output devoted to investment is comparatively high and could only be increased by reducing the proportion of output devoted to consumption. Given the comparatively low standard of living in the former Soviet Union, it would be extremely unpopular and politically difficult to further increase the input of capital goods at the expense of consumption. Also, natural conditions limit the availability of additional farmland. Indeed, occasional attempts to bring more land of marginal quality into crop production has been counterproductive in that yields have been minimal and the land has been lost to grazing.

The alternative to growth through the use of more inputs is to increase the productivity or efficiency of available inputs. But this is universally recognized as a much more complex and difficult means of achieving economic growth. Productivity growth requires, among other things, modern capital equipment, innovation and technological progress, and strong material incentives for workers and managers—none of which have been characteristic of the traditional Soviet planning system. Indeed, labor productivity in the former Soviet Union is estimated to be only 35 to 40 percent that of American workers.

4 Planning Problems The problem of centrally coordinating economic activity becomes much more complex as an economy grows and develops. Early planning under Stalin in the 1930s and 1940s resembled the simple World War II planning of western capitalist nations. A few key production goals were established and resources were centrally directed toward fulfillment of those goals regardless of costs or consumer welfare. But the past success of such "campaign planning" has resulted in a more complex, industrially advanced economy. Products are now more sophisticated and complex and there are more industries for which to plan. The planning techniques which were workable in the Stalinist era were inadequate and inefficient in the more advanced Soviet economy of the past two decades. In a sense, the Soviet economy had outgrown its planning mechanisms.

> Over time the inherent inefficiency of a command-administered economic system has come to dominate its effectiveness in achieving the priority objectives of the central authorities. Methods and institutions that were effective at an earlier, simpler stage of development no longer generate the desired outcomes. The mobilization of resources and effort that produced collectivization, industrialization, and a sizable chemical industry failed to develop modern computer technology, or to modernize consumer goods industries. The administrative superstructure, methods of planning, and plans themselves have become ever less adequate to the needs and flow of economic activity. The natural consequence is an increase in dysfunctional behavior by subordinates, increasingly obvious microeconomic waste and inefficiency, slowing (or declining) economic growth and productivity, and ever more frequent failures to achieve proclaimed priorities.[6]

5 Inadequate Success Indicators Market economies have a single, comprehensive success indicator—profits. Each firm's success or failure is measured by its profits or losses. As we know, profits depend on consumer demand, production efficiency, and product quality.

In contrast, the major success indicator of a Soviet enterprise was its fulfillment of a quantitative production target assigned by the central planners. This generated inefficient practices because production costs, product quality, and product-mix became secondary considerations at best. Achieving least-cost production is nearly impossible without a system of genuine market prices accurately reflecting the relative scarcity of various resources. Product quality was frequently sacrificed by managers and workers who were awarded bonuses for fulfilling quantitative, not qualitative, targets. If meeting production goals of a television or automobile manufacturing plan meant sloppy assembly work, so be it.

Finally, it is difficult for planners to assign quantitative production targets without unintentionally producing ridiculous distortions in output. If an enterprise manufacturing nails specifies its production target in weight (tons of nails), it will tend to produce all large nails. But if its target is a quantity (thousands of nails), it will be motivated to use available inputs to produce all small nails. The obvious problem is that the economy needs *both* large and small nails.

6 Incentive Problems Perhaps the main deficiency of central planning has been the lack of economic incentives. The market systems of western economies have built-in signals resulting in the efficient use of resources. Profits and losses generate incentives for firms and industries to increase or decrease production. If a product is in short supply, its price and profitability will increase and producers will be motivated to expand production. Conversely, surplus supply means falling prices and profits and a reduction in output. Successful innovations in the form of either product quality or production techniques are sought because of their profitability. Greater work effort by labor means higher money incomes which can be translated into a higher real standard of living.

These actions and adjustments do not occur under central planning. The output-mix of the former Soviet economy was determined by the central planners. If their judgments as to the quantities of automobiles, razor blades, underwear, and vodka wanted by the populace at governmentally determined prices were incorrect, there would be persistent shortages and surpluses of products. But the managers who oversaw the production of these goods were rewarded for fulfilling their assigned production goals; they had no incentive to adjust production in response to product shortages or surpluses. And they did not have changes in prices and profitability to signal that more or less of each product was desired. Thus in the former Soviet Union many products were in short supply, while other unwanted goods languished in warehouses.

Incentives to innovate were almost entirely absent; indeed, innovation was often resisted. Soviet enterprises were essentially governmentally owned monopolies. As a result, there was no private gain to managers or workers for improving product quality or developing more efficient production techniques. Historically, government-imposed innovations were resisted by enterprise managers and workers. The reason was that new production processes were usually accompanied by higher and unrealistic production targets, underfulfillment, and loss of bonuses.

Innovation also lagged because there was no competition. New firms could not come into being to introduce better products, superior managerial techniques, or more efficient productive methods. Similarly, the Soviet goal of economic self-sufficiency isolated its enterprises from the competitive pressures of interna-

[6]Richard E. Ericson, "The Classical Soviet-Type Economy: Nature of the System and Implications for Reform," *Journal of Economic Perspectives,* Fall 1991, p. 23.

tional markets. In general, over an extended period Soviet enterprises produced the same products with the same techniques, with both goods and techniques becoming increasingly obsolete by world standards.

Nor were individual workers motivated to work hard, because of a lack of material incentives. Because of the low priority assigned to consumer goods in the Five-year Plans, there was only a limited array of relatively low-quality goods and services available to Soviet workers–consumers. (The price of an automobile is far beyond the means of average factory workers, and for those able to buy, the waiting period may be one to five years.) While hard work might result in promotions and bonuses, the increase in *money* income did not translate into a proportionate increase in *real* income. As we will note later, there was a substantial amount of involuntary saving—a "ruble overhang"—in the Soviet Union because of a lack of consumer goods. Why work hard for additional income if there is nothing to buy with the money you earn? As a Soviet worker once lamented to a western journalist: "The government pretends to pay us and we pretend to work."

THE GORBACHEV REFORMS

The deteriorating Soviet economy of the 1970s and early 1980s prompted President Mikhail Gorbachev to introduce in 1986 a reform program described as **perestroika,** a restructuring of the economy. This economic restructuring was accompanied by **glasnost,** a campaign for greater openness and democratization in both political and economic affairs. Under *glasnost,* workers, consumers, enterprise managers, political leaders, and others were provided greater opportunity to voice complaints and make suggestions for improving the functioning of the economy.

Basically, the **Gorbachev reforms** involved six interrelated elements: (1) the modernization of industry; (2) greater decentralization of decision making; (3) provision for a limited private enterprise sector; (4) improved worker discipline and incentives; (5) a more rational price system; (6) an enlarged role in the international economy.

Modernization was sought through reallocation of investment toward research and development and toward high-tech industries. Decentralization of decision making was intended to keep the planning bureaucracy from interfering in the day-to-day internal operations of individual enterprises. In exchange for greater enterprise autonomy, enterprise success indicators were reoriented from output targets to profitability, thus obligating enterprises to be more conscious of the salability (quality) of their products.

Small-scale private production of some consumer goods and services—such as clothing, furniture, rugs, taxi transport, hairdressing, and appliance repair—was also permitted. But those engaged in such activities also had to hold full-time state jobs or be housewives or retirees. The size of these private enterprises was limited by the Marxist prohibition on hiring someone else's labor.

The Gorbachev reforms also attempted to improve the human factors in production. Actions were taken to dismiss incompetent planners and enterprise managers, trim the size of the planning bureaucracies, and improve worker attitudes and behavior. Campaigns against corruption and alcoholism would reduce inefficiency resulting from theft, absenteeism, industrial accidents, and high worker turnover.

Price reforms would reduce over time the number of prices fixed by central planning with such prices ultimately applying only to what was regarded as the most essential consumer and producer goods. Enterprises were to be able to negotiate sales contracts in much the same manner as capitalist firms.

The reforms also hinted at closer economic relationships with the industrialized nations of the west. A related effort was to encourage joint ventures in the Soviet Union with western firms in a wide variety of activities ranging from fast-food restaurants to construction and operation of petrochemical plants. Such ventures were undoubtedly viewed by the Soviets as an inexpensive means of acquiring western technologies and management skills.

While *perestroika* met with some initial success, it did not comprehensively address the systemic economic problems facing the Soviet Union. In retrospect, *perestroika* was more in the nature of traditional Soviet "campaigns" to elicit better performance within the general framework of the planned economy. It was *not* an overall program of institutional change such as those adopted by Poland and Hungary. Thus, in 1986–1987 the Soviet economy was stagnating; some estimates put its growth rate at only 2 percent per year, while others indicated it did not grow at all. Sharply declining world oil prices also were damaging because the Soviet Union is a major oil exporter. In any event, by 1990 *perestroika* had given way to a greater emphasis on sweeping reforms designed to create a western-style market economy.

QUICK REVIEW 26-2

- ***The failure of central planning in the former Soviet Union was evidenced by diminished growth rates, low-quality goods, and the failure to provide a rising standard of living.***
- ***The recent collapse of the Soviet economy is attributable to a a large military burden; b chronic inefficiencies in agriculture; c the need to expand real output by increasing input productivity rather than increasing the quantity of inputs; d the inability of traditional planning techniques to deal with the growing complexity of the Soviet economy; e inadequate success indicators; and f ineffectual incentives to produce, innovate, and work.***
- ***The Gorbachev reforms of the late 1980s centered on*** **perestroika** ***("restructuring") and*** **glasnost** ***("openness") but failed to provide major systemic change.***

TRANSITION TO A MARKET SYSTEM

The former Soviet republics—particularly Russia—have committed themselves to making the transition to a market economy. What are the components of such a dramatic reform program?

Privatization

If entrepreneurship is to come into existence, private property rights must be established and protected by law. This means that existing government property—farmland, housing, factories, machinery and equipment, stores—must be transferred to private owners. It also means that new private firms must be allowed to form and develop.

It is not yet clear how this can be effectively and equitably accomplished, but there are a number of options. Small enterprises and retail outlets might be sold directly to private individuals or cooperatives through public auctions. Another possibility is employee stock ownership plans where workers, aided by government loans, buy an enterprise and then retire their debt from future earnings. The privatization of large state enterprises may be more difficult. One proposal is for the government to distribute vouchers, each having a designated monetary value, to all citizens. Owners of these vouchers can then pool them in the purchase of enterprises. An interim option is the "commercialization" of Soviet enterprises, meaning that the firm is made financially and managerially independent but remains publicly owned. Privatization is made more complex because it is difficult to determine the economic value of an enterprise in the absence of genuine product and resource prices.

Promotion of Competition

The industrial sector of the former Soviet Union consisted of some 47,000 large state-owned enterprises in which average employment exceeded 800 workers. An estimated 30 to 40 percent of total industrial production comprised products for which there was only one producer. When several enterprises produce a given product, their actions were usually coordinated by the planning process to create a cartel. In short, much Commonwealth production took place under monopoly or near-monopoly conditions.

Realization of a reasonably efficient market economy requires the dismantling of these public monopolies and the creation of antitrust laws to sustain competition. Privatization without "demonopolization" will be of limited benefit to the economy. Existing monopolies must be restructured or split apart as separate, competing firms. For example, a tractor manufacturing enterprise with four plants could be separated into four independent and competing firms. The establishment and guarantee of property rights are prerequisite to the creation and entry of new firms into previously monopolized industries. Joint ventures between Commonwealth and foreign companies provide a further avenue for increasing competition, as does opening the economy to international trade. Recent legislation has opened the door for foreign firms to invest directly in the new Commonwealth.

Limited and Reoriented Role for Government

The transition to a market economy will sharply curtail government's economic role. The government must reduce its involvement to those tasks associated with a market economy: providing an appropriate legal framework; maintaining competition; reducing excessive inequality in the distribution of income and wealth; making market adjustments where spillover costs or benefits are large; providing public goods and services; and stabilizing the economy (Chapter 6).

Many of these functions will be new to the governments within the Commonwealth, at least in the environment of a market system. Unemployment and overt inflation were not evident to Soviet citizens under central planning. Historically, ambitious production plans and overstaffing of enterprises have made for very low unemployment rates while government price-setting has been a direct means of controlling the price level. The task will be to develop monetary and fiscal policies—and institutional arrangements appropriate to their implementation—to indirectly provide macroeconomic stability. Restructuring will likely result in substantial short-run unemployment as inefficient public enterprises are closed or fail to be viable under private ownership. Thus, a priority goal will be to establish a social safety net for Soviet citizens. In particular, a program of unemployment insurance must be established, not only on equity grounds but also to reduce worker resistance to the transition. Similarly, antitrust legislation of some sort will be needed to maintain reasonably competitive markets.

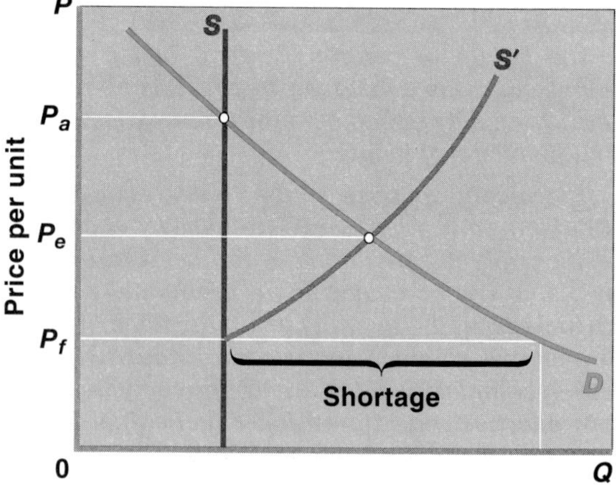

FIGURE 26-1 The effects of government price fixing

Central planners establish below-equilibrium prices such as P_f on many basic consumer goods to make them widely available to everyone. But in fact at such low prices quantity demanded exceeds quantity supplied and this shortage means that many consumers cannot obtain such goods. Assuming no privatization, abandonment of government price fixing would raise price from P_f to P_a. With privatization and an accompanying increase in output as price rises, price would increase from P_f to P_e. In either event, the decontrol of prices can be expected to be inflationary.

Price Reform: Removing Controls

Unlike competitive market prices, the prices established by the government bear no relationship to the economic value of either products or resources. In an effectively functioning competitive market system the price of a product equates, at the margin, the value consumers place on that good and the value of the resources used in its production. When free markets achieve this equality for all goods and services, the economy's scarce resources are being used efficiently to satisfy consumer wants.

But, as noted, in the former Soviet Union both input and output prices were fixed by government and in many instances were not changed for extended periods of time. Because input prices did not measure the relative scarcities of various resources, it was impossible for a firm to minimize real production costs. That is, with fixed prices it is impossible to produce a unit of X in such a way as to minimize sacrifice of alternative goods. Example: Relatively high energy prices have caused firms in market economies to curtail its use. But energy has been underpriced in the former Soviet Union (the world's largest producer of energy) and its industries use two to three times as much energy per unit of output as do leading industrial countries.

A difficult problem arises in making the transition from government- to market-determined prices because historically the prices of many basic consumer goods have been fixed at low levels. The Soviet rationale for this was that low prices would ensure everyone ready access to such goods. As Figure 26-1 shows, this pricing policy helps explain the chronic product shortages and long queues which frustrate consumers in the former Soviet Union. The perfectly inelastic supply curve *S* reflects the fixed output of, say, shoes for which the plan provides. (Disregard supply curve *S*′ for the moment.) The demand curve slopes downward as it would in a market economy. Given *S*, the equilibrium price would be P_a. But in an effort to make shoes accessible to those with lower incomes, the government fixes the price at P_f.

However, Figure 26-1 makes clear that not everyone who wants shoes at price P_f will be able to obtain them. At P_f quantity demanded is substantially greater than quantity supplied, so there is excess demand or, in other words, a shortage. This explains the long, impatient lines of consumers and the empty shelves we saw in television news clips of Soviet shoppers. It is no surprise that black markets—illegal markets where goods are sold at much higher prices than those fixed by the government—were widespread in the former Soviet Union.

Given that Figure 26-1 was characteristic of most Soviet markets, it is obvious that the transition to free markets poses a serious inflationary problem. Without privatization, shoe prices will rise from P_f to P_a when the market for shoes is decontrolled. Similarly, prices will rise for butter, soap, meat, housing, vodka, and a host of other goods. With privatization, this runup of prices will be dampened somewhat by the extra output induced by the rising prices. As shown by supply curve S' in Figure 26-1, private producers will respond to higher prices by increasing quantity supplied. Nevertheless, prices will rise substantially, as from P_f to P_e. An important need during the transition period will be to control inflationary pressures through appropriate macroeconomic policies. The prospect of rampant inflation is an important reason why many Soviet citizens are apprehensive about the transition to a market economy.

In January of 1992 Boris Yeltsin unilaterally decontrolled prices in the Russian Republic. Prices on many products tripled or quadrupled overnight. His strategy is based on the expectation that higher prices will induce farms to supply in the market foodstuffs they are now hoarding and thereby ease growing food shortages. But if inflation continues, the needed food may be withheld in the anticipation of still higher prices.

Joining the World Economy

The Soviet Union was largely isolated from the world economy for almost three-quarters of a century. A key aspect of transition is to open the economy to international trade and finance.

One basic task is to make the ruble a convertible currency, meaning that it must be exchangeable for other foreign currencies. Convertibility is necessary for the former Soviet Union to achieve an enlarged role in international trade and finance. Firms cannot buy from or sell to the former Soviet Union unless a realistic exchange rate is established for the ruble (Chapter 25). Nor can western firms be expected to invest in the former Soviet Union unless they are certain that rubles can be exchanged for dollars. American and other western firms want their profits in dollars, yen, pounds, and marks, not rubles.

Opening the Soviet economy to world trade will be beneficial because world markets are important sources of competition and a means of acquiring much-needed superior technologies from industrially advanced capitalist nations. Liberalized international trade will put pressure on privatized Soviet firms to produce efficiently products which meet world quality standards. Furthermore, free world trade will allow the former Soviet Union to realize the benefits from production based on comparative advantage—income gains which its isolation has long denied it.

Macroeconomic Stability

Unfortunately, the transition to free markets can be accompanied by high rates of inflation. There are several reasons for this.

1 Decontrolling Prices As just discussed (Figure 26-1), the government has kept consumer prices artificially low for decades. Decontrol of these prices will result in a substantially higher price level. If workers respond by demanding and receiving higher nominal wages, a serious and prolonged price-wage spiral could result.

2 Ruble Overhang In what is called the **ruble overhang,** Soviet households have stored massive amounts of currency and deposits at savings banks during years of waiting for scarce consumer goods to become more abundant. Historically, consumer prices fixed at low levels and restricted supplies of consumer goods gave consumers no other choice but to save. This ruble overhang—estimated to be 250 billion rubles—could generate an inflationary surge when prices are decontrolled and more goods begin to appear in consumer markets.

3 Inflationary Finance The most important potential source of inflation is the recent financing of government deficits by printing additional currency. The Soviet government incurred large deficits in the late 1980s and early 1990s, the result of two considerations. First, the main source of government revenue is the *turnover tax,* which is essentially an excise tax of varying amounts on consumer goods. Because of the stagnation and decline of economic activity, revenues from the turnover tax have declined. Second, given the uncertainty as to the future of the Soviet Union as a political entity, the various republics have withheld their tax collections from the central government.

The consequence is that the central government has incurred substantial deficits which it has financed by the expedient of printing and distributing additional rubles. This is the most inflationary form of government finance and a potential cause of hyperinflation. More money chasing a diminishing amount of goods is a classic inflationary scenario. In fact, in late 1991 Soviet economists estimated that inflation was occurring at almost a 100 percent annual rate and accelerating.

The problem is that an environment of high and volatile inflation greatly complicates achieving other components of transition. The purchase of formerly public enterprises by private buyers, the establishing of a convertible ruble, and the encouragement of both domestic and foreign investment to modernize the economy are all more difficult with the uncertainties posed by a rapidly rising price level.

CAN THE TRANSITION BE IMPLEMENTED?

What are the prospects for transforming the former Soviet economy from central planning to a market system? It is not difficult to list obstacles to such a transformation.

Technical Problems

Our discussion of the components of the transition to a market economy has touched on many of the technical economic problems involved. How can the state efficiently and equitably divest itself of public enterprises? How is an effective degree of competition to be achieved and maintained in an economy which has been dominated by public monopolies for some seven decades? Can government create an effective unemployment insurance program, a workable system of antitrust laws, consumer protection legislation, and the legal framework to protect private property and enterprise? Will it be possible to create the institutions and mechanisms needed to implement monetary and fiscal policies? How can the potential inflationary effects of the ruble overhang be offset?

Public Support: Attitudes and Values

The reforms comprising the transition from central planning to a market system must have wide public support. Consider some of the potential difficulties.

1 Bureaucratic Resistance The reforms threaten the jobs and status of many former party members and bureaucrats. These individuals continue in many instances to have positions of power and prestige and therefore have a strong interest in maintaining the status quo. Ironically, there is fear that those most likely to have access to Soviet enterprises and other assets will be those very same bureaucrats who formerly administered the failed system of central planning.

2 Worker Incentives Under a system of capitalist incentives most workers and managers will be required to be more disciplined and to work harder and more productively. This may be difficult to accept in an economy which historically has served consumers–workers poorly. Money wage increases do not provide incentives without corresponding improvements in the quantity and quality of housing, food, and other consumer goods and services.

Some observers say that many citizens in the former Soviet Union and other communist nations have acquired work habits and personality traits which will only change slowly. These include working at a leisurely pace, avoiding responsibility, resistance to innovation and change, stressing output quantity over quality, and promotion based on connections and party affiliation rather than productive efficiency. It may be wishful thinking to assume that the Soviet populace is imbued with a strong work ethic and a latent entrepreneurial spirit, and that these attributes will emerge when the heavy hand of central planning is removed. The Soviet citizenry has been indoctrinated for some seventy years regarding the evils of private property, profits, and capitalist enterprise. The "mental residue" of communism may not be easily removed.

The Political Problem: National Disintegration

At this time (early 1992), the political status of the former Soviet republics is unclear. The Baltic states have declared themselves independent nations and the Georgian Republic may follow suit. It is uncertain at this point as to the nature of the future political alignment, if any, which may evolve among the remaining republics.

What is vital to the success of the transition process is that the republics *not* become separate and distinct *economic* entities. The worst scenario would be that each republic establish its own currency, its own external tariffs and import quotas, its own banking and tax systems and its own economic laws and policies. By becoming distinct economic units the advantages of specialization based on comparative advantage would be partially sacrificed and each political unit would suffer diminished domestic output.

In fact, diminishing trade between the republics in 1991 contributed to the former Soviet Union's economic and political deterioration. Given impending food shortages, the Ukraine (the main agricultural producer among the republics) stopped food shipments to other republics to conserve stocks for its own citizens. Other republics adopted similar policies. Azerbaijan curtailed its shipments of oil-drilling equipment to the Russian Republic and the latter responded by stopping oil shipments to Azerbaijan. An "every republic for itself" policy could be especially devastating because an estimated 40 percent of Soviet industrial production comes from state monopolies. For example, if for some curious reason Ford should decide not to sell its autos in Illinois, there is no doubt that General Motors and Chrysler, along with foreign producers, would be more than pleased to serve the market. But when Azerbaijan cuts off shipments of oil-drilling equipment to Russia, no alternative domestic source of that equipment is available.

A related point is that the transition process will be greatly facilitated by the influx of foreign investment. This will not occur until the former Soviet Union demonstrates political stability and continuity.

The Simultaneity Problem

A more subtle problem is that the components of reform must be pursued, not piecemeal, but more or less simultaneously. Reform components are interlinked; not to move forward on all fronts is to enhance the prospects for failure. Examples: Private ownership will do little to increase productive efficiency unless prices are reformed to accurately measure relative scarcities. Privatization—the selling off of state enterprises—may be helpful in reducing budget deficits. When market prices for inputs and output are unknown, it is extremely difficult to determine the value of an enterprise when it is being privatized. The creation of a more competitive environment depends significantly on the economy being opened to world trade and foreign investment.

Positive Factors

There are also several positive factors which may facilitate the plan-to-market economy transition.

1 Natural Resource Base The former Soviet Union has a generous and varied natural resource base. Although differing significantly in composition, the natural resources of the Commonwealth are roughly comparable with those of the United States. The Commonwealth comprises about one-sixth of the earth's land mass and its resources include gold, diamonds, timber, oil, and natural gas. Its population is 288 million, compared to 252 million for the United States.

2 Peace Dividend The end of the cold war will allow Russia, the Ukraine, and other former Soviet republics to reduce their heavy commitment of resources to the military and to reallocate freed resources to the civilian sector. Westerners estimate that a 50 percent reduction in military spending could save $90 billion per year. Recent arms agreements with the United States and its allies, the withdrawal of Soviet troops from Afghanistan, and reductions in the size of the Red army have been motivated by the desire to revitalize the lagging economy.

3 The "Second Economy" For years the former Soviet Union has had a thriving underground or "second" economy. Black markets where scarce goods sell at two or three times government-fixed prices were widespread. Peasants "borrowed" government fertilizer to use on their "private" plots of ground. Physicians stole medicines for their unofficial private practices. Plant managers hired "expediters" to illegally obtain needed inputs which the planning system failed to supply. The point is that all of these second economy activities reflected a degree of initiative and entrepreneurship which could be legal and useful in a market economy.

4 Democratization Democratization and, more specifically, freedom from the ideological baggage of the Communist Party, is a prerequisite for the transition to capitalism. The Communist Party was created to abolish private property, free enterprise, and genuine markets. It would be unrealistic to expect the Party to reverse these accomplishments. The Soviet Union under *glasnost* has made great strides toward democratization in the past several years. The dissolution of the Communist Party in 1991 was as significant economically as it was politically.

ROLE OF ADVANCED CAPITALIST NATIONS

What might the world's industrialized capitalist nations do to facilitate the Soviet plan-to-market economy metamorphosis?

LAST WORD

OBITUARY: THE SOVIET UNION

Contradictions of the world's first communist state killed Marx's vision of a free and prosperous society.

The Soviet Union is dead. It was 74.

Marketed as utopia, run by slogan and fear, it blended genuine achievement with elaborate facade. It created a system whose top priority seemed to be concealing its own failings.

Foreigners, intimidated by its military prowess and obsessive secrecy, frequently overestimated its strength. Its own citizens, bombarded by buoyant propaganda as they went about their harsh existence, sometimes had no idea if their lives were really growing better or worse.

Irony and artifice were everywhere. The Soviet Union led the world in production of steel, oil, tractors and locomotives, all as it moved inexorably to economic ruin.

Construction crews competed to build whole apartment buildings in a month, a week, a day. Yet the Soviet dream of abolishing "communal apartments," where three or four families had to share a tiny kitchen and toilet, was never achieved.

The Soviets were a nuclear super-power that projected military and diplomatic strength around the world. Yet at home, medical care was poor, citizens' diets poorer, and shoddy goods were the norm.

And a nation that claimed to publish more books and newspapers than any other had a ruthless system of censorship, political control and suppression of free ideas.

What went wrong? Why did a nation rich in natural resources—with a literate, educated work force and one-sixth of the world's land mass to stretch out in—fail to build the vibrant, prosperous, free society that was supposed to be a beacon to the world?

Most Soviets blame, first of all, "scientific socialism," the shaky and untested economic model that Lenin's Communists forced on backward Russia.

It was imposed from above and preserved through brute force. There were huge economic advances at first, but accomplished through intimidation as much as economic logic. After World War II, the "planned economy" operated as a continent-wide shell game, with resources wastefully rushed here and there to maintain an illusion of economic progress.

Since the economy essentially did not work, the leaders who depended on it had to find other ways to preserve their strength and build national pride.

They created a genuine center of accomplishment in the Soviet military, which was denied no human or financial resource. The Soviets also excelled in areas of high technology, mathematics and space; brought electricity, communications and industry to backward zones of their nation; and provided an example of quick, forced economic development that many in the Third World admired and attempted to emulate.

For anyone who was unimpressed by these accomplishments, the Soviets also created a system of terror that silenced political dissidents, religious activists, nationalist agitators and anyone else whose cause might be more appealing than communism.

But perhaps most important of all, the leaders built their strength on a suffocating cradle-to-grave so-

Foreign Aid

In 1991 President Gorbachev appealed to the industrialized countries for \$20 to \$30 billion in aid. The argument for granting this aid was that it would ease the painful transition process when central planning was being dismantled and free enterprise had not yet taken hold. During this critical period the Soviet economy may further deteriorate. In addition, the abortive August 1991 coup indicates clearly that economic collapse can threaten to reverse the Soviet Union's substantial progress toward political democracy and the apparent demise of the cold war.

cial structure that made citizens totally beholden to the state—and then demanded practically nothing of them.

The state provided food, apartments, medicine, education, jobs and old-age pensions. It ran factories, department stores, farms, film studios and excellent orchestras and ballet companies. It may not have provided the weather, but it certainly controlled the news and sports.

This benevolence, such as it was, was practically free of charge. Citizens were judged mainly by political reliability—or political indifference, which also was acceptable.

During Leonid Brezhnev's reign, the situation steadily worsened and hypocrisy was elevated to the level of state policy. Bluster covered the increasing weakness.

Incompetence, sloppiness and corruption at work were widely overlooked. Citizens quickly learned that an effective way to get along was to do the minimum and challenge nothing—neither politics, nor the efficiency of their workplace.

Under such conditions, many believed the Soviet economy—and the country's whole spirit—was heading for a crash long before Mikhail Gorbachev came to power in 1985. He accelerated the slide by public openness about the country's troubles, a tactic that invigorated a few reformers but threw millions into despair and inactivity when facades came down and they realized how far their country had already crumbled.

Gorbachev's attempts at restructuring the economy were too tentative and too late. They could not make up for seven decades of an economic system that did not work, and the intricate structure established to maintain it at all cost.

That cost included stamping out personal initiative and putting political order ahead of everything else—including the welfare of the Soviet people.

Source: Thomas Kent, "Soviets Mixed Achievement, Facade as Dreams Failed," *The Lincoln Star,* Lincoln, Nebraska, December 26, 1991. Reprinted by permission.

The United States and the other market democracies have a great economic stake in the former Soviet Union's transition to democracy and capitalism. If the transition fails, the peace dividend associated with the end of the cold war will not be realized and the possibility of accelerated economic growth through expanded international trade with a free-market Commonwealth will also be sacrificed. The political benefit is that a democratic Commonwealth will isolate the last strongholds of communism—China, Cuba, North Korea, and Vietnam—and perhaps force their leaders toward political and economic reform.

But there are serious reservations concerning aid to the Soviet Union. One argument is that aid is likely to be ineffectual and wasteful until the transition to market capitalism has been accomplished. Aside from humanitarian aid in the form of foodstuffs and medicine, economic aid is not likely to be of much help under existing institutional arrangements.

A second contention is that the Soviet Union has not yet exploited the opportunity it now has to divert vast amounts of resources from the military to the civilian sector. Cutting military spending in half would release resources three or four times as large as the amount of aid Gorbachev requested.

Third, it is pointed out that the Soviet Union is in fact a gigantic $2 trillion economy. Even granting the $30 billion in aid would only amount to about $100 per year per Soviet citizen.

Finally, there is the hard political fact that foreign aid for a long-time cold war foe may not be popular among the voters of industrialized nations who see their own countries troubled with problems of unemployment, poor education, poverty, and drug abuse.

The United States' position has been that at this time it is appropriate to provide food and other humanitarian aid along with technical and educational assistance to Soviet enterprises and political officials, but to withhold unrestricted aid until substantial reform of the economy has been achieved.

In fact, in the spring of 1992 the United States and its G-7 partners (Germany, Japan, France, Britain, Canada, and Italy) have promised Russia a $24 billion aid package. This includes $11 billion in direct aid; $6 billion to provide a fund for stabilizing the ruble; $4.5 billion of IMF and World Bank loans; and $2.5 billion in debt rescheduling (on an estimated $89 billion debt). The United States' share is approximately $5 billion.

Private Investment

As the former Soviet Union attempts to move toward a capitalistic system, will it be able to attract foreign investment to shore up its economy? Given the vast potential market provided by some 288 million citizens, we would expect the answer to be "Yes." Furthermore, it is undoubtedly true that flows of private investment could be extremely helpful to the Soviet economy, perhaps more so than public aid. The reason is that, in addition to providing real capital, profit-seeking private investors will bring in managerial skills, entrepreneurial behavior, and marketing connections.

But in fact there are serious obstacles to foreign firms in doing business in the former Soviet Union. One is determining who is in charge. As the country moves toward decentralization politically, companies must discover whether they should deal with a Commonwealth trade minister in Minsk, officials at the republic level, or both. To whom does a foreign firm pay taxes, and with whom does one sign contracts? Who issues the necessary permits and licenses?

A second problem is that neither suppliers of inputs nor a dependable infrastructure are available. Enterprises manufacturing inputs are still generally committed to selling most of their supplies to the state. How do new "outsiders" acquire necessary resources? Furthermore, Soviet communication and transportation systems are grossly inadequate by world standards. McDonald's spent fourteen years establishing its Moscow fast-food restaurant and its earnings are in rubles rather than dollars.

A third difficulty is the inconvertibility of the ruble. How does an American firm which establishes a successful company in Kiev or St. Petersburg withdraw its profits? The attractive feature of *joint ventures*—businesses in which American firms and Soviet enterprises cooperate in a productive endeavor—is that the convertibility problem may be circumvented. Firms such as Chevron and Amoco which intend to help the former Soviet Union exploit its vast oil reserves can take their earnings in oil rather than currency.

Membership in International Institutions

Historically the Soviet Union has distanced itself from the major international trade and financial institutions such as the International Monetary Fund (IMF), the World Bank, and the General Agreement on Tariffs and Trade (GATT). There is no doubt that membership in these institutions could benefit the Soviet Union. For example, membership in the IMF and World Bank could provide additional sources of economic aid. Membership in GATT would result in lower tariff barriers for Soviet exports. In the spring of 1992 Russia was admitted to the IMF and other republics are expected to follow. IMF and World Bank officials have indicated they would provide $45 to $50 billion in aid to the Commonwealth over the next four years.

QUICK REVIEW 26-3

- ***The former Soviet Union has made the commitment to become a capitalistic system. Ingredients in the transition from planning to markets include: a creating private property and property rights; b promoting competition; c limiting and reformulating government's role; d removing domestic price controls; e opening the economy to international market forces; and f establishing monetary and fiscal policies to stabilize the economy.***
- ***In addition to the technical economic problems associated with the transition, reforms require widespread public support, the maintenance of economic unity among the republics, and more-or-less simultaneous realization of the reform components.***
- ***Factors helpful to the transition include a generous natural resource base, the potential release of large amounts of resources from the military sector, the entrepreneurship implicit in the underground economy, and substantial strides toward political democracy.***
- ***The reform effort in the former Soviet Union may also be assisted by foreign technical and economic aid, private investment by foreign firms, and membership in international trade and lending institutions.***

PROSPECTS

What are the prospects for a successful transition from central planning to markets? At this time there is no definitive answer. The failed August 1991 coup suggests that anarchy and civil war are not beyond imagination. And there is some consensus that the damage done to the Soviet economy by seven decades of communism will not be easily nor quickly undone. The immediate future may bring considerable pain and suffering to citizens in Russia and the other Commonwealth republics. Yet we must keep in mind that the political and economic changes which have occurred in the former Soviet Union in the past several years have been remarkable and justify some measure of optimism.

CHAPTER SUMMARY

1 The labor theory of value is a central principle of Marxian ideology. Capitalists, as property owners, allegedly expropriate most of labor's value as profits or surplus value.
2 Virtually complete state ownership of property resources and central planning historically were the major institutional features of the Soviet economy.
3 Characteristics of Soviet planning included **a** emphasis on industrialization and military strength; **b** overcommitment of resources; **c** economic growth based on additional inputs rather than increased productivity; **d** allocation of resources by bureaucratic rather than market decisions; **e** economic self-sufficiency; and **f** passive macroeconomic policies.
4 The basic problem facing central planners is achieving coordination or internal consistency in their plans to avoid bottlenecks and the chain reaction of production failures which they cause.
5 Diminishing growth rates, shoddy consumer goods, and the inability to provide a promised high standard of living are all evidence of the failure of Soviet central planning.
6 Stagnation of the agricultural sector, a growing labor shortage, and the burden of a large military establishment contributed to the failure of the Soviet economy. However, the primary causes of failure were the inability of central planning to coordinate a more complex economy, the absence of rational success indicators, and the lack of adequate economic incentives.
7 The recent Gorbachev reforms attempted to restructure the economy and introduce greater political "openness," but did not address fundamental systemic deficiencies.
8 To change from central planning to a market economy, the former Soviet Union must move from public to private ownership of property; establish a competitive environment for businesses; restructure government's role to activities appropriate to capitalism; abandon state-determined prices in favor of market-determined prices; bring its economy into nomic policies and institutions to provide employment and price level stability.
9 In addition to resolving the technical economic problems inherent in the transformation of the Soviet economy to a market system, it is also necessary to achieve the support of bureaucrats and workers, preserve economic unity among the republics, and put reforms into effect simultaneously.
10 Reform efforts by the former Soviet republics may be furthered by the Commonwealth's abundant natural resources; the freeing of resources from the military; entrepreneurial talent evident in the underground economy; the democratization of the political system; and the assistance provided by foreign governments, foreign private investment, and international lending and trade institutions.

TERMS AND CONCEPTS

labor theory of value
surplus value
state ownership
central economic planning
Gorbachev reforms
perestroika
glasnost
ruble overhang

QUESTIONS AND STUDY SUGGESTIONS

1 Compare the ideology and institutional framework of the former Soviet economy with that of American capitalism. Contrast the manner in which production is motivated in these two systems.
2 Discuss the problem of coordination which faces central planners. Explain how a planning failure can cause a chain reaction of additional failures.
3 How was the number of automobiles to be produced determined in the former Soviet Union? In the United States? How are the decisions implemented in the two different types of economies?
4 What have been the major characteristics and goals of Soviet central planning?
5 What is the evidence of the failure of Soviet planning? Explain why Soviet economic growth diminished after 1970.
6 Explain why the use of quantitative output targets as the major success indicator for Soviet enterprises contributed to economic inefficiency.
7 Use a supply and demand diagram to explain the persistent shortages of many Soviet consumer goods. Why might the transformation to a market economy be accompanied by inflation? Why were black markets so common in the Soviet Union?
8 What specific changes must be made to transform the Soviet economy to a market system? Why is it important that these changes be introduced simultaneously?

9 Citing both specific obstacles and facilitating factors, do you think that the former Soviet Union will be successful in becoming a capitalistic system?

10 "It has become increasingly difficult for thoughtful men to find meaningful alternatives posed in the traditional choices between socialism and capitalism, planning and the free market, regulation and laissez faire, for they find their actual choices neither simple nor so grand."[7] Explain and evaluate.

[7]Robert A. Dahl and Charles E. Lindblom, *Politics, Economics and Welfare* (New York: Harper & Row, Publishers, Inc., 1953), p. 1.

GLOSSARY

Ability-to-pay principle The belief that those who have greater income (or wealth) should be taxed absolutely and relatively more than those who have less.

Abstraction Elimination of irrelevant and noneconomic facts to obtain an economic principle.

Acreage-allotment program The program which determines the total number of acres that are to be used to produce various agricultural products and allocates these acres among individual farmers who are required to limit their plantings to the number of acres allotted to them if they wish to obtain the Support price for their crops.

Adjustable pegs The device used in the Bretton Woods system ***(see)*** to change Exchange rates in an orderly way to eliminate persistent Payments deficits and surpluses: each nation defined its monetary unit in terms of (pegged it to) gold or the dollar, kept the Rate of exchange for its money stable in the short run, and changed (adjusted) it in the long run when faced with international disequilibrium.

Adverse selection problem A problem which arises when information known to one party to a contract is not known to the other party, causing the latter to incur major costs. Example: Individuals who have the poorest health are more likely to buy health insurance.

AFDC (*See* Aid to families with dependent children.)

Agricultural Adjustment Act The Federal act of 1933 which established the Parity concept ***(see)*** as the cornerstone of American agricultural policy and provided Price supports for farm products, restriction of agricultural production, and the disposal of surplus output.

Aid to families with dependent children (AFDC) A state-administered and partly federally funded program in the United States which provides aid to families in which dependent children do not have the support of a parent because of his or her death, disability, or desertion.

Alcoa case The case decided by the Federal courts in 1945 in which the courts ruled that the possession of monopoly power, no matter how reasonably that power had been used, was a violation of the antitrust laws; and which overturned the Rule of reason ***(see)*** applied in the U.S. Steel case ***(see)***.

Allocative efficiency The apportionment of resources among firms and industries to obtain the production of the products most wanted by society (consumers); the output of each product at which its Marginal cost and Price are equal.

American Federation of Labor (AFL) The organization of affiliated Craft unions formed in 1886.

Applied economics (*See* Policy economics.)

Appreciation of the dollar An increase in the value of the dollar relative to the currency of another nation; a dollar now buys a larger amount of the foreign currency. For example, if the dollar price of a British pound changes from \$3 to \$2, the dollar has appreciated.

Authoritarian capitalism An economic system (method of organization) in which property resources are privately owned and government extensively directs and controls the economy.

Average fixed costs The total Fixed cost ***(see)*** of a Firm divided by its output (the quantity of product produced).

Average product The total output produced per unit of a resource employed (total product divided by the quantity of a resource employed).

Average revenue Total revenue from the sale of a product divided by the quantity of the product sold (demanded); equal to the price at which the product is sold so long as all units of the product are sold at the same price.

Average tax rate Total tax paid divided by total (taxable) income; the tax rate on total (taxable) income.

Average (total) cost The Total cost of a Firm divided by its output (the quantity of product produced); equal to Average fixed cost ***(see)*** plus Average variable cost ***(see)***.

Average variable cost The total Variable cost ***(see)*** of a Firm divided by its output (the quantity of product produced).

Backflows The return of workers to the countries from which they originally migrated.

Balance of payments deficit The sum of the Balance on current account ***(see)*** and the Balance on the capital account ***(see)*** is negative.

Balance of payments surplus The sum of the Balance on current account (*see*) and the Balance on the capital account (*see*) is positive.

Balance on current account The exports of goods (merchandise) and services of a nation less its imports of goods (merchandise) and services plus its Net investment income and Net transfers.

Balance on goods and services The exports of goods (merchandise) and services of a nation less its imports of goods (merchandise) and services.

Balance on the capital account The Capital inflows (*see*) of a nation less its Capital outflows (*see*).

Barrier to entry Anything that artificially prevents the entry of Firms into an industry.

Barter The exchange of one good or service for another good or service.

Benefit-cost analysis Deciding whether to employ resources and the quantity of resources to employ for a project or program (for the production of a good or service) by comparing the marginal benefits with the marginal costs.

Benefit-loss rate The percentage by which subsidy benefits in a Negative income tax plan (*see*) are reduced as earned income rises.

Benefits-received principle The belief that those who receive the benefits of goods and services provided by government should pay the taxes required to finance them.

Big business A business Firm which either produces a large percentage of the total output of an industry, is large (in terms of number of employees or stockholders, sales, assets, or profits) compared with other Firms in the economy, or both.

Bilateral monopoly A market in which there is a single seller (Monopoly) and a single buyer (Monopsony).

Blacklisting The passing from one employer to another of the names of workers who favor the formation of labor unions and who ought not to be hired.

Brain drain The emigration of highly educated, highly skilled workers from a country.

Break-even income The level of Disposable income at which Households plan to consume (spend) all of their income (for consumer goods and services) and to save none of it; also denotes that level of earned income at which subsidy payments become zero in an income maintenance program.

Break-even point Any output which a (competitive) Firm might produce at which its Total cost and Total revenue would be equal; an output at which it has neither an Economic profit nor a loss.

Bretton Woods system The international monetary system developed after World War II in which Adjustable pegs (*see*) were employed, the International Monetary Fund (*see*) helped to stabilize Foreign exchange rates, and gold and the dollar (*see*) were used as International monetary reserves (*see*).

Budget deficit The amount by which the expenditures of the Federal government exceed its revenues in any year.

Budget line A line which shows the different combinations of two products a consumer can purchase with a given money income.

Budget restraint The limit the size of the consumer's income (and the prices that must be paid for the goods and services) imposes on the ability of an individual consumer to obtain goods and services.

Business unionism The belief that the labor union should concern itself with such practical and short-run objectives as higher wages, shorter hours, and improved working conditions and should not concern itself with long-run and idealistic changes in the capitalistic system.

Capital Human-made resources used to produce goods and services; goods which do not directly satisfy human wants; capital goods.

Capital account The section in a nation's International balance of payments (*see*) in which are recorded the Capital inflows (*see*) and the Capital outflows (*see*) of that nation.

Capital account deficit A negative Balance on the capital account (*see*).

Capital account surplus A positive Balance on the capital account (*see*).

Capital gain The gain realized when securities or properties are sold for a price greater than the price paid for them.

Capital goods (*See* Capital.)

Capital inflow The expenditures made by the residents of foreign nations to purchase real and financial capital from the residents of a nation.

Capital-intensive commodity A product which requires a relatively large amount of Capital to produce.

Capital outflow The expenditures made by the residents of a nation to purchase real and financial capital from the residents of foreign nations.

Cartel A formal written or oral agreement among Firms to set the price of the product and the outputs of the individual firms or to divide the market for the product geographically.

Causation A cause-and-effect relationship; one or several events bring about or result in another event.

Cease-and-desist order An order from a court or government agency (commission or board) to a corporation or individual to stop engaging in a specified practice.

Ceiling price (*See* Price ceiling.)

Celler-Kefauver Act The Federal act of 1950 which amended the Clayton Act **(*see*)** by prohibiting the acquisition of the assets of one firm by another firm when the effect would be to lessen competition.

Central economic planning Government determination of the objectives of the economy and the direction of its resources to the attainment of these objectives.

***Ceteris paribus* assumption** (*See* "Other things being equal" assumption.)

Change in amount consumed Increase or decrease in consumption spending that results from an increase or decrease in Disposable income, the Consumption schedule (curve) remaining unchanged; movement from one row (point) to another on the same Consumption schedule (curve).

Circular flow of income The flow of resources from Households to Firms and of products from Firms to Households accompanied in an economy using money by flows of money from Households to Firms and from Firms to Households.

Clayton Act The Federal antitrust act of 1914 which strengthened the Sherman Act **(*see*)** by making it illegal for business firms to engage in certain specified practices.

Clean Air Act of 1990 Legislation embodying a variety of specific measures to deal with air pollution, urban smog, motor vehicle emissions, ozone depletion, and acid rain.

Closed economy An economy which neither exports nor imports goods and services.

Close-down case The circumstance in which a Firm would experience a loss greater than its total Fixed cost if it were to produce any output greater than zero; alternatively, a situation in which a firm would cease to operate when the price at which it can sell its product is less than its Average variable cost.

Closed shop A place of employment at which only workers who are already members of a labor union may be hired.

Coase theorem The idea that Externality problems may be resolved through private negotiations of the affected parties.

Coincidence of wants The item (good or service) which one trader wishes to obtain is the same item which another trader desires to give up and the item which the second trader wishes to acquire is the same item the first trader desires to surrender.

COLA (*See* Cost-of-living adjustment.)

Collective voice The function a union performs for its members as a group when it communicates their problems and grievances to management and presses management for a satisfactory resolution to them.

Collusion A situation in which Firms act together and in agreement (collude) to set the price of the product and the output each firm will produce or to determine the geographic area in which each firm will sell.

Collusive oligopoly Occurs when the few firms composing an oligopolistic industry reach an explicit or unspoken agreement to fix prices, divide a market, or otherwise restrict competition; may take the form of a Cartel **(*see*)**, Gentleman's agreement **(*see*)**, or Price leadership **(*see*)**.

Command economy An economic system (method of organization) in which property resources are publicly owned and Central economic planning **(*see*)** is used to direct and coordinate economic activities.

Communism (*See* Command economy.)

Company union An organization of employees which is dominated by the employer (the company) and does not engage in genuine collective bargaining with the employer.

Comparable worth doctrine The belief that women should receive the same salaries (wages) as men when the levels of skill, effort, and responsibility in their different jobs are the same.

Comparative advantage A lower relative or Comparative cost **(*see*)** than another producer.

Comparative cost The amount the production of one product must be reduced to increase the production of another product; Opportunity cost **(*see*)**.

Competing goods (*See* Substitute goods.)

Competition The presence in a market of a large number of independent buyers and sellers and the freedom of buyers and sellers to enter and leave the market.

Competitive industry's short-run supply curve The horizontal summation of the short-run supply curves of the Firms in a purely competitive industry (*See* Pure competition); a curve which shows the total quantities that will be offered for sale at various prices by the Firms in an industry in the Short run **(*see*)**.

Competitive labor market A market in which a large number of (noncolluding) firms demand a particular type of labor from a large number of nonunionized workers.

Complementary goods Goods or services for which there is an inverse relationship between the price of one and the demand for the other; when the price of one falls (rises) the demand for the other increases (decreases).

Concentration ratio The percentage of the total sales of an industry made by the four (or some other number) largest sellers (Firms) in the industry.

Conglomerate combination A group of Plants **(*see*)** owned by a single Firm and engaged at one or more stages in the production of different products (of products which do not compete with each other).

Conglomerate merger The merger of a Firm in one Industry with a Firm in another Industry (with a Firm that is neither supplier, customer, nor competitor).

Congress of Industrial Organizations (CIO) The organization of affiliated Industrial unions formed in 1936.

Constant-cost industry An industry in which the expansion of the Industry by the entry of new Firms has no effect on the prices the Firms in the industry pay for resources and no effect, therefore, on their cost schedules (curves).

Consumer goods Goods and services which satisfy human wants directly.

Consumer sovereignty Determination by consumers of the types and quantities of goods and services that are produced from the scarce resources of the economy.

Consumption of fixed capital Estimate of the amount of Capital worn out or used up (consumed) in producing the Gross domestic product; depreciation.

Consumption schedule Schedule which shows the amounts Households plan to spend for Consumer goods at different levels of Disposable income.

Corporate income tax A tax levied on the net income (profit) of Corporations.

Corporation A legal entity ("person") chartered by a state or the Federal government, and distinct and separate from the individuals who own it.

Correlation Systematic and dependable association between two sets of data (two kinds of events).

Cost-of-living adjustment An increase in the incomes (wages) of workers which is automatically received by them when there is inflation in the economy and guaranteed by a clause in their labor contracts with their employer.

Cost-plus pricing A procedure used by (oligopolistic) Firms to determine the price they will charge for a product and in which a percentage markup is added to the estimated average cost of producing the product.

Cost ratio The ratio of the decrease in the production of the product to the increase in the production of another product when resources are shifted from the production of the first to the production of the second product; the amount the production of one product decreases when the production of a second product increases by one unit.

Craft union A labor union which limits its membership to workers with a particular skill (craft).

Credit An accounting notation that the value of an asset (such as the foreign money owned by the residents of a nation) has increased.

Criminal-conspiracy doctrine The (now outdated) legal doctrine that combinations of workers (Labor unions) to raise wages were criminal conspiracies and, therefore, illegal.

Cross elasticity of demand The ratio of the percentage change in Quantity demanded of one good to the percentage change in the price of some other good. A negative coefficient indicates the two products are Complementary goods; a positive coefficient indicates Substitute goods.

Crowding model of occupational discrimination A model of labor markets that assumes Occupational discrimination ***(see)*** against women and blacks has kept them out of many occupations and forced them into a limited number of other occupations in which the large Supply of labor (relative to the Demand) results in lower wages and incomes.

Currency appreciation (*See* Exchange rate appreciation.)

Currency depreciation (*See* Exchange rate depreciation.)

Current account The section in a nation's International balance of payments ***(see)*** in which are recorded its exports and imports of goods (merchandise) and services, its net investment income, and its net transfers.

Current account deficit A negative Balance on current account ***(see)***.

Current account surplus A positive Balance on current account ***(see)***.

Customary economy (*See* Traditional economy.)

Debit An accounting notation that the value of an asset (such as the foreign money owned by the residents of a nation) has decreased.

Declining industry An industry in which Economic profits are negative (losses are incurred) and which will, therefore, decrease its output as Firms leave the industry.

Decrease in demand A decrease in the Quantity demanded of a good or service at every price; a shift of the Demand curve to the left.

Decrease in supply A decrease in the Quantity supplied of a good or service at every price; a shift of the Supply curve to the left.

Deduction Reasoning from assumptions to conclusions; a method of reasoning that tests a hypothesis (an assumption) by comparing the conclusions to which it leads with economic facts.

Demand A Demand schedule or a Demand curve (***see*** both).

Demand curve A curve which shows the amounts of a good or service buyers wish to purchase at various prices during some period of time.

Demand schedule A schedule which shows the amounts of a good or service buyers wish to purchase at various prices during some period of time.

Dependent variable A variable which changes as a consequence of a change in some other (independent) variable; the "effect" or outcome.

Depreciation of the dollar A decrease in the value of the dollar relative to another currency; a dollar now buys a smaller amount of the foreign currency. For example, if the dollar price of a British pound changes from $2 to $3, the dollar has depreciated.

Derived demand The demand for a good or service which is dependent on or related to the demand for some other good or service; the demand for a resource which depends on the demand for the products it can be used to produce.

Descriptive economics The gathering or collection of relevant economic facts (data).

Determinants of demand Factors other than its price which determine the quantities demanded of a good or service.

Determinants of supply Factors other than its price which determine the quantities supplied of a good or service.

Devaluation A decrease in the defined value of a currency.

Differentiated oligopoly An Oligopoly in which the firms produce a Differentiated product ***(see)***.

Differentiated product A product which differs physically or in some other way from the similar products produced by other Firms; a product which is similar to but not identical with and, therefore, not a perfect substitute for other products; a product such that buyers are not indifferent to the seller from whom they purchase it so long as the price charged by all sellers is the same.

Dilemma of regulation When a Regulatory agency ***(see)*** must establish the maximum legal price a monopolist may charge, it finds that if it sets the price at the Socially optimal price ***(see)*** this price is below Average cost (and either bankrupts the Firm or requires that it be subsidized) and if it sets the price at the Fair-return price ***(see)*** it has failed to eliminate fully the underallocation of resources that is the consequence of unregulated monopoly.

Directing function of prices (***See*** Guiding function of prices.)

Directly related Two sets of economic data that change in the same direction; when one variable increases (decreases) the other increases (decreases).

Direct relationship The relationship between two variables which change in the same direction, for example, product price and quantity supplied.

Discriminatory discharge The firing of workers who favor formation of labor unions.

Diseconomies of scale Forces which increase the Average cost of producing a product as the Firm expands the size of its Plant (its output) in the Long run ***(see)***.

Disposable income Personal income ***(see)*** less personal taxes; income available for Personal consumption expenditures ***(see)*** and Personal saving ***(see)***.

Division of labor Dividing the work required to produce a product into a number of different tasks which are performed by different workers; Specialization ***(see)*** of workers.

Dollar votes The "votes" which consumers and entrepreneurs in effect cast for the production of the different kinds of consumer and capital goods, respectively, when they purchase them in the markets of the economy.

Domestic capital formation Adding to a nation's stock of Capital by saving part of its own domestic output.

Domestic economic goal Assumed to be full employment with little or no inflation.

Domestic output Gross (or net) domestic product; the total output of final goods and services produced in the economy.

Double taxation Taxation of both corporate net income (profits) and the dividends paid from this net income when they become the Personal income of households.

Dumping The sale of products below cost in a foreign country.

Du Pont cellophane case The antitrust case brought against du Pont in which the U.S. Supreme Court ruled (in 1956) that while du Pont (and one licensee) had a monopoly in the narrowly defined market for cellophane it did not monopolize the more broadly defined market for flexible packaging materials, and was not guilty, therefore, of violating the Sherman Act.

Durable good A consumer good with an expected life (use) of one year or more.

Dynamic progress The development over time of more efficient (less costly) techniques of producing existing products and of improved products; technological progress.

Earnings The money income received by a worker; equal to the Wage (rate) multiplied by the quantity of labor supplied (the amount of time worked) by the worker.

EC European Economic Community (***See*** European Common Market).

Economic analysis Deriving Economic principles ***(see)*** from relevant economic facts.

Economic concentration A description or measure of the degree to which an industry is monopolistic or competitive. (***See*** Concentration ratio.)

Economic cost A payment that must be made to obtain and retain the services of a resource; the income a Firm must provide to a resource supplier to attract the resource away from an alternative use; equal to the quantity of other products that cannot be produced when resources are employed to produce a particular product.

Economic efficiency The relationship between the input of scarce resources and the resulting output of a good or service; production of an output with a given dollar-and-cents value with the smallest total expenditure for resources; obtaining the largest total production of a good or service with resources of a given dollar-and-cents value.

Economic growth (1) An increase in the Production possibilities schedule or curve that results from an increase in resource supplies or an improvement in Technology; (2) an increase either in real output (Gross domestic product) or in real output per capita.

Economic integration Cooperation among and the complete or partial unification of the economies of different nations; the elimination of the barriers to trade among these nations; the bringing together of the markets in each of the separate economies to form one large (a common) market.

Economic law (*See* Economic principle.)

Economic model A simplified picture of reality; an abstract generalization.

Economic perspective A viewpoint which envisions individuals and institutions making rational or purposeful decisions based on a consideration of the benefits and costs associated with their actions.

Economic policy Course of action intended to correct or avoid a problem.

Economic principle Generalization of the economic behavior of individuals and institutions.

Economic profit The Total revenue of a firm less all its Economic costs; also called "pure profit" and "above normal profit."

Economic regulation (*See* Industrial regulation.)

Economic rent The price paid for the use of land and other natural resources, the supply of which is fixed (perfectly inelastic).

Economics Social science concerned with using scarce resources to obtain the maximum satisfaction of the unlimited material wants of society.

Economic theory Deriving economic principles ***(see)*** from relevant economic facts; an Economic principle ***(see)***.

Economies of scale The forces which reduce the Average cost of producing a product as the Firm expands the size of its Plant (its output) in the Long run ***(see)***; the economies of mass production.

Economizing problem Society's material wants are unlimited but the resources available to produce the goods and services that satisfy wants are limited (scarce); the inability of any economy to produce unlimited quantities of goods and services.

Efficiency loss of a tax The loss of net benefits to society because a tax reduces the production and consumption of a taxed good below the allocatively efficient level.

Efficiency wage A wage which minimizes wage costs per unit of output.

Efficient allocation of resources That allocation of the resources of an economy among the production of different products which leads to the maximum satisfaction of the wants of consumers.

Elastic demand The Elasticity coefficient ***(see)*** is greater than one; the percentage change in Quantity demanded is greater than the percentage change in price.

Elasticity coefficient The number obtained when the percentage change in Quantity demanded (or supplied) is divided by the percentage change in the price of the commodity.

Elasticity formula The price elasticity of demand (supply) is equal to

$$\frac{\text{percentage change in quantity demanded (supplied)}}{\text{percentage change in price}}$$

which is equal to

$$\frac{\text{change in quantity demanded (supplied)}}{\text{original quantity demanded (supplied)}}$$

$$\text{divided by } \frac{\text{change in price}}{\text{original price}}$$

Elastic supply The Elasticity coefficient ***(see)*** is greater than one; the percentage change in Quantity supplied is greater than the percentage change in price.

Emission fees Special fees that might be levied against those who discharge pollutants into the environment.

Employment discrimination The employment of whites before blacks (and other minority groups) are employed and the discharge of blacks (and other minority groups) before whites are discharged.

Entrepreneurial ability The human resource which combines the other resources to produce a product, makes nonroutine decisions, innovates, and bears risks.

Equality vs. efficiency tradeoff The decrease in Economic efficiency ***(see)*** that appears to accompany a decrease in Income inequality ***(see)***; the presumption that an increase in Income inequality is required to increase Economic efficiency.

Equalizing differences The differences in the Wages received by workers in different jobs which compensate for nonmonetary differences in the jobs.

Equilibrium position The point at which the Budget line ***(see)*** is tangent to an Indifference curve ***(see)*** in the indifference curve approach to the theory of consumer behavior.

Equilibrium price The price in a competitive market at which the Quantity demanded ***(see)*** and the Quantity supplied **(*see*)** are equal; at which there is neither a shortage nor a surplus; and at which there is no tendency for price to rise or fall.

Equilibrium quantity The Quantity demanded **(*see*)** and Quantity supplied **(*see*)** at the Equilibrium price **(*see*)** in a competitive market.

European Common Market The association of twelve European nations initiated in 1958 to abolish gradually the Tariffs and Import quotas that exist among them, to establish common Tariffs for goods imported from outside the member nations, to allow the eventual free movement of labor and capital among them, and to create other common economic policies.

European Economic Community (EC) (*See* European Common Market.)

Exchange control (*See* Foreign exchange control.)

Exchange rate The Rate of exchange **(*see*)**.

Exchange rate appreciation An increase in the value of a nation's money in foreign exchange markets; an increase in the Rates of exchange for foreign monies.

Exchange rate depreciation A decrease in the value of a nation's money in foreign exchange markets; a decrease in the Rates of exchange for foreign monies.

Exchange rate determinant Any factor other than the Rate of exchange **(*see*)** that determines the demand for and the supply of a currency in the Foreign exchange market **(*see*)**.

Excise tax A tax levied on the expenditure for a specific product or on the quantity of the product purchased.

Exclusion principle The exclusion of those who do not pay for a product from the benefits of the product.

Exclusive unionism The policies employed by a Labor union to restrict the supply of labor by excluding potential members in order to increase the Wages received by its members; the Policies typically employed by a Craft union **(*see*)**.

Exit mechanism Leaving a job and searching for another one in order to improve the conditions under which a worker is employed.

Expanding industry An industry in which Economic profits are obtained by the firms in the industry and which will, therefore, increase its output as new firms enter the industry.

Expansionary fiscal policy An increase in Aggregate demand brought about by an increase in Government expenditures for goods and services, a decrease in Net taxes, or some combination of the two.

Expectations What consumers, business Firms, and others believe will happen or what conditions will be in the future.

Explicit cost The monetary payment a Firm must make to an outsider to obtain a resource.

Exports Goods and services produced in a given nation and sold to customers in other nations.

Export subsidies Government payments which reduce the price of a product to foreign buyers.

Export transactions A sale of a good or service which increases the amount of foreign money held by the citizens, firms, and governments of a nation.

External benefit (*See* Spillover benefit.)

External cost (*See* Spillover cost.)

External debt Public debt **(*see*)** owed to foreign citizens, firms, and institutions.

External economic goal (*See* International economic goal.)

Externality (*See* Spillover.)

Factors of production Economic resources: Land, Capital, Labor, and Entrepreneurial ability.

Fair-return price The price of a product which enables its producer to obtain a Normal profit **(*see*)** and which is equal to the Average cost of producing it.

Fallacy of composition Incorrectly reasoning that what is true for the individual (or part) is therefore necessarily true for the group (or whole).

Fallacy of limited decisions The false notion that there are a limited number of economic decisions to be made so that, if government makes more decisions, there will be fewer private decisions to render.

Farm Act of 1990 Farm legislation which reduces the amount of acreage that is covered by price supports and allows farmers to plant these uncovered acres in alternative crops.

Farm problem The relatively low income of many farmers (compared with incomes in the nonagricultural sectors of the economy) and the tendency for farm income to fluctuate sharply from year to year.

Featherbedding Payment by an employer to a worker for work not actually performed.

Federal Trade Commission (FTC) The commission of five members established by the Federal Trade Commission Act of 1914 to investigate unfair competitive practices of business Firms, to hold hearings of the complaints of such practices, and to issue Cease-and-desist orders **(*see*)** when Firms were found to engage in such practices.

Federal Trade Commission Act The Federal act of 1914 which established the Federal Trade Commission **(*see*)**.

Female labor force participation rate The percentage of the female population of working age in the Labor force **(*see*)**.

Fewness A relatively small number of sellers (or buyers) of a good or service.

Financial capital (*See* Money capital.)

Financing exports and imports The use of Foreign exchange markets by exporters and importers to receive and make payments for goods and services they sell and buy in foreign nations.

Firm An organization that employs resources to produce a good or service for profit and owns and operates one or more Plants **(*see*)**.

(The) firm's short-run supply curve A curve which shows the quantities of a product a Firm in a purely competitive industry (*see* Pure competition) will offer to sell at various prices in the Short run **(*see*)**; the portion of the Firm's short-run Marginal cost **(*see*)** curve which lies above its Average variable cost curve.

Fiscal federalism The system of transfers (grants) by which the Federal government shares its revenues with state and local governments.

Fiscal policy Changes in government spending and tax collections for the purpose of achieving a full-employment and noninflationary domestic output.

Five fundamental economic questions The five questions which every economy must answer: what to produce, how to produce, how to divide the total output, how to maintain Full employment, and how to assure economic flexibility.

Fixed cost Any cost which in total does not change when the Firm changes its output; the cost of Fixed resources **(*see*)**.

Fixed exchange rate A Rate of exchange that is prevented from rising or falling.

Fixed resource Any resource employed by a Firm the quantity of which the firm cannot change.

Flexible exchange rate A rate of exchange that is determined by the demand for and supply of the foreign money and is free to rise or fall.

Floating exchange rate (*See* Flexible exchange rate.)

Food for peace program The program established under the provisions of Public Law 480 which permits less developed nations to buy surplus American agricultural products and pay for them with their own monies (instead of dollars).

Food stamp program A program in the United States which permits low-income persons to purchase for less than their retail value, or to obtain without cost, coupons that can be exchanged for food items at retail stores.

Foreign competition (*See* Import competition.)

Foreign exchange control The control a government may exercise over the quantity of foreign money demanded by its citizens and business firms and over the Rates of exchange in order to limit its outpayments to its inpayments (to eliminate a Payments deficit, ***see***).

Foreign exchange market A market in which the money (currency) used by one nation is used to purchase (is exchanged for) the money used by another nation.

Foreign exchange rate (*See* Rate of exchange.)

Freedom of choice Freedom of owners of property resources and money to employ or dispose of these resources as they see fit, of workers to enter any line of work for which they are qualified, and of consumers to spend their incomes in a manner which they deem to be appropriate (best for them).

Freedom of enterprise Freedom of business Firms to employ economic resources, to use these resources to produce products of the firm's own choosing, and to sell these products in markets of their choice.

Freely floating exchange rates Rates of exchange **(*see*)** which are not controlled and which may, therefore, rise and fall; and which are determined by the demand for and the supply of foreign monies.

Free-rider problem The inability of those who might provide the economy with an economically desirable and indivisible good or service to obtain payment from those who benefit from the good or service because the Exclusion principle **(*see*)** cannot be applied to it.

Free trade The absence of artificial (government imposed) barriers to trade among individuals and firms in different nations.

Fringe benefits The rewards other than Wages that employees receive from their employers and which include pensions, medical and dental insurance, paid vacations, and sick leaves.

Full production The maximum amount of goods and services that can be produced from the employed resources of an economy; the absence of Underemployment **(*see*)**.

Functional distribution of income The manner in which the economy's (the national) income is divided among those who perform different functions (provide the economy with different kinds of resources); the division of National income **(*see*)** into wages and salaries, proprietors' income, corporate profits, interest, and rent.

Game theory A theory which compares the behavior of participants in games of strategy, such as poker and chess, with that of a small group of mutually interdependent firms (an Oligopoly).

GATT (*See* General Agreement on Tariffs and Trade.)

General Agreement on Tariffs and Trade The international agreement reached in 1947 by twenty-three nations (including the United States) in which each nation agreed to give equal and nondiscriminatory treatment to the other nations, to reduce tariff rates by multinational negotiations, and to eliminate Import quotas.

General equilibrium analysis A study of the Market system as a whole; of the interrelations among equilibrium prices, outputs, and employments in all the different markets of the economy.

Generalization Statistical or probability statement; statement of the nature of the relation between two or more sets of facts.

Gentleman's agreement An informal understanding on the price to be charged among the firms in an Oligopoly.

Glasnost A Soviet campaign of the mid-1980s for greater "openness" and democratization in political and economic activities.

GNP (*See* Gross national product.)

Gold export point The rate of exchange for a foreign money above which—when nations participate in the International gold standard ***(see)***—the foreign money will not be purchased and gold will be sent (exported) to the foreign country to make payments there.

Gold flow The movement of gold into or out of a nation.

Gold import point The Rate of exchange for a foreign money below which—when nations participate in the International gold standard ***(see)***—a nation's own money will not be purchased and gold will be sent (imported) into that country by foreigners to make payments there.

Gorbachev's reforms A mid-1980s series of reforms designed to revitalize the Soviet economy. The reforms stressed the modernization of productive facilities, less centralized control, improved worker discipline and productivity, more emphasis on market prices, and an expansion of private economic activity.

Gosbank The state-owned and operated bank in the former U.S.S.R.

Government purchases Disbursements of money by government for which government receives a currently produced good or service in return; the expenditures of all governments in the economy for Final goods ***(see)*** and services.

Government transfer payment The disbursement of money (or goods and services) by government for which government receives no currently produced good or service in return.

Grievance procedure The methods used by a Labor union and the Firm to settle disputes that arise during the life of the collective bargaining agreement between them.

Guaranteed income The minimum income a family (or individual) would receive if a Negative income tax ***(see)*** were to be adopted.

Guiding function of prices The ability of price changes to bring about changes in the quantities of products and resources demanded and supplied (*See* Incentive function of price.)

Herfindahl index A measure of the concentration and competitiveness of an industry; calculated as the sum of the squared market shares of the individual firms.

Homogeneous oligopoly An Oligopoly in which the firms produce a Standardized product ***(see)***.

Horizontal axis The "left–right" or "west–east" axis on a graph or grid.

Horizontal combination A group of Plants ***(see)*** in the same stage of production which are owned by a single Firm ***(see)***.

Horizontal merger The merger of one or more Firms producing the same product into a single Firm.

Household An economic unit (of one or more persons) which provides the economy with resources and uses the money paid to it for these resources to purchase goods and services that satisfy material wants.

Human-capital discrimination The denial to blacks (and other minority groups) of the same quality and quantity of education and training received by whites.

Human-capital investment Any action taken to increase the productivity (by improving the skills and abilities) of workers; expenditures made to improve the education, health, or mobility of workers.

Illegal immigrant A person who unlawfully enters a country.

IMF (*See* International Monetary Fund.)

Immobility The inability or unwillingness of a worker or another resource to move from one geographic area or occupation to another or from a lower-paying to a higher-paying job.

Imperfect competition All markets except Pure competition ***(see)***; Monopoly, Monopsony, Monopolistic competition, Oligopoly, and Oligopsony ***(see all)***.

Implicit cost The monetary income a Firm sacrifices when it employs a resource it owns to produce a product rather than supplying the resource in the market; equal to what the resource could have earned in the best-paying alternative employment.

Import competition Competition which domestic firms encounter from the products and services of foreign suppliers.

Import quota A limit imposed by a nation on the quantity of a good that may be imported during some period of time.

Imports Spending by individuals, Firms, and governments of an economy for goods and services produced in foreign nations.

Import transaction The purchase of a good or service which decreases the amount of foreign money held by citizens, firms, and governments of a nation.

Incentive function of price The inducement which an increase (a decrease) in the price of a commodity offers to sellers of the commodity to make more (less) of it available; and the inducement which an increase (decrease) in price offers to buyers to purchase smaller (larger) quantities; the Guiding function of prices ***(see)***.

Incentive pay plan A compensation scheme which ties worker pay directly to performance. Such plans include piece rates, bonuses, commissions, and profit sharing.

Inclusive unionism A union which attempts to include all workers employed in an industry as members.

Income effect The effect which a change in the price of a product has on the Real income (purchasing power) of a consumer and the resulting effect on the quantity of that product the consumer would purchase after the consequences of the Substitution effect ***(see)*** have been taken into account (eliminated).

Income elasticity of demand The ratio of the percentage change in the Quantity demanded of a good to the percentage change in income; it measures the responsiveness of consumer purchases to income changes.

Income inequality The unequal distribution of an economy's total income among persons or families in the economy.

Income-maintenance system The programs designed to eliminate poverty and to reduce inequality in the distribution of income.

Increase in demand An increase in the Quantity demanded of a good or service at every price; a shift in the Demand curve to the right.

Increase in supply An increase in the Quantity supplied of a good or service at every price; a shift in the Supply curve to the right.

Increasing-cost industry An Industry in which the expansion of the Industry through the entry of new firms increases the prices the Firms in the Industry must pay for resources and, therefore, increases their cost schedules (moves their cost curves upward).

Increasing returns An increase in the Marginal product ***(see)*** of a resource as successive units of the resource are employed.

Independent goods Goods or services such that there is no relationship between the price of one and the demand for the other; when the price of one rises or falls the demand for the other remains constant.

Independent variable The variable which causes a change in some other (dependent) variable.

Indifference curve A curve which shows the different combinations of two products which give a consumer the same satisfaction or Utility ***(see)***.

Indifference map A series of Indifference curves ***(see)***, each of which represents a different level of Utility; and which together show the preferences of the consumer.

Individual demand The Demand schedule ***(see)*** or Demand curve ***(see)*** of a single buyer of a good or service.

Individual supply The Supply schedule ***(see)*** or Supply curve ***(see)*** of a single seller of a good or service.

Induction A method of reasoning that proceeds from facts to Generalization ***(see)***.

Industrial policy Any policy in which government takes a direct and active role in shaping the structure and composition of industry to promote economic growth.

Industrial regulation The older and more traditional type of regulation in which government is concerned with the prices charged and the services provided the public in specific industries; in contrast to Social regulation ***(see)***.

Industrial union A Labor union which accepts as members all workers employed in a particular industry (or by a particular firm) and which contains largely unskilled or semiskilled workers.

Industry The group of (one or more) Firms that produce identical or similar products.

Inelastic demand The Elasticity coefficient ***(see)*** is less than one; the percentage change in price is greater than the percentage change in Quantity demanded.

Inelastic supply The Elasticity coefficient ***(see)*** is less than one; the percentage change in price is greater than the percentage change in Quantity supplied.

Inferior good A good or service of which consumers purchase less (more) at every price when their incomes increase (decrease).

Infrastructure For the economy, the capital goods usually provided by the Public sector for the use of its citizens and Firms (e.g., highways, bridges, transit systems, wastewater treatment facilities, municipal water systems, and airports). For the Firm, the services and facilities which it must have to produce its products, which would be too costly for it to provide for itself, and which are provided by governments or other Firms (e.g., water, electricity, waste treatment, transportation, research, engineering, finance, and banking).

Injunction An order from a court of law that directs a person or organization not to perform a certain act because the act would do irreparable damage to some other person or persons; a restraining order.

In-kind investment Nonfinancial investment ***(see)***.

In-kind transfer The distribution by government of goods and services to individuals and for which the government receives no currently produced good or service in return; a Government transfer payment ***(see)*** made in goods or services rather than in money.

Innovation The introduction of a new product, the use of a new method of production, or the employment of a new form of business organization.

Inpayments The receipts of (its own or foreign) money which the individuals, Firms, and governments of one nation obtain from the sale of goods and services, investment income, Remittances, and Capital inflows from abroad.

Input-output analysis Using an Input-output table ***(see)*** to examine interdependence among different parts (sectors and industries) of the economy and to make economic forecasts and plans.

Input-output table A table which lists (along the left side) the producing sectors and (along the top) the consuming or using sectors of the economy and which shows quantitatively in each of its rows how the output of a producing sector was distributed among consuming sectors and quantitatively in each of its columns the producing sectors from which a consuming sector obtained its inputs during some period of time (a year).

Insurable risk An event, the average occurrence of which can be estimated with considerable accuracy, which would result in a loss that can be avoided by purchasing insurance.

Interest The payment made for the use of money (of borrowed funds).

Interest income Income of those who supply the economy with Capital ***(see)***.

Interest rate The Rate of interest ***(see)***.

Interindustry competition Competition or rivalry between the products produced by Firms in one Industry ***(see)*** and the products produced by Firms in another industry (or in other industries).

Interlocking directorate A situation in which one or more of the members of the board of directors of one Corporation are also on the board of directors of another Corporation; and which is illegal when it reduces competition among the Corporations.

Internal economic goal (*See* Domestic economic goal.)

Internal economies The reduction in the cost of producing or marketing a product that results from an increase in output of the Firm [*see* Economies of (large) scale].

International balance of payments Summary statement of the transactions which took place between the individuals, Firms, and governments of one nation and those in all other nations during the year.

International balance of payments deficit (*See* Balance of payments deficit.)

International balance of payments surplus (*See* Balance of payments surplus.)

International Bank for Reconstruction and Development (*See* World Bank.)

International economic goal Assumed to be a current-account balance of zero.

International gold standard An international monetary system employed in the nineteenth and early twentieth centuries in which each nation defined its money in terms of a quantity of gold, maintained a fixed relationship between its gold stock and money supply, and allowed the free importation and exportation of gold.

International Monetary Fund The international association of nations which was formed after World War II to make loans of foreign monies to nations with temporary Payments deficits ***(see)*** and to administer the Adjustable pegs ***(see)***.

International monetary reserves The foreign monies and such assets as gold a nation may use to settle a Payments deficit ***(see)***.

International value of the dollar The price that must be paid in foreign currency (money) to obtain one American dollar.

Interstate Commerce Commission The commission established in 1887 to regulate the rates and monitor the services of the railroads in the United States.

Interstate Commerce Commission Act The Federal legislation of 1887 which established the Interstate Commerce Commission ***(see)***.

Inverse relationship The relationship between two variables which change in opposite directions, for example, product price and quantity demanded.

Investment Spending for (the production and accumulation of) Capital goods ***(see)*** and additions to inventories.

Investment in human capital (*See* Human-capital investment.)

Invisible hand The tendency of Firms and resource suppliers seeking to further their self-interests in competitive markets to further the best interest of society as a whole (the maximum satisfaction of wants).

Jurisdictional strike Withholding from an employer the labor services of its members by a Labor union that is engaged in a dispute with another Labor union over which is to perform a specific kind of work for the employer.

Kinked demand curve The demand curve which a noncollusive oligopolist sees for its output and which is based on the assumption that rivals will follow a price decrease and will not follow a price increase.

Labor The physical and mental talents (efforts) of people which can be used to produce goods and services.

Labor-intensive commodity A product which requires a relatively large amount of Labor to produce.

Labor-Management Relations Act (*See* Taft-Hartley Act.)

Labor-Management Reporting and Disclosure Act (*See* Landrum-Griffin Act.)

Labor productivity Total output divided by the quantity of labor employed to produce the output; the Average product ***(see)*** of labor or output per worker per hour.

Labor theory of value The Marxian notion that the economic value of any commodity is determined solely by the amount of labor required to produce it.

Labor union A group of workers organized to advance the interests of the group (to increase wages, shorten the hours worked, improve working conditions, etc.).

Laissez faire capitalism (*See* Pure capitalism.)

Land Natural resources ("free gifts of nature") which can be used to produce goods and services.

Land-intensive commodity A product which requires a relatively large amount of Land to produce.

Landrum-Griffin Act The Federal act of 1959 which regulates the elections and finances of Labor unions and guarantees certain rights to their members.

Law of conservation of matter and energy The notion that matter can be changed to other matter or into energy but cannot disappear; all production inputs are ultimately transformed into an equal amount of finished product, energy, and waste (pollution).

Law of demand The inverse relationship between the price and the Quantity demanded ***(see)*** of a good or service during some period of time.

Law of diminishing marginal utility As a consumer increases the consumption of a good or service, the Marginal utility ***(see)*** obtained from each additional unit of the good or service decreases.

Law of diminishing returns When successive equal increments of a Variable resource ***(see)*** are added to the Fixed resources ***(see)***, beyond some level of employment, the Marginal product ***(see)*** of the Variable resource will decrease.

Law of increasing opportunity cost As the amount of a product produced is increased, the Opportunity cost ***(see)***—Marginal cost ***(see)***—of producing an additional unit of the product increases.

Law of supply The direct relationship between the price and the Quantity supplied ***(see)*** of a good or service during some period of time.

Least-cost combination rule (of resources) The quantity of each resource a Firm must employ if it is to produce any output at the lowest total cost; the combination on which the ratio of the Marginal product ***(see)*** of a resource to its Marginal resource cost ***(see)*** (to its price if the resource is employed in a competitive market) is the same for all resources employed.

Legal cartel theory of regulation The hypothesis that industries want to be regulated so that they may form legal Cartels ***(see)*** and that government officials (the government) provide the regulation in return for their political and financial support.

Legal immigrant A person who lawfully enters a country.

Less developed countries (LDCs) Most countries of Africa, Asia, and Latin America which are characterized by a lack of capital goods, primitive production technologies, low literacy rates, high unemployment, rapid population growth, and labor forces heavily committed to agriculture.

Limited liability Restriction of the maximum that may be lost to a predetermined amount; the maximum amount that may be lost by the owners (stockholders) of a Corporation is the amount they paid for their shares of stock.

Loaded terminology Terms which arouse emotions and elicit approval or disapproval.

Loanable funds theory of interest The concept that the supply of and demand for loanable funds determines the equilibrium rate of interest.

Lockout The temporary closing of a place of employment and the halting of production by an employer in order to discourage the formation of a Labor union or to compel a Labor union to modify its demands.

Logrolling The trading of votes by legislators to secure favorable outcomes on decisions to provide public goods and services.

Long run A period of time long enough to enable producers of a product to change the quantities of all the resources they employ; in which all resources and costs are variable and no resources or costs are fixed.

Long-run competitive equilibrium The price at which Firms in Pure competition ***(see)*** neither obtain Economic profit nor suffer losses in the Long run and the total quantity demanded and supplied at that price are equal; a price equal to the minimum long-run average cost of producing the product.

Long-run farm problem The tendency for the incomes of many farmers to decline relative to incomes in the rest of the economy.

Long-run supply A schedule or curve which shows the prices at which a Purely competitive industry will make various quantities of the product available in the Long run.

Lorenz curve A curve which shows the distribution of income in an economy; and when used for this purpose the cumulated percentage of families (income receivers) is measured along the horizontal axis and the cumulated percentage of income is measured along the vertical axis.

Loss-minimizing case The circumstances which result in a loss which is less than its Total fixed cost when a Firm produces the output at which total profit is a maximum (or total loss is a minimum): when the price at which the firm can sell its product is less than Average total cost but greater than Average variable cost.

Macroeconomics The part of economics concerned with the economy as a whole; with such major aggregates as the household, business, and governmental sectors and with totals for the economy.

Managed floating exchange rate An Exchange rate that is allowed to change (float) to eliminate persistent Payments deficits and surpluses and is controlled (managed) to reduce day-to-day fluctuations.

Managerial-opposition hypothesis The explanation that attributes the relative decline of unionism in the United States to the increased and more aggressive opposition of management to unions.

Managerial prerogatives The decisions, often enumerated in the contract between a Labor union and a business Firm, that the management of the Firm has the sole right to make.

Marginal cost The extra (additional) cost of producing one more unit of output; equal to the change in Total cost divided by the change in output (and in the short run to the change in total Variable cost divided by the change in output).

Marginal labor cost The amount by which the total cost of employing Labor increases when a Firm employs one additional unit of Labor (the quantity of other resources employed remaining constant); equal to the change in the total cost of Labor divided by the change in the quantity of Labor employed.

Marginal product The additional output produced when one additional unit of a resource is employed (the quantity of all other resources employed remaining constant); equal to the change in total product divided by the change in the quantity of a resource employed.

Marginal productivity theory of income distribution The contention that the distribution of income is equitable when each unit of each resource receives a money payment equal to its marginal contribution to the firm's revenue (its Marginal revenue product).

Marginal rate of substitution The rate (at the margin) at which a consumer is prepared to substitute one good or service for another and remain equally satisfied (have the same total Utility); and equal to the slope of an Indifference curve ***(see)***.

Marginal resource cost The amount by which the total cost of employing a resource increases when a Firm employs one additional unit of the resource (the quantity of all other resources employed remaining constant); equal to the change in the Total cost of the resource divided by the change in the quantity of the resource employed.

Marginal revenue The change in the Total revenue of the Firm that results from the sale of one additional unit of its product; equal to the change in Total revenue divided by the change in the quantity of the product sold (demanded).

Marginal-revenue–marginal-cost approach The method which finds the total output at which Economic profit ***(see)*** is a maximum (or losses a minimum) by comparing the Marginal revenue ***(see)*** and the Marginal cost ***(see)*** of each additional unit of output.

Marginal revenue product The change in the Total revenue of the Firm when it employs one additional unit of a resource (the quantity of all other resources employed remaining constant); equal to the change in Total revenue divided by the change in the quantity of the resource employed.

Marginal tax rate The fraction of additional (taxable) income that must be paid in taxes.

Marginal utility The extra Utility ***(see)*** a consumer obtains from the consumption of one additional unit of a good or service; equal to the change in total Utility divided by the change in the quantity consumed.

Market Any institution or mechanism that brings together the buyers (demanders) and sellers (suppliers) of a particular good or service.

Market demand (***See*** Total demand.)

Market economy An economy in which only the private decisions of consumers, resource suppliers, and business Firms determine how resources are allocated; the Market system.

Market failure The failure of a market to bring about the allocation of resources that best satisfies the wants of society (that maximizes the satisfaction of wants). In particular, the over- or underallocation of resources to the production of a particular good or service (because of Spillovers or informational problems) and no allocation of resources to the production of Public goods ***(see)***.

Market for externality rights A market in which the Perfectly inelastic supply ***(see)*** of the right to pollute the environment and the demand for the right to pollute would determine the price which a polluter would have to pay for the right.

Market-oriented income stabilization The proposal to shift the goal of farm policy from the enhancement to the stabilization of farm prices and incomes; allow farm prices and incomes to move toward their free-market levels in the long run; and have government stabilize farm prices and incomes from year to year by purchasing farm products when their prices fall below and by selling surplus farm products when their prices rise above their long-run trend of prices.

Market period A period of time in which producers of a product are unable to change the quantity produced in response to a change in its price; in which there is Perfect inelasticity of supply ***(see)***; and in which all resources are Fixed resources ***(see)***.

Market socialism An economic system (method of organization) in which property resources are publicly owned and markets and prices are used to direct and coordinate economic activities.

Market system All the product and resource markets of the economy and the relationships among them; a method which allows the prices determined in these markets to allocate the economy's scarce resources and to communicate and coordinate the decisions made by consumers, business firms, and resource suppliers.

Median-voter model The view that under majority rule the median (middle) voter will be in the dominant position to determine the outcome of an election.

Medicaid A Federal program in the United States which helps to finance the medical expenses of individuals covered by the Supplemental security income ***(see)*** and the Aid to families with dependent children ***(see)*** programs.

Medicare A Federal program which is financed by Payroll taxes ***(see)*** and provides for (1) compulsory hospital insurance for senior citizens and (2) low-cost voluntary insurance to help older Americans pay physicians' fees.

Medium of exchange Money ***(see)***; a convenient means of exchanging goods and services without engaging in Barter ***(see)***; what sellers generally accept and buyers generally use to pay for a good or service.

Microeconomics The part of economics concerned with such individual units within the economy as Industries, Firms, and Households; and with individual markets, particular prices, and specific goods and services.

Minimum wage The lowest Wage (rate) employers may legally pay for an hour of Labor.

Mixed capitalism An economy in which both government and private decisions determine how resources are allocated.

Monetary policy Changing the Money supply ***(see)*** to assist the economy to achieve a full-employment, noninflationary level of total output.

Money Any item which is generally acceptable to sellers in exchange for goods and services.

Money capital Money available to purchase Capital goods ***(see)***.

Money interest rate The Nominal interest rate ***(see)***.

Money wage The amount of money received by a worker per unit of time (hour, day, etc.); nominal wage.

Money wage rate (*See* Money wage.)

Monopolistic competition A market in which many Firms sell a Differentiated product ***(see)***, into which entry is relatively easy, in which the Firm has some control over the price at which the product it produces is sold, and in which there is considerable Nonprice competition ***(see)***.

Monopoly A market in which the number of sellers is so small that each seller is able to influence the total supply and the price of the good or service.

Monopsony A market in which there is only one buyer of the good, service, or resource.

Moral hazard problem The possibility that individuals or institutions will change their behavior in unanticipated ways as the result of a contract or agreement. Example: A bank whose deposits are insured against loss may make riskier loans and investments.

Most-favored-nation clause A clause in a trade agreement between the United States and another nation which provides that the other nation's Imports into the United States will be subjected to the lowest tariff levied then or later on any other nation's Imports into the United States.

MR = MC rule A Firm will maximize its Economic profit (or minimize its losses) by producing the output at which Marginal revenue ***(see)*** and Marginal cost ***(see)*** are equal—provided the price at which it can sell its products is equal to or greater than Average variable cost ***(see)***.

MRP = MRC rule To maximize Economic profit (or minimize losses) a Firm should employ the quantity of a resource at which its Marginal revenue product ***(see)*** is equal to its Marginal resource cost ***(see)***.

Mutual interdependence Situation in which a change in price (or in some other policy) by one Firm will affect the sales and profits of another Firm (or other Firms) and any Firm which makes such a change can expect the other Firm(s) to react in an unpredictable (uncertain) way.

Mutually exclusive goals Goals which conflict and cannot be achieved simultaneously.

National Labor Relations Act (*See* Wagner Act.)

National Labor Relations Board The board established by the Wagner (National Labor Relations) Act ***(see)*** of 1935 to investigate unfair labor practices, issue Cease-and-desist orders ***(see)***, and to conduct elections among employees to determine if they wish to be represented by a Labor union and which union they wish to represent them.

Natural monopoly An industry in which the Economies of scale ***(see)*** are so great that the product can be produced by one Firm at an average cost which is lower than it would be if it were produced by more than one Firm.

Negative income tax The proposal to subsidize families and individuals with money payments when their incomes fall below a Guaranteed income **(*see*)**; the negative tax would decrease as earned income increases. (*See* Benefit-loss rate.)

Negative relationship (*See* Inverse relationship.)

Net American income earned abroad Receipts of resource income from the rest of the world minus payments of resource income to the rest of the world; the difference between GDP **(*see*)** and GNP **(*see*)**.

Net capital movement The difference between the real and financial investments and loans made by individuals and Firms of one nation in the other nations of the world and the investments and loans made by individuals and Firms from other nations in a nation; Capital inflows less Capital outflows.

Net exports Exports **(*see*)** minus Imports **(*see*)**.

Net investment income The interest and dividend income received by the residents of a nation from residents of other nations less the interest and dividend payments made by the residents of that nation to the residents of other nations.

Net transfers The personal and government transfer payments made to residents of foreign nations less the personal and government transfer payments received from residents of foreign nations.

New International Economic Order A series of proposals made by the Less developed countries (LDCs) **(*see*)** for basic changes in their relationships with the advanced industrialized nations that would accelerate the growth of and redistribute world income to the LDCs.

New perspective view of advertising Envisions advertising as a low-cost source of consumer information which increases competition by making consumers more aware of substitute products.

NIT (*See* Negative income tax.)

NLRB (*See* National Labor Relations Board.)

Nominal interest rate The rate of interest expressed in dollars of current value (not adjusted for inflation).

Nominal wage The Money wage **(*see*)**.

Noncollusive oligopoly An Oligopoly **(*see*)** in which the Firms do not act together and in agreement to determine the price of the product and the output each Firm will produce or to determine the geographic area in which each Firm will sell.

Noncompeting groups Groups of workers in the economy that do not compete with each other for employment because the skill and training of the workers in one group are substantially different from those of the workers in other groups.

Nondurable good A Consumer good **(*see*)** with an expected life (use) of less than one year.

Nonexhaustive expenditure An expenditure by government that does not result directly in the employment of economic resources or the production of goods and services; ***see*** Government transfer payment.

Nonfinancial investment An investment which does not require households to save a part of their money incomes; but which uses surplus (unproductive) labor to build Capital goods.

Nonprice competition The means other than decreasing the prices of their products which Firms employ to attempt to increase the sale of their products; and which includes Product differentiation **(*see*)**, advertising, and sales promotion activities.

Nontariff barriers All barriers other than Tariffs **(*see*)** which nations erect to impede trade among nations: Import quotas **(*see*)**, licensing requirements, unreasonable product-quality standards, unnecessary red tape in customs procedures, etc.

Nonunion shop A place of employment at which none of the employees are members of a Labor union (and at which the employer attempts to hire only workers who are not apt to join a union).

Normal good A good or service of which consumers will purchase more (less) at every price when their incomes increase (decrease).

Normal profit Payment that must be made by a Firm to obtain and retain Entrepreneurial ability **(*see*)**; the minimum payment (income) Entrepreneurial ability must (expect to) receive to induce it to perform the entrepreneurial functions for a Firm; an Implicit cost **(*see*)**.

Normative economics That part of economics which pertains to value judgments about what the economy should be like; concerned with economic goals and policies.

Norris-LaGuardia Act The Federal act of 1932 which made it more difficult for employers to obtain Injunctions **(*see*)** against Labor unions in Federal courts and which declared that Yellow-dog contracts **(*see*)** were unenforceable.

NTBs (*See* Nontariff barriers.)

OASDHI (*See* Old age, survivors, and disability health insurance.)

Occupational discrimination The arbitrary restrictions which prevent blacks (and other minority groups) or women from entering the more desirable and higher-paying occupations.

Occupational licensure The laws of state or local governments which require a worker to obtain a license from a licensing board (by satisfying certain specified requirements) before engaging in a particular occupation.

Official reserves The foreign monies (currencies) owned by the central bank of a nation.

Old age, survivors, and disability health insurance The social program in the United States which is financed by Federal Payroll taxes (*see*) on employers and employees and which is designed to replace the Earnings lost when workers retire, die, or become unable to work.

Oligopoly A market in which a few Firms sell either a Standardized or Differentiated product, into which entry is difficult, in which the Firm's control over the price at which it sells its product is limited by Mutual interdependence (*see*) (except when there is collusion among firms), and in which there is typically a great deal of Nonprice competition (*see*).

Oligopsony A market in which there are a few buyers.

OPEC An acronym for the Organization of Petroleum Exporting Countries (*see*).

Open economy An economy which both exports and imports goods and services.

Open shop A place of employment at which the employer may hire either Labor union members or workers who are not (and need not become) members of the union.

Opportunity cost The amount of other products that must be forgone or sacrificed to produce a unit of a product.

Optimal amount of externality reduction That reduction of pollution or other negative externality where society's marginal benefit and marginal cost of reducing the externality are equal.

Organization of Petroleum Exporting Countries The cartel formed in 1970 by thirteen oil-producing countries to control the price at which they sell crude oil to foreign importers and the quantity of oil exported by its members and which accounts for a large proportion of the world's export of oil.

"Other things being equal" assumption Assuming that factors other than those being considered are constant.

Outpayments The expenditures of (its own or foreign) money which the individuals, Firms, and governments of one nation make to purchase goods and services, for Remittances, as investment income, and Capital outflows abroad.

Output effect The impact which a change in the price of a resource has on the output a Firm finds it most profitable to produce and the resulting effect on the quantity of the resource (and the quantities of other resources) employed by the Firm after the consequences of the Substitution effect (*see*) have been taken into account (eliminated).

Paradox of voting A situation where voting by majority rule fails to provide a consistent ranking of society's preferences for public goods or services.

Parity concept The notion that year after year a given output of a farm product should enable a farmer to acquire a constant amount of nonagricultural goods and services.

Parity price The price at which a given amount of an agricultural product would have to be sold to enable a farmer to obtain year after year money income needed to purchase a constant total quantity of nonagricultural goods and services.

Parity ratio The ratio (index) of the price received by farmers from the sale of an agricultural commodity to the (index of the) prices paid by them; used as a rationale for Price supports (*see*).

Partial equilibrium analysis The study of equilibrium prices and equilibrium outputs or employments in a particular market which assumes prices, outputs, and employments in the other markets of the economy remain unchanged.

Partnership An unincorporated business Firm owned and operated by two or more persons.

Patent laws The Federal laws which grant to inventors and innovators the exclusive right to produce and sell a new product or machine for a period of seventeen years.

Payments deficit (*See* Balance of payments deficit.)

Payments surplus (*See* Balance of payments surplus.)

Payroll tax A tax levied on employers of Labor equal to a percentage of all or part of the wages and salaries paid by them; and on employees equal to a percentage of all or part of the wages and salaries received by them.

Perestroika The essential feature of Mikhail Gorbachev's reform program to "restructure" the Soviet economy; includes modernization, decentralization, some privatization, and improved worker incentives.

Perfect elasticity of demand A change in the Quantity demanded requires no change in the price of the commodity; buyers will purchase as much of a commodity as is available at a constant price.

Perfect elasticity of supply A change in the Quantity supplied requires no change in the price of the commodity; sellers will make available as much of the commodity as buyers will purchase at a constant price.

Perfect inelasticity of demand A change in price results in no change in the Quantity demanded of a commodity; the Quantity demanded is the same at all prices.

Perfect inelasticity of supply A change in price results in no change in the Quantity supplied of a commodity; the Quantity supplied is the same at all prices.

Per se violations Collusive actions, such as attempts to fix prices or divide a market, which are violations of the antitrust laws even though the actions are unsuccessful.

Personal distribution of income The manner in which the economy's Personal or Disposable income is divided among different income classes or different households.

Personal income tax A tax levied on the taxable income of individuals (households and unincorporated firms).

Personal saving The Personal income of households less Personal taxes ***(see)*** and Personal consumption expenditures ***(see)***; Disposable income not spent for Consumer goods ***(see)***.

Planned economy An economy in which only government determines how resources are allocated.

Plant A physical establishment (Land and Capital) which performs one or more of the functions in the production (fabrication and distribution) of goods and services.

P = MC rule A firm in Pure competition ***(see)*** will maximize its Economic profit ***(see)*** or minimize its losses by producing the output at which the price of the product is equal to Marginal cost ***(see)***, provided that price is equal to or greater than Average variable cost ***(see)*** in the short run and equal to or greater than Average (total) cost ***(see)*** in the long run.

Policy economics The formulation of courses of action to bring about desired results or to prevent undesired occurrences (to control economic events).

Positive economics The analysis of facts or data to establish scientific generalizations about economic behavior; compare Normative economics.

Positive relationship The relationship between two variables which change in the same direction, for example, product price and quantity supplied.

***Post hoc, ergo propter hoc* fallacy** Incorrectly reasoning that when one event precedes another the first event is the cause of the second.

Potential competition The possibility that new competitors will be induced to enter an industry if firms now in that industry are realizing large economic profits.

Poverty An existence in which the basic needs of an individual or family exceed the means to satisfy them.

Poverty rate The percentage of the population with incomes below the official poverty income levels established by the Federal government.

Preferential hiring A practice (often required by the provisions of a contract between a Labor union and an employer) which requires the employer to hire union members so long as they are available and to hire nonunion workers only when union members are not available.

Preferential tariff treatment Setting Tariffs lower for one nation (or group of nations) than for others.

Price The quantity of money (or of other goods and services) paid and received for a unit of a good or service.

Price ceiling A legally established maximum price for a good or service.

Price-decreasing effect The effect in a competitive market of a decrease in Demand or an increase in Supply upon the Equilibrium price ***(see)***.

Price discrimination The selling of a product (at a given time) to different buyers at different prices when the price differences are not justified by differences in the cost of producing the product for the different buyers; and a practice made illegal by the Clayton Act ***(see)*** when it reduces competition.

Price elasticity of demand The ratio of the percentage change in Quantity demanded of a commodity to the percentage change in its price; the responsiveness or sensitivity of the quantity of a commodity buyers demand to a change in the price of a commodity.

Price elasticity of supply The ratio of the percentage change in Quantity supplied of a commodity to the percentage change in its price; the responsiveness or sensitivity of the quantity of a commodity supplied to a change in the price of a commodity.

Price floor A legally determined price which is above the Equilibrium price.

Price increasing effect The effect in a competitive market of an increase in Demand or a decrease in Supply on the equilibrium price.

Price leadership An informal method which the Firms in an Oligopoly ***(see)*** may employ to set the price of the product they produce: one firm (the leader) is the first to announce a change in price and the other firms (the followers) quickly announce identical (or similar) changes in price.

Price maker A seller (or buyer) of a commodity that is able to affect the price at which the commodity sells by changing the amount it sells (buys).

Price support The minimum price which government allows sellers to receive for a good or service; a price which is a legally established or maintained minimum price.

Price taker A seller (or buyer) of a commodity that is unable to affect the price at which a commodity sells by changing the amount it sells (or buys).

Price war Successive and continued decreases in the prices charged by the firms in an oligopolistic industry by which each firm hopes to increase its sales and revenues and from which firms seldom benefit.

Principal-agent problem A conflict of interest which occurs when agents (workers) pursue their own objectives to the detriment of the principal's (employer's) goals.

Private good A good or service to which the Exclusion principle ***(see)*** is applicable and which is provided by privately owned firms to those who are willing to pay for it.

Private property The right of private persons and Firms to obtain, own, control, employ, dispose of, and bequeath Land, Capital, and other Assets.

Private sector The Households and business firms of the economy.

Product differentiation Physical or other differences between the products produced by different Firms which result in individual buyers preferring (so long as the price charged by all sellers is the same) the product of one Firm to the Products of the other Firms.

Production possibilities curve A curve which shows the different combinations of two goods or services that can be produced in a Full-employment **(*see*)**, Full-production **(*see*)** economy in which the available supplies of resources and technology are constant.

Production possibilities table A table which shows the different combinations of two goods or services that can be produced in a Full-employment **(*see*)**, Full-production **(*see*)** economy in which the available supplies of resources and technology are constant.

Productive efficiency The production of a good in the least costly way; occurs when production takes place at the output where Average total cost is at a minimum and where Marginal product per dollar's worth of each input is the same.

Productivity A measure of average output or real output per unit of input. For example, the productivity of labor may be determined by dividing hours of work into real output.

Product market A market in which Households buy and Firms sell the products they have produced.

Profit **(*See*)** Economic profit and Normal profit; without an adjective preceding it, the income of those who supply the economy with Entrepreneurial ability **(*see*)** or Normal profit.

Profit-maximizing case The circumstances which result in an Economic profit **(*see*)** for a Firm when it produces the output at which Economic profit is a maximum; when the price at which the Firm can sell its product is greater than the Average (total) cost of producing it.

Profit-maximizing rule (combination of resources) The quantity of each resource a Firm must employ if its Economic profit **(*see*)** is to be a maximum or its losses a minimum; the combination in which the Marginal revenue product **(*see*)** of each resource is equal to its Marginal resource cost **(*see*)** (to its price if the resource is employed in a competitive market).

Progressive tax A tax such that the Average tax rate increases as the taxpayer's income increases and decreases as income decreases.

Property tax A tax on the value of property (Capital, Land, stocks and bonds, and other Assets) owned by Firms and Households.

Proportional tax A tax such that the Average tax rate remains constant as the taxpayer's income increases and decreases.

Prosperous industry (*See* Expanding industry.)

Protective tariff A Tariff **(*see*)** designed to protect domestic producers of a good from the competition of foreign producers.

Public assistance programs Programs which pay benefits to those who are unable to earn income (because of permanent handicaps or because they are dependent children) which are financed by general tax revenues, and which are viewed as public charity (rather than earned rights).

Public choice theory Generalizations that describe how government (the Public sector) makes decisions for the use of economic resources.

Public good A good or service to which the Exclusion principle **(*see*)** is not applicable; and which is provided by government if it yields substantial benefits to society.

Public interest theory of regulation The presumption that the purpose of the regulation of an Industry is to protect the public (consumers) from the abuse of the power possessed by Natural monopolies **(*see*)**.

Public sector The part of the economy that contains all its governments; government.

Public-sector failure The failure of the Public sector (government) to resolve socioeconomic problems because it performs its functions in an economically inefficient fashion.

Public utility A Firm which produces an essential good or service, has obtained from a government the right to be the sole supplier of the good or service in the area, and is regulated by that government to prevent the abuse of its monopoly power.

Purchasing power parity The idea that exchange rates between nations equate the purchasing power of various currencies; exchange rates between any two nations adjust to reflect the price level differences between the countries.

Pure capitalism An economic system (method of organization) in which property resources are privately owned and markets and prices are used to direct and coordinate economic activities.

Pure competition (1) A market in which a very large number of Firms sells a Standardized product **(*see*)**, into which entry is very easy, in which the individual seller has no control over the price at which the product sells, and in which there is no Nonprice competition **(*see*)**; (2) a market in which there is a very large number of buyers.

Pure monopoly A market in which one Firm sells a unique product (one for which there are no close substitutes), into which entry is blocked, in which the Firm has considerable control over the price at which the product sells, and in which Nonprice competition **(*see*)** may or may not be found.

Pure profit (*See* Economic profit.)

Pure rate of interest (*See The* rate of interest.)

Quantity-decreasing effect The effect in a competitive market of a decrease in Demand or a decrease in Supply on the Equilibrium quantity ***(see)***.

Quantity demanded The amount of a good or service buyers wish (or a buyer wishes) to purchase at a particular price during some period of time.

Quantity-increasing effect The effect in a competitive market of an increase in Demand or an increase in Supply on the Equilibrium quantity ***(see)***.

Quantity supplied The amount of a good or service sellers offer (or a seller offers) to sell at a particular price during some period of time.

Quasi-public good A good or service to which the Exclusion principle ***(see)*** could be applied, but which has such a large Spillover benefit ***(see)*** that government sponsors its production to prevent an underallocation of resources.

Rate of exchange The price paid in one's own money to acquire one unit of a foreign money; the rate at which the money of one nation is exchanged for the money of another nation.

Rate of interest Price paid for the use of Money or for the use of Capital; interest rate.

Rational An adjective that describes the behavior of any individual who consistently does those things that will enable him or her to achieve the declared objective of the individual; and that describes the behavior of a consumer who uses money income to buy the collection of goods and services that yields the maximum amount of Utility ***(see)***.

Rationing function of price The ability of a price in a competitive market to equalize Quantity demanded and Quantity supplied and to eliminate shortages and surpluses by rising or falling.

Real capital (*See* Capital.)

Real wage The amount of goods and services a worker can purchase with his or her Nominal wage ***(see)***; the purchasing power of the Nominal wage; the Nominal wage adjusted for changes in the Price level.

Real wage rate (*See* Real wage.)

Reciprocal Trade Agreements Act of 1934 The Federal act which gave the President the authority to negotiate agreements with foreign nations and lower American tariff rates by up to 50 percent if the foreign nations would reduce tariff rates on American goods and which incorporated Most-favored-nation clauses ***(see)*** in the agreements reached with these nations.

Regressive tax A tax such that the Average tax rate decreases (increases) as the taxpayer's income increases (decreases).

Regulatory agency An agency (commission or board) established by the Federal or a state government to control for the benefit of the public the prices charged and the services offered (output produced) by a Natural monopoly ***(see)***.

Remittance A gift or grant; a payment for which no good or service is received in return; the funds sent by workers who have legally or illegally entered a foreign nation to their families in the nations from which they have migrated.

Rental income Income received by those who supply the economy with Land ***(see)***.

Rent-seeking behavior The pursuit through government of a transfer of income or wealth to a resource supplier, business, or consumer at someone else's or society's expense.

Resource market A market in which Households sell and Firms buy the services of resources.

Revaluation An increase in the defined value of a currency.

Revenue tariff A Tariff ***(see)*** designed to produce income for the (Federal) government.

Right-to-work law A law which has been enacted in twenty states that makes it illegal in those states to require a worker to join a Labor union in order to retain his or her job with an employer.

Roundabout production The construction and use of Capital ***(see)*** to aid in the production of Consumer goods ***(see)***.

Ruble overhang The large amount of forced savings held by Russian households due to the scarcity of consumer goods; these savings could fuel inflation when Russian prices are decontrolled.

Rule of reason The rule stated and applied in the U.S. Steel case ***(see)*** that only combinations and contracts that unreasonably restrain trade are subject to actions under the antitrust laws and that size and the possession of monopoly were not themselves illegal.

Sales tax A tax levied on expenditures for a broad group of products.

Saving Disposable income not spent for Consumer goods ***(see)***; not spending for consumption; equal to Disposal income minus Personal consumption expenditures ***(see)***.

Scarce resources The fixed (limited) quantities of Land, Capital, Labor, and Entrepreneurial ability ***(see all)*** which are never sufficient to satisfy the material wants of humans because their wants are unlimited.

Schumpeter-Galbraith view (of oligopoly) The belief shared by these two economists that large oligopolistic firms are necessary if there is to be a rapid rate of technological progress (because only this kind of firm has both the means and the incentive to introduce technological changes).

Secondary boycott The refusal of a Labor union to buy or to work with the products produced by another union or a group of nonunion workers.

"Second economy" The semilegal and illegal markets and activities which existed side by side with the legal and official markets and activities in the former U.S.S.R.

Self-interest What each Firm, property owner, worker, and consumer believes is best for itself and seeks to obtain.

Seniority The length of time a worker has been employed by an employer relative to the lengths of time the employer's other workers have been employed; the principle which is used to determine which workers will be laid off when there is insufficient work for them all and who will be rehired when more work becomes available.

Separation of ownership and control Difference between the group that owns the Corporation (the stockholders) and the group that manages it (the directors and officers) and between the interests (goals) of the two groups.

Service That which is intangible (invisible) and for which a consumer, firm, or government is willing to exchange something of value.

Sherman Act The Federal antitrust act of 1890 which made monopoly, restraint of trade, and combinations and conspiracies to monopolize or to restrain trade criminal offenses; and allowed the Federal government or injured parties to take legal action against those committing these offenses.

Shirking Attempts by workers to increase their utility or well-being by neglecting or evading work.

Shortage The amount by which the Quantity demanded of a product exceeds the Quantity supplied at a given (below-equilibrium) price.

Short run A period of time in which producers of a product are able to change the quantity of some but not all of the resources they employ; in which some resources—the Plant ***(see)***—are Fixed resources ***(see)*** and some are Variable resources ***(see)***; in which some costs are Fixed costs ***(see)*** and some are Variable costs ***(see)***; a period of time too brief to allow a Firm to vary its plant capacity but long enough to permit it to change the level at which the plant capacity is used; a period of time not long enough to enable Firms to enter or to leave an Industry ***(see)***.

Short-run competitive equilibrium The price at which the total quantity of a product supplied in the Short run ***(see)*** by a purely competitive industry and the total quantity of the product demanded are equal and which is equal to or greater than the Average variable cost ***(see)*** of producing the product.

Short-run farm problem The sharp year-to-year changes in the prices of agricultural products and in the incomes of farmers.

Simpson-Rodino Act of 1986 Immigration legislation which provides amnesty to qualified illegal aliens; includes penalties for employers who knowingly hire illegal aliens; and allows temporary migrants to harvest perishable crops.

Single-tax movement The attempt of a group which followed the teachings of Henry George to eliminate all taxes except one which would tax all Rental income ***(see)*** at a rate of 100 percent.

Slope of a line The ratio of the vertical change (the rise or fall) to the horizontal change (the run) in moving between two points on a line. The slope of an upward sloping line is positive, reflecting a direct relationship between two variables; the slope of a downward sloping line is negative, reflecting an inverse relationship between two variables.

Smoot-Hawley Tariff Act Passed in 1930, this legislation established some of the highest tariffs in United States history. Its objective was to reduce imports and stimulate the domestic economy.

Socially optimal price The price of a product which results in the most efficient allocation of an economy's resources and which is equal to the Marginal cost ***(see)*** of the last unit of the product produced.

Social regulation The type of regulation in which government is concerned with the conditions under which goods and services are produced, their physical characteristics, and the impact of their production on society; in contrast to Industrial regulation ***(see)***.

Social security programs The programs which replace the earnings lost when people retire or are temporarily unemployed, which are financed by Payroll taxes ***(see)***, and which are viewed as earned rights (rather than charity).

Sole proprietorship An unincorporated business firm owned and operated by a single person.

Special-interest effect Effect on public decision making and the allocation of resources in the economy when government promotes the interests (goals) of small groups to the detriment of society as a whole.

Specialization The use of the resources of an individual, a Firm, a region, or a nation to produce one or a few goods and services.

Spillover A benefit or cost associated with the consumption or production of a good or service which is obtained by or inflicted without compensation on a party other than the buyer or seller of the good or service (***see*** Spillover benefit and Spillover cost).

Spillover benefit The benefit obtained neither by producers nor by consumers of a product but without compensation by a third party (society as a whole).

Spillover cost The cost of producing a product borne neither by producers nor by consumers of the product but without compensation by a third party (society as a whole).

SSI (***See*** Supplemental security income.)

Stabilization fund A stock of money or of a commodity that is used to prevent the price of the commodity from changing by buying (selling) the commodity when its price decreases (increases).

Standardized product A product such that buyers are indifferent to the seller from whom they purchase it so long as the price charged by all sellers is the same; a product such that all units of the product are perfect substitutes for each other (are identical).

State ownership The ownership of property (Land and Capital) by government (the state); in the former U.S.S.R by the central government (the nation).

Strategic trade policy The use of trade barriers to reduce the risk of product development by domestic firms, particularly products involving advanced technology.

Strike The withholding of their labor services by an organized group of workers (a Labor union).

Strikebreaker A person employed by a Firm when its employees are engaged in a strike against the firm.

Structural-change hypothesis The explanation that attributes the relative decline of unionism in the United States to changes in the structure of the economy and of the labor force.

Subsidy A payment of funds (or goods and services) by a government, business firm, or household for which it receives no good or service in return. When made by a government, it is a Government transfer payment ***(see)***.

Substitute goods Goods or services such that there is a direct relationship between the price of one and the Demand for the other; when the price of one falls (rises) the Demand for the other decreases (increases).

Substitution effect (1) The effect which a change in the price of a Consumer good would have on the relative expensiveness of that good and the resulting effect on the quantity of the good a consumer would purchase if the consumer's Real income ***(see)*** remained constant; (2) the effect which a change in the price of a resource would have on the quantity of the resource employed by a firm if the firm did not change its output.

Superfund Law of 1980 Legislation which taxes manufacturers of toxic products and uses these revenues to finance the cleanup of toxic-waste sites; assigns liability for improperly dumped waste to the firms producing, transportings, and dumping that waste.

Superior good (*See* Normal good.)

Supplemental security income A program federally financed and administered which provides a uniform nationwide minimum income for the aged, blind, and disabled who do not qualify for benefits under the Old age, survivors, and disability health insurance ***(see)*** or Unemployment insurance ***(see)*** programs in the United States.

Supply A Supply schedule or a Supply curve ***(see both)***.

Supply curve A curve which shows the amounts of a good or service sellers (a seller) will offer to sell at various prices during some period of time.

Supply schedule A schedule which shows the amounts of a good or service sellers (or seller) will offer at various prices during some period of time.

Support price (*See* Price support.)

Surplus The amount by which the Quantity supplied of a product exceeds the Quantity demanded at a given (above-equilibrium) price.

Surplus value A Marxian term; the amount by which the value of a worker's daily output exceeds his daily wage; the output of workers appropriated by capitalists as profit.

Sympathy strike Withholding from an employer the labor services of its members by a Labor union that does not have a disagreement with the employer but wishes to assist another Labor union that does have a disagreement with the employer.

Tacit collusion Any method used in a Collusive oligopoly ***(see)*** to set prices and outputs or the market area of each firm that does not involve outright (or overt) collusion (formal agreements or secret meetings); and of which Price leadership ***(see)*** is a frequent example.

Taft-Hartley Act The Federal act of 1947 which marked the shift from government sponsorship to government regulation of Labor unions.

Tangent The point at which a line touches, but does not intersect, a curve.

Tariff A tax imposed (only by the Federal government in the United States) on an imported good.

Tax A nonvoluntary payment of money (or goods and services) to a government by a Household or Firm for which the Household or Firm receives no good or service directly in return and which is not a fine imposed by a court for an illegal act.

Tax incidence The income or purchasing power which different persons and groups lose as a result of the imposition of a tax after Tax shifting ***(see)*** has occurred.

Tax shifting The transfer to others of all or part of a tax by charging them a higher price or by paying them a lower price for a good or service.

Tax-transfer disincentives Decreases in the incentives to work, save, invest, innovate, and take risks that allegedly result from high Marginal tax rates and Transfer-payment programs.

Technology The body of knowledge that can be used to produce goods and services from Economic resources.

Terms of trade The rate at which units of one product can be exchanged for units of another product; the Price ***(see)*** of a good or service; the amount of one good or service that must be given up to obtain one unit of another good or service.

Theory of human capital Generalization that Wage differentials ***(see)*** are the result of differences in the amount of Human-capital investment (***see***); and that the incomes of lower-paid workers are increased by increasing the amount of such investment.

The rate of interest The Rate of interest (***see***) which is paid solely for the use of Money over an extended period of time and which excludes the charges made for the riskiness of the loan and its administrative costs; and which is approximately equal to the rate of interest paid on the long-term and virtually riskless bonds of the United States government.

Total cost The sum of Fixed cost (***see***) and Variable cost (***see***).

Total demand The Demand schedule (***see***) or the Demand curve (***see***) of all buyers of a good or service.

Total product The total output of a particular good or service produced by a firm (a group of firms or the entire economy).

Total revenue The total number of dollars received by a Firm (or Firms) from the sale of a product; equal to the total expenditures for the product produced by the Firm (or firms); equal to the quantity sold (demanded) multiplied by the price at which it is sold—by the Average revenue (***see***) from its sale.

Total-revenue test A test to determine whether Demand is Elastic (***see***), Inelastic (***see***), or of Unitary elasticity (***see***) between any two prices: Demand is elastic (inelastic, unit elastic) if the Total revenue (***see***) of sellers of the commodity increases (decreases, remains constant) when the price of the commodity falls; or Total revenue decreases (increases, remains constant) when its price rises.

Total-revenue–total-cost approach The method which finds the output at which Economic profit (***see***) is a maximum or losses a minimum by comparing the Total revenue and the Total costs of a Firm at different outputs.

Total spending The total amount buyers of goods and services spend or plan to spend.

Total supply The Supply schedule (***see***) or the Supply curve (***see***) of all sellers of a good or service.

Trade balance The export of merchandise (goods) of a nation less its imports of merchandise (goods).

Trade controls Tariffs (***see***), export subsidies, Import quotas (***see***), and other means a nation may employ to reduce Imports (***see***) and expand Exports (***see***).

Trade deficit The amount by which a nation's imports of merchandise (goods) exceed its exports of merchandise (goods).

Trade surplus The amount by which a nation's exports of merchandise (goods) exceed its imports of merchandise (goods).

Trading possibilities line A line which shows the different combinations of two products an economy is able to obtain (consume) when it specializes in the production of one product and trades (exports) this product to obtain the other product.

Traditional economy An economic system (method of organization) in which traditions and customs determine how the economy will use its scarce resources.

Traditional view of advertising The position that advertising is persuasive rather than informative; promotes industrial concentration; and is essentially inefficient and wasteful.

Transfer payment A payment of money (or goods and services) by a government or a Firm to a Household or Firm for which the payer receives no good or service directly in return.

Truth in Lending Act Federal law enacted in 1968 that is designed to protect consumers who borrow; and that requires the lender to state in concise and uniform language the costs and terms of the credit (the finance charges and the annual percentage rate of interest).

Tying agreement A promise made by a buyer when allowed to purchase a product from a seller that it will make all of its purchases of certain other products from the same seller; and a practice forbidden by the Clayton Act (***see***).

Underemployment Failure to produce the maximum amount of goods and services that can be produced from the resources employed; failure to achieve Full production (***see***).

Unemployment Failure to use all available Economic resources to produce goods and services; failure of the economy to employ fully its Labor force (***see***).

Unemployment compensation (***See*** Unemployment insurance).

Unemployment insurance The insurance program which in the United States is financed by state Payroll taxes (***see***) on employers and makes income available to workers who are unable to find jobs.

Uninsurable risk An event, the occurrence of which is uncontrollable and unpredictable, which would result in a loss that cannot be avoided by purchasing insurance and must be assumed by an entrepreneur (***See*** Entrepreneurial ability); sometimes called "uncertainty."

Union shop A place of employment at which the employer may hire either labor union members or workers who are not members of the union but who must become members within a specified period of time or lose their jobs.

Unitary elasticity The Elasticity coefficient (***see***) is equal to one; the percentage change in the quantity (demanded or supplied) is equal to the percentage change in price.

United States–Canadian Free-Trade Agreement An accord signed in 1988 to eliminate all trade barriers between the two nations over a ten-year period.

Unit labor cost Labor costs per unit of output; equal to the Nominal wage rate ***(see)*** divided by the Average product ***(see)*** of labor.

Unlimited liability Absence of any limit on the maximum amount that may be lost by an individual and that the individual may become legally required to pay; the amount that may be lost and that a sole proprietor or partner may be required to pay.

Unlimited wants The insatiable desire of consumers (people) for goods and services that will give them pleasure or satisfaction.

Unprosperous industry (*See* Declining industry.)

U.S. Steel case The antitrust action brought by the Federal government against the U.S. Steel Corporation in which the courts ruled (in 1920) that only unreasonable restraints of trade were illegal and size and the possession of monopoly power were not violations of the antitrust laws.

Utility The want-satisfying power of a good or service; the satisfaction or pleasure a consumer obtains from the consumption of a good or service (or from the consumption of a collection of goods and services).

Utility-maximizing rule To obtain the greatest Utility ***(see)*** the consumer should allocate Money income so that the last dollar spent on each good or service yields the same Marginal utility ***(see)***; so that the Marginal utility of each good or service divided by its price is the same for all goods and services.

Value-added tax A tax imposed on the difference between the value of the goods sold by a firm and the value of the goods purchased by the firm from other firms.

Value judgment Opinion of what is desirable or undesirable; belief regarding what ought or ought not to be (regarding what is right or just and wrong or unjust).

Variable cost A cost which in total increases (decreases) when the firm increases (decreases) its output; the cost of Variable resources ***(see)***.

Variable resource Any resource employed by a firm the quantity of which can be increased or decreased (varied).

VAT Value-added tax ***(see)***.

VERs (*See* Voluntary export restrictions.)

Vertical axis The "up–down" or "north–south" axis on a graph or grid.

Vertical combination A group of Plants ***(see)*** engaged in different stages of the production of a final product and owned by a single Firm ***(see)***.

Vertical intercept The point at which a line meets the vertical axis of a graph.

Vertical merger The merger of one or more Firms engaged in different stages of the production of a final product into a single Firm.

Voice mechanism Communication by workers through their union to resolve grievances with an employer.

Voluntary export restrictions The limitations by firms of their exports to particular foreign nations to avoid the erection of other trade barriers by the foreign nations.

Wage The price paid for Labor (for the use or services of Labor, ***see***) per unit of time (per hour, per day, etc.).

Wage differential The difference between the Wage ***(see)*** received by one worker or group of workers and that received by another worker or group of workers.

Wage discrimination The payments to blacks (or other minority groups) of a wage lower than that paid to whites for doing the same work.

Wage rate (*See* Wage.)

Wages The income of those who supply the economy with Labor ***(see)***.

Wagner Act The Federal act of 1935 which established the National Labor Relations Board ***(see)***, guaranteed the rights of Labor unions to organize and to bargain collectively with employers, and listed and prohibited a number of unfair labor practices by employers.

Wastes of monopolistic competition The waste of economic resources resulting from producing an output at which price is more than marginal cost and average cost is more than the minimum average cost.

Welfare programs (*See* Public assistance programs.)

Wheeler-Lea Act The Federal act of 1938 which amended the Federal Trade Commission Act ***(see)*** by prohibiting and giving the commission power to investigate unfair and deceptive acts or practices of commerce (false and misleading advertising and the misrepresentation of products).

Workfare plans Reforms of the welfare system, particularly AFDC, designed to provide education and training for recipients so that they may move from public assistance to gainful employment.

World Bank A bank which lends (and guarantees loans) to less developed nations to assist them to grow; formally, the International Bank for Reconstruction and Development.

X-inefficiency Failure to produce any given output at the lowest average (and total) cost possible.

Yellow-dog contract The (now illegal) contract in which an employee agrees when accepting employment with a Firm that he or she will not become a member of a Labor union while employed by the Firm.

INDEX

A

Ability:
  income inequality and, **382**
  wage differentials and, **267–268**
Ability-to-pay principle, tax apportionment and, **331**
Acid rain, **314**
Acreage allotment programs, **369**
ADA (Airline Deregulation Act of 1978), **353**
Adams, Walter, **155, 234*n.*, 235, 238**
Adjustable-peg system of exchange rates, **457–460**
Administrative costs of social regulation, **355–356**
Advantage, comparative (*see* Comparative advantage)
Adverse selection problem, **318–319**
Advertising:
  monopolistic competition and, **213–217**
  pure monopoly and, **188**
AFC (average fixed cost), **146**
AFDC (Aid to Families with Dependent Children), **318, 390–391, 393**
AFL (American Federation of Labor) **398, 399, 401**
AFL-CIO, **401**
Africa, famine in, **30**
After this, because of this, fallacy, **9**
Age, general equilibrium analysis and, **297–300**
Aggregate(s), **5**
Aggregate demand, trade deficits and, **463–464**
Agricultural Adjustment Act of 1933, **367**
Agricultural cooperatives, antitrust laws and, **350**
Agriculture, **362–375**
  decline in farm population and, **372**
  demand for agricultural products and, **362–365**
    bolstering, **369–370**
  economics of, **362–366**
  farm products and, price elasticity of demand and, **113**
  firms engaged in, **75**
  global, **374–375**
  Soviet, collapse of Soviet system and, **474**
  temporary farm labor immigrants and, **413**
  (*See also* Farm policy)
Aid to Families with Dependent Children (AFDC), **318, 390–391, 393**
Air pollution, **314**
  (*See also* Externalities; Pollution)
Airline Deregulation Act (ADA) of 1978, **353**
Airline industry:
  deregulation of, **353–355**
    price elasticity of demand and, **113**
  price fixing and, **350**
Akerlof, George A., **321**
Alcoa (Aluminum Company of America), **190, 350**
  antitrust case and, **347**
Allis-Chalmers, **228–229**
Allocative efficiency, **22**
  invisible hand and, **181**
  of market system, **85**
  monopolistic competition and, **211**
  oligopoly and, **232**
  pure competition and, **179–181**
Aluminum Company of America (Alcoa), **190, 350**
  antitrust case and, **347**
American Baseball League, **261**
American Federation of Labor (AFL), **398, 399, 401**
American Medical Association, **121, 264**
American Telephone and Telegraph (AT&T), **262, 348, 350**
Amnesty for illegal immigrants, **413**
Amoco, **44–45, 484**
Anheuser Busch, **236**
Antipollution policy, **313–314**
Antitrust laws, **345–351**
  background of, **345–346**
  behavior versus structure and, **347–348**
  collusion and, **230**
  effectiveness of, **348–350**
  market definition and, **348**
  restriction of competition and, **350**
A&P, **71**
Appreciation of currency, **451, 458*n.***
  foreign exchange market and, **64**
Arcon Manufacturing, **44**
Armenia, **470**
ATC (average total cost), **147**
  marginal cost and, **149**
Athletes, wages of, **261–262, 270–271, 378**
  racial discrimination and, **416**
AT&T (American Telephone and Telegraph), **262, 348, 350**
Authoritarian capitalism, **31**
Automation, price elasticity of demand and, **113**
Automobile industry:
  foreign competition and, **77, 235–238**
    restriction of Japanese imports and, **439**
    trade barriers and, **432, 438**
  market for "lemons" and, **320–321**
  as oligopoly, **234–238**
  pollution and, **314**
  social regulation of, **356**
AVC (average variable cost), **146–147**
  marginal cost and, **149**
Average costs, **146–147**
  fixed, **146**
  total, **147, 149**
  variable, **146–147, 149**
Average fixed cost (AFC), **146**
Average product, **143**
Average revenue, **163**
Average tax rate, **99**
Average total cost (ATC), **147**
  marginal cost and, **149**
Average variable cost (AVC), **146–147**
  marginal cost and, **149**
Axes, vertical and horizontal, **14**
Azerbaijan, **470, 481**

B

Baby boom:
  changes in demand and, **52**
  general equilibrium analysis and, **298**
Backflows, immigration and, **415**
Backman, Jules, **229*n.***
Baer, George F., **398*n.***
Balance of payments, **446–450**
  capital account and, **448**
  current account and, **447–448**
  deficits and surpluses and, **449**
  exchange rate systems and, **450–456**
  flexible exchange rates and, **452–453**
  interrelationships between current and capital accounts and, **448**
  official reserves and, **449**
Balance of trade:
  current account and, **447**
  as economic goal, **7**
Balance on capital account, **448**
Balance on current account, **447–448**

Balance on goods and services, **447**
Baltic states, **470, 480**
Bank(s):
  Soviet, **472**
  supply of loanable funds and, **280**
Bargaining, spillovers and, **307–308**
Barriers to entry (*see* Market entry barriers)
Bartering, **41–45**
Bastiat, Frédéric, **441**
Beer industry as oligopoly, **236–237**
Benefit(s):
  marginal:
    marginal benefit = marginal cost rule and, **306**
    optimal amount of externality reduction and, **311–312**
  public sector failure and, **328–329**
  spillover (social), **92–94, 183**
    correcting for, **92–93**
Benefit-cost analysis, **305–306**
Benefit-loss rate, **391–392**
Benefits-received principle, tax apportionment and, **331**
Benham, Alexandra, **216*n.***
Benham, Lee, **216*n.***
Bethlehem Steel, **71**
Bias, **8**
Bilateral monopoly, wages under, **265–266**
Black market:
  price ceilings and, **118–119**
  rationing and, **118**
"Black underclass," **387–388**
Blacklisting, **398**
Boddy, Francis M., **294*n.***
Bond(s), **73, 84–85**
  risk of, **85**
  stocks differentiated from, **84–85**
Bonuses, **272**
Borden, **350**
Boulding, Kenneth E., **4*n.***
Bowen, Howard R., **46*n.***
Break-even income, **391–392**
Bretton Woods system, **457–460**
  demise of, **459–460**
Brezhnev, Leonid, **483**
Brock, James W., **155, 234*n.*, 235, 238**
Browning, Edgar K., **381**
Buchwald, Art, **465**
Budget deficit:
  cutting taxes and, **339**
  farm policy and, **372**
  reducing, **465–466**
  trade deficits and, **465–466**
Budget line, **134–135**
Budget restraint, **126–127**
Budgeting, microeconomic, **28–29**
Bureaucracy:
  public sector failure and, **329–330**
  transition of Soviet economy to market system and, **480**
Business(es), **71–76**
  in circular flow model, **44**
  demand for loanable funds and, **279–280**
Business(es) (continued)
  legal forms of, **71–74**
  (*See also* Corporations; Firms; Private sector)
Business unionism, evolution of, **398–399**
Buyers, inadequate information about, **318–319**
By-products, economies of scale and, **153–154**

C

CAB (Civil Aeronautics Board), **353**
Cady, John F., **216*n.***
Cairns Group, **373**
Campbell, Robert W., **471*n.***
Canada as U.S. trading partner, **76**
  North American Free-Trade Zone and, **438–439**
  U.S.-Canadian Free-Trade Agreement and, **438**
Canner, Glenn B., **118*n.***
Canterbery, E. Ray, **2*n.***
Capital:
  allocation of, interest rates and, **282**
  efficiency of, economies of scale and, **152–153**
  financial, **21**
  real, **21**
  as resource, **20–21**
  wages and, **256**
Capital account, **448**
  balance on, **448**
  interrelationships between current account and, **448**
Capital accumulation, **83**
Capital goods, **21, 23**
  under capitalism, **38–39**
  production possibilities table and, **23**
Capital-intensive goods, international trade and, **424**
Capitalism:
  authoritarian, **31**
  pure (*see* Pure capitalism)
Capitalist nations, role in transition of Soviet economy, **481–484**
Cartels, **228**
  legal cartel theory of regulation and, **352–353**
  (*See also* Organization of Petroleum Exporting Countries)
Causation, correlation differentiated from, **9**
Caves, Richard E., **461*n.***
CBS Records, **77**
CEA (Council of Economic Advisers), **2**
Cease-and-desist orders, **347**
Celler-Kefauver Act of 1950, **347**
Central economic planning, **31**
  Soviet, **471–473**
    collapse of Soviet system and, **474–475**
    coordination problem and, **472–473**
    ends and means and, **471–472**
Ceteris paribus assumption, **5, 15**
Chain stores, **71**
Change in demand, **53**
Change in quantity demanded, **53**
Cheating, collusion and, **224, 229**
Chevron, **44–45, 484**
Chicago Board of Trade, **47, 314**
Choice:
  consumer, **126–127**
    freedom of, **36**
    under pure competition, **183**
  limited, public sector failure and, **329**
  present, future possibilities and, **27–28**
  production possibilities table and, **23**
Chrysler, **77, 234–238**
Cigarette industry, pricing in, **230–231**
Circular flow model:
  government and, **95–96**
  limitations of, **45**
  pure capitalism and, **43–45**
  resource and product markets and, **43–45**
Citizenship, economics for, **2**
Civil Aeronautics Board (CAB), **353**
Clay, Henry, **12*n.***
Clayton Act of 1914, **346–347, 349**
Clean Air Act of 1990, **314**
Clemens, Roger, **378**
Close-down case:
  marginal-revenue–marginal-cost approach and, **170–171**
  total-revenue–total-cost approach and, **165–167**
Closed shop, **400–401**
Clotfelter, Charles T., **101**
Coase theorem, **307**
Coca-Cola, **44, 80**
Cocaine, price elasticity of demand and, **113–114**
COLAs (cost-of-living adjustments), **403**
Collective bargaining, **402–404**
  process of, **402**
  work agreement and, **402–404**
Collective voice, unions and, **407**
Collusion, **350**
  cartels and, **228**
  covert, **228–229**
  obstacles to, **229–230**
  oligopoly and, **224, 227–228**
Colombia, cocaine industry in, **63**
Comanor, William S., **215*n.***
Command economy, **30–31**
  (*See also* Soviet Union)
Commissions, **272**
Common Market, **437–438**
  farm policy and, **372–374**
Commonwealth of Independent States, **470**
  (*See also* Soviet Union)
Communications Workers of America (CWA), **262**
Communism, **30–31**
  Soviet, **470**
    failure of, **473–476**
Company unions, **398**
Comparable worth doctrine, **412**
Comparative advantage, **424–429**
  basic principle of, **424**

Comparative advantage (continued)
comparative costs and, **39–40**
costs and, **39–40, 425, 428–429**
free trade and, **429**
gains from trade and, **40–41, 427–428**
self-sufficiency and, **425–426**
specialization and, **39–41, 426**
terms of trade and, **40, 426–427**
Competition:
advertising as, **214**
automobile industry and, **235–238**
under capitalism, **36–37**
entry and exit and, **37**
foreign (*see* Foreign competition)
global trade and finance and, **77**
government regulation of, **89–90**
imperfect, **161**
import, **221**
industrial concentration and, **345**
interindustry, **221**
industrial concentration and, **345**
"invisible hand" and, **83–85**
large numbers and, **37**
markets under, **47–64, 78**
monopolistic (*see* Monopolistic competition)
nonprice, **209, 212–213, 232**
price, **216–217**
promotion of, transition of Soviet economy to market system and, **477**
pure (*see* Pure competition)
reducing trade deficit and, **466**
regulation of competitive industries and, **352**
restriction of, **350**
social regulation and, **357**
Competitive labor market, wages in, **257–259**
Competitive view of oligopoly, **232–233**
Complementary goods, **52**
cross elasticity of demand and, **116**
Complementary resources, resource demand and, **246–247**
Compliance costs of social regulation, **355, 356**
Composition, fallacy of, **8–9**
trade barriers and, **433**
Compounding, **287**
Comprehensive Trade Act of 1988, **439**
Concentration ratios, oligopoly and, **221–222**
Conglomerate(s), **71**
Conglomerate mergers, **348, 349**
Congress of Industrial Organizations (CIO), **399–401**
Constant-cost industry, **116**
long-run profit maximization and, **175**
supply curve and, **116**
long-run, **177–178**
Constant returns to scale, **154**
Consumer(s):
agricultural price supports and, **368**
consumption by:
personal, expenditures for, **67–71**
trade barriers and, **431**
demand of, **50, 80**
Consumer(s) (continued)
expectations of:
changes in demand and, **52–53**
changes in supply and, **56**
freedom of choice and, **36**
number of, changes in demand and, **52**
preferences of (*see* Preferences)
(*See also* Households)
Consumer behavior, **126–129**
algebraic restatement of, **128–129**
choice and budget restraint and, **126–127**
utility-maximizing rule and, **127–128**
Consumer choice, **126–127**
freedom of, **36**
under pure competition, **183**
Consumer goods, **21**
production possibilities table and, **23**
Consumer Products Safety Commission (CPSC), **355**
Consumer Reports, **319**
Consumer sovereignty, **80**
general equilibrium and, **293**
Consumption:
personal, expenditures for, **67–71**
trade barriers and, **431**
Contestable markets theory, **182**
Contracts:
labor, **400–401**
collective bargaining and, **402–404**
cost-of-living adjustments and, **403**
"tying" (exclusive), **346**
yellow-dog, **398**
Control:
of corporations, separation from ownership, **74**
of exchange rates, **455**
of spillovers, **309**
Cook, Philip J., **101**
Coordination, Soviet, **472–473**
Corporations, **71, 73–74**
financing of, **73, 84–85**
growth of, income shares and, **285–286**
income taxes of, **74, 99, 332, 336**
Correlation, causation differentiated from, **9**
Cost(s):
of agricultural price supports, **368–369**
automobile industry and, **236**
average, **146–147, 149**
benefit-cost analysis and, **305–306**
collusion and, **229**
comparative advantage and, **39–40, 425, 428–429**
of discrimination, **412**
economic, **79, 140–142**
of production, **140–142**
elasticity of resource demand and, **248**
explicit, **141, 282**
fixed, **145, 146**
of health care, **120–121**
implicit, **141, 282**
increasing, comparative advantage and, **428–429**
Cost(s) (continued)
marginal (*see* Marginal cost)
marginal resource cost and, **242–243, 260**
of migration, **415**
monopoly and, **193, 198–199**
oligopoly and, **233**
opportunity (*see* Opportunity costs)
of production (*see* Production costs)
public sector failure and, **328–329**
of regulation, **352**
social, **355–356**
resource pricing and, **241**
spillover (social), **91, 183**
correcting for, **91–92**
total, **145–146, 149, 248**
of trade barriers, **440–441**
variable, **145–147, 149**
Cost curves:
long-run, **150–151**
shifting, **150**
Cost-of-living adjustments (COLAs), **21, 403**
Cost-plus pricing, oligopoly and, **231–232**
Coughlin, Cletus C., **441*n.***
Council of Economic Advisers (CEA), **2**
CPSC (Consumer Products Safety Commission), **355**
Craft unions, **400**
wages and, **263, 269**
Crandall, Robert W., **237*n.*, 356*n.*, 357*n.***
Credit(s):
in current account, **447**
price of (*see* Interest rate)
Credit cards, interest ceilings and, **118**
Crime, price elasticity of demand and, **113–114**
Criminal conspiracy doctrine, **397**
Cross elasticity of demand, **116**
Crowding model of occupational segregation, **410–412**
Currency:
appreciation and depreciation of, **451, 458*n.***
devaluation of, **458**
foreign exchange market and, **63, 64**
revaluation of, **458*n.***
(*See also* Dollar; Money)
Current account, **447–448**
balance on, **447–448**
interrelationships between capital account and, **448**
Curry Company, **204**
Customary economy, **31–32**
CWA (Communication Workers of America), **262**

D

Dahl, Robert A., **486*n.***
De Beers Company, **188, 191**
Debits in current account, **447**
Debt:
public:
government expenditures for interest on, **98**

Debt (continued)
trade deficits and, **464–465**
(*See also* Loan)
Decision(s), limited, fallacy of, **339–341**
Decision making, utility-maximizing rule and, **128**
Declining industry, **79–80**
Decreasing-cost industry, long-run supply curve for, **178–179**
Deduction, **3–4**
Defense:
federal expenditures for, **98**
growth of government and, **97**
Soviet, **471**
collapse of Soviet system and, **474**
transition to market system and, **481**
Deficit:
balance of payments, **449**
budget (*see* Budget deficit)
trade (*see* Trade deficit)
Definitions, **8**
Deindustrialization in United States, **358–359**
Demand, **48–53**
aggregate, trade deficits and, **463–464**
for agricultural products, **362–365**
bolstering, **369–370**
changes in, **51–53, 59–61**
collusion and, **229**
to competitive seller, **162–164**
consumer, **50, 80**
cross elasticity of, **116**
derived, **80, 241–242**
determinants of, **50–51**
economic rent and, **276**
elasticity of (*see* Elasticity of demand)
excess:
market equilibrium and, **57–58**
price ceilings and, **117–120**
income elasticity of, **116–117**
inelastic, **107**
total-revenue test and, **110**
for labor, **258**
elasticity of, unemployment and, **265**
wages and, **262–263**
law of, **48–49, 124–126**
for loanable funds, **279–280**
for marijuana, **63**
market, **48–53**
for labor, **258**
monopoly, **191–193**
perfectly elastic, **107, 162–163**
perfectly inelastic, **107**
price elasticity of (*see* Price elasticity of demand)
for products:
resource demand and, **245**
wages and, **262–263**
for public goods, **304–305**
growth of government and, **97**
for resources (*see* Resource demand)
spillover benefits and, **92–93**
unit elasticity of, **107**
Demand curve, **49–50**
changes in demand and, **53**
Demand curve (continued)
changes in quantity demanded and, **53**
derivation of, **129–130, 137–138**
of firm, monopolistic competition and, **209**
"kinked," **225–227**
marginal utility and, **129–130**
Demand schedule, **48**
marginal resource product as, **243**
Demand shifters, **51**
Democratization, transition of Soviet economy to market system and, **481**
Demographics:
income inequality and, **393**
(*See also* Age; Education and training; Population)
Denzau, Arthur T., **443*n.***
Dependent variable, **14–15**
Depreciation, of currency, **451, 458*n.***
foreign exchange market and, **63**
Deregulation, of airline industry, **113, 353–355**
Derived demand, **80, 241–242**
Descriptive economics, **3, 4**
Devaluation, **458**
Differentiated products, oligopoly and, **220–221**
Dilemma of regulation, **203–204**
Diminishing marginal product, law of, **142–145**
Diminishing marginal utility (*see* Marginal utility, diminishing)
Diminishing returns, law of, **142–145**
Direct relationships, graphing, **14**
Directing function of prices, **82–83**
Discounting, **287**
Discrimination, **409–413**
comparable worth doctrine and, **412**
costs of, **412**
crowding model of, **410–412**
dimensions of, **409–410**
eliminating, **411–412**
employment, **410**
human-capital, **410**
income inequality and, **382–383**
nondiscriminatory factors and, **412**
occupational, **410**
production possibilities curve and, **29**
wage, **410**
Discriminatory discharge, **397–398**
Diseconomies:
external (*see* Externalities; Pollution)
of scale, production costs and, **154**
Dissaving, by households, **69**
Distribution of total output, **81–82**
Dividends, **84**
Division of labor:
under capitalism, **39**
(*See also* Specialization)
Dollar:
appreciation of, **64**
depreciation of, **63**
value of, trade deficit and, **461–462**
Dollar votes, **80, 94*n.***
Domestic demand, for agricultural products, **363–364**
bolstering, **370**
Domestic production, trade barriers and, **431**
Double taxation of corporations, **74**
Doubleday Publishing, **77**
Dumping as argument for trade barriers, **434–435**
Duncan, Greg J., **388*n.***
Duopoly, **223**
du Pont, **190, 349, 350**
cellophane case and, **348**
Durable goods, **70**
Dynamic efficiency, **200–201, 232–233**

E

Eastman Kodak, **350**
Easy money policy, reducing trade deficit and, **466**
EC (European Economic Community), **437–438**
farm policy and, **372–374**
Eckard, E. Woodrow, Jr., **215**
Eckstein, Otto, **330*n.***
Economic costs, **79**
of production, **140–142**
Economic efficiency, as economic goal, **7**
Economic freedom, as economic goal, **7**
Economic goals, **6–7**
complementarity of, **7**
conflicting, **7**
interpretation and, **7**
priorities among, **7**
stating, **7–8**
Economic growth:
as economic goal, **6**
international trade and, **29**
Japanese, **29**
present choices and future possibilities and, **27–28**
production possibilities curve and, **26–29**
reducing trade deficit and, **466**
of United States, **29**
trade deficit and, **462–463**
Economic integration, trade barriers and, **437–439**
Economic planning:
in command economies, **31**
(*See also* Central economic planning)
Economic profits, **79, 141, 282–285**
sources of, **283–284**
Economic regulation, **351–353**
Economic rent, **275–278**
as surplus, **276–277**
Economic Report of the President, **2**
Economic security as economic goal, **7**
Economic theory, **3–6**
abstractions and, **5**
generalizations and, **4**
graphical expression of, **6**
macro and micro, **5–6**
"other things being equal" assumption and, **5**
terminology of, **4**
Economics:
citizenship and, **2**
definition of, **1**

Economics (continued)
descriptive, **3, 4**
efficiency and, **22–25**
empirical, **3, 4**
foundation of, **19–22**
methodology of, **3–8**
normative, **6–8**
personal applications of, **2–3**
perspectives of, **9–11**
policy, **4, 6–8**
positive, **6–8**
Economics textbooks, market for, **216–217**
Economies of scale:
as entry barriers, **189**
industrial concentration and, **345**
monopoly and, **198**
oligopoly and, **222**
production costs and, **151–154, 156–157**
Economizing problem, **19–32**
Economy(ies), **1**
capitalist (*see* Pure capitalism)
command (communist), **30–31**
(*See also* Soviet Union)
effect of monopoly on, **196–201**
external (*see* Externalities; Pollution)
market (*see* Pure capitalism)
mixed, **31**
oil price increases and, **295–297**
stabilization of, **94**
traditional (customary), **31–32**
of United States, impacts of global trade and finance on, **77–78**
world (*see* World economy)
Education and training:
income inequality and, **382, 393**
productivity and, **407**
wage differentials and, **268**
Efficiency:
advertising and, **214–215**
allocative (*see* Allocative efficiency)
dynamic, **200–201, 232–233**
economic, as economic goal, **7**
full employment and full production and, **22**
general equilibrium and, **294**
income inequality and, **384–386**
law of increasing opportunity costs and, **25**
loss of, taxes and, **334–336**
optimal product-mix and, **24**
production possibilities curve and, **23–24**
production possibilities table and, **22–23**
productive (*see* Productive efficiency)
public sector failure and, **329–330**
pure competition and, **179–183**
of regulation, **352**
Soviet, collapse of Soviet system and, **474**
specialization and, **39**
unions and, **405–407**
X-inefficiency and, **198–199**
Efficiency loss of taxes, **334–336**
Efficiency wages, **272**
Egalitarianism, growth of government and, **98**
Eklund, Robert B., Jr., **213*n.***
Elasticity of demand:
cross, **116**
efficiency loss of taxes and, **335–336**
income, **116–117**
for labor, unemployment and, **265**
long-run farm problem and, **365**
price (*see* Price elasticity of demand)
for products, elasticity of resource demand and, **247**
for resources, **247–248**
short-run farm problem and, **362–363**
tax incidence and, **333–334**
total-revenue test and, **109–110**
unit, **107, 110**
Elasticity of supply:
efficiency loss of taxes and, **335–336**
price, **114–116**
tax incidence and, **333–334**
Electrical equipment conspiracy, **228–229**
Elzinga, Kenneth G., **237**
Emission credits, **314**
Empirical economics, **3, 4**
Employee compensation (*see* Wage)
Employment:
discrimination and (*see* Discrimination)
domestic, trade barriers and, **432–433**
full (*see* Full employment)
(*See also* Unemployment; Union; Wage)
English cotton famine, **299–300**
Enterprise, freedom of, **36**
Entrepreneurial ability:
economic profits and, **283**
as resource, **21**
Entry (*see* Market entry; Market entry barriers)
Environmental Protection Agency (EPA), **313, 314**
Environmental quality:
growth of government and, **98**
(*See also* Externalities; Pollution)
EPA (Environmental Protection Agency), **313, 314**
Equalizing differences, wage differentials and, **268**
Equilibrium:
general (*see* General equilibrium analysis)
indifference curve analysis and, **136–137**
market (*see* Market equilibrium)
wages and, **272**
Equilibrium price, **58–61**
changes in supply and demand and, **59–61**
under pure competition, **173–174**
Equilibrium quantity, **58**
changes in supply and demand and, **59–61**
optimal amount of externality reduction and, **311**
Ericson, Richard E., **475*n.***
European Economic Community (EC), **437–438**
farm policy and, **372–374**
Excess capacity, wastes of monopolistic competition and, **211**
Exchange companies, **45**
Exchange rates, **450–461**
adjustable-peg system of, **457–460**
balance of payments and, **452–453**
Bretton Woods system and, **457–460**
changes in, **63–64**
determinants of, **451–452**
fixed, **454–457**
floating (flexible), **450–454**
managed, **460–461**
freely floating, **450–454**
instability and policy and, **77–78**
(*See also* Foreign exchange market)
Excise taxes, **99**
incidence of, **336–337**
price elasticity of demand and, **113**
Exclusion principle, **93**
Exclusive contracts, **346**
Exclusive unionism, wages and, **263**
Exit from market:
under capitalism, **37**
under pure competition, **162, 175–177**
Exit mechanism, unions and, **407**
Expanding industry, **79**
Expectations:
changes in demand and, **52–53**
changes in supply and, **56**
Expenditures:
government, **98, 100–101**
immigration and, **415–417**
of households, **68–71**
personal consumption, **67–71**
Explicit costs, **141, 282**
Export(s):
to less developed countries, trade deficit and, **463**
transaction for, **445**
(*See also* International trade; International trade policies)
Export subsidies, **437**
External economies (*see* Externalities; Pollution)
Externalities, **90–93, 307–316**
benefits of, **92–94, 183**
correcting for, **92–93**
costs of, **91, 183**
correcting for, **91–92**
direct controls and taxes and, **309**
growth of government and, **98**
individual bargaining and, **307–308**
liability rules and lawsuits and, **308–309**
market for externality rights and, **309–310**
pollution as, **312–316**
under pure competition, **183**
society's optimal amount of externality reduction and, **310–312**
(*See also* Environmental quality; Pollution)
Externality rights, market for, **309–310**

F

Factors of production, **21**
Fair Labor Standards Act, **266**
"Fair-return" price, **203**
Fallacies:
of composition, **8–9**
trade barriers and, **433**
of limited decisions, **339–341**
post hoc, ergo propter hoc, **9**
Family Support Act of 1988, **392**
Famine:
production possibilities curve and, **30**
world agriculture and, **374–375**
Fares, airline deregulation and, **353–354**
Farm Act of 1990, **373**
Farm policy, **366–374**
criticisms of, **370–371**
parity concept and, **367–368**
politics of, **371–372**
price supports and, **368–369**
size and rationale for, **366–367**
surpluses and, **369–370**
world trade and, **372–374**
Farming (*see* Agriculture; Farm policy)
Fast-food lines, economic perspective on, **10**
Featherbedding, **400, 405**
Federal budget (*see* Budget deficit; Public debt; Trade deficit)
Federal Communications Commission, **190**
Federal Trade Commission (FTC), **350**
Federal Trade Commission Act of 1914, **347**
Feedback(s), trade barriers and, **433**
Fergus, James T., **118*n.***
Finance:
of corporations, **73, 84–85**
globalized financial markets and, **77**
of government, **96–102**
federal, **98–99**
state and local, **100–102**
inflationary, transition of Soviet economy to market system and, **479–480**
of international trade, **444–446**
nonprice competition and, **232**
of partnerships, **73**
of sole proprietorships, **72**
Financial capital, **21**
Financial markets, globalized, **77**
Firestone Tire, **77**
Firm(s), **71**
demand curve of, monopolistic competition and, **209**
number of, collusion and, **229**
size of, production costs and, **150**
(*See also* Business; Corporations; Private sector)
Fiscal federalism, **102**
Fiscal policy, exchange rates and, **455–457**
Five Fundamental Questions, **78**
Fixed cost, **145**
average, **146**
Fixed exchange rate, gold standard and, **456–457**
Floating (flexible) exchange rates, **450–454**
managed, **460–461**
Fogel, Walter, **417*n.***
Food for Peace program, **370**
Food stamp program, **390**
Ford, **77, 234–238**
Foreign aid, to former Soviet Union, **482–483**
Foreign competition:
automobile industry and, **77, 235–238**
restriction of Japanese imports and, **439**
trade barriers and, **432, 438**
income inequality and, **393**
industrial concentration and, **345**
trade barriers and (*see* Trade barriers)
Foreign demand, for agricultural products, **364**
bolstering, **370**
Foreign enterprises, **75**
Foreign exchange market, **42, 62–64, 423, 444–446**
depreciation and appreciation and, **63–64**
economic consequences of exchange rate changes and, **64**
Foreign investment, direct, reducing trade deficit and, **466**
Foreign labor, cheap, as argument for trade barriers, **435**
Foreign sector, **76–78**
volume, pattern, and linkages of, **76–77**
Franchising, **319**
Free-rider problem, **93**
Free trade, defense of, **429**
Freedom, **339–341**
of choice, **36**
conservative position on, **339**
economic, as economic goal, **7**
of enterprise, **36**
liberal position on, **339–341**
market restraints on, **80**
under market system, **85**
Friedman, Milton, **339*n.***
Fringe benefits, **403, 404**
FTC (Federal Trade Commission), **350**
Fuchs, Victor R., **12*n.***
Full employment:
as economic goal, **7**
efficiency and, **22**
immigration and, **415**
Full production, efficiency and, **22**
Functional distribution of income, **67–68**
Fusfield, Daniel R., **2*n.***

G

G-7 nations, **461**
Gains from trade, comparative advantage and, **40–41, 427–428**
Galbraith, John Kenneth, **12*n.*, 233*n.***
Game theory model, oligopoly and, **223–224**
Gasoline market, inadequate information about sellers in, **317**
GATT (General Agreement on Tariffs and Trade), **436–439**
farm policy and, **373**
Soviet Union and, **484**
GDP (*see* Gross domestic product)
General Agreement on Tariffs and Trade (GATT), **436–439**
farm policy and, **373**
Soviet Union and, **484**
General Electric, **190, 228–229, 350**
General equilibrium analysis, **290–300**
aging population and, **297–300**
input-output analysis and, **294–295**
market interrelationships and, **295–297**
partial equilibrium and, **290–291**
two-industry model of, **291–294**
General Motors, **71, 75–77, 154–155, 190, 231, 234–238, 345, 349**
Generalizations, **4**
Gentlemen's agreements, **229**
Geographic immobility, wage differentials and, **268–269**
Geographic location, monopolistic competition and, **208**
Geographic specialization under capitalism, **39**
George, Henry, **277**
Georgian Republic, **470, 480**
Germany, Nazi, economy of, **31**
Glasnost, **476**
Gold export point, **456**
Gold import point, **456**
Gold standard, **456–457**
demise of, **457**
Goldman, Marshall I., **473*n.***
Gompers, Samuel, **398–399**
Goods, **20**
capital, **21, 23**
under capitalism, **38–39**
production possibilities table and, **23**
capital-intensive, **424**
complementary, **52, 116**
consumer, **21, 23**
durable, **70**
independent, **116**
inferior, **52**
income elasticity of demand and, **116–117**
labor-intensive, **424**
land-intensive, **424**
nondurable, **70**
normal, **52**
income elasticity of demand and, **116**
prices of (*see* Price)
private, **93, 304**
public (social) (*see* Public goods)
related, prices of, **52**
substitute (*see* Substitute goods)
superior (normal), **52, 116**
(*See also* Product)
Gorbachev, Mikhail, **469, 470, 482, 483**
reforms instituted by, **476–477**
Gosbank, **472**
Government, **88–102**
under capitalism, **38**

Government (continued)
in circular flow model, **95–96**
economic functions of, **88–89**
exchange rates and, **455–457**
expenditures of, **98, 100–101**
immigration and, **415–417**
finance of, **96–99**
federal, **98–99**
state and local finance and, **100–102**
fiscal federalism and, **102**
growth of, **96–98**
income redistribution and, **90, 382**
legal and social framework provided by, **89**
maintenance of competition by, **89–90**
public choice theory and, **371–372**
public debt and:
government expenditures for interest on, **98**
trade deficits and, **464–465**
purchases of, **96–97**
receipts of, **98–101**
regulation and (*see* Regulation)
resource reallocation by, **90–94**
trade deficit and, **464–465, 466**
transfers by (*see* Transfer)
transition of Soviet economy to market system and, **477–478**
(*See also* Public sector failure; Tax)
Government enterprises, **75**
Government spending, **98, 100–101**
immigration and, **415–417**
Graphs, **6, 13–17**
constructing, **13–14**
dependent and independent variables and, **14–15**
of direct and inverse relationships, **14**
other variables held constant and, **15**
slope of nonlinear curve and, **16–17**
slope of straight line and, **15–16**
Great Britain, economy of, **32**
Great Depression, demise of gold standard and, **457**
Grievance procedures, **403–404**
Gross domestic product (GDP):
interest rates and, **282**
profits and, **285**
Guaranteed annual income, **391–392**
Guiding function of prices, **82–83**

H

Harrington, Michael, **388*n.***
Haveman, Robert H., **386*n.***
Health care costs, **120–121**
Health insurance, **388–390, 392**
Heilbroner, Robert L., **2*n.*, 87*n.***
Herfindahl index, **221–222, 348–349**
Hewlett-Packard, **155**
Homogeneous products, oligopoly and, **220–221**
Honda, **77**
Horizontal axis, **14**
Horizontal combinations, **71**
Horizontal mergers, **348, 349**
Households:
in circular flow model, **44**
as income receivers, **67–68**
Households (continued)
loanable funds and:
demand for, **280**
supply of, **279**
as spenders, **68–71**
(*See also* Consumer)
Human-capital discrimination, **410**
Human capital investment, wage differentials and, **268**
Hypothesis, **3–4**
Hyundai Motor Company, **77, 238**

I

IBM, **348**
ICC (Interstate Commerce Commission), **352, 355**
ILGWU (International Ladies Garment Workers Union), **262**
Illegal immigrants, **413**
Immigration, **413–417**
aging population and, **299**
cost of migration and, **415**
economics of, **413–415**
fiscal aspects of, **415–417**
full employment versus unemployment and, **415**
history and policy and, **413**
legal and illegal, **413**
remittances and backflows and, **415**
Immigration Reform and Control Act of 1986, **413**
Imperfect competition, **161**
Implicit costs, **141, 282**
Import(s):
decline in, trade barriers and, **431**
job creation from, **433**
transaction for, **445–446**
(*See also* International trade; International trade policies)
Import competition, **221**
Import quotas, **430**
economic impact of, **431–432**
on sugar, **374–375**
Incentive(s):
to cheat, oligopoly and, **224**
income inequality and, **384–385**
to pollute, **313**
for recycling, **316**
Soviet, collapse of Soviet system and, **475–476**
transition of Soviet economy to market system and, **480**
to work, income-maintenance programs and, **390–391**
Incentive function, of resource prices, **276–277**
Incentive pay plan, **272**
Inclusive unionism, wages and, **264–265**
Inco (International Nickel Company of Canada), **190**
Income:
break-even, **391–392**
budget line and, **134**
changes in demand and, **52**
exchange rates and, **451**
farm, stabilization of, **373–374**
guaranteed, **391–392**
Income (continued)
households as receivers of, **67–68**
interest, **21**
lifetime, **381–382**
personal, distribution of, **67, 68, 379**
pollution and, **312**
price elasticity of demand and, **111**
proprietors', **68**
rental, **21**
resource pricing and, **241**
short-run farm problem and, **362–364**
taxable, **98**
Income distribution, **379–386**
broadened income concept and, **381**
causes of, **382–384**
efficiency and, **384–386**
equitable, as economic goal, **7**
functional, **67–68**
general equilibrium and, **293–294**
government intervention in, **90, 382**
industrial concentration and, **344**
inequality of:
causes of, **393**
marginal productivity theory of income distribution and, **251–252**
lifetime income and, **381–382**
Lorenz curve and, **380–381**
marginal productivity theory of, **251–252**
monopoly and, **198**
personal income and, **67, 68, 379**
under pure competition, **181–183**
trends in inequality of, **379–380**
unions and, **408**
Income effect:
demand curve and, **130**
law of demand and, **49, 125**
Income elasticity of demand, **116–117**
Income inequality (*see* Income distribution; Poverty)
Income maintenance system, **388–393**
reform of, **391–393**
Income redistribution, government and, **90, 382**
Income security, federal expenditures for, **98**
Income shares, **285–286**
current, **285**
historical trends in, **285–286**
immigration and, **414–415**
Income taxes:
corporate, **74, 99, 332, 336**
incidence of, **336**
negative, **391–392**
personal, **68–69, 90, 98–99, 332, 336**
Increasing-cost industry, supply curve and, **115–116**
long-run, **178**
Independent goods, cross elasticity of demand and, **116**
Independent variable, **15**
Indifference curve analysis, **134–138**
budget line and, **134–135**
demand curve derivation and, **137–138**
equilibrium at tangency and, **136–137**

Indifference curve analysis (continued)
preferences and, **135–136**
utility measurement and, **137**
Indifference map, **136**
Individual demand, **50**
Induction, **3, 4**
Industrial concentration, **221–222, 343–345**
controversy over, **344–345**
(*See also* Antitrust laws; Regulation)
Industrial policy, need for, **358–359**
Industrial regulation, **351–353**
Industrial relations (*see* Union)
Industrial unions, **400**
wages and, **264**
Industrialization:
in Soviet Union, **471**
taxes and, **338–339**
in United States, **358–359**
Industry(ies), **71**
bigness of, **75–76**
competitive, regulation of, **352**
concentration ratios and, **221–222**
constant-cost (*see* Constant-cost industry)
declining, **79–80**
decreasing-cost, long-run supply curve for, **178–179**
expanding, **79**
increasing-cost, **115–116, 178**
infant-industry argument for trade barriers and, **434**
interindustry competition and, **221**
industrial concentration and, **345**
market concentration and, **156–157**
structure of, **155–157, 221–222**
airline deregulation and, **354–355**
growth and, **285–286**
income inequality and, **393**
types of, **75**
Inefficiency (*see* Efficiency)
Inelastic demand, **107**
total-revenue test and, **110**
Infant-industry argument for trade barriers, **434**
Inferior goods, **52**
income elasticity of demand and, **116–117**
Inflation:
stabilization and, **94**
transition of Soviet economy to market system and, **479–480**
wages and, **408–409**
Information, advertising as, **214**
Information failures, **316–321**
inadequate information about buyers and, **318–319**
inadequate information about products and, **320–321**
inadequate information about sellers and, **317**
solutions to, **319–320**
Injunction, **397**
In-kind transfers, **381**
Input(s), **21**
(*See also* Resource)
Input-output analysis, general equilibrium and, **294–295**
Input-output table, **294–295**
Input substitution, **252**
Instability (*see* Stability)
Institutional immobility, wage differentials and, **269**
Insurance:
adverse selection problem and, **318–319**
health, **390, 392**
health care costs and, **120–121**
risks and, **283–284**
social, **388–389**
unemployment compensation, **389**
Intellectual property rights, **437**
Interdependence, general equilibrium and, **295**
Interest groups, voting and, **325**
Interest income, **21**
Interest rate(s), **278–282**
bond prices and, **85**
ceilings on, for credit cards, **118**
determining, **287**
loanable funds theory of interest and, **279–281**
pure, **281**
range of, **281**
real, exchange rates and, **452**
role of, **282**
Interindustry competition, **221**
industrial concentration and, **345**
Interlocking directorates, **346–347**
International Ladies Garment Workers Union (ILGWU), **262**
International Monetary Fund (IMF), **458**
borrowing from, **458**
pegged exchange rates and, **458**
Soviet Union and, **484**
International Nickel Company of Canada (Inco), **190**
International Telephone and Telegraph, **71**
International trade, **421–441**
barter and, **44–45**
comparative advantage and (*see* Comparative advantage)
economic basis for, **423–424**
farm policy and, **372–374**
financing, **444–446**
General Agreement on Tariffs and Trade and, **373, 436–439, 484**
import competition and, **221**
importance of, **421–423**
income inequality and, **393**
with less developed countries, trade deficit and, **463**
production possibilities curve and, **29–30**
specialization and, **39–41, 424–429**
trade barriers and (*see* Trade barriers)
unique aspects of, **423**
of United States, **76–77, 438–439, 445–446**
volume and pattern of, **421–423**
(*See also* Exchange rates; Foreign competition; Foreign exchange market; Trade deficit)
International trade policies, **436–441**
economic integration and, **437–439**
International trade policies (continued)
exchange rates and, **455**
protectionism and, **439–441**
Interstate Commerce Act, **352–353**
Interstate Commerce Commission (ICC), **352, 355**
Inverse relationships, graphing, **14**
Investment, **21**
foreign, direct, reducing trade deficit and, **466**
in human capital, wage differentials and, **268**
private, in former Soviet Union, **483–484**
profits and, **285**
"Invisible hand," **83–85**
allocative efficiency and, **181**
"Invisible" poor, **388**
Ivy League schools, price fixing and, **349–350**

J

Japan:
automobile import quotas and, **432, 439**
economic growth of, **29**
economy of, **31**
foreign competition from, **236–237**
industrial policy in, **359**
U.S. trade deficit with, **77**
J. C. Penney, **71**
Jewkes, John, ***233n.***
Job Opportunities and Basic Skills program (JOBS), **392**
Johnson & Johnson, **155**
Joint ventures in former Soviet Union, **45, 484**
Jones, Ronald W., ***461n.***
Jurisdictional strikes, **400**

K

Kahn, Lawrence M., **416**
"Kennedy Round," **438**
Kent, Thomas, **483**
Keynes, John Maynard, **2**
Killingsworth, Charles C., ***398n.***
"Kinked" demand curve, noncollusive oligopoly and, **225–227**
Kreps, Juanita M., ***358n.***
Kroger, **71**
Krushchev, Nikita, **469**

L

Labor:
cost of, **248**
demand for, **258**
elasticity of, unemployment and, **265**
wages and, **262–263**
division of, efficiency and, **39**
foreign, cheap, as argument for trade barriers, **435**
marginal product of, **242**
misallocation of, **406**
pricing (*see* Wage determination)
quality of, wages and, **256–257**
specialization of (*see* Specialization)

Labor contract, **400–401**
  collective bargaining and, **402–404**
  cost-of-living adjustments and, **403**
Labor force, women in, **298–299**
Labor-intensive goods, international trade and, **424**
Labor-Management Relations Act of 1947, **400–401**
Labor-Management Reporting and Disclosure Act of 1959, **401**
Labor market:
  aging population and, **298–300**
  competitive, **257–259**
  (*See also* Discrimination; Immigration; Union)
Labor theory of value, **470**
Laissez faire capitalism (*see* Pure capitalism)
Land:
  as resource, **20**
  single tax on, **277–278**
Land-intensive goods, international trade and, **424**
Landrum-Griffin Act of 1959, **401**
Lange, Oskar, **12*n.***
Law (economic):
  of demand, **48–49, 124–126**
    foundation of, **48–49**
    income and substitution effects and, **124–125**
    law of diminishing marginal utility and, **125–126**
  of diminishing marginal product, **142–145**
  of diminishing marginal utility, law of demand and, **125–126**
  of diminishing returns, **142–145**
  of increasing opportunity costs, **25**
    concavity of production possibilities curve and, **25**
    rationale for, **25**
  of supply, **54**
  of variable proportions, **142–145**
  (*See also* Economic theory)
Law of conservation of matter and energy, pollution and, **312–313**
Laws (*see* Legislation; *specific laws*)
Lawsuits, spillovers and, **308–309**
LDCs (less developed countries):
  exports to, trade deficit and, **463**
  oil price increases and, **297**
Leaky-bucket analogy, income inequality and, **386**
Least-cost combination of resources, **81, 248–251**
Legal cartel theory of regulation, **352–353**
Legal environment:
  provided by government, **89**
  (*See also* Legislation; *specific laws*)
Legal immigrants, **413**
Legal prices, **117–120**
Legislation:
  antitrust (*see* Antitrust laws)
  international trade and, **433, 436–437, 439**
  patent laws and, **350**
  right-to-work, **403**

Legislation (continued)
  spillover cost correction and, **91**
  unions and, **397, 399–401**
Leonard, Jonathon S., **357*n.***
Leontieff, Wassily W., **294*n.***
Less developed countries (LDCs):
  exports to, trade deficit and, **463**
  oil price increases and, **297**
Liability:
  limited, of corporations, **73**
  unlimited:
    of partnerships, **73**
    of sole proprietorships, **72**
Liability rules, spillovers and, **308–309**
Licensing:
  as entry barrier, **190**
  occupational, wages and, **263–264**
  of surgeons, **317**
Life of corporations, **74**
Lifetime income, **381–382**
Lilley, William, III, **356*n.***
Limited liability of corporations, **73**
Lindblom, Charles E., **486*n.***
Linder, Staffan B., **132*n.***
Living standards, global trade and finance and, **77**
Loan(s):
  from International Monetary Fund, **458**
  loanable funds theory of interest and, **279–281**
  size of, interest rates and, **281**
Loanable funds theory of interest, **279–281**
Local government, expenditures and receipts of, **100–101**
Location, monopolistic competition and, **208**
Lockout, **398**
Logrolling:
  farm policy and, **371–372**
  voting and, **325–326**
Long run:
  adjustments in, general equilibrium and, **292–293**
  monopolistic competition and, **210–211**
  production costs in, **141–142, 150–156**
  supply curve in, **115–116**
Long-run cost curve, **150–151**
Long-run farm problem, **362, 364–366**
Long-run supply curve
  for constant-cost industry, **177–178**
  for decreasing-cost industry, **178–179**
  for increasing-cost industry, **178**
Lorenz curve, **380–381**
Loss(es):
  monopolistic competition and, **210–211**
  monopoly and, **195–196**
Loss-minimizing case:
  marginal-revenue–marginal-cost approach and, **169–170**
  total-revenue–total-cost approach and, **165**
Luck, income inequality and, **383–384**
Luxuries, **20**
  price elasticity of demand and, **111**

M

McDonald's, **484**
McKenna, Joseph P., **33*n.***
Macroeconomic instability, global trade and finance and, **77–78**
Macroeconomic policies:
  exchange rates and, **455–457**
  Soviet, **472**
  trade deficit and, **466**
Macroeconomics, **5–6**
"Make-work" practices, **400, 405**
Managed floating exchange rates, **460–461**
Management:
  antiunion techniques of, **397–398**
  shock effect and, **407**
  specialization of, economies of scale and, **152**
Managerial opposition hypothesis of unionism's decline, **402**
Managerial prerogatives, **403**
Manufacturing industries, **75**
Marginal benefit (MB), optimal amount of externality reduction and, **311–312**
Marginal benefit = marginal cost rules, **306**
Marginal cost (MC), **147–149**
  average variable cost and average total cost and, **149**
  general equilibrium and, **291**
  marginal benefit = marginal cost rule and, **306**
  marginal product and, **148–149**
  MR = MC rule and, monopoly and, **193–195**
  optimal amount of externality reduction and, **311–312**
  of resources, **242–243, 260**
  short-run supply curve and, **171–173**
Marginal product (MP), **143**
  decline in, elasticity of resource demand and, **247**
  diminishing, law of, **142–145**
  of labor, **242**
  marginal cost and, **148–149**
Marginal productivity, general equilibrium and, **291**
Marginal productivity theory of income distribution, **251–252**
Marginal productivity theory of resource demand, **241–245**
Marginal rate of substitution (MRS), **135–136**
Marginal resource cost (MRC), **242–243**
  MRP = MRC rule and, **243**
  wages and, **260**
Marginal revenue, **163–164**
  monopoly demand and, **191–192**
  MR = MC rule and, monopoly and, **193–195**
Marginal-revenue–marginal-cost approach, to profit maximization in short run, **167–171**
Marginal revenue product (MRP), **242–243**
  as demand schedule, **243**
  labor misallocation and, **406**

Marginal revenue product (MRP) (continued)
MRP = MRC rule and, **243**
of professional athletes, **270**
Marginal tax rates, **99**
Marginal utility, **125**
demand curve and, **129–130**
diminishing:
general equilibrium and, **291**
law of, **125–126**
law of demand and, **49**
total utility versus, **131**
utility-maximizing rule and, **127–128**
Marijuana, price of, **63**
Market(s), **47–64**
adjustments in, general equilibrium and, **293**
automobile industry and, **234**
black, **118–119**
under capitalism, **37–38**
contestable, **182**
definition of, **47–48**
antitrust laws and, **348**
demand and, **48–53**
demand for labor, **258**
for economics textbooks, **216–217**
for externality rights, **309–310**
foreign exchange, **42, 62–64, 423, 444–446**
depreciation and appreciation and, **63–64**
economic consequences of exchange rate changes and, **64**
gasoline, **317**
industrial policy and, **359**
labor (*see* Labor market)
for "lemons," **320–321**
localized, **221**
models of, **160–161**
product, **44**
adjustments in, general equilibrium and, **293**
aging population and, **298**
for recyclable inputs, **315–316**
resource, **44**
adjustments in, general equilibrium and, **293**
market equilibrium and, **61**
resource demand of, **245**
segregation of, price discrimination and, **201**
structure of, antitrust laws and, **348**
supply and, **54–57**
of labor, **258**
(*See also* Supply)
Market-clearing price, **58**
Market concentration, **156–157**
Market demand, **48–53**
for labor, **258**
Market economy (*see* Pure capitalism)
Market entry:
under capitalism, **37**
monopolistic competition and, **209**
in pure competition, **175–176**
under pure competition, **162**
Market entry barriers, **189–191, 217**
automobile industry and, **234**
collusion and, **230**
oligopoly and, **222, 233**

Market entry barriers (continued)
pure monopoly and, **188, 189–191**
Market equilibrium, **57–62**
changes in supply and demand and, **58–61**
"other things being equal" assumption and, **61–62**
rationing function of prices and, **58**
resource market and, **61**
shortages and, **57–58**
surpluses and, **57**
wages and, **258–259, 261**
Market exit:
under capitalism, **37**
in pure competition, **162, 175–177**
Market failure, **90–94**
public goods and, **94**
(*See also* Externalities; Pollution)
Market imperfections:
interest rates and, **281**
wage differentials and, **268–269**
Market intervention, income redistribution and, **90**
Market-oriented income stabilization policy, farm incomes and, **373–374**
Market period, price elasticity of supply and, **114–115**
Market power, income inequality and, **383**
Market share, monopolistic competition and, **208**
Market socialism, **31**
Market system, **78–85**
accommodating change and, **82–83**
allocative efficiency of, **85**
competitive, **78**
determining what to produce and, **78–80**
distributing total output and, **81–82**
freedom under, **85**
"invisible hand" and, **83–85**
organizing production and, **80–81**
in pure capitalism, **30, 43–45**
transition of Soviet economy to, **477–481**
Markup pricing, oligopoly and, **231–232**
Marxian ideology, **470–471**
Maturity, interest rates and, **281**
Mazda, **238**
MB (marginal benefit), optimal amount of externality reduction and, **311–312**
MC (*see* Marginal cost)
Median-voter model, **327–328**
Medicaid, **120, 390, 392**
Medicare, **120, 389**
Medium of exchange, money as, **41**
Mercedes, **77**
Mergers:
antitrust laws and, **348–349**
Herfindahl index and, **348–349**
oligopoly and, **222–223**
MES (minimum efficient scale), **155–157**
Mexico:
North American Free-Trade Zone and, **438–439**
U.S. marijuana supply and, **63**

Microeconomics, **5–6**
Migration, cost of, **415**
Miller, James C., III, **356*n*.**
Miller Brewing Company, **236, 237**
Minimum efficient scale (MES), **155–157**
Minimum wage:
controversy over, **266–267**
price elasticity of demand and, **114**
Mitsubishi, **238**
Mobile Travel Guide, **319**
Models (*see* Economic theory)
Monetary policy:
easy, reducing trade deficit and, **466**
exchange rates and, **455–457**
Money:
under capitalism, **41–43**
paper, **42**
uses of, **41**
(*See also* Currency; Dollar)
Monopolistic competition, **160, 207–217**
concept and occurrence of, **207–209**
economic analysis and, **217**
economics of advertising and, **213–217**
nonprice competition and, **212–213**
price and output determination and, **209–211**
wastes of, **211–212**
Monopoly:
advertising as, **214**
bilateral, wages under, **265–266**
demand and, **191–193**
government regulation of, **89–90**
marginal productivity theory of income distribution and, **252**
natural, **89–90, 155**
productive techniques and, **183**
regulation of, **351–353**
pure (*see* Pure monopoly)
Monopoly power:
economic profit and, **283**
patent laws and, **350**
price discrimination and, **201**
Monopoly profits, **284**
Monopsony:
characteristics of, **259–260**
marginal productivity theory of income distribution and, **252**
wages under, **259–262**
Moral hazard problem, **318**
Most-favored-nation clauses, **436**
Motor vehicles, pollution and, **314**
MP (*see* Marginal product)
MR = MC rule, **167–168**
monopoly and, **193–195**
MRC (marginal resource cost), **242–243**
wages and, **260**
MRP (marginal revenue product), **242–243**
as demand schedule, **243**
of professional athletes, **270**
MRP = MRC rule, **243**
MRS (marginal rate of substitution), **135–136**
Music Corporation of America, **204**

Mutual interdependence, oligopoly and, **223**

N

National Ambient Air Quality Standards, **357**
National Baseball League, **261**
National Basketball Association (NBA), **261**
 racial discrimination in, **416**
National Cash Register, **190**
National defense (*see* Defense)
National Football League, **261**
National Labor Relations Act of 1935, **399–400, 402**
National Labor Relations Board (NLRB), **399–400, 402**
National Park Service (NPS), monopolies and, **204**
Natural monopoly, **89–90, 155**
 productive techniques and, **183**
 regulation of, **351–353**
Natural resources:
 transition of Soviet economy to market system and, **481**
 wages and, **256**
Nazi Germany, economy of, **31**
NBA (National Basketball Association), **261**
 racial discrimination in, **416**
Necessities, **20**
 price elasticity of demand and, **111**
Negative income tax (NIT), **391–392**
Neighborhood effects (*see* Externalities; Pollution)
New perspective on advertising, **214–217**
New York Stock Exchange, **47, 77**
Nicholson, Jack, **378**
Nissan, **77**
NIT (negative income tax), **391–392**
Nixon administration, demise of Bretton Woods system under, **460**
NLRB (National Labor Relations Board), **399–400, 402**
Nominal wages, **256**
Noncompeting groups, wage differentials and, **267–268**
Nondurable goods, **70**
Nonprice competition:
 monopolistic competition and, **209, 212–213**
 oligopoly and, **232**
Nonunion shop, **403**
Normal goods, **52**
 income elasticity of demand and, **116**
Normal profits, **79, 283**
 as costs, **141**
Normative economics, **6**
Norris-La Guardia Act of 1932, **399**
North American Free-Trade Zone, **438–439**
NPS (National Park Service), monopolies and, **204**
NTBs (nontariff barriers), **430**

O

OASDHI (Old Age, Survivors, and Disability Health Insurance), **388–389**
Occupational discrimination, **410**
Occupational licensing, wages and, **263–264**
Occupational Safety and Health Administration (OSHA), **355, 356**
Occupational segregation, **410–412**
Official reserves:
 balance of payments and, **449**
 exchange rates and, **454–455, 458**
Oil prices, automobile industry and, **236**
Okun, Arthur M., **385*n.***
Old Age, Survivors, and Disability Health Insurance (OASDHI), **388–389**
Oligopoly, **161, 220–238**
 automobile industry and, **234–238**
 collusion and cartels and, **227–230**
 concept and occurrence of, **220–223**
 cost-plus pricing and, **231–232**
 definition of, **220–222**
 economic efficiency and, **232–234**
 game theory and, **223–224**
 noncollusive, **225–227**
 nonprice competition and, **232**
 price leadership and, **230–231**
 two-firm, **223**
Oligopsony, **260**
OPEC (*see* Organization of Petroleum Exporting Countries)
Open shop, **403**
Operation Desert Storm, production possibilities curve and, **30. 32**
Opportunity costs:
 increasing, law of, **25**
 marginal, **291**
 of production, **140–142**
Optimal reduction of an externality, **310–312**
Organization of Petroleum Exporting Countries (OPEC):
 collusion and, **228**
 decline of, **230**
 oil price increases and, **228, 236, 295–297**
  balance of payments and, **449**
OSHA (Occupational Safety and Health Administration), **355, 356**
"Other things being equal" assumption, **5, 15**
 law of demand and, **48**
 market equilibrium and, **61–62**
Output:
 agricultural, **363**
 collusion and, **227–228**
 comparative advantage and, **428**
 determination of, monopoly and, **193–196**
 distribution of, **81–82**
 immigration and, **414**
 interest rates and, **282**
 international trade and, **423**
 monopoly and, **197**
 profits and, **285**
 of United States, **21**
Output effect, resource demand and, **246–247**
Ownership:
 of corporations, **74**

Ownership (continued)
 of essential resources as entry barrier, **190–191**
 private, under capitalism, **30, 36**
 of property, income inequality and, **383**
 public:
  in command economies, **30–31**
  of natural monopolies, **351**
 state, in Soviet Union, **471**
Ozone depletion, **314**

P

P = MC rule, **168**
Pabst, **237**
PAC (political action committee), **371**
Packaging, monopolistic competition and, **208**
Paglin, Morton, **382**
Panasonic, **350**
Paper money, **42**
Paradox of voting, **326–327**
Parity concept, **367–368**
Parity ratio, **368**
Partial equilibrium analysis, **290**
Partnerships, **73**
Patent(s) as entry barriers, **190**
Patent laws, **350**
Payroll taxes, **99, 332**
PepsiCo, **44**
Per se violations, **349**
Perestroika, **476**
Perfect competition, resource demand under, **243–245**
Perfectly elastic demand, **107**
 in pure competition, **162–163**
Perfectly elastic supply, **177–178**
Perfectly inelastic demand, **107**
Performance, wages and, **269–272**
Persian Gulf War, production possibilities curve and, **30, 32**
Personal consumption expenditures, **67–71**
Personal distribution of income, **67, 68**
Personal income (PI), distribution of, **67, 68, 379**
Persuasion, advertising and, **214**
Philip Morris Company, **237**
PI (personal income), distribution of, **67, 68, 379**
Piece rates, **272**
Plant, **71**
Polaroid, **190**
Policy:
 antipollution, **313–314**
 evaluation of, **8**
 farm (*see* Farm policy)
 formulation of, **3, 4, 7–8**
 global trade and finance and, **77–78**
 industrial, need for, **358–359**
 international trade, **436–441**
  economic integration and, **437–439**
  protectionism and, **439–441**
 macroeconomic:
  exchange rates and, **455–457**
  Soviet, **472**
  trade deficit and, **466**
 options for, **8**

Policy (continued)
recycling and, **316**
resource pricing and, **241**
Policy economics, **4, 6–8**
economic goals and, **6–7**
policy formulation and, **7–8**
Political logrolling:
farm policy and, **371–372**
voting and, **325–326**
Political votes, **94*n*.**
(*See also* Voting)
Politics:
of farm policy, **371–372**
industrial concentration and, **344–345**
industrial policy and, **359**
international trade and, **423**
transition of Soviet economy to market system and, **480–481**
unions and, **398–399**
(*See also* Public sector failure; Voting)
Pollution, **312–316**
antipollution policy and, **313–314**
causes of, **312–313**
dimensions of problem, **312**
solid-waste disposal and recycling and, **314–316**
(*See also* Externalities)
Pollution rights, **314**
Population:
baby boom and:
changes in demand and, **52**
general equilibrium analysis and, **298**
density of, pollution and, **312**
growth of:
growth of government and, **97**
long-run farm problem and, **365**
Positive economics, **6**
Post hoc, ergo propter hoc fallacy, **9**
Poverty, **386–393**
"black underclass" and, **387–388**
definition of, **386**
income maintenance system and, **388–393**
invisibility of, **388**
trends in, **387**
(*See also* Income distribution)
Poverty rate, **386–387**
Preferences:
changes in, **82–83**
changes in demand and, **51–52**
consumer behavior and, **126**
exchange rates and, **451**
income inequality and, **382**
paradox of voting and, **326**
Price(s):
of bonds, **85**
budget line and, **134–135**
under capitalism, **37–38**
changes in supply and demand and, **52, 55, 56, 59–61**
collusion and, **227–228**
consumer behavior and, **127**
cost-plus, **231–232**
of credit (*see* Interest rate)
determination of, monopoly and, **196**
distribution of total output and, **81–82**
Price(s) (continued)
equilibrium, **58–61**
changes in supply and demand and, **59–61**
under pure competition, **173–174**
exchange rates and, **451–452**
"fair-return," **203**
guiding function of, **82–83**
legal, **117–120**
marginal revenue product and, **242**
of marijuana, **63**
monopoly and, **197**
demand and, **191–192**
noncollusive oligopoly and, **225–227**
of oil:
automobile industry and, **236**
(*See also* Organization of Petroleum Exporting Countries)
price elasticity of demand and, **106–114**
quantity supplied and, **54**
rationing function of, **58**
of related goods, **52**
resource demand and, **246–247**
short-run farm problem and, **362–364**
shortages and, **117–120**
social regulation and, **356–357**
socially optimal, **203**
of substitute products, wages and, **263**
surpluses and, **119–120**
transition of Soviet economy to market system and, **478–479**
Price ceiling, **117–120**
Price competition, **216–217**
Price discrimination, **201–202**
conditions for, **201**
consequences of, **202**
illustrations of, **201**
Price elasticity of demand, **106–114**
determinants of, **110–112**
formula for, **106–108**
graphical analysis of, **108–109**
monopoly and, **193**
practical applications of, **112–114**
total-revenue test and, **109–110**
Price elasticity of supply, **114–116**
Price fixing:
antitrust laws and, **349–350**
by government in Soviet Union, **472**
Price floors, **119–120**
agricultural, **368–369**
criticisms of, **370**
Price leadership:
automobile industry and, **234–235**
oligopoly and, **230–231**
Price level(s), stability of, as economic goal, **7**
Price maker:
monopolist as, **193**
pure monopolist as, **187–188**
Price supports, **119–120**
agricultural, **368–369, 374–375**
criticisms of, **370**
Price takers in pure competition, **161–162**
Price war, **226**
Pricing:
cost-plus, oligopoly and, **231–232**
of labor (*see* Wage determination)
of resources, **241**
Principal-agent problem, **270–272**
Principles (economic):
of comparative advantage, **426**
(*See also* Economic theory)
Private goods, **93, 304**
Private property under capitalism, **30, 36**
Private sector, **67–85**
competitive market system and, **78**
five fundamental questions and, **78**
foreign sector and, **76–78**
industrial distribution and bigness in, **75–76**
legal forms of business enterprise and, **71–74**
market system in (*see* Market system)
(*See also* Business; Consumer; Corporations; Firm; Households)
Privatization, transition of Soviet economy to market system and, **477**
Product(s):
agricultural:
demand for, **362–365, 369–370**
supply of, **364–365, 369**
average, **143**
by-products and, economies of scale and, **153–154**
demand for:
elasticity of, **247**
resource demand and, **245**
wages and, **262–263**
differentiated, **220–221**
homogeneous, **220–221**
inadequate information about, **320–321**
marginal (*see* Marginal product)
marginal revenue (*see* Marginal revenue product)
standardized, in pure competition, **161**
(*See also* Goods)
Product development, nonprice competition and, **213**
Product differentiation, **216**
monopolistic competition and, **208**
nonprice competition and, **213**
oligopoly and, **220–221**
Product markets, **44**
adjustments in, general equilibrium and, **293**
aging population and, **298**
Product-mix, optimal, **24**
Product quality:
automobile industry and, **236**
industrial concentration and, **345**
monopolistic competition and, **208**
Production:
demand for resources and, **240–252**
determining what to produce and, **78–80**
domestic, trade barriers and, **431**
factors of, **21**
full, efficiency and, **22**
least-cost, **81, 248–251**

Production (continued)
natural monopolies and, **183**
organizing, **80–81**
price discrimination and, **202**
roundabout, **38–39**
technological advance and, **183**
war, **29**
Production costs, **140–156**
economic, **140–142**
economies of scale and, **151–154, 156–157**
firm size and, **150**
in long run, **141–142, 150–156**
in short run, **141–150**
Production possibilities curve, **23–24**
economic growth and, **26–28**
law of increasing opportunity costs and, **25**
real-world applications of, **28–30**
Production possibilities table, **22–23**
assumptions and, **22–23**
comparative advantage and, **39–40**
necessity of choice and, **23**
Productive efficiency, **22, 203*n*.**
monopolistic competition and, **211**
oligopoly and, **232**
pure competition and, **179**
Productivity:
economic rent and, **278**
growth of, aging population and, **299–300**
income distribution and, **251–252**
marginal, general equilibrium and, **291**
marginal revenue product and, **242**
resource demand and, **245–246**
unions and, **405–407**
wages and, **256–257, 263**
Productivity slowdown, production possibilities curve and, **29**
Profit(s), **21**
automobile industry and, **234–235**
economic (pure), **79, 141, 282–285**
functions of, **284–285**
sources of, **283–284**
equilibrium price and, **173–174**
expanding industries and, **79**
monopolistic competition and, **210**
monopoly, **284**
normal, **79, 283**
as costs, **141**
oligopoly and, **233**
price discrimination and, **202**
production and, **80–81**
Profit maximization:
in long run, **175–179**
in short run, **164–174**
Profit-maximizing case:
marginal-revenue–marginal-cost approach and, **168–169**
total-revenue–total-cost approach and, **165**
Profit-maximizing combination of resources, **249, 251**
Profit-sharing wage plan, **272**
Progress and Poverty (George), **277**
Progressive tax, **98, 99, 332**
Promotion, monopolistic competition and, **208**
Property ownership (*see* Ownership)
Property right, spillovers and, **308–309**
Property taxes, **101, 332–333**
incidence of, **337**
Proportional tax, **332**
Proprietors' income, **68**
Protection (*see* Trade barriers)
Protective tariffs, **430**
Public assistance programs, **389–393**
reform of, **391–393**
Public choice theory, farm policy and, **371–372**
Public debt:
government expenditures for interest on, **98**
trade deficits and, **464–465**
Public goods, **93–94, 304–307**
allocating resources to, **94**
benefit-cost analysis of, **305–306**
demand for, **304–305**
growth of government and, **97**
measurement problems with, **307**
optimal quantity of, **305**
Public interest theory of regulation, **351–352**
Public regulation (*see* Regulation)
Public sector (*see* Government; Public sector failure; Tax)
Public sector failure, **328–330**
benefits and costs and, **328–329**
bureaucracy and inefficiency and, **329–330**
imperfect institutions and, **330**
limited choice and, **329**
special interests and rent seeking and, **328, 340**
Public services, **93–94**
Public utilities as natural monopolies, **189–190, 351**
Purchasing power parity theory, exchange rates and, **452**
Pure capitalism, **30**
capital goods in, **38–39**
circular flow and, **43–45**
competition in, **36–37**
division of labor in, **39**
freedom of enterprise and choice in, **36**
limited role of government in, **38**
markets and prices in, **37–38**
money in, **41–43**
private property in, **30, 36**
self-interest in, **36**
specialization in, **39–41**
Pure competition, **160–183**
concept and occurrence of, **161–162**
demand to competitive seller in, **162–164**
efficiency and, **179–183**
profit maximization in:
in long run, **175–179**
in short run, **164–174**
technological advance and, **200**
Pure Food and Drug Act of 1906, **89**
Pure monopoly, **160, 187–204**
Pure monopoly (continued)
characteristics of, **187–188**
economic effects of, **196–201**
entry barriers and, **189–191**
examples of, **188**
importance of, **188–189**
monopoly demand and, **191–193**
output and price determination and, **193–196**
price discrimination and, **201–202**
regulation of, **202–204**
technological advance and, **200**
Pure profits, **79, 141, 282–285**
Pure rate of interest, **281**

Q

Quality:
environmental:
growth of government and, **98**
(*See also* Externalities; Pollution)
of labor, wages and, **256–257**
of products (*see* Product quality)
Quantity:
demanded, **53**
equilibrium (*see* Equilibrium quantity)
supplied, changes in, **56–57**
Quasi-public goods, **94**
Quinton, Noel, **271**
Quotas, import, **430**
economic impact of, **431–432**
on sugar, **374–375**

R

Race:
"black underclass" and, **387–388**
(*See also* Discrimination)
Railway Brotherhoods, **263**
Rate of return, **280**
Rational behavior of consumers, **126**
Rationing:
black markets and, **118**
exchange rates and, **455**
during World War II, **117–118**
Rationing function of prices, **58**
RCA, **77**
Real capital, **21**
Real interest rate, exchange rates and, **452**
Real wages, **256**
aging population and, **299**
productivity and, **257**
Recession(s):
collusion and, **229–230**
reducing trade deficit and, **466**
Reciprocal Trade Agreements Act of 1934, **436–437**
Recycling, **314–316**
Regressive Tax, **332**
Regulation:
airline industry deregulation and, **113, 353–355**
dilemma of, **203–204**
economic (industrial), **351–353**
legal cartel theory of, **352–353**
of monopolies, **89–90, 202–204**
natural, **351–353**
public interest theory of, **351–352**

Regulation (continued)
social, **355–358**
Regulatory agencies, **346**
deficiencies of, **352**
Reindustrialization, taxes and, **338–339**
Remittances, immigration and, **415**
Rent(s), economic, **275–278**
as surplus, **276–277**
Rent controls, **118**
Rent-seeking behavior, **328, 340**
farm policy and, **371**
monopoly and, **199**
Rental income, **21**
Republic Steel, **71**
Research and development, oligopoly and, **233**
Reserves, official:
balance of payments and, **449**
exchange rates and, **454–455, 458**
Resources(s):
categories of, **20–21**
demand for (*see* Resource demand)
economic growth and, **26–27**
fixed, production possibilities table and, **23**
marginal resource cost and, **242–243**
wages and, **260**
mobility of, international trade and, **423**
most efficient combination of, **81**
optimal combination of, **248–251**
prices of, **241**
changes in supply and, **55**
(*See also* Wage determination)
scarcity of, **20–22, 45**
(*See also* Capital; Entrepreneurial ability; Labor; Land; Natural resources)
Resource allocation:
government intervention in, **90–94**
industrial concentration and, **344**
labor misallocation and, **406**
monopoly and, **197**
optimal quantity of public good and, **305**
profits and, **285**
to public goods, **94**
resource pricing and, **241**
in Soviet Union, **471–472**
spillover benefits and, **92**
Resource demand, **80, 240–252**
as derived demand, **241–242**
determinants of, **245–247**
elasticity of, **247–248**
marginal resource theory of, **241–245**
market, **245**
under perfect competition, **243–245**
Resource markets, **44**
adjustments in, general equilibrium and, **293**
market equilibrium and, **61**
Resource payments, **21**
Resource pricing:
complexities and significance of, **241**
(*See also* Wage determination)
Retail industries, **75**
chain stores and, **71**
Retaliation as motivation for trade barriers, **433**
Return(s):
diminishing, law of, **142–145**
rate of, **280**
Revenue(s):
average, **163**
marginal, **163–164**
monopoly demand and, **191–192**
MR = MC rule and, monopoly and, **193–194**
from tariffs, **431**
total, **163**
Revenue tariffs, **430**
Richman, Barry M., **473*n.***
Right to bequeath, **36**
Right-to-work laws, **403**
Risk:
of bonds, **85**
economic profit and, **283–284**
income inequality and, **382**
interest rates and, **281**
uninsurable, **283–284**
Rock concerts, price ceilings and, **118–119**
Ross, David, **188*n.*, 199*n.*, 231*n.***
Roundabout production, **38–39**
Royalties, **272**
Ruble overhang, **479**
Rule of reason, **347, 348**
Rule-of-thumb pricing, oligopoly and, **231–232**

S

Safety:
airline deregulation and, **354**
workplace, inadequate information about buyers and, **319**
Safeway, **71**
Sales taxes, **99, 332**
incidence of, **336–337**
Samuelson, Paul A., **341*n.***
Saurman, David S., **213*n.***
Saving:
definition of, **69**
dissaving and, by households, **69**
personal, **69**
reasons for, **69**
Sawers, David, **233*n.***
Scale:
constant returns to, **154**
diseconomies of, production costs and, **154**
economies of (*see* Economies of scale)
minimum efficient, **155–156**
Scalping of concert tickets, **118–119**
Scherer, F. M., **188*n.*, 199*n.*, 231*n.***
Schlitz, **237**
Schumpeter, Joseph, **233*n.***
Schumpeter-Galbraith view:
industrial concentration and, **345**
of oligopoly, **233**
Schwartz, Harry, **471*n.***
Scully, Gerald W., **270**
Secondary boycotts, **400**
Security:
economic, as economic goal, **7**
Security (continued)
income, federal expenditures for, **98**
as reason for saving, **69**
Segregation, occupational, **410–412**
Self-interest under capitalism, **36**
Self-sufficiency:
comparative advantage and, **425–426**
military, as argument for trade barriers, **432**
Soviet, **472**
Sellers:
inadequate information about, **317**
number of, changes in supply and, **56**
pure monopoly and, **187**
Seniority, **403**
productivity and, **407**
wages and, **272**
Service(s), **20, 70**
airline deregulation and, **354**
monopolistic competition and, **208**
public (social), **93–94**
Service industries, **75**
Shepherd, William G., **199*n.*, 206*n.***
Sherer, Peter D., **416**
Sherman Act of 1890, **90, 346–348, 397**
Shirking, **271–272**
Shock effect, **407**
Short run:
adjustments in, general equilibrium and, **291–292**
monopolistic competition and, **210**
production costs in, **141–150**
profit maximization in, **164–174**
supply curve in, **115**
Short-run farm problem, **363–364**
Short-run supply curve, **115**
marginal cost and, **171–173**
Shortages:
market equilibrium and, **57–58**
price ceilings and, **117–120**
Simpson-Rodino Act of 1986, **413**
Single-tax movement, **277–278**
Slope:
of nonlinear curve, **16–17**
of straight line, **15–16**
Smith, Adam, **84*n.*, 268–269, 429**
Smog, **314**
Smoot-Hawley Tariff Act of 1930, **433, 436, 457**
Snider, Delbert A., **459*n.***
Social benefits, **92–94, 183**
correcting for, **92–93**
Social costs, **91, 183**
correcting for, **91–92**
Social environment, provided by government, **89**
Social goods, **93–94**
Social insurance programs, **388–389**
Social regulation, **355–358**
costs and criticisms of, **355–356**
defense of, **357–358**
distinguishing features of, **355**
economic implications of, **356–357**
Social security, **99, 388–389**
Social welfare, welfare programs and, **389–393**

Socially optimal price, **203**
Society:
  agricultural price supports and, **368–369**
  optimal amount of externality reduction, **310–312**
Sociological immobility, wage differentials and, **269**
Sole proprietorships, **72**
Solid-waste disposal, **314–316**
Sommers, Paul M., **271**
Southland Corporation, **350**
Soviet Union:
  disintegration of, **480–481**
  economy of, **31, 32, 469–484**
    central planning and, **471–473**
    failure of communism and, **473–476**
    Gorbachev reforms and, **476–477**
    ideology and institutions and, **470–471**
    prospects for, **484**
    role of capitalist advanced nations and, **481–484**
    transition to market system, **477–481**
  joint ventures with, **45, 484**
  wartime production in, **29**
Sowell, Thomas, **390*n*.**
Special-interest effect, **328, 340**
  farm policy and, **371**
  trade barriers and, **430**
Specialization:
  under capitalism, **39–41**
  disadvantages of, **41**
  economies of scale and, **152**
  efficiency and, **39**
  gains from, **40–41**
  geographic, **39**
  global trade and finance and, **77**
  international (*see* Comparative advantage)
Speculation:
  exchange rates and, **452**
  as reason for saving, **69**
Spending (*see* Consumption; Expenditures)
Spillover benefits, **92–94, 183**
  correcting for, **92–93**
Spillover costs, **91, 183**
  correcting for, **91–92**
SSI (Supplemental Security Income) program, **390**
Stability:
  diversification for, as argument for trade barriers, **433**
  exchange rates and, **454**
  macroeconomic, global trade and finance and, **77–78**
  of Soviet economy, transition to market system and, **479–480**
Stabilization, **94**
  of farm incomes, **373–374**
  inflation and, **94**
  unemployment and, **94**
Standard Oil, **77**
State government:
  expenditures and receipts of, **100**
  lotteries run by, 101
State ownership in Soviet Union, **471**
Steiner, Robert L., **216*n*.**
Stigler, George J., **12*n*., 33*n*., 300**
Stiglitz, Joseph E., **217*n*.**
Stillerman, Richard, **233*n*.**
Stock(s), **73, 74**
  bonds differentiated from, **84–85**
  common, **84**
  dividends and, **84**
Strategic trade policy, **434**
Strikes:
  efficiency and productivity and, **406**
  "health and safety," **401**
  jurisdictional, **400**
  sympathy, **400**
Structural-change hypothesis of unionism's decline, **401–402**
Styling, automobile industry and, **235**
Subsidies, **96**
  changes in supply and, **56**
  of exports, **437**
  spillover benefits and, **93**
Substitute goods, **52**
  cross elasticity of demand and, **116**
  price elasticity of demand and, **110–111**
  prices of, wages and, **263**
  pure monopoly and, **187**
  wages and, **263**
Substitute resources:
  elasticity of resource demand and, **247**
  resource demand and, **246**
Substitution, marginal rate of, **135–136**
Substitution effect:
  demand curve and, **130**
  law of demand and, **49, 125**
  resource demand and, **246–247**
Sugar program, **374–375**
Superfund law of 1980, **313–314**
Superior goods, **52**
  income elasticity of demand and, **116**
Supplemental Security Income (SSI) program, **390**
Supply, **54–57**
  of agricultural products, **364–365**
    restricting, **369**
  changes in, **55–57, 59–61**
  changes in quantity supplied and, **56–57**
  determinants of, **55**
  excess (*see* Surplus)
  law of, **54**
  of loanable funds, **279, 280**
  of marijuana, **63**
  market, of labor, **258**
  perfectly elastic, **177–178**
  perfectly inelastic, economic rent and, **276**
  price elasticity of, **114–116**
  shortages in:
    market equilibrium and, **57–58**
    price ceilings and, **117–120**
  spillover benefits and, **93**
Supply curve, **54–55**
  changes in quantity supplied and, **56–57**
  changes in supply and, **56–57**
  long-run, **115–116, 177–178**
  monopoly and, **195–196**
  short-run, **115, 171–173**
Supply schedule, **54**
Surgeons, licensing of, **317**
Surplus(es):
  agricultural, farm policy and, **368–370**
  balance of payments, **449**
  land rent as, **276–277**
  market equilibrium and, **57**
  price floors and, **119–120**
  trade, **30**
    current account and, **447**
Surplus value, **470–471**
Sweden, economy of, **31**
Sympathy strikes, **400**

T

Taft-Hartley Act of 1947, **400–401**
Tangent lines, **17**
Tariffs, **350, 430**
  economic impact of, **430–431**
  reducing trade deficit and, **466**
  Smoot-Hawley, **433, 436, 457**
Tastes (*see* Preferences)
Tax(es), **330–339**
  allocation of resources to public goods and, **94**
  apportioning burden of, **330–333**
  budget deficit and, **339**
  changes in supply and, **56**
  excise, **99**
    incidence of, **336–337**
    price elasticity of demand and, **113**
  immigration and, **415–417**
  incidence of, **333–338**
  income (*see* Income taxes)
  income inequality and, **393**
  interest rates and, **281**
  payroll, **99, 332**
  personal, **68–69**
  progressive, **98, 99, 332**
  property, **101, 332–333**
    incidence of, **337**
  proportional, **332**
  reform of, **340**
  regressive, **332**
  reindustrialization and, **338–339**
  sales, **99, 332**
    incidence of, **336–337**
  single, on land, **277–278**
  spillovers and, **91–92, 309**
  structure in United States, **337–338**
  turnover, Soviet, **479**
  value-added, **338–339**
Tax incidence, **333–338**
  efficiency loss and, **334–336**
  elasticity and, **333–334**
  in United States, **336–337**
Tax rates:
  average, **99**

Tax rates (continued)
marginal, **99**
Tax Reform Act (TRA) of 1986, **337, 340**
Taxable income, **98**
Technological advance:
automobile industry and, **235**
changes in supply and, **56**
dynamic efficiency and, **200–201**
economic growth and, **27**
economic profit and, **284**
industrial concentration and, **345**
initiating, **83**
long-run farm problem and, **364–365**
oligopoly and, **233–234**
pollution and, **312–313**
productive techniques and, **183**
social regulation and, **357**
wages and, **256**
Technology, fixed, production possibilities table and, **23**
Terminology, loaded, **8**
Terms of trade:
comparative advantage and, **40, 426–427**
exchange rates and, **454**
Theory (*see* Economic theory)
Time:
consumer behavior and, **130–132**
price elasticity of demand and, **111–112**
value of, **130–131**
"Tokyo Round," **438**
Total cost, **145–146**
average, **147, 149**
elasticity of resource demand and, **248**
Total revenue, **163**
Total-revenue–total-cost approach, to profit maximization in short run, **164–167**
Total-revenue test, price elasticity of demand and, **109–110**
Total utility, **126**
marginal utility versus, **131**
Toyota, **77, 238**
TRA (Tax Reform Act of 1986), **337, 340**
Trade:
barter and, **44–45**
free, defense of, **429**
gains from, comparative advantage and, **40–41, 427–428**
international (*see* Exchange rates; Foreign competition; Foreign exchange market; International trade; International trade policies)
terms of:
comparative advantage and, **40, 426–427**
exchange rates and, **454**
Trade balance:
current account and, **447**
as economic goal, **7**
Trade barriers, **350, 430–436**
automobile industry and, **236–237**
cheap-foreign-labor argument for, **435**
Trade barriers (continued)
diversification for stability as argument for, **433**
domestic employment as argument for, **432–433**
economic impact of, **430–432**
infant-industry argument for, **434**
military self-sufficiency argument for, **432**
nontariff, **430**
protection-against-dumping argument for, **434–435**
special-interest effect and, **430**
(*See also* Tariffs)
Trade deficit:
causes of, **461–463**
effects of, **463–465**
production possibilities curve and, **29–30**
reducing, **464–466**
trade barriers and, **439**
of United States, **29–30, 77, 461–466**
Trade surplus, **30**
current account and, **447**
Tradeoff between equality and efficiency, **385–386**
Trading possibilities line, **427–428**
Traditional economy, **31–32**
Traditional view of advertising, **214–217**
Training (*see* Education and training)
Transfer(s), **90**
government finance and, **96, 97**
income inequality and, **393**
in-kind, **381**
Treble damages, **346**
Tregarthen, Timothy, **217*n*.**
Turnover tax, Soviet, **479**
"Tying" contracts, **346**
Tyson, Mike, **378**

U

Ukraine, **481**
Uncertainty:
economic profit and, **283–284**
flexible exchange rate and, **453–454**
Underemployment, **22, 26**
Underground economy, Soviet, **481**
Unemployment, **26**
aging population and, **299**
immigration and, **415**
stabilization and, **94**
wage increases and, **265**
Unemployment compensation, **389**
Uninsurable risks, economic profit and, **283–284**
Union(s), **396–409**
administration of, **400**
antitrust laws and, **350**
antiunion techniques of management and, **397–398**
collective bargaining and, **402–404**
company, **398**
craft, **400**
wages and, **263, 269**
decline of, **401–402**
Union(s) (continued)
efficiency and productivity and, **405–407**
encouragement phase and, **399–400**
evolution of business unionism and, **398–399**
growth of, **286**
income distribution and, **408**
industrial, **400**
wages and, **264**
inflation and, **408–409**
information problems and, **319–320**
intervention phase and, **400–401**
labor contracts and, **400–401**
collective bargaining and, **402–404**
cost-of-living adjustments and, **403**
legislation and, **397, 399–401**
repression phase and, **396–399**
strikes by, **400, 401, 406**
unfair practices of, **400**
wages and, **262–265, 403, 404, 408**
Union shop, **403**
Unit elasticity, **107**
total-revenue test and, **110**
United Automobile Workers, **112**
United Kingdom, economy of, **32**
United Shoe Machinery Company, **190**
United States:
barter transactions in, **45**
budget deficit of (*see* Budget deficit)
control of monopoly in, **89–90**
economic growth of, **29**
trade deficit and, **462–463**
economy of, **32**
impacts of global trade and finance on, **77–78**
export transactions and, **445**
federal finance in, **98–99**
foreign sector and, **76–78**
government of (*see* Government)
import transactions and, **445–446**
income taxes in (*see* Income taxes)
industrial distribution and bigness in, **75–76**
international trade of, **76–77, 438–439, 445–446**
internationalized economy of, **439**
mixed economy of, **31**
need for industrial policy in, **358–359**
North American Free-Trade Zone and, **438–439**
oil price increases and, **296–297**
(*See also* Organization of Petroleum Exporting Countries)
output per capita in, **21**
price of marijuana in, **63**
productivity slowdown in, **29**
public debt of:
government expenditures for interest on, **98**
trade deficits and, **464–465**
restriction of Japanese automobiles imported to, **439**
sugar price supports in, **374–375**
tax incidence in, **336–337**
tax structure in, **337–338**

United States (continued)
trade deficit of, **29–30, 77, 461–466**
U.S.-Canadian Free-Trade Agreement and, **438**
wartime production in, **29**
U.S.-Canadian Free-Trade Agreement, **438**
United States Steel, **71**
antitrust case and, **347**
United Transportation Union (UTU), **252**
Unlimited liability:
of partnerships, **73**
of sole proprietorships, **72**
Urbanization, growth of government and, **97**
"Uruguay Round," **436–437, 439**
USX Corporation, **71**
Util(s), **125**
Utility, **20, 125**
income equality and, **384**
marginal (*see* Marginal utility)
measurement of, **137**
total, **126, 131**
Utility-maximizing rule, **127–128**
UTU (United Transportation Union), **252**

V

Value:
of currency (*see* Currency; Dollar)
labor theory of, **470**
surplus, **470–471**
of time, **130–131**
Value-added tax (VAT), **338–339**
Variable(s):
dependent, **14–15**
independent, **15**
Variable cost, **145**
average, **146–147, 149**
Variable proportions, law of, **142–145**
VAT (value-added tax), **338–339**
VERs (voluntary export restrictions), **430**
Vertical axis, **14**
Vertical combinations, **71**
Vertical intercept, **16**
Vertical mergers, **348, 349**
Vietnam War, production for, **29**
Voice mechanism, unions and, **407**
Voith, Richard, **112*n.***
Volkswagen, **77**
Voluntary export restrictions (VERs), **430**
Votes:
dollar, **80, 94*n.***
political, **94*n.***
Voting, **324–328**
inefficient outcomes of, **324–326**
median-voter model and, **327–328**
paradox of, **326–327**
(*See also* Politics)

W

Wage(s), **21**
cost-of-living adjustments and, **403**
efficiency, **272**
general level of, **256–257**
immigration and, **414**
incentive pay plan and, **272**
meaning of, **256**
minimum:
controversy over, **266–267**
price elasticity of demand and, **114**
nominal, **256**
of professional athletes, **261–262, 270–271, 378**
racial discrimination and, **416**
real, **256**
aging population and, **299**
productivity and, **257**
shock effect and, **407**
unions and, **262–265, 403, 404, 408**
Wage bargaining, price elasticity of demand and, **112**
Wage determination, **255–272**
in bilateral monopoly, **265–266**
in competitive labor market, **257–259**
minimum wage and, **266–267**
in monopsony, **259–262**
performance and, **269–272**
unemployment and, **265**
Wage determination (continued)
unions and, **262–265**
wage differentials and, **267–269**
Wage differentials, **267–269**
Wage discrimination, **410**
Wagner Act of 1935, **399–400, 402**
Wants, unlimited, **19–20**
War:
growth of government and, **97**
production possibilities curve and, **29, 30, 32**
(*See also* World War II)
Waste(s):
advertising as, **214–215**
of monopolistic competition, **210–211**
Weidenbaum, Murray L., **340, 356*n.***
Weiler, E. T., **405*n.***
Welfare programs, **389–393**
reform of, **391–393**
Welfare Reform Act of 1988, **392**
Welfare-to-work programs, **392–393**
Western Union Corporation, **262**
Westinghouse, **228–229**
Wheeler-Lea Act of 1938, **347**
Wholesale industries, **75**
Wilson, Thomas A., **215*n.***
Work rules, **405–406**
Workfare plans, **392–393**
World economy:
agriculture and, **374–375**
oil price increases and, **297**
Soviet joining of, **479**
World War II:
income distribution during, **379**
price controls during, **117–118**
production for, **29**

X

X-inefficiency, **198–199**
Xerox, **190**

Y

Yellow-dog contract, **398**
Yeltsin, Boris, **470, 479**
Yugoslavia, economy of, **31**